AF862012

Accounting Principles Volume 1 ACC 100

Thirteenth Edition

Strayer University

Wiley Custom Learning Solutions

To order books or for customer service, please call 1(800)-CALL-WILEY (225-5945).

Printed in the United States of America.

ISBN 978-1-119-56865-0

V10015269_103119

Table of Contents

Chapters 1-9 and 18, Appendices and Index are originally from *Accounting Principles* 13th Edition by Jerry J. Weygandt, Paul D. Kimmel, and Donald E. Kieso

1 Accounting in Action

2 The Recording Process

3 Adjusting the Accounts

4 Completing the Accounting Cycle

5 Accounting for Merchandising Operations

6 Inventories

7 Accounting Information Systems

8 Fraud, Internal Control, and Cash

9 Accounting for Receivables

18 Financial Analysis: The Big Picture

Checklist of Key Figures Vol 1

Checklist of Key Figures Vol 2

Appendix A: Specimen Financial Statements: Apple Inc.

Appendix B: Specimen Financial Statements: PepsiCo, Inc.

Appendix C: Specimen Financial Statements: The Coca-Cola Company

Appendix D: Specimen Financial Statements: Amazon.com, Inc.

Appendix E: Specimen Financial Statements: Wal-Mart Stores, Inc.

Appendix F: Specimen Financial Statements: Louis Vuitton

Appendix G: Time Value of Money

Appendix H: Just-in-Time Processing and Activity-Based Costing

Company Index

Subject Index

ACCOUNT CLASSIFICATION AND PRESENTATION

Account Title	Classification	Financial Statement	Normal Balance
		A	
Accounts Payable	Current Liability	Balance Sheet	Credit
Accounts Receivable	Current Asset	Balance Sheet	Debit
Accumulated Depreciation—Buildings	Plant Asset—Contra	Balance Sheet	Credit
Accumulated Depreciation—Equipment	Plant Asset—Contra	Balance Sheet	Credit
Advertising Expense	Operating Expense	Income Statement	Debit
Allowance for Doubtful Accounts	Current Asset—Contra	Balance Sheet	Credit
Amortization Expense	Operating Expense	Income Statement	Debit
		B	
Bad Debt Expense	Operating Expense	Income Statement	Debit
Bonds Payable	Long-Term Liability	Balance Sheet	Credit
Buildings	Plant Asset	Balance Sheet	Debit
		C	
Cash	Current Asset	Balance Sheet	Debit
Common Stock	Stockholders' Equity	Balance Sheet	Credit
Copyrights	Intangible Asset	Balance Sheet	Debit
Cost of Goods Sold	Cost of Goods Sold	Income Statement	Debit
		D	
Debt Investments	Current Asset/Long-Term Investment	Balance Sheet	Debit
Depreciation Expense	Operating Expense	Income Statement	Debit
Discount on Bonds Payable	Long-Term Liability—Contra	Balance Sheet	Debit
Dividends	Temporary account closed to Retained Earnings	Retained Earnings Statement	Debit
Dividends Payable	Current Liability	Balance Sheet	Credit
		E	
Equipment	Plant Asset	Balance Sheet	Debit
		F	
Freight-Out	Operating Expense	Income Statement	Debit
		G	
Gain on Disposal of Plant Assets	Other Income	Income Statement	Credit
Goodwill	Intangible Asset	Balance Sheet	Debit
		I	
Income Summary	Temporary account closed to Retained Earnings	Not Applicable	(1)
Income Tax Expense	Income Tax Expense	Income Statement	Debit
Income Taxes Payable	Current Liability	Balance Sheet	Credit
Insurance Expense	Operating Expense	Income Statement	Debit
Interest Expense	Other Expense	Income Statement	Debit
Interest Payable	Current Liability	Balance Sheet	Credit
Interest Receivable	Current Asset	Balance Sheet	Debit
Interest Revenue	Other Income	Income Statement	Credit
Inventory	Current Asset	Balance Sheet (2)	Debit

Account Title	Classification	Financial Statement	Normal Balance
L			
Land	Plant Asset	Balance Sheet	Debit
Loss on Disposal of Plant Assets	Other Expense	Income Statement	Debit
M			
Maintenance and Repairs Expense	Operating Expense	Income Statement	Debit
Mortgage Payable	Long-Term Liability	Balance Sheet	Credit
N			
Notes Payable	Current Liability/ Long-Term Liability	Balance Sheet	Credit
O			
Owner's Capital	Owner's Equity	Owner's Equity and Balance Sheet	Credit
Owner's Drawings	Temporary account closed to Owner's Capital	Owner's Equity	Debit
P			
Patents	Intangible Asset	Balance Sheet	Debit
Paid-in Capital in Excess of Par—Common Stock	Stockholders' Equity	Balance Sheet	Credit
Paid-in Capital in Excess of Par—Preferred Stock	Stockholders' Equity	Balance Sheet	Credit
Preferred Stock	Stockholders' Equity	Balance Sheet	Credit
Premium on Bonds Payable	Long-Term Liability	Balance Sheet	Credit
Prepaid Insurance	Current Asset	Balance Sheet	Debit
Prepaid Rent	Current Asset	Balance Sheet	Debit
R			
Rent Expense	Operating Expense	Income Statement	Debit
Retained Earnings	Stockholders' Equity	Balance Sheet and Retained Earnings Statement	Credit
S			
Salaries and Wages Expense	Operating Expense	Income Statement	Debit
Salaries and Wages Payable	Current Liability	Balance Sheet	Credit
Sales Discounts	Revenue—Contra	Income Statement	Debit
Sales Returns and Allowances	Revenue—Contra	Income Statement	Debit
Sales Revenue	Revenue	Income Statement	Credit
Selling Expenses	Operating Expense	Income Statement	Debit
Service Revenue	Revenue	Income Statement	Credit
Stock Investments	Current Asset/Long-Term Investment	Balance Sheet	Debit
Supplies	Current Asset	Balance Sheet	Debit
Supplies Expense	Operating Expense	Income Statement	Debit
T			
Treasury Stock	Stockholders' Equity—Contra	Balance Sheet	Debit
U			
Unearned Service Revenue	Current Liability	Balance Sheet	Credit
Utilities Expense	Operating Expense	Income Statement	Debit

(1) The normal balance for Income Summary will be credit when there is a net income, debit when there is a net loss. The Income Summary account does not appear on any financial statement.

(2) If a periodic system is used, Inventory also appears on the income statement in the calculation of cost of goods sold.

The following is a sample chart of accounts. It does not represent a comprehensive chart of all the accounts used in this textbook but rather those accounts that are commonly used. This sample chart of accounts is for a company that generates both service revenue as well as sales revenue. It uses the perpetual approach to inventory. If a periodic system was used, the following temporary accounts would be needed to record inventory purchases: Purchases, Freight-In, Purchase Returns and Allowances, and Purchase Discounts.

CHART OF ACCOUNTS

Assets	Liabilities	Owner's and Stockholders' Equity	Revenues	Expenses
Cash	Notes Payable	Owner's Capital	Service Revenue	Advertising Expense
Accounts Receivable	Accounts Payable	Owner's Drawings	Sales Revenue	Amortization Expense
Allowance for Doubtful Accounts	Unearned Service Revenue	Common Stock	Sales Discounts	Bad Debt Expense
Interest Receivable	Salaries and Wages Payable	Paid-in Capital in Excess of Par—Common Stock	Sales Returns and Allowances	Cost of Goods Sold
Inventory	Unearned Rent Revenue	Preferred Stock	Interest Revenue	Depreciation Expense
Supplies	Interest Payable	Paid-in Capital in Excess of Par—Preferred Stock	Gain on Disposal of Plant Assets	Freight-Out
Prepaid Insurance	Dividends Payable	Treasury Stock		Income Tax Expense
Prepaid Rent	Income Taxes Payable	Retained Earnings		Insurance Expense
Land	Bonds Payable	Dividends		Interest Expense
Equipment	Discount on Bonds Payable	Income Summary		Loss on Disposal of Plant Assets
Accumulated Depreciation—Equipment	Premium on Bonds Payable			Maintenance and Repairs Expense
Buildings	Mortgage Payable			Rent Expense
Accumulated Depreciation—Buildings				Salaries and Wages Expense
Copyrights				Supplies Expense
Goodwill				Utilities Expense
Patents				

Accounting Principles

Thirteenth Edition

JERRY J. WEYGANDT PhD, CPA
University of Wisconsin—Madison
Madison, Wisconsin

PAUL D. KIMMEL PhD, CPA
University of Wisconsin—Milwaukee
Milwaukee, Wisconsin

DONALD E. KIESO PhD, CPA
Northern Illinois University
DeKalb, Illinois

WILEY

DEDICATED TO

Our wives,
Enid, Merlynn, and Donna, for their love,
support, and encouragement.

DIRECTOR	Michael McDonald
ACQUISITIONS EDITOR	Lauren Harrell Krassow
LEAD PRODUCT DESIGNER	Ed Brislin
PRODUCT DESIGNER	Matt Origoni
MARKETING MANAGER	Carolyn Wells
EDITORIAL SUPERVISOR	Terry Ann Tatro
EDITORIAL ASSOCIATE	Margaret Thompson
MARKETING ASSISTANT	Ashley Migliaro
EDITORIAL ASSISTANT	Alyce Pellegrino
SENIOR CONTENT MANAGER	Dorothy Sinclair
SENIOR PRODUCTION EDITOR	Elena Saccaro
SENIOR DESIGNER	Wendy Lai
SENIOR PHOTO EDITOR	Mary Ann Price
COVER IMAGE	Kurt Heim/Stocksy

This book was set in Stix Regular by Aptara®, Inc. and printed and bound by Quad Graphics/Versailles. The cover was printed by Quad Graphics/Versailles.

Founded in 1807, John Wiley & Sons, Inc. has been a valued source of knowledge and understanding for more than 200 years, helping people around the world meet their needs and fulfill their aspirations. Our company is built on a foundation of principles that include responsibility to the communities we serve and where we live and work. In 2008, we launched a Corporate Citizenship Initiative, a global effort to address the environmental, social, economic, and ethical challenges we face in our business. Among the issues we are addressing are carbon impact, paper specifications and procurement, ethical conduct within our business and among our vendors, and community and charitable support. For more information, please visit our website: www.wiley.com/go/citizenship.

ISBN-13: 978-1-119-41101-7

The inside back cover will contain printing identification and country of origin if omitted from this page. In addition, if the ISBN on the back cover differs from the ISBN on this page, the one on the back cover is correct.

Printed in America.

V10008183_021219

From the Authors

Dear Student,

WHY THIS COURSE? Remember your biology course in high school? Did you have one of those "invisible man" models (or maybe something more high-tech than that) that gave you the opportunity to look "inside" the human body? This accounting course offers something similar. To understand a business, you have to understand the financial insides of a business organization. An accounting course will help you understand the essential financial components of businesses. Whether you are looking at a large multinational company like **Apple** or **Starbucks** or a single-owner software consulting business or coffee shop, knowing the fundamentals of accounting will help you understand what is happening. As an employee, a manager, an investor, a business owner, or a director of your own personal finances—any of which roles you will have at some point in your life—you will make better decisions for having taken this course.

> "Whether you are looking at a large multinational company like **Apple** or **Starbucks** or a single-owner software consulting business or coffee shop, knowing the fundamentals of accounting will help you understand what is happening."

WHY THIS TEXT? Your instructor has chosen this text for you because of the authors' trusted reputation. The authors have worked hard to write a text that is engaging, timely, and accurate.

HOW TO SUCCEED? We've asked many students and many instructors whether there is a secret for success in this course. The nearly unanimous answer turns out to be not much of a secret: "Do the homework." This is one course where doing is learning. The more time you spend on the homework assignments—using the various tools that this text provides—the more likely you are to learn the essential concepts, techniques, and methods of accounting. Besides the text itself, WileyPLUS also offers various support resources.

Good luck in this course. We hope you enjoy the experience and that you put to good use throughout a lifetime of success the knowledge you obtain in this course. We are sure you will not be disappointed.

Jerry J. Weygandt
Paul D. Kimmel
Donald E. Kieso

Author Commitment

Jerry Weygandt

JERRY J. WEYGANDT, PhD, CPA, is Arthur Andersen Alumni Emeritus Professor of Accounting at the University of Wisconsin—Madison. He holds a Ph.D. in accounting from the University of Illinois. Articles by Professor Weygandt have appeared in *The Accounting Review, Journal of Accounting Research, Accounting Horizons, Journal of Accountancy*, and other academic and professional journals. These articles have examined such financial reporting issues as accounting for price-level adjustments, pensions, convertible securities, stock option contracts, and interim reports. Professor Weygandt is author of other accounting and financial reporting books and is a member of the American Accounting Association, the American Institute of Certified Public Accountants, and the Wisconsin Society of Certified Public Accountants. He has served on numerous committees of the American Accounting Association and as a member of the editorial board of *The Accounting Review*; he also has served as President and Secretary-Treasurer of the American Accounting Association. In addition, he has been actively involved with the American Institute of Certified Public Accountants and has been a member of the Accounting Standards Executive Committee (AcSEC) of that organization. He has served on the FASB task force that examined the reporting issues related to accounting for income taxes and served as a trustee of the Financial Accounting Foundation. Professor Weygandt has received the Chancellor's Award for Excellence in Teaching and the Beta Gamma Sigma Dean's Teaching Award. He is on the board of directors of M & I Bank of Southern Wisconsin. He is the recipient of the Wisconsin Institute of CPA's Outstanding Educator's Award and the Lifetime Achievement Award. In 2001 he received the American Accounting Association's Outstanding Educator Award.

Paul Kimmel

PAUL D. KIMMEL, PhD, CPA, received his bachelor's degree from the University of Minnesota and his doctorate in accounting from the University of Wisconsin. He teaches at the University of Wisconsin—Milwaukee, and has public accounting experience with Deloitte & Touche (Minneapolis). He was the recipient of the UWM School of Business Advisory Council Teaching Award, the Reggie Taite Excellence in Teaching Award and a three-time winner of the Outstanding Teaching Assistant Award at the University of Wisconsin. He is also a recipient of the Elijah Watts Sells Award for Honorary Distinction for his results on the CPA exam. He is a member of the American Accounting Association and the Institute of Management Accountants and has published articles in *The Accounting Review, Accounting Horizons, Advances in Management Accounting, Managerial Finance, Issues in Accounting Education, Journal of Accounting Education*, as well as other journals. His research interests include accounting for financial instruments and innovation in accounting education. He has published papers and given numerous talks on incorporating critical thinking into accounting education, and helped prepare a catalog of critical thinking resources for the Federated Schools of Accountancy.

Don Kieso

DONALD E. KIESO, PhD, CPA, received his bachelor's degree from Aurora University and his doctorate in accounting from the University of Illinois. He has served as chairman of the Department of Accountancy and is currently the KPMG Emeritus Professor of Accountancy at Northern Illinois University. He has public accounting experience with Price Waterhouse & Co. (San Francisco and Chicago) and Arthur Andersen & Co. (Chicago) and research experience with the Research Division of the American Institute of Certified Public Accountants (New York). He has done post doctorate work as a Visiting Scholar at the University of California at Berkeley and is a recipient of NIU's Teaching Excellence Award and four Golden Apple Teaching Awards. Professor Kieso is the author of other accounting and business books and is a member of the American Accounting Association, the American Institute of Certified Public Accountants, and the Illinois CPA Society. He has served as a member of the Board of Directors of the Illinois CPA Society, then AACSB's Accounting Accreditation Committees, the State of Illinois Comptroller's Commission, as Secretary-Treasurer of the Federation of Schools of Accountancy, and as Secretary-Treasurer of the American Accounting Association. Professor Kieso is currently serving on the Board of Trustees and Executive Committee of Aurora University, as a member of the Board of Directors of Kishwaukee Community Hospital, and as Treasurer and Director of Valley West Community Hospital. From 1989 to 1993 he served as a charter member of the national Accounting Education Change Commission. He is the recipient of the Outstanding Accounting Educator Award from the Illinois CPA Society, the FSA's Joseph A. Silvoso Award of Merit, the NIU Foundation's Humanitarian Award for Service to Higher Education, a Distinguished Service Award from the Illinois CPA Society, and in 2003 an honorary doctorate from Aurora University.

Hallmark Features

Accounting Principles, Thirteenth Edition, provides a simple and practical introduction to the fundamentals of accounting. It explains the concepts you need to know. This edition continues this approach by offering even more explanations, illustrations, and homework problems to help students get a firm understanding of the accounting cycle.

DO IT! Exercises

DO IT! Exercises in the body of the text prompt students to stop and review key concepts. They outline the Action Plan necessary to complete the exercise as well as show a detailed solution.

DO IT! 3 | Correcting Entries

Sanchez Company discovered the following errors made in January 2020.

1. A payment of Salaries and Wages Expense of $600 was debited to Supplies and credited to Cash, both for $600.
2. A collection of $3,000 from a client on account was debited to Cash $200 and credited to Service Revenue $200.
3. The purchase of supplies on account for $860 was debited to Supplies $680 and credited to Accounts Payable $680.

Correct the errors without reversing the incorrect entry.

ACTION PLAN

- **Compare the incorrect entry with correct entry.**
- **After comparison, make an entry to correct the accounts.**

Solution

1. Salaries and Wages Expense	600	
Supplies		600
2. Service Revenue	200	
Cash	2,800	
Accounts Receivable		3,000

Review and Practice

Each chapter concludes with a Review and Practice section which includes a review of learning objectives, key terms glossary, practice multiple-choice questions with annotated solutions, practice brief exercises with solutions, practice exercises with solutions, and a practice problem with a solution.

Practice Brief Exercises

Prepare the current assets section of a balance sheet.

3. (LO 4) **Financial Statement** The balance sheet debit column of the worksheet for Miguel Company includes the following accounts: Accounts Receivable $25,000, Prepaid Insurance $7,000, Cash $8,000, Supplies $11,000, and Stock Investments (short-term) $14,000. Prepare the current assets section of the balance sheet, listing the accounts in proper sequence.

Solution

3.

Miguel Company
Partial Balance Sheet

Current assets	
Cash	$ 8,000
Stock investments	14,000
Accounts receivable	25,000
Supplies	11,000
Prepaid insurance	7,000
Total current assets	$65,000

Infographic Learning

Over half of the text is visual, providing students alternative ways of learning about accounting. In addition, a new interior design promotes accessibility.

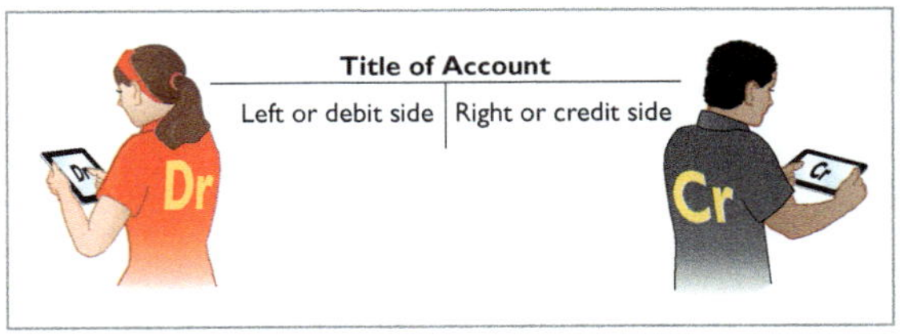

ILLUSTRATION 2.1
Basic form of account

Real-World Decision-Making

Real-world examples that illustrate interesting situations in companies and how accounting information is used are integrated throughout the text, such as in the opening Feature Story as well as the Insight boxes.

People, Planet, and Profit Insight

© Gehringi/iStockphoto

Regaining Goodwill

After falling to unforeseen lows amidst scandals, recalls, and economic crises, the American public's positive perception of the reputation of corporate America is on the rise. Overall corporate reputation is experiencing rehabilitation as the American public gives high marks overall to corporate America, specific industries, and the largest number of individual companies in a dozen years. This is according to the findings of a *Harris Interactive RQ Study*, which measures the reputations of the 60 most visible companies in the United States.

The survey focuses on six reputational dimensions that influence reputation and consumer behavior. Four of these dimensions, along with the five corporations that ranked highest within each, are as follows.

- **Social Responsibility**: (1) Whole Foods Market, (2) Johnson & Johnson, (3) Google, (4) The Walt Disney Company, (5) Procter & Gamble Co.
- **Emotional Appeal**: (1) Johnson & Johnson, (2) Amazon.com, (3) UPS, (4) General Mills, (5) Kraft Foods
- **Financial Performance**: (1) Google, (2) Berkshire Hathaway, (3) Apple, (4) Intel, (5) The Walt Disney Company
- **Products and Services**: (1) Intel Corporation, (2) 3M Company, (3) Johnson & Johnson, (4) Google, (5) Procter & Gamble Co.

Source: www.harrisinteractive.com.

Name two industries today which are probably rated low on the reputational characteristics of "being trusted" and "having high ethical standards." (Go to WileyPLUS for this answer and additional questions.)

Additional Guidance

Throughout the text, marginal notes, such as **Helpful Hints**, **Alternative Terminology**, and **Ethics Notes**, are provided as additional guidance. In addition, more than 100 new solution walkthrough videos are now available in WileyPLUS.

Correcting Entries—An Avoidable Step

Unfortunately, errors may occur in the recording process. Companies should correct errors, **as soon as they discover them**, by journalizing and posting **correcting entries**. If the accounting records are free of errors, no correcting entries are needed.

You should recognize several differences between correcting entries and adjusting entries. First, adjusting entries are an integral part of the accounting cycle. Correcting entries, on the other hand, are unnecessary if the records are error-free. Second, companies journalize and post adjustments **only at the end of an accounting period**. In contrast, companies make correcting entries **whenever they discover an error** (see **Ethics Note**). Finally, adjusting entries always affect at least one balance sheet account and one income statement account. In

ETHICS NOTE

When companies find errors in previously released income statements, they restate those numbers. Perhaps because of the increased scrutiny caused by Sarbanes-Oxley, in a recent year companies filed a record 1,195 restatements

Contents

1 Accounting in Action 1-1

Knowing the Numbers: **Columbia Sportswear** 1-1
Accounting Activities and Users 1-3
Three Activities 1-3
Who Uses Accounting Data 1-4
The Building Blocks of Accounting 1-6
Ethics in Financial Reporting 1-6
Generally Accepted Accounting Principles 1-8
Measurement Principles 1-8
Assumptions 1-9
The Accounting Equation 1-11
Assets 1-11
Liabilities 1-11
Owner's Equity 1-12
Analyzing Business Transactions 1-13
Accounting Transactions 1-14
Transaction Analysis 1-14
Summary of Transactions 1-19
The Four Financial Statements 1-20
Income Statement 1-20
Owner's Equity Statement 1-22
Balance Sheet 1-22
Statement of Cash Flows 1-23
Appendix 1A: Career Opportunities in Accounting 1-24
Public Accounting 1-24
Private Accounting 1-25
Governmental Accounting 1-25
Forensic Accounting 1-25
"Show Me the Money" 1-25
A Look at IFRS 1-47

2 The Recording Process 2-1

Accidents Happen: **MF Global Holdings** 2-1
Accounts, Debits, and Credits 2-2
The Account 2-2
Debits and Credits 2-3
Summary of Debit/Credit Rules 2-6
The Journal 2-7
The Recording Process 2-7
The Journal 2-8
The Ledger and Posting 2-10
The Ledger 2-10
Posting 2-12
Chart of Accounts 2-13
The Recording Process Illustrated 2-13
Summary Illustration of Journalizing and Posting 2-19
The Trial Balance 2-21
Limitations of a Trial Balance 2-22
Locating Errors 2-22
Dollar Signs and Underlining 2-22
A Look at IFRS 2-46

3 Adjusting the Accounts 3-1

Keeping Track of Groupons: **Groupon** 3-1
Accrual-Basis Accounting and Adjusting Entries 3-2
Fiscal and Calendar Years 3-3
Accrual- versus Cash-Basis Accounting 3-3
Recognizing Revenues and Expenses 3-3
The Need for Adjusting Entries 3-5
Types of Adjusting Entries 3-5
Adjusting Entries for Deferrals 3-6
Prepaid Expenses 3-6
Unearned Revenues 3-10
Adjusting Entries for Accruals 3-13
Accrued Revenues 3-13
Accrued Expenses 3-14
Summary of Basic Relationships 3-17
Adjusted Trial Balance and Financial Statements 3-20
Preparing the Adjusted Trial Balance 3-21
Preparing Financial Statements 3-21
Appendix 3A: Alternative Treatment of Deferrals 3-24
Prepaid Expenses 3-25
Unearned Revenues 3-26
Summary of Additional Adjustment Relationships 3-27
Appendix 3B: Financial Reporting Concepts 3-28
Qualities of Useful Information 3-28
Assumptions in Financial Reporting 3-28
Principles in Financial Reporting 3-29
Cost Constraint 3-30
A Look at IFRS 3-58

4 Completing the Accounting Cycle 4-1

Everyone Likes to Win: **Rhino Foods** 4-1
The Worksheet 4-2
Steps in Preparing a Worksheet 4-3
Preparing Financial Statements from a Worksheet 4-10
Preparing Adjusting Entries from a Worksheet 4-11
Closing the Books 4-11

Preparing Closing Entries 4-12
Posting Closing Entries 4-14
Preparing a Post-Closing Trial Balance 4-16
The Accounting Cycle and Correcting Entries 4-19
Summary of the Accounting Cycle 4-19
Reversing Entries—An Optional Step 4-19
Correcting Entries—An Avoidable Step 4-19
Classified Balance Sheet 4-23
Current Assets 4-24
Long-Term Investments 4-25
Property, Plant, and Equipment 4-25
Intangible Assets 4-25
Current Liabilities 4-26
Long-Term Liabilities 4-27
Owner's Equity 4-28
Appendix 4A: Reversing Entries 4-29
Reversing Entries Example 4-29
A Look at IFRS 4-59

5 Accounting for Merchandising Operations 5-1

Buy Now, Vote Later: **REI 5-1**
Merchandising Operations and Inventory Systems 5-3
Operating Cycles 5-3
Flow of Costs 5-4
Recording Purchases under a Perpetual System 5-6
Freight Costs 5-8
Purchase Returns and Allowances 5-9
Purchase Discounts 5-9
Summary of Purchasing Transactions 5-10
Recording Sales Under a Perpetual System 5-11
Sales Returns and Allowances 5-12
Sales Discounts 5-13
The Accounting Cycle for a Merchandising Company 5-15
Adjusting Entries 5-15
Closing Entries 5-15
Summary of Merchandising Entries 5-16
Multiple-Step and Comprehensive Income Statements 5-17
Multiple-Step Income Statement 5-18
Single-Step Income Statement 5-20
Comprehensive Income Statement 5-21
Classified Balance Sheet 5-21
Appendix 5A: Worksheet for a Merchandising Company 5-23
Using a Worksheet 5-23
Appendix 5B: Periodic Inventory System 5-24
Determining Cost of Goods Sold Under a Periodic System 5-25
Recording Merchandise Transactions 5-25
Recording Purchases of Merchandise 5-26
Recording Sales of Merchandise 5-27
Journalizing and Posting Closing Entries 5-28
Using a Worksheet 5-29
A Look at IFRS 5-54

6 Inventories 6-1

"Where Is That Spare Bulldozer Blade?": **Caterpillar 6-1**
Classifying and Determining Inventory 6-2
Classifying Inventory 6-3
Determining Inventory Quantities 6-4
Inventory Methods and Financial Effects 6-7
Specific Identification 6-7
Cost Flow Assumptions 6-8
Financial Statement and Tax Effects of Cost Flow Methods 6-12
Using Inventory Cost Flow Methods Consistently 6-14
Effects of Inventory Errors 6-15
Income Statement Effects 6-15
Balance Sheet Effects 6-16
Inventory Statement Presentation and Analysis 6-17
Presentation 6-17
Lower-of-Cost-or-Net Realizable Value 6-17
Analysis 6-18
Appendix 6A: Inventory Methods and the Perpetual System 6-20
First-In, First-Out (FIFO) 6-20
Last-In, First-Out (LIFO) 6-21
Average-Cost 6-22
Appendix 6B: Estimating Inventories 6-22
Gross Profit Method 6-23
Retail Inventory Method 6-24
A Look at IFRS 6-48

7 Accounting Information Systems 7-1

QuickBooks® Helps This Retailer Sell Guitars: **Intuit 7-1**
Overview of Accounting Information Systems 7-2
Computerized Accounting Systems 7-3
Manual Accounting Systems 7-5
Subsidiary Ledgers 7-5
Subsidiary Ledger Example 7-6
Advantages of Subsidiary Ledgers 7-7
Special Journals 7-8
Sales Journal 7-9
Cash Receipts Journal 7-11
Purchases Journal 7-15
Cash Payments Journal 7-17

Effects of Special Journals on the General Journal 7-20
Cyber Security: A Final Comment 7-21
A Look at IFRS 7-44

8 Fraud, Internal Control, and Cash 8-1

Minding the Money in Madison: **Barriques** 8-1
Fraud and Internal Control 8-3
Fraud 8-3
The Sarbanes-Oxley Act 8-3
Internal Control 8-4
Principles of Internal Control Activities 8-4
Limitations of Internal Control 8-10
Cash Controls 8-11
Cash Receipts Controls 8-12
Cash Disbursements Controls 8-14
Petty Cash Fund 8-16
Control Features of a Bank Account 8-19
Making Bank Deposits 8-19
Writing Checks 8-20
Electronic Funds Transfer (EFT) System 8-21
Bank Statements 8-21
Reconciling the Bank Account 8-22
Reporting Cash 8-27
Cash Equivalents 8-27
Restricted Cash 8-27
A Look at IFRS 8-48

9 Accounting for Receivables 9-1

A Dose of Careful Management Keeps Receivables Healthy: **Whitehall-Robins** 9-1
Recognition of Accounts Receivable 9-2
Types of Receivables 9-3
Recognizing Accounts Receivable 9-3
Valuation and Disposition of Accounts Receivable 9-5
Valuing Accounts Receivable 9-5
Disposing of Accounts Receivable 9-11
Notes Receivable 9-13
Determining the Maturity Date 9-14
Computing Interest 9-15
Recognizing Notes Receivable 9-15
Valuing Notes Receivable 9-16
Disposing of Notes Receivable 9-16
Presentation and Analysis 9-18
Presentation 9-19
Analysis 9-20
A Look at IFRS 9-41

10 Plant Assets, Natural Resources, and Intangible Assets 10-1

How Much for a Ride to the Beach?: **Rent-A-Wreck** 10-1
Plant Asset Expenditures 10-2
Determining the Cost of Plant Assets 10-3
Expenditures During Useful Life 10-5
Depreciation Methods 10-7
Factors in Computing Depreciation 10-7
Depreciation Methods 10-8
Depreciation and Income Taxes 10-13
Revising Periodic Depreciation 10-13
Impairments 10-13
Plant Asset Disposals 10-14
Retirement of Plant Assets 10-15
Sale of Plant Assets 10-15
Natural Resources and Intangible Assets 10-17
Natural Resources 10-17
Depletion 10-17
Intangible Assets 10-18
Accounting for Intangible Assets 10-18
Research and Development Costs 10-21
Statement Presentation and Analysis 10-21
Presentation 10-21
Analysis 10-22
Appendix 10A: Exchange of Plant Assets 10-23
Loss Treatment 10-24
Gain Treatment 10-24
A Look at IFRS 10-46

11 Current Liabilities and Payroll Accounting 11-1

Financing His Dreams: **Wilbert Murdock** 11-1
Accounting for Current Liabilities 11-2
What Is a Current Liability? 11-2
Notes Payable 11-3
Sales Taxes Payable 11-4
Unearned Revenues 11-4
Current Maturities of Long-Term Debt 11-5
Reporting and Analyzing Current Liabilities 11-6
Reporting Uncertainty 11-6
Reporting of Current Liabilities 11-7
Analysis of Current Liabilities 11-8
Accounting for Payroll 11-9
Determining the Payroll 11-10
Recording the Payroll 11-13
Employer Payroll Taxes 11-16
Filing and Remitting Payroll Taxes 11-18
Internal Control for Payroll 11-19
Appendix 11A: Additional Fringe Benefits 11-20

Paid Absences 11-21
Postretirement Benefits 11-21
A Look at IFRS 11-41

12 Accounting for Partnerships 12-1

From Trials to the Top Ten: **Razor & Tie** 12-1
Forming a Partnership 12-2
Characteristics of Partnerships 12-3
Organizations with Partnership Characteristics 12-3
Advantages and Disadvantages of Partnerships 12-5
The Partnership Agreement 12-6
Accounting for a Partnership Formation 12-6
Accounting for Net Income or Net Loss 12-8
Dividing Net Income or Net Loss 12-8
Partnership Financial Statements 12-11
Liquidation of a Partnership 12-12
No Capital Deficiency 12-13
Capital Deficiency 12-15
Appendix 12A: Admissions and Withdrawals of Partners 12-18
Admission of a Partner 12-18
Withdrawal of a Partner 12-21

13 Corporations: Organization and Capital Stock Transactions 13-1

Oh Well, I Guess I'll Get Rich: **Facebook** 13-1
Corporate Form of Organization 13-2
Characteristics of a Corporation 13-3
Forming a Corporation 13-5
Stockholder Rights 13-6
Stock Issue Considerations 13-6
Corporate Capital 13-9
Accounting for Stock Transactions 13-10
Accounting for Common Stock 13-10
Accounting for Preferred Stock 13-12
Accounting for Treasury Stock 13-14
Statement Presentation of Stockholders' Equity 13-17
A Look at IFRS 13-36

14 Corporations: Dividends, Retained Earnings, and Income Reporting 14-1

Owning a Piece of the Action: **Van Meter Inc.** 14-1
Accounting for Dividends and Stock Splits 14-2
Cash Dividends 14-3
Dividend Preferences 14-4
Stock Dividends 14-7
Stock Splits 14-9
Reporting and Analyzing Stockholders' Equity 14-11
Retained Earnings 14-11
Statement Presentation and Analysis 14-13
Corporate Income Statements 14-16
Income Statement Presentation 14-16
Income Statement Analysis 14-16
Appendix 14A: Stockholders' Equity Statement 14-18
Appendix 14B: Book Value per Share 14-18
Book Value per Share 14-18
Book Value versus Market Price 14-20
A Look at IFRS 14-38

15 Long-Term Liabilities 15-1

And Then There Were Two: **Chrysler** 15-1
Major Characteristics of Bonds 15-2
Types of Bonds 15-3
Issuing Procedures 15-3
Bond Trading 15-4
Determining the Market Price of a Bond 15-5
Accounting for Bond Transactions 15-6
Issuing Bonds at Face Value 15-7
Discount or Premium on Bonds 15-7
Issuing Bonds at a Discount 15-8
Issuing Bonds at a Premium 15-9
Redeeming Bonds at Maturity 15-11
Redeeming Bonds before Maturity 15-11
Accounting for Long-Term Notes Payable 15-12
Reporting and Analyzing Long-Term Liabilities 15-14
Presentation 15-14
Use of Ratios 15-14
Debt and Equity Financing 15-15
Lease Liabilities 15-16
Appendix 15A: Straight-Line Amortization 15-17
Amortizing Bond Discount 15-17
Amortizing Bond Premium 15-19
Appendix 15B: Effective-Interest Amortization 15-20
Amortizing Bond Discount 15-20
Amortizing Bond Premium 15-22
A Look at IFRS 15-41

16 Investments 16-1

"Is There Anything Else We Can Buy?": **Time Warner** 16-1
Accounting for Debt Investments 16-2
Why Corporations Invest 16-2

Accounting for Debt Investments 16-4
Accounting for Stock Investments 16-6
Holdings of Less than 20% 16-6
Holdings Between 20% and 50% 16-7
Holdings of More than 50% 16-8
Reporting Investments in Financial Statements 16-10
Debt Securities 16-11
Equity Securities 16-14
Balance Sheet Presentation 16-15
Presentation of Realized and Unrealized Gain or Loss 16-16
A Look at IFRS 16-35

17 Statement of Cash Flows 17-1

Got Cash?: **Microsoft 17-1**
Usefulness and Format of the Statement of Cash Flows 17-3
Usefulness of the Statement of Cash Flows 17-3
Classification of Cash Flows 17-3
Significant Noncash Activities 17-4
Format of the Statement of Cash Flows 17-5
Preparing the Statement of Cash Flows—Indirect Method 17-6
Indirect and Direct Methods 17-7
Indirect Method—Computer Services Company 17-7
Step 1: Operating Activities 17-9
Summary of Conversion to Net Cash Provided by Operating Activities—Indirect Method 17-12
Step 2: Investing and Financing Activities 17-13
Step 3: Net Change in Cash 17-14
Analyzing the Statement of Cash Flows 17-17
Free Cash Flow 17-17
Appendix 17A: Statement of Cash Flows—Direct Method 17-19
Step 1: Operating Activities 17-19
Step 2: Investing and Financing Activities 17-24
Step 3: Net Change in Cash 17-26
Appendix 17B: Worksheet for the Indirect Method 17-26
Preparing the Worksheet 17-27
Appendix 17C: Statement of Cash Flows—T-Account Approach 17-31
A Look at IFRS 17-58

18 Financial Analysis: The Big Picture 18-1

It Pays to Be Patient: **Warren Buffett 18-2**
Sustainable Income and Quality of Earnings 18-3
Sustainable Income 18-3
Quality of Earnings 18-7
Horizontal Analysis and Vertical Analysis 18-9
Horizontal Analysis 18-10
Vertical Analysis 18-12
Ratio Analysis 18-14
Liquidity Ratios 18-15
Solvency Ratios 18-16
Profitability Ratios 18-16
Comprehensive Example of Ratio Analysis 18-17
A Look at IFRS 18-51

19 Managerial Accounting 19-1

Just Add Water . . . and Paddle: **Current Designs 19-1**
Managerial Accounting Basics 19-3
Comparing Managerial and Financial Accounting 19-3
Management Functions 19-3
Organizational Structure 19-5
Managerial Cost Concepts 19-7
Manufacturing Costs 19-7
Product Versus Period Costs 19-8
Illustration of Cost Concepts 19-9
Manufacturing Costs in Financial Statements 19-10
Income Statement 19-11
Cost of Goods Manufactured 19-11
Cost of Goods Manufactured Schedule 19-12
Balance Sheet 19-13
Managerial Accounting Today 19-14
Service Industries 19-14
Focus on the Value Chain 19-15
Balanced Scorecard 19-17
Business Ethics 19-17
Corporate Social Responsibility 19-18

20 Job Order Costing 20-1

Profiting from the Silver Screen: **Disney 20-1**
Cost Accounting Systems 20-3
Process Cost System 20-3
Job Order Cost System 20-3
Job Order Cost Flow 20-4
Accumulating Manufacturing Costs 20-5
Assigning Manufacturing Costs 20-7
Raw Materials Costs 20-8
Factory Labor Costs 20-10
Predetermined Overhead Rates 20-12
Entries for Jobs Completed and Sold 20-15
Assigning Costs to Finished Goods 20-15
Assigning Costs to Cost of Goods Sold 20-16
Summary of Job Order Cost Flows 20-17
Job Order Costing for Service Companies 20-18
Advantages and Disadvantages of Job Order Costing 20-19

Applied Manufacturing Overhead 20-20
Under- or Overapplied Manufacturing Overhead 20-21

21 Process Costing 21-1

The Little Guy Who Could: **Jones Soda 21-1**
Overview of Process Cost Systems 21-3
Uses of Process Cost Systems 21-3
Process Costing for Service Companies 21-4
Similarities and Differences Between Job Order Cost and Process Cost Systems 21-4
Process Cost Flow and Assigning Costs 21-6
Process Cost Flow 21-6
Assigning Manufacturing Costs—Journal Entries 21-6
Equivalent Units 21-9
Weighted-Average Method 21-9
Refinements on the Weighted-Average Method 21-10
The Production Cost Report 21-12
Compute the Physical Unit Flow (Step 1) 21-13
Compute the Equivalent Units of Production (Step 2) 21-13
Compute Unit Production Costs (Step 3) 21-14
Prepare a Cost Reconciliation Schedule (Step 4) 21-15
Preparing the Production Cost Report 21-15
Costing Systems—Final Comments 21-16
Appendix 21A: FIFO Method for Equivalent Units 21-17
Equivalent Units Under FIFO 21-17
Comprehensive Example 21-18
FIFO and Weighted-Average 21-22

22 Cost-Volume-Profit 22-1

Don't Worry—Just Get Big: **Amazon.com 22-1**
Cost Behavior Analysis 22-2
Variable Costs 22-3
Fixed Costs 22-3
Relevant Range 22-5
Mixed Costs 22-6
Mixed Costs Analysis 22-7
High-Low Method 22-7
Importance of Identifying Variable and Fixed Costs 22-9
Cost-Volume-Profit Analysis 22-10
Basic Components 22-10
CVP Income Statement 22-11
Break-Even Analysis 22-14
Mathematical Equation 22-15
Contribution Margin Technique 22-15
Graphic Presentation 22-16
Target Net Income and Margin of Safety 22-18
Target Net Income 22-18
Margin of Safety 22-20
Appendix 22A: Regression Analysis 22-21

23 Incremental Analysis 23-1

Keeping It Clean: **Method Products 23-1**
Decision-Making and Incremental Analysis 23-3
Incremental Analysis Approach 23-3
How Incremental Analysis Works 23-4
Qualitative Factors 23-5
Relationship of Incremental Analysis and Activity-Based Costing 23-5
Types of Incremental Analysis 23-6
Special Orders 23-6
Make or Buy 23-8
Opportunity Cost 23-9
Sell or Process Further 23-10
Single-Product Case 23-11
Multiple-Product Case 23-11
Repair, Retain, or Replace Equipment 23-14
Eliminate Unprofitable Segment or Product 23-15

24 Budgetary Planning 24-1

What's in Your Cupcake?: **BabyCakes NYC 24-1**
Effective Budgeting and the Master Budget 24-3
Budgeting and Accounting 24-3
The Benefits of Budgeting 24-3
Essentials of Effective Budgeting 24-3
The Master Budget 24-6
Sales, Production, and Direct Materials Budgets 24-8
Sales Budget 24-8
Production Budget 24-9
Direct Materials Budget 9-10
Direct Labor, Manufacturing Overhead, and S&A Expense Budgets 24-13
Direct Labor Budget 24-13
Manufacturing Overhead Budget 24-14
Selling and Administrative Expense Budget 24-15
Budgeted Income Statement 24-15
Cash Budget and Budgeted Balance Sheet 24-17
Cash Budget 24-17
Budgeted Balance Sheet 24-20
Budgeting in Nonmanufacturing Companies 24-22
Merchandisers 24-22
Service Companies 24-23
Not-for-Profit Organizations 24-24

25 Budgetary Control and Responsibility Accounting 25-1

Pumpkin Madeleines and a Movie: **Tribeca Grand Hotel** 25-1
Budgetary Control and Static Budget Reports 25-3
Budgetary Control 25-3
Static Budget Reports 25-4
Flexible Budget Reports 25-6
Why Flexible Budgets? 25-7
Developing the Flexible Budget 25-9
Flexible Budget—A Case Study 25-9
Flexible Budget Reports 25-11
Responsibility Accounting and Responsibility Centers 25-13
Controllable versus Noncontrollable Revenues and Costs 25-15
Principles of Performance Evaluation 25-15
Responsibility Reporting System 25-17
Types of Responsibility Centers 25-18
Investment Centers 25-22
Return on Investment (ROI) 25-23
Responsibility Report 25-23
Judgmental Factors in ROI 25-24
Improving ROI 25-24
Appendix 25A: ROI vs. Residual Income 25-26
Residual Income Compared to ROI 25-27
Residual Income Weakness 25-27

26 Standard Costs and Balanced Scorecard 26-1

80,000 Different Caffeinated Combinations: **Starbucks** 26-2
Overview of Standard Costs 26-3
Distinguishing Between Standards and Budgets 26-4
Setting Standard Costs 26-4
Direct Materials Variances 26-7
Analyzing and Reporting Variances 26-7
Calculating Direct Materials Variances 26-9
Direct Labor and Manufacturing Overhead Variances 26-11
Direct Labor Variances 26-11
Manufacturing Overhead Variances 26-14
Variance Reports and Balanced Scorecards 26-16
Reporting Variances 26-16
Income Statement Presentation of Variances 26-16
Balanced Scorecard 26-17
Appendix 26A: Standard Cost Accounting System 26-20
Journal Entries 26-20
Ledger Accounts 26-22
Appendix 26B: Overhead Controllable and Volume Variances 26-23
Overhead Controllable Variance 26-23
Overhead Volume Variance 26-24

27 Planning for Capital Investments 27-1

Floating Hotels: **Holland America Line** 27-2
Capital Budgeting and Cash Payback 27-3
Cash Flow Information 27-3
Illustrative Data 27-4
Cash Payback 27-4
Net Present Value Method 27-6
Equal Annual Cash Flows 27-7
Unequal Annual Cash Flows 27-8
Choosing a Discount Rate 27-9
Simplifying Assumptions 27-9
Comprehensive Example 27-10
Capital Budgeting Challenges and Refinements 27-11
Intangible Benefits 27-11
Profitability Index for Mutually Exclusive Projects 27-13
Risk Analysis 27-14
Post-Audit of Investment Projects 27-15
Internal Rate of Return 27-16
Comparing Discounted Cash Flow Methods 27-17
Annual Rate of Return 27-18

Appendix A Specimen Financial Statements: Apple Inc. A-1

Appendix B Specimen Financial Statements: PepsiCo, Inc. B-1

Appendix C Specimen Financial Statements: The Coca-Cola Company C-1

Appendix D Specimen Financial Statements: Amazon.com, Inc. D-1

Appendix E Specimen Financial Statements: Wal-Mart Stores, Inc. E-1

Appendix F Specimen Financial Statements: Louis Vuitton F-1

Appendix G Time Value of Money G-1

Interest and Future Values G-1
Nature of Interest G-1
Future Value of a Single Amount G-3
Future Value of an Annuity G-5
Present Values G-7
Present Value Variables G-7
Present Value of a Single Amount G-7
Present Value of an Annuity G-9
Time Periods and Discounting G-11
Present Value of a Long-Term Note or Bond G-11
Capital Budgeting Situations G-14
Using Financial Calculators G-15
Present Value of a Single Sum G-16
Present Value of an Annuity G-17
Future Value of a Single Sum G-17
Future Value of an Annuity G-17
Internal Rate of Return G-18
Useful Applications of the Financial Calculator G-18

Appendix H Just-in-Time Processing and Activity-Based Costing H-1

Just-in-Time Processing and Activity-Based Costing H-1
Just-in-Time Processing H-1
Activity-Based Costing H-3
Applying Activity-Based Costing H-4
Identify and Classify Activities and Assign Overhead to Cost Pools (Step 1) H-5
Identify Cost Drivers (Step 2) H-5
Compute Activity-Based Overhead Rates (Step 3) H-6
Allocate Overhead Costs to Products (Step 4) H-6
Comparing Unit Costs H-7
Benefits of ABC H-8
Limitations of ABC H-8

Cases for Managerial Decision-Making
(The full text of these cases is available in WileyPLUS.)

Company Index I-1
Subject Index I-4

Acknowledgments

Accounting Principles has benefited greatly from the input of focus group participants, manuscript reviewers, those who have sent comments by letter or e-mail, ancillary authors, and proofers. We greatly appreciate the constructive suggestions and innovative ideas of reviewers and the creativity and accuracy of the ancillary authors and checkers.

Karen Andrews
Lewis-Clark State College

Sandra Bailey
Oregon Institute of Technology

Shele Bannon
Queensborough Community College

Robert Barta
Suffolk County Community College

Ellen Bartley
St. Joseph's College

LuAnn Bean
Florida Institute of Technology

Quent Below
Roane State Community College

Lila Bergman
Hunter College

Jack Borke
University of Wisconsin—Platteville

Glen Brauchle
Dowling College

Douglas Brown
Forsyth Technical Community College

Ronald Campbell
North Carolina A&T State University

Elizabeth Capener
Dominican University of California

Beth Carraway
Horry-Georgetown Technical College

Jackie Caseu
Cape Fear Community College

Kim Charland
Kansas State University

Sandee Cohen
Columbia College Chicago

Suzanne Cory
St. Mary's University

Paul Cox
Medgar Evers College

Joseph Cunningham
Harford Community College

Kate Demarest
Carroll Community College

Richard Dugger
Kilgore College

Bill Elliott
Oral Roberts University

James Emig
Villanova University

Cole Engel
Fort Hays State University

Larry Falcetto
Emporia State University

Gary Ford
Tompkins Cortland Community College

Alan Foster
J.S. Reynolds Community College

Dale Fowler
Ohio Christian University

George Gardner
Bemidji State University

Willard Garman
University of California, Los Angeles

Heidi Hansel
Kirkwood Community College

Coby Harmon
University of California—Santa Barbara

Derek Jackson
St. Mary's University of Minnesota

Jospeph Jurkowski
D'youville College

Randy Kidd
Metropolitan Community College

Cindy Killian
Wilkes Community College

Shirly Kleiner
Johnson County Community College

David Krug
Johnson County Community College

Christy Land
Catawba Valley Community College

Anita Leslie
York Technical College

Lori Major
Luzerne County Community College

Charles Malone
North Carolina A&T State University

Ken Mark
Kansas City Kansas Community College

Barbara Michal
University of Rio Grande

Jill Misuraca
University of Tampa

Allison Moore
Los Angeles Southwest College

Barbara Muller
Arizona State University

Yvonne Phang
Borough of Manhattan Community College

Brandis Phillips
North Carolina A&T State University

Mary Phillips
North Carolina Central University

Laura Prosser
Black Hills State University

La Vonda Ramey
Schoolcraft College

J. Ramos-Alexander
New Jersey City University

Michelle Randall
Schoolcraft College

Ruthie Reynolds
Tennessee State University

Kathie Rogers
Suffolk Community College

Kent Schneider
East Tennessee State University

Nadia Schwartz
Augustana College

Mehdi Sheikholeslami
Bemidji State University

Alice Sineath
University of Maryland University College

Bradley Smith
Des Moines Area Community College

Emil Soriano
Contra Costa College

Teresa Speck
St. Mary's University of Minnesota

Lynn Stallworth
Appalachian State University

John Stancil
Florida Southern College

Linda Summey
Central Carolina Community College

Joan Van Hise
Fairfield University

Dick Wasson
Southwestern College

Pat Wright
Long Island University

Lori Grady Zaher
Bucks County Community College

Judith Zander
Grossmont College

We thank Benjamin Huegel and Teresa Speck of St. Mary's University for their extensive efforts in the preparation of the homework materials related to Current Designs. We also appreciate the considerable support provided to us by the following people at Current Designs: Mike Cichanowski, Jim Brown, Diane Buswell, and Jake Greseth. We also benefited from the assistance and suggestions provided to us by Joan Van Hise in the preparation of materials related to sustainability.

We appreciate the exemplary support and commitment given to us by editor Lauren Harrell Krassow, marketing manager Carolyn Wells, lead product designer Ed Brislin, editorial supervisor Terry Ann Tatro, editorial associate Margaret Thompson, product designer Matt Origoni, assistant project manager Cyndy Taylor, designer Wendy Lai, photo editor Mary Ann Price, indexer Steve Ingle, senior production editor Elena Saccaro, and Denise Showers at Aptara. All of these professionals provided innumerable services that helped the text take shape.

We will appreciate suggestions and comments from users—instructors and students alike. You can send your thoughts and ideas about the text to us via email at: *AccountingAuthors@yahoo.com.*

Jerry J. Weygandt
Madison, Wisconsin

Paul D. Kimmel
Milwaukee, Wisconsin

Donald E. Kieso
DeKalb, Illinois

CHAPTER 1

© My Good Images/Shutterstock

Accounting in Action

*The **Chapter Preview** describes the purpose of the chapter and highlights major topics.*

Chapter Preview

The following Feature Story about **Columbia Sportswear Company** highlights the importance of having good financial information and knowing how to use it to make effective business decisions. Whatever your pursuits or occupation, the need for financial information is inescapable. You cannot earn a living, spend money, buy on credit, make an investment, or pay taxes without receiving, using, or dispensing financial information. Good decision-making depends on good information.

*The **Feature Story** helps you picture how the chapter topic relates to the real world of accounting and business.*

Feature Story

Knowing the Numbers

Many students who take this course do not plan to be accountants. If you are in that group, you might be thinking, "If I'm not going to be an accountant, why do I need to know accounting?" Well, consider this quote from Harold Geneen, the former chairman of **IT&T**: "To be good at your business, you have to know the numbers—cold." In business, accounting and financial statements are the means for communicating the numbers. If you don't know how to read financial statements, you can't really know your business.

Knowing the numbers is sometimes even a matter of corporate survival. Consider the story of **Columbia Sportswear Company**, headquartered in Portland, Oregon. Gert Boyle's family fled Nazi Germany when she was 13 years old and then purchased a small hat company in Oregon, Columbia Hat

Company. In 1971, Gert's husband, who was then running the company, died suddenly of a heart attack. The company was in the midst of an aggressive expansion, which had taken its sales above $1 million for the first time but which had also left the company financially stressed. Gert took over the small, struggling company with help from her son Tim, who was then a senior at the University of Oregon. Somehow, they kept the company afloat. Today, Columbia has more than 4,000 employees and annual sales in excess of $1 billion. Its brands include Columbia, Mountain Hardwear, Sorel, and Montrail. Gert still heads up the Board of Directors, and Tim is the company's President and CEO.

Columbia doesn't just focus on financial success. The company is very committed to corporate, social, and environmental responsibility. For example, several of its factories have participated in a project to increase health awareness of female factory workers in developing countries. Columbia was also a founding member of the Sustainable Apparel Coalition, which is a group that strives to reduce the environmental and social impact of the apparel industry. In addition, it monitors all of the independent factories that produce its products to ensure that they comply with the company's Standards of Manufacturing Practices. These standards address issues including forced labor, child labor, harassment, wages and benefits, health and safety, and the environment.

Employers such as Columbia Sportswear generally assume that managers in all areas of the company are "financially literate." To help prepare you for that, in this textbook you will learn how to read and prepare financial statements, and how to use basic tools to evaluate financial results.

*The **Chapter Outline** presents the chapter's topics and subtopics, as well as practice opportunities.*

Chapter Outline

LEARNING OBJECTIVES

LO 1 Identify the activities and users associated with accounting.	• Three activities • Who uses accounting data	**DO IT! 1** Basic Concepts
LO 2 Explain the building blocks of accounting: ethics, principles, and assumptions.	• Ethics • GAAP • Measurement principles • Assumptions	**DO IT! 2** Building Blocks of Accounting
LO 3 State the accounting equation, and define its components.	• Assets • Liabilities • Owner's equity	**DO IT! 3** Owner's Equity Effects
LO 4 Analyze the effects of business transactions on the accounting equation.	• Accounting transactions • Transaction analysis • Summary of transactions	**DO IT! 4** Tabular Analysis
LO 5 Describe the four financial statements and how they are prepared.	• Income statement • Owner's equity statement • Balance sheet • Statement of cash flows	**DO IT! 5** Financial Statement Items

Go to the Review and Practice section at the end of the chapter for a review of key concepts and practice applications with solutions.
Visit WileyPLUS with ORION for additional tutorials and practice opportunities.

Accounting Activities and Users

LEARNING OBJECTIVE 1

Identify the activities and users associated with accounting.

What consistently ranks as one of the top career opportunities in business? What frequently rates among the most popular majors on campus? What was the undergraduate degree chosen by **Nike** founder Phil Knight, **Home Depot** co-founder Arthur Blank, former acting director of the **Federal Bureau of Investigation (FBI)** Thomas Pickard, and numerous members of Congress? Accounting.[1] Why did these people choose accounting? They wanted to understand what was happening financially to their organizations. Accounting is the financial information system that provides these insights. In short, to understand your organization, you have to know the numbers.

Accounting consists of three basic activities—it **identifies**, **records**, and **communicates** the economic events of an organization to interested users. Let's take a closer look at these three activities.

__Essential terms__ are printed in blue when they first appear, and are defined in the end-of-chapter __Glossary Review__.

Three Activities

As a starting point to the accounting process, a company **identifies** the **economic events relevant to its business**. Examples of economic events are the sale of snack chips by **PepsiCo**, the provision of cell phone services by **AT&T**, and the payment of wages by **Facebook**.

Once a company like PepsiCo identifies economic events, it **records** those events in order to provide a history of its financial activities. Recording consists of keeping a **systematic, chronological diary of events**, measured in dollars and cents. In recording, PepsiCo also classifies and summarizes economic events.

Finally, PepsiCo **communicates** the collected information to interested users by means of **accounting reports**. The most common of these reports are called **financial statements**. To make the reported financial information meaningful, PepsiCo reports the recorded data in a standardized way. It accumulates information resulting from similar transactions. For example, PepsiCo accumulates all sales transactions over a certain period of time and reports the data as one amount in the company's financial statements. Such data are said to be reported **in the aggregate**. By presenting the recorded data in the aggregate, the accounting process simplifies a multitude of transactions and makes a series of activities understandable and meaningful.

A vital element in communicating economic events is the accountant's ability to **analyze and interpret** the reported information. Analysis involves use of ratios, percentages, graphs, and charts to highlight significant financial trends and relationships. Interpretation involves **explaining the uses, meaning, and limitations of reported data**. Appendices A–E show the financial statements of **Apple Inc.**, **PepsiCo Inc.**, **The Coca-Cola Company**, **Amazon.com, Inc.**, and **Wal-Mart Stores, Inc.**, respectively. (In addition, in the *A Look at IFRS* section at the end of each chapter, the French company **Louis Vuitton Moët Hennessy** is analyzed.) We refer to these statements at various places throughout the textbook. At this point, these financial statements probably strike you as complex and confusing. By the end of this course, you'll be surprised at your ability to understand, analyze, and interpret them.

[1] The appendix to this chapter describes job opportunities for accounting majors and explains why accounting is such a popular major.

Illustration 1.1 summarizes the activities of the accounting process.

ILLUSTRATION 1.1 **The activities of the accounting process**

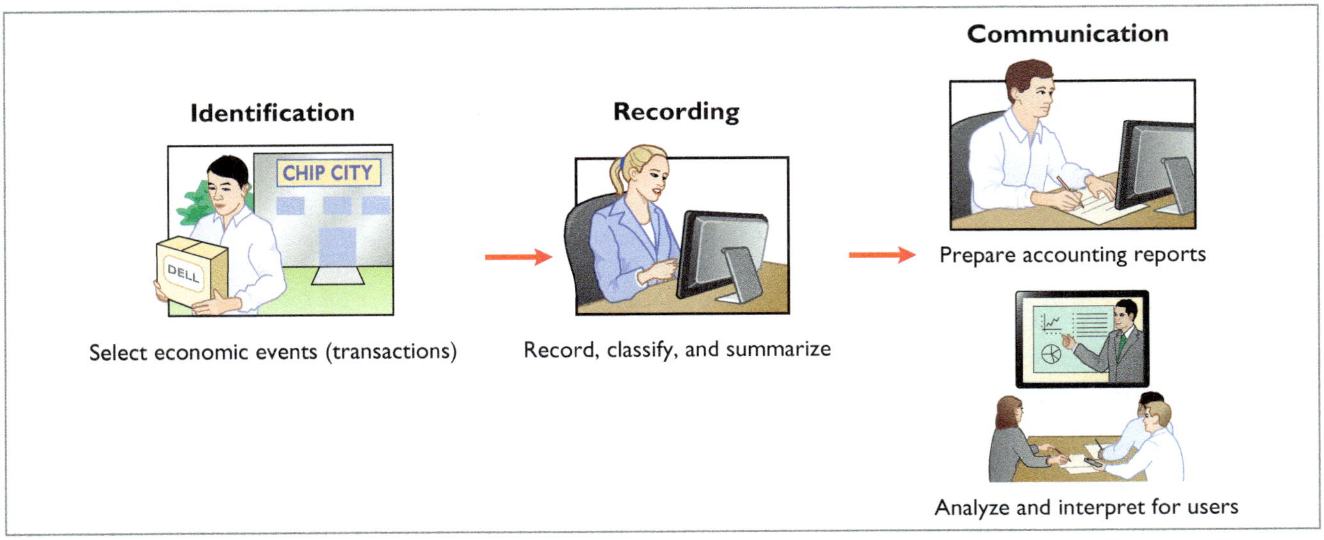

You should understand that the accounting process **includes** the bookkeeping function. **Bookkeeping** usually involves **only** the recording of economic events. It is therefore just one part of the accounting process. In total, accounting involves **the entire process of identifying, recording, and communicating economic events.**[2]

Who Uses Accounting Data

The financial information that users need depends upon the kinds of decisions they make. There are two broad groups of users of financial information: internal users and external users.

Internal Users

Internal users of accounting information are the managers who plan, organize, and run a business. These include marketing managers, production supervisors, finance directors, and company officers. In running a business, internal users must answer many important questions, as shown in **Illustration 1.2**.

ILLUSTRATION 1.2 **Questions that internal users ask**

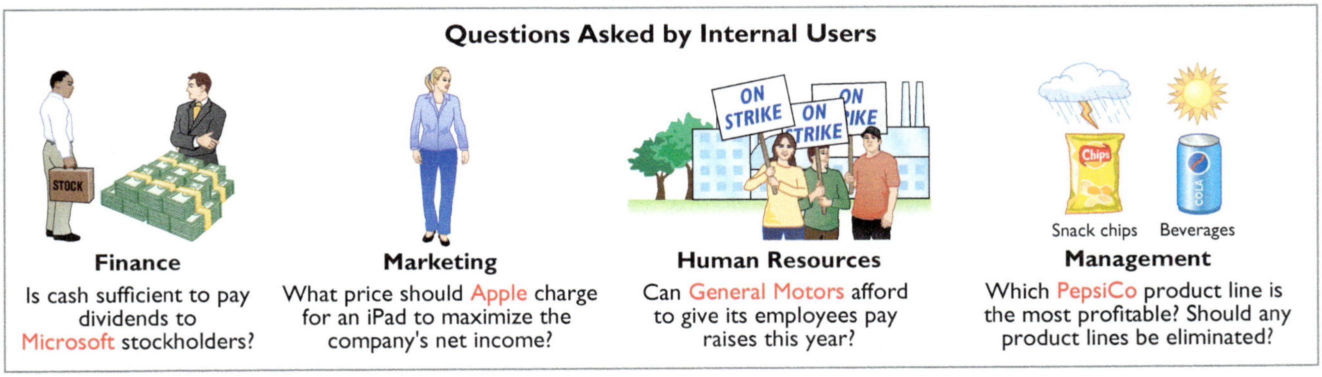

[2]The origins of accounting are generally attributed to the work of Luca Pacioli, an Italian Renaissance mathematician. Pacioli was a close friend and tutor to Leonardo da Vinci and a contemporary of Christopher Columbus. In his 1494 text *Summa de Arithmetica, Geometria, Proportione et Proportionalite*, Pacioli described a system to ensure that financial information was recorded efficiently and accurately.

To answer these and other questions, internal users need detailed information on a timely basis. **Managerial accounting** provides internal reports to help users make decisions about their companies. Examples are financial comparisons of operating alternatives, projections of income from new sales campaigns, and forecasts of cash needs for the next year.

Accounting Across the Organization — Clif Bar & Company

© Dan Moore/iStockphoto

Owning a Piece of the Bar

The original Clif Bar® energy bar was created in 1990 after six months of experimentation by Gary Erickson and his mother in her kitchen. Today, the company has almost 300 employees and is considered one of the leading Landor's Breakaway Brands®. One of **Clif Bar & Company**'s proudest moments was the creation of an employee stock ownership plan (ESOP) in 2010. This plan gives its employees 20% ownership of the company. The ESOP also resulted in Clif Bar enacting an open-book management program, including the commitment to educate all employee-owners about its finances. Armed with basic accounting knowledge, employees are more aware of the financial impact of their actions, which leads to better decisions.

What are the benefits to the company and to the employees of making the financial statements available to all employees? (Go to WileyPLUS for this answer and additional questions.)

Accounting Across the Organization *boxes demonstrate applications of accounting information in various business functions.*

External Users

External users are individuals and organizations outside a company who want financial information about the company. The two most common types of external users are investors and creditors. **Investors** (owners) use accounting information to decide whether to buy, hold, or sell ownership shares of a company. **Creditors** (such as suppliers and bankers) use accounting information to evaluate the risks of granting credit or lending money. **Illustration 1.3** shows some questions that investors and creditors may ask.

ILLUSTRATION 1.3 **Questions that external users ask**

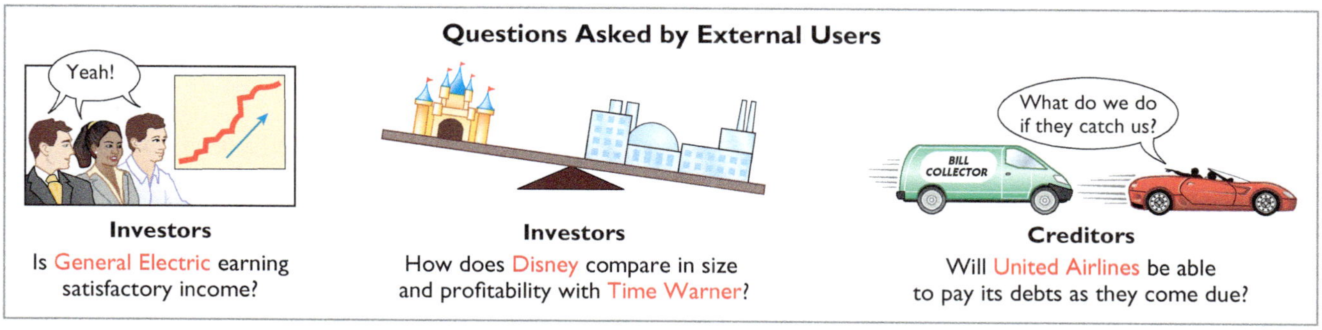

Financial accounting answers these questions. It provides economic and financial information for investors, creditors, and other external users. The information needs of external users vary considerably. **Taxing authorities**, such as the Internal Revenue Service, want to know whether the company complies with tax laws. **Regulatory agencies**, such as the Securities and Exchange Commission or the Federal Trade Commission, want to know whether the company is operating within prescribed rules. **Customers** are interested in whether a company like **Tesla Motors** will continue to honor product warranties and support its product lines. **Labor unions**, such as the **Major League Baseball Players Association**, want to know whether the owners have the ability to pay increased wages and benefits.

*The **DO IT!** exercises ask you to put newly acquired knowledge to work. They outline the **Action Plan** necessary to complete the exercise, and they show a **Solution**.*

DO IT! 1 | Basic Concepts

Indicate whether each of the five statements presented below is true or false. If false, indicate how to correct the statement.

1. The three steps in the accounting process are identification, recording, and communication.
2. Bookkeeping encompasses all steps in the accounting process.
3. Accountants prepare, but do not interpret, financial reports.
4. The two most common types of external users are investors and company officers.
5. Managerial accounting activities focus on reports for internal users.

ACTION PLAN

- **Review the basic concepts discussed.**
- **Develop an understanding of the key terms used.**

Solution

1. True **2.** False. Bookkeeping involves only the recording step. **3.** False. Accountants analyze and interpret information in reports as part of the communication step. **4.** False. The two most common types of external users are investors and creditors. **5.** True.

Related exercise material: **DO IT! 1.1, E1.1, and E1.2.**

The Building Blocks of Accounting

LEARNING OBJECTIVE 2

Explain the building blocks of accounting: ethics, principles, and assumptions.

A doctor follows certain protocols in treating a patient's illness. An architect follows certain structural guidelines in designing a building. Similarly, an accountant follows certain standards in reporting financial information. These standards are based on specific principles and assumptions. For these standards to work, however, a fundamental business concept must be present—ethical behavior.

Ethics in Financial Reporting

People won't gamble in a casino if they think it is "rigged." Similarly, people won't play the stock market if they think prices are rigged. At one time, the financial press was full of articles about financial scandals at **Enron**, **WorldCom**, **HealthSouth**, and **AIG**. As more scandals came to light, a mistrust of financial reporting in general seemed to be developing. One article in the *Wall Street Journal* noted that "repeated disclosures about questionable accounting practices have bruised investors' faith in the reliability of earnings reports, which in turn has sent stock prices tumbling." Imagine trying to carry on a business or invest money if you could not depend on the financial statements to be honestly prepared. Information would have no credibility. There is no doubt that a sound, well-functioning economy depends on accurate and dependable financial reporting.

United States regulators and lawmakers were very concerned that the economy would suffer if investors lost confidence in corporate accounting because of unethical financial reporting. In response, Congress passed the **Sarbanes-Oxley Act (SOX)** to reduce unethical corporate behavior and decrease the likelihood of future corporate scandals (see **Ethics Note**). As a result of SOX, top management must now certify the accuracy of financial information. In addition, penalties for fraudulent financial activity are much more severe. Also, SOX increased the independence requirements of the outside auditors who review the accuracy of corporate financial statements and increased the oversight role of boards of directors.

ETHICS NOTE

Circus-founder P.T. Barnum is alleged to have said, "Trust everyone, but cut the deck." What Sarbanes-Oxley does is to provide measures that (like cutting the deck of playing cards) help ensure that fraud will not occur.

***Ethics Notes** help sensitize you to some of the ethical issues in accounting.*

The standards of conduct by which actions are judged as right or wrong, honest or dishonest, fair or not fair, are **ethics**. Effective financial reporting depends on sound ethical behavior. To sensitize you to ethical situations in business and to give you practice at solving ethical dilemmas, we address ethics in a number of ways in this textbook:

1. A number of the *Feature Stories* and other parts of the textbook discuss the central importance of ethical behavior to financial reporting.
2. *Ethics Insight* boxes and marginal *Ethics Notes* highlight ethics situations and issues in actual business settings.
3. Many of the *People, Planet, and Profit Insight* boxes focus on ethical issues that companies face in measuring and reporting social and environmental issues.
4. At the end of the chapter, an *Ethics Case* simulates a business situation and asks you to put yourself in the position of a decision-maker in that case.

When analyzing these various ethics cases and your own ethical experiences, you should apply the three steps outlined in **Illustration 1.4**.

ILLUSTRATION 1.4 **Steps in analyzing ethics cases and situations**

1. Recognize an ethical situation and the ethical issues involved.
Use your personal ethics to identify ethical situations and issues. Some businesses and professional organizations provide written codes of ethics for guidance in some business situations.

2. Identify and analyze the principal elements in the situation.
Identify the **stakeholders**—persons or groups who may be harmed or benefited. Ask the question: What are the responsibilities and obligations of the parties involved?

3. Identify the alternatives, and weigh the impact of each alternative on various stakeholders.
Select the most ethical alternative, considering all the consequences. Sometimes there will be one right answer. Other situations involve more than one right solution; these situations require an evaluation of each and a selection of the best alternative.

***Insight** boxes provide examples of business situations from various perspectives—ethics, investor, international, and corporate social responsibility. Guideline answers to the critical thinking questions as well as additional questions are available in **WileyPLUS**.*

Ethics Insight Dewey & LeBoeuf LLP

© Alliance/Shutterstock

I Felt the Pressure—Would You?

"I felt the pressure." That's what some of the employees of the now-defunct law firm of **Dewey & LeBoeuf LLP** indicated when they helped to overstate revenue and use accounting tricks to hide losses and cover up cash shortages. These employees worked for the former finance director and former chief financial officer (CFO) of the firm. Here are some of their comments:

- "I was instructed by the CFO to create invoices, knowing they would not be sent to clients. When I created these invoices, I knew that it was inappropriate."
- "I intentionally gave the auditors incorrect information in the course of the audit."

What happened here is that a small group of lower-level employees over a period of years carried out the instructions of their bosses. Their bosses, however, seemed to have no concern as evidenced by various e-mails with one another in which they referred to their financial manipulations as accounting tricks, cooking the books, and fake income.

Source: Ashby Jones, "Guilty Pleas of Dewey Staff Detail the Alleged Fraud," *Wall Street Journal* (March 28, 2014).

Why did these employees lie, and what do you believe should be their penalty for these lies? (Go to WileyPLUS for this answer and additional questions.)

INTERNATIONAL NOTE

Over 115 countries use international standards (called IFRS). For example, all companies in the European Union follow IFRS. The differences between U.S. and international standards are not generally significant.

International Notes highlight differences between U.S. and international accounting standards.

Generally Accepted Accounting Principles

The accounting profession has developed standards that are generally accepted and universally practiced. This common set of standards is called **generally accepted accounting principles (GAAP)**. These standards indicate how to report economic events.

The primary accounting standard-setting body in the United States is the **Financial Accounting Standards Board (FASB)**. The **Securities and Exchange Commission (SEC)** is the agency of the U.S. government that oversees U.S. financial markets and accounting standard-setting bodies. The SEC relies on the FASB to develop accounting standards, which public companies must follow. Many countries outside of the United States have adopted the accounting standards issued by the **International Accounting Standards Board (IASB)**. These standards are called **International Financial Reporting Standards (IFRS)** (see **International Note**).

As markets become more global, it is often desirable to compare the results of companies from different countries that report using different accounting standards. In order to increase comparability, in recent years the two standard-setting bodies have made efforts to reduce the differences between U.S. GAAP and IFRS. This process is referred to as **convergence**. As a result of these convergence efforts, someday there may be a single set of high-quality accounting standards that are used by companies around the world. Because convergence is such an important issue, we highlight any major differences between GAAP and IFRS in *International Notes* (as shown in the margin here) and provide a more in-depth discussion in the *A Look at* IFRS section at the end of each chapter.

International Insight

Toru-Hanai-Pool/Getty Images, Inc.

The Korean Discount

If you think that accounting standards don't matter, consider these events in South Korea. For many years, international investors complained that the financial reports of South Korean companies were inadequate and inaccurate. Accounting practices there often resulted in huge differences between stated revenues and actual revenues. Because investors did not have faith in the accuracy of the numbers, they were unwilling to pay as much for the shares of these companies relative to shares of comparable companies in different countries. This difference in share price was often referred to as the "Korean discount."

In response, Korean regulators decided that companies would have to comply with international accounting standards. This change was motivated by a desire to "make the country's businesses more transparent" in order to build investor confidence and spur economic growth. Many other Asian countries, including China, India, Japan, and Hong Kong, have also decided either to adopt international standards or to create standards that are based on the international standards.

Source: Evan Ramstad, "End to 'Korea Discount'?" *Wall Street Journal* (March 16, 2007).

What is meant by the phrase "make the country's businesses more transparent"? Why would increasing transparency spur economic growth? (Go to WileyPLUS for this answer and additional questions.)

Measurement Principles

HELPFUL HINT

***Relevance* and *faithful representation* are two primary qualities that make accounting information useful for decision-making.**

Helpful Hints further clarify concepts being discussed.

GAAP generally uses one of two measurement principles, the historical cost principle or the fair value principle. Selection of which principle to follow generally relates to trade-offs between relevance and faithful representation (see **Helpful Hint**). **Relevance** means that financial information is capable of making a difference in a decision. **Faithful representation** means that the numbers and descriptions match what really existed or happened—they are factual.

Historical Cost Principle

The **historical cost principle** (or cost principle) dictates that companies record assets at their cost. This is true not only at the time the asset is purchased, but also over the time the asset is held. For example, if **Best Buy** purchases land for $300,000, the company initially reports it in its accounting records at $300,000. But what does Best Buy do if, by the end of the next year, the fair value of the land has increased to $400,000? Under the historical cost principle, it continues to report the land at $300,000.

Fair Value Principle

The **fair value principle** states that assets and liabilities should be reported at fair value (the price received to sell an asset or settle a liability). Fair value information may be more useful than historical cost for certain types of assets and liabilities. For example, certain investment securities are reported at fair value because market price information is usually readily available for these types of assets. In determining which measurement principle to use, companies weigh the factual nature of cost figures versus the relevance of fair value. In general, most companies choose to use cost. Only in situations where assets are actively traded, such as investment securities, do companies apply the fair value principle extensively.

Assumptions

Assumptions provide a foundation for the accounting process. Two main assumptions are the **monetary unit assumption** and the **economic entity assumption**.

Monetary Unit Assumption

The **monetary unit assumption** requires that companies include in the accounting records only transaction data that can be expressed in money terms. This assumption enables accounting to quantify (measure) economic events. The monetary unit assumption is vital to applying the historical cost principle.

This assumption prevents the inclusion of some relevant information in the accounting records. For example, the health of a company's owner, the quality of service, and the morale of employees are not included. The reason: Companies cannot quantify this information in money terms. Though this information is important, companies record only events that can be measured in money.

Economic Entity Assumption

An economic entity can be any organization or unit in society. It may be a company (such as **Crocs, Inc.**), a governmental unit (the state of Ohio), a municipality (Seattle), a school district (St. Louis District 48), or a church (Southern Baptist). The **economic entity assumption** requires that the activities of the entity be kept separate and distinct from the activities of its owner and all other economic entities (see **Ethics Note**). To illustrate, Sally Rider, owner of Sally's Boutique, must keep her personal living costs separate from the expenses of the business. Similarly, **J. Crew** and **Gap Inc.** are segregated into separate economic entities for accounting purposes.

> **ETHICS NOTE**
>
> **The importance of the economic entity assumption is illustrated by scandals involving Adelphia. In this case, senior company employees entered into transactions that blurred the line between the employees' financial interests and those of the company. For example, Adelphia guaranteed over $2 billion of loans to the founding family.**

Proprietorship. A business owned by one person is generally a **proprietorship**. The owner is often the manager/operator of the business. Small service-type businesses (plumbing companies, beauty salons, and auto repair shops), farms, and small retail stores (antique shops, clothing stores, and used-book stores) are often proprietorships. **Usually, only a relatively small amount of money (capital) is necessary to start in business as a proprietorship. The owner (proprietor) receives any profits, suffers any losses, and is personally liable for all debts of the business.** There is no legal distinction between the business as an economic unit and the owner, but the accounting records of the business activities are kept separate from the personal records and activities of the owner.

Partnership. A business owned by two or more persons associated as partners is a **partnership**. In most respects a partnership is like a proprietorship except that more than one owner is involved. Typically, a partnership agreement (written or oral) sets forth such terms as initial investment, duties of each partner, division of net income (or net loss), and settlement to be made upon death or withdrawal of a partner. Each partner generally has unlimited personal liability for the debts of the partnership. **Like a proprietorship, for accounting purposes the partnership transactions must be kept separate from the personal activities of the partners.** Partnerships are often used to organize retail and service-type businesses, including professional practices (lawyers, doctors, architects, and certified public accountants).

Corporation. A business organized as a separate legal entity under state corporation law and having ownership divided into transferable shares of stock is a **corporation**. The holders of the shares (stockholders) **enjoy limited liability**; that is, they are not personally liable for the debts of the corporate entity. Stockholders **may transfer all or part of their ownership shares to other investors at any time** (i.e., sell their shares). The ease with which ownership can change adds to the attractiveness of investing in a corporation. Because ownership can be transferred without dissolving the corporation, the corporation **enjoys an unlimited life**.

Although the combined number of proprietorships and partnerships in the United States is more than five times the number of corporations, the revenue produced by corporations is eight times greater. Most of the largest companies in the United States—for example, **ExxonMobil**, **Ford**, **Wal-Mart Stores, Inc.**, **Citigroup**, and **Apple**—are corporations.

Accounting Across the Organization

Josef Volavka/iStockphoto

Spinning the Career Wheel

How will the study of accounting help you? A working knowledge of accounting is desirable for virtually every field of business. Some examples of how accounting is used in business careers include:

General management: Managers at **Ford Motors**, Massachusetts General Hospital, California State University—Fullerton, a **McDonald's** franchise, and a **Trek** bike shop all need to understand accounting data in order to make wise business decisions.

Marketing: Marketing specialists at **Procter & Gamble** must be sensitive to costs and benefits, which accounting helps them quantify and understand. Making a sale is meaningless unless it is a profitable sale.

Finance: Do you want to be a banker for **Citicorp**, an investment analyst for **Goldman Sachs**, or a stock broker for **Merrill Lynch**? These fields rely heavily on accounting knowledge to analyze financial statements. In fact, it is difficult to get a good job in a finance function without two or three courses in accounting.

Real estate: Are you interested in being a real estate broker for **Prudential Real Estate**? Because a third party—the bank—is almost always involved in financing a real estate transaction, brokers must understand the numbers involved: Can the buyer afford to make the payments to the bank? Does the cash flow from an industrial property justify the purchase price? What are the tax benefits of the purchase?

How might accounting help you? (Go to WileyPLUS for this answer and additional questions.)

DO IT! 2 | Building Blocks of Accounting

Indicate whether each of the five statements presented below is true or false. If false, indicate how to correct the statement.

1. Congress passed the Sarbanes-Oxley Act to reduce unethical behavior and decrease the likelihood of future corporate scandals.
2. The primary accounting standard-setting body in the United States is the Financial Accounting Standards Board (FASB).
3. The historical cost principle dictates that companies record assets at their cost. In later periods, however, the fair value of the asset must be used if fair value is higher than its cost.
4. Relevance means that financial information matches what really happened; the information is factual.
5. A business owner's personal expenses must be separated from expenses of the business to comply with accounting's economic entity assumption.

ACTION PLAN

- **Review the discussion of ethics and financial reporting standards.**
- **Develop an understanding of the key terms used.**

Solution

1. True. **2.** True. **3.** False. The historical cost principle dictates that companies record assets at their cost. Under the historical cost principle, the company must also use cost in later periods. **4.** False. Faithful representation, not relevance, means that financial information matches what really happened; the information is factual. **5.** True.

Related exercise material: **DO IT! 1.2, E1.3, and E1.4.**

The Accounting Equation

LEARNING OBJECTIVE 3

State the accounting equation, and define its components.

The two basic elements of a business are what it owns and what it owes. **Assets** are the resources a business owns. For example, **Alphabet Inc.** has total assets of approximately $167.5 billion. Liabilities and owner's equity are the rights or claims against these resources. Thus, Alphabet has $167.5 billion of claims against its $167.5 billion of assets. Claims of those to whom the company owes money (creditors) are called **liabilities**. Claims of owners are called **owner's equity**. Alphabet has liabilities of $28.5 billion and owners' equity of $139.0 billion.

We can express the relationship of assets, liabilities, and owner's equity as an equation, as shown in **Illustration 1.5**.

Assets	=	Liabilities	+	Owner's Equity

ILLUSTRATION 1.5
The basic accounting equation

This relationship is the **basic accounting equation**. Assets must equal the sum of liabilities and owner's equity. Liabilities appear before owner's equity in the basic accounting equation because they are paid first if a business is liquidated.

The accounting equation applies to all **economic entities** regardless of size, nature of business, or form of business organization. It applies to a small proprietorship such as a corner grocery store as well as to a giant corporation such as **PepsiCo**. The equation provides the **underlying framework** for recording and summarizing economic events.

Let's look in more detail at the categories in the basic accounting equation.

Assets

As noted above, **assets** are resources a business owns. The business uses its assets in carrying out such activities as production and sales. The common characteristic possessed by all assets is **the capacity to provide future services or benefits**. In a business, that service potential or future economic benefit eventually results in cash inflows (receipts). For example, consider Campus Pizza, a local restaurant. It owns a delivery truck that provides economic benefits from delivering pizzas. Other assets of Campus Pizza are tables, chairs, jukebox, cash register, oven, tableware, and, of course, cash.

Liabilities

Liabilities are claims against assets—that is, existing debts and obligations. Businesses of all sizes usually borrow money and purchase merchandise on credit. These economic activities result in payables of various sorts:

- Campus Pizza, for instance, purchases cheese, sausage, flour, and beverages on credit from suppliers. These obligations are called **accounts payable**.

- Campus Pizza also has a **note payable** to First National Bank for the money borrowed to purchase the delivery truck.
- Campus Pizza may also have **salaries and wages payable** to employees and **sales and real estate taxes payable** to the local government.

All of these persons or entities to whom Campus Pizza owes money are its **creditors**.

Creditors may legally force the liquidation of a business that does not pay its debts. In that case, the law requires that creditor claims be paid **before** ownership claims.

Owner's Equity

HELPFUL HINT

In some places, we use the term "owner's equity" and in others we use "owners' equity." ***Owner's*** **(singular, possessive) refers to one owner (the case with a sole proprietorship).** ***Owners'*** **(plural, possessive) refers to multiple owners (the case with partnerships or corporations).**

The ownership claim on total assets is **owner's equity** (see **Helpful Hint**). It is equal to total assets minus total liabilities. Here is why: The assets of a business are claimed by either creditors or owners. To find out what belongs to owners, we subtract the creditors' claims (the liabilities) from assets. The remainder is the owner's claim on the assets—the owner's equity. Since the claims of creditors must be paid **before** ownership claims, owner's equity is often referred to as **residual equity**.

Increases in Owner's Equity

In a proprietorship, owner's investments and revenues increase owner's equity.

Investments by Owner. **Investments by owner** are the assets the owner puts into the business. These investments increase owner's equity. They are recorded in a category called **owner's capital**.

Revenues. **Revenues** are the **increases in assets or decreases in liabilities resulting from the sale of goods or the performance of services in the normal course of business**. Revenues usually result in an increase in an asset. They may arise from different sources and are called different names depending on the nature of the business. Campus Pizza, for instance, has two categories of sales revenues—pizza sales and beverage sales.

Decreases in Owner's Equity

In a proprietorship, owner's drawings and expenses decrease owner's equity.

Drawings. An owner may withdraw cash or other assets for personal use. We use a separate classification called **drawings** to determine the total withdrawals for each accounting period. **Drawings decrease owner's equity.** They are recorded in a category called owner's drawings.

Expenses. **Expenses** are the cost of assets consumed or services used in the process of generating revenue. They are **decreases in owner's equity that result from operating the business**. For example, Campus Pizza recognizes the following expenses: cost of ingredients (meat, flour, cheese, tomato paste, mushrooms, etc.); cost of beverages; salaries and wages expense; utilities expense (electric, gas, and water expense); delivery expense (gasoline, repairs, licenses, etc.); supplies expense (napkins, detergents, aprons, etc.); rent expense; interest expense; and property tax expense.

In summary, owner's equity is increased by an owner's investments and by revenues from business operations. Owner's equity is decreased by an owner's withdrawals of assets and by expenses. **Illustration 1.6** expands the basic accounting equation by showing the items that comprise owner's equity. This format is referred to as the **expanded accounting equation**.

ILLUSTRATION 1.6 Expanded accounting equation

Basic Equation	**Assets**	=	**Liabilities**	+	**Owner's Equity**									
Expanded Equation	**Assets**	=	**Liabilities**	+	**Owner's Capital**	−	**Owner's Drawings**	+	**Revenues**	−	**Expenses**			

DO IT! 3 | Owner's Equity Effects

Classify the following items as investment by owner (I), owner's drawings (D), revenues (R), or expenses (E). Then indicate whether each item increases or decreases owner's equity.

1. Rent Expense.
2. Service Revenue.
3. Drawings.
4. Salaries and Wages Expense.

Solution

1. Rent Expense is an expense (E); it decreases owner's equity. **2.** Service Revenue is revenue (R); it increases owner's equity. **3.** Drawings is owner's drawings (D); it decreases owner's equity. **4.** Salaries and Wages Expense is an expense (E); it decreases owner's equity.

Related exercise material: **BE1.1, BE1.2, BE1.3, BE1.4, BE1.5, BE1.6, DO IT! 1.3, and E1.5.**

ACTION PLAN

- **Understand the sources of revenue.**
- **Understand what causes expenses.**
- **Review the rules for changes in owner's equity.**
- **Recognize that drawings are withdrawals of cash or other assets from the business for personal use.**

Analyzing Business Transactions

LEARNING OBJECTIVE 4

Analyze the effects of business transactions on the accounting equation.

*This **accounting cycle graphic** illustrates the steps companies follow each period to record transactions and eventually prepare financial statements.*

The system of collecting and processing transaction data and communicating financial information to decision-makers is known as the **accounting information system**. Factors that shape an accounting information system include the nature of the company's business, the types of transactions, the size of the company, the volume of data, and the information demands of management and others.

Most businesses use computerized accounting systems—sometimes referred to as electronic data processing (EDP) systems. These systems handle all the steps involved in the recording process, from initial data entry to preparation of the financial statements. In order to remain competitive, companies continually improve their accounting systems to provide accurate and timely data for decision-making. For example, in a recent annual report, **Tootsie Roll** stated, "We also invested in additional processing and data storage hardware during the year. We view information technology as a key strategic tool, and are committed to deploying leading edge technology in this area." In addition, many companies have upgraded their accounting information systems in response to the requirements of Sarbanes-Oxley.

Accounting information systems rely on a process referred to as **the accounting cycle**. As you can see from the graphic above, the accounting cycle begins with the analysis of business transactions and ends with the preparation of a post-closing trial balance. We explain each of the steps, starting in this chapter and continuing in Chapters 2–4.

In this textbook, in order to emphasize the underlying concepts and principles, we focus on a manual accounting system. The accounting concepts and principles do not change whether a system is computerized or manual.

Accounting Transactions

Transactions (**business transactions**) are a business's economic events recorded by accountants. Transactions may be external or internal. **External transactions** involve economic events between the company and some outside enterprise. For example, Campus Pizza's purchase of cooking equipment from a supplier, payment of monthly rent to the landlord, and sale of pizzas to customers are external transactions. **Internal transactions** are economic events that occur entirely within one company. The use of cooking and cleaning supplies are internal transactions for Campus Pizza.

Companies carry on many activities that do not represent business transactions. Examples are hiring employees, responding to e-mails, talking with customers, and placing merchandise orders. Some of these activities may lead to business transactions. Employees will earn wages, and suppliers will deliver ordered merchandise. The company must analyze each event to find out if it affects the components of the accounting equation. If it does, the company will record the transaction. **Illustration 1.7** demonstrates the transaction identification process.

ILLUSTRATION 1.7 **Transaction identification process**

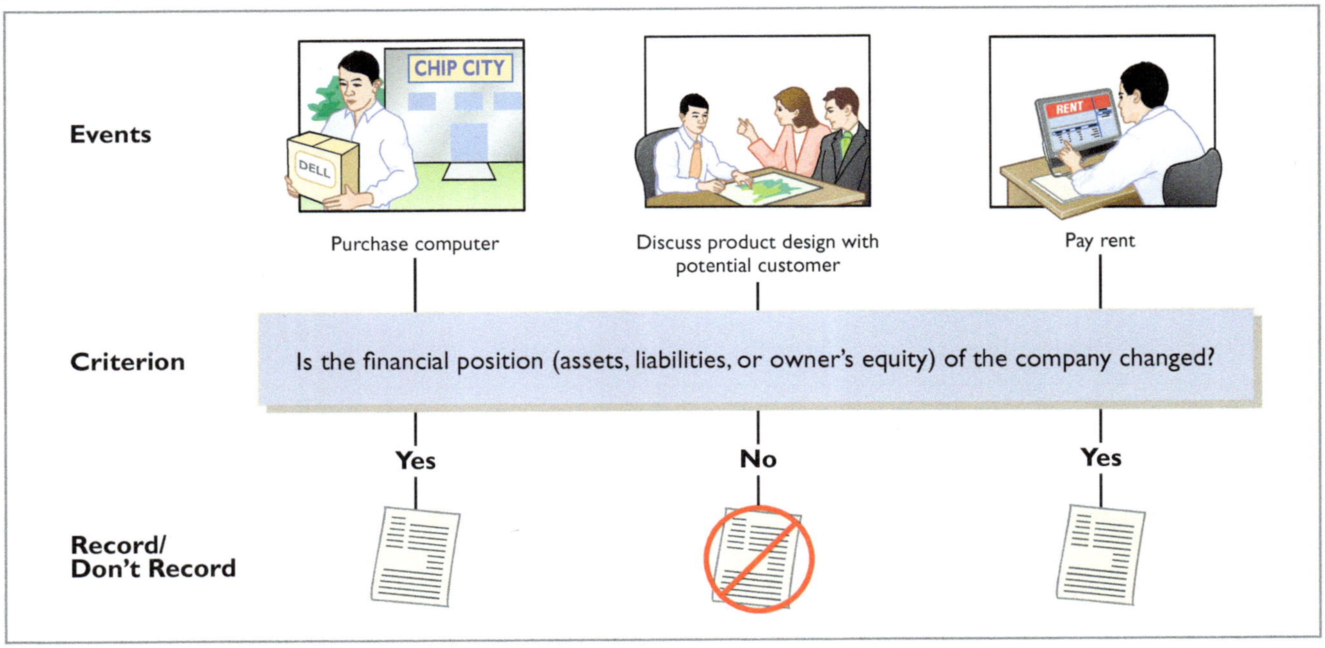

Each transaction must have a dual effect on the accounting equation. For example, if an asset is increased, there must be a corresponding:

- Decrease in another asset, *or*
- Increase in a specific liability, *or*
- Increase in owner's equity.

Two or more items could be affected. For example, as one asset is increased $10,000, another asset could decrease $6,000 and a liability could increase $4,000. Any change in a liability or ownership claim is subject to similar analysis.

HELPFUL HINT

Study these transactions until you are sure you understand them. They are not difficult, but understanding them is important to your success in this course. The ability to analyze transactions in terms of the basic accounting equation is essential in accounting.

Transaction Analysis

To demonstrate how to analyze transactions in terms of the accounting equation, we will review the business activities of Softbyte, a smartphone app development company (see **Helpful Hint**). Softbyte is the creation of Ray Neal, an entrepreneur who wants to create focused apps that inspire and engage users of all ages. Ray was encouraged to start his own business after the success of "FoodAlert," a customizable app he developed that tracks the daily location of local food trucks. The following business transactions occur during Softbyte's first month of operations.

Transaction (1). Investment of Cash by Owner. Ray Neal starts a smartphone app development company which he names Softbyte. On September 1, 2020, he invests $15,000 cash in the business. This transaction results in an equal increase in assets and owner's equity.

Basic Analysis	The asset Cash increases $15,000, and owner's equity (specifically Owner's Capital) increases $15,000.

Equation Analysis

	Assets	=	Liabilities	+	Owner's Equity	
	Cash	=			Owner's Capital	
(1)	+$15,000	=			+$15,000	Initial investment

Observe that the equality of the accounting equation has been maintained. Note that the investments by the owner do not represent revenues, and they are excluded in determining net income. Therefore, it is necessary to make clear that the increase is an investment (increasing Owner's Capital) rather than revenue.

Transaction (2). Purchase of Equipment for Cash. Softbyte purchases computer equipment for $7,000 cash. This transaction results in an equal increase and decrease in total assets, though the composition of assets changes.

Basic Analysis	The asset Cash decreases $7,000, and the asset Equipment increases $7,000.

Equation Analysis

	Assets			=	Liabilities	+	Owner's Equity
	Cash	+	Equipment	=			Owner's Capital
	$15,000						$15,000
(2)	−7,000		+$7,000				
	$ 8,000	+	$7,000	=			$15,000
	$15,000						

Observe that total assets are still $15,000. Owner's equity also remains at $15,000, the amount of Ray Neal's original investment.

Transaction (3). Purchase of Supplies on Credit. Softbyte purchases headsets (and other computer accessories expected to last several months) for $1,600 from Mobile Solutions. Mobile Solutions agrees to allow Softbyte to pay this bill in October. This transaction is a purchase on account (a credit purchase). Assets increase because of the expected future benefits of using the headsets and computer accessories, and liabilities increase by the amount due to Mobile Solutions.

Basic Analysis The asset Supplies increases $1,600, and the liability Accounts Payable increases $1,600.

Equation Analysis

	Assets					=	Liabilities	+	Owner's Equity
	Cash	+	Supplies	+	Equipment	=	Accounts Payable	+	Owner's Capital
	$8,000				$7,000				$15,000
(3)			+$1,600				+$1,600		
	$8,000	+	$1,600	+	$7,000	=	$1,600	+	$15,000
			$16,600					$16,600	

Total assets are now $16,600. This total is matched by a $1,600 creditor's claim and a $15,000 ownership claim.

Transaction (4). Services Performed for Cash. Softbyte receives $1,200 cash from customers for app development services it has performed. This transaction represents Softbyte's principal revenue-producing activity. Recall that **revenue increases owner's equity**.

Basic Analysis The asset Cash increases $1,200, and owner's equity increases $1,200 due to Service Revenue.

Equation Analysis

	Assets					=	Liabilities	+	Owner's Equity			
	Cash	+	Supplies	+	Equipment	=	Accounts Payable	+	Owner's Capital	+	Revenues	
	$8,000		$1,600		$7,000		$1,600		$15,000			
(4)	+1,200										+$1,200	Service Revenue
	$9,200	+	$1,600	+	$7,000	=	$1,600	+	$15,000	+	$1,200	
			$17,800						$17,800			

The two sides of the equation balance at $17,800. Service Revenue is included in determining Softbyte's net income.

Note that we do not have room to give details for each individual revenue and expense account in this illustration. Thus, revenues (and expenses when we get to them) are summarized under one column heading for Revenues and one for Expenses. However, it is important to keep track of the category (account) titles affected (e.g., Service Revenue) as they will be needed when we prepare financial statements later in the chapter.

Transaction (5). Purchase of Advertising on Credit. Softbyte receives a bill for $250 from the *Daily News* for advertising on its online website but postpones payment until a later date. This transaction results in an increase in liabilities and a decrease in owner's equity.

Basic Analysis The liability Accounts Payable increases $250, and owner's equity decreases $250 due to Advertising Expense.

Equation Analysis

	Assets					=	Liabilities	+	Owner's Equity					
	Cash	+	Supplies	+	Equipment	=	Accounts Payable	+	Owner's Capital	+	Revenues	−	Expenses	
	$9,200		$1,600		$7,000		$1,600		$15,000		$1,200			
(5)							+250						−$250	Advertising Expense
	$9,200	+	$1,600	+	$7,000	=	$1,850	+	$15,000	+	$1,200	−	$ 250	
			$17,800						$17,800					

The two sides of the equation still balance at $17,800. Owner's equity decreases when Softbyte incurs the expense. Expenses are not always paid in cash at the time they are incurred. When Softbyte pays at a later date, the liability Accounts Payable will decrease, and the asset Cash will decrease [see Transaction (8)]. The cost of advertising is an expense (rather than an asset) because the company has **used** the benefits. Advertising Expense is included in determining net income.

Transaction (6). Services Performed for Cash and Credit. Softbyte performs $3,500 of app development services for customers. The company receives cash of $1,500 from customers, and it bills the balance of $2,000 on account. This transaction results in an equal increase in assets and owner's equity.

Basic Analysis	Three specific items are affected: The asset Cash increases $1,500, the asset Accounts Receivable increases $2,000, and owner's equity increases $3,500 due to Service Revenue.

Equation Analysis

	Assets				= Liabilities +	Owner's Equity			
	Cash	+ Accounts Receivable	+ Supplies	+ Equipment	= Accounts Payable	+ Owner's Capital	+ Revenues	− Expenses	
	$9,200		$1,600	$7,000	$1,850	$15,000	$1,200	$250	
(6)	+1,500	+$2,000					+3,500		Service Revenue
	$10,700 +	$ 2,000 +	$1,600 +	$7,000	= $1,850	+ $15,000 +	$4,700 −	$250	
	$21,300				$21,300				

Softbyte recognizes $3,500 in revenue when it performs the service. In exchange for this service, it received $1,500 in Cash and Accounts Receivable of $2,000. This Accounts Receivable represents customers' promises to pay $2,000 to Softbyte in the future. When it later receives collections on account, Softbyte will increase Cash and will decrease Accounts Receivable [see Transaction (9)].

Transaction (7). Payment of Expenses. Softbyte pays the following expenses in cash for September: office rent $600, salaries and wages of employees $900, and utilities $200. These payments result in an equal decrease in assets and owner's equity.

Basic Analysis	The asset Cash decreases $1,700, and owner's equity decreases $1,700 due to the specific expense categories (Rent Expense, Salaries and Wages Expense, and Utilities Expense).

Equation Analysis

	Assets				= Liabilities +	Owner's Equity			
	Cash	+ Accounts Receivable	+ Supplies	+ Equipment	= Accounts Payable	+ Owner's Capital	+ Revenues	− Expenses	
	$10,700	$2,000	$1,600	$7,000	$1,850	$15,000	$4,700	$ 250	
(7)	−1,700							−600	Rent Expense
								−900	Sal. and Wages Exp.
								−200	Utilities Exp.
	$9,000 +	$2,000 +	$1,600 +	$7,000	= $1,850	+ $15,000 +	$4,700 −	$1,950	
	$19,600				$19,600				

The two sides of the equation now balance at $19,600. Three lines in the analysis indicate the different types of expenses that have been incurred.

Transaction (8). Payment of Accounts Payable. Softbyte pays its $250 *Daily News* bill in cash. The company previously [in Transaction (5)] recorded the bill as an increase in Accounts Payable and a decrease in owner's equity.

Basic Analysis

This cash payment "on account" decreases the asset Cash by $250 and also decreases the liability Accounts Payable by $250.

Equation Analysis

	Assets							=	Liabilities	+	Owner's Equity				
	Cash	+	Accounts Receivable	+	Supplies	+	Equipment	=	Accounts Payable	+	Owner's Capital	+	Revenues	−	Expenses
	$9,000		$2,000		$1,600		$7,000		$1,850		$15,000		$4,700		$1,950
(8)	−250								−250						
	$8,750	+	$2,000	+	$1,600	+	$7,000	=	$1,600	+	$15,000	+	$4,700	−	$1,950
	$19,350								$19,350						

Observe that the payment of a liability related to an expense that has previously been recorded does not affect owner's equity. The company recorded this expense in Transaction (5) and should not record it again.

Transaction (9). Receipt of Cash on Account. Softbyte receives $600 in cash from customers who had been billed for services [in Transaction (6)]. Transaction (9) does not change total assets, but it changes the composition of those assets.

Basic Analysis

The asset Cash increases $600, and the asset Accounts Receivable decreases $600.

Equation Analysis

	Assets							=	Liabilities	+	Owner's Equity				
	Cash	+	Accounts Receivable	+	Supplies	+	Equipment	=	Accounts Payable	+	Owner's Capital	+	Revenues	−	Expenses
	$8,750		$2,000		$1,600		$7,000		$1,600		$15,000		$4,700		$1,950
(9)	+600		−600												
	$9,350	+	$1,400	+	$1,600	+	$7,000	=	$1,600	+	$15,000	+	$4,700	−	$1,950
	$19,350								$19,350						

Note that the collection of an account receivable for services previously billed and recorded does not affect owner's equity. Softbyte already recorded this revenue in Transaction (6) and should not record it again.

Transaction (10). Withdrawal of Cash by Owner. Ray Neal withdraws $1,300 in cash from the business for his personal use. This transaction results in an equal decrease in assets and owner's equity.

Basic Analysis

The asset Cash decreases $1,300, and owner's equity decreases $1,300 due to owner's withdrawal (Owner's Drawings).

Equation Analysis

	Assets							=	Liabilities	+	Owner's Equity							
	Cash	+	Accounts Receivable	+	Supplies	+	Equipment	=	Accounts Payable	+	Owner's Capital	−	Owner's Drawings	+	Revenues	−	Expenses	
	$9,350		$1,400		$1,600		$7,000		$1,600		$15,000				$4,700		$1,950	
(10)	−1,300												−$1,300					Drawings
	$8,050	+	$1,400	+	$1,600	+	$7,000	=	$1,600	+	$15,000	−	$1,300	+	$4,700	−	$1,950	
	$18,050								$18,050									

Observe that the effect of a cash withdrawal by the owner is the opposite of the effect of an investment by the owner. **Owner's drawings are not expenses.** Expenses are incurred for the purpose of earning revenue. Drawings do not generate revenue. They are a **disinvestment**. Like owner's investment, the company excludes owner's drawings in determining net income.

Summary of Transactions

Illustration 1.8 summarizes the September transactions of Softbyte to show their cumulative effect on the basic accounting equation. It also indicates the transaction number and the specific effects of each transaction.

Illustration 1.8 demonstrates some significant facts:

1. Each transaction is analyzed in terms of its effect on:
    a. The three components of the basic accounting equation (assets, liabilities, and owner's equity).
    b. Specific types (kinds) of items within each component (such as the asset Cash).
2. The two sides of the equation must always be equal.
3. The Owner's Capital, Owner's Drawings, Revenues, and Expenses columns indicate the causes of each change in the owner's claim on assets.

ILLUSTRATION 1.8 **Tabular summary of Softbyte transactions**

	Assets				= Liabilities +	Owner's Equity				
Trans-action	Cash	+ Accounts Receivable	+ Supplies	+ Equipment	= Accounts Payable	+ Owner's Capital	− Owner's Drawings	+ Rev.	− Exp.	
(1)	+$15,000					+ $15,000				Initial invest.
(2)	−7,000			+$7,000						
(3)			+$1,600		+$1,600					
(4)	+1,200							+$1,200		Service Revenue
(5)					+250				−$250	Adver. Expense
(6)	+1,500	+$2,000						+3,500		Service Revenue
(7)	−600								−600	Rent Expense
	−900								−900	Sal./Wages Exp.
	−200								−200	Utilities Expense
(8)	−250				−250					
(9)	+600	−600								
(10)	−1,300						−$1,300			Drawings
	$ 8,050 +	$1,400 +	$1,600 +	$7,000 =	$1,600 +	$15,000 −	$1,300 +	$4,700 −	$1,950	
	$18,050				$18,050					

There! You made it through your first transaction analysis. If you feel a bit shaky on any of the transactions, it might be a good idea at this point to get up, take a short break, and come back again for a brief (10- to 15-minute) review of the transactions, to make sure you understand them before you go on to the next section.

DO IT! 4 | Tabular Analysis

Transactions made by Virmari & Co., a public accounting firm, for the month of August are shown below. Prepare a tabular analysis which shows the effects of these transactions on the expanded accounting equation, similar to that shown in Illustration 1.8.

1. The owner invested $25,000 cash in the business.
2. The company purchased $7,000 of office equipment on credit.
3. The company received $8,000 cash in exchange for services performed.
4. The company paid $850 for this month's rent.
5. The owner withdrew $1,000 cash for personal use.

ACTION PLAN

- **Analyze the effects of each transaction on the accounting equation.**
- **Use appropriate category names (not descriptions).**
- **Keep the accounting equation in balance.**

Solution

	Assets			=	Liabilities	+	Owner's Equity							
Trans-action	Cash	+	Equipment	=	Accounts Payable	+	Owner's Capital	−	Owner's Drawings	+	Revenues	−	Expenses	
(1)	+$25,000						+$25,000							
(2)			+$7,000		+$7,000									
(3)	+8,000										+$8,000			Service Revenue
(4)	−850												−$850	Rent Expense
(5)	−1,000								−$1,000					Drawings
	$31,150	+	$7,000	=	$7,000	+	$25,000	−	$1,000	+	$8,000	−	$850	
	$38,150				$38,150									

Related exercise material: **BE1.7, BE1.9, DO IT! 1.4, E1.6, E1.7, and E1.8.**

The Four Financial Statements

LEARNING OBJECTIVE 5

Describe the four financial statements and how they are prepared.

HELPFUL HINT

The income statement, owner's equity statement, and statement of cash flows are all for a *period* of time, whereas the balance sheet is for a *point* in time.

Companies prepare four financial statements from the summarized accounting data (see **Helpful Hint**):

1. An **income statement** presents the revenues and expenses and resulting net income or net loss for a specific period of time.
2. An **owner's equity statement** summarizes the changes in owner's equity for a specific period of time.
3. A **balance sheet** reports the assets, liabilities, and owner's equity at a specific date.
4. A **statement of cash flows** summarizes information about the cash inflows (receipts) and outflows (payments) for a specific period of time.

These statements provide relevant financial data for internal and external users. **Illustration 1.9** shows the financial statements of Softbyte.

Note that the statements shown in Illustration 1.9 are interrelated:

1. Net income of $2,750 on the **income statement** is added to the beginning balance of owner's capital in the **owner's equity statement**.
2. Owner's capital of $16,450 at the end of the reporting period shown in the **owner's equity statement** is reported on the **balance sheet**.
3. Cash of $8,050 on the **balance sheet** is reported on the **statement of cash flows**.

Also, explanatory notes and supporting schedules are an integral part of every set of financial statements. We illustrate these notes and schedules in later chapters of this textbook.

Be sure to carefully examine the format and content of each statement in Illustration 1.9. We describe the essential features of each in the following sections.

ALTERNATIVE TERMINOLOGY

The income statement is sometimes referred to as the statement of operations, earnings statement, or profit and loss statement.

Alternative Terminology notes introduce synonymous terms you may come across in practice.

Income Statement

The income statement reports the revenues and expenses for a specific period of time (see **Alternative Terminology**). (In Softbyte's case, this is "For the Month Ended September 30, 2020.") Softbyte's income statement is prepared from the data appearing in the owner's equity columns of Illustration 1.8.

ILLUSTRATION 1.9

Financial statements and their interrelationships

The heading of each statement identifies the company, the type of statement, and the specific date or time period covered by the statement.

Note that final sums are double-underlined, and negative amounts (in the statement of cash flows) are presented in parentheses.

The arrows show the interrelationships of the four financial statements.

1. Net income is computed first and is needed to determine the ending balance in owner's equity.
2. The ending balance in owner's equity is needed in preparing the balance sheet.
3. The cash shown on the balance sheet is needed in preparing the statement of cash flows.

Softbyte
Income Statement
For the Month Ended September 30, 2020

Revenues		
Service revenue		$ 4,700
Expenses		
Salaries and wages expense	$900	
Rent expense	600	
Advertising expense	250	
Utilities expense	200	
Total expenses		1,950
Net income		$ 2,750

Softbyte
Owner's Equity Statement
For the Month Ended September 30, 2020

Owner's capital, September 1		$ –0–
Add: Investments	$15,000	
Net income	2,750	17,750
		17,750
Less: Drawings		1,300
Owner's capital, September 30		$ 16,450

Softbyte
Balance Sheet
September 30, 2020

Assets	
Cash	$ 8,050
Accounts receivable	1,400
Supplies	1,600
Equipment	7,000
Total assets	$ 18,050
Liabilities and Owner's Equity	
Liabilities	
Accounts payable	$ 1,600
Owner's equity	
Owner's capital	16,450
Total liabilities and owner's equity	$ 18,050

Softbyte
Statement of Cash Flows
For the Month Ended September 30, 2020

Cash flows from operating activities		
Cash receipts from revenues		$ 3,300
Cash payments for expenses		(1,950)
Net cash provided by operating activities		1,350
Cash flows from investing activities		
Purchase of equipment		(7,000)
Cash flows from financing activities		
Investments by owner	$15,000	
Drawings by owner	(1,300)	13,700
Net increase in cash		8,050
Cash at the beginning of the period		0
Cash at the end of the period		$ 8,050

The income statement lists revenues first, followed by expenses. Finally the statement shows net income (or net loss). **Net income** results when revenues exceed expenses. A **net loss** occurs when expenses exceed revenues.

Although practice varies, we have chosen in our illustrations and homework solutions to list expenses in order of magnitude. (We will consider alternative formats for the income statement in later chapters.)

Note that the income statement does **not** include investment and withdrawal transactions between the owner and the business in measuring net income. For example, as explained earlier, Ray Neal's withdrawal of cash from Softbyte was not regarded as a business expense.

Owner's Equity Statement

The owner's equity statement reports the changes in owner's equity for a specific period of time. The time period is the same as that covered by the income statement (in Softbyte's case, this is "For the Month Ended September 30, 2020"). Data for the preparation of the owner's equity statement come from the owner's equity columns of the tabular summary (Illustration 1.8) and from the income statement. The first line of the statement shows the beginning owner's equity amount (which was zero at the start of the business). Then come the owner's investments, net income (or loss), and the owner's drawings. This statement indicates **why** owner's equity has increased or decreased during the period.

What if Softbyte had reported a net loss in its first month? Let's assume that during the month of September 2020, Softbyte lost $10,000. **Illustration 1.10** shows the presentation of a net loss in the owner's equity statement.

ILLUSTRATION 1.10
Presentation of net loss

Softbyte
Owner's Equity Statement
For the Month Ended September 30, 2020

Owner's capital, September 1		$ –0–
Add: Investments		15,000
		15,000
Less: Drawings	$ 1,300	
Net loss	**10,000**	11,300
Owner's capital, September 30		$ 3,700

If the owner makes any additional investments, the company reports them in the owner's equity statement as investments.

Balance Sheet

Softbyte's balance sheet reports the assets, liabilities, and owner's equity at a specific date (in Softbyte's case, September 30, 2020). The company prepares the balance sheet from the column headings of the tabular summary (Illustration 1.8) and the month-end data shown in its last line.

Observe that the balance sheet lists assets at the top, followed by liabilities and owner's equity. Total assets must equal total liabilities and owner's equity. Softbyte reports only one liability—accounts payable—in its balance sheet. In most cases, there will be more than one liability. When two or more liabilities are involved, a customary way of listing is as shown in **Illustration 1.11**.

ILLUSTRATION 1.11
Presentation of liabilities

Liabilities	
Notes payable	$10,000
Accounts payable	63,000
Salaries and wages payable	18,000
Total liabilities	**$91,000**

The balance sheet is a snapshot of the company's financial condition at a specific moment in time (usually the month-end or year-end).

Statement of Cash Flows

The primary purpose of a statement of cash flows is to provide financial information about the cash receipts and cash payments of a company for a specific period of time (see **Helpful Hint**). To help investors, creditors, and others in their analysis of a company's cash position, the statement of cash flows reports the cash effects of a company's operating, investing, and financing activities. In addition, the statement shows the net increase or decrease in cash during the period, and the amount of cash at the end of the period.

Reporting the sources, uses, and change in cash is useful because investors, creditors, and others want to know what is happening to a company's most liquid resource. The statement of cash flows provides answers to the following simple but important questions.

HELPFUL HINT

The statement of cash flows helps users determine if the company generates enough cash from operations to fund its investing and financing activities.

1. Where did cash come from during the period?
2. What was cash used for during the period?
3. What was the change in the cash balance during the period?

As shown in Softbyte's statement of cash flows in Illustration 1.9, cash increased $8,050 during the period. Net cash provided by operating activities increased cash $1,350 (cash receipts from revenue less cash payments for expenses). Cash flow from investing activities decreased cash $7,000 (purchase of equipment). And cash flow from financing activities increased cash $13,700 (investment by owner less drawings by owner). At this time, you need not be concerned with how these amounts are determined. Chapter 17 will examine the statement of cash flows in detail.

People, Planet, and Profit Insight

© Marek Uliasz/iStockphoto

Beyond Financial Statements

Should we expand our financial statements beyond the income statement, owner's equity statement, balance sheet, and statement of cash flows? Some believe we should take into account ecological and social performance, in addition to financial results, in evaluating a company. The argument is that a company's responsibility lies with anyone who is influenced by its actions. In other words, a company should be interested in benefiting many different parties, instead of only maximizing stockholders' interests.

A socially responsible business does not exploit or endanger any group of individuals. It follows fair trade practices, provides safe environments for workers, and bears responsibility for environmental damage. Granted, measurement of these factors is difficult. How to report this information is also controversial. But many interesting and useful efforts are underway. Throughout this textbook, we provide additional insights into how companies are attempting to meet the challenge of measuring and reporting their contributions to society, as well as their financial results, to stockholders.

Why might a company's stockholders be interested in its environmental and social performance? (Go to WileyPLUS for this answer and additional questions.)

DO IT! 5 | Financial Statement Items

Presented below is selected information related to Flanagan Company at December 31, 2020. Flanagan reports financial information monthly.

Equipment	$10,000	Utilities Expense	$ 4,000
Cash	8,000	Accounts Receivable	9,000
Service Revenue	36,000	Salaries and Wages Expense	7,000
Rent Expense	11,000	Notes Payable	16,500
Accounts Payable	2,000	Owner's Drawings	5,000

a. Determine the total assets of Flanagan Company at December 31, 2020.

b. Determine the net income that Flanagan Company reported for December 2020.

c. Determine the owner's equity of Flanagan Company at December 31, 2020.

ACTION PLAN

- **Remember the basic accounting equation: assets must equal liabilities plus owner's equity.**
- **Review previous financial statements to determine how total assets, net income, and owner's equity are computed.**

Solution

a. The total assets are $27,000, comprised of Cash $8,000, Accounts Receivable $9,000, and Equipment $10,000.

b. Net income is $14,000, computed as follows.

Revenues		
Service revenue		$36,000
Expenses		
Rent expense	$11,000	
Salaries and wages expense	7,000	
Utilities expense	4,000	
Total expenses		22,000
Net income		$14,000

c. The ending owner's equity of Flanagan Company is $8,500. By rewriting the accounting equation, we can compute owner's equity as assets minus liabilities, as follows.

Total assets [as computed in (a)]		$27,000
Less: Liabilities		
Notes payable	$16,500	
Accounts payable	2,000	18,500
Owner's equity		$ 8,500

Note that it is not possible to determine the company's owner's equity in any other way because the beginning total for owner's equity is not provided.

Related exercise material: **BE1.10, BE1.11, DO IT! 1.5, E1.9, E1.10, E1.11, E1.12, E1.13, E1.14, E1.15, E1.16 , E1.17, and E1.18**

Appendix 1A Career Opportunities in Accounting

LEARNING OBJECTIVE *6

Explain the career opportunities in accounting.

Why is accounting such a popular major and career choice? First, there are a lot of jobs. In many cities in recent years, the demand for accountants exceeded the supply. Not only are there a lot of jobs, but there are a wide array of opportunities. As one accounting organization observed, "accounting is one degree with 360 degrees of opportunity."

Accounting is also hot because it is obvious that accounting matters. Interest in accounting has increased, ironically, because of the attention caused by the accounting failures of companies such as **Enron** and **WorldCom**. These widely publicized scandals revealed the important role that accounting plays in society. Most people want to make a difference, and an accounting career provides many opportunities to contribute to society. Finally, the Sarbanes-Oxley Act (SOX) significantly increased the accounting and internal control requirements for corporations. This dramatically increased demand for professionals with accounting training.

Accountants are in such demand that it is not uncommon for accounting students to have accepted a job offer a year before graduation. As the following discussion reveals, the job options of people with accounting degrees are virtually unlimited.

Public Accounting

Individuals in **public accounting** offer expert service to the general public, in much the same way that doctors serve patients and lawyers serve clients. A major portion of public accounting involves **auditing**. In auditing, a certified public accountant (CPA) examines company financial statements and provides an opinion as to how accurately the financial statements present the company's results and financial position. Analysts, investors, and creditors rely heavily on these "audit opinions," which CPAs have the exclusive authority to issue.

Taxation is another major area of public accounting. The work that tax specialists perform includes tax advice and planning, preparing tax returns, and representing clients before governmental agencies such as the Internal Revenue Service.

A third area in public accounting is **management consulting**. It ranges from installing basic accounting software or highly complex enterprise resource planning systems, to performing support services for major marketing projects and merger and acquisition activities.

Many CPAs are entrepreneurs. They form small- or medium-sized practices that frequently specialize in tax or consulting services.

Private Accounting

Instead of working in public accounting, you might choose to be an employee of a for-profit company such as **Starbucks**, **Alphabet**, or **PepsiCo**. In **managerial (or private) accounting**, you would be involved in activities such as cost accounting (finding the cost of producing specific products), budgeting, accounting information system design and support, and tax planning and preparation. You might also be a member of your company's internal audit team. In response to SOX, the internal auditors' job of reviewing the company's operations to ensure compliance with company policies and to increase efficiency has taken on increased importance.

Alternatively, many accountants work for not-for-profit organizations such as the **Red Cross** or the **Bill and Melinda Gates Foundation**, or for museums, libraries, or performing arts organizations.

Governmental Accounting

Another option is to pursue one of the many accounting opportunities in governmental agencies. For example, the Internal Revenue Service (IRS), Federal Bureau of Investigation (FBI), and the Securities and Exchange Commission (SEC) all employ accountants. The FBI has a stated goal that at least 15% of its new agents should be CPAs. There is also a very high demand for accounting educators at public colleges and universities and in state and local governments.

Forensic Accounting

Forensic accounting uses accounting, auditing, and investigative skills to conduct investigations into theft and fraud. It is listed among the top 20 career paths of the future. The job of forensic accountants is to catch the perpetrators of the estimated $600 billion per year of theft and fraud occurring at U.S. companies. This includes tracing money-laundering and identity-theft activities as well as tax evasion. Insurance companies hire forensic accountants to detect frauds such as arson, and law offices employ forensic accountants to identify marital assets in divorces. Forensic accountants often have FBI, IRS, or similar government experience.

"Show Me the Money"

How much can a new accountant make? Take a look at the average salaries for college graduates in public and private accounting listed in **Illustration 1A.1**. Keep in mind if you also have a CPA license, you'll make 10–15% more when you start out.

ILLUSTRATION 1A.1
Salary estimates for jobs in public and corporate accounting

Employer	Jr. Level (0–3 yrs.)	Sr. Level (4–6 yrs.)
Public accounting (large firm)	$63,250–$83,250	$78,500–$106,500
Public accounting (small firm)	$51,500–$60,500	$63,750–$ 81,500
Corporate accounting (large company)	$53,750–$69,500	$68,750–$ 87,750
Corporate accounting (small company)	$45,000–$59,000	$57,500–$ 70,000

Illustration 1A.2 offers some examples of upper-level salaries for managers in corporate accounting. Note that geographic region, experience, education, CPA certification, and company size each play a role in determining salary.

ILLUSTRATION 1A.2
Upper-level management salaries in corporate accounting

Position	Large Company	Small to Medium Company
Chief financial officer	$207,000–$465,750	$105,250–$208,750
Corporate controller	$140,000–$224,750	$ 92,000–$161,250
Tax manager	$112,000–$158,250	$ 88,000–$124,750

The Review and Practice section provides opportunities for students to review key concepts and terms as well as complete multiple-choice questions, exercises, and a comprehensive problem. Detailed solutions are also included.

Review and Practice

Learning Objectives Review

1 Identify the activities and users associated with accounting.

Accounting is an information system that identifies, records, and communicates the economic events of an organization to interested users. The major users and uses of accounting are as follows. (a) Management uses accounting information to plan, organize, and run the business. (b) Investors (owners) decide whether to buy, hold, or sell their financial interests on the basis of accounting data. (c) Creditors (suppliers and bankers) evaluate the risks of granting credit or lending money on the basis of accounting information. Other groups that use accounting information are taxing authorities, regulatory agencies, customers, and labor unions.

2 Explain the building blocks of accounting: ethics, principles, and assumptions.

Ethics are the standards of conduct by which actions are judged as right or wrong. Effective financial reporting depends on sound ethical behavior.

Generally accepted accounting principles are a common set of standards used by accountants. The primary accounting standard-setting body in the United States is the Financial Accounting Standards Board. The monetary unit assumption requires that companies include in the accounting records only transaction data that can be expressed in terms of money. The economic entity assumption requires that the activities of each economic entity be kept separate from the activities of its owner(s) and other economic entities.

3 State the accounting equation, and define its components.

The basic accounting equation is:

Assets = Liabilities + Owner's Equity

Assets are resources a business owns. Liabilities are creditorship claims on total assets. Owner's equity is the ownership claim on total assets.

The expanded accounting equation is:

Assets = Liabilities + Owner's Capital – Owner's Drawings + Revenues – Expenses

Investments by owners (assets the owner puts into the business) are recorded in a category called owner's capital. Owner's drawings are the withdrawal of assets by the owner for personal use. Revenues are the gross increase in owner's equity from business activities for the purpose of earning income. Expenses are the costs of assets consumed or services used in the process of earning revenue.

4 Analyze the effects of business transactions on the accounting equation.

Each business transaction must have a dual effect on the accounting equation. For example, if an individual asset increases, there must be a corresponding (1) decrease in another asset, (2) increase in a specific liability, or (3) increase in owner's equity.

5 Describe the four financial statements and how they are prepared.

An income statement presents the revenues and expenses, and resulting net income or net loss, for a specific period of time. An owner's equity statement summarizes the changes in owner's equity for a specific period of time. A balance sheet reports the assets, liabilities, and owner's equity at a specific date. A statement of cash flows summarizes information about the cash inflows (receipts) and outflows (payments) for a specific period of time.

***6 Explain the career opportunities in accounting.**

Accounting offers many different jobs in fields such as public and private accounting, governmental, and forensic accounting. Accounting is a popular major because there are many different types of jobs, with unlimited potential for career advancement.

Glossary Review

Accounting The information system that identifies, records, and communicates the economic events of an organization to interested users. (p. 1-3).

Accounting information system The system of collecting and processing transaction data and communicating financial information to decision-makers. (p. 1-13)

Assets Resources a business owns. (p. 1-11).

***Auditing** The examination of financial statements by a certified public accountant in order to express an opinion as to the fairness of presentation. (p. 1-25).

Balance sheet A financial statement that reports the assets, liabilities, and owner's equity at a specific date. (p. 1-20).

Basic accounting equation Assets = Liabilities + Owner's equity. (p. 1-11).

Bookkeeping A part of the accounting process that involves only the recording of economic events. (p. 1-4).

Convergence The process of reducing the differences between U.S. GAAP and IFRS. (p. 1-8).

Corporation A business organized as a separate legal entity under state corporation law, having ownership divided into transferable shares of stock. (p. 1-10).

Drawings Withdrawal of cash or other assets from an unincorporated business for the personal use of the owner(s). (p. 1-12).

Economic entity assumption An assumption that requires that the activities of the entity be kept separate and distinct from the activities of its owner and all other economic entities. (p. 1-9).

Ethics The standards of conduct by which actions are judged as right or wrong, honest or dishonest, fair or not fair. (p. 1-7).

Expanded accounting equation Assets = Liabilities + Owner's capital – Owner's drawings + Revenues – Expenses. (p. 1-12).

Expenses The cost of assets consumed or services used in the process of generating revenue. (p. 1-12).

Fair value principle An accounting principle stating that assets and liabilities should be reported at fair value (the price received to sell an asset or settle a liability). (p. 1-9).

Faithful representation Numbers and descriptions match what really existed or happened—they are factual. (p. 1-8).

Financial accounting The field of accounting that provides economic and financial information for investors, creditors, and other external users. (p. 1-5).

Financial Accounting Standards Board (FASB) A private organization that establishes generally accepted accounting principles (GAAP) in the United States. (p. 1-8).

***Forensic accounting** An area of accounting that uses accounting, auditing, and investigative skills to conduct investigations into theft and fraud. (p. 1-25).

Generally accepted accounting principles (GAAP) Common standards that indicate how to report economic events. (p. 1-8).

Historical cost principle An accounting principle that states that companies should record assets at their cost. (p. 1-8).

Income statement A financial statement that presents the revenues and expenses and resulting net income or net loss of a company for a specific period of time. (p. 1-20).

International Accounting Standards Board (IASB) An accounting standard-setting body that issues standards adopted by many countries outside of the United States. (p. 1-8).

International Financial Reporting Standards (IFRS) International accounting standards set by the International Accounting Standards Board (IASB). (p. 1-8).

Investments by owner The assets an owner puts into the business. (p. 1-12).

Liabilities Creditor claims against total assets. (p. 1-11).

***Management consulting** An area of public accounting ranging from development of accounting and computer systems to support services for marketing projects and merger and acquisition activities. (p. 1-25).

Managerial accounting The field of accounting that provides internal reports to help users make decisions about their companies. (p. 1-5).

Monetary unit assumption An assumption stating that companies include in the accounting records only transaction data that can be expressed in terms of money. (p. 1-9).

Net income The amount by which revenues exceed expenses. (p. 1-22).

Net loss The amount by which expenses exceed revenues. (p. 1-22).

Owner's equity The ownership claim on total assets. (p. 1-12).

Owner's equity statement A financial statement that summarizes the changes in owner's equity for a specific period of time. (p. 1-20).

Partnership A business owned by two or more persons associated as partners. (p. 1-9).

Proprietorship A business owned by one person. (p. 1-9).

***Public accounting** An area of accounting in which the accountant offers expert service to the general public. (p. 1-24).

Relevance Financial information that is capable of making a difference in a decision. (p. 1-8).

Revenues The increases in assets or decreases in liabilities resulting from the sale of goods or the performance of services in the normal course of business. (p. 1-12).

Sarbanes-Oxley Act (SOX) Law passed by Congress intended to reduce unethical corporate behavior. (p. 1-6).

Securities and Exchange Commission (SEC) A governmental agency that oversees U.S. financial markets and accounting standard-setting bodies. (p. 1-8).

Statement of cash flows A financial statement that summarizes information about the cash inflows (receipts) and cash outflows (payments) for a specific period of time. (p. 1-20).

***Taxation** An area of public accounting involving tax advice, tax planning, preparing tax returns, and representing clients before governmental agencies. (p. 1-25).

Transactions The economic events of a business that are recorded by accountants. (p. 1-14).

Practice Multiple-Choice Questions

1. **(LO 1)** Which of the following is **not** a step in the accounting process?

   a. Identification. **c.** Recording.
   b. Economic entity. **d.** Communication.

2. **(LO 1)** Which of the following statements about users of accounting information is **incorrect**?

   a. Management is an internal user.
   b. Taxing authorities are external users.
   c. Present creditors are external users.
   d. Regulatory authorities are internal users.

3. **(LO 2)** The historical cost principle states that:

   a. assets should be initially recorded at cost and adjusted when the fair value changes.
   b. activities of an entity are to be kept separate and distinct from its owner.
   c. assets should be recorded at their cost.
   d. only transaction data capable of being expressed in terms of money be included in the accounting records.

4. **(LO 2)** Which of the following statements about basic assumptions is **correct**?

   a. Basic assumptions are the same as accounting principles.
   b. The economic entity assumption states that there should be a particular unit of accountability.
   c. The monetary unit assumption enables accounting to measure employee morale.
   d. Partnerships are not economic entities.

5. **(LO 2)** The three types of business entities are:

   a. proprietorships, small businesses, and partnerships.
   b. proprietorships, partnerships, and corporations.
   c. proprietorships, partnerships, and large businesses.
   d. financial, manufacturing, and service companies.

6. **(LO 3)** Net income will result during a time period when:

   a. assets exceed liabilities.
   b. assets exceed revenues.
   c. expenses exceed revenues.
   d. revenues exceed expenses.

7. **(LO 3)** As of December 31, 2020, Kent Company has assets of $3,500 and owner's equity of $2,000. What are the liabilities for Kent Company as of December 31, 2020?

   a. $1,500. **c.** $2,500.
   b. $1,000. **d.** $2,000.

8. **(LO 4)** Performing services on account will have the following effects on the components of the basic accounting equation:

   a. increase assets and decrease owner's equity.
   b. increase assets and increase owner's equity.
   c. increase assets and increase liabilities.
   d. increase liabilities and increase owner's equity.

9. **(LO 4)** Which of the following events is **not** recorded in the accounting records?

   a. Equipment is purchased on account.
   b. An employee is terminated.
   c. A cash investment is made into the business.
   d. The owner withdraws cash for personal use.

10. **(LO 4)** During 2020, Bruske Company's assets decreased $50,000 and its liabilities decreased $50,000. Its owner's equity therefore:

    a. increased $50,000. **c.** decreased $100,000.
    b. decreased $50,000. **d.** did not change.

11. **(LO 4)** Payment of an account payable affects the components of the accounting equation in the following way.

    a. Decreases owner's equity and decreases liabilities.
    b. Increases assets and decreases liabilities.
    c. Decreases assets and increases owner's equity.
    d. Decreases assets and decreases liabilities.

12. **(LO 5)** Which of the following statements is **false**?

    a. A statement of cash flows summarizes information about the cash inflows (receipts) and outflows (payments) for a specific period of time.
    b. A balance sheet reports the assets, liabilities, and owner's equity at a specific date.
    c. An income statement presents the revenues, expenses, changes in owner's equity, and resulting net income or net loss for a specific period of time.
    d. An owner's equity statement summarizes the changes in owner's equity for a specific period of time.

13. **(LO 5)** On the last day of the period, Alan Cesska Company buys a $900 machine on credit. This transaction will affect the:

    a. income statement only.

b. balance sheet only.

c. income statement and owner's equity statement only.

d. income statement, owner's equity statement, and balance sheet.

14. (LO 5) The financial statement that reports assets, liabilities, and owner's equity is the:

a. income statement.

b. owner's equity statement.

c. balance sheet.

d. statement of cash flows.

*15. (LO 6) Services performed by a public accountant include:

a. auditing, taxation, and management consulting.

b. auditing, budgeting, and management consulting.

c. auditing, budgeting, and cost accounting.

d. auditing, budgeting, and management consulting.

Solutions

1. **b.** Economic entity is not one of the steps in the accounting process. The other choices are true because (a) identification is the first step in the accounting process, (c) recording is the second step in the accounting process, and (d) communication is the third and final step in the accounting process.

2. **d.** Regulatory authorities are external, not internal, users of accounting information. The other choices are true statements.

3. **c.** The historical cost principle states that assets should be recorded at their cost. The other choices are incorrect because (a) the historical cost principle does not say that assets should be adjusted for changes in fair value, (b) describes the economic entity assumption, and (d) describes the monetary unit assumption.

4. **b.** The economic entity assumption states that there should be a particular unit of accountability. The other choices are incorrect because (a) basic assumptions are not the same as accounting principles, (c) the monetary unit assumption allows accounting to measure economic events, and (d) partnerships are economic entities.

5. **b.** Proprietorships, partnerships, and corporations are the three types of business entities. Choices (a) and (c) are incorrect because small and large businesses only denote the sizes of businesses. Choice (d) is incorrect because financial, manufacturing, and service companies are types of businesses, not business entities.

6. **d.** Net income results when revenues exceed expenses. The other choices are incorrect because (a) assets and liabilities are not used in the computation of net income; (b) revenues, not assets, are included in the computation of net income; and (c) when expenses exceed revenues, a net loss results.

7. **a.** Using a variation of the basic accounting equation, Assets − Owner's equity = Liabilities, $3,500 − $2,000 = $1,500. Therefore, choices (b) $1,000, (c) $2,500, and (d) $2,000 are incorrect.

8. **b.** When services are performed on account, assets are increased and owner's equity is increased. The other choices are incorrect because when services are performed on account (a) owner's equity is increased, not decreased; (c) liabilities are not affected; and (d) owner's equity is increased and liabilities are not affected.

9. **b.** If an employee is terminated, this represents an activity of a company, not a business transaction. Assets, liabilities, and owner's equity are not affected. Thus, there is no effect on the accounting equation. The other choices are incorrect because they are all recorded: (a) when equipment is purchased on account, both assets and liabilities increase; (c) when a cash investment is made into a business, both assets and owner's equity increase; and (d) when an owner withdraws cash for personal use, both assets and owner's equity decrease.

10. **d.** In this situation, owner's equity does not change because only assets and liabilities decreased $50,000. Therefore, the other choices are incorrect.

11. **d.** Payment of an account payable results in an equal decrease of assets (cash) and liabilities (accounts payable). The other choices are incorrect because payment of an account payable (a) does not affect owner's equity, (b) does not increase assets, and (c) does not affect owner's equity.

12. **c.** An income statement represents the revenues, expenses, and the resulting net income or net loss for a specific period of time but not the changes in owner's equity. The other choices are true statements.

13. **b.** This transaction will cause assets to increase by $900 and liabilities to increase by $900. The other choices are incorrect because this transaction (a) will have no effect on the income statement, (c) will have no effect on the income statement or the owner's equity statement, and (d) will affect the balance sheet but not the income statement or the owner's equity statement.

14. **c.** The balance sheet is the statement that reports assets, liabilities and owner's equity. The other choices are incorrect because (a) the income statement reports revenues and expenses, (b) the owner's equity statement reports details about owner's equity, and (d) the statement of cash flows reports inflows and outflows of cash.

*15. **a.** Auditing, taxation, and management consulting are all services performed by public accountants. The other choices are incorrect because public accountants do not perform budgeting or cost accounting.

Practice Brief Exercises

1. (LO 3) At the beginning of the year, Ortiz Company had total assets of $900,000 and total liabilities of $440,000. Answer the following questions.

Use basic accounting equation.

a. If total assets decreased $100,000 during the year and total liabilities increased $80,000 during the year, what is the amount of owner's equity at the end of the year?

b. During the year, total liabilities decreased $100,000 and owner's equity increased $200,000. What is the amount of total assets at the end of the year?

c. If total assets increased $50,000 during the year and owner's equity increased $60,000 during the year, what is the amount of total liabilities at the end of the year?

Solution

1. **a.** ($900,000 – $440,000) – $100,000 – $80,000 = $280,000 owner's equity
   b. $900,000 – $100,000 + $200,000 = $1,000,000 total assets
   c. $440,000 – $60,000 + $50,000 = $430,000 total liabilities

Determine effect of transactions on basic accounting equation

2. **(LO 4)** Presented below are three business transactions. List the letters (a), (b), and (c) with columns for assets, liabilities and owner's equity. For each column, indicate whether the transactions increased (+), decreased (–), or had no effect (NE) on assets, liabilities, and owner's equity.
   a. Purchased equipment on account.
   b. Withdrawal of cash by owner.
   c. Paid expenses in cash.

Solution

	Assets	Liabilities	Owner's Equity
2. a.	+	+	NE
b.	–	NE	–
c.	–	NE	–

Determine effect of transactions on basic accounting equation.

3. **(LO 4)** Follow the same format as in **Practice Brief Exercise 2.** Determine the effect on assets, liabilities, and owner's equity of the following three transactions.
   a. Performed accounting services for clients for cash.
   b. Borrowed cash from a bank on a note payable.
   c. Paid cash for rent for the month.

Solution

	Assets	Liabilities	Owner's Equity
3. a.	+	NE	+
b.	+	+	NE
c.	–	NE	–

Determine where items appear on financial statements.

4. **(LO 5)** **Financial Statement** Indicate whether the following items would appear on the income statement (IS), balance sheet (BS), or owner's equity statement (OE).
   a. Owner's capital.
   b. Cash.
   c. Salaries and wages expense.
   d. Service revenue.
   e. Accounts payable.

Solution

4. **a.** Owner's capital	OE, BS
b. Cash	BS
c. Salaries and wages expense	IS
d. Service revenue	IS
e. Accounts payable	BS

5. (LO 5) **Financial Statement** Presented below in alphabetical order are balance sheet items for Feagler Company at December 31, 2020. Carole Feagler is the owner of the company. Prepare a balance sheet following the format of Illustration 1.9.

Prepare a balance sheet.

Accounts receivable	$12,500
Cash	38,000
Notes payable	40,000
Owner's capital	10,500

Solution

5.

Feagler Company
Balance Sheet
December 31, 2020

Assets

Cash	$38,000
Accounts receivable	12,500
Total assets	$50,500

Liabilities and Owner's Equity

Liabilities	
Notes payable	$40,000
Owner's equity	
Owner's capital	10,500
Total liabilities and owner's equity	$50,500

Practice Exercises

1. (LO 3, 4) Selected transactions for Fabulous Flora Company are listed below.

Analyze the effect of transactions.

1. Made cash investment to start business.
2. Purchased equipment on account.
3. Paid salaries.
4. Billed customers for services performed.
5. Received cash from customers billed in (4).
6. Withdrew cash for owner's personal use.
7. Incurred advertising expense on account.
8. Purchased additional equipment for cash.
9. Received cash from customers when service was performed.

Instructions

List the numbers of the above transactions and describe the effect of each transaction on assets, liabilities, and owner's equity. For example, the first answer is: (1) Increase in assets and increase in owner's equity.

Solution

1. 1. Increase in assets and increase in owner's equity.
   2. Increase in assets and increase in liabilities.
   3. Decrease in assets and decrease in owner's equity.
   4. Increase in assets and increase in owner's equity.
   5. Increase in assets and decrease in assets.
   6. Decrease in assets and decrease in owner's equity.

7. Increase in liabilities and decrease in owner's equity.
8. Increase in assets and decrease in assets.
9. Increase in assets and increase in owner's equity.

Analyze the effect of transactions on assets, liabilities, and owner's equity.

2. **(LO 3, 4)** Alma's Payroll Services Company entered into the following transactions during May 2020.

1. Purchased computers for $15,000 from Bytes of Data on account.
2. Paid $3,000 cash for May rent on storage space.
3. Received $12,000 cash from customers for contracts billed in April.
4. Performed payroll services for Magic Construction Company for $2,500 cash.
5. Paid Northern Ohio Power Co. $7,000 cash for energy usage in May.
6. Alma invested an additional $25,000 in the business.
7. Paid Bytes of Data for the computers purchased in (1) above.
8. Incurred advertising expense for May of $900 on account.

Instructions

Indicate with the appropriate letter whether each of the transactions above results in:

a. an increase in assets and a decrease in assets.
b. an increase in assets and an increase in owner's equity.
c. an increase in assets and an increase in liabilities.
d. a decrease in assets and a decrease in owner's equity.
e. a decrease in assets and a decrease in liabilities.
f. an increase in liabilities and a decrease in owner's equity.
g. an increase in owner's equity and a decrease in liabilities.

Solution

2. **1.** c	**3.** a	**5.** d	**7.** e
2. d	**4.** b	**6.** b	**8.** f

Practice Problem

Prepare a tabular presentation and financial statements.

(LO 4, 5) Joan Robinson opens her own law office on July 1, 2020. During the first month of operations, the following transactions occurred.

1. Joan invested $11,000 in cash in the law practice.
2. Paid $800 for July rent on office space.
3. Purchased equipment on account $3,000.
4. Performed legal services for clients for cash $1,500.
5. Borrowed $700 cash from a bank on a note payable.
6. Performed legal services for client on account $2,000.
7. Paid monthly expenses: salaries and wages $500, utilities $300, and advertising $100.
8. Joan withdrew $1,000 cash for personal use.

Instructions

a. Prepare a tabular summary of the transactions.
b. **Financial Statement** Prepare the income statement, owner's equity statement, and balance sheet at July 31, 2020, for Joan Robinson, Attorney.

Solution

a.

Trans-action	Cash	+	Accounts Receivable	+	Equipment	=	Notes Payable	+	Accounts Payable	+	Owner's Capital	−	Owner's Drawings	+	Revenues	−	Expenses
	Assets					=	**Liabilities**			+	**Owner's Equity**						
1.	+$11,000					=					+$11,000						
2.	−800																−$800
3.					+$3,000	=			+$3,000								
4.	+1,500														+$1,500		
5.	+700						+$700										
6.			+$2,000												+2,000		
7.	−500																−500
	−300																−300
	−100																−100
8.	−1,000												−$1,000				
	$10,500	+	$2,000	+	$3,000	=	$700	+	$3,000	+	$11,000	−	$1,000	+	$3,500	−	$1,700
	$15,500						$15,500										

b.

Joan Robinson, Attorney
Income Statement
For the Month Ended July 31, 2020

Revenues		
Service revenue		$3,500
Expenses		
Rent expense	$800	
Salaries and wages expense	500	
Utilities expense	300	
Advertising expense	100	
Total expenses		1,700
Net income		$1,800

Joan Robinson, Attorney
Owner's Equity Statement
For the Month Ended July 31, 2020

Owner's capital, July 1		$ 0
Add: Investments	$11,000	
Net income	1,800	12,800
		12,800
Less: Drawings		1,000
Owner's capital, July 31		$11,800

Joan Robinson, Attorney
Balance Sheet
July 31, 2020

Assets	
Cash	$10,500
Accounts receivable	2,000
Equipment	3,000
Total assets	$15,500
Liabilities and Owner's Equity	
Liabilities	
Notes payable	$ 700
Accounts payable	3,000
Total liabilities	3,700
Owner's equity	
Owner's capital	11,800
Total liabilities and owner's equity	$15,500

WileyPLUS

Brief Exercises, DO IT! Exercises, Exercises, Problems, and many additional resources are available for practice in WileyPLUS.

Note: All asterisked Questions, Exercises, and Problems relate to material in the appendix to the chapter.

Questions

1. "Accounting is ingrained in our society and it is vital to our economic system." Do you agree? Explain.

2. Identify and describe the steps in the accounting process.

3. (a) Who are internal users of accounting data? (b) How does accounting provide relevant data to these users?

4. What uses of financial accounting information are made by (a) investors and (b) creditors?

5. "Bookkeeping and accounting are the same." Do you agree? Explain.

6. Benton Travel Agency purchased land for $90,000 cash on December 10, 2020. At December 31, 2020, the land's value has increased to $92,000. What amount should be reported for land on Benton's balance sheet at December 31, 2020? Explain.

7. What is the monetary unit assumption?

8. What is the economic entity assumption?

9. What are the three basic forms of business organizations for profit-oriented enterprises?

10. Helen Rupp is the owner of a successful printing shop. Recently, her business has been increasing, and Helen has been thinking about changing the organization of her business from a proprietorship to a corporation. Discuss some of the advantages Helen would enjoy if she were to incorporate her business.

11. What is the basic accounting equation?

12. **a.** Define the terms assets, liabilities, and owner's equity.

 b. What items affect owner's equity?

13. Which of the following items are liabilities of Siebers Jewelry Stores?

 a. Cash.

 b. Accounts payable.

 c. Owner's drawings.

 d. Accounts receivable.

 e. Supplies.

 f. Equipment.

 g. Salaries and wages payable.

 h. Service revenue.

 i. Rent expense.

14. Can a business enter into a transaction in which only the left side of the basic accounting equation is affected? If so, give an example.

15. Are the following events recorded in the accounting records? Explain your answer in each case.

 a. The owner of the company dies.

 b. Supplies are purchased on account.

 c. An employee is fired.

 d. The owner of the business withdraws cash from the business for personal use.

16. Indicate how the following business transactions affect the basic accounting equation.

 a. Paid cash for janitorial services.

 b. Purchased equipment for cash.

 c. Invested cash in the business.

 d. Paid accounts payable in full.

17. Listed below are some items found in the financial statements of Tony Gruber Co. Indicate in which financial statement(s) the following items would appear.

 a. Service revenue.

 b. Equipment.

 c. Advertising expense.

 d. Accounts receivable.

 e. Owner's capital.

 f. Salaries and wages payable.

18. In February 2020, Ola Gott invested an additional $12,000 in her business, Gott's Pharmacy, which is organized as a proprietorship. Gott's accountant, Sal Costa, recorded this receipt as an increase in cash and revenues. Is this treatment appropriate? Why or why not?

19. "A company's net income appears directly on the income statement and the owner's equity statement, and it is included indirectly in the company's balance sheet." Do you agree? Explain.

20. Bayler Enterprises had a capital balance of $186,000 at the beginning of the period. At the end of the accounting period, the capital balance was $189,000.

 a. Assuming no additional investment or withdrawals during the period, what is the net income for the period?

 b. Assuming an additional investment of $13,000 but no withdrawals during the period, what is the net income for the period?

21. Summarized operations for Bayles Co. for the month of July are as follows.

 Revenues recognized: for cash $20,000; on account $70,000.

 Expenses incurred: for cash $26,000; on account $40,000.

 Indicate for Bayles Co. (a) the total revenues, (b) the total expenses, and (c) net income for the month of July.

22. The basic accounting equation is Assets = Liabilities + Owner's equity. Replacing the words in that equation with dollar amounts, what is **Apple**'s accounting equation at September 26, 2015? (*Hint:* Owner's equity is equivalent to shareholders' equity.)

Brief Exercises

BE1.1 (LO 3) Presented below is the basic accounting equation. Determine the missing amounts.

Use basic accounting equation.

	Assets	=	Liabilities	+	Owner's Equity
a.	$90,000		$50,000		?
b.	?		$44,000		$70,000
c.	$94,000		?		$53,000

BE1.2 (LO 3) Given the accounting equation, answer each of the following questions.

Use basic accounting equation.

a. The liabilities of Berber Company are $120,000 and the owner's equity is $230,000. What is the amount of Berber Company's total assets?

b. The total assets of Berber Company are $190,000 and its owner's equity is $89,000. What is the amount of its total liabilities?

c. The total assets of Berber Company are $900,000 and its liabilities are equal to one-half of its total assets. What is the amount of Berber Company's owner's equity?

BE1.3 (LO 3) At the beginning of the year, Gilles Company had total assets of $800,000 and total liabilities of $300,000. Answer the following questions.

Use basic accounting equation.

a. If total assets increased $150,000 during the year and total liabilities decreased $60,000, what is the amount of owner's equity at the end of the year?

b. During the year, total liabilities increased $100,000 and owner's equity decreased $70,000. What is the amount of total assets at the end of the year?

c. If total assets decreased $80,000 and owner's equity increased $120,000 during the year, what is the amount of total liabilities at the end of the year?

BE1.4 (LO 3) Use the expanded accounting equation to answer each of the following questions.

Solve expanded accounting equation.

a. The liabilities of Platt Company are $90,000. Owner's capital is $150,000; drawings are $40,000; revenues, $450,000; and expenses, $340,000. What is the amount of Platt Company's total assets?

b. The total assets of Sierra Company are $57,000. Owner's capital is $35,000; drawings are $7,000; revenues, $52,000; and expenses, $35,000. What is the amount of the company's total liabilities?

c. The total assets of Birch Co. are $660,000 and its liabilities are equal to two-thirds of its total assets. What is the amount of Birch Co.'s owner's equity?

BE1.5 (LO 3) Indicate whether each of the following items is an asset (A), liability (L), or part of owner's equity (OE).

Identify assets, liabilities, and owner's equity.

________ **a.** Accounts receivable	________ **d.** Supplies
________ **b.** Salaries and wages payable	________ **e.** Owner's capital
________ **c.** Equipment	________ **f.** Notes payable

BE1.6 (LO 3) Classify each of the following items as owner's drawings (D), revenue (R), or expense (E).

Classify items affecting owner's equity.

________ **a.** Advertising expense	________ **e.** Owner's drawings
________ **b.** Service revenue	________ **f.** Rent revenue
________ **c.** Insurance expense	________ **g.** Utilities expense
________ **d.** Salaries and wages expense	

BE1.7 (LO 4) Presented below are three business transactions. On a sheet of paper, list the letters (a), (b), and (c) with columns for assets, liabilities, and owner's equity. For each column, indicate whether the transactions increased (+), decreased (–), or had no effect (NE) on assets, liabilities, and owner's equity.

Determine effect of transactions on basic accounting equation.

a. Purchased supplies on account.

b. Received cash for performing a service.

c. Paid expenses in cash.

BE1.8 (LO 4) Follow the same format as in BE1.7. Determine the effect on assets, liabilities, and owner's equity of the following three transactions.

Determine effect of transactions on basic accounting equation.

a. Invested cash in the business.

b. Withdrawal of cash by owner.

c. Received cash from a customer who had previously been billed for services performed.

Determine effect of transactions on basic owner's equity.

BE1.9 (LO 4) Presented below are three transactions. Mark each transaction as affecting owner's investment (I), owner's drawings (D), revenue (R), expense (E), or not affecting owner's equity (NOE).

________ **a.** Received cash for services performed

________ **b.** Paid cash to purchase equipment

________ **c.** Paid employee salaries

Prepare a balance sheet.

BE1.10 (LO 5) Financial Statement In alphabetical order below are balance sheet items for Smyth Company at December 31, 2020. Kathy Smyth is the owner of Smyth Company. Prepare a balance sheet, following the format of Illustration 1.9.

Accounts payable	$90,000
Accounts receivable	62,500
Cash	49,000
Owner's capital	21,500

Determine where items appear on financial statements.

BE1.11 (LO 5) Financial Statement Indicate whether the following items would appear on the income statement (IS), balance sheet (BS), or owner's equity statement (OE).

________ **a.** Notes payable

________ **b.** Advertising expense

________ **c.** Owner's capital

________ **d.** Cash

________ **e.** Service revenue

DO IT! Exercises

Review basic concepts.

DO IT! 1.1 (LO 1) Indicate whether each of the five statements presented below is true or false.

1. The three steps in the accounting process are identification, recording, and examination.
2. The accounting process includes the bookkeeping function.
3. Managerial accounting provides reports to help investors and creditors evaluate a company.
4. The two most common types of external users are investors and creditors.
5. Internal users include human resources managers.

Identify building blocks of accounting.

DO IT! 1.2 (LO 2) Indicate whether each of the five statements presented below is true or false.

1. Congress passed the Sarbanes-Oxley Act to ensure that investors invest only in companies that will be profitable.
2. The standards of conduct by which actions are judged as loyal or disloyal are ethics.
3. The primary accounting standard-setting body in the United States is the Securities and Exchange Commission (SEC).
4. The historical cost principle dictates that companies record assets at their cost and continue to report them at their cost over the time the assets are held.
5. The monetary unit assumption requires that companies record only transactions that can be measured in money.

Evaluate effects of transactions on owner's equity.

DO IT! 1.3 (LO 3) Classify the following items as investment by owner (I), owner's drawings (D), revenues (R), or expenses (E). Then indicate whether each item increases or decreases owner's equity.

1. Drawings.
2. Rent revenue.
3. Advertising expense.
4. Owner puts personal assets into the business.

Prepare tabular analysis.

DO IT! 1.4 (LO 4) Transactions made by A. Marti and Co., a law firm, for the month of March are shown below. Prepare a tabular analysis which shows the effects of these transactions on the expanded accounting equation, similar to that shown in Illustration 1.8.

1. The company performed $20,000 of services for customers, on credit.
2. The company received $20,000 in cash from customers who had been billed for services (in transaction 1).
3. The company received a bill for $3,200 of advertising but will not pay it until a later date.
4. A. Marti withdrew $2,500 cash from the business for personal use.

DO IT! 1.5 (LO 5) Presented below is selected information related to Kirby Company at December 31, 2020. Kirby reports financial information monthly.

Determine specific amounts on the financial statements.

Accounts Payable	$ 3,000	Salaries and Wages Expense	$16,500
Cash	6,500	Notes Payable	25,000
Advertising Expense	6,000	Rent Expense	10,500
Service Revenue	53,500	Accounts Receivable	13,500
Equipment	29,000	Owner's Drawings	7,500

a. Determine the total assets of Kirby Company at December 31, 2020.

b. Determine the net income that Kirby Company reported for December 2020.

c. Determine the owner's equity of Kirby Company at December 31, 2020.

Exercises

E1.1 (LO 1) Genesis Company performs the following accounting tasks during the year.

Classify the three activities of accounting.

________Analyzing and interpreting information.
________Classifying economic events.
________Explaining uses, meaning, and limitations of data.
________Keeping a systematic chronological diary of events.
________Measuring events in dollars and cents.
________Preparing accounting reports.
________Reporting information in a standard format.
________Selecting economic activities relevant to the company.
________Summarizing economic events.

Accounting is "an information system that **identifies**, **records**, and **communicates** the economic events of an organization to interested users."

Instructions

Categorize the accounting tasks performed by Genesis as relating to either the identification (I), recording (R), or communication (C) aspects of accounting.

E1.2 (LO 1) **a.** The following are users of financial statements.

Identify users of accounting information.

________Customers
________Internal Revenue Service
________Labor unions
________Marketing manager
________Production supervisor
________Securities and Exchange Commission
________Store manager
________Suppliers
________Vice president of finance

Instructions

Identify the users as being either **external users** or **internal users**.

b. The following questions could be asked by an internal user or an external user.

________Can we afford to give our employees a pay raise?
________Did the company earn a satisfactory income?
________Do we need to borrow in the near future?
________How does the company's profitability compare to other companies?
________What does it cost us to manufacture each unit produced?
________Which product should we emphasize?
________Will the company be able to pay its short-term debts?

Instructions

Identify each of the questions as being more likely asked by an **internal user** or an **external user**.

Discuss ethics and the historical cost principle.

E1.3 (LO 2) Angela Duffy, president of Duffy Company, has instructed Jana Barth, the head of the accounting department for Duffy Company, to report the company's land in the company's accounting reports at its fair value of $170,000 instead of its cost of $100,000. Duffy says, "Showing the land at $170,000 will make our company look like a better investment when we try to attract new investors next month."

Instructions

Explain the ethical situation involved for Jana Barth, identifying the stakeholders and the alternatives.

Use accounting concepts.

E1.4 (LO 2) The following situations involve accounting principles and assumptions.

1. Sosa Company owns buildings that are worth substantially more than they originally cost. In an effort to provide more relevant information, Sosa reports the buildings at fair value in its accounting reports.
2. Mays Company includes in its accounting records only transaction data that can be expressed in terms of money.
3. Curt Russell, owner of Curt's Photography, records his personal living costs as expenses of the business.

Instructions

For each of the three situations, say if the accounting method used is correct or incorrect. If correct, identify which principle or assumption supports the method used. If incorrect, identify which principle or assumption has been violated.

Classify accounts as assets, liabilities, and owner's equity.

E1.5 (LO 3) Diehl Cleaners has the following balance sheet items.

Accounts payable	Accounts receivable
Cash	Notes payable
Equipment	Salaries and wages payable
Supplies	Owner's capital

Instructions

Classify each item as an asset, liability, or owner's equity.

Analyze the effect of transactions.

E1.6 (LO 4) Selected transactions for Poway Landscaping Company are listed below.

1. Made cash investment to start business.
2. Paid monthly rent.
3. Purchased equipment on account.
4. Billed customers for services performed.
5. Withdrew cash for owner's personal use.
6. Received cash from customers billed in (4).
7. Incurred advertising expense on account.
8. Purchased additional equipment for cash.
9. Received cash from customers when service was performed.

Instructions

List the numbers of the above transactions and describe the effect of each transaction on assets, liabilities, and owner's equity. For example, the first answer is: (1) Increase in assets and increase in owner's equity.

Analyze the effect of transactions on assets, liabilities, and owner's equity.

E1.7 (LO 4) Falske Computer Timeshare Company entered into the following transactions during May 2020.

1. Purchased computers for $20,000 from Digital Equipment on account.
2. Paid $4,000 cash for May rent on storage space.
3. Received $17,000 cash from customers for contracts billed in April.
4. Performed computer services for Viking Construction Company for $4,000 cash.
5. Paid Tri-State Power Co. $11,000 cash for energy usage in May.

6. Falske invested an additional $29,000 in the business.
7. Paid Digital Equipment for the computers purchased in (1) above.
8. Incurred advertising expense for May of $1,200 on account.

Instructions

Indicate with the appropriate letter whether each of the transactions above results in:

a. An increase in assets and a decrease in assets.

b. An increase in assets and an increase in owner's equity.

c. An increase in assets and an increase in liabilities.

d. A decrease in assets and a decrease in owner's equity.

e. A decrease in assets and a decrease in liabilities.

f. An increase in liabilities and a decrease in owner's equity.

g. An increase in owner's equity and a decrease in liabilities.

Analyze transactions and compute net income.

E1.8 (LO 4) **Writing** An analysis of the transactions made by Peat Deloitte & Co., a certified public accounting firm, for the month of August is shown below. The expenses were $560 for rent, $4,800 for salaries and wages, and $400 for utilities.

	Cash	+	Accounts Receivable	+	Supplies	+	Equipment	=	Accounts Payable	+	Owner's Capital	−	Owner's Drawings	+	Revenues	−	Expenses
1.	+$15,000										+$15,000						
2.	−2,000						+$5,000		+$3,000								
3.	−750				+$750												
4.	+4,000		+$4,500												+$8,500		
5.	−1,500								−1,500								
6.	−2,000												−$2,000				
7.	−560																−$560
8.	+450		−450														
9.	−4,800																−4,800
10.									+400								−400

Instructions

a. Describe each transaction that occurred for the month.

b. Determine how much owner's equity increased for the month.

c. Compute the amount of net income for the month.

Prepare financial statements.

E1.9 (LO 5) **Financial Statement** An analysis of transactions for Peat DeLoitte & Co. was presented in E1.8.

Instructions

Prepare an income statement and an owner's equity statement for August and a balance sheet at August 31, 2020. Assume that August is the company's first month of business.

Determine net income (or loss).

E1.10 (LO 5) Hawke Company had the following assets and liabilities on the dates indicated.

December 31	Total Assets	Total Liabilities
2019	$400,000	$250,000
2020	$460,000	$300,000
2021	$590,000	$400,000

Hawke began business on January 1, 2019, with an investment of $100,000.

Instructions

From an analysis of the change in owner's equity during the year, compute the net income (or loss) for:

a. 2019, assuming Hawke's drawings were $12,000 for the year.

b. 2020, assuming Hawke made an additional investment of $34,000 and had no drawings in 2020.

c. 2021, assuming Hawke made an additional investment of $12,000 and had drawings of $25,000 in 2021.

Analyze financial statements items.

E1.11 (LO 5) Two items are omitted from each of the following summaries of balance sheet and income statement data for two proprietorships for the year 2020, Greene's Goods and Solar Enterprises.

	Greene's Goods	Solar Enterprises
Beginning of year:		
Total assets	$110,000	$129,000
Total liabilities	85,000	(c)
Total owner's equity	(a)	80,000
End of year:		
Total assets	160,000	180,000
Total liabilities	120,000	50,000
Total owner's equity	40,000	130,000
Changes during year in owner's equity:		
Additional investment	(b)	25,000
Drawings	37,000	(d)
Total revenues	220,000	100,000
Total expenses	175,000	60,000

Instructions

Determine the missing amounts.

Prepare income statement and owner's equity statement.

E1.12 (LO 5) **Financial Statement** The following information relates to Fleete Co. for the year 2020.

Owner's capital, January 1, 2020	$42,000	Advertising expense	$ 1,800
Owner's drawings during 2020	6,000	Rent expense	10,400
Service revenue	63,600	Utilities expense	3,100
Salaries and wages expense	30,200		

Instructions

After analyzing the data, prepare an income statement and an owner's equity statement for the year ending December 31, 2020.

Correct an incorrectly prepared balance sheet.

E1.13 (LO 5) **Financial Statement** Abby Roland is the bookkeeper for Cheng Company. Abby has been trying to determine the correct balance sheet for Cheng Company. Cheng's balance sheet is shown below.

Cheng Company
Balance Sheet
December 31, 2020

Assets		Liabilities	
Cash	$15,000	Accounts payable	$21,000
Supplies	8,000	Accounts receivable	(6,500)
Equipment	46,000	Owner's capital	67,500
Owner's drawings	13,000	Total liabilities and	
Total assets	$82,000	owner's equity	$82,000

Instructions

Prepare a correct balance sheet.

Compute net income and prepare a balance sheet.

E1.14 (LO 5) **Financial Statement** Saira Morrow is the sole owner of Buena Vista Park, a public camping ground near the Crater Lake National Recreation Area. Saira has compiled the following financial information as of December 31, 2020.

Revenues during 2020—camping fees	$140,000	Fair value of equipment	$140,000
Revenues during 2020—general store	65,000	Notes payable	60,000
Accounts payable	11,000	Expenses during 2020	160,000
Cash on hand	23,000	Accounts receivable	17,500
Original cost of equipment	115,500		

Instructions

a. Determine Saira Morrow's net income from Buena Vista Park for 2020.

b. Prepare a balance sheet for Buena Vista Park as of December 31, 2020.

E1.15 (LO 5) **Financial Statement** Presented below is financial information related to the 2020 operations of Sea Legs Cruise Company.

Prepare an income statement.

Maintenance and repairs expense	$ 95,000
Utilities expense	13,000
Salaries and wages expense	142,000
Advertising expense	24,500
Ticket revenue	410,000

Instructions

Prepare the 2020 income statement for Sea Legs Cruise Company.

E1.16 (LO 5) **Financial Statement** Presented below is information related to the sole proprietorship of Helen Archer, attorney.

Prepare an owner's equity statement.

Legal service revenue—2020	$330,000
Total expenses—2020	211,000
Assets, January 1, 2020	98,000
Liabilities, January 1, 2020	62,000
Assets, December 31, 2020	168,000
Liabilities, December 31, 2020	100,000
Drawings—2020	?

Instructions

Prepare the 2020 owner's equity statement for Helen Archer's legal practice.

E1.17 (LO 5) **Financial Statement** This information is for Paulo Company for the year ended December 31, 2020.

Prepare a cash flow statement.

Cash received from revenues from customers	$600,000
Cash received from investment by owner	280,000
Cash paid for new equipment	115,000
Cash drawings by owner paid	18,000
Cash paid for expenses	430,000
Cash balance 1/1/20	30,000

Instructions

Prepare the 2020 statement of cash flows for Paulo Company.

E1.18 (LO 5) The statement of cash flows classifies each transaction as an operating activity, an investing activity, or a financing activity. Operating activities are the types of activities the company performs to generate profits. Investing activities include the purchase of long-lived assets such as equipment or the purchase of investment securities. Financing activities are borrowing money, investment by owner, and cash drawings by owner.

Identify cash flow activities.

Presented below are the following transactions.

1. Owner invested $20,000 cash.
2. Issued note payable for $12,000 cash.
3. Purchased office equipment for $11,000 cash.
4. Received $15,000 cash for services performed.
5. Paid $1,000 cash for rent.
6. Paid $600 cash drawings to owner.
7. Paid $5,700 cash for salaries.

Instructions

Classify each of these transactions as operating, investing, or financing activities.

Problems: Set A

Analyze transactions and compute net income.

Excel

P1.1A (LO 3, 4) On April 1, Julie Spengel established Spengel's Travel Agency. The following transactions were completed during the month.

1. Invested $15,000 cash to start the agency.
2. Paid $600 cash for April office rent.
3. Purchased equipment for $3,000 cash.
4. Incurred $700 of advertising costs in the *Chicago Tribune,* on account.
5. Paid $900 cash for office supplies.
6. Performed services worth $10,000: $3,000 cash is received from customers, and the balance of $7,000 is billed to customers on account.
7. Withdrew $600 cash for personal use.
8. Paid *Chicago Tribune* $500 of the amount due in transaction (4).
9. Paid employees' salaries $2,500.
10. Received $4,000 in cash from customers who have previously been billed in transaction (6).

***Check figures** provide a key number to let you know you are on the right track.*

a. Total assets $20,800

b. Net income $6,200

Instructions

a. Prepare a tabular analysis of the transactions using the following column headings: Cash, Accounts Receivable, Supplies, Equipment, Accounts Payable, Owner's Capital, Owner's Drawings, Revenues, and Expenses.

b. From an analysis of the owner's equity columns, compute the net income or net loss for April.

Analyze transactions and prepare income statement, owner's equity statement, and balance sheet.

Excel

P1.2A (LO 4, 5) **Financial Statement** Sonya Jared opened a law office on July 1, 2020. On July 31, the balance sheet showed Cash $5,000, Accounts Receivable $1,500, Supplies $500, Equipment $6,000, Accounts Payable $4,200, and Owner's Capital $8,800. During August, the following transactions occurred.

1. Collected $1,200 of accounts receivable.
2. Paid $2,800 cash on accounts payable.
3. Recognized revenue of $7,500 of which $4,000 is collected in cash and the balance is due in September.
4. Purchased additional equipment for $2,000, paying $400 in cash and the balance on account.
5. Paid salaries $2,800, rent for August $900, and advertising expenses $400.
6. Withdrew $700 in cash for personal use.
7. Received $2,000 from Standard Federal Bank—money borrowed on a note payable.
8. Incurred utility expenses for month on account $270.

Instructions

a. Total assets $16,500

b. Net income $3,130
Ending capital $11,230

a. Prepare a tabular analysis of the August transactions beginning with July 31 balances. The column headings should be as follows: Cash + Accounts Receivable + Supplies + Equipment = Notes Payable + Accounts Payable + Owner's Capital − Owner's Drawings + Revenues − Expenses.

b. Prepare an income statement for August, an owner's equity statement for August, and a balance sheet at August 31.

Prepare income statement, owner's equity statement, and balance sheet.

P1.3A (LO 5) **Financial Statement** On June 1, Cindy Godfrey started Divine Designs Co., a company that provides craft opportunities, by investing $12,000 cash in the business. Following are the assets and liabilities of the company at June 30 and the revenues and expenses for the month of June.

Cash	$10,150	Service Revenue	$6,500
Accounts Receivable	2,800	Advertising Expense	500
Supplies	2,000	Rent Expense	1,600
Equipment	10,000	Gasoline Expense	200
Notes Payable	9,000	Utilities Expense	150
Accounts Payable	1,200		

Cindy made no additional investment in June but withdrew $1,300 in cash for personal use during the month.

Instructions

a. Net income $4,050
Owner's equity $14,750
Total assets $24,950
b. Owner's equity $15,500

a. Prepare an income statement and owner's equity statement for the month of June and a balance sheet at June 30, 2020.

b. Prepare an income statement and owner's equity statement for June assuming the following data are not included above: (1) $900 of services were performed and billed but not collected at June 30, and (2) $150 of gasoline expense was incurred but not paid.

Analyze transactions and prepare financial statements.

P1.4A (LO 4, 5) **Financial Statement** Maisie Taft started her own consulting firm, Maisie Consulting, on May 1, 2020. The following transactions occurred during the month of May.

May	1	Maisie invested $7,000 cash in the business.
	2	Paid $900 for office rent for the month.
	3	Purchased $800 of supplies on account.
	5	Paid $125 to advertise in the *County News*.
	9	Received $4,000 cash for services performed.
	12	Withdrew $1,000 cash for personal use.
	15	Performed $6,400 of services on account.
	17	Paid $2,500 for employee salaries.
	20	Made a partial payment of $600 for the supplies purchased on account on May 3.
	23	Received a cash payment of $4,000 for services performed on account on May 15.
	26	Borrowed $5,000 from the bank on a note payable.
	29	Purchased equipment for $4,200 on account.
	30	Paid $275 for utilities.

Instructions

a. Show the effects of the previous transactions on the accounting equation using the following format.

a. Total assets $22,000

	Assets								Liabilities				Owner's Equity						
			Accounts						Notes		Accounts		Owner's		Owner's				
Date	Cash	+	Receivable	+	Supplies	+	Equipment	=	Payable	+	Payable	+	Capital	−	Drawings	+	Revenues	−	Expenses

b. Prepare an income statement for the month of May.

c. Prepare a balance sheet at May 31, 2020.

b. Net income $6,600
c. Cash $14,600

Determine financial statement amounts and prepare owner's equity statement.

P1.5A (LO 4, 5) **Writing** **Financial Statement** Financial statement information about four different companies is as follows.

	Alpha Company	Beta Company	Psi Company	Omega Company
January 1, 2020				
Assets	$ 80,000	$ 90,000	(g)	$150,000
Liabilities	41,000	(d)	80,000	(j)
Owner's equity	(a)	40,000	49,000	90,000
December 31, 2020				
Assets	(b)	112,000	170,000	(k)
Liabilities	60,000	72,000	(h)	100,000
Owner's equity	50,000	(e)	82,000	151,000
Owner's equity changes in year				
Additional investment	(c)	8,000	10,000	15,000
Drawings	15,000	(f)	12,000	10,000
Total revenues	350,000	410,000	(i)	500,000
Total expenses	333,000	385,000	350,000	(l)

Instructions

a. Determine the missing amounts. (*Hint:* For example, to solve for (a), Assets − Liabilities = Owner's equity = $39,000.)

b. Prepare the owner's equity statement for Alpha Company.

c. Write a memorandum explaining the sequence for preparing financial statements and the interrelationship of the owner's equity statement to the income statement and balance sheet.

Continuing Case

*The **Cookie Creations** case starts in this chapter and continues through Chapter 18. The business begins as a sole proprietorship and then evolves into a partnership and finally a corporation. You also can find this case in WileyPLUS.*

Cookie Creations

© leungchopan/ Shutterstock

CC1 Natalie Koebel spent much of her childhood learning the art of cookie-making from her grandmother. They passed many happy hours mastering every type of cookie imaginable and later creating new recipes that were both healthy and delicious. Now at the start of her second year in college, Natalie is investigating various possibilities for starting her own business as part of the requirements of the entrepreneurship program in which she is enrolled.

A long-time friend insists that Natalie has to include cookies in her business plan. After a series of brainstorming sessions, Natalie settles on the idea of operating a cookie-making school. She will start on a part-time basis and offer her services in people's homes. Now that she has started thinking about it, the possibilities seem endless. During the fall, she will concentrate on holiday cookies. She will offer individual lessons and group sessions (which will probably be more entertainment than education for the participants). Natalie also decides to include children in her target market.

The first difficult decision is coming up with the perfect name for her business. Natalie settles on "Cookie Creations" and then moves on to more important issues.

Instructions

a. What form of business organization—proprietorship, partnership, or corporation—do you recommend that Natalie use for her business? Discuss the benefits and weaknesses of each form and give the reasons for your choice.

b. Will Natalie need accounting information? If yes, what information will she need and why? How often will she need this information?

c. Identify specific asset, liability, and owner's equity accounts that Cookie Creations will likely use to record its business transactions.

d. Should Natalie open a separate bank account for the business? Why or why not?

Ethics Case

EC1 After numerous campus interviews, Travis Chase, a senior at Great Northern College, received two office interview invitations from the Baltimore offices of two large firms. Both firms offered to cover his out-of-pocket expenses (travel, hotel, and meals). He scheduled the interviews for both firms on the same day, one in the morning and one in the afternoon. At the conclusion of each interview, he submitted to both firms his total out-of-pocket expenses for the trip to Baltimore: mileage $112 (280 miles at $0.40), hotel $130, meals $36, and parking and tolls $18, for a total of $296. He believes this approach is appropriate. If he had made two trips, his cost would have been two times $296. He is also certain that neither firm knew he had visited the other on that same trip. Within 10 days, Travis received two checks in the mail, each in the amount of $296.

Instructions

a. Who are the stakeholders (affected parties) in this situation?

b. What are the ethical issues in this case?

c. What would you do in this situation?

Expand Your Critical Thinking

Financial Reporting Problem: Apple Inc.

CT1.1 The financial statements of **Apple Inc.** for 2015 are presented in Appendix A. The complete annual report, including the notes to the financial statements, is available at the company's website.

Instructions

Refer to Apple's financial statements and answer the following questions.

a. What were Apple's total assets at September 26, 2015? At September 27, 2014?

b. How much cash (and cash equivalents) did Apple have on September 26, 2015?

c. What amount of accounts payable did Apple report on September 26, 2015? On September 27, 2014?

d. What were Apple's net sales in 2013? In 2014? In 2015?

e. What is the amount of the change in Apple's net income from 2014 to 2015?

Comparative Analysis Problem: PepsiCo, Inc. vs. The Coca-Cola Company

CT1.2 PepsiCo, Inc.'s financial statements are presented in Appendix B. Financial statements of **The Coca-Cola Company** are presented in Appendix C. The complete annual reports of PepsiCo and Coca-Cola, including the notes to the financial statements, are available at each company's respective website.

Instructions

a. Based on the information contained in these financial statements, determine the following for each company.

1. Total assets at December 26, 2015, for PepsiCo and for Coca-Cola at December 31, 2015.
2. Accounts (notes) receivable, net at December 26, 2015, for PepsiCo and at December 31, 2015, for Coca-Cola.
3. Net revenues for year ended in 2015.
4. Net income for year ended in 2015.

b. What conclusions concerning the two companies can be drawn from these data?

Comparative Analysis Problem: Amazon.com, Inc. vs. Wal-Mart Stores, Inc.

CT1.3 Amazon.com, Inc.'s financial statements are presented in Appendix D. Financial statements of **Wal-Mart Stores, Inc.** are presented in Appendix E. The complete annual reports of Amazon and Wal-Mart, including the notes to the financial statements, are available at each company's respective website.

Instructions

a. Based on the information contained in these financial statements, determine the following for each company.

1. Total assets at December 31, 2015, for Amazon and for Wal-Mart at January 31, 2016.
2. Receivables (net) at December 31, 2015, for Amazon and for Wal-Mart at January 31, 2016.
3. Net sales (product only) for year ended in 2015 (2016 for Wal-Mart).
4. Net income for the year ended in 2015 (2016 for Wal-Mart).

b. What conclusions concerning these two companies can be drawn from these data?

Real-World Focus

CT1.4 This exercise will familiarize you with the skills needed (other than accounting skills) to be a successful accountant.

Instructions

Search the Internet for "start here go places" to access free accounting resources for future CPAs and then answer the following questions.

a. What are the four skill sets that are useful for success in accounting?

b. Why are these skill sets useful for a successful accounting career?

Decision-Making Across the Organization

CT1.5 Anya and Nick Ramon, local golf stars, opened the Chip-Shot Driving Range on March 1, 2020, by investing $25,000 of their cash savings in the business. A caddy shack was constructed for cash at a cost of $8,000, and $800 was spent on golf balls and golf clubs. The Ramons leased five acres of land at a cost of $1,000 per month and paid the first month's rent. During the first month, advertising costs totaled $750, of which $100 was unpaid at March 31, and $400 was paid to members of the high-school golf team for retrieving golf balls. All revenues from customers were deposited in the company's bank account. On March 15, Anya and Nick withdrew a total of $1,000 in cash for personal living expenses. A $120 utility bill was received on March 31 but was not paid. On March 31, the balance in the company's bank account was $18,900.

Anya and Nick thought they had a pretty good first month of operations. But, their estimates of profitability ranged from a loss of $6,100 to net income of $2,480.

Instructions

With the class divided into groups, answer the following.

a. How could the Ramons have concluded that the business operated at a loss of $6,100? Was this a valid basis on which to determine net income?

b. How could the Ramons have concluded that the business operated at a net income of $2,480? (*Hint:* Prepare a balance sheet at March 31.) Was this a valid basis on which to determine net income?

c. Without preparing an income statement, determine the actual net income for March.

d. What was the revenue recognized in March?

Communication Activity

CT1.6 Amy Sawyer, the bookkeeper for New Hampshire Company, has been trying to determine the correct balance sheet for the company. The company's balance sheet is shown below.

New Hampshire Company
Balance Sheet
For the Month Ended December 31, 2020

Assets		Liabilities	
Equipment	$25,500	Owner's capital	$26,000
Cash	9,000	Accounts receivable	(5,000)
Supplies	3,000	Owner's drawings	(2,000)
Accounts payable	(8,000)	Notes payable	10,500
	$29,500		$29,500

Instructions

Explain to Amy Sawyer in a memo why the original balance sheet is incorrect, and what should be done to correct it.

All About You

CT1.7 Some people are tempted to make their finances look worse to get financial aid. Companies sometimes also manage their financial numbers in order to accomplish certain goals. Earnings management is the planned timing of revenues, expenses, gains, and losses to smooth out bumps in net income. In managing earnings, companies' actions vary from being within the range of ethical activity to being both unethical and illegal attempts to mislead investors and creditors.

Instructions

Provide responses for each of the following questions.

a. Discuss whether you think each of the following actions (adapted from the FAFSA website) to increase the chances of receiving financial aid is ethical.

1. Spend the student's assets and income first, before spending parents' assets and income.
2. Accelerate necessary expenses to reduce available cash. For example, if you need a new car, buy it before applying for financial aid.
3. State that a truly financially dependent child is independent.
4. Have a parent take an unpaid leave of absence for long enough to get below the "threshold" level of income.

b. What are some reasons why a **company** might want to overstate its earnings?

c. What are some reasons why a **company** might want to understate its earnings?

d. Under what circumstances might an otherwise ethical person decide to illegally overstate or understate earnings?

Considering People, Planet, and Profit

CT1.8 Although **Clif Bar & Company** is not a public company, it does share its financial information with its employees as part of its open-book management approach. Further, although it does not publicly share its financial information, it does provide a different form of an annual report to external users. In this report, the company provides information regarding its sustainability efforts.

Instructions

Go to the Who We Are page at the Clif Bar website and identify the five aspirations.

FASB Codification Activity

CT1.9 The FASB has developed the Financial Accounting Standards Board Accounting Standards Codification (or more simply "the Codification"). The FASB's primary goal in developing the Codification is to provide in one place all the authoritative literature related to a particular topic. To provide easy access to the Codification, the FASB also developed the Financial Accounting Standards Board Codification Research System (CRS). CRS is an online, real-time database that provides easy access to the Codification. The Codification and the related CRS provide a topically organized structure, subdivided into topic, subtopics, sections, and paragraphs, using a numerical index system.

You may find this system useful in your present and future studies, and so we have provided an opportunity to use this online system as part of the *Expand Your Critical Thinking* section.

Instructions

Academic access to the FASB Codification is available through university subscriptions, obtained from the American Accounting Association, for an annual fee of $150. This subscription covers an unlimited number of students within a single institution. Once this access has been obtained by your school, you should log in and familiarize yourself with the resources that are accessible at the FASB Codification site.

A Look at IFRS

LEARNING OBJECTIVE 7

Describe the impact of international accounting standards on U.S. financial reporting.

Most agree that there is a need for one set of international accounting standards. Here is why:

Multinational corporations. Today's companies view the entire world as their market. For example, **Coca-Cola**, **Intel**, and **McDonald's** generate more than 50% of their sales outside the United States. Many foreign companies, such as **Toyota**, **Nestlé**, and **Sony**, find their largest market to be the United States.

Mergers and acquisitions. The mergers between **Fiat/Chrysler** and **Vodafone/Mannesmann** suggest that we will see even more such business combinations of companies from different countries in the future.

Information technology. As communication barriers continue to topple through advances in technology, companies and individuals in different countries and markets are becoming more comfortable buying and selling goods and services from one another.

Financial markets. Financial markets are of international significance today. Whether it is currency, equity securities (stocks), bonds, or derivatives, there are active markets throughout the world trading these types of instruments.

Key Points

Following are the key similarities and differences between GAAP and IFRS as related to accounting fundamentals.

Similarities

- The basic techniques for recording business transactions are the same for U.S. and international companies.
- Both international and U. S. accounting standards emphasize transparency in financial reporting. Both sets of standards are primarily driven by meeting the needs of investors and creditors.
- The three most common forms of business organizations, proprietorships, partnerships, and corporations, are also found in countries that use international accounting standards.

Differences

- International standards are referred to as International Financial Reporting Standards (IFRS), developed by the International Accounting Standards Board. Accounting standards in the United States are referred to as generally accepted accounting principles (GAAP) and are developed by the Financial Accounting Standards Board.
- IFRS tends to be simpler in its accounting and disclosure requirements; some people say it is more "principles-based." GAAP is more detailed; some people say it is more "rules-based."
- The internal control standards applicable to Sarbanes-Oxley (SOX) apply only to large public companies listed on U.S. exchanges. There is continuing debate as to whether non-U.S. companies should have to comply with this extra layer of regulation.

Looking to the Future

Both the IASB and the FASB are hard at work developing standards that will lead to the elimination of major differences in the way certain transactions are accounted for and reported.

IFRS Practice

IFRS Self-Test Questions

1. Which of the following is **not** a reason why a single set of high-quality international accounting standards would be beneficial?
   - **a.** Mergers and acquisition activity.
   - **b.** Financial markets.
   - **c.** Multinational corporations.
   - **d.** GAAP is widely considered to be a superior reporting system.
2. The Sarbanes-Oxley Act determines:
   - **a.** international tax regulations.
   - **b.** internal control standards as enforced by the IASB.
   - **c.** internal control standards of U.S. publicly traded companies.
   - **d.** U.S. tax regulations.
3. IFRS is considered to be more:
   - **a.** principles-based and less rules-based than GAAP.
   - **b.** rules-based and less principles-based than GAAP.
   - **c.** detailed than GAAP.
   - **d.** None of the above.

IFRS Exercises

IFRS1.1 Who are the two key international players in the development of international accounting standards? Explain their role.

IFRS1.2 What is the benefit of a single set of high-quality accounting standards?

International Financial Reporting Problem: Louis Vuitton

IFRS1.3 The financial statements of **Louis Vuitton** are presented in Appendix F. The complete annual report, including the notes to its financial statements, is available at the company's website.

Instructions

Visit Louis Vuitton's corporate website and answer the following questions from the company's 2015 annual report.

- **a.** What accounting firm performed the audit of Louis Vuitton's financial statements?
- **b.** What is the address of the company's corporate headquarters?
- **c.** What is the company's reporting currency?

Answers to IFRS Self-Test Questions

1. d **2.** c **3.** a

CHAPTER 2

© Nick Laham/Getty Images, Inc.

The Recording Process

Chapter Preview

In Chapter 1, we analyzed business transactions in terms of the accounting equation, and we presented the cumulative effects of these transactions in tabular form. Imagine a company like **MF Global** (as in the following Feature Story) using the same tabular format as Softbyte to keep track of its transactions. In a single day, MF Global engaged in thousands of business transactions. To record each transaction this way would be impractical, expensive, and unnecessary. Instead, companies use a set of procedures and records to keep track of transaction data more easily. This chapter introduces and illustrates these basic procedures and records.

Feature Story

Accidents Happen

How organized are you financially? Take a short quiz. Answer yes or no to each question:

- Does your wallet contain so many cash machine receipts that you've been declared a walking fire hazard?
- Do you wait until your debit card is denied before checking the status of your funds?
- Was Aaron Rodgers (the quarterback for the **Green Bay Packers**) playing high school football the last time you verified the accuracy of your bank account?

If you think it is hard to keep track of the many transactions that make up your life, imagine how difficult it is for a big corporation to do so. Not only that, but now consider how important it is for a large company to have good accounting records, especially if it has control of your life savings. **MF Global Holdings Ltd** was such a company. As a large investment broker, it held billions of dollars of investments for clients. If you had your life savings invested at MF Global, you might be slightly displeased if you heard this from one of its representatives: "You know, I kind of remember an account for someone with a name like yours—now what did we do with that?"

Unfortunately, that is almost exactly what happened to MF Global's clients shortly before it filed for bankruptcy. During the days immediately following the bankruptcy filing, regulators and auditors struggled to piece things together. In the words of one regulator, "Their books are a disaster . . . we're trying to figure out what numbers are real numbers." One company that considered buying an interest in MF Global walked away from the deal because it "couldn't get a sense of what was on the balance sheet." That company said the information that should have been instantly available instead took days to produce.

It now appears that MF Global did not properly segregate customer accounts from company accounts. And, because of its sloppy recordkeeping, customers were not protected when the company had financial troubles. Total customer losses were approximately $1 billion. As you can see, accounting matters!

Source: S. Patterson and A. Lucchetti, "Inside the Hunt for MF Global Cash," *Wall Street Journal Online* (November 11, 2011).

Chapter Outline

LEARNING OBJECTIVES

LO 1 Describe how accounts, debits, and credits are used to record business transactions.	• The account • Debits and credits • Summary of debit/credit rules	**DO IT! 1** Normal Account Balances
LO 2 Indicate how a journal is used in the recording process.	• The recording process • The journal	**DO IT! 2** Recording Business Activities
LO 3 Explain how a ledger and posting help in the recording process.	• The ledger • Posting • Chart of accounts • The recording process illustrated • Summary illustration of journalizing and posting	**DO IT! 3** Posting
LO 4 Prepare a trial balance.	• Limitations of a trial balance • Locating errors • Dollar signs and underlining	**DO IT! 4** Trial Balance

Go to the Review and Practice section at the end of the chapter for a review of key concepts and practice applications with solutions.
Visit WileyPLUS with ORION for additional tutorials and practice opportunities.

Accounts, Debits, and Credits

LEARNING OBJECTIVE 1

Describe how accounts, debits, and credits are used to record business transactions.

The Account

An **account** is an individual accounting record of increases and decreases in a specific asset, liability, or owner's equity item. For example, Softbyte (the company discussed in Chapter 1) would have separate accounts for Cash, Accounts Receivable, Accounts Payable, Service

Revenue, Salaries and Wages Expense, and so on. (Note that whenever we are referring to a specific account, we capitalize the name.)

In its simplest form, an account consists of three parts: (1) a title, (2) a left or debit side, and (3) a right or credit side. Because the format of an account resembles the letter T, we refer to it as a **T-account**. **Illustration 2.1** shows the basic form of an account.

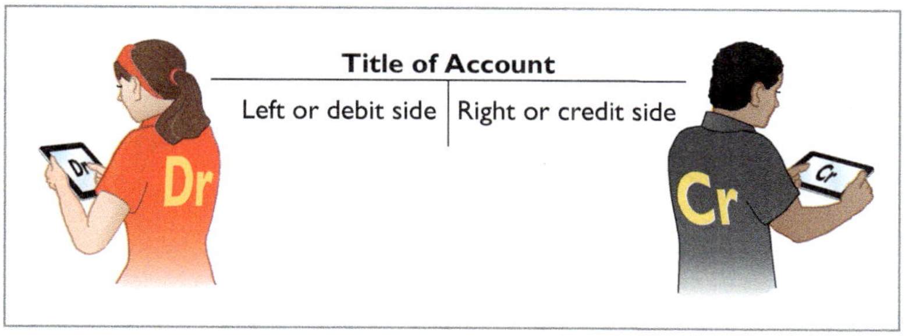

ILLUSTRATION 2.1
Basic form of account

We use this form often throughout this book to explain basic accounting relationships.

Debits and Credits

The term **debit** indicates the left side of an account, and **credit** indicates the right side. They are commonly abbreviated as **Dr.** for debit and **Cr.** for credit. They **do not** mean increase or decrease, as is commonly thought. We use the terms **debit** and **credit** repeatedly in the recording process to describe **where** entries are made in accounts. For example, the act of entering an amount on the left side of an account is called **debiting** the account. Making an entry on the right side is **crediting** the account.

When comparing the totals of the two sides, an account shows a **debit balance** if the total of the debit amounts exceeds the credits. An account shows a **credit balance** if the credit amounts exceed the debits. Note the position of the debit side and credit side in Illustration 2.1.

The procedure of recording debits and credits in an account is shown in **Illustration 2.2** for the transactions affecting the Cash account of Softbyte. The data are taken from the Cash column of the tabular summary in Illustration 1.8.

ILLUSTRATION 2.2
Tabular summary and account form for Softbyte's Cash account

Tabular Summary

Cash
$15,000
−7,000
1,200
1,500
−1,700
−250
600
−1,300
$ 8,050

Account Form

Cash			
(Debits)	15,000	**(Credits)**	7,000
	1,200		1,700
	1,500		250
	600		1,300
Balance **(Debit)**	8,050		

Every positive item in the tabular summary represents a receipt of cash. Every negative amount represents a payment of cash. **Notice that in the account form, we record the increases in cash as debits and the decreases in cash as credits.** For example, the $15,000 receipt of cash (in blue) is debited to Cash, and the –$7,000 payment of cash (in red) is credited to Cash.

Having increases on one side and decreases on the other reduces recording errors and helps in determining the totals of each side of the account as well as the account balance. The balance is determined by netting the two sides (subtracting one amount from the other). The account balance, a debit of $8,050, indicates that Softbyte had $8,050 more increases than decreases in cash. In other words, Softbyte started with a balance of zero and now has $8,050 in its Cash account.

Debit and Credit Procedure

INTERNATIONAL NOTE

Rules for accounting for specific events sometimes differ across countries. Despite the differences, the double-entry accounting system is the basis of accounting systems worldwide.

In Chapter 1, you learned the effect of a transaction on the basic accounting equation. Remember that each transaction must affect two or more accounts to keep the basic accounting equation in balance. In other words, for each transaction, debits must equal credits. The equality of debits and credits provides the basis for the **double-entry system** of recording transactions (see **International Note**).

Under the double-entry system, the dual (two-sided) effect of each transaction is recorded in appropriate accounts. This system provides a logical method for recording transactions and also helps ensure the accuracy of the recorded amounts as well as the detection of errors. If every transaction is recorded with equal debits and credits, the sum of all the debits to the accounts must equal the sum of all the credits.

The double-entry system for determining the equality of the accounting equation is much more efficient than the plus/minus procedure used in Chapter 1. The following discussion illustrates debit and credit procedures in the double-entry system.

Dr./Cr. Procedures for Assets and Liabilities

In Illustration 2.2 for Softbyte, increases in Cash—an asset—are entered on the left side, and decreases in Cash are entered on the right side. We know that both sides of the basic equation (Assets = Liabilities + Owner's Equity) must be equal. It therefore follows that increases and decreases in liabilities have to be recorded **opposite from** increases and decreases in assets. Thus, increases in liabilities are entered on the right or credit side, and decreases in liabilities are entered on the left or debit side. The effects that debits and credits have on assets and liabilities are summarized in **Illustration 2.3**.

ILLUSTRATION 2.3

Debit and credit effects—assets and liabilities

Debits	Credits
Increase assets	Decrease assets
Decrease liabilities	Increase liabilities

Asset accounts normally show debit balances. That is, debits to a specific asset account should exceed credits to that account. Likewise, **liability accounts normally show credit balances**. That is, credits to a liability account should exceed debits to that account. The **normal balance** of an account is on the side where an increase in the account is recorded. **Illustration 2.4** shows the normal balances for assets and liabilities.

ILLUSTRATION 2.4

Normal balances—assets and liabilities

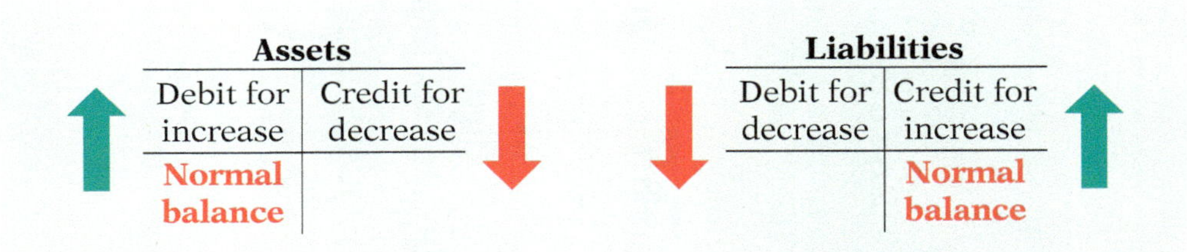

Knowing the normal balance in an account may help you trace errors. For example, a credit balance in an asset account such as Land or a debit balance in a liability account such as Salaries and Wages Payable usually indicates an error. Occasionally, though, an abnormal balance may be correct. The Cash account, for example, will have a credit balance when a company has overdrawn its bank balance by spending more than it has in its account.

Dr./Cr. Procedures for Owner's Equity

As Chapter 1 indicated, owner's investments and revenues increase owner's equity. Owner's drawings and expenses decrease owner's equity. Companies keep accounts for each of these types of transactions.

Owner's Capital. Investments by owners are credited to the Owner's Capital account. Credits increase this account, and debits decrease it. When an owner invests cash in the business, the company debits (increases) Cash and credits (increases) Owner's Capital. When the owner's investment in the business is reduced, Owner's Capital is debited (decreased).

Illustration 2.5 shows the rules of debit and credit for the Owner's Capital account.

Debits	Credits
Decrease Owner's Capital	Increase Owner's Capital

ILLUSTRATION 2.5
Debit and credit effects—Owner's Capital

We can diagram the normal balance in Owner's Capital as shown in **Illustration 2.6**.

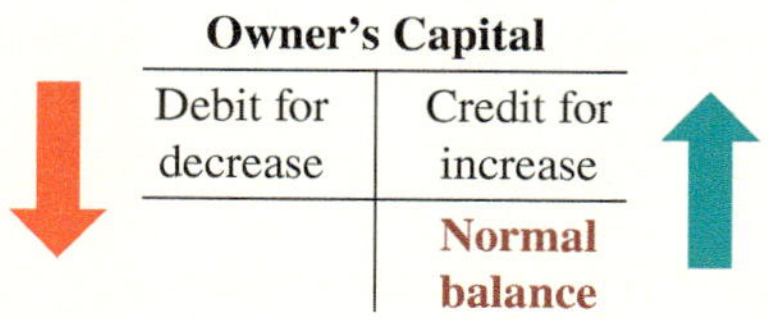

ILLUSTRATION 2.6
Normal balance—Owner's Capital

Owner's Drawings. An owner may withdraw cash or other assets for personal use. Withdrawals could be debited directly to Owner's Capital to indicate a decrease in owner's equity. However, it is preferable to use a separate account, called Owner's Drawings. This separate account makes it easier to determine total withdrawals for each accounting period. Owner's Drawings is increased by debits and decreased by credits. Normally, the drawings account will have a debit balance.

Illustration 2.7 shows the rules of debit and credit for the Owner's Drawings account.

Debits	Credits
Increase Owner's Drawings	Decrease Owner's Drawings

ILLUSTRATION 2.7
Debit and credit effects—Owner's Drawings

We can diagram the normal balance as shown in **Illustration 2.8**.

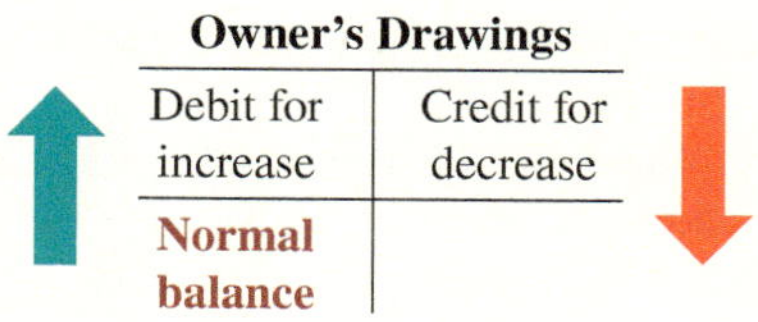

ILLUSTRATION 2.8
Normal balance—Owner's Drawings

The Owner's Drawings account decreases owner's equity. It is not an income statement account like revenues and expenses.

Revenues and Expenses. The purpose of earning revenues is to benefit the owner(s) of the business. When a company recognizes revenues, owner's equity increases. Therefore, **the effect of debits and credits on revenue accounts is the same as their effect on Owner's Capital**. That is, revenue accounts are increased by credits and decreased by debits (see **Helpful Hint**).

Expenses have the opposite effect. Expenses decrease owner's equity. Since expenses decrease net income and revenues increase it, it is logical that the increase and decrease sides of expense accounts should be the opposite of revenue accounts. Thus, expense accounts are increased by debits and decreased by credits. **Illustration 2.9** shows the rules of debits and credits for revenues and expenses.

HELPFUL HINT

Because revenues increase owner's equity, a revenue account has the same debit/credit rules as the Owner's Capital account. Expenses have the opposite effect.

ILLUSTRATION 2.9

Debit and credit effects—revenues and expenses

Debits	Credits
Decrease revenues	Increase revenues
Increase expenses	Decrease expenses

Credits to revenue accounts should exceed debits. Debits to expense accounts should exceed credits. Thus, revenue accounts normally show credit balances, and expense accounts normally show debit balances. **Illustration 2.10** shows the normal balances for revenues and expenses.

ILLUSTRATION 2.10

Normal balances—revenues and expenses

Revenues	
Debit for decrease	Credit for increase
	Normal balance

Expenses	
Debit for increase	Credit for decrease
Normal balance	

Investor Insight Chicago Cubs

Jonathan Daniel/Getty Images, Inc.

Keeping Score

The **Chicago Cubs** baseball team probably has these major revenue and expense accounts:

Revenues	Expenses
Admissions (ticket sales)	Players' salaries
Concessions	Administrative salaries
Television and radio	Travel
Advertising	Ballpark maintenance

Do you think that the Chicago Bears football team would be likely to have the same major revenue and expense accounts as the Cubs? (Go to WileyPLUS for this answer and additional questions.)

HELPFUL HINT

You may want to bookmark Illustration 2.11. You probably will refer to it often.

Summary of Debit/Credit Rules

Illustration 2.11 shows a summary of the debit/credit rules and effects on each type of account. Study this diagram carefully. It will help you understand the fundamentals of the double-entry system (see **Helpful Hint**).

ILLUSTRATION 2.11 **Summary of debit/credit rules**

Basic Equation: Assets = Liabilities + Owner's Equity

Expanded Equation and **Debit / Credit Effects**:

Assets		=	Liabilities		+	Owner's Capital		−	Owner's Drawings		+	Revenues		−	Expenses	
Dr. +	Cr. −		Dr. −	Cr. +		Dr. −	Cr. +		Dr. +	Cr. −		Dr. −	Cr. +		Dr. +	Cr. −

DO IT! 1 | Normal Account Balances

Kate Browne has just rented space in a shopping mall. In this space, she will open a hair salon to be called "Hair It Is." A friend has advised Kate to set up a double-entry set of accounting records in which to record all of her business transactions.

Identify the balance sheet accounts that Kate will likely need to record the transactions needed to open her business. Indicate whether the normal balance of each account is a debit or a credit.

Solution

Kate would likely need the following accounts in which to record the transactions necessary to ready her hair salon for opening day:

Cash (debit balance)
Equipment (debit balance)
Supplies (debit balance)
Accounts Payable (credit balance)
If she borrows money: Notes Payable (credit balance)
Owner's Capital (credit balance)

Related exercise material: **BE2.1, BE2.2, DO IT! 2.1, E2.1, E2.2, and E2.4.**

ACTION PLAN

- **Determine the types of accounts needed. Kate will need asset accounts for each different type of asset she invests in the business and liability accounts for any debts she incurs.**
- **Understand the types of owner's equity accounts. Only Owner's Capital will be needed when Kate begins the business. Other owner's equity accounts will be needed later.**

The Journal

LEARNING OBJECTIVE 2

Indicate how a journal is used in the recording process.

The Recording Process

Although it is possible to enter transaction information directly into the accounts, few businesses do so. Practically every business uses the basic steps shown in **Illustration 2.12** in the recording process (an integral part of the accounting cycle):

1. Analyze each transaction in terms of its effect on the accounts.
2. Enter the transaction information in a journal.
3. Transfer the journal information to the appropriate accounts in the ledger.

ILLUSTRATION 2.12 **The recording process**

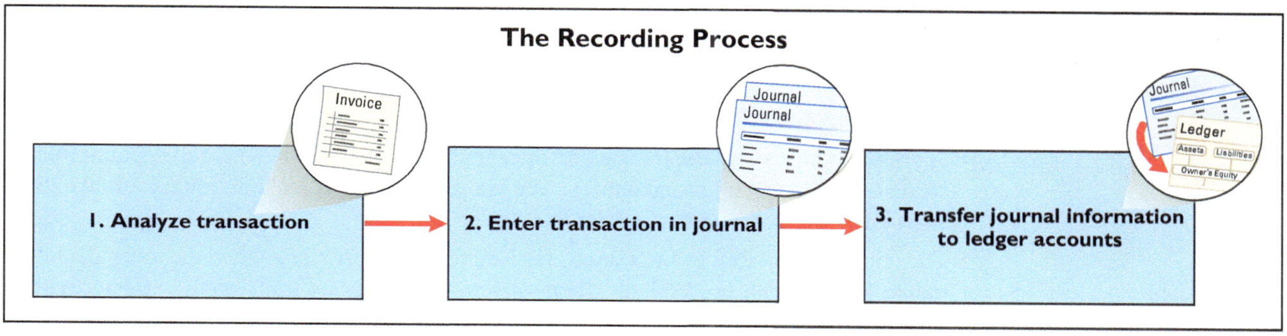

The steps in the recording process occur repeatedly. In Chapter 1, we illustrated the first step, the analysis of transactions, and will give further examples in this and later chapters. The other two steps in the recording process are explained in the next sections.

The Journal

Companies initially record transactions in chronological order (the order in which they occur). Thus, the **journal** is referred to as the book of original entry. For each transaction, the journal shows the debit and credit effects on specific accounts.

Companies may use various kinds of journals, but every company has the most basic form of journal, a **general journal**. Typically, a general journal has spaces for dates, account titles and explanations, references, and two amount columns. See the format of the journal in Illustration 2.13. *Whenever we use the term "journal" in this textbook, we mean the general journal unless we specify otherwise.*

The journal makes several significant contributions to the recording process:

1. It discloses in one place the **complete effects of a transaction**.
2. It provides a **chronological record** of transactions.
3. It helps to **prevent or locate errors** because the debit and credit amounts for each entry can be easily compared.

Journalizing

Entering transaction data in the journal is known as **journalizing**. Companies make separate journal entries for each transaction. A complete entry consists of (1) the date of the transaction, (2) the accounts and amounts to be debited and credited, and (3) a brief explanation of the transaction.

Illustration 2.13 shows the technique of journalizing, using the first two transactions of Softbyte. Recall that on September 1, Ray Neal invested $15,000 cash in the business, and Softbyte purchased computer equipment for $7,000 cash. The number J1 indicates that these two entries are recorded on the first page of the journal. **Illustration 2.13** shows the standard form of journal entries for these two transactions. (The boxed numbers correspond to explanations in the list below the illustration.)

ILLUSTRATION 2.13

Technique of journalizing

GENERAL JOURNAL J1

Date	Account Titles and Explanation	Ref.	Debit	Credit
2020		[5]		
Sept. 1	[2] Cash		15,000	
[1]	[3] Owner's Capital			15,000
	[4] (Owner's investment of cash in business)			
1	Equipment		7,000	
	Cash			7,000
	(Purchase of equipment for cash)			

[1] The date of the transaction is entered in the Date column.

[2] The debit account title (that is, the account to be debited) is entered first at the extreme left margin of the column headed "Account Titles and Explanation," and the amount of the debit is recorded in the Debit column.

[3] The credit account title (that is, the account to be credited) is indented and entered on the next line in the column headed "Account Titles and Explanation," and the amount of the credit is recorded in the Credit column.

[4] A brief explanation of the transaction appears on the line below the credit account title. A space is left between journal entries. The blank space separates individual journal entries and makes the entire journal easier to read.

[5] The column titled Ref. (which stands for Reference) is left blank when the journal entry is made. This column is used later when the journal entries are transferred to the individual accounts.

It is important to use correct and specific account titles in journalizing. Erroneous account titles lead to incorrect financial statements. However, some flexibility exists initially in selecting account titles. The main criterion is that each title must appropriately describe the content of the account. Once a company chooses the specific title to use, it should record under that account title all later transactions involving the account. *In homework problems, you should use specific account titles when they are given.* When account titles are not given, you may select account titles that identify the nature and content of each account. The account titles used in journalizing should not contain explanations such as Cash Paid or Cash Received.

Simple and Compound Entries

Some entries involve only two accounts, one debit and one credit. (See, for example, the entries in Illustration 2.13.) This type of entry is called a **simple entry**. Some transactions, however, require more than two accounts in journalizing. An entry that requires three or more accounts is a **compound entry**. To illustrate, assume that on July 1, Butler Company purchases a delivery truck costing $14,000. It pays $8,000 cash now and agrees to pay the remaining $6,000 on account (to be paid later). **Illustration 2.14** shows the compound entry.

ILLUSTRATION 2.14
Compound journal entry

GENERAL JOURNAL — J1

Date	Account Titles and Explanation	Ref.	Debit	Credit
2020				
July 1	Equipment		14,000	
	Cash			8,000
	Accounts Payable			6,000
	(Purchased truck for cash with balance on account)			

In a compound entry, the standard format requires that all debits be listed before the credits.

Accounting Across the Organization — Hain Celestial Group

Keith Homan/Shutterstock

It Starts with the Transaction

Recording financial transactions in a company's records should be straightforward. If a company determines that a transaction involves revenue, it records revenue. If it has an expense, then it records an expense. However, sometimes this is difficult to do. For example, for more than a year, **Hain Celestial Group** (an organic food company) did not provide income information to investors and regulators. The reason was that the company discovered revenue irregularities and said it could not release financial results until it determined when and how to record revenue for certain transactions. When Hain missed four deadlines for reporting earnings information, the food company suffered a 34% drop in its stock price. As one analyst noted, it was hard to fathom why a seemingly simple revenue recognition issue took one year to resolve.

In other situations, outright fraud may occur. For example, regulators charged **Obsidian Energy** for fraudulently moving millions of dollars in expenses from operating expenses to capital expenditure accounts. By understating reported operating expenses, Obsidian made it appear that it was efficiently managing its costs as well as increasing its income.

These examples demonstrate that "getting the basic transaction right" is the foundation for relevant and reliable financial statements. Starting with an incorrect or inappropriate transaction leads to distortions in the financial statements.

Sources: Shawn Tully, "The Mystery of Hain Celestial's Accounting," *Fortune.com* (August 20, 2016); and Kelly Cryderman, "U.S. Charges Obsidian, Formerly Penn West, with Accounting Fraud," *The Globe and Mail* (June 28, 2017).

Why is it important for companies to record financial transactions completely and accurately? (Go to WileyPLUS for this answer and additional questions.)

DO IT! 2 | Recording Business Activities

Kate Browne engaged in the following activities in establishing her salon, Hair It Is:

1. Opened a bank account in the name of Hair It Is and deposited $20,000 of her own money in this account as her initial investment.
2. Purchased equipment on account (to be paid in 30 days) for a total cost of $4,800.
3. Interviewed three people for the position of hair stylist.

Prepare the journal entries to record the transactions.

ACTION PLAN

- **Understand which activities need to be recorded and which do not. Any that affect assets, liabilities, or owner's equity should be recorded in a journal.**
- **Analyze the effects of transactions on asset, liability, and owner's equity accounts.**

Solution

The three activities would be recorded as follows.

1. Cash	20,000	
Owner's Capital		20,000
(Owner's investment of cash in business)		
2. Equipment	4,800	
Accounts Payable		4,800
(Purchase of equipment on account)		

3. No entry because no transaction has occurred.

Related exercise material: **BE2.3, BE2.4, BE2.5, BE2.6, DO IT! 2.2, E2.3, E2.5, E2.6, E2.7, E2.8, and E2.9.**

The Ledger and Posting

LEARNING OBJECTIVE 3

Explain how a ledger and posting help in the recording process.

The Ledger

The entire group of accounts maintained by a company is the **ledger**. The ledger provides the balance in each of the accounts as well as keeps track of changes in these balances.

Companies may use various kinds of ledgers, but every company has a general ledger. A **general ledger** contains all the asset, liability, and owner's equity accounts, as shown in **Illustration 2.15**. *Whenever we use the term "ledger" in this textbook, we are referring to the general ledger unless we specify otherwise.*

ILLUSTRATION 2.15

The general ledger, which contains all of a company's accounts

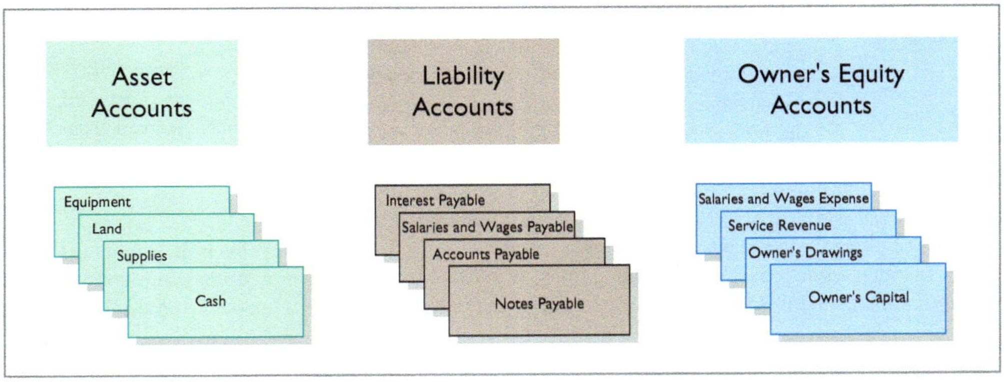

Companies arrange the ledger in the sequence in which they present the accounts in the financial statements, beginning with the balance sheet accounts. First in order are the asset accounts, followed by liability accounts, owner's capital, owner's drawings, revenues, and expenses. Each account is numbered for easier identification.

The ledger provides the balance in each of the accounts. For example, the Cash account shows the amount of cash available to meet current obligations. The Accounts Receivable account shows amounts due from customers. Accounts Payable shows amounts owed to creditors.

Ethics Insight Credit Suisse Group

© Nuno Silva/iStockphoto

A Convenient Overstatement

Sometimes a company's investment securities suffer a permanent decline in value below their original cost. When this occurs, the company is supposed to reduce the recorded value of the securities on its balance sheet ("write them down" in common financial lingo) and record a loss. It appears, however, that during the financial crisis of 2008, employees at some financial institutions chose to look the other way as the value of their investments skidded.

A number of Wall Street traders that worked for the investment bank **Credit Suisse Group** were charged with intentionally overstating the value of securities that had suffered declines of approximately $2.85 billion. One reason that they may have been reluctant to record the losses is out of fear that the company's shareholders and clients would panic if they saw the magnitude of the losses. However, personal self-interest might have been equally to blame—the bonuses of the traders were tied to the value of the investment securities.

Source: S. Pulliam, J. Eaglesham, and M. Siconolfi, "U.S. Plans Changes on Bond Fraud," *Wall Street Journal Online* (February 1, 2012).

What incentives might employees have had to overstate the value of these investment securities on the company's financial statements? (Go to WileyPLUS for this answer and additional questions.)

Standard Form of Account

The simple T-account form used in accounting textbooks is often very useful for illustration purposes. However, in practice, the account forms used in ledgers are much more structured. **Illustration 2.16** shows a typical form, using assumed data from a cash account.

ILLUSTRATION 2.16

Three-column form of account

CASH						NO. 101
Date		**Explanation**	**Ref.**	**Debit**	**Credit**	**Balance**
2020						
June	1			25,000		25,000
	2				8,000	17,000
	3			4,200		21,200
	9			7,500		28,700
	17				11,700	17,000
	20				250	16,750
	30				7,300	9,450

This format is called the **three-column form of account**. It has three money columns—debit, credit, and balance. The balance in the account is determined after each transaction. Companies use the explanation space and reference columns to provide special information about the transaction.

Posting

The procedure of transferring journal entries to the ledger accounts is called **posting**. This phase of the recording process accumulates the effects of journalized transactions into the individual accounts. Posting involves the following steps.

1. In the **ledger**, in the appropriate columns of the account(s) debited, enter the date, journal page, and debit amount shown in the journal.
2. In the reference column of the **journal**, write the account number to which the debit amount was posted.
3. In the **ledger**, in the appropriate columns of the account(s) credited, enter the date, journal page, and credit amount shown in the journal.
4. In the reference column of the **journal**, write the account number to which the credit amount was posted.

Illustration 2.17 shows these four steps using Softbyte's first journal entry. The boxed numbers indicate the sequence of the steps.

ILLUSTRATION 2.17

Posting a journal entry

GENERAL JOURNAL J1

Date	Account Titles and Explanation	Ref.	Debit	Credit
2020 Sept. 1	Cash	101	15,000	
	Owner's Capital	301		15,000
	(Owner's investment of cash in business)			

GENERAL LEDGER

Cash No. 101

Date	Explanation	Ref.	Debit	Credit	Balance
2020 Sept. 1		J1	15,000		15,000

Owner's Capital No. 301

Date	Explanation	Ref.	Debit	Credit	Balance
2020 Sept. 1		J1		15,000	15,000

Key: [1] Post to debit account–date, journal page number, and amount.
[2] Enter debit account number in journal reference column.
[3] Post to credit account–date, journal page number, and amount.
[4] Enter credit account number in journal reference column.

Posting should be performed in chronological order. That is, the company should post all the debits and credits of one journal entry before proceeding to the next journal entry. Postings should be made on a timely basis to ensure that the ledger is up-to-date. *In homework problems, you can journalize all transactions before posting any of the journal entries.*

The reference column of a ledger account indicates the journal page from which the transaction was posted. (After the last entry has been posted, the accountant should scan the reference column **in the journal**, to confirm that all postings have been made.) The explanation space of the ledger account is used infrequently because an explanation already appears in the journal.

Chart of Accounts

The number and type of accounts differ for each company. The number of accounts depends on the amount of detail management desires. For example, the management of one company may want a single account for all types of utility expense. Another may keep separate expense accounts for each type of utility, such as gas, electricity, and water. Similarly, a small company like Softbyte will have fewer accounts than a corporate giant like **Dell**. Softbyte may be able to manage and report its activities in 20 to 30 accounts, while Dell may require thousands of accounts to keep track of its worldwide activities.

Most companies have a **chart of accounts**. This chart lists the accounts and the account numbers that identify their location in the ledger. The numbering system that identifies the accounts usually starts with the balance sheet accounts and follows with the income statement accounts.

In this and the next two chapters, we explain the accounting for Pioneer Advertising (a service company). Accounts 101–199 indicate asset accounts; 200–299 indicate liabilities; 301–350 indicate owner's equity accounts; 400–499, revenues; 601–799, expenses; 800–899, other revenues; and 900–999, other expenses. **Illustration 2.18** shows Pioneer's chart of accounts. Accounts listed in red are used in this chapter; accounts shown in black are explained in later chapters.

ILLUSTRATION 2.18
Chart of accounts

Pioneer Advertising
Chart of Accounts

Assets	Owner's Equity
101 Cash	301 Owner's Capital
112 Accounts Receivable	306 Owner's Drawings
126 Supplies	350 Income Summary
130 Prepaid Insurance	**Revenues**
157 Equipment	400 Service Revenue
158 Accumulated Depreciation—Equipment	
Liabilities	**Expenses**
200 Notes Payable	631 Supplies Expense
201 Accounts Payable	711 Depreciation Expense
209 Unearned Service Revenue	722 Insurance Expense
212 Salaries and Wages Payable	726 Salaries and Wages Expense
230 Interest Payable	729 Rent Expense
	732 Utilities Expense
	905 Interest Expense

You will notice that there are gaps in the numbering system of the chart of accounts for Pioneer. Companies leave gaps to permit the insertion of new accounts as needed during the life of the business.

The Recording Process Illustrated

Illustrations 2.19 through **2.28** show the basic steps in the recording process, using the October transactions of Pioneer Advertising (see **Helpful Hint**). Pioneer's accounting period is a month. In these illustrations, a basic analysis, an equation analysis, and a debit-credit analysis precede the journal entry and posting of each transaction. For simplicity, we use the T-account form to show the posting instead of the standard account form.

HELPFUL HINT

The Accounting Cycle Tutorial in WileyPLUS provides an interactive presentation of the accounting cycle using these transaction analyses.

Study these transaction analyses carefully. **The purpose of transaction analysis is first to identify the type of account involved, and then to determine whether to make a debit**

or a credit to the account. You should always perform this type of analysis before preparing a journal entry. Doing so will help you understand the journal entries discussed in this chapter as well as more complex journal entries in later chapters (see **Helpful Hint**).

ILLUSTRATION 2.19
Investment of cash by owner

Cash flow analyses show the impact of each transaction on cash.

Cash Flows
+10,000

Transaction: On October 1, C. R. Byrd invests $10,000 cash in an advertising company called Pioneer Advertising.

Basic Analysis: The asset Cash increases $10,000; owner's equity (specifically, Owner's Capital) increases $10,000.

Equation Analysis:

Assets	=	Liabilities	+	Owner's Equity
Cash	=			Owner's Capital
+$10,000				+$10,000

Debit–Credit Analysis: Debits increase assets: debit Cash $10,000. Credits increase owner's equity: credit Owner's Capital $10,000.

Journal Entry:

Oct. 1	Cash	101	10,000	
	Owner's Capital	301		10,000
	(Owner's investment of cash in business)			

Posting:

Cash		101
Oct. 1	10,000	

Owner's Capital		301
	Oct. 1	10,000

HELPFUL HINT

Follow these steps:

1. Determine what type of account is involved.
2. Determine what items increased or decreased and by how much.
3. Translate the increases and decreases into debits and credits.

ILLUSTRATION 2.20
Purchase of office equipment

Cash Flows
no effect

Transaction: On October 1, Pioneer purchases office equipment costing $5,000 by signing a 3-month, 12%, $5,000 note payable.

Basic Analysis: The asset Equipment increases $5,000; the liability Notes Payable increases $5,000.

Equation Analysis:

Assets	=	Liabilities	+	Owner's Equity
Equipment	=	Notes Payable		
+$5,000		+$5,000		

Debit–Credit Analysis: Debits increase assets: debit Equipment $5,000. Credits increase liabilities: credit Notes Payable $5,000.

Journal Entry:

Oct. 1	Equipment	157	5,000	
	Notes Payable	200		5,000
	(Issued 3-month, 12% note for office equipment)			

Posting:

Equipment		157
Oct. 1	5,000	

Notes Payable		200
	Oct. 1	5,000

ILLUSTRATION 2.21

Receipt of cash for future service

Transaction

On October 2, Pioneer receives a $1,200 cash advance from R. Knox, a client, for advertising services that are expected to be completed by December 31.

Basic Analysis

The asset Cash increases $1,200; the liability Unearned Service Revenue increases $1,200 because the service has not been performed yet. That is, when Pioneer receives an advance payment, it should record an unearned revenue (a liability) in order to recognize the obligation that exists.

Equation Analysis

Assets	=	**Liabilities**	+	**Owner's Equity**
Cash	=	Unearned Service Revenue		
+$1,200		+$1,200		

Debit–Credit Analysis

Debits increase assets: debit Cash $1,200.
Credits increase liabilities: credit Unearned Service Revenue $1,200.

Journal Entry

Oct. 2	Cash	101	1,200	
	Unearned Service Revenue	209		1,200
	(Received cash from R. Knox for future services)			

Posting

Cash			101
Oct. 1	10,000		
2	1,200		

Unearned Service Revenue			209
		Oct. 2	1,200

Many liabilities have the word "payable" in their title. But, note that Unearned Service Revenue is considered a liability even though the word *payable* is not used.

Cash Flows
+1,200

ILLUSTRATION 2.22

Payment of monthly rent

Transaction

On October 3, Pioneer pays office rent for October in cash, $900.

Basic Analysis

The expense account Rent Expense increases $900 because the payment pertains only to the current month; the asset Cash decreases $900.

Equation Analysis

Assets	=	**Liabilities**	+	**Owner's Equity**
Cash	=			Rent Expense
-$900				-$900

Debit–Credit Analysis

Debits increase expenses: debit Rent Expense $900.
Credits decrease assets: credit Cash $900.

Journal Entry

Oct. 3	Rent Expense	729	900	
	Cash	101		900
	(Paid cash for October office rent)			

Posting

Cash			101
Oct. 1	10,000	Oct. 3	900
2	1,200		

Rent Expense			729
Oct. 3	900		

Cash Flows
−900

ILLUSTRATION 2.23

Payment for insurance

Cash Flows
−600

Transaction	On October 4, Pioneer pays $600 for a one-year insurance policy that will expire next year on September 30.
Basic Analysis	The asset Prepaid Insurance increases $600 because the payment extends to more than the current month; the asset Cash decreases $600. Payments of expenses that will benefit more than one accounting period are prepaid expenses or prepayments. When a company makes a payment, it debits an asset account in order to show the service or benefit that will be received in the future.
Equation Analysis	**Assets** (Cash + Prepaid Insurance) = **Liabilities** + **Owner's Equity** Cash: -$600; Prepaid Insurance: +$600
Debit–Credit Analysis	Debits increase assets: debit Prepaid Insurance $600. Credits decrease assets: credit Cash $600.

Journal Entry

Date	Account	Ref.	Debit	Credit
Oct. 4	Prepaid Insurance	130	600	
	Cash	101		600
	(Paid one-year policy; effective date October 1)			

Posting

Cash 101

Oct. 1	10,000	Oct. 3	900
2	1,200	4	600

Prepaid Insurance 130

Oct. 4	600		

ILLUSTRATION 2.24

Purchase of supplies on credit

Cash Flows
no effect

Transaction	On October 5, Pioneer purchases an estimated 3-month supply of advertising materials on account from Aero Supply for $2,500.
Basic Analysis	The asset Supplies increases $2,500; the liability Accounts Payable increases $2,500.
Equation Analysis	**Assets** (Supplies) = **Liabilities** (Accounts Payable) + **Owner's Equity** Supplies: +$2,500 = Accounts Payable: +$2,500
Debit–Credit Analysis	Debits increase assets: debit Supplies $2,500. Credits increase liabilities: credit Accounts Payable $2,500.

Journal Entry

Date	Account	Ref.	Debit	Credit
Oct. 5	Supplies	126	2,500	
	Accounts Payable	201		2,500
	(Purchased supplies on account from Aero Supply)			

Posting

Supplies 126

Oct. 5	2,500		

Accounts Payable 201

		Oct. 5	2,500

ILLUSTRATION 2.25

Hiring of employees

Event

On October 9, Pioneer hires four employees to begin work on October 15. Each employee is to receive a weekly salary of $500 for a 5-day work week, payable every 2 weeks—first payment made on October 26.

Basic Analysis

A business transaction has not occurred. There is only an agreement between the employer and the employees to enter into a business transaction beginning on October 15. Thus, a debit–credit analysis is not needed because there is no accounting entry (see October 26 transaction for first entry).

Cash Flows
no effect

ILLUSTRATION 2.26

Withdrawal of cash by owner

Transaction

On October 20, C. R. Byrd withdraws $500 cash for personal use.

Basic Analysis

The owner's equity account Owner's Drawings increases $500; the asset Cash decreases $500.

Equation Analysis

Assets	=	**Liabilities**	+	**Owner's Equity**
Cash	=			Owner's Drawings
-$500				-$500

Debit–Credit Analysis

Debits increase drawings: debit Owner's Drawings $500.
Credits decrease assets: credit Cash $500.

Journal Entry

Oct. 20	Owner's Drawings	306	500	
	Cash	101		500
	(Withdrew cash for personal use)			

Posting

Cash			101
Oct. 1	10,000	Oct. 3	900
2	1,200	4	600
		20	500

Owner's Drawings			306
Oct. 20	500		

Cash Flows
−500

ILLUSTRATION 2.27
Payment of salaries

Cash Flows
−4,000

Transaction
On October 26, Pioneer owes employee salaries of $4,000 and pays them in cash (see October 9 event).

Basic Analysis
The expense account Salaries and Wages Expense increases $4,000; the asset Cash decreases $4,000.

Equation Analysis

Assets	=	Liabilities	+	Owner's Equity
Cash	=			Salaries and Wages Expense
-$4,000				-$4,000

Debit–Credit Analysis
Debits increase expenses: debit Salaries and Wages Expense $4,000.
Credits decrease assets: credit Cash $4,000.

Journal Entry

Oct. 26	Salaries and Wages Expense	726	4,000	
	Cash	101		4,000
	(Paid salaries to date)			

Posting

Cash			101
Oct. 1	10,000	Oct. 3	900
2	1,200	4	600
		20	500
		26	4,000

Salaries and Wages Expense			726
Oct. 26	4,000		

ILLUSTRATION 2.28
Receipt of cash for services performed

Cash Flows
+10,000

Transaction
On October 31, Pioneer receives $10,000 in cash from Copa Company for advertising services performed in October.

Basic Analysis
The asset Cash increases $10,000; the revenue account Service Revenue increases $10,000.

Equation Analysis

Assets	=	Liabilities	+	Owner's Equity
Cash	=			Service Revenue
+$10,000				+$10,000

Debit–Credit Analysis
Debits increase assets: debit Cash $10,000.
Credits increase revenues: credit Service Revenue $10,000.

Journal Entry

Oct. 31	Cash	101	10,000	
	Service Revenue	400		10,000
	(Received cash for services performed)			

Posting

Cash			101
Oct. 1	10,000	Oct. 3	900
2	1,200	4	600
31	10,000	20	500
		26	4,000

Service Revenue			400
		Oct. 31	10,000

Summary Illustration of Journalizing and Posting

Illustration 2.29 shows the journal for Pioneer Advertising for October.

ILLUSTRATION 2.29
General journal entries

GENERAL JOURNAL — PAGE J1

Date	Account Titles and Explanation	Ref.	Debit	Credit
2020				
Oct. 1	Cash	101	10,000	
	Owner's Capital	301		10,000
	(Owner's investment of cash in business)			
1	Equipment	157	5,000	
	Notes Payable	200		5,000
	(Issued 3-month, 12% note for office equipment)			
2	Cash	101	1,200	
	Unearned Service Revenue	209		1,200
	(Received cash from R. Knox for future services)			
3	Rent Expense	729	900	
	Cash	101		900
	(Paid cash for October office rent)			
4	Prepaid Insurance	130	600	
	Cash	101		600
	(Paid one-year policy; effective date October 1)			
5	Supplies	126	2,500	
	Accounts Payable	201		2,500
	(Purchased supplies on account from Aero Supply)			
20	Owner's Drawings	306	500	
	Cash	101		500
	(Withdrew cash for personal use)			
26	Salaries and Wages Expense	726	4,000	
	Cash	101		4,000
	(Paid salaries to date)			
31	Cash	101	10,000	
	Service Revenue	400		10,000
	(Received cash for services performed)			

Illustration 2.30 shows the ledger, with all balances in red.

ILLUSTRATION 2.30 General ledger

GENERAL LEDGER

Cash — No. 101

Date	Explanation	Ref.	Debit	Credit	Balance
2020					
Oct. 1		J1	10,000		10,000
2		J1	1,200		11,200
3		J1		900	10,300
4		J1		600	9,700
20		J1		500	9,200
26		J1		4,000	5,200
31		J1	10,000		15,200

Supplies — No. 126

Date	Explanation	Ref.	Debit	Credit	Balance
2020					
Oct. 5		J1	2,500		2,500

Prepaid Insurance — No. 130

Date	Explanation	Ref.	Debit	Credit	Balance
2020					
Oct. 4		J1	600		600

Equipment — No. 157

Date	Explanation	Ref.	Debit	Credit	Balance
2020					
Oct. 1		J1	5,000		5,000

Notes Payable — No. 200

Date	Explanation	Ref.	Debit	Credit	Balance
2020					
Oct. 1		J1		5,000	5,000

Accounts Payable — No. 201

Date	Explanation	Ref.	Debit	Credit	Balance
2020					
Oct. 5		J1		2,500	2,500

Unearned Service Revenue — No. 209

Date	Explanation	Ref.	Debit	Credit	Balance
2020					
Oct. 2		J1		1,200	1,200

Owner's Capital — No. 301

Date	Explanation	Ref.	Debit	Credit	Balance
2020					
Oct. 1		J1		10,000	10,000

Owner's Drawings — No. 306

Date	Explanation	Ref.	Debit	Credit	Balance
2020					
Oct. 20		J1	500		500

Service Revenue — No. 400

Date	Explanation	Ref.	Debit	Credit	Balance
2020					
Oct. 31		J1		10,000	10,000

Salaries and Wages Expense — No. 726

Date	Explanation	Ref.	Debit	Credit	Balance
2020					
Oct. 26		J1	4,000		4,000

Rent Expense — No. 729

Date	Explanation	Ref.	Debit	Credit	Balance
2020					
Oct. 3		J1	900		900

DO IT! 3 | Posting

Kate Browne recorded the following transactions in a general journal during the month of March.

Mar. 4	Cash	2,280	
	Service Revenue		2,280
15	Salaries and Wages Expense	400	
	Cash		400
19	Utilities Expense	92	
	Cash		92

Post these entries to the Cash account of the general ledger to determine its ending balance. The beginning balance of Cash on March 1 was $600.

ACTION PLAN

- **Recall that posting involves transferring the journalized debits and credits to specific accounts in the ledger.**
- **Determine the ending balance by netting the total debits and credits.**

Solution

Cash

3/1 Bal.	600	3/15	400
3/4	2,280	3/19	92
3/31 Bal.	2,388		

Related exercise material: **BE2.7, BE2.8, DO IT! 2.3, E2.11, and E2.14.**

The Trial Balance

LEARNING OBJECTIVE 4

Prepare a trial balance.

A **trial balance** is a list of accounts and their balances at a given time. Companies usually prepare a trial balance at the end of an accounting period. They list accounts in the order in which they appear in the ledger. Debit balances appear in the left column and credit balances in the right column. The totals of the two columns must equal.

The trial balance proves the mathematical equality of debits and credits after posting. Under the double-entry system, this equality occurs when the sum of the debit account balances equals the sum of the credit account balances. **A trial balance may also uncover errors in journalizing and posting.** For example, a trial balance may well have detected the error at MF Global discussed in the Feature Story. **In addition, a trial balance is useful in the preparation of financial statements**, as we will explain in the next two chapters.

The steps for preparing a trial balance are:

1. List the account titles and their balances in the appropriate debit or credit column.
2. Total the debit and credit columns.
3. Verify the equality of the two columns.

Illustration 2.31 shows the trial balance prepared from Pioneer Advertising's ledger. Note that the total debits equal the total credits.

ILLUSTRATION 2.31
A Trial balance

Pioneer Advertising
Trial Balance
October 31, 2020

	Debit	Credit
Cash	$15,200	
Supplies	2,500	
Prepaid Insurance	600	
Equipment	5,000	
Notes Payable		$ 5,000
Accounts Payable		2,500
Unearned Service Revenue		1,200
Owner's Capital		10,000
Owner's Drawings	500	
Service Revenue		10,000
Salaries and Wages Expense	4,000	
Rent Expense	900	
	$28,700	$28,700

Note that the order of presentation in the trial balance is:

Assets
Liabilities
Owner's equity
Revenues
Expenses

A trial balance is a necessary checkpoint for uncovering certain types of errors. For example, if only the debit portion of a journal entry has been posted, the trial balance would bring this error to light.

Limitations of a Trial Balance

ETHICS NOTE

An error is the result of an unintentional mistake; it is neither ethical nor unethical. An irregularity is an intentional misstatement, which is viewed as unethical.

A trial balance does not guarantee freedom from recording errors, however (see **Ethics Note**). Numerous errors may exist even though the totals of the trial balance columns agree. For example, the trial balance may balance even when:

1. A transaction is not journalized.
2. A correct journal entry is not posted.
3. A journal entry is posted twice.
4. Incorrect accounts are used in journalizing or posting.
5. Offsetting errors are made in recording the amount of a transaction.

As long as equal debits and credits are posted, even to the wrong account or in the wrong amount, the total debits will equal the total credits. **The trial balance does not prove that the company has recorded all transactions or that the ledger is correct.**

Locating Errors

Errors in a trial balance generally result from mathematical mistakes, incorrect postings, or simply transcribing data incorrectly. What do you do if you are faced with a trial balance that does not balance? First, determine the amount of the difference between the two columns of the trial balance. After this amount is known, the following steps are often helpful:

1. If the error is $1, $10, $100, or $1,000, re-add the trial balance columns and recompute the account balances.
2. If the error is divisible by 2, scan the trial balance to see whether a balance equal to half the error has been entered in the wrong column.
3. If the error is divisible by 9, retrace the account balances on the trial balance to see whether they are incorrectly copied from the ledger. For example, if a balance was $12 and it was listed as $21, a $9 error has been made. Reversing the order of numbers is called a **transposition error**.
4. If the error is not divisible by 2 or 9, scan the ledger to see whether an account balance in the amount of the error has been omitted from the trial balance, and scan the journal to see whether a posting of that amount has been omitted.

Dollar Signs and Underlining

Note that dollar signs do not appear in journals or ledgers. Dollar signs are typically used only in the trial balance and the financial statements. Generally, a dollar sign is shown only for the first item in the column and for the total of that column. A single line (a totaling rule) is placed under the column of figures to be added or subtracted. Total amounts are double-underlined to indicate they are final sums.

Investor Insight Fannie Mae

Enviromatic/iStockphoto

Why Accuracy Matters

While most companies record transactions very carefully, the reality is that mistakes still happen. For example, bank regulators fined **Bank One Corporation** (now **Chase**) $1.8 million because they felt that the unreliability of the bank's accounting system caused it to violate regulatory requirements.

Also, in recent years **Fannie Mae**, the government-chartered mortgage association, announced a series of large accounting errors. These announcements caused alarm among investors, regulators, and politicians because they fear that the errors may suggest larger, undetected problems. This is important because the home-mortgage market depends on Fannie Mae to buy hundreds of billions of dollars of mortgages each year from banks, thus enabling the banks to issue new mortgages.

Finally, before a major overhaul of its accounting system, the financial records of **Waste Management Inc.** were in such disarray that of the company's 57,000 employees, 10,000 were receiving pay slips that were in error.

The Sarbanes-Oxley Act was created to minimize the occurrence of errors like these by increasing every employee's responsibility for accurate financial reporting.

In order for these companies to prepare and issue financial statements, their accounting equations (debits and credits) must have been in balance at year-end. How could these errors or misstatements have occurred? (Go to WileyPLUS for this answer and additional questions.)

DO IT! 4 | Trial Balance

The following accounts come from the ledger of SnowGo Company at December 31, 2020.

157	Equipment	$88,000	301	Owner's Capital	$20,000
306	Owner's Drawings	8,000	212	Salaries and Wages Payable	2,000
201	Accounts Payable	22,000	200	Notes Payable (due in 3 months)	19,000
726	Salaries and Wages Expense	42,000	732	Utilities Expense	3,000
112	Accounts Receivable	4,000	130	Prepaid Insurance	6,000
400	Service Revenue	95,000	101	Cash	7,000

Prepare a trial balance in good form.

ACTION PLAN

- **Determine normal balances and list accounts in the order they appear in the ledger.**
- **Accounts with debit balances appear in the left column, and those with credit balances in the right column.**
- **Total the debit and credit columns to prove equality.**

Solution

SnowGo Company
Trial Balance
December 31, 2020

	Debit	Credit
Cash	$ 7,000	
Accounts Receivable	4,000	
Prepaid Insurance	6,000	
Equipment	88,000	
Notes Payable		$ 19,000
Accounts Payable		22,000
Salaries and Wages Payable		2,000
Owner's Capital		20,000
Owner's Drawings	8,000	
Service Revenue		95,000
Utilities Expense	3,000	
Salaries and Wages Expense	42,000	
	$158,000	$158,000

Related exercise material: **BE2.9, BE2.10, DO IT! 2.4, E2.11, E2.12, E2.13, E2.15, and E2.16.**

Review and Practice

Learning Objectives Review

1 Describe how accounts, debits, and credits are used to record business transactions.

An account is a record of increases and decreases in specific asset, liability, and owner's equity items. The terms debit and credit are synonymous with left and right. Assets, drawings, and expenses are increased by debits and decreased by credits. Liabilities, owner's capital, and revenues are increased by credits and decreased by debits.

2 Indicate how a journal is used in the recording process.

The basic steps in the recording process are (a) analyze each transaction for its effects on the accounts, (b) enter the transaction information in a journal, and (c) transfer the journal information to the appropriate accounts in the ledger.

The initial accounting record of a transaction is entered in a journal before the data are entered in the accounts. A journal (a) discloses in one place the complete effects of a transaction, (b) provides a chronological record of transactions, and (c) prevents or locates errors because the debit and credit amounts for each entry can be easily compared.

3 Explain how a ledger and posting help in the recording process.

The ledger is the entire group of accounts maintained by a company. The ledger provides the balance in each of the accounts as well as keeps track of changes in these balances. Posting is the transfer of journal entries to the ledger accounts. This phase of the recording process accumulates the effects of journalized transactions in the individual accounts.

4 Prepare a trial balance.

A trial balance is a list of accounts and their balances at a given time. Its primary purpose is to prove the equality of debits and credits after posting. A trial balance also uncovers errors in journalizing and posting and is useful in preparing financial statements.

Glossary Review

Account A record of increases and decreases in specific asset, liability, or owner's equity items. (p. 2-2).

Chart of accounts A list of accounts and the account numbers that identify their location in the ledger. (p. 2-13).

Compound entry A journal entry that involves three or more accounts. (p. 2-9).

Credit The right side of an account. (p. 2-3).

Debit The left side of an account. (p. 2-3).

Double-entry system A system that records in appropriate accounts the dual effect of each transaction. (p. 2-4).

General journal The most basic form of journal. (p. 2-8).

General ledger A ledger that contains all asset, liability, and owner's equity accounts. (p. 2-10).

Journal An accounting record in which transactions are initially recorded in chronological order. (p. 2-8).

Journalizing The entering of transaction data in the journal. (p. 2-8).

Ledger The entire group of accounts maintained by a company. (p. 2-10).

Normal balance An account balance on the side where an increase in the account is recorded. (p. 2-4).

Posting The procedure of transferring journal entries to the ledger accounts. (p. 2-12).

Simple entry A journal entry that involves only two accounts. (p. 2-9).

T-account The basic form of an account, consisting of (1) a title, (2) a left or debit side, and (3) a right or credit side. (p. 2-3).

Three-column form of account A form with columns for debit, credit, and balance amounts in an account. (p. 2-11).

Trial balance A list of accounts and their balances at a given time. (p. 2-21).

Practice Multiple-Choice Questions

1. **(LO 1)** Which of the following statements about an account is **true**?
   - **a.** The right side of an account is the debit, or increase, side.
   - **b.** An account is an individual accounting record of increases and decreases in specific asset, liability, and owner's equity items.
   - **c.** There are separate accounts for specific assets and liabilities but only one account for owner's equity items.
   - **d.** The left side of an account is the credit, or decrease, side.

2. **(LO 1)** Debits:
   a. increase both assets and liabilities.
   b. decrease both assets and liabilities.
   c. increase assets and decrease liabilities.
   d. decrease assets and increase liabilities.

3. **(LO 1)** A revenue account:
   a. is increased by debits.
   b. is decreased by credits.
   c. has a normal balance of a debit.
   d. is increased by credits.

4. **(LO 1)** Accounts that normally have debit balances are:
   a. assets, expenses, and revenues.
   b. assets, expenses, and owner's capital.
   c. assets, liabilities, and owner's drawings.
   d. assets, owner's drawings, and expenses.

5. **(LO 1)** The expanded accounting equation is:
   a. Assets + Liabilities = Owner's Capital + Owner's Drawings + Revenues + Expenses.
   b. Assets = Liabilities + Owner's Capital + Owner's Drawings + Revenues – Expenses.
   c. Assets = Liabilities – Owner's Capital – Owner's Drawings – Revenues – Expenses.
   d. Assets = Liabilities + Owner's Capital – Owner's Drawings + Revenues – Expenses.

6. **(LO 2)** Which of the following is **not** part of the recording process?
   a. Analyzing transactions.
   b. Preparing an income statement.
   c. Entering transactions in a journal.
   d. Posting journal entries.

7. **(LO 2)** Which of the following statements about a journal is **false**?
   a. It is not a book of original entry.
   b. It provides a chronological record of transactions.
   c. It helps to locate errors because the debit and credit amounts for each entry can be readily compared.
   d. It discloses in one place the complete effect of a transaction.

8. **(LO 2)** The purchase of supplies on account should result in:
   a. a debit to Supplies Expense and a credit to Cash.
   b. a debit to Supplies Expense and a credit to Accounts Payable.
   c. a debit to Supplies and a credit to Accounts Payable.
   d. a debit to Supplies and a credit to Accounts Receivable.

9. **(LO 3)** The order of the accounts in the ledger is:
   a. assets, revenues, expenses, liabilities, owner's capital, owner's drawings.
   b. assets, liabilities, owner's capital, owner's drawings, revenues, expenses.
   c. owner's capital, assets, revenues, expenses, liabilities, owner's drawings.
   d. revenues, assets, expenses, liabilities, owner's capital, owner's drawings.

10. **(LO 3)** A ledger:
   a. contains only asset and liability accounts.
   b. should show accounts in alphabetical order.
   c. is a collection of the entire group of accounts maintained by a company.
   d. is a book of original entry.

11. **(LO 3)** Posting:
   a. normally occurs before journalizing.
   b. transfers ledger transaction data to the journal.
   c. is an optional step in the recording process.
   d. transfers journal entries to ledger accounts.

12. **(LO 3)** Before posting a payment of $5,000, the Accounts Payable of Senator Company had a normal balance of $16,000. The balance after posting this transaction was:
   a. $21,000. **c.** $11,000.
   b. $5,000. **d.** Cannot be determined.

13. **(LO 4)** A trial balance:
   a. is a list of accounts with their balances at a given time.
   b. proves the journalized transactions are correct.
   c. will not balance if a correct journal entry is posted twice.
   d. proves that all transactions have been recorded.

14. **(LO 4)** A trial balance will not balance if:
   a. a correct journal entry is posted twice.
   b. the purchase of supplies on account is debited to Supplies and credited to Cash.
   c. a $100 cash drawing by the owner is debited to Owner's Drawings for $1,000 and credited to Cash for $100.
   d. a $450 payment on account is debited to Accounts Payable for $45 and credited to Cash for $45.

15. **(LO 4)** The trial balance of Jeong Company had accounts with the following normal balances: Cash $5,000, Service Revenue $85,000, Salaries and Wages Payable $4,000, Salaries and Wages Expense $40,000, Rent Expense $10,000, Owner's Capital $42,000, Owner's Drawings $15,000, and Equipment $61,000. In preparing a trial balance, the total in the debit column is:
   a. $131,000. **c.** $91,000.
   b. $216,000. **d.** $116,000.

Solutions

1. **b.** An account is an individual accounting record of increases and decreases in specific asset, liability, and owner's equity items. The other choices are incorrect because (a) the right side of the account is the credit side, not the debit side, and can be the increase or the decrease side, depending on the specific classification account; (c) there are also separate accounts for different owner's equity items; and (d) the left side of the account is the debit side, not the credit side, and can be either the decrease or the increase side, depending on the specific classification account.

2. **c.** Debits increase assets but they decrease liabilities. The other choices are incorrect because debits (a) decrease, not increase, liabilities; (b) increase, not decrease, assets; and (d) increase, not decrease, assets and decrease, not increase, liabilities.

3. **d.** A revenue account is increased by credits. The other choices are incorrect because a revenue account (a) is increased by credits, not debits; (b) is decreased by debits, not credits; and (c) has a normal balance of a credit, not a debit.

4. **d.** Assets, owner's drawings, and expenses all have normal debit balances. The other choices are incorrect because (a) revenues have normal credit balances, (b) owner's capital has a normal credit balance, and (c) liabilities have normal credit balances.

5. **d.** The expanded accounting equation is Assets = Liabilities + Owner's Capital − Owner's Drawings + Revenue − Expenses. The other choices are incorrect because (a) both Owner's Drawings and Expenses must be subtracted, not added, and Liabilities should be added to the right side of equation, not to the left side; (b) Owner's Drawings must be subtracted, not added; and (c) Owner's Capital and Revenues must be added, not subtracted.

6. **b.** Preparing an income statement is not part of the recording process. Choices (a) analyzing transactions, (c) entering transactions in a journal, and (d) posting journal entries are all part of the recording process.

7. **a.** The journal is a book of original entry. The other choices are all true statements.

8. **c.** The purchase of supplies on account results in a debit to Supplies and a credit to Accounts Payable. The other choices are incorrect because the purchase of supplies on account results in (a) a debit to Supplies, not Supplies Expense, and a credit to Accounts Payable, not Cash; (b) a debit to Supplies, not Supplies Expense; and (d) a credit to Accounts Payable, not Accounts Receivable.

9. **b.** The correct order of the accounts in the ledger is assets, liabilities, owner's capital, owner's drawing, revenues, expenses. The other choices are incorrect because they do not reflect this order. The order of the accounts in the ledger is (1) balance sheet accounts: assets, liabilities, and owner's equity accounts (owner's capital and owner's drawings); and then (2) income statement accounts: revenues and expenses.

10. **c.** A ledger is a collection of all the accounts maintained by a company. The other choices are incorrect because a ledger (a) contains all account types—assets, liabilities, and owner's equity—not just assets and liability accounts; (b) usually shows accounts in account number order, not alphabetical order; and (d) is not a book of original entry because entries made in the ledger come from the journals (the books of original entry).

11. **d.** Posting transfers journal entries to ledger accounts. The other choices are incorrect because posting (a) occurs after journalizing, (b) transfers journal transaction data to the ledger; and (c) is not an optional step in the recording process.

12. **c.** The balance is $11,000 ($16,000 normal balance − $5,000 payment), not (a) $21,000 or (b) $5,000. Choice (d) is incorrect because the balance can be determined.

13. **a.** A trial balance is a list of accounts with their balances at a given time. The other choices are incorrect because (b) the trial balance does not prove that journalized transactions are mathematically correct; (c) if a journal entry is posted twice, the trial balance will still balance; and (d) the trial balance does not prove that all transactions have been recorded.

14. **c.** The trial balance will not balance in this case because the debit of $1,000 to Owner's Drawings is not equal to the credit of $100 to Cash. The other choices are incorrect because (a) if a correct journal entry is posted twice, the trial balance will still balance; (b) if the purchase of supplies on account is debited to Supplies and credited to Cash, Cash and Accounts Payable will be understated but the trial balance will still balance; and (d) since the debit and credit amounts are the same, the trial balance will still balance but both Accounts Payable and Cash will be overstated.

15. **a.** The total debit column = $5,000 (Cash) + $40,000 (Salaries and Wages Expense) + $10,000 (Rent Expense) + $15,000 (Owner's Drawings) + $61,000 (Equipment) = $131,000. The normal balance for Assets, Expenses, and Owner's Drawings is a debit. The other choices are incorrect because (b) revenue of $85,000 should not be included in the total of $216,000 and its normal balance is a credit; (c) the total of $91,000 is missing the Salaries and Wages Expense of $40,000, which has a normal balance of a debit; and (d) the total of $116,000 is missing the Owner's Drawings of $15,000, which has a normal balance of a debit.

Practice Brief Exercises

Identify accounts to be debited and credited.

1. **(LO 1)** Transactions for the Warren Potter Company for the month of May are presented below. Identify the accounts to be debited and credited for each transaction.

May	1	Warren Potter invested $22,000 in the business.
	6	Paid office rent of $900.
	12	Performed consulting services and billed client $4,400.
	18	Purchased equipment on account for $1,200.

Solution

1.

		Account Debited	Account Credited
May	1	Cash	Owner's Capital
	6	Rent Expense	Cash
	12	Accounts Receivable	Service Revenue
	18	Equipment	Accounts Payable

Journalize transactions.

2. **(LO 2)** Using the data from **Practice Brief Exercise 1**, journalize the transactions (omit explanations).

Solution

2.

May 1	Cash	22,000	
	Owner's Capital		22,000
6	Rent Expense	900	
	Cash		900
12	Accounts Receivable	4,400	
	Service Revenue		4,400
18	Equipment	1,200	
	Accounts Payable		1,200

3. **(LO 3)** Selected transactions for Carlos Santana Company are presented in journal form below. Post the transactions to T-accounts. Make one T-account for each and determine each account's ending balance.

Post journal entries to T-accounts.

J1

Date	Account Titles and Explanation	Ref.	Debit	Credit
June 6	Cash		22,000	
	Owner's Capital			22,000
	(Owner's investment of cash in business)			
13	Accounts Receivable		8,200	
	Service Revenue			8,200
	(Billed for services performed)			
14	Cash		3,700	
	Accounts Receivable			3,700
	(Received cash in payment of account)			

Solution

3.

Cash

6/6	22,000		
6/14	3,700		
	Bal. 25,700		

Accounts Receivable

6/13	8,200	6/14	3,700
	Bal. 4,500		

Service Revenue

		6/13	8,200
			Bal. 8,200

Owner's Capital

		6/6	22,000
			Bal. 22,000

4. **(LO 3)** Selected journal entries for Carlos Santana Company are presented in **Practice Brief Exercise 3.** Post the transactions using the standard form of account.

Post journal entries to standard form of account.

Solution

4. **Cash**

Date	Explanation	Ref.	Debit	Credit	Balance
June 6		J1	22,000		22,000
14		J1	3,700		25,700

Accounts Receivable

Date	Explanation	Ref.	Debit	Credit	Balance
June 13		J1	8,200		8,200
14		J1		3,700	4,500

Service Revenue

Date	Explanation	Ref.	Debit	Credit	Balance
June 13		J1		8,200	8,200

Owner's Capital

Date	Explanation	Ref.	Debit	Credit	Balance
June 6		J1		22,000	22,000

Prepare a trial balance.

5. **(LO 4)** From the ledger accounts below, prepare a trial balance for Bundy Company at December 31, 2020. List the accounts in the order shown in the textbook. All account balances are normal.

Accounts Receivable	$10,000	Salaries and Wages Expense	$ 2,300
Supplies	4,100	Rent Expense	1,200
Accounts Payable	3,500	Owner's Capital	10,200
Owner's Drawing	1,100	Cash	6,000
Service Revenue	11,000		

Solution

5.

Bundy Company
Trial Balance
December 31, 2020

	Debit	Credit
Cash	$ 6,000	
Accounts Receivable	10,000	
Supplies	4,100	
Accounts Payable		$ 3,500
Owner's Capital		10,200
Owner's Drawings	1,100	
Service Revenue		11,000
Salaries and Wages Expense	2,300	
Rent Expense	1,200	
	$24,700	$24,700

Practice Exercises

Analyze and journalize transactions.

1. **(LO 2)** Presented below is information related to Hammond Real Estate Agency.

Oct. 1 Lia Berge begins business as a real estate agent with a cash investment of $30,000.
2 Paid rent, $700, on office space.
3 Purchases office equipment for $2,800, on account.
6 Sells a house and lot for Hal Smith; bills Hal Smith $4,400 for realty services performed.
27 Pays $1,100 on the balance related to the transaction of October 3.
30 Receives bill for October utilities, $130 (not paid at this time).

Instructions

Journalize the transactions. (You may omit explanations)

Solution

1. **GENERAL JOURNAL**

Date	Account Titles and Explanation	Ref.	Debit	Credit
Oct. 1	Cash		30,000	
	Owner's Capital			30,000
2	Rent Expense		700	
	Cash			700
3	Equipment		2,800	
	Accounts Payable			2,800
6	Accounts Receivable		4,400	
	Service Revenue			4,400
27	Accounts Payable		1,100	
	Cash			1,100
30	Utilities Expense		130	
	Accounts Payable			130

2. **(LO 2, 4)** The T-accounts below summarize the ledger of Depot Company at the end of the first month of operations.

Journalize transactions from account data and prepare a trial balance.

Cash No. 101

4/1	16,000	4/15	700
4/12	1,200	4/25	1,600
4/29	900		
4/30	1,600		

Unearned Service Revenue No. 209

		4/30	1,600

Accounts Receivable No. 112

4/7	2,900	4/29	900

Owner's Capital No. 301

		4/1	16,000

Supplies No. 126

4/4	1,900		

Service Revenue No. 400

		4/7	2,900
		4/12	1,200

Accounts Payable No. 201

4/25	1,600	4/4	1,900

Salaries and Wages Expense No. 726

4/15	700		

Instructions

a. Prepare the complete general journal (including explanations) from which the postings to Cash were made.

b. Prepare a trial balance at April 30, 2020.

Solution

2. **a.**

GENERAL JOURNAL

Date	Account Titles and Explanation	Ref.	Debit	Credit
Apr. 1	Cash		16,000	
	Owner's Capital			16,000
	(Owner's investment of cash in business)			
4	Supplies		1,900	
	Accounts Payable			1,900
	(Purchased supplies on account)			
7	Accounts Receivable		2,900	
	Service Revenue			2,900
	(Billed customers for services performed)			
12	Cash		1,200	
	Service Revenue			1,200
	(Received cash for services performed)			
15	Salaries and Wages Expense		700	
	Cash			700
	(Paid salaries to date)			
25	Accounts Payable		1,600	
	Cash			1,600
	(Paid creditors on account)			
29	Cash		900	
	Accounts Receivable			900
	(Received cash in payment of account)			
30	Cash		1,600	
	Unearned Service Revenue			1,600
	(Received cash for future services)			

b.

Depot Company
Trial Balance
April 30, 2020

	Debit	Credit
Cash	$17,400	
Accounts Receivable	2,000	
Supplies	1,900	

Accounts Payable		$ 300
Unearned Service Revenue		1,600
Owner's Capital		16,000
Service Revenue		4,100
Salaries and Wages Expense	700	
	$22,000	$22,000

Practice Problem

Journalize transactions, post, and prepare a trial balance.

(LO 1, 2, 3, 4) Bob Sample opened the Campus Laundromat on September 1, 2020. During the first month of operations, the following transactions occurred.

Sept.	1	Bob invested $20,000 cash in the business.
	2	The company paid $1,000 cash for store rent for September.
	3	Purchased washers and dryers for $25,000, paying $10,000 in cash and signing a $15,000, 6-month, 12% note payable.
	4	Paid $1,200 for a one-year accident insurance policy.
	10	Received a bill from the *Daily News* for online advertising of the opening of the laundromat $200.
	20	Bob withdrew $700 cash for personal use.
	30	The company determined that cash receipts for laundry services for the month were $6,200.

The chart of accounts for the company is the same as that for Pioneer Advertising plus No. 610 Advertising Expense.

Instructions

a. Journalize the September transactions. (Use J1 for the journal page number.)

b. Open ledger accounts and post the September transactions.

c. Prepare a trial balance at September 30, 2020.

Solution

a. GENERAL JOURNAL — J1

Date	Account Titles and Explanation	Ref.	Debit	Credit
2020				
Sept. 1	Cash	101	20,000	
	Owner's Capital	301		20,000
	(Owner's investment of cash in business)			
2	Rent Expense	729	1,000	
	Cash	101		1,000
	(Paid September rent)			
3	Equipment	157	25,000	
	Cash	101		10,000
	Notes Payable	200		15,000
	(Purchased laundry equipment for cash and 6-month, 12% note payable)			
4	Prepaid Insurance	130	1,200	
	Cash	101		1,200
	(Paid one-year insurance policy)			
10	Advertising Expense	610	200	
	Accounts Payable	201		200
	(Received bill from *Daily News* for advertising)			
20	Owner's Drawings	306	700	
	Cash	101		700
	(Withdrew cash for personal use)			
30	Cash	101	6,200	
	Service Revenue	400		6,200
	(Received cash for services performed)			

b.

GENERAL LEDGER

Cash — **No. 101**

Date		Explanation	Ref.	Debit	Credit	Balance
2020						
Sept.	1		J1	20,000		20,000
	2		J1		1,000	19,000
	3		J1		10,000	9,000
	4		J1		1,200	7,800
	20		J1		700	7,100
	30		J1	6,200		13,300

Prepaid Insurance — **No. 130**

Date		Explanation	Ref.	Debit	Credit	Balance
2020						
Sept.	4		J1	1,200		1,200

Equipment — **No. 157**

Date		Explanation	Ref.	Debit	Credit	Balance
2020						
Sept.	3		J1	25,000		25,000

Notes Payable — **No. 200**

Date		Explanation	Ref.	Debit	Credit	Balance
2020						
Sept.	3		J1		15,000	15,000

Accounts Payable — **No. 201**

Date		Explanation	Ref.	Debit	Credit	Balance
2020						
Sept.	10		J1		200	200

Owner's Capital — **No. 301**

Date		Explanation	Ref.	Debit	Credit	Balance
2020						
Sept.	1		J1		20,000	20,000

Owner's Drawings — **No. 306**

Date		Explanation	Ref.	Debit	Credit	Balance
2020						
Sept.	20		J1	700		700

Service Revenue — **No. 400**

Date		Explanation	Ref.	Debit	Credit	Balance
2020						
Sept.	30		J1		6,200	6,200

Advertising Expense — **No. 610**

Date		Explanation	Ref.	Debit	Credit	Balance
2020						
Sept.	10		J1	200		200

Rent Expense — **No. 729**

Date		Explanation	Ref.	Debit	Credit	Balance
2020						
Sept.	2		J1	1,000		1,000

c.

Campus Laundromat
Trial Balance
September 30, 2020

	Debit	Credit
Cash	$13,300	
Prepaid Insurance	1,200	
Equipment	25,000	
Notes Payable		$15,000
Accounts Payable		200
Owner's Capital		20,000
Owner's Drawings	700	
Service Revenue		6,200
Advertising Expense	200	
Rent Expense	1,000	
	$41,400	$41,400

WileyPLUS

Brief Exercises, DO IT! Exercises, Exercises, Problems, and many additional resources are available for practice in WileyPLUS.

Questions

1. Describe the parts of a T-account.

2. "The terms debit and credit mean increase and decrease, respectively." Do you agree? Explain.

3. Pete Harcourt, a fellow student, contends that the double-entry system means each transaction must be recorded twice. Is Pete correct? Explain.

4. Melissa Estes, a beginning accounting student, believes debit balances are favorable and credit balances are unfavorable. Is Melissa correct? Discuss.

5. State the rules of debit and credit as applied to (a) asset accounts, (b) liability accounts, and (c) the owner's equity accounts (revenue, expenses, owner's drawings, and owner's capital).

6. What is the normal balance for each of the following accounts? (a) Accounts Receivable. (b) Cash. (c) Owner's Drawings. (d) Accounts Payable. (e) Service Revenue. (f) Salaries and Wages Expense. (g) Owner's Capital.

7. Indicate whether each of the following accounts is an asset, a liability, or an owner's equity account and whether it has a normal debit or credit balance: (a) Accounts Receivable, (b) Accounts Payable, (c) Equipment, (d) Owner's Drawings, and (e) Supplies.

8. For the following transactions, indicate the account debited and the account credited.

   a. Supplies are purchased on account.

   b. Cash is received on signing a note payable.

   c. Employees are paid salaries in cash.

9. Indicate whether the following accounts generally will have (a) debit entries only, (b) credit entries only, or (c) both debit and credit entries.

   1. Cash.

   2. Accounts Receivable.

   3. Owner's Drawings.

   4. Accounts Payable.

   5. Salaries and Wages Expense.

   6. Service Revenue.

10. What are the basic steps in the recording process?

11. What are the advantages of using a journal in the recording process?

12. **a.** When entering a transaction in the journal, should the debit or credit be written first?

    b. Which should be indented, the debit or credit?

13. Describe a compound entry, and provide an example.

14. **a.** Should business transaction debits and credits be recorded directly in the ledger accounts?

    b. What are the advantages of first recording transactions in the journal and then posting to the ledger?

15. The account number is entered as the last step in posting the amounts from the journal to the ledger. What is the advantage of this step?

16. Journalize the following business transactions.

    a. Wes Lee invests $7,000 cash in the business.

    b. Insurance of $800 is paid for the year.

    c. Supplies of $2,000 are purchased on account.

    d. Cash of $8,500 is received for services performed.

17. **a.** What is a ledger?

    b. What is a chart of accounts and why is it important?

18. What is a trial balance and what are its purposes?

19. Victor Grimm is confused about how accounting information flows through the accounting system. He believes the flow of information is as follows.

    a. Debits and credits posted to the ledger.

    b. Business transaction occurs.

    c. Information entered in the journal.

    d. Financial statements are prepared.

    e. Trial balance is prepared.

    Is Victor correct? If not, indicate to Victor the proper flow of the information.

20. Two students are discussing the use of a trial balance. They wonder whether the following errors, each considered separately, would prevent the trial balance from balancing.

    a. The bookkeeper debited Cash for $600 and credited Salaries and Wages Expense for $600 for payment of wages.

    b. Cash collected on account was debited to Cash for $800 and Service Revenue was credited for $80.

    What would you tell them?

21. What are the normal balances for **Apple**'s Cash, Accounts Payable, and Interest Expense accounts?

Brief Exercises

Indicate debit and credit effects and normal balance.

BE2.1 (LO 1) For each of the following accounts, indicate the effects of (a) a debit and (b) a credit on the accounts and (c) the normal balance of the account.

1. Accounts Payable.

2. Advertising Expense.

3. Service Revenue.

4. Accounts Receivable.

5. Owner's Capital.

6. Owner's Drawings.

BE2.2 (LO 1) Transactions for the Oleg Thorn Company for the month of June are presented below. Identify the accounts to be debited and credited for each transaction.

Identify accounts to be debited and credited.

June	1	Oleg Thorn invests $5,000 cash in a small welding business of which he is the sole proprietor.
	2	Purchases equipment on account for $3,600.
	3	$800 cash is paid to landlord for June rent.
	12	Sends a bill to K. Johnsen for $400 after completing welding work done on account.

BE2.3 (LO 2) Using the data in BE2.2, journalize the transactions. (You may omit explanations.)

Journalize transactions.

BE2.4 (LO 2) Writing Shea Jonas, a fellow student, is unclear about the basic steps in the recording process. Identify and briefly explain the steps in the order in which they occur.

Identify and explain steps in recording process.

BE2.5 (LO 2) M. Gonzales has the following transactions during August of the current year. Indicate (a) the effect on the accounting equation and (b) the debit-credit analysis illustrated in the textbook.

Indicate basic and debit-credit analysis.

Aug.	1	Opens an office as a financial advisor, investing $9,000 in cash.
	4	Pays insurance in advance for 6 months, $2,100 cash.
	16	Receives $3,600 from clients for services performed.
	27	Pays secretary $1,000 salary.

BE2.6 (LO 2) Using the data in BE2.5, journalize the transactions. (You may omit explanations.)

Journalize transactions.

BE2.7 (LO 3) Selected transactions for the Walt Bryce Company are presented in journal form below. Post the transactions to T-accounts. Make one T-account for each item and determine each account's ending balance.

Post journal entries to T-accounts.

J1

Date		Account Titles and Explanation	Ref.	Debit	Credit
May	5	Accounts Receivable		5,400	
		Service Revenue			5,400
		(Billed for services performed)			
	12	Cash		4,200	
		Accounts Receivable			4,200
		(Received cash in payment of account)			
	15	Cash		3,000	
		Service Revenue			3,000
		(Received cash for services performed)			

BE2.8 (LO 3) Selected journal entries for the Walt Bryce Company are presented in BE2.7. Post the transactions using the standard form of account.

Post journal entries to standard form of account.

BE2.9 (LO 4) From the ledger balances given below, prepare a trial balance for the Amaro Company at June 30, 2020. List the accounts in the order shown in the textbook. All account balances are normal.

Accounts Payable $8,100, Cash $5,800, Owner's Capital $15,000, Owner's Drawings $1,200, Equipment $17,000, Service Revenue $10,000, Accounts Receivable $3,000, Salaries and Wages Expense $5,100, and Rent Expense $1,000.

Prepare a trial balance.

BE2.10 (LO 4) An inexperienced bookkeeper prepared the following trial balance. Prepare a correct trial balance, assuming all account balances are normal.

Prepare a correct trial balance.

Shaushank Company
Trial Balance
December 31, 2020

	Debit	Credit
Cash	$10,600	
Prepaid Insurance		$ 3,500
Accounts Payable		3,000
Unearned Service Revenue	2,200	
Owner's Capital		9,000
Owner's Drawings		4,500
Service Revenue		25,400
Salaries and Wages Expense	18,600	
Rent Expense		2,400
	$31,400	$47,800

DO IT! Exercises

Identify normal balances.

DO IT! 2.1 (LO 1) Tom Rast has just rented space in a strip mall. In this space, he will open a photography studio, to be called "Picture This!" A friend has advised Tom to set up a double-entry set of accounting records in which to record all of his business transactions.

Identify the balance sheet accounts that Tom will likely need to record the transactions needed to open his business. Indicate whether the normal balance of each account is a debit or credit.

Record business activities.

DO IT! 2.2 (LO 2) Ron Tost engaged in the following activities in establishing his photography studio, Shutter Bug:

1. Opened a bank account in the name of Shutter Bug and deposited $6,500 of his own money into this account as his initial investment.
2. Purchased photography supplies at a total cost of $1,200. The business paid $400 in cash and the balance is on account.
3. Obtained estimates on the cost of photography equipment from three different manufacturers.

Prepare the journal entries to record the transactions. (You may omit explanations.)

Post transactions.

DO IT! 2.3 (LO 3) Tom Rast recorded the following transactions during the month of April.

April 3	Cash	3,400	
	Service Revenue		3,400
April 16	Rent Expense	700	
	Cash		700
April 20	Salaries and Wages Expense	250	
	Cash		250

Post these entries to the Cash T-account of the general ledger to determine the ending balance in cash. The beginning balance in cash on April 1 was $1,600.

Prepare a trial balance.

DO IT! 2.4 (LO 4) The following accounts are taken from the ledger of Macon Company at December 31, 2020.

200	Notes Payable	$20,000	101	Cash	$ 6,000
301	Owner's Capital	28,000	126	Supplies	7,000
157	Equipment	80,000	729	Rent Expense	4,000
306	Owner's Drawings	9,000	212	Salaries and Wages Payable	3,000
726	Salaries and Wages Expense	38,000	201	Accounts Payable	11,000
400	Service Revenue	90,000	112	Accounts Receivable	8,000

Prepare a trial balance in good form.

Exercises

Analyze statements about accounting and the recording process.

E2.1 (LO 1) Kim Yi has prepared the following list of statements about accounts.

1. An account is an accounting record of either a specific asset or a specific liability.
2. An account shows only increases, not decreases, in the item it relates to.
3. Some items, such as Cash and Accounts Receivable, are combined into one account.
4. An account has a left, or credit side, and a right, or debit side.
5. A simple form of an account consisting of just the account title, the left side, and the right side, is called a T-account.

Instructions

Identify each statement as true or false. If false, indicate how to correct the statement.

E2.2 (LO 1) Selected transactions for M. Acosta, an interior decorator, in her first month of business, are as follows.

Identify debits, credits, and normal balances.

Jan.	2	Invested $10,000 cash in business.
	3	Purchased used car for $3,000 cash for use in business.
	9	Purchased supplies on account for $600.
	11	Billed customers $2,400 for services performed.
	16	Paid $350 cash for advertising.
	20	Received $900 cash from customers billed on January 11.
	23	Paid creditor $300 cash on balance owed.
	28	Withdrew $1,000 cash for personal use by owner.

Instructions

For each transaction, indicate the following.

a. The basic type of account debited and credited (asset, liability, owner's equity).

b. The specific account debited and credited (Cash, Rent Expense, Service Revenue, etc.).

c. Whether the specific account is increased or decreased.

d. The normal balance of the specific account.

Use the following format, in which the January 2 transaction is given as an example.

	Account Debited				Account Credited			
Date	**(a) Basic Type**	**(b) Specific Account**	**(c) Effect**	**(d) Normal Balance**	**(a) Basic Type**	**(b) Specific Account**	**(c) Effect**	**(d) Normal Balance**
Jan. 2	Asset	Cash	Increase	Debit	Owner's Equity	Owner's Capital	Increase	Credit

E2.3 (LO 2) Data for M. Acosta, interior decorator, are presented in E2.2.

Journalize transactions.

Instructions

Journalize the transactions using journal page J1. (You may omit explanations.)

E2.4 (LO 1) The following information relates to Royale Real Estate Agency.

Analyze transactions and determine their effect on accounts.

Oct.	1	James Royale begins business as a real estate agent with a cash investment of $17,000.
	2	Hires an administrative assistant.
	3	Purchases office furniture for $1,900, on account.
	6	Sells a house and lot for C. Rouse; bills C. Rouse $3,800 for realty services performed.
	27	Pays $1,300 on the balance related to the transaction of October 3.
	30	Pays the administrative assistant $2,500 in salary for October.

Instructions

Prepare the debit-credit analysis for each transaction as illustrated in the textbook.

E2.5 (LO 2) Transaction data for Royale Real Estate Agency are presented in E2.4.

Journalize transactions.

Instructions

Journalize the transactions. (You may omit explanations.)

E2.6 (LO 1, 2) Lennon Industries had the following transactions.

Analyze transactions and journalize.

1. Borrowed $5,000 from the bank by signing a note.

2. Paid $3,900 cash for a computer.

3. Purchased $650 of supplies on account.

Instructions

a. Indicate what accounts are increased and decreased by each transaction.

b. Journalize each transaction. (Omit explanations.)

Analyze transactions and journalize.

E2.7 (LO 1, 2) Halladay Enterprises had the following selected transactions.

1. Bo Halladay invested $4,000 cash in the business.
2. Paid office rent of $840.
3. Performed consulting services and billed a client $5,200.
4. Bo Halladay withdrew $750 cash for personal use.

Instructions

a. Indicate the effect each transaction has on the accounting equation (Assets = Liabilities + Owner's Equity), using plus and minus signs.

b. Journalize each transaction. (Omit explanations.)

Journalize a series of transactions.

E2.8 (LO 2) Selected transactions for Sophie's Dog Care are as follows during the month of March.

March	1	Paid monthly rent of $1,200.
	3	Performed services for $160 on account.
	5	Performed services for cash of $75.
	8	Purchased equipment for $600. The company paid cash of $90 and the balance was on account.
	12	Received cash from customers billed on March 3.
	14	Paid salaries and wages to employees of $525.
	22	Paid utilities of $72.
	24	Borrowed $1,500 from Grafton State Bank by signing a note.
	27	Paid $220 to repair service for plumbing repairs.
	28	Paid balance amount owed from equipment purchase on March 8.
	30	Paid $1,800 for six months of insurance.

Instructions

Journalize the transactions. (Omit explanations.)

Record journal entries.

E2.9 (LO 2) On April 1, Adventures Travel Agency began operations. The following transactions were completed during the month.

1. Owner invested $24,000 in the business.
2. Obtained a bank loan for $7,000 by issuing a note payable.
3. Paid $11,000 cash to buy equipment.
4. Paid $1,200 cash for April office rent.
5. Paid $1,450 for supplies.
6. Purchased $600 of advertising in the *Daily Herald*, on account.
7. Performed services for $18,000: cash of $2,000 was received from customers, and the balance of $16,000 was billed to customers on account.
8. Cash withdrawal of $400 by owner for personal use.
9. Paid the utility bill for the month, $2,000.
10. Paid *Daily Herald* the amount due in transaction (6).
11. Paid $40 of interest on the bank loan obtained in transaction (2).
12. Paid employees' salaries and wages, $6,400.
13. Received $12,000 cash from customers billed in transaction (7).

Instructions

Journalize the transactions. (Omit explanations).

Analyze statements about the ledger.

E2.10 (LO 3) Alma Ortiz has prepared the following list of statements about the general ledger.

1. The general ledger contains all the asset and liability accounts but no owner's equity accounts.
2. The general ledger is sometimes referred to as simply the ledger.
3. The accounts in the general ledger are arranged in alphabetical order.
4. Each account in the general ledger is numbered for easier identification.
5. The general ledger is a book of original entry.

Instructions

Identify each statement as true or false. If false, indicate how to correct the statement.

E2.11 (LO 3, 4) Selected transactions from the journal of June Feldman, investment broker, are presented below.

Post journal entries and prepare a trial balance.

Date	Account Titles and Explanation	Ref.	Debit	Credit
Aug. 1	Cash		5,000	
	Owner's Capital			5,000
	(Owner's investment of cash in business)			
10	Cash		2,600	
	Service Revenue			2,600
	(Received cash for services performed)			
12	Equipment		5,000	
	Cash			2,300
	Notes Payable			2,700
	(Purchased equipment for cash and notes payable)			
25	Accounts Receivable		1,700	
	Service Revenue			1,700
	(Billed clients for services performed)			
31	Cash		900	
	Accounts Receivable			900
	(Receipt of cash on account)			

Instructions

a. Post the transactions to T-accounts.

b. Prepare a trial balance at August 31, 2020.

E2.12 (LO 2, 4) The T-accounts below summarize the ledger of Negrete Landscaping Company at the end of the first month of operations.

Journalize transactions from account data and prepare a trial balance.

Cash — No. 101

4/1	14,000	4/15	1,300
4/12	900	4/25	1,500
4/29	400		
4/30	1,000		

Accounts Receivable — No. 112

4/7	3,000	4/29	400

Supplies — No. 126

4/4	1,800		

Accounts Payable — No. 201

4/25	1,500	4/4	1,800

Unearned Service Revenue — No. 209

		4/30	1,000

Owner's Capital — No. 301

		4/1	14,000

Service Revenue — No. 400

		4/7	3,000
		4/12	900

Salaries and Wages Expense — No. 726

4/15	1,300		

Instructions

a. Prepare the complete general journal (including explanations) from which the postings to Cash were made.

b. Prepare a trial balance at April 30, 2020.

Journalize transactions from account data and prepare a trial balance.

E2.13 (LO 2, 4) Presented below is the ledger for Shumway Co.

Cash No. 101

10/1	3,000	10/4	400
10/10	750	10/12	1,500
10/10	4,000	10/15	350
10/20	500	10/30	300
10/25	2,000	10/31	500

Accounts Receivable No. 112

10/6	800	10/20	500
10/20	940		

Supplies No. 126

10/4	400		

Equipment No. 157

10/3	2,000		

Notes Payable No. 200

		10/10	4,000

Accounts Payable No. 201

10/12	1,500	10/3	2,000

Owner's Capital No. 301

		10/1	3,000
		10/25	2,000

Owner's Drawings No. 306

10/30	300		

Service Revenue No. 400

		10/6	800
		10/10	750
		10/20	940

Salaries and Wages Expense No. 726

10/31	500		

Rent Expense No. 729

10/15	350		

Instructions

a. Reproduce the journal entries for the transactions that occurred on October 1, 10, and 20, and provide explanations for each.

b. Determine the October 31 balance for each of the accounts above, and prepare a trial balance at October 31, 2020.

Prepare journal entries and post using standard account form.

E2.14 (LO 2, 3) Selected transactions for Bonnie Donne Company during its first month in business are presented below.

Sept.	1	Invested $10,000 cash in the business.
	5	Purchased equipment for $14,000 paying $4,000 in cash and the balance on account.
	25	Paid $3,000 cash on balance owed for equipment.
	30	Withdrew $900 cash for personal use.

Donne's chart of accounts shows No. 101 Cash, No. 157 Equipment, No. 201 Accounts Payable, No. 301 Owner's Capital, and No. 306 Owner's Drawings.

Instructions

a. Journalize the transactions on page J1 of the journal. (Omit explanations.)

b. Post the transactions using the standard account form.

Analyze errors and their effects on trial balance.

E2.15 (LO 4) The bookkeeper for J.L. Kang Equipment Repair made a number of errors in journalizing and posting, as described below.

1. A credit posting of $525 to Accounts Receivable was omitted.
2. A debit posting of $750 for Prepaid Insurance was debited to Insurance Expense.
3. A collection from a customer of $100 in payment of its account owed was journalized and posted as a debit to Cash $100 and a credit to Service Revenue $100.
4. A credit posting of $415 to Property Taxes Payable was made twice.
5. A cash purchase of supplies for $250 was journalized and posted as a debit to Supplies $25 and a credit to Cash $25.
6. A debit of $625 to Advertising Expense was posted as $652.

Instructions

For each error:

a. Indicate whether the trial balance will balance.

b. If the trial balance will not balance, indicate the amount of the difference.

c. Indicate the trial balance column that will have the larger total.

Consider each error separately. Use the following form, in which error (1) is given as an example.

Error	(a) In Balance	(b) Difference	(c) Larger Column
(1)	No	$525	debit

E2.16 (LO 4) The accounts in the ledger of Prompt Delivery Service contain the following balances on July 31, 2020.

Prepare a trial balance.

Accounts Receivable	$ 7,640	Prepaid Insurance	$ 1,968
Accounts Payable	8,394	Maintenance and Repairs Expense	961
Cash	?	Service Revenue	10,610
Equipment	45,360	Owner's Drawings	700
Gasoline Expense	758	Owner's Capital	38,000
Utilities Expense	523	Salaries and Wages Expense	4,428
Notes Payable	17,000	Salaries and Wages Payable	815

Instructions

Prepare a trial balance with the accounts arranged as illustrated in the chapter and fill in the missing amount for Cash.

E2.17 (LO 2, 3, 4) Beyers Security Company provides security services. Selected transactions for Beyers are presented below.

Journalize transactions, post transactions to T-accounts, and prepare trial balance.

Oct.	1	Invested $66,000 cash in the business.
	2	Hired part-time security consultant. Salary will be $2,000 per month. First day of work will be October 15.
	4	Paid one month of rent for building for $2,000.
	7	Purchased equipment for $18,000, paying $4,000 cash and the balance on account.
	8	Paid $500 for advertising.
	10	Received bill for equipment repair cost of $390.
	12	Provided security services for event for $3,200 on account.
	16	Purchased supplies for $410 on account.
	21	Paid balance due from October 7 purchase of equipment.
	24	Received and paid utility bill for $148.
	27	Received payment from customer for October 12 services performed.
	31	Paid employee salaries and wages of $5,100.

Instructions

a. Journalize the transactions. Do not provide explanations.

b. Post the transactions to T-accounts.

c. Prepare a trial balance at October 31, 2020. (*Hint:* Compute ending balances of T-accounts first.)

Problems: Set A

P2.1A (LO 1, 2) Holz Disc Golf Course was opened on March 1 by Ian Holz. The following selected events and transactions occurred during March.

Journalize a series of transactions.

GLS

Mar.	1	Invested $20,000 cash in the business.
	3	Purchased Rainbow Golf Land for $15,000 cash. The price consists of land $12,000, shed $2,000, and equipment $1,000. (Make one compound entry.)
	5	Paid advertising expenses of $900.
	6	Paid cash $600 for a one-year insurance policy.
	10	Purchased golf discs and other equipment for $1,050 from Stevenson Company payable in 30 days.

Mar. 18 Received $1,100 in cash for golf fees (Holz records golf fees as service revenue).
19 Sold 150 coupon books for $10 each. Each book contains 4 coupons that enable the holder to play one round of disc golf.
25 Withdrew $800 cash for personal use.
30 Paid salaries of $250.
30 Paid Stevenson Company in full.
31 Received $2,700 cash for golf fees.

Holz Disc Golf uses the following accounts: Cash, Prepaid Insurance, Land, Buildings, Equipment, Accounts Payable, Unearned Service Revenue, Owner's Capital, Owner's Drawings, Service Revenue, Advertising Expense, and Salaries and Wages Expense.

Instructions

Journalize the March transactions.

Journalize transactions, post, and prepare a trial balance.

GLS

P2.2A (LO 1, 2, 3, 4) Vera Ernst is a licensed dentist. During the first month of the operation of her business, the following events and transactions occurred.

April 1 Invested $20,000 cash in her business.
1 Hired a secretary-receptionist at a salary of $700 per week payable monthly.
2 Paid office rent for the month $1,500.
3 Purchased dental supplies on account from Dazzle Company $4,000.
10 Performed dental services and billed insurance companies $5,100.
11 Received $1,000 cash advance from Leah Mataruka for an implant.
20 Received $2,100 cash for services performed from Michael Santos.
30 Paid secretary-receptionist for the month $2,800.
30 Paid $2,600 to Dazzle for accounts payable due.

Vera uses the following chart of accounts: No. 101 Cash, No. 112 Accounts Receivable, No. 126 Supplies, No. 201 Accounts Payable, No. 209 Unearned Service Revenue, No. 301 Owner's Capital, No. 400 Service Revenue, No. 726 Salaries and Wages Expense, and No. 729 Rent Expense.

Instructions

a. Journalize the transactions.

b. Post to the ledger accounts.

c. Prepare a trial balance on April 30, 2020.

c. Trial balance totals $29,600

Journalize transactions, post, and prepare a trial balance.

P2.3A (LO 1, 2, 3, 4) Maquoketa Services was formed on May 1, 2020. The following transactions took place during the first month.

Transactions on May 1:

1. Jay Bradford invested $40,000 cash in the company, as its sole owner.
2. Hired two employees to work in the warehouse. They will each be paid a salary of $3,050 per month.
3. Signed a 2-year rental agreement on a warehouse; paid $24,000 cash in advance for the first year.
4. Purchased furniture and equipment costing $30,000. A cash payment of $10,000 was made immediately; the remainder will be paid in 6 months.
5. Paid $1,800 cash for a one-year insurance policy on the furniture and equipment.

Transactions during the remainder of the month:

6. Purchased basic office supplies for $420 cash.
7. Purchased more office supplies for $1,500 on account.
8. Total revenues earned were $20,000—$8,000 cash and $12,000 on account.
9. Paid $400 to suppliers for accounts payable due.
10. Received $3,000 from customers in payment of accounts receivable.
11. Received utility bills in the amount of $380, to be paid next month.
12. Paid the monthly salaries of the two employees, totaling $6,100.

Instructions

a. Prepare journal entries to record each of the events listed. (Omit explanations.)

b. Post the journal entries to T-accounts.

c. Prepare a trial balance as of May 31, 2020.

c. Trial balance totals $81,480

P2.4A (LO 4) The following trial balance of Sergei Asbrecht Co. does not balance.

Prepare a correct trial balance.

Excel

Sergei Asbrecht Co.
Trial Balance
June 30, 2020

	Debit	**Credit**
Cash		$ 3,140
Accounts Receivable	$ 2,812	
Supplies	1,200	
Equipment	2,600	
Accounts Payable		3,666
Unearned Service Revenue	1,100	
Owner's Capital		8,000
Owner's Drawings	800	
Service Revenue		2,480
Salaries and Wages Expense	3,200	
Utilities Expense	810	
	$12,522	$17,286

Each of the listed accounts has a normal balance per the general ledger. An examination of the ledger and journal reveals the following errors.

1. Cash received from a customer in payment of its account was debited for $850, and Accounts Receivable was credited for the same amount. The actual collection was for $580.
2. The purchase of a computer on account for $710 was recorded as a debit to Supplies for $710 and a credit to Accounts Payable for $710.
3. Services were performed on account for a client for $980. Accounts Receivable was debited for $980, and Service Revenue was credited for $98.
4. A debit posting to Salaries and Wages Expense of $900 was omitted.
5. A payment of a balance due for $306 was credited to Cash for $306 and credited to Accounts Payable for $360.
6. The withdrawal of $600 cash for Sergei's personal use was debited to Salaries and Wages Expense for $600 and credited to Cash for $600.

Instructions

Prepare a correct trial balance. (*Hint:* It helps to prepare the correct journal entry for the transaction described and compare it to the mistake made.)

Trial balance totals $15,462

P2.5A (LO 1, 2, 3, 4) The Starr Theater, owned by Meg Vargo, will begin operations in March. The Starr will be unique in that it will show only triple features of sequential theme movies. As of March 1, the ledger of Starr showed No. 101 Cash $3,000, No. 140 Land $24,000, No. 145 Buildings (concession stand, projection room, ticket booth, and screen) $10,000, No. 157 Equipment $10,000, No. 201 Accounts Payable $7,000, and No. 301 Owner's Capital $40,000. During the month of March, the following events and transactions occurred.

Journalize transactions, post, and prepare a trial balance.

GLS

Mar.	2	Rented the three *Indiana Jones* movies to be shown for the first 3 weeks of March. The film rental was $3,500; $1,500 was paid in cash and $2,000 will be paid on March 10.
	3	Ordered the *Lord of the Rings* movies to be shown the last 10 days of March. It will cost $200 per night.
	9	Received $4,300 cash from admissions.
	10	Paid balance due on *Indiana Jones* movies rental and $2,100 on March 1 accounts payable.
	11	Starr Theater contracted with Adam Ladd to operate the concession stand. Ladd is to pay 15% of gross concession receipts, payable monthly, for the rental of the concession stand.
	12	Paid advertising expenses $900.
	20	Received $5,000 cash from customers for admissions.
	20	Received the *Lord of the Rings* movies and paid the rental fee of $2,000.
	31	Paid salaries of $3,100.
	31	Received statement from Adam Ladd showing gross receipts from concessions of $6,000 and the balance due to Starr Theater of $900 ($6,000 × 15%) for March. Ladd paid one-half the balance due and will remit the remainder on April 5.
	31	Received $9,000 cash from customers for admissions.

In addition to the accounts identified above, the chart of accounts includes No. 112 Accounts Receivable, No. 400 Service Revenue, No. 429 Rent Revenue, No. 610 Advertising Expense, No. 726 Salaries and Wages Expense, and No. 729 Rent Expense.

Instructions

a. Enter the beginning balances in the ledger. Insert a check mark (✓) in the reference column of the ledger for the beginning balance.

b. Journalize the March transactions. Starr records admission revenue as service revenue, rental of the concession stand as rent revenue, and film rental expense as rent expense.

c. Post the March journal entries to the ledger. Assume that all entries are posted from page 1 of the journal.

d. Trial balance totals $64,100

d. Prepare a trial balance on March 31, 2020.

Continuing Case

Cookie Creations

(*Note:* This is a continuation of the Cookie Creations case from Chapter 1.)

© leungchopan/ Shutterstock

CC2 After researching the different forms of business organization. Natalie Koebel decides to operate "Cookie Creations" as a proprietorship. She then starts the process of getting the business running. In November 2019, the following activities take place.

Nov.	8	Natalie cashes her U.S. Savings Bonds and receives $520, which she deposits in her personal bank account.
	8	She opens a bank account under the name "Cookie Creations" and transfers $500 from her personal account to the new account.
	11	Natalie pays $65 for advertising.
	13	She buys baking supplies, such as flour, sugar, butter, and chocolate chips, for $125 cash. (*Hint:* Use Supplies account.)
	14	Natalie starts to gather some baking equipment to take with her when teaching the cookie classes. She has an excellent top-of-the-line food processor and mixer that originally cost her $750. Natalie decides to start using it only in her new business. She estimates that the equipment is currently worth $300. She invests the equipment in the business.
	16	Natalie realizes that her initial cash investment is not enough. Her grandmother lends her $2,000 cash, for which Natalie signs a note payable in the name of the business. Natalie deposits the money in the business bank account. (*Hint:* The note does not have to be repaid for 24 months. As a result, the note payable should be reported in the accounts as the last liability and also on the balance sheet as the last liability.)
	17	She buys more baking equipment for $900 cash.
	20	She teaches her first class and collects $125 cash.
	25	Natalie books a second class for December 4 for $150. She receives $30 cash in advance as a down payment.
	30	Natalie pays $1,320 for a one-year insurance policy that will expire on December 1, 2020.

Instructions

a. Prepare journal entries to record the November transactions.

b. Post the journal entries to general ledger accounts.

c. Prepare a trial balance at November 30.

Ethics Cases

EC2.1 Ellynn Kole is the assistant chief accountant at Doman Company, a manufacturer of computer chips and cellular phones. The company presently has total sales of $20 million. It is the end of the first quarter. Ellynn is hurriedly trying to prepare a trial balance so that quarterly financial statements can be prepared and released to management and the regulatory agencies. The total credits on the trial balance exceed the debits by $1,000. In order to meet the 4 p.m. deadline, Ellynn decides to force the debits and credits into balance by adding the amount of the difference to the Equipment account. She chooses

Equipment because it is one of the larger account balances; percentage-wise, it will be the least misstated. Ellynn "plugs" the difference! She believes that the difference will not affect anyone's decisions. She wishes that she had another few days to find the error but realizes that the financial statements are already late.

Instructions

a. Who are the stakeholders in this situation?

b. What are the ethical issues involved in this case?

c. What are Ellynn's alternatives?

EC2.2 If you haven't already done so, in the not-too-distant future you will prepare a résumé. In some ways, your résumé is like a company's annual report. Its purpose is to enable others to evaluate your past, in an effort to predict your future.

A résumé is your opportunity to create a positive first impression. It is important that it be impressive—but it should also be accurate. In order to increase their job prospects, some people are tempted to "inflate" their résumés by overstating the importance of some past accomplishments or positions. In fact, you might even think that "everybody does it" and that if you don't do it, you will be at a disadvantage.

David Edmondson, the president and CEO of well-known electronics retailer **Radio Shack**, overstated his accomplishments by claiming that he had earned a bachelor's of science degree, when in fact he had not. Apparently, his employer had not done a background check to ensure the accuracy of his résumé. Should Radio Shack have fired him?

> **YES:** Radio Shack is a publicly traded company. Investors, creditors, employees, and others doing business with the company will not trust it if its leader is known to have poor integrity. The "tone at the top" is vital to creating an ethical organization.
>
> **NO:** Mr. Edmondson had been a Radio Shack employee for 11 years. He had served the company in a wide variety of positions, and had earned the position of CEO through exceptional performance. While the fact that he lied 11 years earlier on his résumé was unfortunate, his service since then made this past transgression irrelevant. In addition, the company was in the midst of a massive restructuring, which included closing 700 of its 7,000 stores. It could not afford additional upheaval at this time.

Instructions

Write a response indicating your position regarding this situation. Provide support for your view.

Expand Your Critical Thinking

Financial Reporting Problem: Apple Inc.

CT2.1 The financial statements of **Apple Inc.** are presented in Appendix A. The complete annual report, including the notes to the financial statements, is available at the company's website.

Apple's financial statements contain the following selected accounts, stated in millions of dollars.

Accounts Payable	Cash and Cash Equivalents
Accounts Receivable	Research and Development Expense
Property, Plant, and Equipment	Inventories

Instructions

a. Answer the following questions.

1. What is the increase and decrease side for each account?
2. What is the normal balance for each account?

b. Identify the probable other account in the transaction and the effect on that account when:

1. Accounts Receivable is decreased.
2. Accounts Payable is decreased.
3. Inventories are increased.

c. Identify the other account(s) that ordinarily would be involved when:

1. Research and Development Expense is increased.
2. Property, Plant, and Equipment is increased.

Comparative Analysis Problem: PepsiCo, Inc. vs. The Coca-Cola Company

CT2.2 PepsiCo, Inc.'s financial statements are presented in Appendix B. Financial statement of **The Coca-Cola Company** are presented in Appendix C. The complete annual reports of PepsiCo and Coca-Cola, including the notes to the financial statements, are available at each company's respective website.

Instructions

a. Based on the information contained in the financial statements, determine the normal balance of the listed accounts for each company.

PepsiCo	Coca-Cola
1. Inventory	1. Accounts Receivable
2. Property, Plant, and Equipment	2. Cash and Cash Equivalents
3. Accounts Payable	3. Cost of Goods Sold (expense)
4. Interest Expense	4. Sales (revenue)

b. Identify the other account ordinarily involved when:

1. Accounts Receivable is increased.

2. Salaries and Wages Payable is decreased.

3. Property, Plant, and Equipment is increased.

4. Interest Expense is increased.

Comparative Analysis Problem: Amazon.com, Inc. vs. Wal-Mart Stores, Inc.

CT2.3 Amazon.com, Inc.'s financial statements are presented in Appendix D. Financial statements of **Wal-Mart Stores, Inc.** are presented in Appendix E. The complete annual reports of Amazon and Wal-Mart, including the notes to the financial statements, are available at each company's respective website.

Instructions

a. Based on the information contained in the financial statements, determine the normal balance of the listed accounts for each company.

Amazon	Wal-Mart
1. Interest Expense	1. Net Product Revenues
2. Cash and Cash Equivalents	2. Inventories
3. Accounts Payable	3. Cost of Sales

b. Identify the other account ordinarily involved when:

1. Accounts Receivable is increased.

2. Interest Expense is increased.

3. Salaries and Wages Payable is decreased.

4. Service Revenue is increased.

Real-World Focus

CT2.4 Much information about specific companies is available on the Internet. Such information includes basic descriptions of the company's location, activities, industry, financial health, and financial performance.

Instructions

Go to the **Yahoo! Finance** website and then answer the following questions.

a. What is the company's industry?

b. What is the company's total sales?

c. What is the company's net income?

d. What are the names of four of the company's competitors?

e. Choose one of these competitors.

f. What is this competitor's name? What are its sales? What is its net income?

g. Which of these two companies is larger by size of sales? Which one reported higher net income?

CT2.5 The January 27, 2011, edition of the *New York Times* contains an article by Richard Sandomir entitled "N.F.L. Finances, as Seen Through Packers' Records." The author of the article discusses the fact that the **Green Bay Packers** are the only NFL team that publicly publishes its annual report.

Instructions

Read the article and answer the following questions.

a. Why are the Green Bay Packers the only professional football team to publish and distribute an annual report?

b. Why is the football players' labor union particularly interested in the Packers' annual report?

c. In addition to the players' labor union, what other outside party might be interested in the annual report?

d. Even though the Packers' revenue increased in recent years, the company's operating profit fell significantly. How does the article explain this decline?

Communication Activity

CT2.6 Melia's Maid Company offers home-cleaning service. Two recurring transactions for the company are billing customers for services performed and paying employee salaries. For example, on March 15, bills totaling $6,000 were sent to customers and $2,000 was paid in salaries to employees.

Instructions

Write a memo to your instructor that explains and illustrates the steps in the recording process for each of the March 15 transactions. Use the format illustrated in the textbook.

All About You

CT2.7 Every company needs to plan in order to move forward. Its top management must consider where it wants the company to be in three to five years. Like a company, you need to think about where you want to be three to five years from now, and you need to start taking steps now in order to get there.

Instructions

Provide responses to each of the following items.

a. Where would you like to be working in three to five years? Describe your plan for getting there by identifying between five and 10 specific steps that you need to take.

b. In order to get the job you want, you will need a résumé. Your résumé is the equivalent of a company's annual report. It needs to provide relevant and reliable information about your past accomplishments so that employers can decide whether to "invest" in you. Do a search on the Internet to find a good résumé format. What are the basic elements of a résumé?

c. A company's annual report provides information about a company's accomplishments. In order for investors to use the annual report, the information must be reliable; that is, users must have faith that the information is accurate and believable. How can you provide assurance that the information on your résumé is reliable?

d. Prepare a résumé assuming that you have accomplished the five to 10 specific steps you identified in part (a). Also, provide evidence that would give assurance that the information is reliable.

Considering People, Planet, and Profit

CT2.8 Auditors provide a type of certification of corporate financial statements. Certification is used in many other aspects of business as well. For example, it plays a critical role in the sustainability movement. The February 7, 2012, issue of the *New York Times* contained an article by S. Amanda Caudill entitled "Better Lives in Better Coffee," which discusses the role of certification in the coffee business.

Instructions

Conduct an Internet search to locate and read the article, and then answer the following questions.

a. The article mentions three different certification types that coffee growers can obtain from three different certification bodies. Using financial reporting as an example, what potential problems might the existence of multiple certification types present to coffee purchasers?

b. According to the author, which certification is most common among coffee growers? What are the possible reasons for this?

c. What social and environmental benefits are coffee certifications trying to achieve? Are there also potential financial benefits to the parties involved?

A Look at IFRS

LEARNING OBJECTIVE 5

Compare the procedures for the recording process under GAAP and IFRS.

International companies use the same set of procedures and records to keep track of transaction data. Thus, the material in Chapter 2 dealing with the account, general rules of debit and credit, and steps in the recording process—the journal, ledger, and chart of accounts—is the same under both GAAP and IFRS.

Key Points

Following are the key similarities and differences between GAAP and IFRS as related to the recording process.

Similarities

- Transaction analysis is the same under IFRS and GAAP.
- Both the IASB and the FASB go beyond the basic definitions provided in the textbook for the key elements of financial statements, that is assets, liabilities, equity, revenue, and expenses. The implications of the expanded definitions are discussed in more advanced accounting courses.
- As shown in the textbook, dollar signs are typically used only in the trial balance and the financial statements. The same practice is followed under IFRS, using the currency of the country where the reporting company is headquartered.
- A trial balance under IFRS follows the same format as shown in the textbook.

Differences

- IFRS relies less on historical cost and more on fair value than do FASB standards.
- Internal controls are a system of checks and balances designed to prevent and detect fraud and errors. While most public U.S. companies have these systems in place, many non-U.S. companies have never completely documented the controls nor had an independent auditors attest to their effectiveness.

Looking to the Future

The basic recording process shown in this textbook is followed by companies across the globe. It is unlikely to change in the future. The definitional structure of assets, liabilities, equity, revenues, and expenses may change over time as the IASB and FASB evaluate their overall conceptual framework for establishing accounting standards.

IFRS Practice

IFRS Self-Test Questions

1. Which statement is **correct** regarding IFRS?
   a. IFRS reverses the rules of debits and credits, that is, debits are on the right and credits are on the left.
   b. IFRS uses the same process for recording transactions as GAAP.
   c. The chart of accounts under IFRS is different because revenues follow assets.
   d. None of the above statements are correct.
2. The expanded accounting equation under IFRS is as follows:
   a. Assets = Liabilities + Owner's Capital + Owner's Drawings + Revenues – Expenses.
   b. Assets + Liabilities = Owner's Capital + Owner's Drawings + Revenues – Expenses.
   c. Assets = Liabilities + Owner's Capital – Owner's Drawings + Revenues – Expenses.
   d. Assets = Liabilities + Owner's Capital + Owner's Drawings – Revenues – Expenses.
3. A trial balance:
   a. is the same under IFRS and GAAP.
   b. proves that transactions are recorded correctly.
   c. proves that all transactions have been recorded.
   d. will not balance if a correct journal entry is posted twice.
4. One difference between IFRS and GAAP is that:
   a. GAAP uses accrual-accounting concepts and IFRS uses primarily the cash basis of accounting.
   b. IFRS uses a different posting process than GAAP.

c. IFRS uses more fair value measurements than GAAP.

d. the limitations of a trial balance are different between IFRS and GAAP.

5. The general policy for using proper currency signs (dollar, yen, pound, etc.) is the same for both IFRS and this textbook. This policy is as follows:

a. Currency signs only appear in ledgers and journal entries.

b. Currency signs are only shown in the trial balance.

c. Currency signs are shown for all compound journal entries.

d. Currency signs are shown in trial balances and financial statements.

International Financial Reporting Problem: Louis Vuitton

IFRS2.1 The financial statements of **Louis Vuitton** are presented in Appendix F. The complete annual report, including the notes to its financial statements, is available at the company's website.

Instructions

Describe in which statement each of the following items is reported, and the position in the statement (e.g., current asset).

a. Other operating income and expenses.

b. Cash and cash equivalents.

c. Trade accounts payable.

d. Cost of net financial debt.

Answers to IFRS Self-Test Questions

1. b **2.** c **3.** a **4.** c **5.** d

CHAPTER **3**

Rudy Archuleta/Redux Pictures

Adjusting the Accounts

Chapter Preview

In Chapter 1, you learned a neat little formula: Net income = Revenues − Expenses. In Chapter 2, you learned some rules for recording revenue and expense transactions. Guess what? Things are not really that nice and neat. In fact, it is often difficult for companies to determine in what time period they should report some revenues and expenses. In other words, in measuring net income, timing is everything.

Feature Story

Keeping Track of Groupons

Who doesn't like buying things at a discount? That's why it's not surprising that three years after it started as a company, **Groupon, Inc.** was estimated to be worth $16 billion. This translates into an average increase in value of almost $15 million per day.

Now consider that Groupon had previously been estimated to be worth even more than that. What happened? Well, accounting regulators and investors began to question the way that Groupon had accounted for some of its transactions. Groupon sells coupons ("groupons"), so how hard can it be to accurately account for that? It turns out that accounting for coupons is not as easy as you might think.

First, consider what happens when Groupon makes a sale. Suppose it sells a groupon for $30 for Highrise Hamburgers. When it receives the $30 from the customer, it must turn over half of that amount ($15) to Highrise Hamburgers. So should Groupon record revenue for the full $30 or just $15? Until recently, Groupon recorded the full $30. But, in response to an SEC ruling on the issue, Groupon now records revenue of $15 instead.

A second issue is a matter of timing. When should Groupon record this $15 revenue? Should it record the revenue when it sells the groupon, or must it wait until the customer uses the groupon at Highrise Hamburgers? You can find the answer to this question in the notes to Groupon's financial statements. It recognizes the revenue once "the number of customers who purchase the daily deal exceeds the predetermined threshold, the Groupon has been electronically delivered to the purchaser and a listing of Groupons sold has been made available to the merchant."

The accounting becomes even more complicated when you consider the company's loyalty programs. Groupon offers free or discounted groupons to its subscribers for doing things such as referring new customers or participating in promotions. These groupons are to be used for future purchases, yet the company must record the expense at the time the customer receives the groupon. The cost of these programs is huge for Groupon, so the timing of this expense can definitely affect its reported income.

Finally, Groupon, like all other companies, relies on many estimates in its financial reporting. For example, Groupon reports that "estimates are utilized for, but not limited to, stock-based compensation, income taxes, valuation of acquired goodwill and intangible assets, customer refunds, contingent liabilities and the depreciable lives of fixed assets." It notes that "actual results could differ materially from those estimates." So, next time you use a coupon, think about what that means for the company's accountants!

Chapter Outline

LEARNING OBJECTIVES

LO 1 Explain the accrual basis of accounting and the reasons for adjusting entries.	• Fiscal and calendar years • Accrual- vs. cash-basis accounting • Recognizing revenues and expenses • Need for adjusting entries • Types of adjusting entries	**DO IT! 1** Timing Concepts
LO 2 Prepare adjusting entries for deferrals.	• Prepaid expenses • Unearned revenues	**DO IT! 2** Adjusting Entries for Deferrals
LO 3 Prepare adjusting entries for accruals.	• Accrued revenues • Accrued expenses • Summary of basic relationships	**DO IT! 3** Adjusting Entries for Accruals
LO 4 Describe the nature and purpose of an adjusted trial balance.	• Preparing the adjusted trial balance • Preparing financial statements	**DO IT! 4** Trial Balance

Go to the Review and Practice section at the end of the chapter for a review of key concepts and practice applications with solutions.
Visit WileyPLUS with ORION for additional tutorials and practice opportunities.

Accrual-Basis Accounting and Adjusting Entries

LEARNING OBJECTIVE 1

Explain the accrual basis of accounting and the reasons for adjusting entries.

If we could wait to prepare financial statements until a company ended its operations, no adjustments would be needed. At that point, we could easily determine its final balance sheet and the amount of lifetime income it earned.

However, most companies need feedback about how well they are performing during a period of time. For example, management usually wants monthly financial statements. The Internal Revenue Service requires all businesses to file annual tax returns. Therefore, **accountants**

divide the economic life of a business into artificial time periods. This convenient assumption is referred to as the **time period assumption** (see **Alternative Terminology**).

Many business transactions affect more than one of these arbitrary time periods. For example, the airplanes purchased by **Southwest Airlines** five years ago are still in use today. It would not make sense to expense the full cost of the airplanes at the time of purchase because they will be used for many subsequent periods. Instead, companies must therefore allocate the costs to the periods of use (how much of the cost of an airplane contributed to operations this year?).

ALTERNATIVE TERMINOLOGY

The time period assumption is also called the *periodicity assumption.*

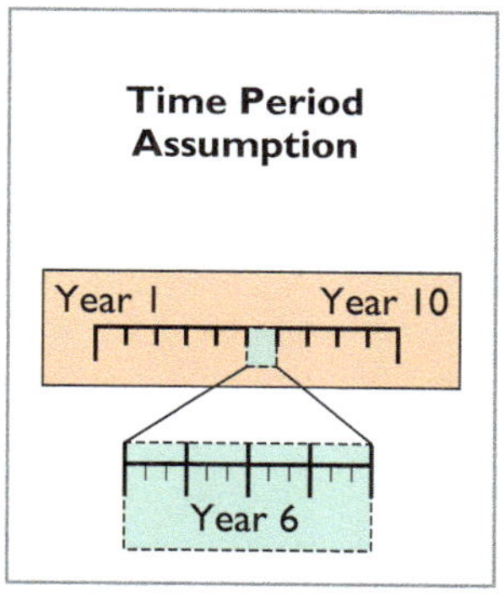

Fiscal and Calendar Years

Both small and large companies prepare financial statements periodically in order to assess their financial condition and results of operations. **Accounting time periods are generally a month, a quarter, or a year.** Monthly and quarterly time periods are called **interim periods**. Most large companies must prepare both quarterly and annual financial statements.

An accounting time period that is one year in length is a **fiscal year**. A fiscal year usually begins with the first day of a month and ends 12 months later on the last day of a month. Many businesses use the **calendar year** (January 1 to December 31) as their accounting period. Some do not. Companies whose fiscal year differs from the calendar year include **Delta Air Lines**, June 30, and **The Walt Disney Company**, September 30. Sometimes a company's year-end will vary from year to year. For example, **PepsiCo**'s fiscal year ends on the Friday closest to December 31, which was December 27 in 2014 and December 26 in 2015.

Accrual- versus Cash-Basis Accounting

What you will learn in this chapter is **accrual-basis accounting**. Under the accrual basis, companies record transactions that change a company's financial statements **in the periods in which the events occur**. For example, using the accrual basis to determine net income means companies recognize revenues when they perform services (rather than when they receive cash). It also means recognizing expenses when incurred (rather than when paid).

An alternative to the accrual basis is the cash basis. Under **cash-basis accounting**, companies record revenue at the time they receive cash. They record an expense at the time they pay out cash. The cash basis seems appealing due to its simplicity, but it often produces misleading financial statements. For example, it fails to record revenue for a company that has performed services but has not yet received payment. As a result, the cash basis may not recognize revenue in the period that a performance obligation is satisfied.

Accrual-basis accounting is therefore in accordance with generally accepted accounting principles (GAAP). Individuals and some small companies, however, do use cash-basis accounting. The cash basis is justified for small businesses because they often have few receivables and payables. Medium and large companies use accrual-basis accounting.

Recognizing Revenues and Expenses

It can be difficult to determine when to report revenues and expenses. The revenue recognition principle and the expense recognition principle help in this task.

Revenue Recognition Principle

When a company agrees to perform a service or sell a product to a customer, it has a **performance obligation**. When the company meets this performance obligation, it recognizes revenue. The **revenue recognition principle** therefore requires that companies recognize revenue in the accounting period in which the performance obligation is satisfied. A company satisfies its performance obligation by performing a service or providing a good to a customer.

To illustrate, assume that Dave's Dry Cleaning cleans clothing on June 30 but customers do not claim and pay for their clothes until the first week of July. Dave's should record revenue in June when it performed the service (satisfied the performance obligation) rather than in July when it received the cash. At June 30, Dave's would report a receivable on its balance sheet and revenue in its income statement for the service performed.

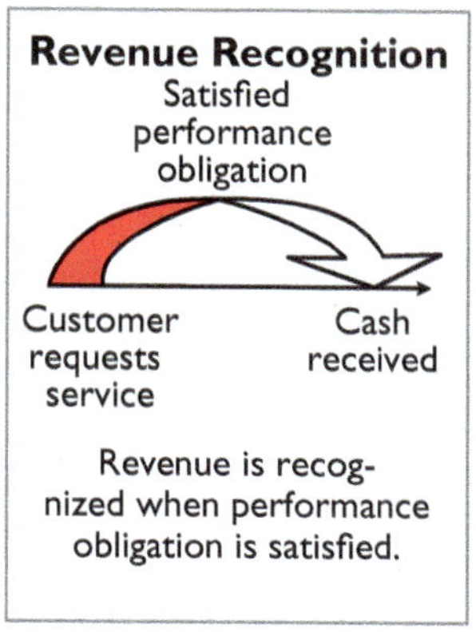

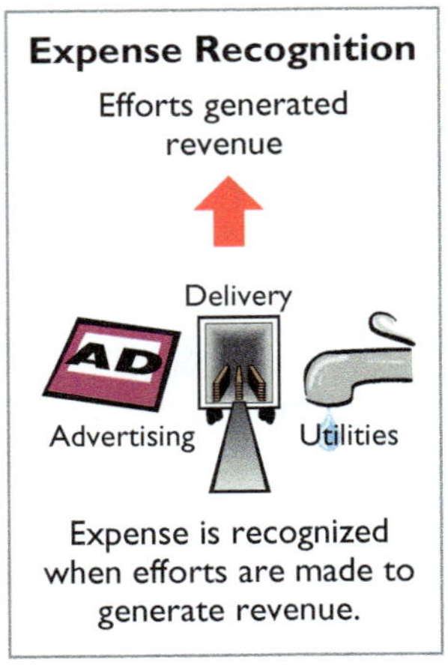

Expense Recognition Principle

Accountants follow a simple rule in recognizing expenses: "Let the expenses follow the revenues." Thus, expense recognition is tied to revenue recognition. In the dry cleaning example, this means that Dave's should report the salary expense incurred in performing the June 30 cleaning service in the same period in which it recognizes the service revenue. The critical issue in expense recognition is when the expense makes its contribution to revenue. This may or may not be the same period in which the expense is paid. If Dave's does not pay the salary incurred on June 30 until July, it would report salaries payable on its June 30 balance sheet.

This practice of expense recognition is referred to as the **expense recognition principle**. It requires that companies recognize expenses in the period in which they make efforts (consume assets or incur liabilities) to generate revenue. The term matching is sometimes used in expense recognition to indicate the relationship between the effort expended and the revenue generated. **Illustration 3.1** summarizes the revenue and expense recognition principles.

ILLUSTRATION 3.1 **GAAP relationships in revenue and expense recognition**

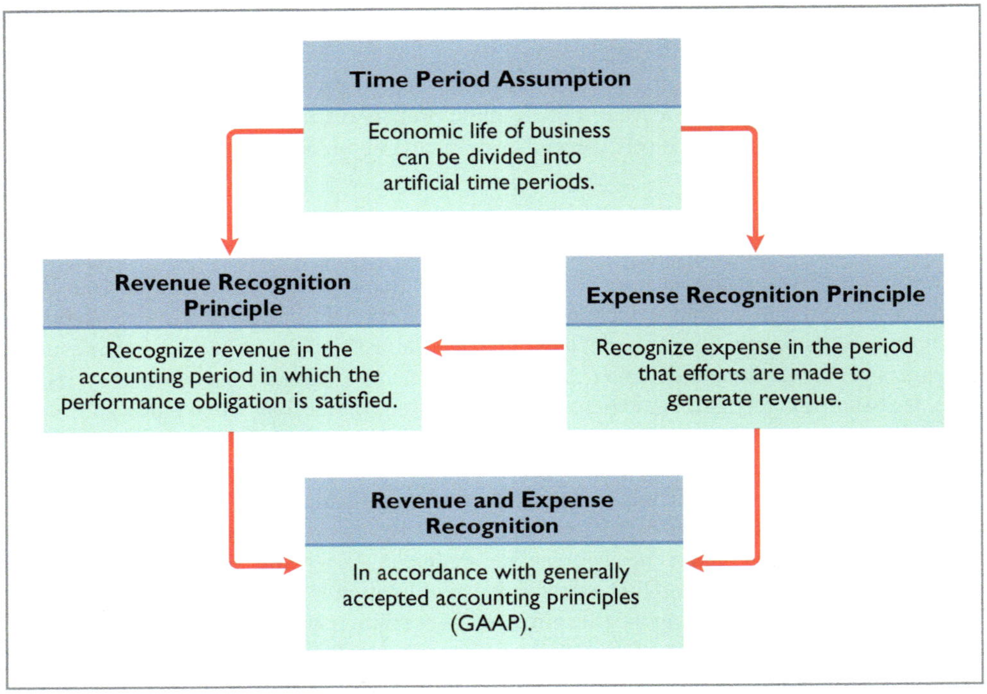

Investor Insight Apple Inc.

PhotoAlto/James Hardy/Getty Images, Inc.

Reporting Revenue Accurately

Until recently, electronics manufacturer **Apple** was required to spread the revenues from iPhone sales over the two year period following the sale of the phone. Accounting standards required this because Apple was obligated to provide software updates after the phone was sold. Since Apple had service obligations after the initial date of sale, it was forced to spread the revenue over a two-year period.

As a result, the rapid growth of iPhone sales was not fully reflected in the revenue amounts reported in Apple's income statement. A new accounting standard now enables Apples to report much more of its iPhone revenue at the point of sale. It was estimated that under the new rule revenues would have been about 17% higher and earnings per share almost 50% higher.

In the past, why was it argued that Apple should spread the recognition of iPhone revenue over a two-year period, rather than recording it upfront? (Go to WileyPLUS for this answer and additional questions.)

The Need for Adjusting Entries

In order for revenues to be recorded in the period in which services are performed and for expenses to be recognized in the period in which they are incurred, companies make adjusting entries. **Adjusting entries ensure that the revenue recognition and expense recognition principles are followed** (see **International Note**).

Adjusting entries are necessary because the **trial balance**—the first pulling together of the transaction data—may not contain up-to-date and complete data. This is true for several reasons:

1. Some events are not recorded daily because it is not efficient to do so. Examples are the use of supplies and the earning of wages by employees.
2. Some costs are not recorded during the accounting period because these costs expire with the passage of time rather than as a result of recurring daily transactions. Examples are charges related to the use of buildings and equipment, rent, and insurance.
3. Some items may be unrecorded. An example is a utility service bill that will not be received until the next accounting period.

INTERNATIONAL NOTE

Internal controls are a system of checks and balances designed to detect and prevent fraud and errors. The Sarbanes-Oxley Act requires U.S. companies to enhance their systems of internal control. However, many foreign companies do not have to meet strict internal control requirements. Some U.S. companies believe that this gives foreign firms an unfair advantage because developing and maintaining internal controls can be very expensive.

Adjusting entries are required every time a company prepares financial statements. The company analyzes each account in the trial balance to determine whether it is complete and up-to-date for financial statement purposes. **Every adjusting entry will include one income statement account and one balance sheet account.**

Types of Adjusting Entries

Adjusting entries are classified as either **deferrals** or **accruals**. As **Illustration 3.2** shows, each of these classes has two subcategories.

Deferrals:

1. **Prepaid expenses**: Expenses paid in cash before they are used or consumed.
2. **Unearned revenues**: Cash received before services are performed.

Accruals:

1. **Accrued revenues**: Revenues for services performed but not yet received in cash or recorded.
2. **Accrued expenses**: Expenses incurred but not yet paid in cash or recorded.

ILLUSTRATION 3.2
Categories of adjusting entries

Subsequent sections give examples of each type of adjustment. Each example is based on the October 31 trial balance of Pioneer Advertising from Chapter 2, reproduced in **Illustration 3.3**.

Pioneer Advertising
Trial Balance
October 31, 2020

	Debit	Credit
Cash	$15,200	
Supplies	2,500	
Prepaid Insurance	600	
Equipment	5,000	
Notes Payable		$ 5,000
Accounts Payable		2,500
Unearned Service Revenue		1,200
Owner's Capital		10,000
Owner's Drawings	500	
Service Revenue		10,000
Salaries and Wages Expense	4,000	
Rent Expense	900	
	$28,700	**$28,700**

ILLUSTRATION 3.3
Trial balance

We assume that Pioneer uses an accounting period of one month. Thus, monthly adjusting entries are made. The entries are dated October 31.

DO IT! 1 | Timing Concepts

Below is a list of timing concepts in the left column, with a description of the concept in the right column. There are more descriptions provided than concepts. Match the description to the concept.

1. ____Accrual-basis accounting.

2. ____Calendar year.

3. ____Time period assumption.

4. ____Expense recognition principle.

(a) Monthly and quarterly time periods.

(b) Efforts (expenses) should be recognized in the period in which a company uses assets or incurs liabilities to generate results (revenues).

(c) Accountants divide the economic life of a business into artificial time periods.

(d) Companies record revenues when they receive cash and record expenses when they pay out cash.

(e) An accounting time period that starts on January 1 and ends on December 31.

(f) Companies record transactions in the period in which the events occur.

ACTION PLAN

- **Review the definitions of the timing concepts in the Glossary Review section.**
- **Study carefully the revenue recognition principle, the expense recognition principle, and the time period assumption.**

Solution

1. f **2.** e **3.** c **4.** b

Related exercise material: **BE3.1, BE3.2, DO IT! 3.1, E3.1, E3.2, and E3.3.**

Adjusting Entries for Deferrals

LEARNING OBJECTIVE 2

Prepare adjusting entries for deferrals.

To defer means to postpone or delay. **Deferrals** are expenses or revenues that are recognized at a date later than the point when cash was originally exchanged. The two types of deferrals are prepaid expenses and unearned revenues.

Prepaid Expenses

When companies record payments of expenses that will benefit more than one accounting period, they record an asset called **prepaid expenses** or **prepayments**. When expenses are prepaid, an asset account is increased (debited) to show the service or benefit that the company will receive in the future. Examples of common prepayments are insurance, supplies, advertising, and rent. In addition, companies make prepayments when they purchase buildings and equipment.

Prepaid expenses are costs that expire either with the passage of time (e.g., rent and insurance) **or through use** (e.g., supplies). The expiration of these costs does not require daily entries, which would be impractical and unnecessary. Accordingly, companies postpone the recognition of such cost expirations until they prepare financial statements. At each statement date, they make adjusting entries to record the expenses applicable to the current accounting period and to show the remaining amounts in the asset accounts.

Prior to adjustment, assets are overstated and expenses are understated. Therefore, as shown in **Illustration 3.4**, **an adjusting entry for prepaid expenses results in an increase (a debit) to an expense account and a decrease (a credit) to an asset account**.

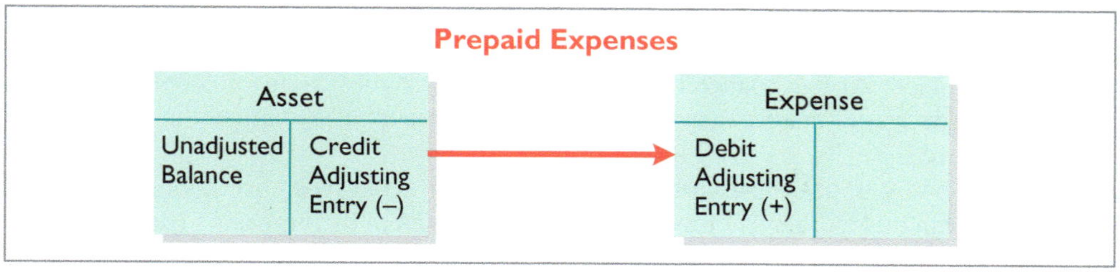

ILLUSTRATION 3.4
Adjusting entries for prepaid expenses

Let's look in more detail at some specific types of prepaid expenses, beginning with supplies.

Supplies

The purchase of supplies, such as paper and envelopes, results in an increase (a debit) to an asset account. During the accounting period, the company uses supplies. Rather than record supplies expense as the supplies are used, companies recognize supplies expense at the **end** of the accounting period. At the end of the accounting period, the company counts the remaining supplies. As shown in Illustration 3.5, the difference between the unadjusted balance in the Supplies (asset) account and the actual cost of supplies on hand represents the supplies used (an expense) for that period.

Recall from Chapter 2 that Pioneer Advertising purchased supplies costing $2,500 on October 5. Pioneer recorded the purchase by increasing (debiting) the asset Supplies. This account shows a balance of $2,500 in the October 31 trial balance. An inventory count at the close of business on October 31 reveals that $1,000 of supplies are still on hand. Thus, the cost of supplies used is $1,500 ($2,500 – $1,000). This use of supplies decreases an asset, Supplies. It also decreases owner's equity by increasing an expense account, Supplies Expense. This is shown in **Illustration 3.5**.

Supplies

Oct. 5

Supplies purchased; record asset

Oct. 31
Supplies used; record supplies expense

ILLUSTRATION 3.5 **Adjustment for supplies**

Basic Analysis

The expense Supplies Expense is increased $1,500; the asset Supplies is decreased $1,500.

Equation Analysis

	Assets	=	Liabilities	+	Owner's Equity
(1)	Supplies	=			Supplies Expense
	–$1,500				–$1,500

Debit–Credit Analysis

Debits increase expenses: debit Supplies Expense $1,500.
Credits decrease assets: credit Supplies $1,500.

Journal Entry

Oct. 31	Supplies Expense	631	1,500	
	Supplies	126		1,500
	(To record supplies used)			

Posting

Supplies			126
Oct. 5	2,500	Oct. 31	Adj. 1,500
Oct. 31	Bal. 1,000		

Supplies Expense			631
Oct. 31	Adj. 1,500		
Oct. 31	Bal. 1,500		

After adjustment, the asset account Supplies shows a balance of $1,000, which is equal to the cost of supplies on hand at the statement date. In addition, Supplies Expense shows a balance of $1,500, which equals the cost of supplies used in October. **If Pioneer does not make the adjusting entry, October expenses are understated and net income is overstated by $1,500. Moreover, both assets and owner's equity will be overstated by $1,500 on the October 31 balance sheet.**

Insurance

Oct. 4

Insurance purchased; record asset

Insurance Policy			
Oct $50	Nov $50	Dec $50	Jan $50
Feb $50	March $50	April $50	May $50
June $50	July $50	Aug $50	Sept $50
I YEAR $600			

Oct. 31
Insurance expired; record insurance expense

Insurance

Companies purchase insurance to protect themselves from losses due to fire, theft, and unforeseen events. Insurance must be paid in advance, often for multiple months. The cost of insurance (premiums) paid in advance is recorded as an increase (debit) in the asset account Prepaid Insurance. At the financial statement date, companies increase (debit) Insurance Expense and decrease (credit) Prepaid Insurance for the cost of insurance that has expired during the period.

On October 4, Pioneer Advertising paid $600 for a one-year fire insurance policy. Coverage began on October 1. Pioneer recorded the payment by increasing (debiting) Prepaid Insurance. This account shows a balance of $600 in the October 31 trial balance. Insurance of $50 ($600 ÷ 12) expires each month. The expiration of prepaid insurance decreases an asset, Prepaid Insurance. It also decreases owner's equity by increasing an expense account, Insurance Expense.

As shown in **Illustration 3.6**, the asset Prepaid Insurance shows a balance of $550, which represents the unexpired cost for the remaining 11 months of coverage. At the same time, the balance in Insurance Expense equals the insurance cost that expired in October. **If Pioneer does not make this adjustment, October expenses are understated by $50 and net income is overstated by $50. Moreover, both assets and owner's equity will be overstated by $50 on the October 31 balance sheet.**

ILLUSTRATION 3.6 **Adjustment for insurance**

Basic Analysis: The expense Insurance Expense is increased $50; the asset Prepaid Insurance is decreased $50.

Equation Analysis:

	Assets	=	Liabilities	+	Owner's Equity
(2)	Prepaid Insurance	=			Insurance Expense
	−$50				−$50

Debit–Credit Analysis: Debits increase expenses: debit Insurance Expense $50.
Credits decrease assets: credit Prepaid Insurance $50.

Journal Entry:

Oct. 31	Insurance Expense	722	50	
	Prepaid Insurance	130		50
	(To record insurance expired)			

Posting:

Prepaid Insurance			130
Oct. 4	600	Oct. 31	Adj. 50
Oct. 31	Bal. 550		

Insurance Expense			722
Oct. 31	Adj. 50		
Oct. 31	Bal. 50		

Depreciation

A company typically owns a variety of assets that have long lives, such as buildings, equipment, and motor vehicles. The period of service is referred to as the **useful life** of the asset. Because a building is expected to be of service for many years, it is recorded as an asset, rather than an expense, on the date it is acquired. As explained in Chapter 1, companies record such assets **at cost**, as required by the historical cost principle. To follow the expense recognition principle, companies allocate a portion of this cost as an expense during each period of the asset's useful life. **Depreciation** is the process of allocating the cost of an asset to expense over its useful life.

Need for Adjustment. The acquisition of long-lived assets is essentially a long-term prepayment for the use of an asset. An adjusting entry for depreciation is needed to recognize the cost that has been used (an expense) during the period and to report the unused cost (an asset) at the end of the period. One very important point to understand: **Depreciation is an allocation concept, not a valuation concept.** That is, depreciation **allocates an asset's cost to the periods in which it is used. Depreciation does not attempt to report the actual change in the value of the asset.**

For Pioneer Advertising, assume that depreciation on the equipment is $480 a year, or $40 per month. As shown in **Illustration 3.7**, rather than decrease (credit) the asset account directly, Pioneer instead credits Accumulated Depreciation—Equipment. Accumulated Depreciation is called a **contra asset account**. Such an account is offset against an asset account on the balance sheet (see **Helpful Hint**). Thus, the Accumulated Depreciation—Equipment account offsets the asset Equipment. **This account keeps track of the total amount of depreciation expense taken over the life of the asset.** To keep the accounting equation in balance, Pioneer decreases owner's equity by increasing an expense account, Depreciation Expense.

Depreciation

Oct. 1

Equipment purchased; record asset

Equipment			
Oct $40	Nov $40	Dec $40	Jan $40
Feb $40	March $40	April $40	May $40
June $40	July $40	Aug $40	Sept $40
Depreciation = $480/year			

Oct. 31

Depreciation recognized; record depreciation expense

HELPFUL HINT

All contra accounts have increases, decreases, and normal balances opposite to the account to which they relate.

ILLUSTRATION 3.7 **Adjustment for depreciation**

Basic Analysis

The expense Depreciation Expense is increased $40; the contra asset Accumulated Depreciation—Equipment is increased $40.

Equation Analysis

Assets	=	Liabilities	+	Owner's Equity
Accumulated Depreciation—Equipment	=			Depreciation Expense
−$40				−$40

Debit–Credit Analysis

Debits increase expenses: debit Depreciation Expense $40.
Credits increase contra assets: credit Accumulated Depreciation—Equipment $40.

Journal Entry

Oct. 31	Depreciation Expense	711	40	
	Accumulated Depreciation—Equipment	158		40
	(To record monthly depreciation)			

Posting

Equipment			157
Oct. 1	5,000		
Oct. 31	Bal. 5,000		

Accumulated Depreciation—Equipment			158
		Oct. 31	Adj. 40
		Oct. 31	Bal. 40

Depreciation Expense			711
Oct. 31	Adj. 40		
Oct. 31	Bal. 40		

The balance in the Accumulated Depreciation—Equipment account will increase $40 each month, and the balance in Equipment remains $5,000.

Statement Presentation. As indicated, Accumulated Depreciation—Equipment is a contra asset account. It is offset against Equipment on the balance sheet. The normal balance of a contra asset account is a credit. A theoretical alternative to using a contra asset account would be to decrease (credit) the asset account by the amount of depreciation each period. But using the contra account is preferable for a simple reason: It discloses **both** the original cost of the equipment **and** the total cost that has been expensed to date. Thus, in the balance sheet, Pioneer deducts Accumulated Depreciation—Equipment from the related asset account, as shown in **Illustration 3.8**.

ILLUSTRATION 3.8

Balance sheet presentation of accumulated depreciation

Equipment	$5,000
Less: Accumulated depreciation—equipment	40
	$4,960

ALTERNATIVE TERMINOLOGY

Book value is also referred to as *carrying value*.

Book value is the difference between the cost of any depreciable asset and its related accumulated depreciation (see **Alternative Terminology**). In Illustration 3.8, the book value of the equipment at the balance sheet date is $4,960. The book value and the fair value of the asset are generally two different values. As noted earlier, **the purpose of depreciation is not valuation but a means of cost allocation**.

Depreciation expense identifies the portion of an asset's cost that expired during the period (in this case, in October). The accounting equation shows that **without this adjusting entry, total assets, total owner's equity, and net income are overstated by $40 and depreciation expense is understated by $40**.

Illustration 3.9 summarizes the accounting for prepaid expenses.

ILLUSTRATION 3.9

Accounting for prepaid expenses

Accounting for Prepaid Expenses

Examples	Reason for Adjustment	Accounts Before Adjustment	Adjusting Entry
Insurance, supplies, advertising, rent, depreciation	Prepaid expenses originally recorded in asset accounts have been used.	Assets overstated. Expenses understated.	Dr. Expenses Cr. Assets or Contra Assets

Unearned Revenues

When companies receive cash before services are performed, they record a liability by increasing (crediting) a liability account called **unearned revenues**. In other words, a **company now has a performance obligation** (liability) to transfer a service to one of its customers. Items like rent, magazine subscriptions, and customer deposits for future service may result in unearned revenues. Airlines such as **United**, **Southwest**, and **Delta**, for instance, treat receipts from the sale of tickets as unearned revenue until the flight service is provided.

Unearned revenues are the opposite of prepaid expenses. Indeed, unearned revenue on the books of one company is likely to be a prepaid expense on the books of the company that has made the advance payment. For example, if identical accounting periods are assumed, a landlord will have unearned rent revenue when a tenant has prepaid rent.

When a company receives payment for services to be performed in a future accounting period, it increases (credits) an unearned revenue (a liability) account to recognize the liability that exists. The company subsequently recognizes revenues when it performs the service (see **Illustration 3.10**).

ILLUSTRATION 3.10

Adjusting entries for unearned revenues

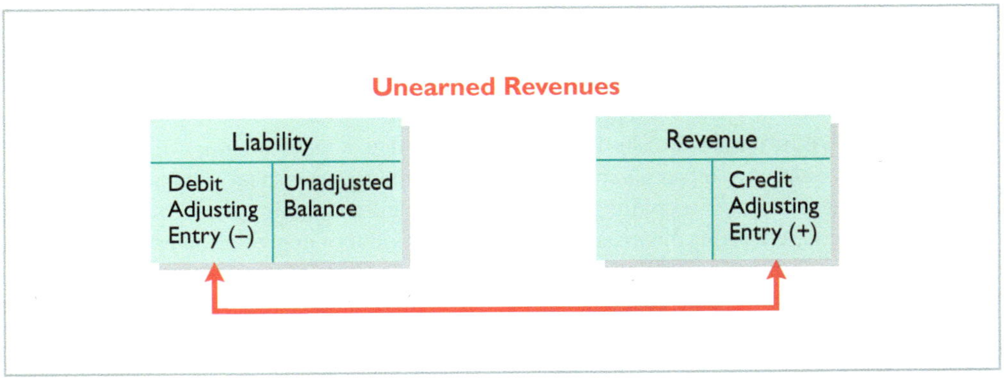

During the accounting period, it is not practical to make daily entries as the company performs services. Instead, the company delays recognition of revenue until the adjustment process. Then, the company makes an adjusting entry to record the revenue for services performed during the period and to show the liability that remains at the end of the accounting period. Typically, prior to adjustment, liabilities are overstated and revenues are understated. Therefore, **the adjusting entry for unearned revenues results in a decrease (a debit) to a liability account and an increase (a credit) to a revenue account**.

Pioneer Advertising received $1,200 on October 2 from R. Knox for advertising services expected to be completed by December 31. Pioneer credited the payment to Unearned Service Revenue. This liability account shows a balance of $1,200 in the October 31 trial balance. From an evaluation of the services Pioneer performed for Knox during October, the company determines that it should recognize $400 of revenue in October. The liability (Unearned Service Revenue) is therefore decreased, and owner's equity (Service Revenue) is increased.

As shown in **Illustration 3.11**, the liability Unearned Service Revenue now shows a balance of $800. That amount represents the remaining advertising services Pioneer is obligated to perform in the future. At the same time, Service Revenue shows total revenue recognized in October of $10,400. **Without this adjustment, revenues and net income are understated by $400 in the income statement. Moreover, liabilities will be overstated and owner's equity will be understated by $400 on the October 31 balance sheet.**

ILLUSTRATION 3.11 **Service revenue accounts after adjustment**

Basic Analysis

The liability Unearned Service Revenue is decreased $400; the revenue Service Revenue is increased $400.

Equation Analysis

Assets	=	Liabilities	+	Owner's Equity
		Unearned Service Revenue		Service Revenue
		−$400		+$400

Debit–Credit Analysis

Debits decrease liabilities: debit Unearned Service Revenue $400.
Credits increase revenues: credit Service Revenue $400.

Journal Entry

Oct. 31	Unearned Service Revenue	209	400	
	Service Revenue	400		400
	(To record revenue for services performed)			

Posting

Unearned Service Revenue 209			
Oct. 31	Adj. 400	Oct. 2	1,200
		Oct. 31	Bal. 800

Service Revenue 400			
		Oct. 31	10,000
		31	Adj. 400
		Oct. 31	Bal. 10,400

Illustration 3.12 summarizes the accounting for unearned revenues.

ILLUSTRATION 3.12 **Accounting for unearned revenues**

Accounting for Unearned Revenues

Examples	Reason for Adjustment	Accounts Before Adjustment	Adjusting Entry
Rent, magazine subscriptions, customer deposits for future service	Unearned revenues recorded in liability accounts are now recognized as revenue for services performed.	Liabilities overstated. Revenues understated.	Dr. Liabilities Cr. Revenues

Accounting Across the Organization Best Buy

© Skip ODonnell/iStockphoto

Turning Gift Cards into Revenue

Those of you who are marketing majors (and even most of you who are not) know that gift cards are among the hottest marketing tools in merchandising today. Customers purchase gift cards and give them to someone for later use. In a recent year, gift-card sales were expected to exceed $124 billion.

Although these programs are popular with marketing executives, they create accounting questions. Should revenue be recorded at the time the gift card is sold, or when it is exercised? How should expired gift cards be accounted for? In a recent balance sheet, **Best Buy** reported unearned revenue related to gift cards of $427 million.

Source: "2014 Gift Card Sales to Top $124 Billion, but Growth Slowing," *PR Newswire* (December 10, 2014).

Suppose that Robert Jones purchases a $100 gift card at Best Buy on December 24, 2019, and gives it to his wife, Mary Jones, on December 25, 2019. On January 3, 2020, Mary uses the card to purchase $100 worth of CDs. When do you think Best Buy should recognize revenue and why? (Go to WileyPLUS for this answer and additional questions.)

DO IT! 2 | Adjusting Entries for Deferrals

The ledger of Hammond Company, on March 31, 2020, includes these selected accounts before adjusting entries are prepared.

	Debit	Credit
Prepaid Insurance	$ 3,600	
Supplies	2,800	
Equipment	25,000	
Accumulated Depreciation—Equipment		$5,000
Unearned Service Revenue		9,200

An analysis of the accounts shows the following.

1. Insurance expires at the rate of $100 per month.
2. Supplies on hand total $800.
3. The equipment depreciates $200 a month.
4. During March, services were performed for $4,000 of the unearned service revenue reported.

Prepare the adjusting entries for the month of March.

ACTION PLAN

- **Make adjusting entries at the end of the period for revenues recognized and expenses incurred in the period.**
- **Don't forget to make adjusting entries for deferrals. Failure to adjust for deferrals leads to overstatement of the asset or liability and understatement of the related expense or revenue.**

Solution

1. Insurance Expense	100	
Prepaid Insurance		100
(To record insurance expired)		
2. Supplies Expense ($2,800 – $800)	2,000	
Supplies		2,000
(To record supplies used)		
3. Depreciation Expense	200	
Accumulated Depreciation—Equipment		200
(To record monthly depreciation)		
4. Unearned Service Revenue	4,000	
Service Revenue		4,000
(To record revenue for services performed)		

Related exercise material: **BE3.2, BE3.3, BE3.4, BE3.5, BE3.6, and DO IT! 3.2.**

Adjusting Entries for Accruals

LEARNING OBJECTIVE 3

Prepare adjusting entries for accruals.

The second category of adjusting entries is **accruals**. Prior to an accrual adjustment, the revenue account (and the related asset account) or the expense account (and the related liability account) are understated. Thus, the adjusting entry for accruals will **increase both a balance sheet and an income statement account**.

Accrued Revenues

Revenues for services performed but not yet recorded at the statement date are **accrued revenues**. Accrued revenues may accumulate (accrue) with the passing of time, as in the case of interest revenue. These are unrecorded because the earning of interest does not involve daily transactions. Companies do not record interest revenue on a daily basis because it is often impractical to do so. Accrued revenues also may result from services that have been performed but not yet billed nor collected, as in the case of commissions and fees. These may be unrecorded because only a portion of the total service has been performed and the clients will not be billed until the service has been completed.

An adjusting entry records the receivable that exists at the balance sheet date and the revenue for the services performed during the period. Prior to adjustment, both assets and revenues are understated. As shown in **Illustration 3.13**, **an adjusting entry for accrued revenues results in an increase (a debit) to an asset account and an increase (a credit) to a revenue account**.

ILLUSTRATION 3.13 **Adjusting entries for accrued revenues**

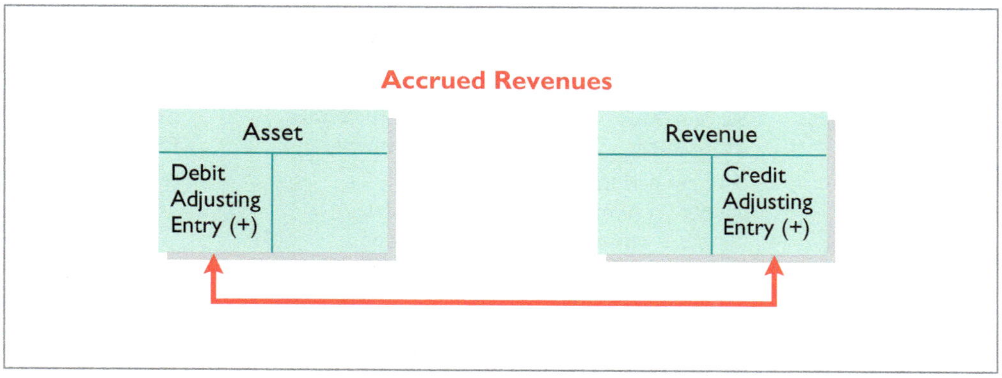

In October, Pioneer Advertising performed services worth $200 that were not billed to clients on or before October 31. Because these services were not billed, they were not recorded. The accrual of unrecorded service revenue increases an asset account, Accounts Receivable. It also increases owner's equity by increasing a revenue account, Service Revenue, as shown in **Illustration 3.14**.

ILLUSTRATION 3.14 Adjustment for accrued revenue

Basic Analysis

The asset Accounts Receivable is increased $200; the revenue Service Revenue is increased $200.

Equation Analysis

Assets	=	Liabilities	+	Owner's Equity
Accounts Receivable				Service Revenue
+$200				+$200

Debit–Credit Analysis

Debits increase assets: debit Accounts Receivable $200.
Credits increase revenues: credit Service Revenue $200.

Journal Entry

Oct. 31	Accounts Receivable	112	200	
	Service Revenue	400		200
	(To record revenue for services performed)			

Posting

Accounts Receivable		112
Oct. 31	Adj. 200	
Oct. 31	Bal. 200	

Service Revenue			400
	Oct. 31		10,000
	31		400
	31	Adj.	200
	Oct. 31	Bal.	10,600

Equation analyses summarize the effects of transactions on the three elements of the accounting equation, as well as the effect on cash flows.

A	=	L	+	OE
+200				
−200				

Cash Flows
+200

The asset Accounts Receivable shows that clients owe Pioneer $200 at the balance sheet date. The balance of $10,600 in Service Revenue represents the total revenue for services performed by Pioneer during the month ($10,000 + $400 + $200). **Without the adjusting entry, assets and owner's equity on the balance sheet and revenues and net income on the income statement are understated.**

On November 10, Pioneer receives cash of $200 for the services performed in October and makes the following entry.

Nov. 10	Cash	200	
	Accounts Receivable		200
	(To record cash collected on account)		

The company records the collection of the receivables by a debit (increase) to Cash and a credit (decrease) to Accounts Receivable.

Illustration 3.15 summarizes the accounting for accrued revenues.

ILLUSTRATION 3.15 Accounting for accrued revenues

Accounting for Accrued Revenues

Examples	Reason for Adjustment	Accounts Before Adjustment	Adjusting Entry
Interest, rent, services	Services performed but not yet received in cash or recorded.	Assets understated. Revenues understated.	Dr. Assets Cr. Revenues

ETHICS NOTE

A report released by Fannie Mae's board of directors stated that improper adjusting entries at the mortgage-finance company resulted in delayed recognition of expenses caused by interest rate changes. The motivation for such accounting apparently was the desire to hit earnings estimates.

Accrued Expenses

Expenses incurred but not yet paid or recorded at the statement date are called **accrued expenses**. Interest, taxes, and salaries are common examples of accrued expenses.

Companies make adjustments for accrued expenses to record the obligations that exist at the balance sheet date and to recognize the expenses that apply to the current accounting period (see **Ethics Note**). Prior to adjustment, both liabilities and expenses are understated. Therefore, as **Illustration 3.16** shows, **an adjusting entry for accrued expenses results in an increase (a debit) to an expense account and an increase (a credit) to a liability account**.

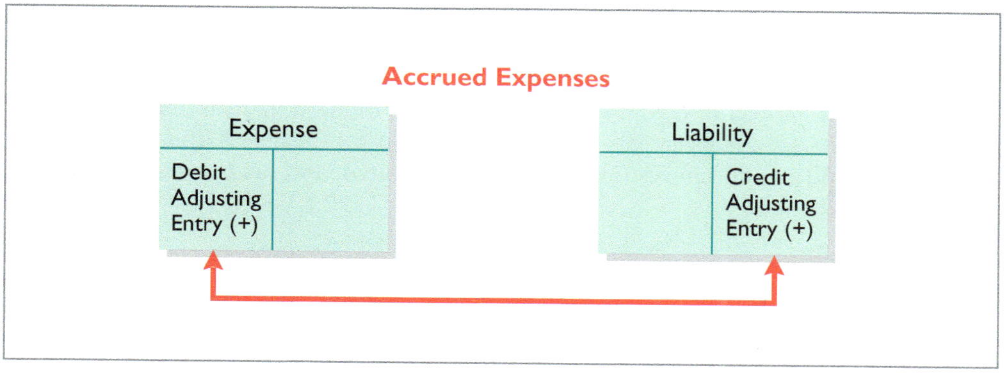

ILLUSTRATION 3.16
Adjusting entries for accrued expenses

Let's look in more detail at some specific types of accrued expenses, beginning with accrued interest.

Accrued Interest

Pioneer Advertising signed a three-month note payable in the amount of $5,000 on October 1. The note requires Pioneer to pay interest at an annual rate of 12%.

The amount of the interest recorded is determined by three factors: (1) the face value of the note; (2) the interest rate, which is always expressed as an annual rate; and (3) the length of time the note is outstanding. For Pioneer, the total interest due on the $5,000 note at its maturity date three months in the future is $150 ($5,000 × 12% × $\frac{3}{12}$), or $50 for one month. **Illustration 3.17** shows the formula for computing interest and its application to Pioneer for the month of October (see **Helpful Hint**).

> **HELPFUL HINT**
> **In computing interest, we express the time period as a fraction of a year.**

ILLUSTRATION 3.17
Formula for computing interest

Face Value of Note	×	Annual Interest Rate	×	Time in Terms of One Year	=	Interest
$5,000	×	12%	×	$\frac{1}{12}$	=	$50

As **Illustration 3.18** shows, the accrual of interest at October 31 increases a liability account, Interest Payable. It also decreases owner's equity by increasing an expense account, Interest Expense.

ILLUSTRATION 3.18 **Adjustment for accrued interest**

Basic Analysis
The expense Interest Expense is increased $50; the liability Interest Payable is increased $50.

Equation Analysis

Assets	=	Liabilities	+	Owner's Equity
		Interest Payable		Interest Expense
		+$50		−$50

Debit–Credit Analysis
Debits increase expenses: debit Interest Expense $50.
Credits increase liabilities: credit Interest Payable $50.

Journal Entry

Oct. 31	Interest Expense	905	50	
	Interest Payable	230		50
	(To record interest on notes payable)			

Posting

Interest Expense		905	
Oct. 31	Adj. 50		
Oct. 31	Bal. 50		

Interest Payable			230
		Oct. 31	Adj. 50
		Oct. 31	Bal. 50

Interest Expense shows the interest charges for the month of October. Interest Payable shows the amount of interest the company owes at the statement date. Pioneer will not pay the interest until the note comes due at the end of three months. Companies use the Interest Payable account, instead of crediting Notes Payable, to disclose the two different types of obligations—interest and principal—in the accounts and statements. **Without this adjusting entry, liabilities and interest expense are understated, and net income and owner's equity are overstated.**

Accrued Salaries and Wages

Companies pay for some types of expenses, such as employee salaries and wages, after the services have been performed. Pioneer Advertising paid salaries and wages on October 26 for its employees' first two weeks of work. The next payment of salaries will not occur until November 9. As **Illustration 3.19** shows, three working days remain in October (October 29–31).

ILLUSTRATION 3.19

Calendar showing Pioneer's pay periods

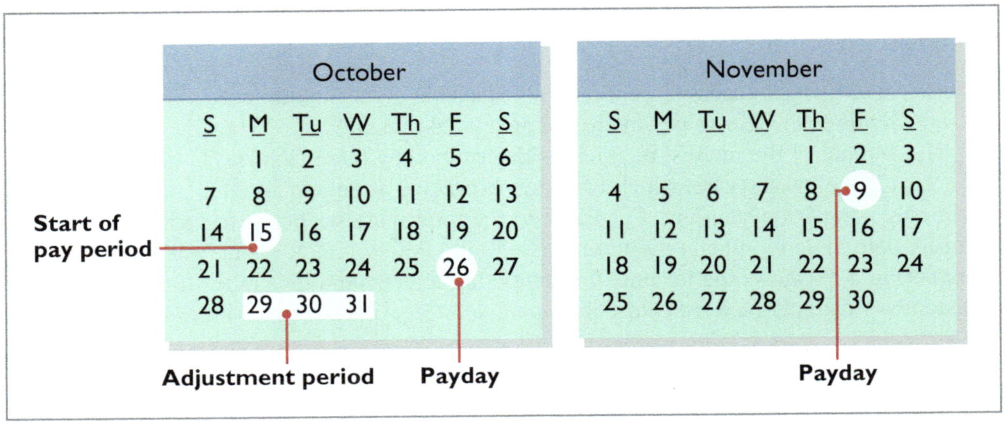

At October 31, the salaries and wages for these three days represent an accrued expense and a related liability to Pioneer. The employees receive total salaries and wages of $2,000 for a five-day work week, or $400 per day. Thus, accrued salaries and wages at October 31 are $1,200 ($400 × 3). This accrual increases a liability, Salaries and Wages Payable. It also decreases owner's equity by increasing an expense account, Salaries and Wages Expense, as shown in **Illustration 3.20**.

ILLUSTRATION 3.20 **Adjustment for accrued salaries and wages**

Basic Analysis

The expense Salaries and Wages Expense is increased $1,200; the liability Salaries and Wages Payable is increased $1,200.

Equation Analysis

Assets	=	Liabilities	+	Owner's Equity
		Salaries and Wages Payable		Salaries and Wages Expense
		+$1,200		−$1,200

Debit–Credit Analysis

Debits increase expenses: debit Salaries and Wages Expense $1,200.
Credits increase liabilities: credit Salaries and Wages Payable $1,200.

Journal Entry

Date	Account	Ref.	Debit	Credit
Oct. 31	Salaries and Wages Expense	726	1,200	
	Salaries and Wages Payable	212		1,200
	(To record accrued salaries and wages)			

Posting

Salaries and Wages Expense 726

Debit		Credit
Oct. 26	4,000	
31 Adj.	1,200	
Oct. 31 Bal.	5,200	

Salaries and Wages Payable 212

Debit	Credit	
	Oct. 31 Adj.	1,200
	Oct. 31 Bal.	1,200

After this adjustment, the balance in Salaries and Wages Expense of \$5,200 (13 days × \$400) is the actual salary and wages expense for October. The balance in Salaries and Wages Payable of \$1,200 is the amount of the liability for salaries and wages Pioneer owes as of October 31. **Without the \$1,200 adjustment for salaries and wages, Pioneer's expenses are understated \$1,200 and its liabilities are understated \$1,200.**

Pioneer pays salaries and wages every two weeks. Consequently, the next payday is November 9, when the company will again pay total salaries and wages of \$4,000. The payment consists of \$1,200 of salaries and wages payable at October 31 plus \$2,800 of salaries and wages expense for November (7 working days, as shown in the November calendar × \$400). Therefore, Pioneer makes the following entry on November 9.

Nov. 9	Salaries and Wages Payable	1,200	
	Salaries and Wages Expense	2,800	
	Cash		4,000
	(To record November 9 payroll)		

A	=	L	+	OE
		−1,200		
				−2,800
−4,000				

Cash Flows
−4,000

This entry eliminates the liability for Salaries and Wages Payable that Pioneer recorded in the October 31 adjusting entry, and it records the proper amount of Salaries and Wages Expense for the period between November 1 and November 9.

Illustration 3.21 summarizes the accounting for accrued expenses.

ILLUSTRATION 3.21
Accounting for accrued expenses

Accounting for Accrued Expenses

Examples	Reason for Adjustment	Accounts Before Adjustment	Adjusting Entry
Interest, rent, salaries	Expenses have been incurred but not yet paid in cash or recorded.	Expenses understated. Liabilities understated.	Dr. Expenses Cr. Liabilities

People, Planet, and Profit Insight

© Nathan Gleave/iStockphoto

Got Junk?

Do you have an old computer or two that you no longer use? How about an old TV that needs replacing? Many people do. Approximately 163,000 computers and televisions become obsolete each day. Yet, in a recent year, only 11% of computers were recycled. It is estimated that 75% of all computers ever sold are sitting in storage somewhere, waiting to be disposed of. Each of these old TVs and computers is loaded with lead, cadmium, mercury, and other toxic chemicals. If you have one of these electronic gadgets, you have a responsibility, and a probable cost, for disposing of it. Companies have the same problem, but their discarded materials may include lead paint, asbestos, and other toxic chemicals.

What accounting issue might this cause for companies? (Go to WileyPLUS for this answer and additional questions.)

Summary of Basic Relationships

Illustration 3.22 summarizes the four basic types of adjusting entries. Take some time to study and analyze the adjusting entries. Be sure to note that **each adjusting entry affects one balance sheet account and one income statement account**.

ILLUSTRATION 3.22
Summary of adjusting entries

Type of Adjustment	Accounts Before Adjustment	Adjusting Entry
Prepaid expenses	Assets overstated. Expenses understated.	Dr. Expenses Cr. Assets or Contra Assets
Unearned revenues	Liabilities overstated. Revenues understated.	Dr. Liabilities Cr. Revenues
Accrued revenues	Assets understated. Revenues understated.	Dr. Assets Cr. Revenues
Accrued expenses	Expenses understated. Liabilities understated.	Dr. Expenses Cr. Liabilities

Illustrations 3.23 and 3.24 show the journalizing and posting of adjusting entries for Pioneer Advertising on October 31. The ledger identifies all adjustments by the reference J2 because they have been recorded on page 2 of the general journal. The company may insert a center caption "Adjusting Entries" between the last transaction entry and the first adjusting entry in the journal. When you review the general ledger in Illustration 3.24, note that the entries highlighted in red are the adjustments.

ILLUSTRATION 3.23
General journal showing adjusting entries

GENERAL JOURNAL — J2

Date	Account Titles and Explanation	Ref.	Debit	Credit
2020	Adjusting Entries			
Oct. 31	Supplies Expense	631	1,500	
	Supplies	126		1,500
	(To record supplies used)			
31	Insurance Expense	722	50	
	Prepaid Insurance	130		50
	(To record insurance expired)			
31	Depreciation Expense	711	40	
	Accumulated Depreciation—Equipment	158		40
	(To record monthly depreciation)			
31	Unearned Service Revenue	209	400	
	Service Revenue	400		400
	(To record revenue for services performed)			
31	Accounts Receivable	112	200	
	Service Revenue	400		200
	(To record revenue for services performed)			
31	Interest Expense	905	50	
	Interest Payable	230		50
	(To record interest on notes payable)			
31	Salaries and Wages Expense	726	1,200	
	Salaries and Wages Payable	212		1,200
	(To record accrued salaries and wages)			

(1) Adjusting entries should not involve debits or credits to Cash.
(2) Evaluate whether the adjustment makes sense. For example, an adjustment to recognize supplies used should increase Supplies Expense.
(3) Double-check all computations.
(4) Each adjusting entry affects one balance sheet account and one income statement account.

ILLUSTRATION 3.24 General ledger after adjustment

GENERAL LEDGER

Cash — No. 101

Date	Explanation	Ref.	Debit	Credit	Balance
2020					
Oct. 1		J1	10,000		10,000
2		J1	1,200		11,200
3		J1		900	10,300
4		J1		600	9,700
20		J1		500	9,200
26		J1		4,000	5,200
31		J1	10,000		15,200

Accounts Receivable — No. 112

Date	Explanation	Ref.	Debit	Credit	Balance
2020					
Oct. 31	**Adj. entry**	**J2**	**200**		**200**

Supplies — No. 126

Date	Explanation	Ref.	Debit	Credit	Balance
2020					
Oct. 5		J1	2,500		2,500
31	**Adj. entry**	**J2**		**1,500**	**1,000**

Prepaid Insurance — No. 130

Date	Explanation	Ref.	Debit	Credit	Balance
2020					
Oct. 4		J1	600		600
31	**Adj. entry**	**J2**		**50**	**550**

Equipment — No. 157

Date	Explanation	Ref.	Debit	Credit	Balance
2020					
Oct. 1		J1	5,000		5,000

Accumulated Depreciation—Equipment — No. 158

Date	Explanation	Ref.	Debit	Credit	Balance
2020					
Oct. 31	**Adj. entry**	**J2**		**40**	**40**

Notes Payable — No. 200

Date	Explanation	Ref.	Debit	Credit	Balance
2020					
Oct. 1		J1		5,000	5,000

Accounts Payable — No. 201

Date	Explanation	Ref.	Debit	Credit	Balance
2020					
Oct. 5		J1		2,500	2,500

Unearned Service Revenue — No. 209

Date	Explanation	Ref.	Debit	Credit	Balance
2020					
Oct. 2		J1		1,200	1,200
31	**Adj. entry**	**J2**	**400**		**800**

Salaries and Wages Payable — No. 212

Date	Explanation	Ref.	Debit	Credit	Balance
2020					
Oct. 31	**Adj. entry**	**J2**		**1,200**	**1,200**

Interest Payable — No. 230

Date	Explanation	Ref.	Debit	Credit	Balance
2020					
Oct. 31	**Adj. entry**	**J2**		**50**	**50**

Owner's Capital — No. 301

Date	Explanation	Ref.	Debit	Credit	Balance
2020					
Oct. 1		J1		10,000	10,000

Owner's Drawings — No. 306

Date	Explanation	Ref.	Debit	Credit	Balance
2020					
Oct. 20		J1	500		500

Service Revenue — No. 400

Date	Explanation	Ref.	Debit	Credit	Balance
2020					
Oct. 31		J1		10,000	10,000
31	**Adj. entry**	**J2**		**400**	**10,400**
31	**Adj. entry**	**J2**		**200**	**10,600**

Supplies Expense — No. 631

Date	Explanation	Ref.	Debit	Credit	Balance
2020					
Oct. 31	**Adj. entry**	**J2**	**1,500**		**1,500**

Depreciation Expense — No. 711

Date	Explanation	Ref.	Debit	Credit	Balance
2020					
Oct. 31	**Adj. entry**	**J2**	**40**		**40**

Insurance Expense — No. 722

Date	Explanation	Ref.	Debit	Credit	Balance
2020					
Oct. 31	**Adj. entry**	**J2**	**50**		**50**

Salaries and Wages Expense — No. 726

Date	Explanation	Ref.	Debit	Credit	Balance
2020					
Oct. 26		J1	4,000		4,000
31	**Adj. entry**	**J2**	**1,200**		**5,200**

Rent Expense — No. 729

Date	Explanation	Ref.	Debit	Credit	Balance
2020					
Oct. 3		J1	900		900

Interest Expense — No. 905

Date	Explanation	Ref.	Debit	Credit	Balance
2020					
Oct. 31	**Adj. entry**	**J2**	**50**		**50**

DO IT! 3 | Adjusting Entries for Accruals

Micro Computer Services began operations on August 1, 2020. At the end of August 2020, management prepares monthly financial statements. The following information relates to August.

1. At August 31, the company owed its employees $800 in salaries and wages that will be paid on September 1.
2. On August 1, the company borrowed $30,000 from a local bank on a 15-year mortgage. The annual interest rate is 10%.
3. Revenue for services performed but unrecorded for August totaled $1,100.

Prepare the adjusting entries needed at August 31, 2020.

ACTION PLAN

- **Make adjusting entries at the end of the period to recognize revenues for services performed and for expenses incurred.**
- **Don't forget to make adjusting entries for accruals. Adjusting entries for accruals will increase both a balance sheet and an income statement account.**

Solution

1. Salaries and Wages Expense	800	
Salaries and Wages Payable		800
(To record accrued salaries)		
2. Interest Expense	250	
Interest Payable		250
(To record accrued interest: $\$30{,}000 \times 10\% \times \frac{1}{12} = \$250$)		
3. Accounts Receivable	1,100	
Service Revenue		1,100
(To record revenue for services performed)		

Related exercise material: **BE3.7, DO IT! 3.3, E3.5, E3.6, E3.7, E3.8 and E3.9.**

Adjusted Trial Balance and Financial Statements

LEARNING OBJECTIVE 4

Describe the nature and purpose of an adjusted trial balance.

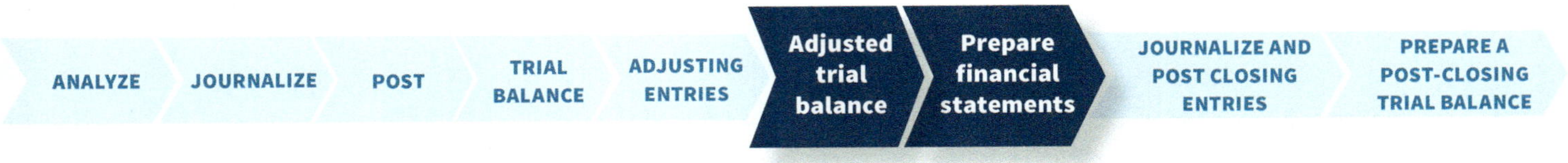

After a company has journalized and posted all adjusting entries, it prepares another trial balance from the ledger accounts. This trial balance is called an **adjusted trial balance**. It shows the balances of all accounts, including those adjusted, at the end of the accounting period. The purpose of an adjusted trial balance is to **prove the equality** of the total debit balances and the total credit balances in the ledger after all adjustments. Because the accounts contain all data needed for financial statements, the adjusted trial balance is the **primary basis for the preparation of financial statements**.

Preparing the Adjusted Trial Balance

Illustration 3.25 presents the adjusted trial balance for Pioneer Advertising prepared from the ledger accounts in Illustration 3.24. The amounts affected by the adjusting entries are highlighted in red. Compare these amounts to those in the unadjusted trial balance in Illustration 3.3. In this comparison, you will see that there are more accounts in the adjusted trial balance as a result of the adjusting entries made at the end of the month.

ILLUSTRATION 3.25
Adjusted trial balance

Pioneer Advertising
Adjusted Trial Balance
October 31, 2020

	Debit	Credit
Cash	$15,200	
Accounts Receivable	**200**	
Supplies	**1,000**	
Prepaid Insurance	**550**	
Equipment	5,000	
Accumulated Depreciation—Equipment		**$ 40**
Notes Payable		5,000
Accounts Payable		2,500
Interest Payable		**50**
Unearned Service Revenue		**800**
Salaries and Wages Payable		**1,200**
Owner's Capital		10,000
Owner's Drawings	500	
Service Revenue		**10,600**
Salaries and Wages Expense	**5,200**	
Supplies Expense	**1,500**	
Rent Expense	900	
Insurance Expense	**50**	
Interest Expense	**50**	
Depreciation Expense	**40**	
	$30,190	**$30,190**

Preparing Financial Statements

Companies can prepare financial statements directly from the adjusted trial balance. **Illustrations 3.26** and **3.27** present the interrelationships of data in the adjusted trial balance and the financial statements.

As Illustration 3.26 shows, companies prepare the income statement from the revenue and expense accounts. Next, they use the owner's capital and drawings accounts and the net income (or net loss) from the income statement to prepare the owner's equity statement.

ILLUSTRATION 3.26 **Preparation of the income statement and owner's equity statement from the adjusted trial balance**

Pioneer Advertising
Adjusted Trial Balance
October 31, 2020

Account	Debit	Credit
Cash	$15,200	
Accounts Receivable	200	
Supplies	1,000	
Prepaid Insurance	550	
Equipment	5,000	
Accumulated Depreciation—Equipment		$ 40
Notes Payable		5,000
Accounts Payable		2,500
Unearned Service Revenue		800
Salaries and Wages Payable		1,200
Interest Payable		50
Owner's Capital		10,000
Owner's Drawings	500	
Service Revenue		10,600
Salaries and Wages Expense	5,200	
Supplies Expense	1,500	
Rent Expense	900	
Insurance Expense	50	
Interest Expense	50	
Depreciation Expense	40	
	$30,190	$30,190

Pioneer Advertising
Income Statement
For the Month Ended October 31, 2020

Revenues		
Service revenue		$10,600
Expenses		
Salaries and wages expense	$5,200	
Supplies expense	1,500	
Rent expense	900	
Insurance expense	50	
Interest expense	50	
Depreciation expense	40	
Total expenses		7,740
Net income		$ 2,860

Pioneer Advertising
Owner's Equity Statement
For the Month Ended October 31, 2020

Owner's capital, October 1	$ -0-
Add: Investments	10,000
	10,000
Net income	2,860
	12,860
Owner's drawings	500
Owner's capital, October 31	$12,360

To balance sheet

As Illustration 3.27 shows, companies then prepare the balance sheet from the asset and liability accounts and the ending owner's capital balance as reported in the owner's equity statement.

ILLUSTRATION 3.27 Preparation of the balance sheet from the adjusted trial balance

Pioneer Advertising
Adjusted Trial Balance
October 31, 2020

Account	Debit	Credit
Cash	$15,200	
Accounts Receivable	200	
Supplies	1,000	
Prepaid Insurance	550	
Equipment	5,000	
Accumulated Depreciation—Equipment		$ 40
Notes Payable		5,000
Accounts Payable		2,500
Unearned Service Revenue		800
Salaries and Wages Payable		1,200
Interest Payable		50
Owner's Capital		10,000
Owner's Drawings	500	
Service Revenue		10,600
Salaries and Wages Expense	5,200	
Supplies Expense	1,500	
Rent Expense	900	
Insurance Expense	50	
Interest Expense	50	
Depreciation Expense	40	
	$30,190	$30,190

Pioneer Advertising
Balance Sheet
October 31, 2020

Assets

Cash		$15,200
Accounts receivable		200
Supplies		1,000
Prepaid insurance		550
Equipment	$5,000	
Less: Accumulated depreciation—equip.	40	4,960
Total assets		$21,910

Liabilities and Owner's Equity

Liabilities	
Notes payable	$ 5,000
Accounts payable	2,500
Unearned service revenue	800
Salaries and wages payable	1,200
Interest payable	50
Total liabilities	9,550
Owner's equity	
Owner's capital	12,360
Total liabilities and owner's equity	$21,910

Capital balance at Oct. 31 from owner's equity statement in Illustration 3.26

DO IT! 4 | Trial Balance

Skolnick Co. was organized on April 1, 2020. The company prepares quarterly financial statements. The adjusted trial balance amounts at June 30 are shown below.

	Debit		Credit
Cash	$ 6,700	Accumulated Depreciation—Equipment	$ 850
Accounts Receivable	600	Notes Payable	5,000
Prepaid Rent	900	Accounts Payable	1,510
Supplies	1,000	Salaries and Wages Payable	400
Equipment	15,000	Interest Payable	50
Owner's Drawings	600	Unearned Rent Revenue	500
Salaries and Wages Expense	9,400	Owner's Capital	14,000
Rent Expense	1,500	Service Revenue	14,200
Depreciation Expense	850	Rent Revenue	800
Supplies Expense	200		
Utilities Expense	510		
Interest Expense	50		
	$37,310		$37,310

a. Determine the net income for the quarter April 1 to June 30.

b. Determine the total assets and total liabilities at June 30, 2020, for Skolnick Co.

c. Determine the amount of owner's capital at June 30, 2020.

ACTION PLAN

- **In an adjusted trial balance, all asset, liability, revenue, and expense accounts are properly stated.**
- **To determine the ending balance in Owner's Capital, add net income and subtract dividends.**

Solution

a. The net income is determined by adding revenues and subtracting expenses. The net income is computed as follows.

Revenues		
Service revenue	$14,200	
Rent revenue	800	
Total revenues		$15,000
Expenses		
Salaries and wages expense	9,400	
Rent expense	1,500	
Depreciation expense	850	
Utilities expense	510	
Supplies expense	200	
Interest expense	50	
Total expenses		12,510
Net income		$ 2,490

b. Total assets and liabilities are computed as follows.

Assets			Liabilities	
Cash		$ 6,700	Notes payable	$5,000
Accounts receivable		600	Accounts payable	1,510
Supplies		1,000	Unearned rent revenue	500
Prepaid rent		900		
Equipment	$15,000		Salaries and wages payable	400
Less: Accumulated depreciation—equipment	850	14,150	Interest payable	50
Total assets		$23,350	Total liabilities	$7,460

c.

Owner's capital, April 1	$ 0
Add: Investments	14,000
Net income	2,490
Less: Owner's drawings	600
Owner's capital, June 30	$15,890

Related exercise material: **BE3.9, BE3.10, DO IT! 3.4, and E3.11.**

Appendix 3A Alternative Treatment of Deferrals

LEARNING OBJECTIVE *5

Prepare adjusting entries for the alternative treatment of deferrals.

In discussing adjusting entries for prepaid expenses and unearned revenues, we illustrated transactions for which companies made the initial entries to balance sheet accounts. In the case of prepaid expenses, the company debited the prepayment to an asset account. In the case of unearned revenue, the company credited a liability account to record the cash received.

Some companies use an alternative treatment. (1) When a company prepays an expense, it debits that amount to an expense account. (2) When it receives payment for future services, it credits the amount to a revenue account. In this appendix, we describe the circumstances that justify such entries and the different adjusting entries that may be required. This alternative treatment of prepaid expenses and unearned revenues has the same effect on the financial statements as the procedures described in the chapter.

Prepaid Expenses

Prepaid expenses become expired costs either through the passage of time (e.g., insurance) or through consumption (e.g., advertising supplies). If at the time of purchase the company expects to consume the supplies before the next financial statement date, **it may choose to debit (increase) an expense account rather than an asset account. This alternative treatment is simply more convenient.**

Assume that Pioneer Advertising expects that it will use before the end of the month all of the supplies purchased on October 5. A debit of $2,500 to Supplies Expense (rather than to the asset account Supplies) on October 5 will eliminate the need for an adjusting entry on October 31. At October 31, the Supplies Expense account will show a balance of $2,500, which is the cost of supplies used between October 5 and October 31.

But what if the company does not use all the supplies? For example, what if an inventory of $1,000 of advertising supplies remains on October 31? Obviously, the company would need to make an adjusting entry. Prior to adjustment, the expense account Supplies Expense is overstated $1,000, and the asset account Supplies is understated $1,000. Thus, Pioneer makes the following adjusting entry.

Oct. 31	Supplies	1,000	
	Supplies Expense		1,000
	(To record supplies inventory)		

A	=	L	+	OE
+1,000				+1,000 Exp

Cash Flows
no effect

Illustration 3A.1 shows the accounts after the company posts the adjusting entry.

Supplies

10/31	**Adj.**	**1,000**	

Supplies Expense

10/5		2,500	10/31	**Adj.**	**1,000**
10/31	**Bal.**	**1,500**			

ILLUSTRATION 3A.1
Prepaid expenses accounts after adjustment

After adjustment, the asset account Supplies shows a balance of $1,000, which is equal to the cost of supplies on hand at October 31. In addition, Supplies Expense shows a balance of $1,500. This is equal to the cost of supplies used between October 5 and October 31. Without the adjusting entry, expenses are overstated and net income is understated by $1,000 in the October income statement. Also, both assets and owner's equity are understated by $1,000 on the October 31 balance sheet.

Illustration 3A.2 compares the entries and accounts for advertising supplies in the two adjustment approaches.

Prepayment Initially Debited to Asset Account (per chapter)				**Prepayment Initially Debited to Expense Account (per appendix)**			
Oct. 5	Supplies	2,500		Oct. 5	Supplies Expense	2,500	
	Accounts Payable		2,500		Accounts Payable		2,500
Oct. 31	Supplies Expense	1,500		Oct. 31	Supplies	1,000	
	Supplies		1,500		Supplies Expense		1,000

ILLUSTRATION 3A.2
Adjustment approaches—a comparison

After Pioneer posts the entries, the accounts appear as shown in **Illustration 3A.3**.

ILLUSTRATION 3A.3

Comparison of accounts

(per chapter)

Supplies

10/5		2,500	10/31	**Adj.**	**1,500**
10/31	**Bal.**	**1,000**			

Supplies Expense

10/31	**Adj.**	**1,500**			

(per appendix)

Supplies

10/31	**Adj.**	**1,000**			

Supplies Expense

10/5		2,500	10/31	**Adj.**	**1,000**
10/31	**Bal.**	**1,500**			

Note that the account balances under each alternative are the same at October 31: Supplies $1,000 and Supplies Expense $1,500.

Unearned Revenues

Unearned revenues are recognized as revenue at the time services are performed. Similar to the case for prepaid expenses, companies may credit (increase) a revenue account when they receive cash for future services.

To illustrate, assume that Pioneer Advertising received $1,200 for future services on October 2. Pioneer expects to perform the services before October 31.[1] In such a case, the company credits Service Revenue. If Pioneer in fact performs the service before October 31, no adjustment is needed.

HELPFUL HINT

The required adjusted balances here are Service Revenue $400 and Unearned Service Revenue $800.

However, if at the statement date Pioneer has not performed $800 of the services, it would make an adjusting entry (see **Helpful Hint**). Without the entry, the revenue account Service Revenue is overstated $800, and the liability account Unearned Service Revenue is understated $800. Thus, Pioneer makes the following adjusting entry.

A	=	L	+	OE
				−800 Rev
		+800		

Cash Flows
no effect

Oct. 31	Service Revenue	800	
	Unearned Service Revenue		800
	(To record unearned service revenue)		

Illustration 3A.4 shows the accounts after Pioneer posts the adjusting entry.

ILLUSTRATION 3A.4

Unearned service revenue accounts after adjustment

Unearned Service Revenue

			10/31	**Adj.**	**800**

Service Revenue

10/31	**Adj.**	**800**	10/2		1,200
			10/31	**Bal.**	**400**

The liability account Unearned Service Revenue shows a balance of $800. This equals the services that will be performed in the future. In addition, the balance in Service Revenue equals the services performed in October. Without the adjusting entry, both revenues and net income are overstated by $800 in the October income statement. Also, liabilities are understated by $800 and owner's equity is overstated by $800 on the October 31 balance sheet.

[1]This example focuses only on the alternative treatment of unearned revenues. For simplicity, we have ignored the entries to Service Revenue pertaining to the immediate recognition of revenue ($10,000) and the adjusting entry for accrued revenue ($200).

Illustration 3A.5 compares the entries and accounts for initially recording unearned service revenue in (1) a liability account or (2) a revenue account.

ILLUSTRATION 3A.5

Adjustment approaches—a comparison

Unearned Service Revenue Initially Credited to Liability Account (per chapter)				Unearned Service Revenue Initially Credited to Revenue Account (per appendix)			
Oct. 2	Cash	1,200		Oct. 2	Cash	1,200	
	Unearned Service Revenue		1,200		Service Revenue		1,200
Oct. 31	Unearned Service Revenue	400		Oct. 31	Service Revenue	800	
	Service Revenue		400		Unearned Service Revenue		800

After Pioneer posts the entries, the accounts appear as shown in **Illustration 3A.6**.

ILLUSTRATION 3A.6

Comparison of accounts

(per chapter) Unearned Service Revenue

10/31 **Adj.**	**400**	10/2	1,200
		10/31 **Bal.**	**800**

Service Revenue

		10/31 **Adj.**	**400**

(per appendix) Unearned Service Revenue

		10/31 **Adj.**	**800**

Service Revenue

10/31 **Adj.**	**800**	10/2	1,200
		10/31 **Bal.**	**400**

Note that the balances in the accounts are the same under the two alternatives: Unearned Service Revenue $800 and Service Revenue $400.

Summary of Additional Adjustment Relationships

Illustration 3A.7 provides a summary of basic relationships for deferrals.

ILLUSTRATION 3A.7 **Summary of basic relationships for deferrals**

Type of Adjustment	Reason for Adjustment	Account Balances before Adjustment	Adjusting Entry
1. Prepaid expenses	(a) Prepaid expenses initially recorded in asset accounts have been used.	Assets overstated. Expenses understated.	Dr. Expenses Cr. Assets
	(b) **Prepaid expenses initially recorded in expense accounts have not been used.**	**Assets understated. Expenses overstated.**	**Dr. Assets Cr. Expenses**
2. Unearned revenues	(a) Unearned revenues initially recorded in liability accounts are now recognized as revenue.	Liabilities overstated. Revenues understated.	Dr. Liabilities Cr. Revenues
	(b) **Unearned revenues initially recorded in revenue accounts are still unearned.**	**Liabilities understated. Revenues overstated.**	**Dr. Revenues Cr. Liabilities**

Alternative adjusting entries **do not apply** to accrued revenues and accrued expenses because **no entries occur before companies make these types of adjusting entries**.

Appendix 3B Financial Reporting Concepts

LEARNING OBJECTIVE *6

Discuss financial reporting concepts.

This appendix provides a summary of the concepts in action used in this textbook. In addition, it provides other useful concepts which accountants use as a basis for recording and reporting financial information.

Qualities of Useful Information

Recently, the FASB completed the first phase of a project in which it developed a conceptual framework to serve as the basis for future accounting standards. The framework begins by stating that the primary objective of financial reporting is to provide financial information that is **useful** to investors and creditors for making decisions about providing capital. Useful information should possess two fundamental qualities, relevance and faithful representation, as shown in **Illustration 3B.1**.

ILLUSTRATION 3B.1
Fundamental qualities of useful information

Relevance Accounting information has **relevance** if it would make a difference in a business decision. Information is considered relevant if it provides information that has **predictive value**, that is, helps provide accurate expectations about the future, and has **confirmatory value**, that is, confirms or corrects prior expectations. **Materiality** is a company-specific aspect of relevance. An item is material when its **size** makes it likely to influence the decision of an investor or creditor.

Faithful Representation **Faithful representation** means that information accurately depicts what really happened. To provide a faithful representation, information must be **complete** (nothing important has been omitted), **neutral** (is not biased toward one position or another), and **free from error**.

Enhancing Qualities

In addition to the two fundamental qualities, the FASB also describes a number of enhancing qualities of useful information. These include **comparability**, **verifiability**, **timeliness**, and **understandability**. In accounting, **comparability** results when different companies use the same accounting principles. Another type of comparability is consistency. **Consistency** means that a company uses the same accounting principles and methods from year to year. Information is **verifiable** if independent observers, using the same methods, obtain similar results. For accounting information to have relevance, it must be **timely**. That is, it must be available to decision-makers before it loses its capacity to influence decisions. For example, public companies like **Google** or **Best Buy** provide their annual reports to investors within 60 days of their year-end. Information has the quality of **understandability** if it is presented in a clear and concise fashion, so that reasonably informed users of that information can interpret it and comprehend its meaning.

Assumptions in Financial Reporting

To develop accounting standards, the FASB relies on some key assumptions, as shown in **Illustration 3B.2**. These include assumptions about the monetary unit, economic entity, time period, and going concern.

ILLUSTRATION 3B.2

Key assumptions in financial reporting

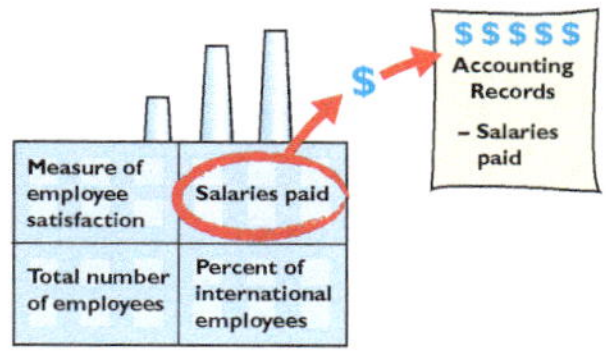

Monetary Unit Assumption The **monetary unit assumption** requires that only those things that can be expressed in money are included in the accounting records. This means that certain important information needed by investors, creditors, and managers, such as customer satisfaction, is not reported in the financial statements. This assumption relies on the monetary unit remaining relatively stable in value.

Economic Entity Assumption The **economic entity assumption** states that every economic entity can be separately identified and accounted for. In order to assess a company's performance and financial position accurately, it is important to not blur company transactions with personal transactions (especially those of its managers) or transactions of other companies.

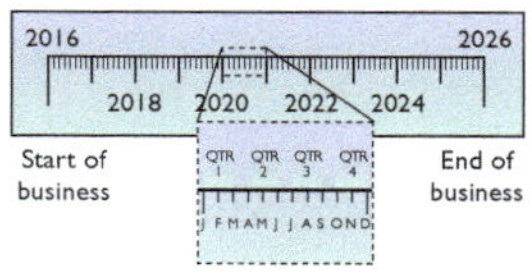

Time Period Assumption Notice that the income statement, retained earnings statement, and statement of cash flows all cover periods of one year, and the balance sheet is prepared at the end of each year. The **time period assumption** states that the life of a business can be divided into artificial time periods and that useful reports covering those periods can be prepared for the business.

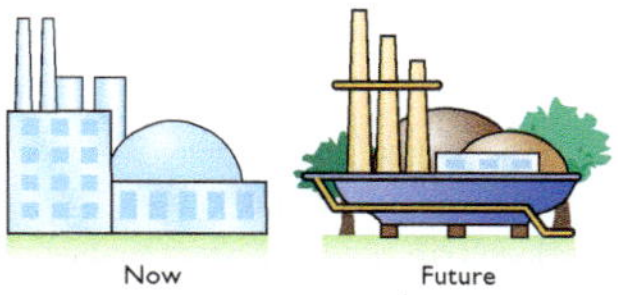

Going Concern Assumption The **going concern assumption** states that the business will remain in operation for the foreseeable future. Of course, many businesses do fail, but in general it is reasonable to assume that the business will continue operating.

Principles in Financial Reporting

Measurement Principles

GAAP generally uses one of two measurement principles, the historical cost principle or the fair value principle. Selection of which principle to follow generally relates to trade-offs between relevance and faithful representation.

Historical Cost Principle. The **historical cost principle** (or cost principle, discussed in Chapter 1) dictates that companies record assets at their cost. This is true not only at the time the asset is purchased but also over the time the asset is held. For example, if land that was purchased for $30,000 increases in value to $40,000, it continues to be reported at $30,000.

Fair Value Principle. The **fair value principle** (discussed in Chapter 1) indicates that assets and liabilities should be reported at fair value (the price received to sell an asset or settle a liability). Fair value information may be more useful than historical cost for certain types of assets and liabilities. For example, certain investment securities are reported at fair value because market price information is often readily available for these types of assets. In choosing between cost and fair value, two qualities that make accounting information useful for decision-making are used—relevance and faithful representation. In determining which measurement principle to use, the factual nature of cost figures are weighed versus the relevance of fair value. In general, most assets follow the historical cost principle because fair values may not be representationally faithful. Only in situations where assets are actively traded, such as investment securities, is the fair value principle applied.

Revenue Recognition Principle

The **revenue recognition principle** requires that companies recognize revenue in the accounting period in which the performance obligation is satisfied. As discussed earlier in the chapter, in a service company, revenue is recognized at the time the service is performed. In a merchandising company, the performance obligation is generally satisfied when the goods transfer from the seller to the buyer (discussed in Chapter 5). At this point, the sales transaction is complete and the sales price established.

Expense Recognition Principle

The **expense recognition principle** (discussed earlier in the chapter) dictates that companies recognize expense in the period in which they make efforts to generate revenue. Thus, expenses follow revenues.

Full Disclosure Principle

The **full disclosure principle** (discussed in Chapter 11) requires that companies disclose all circumstances and events that would make a difference to financial statement users. If an important item cannot reasonably be reported directly in one of the four types of financial statements, then it should be discussed in notes that accompany the statements.

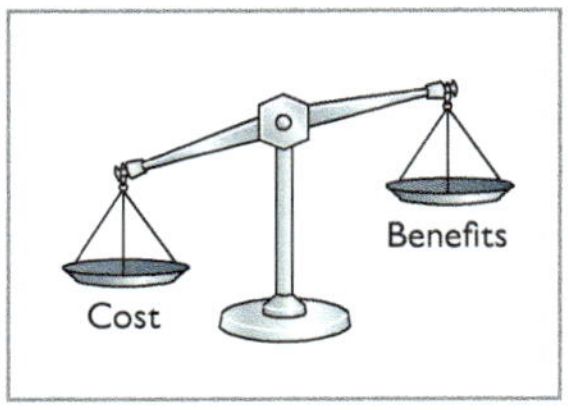

Cost Constraint

Providing information is costly. In deciding whether companies should be required to provide a certain type of information, accounting standard-setters consider the **cost constraint**. It weighs the cost that companies will incur to provide the information against the benefit that financial statement users will gain from having the information available.

Review and Practice

Learning Objectives Review

1 Explain the accrual basis of accounting and the reasons for adjusting entries.

The time period assumption assumes that the economic life of a business is divided into artificial time periods. Accrual-basis accounting means that companies record events that change a company's financial statements in the periods in which those events occur, rather than in the periods in which the company receives or pays cash.

Companies make adjusting entries at the end of an accounting period. Such entries ensure that companies recognize revenues in the period in which the performance obligation is satisfied and recognize expenses in the period in which they are incurred. The major types of adjusting entries are deferrals (prepaid expenses and unearned revenues) and accruals (accrued revenues and accrued expenses).

2 Prepare adjusting entries for deferrals.

Deferrals are either prepaid expenses or unearned revenues. Companies make adjusting entries for deferrals to record the portion of the prepayment that represents the expense incurred or the revenue for services performed in the current accounting period.

3 Prepare adjusting entries for accruals.

Accruals are either accrued revenues or accrued expenses. Companies make adjusting entries for accruals to record revenues for services performed and expenses incurred in the current accounting period that have not been recognized through daily entries.

4 Describe the nature and purpose of an adjusted trial balance.

An adjusted trial balance shows the balances of all accounts, including those that have been adjusted, at the end of an accounting period. Its purpose is to prove the equality of the total debit balances and total credit balances in the ledger after all adjustments.

*5 Prepare adjusting entries for the alternative treatment of deferrals.

Companies may initially debit prepayments to an expense account. Likewise, they may credit unearned revenues to a revenue account. At the end of the period, these accounts may be overstated. The adjusting entries for prepaid expenses are a debit to an asset account and a credit to an expense account. Adjusting entries for unearned revenues are a debit to a revenue account and a credit to a liability account.

*6 Discuss financial reporting concepts.

To be judged useful, information should have the primary characteristics of relevance and faithful representation. In addition, it should be comparable, consistent, verifiable, timely, and understandable.

The **monetary unit assumption** requires that companies include in the accounting records only transaction data that can be expressed in terms of money. The **economic entity assumption** states that economic events can be identified with a particular unit of accountability. The **time period assumption** states that the economic life of a business can be divided into artificial time periods and that meaningful accounting reports can be prepared for each period. The **going concern assumption** states that the company will continue in operation long enough to carry out its existing objectives and commitments.

The **historical cost principle** states that companies should record assets at their cost. The **fair value principle** indicates that assets and liabilities should be reported at fair value. The **revenue recognition principle** requires that companies recognize revenue in the accounting period in which the performance obligation is satisfied. The **expense recognition principle** dictates that efforts (expenses) be matched with results (revenues). The **full disclosure principle** requires that companies disclose circumstances and events that matter to financial statement users.

The **cost constraint** weighs the cost that companies incur to provide a type of information against its benefits to financial statement users.

Glossary Review

Accrual-basis accounting Accounting basis in which companies record transactions that change a company's financial statements in the periods in which the events occur. (p. 3-3).

Accruals Adjusting entries for either accrued revenues or accrued expenses. (p. 3-5).

Accrued expenses Expenses incurred but not yet paid in cash or recorded. (p. 3-14).

Accrued revenues Revenues for services performed but not yet received in cash or recorded. (p. 3-13).

Adjusted trial balance A list of accounts and their balances after the company has made all adjustments. (p. 3-20).

Adjusting entries Entries made at the end of an accounting period to ensure that companies follow the revenue recognition and expense recognition principles. (p. 3-5).

Book value The difference between the cost of a depreciable asset and its related accumulated depreciation. (p. 3-10).

Calendar year An accounting period that extends from January 1 to December 31. (p. 3-3).

Cash-basis accounting Accounting basis in which companies record revenue when they receive cash and an expense when they pay out cash. (p. 3-3).

***Comparability** Ability to compare the accounting information of different companies because they use the same accounting principles. (p. 3-28).

***Consistency** Use of the same accounting principles and methods from year to year within a company. (p. 3-28).

Contra asset account An account offset against an asset account on the balance sheet. (p. 3-9).

***Cost constraint** Constraint that weighs the cost that companies will incur to provide the information against the benefit that financial statement users will gain from having the information available. (p. 3-30).

Deferrals Adjusting entries for either prepaid expenses or unearned revenues. (p. 3-5).

Depreciation The process of allocating the cost of an asset to expense over its useful life. (p. 3-9).

***Economic entity assumption** An assumption that every economic entity can be separately identified and accounted for. (p. 3-29).

Expense recognition principle (matching principle) The principle that companies recognize expense in the period in which they make efforts (consume assets or incur liabilities) to generate revenue. (pp. 3-4, 3-30).

***Fair value principle** Assets and liabilities should be reported at fair value (the price received to sell an asset or settle a liability). (p. 3-29).

***Faithful representation** Information that accurately depicts what really happened. (p. 3-28).

Fiscal year An accounting period that is one year in length. (p. 3-3).

***Full disclosure principle** Accounting principle that dictates that companies disclose circumstances and events that make a difference to financial statement users. (p. 3-30).

***Going concern assumption** The assumption that the company will continue in operation for the foreseeable future. (p. 3-29).

***Historical cost principle** An accounting principle that states that companies should record assets at their cost. (p. 3-29).

Interim periods Monthly or quarterly accounting time periods. (p. 3-3).

***Materiality** A company-specific aspect of relevance. An item is material when its size makes it likely to influence the decision of an investor or creditor. (p. 3-28).

***Monetary unit assumption** An assumption that requires that only those things that can be expressed in money are included in the accounting records. (p. 3-29).

Prepaid expenses (prepayments) Expenses paid in cash before they are used or consumed. (p. 3-6).

***Relevance** The quality of information that indicates the information makes a difference in a decision. (p. 3-28).

Revenue recognition principle The principle that companies recognize revenue in the accounting period in which the performance obligation is satisfied. (pp. 3-3, 3-30).

***Timely** Information that is available to decision-makers before it loses its capacity to influence decisions. (p. 3-28).

Time period assumption An assumption that accountants can divide the economic life of a business into artificial time periods. (pp. 3-3, 3-29).

***Understandability** Information presented in a clear and concise fashion so that users can interpret it and comprehend its meaning. (p. 3-28).

Unearned revenues A liability recorded for cash received before services are performed. (p. 3-10).

Useful life The length of service of a long-lived asset. (p. 3-8).

***Verifiable** The quality of information that occurs when independent observers, using the same methods, obtain similar results. (p. 3-28).

Practice Multiple-Choice Questions

1. **(LO 1)** The revenue recognition principle states that:
   - **a.** revenue should be recognized in the accounting period in which a performance obligation is satisfied.
   - **b.** expenses should be matched with revenues.
   - **c.** the economic life of a business can be divided into artificial time periods.
   - **d.** the fiscal year should correspond with the calendar year.

2. **(LO 1)** The time period assumption states that:
   - **a.** companies must wait until the calendar year is completed to prepare financial statements.
   - **b.** companies use the fiscal year to report financial information.
   - **c.** the economic life of a business can be divided into artificial time periods.
   - **d.** companies record information in the time period in which the events occur.

3. **(LO 1)** Which of the following statements about the accrual basis of accounting is **false**?
   - **a.** Events that change a company's financial statements are recorded in the periods in which the events occur.
   - **b.** Revenue is recognized in the period in which services are performed.
   - **c.** This basis is in accordance with generally accepted accounting principles.
   - **d.** Revenue is recorded only when cash is received, and expense is recorded only when cash is paid.

4. **(LO 1)** The principle or assumption dictating that efforts (expenses) should be recognized in the period in which a company consumes assets or incurs liabilities to generate revenue is the:
   - **a.** expense recognition principle.
   - **b.** cost assumption.
   - **c.** time period assumption.
   - **d.** revenue recognition principle.

5. **(LO 1)** Adjusting entries are made to ensure that:
   - **a.** expenses are recognized in the period in which they are incurred.
   - **b.** revenues are recorded in the period in which services are performed.
   - **c.** balance sheet and income statement accounts have correct balances at the end of an accounting period.
   - **d.** All the responses above are correct.

6. **(LO 1)** Each of the following is a major type (or category) of adjusting entries **except**:
   - **a.** prepaid expenses.
   - **b.** accrued revenues.
   - **c.** accrued expenses.
   - **d.** recognized revenues.

7. **(LO 2)** The trial balance shows Supplies $1,350 and Supplies Expense $0. If $600 of supplies are on hand at the end of the period, the adjusting entry is:

a. Supplies	600	
Supplies Expense		600
b. Supplies	750	
Supplies Expense		750
c. Supplies Expense	750	
Supplies		750
d. Supplies Expense	600	
Supplies		600

8. **(LO 2)** Adjustments for prepaid expenses:
   - **a.** decrease assets and increase revenues.
   - **b.** decrease expenses and increase assets.
   - **c.** decrease assets and increase expenses.
   - **d.** decrease revenues and increase assets.

9. **(LO 2)** Accumulated Depreciation is:
   - **a.** a contra asset account.
   - **b.** an expense account.
   - **c.** an owner's equity account.
   - **d.** a liability account.

10. **(LO 2)** Rivera Company computes depreciation on delivery equipment at $1,000 for the month of June. The adjusting entry to record this depreciation is as follows.

a. Depreciation Expense	1,000	
Accumulated Depreciation—Rivera Company		1,000
b. Depreciation Expense	1,000	
Equipment		1,000
c. Depreciation Expense	1,000	
Accumulated Depreciation—Equipment		1,000
d. Equipment Expense	1,000	
Accumulated Depreciation—Equipment		1,000

11. **(LO 2)** Adjustments for unearned revenues:
   - **a.** decrease liabilities and increase revenues.
   - **b.** have an assets-and-revenues-account relationship.
   - **c.** increase assets and increase revenues.
   - **d.** decrease revenues and decrease assets.

12. **(LO 3)** Adjustments for accrued revenues:
   - **a.** have a liabilities-and-revenues-account relationship.
   - **b.** have an assets-and-revenues-account relationship.
   - **c.** decrease assets and revenues.
   - **d.** decrease liabilities and increase revenues.

13. (LO 3) Anika Wilson earned a salary of $400 for the last week of September. She will be paid on October 1. The adjusting entry for Anika's employer at September 30 is:

a. No entry is required.

b. Salaries and Wages Expense	400	
Salaries and Wages Payable		400
c. Salaries and Wages Expense	400	
Cash		400
d. Salaries and Wages Payable	400	
Cash		400

14. (LO 4) Which of the following statements is **incorrect** concerning the adjusted trial balance?

a. An adjusted trial balance proves the equality of the total debit balances and the total credit balances in the ledger after all adjustments are made.

b. The adjusted trial balance provides the primary basis for the preparation of financial statements.

c. The adjusted trial balance lists the account balances segregated by assets and liabilities.

d. The adjusted trial balance is prepared after the adjusting entries have been journalized and posted.

*15. (LO 5) The trial balance shows Supplies $0 and Supplies Expense $1,500. If $800 of supplies are on hand at the end of the period, the adjusting entry is:

a. debit Supplies $800 and credit Supplies Expense $800.

b. debit Supplies Expense $800 and credit Supplies $800.

c. debit Supplies $700 and credit Supplies Expense $700.

d. debit Supplies Expense $700 and credit Supplies $700.

*16. (LO 6) Neutrality is an ingredient of:

	Faithful Representation	Relevance
a.	Yes	Yes
b.	No	No
c.	Yes	No
d.	No	Yes

*17. (LO 6) Which item is a constraint in financial accounting?

a. Comparability.
b. Materiality.
c. Cost.
d. Consistency.

Solutions

1. **a.** Revenue should be recognized in the accounting period in which a performance obligation is satisfied. The other choices are incorrect because (b) defines the expense recognition principle, (c) describes the time period assumption, and (d) a company's fiscal year does not need to correspond with the calendar year.

2. **c.** The economic life of a business can be divided into artificial time periods. The other choices are incorrect because (a) companies report their activities on a more frequent basis and not necessarily based on a calendar year; (b) companies report financial information more frequently than annually, such as monthly or quarterly, in order to evaluate results of operations; and (d) describes accrual-basis accounting.

3. **d.** Under the accrual basis of accounting, revenue is recognized when the performance obligation is satisfied, not when cash is received, and expense is recognized when incurred, not when cash is paid. The other choices are all true statements.

4. **a.** The expense recognition principle dictates that companies recognize expense in the period in which they make efforts to generate revenue. The other choices are incorrect because (b) there is no cost assumption, but the historical cost principle states that assets should be recorded at their cost; (c) the time period assumption states that the economic life of a business can be divided into artificial time periods; and (d) the revenue recognition principle indicates that revenue should be recognized in the accounting period in which a performance obligation is satisfied.

5. **d.** Adjusting entries are made for the reasons noted in choices (a), (b), and (c). The other choices are true statements, but (d) is the best answer.

6. **d.** Unearned revenues, not recognized revenues, is one of the major categories of adjusting entries. The other choices all list one of the major categories of adjusting entries.

7. **c.** Debiting Supplies Expense for $750 and crediting Supplies for $750 ($1,350 – $600) will decrease Supplies and increase Supplies Expense. The other choices are incorrect because (a) will increase Supplies and decrease Supplies Expense and also for the wrong amounts, (b) will increase Supplies and decrease Supplies Expense, and (d) will cause Supplies to have an incorrect balance of $750 ($1,350 – $600) and Supplies Expense to have an incorrect balance of $600 ($0 + $600).

8. **c.** Adjustments for prepaid expenses decrease assets and increase expenses. The other choices are incorrect because an adjusting entry for prepaid expenses (a) increases expenses, not revenues; (b) increases, not decreases, expenses and decreases, not increases, assets; and (d) increases expenses, not decreases, revenues and decreases, not increases, assets.

9. **a.** Accumulated Depreciation is a contra asset account; it is offset against an asset account on the balance sheet. The other choices are incorrect because Accumulated Depreciation is not (b) an expense account nor located on the income statement, (c) an owner's equity account, or (d) a liability account.

10. **c.** The adjusting entry is to debit Depreciation Expense and credit Accumulated Depreciation—Equipment. The other choices are incorrect because (a) the contra asset account title includes the asset being depreciated, not the company name; (b) the credit should be to the contra asset account, not directly to the asset; and (d) the debit for this entry should be Depreciation Expense, not Equipment Expense.

11. **a.** Adjustments for unearned revenues will consist of a debit (decrease) to unearned revenues (a liability) and a credit (increase) to a revenue account. Choices (b), (c), and (d) are incorrect because adjustments for unearned revenues will increase revenues but will have no effect on assets.

12. **b.** Adjustments for accrued revenues will have an assets-and-revenues-account relationship. Choices (a) and (d) are incorrect because adjustments for accrued revenues have no effect on liabilities. Choice (c) is incorrect because these adjustments will increase, not decrease, both assets and revenues.

13. **b.** The adjusting entry should be to debit Salaries and Wages Expense for $400 and credit Salaries and Wages Payable for $400.

The other choices are incorrect because (a) if an adjusting entry is not made, the amount of money owed (liability) that is shown on the balance sheet will be understated and the amount of salaries and wages expense will also be understated; (c) the credit account is incorrect as adjusting entries never affect cash; and (d) the debit account should be Salaries and Wages Expense and the credit account should be Salaries and Wages Payable. Adjusting entries never affect cash.

14. **c.** The accounts on the trial balance can be segregated by the balance in the account—either debit or credit—not whether they are assets or liabilities. All accounts in the ledger are included in the adjusted trial balance, not just assets and liabilities. The other choices are all true statements.

*15. **a.** This adjusting entry correctly states the Supplies account at $800 ($0 + $800) and the Supplies Expense account at $700 ($1,500 – $800). The other choices are incorrect because (b) will cause the Supplies account to have a credit balance (assets have a normal debit balance) and the Supplies Expense account to be stated at $2,300, which is too high; (c) will result in a $700 balance in the Supplies account ($100 too low) and an $800 balance in the Supplies Expense account ($100 too high); and (d) will cause the Supplies account to have a credit balance (assets have a normal debit balance) and the Supplies Expense account to be stated at $2,200, which is too high.

*16. **c.** Neutrality is one of the enhancing qualities that makes information more representationally faithful, not relevant. Therefore, choices (a), (b), and (d) are incorrect.

*17. **c.** Cost is a constraint in financial accounting. The other choices are all enhancing qualities of useful information.

Practice Brief Exercises

Indicate why adjusting entries are needed.

1. **(LO 1)** The ledger of Dey Company includes the following accounts. Explain why each account may need adjustment.

a. Supplies.
b. Unearned Service Revenue.
c. Salaries and Wages Payable.
d. Interest Payable.

Solution

1. **a.** Supplies: to recognize supplies used during the period.
b. Unearned Service Revenue: to record revenue generated for services performed.
c. Salaries and Wages Payable: to recognize salaries and wages accrual to employees at the end of a reporting period.
d. Interest Payable: to recognize interest accrued but unpaid on notes payable.

Prepare adjusting entry for depreciation.

2. **(LO 2)** **Financial Statement** At the end of its first year, the trial balance of Denton Company shows Equipment of $40,000 and zero balances in Accumulated Depreciation—Equipment and Depreciation Expense. Depreciation for the year is estimated to be $8,000. Prepare the adjusting entry for depreciation at December 31, post the adjustments to T-accounts, and indicate the balance sheet presentation of the equipment at December 31.

Solution

2. Dec. 31	Depreciation Expense	8,000	
	Accumulated Depreciation—Equipment		8,000

Depreciation Expense

12/31	8,000		

Accum. Depreciation—Equipment

		12/31	8,000

Balance Sheet:

Equipment	$40,000	
Less: Accumulated Depreciation—Equipment	8,000	$32,000

Prepare adjusting entries for accruals.

3. **(LO 3)** You are asked to prepare the following accrued adjusting entries at December 31.

1. Services performed but not recorded are $4,200.
2. Utility expenses incurred but not paid are $660.
3. Salaries and wages earned by employees of $3,000 are unpaid.

Use the following account titles: Accounts Payable, Accounts Receivable, Service Revenue, Salaries and Wages Expense, Salaries and Wages Payable, and Utility Expense.

Solution

3.

Dec. 31	Accounts Receivable	4,200	
	Service Revenue		4,200
31	Utility Expense	660	
	Accounts Payable		660
31	Salaries and Wage Expense	3,000	
	Salaries and Wages Payable		3,000

Analyze accounts in an unadjusted trial balance.

4. (LO 1, 2, 3) The trial balance for Blair Company includes the following balance sheet accounts. Identify the accounts that may require adjustment. For each account that requires adjustment, indicate (a) the type of adjusting entry (prepaid expense, unearned revenue, accrued revenue, or accrued expense) and (b) the related account in the adjusting entry.

Accounts Receivable	Interest Payable
Supplies	Unearned Service Revenue
Prepaid Insurance	

Solution

4.

Account	Type of Adjustment	Related Account
Accounts Receivable	Accrued Revenue	Service Revenue
Supplies	Prepaid Expense	Supplies Expense
Prepaid Insurance	Prepaid Expense	Insurance Expense
Interest Payable	Accrued Expense	Interest Expense
Unearned Service Revenue	Unearned Revenue	Service Revenue

Prepare an income statement from an adjusted trial balance.

5. (LO 4) **Financial Statement** The adjusted trial balance of Harmony Company includes the following accounts at December 31, 2020: Cash $12,000, Owner's Capital $22,000, Owner's Drawing $3,000, Service Revenue $41,000, Rent Expense $900, Salaries and Wages Expense $6,000, Supplies Expense $700, and Depreciation Expense $1,800. Prepare an income statement for the year.

Solution

5.

Harmony Company
Income Statement
For the Year Ended December 31, 2020

Revenues		
Service revenue		$41,000
Expenses		
Salaries and wages expense	$6,000	
Rent expense	900	
Depreciation expense	1,800	
Supplies expense	700	
Total expenses		9,400
Net income		$31,600

Practice Exercises

Prepare adjusting entries.

1. (LO 2, 3) Evan Watts, D.D.S., opened a dental practice on January 1, 2020. During the first month of operations, the following transactions occurred.

1. Watts performed services for patients totaling $2,400. These services have not yet been recorded.
2. Utility expenses incurred but not paid prior to January 31 totaled $400.
3. Purchased dental equipment on January 1 for $80,000, paying $20,000 in cash and signing a $60,000, 3-year note payable. The equipment depreciates $500 per month. Interest is $600 per month.
4. Purchased a one-year malpractice insurance policy on January 1 for $12,000.
5. Purchased $2,600 of dental supplies. On January 31, determined that $900 of supplies were on hand.

Instructions

Prepare the adjusting entries on January 31. Account titles are Accumulated Depreciation—Equipment, Depreciation Expense, Service Revenue, Accounts Receivable, Insurance Expense, Interest Expense, Interest Payable, Prepaid Insurance, Supplies, Supplies Expense, Utilities Expense, and Utilities Payable.

Solution

1.

Jan. 31	Accounts Receivable	2,400	
	Service Revenue		2,400
	Utilities Expense	400	
	Utilities Payable		400
	Depreciation Expense	500	
	Accumulated Depreciation—Equipment		500
	Interest Expense	600	
	Interest Payable		600
	Insurance Expense ($12,000 ÷ 12)	1,000	
	Prepaid Insurance		1,000
	Supplies Expense ($2,600 – $900)	1,700	
	Supplies		1,700

Prepare correct income statement.

2. **(LO 2, 3, 4)** **Financial Statement** The income statement of Venden Co. for the month of July shows net income of $4,000 based on Service Revenue $8,700, Salaries and Wages Expense $2,500, Supplies Expense $1,700, and Utilities Expense $500. In reviewing the statement, you discover the following.

1. Insurance expired during July of $700 was omitted.
2. Supplies expense includes $250 of supplies that are still on hand at July 31.
3. Depreciation on equipment of $300 was omitted.
4. Accrued but unpaid wages at July 31 of $400 were not included.
5. Services performed but unrecorded totaled $650.

Instructions

Prepare a correct income statement for July 2020.

Solution

2.

Venden Co.
Income Statement
For the Month Ended July 31, 2020

Revenues		
Service revenue ($8,700 + $650)		$9,350
Expenses		
Salaries and wages expense ($2,500 + $400)	$2,900	
Supplies expense ($1,700 – $250)	1,450	
Utilities expense	500	
Insurance expense	700	
Depreciation expense	300	
Total expenses		5,850
Net income		$3,500

Practice Problem

Prepare adjusting entries from selected data.

(LO 2, 3) The Green Thumb Lawn Care Company began operations on April 1. At April 30, the trial balance shows the following balances for selected accounts.

Prepaid Insurance	$ 3,600
Equipment	28,000
Notes Payable	20,000
Unearned Service Revenue	4,200
Service Revenue	1,800

Analysis reveals the following additional data.

1. Prepaid insurance is the cost of a 2-year insurance policy, effective April 1.
2. Depreciation on the equipment is $500 per month.
3. The note payable is dated April 1. It is a 6-month, 12% note.
4. Seven customers paid for the company's 6-month lawn service package of $600 beginning in April. The company performed services for these customers in April.
5. Lawn services performed for other customers but not recorded at April 30 totaled $1,500.

Instructions

Prepare the adjusting entries for the month of April. Show computations.

Solution

GENERAL JOURNAL **J1**

Date		Account Titles and Explanation	Ref.	Debit	Credit
		Adjusting Entries			
Apr.	30	Insurance Expense		150	
		Prepaid Insurance			150
		(To record insurance expired: $3,600 ÷ 24 = $150 per month)			
	30	Depreciation Expense		500	
		Accumulated Depreciation—Equipment			500
		(To record monthly depreciation)			
	30	Interest Expense		200	
		Interest Payable			200
		(To record interest on notes payable: $20,000 × 12% × 1/12 = $200)			
	30	Unearned Service Revenue		700	
		Service Revenue			700
		(To record revenue for services performed: $600 ÷ 6 = $100; $100 per month × 7 = $700)			
	30	Accounts Receivable		1,500	
		Service Revenue			1,500
		(To record revenue for services performed)			

WileyPLUS

Brief Exercises, DO IT! Exercises, Exercises, Problems, and many additional resources are available for practice in WileyPLUS.

Note: All asterisked Questions, Exercises, and Problems relate to material in the appendices to the chapter.

Questions

1. **a.** How does the time period assumption affect an accountant's analysis of business transactions?

   b. Explain the terms fiscal year, calendar year, and interim periods.

2. Define two generally accepted accounting principles that relate to adjusting the accounts.

3. Susan Hardy, a lawyer, accepts a legal engagement in March, performs the work in April, and is paid in May. If Hardy's law firm prepares monthly financial statements, when should it recognize revenue from this engagement? Why?

4. Why do accrual-basis financial statements provide more useful information than cash-basis statements?

5. In completing the engagement in Question 3, Hardy pays no costs in March, $2,000 in April, and $2,500 in May (incurred in April). How much expense should the firm deduct from revenues in the month when it recognizes the revenue? Why?

6. "Adjusting entries are required by the historical cost principle of accounting." Do you agree? Explain.

7. Why may a trial balance not contain up-to-date and complete financial information?

8. Distinguish between the two categories of adjusting entries, and identify the types of adjustments applicable to each category.

9. What is the debit/credit effect of a prepaid expense adjusting entry?

10. "Depreciation is a valuation process that results in the reporting of the fair value of the asset." Do you agree? Explain.

11. Explain the differences between depreciation expense and accumulated depreciation.

12. G. Phillips Company purchased equipment for $18,000. By the current balance sheet date, $6,000 had been depreciated. Indicate the balance sheet presentation of the data.

13. What is the debit/credit effect of an unearned revenue adjusting entry?

14. Whistler Corp. performed services for a customer but has not yet recorded payment, nor has it recorded any entry related to the work. Which of the following accounts are involved in the adjusting entry: (a) asset, (b) liability, (c) revenue, or (d) expense? For the accounts selected, indicate whether they would be debited or credited in the entry.

15. A company fails to recognize an expense incurred but not paid. Indicate which of the following accounts is debited and which is credited in the adjusting entry: (a) asset, (b) liability, (c) revenue, or (d) expense.

16. A company makes an accrued revenue adjusting entry for $900 and an accrued expense adjusting entry for $700. How much was net income understated prior to these entries? Explain.

17. On January 9, a company pays $5,000 for salaries and wages of which $2,000 was reported as Salaries and Wages Payable on December 31. Give the entry to record the payment.

18. For each of the following items before adjustment, indicate the type of adjusting entry (prepaid expense, unearned revenue, accrued revenue, or accrued expense) that is needed to correct the misstatement. If an item could result in more than one type of adjusting entry, indicate each of the types.

    a. Assets are understated.
    b. Liabilities are overstated.
    c. Liabilities are understated.
    d. Expenses are understated.
    e. Assets are overstated.
    f. Revenue is understated.

19. One-half of the adjusting entry is given below. Indicate the account title for the other half of the entry.

    a. Salaries and Wages Expense is debited.
    b. Depreciation Expense is debited.
    c. Interest Payable is credited.
    d. Supplies is credited.
    e. Accounts Receivable is debited.
    f. Unearned Service Revenue is debited.

20. "An adjusting entry may affect more than one balance sheet or income statement account." Do you agree? Why or why not?

21. Why is it possible to prepare financial statements directly from an adjusted trial balance?

*22. Dashan Company debits Supplies Expense for all purchases of supplies and credits Rent Revenue for all advanced rentals. For each type of adjustment, give the adjusting entry.

*23. **a.** What is the primary objective of financial reporting?

   b. Identify the characteristics of useful accounting information.

*24. Dan Fineman, the president of King Company, is pleased. King substantially increased its net income in 2020 while keeping its unit inventory relatively the same. Howard Gross, chief accountant, cautions Dan, however. Gross says that since King changed its method of inventory valuation, there is a consistency problem and it is difficult to determine whether King is better off. Is Gross correct? Why or why not?

*25. What is the distinction between comparability and consistency?

*26. Describe the constraint inherent in the presentation of accounting information.

*27. Quinn Becker is president of Better Books. She has no accounting background. Becker cannot understand why fair value is not used as the basis for all accounting measurement and reporting. Discuss.

*28. What is the economic entity assumption? Give an example of its violation.

Brief Exercises

Indicate why adjusting entries are needed.

BE3.1 (LO 1) The ledger of Althukair Company includes the following accounts. Explain why each account may require adjustment.

a. Prepaid Insurance.
b. Depreciation Expense.
c. Unearned Service Revenue.
d. Interest Payable.

BE3.2 (LO 1, 2) Gee Company accumulates the following adjustment data at December 31. Indicate (a) the type of adjustment (prepaid expense, accrued revenue, and so on), and (b) the status of accounts before adjustment (for example, "assets understated and revenues understated").

Identify the major types of adjusting entries.

1. Supplies of $150 are on hand.
2. Services performed but not recorded total $900.
3. Interest of $200 has accumulated on a note payable.
4. Rent collected in advance totaling $850 has been earned.

BE3.3 (LO 2) Schramel Advertising Company's trial balance at December 31 shows Supplies $6,700 and Supplies Expense $0. On December 31, there are $2,100 of supplies on hand. Prepare the adjusting entry at December 31, and using T-accounts, enter the balances in the accounts, post the adjusting entry, and indicate the adjusted balance in each account.

Prepare adjusting entry for supplies.

BE3.4 (LO 2) At the end of its first year, the trial balance of Wolowitz Company shows Equipment $30,000 and zero balances in Accumulated Depreciation—Equipment and Depreciation Expense. Depreciation for the year is estimated to be $3,750. Prepare the annual adjusting entry for depreciation at December 31, post the adjustments to T-accounts, and indicate the balance sheet presentation of the equipment at December 31.

Prepare adjusting entry for depreciation.

BE3.5 (LO 2) On July 1, 2019, Major Co. pays $15,120 to Mesa Insurance Co. for a 4-year insurance contract. Both companies have fiscal years ending December 31. For Major Co., journalize and post the entry on July 1 and the annual adjusting entry on December 31.

Prepare adjusting entry for prepaid expense.

BE3.6 (LO 2) Using the data in BE3.5, journalize and post the entry on July 1 and the adjusting entry on December 31 for Mesa Insurance Co. Mesa uses the accounts Unearned Service Revenue and Service Revenue.

Prepare adjusting entry for unearned revenue.

BE3.7 (LO 3) The bookkeeper for Abduli Company asks you to prepare the following accrued adjusting entries at December 31.

Prepare adjusting entries for accruals.

1. Interest on notes payable of $400 is accrued.
2. Services performed but not recorded total $2,300.
3. Salaries earned by employees of $900 have not been recorded.

Use the following account titles: Service Revenue, Accounts Receivable, Interest Expense, Interest Payable, Salaries and Wages Expense, and Salaries and Wages Payable.

BE3.8 (LO 1, 2, 3) The trial balance of Beowulf Company includes the following balance sheet accounts, which may require adjustment. For each account that requires adjustment, indicate (a) the type of adjusting entry (prepaid expense, unearned revenue, accrued revenue, or accrued expense) and (b) the related account in the adjusting entry.

Analyze accounts in an unadjusted trial balance.

Accounts Receivable	Interest Payable
Prepaid Insurance	Unearned Service Revenue
Accumulated Depreciation—Equipment	

BE3.9 (LO 4) **Financial Statement** The adjusted trial balance of Miller Company at December 31, 2020, includes the following accounts: Owner's Capital $16,400, Owner's Drawings $7,000, Service Revenue $39,000, Salaries and Wages Expense $16,000, Insurance Expense $2,000, Rent Expense $4,000, Supplies Expense $1,500, and Depreciation Expense $1,300. Prepare an income statement for the year.

Prepare an income statement from an adjusted trial balance.

BE3.10 (LO 4) **Financial Statement** Partial adjusted trial balance data for Miller Company is presented in BE3.9. The balance in Owner's Capital is the balance as of January 1. Prepare an owner's equity statement for the year assuming net income is $14,200 for the year.

Prepare an owner's equity statement from an adjusted trial balance.

***BE3.11 (LO 5)** Eckholm Company records all prepayments in income statement accounts. At April 30, the trial balance shows Supplies Expense $2,800, Service Revenue $9,200, and zero balances in related

Prepare adjusting entries under alternative treatment of deferrals.

balance sheet accounts. Prepare the adjusting entries at April 30 assuming (a) $400 of supplies on hand and (b) $3,000 of service revenue should be reported as unearned.

Identify characteristics of useful information.

***BE3.12 (LO 6)** The accompanying chart shows the qualitative characteristics of useful accounting information. Fill in the blanks.

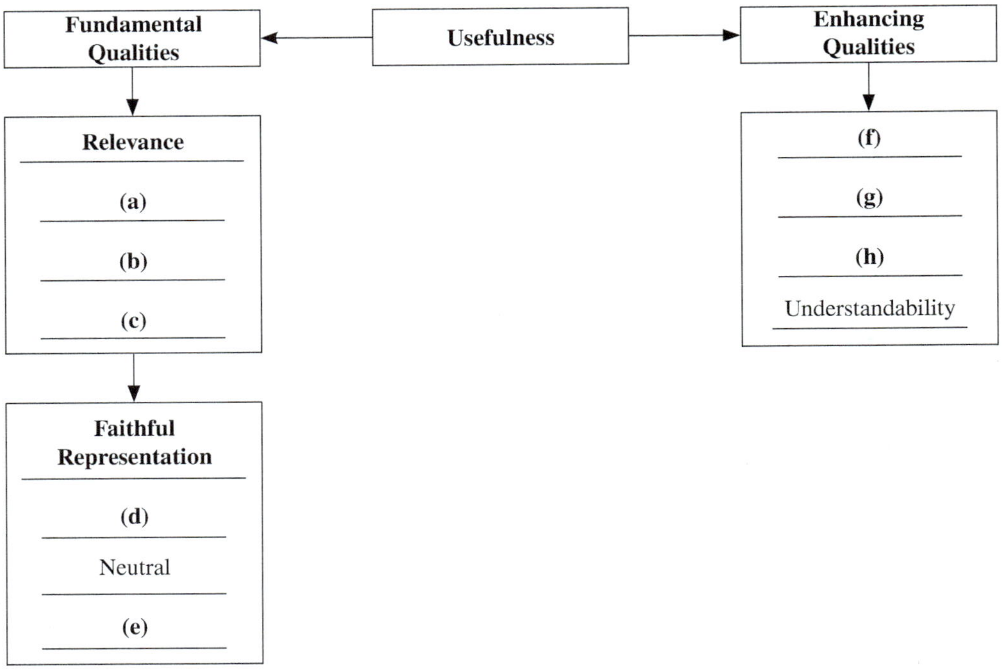

Identify characteristics of useful information.

***BE3.13 (LO 6)** Given the characteristics of useful accounting information, complete each of the following statements.

a. For information to be _____, it should have predictive value, confirmatory value, and be material.

b. _____ is the quality of information that gives assurance that the information accurately depicts what really happened.

c. _____ means using the same accounting principles and methods from year to year within a company.

Identify characteristics of useful information.

***BE3.14 (LO 6)** Here are some qualitative characteristics of useful accounting information:

1. Predictive value.
2. Neutral.
3. Verifiable.
4. Timely.

Match each qualitative characteristic to one of the following statements.

_______ **a.** Accounting information should help provide accurate expectations about future events.

_______ **b.** Accounting information cannot be selected, prepared, or presented to favor one set of interested users over another.

_______ **c.** The quality of information that occurs when independent observers, using the same methods, obtain similar results.

_______ **d.** Accounting information must be available to decision-makers before it loses its capacity to influence their decisions.

Define full disclosure principle.

***BE3.15 (LO 6)** Select the response that completes the following statement correctly. The full disclosure principle dictates that:

a. financial statements should disclose all assets at their cost.

b. financial statements should disclose only those events that can be measured in currency.

c. financial statements should disclose all events and circumstances that would matter to users of financial statements.

d. financial statements should not be relied on unless an auditor has expressed an unqualified opinion on them.

DO IT! Exercises

DO IT! 3.1 (LO 1) Below is a list of concepts in the left column, with a description of the concept in the right column. There are more descriptions provided than concepts. Match the description of the concept to the concept.

Identify timing concepts.

1. ____ Cash-basis accounting.
2. ____ Fiscal year.
3. ____ Revenue recognition principle.
4. ____ Expense recognition principle.

a. Monthly and quarterly time periods.

b. Accountants divide the economic life of a business into artificial time periods.

c. Efforts (expenses) should be recognized in the period in which a company uses assets or incurs liabilities to generate accomplishments (revenues).

d. Companies record revenues when they receive cash and record expenses when they pay out cash.

e. An accounting time period that is one year in length.

f. An accounting time period that starts on January 1 and ends on December 31.

g. Companies record transactions in the period in which the events occur.

h. Recognize revenue in the accounting period in which a performance obligation is satisfied.

DO IT! 3.2 (LO 2) The ledger of Milton, Inc. on March 31, 2020, includes the following selected accounts before adjusting entries.

Prepare adjusting entries for deferrals.

	Debit	Credit
Prepaid Insurance	$ 2,400	
Supplies	2,500	
Equipment	30,000	
Unearned Service Revenue		$9,000

An analysis of the accounts shows the following.

1. Insurance expires at the rate of $400 per month.
2. Supplies on hand total $1,600.
3. The equipment depreciates $480 per month.
4. During March, services were performed for two-fifths of the unearned service revenue.

Prepare the adjusting entries for the month of March.

DO IT! 3.3 (LO 3) Fiske Computer Services began operations in July 2020. At the end of the month, the company prepares monthly financial statements. It has the following information for the month.

Prepare adjusting entries for accruals.

1. At July 31, the company owed employees $1,300 in salaries that the company will pay in August.
2. On July 1, the company borrowed $20,000 from a local bank on a 10-year note. The annual interest rate is 6%.
3. Service revenue unrecorded in July totaled $2,400.

Prepare the adjusting entries needed at July 31, 2020.

DO IT! 3.4 (LO 4) **Financial Statement** Ming Company was organized on April 1, 2020. The company prepares quarterly financial statements. The adjusted trial balance amounts at June 30 are as follows.

Calculate amounts from trial balance.

	Debit		Credit
Cash	$ 5,360	Accumulated Depreciation—Equipment	$ 700
Accounts Receivable	580	Notes Payable	4,000
Prepaid Rent	1,120	Accounts Payable	790
Supplies	920	Salaries and Wages Payable	300
Equipment	12,000	Interest Payable	40
Owner's Drawings	500	Unearned Rent Revenue	400
Salaries and Wages Expense	7,400	Owner's Capital	11,200
Rent Expense	1,200	Service Revenue	11,360
Depreciation Expense	700	Rent Revenue	1,600
Supplies Expense	160		$30,390
Utilities Expense	410		
Interest Expense	40		
	$30,390		

a. Determine the net income for the quarter April 1 to June 30.

b. Determine the total assets and total liabilities at June 30, 2020, for Ming Company.

c. Determine the amount that appears for Owner's Capital at June 30, 2020.

Exercises

Explain the time period assumption.

E3.1 (LO 1) Chloe Davis has prepared the following list of statements about the time period assumption.

1. Adjusting entries would not be necessary if a company's life were not divided into artificial time periods.
2. The IRS requires companies to file annual tax returns.
3. Accountants divide the economic life of a business into artificial time periods, but each transaction affects only one of these periods.
4. Accounting time periods are generally a month, a quarter, or a year.
5. A time period lasting one year is called an interim period.
6. All fiscal years are calendar years, but not all calendar years are fiscal years.

Instructions

Identify each statement as true or false. If false, indicate how to correct the statement.

Distinguish between cash and accrual basis of accounting.

E3.2 (LO 1) Writing On numerous occasions, proposals have surfaced to put the federal government on the accrual basis of accounting. This is no small issue. If this basis were used, it would mean that billions in unrecorded liabilities would have to be booked, and the federal deficit would increase substantially.

Instructions

a. What is the difference between accrual-basis accounting and cash-basis accounting?

b. Why would politicians prefer the cash basis over the accrual basis?

c. Write a letter to your senator explaining why the federal government should adopt the accrual basis of accounting.

Compute cash and accrual accounting income.

E3.3 (LO 1) Carillo Industries collected $108,000 from customers in 2020. Of the amount collected, $25,000 was for services performed in 2019. In addition, Carillo performed services worth $36,000 in 2020, which will not be collected until 2021.

Carillo Industries also paid $72,000 for expenses in 2020. Of the amount paid, $30,000 was for expenses incurred on account in 2019. In addition, Carillo incurred $42,000 of expenses in 2020, which will not be paid until 2021.

Instructions

a. Compute 2020 cash-basis net income.

b. Compute 2020 accrual-basis net income.

E3.4 (LO 1, 2, 3) Luong Corporation encounters the following situations:

Identify the type of adjusting entry needed.

1. Luong collects $1,300 from a customer in 2020 for services to be performed in 2021.
2. Luong incurs utility expense which is not yet paid in cash or recorded.
3. Luong's employees worked 3 days in 2020 but will not be paid until 2021.
4. Luong performs services for customers but has not yet received cash or recorded the transaction.
5. Luong paid $2,800 rent on December 1 for the 4 months starting December 1.
6. Luong received cash for future services and recorded a liability until the service was performed.
7. Luong performed consulting services for a client in December 2020. On December 31, it had not billed the client for services provided of $1,200.
8. Luong paid cash for an expense and recorded an asset until the item was used up.
9. Luong purchased $900 of supplies in 2020; at year-end, $400 of supplies remain unused.
10. Luong purchased equipment on January 1, 2020; the equipment will be used for 5 years.
11. Luong borrowed $12,000 on October 1, 2020, signing an 8% one-year note payable.

Instructions

Identify what type of adjusting entry (prepaid expense, unearned revenue, accrued expense, or accrued revenue) is needed in each situation at December 31, 2020.

E3.5 (LO 2, 3) Devin Wolf Company has the following balances in selected accounts on December 31, 2020.

Prepare adjusting entries from selected data.

Accounts Receivable	$ –0–
Accumulated Depreciation—Equipment	–0–
Equipment	7,000
Interest Payable	–0–
Notes Payable	10,000
Prepaid Insurance	2,100
Salaries and Wages Payable	–0–
Supplies	2,450
Unearned Service Revenue	32,000

All the accounts have normal balances. The information below has been gathered at December 31, 2020.

1. Devin Wolf Company borrowed $10,000 by signing a 9%, one-year note on September 1, 2020.
2. A count of supplies on December 31, 2020, indicates that supplies of $900 are on hand.
3. Depreciation on the equipment for 2020 is $1,000.
4. Devin Wolf Company paid $2,100 for 12 months of insurance coverage on June 1, 2020.
5. On December 1, 2020, Devin Wolf collected $32,000 for consulting services to be performed from December 1, 2020, through March 31, 2021.
6. Devin Wolf performed consulting services for a client in December 2020. The client will be billed $4,200.
7. Devin Wolf Company pays its employees total salaries of $9,000 every Monday for the preceding 5-day week (Monday through Friday). On Monday, December 29, employees were paid for the week ending December 26. All employees worked the last 3 days of 2020.

Instructions

Prepare adjusting entries for the seven items described above.

E3.6 (LO 2, 3, 4) Mendoza Company accumulates the following adjustment data at December 31.

Identify types of adjustments and account relationships.

1. Services performed but unbilled total $3,000.
2. Supplies of $300 have been used.
3. Utility expenses of $552 are unpaid.
4. Services performed of $260 collected in advance.
5. Salaries of $800 are unpaid.
6. Prepaid insurance totaling $350 has expired.

Instructions

For each of the above items indicate the following.

a. The type of adjustment (prepaid expense, unearned revenue, accrued revenue, or accrued expense).

b. The status of accounts before adjustment (overstatement or understatement).

Prepare adjusting entries from selected account data.

E3.7 (LO 2, 3) The ledger of Passehl Rental Agency on March 31 of the current year includes the selected accounts, shown below, before adjusting entries have been prepared.

	Debit	Credit
Prepaid Insurance	$ 3,600	
Supplies	2,800	
Equipment	25,000	
Accumulated Depreciation—Equipment		$ 8,400
Notes Payable		20,000
Unearned Rent Revenue		10,200
Rent Revenue		60,000
Interest Expense	–0–	
Salaries and Wages Expense	14,000	

An analysis of the accounts shows the following.

1. The equipment depreciates $400 per month.
2. One-third of the unearned rent revenue was earned during the quarter.
3. Interest of $500 is accrued on the notes payable.
4. Supplies on hand total $750.
5. Insurance expires at the rate of $300 per month.

Instructions

Prepare the adjusting entries at March 31, assuming that adjusting entries are made **quarterly**. Additional accounts are Depreciation Expense, Insurance Expense, Interest Payable, and Supplies Expense.

Prepare adjusting entries.

E3.8 (LO 2, 3) Lorena Manzone, D.D.S., opened a dental practice on January 1, 2020. During the first month of operations, the following transactions occurred.

1. Performed services for patients who had dental plan insurance. At January 31, $785 of such services were performed but not yet recorded.
2. Utility expenses incurred but not paid prior to January 31 totaled $650.
3. Purchased dental equipment on January 1 for $80,000, paying $30,000 in cash and signing a $50,000, 3-year note payable. The equipment depreciates $400 per month. Interest is $500 per month.
4. Purchased a one-year malpractice insurance policy on January 1 for $24,000.
5. Purchased $1,600 of dental supplies. On January 31, determined that $400 of supplies were on hand.

Instructions

Prepare the adjusting entries on January 31. Account titles are Accumulated Depreciation—Equipment, Depreciation Expense, Service Revenue, Accounts Receivable, Insurance Expense, Interest Expense, Interest Payable, Prepaid Insurance, Supplies, Supplies Expense, Utilities Expense, and Utilities Payable.

Prepare adjusting entries.

E3.9 (LO 2, 3) The trial balance for Pioneer Advertising is shown in Illustration 3.3. Instead of the adjusting entries shown in the textbook at October 31, assume the following adjustment data.

1. Supplies on hand at October 31 total $500.
2. Expired insurance for the month is $120.
3. Depreciation for the month is $50.
4. Services related to unearned service revenue in October worth $600 were performed.
5. Services performed but not recorded at October 31 are $360.
6. Interest accrued at October 31 is $95.
7. Accrued salaries at October 31 are $1,625.

Instructions

Prepare the adjusting entries for the items above.

Prepare correct income statement.

Excel

E3.10 (LO 1, 2, 3, 4) Financial Statement The income statement of Lundeen Co. for the month of July shows net income of $1,400 based on Service Revenue $5,500, Salaries and Wages Expense $2,300, Supplies Expense $1,200, and Utilities Expense $600. In reviewing the statement, you discover the following.

1. Insurance expired during July of $500 was omitted.
2. Supplies expense includes $250 of supplies that are still on hand at July 31.
3. Depreciation on equipment of $150 was omitted.
4. Accrued but unpaid salaries and wages at July 31 of $400 were not included.
5. Services performed but unrecorded totaled $650.

Instructions

Prepare a correct income statement for July 2020.

Analyze adjusted data.

Excel

E3.11 (LO 1, 2, 3, 4) A partial adjusted trial balance of Frangesch Company at January 31, 2020, shows the following.

Frangesch Company
Adjusted Trial Balance
January 31, 2020

	Debit	Credit
Supplies	$ 850	
Prepaid Insurance	2,400	
Salaries and Wages Payable		$ 920
Unearned Service Revenue		750
Supplies Expense	950	
Insurance Expense	400	
Salaries and Wages Expense	2,900	
Service Revenue		2,000

Instructions

Answer the following questions, assuming the year begins January 1.

a. If the amount in Supplies Expense is the January 31 adjusting entry and $1,000 of supplies was purchased in January, what was the balance in Supplies on January 1?

b. If the amount in Insurance Expense is the January 31 adjusting entry and the original insurance premium was for one year, what was the total premium and when was the policy purchased?

c. If $3,800 of salaries was paid in January, what was the balance in Salaries and Wages Payable at December 31, 2019?

Journalize basic transactions and adjusting entries.

E3.12 (LO 2, 3) Selected accounts of Shannon Company are shown as follows.

Supplies Expense

7/31	900		

Supplies

7/1 Bal.	1,100	7/31	900
7/10	650		

Salaries and Wages Payable

		7/31	1,200

Accounts Receivable

7/31	500		

Unearned Service Revenue

7/31	1,150	7/1 Bal.	1,500
		7/20	1,000

Salaries and Wages Expense

7/15	1,200		
7/31	1,200		

Service Revenue

		7/14	2,200
		7/31	1,150
		7/31	500

Instructions

After analyzing the accounts, journalize (a) the July transactions and (b) the adjusting entries that were made on July 31. (*Hint:* July transactions were for cash.)

Prepare adjusting entries from selected account data.

E3.13 (LO 2, 3) The ledger of Armour Lake Lumber Supply on July 31, 2020, includes the selected accounts below before adjusting entries have been prepared.

	Debit	Credit
Notes Payable		$ 20,000
Supplies	$ 24,000	
Prepaid Rent	3,600	
Buildings	250,000	
Accumulated Depreciation—Buildings		140,000
Unearned Service Revenue		11,500

An analysis of the company's accounts shows the following.

1. The notes payable pays interest at a rate of 6% per year.
2. Supplies on hand at the end of the month totaled $18,600.
3. The balance in Prepaid Rent represents 4 months of rent costs.
4. Employees were owed $3,100 related to unpaid salaries and wages.
5. Depreciation on buildings is $6,000 per year.
6. During the month, the company satisfied obligations worth $4,700 related to the Unearned Services Revenue.
7. Unpaid maintenance and repairs costs were $2,300.

Instructions

Prepare the adjusting entries at July 31 assuming that adjusting entries are made monthly. Use additional accounts as needed.

Determine effect of adjusting entries.

E3.14 (LO 2, 3) On December 31, 2020, Waters Company prepared an income statement and balance sheet, but failed to take into account three adjusting entries. The balance sheet showed total assets $150,000, total liabilities $70,000, and owner's equity $80,000. The incorrect income statement showed net income of $70,000.

The data for the three adjusting entries were:

1. Salaries and wages amounting to $10,000 for the last 2 days in December were not paid and not recorded. The next payroll will be in January.
2. Rent payments of $8,000 was received for two months in advance on December 1. The entire amount was credited to Unearned Rent Revenue when paid.
3. Depreciation expense for 2020 is $9,000.

Instructions

Complete the following table to correct the financial statement amounts shown (indicate deductions with parentheses).

Item	Net Income	Total Assets	Total Liabilities	Owner's Equity
Incorrect balances	$70,000	$150,000	$70,000	$80,000
Effects of:				
Salaries and Wages	______	______	______	______
Rent Revenue	______	______	______	______
Depreciation	______	______	______	______
Correct balances	______	______	______	______

Prepare and post transaction and adjusting entries for prepayments.

E3.15 (LO 2) Action Quest Games Co. adjusts its accounts annually. The following information is available for the year ended December 31, 2020.

1. Purchased a 1-year insurance policy on June 1 for $1,800 cash.
2. Paid $6,500 on August 31 for 5 months' rent in advance.
3. On September 4, received $3,600 cash in advance from a company to sponsor a game each month for a total of 9 months for the most improved students at a local school.
4. Signed a contract for cleaning services starting December 1 for $1,000 per month. Paid for the first 2 months on November 30. (*Hint:* Use the account Prepaid Cleaning to record prepayments.)
5. On December 5, received $1,500 in advance from a gaming club. Determined that on December 31, $475 of these games had not yet been played.

Instructions

a. For each of the above transactions, prepare the journal entry to record the initial transaction.

b. For each of the above transactions, prepare the adjusting journal entry that is required on December 31, (*Hint:* Use the account Service Revenue for item 3 and Repairs and Maintenance Expense for item 4.)

c. Post the journal entries in parts (a) and (b) to T-accounts and determine the final balance in each account balance. (*Note:* Posting to the Cash account is not required.)

E3.16 (LO 3) Greenock Company has the following information available for accruals for the year ended December 31, 2020. The company adjusts its accounts annually.

Prepare adjusting and subsequent entries for accruals.

1. The December utility bill for $425 was unrecorded on December 31. Greenock paid the bill on January 11.
2. Greenock is open 7 days a week and employees are paid a total of $3,500 every Monday for a 7-day (Monday–Sunday) workweek. December 31 is a Thursday, so employees will have worked 4 days (Monday, December 28–Thursday, December 31) that they have not been paid for by year-end. Employees will be paid next on January 4.
3. Greenock signed a $48,000, 5% bank loan on November 1, 2019, due in 2 years. Interest is payable on the first day of each following month.
4. Greenock receives a fee from Pizza Shop next door for all pizzas sold to customers using Greenock's facility. The amount owed for December is $300, which Pizza Shop will pay on January 4. (*Hint:* Use the Service Revenue account.)
5. Greenock rented some of its unused warehouse space to a client for $6,000 a month, payable the first day of the following month. It received the rent for the month of December on January 2.

Instructions

a. For each situation, prepare the adjusting entry required at December 31. (Round all calculations to the nearest dollar.)

b. For each situation, prepare the journal entry to record the subsequent cash transaction in 2021.

E3.17 (LO 2, 3, 4) The trial balances before and after adjustment for Renfro Company at the end of its fiscal year are presented below.

Prepare adjusting entries from analysis of trial balances.

Renfro Company
Trial Balance
August 31, 2020

	Before Adjustment		After Adjustment	
	Dr.	**Cr.**	**Dr.**	**Cr.**
Cash	$10,400		$10,400	
Accounts Receivable	8,800		11,200	
Supplies	2,300		700	
Prepaid Insurance	4,000		2,500	
Equipment	14,000		14,000	
Accumulated Depreciation—Equipment		$ 3,600		$ 4,500
Accounts Payable		5,800		5,800
Salaries and Wages Payable		–0–		1,100
Unearned Rent Revenue		1,500		400
Owner's Capital		15,600		15,600
Service Revenue		34,000		36,400
Rent Revenue		11,000		12,100
Salaries and Wages Expense	17,000		18,100	
Supplies Expense	–0–		1,600	
Rent Expense	15,000		15,000	
Insurance Expense	–0–		1,500	
Depreciation Expense	–0–		900	
	$71,500	$71,500	$75,900	$75,900

Instructions

Prepare the adjusting entries that were made.

Prepare financial statements from adjusted trial balance.

E3.18 (LO 4) **Financial Statement** The adjusted trial balance for Renfro Company is given in E3.17.

Instructions

Prepare the income and owner's equity statements for the year and the balance sheet at August 31.

Record transactions on accrual basis; convert revenue to cash receipts.

E3.19 (LO 2, 3) The following data are taken from the comparative balance sheets of Bundies Billiards Club, which prepares its financial statements using the accrual basis of accounting.

December 31	2020	2019
Accounts receivable from members	$16,000	$ 8,000
Unearned service revenue	17,000	25,000

Members are billed based upon their use of the club's facilities. Unearned service revenues arise from the sale of gift certificates, which members can apply to their future use of club facilities. The 2020 income statement for the club showed that service revenue of $161,000 was earned during the year.

Instructions

(*Hint:* You will probably find it helpful to use T-accounts to analyze these data.)

a. Prepare journal entries for each of the following events that took place during 2020.

1. Accounts receivable from 2019 were all collected.
2. Gift certificates outstanding at the end of 2019 were all redeemed.
3. An additional $38,000 worth of gift certificates were sold during 2020. A portion of these was used by the recipients during the year; the remainder was still outstanding at the end of 2020.
4. Services performed for members for 2020 were billed to members.
5. Accounts receivable for 2020 (i.e., those billed in item [4] above) were partially collected.

b. Determine the amount of cash received by the club, with respect to member services, during 2020.

Journalize adjusting entries.

***E3.20 (LO 5)** Bob Zeller Company has the following balances in selected accounts on December 31, 2020.

Service Revenue	$40,000
Insurance Expense	2,400
Supplies Expense	2,450

All the accounts have normal balances. Bob Zeller Company debits prepayments to expense accounts when paid, and credits unearned revenues to revenue accounts when received. The following information below has been gathered at December 31, 2020.

1. Bob Zeller Company paid $2,400 for 12 months of insurance coverage on June 1, 2020.
2. On December 1, 2020, Bob Zeller Company collected $40,000 for consulting services to be performed from December 1, 2020, through March 31, 2021.
3. A count of supplies on December 31, 2020, indicates that supplies of $600 are on hand.

Instructions

Prepare the adjusting entries needed at December 31, 2020.

Journalize transactions and adjusting entries.

***E3.21 (LO 5)** At Sekon Company, prepayments are debited to expense when paid, and unearned revenues are credited to revenue when cash is received. During January of the current year, the following transactions occurred.

Jan.	2	Paid $1,920 for fire insurance protection for the year.
	10	Paid $1,700 for supplies.
	15	Received $6,100 for services to be performed in the future.

On January 31, it is determined that $2,100 of the services were performed and that there are $650 of supplies on hand.

Instructions

a. Journalize and post the January transactions. (Use T-accounts.)

b. Journalize and post the adjusting entries at January 31.

c. Determine the ending balance in each of the accounts.

***E3.22 (LO 6)** Presented below are the assumptions and principles discussed in this chapter.

Identify accounting assumptions and principles.

1. Full disclosure principle.
2. Going concern assumption.
3. Monetary unit assumption.
4. Time period assumption.
5. Historical cost principle.
6. Economic entity assumption.

Instructions

Identify by number the accounting assumption or principle that is described below. Do not use a number more than once.

_______ **a.** Is the rationale for why plant assets are not reported at liquidation value. (*Note:* Do not use the historical cost principle.)

_______ **b.** Indicates that personal and business recordkeeping should be separately maintained.

_______ **c.** Assumes that the monetary unit is the "measuring stick" used to report on financial performance.

_______ **d.** Separates financial information into time periods for reporting purposes.

_______ **e.** Measurement basis used when a reliable estimate of fair value is not available.

_______ **f.** Dictates that companies should disclose all circumstances and events that make a difference to financial statement users.

***E3.23 (LO 6)** Weber Co. had three major business transactions during 2020.

Identify the assumption or principle that has been violated.

a. Reported at its fair value of $260,000 merchandise inventory with a cost of $208,000.

b. The president of Weber Co., Austin Weber, purchased a truck for personal use and charged it to his expense account.

c. Weber Co. wanted to make its 2020 income look better, so it added 2 more weeks to the year (a 54-week year). Previous years were 52 weeks.

Instructions

In each situation, identify the assumption or principle that has been violated, if any, and discuss what the company should have done.

***E3.24 (LO 6)** The following characteristics, assumptions, principles, or constraint guide the FASB when it creates accounting standards.

Identity financial accounting concepts and principles.

Relevance	Expense recognition principle
Faithful representation	Time period assumption
Comparability	Going concern assumption
Consistency	Historical cost principle
Monetary unit assumption	Full disclosure principle
Economic entity assumption	Materiality

Match each item above with a description below.

1. _______ Ability to easily evaluate one company's results relative to another's.

2. _______ Requirement that a company will continue to operate for the foreseeable future.

3. _______ The judgment concerning whether an item's size is large enough to matter to decision-makers.

4. _______ The reporting of all information that would make a difference to financial statement users.

5. _______ The practice of preparing financial statements at regular intervals.

6. _______ The quality of information that indicates the information makes a difference in a decision.

7. _______ A belief that items should be reported on the balance sheet at the price that was paid to acquire them.

8. _______ A company's use of the same accounting principles and methods from year to year.

9. _______ Tracing accounting events to particular companies.

10. _______ The desire to minimize bias in financial statements.

11. _______ Reporting only those things that can be measured in monetary units.

12. _______ Dictates that efforts (expenses) be recognized in the period in which a company generates results (revenues).

Comment on the objective and qualitative characteristics of accounting information.

***E3.25 (LO 6) Writing** Speyeware International Inc., headquartered in Vancouver, Canada, specializes in Internet safety and computer security products for both the home and commercial markets. In a recent balance sheet, it reported a deficit of US$5,678,288. It has reported only net losses since its inception. In spite of these losses, Speyeware's shares of stock have traded anywhere from a high of $3.70 to a low of $0.32 on the Canadian Venture Exchange.

Speyeware's financial statements have historically been prepared in Canadian dollars. Recently, the company adopted the U.S. dollar as its reporting currency.

Instructions

a. What is the objective of financial reporting? How does this objective meet or not meet Speyeware's investors' needs?

b. Why would investors want to buy Speyeware's shares if the company has consistently reported losses over the last few years? Include in your answer an assessment of the relevance of the information reported on Speyeware's financial statements.

c. Comment on how the change in reporting information from Canadian dollars to U.S. dollars likely affected the readers of Speyeware's financial statements. Include in your answer an assessment of the comparability of the information.

Comment on the objective and qualitative characteristics of financial reporting.

***E3.26 (LO 6) Writing** A friend of yours, Mindy Gare, recently completed an undergraduate degree in science and has just started working with a biotechnology company. Mindy tells you that the owners of the business are trying to secure new sources of financing which are needed in order for the company to proceed with development of a new healthcare product. Mindy said that her boss told her that the company must put together a report to present to potential investors.

Mindy thought that the company should include in this package the detailed scientific findings related to the Phase I clinical trials for this product. She said, "I know that the biotech industry sometimes has only a 10% success rate with new products, but if we report all the scientific findings, everyone will see what a sure success this is going to be! The president was talking about the importance of following some set of accounting principles. Why do we need to look at some accounting rules? What they need to realize is that we have scientific results that are quite encouraging, some of the most talented employees around, and the start of some really great customer relationships. We haven't made any sales yet, but we will. We just need the funds to get through all the clinical testing and get government approval for our product. Then these investors will be quite happy that they bought in to our company early!"

Instructions

a. What is accounting information?

b. Comment on how Mindy's suggestions for what should be reported to prospective investors conforms to the qualitative characteristics of accounting information. Do you think that the things that Mindy wants to include in the information for investors will conform to financial reporting guidelines?

Problems: Set A

Prepare adjusting entries, post to ledger accounts, and prepare an adjusted trial balance.

P3.1A (LO 2, 3, 4) Logan Krause started her own consulting firm, Krause Consulting, on May 1, 2020. The trial balance at May 31 is as follows.

Krause Consulting
Trial Balance
May 31, 2020

Account Number		Debit	Credit
101	Cash	$ 4,500	
112	Accounts Receivable	6,000	
126	Supplies	1,900	
130	Prepaid Insurance	3,600	
149	Equipment	11,400	
201	Accounts Payable		$ 4,500
209	Unearned Service Revenue		2,000
301	Owner's Capital		18,700
400	Service Revenue		9,500
726	Salaries and Wages Expense	6,400	
729	Rent Expense	900	
		$34,700	$34,700

In addition to those accounts listed on the trial balance, the chart of accounts for Krause Consulting also contains the following accounts and account numbers: No. 150 Accumulated Depreciation—Equipment, No. 212 Salaries and Wages Payable, No. 631 Supplies Expense, No. 717 Depreciation Expense, No. 722 Insurance Expense, and No. 732 Utilities Expense.

Other data:

1. $900 of supplies have been used during the month.
2. Utilities expense incurred but not paid on May 31, 2020, $250.
3. The insurance policy is for 2 years.
4. $400 of the balance in the unearned service revenue account remains unearned at the end of the month.
5. May 31 is a Wednesday, and employees are paid on Fridays. Krause Consulting has two employees, who are paid $920 each for a 5-day work week.
6. The office furniture has a 5-year life with no salvage value. It is being depreciated at $190 per month for 60 months.
7. Invoices representing $1,700 of services performed during the month have not been recorded as of May 31.

Instructions

a. Prepare the adjusting entries for the month of May. Use J4 as the page number for your journal.

b. Post the adjusting entries to the ledger accounts. Enter the totals from the trial balance as beginning account balances and place a check mark in the posting reference column.

c. Prepare an adjusted trial balance at May 31, 2020.

c. Adj. trial balance $37,944

P3.2A (LO 2, 3, 4) Financial Statement Hank's Hotel opened for business on May 1, 2020. Its trial balance before adjustment on May 31 is as follows.

Prepare adjusting entries, post, and prepare adjusted trial balance and financial statements.

GLS

Hank's Hotel
Trial Balance
May 31, 2020

Account Number		Debit	Credit
101	Cash	$ 3,400	
126	Supplies	2,080	
130	Prepaid Insurance	2,400	
140	Land	12,000	
141	Buildings	60,000	
149	Equipment	15,000	
201	Accounts Payable		$ 4,700
208	Unearned Rent Revenue		3,300
275	Mortgage Payable		40,000
301	Owner's Capital		41,380
429	Rent Revenue		10,300
610	Advertising Expense	600	
726	Salaries and Wages Expense	3,300	
732	Utilities Expense	900	
		$99,680	$99,680

In addition to those accounts listed on the trial balance, the chart of accounts for Hank's Hotel also contains the following accounts and account numbers: No. 142 Accumulated Depreciation—Buildings, No. 150 Accumulated Depreciation—Equipment, No. 212 Salaries and Wages Payable, No. 230 Interest Payable, No. 619 Depreciation Expense, No. 631 Supplies Expense, No. 718 Interest Expense, and No. 722 Insurance Expense.

Other data:

1. Prepaid insurance is a 1-year policy starting May 1, 2020.
2. A count of supplies shows $750 of unused supplies on May 31.
3. Annual depreciation is $3,600 on the buildings and $1,500 on equipment.
4. The mortgage interest rate is 6%. (The mortgage was taken out on May 1.)
5. Two-thirds of the unearned rent revenue has been earned.
6. Salaries of $750 are accrued and unpaid at May 31.

c. Adj. trial balance $101,055

d. Net income $4,795
Ending capital $46,175
Total assets $92,925

Instructions

a. Journalize the adjusting entries on May 31.

b. Prepare a ledger using the three-column form of account. Enter the trial balance amounts and post the adjusting entries. (Use J1 as the posting reference.)

c. Prepare an adjusted trial balance on May 31.

d. Prepare an income statement and an owner's equity statement for the month of May and a balance sheet at May 31.

Prepare adjusting entries and financial statements.

P3.3A (LO 2, 3, 4) **Financial Statement** Alena Co. was organized on July 1, 2020. Quarterly financial statements are prepared. The unadjusted and adjusted trial balances as of September 30 are shown below.

Alena Co.
Trial Balance
September 30, 2020

	Unadjusted		Adjusted	
	Dr.	**Cr.**	**Dr.**	**Cr.**
Cash	$ 8,700		$ 8,700	
Accounts Receivable	10,400		11,500	
Supplies	1,500		650	
Prepaid Rent	2,200		500	
Equipment	18,000		18,000	
Accumulated Depreciation—Equipment		$ –0–		$ 700
Notes Payable		10,000		10,000
Accounts Payable		2,500		2,500
Salaries and Wages Payable		–0–		725
Interest Payable		–0–		100
Unearned Rent Revenue		1,900		450
Owner's Capital		22,000		22,000
Owner's Drawings	1,600		1,600	
Service Revenue		16,000		17,100
Rent Revenue		1,410		2,860
Salaries and Wages Expense	8,000		8,725	
Rent Expense	1,900		3,600	
Depreciation Expense			700	
Supplies Expense			850	
Utilities Expense	1,510		1,510	
Interest Expense			100	
	$53,810	$53,810	$56,435	$56,435

Instructions

b. Net income $4,475
Ending capital $24,875
Total assets $38,650

a. Journalize the adjusting entries that were made.

b. Prepare an income statement and an owner's equity statement for the 3 months ending September 30 and a balance sheet at September 30.

c. If the note bears interest at 12%, how many months has it been outstanding?

Prepare adjusting entries.

P3.4A (LO 2, 3) A review of the ledger of Gina Company at December 31, 2020, produces the following data pertaining to the preparation of annual adjusting entries.

1. Insurance expense $4,840

1. Prepaid Insurance $10,440. The company has separate insurance policies on its buildings and its motor vehicles. Policy B4564 on the building was purchased on April 1, 2019, for $7,920. The policy has a term of 3 years. Policy A2958 on the vehicles was purchased on January 1, 2020, for $4,400. This policy has a term of 2 years.

2. Rent revenue $75,500

2. Unearned Rent Revenue $429,000. The company began subleasing office space in its new building on November 1. At December 31, the company had the following rental contracts that are paid in full for the entire term of the lease.

Date	Term (in months)	Monthly Rent	Number of Leases
Nov. 1	9	$5,000	5
Dec. 1	6	$8,500	3

3. Notes Payable $120,000. This balance consists of a note for 9 months at an annual interest rate of 6%, dated November 1.

4. Salaries and Wages Payable $0. There are eight salaried employees. Salaries are paid every Friday for the current week. Five employees receive a salary of $700 each per week, and three employees earn $500 each per week. Assume December 31 is a Tuesday. Employees do not work weekends. All employees worked the last 2 days of December.

3. Interest expense $1,200

4. Salaries and wages expense $2,000

Instructions

Prepare the adjusting entries at December 31, 2020.

P3.5A (LO 2, 3, 4) **Financial Statement** On November 1, 2020, the account balances of Hamm Equipment Repair were as follows.

Journalize transactions and follow through accounting cycle to preparation of financial statements.

GLS

No.		Debit	No.		Credit
101	Cash	$ 2,400	154	Accumulated Depreciation—Equipment	$ 2,000
112	Accounts Receivable	4,250	201	Accounts Payable	2,600
126	Supplies	1,800	209	Unearned Service Revenue	1,200
153	Equipment	12,000	212	Salaries and Wages Payable	700
			301	Owner's Capital	13,950
		$20,450			$20,450

During November, the following summary transactions were completed.

Nov.	8	Paid $1,700 for salaries due employees, of which $700 is for October salaries.
	10	Received $3,620 cash from customers on account.
	12	Received $3,100 cash for services performed in November.
	15	Purchased equipment on account $2,000.
	17	Purchased supplies on account $700.
	20	Paid creditors on account $2,700.
	22	Paid November rent $400.
	25	Paid salaries $1,700.
	27	Performed services on account and billed customers for these services $2,200.
	29	Received $600 from customers for future service.

Adjustment data consist of:

1. Supplies on hand $1,400.
2. Accrued salaries payable $350.
3. Depreciation for the month is $200.
4. Services related to unearned service revenue of $1,220 were performed.

Instructions

a. Enter the November 1 balances in the ledger accounts.

b. Journalize the November transactions.

c. Post to the ledger accounts. Use J1 for the posting reference. Use the following additional accounts: No. 407 Service Revenue, No. 615 Depreciation Expense, No. 631 Supplies Expense, No. 726 Salaries and Wages Expense, and No. 729 Rent Expense.

d. Prepare a trial balance at November 30.

e. Journalize and post adjusting entries.

f. Prepare an adjusted trial balance.

g. Prepare an income statement and an owner's equity statement for November and a balance sheet at November 30.

d. Trial balance $25,650

f. Adj. trial balance $26,200

g. Net income $1,770; Ending capital $15,720 Total assets $19,250

***P3.6A (LO 2, 3, 4, 5)** **Financial Statement** Gabriel's Graphics Company was organized on January 1, 2020, by Gabriel Mediña. At the end of the first 6 months of operations, the trial balance contained the following accounts.

Prepare adjusting entries, adjusted trial balance, and financial statements using appendix.

	Debit		Credit
Cash	$ 8,600	Notes Payable	$ 20,000
Accounts Receivable	14,000	Accounts Payable	9,000
Equipment	45,000	Owner's Capital	22,000
Insurance Expense	2,700	Sales Revenue	52,100
Salaries and Wages Expense	30,000	Service Revenue	6,000
Supplies Expense	3,700		
Advertising Expense	1,900		
Rent Expense	1,500		
Utilities Expense	1,700		
	$109,100		$109,100

Analysis reveals the following additional data.

1. The $3,700 balance in Supplies Expense represents supplies purchased in January. At June 30, $1,300 of supplies are on hand.
2. The note payable was issued on February 1. It is a 6%, 6-month note.
3. The balance in Insurance Expense is the premium on a one-year policy, dated April 1, 2020.
4. Service revenues are credited to revenue when received. At June 30, services revenue of $1,300 are unearned.
5. Revenue for services performed but unrecorded at June 30 totals $2,000.
6. Depreciation is $2,250 per year.

Instructions

a. Journalize the adjusting entries at June 30. (Assume adjustments are recorded every 6 months.)

b. Prepare an adjusted trial balance.

c. Prepare an income statement and owner's equity statement for the 6 months ended June 30 and a balance sheet at June 30.

b. Adj. trial balance $112,725

c. Net income $19,000
Ending capital $41,000
Total assets $71,800

Continuing Case

Cookie Creations

(*Note:* This is a continuation of the Cookie Creations case from Chapters 1 and 2. Use the information from the previous chapters and follow the instructions below using the general ledger accounts you have already prepared.)

© leungchopan/ Shutterstock

CC3 It is the end of November and Natalie has been in touch with her grandmother. Her grandmother asked Natalie how well things went in her first month of business. Natalie, too, would like to know if she has been profitable or not during November. Natalie realizes that in order to determine Cookie Creations' income, she must first make adjustments.

Natalie puts together the following additional information.

1. A count reveals that $35 of baking supplies were used during November.
2. Natalie estimates that all of her baking equipment will have a useful life of 5 years or 60 months. (Assume Natalie decides to record a full month's worth of depreciation, regardless of when the equipment was obtained by the business.)
3. Natalie's grandmother has decided to charge interest of 6% on the note payable extended on November 16. The loan plus interest is to be repaid in 24 months. (Assume that half a month of interest accrued during November.)
4. On November 30, a friend of Natalie's asks her to teach a class at the neighborhood school. Natalie agrees and teaches a group of 35 first-grade students how to make gingerbread cookies. The next

day, Natalie prepares an invoice for $300 and leaves it with the school principal. The principal says that he will pass the invoice along to the head office, and it will be paid sometime in December.

5. Natalie receives a utilities bill for $45. The bill is for utilities consumed by Natalie's business during November and is due December 15.

Instructions

Using the information that you have gathered through Chapter 2, and based on the new information above, do the following.

a. Prepare and post the adjusting journal entries.

b. Prepare an adjusted trial balance.

c. Using the adjusted trial balance, calculate Cookie Creations' net income or net loss for the month of November. Do not prepare an income statement.

Ethics Case

EC3 Russell Company is a pesticide manufacturer. Its sales declined greatly this year due to the passage of legislation outlawing the sale of several of Russell's chemical pesticides. In the coming year, Russell will have environmentally safe and competitive chemicals to replace these discontinued products. Sales in the next year are expected to greatly exceed any prior year's. The decline in sales and profits appears to be a one-year aberration. But even so, the company president fears a large dip in the current year's profits. He believes that such a dip could cause a significant drop in the market price of Russell's stock and make the company a takeover target.

To avoid this possibility, the company president calls in Zoe Baas, controller, to discuss this period's year-end adjusting entries. He urges her to accrue every possible revenue and to defer as many expenses as possible. He says to Zoe, "We need the revenues this year, and next year can easily absorb expenses deferred from this year. We can't let our stock price be hammered down!" Zoe didn't get around to recording the adjusting entries until January 17, but she dated the entries December 31 as if they were recorded then. Zoe also made every effort to comply with the president's request.

Instructions

a. Who are the stakeholders in this situation?

b. What are the ethical considerations of (1) the president's request and (2) Zoe dating the adjusting entries December 31?

c. Can Zoe accrue revenues and defer expenses and still be ethical?

Expand Your Critical Thinking

Financial Reporting Problem: Apple Inc.

CT3.1 The financial statements of **Apple Inc.** are presented in Appendix A at the end of this textbook. The complete annual report, including the notes to the financial statements, is available at the company's website.

Instructions

a. Using the consolidated financial statements and related information, identify items that may result in adjusting entries for prepayments.

b. Using the consolidated financial statements and related information, identify items that may result in adjusting entries for accruals.

c. What has been the trend since 2013 for net income?

Comparative Analysis Problem: PepsiCo, Inc. vs. The Coca-Cola Company

CT3.2 **PepsiCo, Inc.**'s financial statements are presented in Appendix B. Financial statements of **The Coca-Cola Company** are presented in Appendix C. The complete annual reports of PepsiCo and Coca-Cola, including the notes to the financial statements, are available at each company's respective website.

Instructions

Based on information contained in these financial statements, determine the following for each company.

a. Net increase (decrease) in property, plant, and equipment (net) from 2014 to 2015.

b. Increase (decrease) in selling, general, and administrative expenses from 2014 to 2015.

c. Increase (decrease) in long-term debt (obligations) from 2014 to 2015.

d. Increase (decrease) in net income from 2014 to 2015.

e. Increase (decrease) in cash and cash equivalents from 2014 to 2015.

Comparative Analysis Problem: Amazon.com, Inc. vs. Wal-Mart Stores, Inc.

CT3.3 **Amazon.com, Inc.**'s financial statements are presented in Appendix D. Financial statements of **Wal-Mart Stores, Inc.** are presented in Appendix E. The complete annual reports of Amazon and Wal-Mart, including the notes to the financial statements, are available at each company's respective website.

Instructions

Based on information contained in these financial statements, determine the following for each company.

1. **a.** Increase (decrease) in interest expense from 2014 to 2015.

   b. Increase (decrease) in net income from 2014 to 2015.

   c. Increase (decrease) in cash flow from operations from 2014 to 2015.

2. Cash flow from operations and net income for each company is different. What are some possible reasons for these differences?

Real-World Focus

CT3.4 No financial decision-maker should ever rely solely on the financial information reported in the annual report to make decisions. It is important to keep abreast of financial news. This activity demonstrates how to search for financial news on the Internet.

Instructions

Conduct an Internet search and select an article that sounds interesting to you and that would be relevant to an investor in **Wal-Mart**, **Target Corp.**, or **Kmart**.

a. What was the source of the article (e.g., Reuters, Businesswire, Prnewswire)?

b. Assume that you are a personal financial planner and that one of your clients owns stock in the company. Write a brief memo to your client summarizing the article and explaining the implications of the article for his or her investment.

Decision-Making Across the Organization

CT3.5 **Financial Statement** Happy Camper Park was organized on April 1, 2019, by Erica Hatt. Erica is a good manager but a poor accountant. From the trial balance prepared by a part-time bookkeeper, Erica prepared the following income statement for the quarter that ended March 31, 2020.

Happy Camper Park
Income Statement
For the Quarter Ended March 31, 2020

Revenues		
Rent revenue		$90,000
Operating expenses		
Advertising	$ 5,200	
Salaries and wages	29,800	
Utilities	900	
Depreciation	800	
Maintenance and repairs	4,000	
Total operating expenses		40,700
Net income		$49,300

Erica thought that something was wrong with the statement because net income had never exceeded $20,000 in any one quarter. Knowing that you are an experienced accountant, she asks you to review the income statement and other data.

You first look at the trial balance. In addition to the account balances reported above in the income statement, the ledger contains the following additional selected balances at March 31, 2020.

Supplies	$ 6,200
Prepaid Insurance	7,200
Notes Payable	12,000

You then make inquiries and discover the following.

1. Rent revenues include advanced rentals for summer occupancy $15,000.
2. There were $1,700 of supplies on hand at March 31.
3. Prepaid insurance resulted from the payment of a one-year policy on January 1, 2020.
4. The mail on April 1, 2020, brought the following bills: advertising for week of March 24, $110; repairs made March 10, $260; and utilities, $180.
5. Salaries and wages expense total $300 per day. At March 31, 2 days' salaries and wages have been incurred but not paid.
6. The note payable is a 3-month, 10% note dated January 1, 2020.

Instructions

With the class divided into groups, answer the following.

a. Prepare a correct income statement for the quarter ended March 31, 2020.

b. Explain to Erica the generally accepted accounting principles that she did not recognize in preparing her income statement and their effect on her results.

Communication Activity

CT3.6 In reviewing the accounts of Terri Kahn Co. at the end of the year, you discover that adjusting entries have not been made.

Instructions

Write a memo to Terri Kahn, the owner of Terri Kahn Co., that explains the following: the nature and purpose of adjusting entries, why adjusting entries are needed, and the types of adjusting entries that may be made.

All About You

CT3.7 Companies must report or disclose in their financial statement information about all liabilities, including potential liabilities related to environmental cleanup. There are many situations in which you will be asked to provide personal financial information about your assets, liabilities, revenue, and expenses. Sometimes you will face difficult decisions regarding what to disclose and how to disclose it.

Instructions

Suppose that you are putting together a loan application to purchase a home. Based on your income and assets, you qualify for the mortgage loan, but just barely. How would you address each of the following situations in reporting your financial position for the loan application? Provide responses for each of the following situations.

a. You signed a guarantee for a bank loan that a friend took out for $25,000. If your friend doesn't pay, you will have to pay. Your friend has made all of the payments so far, and it appears he will be able to pay in the future.

b. You were involved in an auto accident in which you were at fault. There is the possibility that you may have to pay as much as $60,000 as part of a settlement. The issue will not be resolved before the bank processes your mortgage request.

c. The company for which you work isn't doing very well, and it has recently laid off employees. You are still employed, but it is quite possible that you will lose your job in the next few months.

Considering People, Planet, and Profit

CT3.8 Many companies have potential pollution or environmental-disposal problems—not only for electronic gadgets, but also for the lead paint or asbestos they sold. How do we fit these issues into the accounting equation? Are these costs and related liabilities that companies should report?

> **YES:** As more states impose laws holding companies responsible, and as more courts levy pollution-related fines, it becomes increasingly likely that companies will have to pay large amounts in the future.
>
> **NO:** The amounts still are too difficult to estimate. Putting inaccurate estimates on the financial statements reduces their usefulness. Instead, why not charge the costs later, when the actual environmental cleanup or disposal occurs, at which time the company knows the actual cost?

Instructions

Write a response indicating your position regarding this situation. Provide support for your view.

FASB Codification Activity

CT3.9 If your school has a subscription to the FASB Codification, log in and prepare responses to the following.

Instructions

Access the glossary ("Master Glossary") to answer the following.

a. What is the definition of revenue?

b. What is the definition of compensation?

A Look at IFRS

LEARNING OBJECTIVE 7

Compare the procedures for adjusting entries under GAAP and IFRS.

It is often difficult for companies to determine in what time period they should report particular revenues and expenses. Both the IASB and FASB are working on a joint project to develop a common conceptual framework that will enable companies to better use the same principles to record transactions consistently over time.

Key Points

Following are the key similarities and differences between GAAP and IFRS as related to accrual accounting.

Similarities

- In this chapter, you learned accrual-basis accounting applied under GAAP. Companies applying IFRS also use accrual-basis accounting to ensure that they record transactions that change a company's financial statements in the period in which events occur.
- Similar to GAAP, cash-basis accounting is not in accordance with IFRS.
- IFRS also divides the economic life of companies into artificial time periods. Under both GAAP and IFRS, this is referred to as the **time period assumption**.
- The **general** revenue recognition principle required by GAAP that is used in this textbook is similar to that used under IFRS.
- Revenue recognition fraud is a major issue in U.S. financial reporting. The same situation occurs in other countries, as evidenced by revenue recognition breakdowns at Dutch software company **Baan NV**, Japanese electronics giant **NEC**, and Dutch grocer **Ahold NV**.

Differences

- Under IFRS, revaluation (using fair value) of items such as land and buildings is permitted. IFRS allows depreciation based on revaluation of assets, which is not permitted under GAAP.
- The terminology used for revenues and gains, and expenses and losses, differs somewhat between IFRS and GAAP. For example, income under IFRS includes both revenues, which arise during the normal course of operating activities, and gains, which arise from activities outside of the normal sales of goods and services. The term income is not used this way under GAAP. Instead, under GAAP income refers to the net difference between revenues and expenses.
- Under IFRS, expenses include both those costs incurred in the normal course of operations as well as losses that are not part of normal operations. This is in contrast to GAAP, which defines each separately.

Looking to the Future

The IASB and FASB are completing a joint project on revenue recognition. The purpose of this project is to develop comprehensive guidance on when to recognize revenue. It is hoped that this approach will lead to more consistent accounting in this area.

IFRS Practice

IFRS Self-Test Questions

1. IFRS:
   a. uses accrual accounting.
   b. uses cash-basis accounting.
   c. allows revenue to be recognized when a customer makes an order.
   d. requires that revenue not be recognized until cash is received.
2. Which of the following statements is **false**?
   a. IFRS employs the time period assumption.
   b. IFRS employs accrual accounting.
   c. IFRS requires that revenues and costs must be capable of being measured reliably.
   d. IFRS uses the cash basis of accounting.
3. As a result of the revenue recognition project by the FASB and IASB:
   a. revenue recognition places more emphasis on when the performance obligation is satisfied.
   b. revenue recognition places more emphasis on when revenue is realized.
   c. revenue recognition places more emphasis on when expenses are incurred.
   d. revenue is no longer recorded unless cash has been received.
4. Which of the following is **false**?
   a. Under IFRS, the term income describes both revenues and gains.
   b. Under IFRS, the term expenses includes losses.
   c. Under IFRS, companies do not engage in the adjusting process.
   d. Under IFRS, revenue recognition fraud is a major issue.
5. Accrual-basis accounting:
   a. is optional under IFRS.
   b. results in companies recording transactions that change a company's financial statements in the period in which events occur.
   c. has been eliminated as a result of the IASB/FASB joint project on revenue recognition.
   d. is not consistent with the IASB conceptual framework.

International Financial Reporting Problem: Louis Vuitton

IFRS3.1 The financial statements of **Louis Vuitton** are presented in Appendix F. The complete annual report, including the notes to its financial statements, is available at the company's website.

Instructions

Visit Louis Vuitton's corporate website and answer the following questions from Louis Vuitton's 2015 annual report.

a. From the notes to the financial statements, how does the company determine the amount of revenue to record at the time of a sale?

b. From the notes to the financial statements, how does the company determine the provision for product returns?

c. Using the consolidated income statement and consolidated statement of financial position, identify items that may result in adjusting entries for deferrals.

d. Using the consolidated income statement, identify two items that may result in adjusting entries for accruals.

Answers to IFRS Self-Test Questions

1. a **2.** d **3.** a **4.** c **5.** b

CHAPTER 4

Comstock/Getty Images, Inc.

Completing the Accounting Cycle

Chapter Preview

As the following Feature Story highlights, at **Rhino Foods, Inc.**, financial statements help employees understand what is happening in the business. In Chapter 3, we prepared financial statements directly from the adjusted trial balance. However, with so many details involved in the end-of-period accounting procedures, it is easy to make errors. One way to minimize errors in the records and to simplify the end-of-period procedures is to use a worksheet.

In this chapter, we will explain the role of the worksheet in accounting. We also will study the remaining steps in the accounting cycle, especially the closing process, again using Pioneer Advertising as an example. Then, we will consider correcting entries and classified balance sheets.

Feature Story

Everyone Likes to Win

When Ted Castle was a hockey coach at the University of Vermont, his players were self-motivated by their desire to win. Hockey was a game you usually either won or lost. But at **Rhino Foods, Inc.**, a bakery-foods company he founded in Burlington, Vermont, he discovered that manufacturing-line workers were not so self-motivated. Ted thought, what if he turned the food-making business into a game, with rules, strategies, and trophies?

In a game, knowing the score is all-important. Ted felt that only if the employees know the score—know exactly how the business is doing daily, weekly, monthly—could he turn food-making into a game. But Rhino is a closely held, family-owned business, and its financial statements and profits were confidential. Ted wondered, should he open Rhino's books to the employees?

A consultant put Ted's concerns in perspective when he said, "Imagine you're playing touch football. You play for an hour or two, and the whole time I'm sitting there with a book, keeping score. All of a sudden I blow the whistle, and I say, 'OK, that's it. Everybody go home.' I close my book and walk away. How would you feel?" Ted opened his books and revealed the financial statements to his employees.

The next step was to teach employees the rules and strategies of how to "win" at making food. The first lesson: "Your opponent at Rhino is expenses. You must cut and control expenses." Ted and his staff distilled those lessons into daily scorecards—production reports and income statements—that keep Rhino's employees up-to-date on the game. At noon each day, Ted posts the previous day's results at the entrance to the production room. Everyone checks whether they made or lost money on what they produced the day before. And it's not just an academic exercise: There's a bonus check for each employee at the end of every four-week "game" that meets profitability guidelines.

Rhino has flourished since the first game. Employment has increased from 20 to 130 people, while both revenues and profits have grown dramatically.

Chapter Outline

LEARNING OBJECTIVES

LO 1 Prepare a worksheet.	• Steps in preparing a worksheet • Preparing financial statements from a worksheet • Preparing adjusting entries from a worksheet	**DO IT! 1** Worksheet
LO 2 Prepare closing entries and a post-closing trial balance.	• Preparing closing entries • Posting closing entries • Preparing a post-closing trial balance	**DO IT! 2** Closing Entries
LO 3 Explain the steps in the accounting cycle and how to prepare correcting entries.	• Summary of the accounting cycle • Reversing entries • Correcting entries	**DO IT! 3** Correcting Entries
LO 4 Identify the sections of a classified balance sheet.	• Current assets • Long-term investments • Property, plant, and equipment • Intangible assets • Current liabilities • Long-term liabilities • Owner's equity	**DO IT! 4** Balance Sheet Classifications

Go to the Review and Practice section at the end of the chapter for a review of key concepts and practice applications with solutions.
Visit WileyPLUS with ORION for additional tutorials and practice opportunities.

The Worksheet

LEARNING OBJECTIVE 1

Prepare a worksheet.

A **worksheet** is a multiple-column form used in the adjustment process and in preparing financial statements. As its name suggests, the worksheet is a working tool. **It is not a**

permanent accounting record. It is neither a journal nor a part of the general ledger. The worksheet is merely a device used in preparing adjusting entries and the financial statements. Companies generally computerize worksheets using an electronic spreadsheet program such as **Microsoft** Excel.

Illustration 4.1 shows the basic form of a worksheet and the five steps for preparing it. Each step is performed in sequence. **The use of a worksheet is optional.** When a company chooses to use one, it prepares financial statements directly from the worksheet. It enters the adjustments in the worksheet columns and then journalizes and posts the adjustments after it has prepared the financial statements. Thus, worksheets make it possible to provide the financial statements to management and other interested parties at an earlier date.

Steps in Preparing a Worksheet

We will use the October 31 trial balance and adjustment data of Pioneer Advertising from Chapter 3 to illustrate how to prepare a worksheet. In the following pages, we describe and then demonstrate each step of the process.

ILLUSTRATION 4.1

Form and procedure for a worksheet

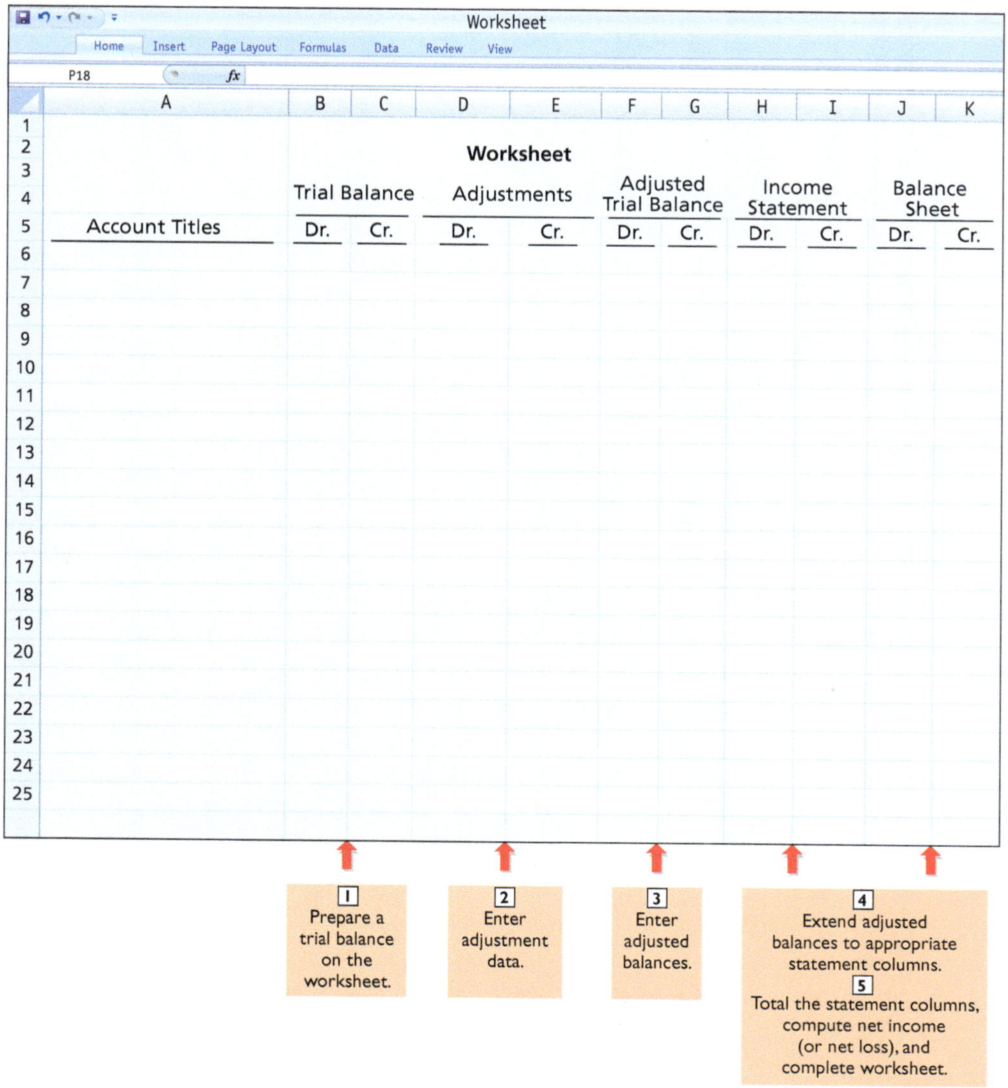

Step 1 Prepare a Trial Balance on the Worksheet

The first step in preparing a worksheet is to enter all ledger accounts with balances in the account titles column and then enter debit and credit amounts from the ledger in the trial balance columns. **Illustration 4.2** shows the worksheet trial balance for Pioneer Advertising. This trial balance is the same one that appears in Illustration 2.31 and Illustration 3.3.

ILLUSTRATION 4.2 **Preparing a trial balance**

Pioneer Advertising

Home Insert Page Layout Formulas Data Review View

P18 fx

Pioneer Advertising
Worksheet
For the Month Ended October 31, 2020

	Trial Balance		Adjustments		Adjusted Trial Balance		Income Statement		Balance Sheet	
Account Titles	Dr.	Cr.	Dr.	Cr.	Dr.	Cr.	Dr.	Cr.	Dr.	Cr.
Cash	15,200									
Supplies	2,500									
Prepaid Insurance	600									
Equipment	5,000									
Notes Payable		5,000								
Accounts Payable		2,500								
Unearned Service Revenue		1,200								
Owner's Capital		10,000								
Owner's Drawings	500									
Service Revenue		10,000								
Salaries and Wages Expense	4,000									
Rent Expense	900									
Totals	28,700	28,700								

Include all accounts with balances from ledger.

Trial balance amounts come directly from ledger accounts.

Step 2 Enter the Adjustments in the Adjustments Columns

As shown in **Illustration 4.3**, the second step when using a worksheet is to enter all adjustments in the adjustments columns. In entering the adjustments, use applicable trial balance accounts. If additional accounts are needed, insert them on the lines immediately below the trial balance totals. A different letter identifies the debit and credit for each adjusting entry. The term used to describe this process is **keying**. **Companies do not journalize the adjustments until after they complete the worksheet and prepare the financial statements.**

The adjustments for Pioneer Advertising are the same as the adjustments in Illustration 3.23. They are keyed in the adjustments columns of the worksheet as follows.

a. Pioneer debits an additional account, Supplies Expense, $1,500 for the cost of supplies used, and credits Supplies $1,500.

b. Pioneer debits an additional account, Insurance Expense, $50 for the insurance that has expired, and credits Prepaid Insurance $50.

c. The company needs two additional depreciation accounts. It debits Depreciation Expense $40 for the month's depreciation, and credits Accumulated Depreciation—Equipment $40.

d. Pioneer debits Unearned Service Revenue $400 for services performed, and credits Service Revenue $400.

e. Pioneer debits an additional account, Accounts Receivable, $200 for services performed but not billed, and credits Service Revenue $200.

f. The company needs two additional accounts relating to interest. It debits Interest Expense $50 for accrued interest, and credits Interest Payable $50.

g. Pioneer debits Salaries and Wages Expense $1,200 for accrued salaries, and credits an additional account, Salaries and Wages Payable, $1,200.

After Pioneer has entered all the adjustments, the adjustments columns are totaled to prove their equality.

ILLUSTRATION 4.3 **Entering the adjustments in the adjustments columns**

Pioneer Advertising

Home Insert Page Layout Formulas Data Review View

P18 fx

Pioneer Advertising
Worksheet
For the Month Ended October 31, 2020

	A	B	C	D	E	F	G	H	I	J	K
5–6		Trial Balance		Adjustments		Adjusted Trial Balance		Income Statement		Balance Sheet	
7	Account Titles	Dr.	Cr.	Dr.	Cr.	Dr.	Cr.	Dr.	Cr.	Dr.	Cr.
8	Cash	15,200									
9	Supplies	2,500			(a) 1,500						
10	Prepaid Insurance	600			(b) 50						
11	Equipment	5,000									
12	Notes Payable		5,000								
13	Accounts Payable		2,500								
14	Unearned Service Revenue		1,200	(d) 400							
15	Owner's Capital		10,000								
16	Owner's Drawings	500									
17	Service Revenue		10,000		(d) 400						
18					(e) 200						
19	Salaries and Wages Expense	4,000		(g) 1,200							
20	Rent Expense	900									
21	Totals	28,700	28,700								
22											
23											
24	Supplies Expense			(a) 1,500							
25	Insurance Expense			(b) 50							
26	Accum. Depreciation—										
27	Equipment				(c) 40						
28	Depreciation Expense			(c) 40							
29	Accounts Receivable			(e) 200							
30	Interest Expense			(f) 50							
31	Interest Payable				(f) 50						
32	Salaries and Wages Payable				(g) 1,200						
33	Totals			3,440	3,440						
34											
35											
36											

Add additional accounts as needed to complete the adjustments:
(a) Supplies Used.
(b) Insurance Expired.
(c) Depreciation Expensed.
(d) Service Revenue Recognized.
(e) Service Revenue Accrued.
(f) Interest Accrued.
(g) Salaries Accrued.

Enter adjustment amounts in appropriate columns, and use letters to cross-reference the debit and credit adjustments.

Total adjustments columns and check for equality.

Step 3 Enter Adjusted Balances in the Adjusted Trial Balance Columns

As shown in **Illustration 4.4**, Pioneer Advertising next determines the adjusted balance of an account by combining the amounts entered in the first four columns of the worksheet for each account. For example, the Prepaid Insurance account in the trial balance columns has a $600 debit balance and a $50 credit in the adjustments columns. The result is a $550 debit balance recorded in the adjusted trial balance columns. **For each account, the amount in the adjusted trial balance columns is the balance that will appear in the ledger after journalizing and posting the adjusting entries.** The balances in these columns are the same as those in the adjusted trial balance in Illustration 3.25.

After Pioneer has entered all account balances in the adjusted trial balance columns, the columns are totaled to prove their equality. If the column totals do not agree, the financial statement columns will not balance and the financial statements will be incorrect.

ILLUSTRATION 4.4 **Entering adjusted balances in the adjusted trial balance columns**

Pioneer Advertising
Worksheet
For the Month Ended October 31, 2020

Account Titles	Trial Balance Dr.	Trial Balance Cr.	Adjustments Dr.	Adjustments Cr.	Adjusted Trial Balance Dr.	Adjusted Trial Balance Cr.	Income Statement Dr.	Income Statement Cr.	Balance Sheet Dr.	Balance Sheet Cr.
Cash	15,200				15,200					
Supplies	2,500			(a) 1,500	1,000					
Prepaid Insurance	600			(b) 50	550					
Equipment	5,000				5,000					
Notes Payable		5,000				5,000				
Accounts Payable		2,500				2,500				
Unearned Service Revenue		1,200	(d) 400			800				
Owner's Capital		10,000				10,000				
Owner's Drawings	500				500					
Service Revenue		10,000		(d) 400		10,600				
				(e) 200						
Salaries and Wages Expense	4,000		(g) 1,200		5,200					
Rent Expense	900				900					
Totals	28,700	28,700								
Supplies Expense			(a) 1,500		1,500					
Insurance Expense			(b) 50		50					
Accum. Depreciation— Equipment				(c) 40		40				
Depreciation Expense			(c) 40		40					
Accounts Receivable			(e) 200		200					
Interest Expense			(f) 50		50					
Interest Payable				(f) 50		50				
Salaries and Wages Payable				(g) 1,200		1,200				
Totals			3,440	3,440	30,190	30,190				

Combine trial balance amounts with adjustment amounts to obtain the adjusted trial balance.

Total adjusted trial balance columns and check for equality.

Step 4 Extend Adjusted Trial Balance Amounts to Appropriate Financial Statement Columns

HELPFUL HINT

Every adjusted trial balance amount must be extended to one of the four statement columns.

As shown in **Illustration 4.5**, the fourth step is to extend adjusted trial balance amounts to the income statement and balance sheet columns of the worksheet (see **Helpful Hint**). Pioneer Advertising enters balance sheet accounts in the appropriate balance sheet debit and credit columns. For instance, it enters Cash in the balance sheet debit column, and Notes Payable in the balance sheet credit column. Pioneer extends Accumulated Depreciation—Equipment to the balance sheet credit column. The reason is that accumulated depreciation is a contra asset account with a credit balance.

Because the worksheet does not have columns for the owner's equity statement, Pioneer extends the balance in owner's capital to the balance sheet credit column. In addition, it extends the balance in owner's drawings to the balance sheet debit column because it is an owner's equity account with a debit balance.

The company enters the expense and revenue accounts such as Salaries and Wages Expense and Service Revenue in the appropriate income statement columns.

ILLUSTRATION 4.5 **Extending the adjusted trial balance amounts to appropriate financial statement columns**

Pioneer Advertising
Worksheet
For the Month Ended October 31, 2020

		Trial Balance		Adjustments		Adjusted Trial Balance		Income Statement		Balance Sheet	
	Account Titles	Dr.	Cr.	Dr.	Cr.	Dr.	Cr.	Dr.	Cr.	Dr.	Cr.
8	Cash	15,200				15,200				15,200	
9	Supplies	2,500			(a) 1,500	1,000				1,000	
10	Prepaid Insurance	600			(b) 50	550				550	
11	Equipment	5,000				5,000				5,000	
12	Notes Payable		5,000				5,000				5,000
13	Accounts Payable		2,500				2,500				2,500
14	Unearned Service Revenue		1,200	(d) 400			800				800
15	Owner's Capital		10,000				10,000				10,000
16	Owner's Drawings	500				500				500	
17	Service Revenue		10,000		(d) 400		10,600		10,600		
18					(e) 200						
19	Salaries and Wages Expense	4,000		(g) 1,200		5,200		5,200			
20	Rent Expense	900				900		900			
21	Totals	28,700	28,700								
22											
23											
24	Supplies Expense			(a) 1,500		1,500		1,500			
25	Insurance Expense			(b) 50		50		50			
26	Accum. Depreciation—										
27	Equipment				(c) 40		40				40
28	Depreciation Expense			(c) 40		40		40			
29	Accounts Receivable			(e) 200		200				200	
30	Interest Expense			(f) 50		50		50			
31	Interest Payable				(f) 50		50				50
32	Salaries and Wages Payable				(g) 1,200		1,200				1,200
33	Totals			3,440	3,440	30,190	30,190				

Extend all revenue and expense account balances to the income statement columns.

Extend all asset and liability account balances, as well as owner's capital and drawings account balances, to the balance sheet columns.

Step 5 Total the Statement Columns, Compute the Net Income (or Net Loss), and Complete the Worksheet

As shown in **Illustration 4.6**, Pioneer Advertising must now total each of the financial statement columns. The net income or loss for the period is the difference between the totals of the two income statement columns. If total credits exceed total debits, the result is net income. In such a case, the company inserts the words "Net Income" in the account titles space. It then enters the amount in the income statement debit column and the balance sheet credit column. **The debit amount balances the income statement columns; the credit amount balances the balance sheet columns.** In addition, the credit in the balance sheet column indicates the increase in owner's equity resulting from net income.

What if total debits in the income statement columns exceed total credits? In that case, Pioneer has a net loss. It enters the amount of the net loss in the income statement credit column and the balance sheet debit column.

After entering the net income or net loss, Pioneer determines new column totals. The totals shown in the debit and credit income statement columns will match. So will the totals shown in the debit and credit balance sheet columns. If either the income statement columns or the balance sheet columns are not equal after the net income or net loss has been entered, there is an error in the worksheet.

ILLUSTRATION 4.6 **Computing net income or net loss and completing the worksheet**

Pioneer Advertising

Pioneer Advertising
Worksheet
For the Month Ended October 31, 2020

	A	B	C	D	E	F	G	H	I	J	K
		Trial Balance		Adjustments		Adjusted Trial Balance		Income Statement		Balance Sheet	
7	Account Titles	Dr.	Cr.	Dr.	Cr.	Dr.	Cr.	Dr.	Cr.	Dr.	Cr.
8	Cash	15,200				15,200				15,200	
9	Supplies	2,500			(a) 1,500	1,000				1,000	
10	Prepaid Insurance	600			(b) 50	550				550	
11	Equipment	5,000				5,000				5,000	
12	Notes Payable		5,000				5,000				5,000
13	Accounts Payable		2,500				2,500				2,500
14	Unearned Service Revenue		1,200	(d) 400			800				800
15	Owner's Capital		10,000				10,000				10,000
16	Owner's Drawings	500				500				500	
17	Service Revenue		10,000		(d) 400		10,600		10,600		
18					(e) 200						
19	Salaries and Wages Expense	4,000		(g) 1,200		5,200		5,200			
20	Rent Expense	900				900		900			
21	Totals	28,700	28,700								
22											
23											
24	Supplies Expense			(a) 1,500		1,500		1,500			
25	Insurance Expense			(b) 50		50		50			
26	Accum. Depreciation—										
27	Equipment				(c) 40		40				40
28	Depreciation Expense			(c) 40		40		40			
29	Accounts Receivable			(e) 200		200				200	
30	Interest Expense			(f) 50		50		50			
31	Interest Payable				(f) 50		50				50
32	Salaries and Wages Payable				(g) 1,200		1,200				1,200
33	Totals			3,440	3,440	30,190	30,190	7,740	10,600	22,450	19,590
34											
35	Net Income							2,860			2,860
36	Totals							10,600	10,600	22,450	22,450

The difference between the totals of the two income statement columns determines net income or net loss.

Net income is extended to the credit column of the balance sheet columns. (Net loss would be extended to the debit column.)

Preparing Financial Statements from a Worksheet

After a company has completed a worksheet, it has at hand all the data required for preparation of financial statements. The income statement is prepared from the income statement columns. The owner's equity statement and balance sheet are prepared from the balance sheet columns. **Illustration 4.7** shows the financial statements prepared from Pioneer Advertising's

ILLUSTRATION 4.7

Financial statements from a worksheet

Pioneer Advertising
Income Statement
For the Month Ended October 31, 2020

Revenues		
Service revenue		$10,600
Expenses		
Salaries and wages expense	$5,200	
Supplies expense	1,500	
Rent expense	900	
Insurance expense	50	
Interest expense	50	
Depreciation expense	40	
Total expenses		7,740
Net income		$ 2,860

Pioneer Advertising
Owner's Equity Statement
For the Month Ended October 31, 2020

Owner's capital, October 1		$ -0-
Add: Investments	$10,000	
Net income	2,860	12,860
		12,860
Less: Drawings		500
Owner's capital, October 31		$12,360

Pioneer Advertising
Balance Sheet
October 31, 2020

Assets		
Cash		$15,200
Accounts receivable		200
Supplies		1,000
Prepaid insurance		550
Equipment	$5,000	
Less: Accumulated depreciation—equipment	40	4,960
Total assets		$21,910
Liabilities and Owner's Equity		
Liabilities		
Notes payable	$5,000	
Accounts payable	2,500	
Interest payable	50	
Unearned service revenue	800	
Salaries and wages payable	1,200	
Total liabilities		$ 9,550
Owner's equity		
Owner's capital		12,360
Total liabilities and owner's equity		$21,910

worksheet. At this point, the company has not journalized or posted adjusting entries. Therefore, ledger balances for some accounts are not the same as the financial statement amounts.

The amount shown for owner's capital on the worksheet is the account balance **before considering drawings and net income (or loss)**. When the owner has made no additional investments of capital during the period, this worksheet amount for owner's capital is the balance at the beginning of the period.

Using a worksheet, companies can prepare financial statements before they journalize and post adjusting entries. **However, the completed worksheet is not a substitute for formal financial statements.** The format of the data in the financial statement columns of the worksheet is not the same as the format of the financial statements. **A worksheet is essentially a working tool of the accountant**; companies do not distribute it to management and other parties.

Preparing Adjusting Entries from a Worksheet

A worksheet is not a journal, and it cannot be used as a basis for posting to ledger accounts. To adjust the accounts, the company must journalize the adjustments and post them to the ledger. **The adjusting entries are prepared from the adjustments columns of the worksheet.** The reference letters in the adjustments columns and the explanations of the adjustments at the bottom of the worksheet help identify the adjusting entries (see **Helpful Hint**). The journalizing and posting of adjusting entries **follows** the preparation of financial statements when a worksheet is used. The adjusting entries on October 31 for Pioneer Advertising are the same as those shown in Illustration 3.23.

HELPFUL HINT

Note that writing the explanation to the adjustment at the bottom of the worksheet is not required.

DO IT! 1 | Worksheet

Susan Elbe is preparing a worksheet. Explain to Susan how she should extend the following adjusted trial balance accounts to the financial statement columns of the worksheet.

Cash	Owner's Drawings
Accumulated Depreciation—Equipment	Service Revenue
Accounts Payable	Salaries and Wages Expense

Solution

Income statement debit column—Salaries and Wages Expense
Income statement credit column—Service Revenue
Balance sheet debit column—Cash; Owner's Drawings
Balance sheet credit column—Accumulated Depreciation—Equipment; Accounts Payable

Related exercise material: **BE4.1, BE4.2, BE4.3, DO IT! 4.1, E4.1, E4.2, E4.3, E4.5, and E4.6.**

ACTION PLAN

- **Balance sheet: Extend assets to debit column. Extend liabilities to credit column. Extend contra assets to credit column. Extend drawings account to debit column.**
- **Income statement: Extend expenses to debit column. Extend revenues to credit column.**

Closing the Books

LEARNING OBJECTIVE 2

Prepare closing entries and a post-closing trial balance.

ANALYZE → JOURNALIZE → POST → TRIAL BALANCE → ADJUSTING ENTRIES → ADJUSTED TRIAL BALANCE → PREPARE FINANCIAL STATEMENTS → **Journalize and post closing entries** → **Prepare a post-closing trial balance**

At the end of the accounting period, the company makes the accounts ready for the next period. This is called **closing the books**. In closing the books, the company distinguishes between temporary and permanent accounts.

ALTERNATIVE TERMINOLOGY

Temporary accounts are sometimes called *nominal accounts*, and permanent accounts are sometimes called *real accounts*.

Temporary accounts relate only to a given accounting period. They include all income statement accounts and the owner's drawings account. **The company closes all temporary accounts at the end of the period.**

In contrast, **permanent accounts** relate to one or more future accounting periods. They consist of all balance sheet accounts, including the owner's capital account. **Permanent accounts are not closed from period to period.** Instead, the company carries forward the balances of permanent accounts into the next accounting period. **Illustration 4.8** identifies the accounts in each category (see **Alternative Terminology**).

ILLUSTRATION 4.8

Temporary versus permanent accounts

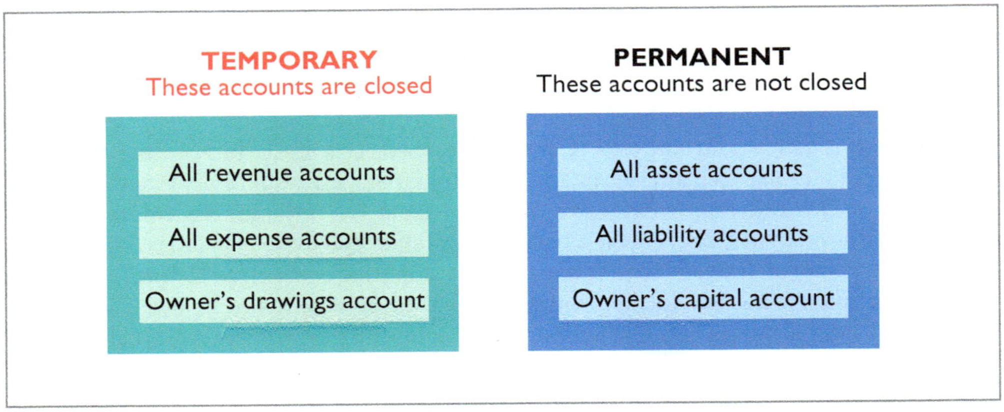

Preparing Closing Entries

At the end of the accounting period, the company transfers temporary account balances to the permanent owner's equity account, Owner's Capital, by means of closing entries.[1]

Closing entries formally recognize in the ledger the transfer of net income (or net loss) and owner's drawings to owner's capital. The owner's equity statement shows the results of these entries. **Closing entries also produce a zero balance in each temporary account.** The temporary accounts are then ready to accumulate data in the next accounting period separate from the data of prior periods. Permanent accounts are not closed.

Journalizing and posting closing entries is a required step in the accounting cycle (see Illustration 4.15). The company performs this step after it has prepared financial statements. In contrast to the steps in the cycle that you have already studied, companies generally journalize and post closing entries **only at the end of the annual accounting period**. Thus, all temporary accounts will contain data for the entire accounting period.

In preparing closing entries, companies could close each income statement account directly to owner's capital. However, to do so would result in excessive detail in the permanent Owner's Capital account. Instead, companies close the revenue and expense accounts to another temporary account, **Income Summary**, and then transfer the resulting net income or net loss from this account to owner's capital.

Companies **record closing entries in the general journal**. A center caption, Closing Entries, inserted in the journal between the last adjusting entry and the first closing entry, identifies these entries. Then the company posts the closing entries to the ledger accounts.

Companies generally prepare closing entries directly from the adjusted balances in the ledger. They could prepare separate closing entries for each nominal account, but the following four entries accomplish the desired result more efficiently:

1. Debit each revenue account for its balance, and credit Income Summary for total revenues.

[1]We explain closing entries for a partnership and for a corporation in Chapters 12 and 13, respectively.

2. Debit Income Summary for total expenses, and credit each expense account for its balance.
3. Debit Income Summary and credit Owner's Capital for the amount of net income.
4. Debit Owner's Capital for the balance in the Owner's Drawings account, and credit Owner's Drawings for the same amount (see **Helpful Hint**).

HELPFUL HINT

Owner's Drawings is closed directly to Owner's Capital and not to Income Summary. Owner's Drawings is not an expense.

Illustration 4.9 presents a diagram of the closing process. In it, the boxed numbers refer to the four entries required in the closing process.

ILLUSTRATION 4.9 **Diagram of closing process—proprietorship**

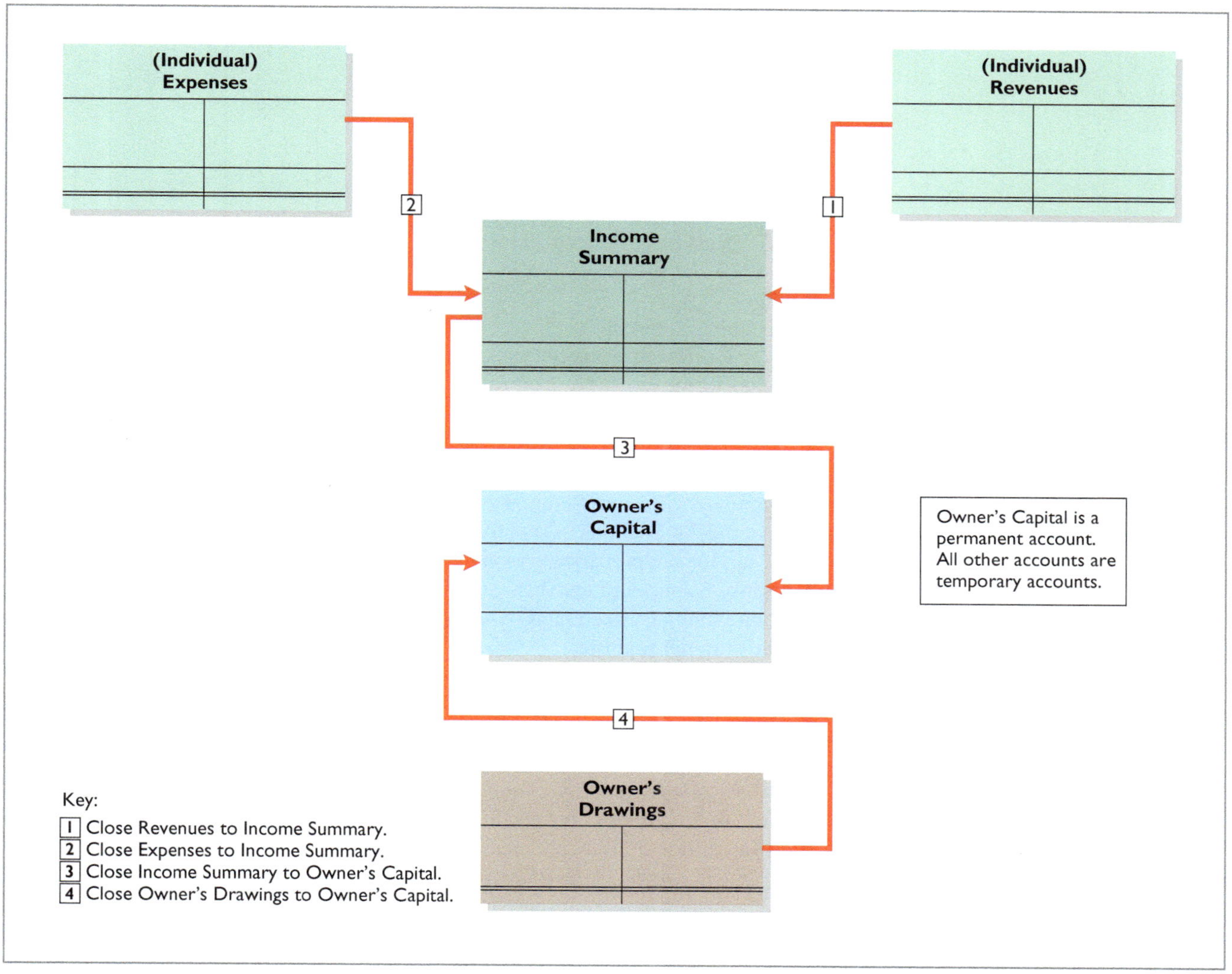

If there were a net loss (because expenses exceeded revenues), entry 3 in Illustration 4.9 would be reversed: there would be a credit to Income Summary and a debit to Owner's Capital.

Closing Entries Illustrated

In practice, companies generally prepare closing entries only at the end of the annual accounting period. However, to illustrate the journalizing and posting of closing entries, we will assume that Pioneer Advertising closes its books monthly. **Illustration 4.10** shows the closing entries at October 31. (The numbers in parentheses before each entry correspond to the four entries diagrammed in Illustration 4.9.)

ILLUSTRATION 4.10

Closing entries journalized

GENERAL JOURNAL J3

Date	Account Titles and Explanation	Ref.	Debit	Credit
	Closing Entries			
2020	(1)			
Oct. 31	Service Revenue	400	10,600	
	Income Summary	350		10,600
	(To close revenue account)			
	(2)			
31	Income Summary	350	7,740	
	Supplies Expense	631		1,500
	Depreciation Expense	711		40
	Insurance Expense	722		50
	Salaries and Wages Expense	726		5,200
	Rent Expense	729		900
	Interest Expense	905		50
	(To close expense accounts)			
	(3)			
31	Income Summary	350	2,860	
	Owner's Capital	301		2,860
	(To close net income to capital)			
	(4)			
31	Owner's Capital	301	500	
	Owner's Drawings	306		500
	(To close drawings to capital)			

Note that the amounts for Income Summary in entries (1) and (2) are the totals of the income statement credit and debit columns, respectively, in the worksheet.

A couple of cautions in preparing closing entries. (1) Avoid unintentionally doubling the revenue and expense balances rather than zeroing them. (2) Do not close Owner's Drawings through the Income Summary account. **Owner's Drawings is not an expense, and it is not a factor in determining net income.**

Posting Closing Entries

Illustration 4.11 shows the posting of the closing entries and the underlining (ruling) of the accounts. Note that all temporary accounts have zero balances after posting the closing entries. In addition, notice that the balance in owner's capital (Owner's Capital) represents the total equity of the owner at the end of the accounting period. This balance is shown on the balance sheet and is the ending capital reported on the owner's equity statement, as shown in Illustration 4.7. Pioneer Advertising uses the Income Summary account only in closing. It does not journalize and post entries to this account during the year (see **Helpful Hint**).

HELPFUL HINT

The balance in Income Summary before it is closed must equal the net income or net loss for the period.

As part of the closing process, Pioneer totals, balances, and double-underlines its temporary accounts—revenues, expenses, and Owner's Drawings, as shown in T-account form in Illustration 4.11. It does not close its permanent accounts—assets, liabilities, and Owner's Capital. Instead, Pioneer draws a single underline beneath the current-period entries for the permanent accounts. The account balance is then entered below the single underline and is carried forward to the next period (for example, see Owner's Capital).

ILLUSTRATION 4.11 **Posting of closing entries**

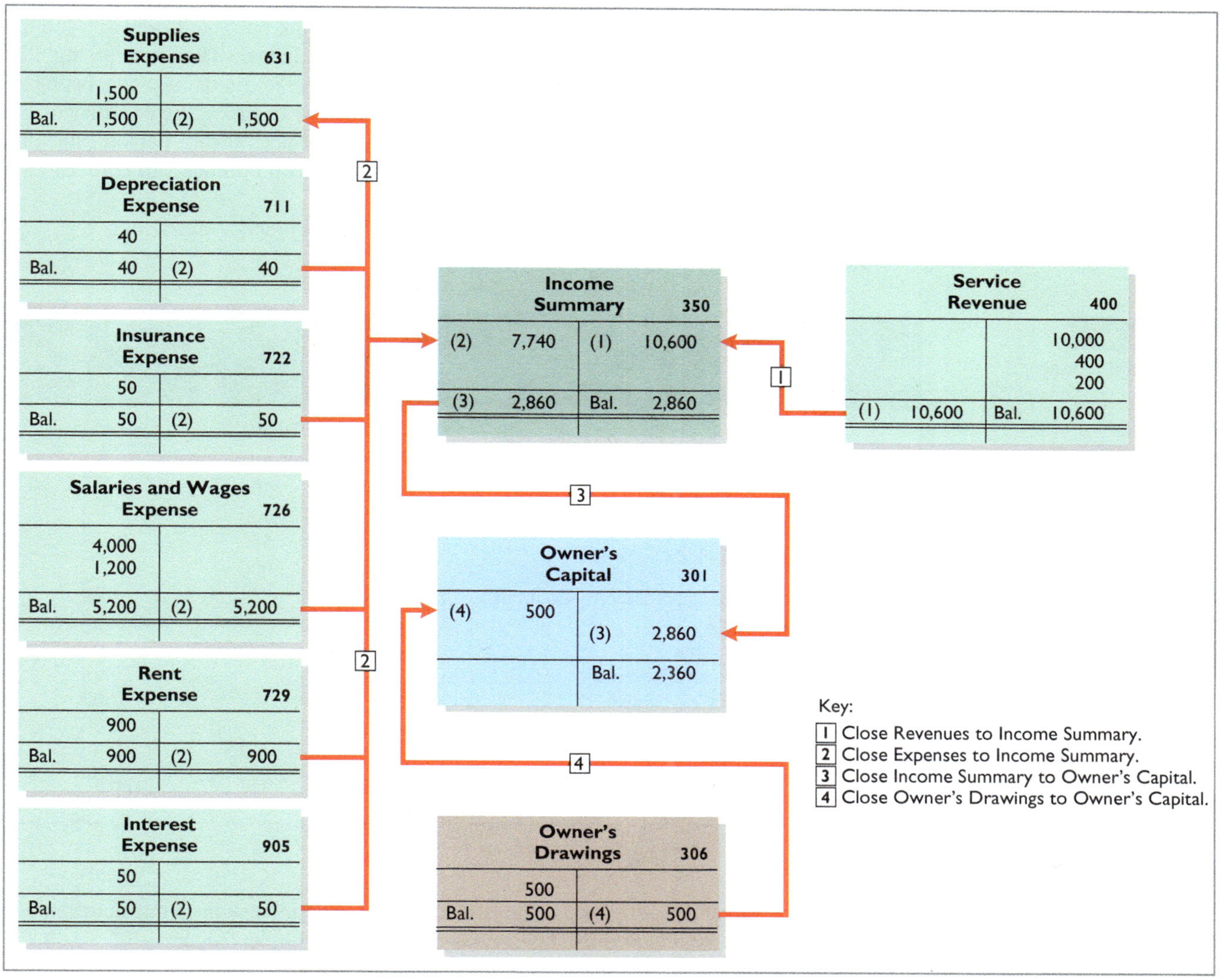

Accounting Across the Organization   Cisco Systems

© Steve Cole/iStockphoto

Performing the Virtual Close

Technology has dramatically shortened the closing process. Recent surveys have reported that the average company now takes only six to seven days to close, rather than the previous 20 days. But a few companies do much better. **Cisco Systems** can perform a "virtual close"—closing within 24 hours on any day in the quarter. The same is true at **Lockheed Martin Corp.**, which improved its closing time by 85% in just the last few years. Not very long ago, it took 14 to 16 days. Managers at these companies emphasize that this increased speed has not reduced the accuracy and completeness of the data.

This is not just showing off. Knowing exactly where you are financially all of the time allows the company to respond faster than its competitors. It also means that the hundreds of people who used to spend 10 to 20 days a quarter tracking transactions can now be more usefully employed on things such as mining data for business intelligence to find new business opportunities.

Source: "Reporting Practices: Few Do It All," *Financial Executive* (November 2003), p. 11.

Who else benefits from a shorter closing process? (Go to WileyPLUS for this answer and additional questions.)

Preparing a Post-Closing Trial Balance

After Pioneer Advertising has journalized and posted all closing entries, it prepares another trial balance, called a **post-closing trial balance**, from the ledger. The post-closing trial balance lists permanent accounts and their balances after the journalizing and posting of closing entries. The purpose of the post-closing trial balance is **to prove the equality of the permanent account balances carried forward into the next accounting period**. Since all temporary accounts will have zero balances, **the post-closing trial balance will contain only permanent—balance sheet—accounts**.

Illustration 4.12 shows the post-closing trial balance for Pioneer Advertising.

ILLUSTRATION 4.12
Post-closing trial balance

Pioneer Advertising
Post-Closing Trial Balance
October 31, 2020

	Debit	Credit
Cash	$15,200	
Accounts Receivable	200	
Supplies	1,000	
Prepaid Insurance	550	
Equipment	5,000	
Accumulated Depreciation—Equipment		$ 40
Notes Payable		5,000
Accounts Payable		2,500
Unearned Service Revenue		800
Salaries and Wages Payable		1,200
Interest Payable		50
Owner's Capital		12,360
	$21,950	$21,950

Pioneer prepares the post-closing trial balance from the permanent accounts in the ledger. Illustration 4.13 shows the permanent accounts in Pioneer's general ledger.

ILLUSTRATION 4.13 General ledger, permanent accounts

(Permanent Accounts Only)

GENERAL LEDGER

Cash — No. 101

Date	Explanation	Ref.	Debit	Credit	Balance
2020					
Oct. 1		J1	10,000		10,000
2		J1	1,200		11,200
3		J1		900	10,300
4		J1		600	9,700
20		J1		500	9,200
26		J1		4,000	5,200
31		J1	10,000		**15,200**

Accounts Receivable — No. 112

Date	Explanation	Ref.	Debit	Credit	Balance
2020					
Oct. 31	Adj. entry	J2	**200**		**200**

Supplies — No. 126

Date	Explanation	Ref.	Debit	Credit	Balance
2020					
Oct. 5		J1	2,500		2,500
31	Adj. entry	J2		**1,500**	**1,000**

Prepaid Insurance — No. 130

Date	Explanation	Ref.	Debit	Credit	Balance
2020					
Oct. 4		J1	600		600
31	Adj. entry	J2		**50**	**550**

Equipment — No. 157

Date	Explanation	Ref.	Debit	Credit	Balance
2020					
Oct. 1		J1	5,000		**5,000**

Accumulated Depreciation—Equipment — No. 158

Date	Explanation	Ref.	Debit	Credit	Balance
2020					
Oct. 31	Adj. entry	J2		**40**	**40**

Notes Payable — No. 200

Date	Explanation	Ref.	Debit	Credit	Balance
2020					
Oct. 1		J1		5,000	**5,000**

Accounts Payable — No. 201

Date	Explanation	Ref.	Debit	Credit	Balance
2020					
Oct. 5		J1		2,500	**2,500**

Unearned Service Revenue — No. 209

Date	Explanation	Ref.	Debit	Credit	Balance
2020					
Oct. 2		J1		1,200	1,200
31	Adj. entry	J2	400		**800**

Salaries and Wages Payable — No. 212

Date	Explanation	Ref.	Debit	Credit	Balance
2020					
Oct. 31	Adj. entry	J2		**1,200**	**1,200**

Interest Payable — No. 230

Date	Explanation	Ref.	Debit	Credit	Balance
2020					
Oct. 31	Adj. entry	J2		**50**	**50**

Owner's Capital — No. 301

Date	Explanation	Ref.	Debit	Credit	Balance
2020					
Oct. 1		J1		10,000	10,000
31	**Closing entry**	**J3**		**2,860**	**12,860**
31	**Closing entry**	**J3**	**500**		**12,360**

Note: The permanent accounts for Pioneer Advertising are shown here. Illustration 4.14 shows the temporary accounts. Both permanent and temporary accounts are part of the general ledger. They are segregated here to aid in learning.

A post-closing trial balance provides evidence that the company has properly journalized and posted the closing entries. It also shows that the accounting equation is in balance at the end of the accounting period. However, like the trial balance, it does not prove that Pioneer has recorded all transactions or that the ledger is correct. For example, the post-closing trial balance still will balance even if a transaction is not journalized and posted or if a transaction is journalized and posted twice.

The remaining accounts in the general ledger are temporary accounts, shown in **Illustration 4.14**. After Pioneer correctly posts the closing entries, each temporary account has a zero balance. These accounts are double-underlined to finalize the closing process.

ILLUSTRATION 4.14 General ledger, temporary accounts

(Temporary Accounts Only)

GENERAL LEDGER

Owner's Drawings No. 306

Date	Explanation	Ref.	Debit	Credit	Balance
2020					
Oct. 20		J1	500		500
31	**Closing entry**	**J3**		**500**	**–0–**

Income Summary No. 350

Date	Explanation	Ref.	Debit	Credit	Balance
2020					
Oct. 31	**Closing entry**	**J3**		**10,600**	**10,600**
31	**Closing entry**	**J3**	**7,740**		**2,860**
31	**Closing entry**	**J3**	**2,860**		**–0–**

Service Revenue No. 400

Date	Explanation	Ref.	Debit	Credit	Balance
2020					
Oct. 31		J1		10,000	10,000
31	Adj. entry	J2		400	10,400
31	Adj. entry	J2		200	10,600
31	**Closing entry**	**J3**	**10,600**		**–0–**

Supplies Expense No. 631

Date	Explanation	Ref.	Debit	Credit	Balance
2020					
Oct. 31	Adj. entry	J2	1,500		1,500
31	**Closing entry**	**J3**		**1,500**	**–0–**

Depreciation Expense No. 711

Date	Explanation	Ref.	Debit	Credit	Balance
2020					
Oct. 31	Adj. entry	J2	**40**		40
31	**Closing entry**	**J3**		**40**	**–0–**

Insurance Expense No. 722

Date	Explanation	Ref.	Debit	Credit	Balance
2020					
Oct. 31	Adj. entry	J2	**50**		50
31	**Closing entry**	**J3**		**50**	**–0–**

Salaries and Wages Expense No. 726

Date	Explanation	Ref.	Debit	Credit	Balance
2020					
Oct. 26		J1	4,000		4,000
31	Adj. entry	J2	**1,200**		5,200
31	**Closing entry**	**J3**		**5,200**	**–0–**

Rent Expense No. 729

Date	Explanation	Ref.	Debit	Credit	Balance
2020					
Oct. 3		J1	900		900
31	**Closing entry**	**J3**		**900**	**–0–**

Interest Expense No. 905

Date	Explanation	Ref.	Debit	Credit	Balance
2020					
Oct. 31	Adj. entry	J2	**50**		50
31	**Closing entry**	**J3**		**50**	**–0–**

Note: The temporary accounts for Pioneer Advertising are shown here. Illustration 4.13 shows the permanent accounts. Both permanent and temporary accounts are part of the general ledger. They are segregated here to aid in learning.

DO IT! 2 | Closing Entries

Hancock Company has the following balances in selected accounts of its adjusted trial balance.

Accounts Payable	$27,000	Owner's Drawings	$15,000
Service Revenue	98,000	Owner's Capital	42,000
Rent Expense	22,000	Accounts Receivable	38,000
Salaries and Wages Expense	51,000	Supplies Expense	7,000

Prepare the closing entries at December 31.

ACTION PLAN

- **Close revenue and expense accounts to Income Summary.**
- **Close Income Summary to Owner's Capital.**
- **Close Owner's Drawings to Owner's Capital.**

Solution

Dec. 31	Service Revenue	98,000	
	Income Summary		98,000
	(To close revenue account to Income Summary)		
31	Income Summary	80,000	
	Salaries and Wages Expense		51,000
	Rent Expense		22,000
	Supplies Expense		7,000
	(To close expense accounts to Income Summary)		

31	Income Summary ($98,000 – $80,000)	18,000	
	Owner's Capital		18,000
	(To close net income to owner's capital)		
31	Owner's Capital	15,000	
	Owner's Drawings		15,000
	(To close owner's drawings to owner's capital)		

Related exercise material: **BE4.4, BE4.5, BE4.6, DO IT! 4.2, E4.4, E4.7, E4.8, and E4.11.**

The Accounting Cycle and Correcting Entries

LEARNING OBJECTIVE 3

Explain the steps in the accounting cycle and how to prepare correcting entries.

Summary of the Accounting Cycle

Illustration 4.15 summarizes the steps in the accounting cycle. You can see that the cycle begins with the analysis of business transactions and ends with the preparation of a post-closing trial balance. Companies perform the steps in the cycle in sequence and repeat them in each accounting period.

Steps 1–3 may occur daily during the accounting period. Companies perform Steps 4–7 on a periodic basis, such as monthly, quarterly, or annually. Steps 8 and 9—closing entries and a post-closing trial balance—usually take place only at the end of a company's **annual** accounting period.

There are also two **optional steps** in the accounting cycle. As you have seen, companies may use a worksheet in preparing adjusting entries and financial statements. In addition, they may use reversing entries, as explained below.

Reversing Entries—An Optional Step

Some accountants prefer to reverse certain adjusting entries by making a **reversing entry** at the beginning of the next accounting period. A reversing entry is the exact opposite of the adjusting entry made in the previous period. **Use of reversing entries is an optional bookkeeping procedure; it is not a required step in the accounting cycle.** Accordingly, we have chosen to cover this topic in an appendix at the end of the chapter.

Correcting Entries—An Avoidable Step

Unfortunately, errors may occur in the recording process. Companies should correct errors, **as soon as they discover them**, by journalizing and posting **correcting entries**. If the accounting records are free of errors, no correcting entries are needed.

You should recognize several differences between correcting entries and adjusting entries. First, adjusting entries are an integral part of the accounting cycle. Correcting entries, on the other hand, are unnecessary if the records are error-free. Second, companies journalize and post adjustments **only at the end of an accounting period**. In contrast, companies make correcting entries **whenever they discover an error** (see **Ethics Note**). Finally, adjusting entries always affect at least one balance sheet account and one income statement account. In

ETHICS NOTE

When companies find errors in previously released income statements, they restate those numbers. Perhaps because of the increased scrutiny caused by Sarbanes-Oxley, in a recent year companies filed a record 1,195 restatements

ILLUSTRATION 4.15

Required steps in the accounting cycle

THE ACCOUNTING CYCLE

1. ANALYZE BUSINESS TRANSACTIONS

Equation Analysis

	Assets				= Liabilities	+ Owner's Equity			
	Cash	+ Accounts Receivable	+ Supplies	+ Equipment	= Accounts Payable	+ Owner's Capital	+ Revenues	− Expenses	
	$9,200		$1,600	$7,000	$1,850	$15,000	$1,200	$250	
(6)	+1,500	+$2,000					+3,500		Service Revenue
	$10,700 +	$2,000 +	$1,600 +	$7,000	= $1,850	+ $15,000 +	$4,700 −	$250	
	$21,300				$21,300				

2. JOURNALIZE THE TRANSACTIONS

GENERAL JOURNAL — PAGE J1

Date	Account Titles and Explanation	Ref.	Debit	Credit
2020				
Oct. 1	Cash	101	10,000	
	Owner's Capital	301		10,000
	(Owner's investment of cash in business)			
1	Equipment	157	5,000	
	Notes Payable	200		5,000
	(Issued 3-month, 12% note for office equipment)			
2	Cash	101	1,200	
	Unearned Service Revenue	209		1,200
	(Received cash from R. Knox for future services)			

3. POST TO THE LEDGER ACCOUNTS

GENERAL LEDGER

Cash — No. 101

Date	Explanation	Ref.	Debit	Credit	Balance
2020					
Oct. 1		J1	10,000		10,000
2		J1	1,200		11,200
3		J1		900	10,300
4		J1		600	9,700
20		J1		500	9,200
26		J1		4,000	5,200
31		J1	10,000		15,200

Supplies — No. 126

Date	Explanation	Ref.	Debit	Credit	Balance
2020					
Oct. 5		J1	2,500		2,500

Accounts Payable — No. 201

Date	Explanation	Ref.	Debit	Credit	Balance
2020					
Oct. 5		J1		2,500	2,500

Unearned Service Revenue — No. 209

Date	Explanation	Ref.	Debit	Credit	Balance
2020					
Oct. 2		J1		1,200	1,200

Owner's Capital — No. 301

Date	Explanation	Ref.	Debit	Credit	Balance
2020					
Oct. 1		J1		10,000	10,000

Owner's Drawings — No. 306

4. PREPARE A TRIAL BALANCE

Pioneer Advertising
Trial Balance
October 31, 2020

	Debit	Credit
Cash	$15,200	
Supplies	2,500	
Prepaid Insurance	600	
Equipment	5,000	
Notes Payable		$ 5,000
Accounts Payable		2,500
Unearned Service Revenue		1,200
Owner's Capital		10,000
Owner's Drawings	500	
Service Revenue		10,000

5. JOURNALIZE AND POST ADJUSTING ENTRIES: DEFERRALS/ACCRUALS

GENERAL JOURNAL — J2

Date	Account Titles and Explanation	Ref.	Debit	Credit
2020	Adjusting Entries			
Oct. 31	Supplies Expense	631	1,500	
31	I			
31	I			

GENERAL LEDGER

Cash — No. 101

Date	Explanation	Ref.	Debit	Credit	Balance
2020					
Oct. 1		J1	10,000		10,000
2		J1	1,200		11,200
3		J1		900	10,300
4		J1		600	9,700
20		J1		500	9,200
26		J1		4,000	5,200

Interest Payable — No. 230

Date	Explanation	Ref.	Debit	Credit	Balance
2020					
Oct. 31	Adj. entry	J2		50	50

Owner's Capital — No. 301

Date	Explanation	Ref.	Debit	Credit	Balance
2020					
Oct. 1		J1		10,000	10,000

6. PREPARE AN ADJUSTED TRIAL BALANCE

Pioneer Advertising
Adjusted Trial Balance
October 31, 2020

	Debit	Credit
Cash	$15,200	
Accounts Receivable	200	
Supplies	1,000	
Prepaid Insurance	550	
Equipment	5,000	
Accumulated Depreciation—Equipment		$ 40
Notes Payable		5,000
Accounts Payable		2,500
Interest Payable		50
Unearned Service Revenue		800
Salaries and Wages Payable		1,200

7. PREPARE FINANCIAL STATEMENTS

Pioneer Advertising
Income Statement
For the Month Ended October 31, 2020

Reven
Servi

Pioneer Advertising
Owner's Equity Statement
For the Month Ended October 31, 2020

Pioneer Advertising
Balance Sheet
October 31, 2020

Assets

Cash	$15,200
Accounts receivable	200
Supplies	1,000
Prepaid insurance	550

8. JOURNALIZE AND POST CLOSING ENTRIES

GENERAL JOURNAL — J3

Date	Account Titles and Explanation	Ref.	Debit	Credit
	Closing Entries			
2020	(1)			
Oct. 31	Service Revenue	400	10,600	
	Income Summary	350		10,600
	(To close revenue account)			
	(2)			
31	Income Summary	350	7,740	
	Supplies Expense	631		1,500
	Depreciation Expense	711		40
	Insurance Expense	722		50
	Salaries and Wages Expense	726		5,200
	Rent Expense	729		900

9. PREPARE A POST-CLOSING TRIAL BALANCE

Pioneer Advertising
Post-Closing Trial Balance
October 31, 2020

	Debit	Credit
Cash	$15,200	
Accounts Receivable	200	
Supplies	1,000	
Prepaid Insurance	550	
Equipment	5,000	
Accumulated Depreciation—Equipment		$ 40
Notes Payable		5,000
Accounts Payable		2,500
Unearned Service Revenue		800
Salaries and Wages Payable		1,200

contrast, correcting entries may involve any combination of accounts in need of correction. **Correcting entries must be posted before closing entries.**

To determine the correcting entry, it is useful to compare the incorrect entry with the correct entry. Doing so helps identify the accounts and amounts that should—and should not—be corrected. After comparison, the accountant makes an entry to correct the accounts. The following two cases for Mercato Co. illustrate this approach.

Case 1

On May 10, Mercato Co. journalized and posted a $50 cash collection on account from a customer as a debit to Cash $50 and a credit to Service Revenue $50. The company discovered the error on May 20, when the customer paid the remaining balance in full (see **Illustration 4.16**).

Incorrect Entry (May 10)			Correct Entry (May 10)		
Cash	50		Cash	50	
Service Revenue		50	Accounts Receivable		50

ILLUSTRATION 4.16

Comparison of entries

Comparison of the incorrect entry with the correct entry reveals that the debit to Cash $50 is correct. However, the $50 credit to Service Revenue should have been credited to Accounts Receivable. As a result, both Service Revenue and Accounts Receivable are overstated in the ledger. Mercato makes the correcting entry shown in **Illustration 4.17**.

	Correcting Entry		
May 20	Service Revenue	50	
	Accounts Receivable		50
	(To correct entry of May 10)		

ILLUSTRATION 4.17

Correcting entry

A	=	L	+	OE
				−50 Rev
−50				

Cash Flows
no effect

Case 2

On May 18, Mercato purchased on account equipment costing $450. The transaction was journalized and posted as a debit to Equipment $45 and a credit to Accounts Payable $45. The error was discovered on June 3, when Mercato received the monthly statement for May from the creditor (see **Illustration 4.18**).

Incorrect Entry (May 18)			Correct Entry (May 18)		
Equipment	45		Equipment	450	
Accounts Payable		45	Accounts Payable		450

ILLUSTRATION 4.18

Comparison of entries

Comparison of the two entries shows that two accounts are incorrect. Equipment is understated $405, and Accounts Payable is understated $405. Mercato makes the correcting entry shown in **Illustration 4.19**.

	Correcting Entry		
June 3	Equipment	405	
	Accounts Payable		405
	(To correct entry of May 18)		

ILLUSTRATION 4.19

Correcting entry

A	=	L	+	OE
+405				
		+405		

Cash Flows
no effect

Instead of preparing a correcting entry, **it is possible to reverse the incorrect entry and then prepare the correct entry**. This approach will result in more entries and postings than a correcting entry, but it will accomplish the desired result.

Accounting Across the Organization Yale Express

© Christian Lagereek/iStockphoto

Lost in Transportation

Yale Express, a short-haul trucking firm, turned over much of its cargo to local truckers to complete deliveries. Yale collected the entire delivery charge. When billed by the local trucker, Yale sent payment for the final phase to the local trucker. Yale used a cutoff period of 20 days into the next accounting period in making its adjusting entries for accrued liabilities. That is, it waited 20 days to receive the local truckers' bills to determine the amount of the unpaid but incurred delivery charges as of the balance sheet date.

On the other hand, **Republic Carloading**, a nationwide, long-distance freight forwarder, frequently did not receive transportation bills from truckers to whom it passed on cargo until months after the year-end. In making its year-end adjusting entries, Republic waited for months in order to include all of these outstanding transportation bills.

When Yale Express merged with Republic Carloading, Yale's vice president employed the 20-day cutoff procedure for both firms. As a result, millions of dollars of Republic's accrued transportation bills went unrecorded. When the company detected the error and made correcting entries, these and other errors changed a reported profit of $1.14 million into a loss of $1.88 million!

What might Yale Express's vice president have done to produce more accurate financial statements without waiting months for Republic's outstanding transportation bills? (Go to WileyPLUS for this answer and additional questions.)

DO IT! 3 | Correcting Entries

Sanchez Company discovered the following errors made in January 2020.

1. A payment of Salaries and Wages Expense of $600 was debited to Supplies and credited to Cash, both for $600.
2. A collection of $3,000 from a client on account was debited to Cash $200 and credited to Service Revenue $200.
3. The purchase of supplies on account for $860 was debited to Supplies $680 and credited to Accounts Payable $680.

Correct the errors without reversing the incorrect entry.

ACTION PLAN

- **Compare the incorrect entry with correct entry.**
- **After comparison, make an entry to correct the accounts.**

Solution

1. Salaries and Wages Expense	600	
Supplies		600
2. Service Revenue	200	
Cash	2,800	
Accounts Receivable		3,000
3. Supplies ($860 − $680)	180	
Accounts Payable		180

Related exercise material: **BE4.9, DO IT! 4.3, E4.12, and E4.13.**

Classified Balance Sheet

LEARNING OBJECTIVE 4

Identify the sections of a classified balance sheet.

The balance sheet presents a snapshot of a company's financial position at a point in time. To improve users' understanding of a company's financial position, companies often use a classified balance sheet. A **classified balance sheet** groups together similar assets and similar liabilities, using a number of standard classifications and sections. This is useful because items within a group have similar economic characteristics. A classified balance sheet generally contains the standard classifications listed in **Illustration 4.20**.

Assets	Liabilities and Owner's Equity
Current assets	Current liabilities
Long-term investments	Long-term liabilities
Property, plant, and equipment	Owner's (Stockholders') equity
Intangible assets	

ILLUSTRATION 4.20

Standard balance sheet classifications

These groupings help financial statement readers determine such things as (1) whether the company has enough assets to pay its debts as they come due, and (2) the claims of short- and long-term creditors on the company's total assets. Many of these groupings can be seen in the balance sheet of Franklin Company shown in **Illustration 4.21** (see **Helpful Hint**). In the sections that follow, we explain each of these groupings.

HELPFUL HINT

Recall that the basic accounting equation is Assets = Liabilities + Owner's Equity.

ILLUSTRATION 4.21

Classified balance sheet

Franklin Company
Balance Sheet
October 31, 2020

Assets			
Current assets			
Cash		$ 6,600	
Debt investments		2,000	
Accounts receivable		7,000	
Notes receivable		1,000	
Inventory		3,000	
Supplies		2,100	
Prepaid insurance		400	
Total current assets			$22,100
Long-term investments			
Stock investments		5,200	
Investment in real estate		2,000	7,200
Property, plant, and equipment			
Land		10,000	
Equipment	$24,000		
Less: Accumulated depreciation—equipment	5,000	19,000	29,000
Intangible assets			
Patents			3,100
Total assets			$61,400

ILLUSTRATION 4.21
(continued)

Liabilities and Owner's Equity

Current liabilities		
Notes payable	$11,000	
Accounts payable	2,100	
Unearned service revenue	900	
Salaries and wages payable	1,600	
Interest payable	450	
Total current liabilities		$16,050
Long-term liabilities		
Mortgage payable	10,000	
Notes payable	1,300	
Total long-term liabilities		11,300
Total liabilities		27,350
Owner's equity		
Owner's capital		34,050
Total liabilities and owner's equity		$61,400

Current Assets

Current assets are assets that a company expects to convert to cash or use up within one year or its operating cycle, whichever is longer. In Illustration 4.21, Franklin Company had current assets of $22,100. For most businesses, the cutoff for classification as current assets is one year from the balance sheet date. For example, accounts receivable are current assets because the company will collect them and convert them to cash within one year. Supplies is a current asset because the company expects to use them up in operations within one year.

Some companies use a period longer than one year to classify assets and liabilities as current because they have an operating cycle longer than one year. The **operating cycle** of a company is the average time that it takes to purchase inventory, sell it on account, and then collect cash from customers. For most businesses, this cycle takes less than a year so they use a one-year cutoff. But for some businesses, such as vineyards or airplane manufacturers, this period may be longer than a year. **Except where noted, we will assume that companies use one year to determine whether an asset or liability is current or long-term.**

Common types of current assets are (1) cash, (2) investments (such as short-term U.S. government securities), (3) receivables (notes receivable, accounts receivable, and interest receivable), (4) inventories, and (5) prepaid expenses (supplies and insurance). **On the balance sheet, companies usually list these items in the order in which they expect to convert them into cash.** Illustration 4.22 presents the current assets of **Southwest Airlines Co.**

ILLUSTRATION 4.22
Current assets section

Real World

Southwest Airlines Co.
Balance Sheet (partial)
(in millions)

Current assets	
Cash and cash equivalents	$1,355
Short-term investments	1,797
Accounts receivable	419
Inventories	467
Prepaid expenses and other current assets	418
Total current assets	$4,456

As we explain later in the chapter, a company's current assets are important in assessing its short-term debt-paying ability.

Long-Term Investments

Long-term investments are generally (1) investments in stocks and bonds of other companies that are normally held for many years, (2) long-term assets such as land or buildings that a company is not currently using in its operating activities, and (3) long-term notes receivable (see **Alternative Terminology**). In Illustration 4.21, Franklin Company reported total long-term investments of $7,200 on its balance sheet. **Alphabet Inc.** reported long-term investments in its balance sheet, as shown in **Illustration 4.23**.

ALTERNATIVE TERMINOLOGY

Long-term investments are often referred to simply as *investments*.

ILLUSTRATION 4.23

Long-term investments section

Real World

Alphabet Inc.
Balance Sheet (partial)
(in millions)

Long-term investments	
Non-marketable equity investments	$1,469

Property, Plant, and Equipment

Property, plant, and equipment are assets with relatively long useful lives that a company is currently using in operating the business. This category includes land, buildings, machinery and equipment, delivery equipment, and furniture (see **Alternative Terminology**). In Illustration 4.21, Franklin Company reported property, plant, and equipment of $29,000.

Depreciation is the practice of allocating the cost of assets to a number of years. Companies do this by systematically assigning a portion of an asset's cost as an expense each year (rather than expensing the full purchase price in the year of purchase). The assets that the company depreciates are reported on the balance sheet at cost less accumulated depreciation. The **accumulated depreciation** account shows the total amount of depreciation that the company has expensed thus far in the asset's life. In Illustration 4.21, Franklin Company reported accumulated depreciation of $5,000. **Illustration 4.24** presents the property, plant, and equipment of **Tesla Motors, Inc**.

ALTERNATIVE TERMINOLOGY

Property, plant, and equipment is sometimes called *fixed assets* or *plant assets*.

ILLUSTRATION 4.24

Property, plant, and equipment section

Real World

Tesla Motors, Inc.
Balance Sheet (partial)
(in thousands)

Property, plant, and equipment	
Machinery, equipment and office furniture	$ 322,394
Tooling	230,385
Leasehold improvements	94,763
Building and building improvements	67,707
Land	45,020
Computer equipment and software	42,073
Construction in progress	76,294
	878,636
Less: Accumulated depreciation	140,142
Total	$ 738,494

Intangible Assets

Many companies have long-lived assets that do not have physical substance yet often are very valuable. We call these assets **intangible assets** (see **Helpful Hint**). One significant intangible asset is goodwill. Others include patents, copyrights, and trademarks or trade names that give

HELPFUL HINT

Sometimes intangible assets are reported under a broader heading called "*Other assets*."

the company **exclusive right** of use for a specified period of time. In Illustration 4.21, Franklin Company reported intangible assets of $3,100. **Illustration 4.25** shows the intangible assets of media and theme-park giant **The Walt Disney Company** in a recent year.

ILLUSTRATION 4.25
Intangible assets section

Real World

The Walt Disney Company
Balance Sheet (partial)
(in millions)

Intangible assets and goodwill	
Character/franchise intangibles and copyrights	$ 5,830
Other amortizable intangible assets	903
Accumulated amortization	(1,204)
Net amortizable intangible assets	5,529
FCC licenses	667
Trademarks	1,218
Other indefinite lived intangible assets	20
	7,434
Goodwill	27,881
	$35,315

People, Planet, and Profit Insight

© Gehringi/iStockphoto

Regaining Goodwill

After falling to unforeseen lows amidst scandals, recalls, and economic crises, the American public's positive perception of the reputation of corporate America is on the rise. Overall corporate reputation is experiencing rehabilitation as the American public gives high marks overall to corporate America, specific industries, and the largest number of individual companies in a dozen years. This is according to the findings of a *Harris Interactive RQ Study,* which measures the reputations of the 60 most visible companies in the United States.

The survey focuses on six reputational dimensions that influence reputation and consumer behavior. Four of these dimensions, along with the five corporations that ranked highest within each, are as follows.

- **Social Responsibility**: (1) Whole Foods Market, (2) Johnson & Johnson, (3) Google, (4) The Walt Disney Company, (5) Procter & Gamble Co.
- **Emotional Appeal**: (1) Johnson & Johnson, (2) Amazon.com, (3) UPS, (4) General Mills, (5) Kraft Foods
- **Financial Performance**: (1) Google, (2) Berkshire Hathaway, (3) Apple, (4) Intel, (5) The Walt Disney Company
- **Products and Services**: (1) Intel Corporation, (2) 3M Company, (3) Johnson & Johnson, (4) Google, (5) Procter & Gamble Co.

Source: www.harrisinteractive.com.

Name two industries today which are probably rated low on the reputational characteristics of "being trusted" and "having high ethical standards." (Go to WileyPLUS for this answer and additional questions.)

ETHICS NOTE

A company that has more current assets than current liabilities can increase the ratio of current assets to current liabilities by using cash to pay off some current liabilities. This gives the appearance of being more liquid. Do you think this move is ethical?

Current Liabilities

In the liabilities and owner's equity section of the balance sheet, the first grouping is current liabilities. **Current liabilities** are obligations that the company is to pay within the coming year or its operating cycle, whichever is longer (see **Ethics Note**). Common examples are accounts payable, salaries and wages payable, notes payable, interest payable, and income taxes payable. Also included as current liabilities are current maturities of long-term obligations—payments to be made within the next year on long-term obligations. In Illustration 4.21, Franklin Company reported five different types of current liabilities, for a total of

$16,050. **Illustration 4.26** shows the current liabilities section adapted from the balance sheet of **Marcus Corporation**.

Real World

Marcus Corporation
Balance Sheet (partial)
(in thousands)

Current liabilities	
Notes payable	$ 239
Accounts payable	24,242
Current maturities of long-term debt	57,250
Other current liabilities	27,477
Income taxes payable	11,215
Salaries and wages payable	6,720
Total current liabilities	$127,143

ILLUSTRATION 4.26
Current liabilities section

Users of financial statements look closely at the relationship between current assets and current liabilities. This relationship is important in evaluating a company's **liquidity**—its ability to pay obligations expected to be due within the next year. When current assets exceed current liabilities, the likelihood for paying the liabilities is favorable. When the reverse is true, short-term creditors may not be paid, and the company may ultimately be forced into bankruptcy.

Accounting Across the Organization REL Consultancy Group

© Jorge Salcedo/iStockphoto

Can a Company Be Too Liquid?

There actually is a point where a company can be too liquid—that is, it can have too much working capital (current assets less current liabilities). While it is important to be liquid enough to be able to pay short-term bills as they come due, a company does not want to tie up its cash in extra inventory or receivables that are not earning the company money.

By one estimate from the **REL Consultancy Group**, the thousand largest U.S. companies have on their books cumulative excess working capital of $764 billion. Based on this figure, companies could have reduced debt by 36% or increased net income by 9%. Given that managers throughout a company are interested in improving profitability, it is clear that they should have an eye toward managing working capital. They need to aim for a "Goldilocks solution"—not too much, not too little, but just right.

Source: K. Richardson, "Companies Fall Behind in Cash Management," *Wall Street Journal* (June 19, 2007).

What can various company managers do to ensure that working capital is managed efficiently to maximize net income? (Go to WileyPLUS for this answer and additional questions.)

Long-Term Liabilities

Long-term liabilities are obligations that a company expects to pay **after** one year. Liabilities in this category include bonds payable, mortgages payable, long-term notes payable, lease liabilities, and pension liabilities. Many companies report long-term debt maturing after one year as a single amount in the balance sheet and show the details of the debt in notes that accompany the financial statements. Others list the various types of long-term liabilities. In Illustration 4.21, Franklin Company reported long-term liabilities of $11,300. **Illustration 4.27** shows the long-term liabilities that **Nike, Inc.** reported in its balance sheet in a recent year.

ILLUSTRATION 4.27
Long-term liabilities section

Real World

Nike, Inc.
Balance Sheet (partial)
(in millions)

Long-term liabilities	
Bonds payable	$1,106
Notes payable	51
Deferred income taxes and other	1,544
Total long-term liabilities	$2,701

Owner's Equity

The content of the owner's equity section varies with the form of business organization. In a proprietorship, there is one capital account. In a partnership, there is a capital account for each partner. Corporations divide owners' equity into two accounts—Common Stock (sometimes referred to as Capital Stock) and Retained Earnings. Corporations record stockholders' investments in the company by debiting an asset account and crediting the Common Stock account. They record in the Retained Earnings account income retained for use in the business. Corporations combine the Common Stock and Retained Earnings accounts and report them on the balance sheet as **stockholders' equity**. (We discuss these corporation accounts in later chapters.) **Nordstrom, Inc.** recently reported its stockholders' equity section as shown in **Illustration 4.28**.

ILLUSTRATION 4.28
Stockholders' equity section

Real World

Nordstrom, Inc.
Balance Sheet (partial)
(in thousands)

Stockholders' equity	
Common stock, 271,331 shares	$ 685,934
Retained earnings	1,406,747
Total stockholders' equity	$2,092,681

DO IT! 4 | Balance Sheet Classifications

The following accounts were taken from the financial statements of Callahan Company.

________ Salaries and wages payable
________ Service revenue
________ Interest payable
________ Goodwill
________ Debt investments (short-term)
________ Mortgage payable (due in 3 years)
________ Stock investments (long-term)
________ Equipment
________ Accumulated depreciation—equipment
________ Depreciation expense
________ Owner's capital
________ Unearned service revenue

Match each of the following to its proper balance sheet classification, shown below. If the item would not appear on a balance sheet, use "NA."

Current assets (CA)
Long-term investments (LTI)
Property, plant, and equipment (PPE)
Intangible assets (IA)
Current liabilities (CL)
Long-term liabilities (LTL)
Owner's equity (OE)

ACTION PLAN

- **Analyze whether each financial statement item is an asset, liability, or owner's equity.**
- **Determine if asset and liability items are short-term or long-term.**

Solution

__CL__ Salaries and wages payable
__NA__ Service revenue
__CL__ Interest payable
__IA__ Goodwill
__CA__ Debt investments (short-term)
__LTL__ Mortgage payable (due in 3 years)
__LTI__ Stock investments (long-term)
__PPE__ Equipment
__PPE__ Accumulated depreciation—equipment
__NA__ Depreciation expense
__OE__ Owner's capital
__CL__ Unearned service revenue

Related exercise material: **BE4.11, DO IT! 4.4, E4.14, E4.15, E4.16, and E4.17.**

Appendix 4A Reversing Entries

LEARNING OBJECTIVE *5

Prepare reversing entries.

After preparing the financial statements and closing the books, it is often helpful to reverse some of the adjusting entries before recording the regular transactions of the next period. Such entries are **reversing entries**. Companies make **a reversing entry at the beginning of the next accounting period**. Each reversing entry **is the exact opposite of the adjusting entry made in the previous period**. The recording of reversing entries is an **optional step** in the accounting cycle.

The purpose of reversing entries is to simplify the recording of a subsequent transaction related to an adjusting entry. For example, in Chapter 3, the payment of salaries after an adjusting entry resulted in two debits: one to Salaries and Wages Payable and the other to Salaries and Wages Expense. With reversing entries, the company can debit the entire subsequent payment to Salaries and Wages Expense. **The use of reversing entries does not change the amounts reported in the financial statements.** What it does is simplify the recording of subsequent transactions.

Reversing Entries Example

Companies most often use reversing entries to reverse two types of adjusting entries: accrued revenues and accrued expenses. To illustrate the optional use of reversing entries for accrued expenses, we will use the salaries expense transactions for Pioneer Advertising as illustrated in Chapters 2, 3, and 4. The transaction and adjustment data are as follows.

1. October 26 (initial salary entry): Pioneer pays $4,000 of salaries and wages earned between October 15 and October 26.
2. October 31 (adjusting entry): Salaries and wages earned between October 29 and October 31 are $1,200. The company will pay these in the November 9 payroll.
3. November 9 (subsequent salary entry): Salaries and wages paid are $4,000. Of this amount, $1,200 applied to accrued salaries and wages payable and $2,800 was earned between November 1 and November 9.

Illustration 4A.1 shows the entries with and without reversing entries.

ILLUSTRATION 4A.1 Comparative entries—without and with reversing

Without Reversing Entries (per chapter)				With Reversing Entries (per appendix)			
	Initial Salary Entry				Initial Salary Entry		
Oct. 26	Salaries and Wages Expense	4,000		Oct. 26	(Same entry)		
	Cash		4,000				
	Adjusting Entry				Adjusting Entry		
Oct. 31	Salaries and Wages Expense	1,200		Oct. 31	(Same entry)		
	Salaries and Wages Payable		1,200				
	Closing Entry				Closing Entry		
Oct. 31	Income Summary	5,200		Oct. 31	(Same entry)		
	Salaries and Wages Expense		5,200				
	Reversing Entry				Reversing Entry		
Nov. 1	No reversing entry is made.			Nov. 1	**Salaries and Wages Payable**	**1,200**	
					Salaries and Wages Expense		**1,200**
	Subsequent Salary Entry				Subsequent Salary Entry		
Nov. 9	Salaries and Wages Payable	1,200		Nov. 9	**Salaries and Wages Expense**	**4,000**	
	Salaries and Wages Expense	2,800			**Cash**		**4,000**
	Cash		4,000				

The first three entries are the same whether or not Pioneer uses reversing entries. The last two entries are different. The November 1 **reversing entry** eliminates the $1,200 balance in Salaries and Wages Payable created by the October 31 adjusting entry. The reversing entry also creates a $1,200 credit balance in the Salaries and Wages Expense account. As you know, it is unusual for an expense account to have a credit balance. The balance is correct in this instance, though, because it anticipates that the entire amount of the first salaries and wages payment in the new accounting period will be debited to Salaries and Wages Expense. This debit will eliminate the credit balance. The resulting debit balance in the expense account will equal the salaries and wages expense incurred in the new accounting period ($2,800 in this example).

If Pioneer makes reversing entries, it can debit all cash payments of expenses to the expense account. This means that on November 9 (and every payday) Pioneer can debit Salaries and Wages Expense for the amount paid, without regard to any accrued salaries and wages payable. Being able to make the **same entry each time** simplifies the recording process. The company can record subsequent transactions as if the related adjusting entry had never been made.

Illustration 4A.2 shows the posting of the entries with reversing entries.

ILLUSTRATION 4A.2 Postings with reversing entries

Salaries and Wages Expense

10/26	Paid	4,000			
31	Adjusting	1,200			
		5,200	10/31	Closing	5,200
11/9	Paid	4,000	**11/1**	**Reversing**	**1,200**

Salaries and Wages Payable

11/1	**Reversing**	**1,200**	10/31	Adjusting	1,200

A company can also use reversing entries for accrued revenue adjusting entries. For Pioneer, the adjusting entry was Accounts Receivable (Dr.) $200 and Service Revenue (Cr.) $200. Thus, the reversing entry on November 1 is:

A	=	L	+	OE
				−200 Rev
+200				

Cash Flows
no effect

Nov. 1	Service Revenue	200	
	Accounts Receivable		200
	(To reverse October 31 adjusting entry)		

When Pioneer collects the accrued service revenue, it debits Cash and credits Service Revenue.

Review and Practice

Learning Objectives Review

1 Prepare a worksheet.

The steps in preparing a worksheet are as follows. (a) Prepare a trial balance on the worksheet. (b) Enter the adjustments in the adjustments columns. (c) Enter adjusted balances in the adjusted trial balance columns. (d) Extend adjusted trial balance amounts to appropriate financial statement columns. (e) Total the statement columns, compute net income (or net loss), and complete the worksheet.

2 Prepare closing entries and a post-closing trial balance.

Closing the books occurs at the end of an accounting period. The process is to journalize and post closing entries and then underline and balance all accounts. In closing the books, companies make separate entries to close revenues and expenses to Income Summary, Income Summary to Owner's Capital, and Owner's Drawings to Owner's Capital. Only temporary accounts are closed. A post-closing trial balance contains the balances in permanent accounts that are carried forward to the next accounting period. The purpose of this trial balance is to prove the equality of these balances.

3 Explain the steps in the accounting cycle and how to prepare correcting entries.

The required steps in the accounting cycle are (1) analyze business transactions, (2) journalize the transactions, (3) post to ledger accounts, (4) prepare a trial balance, (5) journalize and post adjusting entries, (6) prepare an adjusted trial balance, (7) prepare financial statements, (8) journalize and post closing entries, and (9) prepare a post-closing trial balance.

One way to determine the correcting entry is to compare the incorrect entry with the correct entry. After comparison, the company makes a correcting entry to correct the accounts. An alternative to a correcting entry is to reverse the incorrect entry and then prepare the correct entry.

4 Identify the sections of a classified balance sheet.

A classified balance sheet categorizes assets as current assets; long-term investments; property, plant, and equipment; and intangibles. Liabilities are classified as either current or long-term. There is also an owner's (owners') equity section, which varies with the form of business organization.

***5 Prepare reversing entries.**

Reversing entries are the opposite of the adjusting entries made in the preceding period. Some companies choose to make reversing entries at the beginning of a new accounting period to simplify the recording of later transactions related to the adjusting entries. In most cases, only accrued adjusting entries are reversed.

Glossary Review

Classified balance sheet A balance sheet that contains standard classifications or sections. (p. 4-23).

Closing entries Entries made at the end of an accounting period to transfer the balances of temporary accounts to a permanent owner's equity account, Owner's Capital. (p. 4-12).

Correcting entries Entries to correct errors made in recording transactions. (p. 4-19).

Current assets Assets that a company expects to convert to cash or use up within one year or its operating cycle, whichever is longer. (p. 4-24).

Current liabilities Obligations that a company expects to pay within the coming year or its operating cycle, whichever is longer. (p. 4-26).

Income Summary A temporary account used in closing revenue and expense accounts. (p. 4-12).

Intangible assets Long-lived assets that do not have physical substance. (p. 4-25).

Liquidity The ability of a company to pay obligations expected to be due within the next year. (p. 4-27).

Long-term investments Generally, (1) investments in stocks and bonds of other companies that companies normally hold for many years; (2) long-term assets, such as land and buildings, not currently being used in operating activities; and (3) long-term notes receivable. (p. 4-25).

Long-term liabilities Obligations that a company expects to pay after one year. (p. 4-27).

Operating cycle The average time that it takes to purchase inventory, sell it on account, and then collect cash from customers. (p. 4-24).

Permanent (real) accounts Accounts that relate to one or more future accounting periods. Consist of all balance sheet accounts. Balances are carried forward to the next accounting period. (p. 4-12).

Post-closing trial balance A list of permanent accounts and their balances after a company has journalized and posted closing entries. (p. 4-16).

Property, plant, and equipment Assets with relatively long useful lives and currently being used in operations. (p. 4-25).

Reversing entry An entry, made at the beginning of the next accounting period that is the exact opposite of the adjusting entry made in the previous period. (p. 4-19).

Stockholders' equity The ownership claim of shareholders on total assets. It is to a corporation what owner's equity is to a proprietorship. (p. 4-28).

Temporary (nominal) accounts Accounts that relate only to a given accounting period. Consist of all income statement accounts and owner's drawings account. All temporary accounts are closed at end of the accounting period. (p. 4-12).

Worksheet A multiple-column form that may be used in making adjustments and in preparing financial statements. (p. 4-2).

Practice Multiple-Choice Questions

1. **(LO 1)** Which of the following statements is **incorrect** concerning the worksheet?
   - **a.** The worksheet is essentially a working tool of the accountant.
   - **b.** The worksheet is distributed to management and other interested parties.
   - **c.** The worksheet cannot be used as a basis for posting to ledger accounts.
   - **d.** Financial statements can be prepared directly from the worksheet before journalizing and posting the adjusting entries.

2. **(LO 1)** In a worksheet, net income is entered in the following columns:
   - **a.** income statement (Dr) and balance sheet (Dr).
   - **b.** income statement (Cr) and balance sheet (Dr).
   - **c.** income statement (Dr) and balance sheet (Cr).
   - **d.** income statement (Cr) and balance sheet (Cr).

3. **(LO 1)** In the unadjusted trial balance of its worksheet for the year ended December 31, 2020, Knox Company reported Equipment of $120,000. The year-end adjusting entries require an adjustment of

$15,000 for depreciation expense for the equipment. After the adjusted trial balance is completed, what amount should be shown in the financial statement columns?

- **a.** A debit of $105,000 for Equipment in the balance sheet column.
- **b.** A credit of $15,000 for Depreciation Expense in the income statement column.
- **c.** A debit of $120,000 for Equipment in the balance sheet column.
- **d.** A debit of $15,000 for Accumulated Depreciation—Equipment in the balance sheet column.

4. **(LO 2)** An account that will have a zero balance after closing entries have been journalized and posted is:

- **a.** Service Revenue.
- **b.** Supplies.
- **c.** Prepaid Insurance.
- **d.** Accumulated Depreciation—Equipment.

5. **(LO 2)** When a net loss has occurred, Income Summary is:

- **a.** debited and Owner's Capital is credited.
- **b.** credited and Owner's Capital is debited.
- **c.** debited and Owner's Drawings is credited.
- **d.** credited and Owner's Drawings is debited.

6. **(LO 2)** The closing process involves separate entries to close (1) expenses, (2) drawings, (3) revenues, and (4) income summary. The correct sequencing of the entries is:

- **a.** (4), (3), (2), (1).
- **b.** (1), (2), (3), (4).
- **c.** (3), (1), (4), (2).
- **d.** (3), (2), (1), (4).

7. **(LO 2)** Which types of accounts will appear in the post-closing trial balance?

- **a.** Permanent (real) accounts.
- **b.** Temporary (nominal) accounts.
- **c.** Accounts shown in the income statement columns of a worksheet.
- **d.** None of these answer choices is correct.

8. **(LO 3)** All of the following are required steps in the accounting cycle **except**:

- **a.** journalizing and posting closing entries.
- **b.** preparing financial statements.
- **c.** journalizing the transactions.
- **d.** preparing a worksheet.

9. **(LO 3)** The proper order of the following steps in the accounting cycle is:

- **a.** prepare unadjusted trial balance, journalize transactions, post to ledger accounts, journalize and post adjusting entries.
- **b.** journalize transactions, prepare unadjusted trial balance, post to ledger accounts, journalize and post adjusting entries.
- **c.** journalize transactions, post to ledger accounts, prepare unadjusted trial balance, journalize and post adjusting entries.
- **d.** prepare unadjusted trial balance, journalize and post adjusting entries, journalize transactions, post to ledger accounts.

10. **(LO 3)** When Lopez Company purchased supplies worth $600, it incorrectly recorded a credit to Supplies for $6,000 and a debit to Cash for $6,000. Before correcting this error:

- **a.** Cash is overstated and Supplies is overstated.
- **b.** Cash is understated and Supplies is understated.
- **c.** Cash is understated and Supplies is overstated.
- **d.** Cash is overstated and Supplies is understated.

11. **(LO 3)** Cash of $100 received at the time the service was performed was journalized and posted as a debit to Cash $100 and a credit to Accounts Receivable $100. Assuming the incorrect entry is not reversed, the correcting entry is:

- **a.** debit Service Revenue $100 and credit Accounts Receivable $100.
- **b.** debit Accounts Receivable $100 and credit Service Revenue $100.
- **c.** debit Cash $100 and credit Service Revenue $100.
- **d.** debit Accounts Receivable $100 and credit Cash $100.

12. **(LO 4)** The correct order of presentation in a classified balance sheet for the following current assets is:

- **a.** accounts receivable, cash, prepaid insurance, inventory.
- **b.** cash, inventory, accounts receivable, prepaid insurance.
- **c.** cash, accounts receivable, inventory, prepaid insurance.
- **d.** inventory, cash, accounts receivable, prepaid insurance.

13. **(LO 4)** A company has purchased a tract of land. It expects to build a production plant on the land in approximately 5 years. During the 5 years before construction, the land will be idle. The land should be reported as:

- **a.** property, plant, and equipment.
- **b.** land expense.
- **c.** a long-term investment.
- **d.** an intangible asset.

14. **(LO 4)** In a classified balance sheet, assets are usually classified using the following categories:

- **a.** current assets; long-term assets; property, plant, and equipment; and intangible assets.
- **b.** current assets; long-term investments; property, plant, and equipment; and tangible assets.
- **c.** current assets; long-term investments; tangible assets; and intangible assets.
- **d.** current assets; long-term investments; property, plant, and equipment; and intangible assets.

15. **(LO 4)** Current assets are listed:

- **a.** by expected conversion to cash.
- **b.** by importance.
- **c.** by longevity.
- **d.** alphabetically.

*16. **(LO 5)** On December 31, Harvey Kohl Company correctly made an adjusting entry to recognize $2,000 of accrued salaries payable. On January 8 of the next year, total salaries of $3,800 were paid. Assuming the correct reversing entry was made on January 1, the entry on January 8 will result in a credit to Cash $3,800 and the following debit(s):

a. Salaries and Wages Payable $1,800 and Salaries and Wages Expense $2,000.

b. Salaries and Wages Payable $2,000 and Salaries and Wages Expense $1,800.

c. Salaries and Wages Expense $3,800.

d. Salaries and Wages Payable $3,800.

Solutions

1. **b.** The worksheet is a working tool of the accountant; it is not distributed to management and other interested parties. The other choices are all true statements.

2. **c.** Net income is entered in the Dr column of the income statement and the Cr column of the balance sheet. The other choices are incorrect because net income is entered in the (a) Cr (not Dr) column of the balance sheet, (b) Dr (not Cr) column of the income statement and in the Cr (not Dr) column of the balance sheet, and (d) Dr (not Cr) column of the income statement.

3. **c.** A debit of $120,000 for Equipment would appear in the balance sheet column. The other choices are incorrect because (a) Equipment, less accumulated depreciation of $15,000, would total $105,000 under assets on the balance sheet, not on the worksheet; (b) a debit, not credit, for Depreciation Expense would appear in the income statement column; and (d) a credit, not debit, of $15,000 for Accumulated Depreciation—Equipment would appear in the balance sheet column.

4. **a.** The Service Revenue account will have a zero balance after closing entries have been journalized and posted because it is a temporary account. The other choices are incorrect because (b) Supplies, (c) Prepaid Insurance, and (d) Accumulated Depreciation—Equipment are all permanent accounts and therefore not closed in the closing process.

5. **b.** The effect of a net loss is a credit to Income Summary and a debit to Owner's Capital. The other choices are incorrect because (a) Income Summary is credited, not debited, and Owner's Capital is debited, not credited; (c) Income Summary is credited, not debited, and Owner's Drawings is not affected; and (d) Owner's Capital, not Owner's Drawings, is debited.

6. **c.** The correct order is (3) revenues, (1) expenses, (4) income summary, and (2) drawings. Therefore, choices (a), (b), and (d) are incorrect.

7. **a.** Permanent accounts appear in the post-closing trial balance. The other choices are incorrect because (b) temporary accounts and (c) income statement accounts are closed to a zero balance and are therefore not included in the post-closing trial balance. Choice (d) is wrong as there is only one correct answer for this question.

8. **d.** Preparing a worksheet is not a required step in the accounting cycle. The other choices are all required steps in the accounting cycle.

9. **c.** The proper order of the steps in the accounting cycle is (1) journalize transactions, (2) post to ledger accounts, (3) prepare unadjusted trial balance, and (4) journalize and post adjusting entries. Therefore, choices (a), (b), and (d) are incorrect.

10. **d.** This entry causes Cash to be overstated and Supplies to be understated. Supplies should have been debited (increasing supplies) and Cash should have been credited (decreasing cash). The other choices are incorrect because (a) Supplies is understated, not overstated; (b) Cash is overstated, not understated; and (c) Cash is overstated, not understated, and Supplies is understated, not overstated.

11. **b.** The correcting entry is to debit Accounts Receivable $100 and credit Service Revenue $100. The other choices are incorrect because (a) Service Revenue should be credited, not debited, and Accounts Receivable should be debited, not credited; (c) Service Revenue should be credited for $100, and Cash should not be included in the correcting entry as it was recorded properly; and (d) Accounts Receivable should be debited for $100 and Cash should not be included in the correcting entry as it was recorded properly.

12. **c.** Companies list current assets on balance sheet in the order of liquidity: cash, accounts receivable, inventory, and prepaid insurance. Therefore, choices (a), (b), and (d) are incorrect.

13. **c.** Long-term investments include long-term assets such as land that a company is not currently using in its operating activities. The other choices are incorrect because (a) land would be reported as property, plant, and equipment only if it is being currently used in the business; (b) land is an asset, not an expense; and (d) land has physical substance and thus is a tangible property.

14. **d.** These are the categories usually used in a classified balance sheet. The other choices are incorrect because the categories (a) "long-term assets" and (b) and (c) "tangible assets" are generally not used.

15. **a.** Current assets are listed in order of their liquidity, not (b) by importance, (c) by longevity, or (d) alphabetically.

*16. **c.** The use of reversing entries simplifies the recording of the first payroll following the end of the year by eliminating the need to make an entry to the Salaries and Wages Payable account. The other choices are incorrect because (a) Salaries and Wages Payable is not part of the payroll entry on January 8, and the debit to Salaries and Wages Expense should be for $3,800, not $2,000; and (b) and (d) the Salaries and Wages Expense account, not the Salaries and Wages Payable account, should be debited.

Practice Brief Exercises

Prepare closing entries from ledger balances.

1. **(LO 2)** The ledger of Quintana Company contains the following balances: Owner's Capital $40,000, Owner's Drawings $3,000, Service Revenue $65,000, Salaries and Wages Expense $39,000, and Maintenance and Repairs Expense $9,000. Prepare the closing entries at December 31.

Solution

1.

Dec. 31	Service Revenue	65,000	
	Income Summary		65,000
31	Income Summary	48,000	
	Salaries and Wages Expense		39,000
	Maintenance and Repairs Expense		9,000
31	Income Summary	17,000	
	Owner's Capital		17,000
31	Owner's Capital	3,000	
	Owner's Drawing		3,000

Prepare correcting entries.

2. **(LO 3)** At Shields Company, the following errors were discovered after the transactions had been journalized and posted. Prepare the correcting entries.

a. A cash sale to a customer for $780 was recorded as a debit to Cash $780 and a credit to Accounts Receivable $780.

b. The purchase of equipment on account for $1,730 was recorded as a debit to Equipment $1,370 and a credit to Accounts Payable $1,370.

Solution

2. a.	Accounts Receivable	780	
	Service Revenue		780
b.	Equipment ($1,730 – $1,370)	360	
	Accounts Payable		360

Prepare the current assets section of a balance sheet.

3. **(LO 4)** **Financial Statement** The balance sheet debit column of the worksheet for Miguel Company includes the following accounts: Accounts Receivable $25,000, Prepaid Insurance $7,000, Cash $8,000, Supplies $11,000, and Stock Investments (short-term) $14,000. Prepare the current assets section of the balance sheet, listing the accounts in proper sequence.

Solution

3.

Miguel Company
Partial Balance Sheet

Current assets	
Cash	$ 8,000
Stock investments	14,000
Accounts receivable	25,000
Supplies	11,000
Prepaid insurance	7,000
Total current assets	$65,000

Practice Exercises

Journalize and post closing entries, and prepare a post-closing trial balance.

1. **(LO 2)** Hercules Company ended its fiscal year on August 31, 2020. The company's adjusted trial balance as of the end of its fiscal year is as shown below.

Hercules Company
Adjusted Trial Balance
August 31, 2020

No.	Account Titles	Debit	Credit
101	Cash	$10,900	
112	Accounts Receivable	6,200	
157	Equipment	10,600	
167	Accumulated Depr.—Equip.		$ 5,400
201	Accounts Payable		2,800
208	Unearned Rent Revenue		1,200
301	Owner's Capital		31,700
306	Owner's Drawings	12,000	
404	Service Revenue		42,400
429	Rent Revenue		6,100
711	Depreciation Expense	2,700	
720	Salaries and Wages Expense	37,100	
732	Utilities Expense	10,100	
		$89,600	$89,600

Instructions

a. Prepare the closing entries using page J15 in a general journal.

b. Post to Owner's Capital and No. 350 Income Summary accounts. (Use the three-column form.)

c. Prepare a post-closing trial balance at August 31, 2020.

Solution

1. a.

GENERAL JOURNAL **J15**

Date	Account Titles	Ref.	Debit	Credit
Aug. 31	Service Revenue	404	42,400	
	Rent Revenue	429	6,100	
	Income Summary	350		48,500
	(To close revenue accounts)			
31	Income Summary	350	49,900	
	Salaries and Wages Expense	720		37,100
	Utilities Expense	732		10,100
	Depreciation Expense	711		2,700
	(To close expense accounts)			
31	Owner's Capital ($49,900 – $48,500)	301	1,400	
	Income Summary	350		1,400
	(To close net loss to capital)			
31	Owner's Capital	301	12,000	
	Owner's Drawings	306		12,000
	(To close drawings to capital)			

b.

Owner's Capital **No. 301**

Date	Explanation	Ref.	Debit	Credit	Balance
Aug. 31	Balance				31,700
31	Close net loss	J15	1,400		30,300
31	Close drawings	J15	12,000		18,300

Income Summary **No. 350**

Date	Explanation	Ref.	Debit	Credit	Balance
Aug. 31	Close revenue	J15		48,500	48,500
31	Close expenses	J15	49,000		(1,400)
31	Close net loss	J15		1,400	0

c.

Hercules Company
Post-Closing Trial Balance
August 31, 2020

	Debit	Credit
Cash	$10,900	
Accounts Receivable	6,200	
Equipment	10,600	
Accumulated Depreciation—Equipment		$ 5,400
Accounts Payable		2,800
Unearned Rent Revenue		1,200
Owner's Capital		18,300
	$27,700	$27,700

Prepare financial statements.

2. (LO 4) Financial Statement The adjusted trial balance for Hercules Company is presented in **Practice Exercise 1**.

Instructions

a. Prepare an income statement and an owner's equity statement for the year ended August 31, 2020. Hercules did not make any capital investments during the year.

b. Prepare a classified balance sheet at August 31, 2020.

Solution

2. **a.**

Hercules Company
Income Statement
For the Year Ended August 31, 2020

Revenues		
Service revenue	$42,400	
Rent revenue	6,100	
Total revenues		$48,500
Expenses		
Salaries and wages expense	37,100	
Utilities expense	10,100	
Depreciation expense	2,700	
Total expenses		49,900
Net loss		$ (1,400)

Hercules Company
Owner's Equity Statement
For the Year Ended August 31, 2020

Owner's capital, September 1, 2019		$ 31,700
Less: Net loss	$ 1,400	
Owner's drawings	12,000	13,400
Owner's capital, August 31, 2020		$ 18,300

b.

Hercules Company
Balance Sheet
August 31, 2020

Assets		
Current assets		
Cash	$10,900	
Accounts receivable	6,200	
Total current assets		$17,100
Property, plant, and equipment		
Equipment	10,600	
Less: Accumulated depreciation—equip.	5,400	5,200
Total assets		$22,300
Liabilities and Owner's Equity		
Current liabilities		
Accounts payable	$ 2,800	
Unearned rent revenue	1,200	
Total current liabilities		$ 4,000
Owner's equity		
Owner's capital		18,300
Total liabilities and owner's equity		$22,300

Practice Problem

(LO 1, 2, 4) **Financial Statement** At the end of its first month of operations, Pampered Pet Service has the following unadjusted trial balance.

Prepare worksheet and classified balance sheet, and journalize closing entries.

Pampered Pet Service
August 31, 2020
Trial Balance

	Debit	Credit
Cash	$ 5,400	
Accounts Receivable	2,800	
Supplies	1,300	
Prepaid Insurance	2,400	
Equipment	60,000	
Notes Payable		$40,000
Accounts Payable		2,400
Owner's Capital		30,000
Owner's Drawings	1,000	
Service Revenue		4,900
Salaries and Wages Expense	3,200	
Utilities Expense	800	
Advertising Expense	400	
	$77,300	$77,300

Other data:

1. Insurance expires at the rate of $200 per month.
2. $1,000 of supplies are on hand at August 31.
3. Monthly depreciation on the equipment is $900.
4. Interest of $500 on the notes payable has accrued during August.

Instructions

a. Prepare a worksheet.

b. Prepare a classified balance sheet assuming $35,000 of the notes payable are long-term.

c. Journalize the closing entries.

Solution

a.

Pampered Pet Service
Worksheet for the Month Ended August 31, 2020

	Trial Balance		Adjustments		Adjusted Trial Balance		Income Statement		Balance Sheet	
Account Titles	**Dr.**	**Cr.**	**Dr.**	**Cr.**	**Dr.**	**Cr.**	**Dr.**	**Cr.**	**Dr.**	**Cr.**
Cash	5,400				5,400				5,400	
Accounts Receivable	2,800				2,800				2,800	
Supplies	1,300			(b) 300	1,000				1,000	
Prepaid Insurance	2,400			(a) 200	2,200				2,200	
Equipment	60,000				60,000				60,000	
Notes Payable		40,000				40,000				40,000
Accounts Payable		2,400				2,400				2,400
Owner's Capital		30,000				30,000				30,000
Owner's Drawings	1,000				1,000				1,000	
Service Revenue		4,900				4,900		4,900		
Salaries and Wages Expense	3,200				3,200		3,200			
Utilities Expense	800				800		800			
Advertising Expense	400				400		400			
Totals	77,300	77,300								
Insurance Expense			(a) 200		200		200			
Supplies Expense			(b) 300		300		300			
Depreciation Expense			(c) 900		900		900			
Accumulated Depreciation—Equipment				(c) 900		900				900
Interest Expense			(d) 500		500		500			
Interest Payable				(d) 500		500				500
Totals			1,900	1,900	78,700	78,700	6,300	4,900	72,400	73,800
Net Loss								1,400	1,400	
Totals							6,300	6,300	73,800	73,800

Explanation: (a) insurance expired, (b) supplies used, (c) depreciation expensed, and (d) interest accrued.

b.

Pampered Pet Service
Balance Sheet
August 31, 2020

Assets

Current assets		
Cash	$ 5,400	
Accounts receivable	2,800	
Supplies	1,000	
Prepaid insurance	2,200	
Total current assets		$11,400
Property, plant, and equipment		
Equipment	60,000	
Less: Accumulated depreciation—equipment	900	59,100
Total assets		$70,500

Liabilities and Owner's Equity

Current liabilities		
Notes payable	$ 5,000	
Accounts payable	2,400	
Interest payable	500	
Total current liabilities		$ 7,900
Long-term liabilities		
Notes payable		35,000
Total liabilities		42,900
Owner's equity		
Owner's capital		27,600*
Total liabilities and owner's equity		$70,500

*Owner's capital $30,000 less drawings $1,000 and net loss $1,400.

c.

Aug. 31	Service Revenue	4,900	
	Income Summary		4,900
	(To close revenue account)		
31	Income Summary	6,300	
	Salaries and Wages Expense		3,200
	Depreciation Expense		900
	Utilities Expense		800
	Interest Expense		500
	Advertising Expense		400
	Supplies Expense		300
	Insurance Expense		200
	(To close expense accounts)		
31	Owner's Capital ($6,300 – $4,900)	1,400	
	Income Summary		1,400
	(To close net loss to capital)		
31	Owner's Capital	1,000	
	Owner's Drawings		1,000
	(To close drawings to capital)		

WileyPLUS

Brief Exercises, DO IT! Exercises, Exercises, Problems, and many additional resources are available for practice in WileyPLUS.

Note: All asterisked Questions, Exercises, and Problems relate to material in the appendix to the chapter.

Questions

1. "A worksheet is a permanent accounting record and its use is required in the accounting cycle." Do you agree? Explain.

2. Explain the purpose of the worksheet.

3. What is the relationship, if any, between the amount shown in the adjusted trial balance column for an account and that account's ledger balance?

4. If a company's revenues are $125,000 and its expenses are $113,000, in which financial statement columns of the worksheet will the net income of $12,000 appear? When expenses exceed revenues, in which columns will the difference appear?

5. Why is it necessary to prepare formal financial statements if all of the data are in the statement columns of the worksheet?

6. Identify the account(s) debited and credited in each of the four closing entries, assuming the company has net income for the year.

7. Describe the nature of the Income Summary account and identify the types of summary data that may be posted to this account.

8. What are the content and purpose of a post-closing trial balance?

9. Which of the following accounts would not appear in the post-closing trial balance? Interest Payable, Equipment, Depreciation Expense, Owner's Drawings, Unearned Service Revenue, Accumulated Depreciation—Equipment, and Service Revenue.

10. Distinguish between a reversing entry and an adjusting entry. Are reversing entries required?

11. Indicate, in the sequence in which they are made, the three required steps in the accounting cycle that involve journalizing.

12. Identify, in the sequence in which they are prepared, the three trial balances that are used in the accounting cycles.

13. How do correcting entries differ from adjusting entries?

14. What standard classifications are used in preparing a classified balance sheet?

15. What is meant by the term "operating cycle?"

16. Define current assets. What basis is used for arranging individual items within the current assets section?

17. Distinguish between long-term investments and property, plant, and equipment.

18. (a) What is the term used to describe the owner's equity section of a corporation? (b) Identify the two owners' equity accounts in a corporation and indicate the purpose of each.

19. Using **Apple**'s annual report, determine its current liabilities at September 27, 2014, and September 26, 2015. Were current liabilities higher or lower than current assets in these two years?

*20. Cigale Company prepares reversing entries. If the adjusting entry for interest payable is reversed, what type of an account balance, if any, will there be in Interest Payable and Interest Expense after the reversing entry is posted?

*21. At December 31, accrued salaries payable totaled $3,500. On January 10, total salaries of $8,000 are paid. (a) Assume that reversing entries are made at January 1. Give the January 10 entry, and indicate the Salaries and Wages Expense account balance after the entry is posted. (b) Repeat part (a) assuming reversing entries are not made.

Brief Exercises

List the steps in preparing a worksheet.

BE4.1 (LO 1) The steps in using a worksheet are presented in random order below. List the steps in the proper order by placing numbers 1–5 in the blank spaces.

a. _____ Prepare a trial balance on the worksheet.

b. _____ Enter adjusted balances.

c. _____ Extend adjusted balances to appropriate statement columns.

d. _____ Total the statement columns, compute net income (loss), and complete the worksheet.

e. _____ Enter adjustment data.

Prepare partial worksheet.

BE4.2 (LO 1) The ledger of Walters Company includes the following unadjusted balances: Prepaid Insurance $3,000, Service Revenue $60,000, and Salaries and Wages Expense $25,000. Adjusting entries are required for (a) expired insurance $1,800, (b) services performed $1,100 are billed and not yet collected, and (c) accrued salaries payable $900. Enter the unadjusted balances and adjustments into a worksheet and complete the worksheet for all accounts. (*Note:* You will need to add the following accounts: Accounts Receivable, Salaries and Wages Payable, and Insurance Expense.)

Identify worksheet columns for selected accounts.

BE4.3 (LO 1) The following selected accounts appear in the adjusted trial balance columns of the worksheet for Ashram Company: Accumulated Depreciation, Depreciation Expense, Owner's Capital, Owner's Drawings, Service Revenue, Supplies, and Accounts Payable. Indicate the financial statement column (income statement Dr., balance sheet Cr., etc.) to which each balance should be extended.

Prepare closing entries from ledger balances.

BE4.4 (LO 2) The ledger of Pitt Company contains the following balances: Owner's Capital $30,000, Owner's Drawings $2,000, Service Revenue $58,000, Salaries and Wages Expense $39,000, and Supplies Expense $7,000. Prepare the closing entries at December 31.

Post closing entries; underline and balance T-accounts.

BE4.5 (LO 2) Using the data in BE4.4, enter the balances in T-accounts, post the closing entries, and underline and balance the accounts.

Journalize and post closing entries using the three-column form of account.

BE4.6 (LO 2) The income statement for Salt Creek Golf Club for the month ending July 31 shows Service Revenue $17,800, Salaries and Wages Expense $9,600, Maintenance and Repairs Expense $2,500, and Net Income $5,700. Prepare the entries to close the revenue and expense accounts. Post the entries to the revenue and expense accounts, and complete the closing process for these accounts using the three-column form of account.

Identify post-closing trial balance accounts.

BE4.7 (LO 2) Using the data in BE4.3, identify the accounts that would be included in a post-closing trial balance.

BE4.8 (LO 3) The steps in the accounting cycle are listed in random order below. List the steps in proper sequence, assuming no worksheet is prepared, by placing numbers 1–9 in the blank spaces.

List the required steps in the accounting cycle in sequence.

a. ________ Prepare a trial balance.
b. ________ Journalize the transactions.
c. ________ Journalize and post closing entries.
d. ________ Prepare financial statements.
e. ________ Journalize and post adjusting entries.
f. ________ Post to ledger accounts.
g. ________ Prepare a post-closing trial balance.
h. ________ Prepare an adjusted trial balance.
i. ________ Analyze business transactions.

BE4.9 (LO 3) At Raymond Company, the following errors were discovered after the transactions had been journalized and posted. Prepare the correcting entries.

Prepare correcting entries.

1. A collection on account from a customer for $870 was recorded as a debit to Cash $870 and a credit to Service Revenue $870.
2. The purchase of store supplies on account for $1,510 was recorded as a debit to Supplies $1,150 and a credit to Accounts Payable $1,150.

BE4.10 (LO 4) **Financial Statement** The balance sheet debit column of the worksheet for Jolie Company includes the following accounts: Accounts Receivable $12,500, Prepaid Insurance $4,500, Cash $4,100, Supplies $5,200, and Debt Investments (short-term) $7,600. Prepare the current assets section of the balance sheet, listing the accounts in proper sequence.

Prepare the current assets section of a balance sheet.

BE4.11 (LO 4) The following are the major balance sheet classifications:

Classify accounts on balance sheet.

Current assets (CA)	Current liabilities (CL)
Long-term investments (LTI)	Long-term liabilities (LTL)
Property, plant, and equipment (PPE)	Owner's equity (OE)
Intangible assets (IA)	

Match each of the following accounts to its proper balance sheet classification.

________ Accounts payable	________ Income taxes payable
________ Accounts receivable	________ Debt investments (long-term)
________ Accumulated depreciation—buildings	________ Land
________ Buildings	________ Inventory
________ Cash	________ Patents
________ Copyrights	________ Supplies

***BE4.12 (LO 5)** At October 31, Miras Company made an accrued expense adjusting entry of $3,300 for salaries. Prepare the reversing entry on November 1, and indicate the balances in Salaries and Wages Payable and Salaries and Wages Expense after posting the reversing entry.

Prepare reversing entries.

DO IT! Exercises

DO IT! 4.1 (LO 1) Jordan Carr is preparing a worksheet. Explain to Jordan how he should extend the following adjusted trial balance accounts to the financial statement columns of the worksheet.

Prepare a worksheet.

Service Revenue	Accounts Receivable
Notes Payable	Accumulated Depreciation
Owner's Capital	Utilities Expense

DO IT! 4.2 (LO2) Paloma Company shows the following balances in selected accounts of its adjusted trial balance.

Prepare closing entries.

Supplies	$32,000	Service Revenue	$108,000
Supplies Expense	6,000	Salaries and Wages Expense	40,000
Accounts Receivable	12,000	Utilities Expense	8,000
Owner's Drawings	22,000	Rent Expense	18,000
Owner's Capital	70,000		

Prepare the closing entries at December 31.

Prepare correcting entries.

DO IT! 4.3 (LO 3) Hanson Company has an inexperienced accountant. During the first month on the job, the accountant made the following errors in journalizing transactions. All entries were posted as made.

1. The purchase of supplies for $650 cash was debited to Equipment $210 and credited to Cash $210.
2. A $500 withdrawal of cash for B. Hanson's personal use was debited to Salaries and Wages Expense $900 and credited to Cash $900.
3. A payment on account of $820 to a creditor was debited to Accounts Payable $280 and credited to Cash $280.

Prepare the correcting entries.

Match accounts to balance sheet classifications.

DO IT! 4.4 (LO 4) The following accounts were taken from the financial statements of Giles Company.

________	Interest revenue	________	Owner's capital
________	Utilities payable	________	Accumulated depreciation—equipment
________	Accounts payable	________	Equipment
________	Supplies	________	Salaries and wages expense
________	Bonds payable	________	Debt investments (long-term)
________	Goodwill	________	Unearned rent revenue

Match each of the accounts to its proper balance sheet classification, as shown below. If the item would not appear on a balance sheet, use "NA."

Current assets (CA)	Current liabilities (CL)
Long-term investments (LTI)	Long-term liabilities (LTL)
Property, plant, and equipment (PPE)	Owner's equity (OE)
Intangible assets (IA)	

Exercises

Complete the worksheet.

E4.1 (LO 1, 3) The trial balance columns of the worksheet for Dixon Company at June 30, 2020, are as follows.

Dixon Company
Worksheet
For the Month Ended June 30, 2020

	Trial Balance	
Account Titles	**Dr.**	**Cr.**
Cash	2,320	
Accounts Receivable	2,440	
Supplies	1,880	
Accounts Payable		1,120
Unearned Service Revenue		240
Owner's Capital		3,600
Service Revenue		2,400
Salaries and Wages Expense	560	
Miscellaneous Expense	160	
	7,360	7,360

Other data:

1. A physical count reveals $500 of supplies on hand.
2. $100 of the unearned revenue is still unearned at month-end.
3. Accrued salaries are $210.

Instructions

Enter the trial balance on a worksheet and complete the worksheet.

E4.2 (LO 1) The adjusted trial balance columns of the worksheet for Auburn Company are as follows.

Complete the worksheet.

Excel

Auburn Company
Worksheet (partial)
For the Month Ended April 30, 2020

Account Titles	Adjusted Trial Balance Dr.	Adjusted Trial Balance Cr.	Income Statement Dr.	Income Statement Cr.	Balance Sheet Dr.	Balance Sheet Cr.
Cash	10,000					
Accounts Receivable	7,840					
Prepaid Rent	2,280					
Equipment	23,050					
Accumulated Depreciation—Equip.		4,900				
Notes Payable		5,700				
Accounts Payable		4,920				
Owner's Capital		27,960				
Owner's Drawings	3,650					
Service Revenue		15,590				
Salaries and Wages Expense	10,840					
Rent Expense	760					
Depreciation Expense	650					
Interest Expense	57					
Interest Payable		57				
Totals	59,127	59,127				

Instructions

Complete the worksheet.

E4.3 (LO 1, 4) **Financial Statement** Worksheet data for Auburn Company are presented in E4.2. The owner did not make any additional investments in the business in April.

Prepare financial statements from worksheet.

Excel

Instructions

Prepare an income statement, an owner's equity statement, and a classified balance sheet.

E4.4 (LO 2) Worksheet data for Auburn Company are presented in E4.2.

Journalize and post closing entries and prepare a post-closing trial balance.

Instructions

a. Journalize the closing entries at April 30.

b. Post the closing entries to Income Summary and Owner's Capital. Use T-accounts.

c. Prepare a post-closing trial balance at April 30.

E4.5 (LO 1) The adjustments columns of the worksheet for Becker Company are shown below.

Prepare adjusting entries from a worksheet, and extend balances to worksheet columns.

Account Titles	Adjustments Debit	Adjustments Credit
Accounts Receivable	1,100	
Prepaid Insurance		300
Accumulated Depreciation—Equipment		900
Salaries and Wages Payable		500
Service Revenue		1,100
Salaries and Wages Expense	500	
Insurance Expense	300	
Depreciation Expense	900	
	2,800	2,800

Instructions

a. Prepare the adjusting entries.

b. Assuming the adjusted trial balance amount for each account is normal, indicate the financial statement column to which each balance should be extended.

Derive adjusting entries from worksheet data.

E4.6 (LO 1) Selected worksheet data for Bonita Company are presented below.

Account Titles	Trial Balance Dr.	Trial Balance Cr.	Adjusted Trial Balance Dr.	Adjusted Trial Balance Cr.
Accounts Receivable	?		34,000	
Prepaid Insurance	26,000		20,000	
Supplies	7,000		?	
Accumulated Depreciation—Equipment		12,000		?
Salaries and Wages Payable		?		5,600
Service Revenue		88,000		97,000
Insurance Expense			?	
Depreciation Expense			10,000	
Supplies Expense			4,500	
Salaries and Wages Expense	?		49,000	

Instructions

a. Fill in the missing amounts.

b. Prepare the adjusting entries that were made.

Prepare closing entries, and prepare a post-closing trial balance.

E4.7 (LO 2) Victoria Lee Company had the following adjusted trial balance.

Victoria Lee Company
Adjusted Trial Balance
For the Month Ended June 30, 2020

Account Titles	Adjusted Trial Balance Debit	Adjusted Trial Balance Credit
Cash	$ 3,712	
Accounts Receivable	3,904	
Supplies	480	
Accounts Payable		$ 1,382
Unearned Service Revenue		160
Owner's Capital		5,760
Owner's Drawings	550	
Service Revenue		4,300
Salaries and Wages Expense	1,260	
Miscellaneous Expense	256	
Supplies Expense	1,900	
Salaries and Wages Payable		460
	$12,062	$12,062

Instructions

a. Prepare closing entries at June 30, 2020.

b. Prepare a post-closing trial balance.

Journalize and post closing entries, and prepare a post-closing trial balance.

E4.8 (LO 2) Phoebe Company ended its fiscal year on July 31, 2020. The company's adjusted trial balance as of the end of its fiscal year is as follows.

Phoebe Company
Adjusted Trial Balance
July 31, 2020

No.	Account Titles	Debit	Credit
101	Cash	$ 9,840	
112	Accounts Receivable	8,780	
157	Equipment	15,900	
158	Accumulated Depreciation—Equip.		$ 7,400
201	Accounts Payable		4,220
208	Unearned Rent Revenue		1,800
301	Owner's Capital		45,200
306	Owner's Drawings	16,000	
400	Service Revenue		64,000
429	Rent Revenue		6,500
711	Depreciation Expense	8,000	
726	Salaries and Wages Expense	55,700	
732	Utilities Expense	14,900	
		$129,120	$129,120

Instructions

a. Prepare the closing entries using page J15.

b. Post to Owner's Capital and No. 350 Income Summary accounts. (Use the three-column form.)

c. Prepare a post-closing trial balance at July 31.

E4.9 (LO 4) **Financial Statement** The adjusted trial balance for Phoebe Company is presented in E4.8.

Prepare financial statements.

Instructions

a. Prepare an income statement and an owner's equity statement for the year. Phoebe did not make any capital investments during the year.

b. Prepare a classified balance sheet at July 31.

E4.10 (LO 3) Ray Louis has prepared the following list of statements about the accounting cycle.

Answer questions related to the accounting cycle.

1. "Journalize the transactions" is the first step in the accounting cycle.
2. Reversing entries are a required step in the accounting cycle.
3. Correcting entries do not have to be part of the accounting cycle.
4. If a worksheet is prepared, some steps of the accounting cycle are incorporated into the worksheet.
5. The accounting cycle begins with the analysis of business transactions and ends with the preparation of a post-closing trial balance.
6. All steps of the accounting cycle occur daily during the accounting period.
7. The step of "post to the ledger accounts" occurs before the step of "journalize the transactions."
8. Closing entries must be prepared before financial statements can be prepared.

Instructions

Identify each statement as true or false. If false, indicate how to correct the statement.

E4.11 (LO 2) Selected accounts for Tamora's Salon are presented below. All June 30 postings are from closing entries.

Prepare closing entries.

Salaries and Wages Expense

6/10	3,200		
6/28	5,600		
Bal.	8,800	6/30	8,800

Service Revenue

		6/15	9,700
		6/24	8,400
6/30	18,100	Bal.	18,100

Owner's Capital

6/30	2,500	6/1	12,000
		6/30	5,000
		Bal.	14,500

Supplies Expense

6/12	600		
6/24	700		
Bal.	1,300	6/30	1,300

Rent Expense

6/1	3,000		
Bal.	3,000	6/30	3,000

Owner's Drawings

6/13	1,000		
6/25	1,500		
Bal.	2,500	6/30	2,500

Instructions

a. Prepare the closing entries that were made.

b. Post the closing entries to Income Summary.

Prepare correcting entries.

E4.12 (LO 3) Blair Natt Company discovered the following errors made in January 2020.

1. A payment of Salaries and Wages Expense of $700 was debited to Equipment and credited to Cash, both for $700.
2. A collection of $1,500 from a client on account was debited to Cash $150 and credited to Service Revenue $150.
3. The purchase of equipment on account for $670 was debited to Equipment $760 and credited to Accounts Payable $760.

Instructions

a. Correct the errors by reversing the incorrect entry and preparing the correct entry.

b. Correct the errors without reversing the incorrect entry.

Prepare correcting entries.

E4.13 (LO 3) Patel Company has an inexperienced accountant. During the first 2 weeks on the job, the accountant made the following errors in journalizing transactions. All entries were posted as made.

1. A payment on account of $750 to a creditor was debited to Accounts Payable $570 and credited to Cash $570.
2. The purchase of supplies on account for $560 was debited to Equipment $56 and credited to Accounts Payable $56.
3. A $500 withdrawal of cash for N. Patel's personal use was debited to Salaries and Wages Expense $500 and credited to Cash $500.

Instructions

Prepare the correcting entries.

Prepare a classified balance sheet.

E4.14 (LO 4) **Writing** **Financial Statement** The adjusted trial balance for Carter Bowling Alley at December 31, 2020, contains the following accounts.

	Debit		Credit
Buildings	$128,800	Owner's Capital	$113,000
Accounts Receivable	14,520	Accumulated Depreciation—Buildings	42,600
Prepaid Insurance	4,680	Accounts Payable	12,300
Cash	18,040	Notes Payable	97,780
Equipment	62,400	Accumulated Depreciation—Equipment	18,720
Land	65,000	Interest Payable	3,800
Insurance Expense	780	Service Revenue	17,180
Depreciation Expense	7,360		$305,380
Interest Expense	3,800		
	$305,380		

Instructions

a. Prepare a classified balance sheet; assume that $30,000 of the note payable will be paid in 2021.

b. Comment on the liquidity of the company.

Classify accounts on balance sheet.

E4.15 (LO 4) The following are the major balance sheet classifications.

Current assets (CA)
Long-term investments (LTI)
Property, plant, and equipment (PPE)
Intangible assets (IA)
Current liabilities (CL)
Long-term liabilities (LTL)
Owner's equity (OE)

Instructions

Classify each of the following accounts taken from Faust Company's balance sheet.

________ Accounts payable
________ Accounts receivable
________ Cash
________ Owner's capital
________ Patents
________ Salaries and wages payable
________ Inventory
________ Stock investments (to be sold in 7 months)
________ Accumulated depreciation—equipment
________ Buildings
________ Land (in use)
________ Notes payable (due in 2 years)
________ Supplies
________ Equipment
________ Prepaid expenses

E4.16 (LO 4) **Financial Statement** The following items were taken from the financial statements of P. Jimenez Company. (All amounts are in thousands.)

Prepare a classified balance sheet.

Long-term debt	$ 1,000	Accumulated depreciation—equipment	$ 5,655
Prepaid insurance	650	Accounts payable	1,214
Equipment	11,500	Notes payable (due after 2021)	400
Stock investments (long-term)	264	Owner's capital	12,955
Debt investments (short-term)	3,690	Accounts receivable	1,696
Notes payable (due in 2021)	500	Inventory	1,256
Cash	2,668		

Instructions

Prepare a classified balance sheet in good form as of December 31, 2020.

E4.17 (LO 4) **Financial Statement** These financial statement items are for Basten Company at year-end, July 31, 2020.

Prepare financial statements.

Salaries and wages payable	$ 2,080	Notes payable (long-term)	$ 1,800
Salaries and wages expense	48,700	Cash	14,200
Utilities expense	22,600	Accounts receivable	9,780
Equipment	34,400	Accumulated depreciation—equipment	6,000
Accounts payable	4,100	Owner's drawings	3,000
Service revenue	63,000	Depreciation expense	4,000
Rent revenue	8,500	Owner's capital (beginning of the year)	51,200

Instructions

a. Prepare an income statement and an owner's equity statement for the year. The owner did not make any new investments during the year.

b. Prepare a classified balance sheet at July 31.

***E4.18 (LO 5)** Krantz Company pays salaries of $15,000 every Monday for the preceding 5-day week (Monday through Friday). Assume December 31 falls on a Tuesday, so Krantz's employees have worked 2 days without being paid at the end of the fiscal year.

Use reversing entries.

Instructions

a. Assume the company does not use reversing entries. Prepare the December 31 adjusting entry and the entry on Monday, January 6, when Krantz pays the payroll.

b. Assume the company does use reversing entries. Prepare the December 31 adjusting entry, the January 1 reversing entry, and the entry on Monday, January 6, when Krantz pays the payroll.

***E4.19 (LO 2, 5)** On December 31, the adjusted trial balance of Shihata Employment Agency shows the following selected data.

Prepare closing and reversing entries.

Accounts Receivable	$24,500	Service Revenue	$92,500
Interest Expense	7,700	Interest Payable	2,200

Analysis shows that adjusting entries were made to (1) accrue $5,000 of service revenue and (2) accrue $2,200 interest expense.

Instructions

a. Prepare the closing entries for the temporary accounts shown above at December 31.

b. Prepare the reversing entries on January 1.

c. Post the entries in (a) and (b). Underline and balance the accounts. (Use T-accounts.)

d. Prepare the entries to record (1) the collection of the accrued revenue on January 10 and (2) the payment of all interest due ($3,000) on January 15.

e. Post the entries in (d) to the temporary accounts.

Problems: Set A

P4.1A (LO 1, 2, 4) **Financial Statement** The trial balance columns of the worksheet for Warren Roofing at March 31, 2020, are as follows.

Prepare a worksheet, financial statements, and adjusting and closing entries.

Excel

Warren Roofing
Worksheet
For the Month Ended March 31, 2020

Account Titles	Trial Balance Dr.	Trial Balance Cr.
Cash	4,500	
Accounts Receivable	3,200	
Supplies	2,000	
Equipment	11,000	
Accumulated Depreciation—Equipment		1,250
Accounts Payable		2,500
Unearned Service Revenue		550
Owner's Capital		12,900
Owner's Drawings	1,100	
Service Revenue		6,300
Salaries and Wages Expense	1,300	
Miscellaneous Expense	400	
	23,500	23,500

Other data:

1. A physical count reveals only $480 of roofing supplies on hand.
2. Depreciation for March is $250.
3. Unearned revenue amounted to $260 at March 31.
4. Accrued salaries are $700.

Instructions

a. Adjusted trial balance $24,450
b. Net income $2,420
Total assets $17,680

a. Enter the trial balance on a worksheet and complete the worksheet.

b. Prepare an income statement and owner's equity statement for the month of March and a classified balance sheet at March 31. T. Warren made an additional investment in the business of $10,000 in March.

c. Journalize the adjusting entries from the adjustments columns of the worksheet.

d. Journalize the closing entries from the financial statement columns of the worksheet.

Complete worksheet; prepare financial statements, closing entries, and post-closing trial balance.

GLS

P4.2A (LO 1, 2, 4) Financial Statement The adjusted trial balance columns of the worksheet for Nguyen Company, owned by C. Nguyen, are as follows.

Nguyen Company
Worksheet
For the Year Ended December 31, 2020

Account No.	Account Titles	Adjusted Trial Balance Dr.	Adjusted Trial Balance Cr.
101	Cash	5,300	
112	Accounts Receivable	10,800	
126	Supplies	1,500	
130	Prepaid Insurance	2,000	
157	Equipment	27,000	
158	Accumulated Depreciation—Equipment		5,600
200	Notes Payable		15,000
201	Accounts Payable		6,100
212	Salaries and Wages Payable		3,600
230	Interest Payable		600
301	Owner's Capital		13,000
306	Owner's Drawings	7,600	
400	Service Revenue		61,000
610	Advertising Expense	9,000	
631	Supplies Expense	4,000	
711	Depreciation Expense	5,600	
722	Insurance Expense	3,500	
726	Salaries and Wages Expense	28,000	
905	Interest Expense	600	
	Totals	104,900	104,900

Instructions

a. Complete the worksheet by extending the balances to the financial statement columns.

b. Prepare an income statement, owner's equity statement, and a classified balance sheet. (*Note:* $4,000 of the notes payable become due in 2021.) C. Nguyen did not make any additional investments in the business during the year.

c. Prepare the closing entries. Use J14 for the journal page.

d. Post the closing entries. Use the three-column form of account. Income Summary is No. 350.

e. Prepare a post-closing trial balance.

a. Net income $10,300
b. Current assets $19,600
Current liabilities $14,300
e. Post-closing trial balance $46,600

P4.3A (LO 1, 2, 4) Financial Statement The completed financial statement columns of the worksheet for Bray Company are shown as follows.

Prepare financial statements, closing entries, and post-closing trial balance.

Bray Company
Worksheet
For the Year Ended December 31, 2020

Account No.	Account Titles	Income Statement Dr.	Income Statement Cr.	Balance Sheet Dr.	Balance Sheet Cr.
101	Cash			8,800	
112	Accounts Receivable			10,800	
130	Prepaid Insurance			2,800	
157	Equipment			24,000	
158	Accumulated Depreciation—Equip.				4,200
201	Accounts Payable				9,000
212	Salaries and Wages Payable				2,400
301	Owner's Capital				19,500
306	Owner's Drawings			11,000	
400	Service Revenue		60,000		
622	Maintenance and Repairs Expense	1,700			
711	Depreciation Expense	2,800			
722	Insurance Expense	1,800			
726	Salaries and Wages Expense	30,000			
732	Utilities Expense	1,400			
	Totals	37,700	60,000	57,400	35,100
	Net Income	22,300			22,300
		60,000	60,000	57,400	57,400

Instructions

a. Prepare an income statement, an owner's equity statement, and a classified balance sheet.

b. Prepare the closing entries. L. Bray did not make any additional investments during the year.

c. Post the closing entries and underline and balance the accounts. (Use T-accounts.) Income Summary is account No. 350.

d. Prepare a post-closing trial balance.

a. Ending capital $30,800
Total current assets $22,400
d. Post-closing trial balance $46,400

P4.4A (LO 1, 2, 4) Financial Statement Rusthe Management Services began business on January 1, 2020, with a capital investment of $120,000. The company manages condominiums for owners (Service Revenue) and rents space in its own office building (Rent Revenue). The trial balance and adjusted trial balance columns of the worksheet at the end of the first year are as follows.

Complete worksheet; prepare classified balance sheet, entries, and post-closing trial balance.

Rusthe Management Services
Worksheet
For the Year Ended December 31, 2020

Account Titles	Trial Balance Dr.	Trial Balance Cr.	Adjusted Trial Balance Dr.	Adjusted Trial Balance Cr.
Cash	13,800		13,800	
Accounts Receivable	28,300		28,300	
Prepaid Insurance	3,600		2,100	
Land	67,000		67,000	
Buildings	127,000		127,000	

Account Titles	Trial Balance Dr.	Trial Balance Cr.	Adjusted Trial Balance Dr.	Adjusted Trial Balance Cr.
Equipment	59,000		59,000	
Accounts Payable		12,500		12,500
Unearned Rent Revenue		6,000		1,000
Mortgage Payable		120,000		120,000
Owner's Capital		144,000		144,000
Owner's Drawings	22,000		22,000	
Service Revenue		90,700		90,700
Rent Revenue		29,000		34,000
Salaries and Wages Expense	42,000		42,000	
Advertising Expense	20,500		20,500	
Utilities Expense	19,000		19,000	
Totals	402,200	402,200		
Insurance Expense			1,500	
Depreciation Expense			6,600	
Accumulated Depreciation—Buildings				3,000
Accumulated Depreciation—Equipment				3,600
Interest Expense			10,000	
Interest Payable				10,000
Totals			418,800	418,800

Instructions

a. Net income $25,100

b. Total current assets $44,200

e. Post-closing trial balance $297,200

a. Prepare a complete worksheet.

b. Prepare a classified balance sheet. (*Note:* $45,000 of the mortgage note payable is due for payment next year.)

c. Journalize the adjusting entries.

d. Journalize the closing entries.

e. Prepare a post-closing trial balance.

Complete all steps in accounting cycle.

GLS

P4.5A (LO 1, 2, 4) Anya Clark opened Anya's Cleaning Service on July 1, 2020. During July, the following transactions were completed.

July	1	Anya invested $20,000 cash in the business.
	1	Purchased used truck for $12,000, paying $4,000 cash and the balance on account.
	3	Purchased cleaning supplies for $2,100 on account.
	5	Paid $1,800 cash on a 1-year insurance policy effective July 1.
	12	Billed customers $4,500 for cleaning services.
	18	Paid $1,500 cash on amount owed on truck and $1,400 on amount owed on cleaning supplies.
	20	Paid $2,800 cash for employee salaries.
	21	Collected $3,400 cash from customers billed on July 12.
	25	Billed customers $6,000 for cleaning services.
	31	Paid $350 for the monthly gasoline bill for the truck.
	31	Withdraw $5,600 cash for personal use.

The chart of accounts for Anya's Cleaning Service contains the following accounts: No. 101 Cash, No. 112 Accounts Receivable, No. 126 Supplies, No. 130 Prepaid Insurance, No. 157 Equipment, No. 158 Accumulated Depreciation—Equipment, No. 201 Accounts Payable, No. 212 Salaries and Wages Payable, No. 301 Owner's Capital, No. 306 Owner's Drawings, No. 350 Income Summary, No. 400 Service Revenue, No. 631 Supplies Expense, No. 633 Gasoline Expense, No. 711 Depreciation Expense, No. 722 Insurance Expense, and No. 726 Salaries and Wages Expense.

Instructions

a. Journalize and post the July transactions. Use page J1 for the journal and the three-column form of account.

b. Trial balance $37,700

c. Adjusted trial balance $41,900

b. Prepare a trial balance at July 31 on a worksheet.

c. Enter the following adjustments on the worksheet and complete the worksheet.

1. Unbilled and uncollected revenue for services performed at July 31 were $2,700.
2. Depreciation on equipment for the month was $500.

3. One-twelfth of the insurance expired.
4. An inventory count shows $600 of cleaning supplies on hand at July 31.
5. Accrued but unpaid employee salaries were $1,000.

d. Prepare the income statement and owner's equity statement for July and a classified balance sheet at July 31.

d. Net income $6,900
Total assets $29,500

e. Journalize and post adjusting entries. Use page J2 for the journal.

f. Journalize and post closing entries and complete the closing process. Use page J3 for the journal.

g. Prepare a post-closing trial balance at July 31.

g. Post-closing trial balance $30,000

Analyze errors and prepare correcting entries and trial balance.

P4.6A (LO 3) Horace Culpepper, CPA, was retained by Pulsar Cable to prepare financial statements for April 2020. Horace accumulated all the ledger balances per Pulsar's records and found the following.

Pulsar Cable
Trial Balance
April 30, 2020

	Debit	Credit
Cash	$ 4,100	
Accounts Receivable	3,200	
Supplies	800	
Equipment	10,800	
Accumulated Depreciation—Equip.		$ 1,350
Accounts Payable		2,100
Salaries and Wages Payable		700
Unearned Service Revenue		890
Owner's Capital		12,900
Service Revenue		5,650
Salaries and Wages Expense	3,300	
Advertising Expense	600	
Miscellaneous Expense	290	
Depreciation Expense	500	
	$23,590	$23,590

Horace Culpepper then reviewed the records and found the following errors.

1. Cash received from a customer on account was recorded as $950 instead of $590.
2. A payment of $75 for advertising expense was entered as a debit to Miscellaneous Expense $75 and a credit to Cash $75.
3. The first salary payment in April was for $1,900, which included $900 of salaries payable on March 31. The payment was recorded as a debit to Salaries and Wages Expense $1,900 and a credit to Cash $1,900. (No reversing entries were made on April 1.)
4. The purchase on account of a printer costing $510 was recorded as a debit to Supplies and a credit to Accounts Payable for $510.
5. A cash payment of repair expense on equipment for $96 was recorded as a debit to Equipment $69 and a credit to Cash $69.

Instructions

a. Prepare an analysis of each error showing (1) the incorrect entry, (2) the correct entry, and (3) the correcting entry. Items 4 and 5 occurred on April 30, 2020.

b. Prepare a correct trial balance.

b. Trial balance $22,890

Continuing Case

Cookie Creations

(*Note:* This is a continuation of the Cookie Creations case from Chapters 1 through 3.)

CC4 Natalie had a very busy December. At the end of the month, after journalizing and posting the December transactions and adjusting entries, Natalie prepared the following adjusted trial balance.

© leungchopan/ Shutterstock

Cookie Creations
Adjusted Trial Balance
December 31, 2019

	Debit	Credit
Cash	$1,180	
Accounts Receivable	875	
Supplies	350	
Prepaid Insurance	1,210	
Equipment	1,200	
Accumulated Depreciation—Equipment		$ 40
Accounts Payable		75
Salaries and Wages Payable		56
Interest Payable		15
Unearned Service Revenue		300
Notes Payable		2,000
Owner's Capital		800
Owner's Drawings	500	
Service Revenue		4,515
Salaries and Wages Expense	1,006	
Utilities Expense	125	
Advertising Expense	165	
Supplies Expense	1,025	
Depreciation Expense	40	
Insurance Expense	110	
Interest Expense	15	
	$7,801	$7,801

Instructions

Using the information in the adjusted trial balance, do the following.

a. Prepare an income statement and an owner's equity statement for the 2 months ended December 31, 2019, and a classified balance sheet at December 31, 2019. The note payable has a stated interest rate of 6%, and the principal and interest are due on November 16, 2021.

b. Natalie has decided that her year-end will be December 31, 2019. Prepare and post closing entries as of December 31, 2019.

c. Prepare a post-closing trial balance.

Ethics Case

EC4 As the controller of Take No Prisoners Perfume Company, you discover a misstatement that overstated net income in the prior year's financial statements. The misleading financial statements appear in the company's annual report which was issued to banks and other creditors less than a month ago. After much thought about the consequences of telling the president, Mike Flanary, about this misstatement, you gather your courage to inform him. Mike says, "Hey! What they don't know won't hurt them. But, just so we set the record straight, we'll adjust this year's financial statements for last year's misstatement. We can absorb that misstatement better in this year than in last year anyway! Just don't make such a mistake again."

Instructions

a. Who are the stakeholders in this situation?

b. What are the ethical issues in this situation?

c. What would you do as a controller in this situation?

Comprehensive Accounting Cycle Review

Complete all steps in accounting cycle. GLS

ACR4.1 **Financial Statement** Mike Greenberg opened Kleene Window Washing Co. on July 1, 2020. During July, the following transactions were completed.

July	1	Owner invested $12,000 cash in the company.
	1	Purchased used truck for $8,000, paying $2,000 cash and the balance on account.
	3	Purchased cleaning supplies for $900 on account.
	5	Paid $1,800 cash on a 1-year insurance policy effective July 1.
	12	Billed customers $3,700 for cleaning services performed.
	18	Paid $1,000 cash on amount owed on truck and $500 on amount owed on cleaning supplies.
	20	Paid $2,000 cash for employee salaries.
	21	Collected $1,600 cash from customers billed on July 12.
	25	Billed customers $2,500 for cleaning services performed.
	31	Paid $290 for maintenance of the truck during month.
	31	Owner withdrew $600 cash from the company.

The chart of accounts for Kleene Window Washing contains the following accounts: Cash, Accounts Receivable, Supplies, Prepaid Insurance, Equipment, Accumulated Depreciation—Equipment, Accounts Payable, Salaries and Wages Payable, Owner's Capital, Owner's Drawings, Income Summary, Service Revenue, Maintenance and Repairs Expense, Supplies Expense, Depreciation Expense, Insurance Expense, and Salaries and Wages Expense.

Instructions

a. Journalize the July transactions.

b. Post to the ledger accounts. (Use T-accounts.)

c. Prepare a trial balance at July 31.

d. Journalize the following adjustments.

1. Services performed but unbilled and uncollected at July 31 were $1,700.
2. Depreciation on equipment for the month was $180.
3. One-twelfth of the insurance expired.
4. A count shows $320 of cleaning supplies on hand at July 31.
5. Accrued but unpaid employee salaries were $400.

e. Post adjusting entries to the T-accounts.

f. Prepare an adjusted trial balance.

g. Prepare the income statement and an owner's equity statement for July and a classified balance sheet at July 31.

h. Journalize and post closing entries and complete the closing process.

i. Prepare a post-closing trial balance at July 31.

f. Cash $5,410

g. Tot. assets $21,500

ACR4.2 **Financial Statement** Lars Linken opened Lars Cleaners on March 1, 2020. During March, the following transactions were completed.

Complete all steps in accounting cycle.

GLS

Mar.	1	Owner invested $15,000 cash in the company.
	1	Borrowed $6,000 cash by signing a 6-month, 6%, $6,000 note payable. Interest will be paid the first day of each subsequent month.
	1	Purchased used truck for $8,000 cash.
	2	Paid $1,500 cash to cover rent from March 1 through May 31.
	3	Paid $2,400 cash on a 6-month insurance policy effective March 1.
	6	Purchased cleaning supplies for $2,000 on account.
	14	Billed customers $3,700 for cleaning services performed.
	18	Paid $500 on amount owed on cleaning supplies.
	20	Paid $1,750 cash for employee salaries.
	21	Collected $1,600 cash from customers billed on March 14.
	28	Billed customers $4,200 for cleaning services performed.
	31	Paid $350 for gas and oil used in truck during month (use Maintenance and Repairs Expense).
	31	Owner withdrew $900 cash from the company.

The chart of accounts for Lars Cleaners contains the following accounts: Cash, Accounts Receivable, Supplies, Prepaid Insurance, Prepaid Rent, Equipment, Accumulated Depreciation—Equipment, Accounts Payable, Salaries and Wages Payable, Notes Payable, Interest Payable, Owner's Capital, Owner's Drawings, Income Summary, Service Revenue, Maintenance and Repairs Expense, Supplies Expense, Depreciation Expense, Insurance Expense, Salaries and Wages Expense, Rent Expense, and Interest Expense.

Instructions

a. Journalize the March transactions.

b. Post to the ledger accounts. (Use T-accounts.)

c. Prepare a trial balance at March 31.

d. Journalize the following adjustments.

1. Services performed but unbilled and uncollected at March 31 were $200.
2. Depreciation on equipment for the month was $250.
3. One-sixth of the insurance expired.
4. An inventory count shows $280 of cleaning supplies on hand at March 31.
5. Accrued but unpaid employee salaries were $1,080.
6. One month of the prepaid rent has expired.
7. One month of interest expense related to the note payable has accrued and will be paid April 1. (*Hint:* Use the formula from Illustration 3.17 to compute interest.)

e. Post adjusting entries to the T-accounts.

f. Tot. adj. trial balance $31,960

g. Tot. assets $24,730

f. Prepare an adjusted trial balance.

g. Prepare the income statement and an owner's equity statement for March and a classified balance sheet at March 31.

h. Journalize and post closing entries and complete the closing process.

i. Prepare a post-closing trial balance at March 31.

Journalize transactions and follow through accounting cycle to preparation of financial statements.

GLS

ACR4.3 **Financial Statement** On August 1, 2020, the following were the account balances of B&B Repair Services.

	Debit		Credit
Cash	$ 6,040	Accumulated Depreciation—Equipment	$ 600
Accounts Receivable	2,910	Accounts Payable	2,300
Notes Receivable	4,000	Unearned Service Revenue	1,260
Supplies	1,030	Salaries and Wages Payable	1,420
Equipment	10,000	Owner's Capital	18,400
	$23,980		$23,980

During August, the following summary transactions were completed.

Aug.	1	Paid $400 cash for advertising in local newspapers. Advertising flyers will be included with newspapers delivered during August and September.
	3	Paid August rent $380.
	5	Received $1,200 cash from customers in payment on account.
	10	Paid $3,120 for salaries due employees, of which $1,700 is for August and $1,420 is for July salaries payable.
	12	Received $2,800 cash for services performed in August.
	15	Purchased store equipment on account $2,000.
	20	Paid creditors $2,000 of accounts payable due.
	22	Purchased supplies on account $800.
	25	Paid $2,900 cash for employees' salaries.
	27	Billed customers $3,760 for services performed.
	29	Received $780 from customers for services to be performed in the future.

Adjustment data:

1. A count shows supplies on hand of $960.
2. Accrued but unpaid employees' salaries are $1,540.
3. Depreciation on equipment for the month is $320.
4. Services were performed to satisfy $800 of unearned service revenue.
5. One month's worth of advertising services has been received.
6. One month of interest revenue related to the $4,000 note receivable has accrued. The 4-month note has a 6% annual interest rate. (*Hint:* Use the formula from Illustration 3.17 to compute interest.)

Instructions

a. Enter the August 1 balances in the ledger accounts. (Use T-accounts.)

b. Journalize the August transactions.

c. Post to the ledger accounts. B&B's chart of accounts includes Prepaid Advertising, Interest Receivable, Service Revenue, Interest Revenue, Advertising Expense, Depreciation Expense, Supplies Expense, Salaries and Wages Expense, and Rent Expense.

d. Prepare a trial balance at August 31.

e. Journalize and post adjusting entries.

f. Prepare an adjusted trial balance.

g. Prepare an income statement and an owner's equity statement for August and a classified balance sheet at August 31.

h. Journalize and post closing entries and complete the closing process.

i. Prepare a post-closing trial balance at August 31.

f. Cash $2,020
Tot. adj. trial balance $32,580

g. Net loss $530

ACR4.4 **Financial Statement** At June 30, 2020, the end of its most recent fiscal year, Green River Computer Consultants' post-closing trial balance was as follows:

Record and post transaction, adjusting, and closing journal entries; prepare adjusted trial balance and financial statements.

	Debit	Credit
Cash	$5,230	
Accounts receivable	1,200	
Supplies	690	
Accounts payable		$ 400
Unearned service revenue		1,120
Owner's capital		5,600
	$7,120	$7,120

The company underwent a major expansion in July. New staff was hired and more financing was obtained. Green River conducted the following transactions during July 2020, and adjusts its accounts monthly.

July	1	Purchased equipment, paying $4,000 cash and signing a 2-year note payable for $20,000. The equipment has a 4-year useful life. The note has a 6% interest rate which is payable on the first day of each following month.
	2	Owner invested $50,000 cash in the company.
	3	Paid $3,600 cash for a 12-month insurance policy effective July 1.
	3	Paid the first 2 (July and August 2020) months' rent for an annual lease of office space for $4,000 per month.
	6	Paid $3,800 for supplies.
	9	Visited client offices and agreed on the terms of a consulting project. Green River will bill the client, Connor Productions, on the 20th of each month for services performed.
	10	Collected $1,200 cash on account from Milani Brothers. This client was billed in June when Green River performed the service.
	13	Performed services for Fitzgerald Enterprises. This client paid $1,120 in advance last month. All services relating to this payment are now completed.
	14	Paid $400 cash for a utility bill. This related to June utilities that were accrued at the end of June.
	16	Met with a new client, Thunder Bay Technologies. Received $12,000 cash in advance for future services to be performed.
	18	Paid semi-monthly salaries for $11,000.
	20	Performed services worth $28,000 on account and billed customers.
	20	Received a bill for $2,200 for advertising services received during July. The amount is not due until August 15.
	23	Performed the first phase of the project for Thunder Bay Technologies. Recognized $10,000 of revenue from the cash advance received July 16.
	27	Received $15,000 cash from customers billed on July 20.

Adjustment data:

1. Adjustment of prepaid insurance.
2. Adjustment of prepaid rent.
3. Supplies used, $1,250.
4. Equipment depreciation, $500 per month.
5. Accrual of interest on note payable. (*Hint:* Use the formula from Illustration 3.17 to compute interest.)
6. Salaries for the second half of July, $11,000, to be paid on August 1.

7. Estimated utilities expense for July, $800 (invoice will be received in August).
8. Income tax for July, $1,200, will be paid in August. (*Hint:* Use the accounts Income Tax Expense and Income Taxes Payable.)

The chart of accounts for Green River Computer Consultants contains the following accounts: Cash, Accounts Receivable, Supplies, Prepaid Insurance. Prepaid Rent, Equipment, Accumulated Depreciation—Equipment, Accounts Payable, Notes Payable, Interest Payable, Income Taxes Payable, Salaries and Wages Payable, Unearned Service Revenue, Owner's Capital, Owner's Drawings, Income Summary, Service Revenue, Supplies Expense, Depreciation Expense, Insurance Expense, Salaries and Wages Expense, Advertising Expense, Income Tax Expense, Interest Expense, Rent Expense, and Utilities Expense.

Instructions

a. Enter the July 1 balances in the ledger accounts. (Use T-accounts.)
b. Journalize the July transactions.
c. Post to the ledger accounts.
d. Prepare a trial balance at July 31.
e. Journalize and post adjusting entries for the month ending July 31.
f. Prepare an adjusted trial balance.
g. Prepare an income statement and an owner's equity statement for July and a classified balance sheet at July 31.
h. Journalize and post closing entries and complete the closing process.
i. Prepare a post-closing trial balance at July 31.

g. Net income $6,770
Tot. assets $99,670

Expand Your Critical Thinking

Financial Reporting Problem: Apple Inc.

CT4.1 The financial statements of **Apple Inc.** are presented in Appendix A at the end of this textbook. The complete annual report, including the notes to the financial statements, is available at the company's website.

Instructions

Answer the questions below using Apple's Consolidated Balance Sheets.

a. What were Apple's total current assets at September 26, 2015, and September 27, 2014?
b. Are assets that Apple included under current assets listed in proper order? Explain.
c. How are Apple's assets classified?
d. What was Apple's "Cash and cash equivalents" at September 26, 2015?
e. What were Apple's total current liabilities at September 26, 2015, and September 27, 2014?

Comparative Analysis Problem: PepsiCo, Inc. vs. The Coca-Cola Company

CT4.2 PepsiCo, Inc.'s financial statements are presented in Appendix B. Financial statements of **The Coca-Cola Company** are presented in Appendix C. The complete annual reports of PepsiCo and Coca-Cola, including the notes to the financial statements, are available at each company's respective website.

Instructions

a. Based on the information contained in these financial statements, determine each of the following for PepsiCo at December 26, 2015, and for Coca-Cola at December 31, 2015.
   1. Total current assets.
   2. Net amount of property, plant, and equipment (land, buildings, and equipment).
   3. Total current liabilities.
   4. Total equity.
b. What conclusions concerning the companies' respective financial positions can be drawn?

Comparative Analysis Problem: Amazon.com, Inc. vs. Wal-Mart Stores, Inc.

CT4.3 **Amazon.com, Inc.**'s financial statements are presented in Appendix D. Financial statements of **Wal-Mart Stores, Inc.** are presented in Appendix E. The complete annual reports of Amazon and Wal-Mart, including the notes to the financial statements, are available at each company's respective website.

Instructions

a. Based on the information contained in these financial statements, determine the following for Amazon at December 31, 2015, and Wal-Mart at January 31, 2016.

1. Total current assets.
2. Net amount of property and equipment (fixed assets), net.
3. Total current liabilities.
4. Total equity.

b. What conclusions concerning these two companies can be drawn from these data?

Real-World Focus

CT4.4 Most companies have established home pages on the Internet, but each might offer different types of information.

Instructions

Examine the home pages of any two companies and then answer the following questions.

a. What type of information is available?

b. Is any accounting-related information presented?

c. Would you describe the home page as informative, promotional, or both? Why?

Decision-Making Across the Organization

CT4.5 Whitegloves Janitorial Service was started 2 years ago by Jenna Olson. Because business has been exceptionally good, Jenna decided on July 1, 2020, to expand operations by acquiring an additional truck and hiring two more assistants. To finance the expansion, Jenna obtained on July 1, 2020, a $25,000, 10% bank loan, payable $10,000 on July 1, 2021, and the balance on July 1, 2022. The terms of the loan require the borrower to have $10,000 more current assets than current liabilities at December 31, 2020. If these terms are not met, the bank loan will be refinanced at 15% interest. At December 31, 2020, the accountant for Whitegloves Janitorial Service prepared the balance sheet shown below.

Whitegloves Janitorial Service
Balance Sheet
December 31, 2020

Assets		Liabilities and Owner's Equity	
Current assets		Current liabilities	
Cash	$ 6,500	Notes payable	$10,000
Accounts receivable	9,000	Accounts payable	2,500
Supplies	5,200	Total current liabilities	12,500
Prepaid insurance	4,800	Long-term liability	
Total current assets	25,500	Notes payable	15,000
Property, plant, and equipment		Total liabilities	27,500
Equipment (net)	22,000	Owner's equity	
Delivery trucks (net)	34,000	Owner's capital	54,000
Total property, plant, and equipment	56,000		
Total assets	$81,500	Total liabilities and owner's equity	$81,500

Jenna presented the balance sheet to the bank's loan officer on January 2, 2021, confident that the company had met the terms of the loan. The loan officer was not impressed. She said, "We need financial statements audited by a CPA." A CPA was hired and immediately realized that the balance sheet had been prepared from a trial balance and not from an adjusted trial balance. The adjustment data at the balance sheet date consisted of the following.

1. Unbilled janitorial services performed were $3,700.
2. Janitorial supplies on hand were $2,500.
3. Prepaid insurance was a 3-year policy dated January 1, 2020.
4. December expenses incurred but unpaid at December 31, $500.
5. Interest on the bank loan was not recorded.
6. The amounts for property, plant, and equipment presented in the balance sheet were reported net of accumulated depreciation (cost less accumulated depreciation). These amounts were $4,000 for cleaning equipment and $5,000 for delivery trucks as of January 1, 2020. Depreciation for 2020, still unrecorded, was $2,000 for cleaning equipment and $5,000 for delivery trucks.

Instructions

With the class divided into groups, answer the following.

a. Prepare a correct balance sheet.

b. Were the terms of the bank loan met? Explain.

Communication Activity

CT4.6 The accounting cycle is important in understanding the accounting process.

Instructions

Write a memo to your instructor that lists the steps of the accounting cycle in the order they should be completed. End with a paragraph that explains the optional steps in the cycle.

All About You

CT4.7 Companies prepare balance sheets in order to know their financial position at a specific point in time. This enables them to make a comparison to their position at previous points in time, and gives them a basis for planning for the future. In order to evaluate your financial position, you need to prepare a personal balance sheet. Assume that you have compiled the following information regarding your finances. (*Note:* Some of the items might not be used in your personal balance sheet.)

Amount owed on student loan balance (long-term)	$ 5,000
Balance in checking account	1,200
Certificate of deposit (6-month)	3,000
Annual earnings from part-time job	11,300
Automobile	7,000
Balance on automobile loan (current portion)	1,500
Balance on automobile loan (long-term portion)	4,000
Home computer	800
Amount owed to you by younger brother	300
Balance in money market account	1,800
Annual tuition	6,400
Video and stereo equipment	1,250
Balance owed on credit card (current portion)	150
Balance owed on credit card (long-term portion)	1,650

Instructions

Prepare a personal balance sheet using the format you have learned for a classified balance sheet for a company. For the capital account, use Owner's Capital.

FASB Codification Activity

CT4.8 If your school has a subscription to the FASB Codification, log in and prepare responses to the following.

Instructions

a. Access the glossary ("Master Glossary") at the FASB Codification website to answer the following.

   1. What is the definition of current assets?

   2. What is the definition of current liabilities?

b. A company wants to offset its accounts payable against its cash account and show a cash amount net of accounts payable on its balance sheet. Identify the criteria (found in the FASB Codification) under which a company has the right of set off. Does the company have the right to offset accounts payable against the cash account?

A Look at IFRS

LEARNING OBJECTIVE 6

Compare the procedures for the closing process under GAAP and IFRS.

The classified balance sheet, although generally required internationally, contains certain variations in format when reporting under IFRS.

Key Points

Following are the key similarities and differences between GAAP and IFRS related to the closing process and the financial statements.

Similarities

- The procedures of the closing process are applicable to all companies, whether they are using IFRS or GAAP.
- IFRS generally requires a classified statement of financial position similar to the classified balance sheet under GAAP.
- IFRS follows the same guidelines as GAAP for distinguishing between current and non-current assets and liabilities.

Differences

- IFRS recommends but does not require the use of the title "statement of financial position" rather than balance sheet.
- The format of statement of financial position information is often presented differently under IFRS. Although no specific format is required, many companies that follow IFRS present statement of financial position information in this order:
  - ♦ Non-current assets
  - ♦ Current assets
  - ♦ Equity
  - ♦ Non-current liabilities
  - ♦ Current liabilities
- Under IFRS, current assets are usually listed in the reverse order of liquidity. For example, under GAAP cash is listed first, but under IFRS it is listed last.
- IFRS has many differences in terminology from what are shown in your textbook. For example, in the following sample statement of financial position, notice in the investment category that stock is called shares.

Franklin Company
Statement of Financial Position
October 31, 2020

Assets			
Intangible assets			
Patents			$ 3,100
Property, plant, and equipment			
Land		$10,000	
Equipment	$24,000		
Less: Accumulated depreciation	5,000	19,000	29,000
Long-term investments			
Share investments		5,200	
Investment in real estate		2,000	7,200
Current assets			
Prepaid insurance		400	
Supplies		2,100	
Inventory		3,000	
Notes receivable		1,000	
Accounts receivable		7,000	
Debt investments		2,000	
Cash		6,600	22,100
Total assets			$61,400
Equity and Liabilities			
Equity			
Owner's capital			$34,050
Non-current liabilities			
Mortgage payable		$10,000	
Notes payable		1,300	11,300
Current liabilities			
Notes payable		11,000	
Accounts payable		2,100	
Salaries and wages payable		1,600	
Unearned service revenue		900	
Interest payable		450	16,050
Total equity and liabilities			$61,400

- Both GAAP and IFRS are increasing the use of fair value to report assets. However, at this point IFRS has adopted it more broadly. As examples, under IFRS, companies can apply fair value to property, plant, and equipment, and in some cases intangible assets.

Looking to the Future

The IASB and the FASB are working on a project to converge their standards related to financial statement presentation. A key feature of the proposed framework is that each of the statements will be organized in the same format, to separate an entity's financing activities from its operating and investing activities and, further, to separate financing activities into transactions with owners and creditors. Thus, the same classifications used in the statement of financial position would also be used in the income statement and the statement of cash flows. The project has three phases. You can follow the joint financial presentation project at the FASB website.

IFRS Practice

IFRS Self-Test Questions

1. A company has purchased a tract of land and expects to build a production plant on the land in approximately 5 years. During the 5 years before construction, the land will be idle. Under IFRS, the land should be reported as:
   a. land expense.
   b. property, plant, and equipment.
   c. an intangible asset.
   d. a long-term investment.
2. Current assets under IFRS are listed generally:
   a. by importance.
   b. in the reverse order of their expected conversion to cash.
   c. by longevity.
   d. alphabetically.
3. Companies that use IFRS:
   a. may report all their assets on the statement of financial position at fair value.
   b. may offset assets against liabilities and show net assets and net liabilities on their statements of financial position, rather than the underlying detailed line items.
   c. may report non-current assets before current assets on the statement of financial position.
   d. do not have any guidelines as to what should be reported on the statement of financial position.
4. Companies that follow IFRS to prepare a statement of financial position generally use the following order of classification:
   a. current assets, current liabilities, non-current assets, non-current liabilities, equity.
   b. non-current assets, non-current liabilities, current assets, current liabilities, equity.
   c. non-current assets, current assets, equity, non-current liabilities, current liabilities.
   d. equity, non-current assets, current assets, non-current liabilities, current liabilities.

IFRS Exercises

IFRS4.1 In what ways does the format of a statement of financial of position under IFRS often differ from a balance sheet presented under GAAP?

IFRS4.2 What term is commonly used under IFRS in reference to the balance sheet?

IFRS4.3 The statement of financial position for Wallby Company includes the following accounts (in British pounds): Accounts Receivable £12,500, Prepaid Insurance £3,600, Cash £15,400, Supplies £5,200, and Debt Investments (short-term) £6,700. Prepare the current assets section of the statement of financial position, listing the accounts in proper sequence.

IFRS4.4 The following information is available for Sutter Bowling Alley at December 31, 2020.

Buildings	$128,800	Owner's Capital	$115,000
Accounts Receivable	14,520	Accumulated Depreciation—Buildings	42,600
Prepaid Insurance	4,680	Accounts Payable	12,300
Cash	18,040	Notes Payable	97,780
Equipment	62,400	Accumulated Depreciation—Equipment	18,720
Land	64,000	Interest Payable	2,600
Insurance Expense	780	Bowling Revenues	14,180
Depreciation Expense	7,360		
Interest Expense	2,600		

Prepare a classified statement of financial position. Assume that $13,900 of the notes payable will be paid in 2021.

International Comparative Analysis Problem: Apple vs. Louis Vuitton

IFRS4.5 The financial statements of **Louis Vuitton** are presented in Appendix F. The complete annual report, including the notes to its financial statements, is available at the company's website.

Instructions

Identify five differences in the format of the statement of financial position used by Louis Vuitton compared to a company, such as **Apple**, that follows GAAP. (Apple's financial statements are available in Appendix A.)

Answers to IFRS Self-Test Questions

1. d **2.** b **3.** c **4.** c

CHAPTER 5

© omgimages/iStockphoto

Accounting for Merchandising Operations

Chapter Preview

Merchandising is one of the largest and most influential industries in the United States. It is likely that a number of you will work for a merchandiser. Therefore, understanding the financial statements of merchandising companies is important. In this chapter, you will learn the basics about reporting merchandising transactions. In addition, you will learn how to prepare and analyze a commonly used form of the income statement—the multiple-step income statement.

Feature Story

Buy Now, Vote Later

Have you ever shopped for outdoor gear at an **REI (Recreational Equipment Incorporated)** store? If so, you might have been surprised if a salesclerk asked if you were a member. A member? What do you mean a member? REI is a consumer cooperative, or "co-op" for short. To figure out what that means, consider this quote from the company's annual stewardship report:

As a cooperative, the Company is owned by its members. Each member is entitled to one vote in the election of the Company's Board of Directors. Since January 1, 2008, the nonrefundable, nontransferable, one-time membership fee has been 20 dollars. As of December 31, 2010, there were approximately 10.8 million members.

Voting rights? Now that's something you don't get from shopping at **Wal-Mart**. REI members get other benefits as well, including sharing in the company's profits through a dividend at the end of the year. The more you spend, the bigger your dividend.

Since REI is a co-op, you might also wonder whether management's incentives might be a little different than at other stores. Management is still concerned about making a profit as it ensures the long-term viability of the company. REI's members also want the company to be run efficiently, so that prices remain low. In order for its members to evaluate just how well management is doing, REI publishes an audited annual report, just like publicly traded companies do.

How well is this business model working for REI? Well, it has consistently been rated as one of the best places to work in the United States by *Fortune* magazine. It is one of only five companies named each year since the list was created in 1998. Also, REI had sustainable business practices long before social responsibility became popular at other companies. The CEO's stewardship report states "we reduced the absolute amount of energy we use despite opening four new stores and growing our business; we grew the amount of FSC-certified paper we use to 58.4 percent of our total paper footprint—including our cash register receipt paper; we facilitated 2.2 million volunteer hours and we provided $3.7 million to more than 330 conservation and recreation nonprofits."

So, while REI, like other retailers, closely monitors its financial results, it also strives to succeed in other areas. And, with over 10 million votes at stake, REI's management knows that it has to deliver.

Chapter Outline

LEARNING OBJECTIVES

LO 1 Describe merchandising operations and inventory systems.	• Operating cycles • Flow of costs	**DO IT! 1** Merchandising Operations and Inventory Systems
LO 2 Record purchases under a perpetual inventory system.	• Freight costs • Purchase returns and allowances • Purchase discounts • Summary of purchasing transactions	**DO IT! 2** Purchase Transactions
LO 3 Record sales under a perpetual inventory system.	• Sales returns and allowances • Sales discounts	**DO IT! 3** Sales Transactions
LO 4 Apply the steps in the accounting cycle to a merchandising company.	• Adjusting entries • Closing entries • Summary of merchandising entries	**DO IT! 4** Closing Entries
LO 5 Prepare a multiple-step income statement and a comprehensive income statement.	• Multiple-step income statement • Single-step income statement • Comprehensive income statement • Classified balance sheet	**DO IT! 5** Multiple-Step Income Statement

Go to the Review and Practice section at the end of the chapter for a review of key concepts and practice applications with solutions.
Visit WileyPLUS with ORION for additional tutorials and practice opportunities.

Merchandising Operations and Inventory Systems

LEARNING OBJECTIVE 1

Describe merchandising operations and inventory systems.

REI, **Wal-Mart**, and **Amazon.com** are called merchandising companies because they buy and sell merchandise rather than perform services as their primary source of revenue. Merchandising companies that purchase and sell directly to consumers are called **retailers**. Merchandising companies that sell to retailers are known as **wholesalers**. For example, retailer **Walgreens** might buy goods from wholesaler **McKesson**. Retailer **Office Depot** might buy office supplies from wholesaler **United Stationers**. The primary source of revenue for merchandising companies is the sale of merchandise, often referred to simply as **sales revenue** or **sales**. A merchandising company has two categories of expenses: cost of goods sold and operating expenses.

Cost of goods sold is the total cost of merchandise sold during the period. This expense is directly related to the revenue recognized from the sale of goods. **Illustration 5.1** shows the income measurement process for a merchandising company. The items in the two blue boxes are unique to a merchandising company; they are not used by a service company.

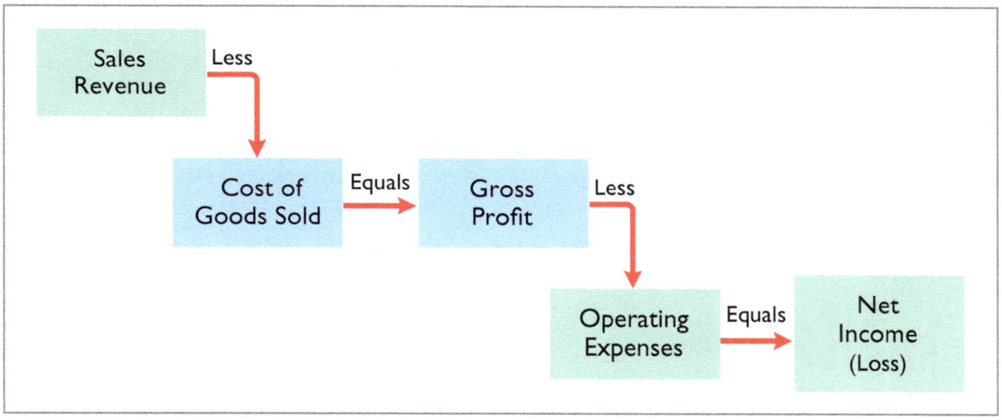

ILLUSTRATION 5.1

Income measurement process for a merchandising company

Operating Cycles

The operating cycle of a merchandising company ordinarily is longer than that of a service company. The purchase of merchandise inventory and its eventual sale lengthen the cycle. **Illustration 5.2** shows the operating cycle of a service company.

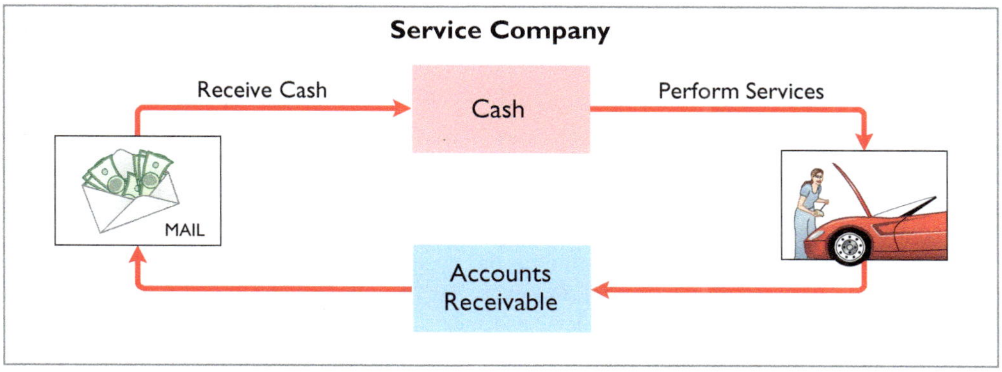

ILLUSTRATION 5.2

Operating cycle for a service company

Illustration 5.3 shows the operating cycle of a merchandising company.

ILLUSTRATION 5.3

Operating cycle for a merchandising company

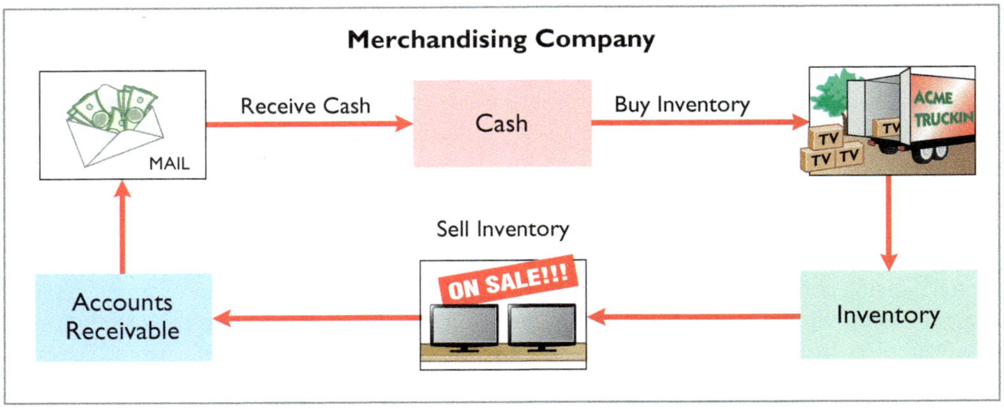

Note that the added asset account for a merchandising company is the Inventory account. Companies report inventory as a current asset on the balance sheet.

Flow of Costs

The flow of costs for a merchandising company is as follows. Beginning inventory plus the cost of goods purchased is the cost of goods available for sale. As goods are sold, they are assigned to cost of goods sold. Those goods that are not sold by the end of the accounting period represent ending inventory. **Illustration 5.4** describes these relationships. Companies use one of two systems to account for inventory: a **perpetual inventory system** or a **periodic inventory system**.

ILLUSTRATION 5.4

Flow of costs

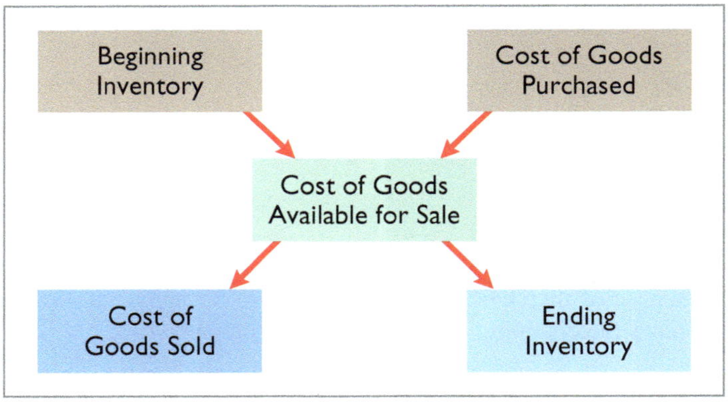

Perpetual System

In a **perpetual inventory system**, companies keep detailed records of the cost of each inventory purchase and sale (see **Helpful Hint**). These records continuously—perpetually—show the inventory that should be on hand for every item. For example, a **Ford** dealership has separate inventory records for each automobile, truck, and van on its lot and showroom floor. Similarly, a **Kroger** grocery store uses bar codes and optical scanners to keep a daily running record of every box of cereal and every jar of jelly that it buys and sells. Under a perpetual inventory system, a company determines the cost of goods sold **each time a sale occurs**.

HELPFUL HINT

Even under perpetual inventory systems, companies take a physical inventory count. This is done as a control procedure to verify inventory levels, in order to detect theft or "shrinkage."

Periodic System

In a **periodic inventory system**, companies do not keep detailed inventory records of the goods on hand throughout the period. Instead, they determine the cost of goods sold **only at the end of the accounting period**—that is, periodically. At that point, the company takes a physical inventory count to determine the cost of goods on hand.

To determine the cost of goods sold under a periodic inventory system, the following steps are necessary:

1. Determine the cost of goods on hand at the beginning of the accounting period.
2. Add to it the cost of goods purchased.
3. Subtract the cost of goods on hand as determined by the physical inventory count at the end of the accounting period.

Illustration 5.5 compares the sequence of activities and the timing of the cost of goods sold computation under the two inventory systems.

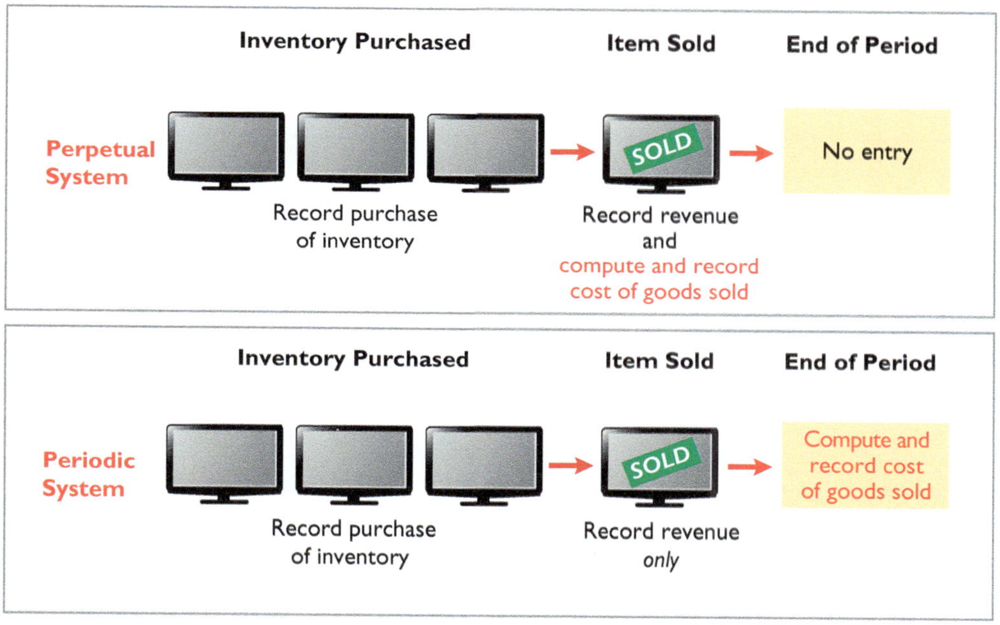

ILLUSTRATION 5.5
Comparing perpetual and periodic inventory systems

Advantages of the Perpetual System

Companies that sell merchandise with high unit values, such as automobiles, furniture, and major home appliances, have traditionally used perpetual systems. The growing use of computers and electronic scanners has enabled many more companies to install perpetual inventory systems. The perpetual inventory system is so named because the accounting records continuously—perpetually—show the quantity and cost of the inventory that should be on hand at any time.

A perpetual inventory system provides better control over inventories than a periodic system. Since the inventory records show the quantities that should be on hand, the company can count the goods at any time to see whether the amount of goods actually on hand agrees with the inventory records. If shortages are uncovered, the company can investigate immediately. Although a perpetual inventory system requires both additional clerical work and expense to maintain the subsidiary records, a computerized system can minimize this cost. Much of **Amazon.com**'s success is attributed to its sophisticated inventory system.

Some businesses find it either unnecessary or uneconomical to invest in a sophisticated, computerized perpetual inventory system such as Amazon's. Many small merchandising businesses now use basic accounting software which provides some of the essential benefits of a perpetual inventory system. Also, managers of some small businesses still find that they can control their merchandise and manage day-to-day operations using a periodic inventory system.

Because of the widespread use of the perpetual inventory system, we illustrate it in this chapter. We discuss and illustrate the periodic system in Appendix 5B.

Investor Insight Morrow Snowboards, Inc.

© Ben Blankenburg/iStockphoto

Improving Stock Appeal

Investors are often eager to invest in a company that has a hot new product. However, when snowboard-maker **Morrow Snowboards, Inc.** issued shares of stock to the public for the first time, some investors expressed reluctance to invest in Morrow because of a number of accounting control problems. To reduce investor concerns, Morrow implemented a perpetual inventory system to improve its control over inventory. In addition, the company stated that it would perform a physical inventory count every quarter until it felt that its perpetual inventory system was reliable.

If a perpetual system keeps track of inventory on a daily basis, why do companies ever need to do a physical count? (Go to WileyPLUS for this answer and additional questions.)

DO IT! 1 | Merchandising Operations and Inventory Systems

Indicate whether the following statements are true or false. If false, indicate how to correct the statement.

1. The primary source of revenue for a merchandising company results from performing services for customers.
2. The operating cycle of a service company is usually shorter than that of a merchandising company.
3. Sales revenue less cost of goods sold equals gross profit.
4. Ending inventory plus the cost of goods purchased equals cost of goods available for sale.

ACTION PLAN

- **Review merchandising concepts.**
- **Understand the flow of costs in a merchandising company.**

Solution

1. False. The primary source of revenue for a service company results from performing services for customers. **2.** True. **3.** True. **4.** False. Beginning inventory plus the cost of goods purchased equals cost of goods available for sale.

Related exercise material: **BE5.1, BE5.2, DO IT! 5.1, and E5.1.**

Recording Purchases under a Perpetual System

LEARNING OBJECTIVE 2

Record purchases under a perpetual inventory system.

Companies purchase inventory using cash or credit (on account). They normally record purchases when they receive the goods from the seller. Every purchase should be supported by business documents that provide written evidence of the transaction. Each cash purchase should be supported by a canceled check or a cash register receipt indicating the items purchased and amounts paid. Companies record cash purchases by an increase in Inventory and a decrease in Cash.

A **purchase invoice** should support each credit purchase. This invoice indicates the total purchase price and other relevant information. However, the purchaser does not prepare a separate purchase invoice. Instead, the purchaser uses as a purchase invoice a copy of the sales invoice sent by the seller. In **Illustration 5.6**, for example, Sauk Stereo (the buyer) uses as a purchase invoice the sales invoice prepared by PW Audio Supply (the seller) (see **Helpful Hint**).

ILLUSTRATION 5.6

Sales invoice used as purchase invoice by Sauk Stereo

INVOICE NO. 731

PW AUDIO SUPPLY
27 CIRCLE DRIVE
HARDING, MICHIGAN 48281

SOLD TO
Firm Name: Sauk Stereo
Attention of: James Hoover, Purchasing Agent
Address: 125 Main Street
Chelsea (City) Illinois (State) 60915 (Zip)

Date 5/4/20	Salesperson Malone	Terms 2/10, n/30	FOB Shipping Point	
Catalog No.	**Description**	**Quantity**	**Price**	**Amount**
X572Y9820	Printed Circuit Board-prototype	1	2,300	$2,300
A2547Z45	Production Model Circuits	5	300	1,500

IMPORTANT: ALL RETURNS MUST BE MADE WITHIN 10 DAYS — **TOTAL** $3,800

HELPFUL HINT

To better understand the contents of this invoice, identify these items:

1. Seller
2. Invoice date
3. Purchaser
4. Salesperson
5. Credit terms
6. Freight terms
7. Goods sold: catalog number, description, quantity, price per unit
8. Total invoice amount

Sauk Stereo makes the following journal entry to record its purchase from PW Audio Supply on account. The entry increases (debits) Inventory and increases (credits) Accounts Payable.

May 4	Inventory	3,800	
	Accounts Payable		3,800
	(To record goods purchased on account from PW Audio Supply)		

A	=	L	+	OE
+3,800				
		+3,800		

Cash Flows
no effect

Under the perpetual inventory system, companies record purchases of merchandise for sale in the Inventory account. Thus, **REI** would increase (debit) Inventory for clothing, sporting goods, and anything else purchased for resale to customers.

Not all purchases are debited to Inventory, however. Companies record purchases of assets acquired for use and not for resale, such as supplies, equipment, and similar items, as increases to specific asset accounts rather than to Inventory. For example, to record the purchase of materials used to make shelf signs or for cash register receipt paper, REI would increase (debit) Supplies.

Freight Costs

The sales agreement should indicate who—the seller or the buyer—is to pay for transporting the goods to the buyer's place of business. When a common carrier such as a railroad, trucking company, or airline transports the goods, the carrier prepares a freight bill in accord with the sales agreement.

Freight terms are expressed as either FOB shipping point or FOB destination. The letters FOB mean **free on board**. Thus, **FOB shipping point** means that the seller places the goods free on board the carrier, and the buyer pays the freight costs. Conversely, **FOB destination** means that the seller places the goods free on board to the buyer's place of business, and the seller pays the freight. For example, the sales invoice in Illustration 5.6 indicates FOB shipping point. Thus, the buyer (Sauk Stereo) pays the freight charges. **Illustration 5.7** illustrates these shipping terms.

ILLUSTRATION 5.7 **Shipping terms**

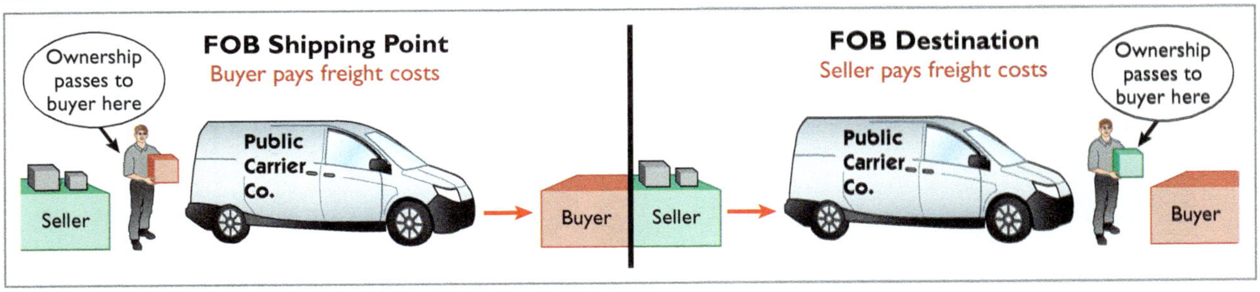

Freight Costs Incurred by the Buyer

When the buyer incurs the transportation costs, these costs are considered part of the cost of purchasing inventory. Therefore, the buyer debits (increases) the Inventory account. For example, if Sauk Stereo (the buyer) pays Public Carrier Co. $150 for freight charges on May 6, the entry on Sauk Stereo's books is:

A	=	L	+	OE
+150				
−150				

Cash Flows
−150

May 6	Inventory	150	
	Cash		150
	(To record payment of freight on goods purchased)		

Thus, any freight costs incurred by the buyer are part of the cost of merchandise purchased. The reason: Inventory cost should include all costs to acquire the inventory, including freight necessary to deliver the goods to the buyer. Companies recognize these costs as cost of goods sold when inventory is sold.

Freight Costs Incurred by the Seller

In contrast, **freight costs incurred by the seller on outgoing merchandise are an operating expense to the seller**. These costs increase an expense account titled Freight-Out (sometimes called Delivery Expense). For example, if the freight terms on the invoice in Illustration 5.6 had required PW Audio Supply (the seller) to pay the freight charges, the entry by PW Audio Supply would be:

A	=	L	+	OE
				−150 Exp
−150				

Cash Flows
−150

May 4	Freight-Out (or Delivery Expense)	150	
	Cash		150
	(To record payment of freight on goods sold)		

When the seller pays the freight charges, the seller will usually establish a higher invoice price for the goods to cover the shipping expense.

Purchase Returns and Allowances

A purchaser may be dissatisfied with the merchandise received because the goods are damaged or defective, of inferior quality, or do not meet the purchaser's specifications. In such cases, the purchaser may return the goods to the seller for credit if the sale was made on credit, or for a cash refund if the purchase was for cash. This transaction is known as a **purchase return**. Alternatively, the purchaser may choose to keep the merchandise if the seller is willing to grant an allowance (deduction) from the purchase price. This transaction is known as a **purchase allowance**.

Assume that Sauk Stereo returned goods costing $300 to PW Audio Supply on May 8. The following entry by Sauk Stereo for the returned merchandise decreases (debits) Accounts Payable and decreases (credits) Inventory.

May 8	Accounts Payable	300	
	Inventory		300
	(To record return of goods purchased from PW Audio Supply)		

A	=	L	+	OE
		−300		
−300				

Cash Flows
no effect

Because Sauk Stereo increased Inventory when the goods were received, Inventory is decreased when Sauk Stereo returns the goods.

Suppose instead that Sauk Stereo chose to keep the goods after being granted a $50 allowance (reduction in price). It would reduce (debit) Accounts Payable and reduce (credit) Inventory for $50.

Purchase Discounts

The credit terms of a purchase on account may permit the buyer to claim a cash discount for prompt payment. The buyer calls this cash discount a **purchase discount**. This incentive offers advantages to both parties. The purchaser saves money, and the seller is able to shorten the operating cycle by converting the accounts receivable into cash.

Credit terms specify the amount of the cash discount and time period in which it is offered. They also indicate the time period in which the purchaser is expected to pay the full invoice price. In the sales invoice in Illustration 5.6, credit terms are 2/10, n/30, which is read "two-ten, net thirty" (see **Helpful Hint**). This means that the buyer may take a 2% cash discount on the invoice price, less ("net of") any returns or allowances, if payment is made within 10 days of the invoice date (the **discount period**). Otherwise, the invoice price, less any returns or allowances, is due 30 days from the invoice date.

HELPFUL HINT

The term *net* in "net 30" means the remaining amount due after subtracting any sales returns and allowances and partial payments.

Alternatively, the discount period may extend to a specified number of days following the month in which the sale occurs. For example, 1/10 EOM (end of month) means that a 1% discount is available if the invoice is paid within the first 10 days of the next month.

When the seller elects not to offer a cash discount for prompt payment, credit terms will specify only the maximum time period for paying the balance due. For example, the invoice may state the time period as n/30, n/60, or n/10 EOM. This means, respectively, that the buyer must pay the net amount in 30 days, 60 days, or within the first 10 days of the next month.

When the buyer pays an invoice within the discount period, the amount of the discount decreases Inventory. Why? Because companies record inventory at cost and, by paying within the discount period, the buyer has reduced its cost. To illustrate, assume Sauk Stereo pays the balance due of $3,500 (gross invoice price of $3,800 less purchase returns and allowances of $300) on May 14, the last day of the discount period. Since the terms are 2/10, n/30, the cash discount is $70 ($3,500 × 2%), and Sauk Stereo pays $3,430 ($3,500 − $70). The entry Sauk Stereo makes to record its May 14 payment decreases (debits) Accounts Payable by

A	=	L	+	OE
		−3,500		
−3,430				
−70				

Cash Flows
−3,430

the amount of the gross invoice price, reduces (credits) Inventory by the $70 discount, and reduces (credits) Cash by the net amount owed.

May 14	Accounts Payable	3,500	
	Cash		3,430
	Inventory		70
	(To record payment within discount period)		

A	=	L	+	OE
		−3500		
−3,500				

Cash Flows
−3,500

If Sauk Stereo failed to take the discount and instead made full payment of $3,500 on June 3, it would debit Accounts Payable and credit Cash for $3,500 each.

June 3	Accounts Payable	3,500	
	Cash		3,500
	(To record payment with no discount taken)		

A merchandising company usually should take all available discounts. Passing up the discount may be viewed as **paying interest** for use of the money. For example, passing up the discount offered by PW Audio Supply would be comparable to Sauk Stereo paying an interest rate of 2% for the use of $3,500 for 20 days. This is the equivalent of an annual interest rate of approximately 36.5% (2% × 365/20). Obviously, it would be better for Sauk Stereo to borrow at prevailing bank interest rates of 6% to 10% than to lose the discount.

Summary of Purchasing Transactions

The following T-account (with transaction descriptions in red) provides a summary of the effect of the previous transactions on Inventory. Sauk Stereo originally purchased $3,800 worth of inventory on account for resale. It then returned $300 of goods. It paid $150 in freight charges, and finally, it received a $70 discount off the balance owed because it paid within the discount period. This results in a balance in Inventory of $3,580.

	Inventory				
Purchase	May 4	3,800	May 8	300	**Purchase return**
Freight-in	6	150	14	70	**Purchase discount**
Balance		3,580			

DO IT! 2 | Purchase Transactions

On September 5, De La Hoya Company buys merchandise on account from Junot Diaz Company. The purchase price of the goods paid by De La Hoya is $1,500, and the cost to Diaz Company was $800. On September 8, De La Hoya returns defective goods with a selling price of $200. Record the transactions on the books of De La Hoya Company.

ACTION PLAN

- **Purchaser records goods at cost.**
- **When goods are returned, purchaser reduces Inventory.**

Solution

Sept. 5	Inventory	1,500	
	Accounts Payable		1,500
	(To record goods purchased on account)		
8	Accounts Payable	200	
	Inventory		200
	(To record return of defective goods)		

Related exercise material: **BE5.3, BE5.5, DO IT! 5.2, E5.2, E5.3, and E5.4.**

Recording Sales Under a Perpetual System

LEARNING OBJECTIVE 3

Record sales under a perpetual inventory system.

In accordance with the revenue recognition principle, companies record sales revenue when the performance obligation is satisfied. Typically, the performance obligation is satisfied when the goods transfer from the seller to the buyer. At this point, the sales transaction is complete and the sales price established.

Sales may be made on credit or for cash. A **business document** should support every sales transaction, to provide written evidence of the sale. **Cash register documents** provide evidence of cash sales. A **sales invoice**, like the one shown in Illustration 5.6, provides support for a credit sale. The original copy of the invoice goes to the customer, and the seller keeps a copy for use in recording the sale. The invoice shows the date of sale, customer name, total sales price, and other relevant information.

The seller makes two entries for each sale. **The first entry records the sale**: The seller increases (debits) Cash (or Accounts Receivable if a credit sale) and also increases (credits) Sales Revenue. **The second entry records the cost of the merchandise sold**: The seller increases (debits) Cost of Goods Sold and also decreases (credits) Inventory for the cost of those goods. As a result, the Inventory account will show at all times the amount of inventory that should be on hand.

To illustrate a credit sales transaction, PW Audio Supply records its May 4 sale of $3,800 to Sauk Stereo (see Illustration 5.6) as follows (assume the merchandise cost PW Audio Supply $2,400).

May 4	Accounts Receivable	3,800	
	Sales Revenue		3,800
	(To record credit sale to Sauk Stereo per invoice #731)		
4	Cost of Goods Sold	2,400	
	Inventory		2,400
	(To record cost of merchandise sold on invoice #731 to Sauk Stereo)		

A	=	L	+	OE
+3,800				+3,800 Rev

Cash Flows
no effect

A	=	L	+	OE
−2,400				−2,400 Exp

Cash Flows
no effect

For internal decision-making purposes, merchandising companies may use more than one sales account. For example, PW Audio Supply may decide to keep separate sales accounts for its sales of TVs, Blu-ray players, and headsets. **REI** might use separate accounts for camping gear, children's clothing, and ski equipment—or it might have even more narrowly defined accounts. By using separate sales accounts for major product lines, rather than a single combined sales account, company management can more closely monitor sales trends and respond to changes in sales patterns more strategically. For example, if TV sales are increasing while Blu-ray player sales are decreasing, PW Audio Supply might reevaluate both its advertising and pricing policies on these items to ensure they are optimal.

On its income statement presented to outside investors, a merchandising company normally would provide only a single sales figure—the sum of all of its individual sales accounts. This is done for two reasons. First, providing detail on all of its individual sales accounts would add considerable length to its income statement. Second, companies do not want their competitors to know the details of their operating results. However, **Microsoft** recently expanded its disclosure of revenue from three to five types. The reason: The additional categories enabled financial statement users to better evaluate the growth of the company's consumer and Internet businesses (see **Ethics Note**).

ETHICS NOTE

Many companies are trying to improve the quality of their financial reporting. For example, General Electric now provides more detail on its revenues and operating profits.

Anatomy of a Fraud[1]

Holly Harmon was a cashier at a national superstore for only a short time when she began stealing merchandise using three methods. Under the first method, her husband or friends took UPC labels from cheaper items and put them on more expensive items. Holly then scanned the goods at the register. Using the second method, Holly scanned an item at the register but then voided the sale and left the merchandise in the shopping cart. A third approach was to put goods into large plastic containers. She scanned the plastic containers but not the goods within them. After Holly quit, a review of past surveillance tapes enabled the store to observe the thefts and to identify the participants.

Total take: $12,000

The Missing Controls

Human resource controls. A background check would have revealed Holly's previous criminal record. She would not have been hired as a cashier.

Physical controls. Software can flag high numbers of voided transactions or a high number of sales of low-priced goods. Random comparisons of video records with cash register records can ensure that the goods reported as sold on the register are the same goods that are shown being purchased on the video recording. Finally, employees should be aware that they are being monitored.

Source: Adapted from Wells, *Fraud Casebook* (2007), pp. 251–259.

At the end of "Anatomy of a Fraud" stories, which describe some recent real-world frauds, we discuss the missing control activities that would likely have prevented or uncovered the fraud.

Sales Returns and Allowances

We now look at the "flip side" of purchase returns and allowances, which the seller records as **sales returns and allowances**. These are transactions where the seller either accepts goods back from the buyer (a return) or grants a reduction in the purchase price (an allowance) so the buyer will keep the goods. PW Audio Supply's entries to record credit for returned goods involve (1) an increase (debit) in Sales Returns and Allowances (a contra account to Sales Revenue) and a decrease (credit) in Accounts Receivable at the $300 selling price, and (2) an increase (debit) in Inventory (assume a $140 cost) and a decrease (credit) in Cost of Goods Sold, as shown below (assuming that the goods were not defective).

A	=	L	+	OE
				−300 Rev
−300				

Cash Flows
no effect

May 8	Sales Returns and Allowances	300	
	Accounts Receivable		300
	(To record credit granted to Sauk Stereo for returned goods)		

A	=	L	+	OE
+140				
				+140 Exp

Cash Flows
no effect

8	Inventory	140	
	Cost of Goods Sold		140
	(To record cost of goods returned)		

If Sauk Stereo returns goods because they are damaged or defective, then PW Audio Supply's entry to Inventory and Cost of Goods Sold should be for the fair value of the returned goods, rather than their cost. For example, if the returned goods were defective and had a fair value of $50, PW Audio Supply would debit Inventory for $50 and credit Cost of Goods Sold for $50.

[1]The "Anatomy of a Fraud" stories in this textbook are adapted from *Fraud Casebook: Lessons from the Bad Side of Business*, edited by Joseph T. Wells (Hoboken, NJ: John Wiley & Sons, Inc., 2007). Used by permission. The names of some of the people and organizations in the stories are fictitious, but the facts in the stories are true.

What happens if the goods are not returned but the seller grants the buyer an allowance by reducing the purchase price? In this case, the seller debits Sales Returns and Allowances and credits Accounts Receivable for the amount of the allowance. An allowance has no impact on Inventory or Cost of Goods Sold.

Sales Returns and Allowances is a **contra revenue account** to Sales Revenue. This means that it is offset against a revenue account on the income statement. The normal balance of Sales Returns and Allowances is a debit. Companies use a contra account, instead of debiting Sales Revenue, to disclose in the accounts and in the income statement the amount of sales returns and allowances. Disclosure of this information is important to management. Excessive returns and allowances may suggest problems—inferior merchandise, inefficiencies in filling orders, errors in billing customers, or delivery or shipment mistakes. Moreover, a decrease (debit) recorded directly to Sales Revenue would obscure the relative importance of sales returns and allowances as a percentage of sales. It also could distort comparisons between total sales in different accounting periods.

At the end of the accounting period, if the company anticipates that sales returns and allowances will be material, the company should make an adjusting entry to estimate the amount of returns. In some industries, such as those relating to the sale of books and periodicals, returns are often material. The accounting for situations where returns must be estimated is addressed in advanced accounting courses.

Accounting Across the Organization — Costco Wholesale Corp.

© Jacob Wackerhausen/iStockphoto

The Point of No Returns?

In most industries, sales returns are relatively minor. But returns of consumer electronics can really take a bite out of profits. Recently, the marketing executives at **Costco Wholesale Corp.** faced a difficult decision. Costco has always prided itself on its generous return policy. Most goods have had an unlimited grace period for returns. However, a new policy requires that certain electronics must be returned within 90 days of their purchase. The reason? The cost of returned products such as high-definition TVs, computers, and iPods cut an estimated 8¢ per share off Costco's earnings per share, which was $2.30.

Source: Kris Hudson, "Costco Tightens Policy on Returning Electronics," *Wall Street Journal* (February 27, 2007), p. B4.

If a company expects significant returns, what are the implications for revenue recognition? (Go to WileyPLUS for this answer and additional questions.)

Sales Discounts

As mentioned in our discussion of purchase transactions, the seller may offer the customer a cash discount—called by the seller a **sales discount**—for the prompt payment of the balance due. Like a purchase discount, a sales discount is based on the invoice price less returns and allowances, if any. The seller increases (debits) the Sales Discounts account for discounts that are taken. For example, PW Audio Supply makes the following entry to record the cash receipt on May 14 from Sauk Stereo within the discount period.

May 14	Cash	3,430	
	Sales Discounts	70	
	Accounts Receivable		3,500
	(To record collection within 2/10, n/30 discount period from Sauk Stereo)		

A	=	L	+	OE
+3,430				
				−70 Rev
−3,500				

Cash Flows
+3,430

Like Sales Returns and Allowances, Sales Discounts is a **contra revenue account** to Sales Revenue. Its normal balance is a debit. PW Audio Supply uses this account, instead of debiting Sales Revenue, to disclose the amount of cash discounts taken by customers. If Sauk

Stereo does not take the discount, PW Audio Supply increases (debits) Cash for $3,500 and decreases (credits) Accounts Receivable for the same amount at the date of collection.

At the end of the accounting period, if the amount of potential discounts is material, the company should make an adjusting entry to estimate the discounts. This would not usually be the case for sales discounts but might be necessary for other types of discounts such as volume discounts, which are addressed in more advanced accounting courses.

The following T-accounts summarize the three sales-related transactions and show their combined effect on net sales.

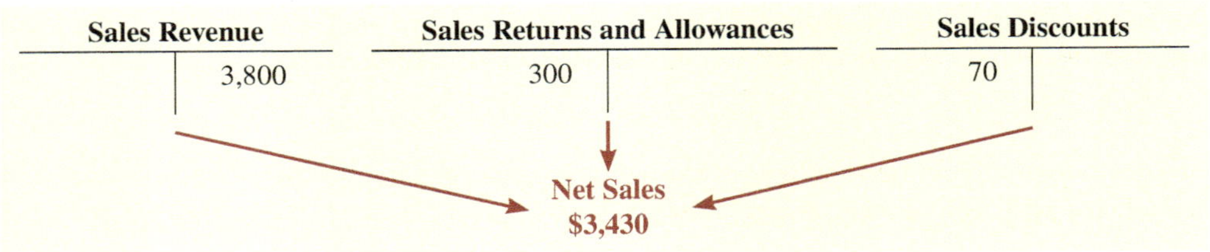

People, Planet, and Profit Insight PepsiCo

Helen Sessions/Alamy

Selling Green

Here is a question an executive of **PepsiCo** was asked: Should PepsiCo market green? The executive indicated that the company should, as he believes it's the No. 1 thing consumers all over the world care about. Here are some of his thoughts on this issue:

"Sun Chips are part of the food business I run. It's a 'healthy snack.' We decided that Sun Chips, if it's a healthy snack, should be made in facilities that have a net-zero footprint. In other words, I want off the electric grid everywhere we make Sun Chips. We did that. Sun Chips should be made in a facility that puts back more water than it uses. It does that. And we partnered with our suppliers and came out with the world's first compostable chip package.

Now, there was an issue with this package: It was louder than the New York subway, louder than jet engines taking off. What would a company that's committed to green do: walk away or stay committed? If your people are passionate, they're going to fix it for you as long as you stay committed. Six months later, the compostable bag has half the noise of our current package.

So the view today is: we should market green, we should be proud to do it . . . it has to be a 360-degree process, both internal and external. And if you do that, you can monetize environmental sustainability for the shareholders."

Source: "Four Problems—and Solutions," *Wall Street Journal* (March 7, 2011), p. R2.

What is meant by "monetize environmental sustainability" for shareholders? (Go to WileyPLUS for this answer and additional questions.)

DO IT! 3 | Sales Transactions

On September 5, De La Hoya Company buys merchandise on account from Junot Diaz Company. The selling price of the goods is $1,500, and the cost to Diaz Company was $800. On September 8, De La Hoya returns defective goods with a selling price of $200 and a fair value of $30. Record the transactions on the books of Junot Diaz Company.

Solution

Sept. 5	Accounts Receivable	1,500	
	Sales Revenue		1,500
	(To record credit sale)		
5	Cost of Goods Sold	800	
	Inventory		800
	(To record cost of goods sold on account)		

ACTION PLAN

- **Seller records both the sale and the cost of goods sold at the time of the sale.**
- **When goods are returned, the seller records the return in a contra account, Sales Returns and Allowances, and reduces Accounts Receivable.**

8	Sales Returns and Allowances	200	
	Accounts Receivable		200
	(To record credit granted for receipt of returned goods)		
8	Inventory	30	
	Cost of Goods Sold		30
	(To record fair value of goods returned)		

Related exercise material: **BE5.3, BE5.4, DO IT! 5.3, E5.3, E5.4, and E5.5.**

ACTION PLAN (*cont.*)

- **Any goods returned increase Inventory and reduce Cost of Goods Sold. Defective or damaged inventory is recorded at fair value (scrap value).**

The Accounting Cycle for a Merchandising Company

LEARNING OBJECTIVE 4

Apply the steps in the accounting cycle to a merchandising company.

Up to this point, we have illustrated the basic entries for transactions relating to purchases and sales in a perpetual inventory system. Now we consider the remaining steps in the accounting cycle for a merchandising company. Each of the required steps described in Chapter 4 for service companies apply to merchandising companies. Appendix 5A to this chapter shows use of a worksheet by a merchandiser (an optional step).

Adjusting Entries

A merchandising company generally has the same types of adjusting entries as a service company. However, a merchandiser using a perpetual system will require one additional adjustment to make the records agree with the actual inventory on hand. Here's why. At the end of each period, for control purposes, a merchandising company that uses a perpetual system will take a physical count of its goods on hand. The company's unadjusted balance in Inventory usually does not agree with the actual amount of inventory on hand. The perpetual inventory records may be incorrect due to recording errors, theft, or waste. Thus, the company needs to adjust the perpetual records to make the recorded inventory amount agree with the inventory on hand. **This involves adjusting Inventory and Cost of Goods Sold.**

For example, suppose that PW Audio Supply has an unadjusted balance of $40,500 in Inventory. Through a physical count, PW Audio Supply determines that its actual merchandise inventory at December 31 is $40,000. The company would make an adjusting entry as follows.

Dec. 31	Cost of Goods Sold	500	
	Inventory ($40,500 – $40,000)		500
	(To adjust inventory to physical count)		

A	=	L	+	OE
–500				–500 Exp

Cash Flows
no effect

Closing Entries

A merchandising company, like a service company, closes to Income Summary all accounts that affect net income. In journalizing, the company credits all temporary accounts with debit balances, and debits all temporary accounts with credit balances, as the following shows for PW Audio Supply (see **Helpful Hint**). Note that PW Audio Supply closes Cost of Goods Sold to Income Summary.

HELPFUL HINT

The easiest way to prepare the first two closing entries is to identify the temporary accounts by their balances and then prepare one entry for the credits and one for the debits.

Dec. 31	Sales Revenue	480,000	
	Income Summary		480,000
	(To close income statement accounts with credit balances)		

31	Income Summary	450,000	
	Sales Returns and Allowances		12,000
	Sales Discounts		8,000
	Cost of Goods Sold		316,000
	Salaries and Wages Expense		64,000
	Freight-Out		7,000
	Advertising Expense		16,000
	Utilities Expense		17,000
	Depreciation Expense		8,000
	Insurance Expense		2,000
	(To close income statement accounts with debit balances)		
31	Income Summary	30,000	
	Owner's Capital		30,000
	(To close net income to capital)		
31	Owner's Capital	15,000	
	Owner's Drawings		15,000
	(To close drawings to capital)		

After PW Audio Supply has posted the closing entries, all temporary accounts have zero balances. Also, Owner's Capital has a balance that is carried over to the next period.

Summary of Merchandising Entries

Illustration 5.8 summarizes the entries for the merchandising accounts using a perpetual inventory system.

ILLUSTRATION 5.8 **Daily recurring and adjusting and closing entries**

	Transactions	Daily Recurring Entries	Dr.	Cr.
Sales Transactions	Selling merchandise to customers.	Cash or Accounts Receivable	XX	
		Sales Revenue		XX
		Cost of Goods Sold	XX	
		Inventory		XX
	Granting sales returns or allowances to customers.	Sales Returns and Allowances	XX	
		Cash or Accounts Receivable		XX
		Inventory	XX	
		Cost of Goods Sold		XX
	Paying freight costs on sales; FOB destination.	Freight-Out	XX	
		Cash		XX
	Receiving payment from customers within discount period.	Cash	XX	
		Sales Discounts	XX	
		Accounts Receivable		XX
Purchase Transactions	Purchasing merchandise for resale.	Inventory	XX	
		Cash or Accounts Payable		XX
	Paying freight costs on merchandise purchased; FOB shipping point.	Inventory	XX	
		Cash		XX
	Receiving purchase returns or allowances from suppliers.	Cash or Accounts Payable	XX	
		Inventory		XX
	Paying suppliers within discount period.	Accounts Payable	XX	
		Inventory		XX
		Cash		XX

ILLUSTRATION 5.8 *(Continued)*

Events	Adjusting and Closing Entries		
Adjust because book amount is higher than the inventory amount determined to be on hand.	Cost of Goods Sold	XX	
	Inventory		XX
Closing temporary accounts with credit balances.	Sales Revenue	XX	
	Income Summary		XX
Closing temporary accounts with debit balances.	Income Summary	XX	
	Sales Returns and Allowances		XX
	Sales Discounts		XX
	Cost of Goods Sold		XX
	Freight-Out		XX
	Expenses		XX

DO IT! 4 | Closing Entries

The trial balance of Celine's Sports Wear Shop at December 31 shows Inventory $25,000, Sales Revenue $162,400, Sales Returns and Allowances $4,800, Sales Discounts $3,600, Cost of Goods Sold $110,000, Rent Revenue $6,000, Freight-Out $1,800, Rent Expense $8,800, and Salaries and Wages Expense $22,000. Prepare the closing entries for the above accounts.

ACTION PLAN

- **Close all temporary accounts with credit balances to Income Summary by debiting these accounts.**
- **Close all temporary accounts with debit balances, except drawings, to Income Summary by crediting these accounts.**

Solution

The two closing entries are:

Dec. 31	Sales Revenue	162,400	
	Rent Revenue	6,000	
	Income Summary		168,400
	(To close accounts with credit balances)		
31	Income Summary	151,000	
	Cost of Goods Sold		110,000
	Sales Returns and Allowances		4,800
	Sales Discounts		3,600
	Freight-Out		1,800
	Rent Expense		8,800
	Salaries and Wages Expense		22,000
	(To close accounts with debit balances)		

Related exercise material: **BE5.6, BE5.7, DO IT! 5.4, E5.6, E5.7, and E5.8.**

Multiple-Step and Comprehensive Income Statements

LEARNING OBJECTIVE 5

Prepare a multiple-step income statement and a comprehensive income statement.

Merchandising companies widely use the classified balance sheet introduced in Chapter 4 and one of two forms for the income statement. This section explains the use of these financial statements by merchandisers.

Multiple-Step Income Statement

The **multiple-step income statement** is so named because it shows several steps in determining net income. Two of these steps relate to the company's principal operating activities. A multiple-step statement also distinguishes between **operating** and **nonoperating activities**. Finally, the statement highlights intermediate components of income and shows subgroupings of expenses.

Income Statement Presentation of Sales

The multiple-step income statement begins by presenting **sales revenue**. It then deducts contra revenue accounts—sales returns and allowances, and sales discounts—from sales revenue to arrive at **net sales**. **Illustration 5.9** presents the sales section for PW Audio Supply, using assumed data.

ILLUSTRATION 5.9
Computation of net sales

PW Audio Supply
Income Statement (partial)

Sales		
Sales revenue		$480,000
Less: Sales returns and allowances	$12,000	
Sales discounts	8,000	20,000
Net sales		**$460,000**

Gross Profit

ALTERNATIVE TERMINOLOGY
Gross profit is sometimes referred to as *gross margin*.

From Illustration 5.1, you learned that companies deduct cost of goods sold from sales revenue to determine **gross profit** (see **Alternative Terminology**). For this computation, companies use **net sales** (which takes into consideration Sales Returns and Allowances and Sales Discounts) as the amount of sales revenue. On the basis of the sales data in Illustration 5.9 (net sales of $460,000) and cost of goods sold under the perpetual inventory system (assume $316,000), PW Audio Supply's gross profit is $144,000, computed as shown in **Illustration 5.10**.

ILLUSTRATION 5.10
Computation of gross profit

Net sales	$460,000
Cost of goods sold	316,000
Gross profit	**$144,000**

We also can express a company's gross profit as a percentage, called the **gross profit rate**. To do so, we divide the amount of gross profit by net sales. For PW Audio Supply, the **gross profit rate** is 31.3%, computed as shown in **Illustration 5.11**.

ILLUSTRATION 5.11
Gross profit rate formula and computation

Gross Profit	÷	Net Sales	=	Gross Profit Rate
$144,000	÷	$460,000	=	31.3%

Analysts generally consider the gross profit **rate** to be more useful than the gross profit **amount**. The rate expresses a more meaningful (qualitative) relationship between net sales and gross profit. For example, a gross profit of $1,000,000 may sound impressive. But if it is the result of a gross profit rate of only 7%, it is not so impressive. The gross profit rate tells how many cents of each sales dollar go to gross profit.

Gross profit represents the **merchandising profit** of a company. It is not a measure of the overall profitability because operating expenses are not yet deducted. But managers and other interested parties closely watch the amount and trend of gross profit. They compare current gross profit with amounts reported in past periods. They also compare the company's gross profit rate with rates of competitors and with industry averages. Such comparisons provide information about the effectiveness of a company's purchasing function and the soundness of its pricing policies.

Operating Expenses and Net Income

Operating expenses are the next component in measuring net income for a merchandising company. They are the expenses incurred in the process of earning sales revenue. These expenses are similar in merchandising and service companies. Companies sometimes segregate operating expenses into selling expenses and administrative expenses to provide additional information. Selling expenses include such items as expenses for sales salaries and advertising. Administrative expenses include such items as insurance expense and utility expense.

At PW Audio Supply, operating expenses were $114,000. The company determines its net income by subtracting operating expenses from gross profit. Thus, net income is $30,000, as **Illustration 5.12** shows.

Gross profit	$144,000
Operating expenses	**114,000**
Net income	$ 30,000

ILLUSTRATION 5.12

Operating expenses in computing net income

The net income amount is the so-called "bottom line" of a company's income statement.

Nonoperating Activities

Nonoperating activities consist of various revenues and expenses and gains and losses that are unrelated to the company's main line of operations. When nonoperating items are included, the label "**Income from operations**" (or "Operating income") precedes them. This label clearly identifies the results of the company's normal operations, an amount determined by subtracting cost of goods sold and operating expenses from net sales. The results of nonoperating activities are shown in the categories "**Other revenues and gains**" and "**Other expenses and losses**." **Illustration 5.13** lists examples of each.

Other Revenues and Gains
Interest revenue from notes receivable and marketable securities.
Dividend revenue from investments in common stock.
Rent revenue from subleasing a portion of the store.
Gain from the sale of property, plant, and equipment.
Other Expenses and Losses
Interest expense on notes and loans payable.
Casualty losses from recurring causes, such as vandalism and accidents.
Loss from the sale or abandonment of property, plant, and equipment.
Loss from strikes by employees and suppliers.

ILLUSTRATION 5.13

Other items of nonoperating activities

Merchandising companies report the nonoperating activities in the income statement immediately after the company's operating activities. **Illustration 5.14** shows these sections for PW Audio Supply, using assumed data.

The distinction between operating and nonoperating activities is crucial to many external users of financial data. These users view operating income as sustainable and many nonoperating activities as non-recurring (see **Ethics Note**). Therefore, when forecasting next year's income, analysts put the most weight on this year's operating income and less weight on this year's nonoperating activities.

ETHICS NOTE

Companies manage earnings in various ways. ConAgra Foods recorded a non-recurring gain for $186 million from the sale of Pilgrim's Pride stock to help meet an earnings projection for the quarter.

ILLUSTRATION 5.14

Multiple-step income statement

PW Audio Supply
Income Statement
For the Year Ended December 31, 2020

	Sales		
	Sales revenue		$480,000
Calculation of gross profit	Less: Sales returns and allowances	$12,000	
	Sales discounts	8,000	20,000
	Net sales		460,000
	Cost of goods sold		316,000
	Gross profit		144,000
	Operating expenses		
	Salaries and wages expense	64,000	
	Utilities expense	17,000	
Calculation of income from operations	Advertising expense	16,000	
	Depreciation expense	8,000	
	Freight-out	7,000	
	Insurance expense	2,000	
	Total operating expenses		114,000
	Income from operations		30,000
	Other revenues and gains		
	Interest revenue	3,000	
	Gain on disposal of plant assets	600	3,600
Results of nonoperating activities			
	Other expenses and losses		
	Interest expense	1,800	
	Casualty loss from vandalism	200	2,000
	Net income		$ 31,600

Ethics Insight IBM

ImageRite/Getty Images, Inc.

Disclosing More Details

After **Enron**, increased investor criticism and regulator scrutiny forced many companies to improve the clarity of their financial disclosures. For example, **IBM** began providing more detail regarding its "Other gains and losses." It had previously included these items in its selling, general, and administrative expenses, with little disclosure. For example, previously if IBM sold off one of its buildings at a gain, it would include this gain in the selling, general and administrative expense line item, thus reducing that expense. This made it appear that the company had done a better job of controlling operating expenses than it actually had.

As another example, when **eBay** sold the remainder of its investment in **Skype** to **Microsoft**, it reported a gain in "Other revenues and gains" of $1.7 billion. Since eBay's total income from operations was $2.4 billion, it was very important that the gain from the Skype sale not be buried in operating income.

Why have investors and analysts demanded more accuracy in isolating "Other gains and losses" from operating items? (Go to WileyPLUS for this answer and additional questions.)

Single-Step Income Statement

Another income statement format is the **single-step income statement**. The statement is so named because only one step—subtracting total expenses from total revenues—is required in determining net income.

In a single-step statement, all data are classified into two categories: (1) **revenues**, which include both operating revenues and other revenues and gains; and (2) **expenses**, which include cost of goods sold, operating expenses, and other expenses and losses. **Illustration 5.15** shows a single-step statement for PW Audio Supply.

ILLUSTRATION 5.15

Single-step income statement

PW Audio Supply Income Statement For the Year Ended December 31, 2020		
Revenues		
Net sales		$460,000
Interest revenue		3,000
Gain on disposal of plant assets		600
Total revenues		463,600
Expenses		
Cost of goods sold	$316,000	
Operating expenses	114,000	
Interest expense	1,800	
Casualty loss from vandalism	200	
Total expenses		432,000
Net income		$ 31,600

There are two primary reasons for using the single-step format. (1) A company does not realize any type of profit or income until total revenues exceed total expenses, so it makes sense to divide the statement into these two categories. (2) The format is simpler and easier to read. *For homework problems, however, you should use the single-step format only when specifically instructed to do so.*

Comprehensive Income Statement

Chapter 1 discussed the fair value principle. Accounting standards require companies to adjust the recorded values of certain types of assets and liabilities to their fair values at the end of each reporting period. In some instances, the unrealized gains or losses that result from adjusting recorded amounts to fair value are included in net income. However, in other cases, these unrealized gains and losses are not included in net income. Instead, these excluded items are reported as part of a more inclusive earnings measure, called **comprehensive income**. Examples of such items include certain adjustments to pension plan assets, gains and losses on foreign currency translation, and unrealized gains and losses on certain types of investments. Items that are excluded from net income but included in comprehensive income are either reported in a combined statement of net income and comprehensive income, or in a separate comprehensive income statement. The **comprehensive income statement** presents items that are not included in the determination of net income, referred to as other comprehensive income. **Illustration 5.16** shows how comprehensive income is presented in a separate comprehensive income statement. It assumes that PW Audio Supply had an unrealized gain of $2,300. *Use this format when preparing your homework.*

ILLUSTRATION 5.16

Combined statement of net income and comprehensive income

PW Audio Supply Comprehensive Income Statement For the Year Ended December 31, 2020	
Net income	$31,600
Other comprehensive income	
Unrealized holding gain on investment securities	2,300
Comprehensive income	$33,900

Classified Balance Sheet

In the balance sheet, merchandising companies report inventory as a current asset immediately below accounts receivable. Recall from Chapter 4 that companies generally list current asset items in the order of their closeness to cash (liquidity). Inventory is less close to cash than accounts receivable because the goods must first be sold and then collection made from the customer. **Illustration 5.17** presents the assets section of a classified balance sheet for PW Audio Supply (see **Helpful Hint**).

ILLUSTRATION 5.17 **Assets section of a classified balance sheet**

PW Audio Supply
Balance Sheet (Partial)
December 31, 2020

Assets		
Current assets		
Cash		$ 9,500
Accounts receivable		16,100
Inventory		40,000
Prepaid insurance		1,800
Total current assets		67,400
Property, plant, and equipment		
Equipment	$80,000	
Less: Accumulated depreciation—equipment	24,000	56,000
Total assets		$123,400

HELPFUL HINT

The $40,000 is the cost of the inventory on hand, not its expected selling price.

DO IT! 5 | Multiple-Step Income Statement

The following information is available for Art Center for the year ended December 31, 2020.

Other revenues and gains	$ 8,000	Sales revenue	$462,000
Other expenses and losses	3,000	Operating expenses	187,000
Cost of goods sold	147,000	Sales discounts	20,000
		Other comprehensive loss	10,000

Prepare a multiple-step income statement and comprehensive income statement for Art Center.

ACTION PLAN

- **Subtract cost of goods sold from net sales to determine gross profit.**
- **Subtract operating expenses from gross profit to determine income from operations.**
- **Add/subtract nonoperating items to determine net income.**

Solution

Art Center
Income Statement
For the Year Ended December 31, 2020

Sales		
Sales revenue		$462,000
Sales discounts		20,000
Net sales		442,000
Cost of goods sold		147,000
Gross profit		295,000
Operating expenses		187,000
Income from operations		108,000
Other revenues and gains	$8,000	
Other expenses and losses	3,000	5,000
Net income		$113,000

Art Center
Comprehensive Income Statement
For the Year Ended December 31, 2020

Net income	$113,000
Other comprehensive loss	10,000
Comprehensive income	$103,000

Related exercise material: **BE5.8, BE5.9, DO IT! 5.5, E5.9, E5.10, E5.12, E5.13, and E5.14.**

Appendix 5A Worksheet for a Merchandising Company

LEARNING OBJECTIVE *6

Prepare a worksheet for a merchandising company.

Using a Worksheet

As indicated in Chapter 4, a worksheet enables companies to prepare financial statements before they journalize and post adjusting entries. The steps in preparing a worksheet for a merchandising company are the same as for a service company. **Illustration 5A.1** shows the worksheet for PW Audio Supply (excluding nonoperating items). The unique accounts for a merchandiser using a **perpetual inventory system** are in red.

ILLUSTRATION 5A.1 **Worksheet for merchandising company—perpetual inventory system**

PW Audio Supply

PW Audio Supply
Worksheet
For the Year Ended December 31, 2020

	A	B	C	D	E	F	G	H	I	J	K
5–6		Trial Balance		Adjustments		Adjusted Trial Balance		Income Statement		Balance Sheet	
7	Accounts	Dr.	Cr.	Dr.	Cr.	Dr.	Cr.	Dr.	Cr.	Dr.	Cr.
8	Cash	9,500				9,500				9,500	
9	Accounts Receivable	16,100				16,100				16,100	
10	Inventory	40,500			(a) 500	40,000				40,000	
11	Prepaid Insurance	3,800			(b) 2,000	1,800				1,800	
12	Equipment	80,000				80,000				80,000	
13	Accumulated Depreciation—Equipment		16,000		(c) 8,000		24,000				24,000
14	Accounts Payable		20,400				20,400				20,400
15	Owner's Capital		83,000				83,000				83,000
16	Owner's Drawings	15,000				15,000				15,000	
17	Sales Revenue		480,000				480,000		480,000		
18	Sales Returns and Allowances	12,000				12,000		12,000			
19	Sales Discounts	8,000				8,000		8,000			
20	Cost of Goods Sold	315,500		(a) 500		316,000		316,000			
21	Freight-Out	7,000				7,000		7,000			
22	Advertising Expense	16,000				16,000		16,000			
23	Salaries and Wages Expense	59,000		(d) 5,000		64,000		64,000			
24	Utilities Expense	17,000				17,000		17,000			
25	Totals	599,400	599,400								
26	Insurance Expense			(b) 2,000		2,000		2,000			
27	Depreciation Expense			(c) 8,000		8,000		8,000			
28	Salaries and Wages Payable				(d) 5,000		5,000				5,000
29	Totals			15,500	15,500	612,400	612,400	450,000	480,000	162,400	132,400
30	Net Income							30,000			30,000
31	Totals							480,000	480,000	162,400	162,400

Key: (a) Adjustment to inventory on hand. (b) Insurance expired. (c) Depreciation expense. (d) Salaries and wages accrued.

Trial Balance Columns

Data for the trial balance come from the ledger balances of PW Audio Supply at December 31. The amount shown for Inventory, $40,500, is the year-end inventory amount from the perpetual inventory system.

Adjustments Columns

A merchandising company generally has the same types of adjustments as a service company. As you see in the worksheet, adjustments (b), (c), and (d) are for insurance, depreciation, and salaries. Pioneer Advertising, as illustrated in Chapters 3 and 4, also had these adjustments. Adjustment (a) was required to adjust the perpetual inventory carrying amount to the actual count.

After PW Audio Supply enters all adjustments data on the worksheet, it establishes the equality of the adjustments column totals. It then extends the balances in all accounts to the adjusted trial balance columns.

Adjusted Trial Balance

The adjusted trial balance shows the balance of all accounts after adjustment at the end of the accounting period.

Income Statement Columns

Next, the merchandising company transfers the accounts and balances that affect the income statement from the adjusted trial balance columns to the income statement columns. PW Audio Supply shows Sales Revenue of $480,000 in the credit column. It shows the contra revenue accounts Sales Returns and Allowances $12,000 and Sales Discounts $8,000 in the debit column. The difference of $460,000 is the net sales shown on the income statement (Illustration 5.14).

Finally, the company totals all the credits in the income statement column and compares those totals to the total of the debits in the income statement column. If the credits exceed the debits, the company has net income. PW Audio Supply has net income of $30,000. If the debits exceed the credits, the company would report a net loss.

Balance Sheet Columns

The major difference between the balance sheets of a service company and a merchandiser is inventory. PW Audio Supply shows the ending inventory amount of $40,000 in the balance sheet debit column. The information to prepare the owner's equity statement is also found in these columns. That is, the Owner's Capital account is $83,000. Owner's Drawings are $15,000. Net income results when the total of the debit column exceeds the total of the credit column in the balance sheet columns. A net loss results when the total of the credits exceeds the total of the debit balances.

Appendix 5B Periodic Inventory System

LEARNING OBJECTIVE *7

Record purchases and sales under a periodic inventory system.

As described in this chapter, companies may use one of two basic systems of accounting for inventories: (1) the perpetual inventory system or (2) the periodic inventory system. In the chapter, we focused on the characteristics of the perpetual inventory system. In this appendix, we discuss and illustrate the **periodic inventory system**. One key difference between the two systems is the point at which the company computes cost of goods sold. For a visual reminder of this difference, refer back to Illustration 5.5.

Determining Cost of Goods Sold Under a Periodic System

Determining cost of goods sold is different when a periodic inventory system is used rather than a perpetual system. As you have seen, a company using a **perpetual system** makes an entry to record cost of goods sold and to reduce inventory each time a sale is made. A company using a **periodic system** does not determine cost of goods sold until the end of the period. At the end of the period, the company performs a count to determine the ending balance of inventory. It then **calculates cost of goods sold by subtracting ending inventory from the cost of goods available for sale**. Cost of goods available for sale is the sum of beginning inventory plus purchases, as shown in **Illustration 5B.1**.

ILLUSTRATION 5B.1
Basic formula for cost of goods sold using the periodic system

	Beginning Inventory
+	Cost of Goods Purchased
	Cost of Goods Available for Sale
−	Ending Inventory
	Cost of Goods Sold

Another difference between the two approaches is that the perpetual system directly adjusts the Inventory account for any transaction that affects inventory (such as freight costs, returns, and discounts). The periodic system does not do this. Instead, it creates different accounts for purchases, freight costs, returns, and discounts. These various accounts are shown in **Illustration 5B.2**, which presents the calculation of cost of goods sold for PW Audio Supply using the periodic approach (see **Helpful Hint**).

ILLUSTRATION 5B.2
Cost of goods sold for a merchandiser using a periodic inventory system

PW Audio Supply
Cost of Goods Sold
For the Year Ended December 31, 2020

Cost of goods sold			
Inventory, January 1			**$ 36,000**
Purchases		$325,000	
Less: Purchase returns and allowances	$10,400		
Purchase discounts	6,800	17,200	
Net purchases		307,800	
Add: Freight-in		12,200	
Cost of goods purchased			**320,000**
Cost of goods available for sale			356,000
Less: Inventory, December 31			**40,000**
Cost of goods sold			**$316,000**

HELPFUL HINT

The far right column identifies the primary items that make up cost of goods sold of $316,000. The middle column explains cost of goods purchased of $320,000. The left column reports contra purchase items of $17,200.

Note that the basic elements from Illustration 5B.1 are highlighted in Illustration 5B.2. You will learn more in Chapter 6 about how to determine cost of goods sold using the periodic system.

The use of the periodic inventory system does not affect the form of presentation in the balance sheet. As under the perpetual system, a company reports inventory in the current assets section.

Recording Merchandise Transactions

In a **periodic inventory system**, companies record revenues from the sale of merchandise when sales are made, just as in a perpetual system. Unlike the perpetual system, however, companies **do not attempt on the date of sale to record the cost of the merchandise sold.**

Instead, they take a physical inventory count at the **end of the period** to determine (1) the cost of the merchandise then on hand and (2) the cost of the goods sold during the period. And, **under a periodic system, companies record purchases of merchandise in the Purchases account rather than in the Inventory account**. Purchase returns and allowances, purchase discounts, and freight costs on purchases are recorded in separate accounts.

To illustrate the recording of merchandise transactions under a periodic inventory system, we will use purchase/sales transactions between PW Audio Supply and Sauk Stereo, as illustrated for the perpetual inventory system in this chapter.

Recording Purchases of Merchandise

HELPFUL HINT

Be careful not to debit purchases of equipment or supplies to a Purchases account.

On the basis of the sales invoice (Illustration 5.6) and receipt of the merchandise ordered from PW Audio Supply, Sauk Stereo records the $3,800 purchase as follows (see **Helpful Hint**).

May 4	Purchases	3,800	
	Accounts Payable		3,800
	(To record goods purchased on account from PW Audio Supply)		

Purchases is a temporary account whose normal balance is a debit.

Freight Costs

When the purchaser directly incurs the freight costs, it debits the account Freight-In (or Transportation-In). For example, if Sauk Stereo pays Public Carrier Co. $150 for freight charges on its purchase from PW Audio Supply on May 6, the entry on Sauk Stereo's books is as follows.

May 6	Freight-In (Transportation-In)	150	
	Cash		150
	(To record payment of freight on goods purchased)		

Like Purchases, Freight-In is a temporary account whose normal balance is a debit. **Freight-In is part of cost of goods purchased.** The reason is that cost of goods purchased should include any freight charges necessary to bring the goods to the purchaser. Freight costs are not subject to a purchase discount. Purchase discounts apply only to the invoice cost of the merchandise.

Purchase Returns and Allowances

Sauk Stereo returns goods costing $300 to PW Audio Supply and prepares the following entry to recognize the return.

May 8	Accounts Payable	300	
	Purchase Returns and Allowances		300
	(To record return of goods purchased from PW Audio Supply)		

Purchase Returns and Allowances is a temporary account whose normal balance is a credit.

Purchase Discounts

On May 14, Sauk Stereo pays the balance due on account to PW Audio Supply, taking the 2% cash discount allowed by PW Audio Supply for payment within 10 days. Sauk Stereo records the payment and discount as follows.

May 14	Accounts Payable ($3,800 – $300)	3,500	
	Purchase Discounts ($3,500 × .02)		70
	Cash		3,430
	(To record payment within the discount period)		

Purchase Discounts is a temporary account whose normal balance is a credit.

Recording Sales of Merchandise

The seller, PW Audio Supply, records the sale of $3,800 of merchandise to Sauk Stereo on May 4 (sales invoice No. 731, Illustration 5.6) as follows.

May 4	Accounts Receivable	3,800	
	Sales Revenue		3,800
	(To record credit sales per invoice #731 to Sauk Stereo)		

Sales Returns and Allowances

To record the returned goods received from Sauk Stereo on May 8, PW Audio Supply records the $300 sales return as follows.

May 8	Sales Returns and Allowances	300	
	Accounts Receivable		300
	(To record credit granted to Sauk Stereo for returned goods)		

Sales Discounts

On May 14, PW Audio Supply receives payment of $3,430 on account from Sauk Stereo. PW Audio Supply honors the 2% cash discount and records the payment of Sauk Stereo's account receivable in full as follows.

May 14	Cash	3,430	
	Sales Discounts ($3,500 × .02)	70	
	Accounts Receivable ($3,800 – $300)		3,500
	(To record collection within 2/10, n/30 discount period from Sauk Stereo)		

Comparison of Entries—Perpetual vs. Periodic

Illustration 5B.3 summarizes the periodic inventory entries shown in this appendix and compares them to the perpetual system entries from the chapter. Entries that differ in the two systems are shown in color.

ILLUSTRATION 5B.3 **Comparison of entries for perpetual and periodic inventory systems**

ENTRIES ON SAUK STEREO'S BOOKS

	Transaction	Perpetual Inventory System			Periodic Inventory System		
May 4	Purchase of merchandise on credit.	**Inventory**	**3,800**		**Purchases**	**3,800**	
		Accounts Payable		3,800	Accounts Payable		3,800
6	Freight costs on purchases.	**Inventory**	**150**		**Freight-In**	**150**	
		Cash		150	Cash		150
8	Purchase returns and allowances.	Accounts Payable	300		Accounts Payable	300	
		Inventory		**300**	**Purchase Returns and Allowances**		**300**
14	Payment on account with a discount.	Accounts Payable	3,500		Accounts Payable	3,500	
		Cash		3,430	Cash		3,430
		Inventory		**70**	**Purchase Discounts**		**70**

ILLUSTRATION 5B.3 *(Continued)*

ENTRIES ON PW AUDIO SUPPLY'S BOOKS

Transaction		Perpetual Inventory System			Periodic Inventory System		
May 4	Sale of merchandise on credit.	Accounts Receivable	3,800		Accounts Receivable	3,800	
		Sales Revenue		3,800	Sales Revenue		3,800
		Cost of Goods Sold	**2,400**		**No entry for cost of goods sold**		
		Inventory		**2,400**			
8	Return of merchandise sold.	Sales Returns and Allowances	300		Sales Returns and Allowances	300	
		Accounts Receivable		300	Accounts Receivable		300
		Inventory	**140**		**No entry**		
		Cost of Goods Sold		**140**			
14	Cash received on account with a discount.	Cash	3,430		Cash	3,430	
		Sales Discounts	70		Sales Discounts	70	
		Accounts Receivable		3,500	Accounts Receivable		3,500

Journalizing and Posting Closing Entries

For a merchandising company, like a service company, all accounts that affect the determination of net income are closed to Income Summary. Data for the preparation of closing entries may be obtained from the income statement columns of the worksheet. In journalizing, all debit column amounts are credited, and all credit columns amounts are debited. To close the merchandise inventory in a periodic inventory system:

1. The beginning inventory balance is debited to Income Summary and credited to Inventory.
2. The ending inventory balance is debited to Inventory and credited to Income Summary.

The two entries for PW Audio Supply are as follows.

	(1)		
Dec. 31	Income Summary	36,000	
	Inventory		36,000
	(To close beginning inventory)		
	(2)		
31	Inventory	40,000	
	Income Summary		40,000
	(To record ending inventory)		

Illustration 5B.4 shows the Inventory and Income Summary accounts after posting.

ILLUSTRATION 5B.4

Posting closing entries for merchandise inventory

Inventory

1/1	Bal.	36,000	12/31	Close	36,000
12/31	Close	40,000			
12/31	Bal.	40,000			

Income Summary

12/31	Close	36,000	12/31	Close	40,000

HELPFUL HINT

Except for merchandise inventory, the easiest way to prepare the first two closing entries is to identify the temporary accounts by their balances and then prepare one entry for the credits and one for the debits.

Often, the closing of inventory is included with other closing entries, as shown below for PW Audio Supply (see **Helpful Hint**). (*Close inventory with other accounts in homework problems unless stated otherwise.*)

Dec. 31	**Inventory (Dec. 31)**	**40,000**	
	Sales Revenue	480,000	
	Purchase Returns and Allowances	10,400	
	Purchase Discounts	6,800	
	Income Summary		537,200
	(To record ending inventory and close accounts with credit balances)		

31	Income Summary	507,200	
	Inventory (Jan. 1)		**36,000**
	Sales Returns and Allowances		12,000
	Sales Discounts		8,000
	Purchases		325,000
	Freight-In		12,200
	Salaries and Wages Expense		64,000
	Freight-Out		7,000
	Advertising Expense		16,000
	Utilities Expense		17,000
	Depreciation Expense		8,000
	Insurance Expense		2,000
	(To close beginning inventory and other income statement accounts with debit balances)		
31	Income Summary	30,000	
	Owner's Capital		30,000
	(To transfer net income to capital)		
31	Owner's Capital	15,000	
	Owner's Drawings		15,000
	(To close drawings to capital)		

After the closing entries are posted, all temporary accounts have zero balances. In addition, Owner's Capital has a credit balance of $98,000: beginning balance + net income – drawings ($83,000 + $30,000 – $15,000).

Using a Worksheet

As indicated in Chapter 4, a worksheet enables companies to prepare financial statements before journalizing and posting adjusting entries. The steps in preparing a worksheet for a merchandising company are the same as they are for a service company.

Trial Balance Columns

Data for the trial balance come from the ledger balances of PW Audio Supply at December 31. The amount shown for Inventory, $36,000, is the beginning inventory amount from the periodic inventory system.

Adjustments Columns

A merchandising company generally has the same types of adjustments as a service company. As you see in the worksheet in **Illustration 5B.5**, adjustments (a), (b), and (c) are for insurance, depreciation, and salaries and wages. These adjustments were also required for Pioneer Advertising, as illustrated in Chapters 3 and 4. The unique accounts for a merchandiser using a **periodic inventory system** are shown in capital red letters. Note, however, that the worksheet excludes nonoperating items.

After all adjustment data are entered on the worksheet, the equality of the adjustment column totals is established. The balances in all accounts are then extended to the adjusted trial balance columns.

Income Statement Columns

Next, PW Audio Supply transfers the accounts and balances that affect the income statement from the adjusted trial balance columns to the income statement columns. The company shows Sales Revenue of $480,000 in the credit column. It shows the contra revenue accounts, Sales Returns and Allowances of $12,000 and Sales Discounts of $8,000 in the debit column. The difference of $460,000 is the net sales shown on the income statement (Illustration 5.9).

ILLUSTRATION 5B.5 Worksheet for merchandising company—periodic inventory system

PW Audio Supply

Home Insert Page Layout Formulas Data Review View

P18 fx

PW Audio Supply
Worksheet
For the Year Ended December 31, 2020

	Accounts	Trial Balance Dr.	Trial Balance Cr.	Adjustments Dr.	Adjustments Cr.	Adjusted Trial Balance Dr.	Adjusted Trial Balance Cr.	Income Statement Dr.	Income Statement Cr.	Balance Sheet Dr.	Balance Sheet Cr.
8	Cash	9,500				9,500				9,500	
9	Accounts Receivable	16,100				16,100				16,100	
10	INVENTORY	36,000				36,000		36,000	40,000	40,000	
11	Prepaid Insurance	3,800			(a) 2,000	1,800				1,800	
12	Equipment	80,000				80,000				80,000	
13	Accumulated Depreciation—Equipment		16,000		(b) 8,000		24,000				24,000
14	Accounts Payable		20,400				20,400				20,400
15	Owner's Capital		83,000				83,000				83,000
16	Owner's Drawings	15,000				15,000				15,000	
17	SALES REVENUE		480,000				480,000		480,000		
18	SALES RETURNS AND ALLOWANCES	12,000				12,000		12,000			
19	SALES DISCOUNTS	8,000				8,000		8,000			
20	PURCHASES	325,000				325,000		325,000			
21	PURCHASE RETURNS AND ALLOWANCES		10,400				10,400		10,400		
22	PURCHASE DISCOUNTS		6,800				6,800		6,800		
23	FREIGHT-IN	12,200				12,200		12,200			
24	Freight-Out	7,000				7,000		7,000			
25	Advertising Expense	16,000				16,000		16,000			
26	Salaries and Wages Expense	59,000		(c) 5,000		64,000		64,000			
27	Utilities Expense	17,000				17,000		17,000			
28	Totals	616,600	616,600								
29	Insurance Expense			(a) 2,000		2,000		2,000			
30	Depreciation Expense			(b) 8,000		8,000		8,000			
31	Salaries and Wages Payable				(c) 5,000		5,000				5,000
32	Totals			15,000	15,000	629,600	629,600	507,200	537,200	162,400	132,400
33	Net Income							30,000			30,000
34	Totals							537,200	537,200	162,400	162,400

Key: (a) Insurance expired. (b) Depreciation expense. (c) Salaries and wages accrued.

Similarly, Purchases of $325,000 and Freight-In of $12,200 are extended to the debit column. The contra purchase accounts, Purchase Returns and Allowances of $10,400 and Purchase Discounts of $6,800, are extended to the credit columns.

The worksheet procedures for the Inventory account merit specific comment. The procedures are:

1. The beginning balance, $36,000, is extended from the adjusted trial balance column to the **income statement debit column**. From there, it can be added in reporting cost of goods available for sale in the income statement.
2. The ending inventory, $40,000, is added to the worksheet by an **income statement credit and a balance sheet debit**. The credit makes it possible to deduct ending inventory from

the cost of goods available for sale in the income statement to determine cost of goods sold. The debit means the ending inventory can be reported as an asset on the balance sheet.

Illustration 5B.6 shows these two procedures.

		Income Statement		Balance Sheet	
		Dr.	Cr.	Dr.	Cr.
Inventory	(1)	**36,000**	**40,000** ←(2)→	**40,000**	

ILLUSTRATION 5B.6
Worksheet procedures for inventories

The computation for cost of goods sold, taken from the income statement column in Illustration 5B.5, is as shown in **Illustration on 5B.7** (see **Helpful Hint**).

Debit Column		Credit Column	
Beginning inventory	$ 36,000	Ending inventory	$40,000
Purchases	325,000	Purchase returns and allowances	10,400
Freight-in	12,200	Purchase discounts	6,800
Total debits	373,200	Total credits	$57,200
Less: Total credits	57,200		
Cost of goods sold	$316,000		

ILLUSTRATION 5B.7
Computation of cost of goods sold from worksheet columns

HELPFUL HINT
In a periodic system, cost of goods sold is a computation—it is not a separate account with a balance.

Finally, PW Audio Supply totals all the credits in the income statement column and compares these totals to the total of the debits in the income statement column. If the credits exceed the debits, the company has net income. PW Audio Supply has net income of $30,000. If the debits exceed the credits, the company would report a net loss.

Balance Sheet Columns

The major difference between the balance sheets of a service company and a merchandising company is inventory. PW Audio Supply shows ending inventory of $40,000 in the balance sheet debit column. The information to prepare the owner's equity statement is also found in these columns. That is, the Owner's Capital account is $83,000. Owner's Drawings are $15,000. Net income results when the total of the debit column exceeds the total of the credit column in the balance sheet columns. A net loss results when the total of the credits exceeds the total of the debit balances.

Review and Practice

Learning Objectives Review

1 Describe merchandising operations and inventory systems.

Because of inventory, a merchandising company has sales revenue, cost of goods sold, and gross profit. To account for inventory, a merchandising company must choose between a perpetual and a periodic inventory system.

2 Record purchases under a perpetual inventory system.

The company debits the Inventory account for all purchases of merchandise and freight-in, and credits it for purchase discounts and purchase returns and allowances.

3 Record sales under a perpetual inventory system.

When a merchandising company sells inventory, it debits Accounts Receivable (or Cash) and credits Sales Revenue for the **selling price** of the merchandise. At the same time, it debits Cost of Goods Sold and credits Inventory for the **cost** of the inventory items sold. Sales Returns and Allowances and Sales Discounts are debited and are contra revenue accounts.

4 Apply the steps in the accounting cycle to a merchandising company.

Each of the required steps in the accounting cycle for a service company applies to a merchandising company. A worksheet is again an optional step. Under a perpetual inventory system, the company must adjust the Inventory account to agree with the physical count.

5 Prepare a multiple-step income statement and a comprehensive income statement.

A multiple-step income statement shows numerous steps in determining net income, including nonoperating activities sections. A single-step income statement classifies all data under two categories, revenues or expenses, and determines net income in one step. A comprehensive income statement adds or subtracts any items of other comprehensive income to net income to arrive at comprehensive income.

***6 Prepare a worksheet for a merchandising company.**

The steps in preparing a worksheet for a merchandising company are the same as for a service company. The unique accounts for a merchandiser are Inventory, Sales Revenue, Sales Returns and Allowances, Sales Discounts, and Cost of Goods Sold.

***7 Record purchases and sales under a periodic inventory system.**

In recording purchases under a periodic system, companies must make entries for (a) cash and credit purchases, (b) purchase returns and allowances, (c) purchase discounts, and (d) freight costs. In recording sales, companies must make entries for (a) cash and credit sales, (b) sales returns and allowances, and (c) sales discounts.

Glossary Review

Comprehensive income An income measure that includes gains and losses that are excluded from the determination of net income. (p. 5-21).

Comprehensive income statement A statement that presents items that are not included in the determination of net income, referred to as other comprehensive income. (p. 5-21).

Contra revenue account An account that is offset against a revenue account on the income statement. (p. 5-13).

Cost of goods sold The total cost of merchandise sold during the period. (p. 5-3).

FOB destination Freight terms indicating that the seller places the goods free on board to the buyer's place of business, and the seller pays the freight. (p. 5-8).

FOB shipping point Freight terms indicating that the seller places goods free on board the carrier, and the buyer pays the freight costs. (p. 5-8).

Gross profit The excess of net sales over the cost of goods sold. (p. 5-18).

Gross profit rate Gross profit expressed as a percentage, by dividing the amount of gross profit by net sales. (p. 5-18).

Income from operations Income from a company's principal operating activity; determined by subtracting cost of goods sold and operating expenses from net sales. (p. 5-19).

Multiple-step income statement An income statement that shows several steps in determining net income. (p. 5-18).

Net sales Sales revenue less sales returns and allowances and less sales discounts. (p. 5-18).

Nonoperating activities Various revenues, expenses, gains, and losses that are unrelated to a company's main line of operations. (p. 5-19).

Operating expenses Expenses incurred in the process of earning sales revenue. (p. 5-19).

Other expenses and losses A nonoperating-activities section of the income statement that shows expenses and losses unrelated to the company's main line of operations. (p. 5-19).

Other revenues and gains A nonoperating-activities section of the income statement that shows revenues and gains unrelated to the company's main line of operations. (p. 5-19).

Periodic inventory system An inventory system under which the company does not keep detailed inventory records throughout the accounting period but determines the cost of goods sold only at the end of an accounting period. (p. 5-5).

Perpetual inventory system An inventory system under which the company keeps detailed records of the cost of each inventory purchase and sale, and the records continuously show the inventory that should be on hand. (p. 5-4).

Purchase allowance A deduction made to the selling price of merchandise, granted by the seller so that the buyer will keep the merchandise. (p. 5-9).

Purchase discount A cash discount claimed by a buyer for prompt payment of a balance due. (p. 5-9).

Purchase invoice A document that supports each credit purchase. (p. 5-7).

Purchase return A return of goods from the buyer to the seller for a cash or credit refund. (p. 5-9).

Sales discount A reduction given by a seller for prompt payment of a credit sale. (p. 5-13).

Sales invoice A document that supports each credit sale. (p. 5-11).

Sales returns and allowances Purchase returns and allowances from the seller's perspective. See *Purchase return* and *Purchase allowance*, above. (p. 5-12).

Sales revenue (Sales) The primary source of revenue in a merchandising company. (p. 5-3).

Single-step income statement An income statement that shows only one step in determining net income. (p. 5-20).

Practice Multiple-Choice Questions

1. **(LO 1)** Gross profit will result if:
   - **a.** operating expenses are less than net income.
   - **b.** net sales are greater than operating expenses.
   - **c.** net sales are greater than cost of goods sold.
   - **d.** operating expenses are greater than cost of goods sold.

2. **(LO 2)** Under a perpetual inventory system, when goods are purchased for resale by a company:
   - **a.** purchases on account are debited to Inventory.
   - **b.** purchases on account are debited to Purchases.
   - **c.** purchase returns are debited to Purchase Returns and Allowances.
   - **d.** freight costs are debited to Freight-Out.

3. **(LO 3)** The sales accounts that normally have a debit balance are:
   - **a.** Sales Discounts.
   - **b.** Sales Returns and Allowances.
   - **c.** Both (a) and (b).
   - **d.** Neither (a) nor (b).

4. **(LO 3)** A credit sale of $750 is made on June 13, terms 2/10, net/30. A return of $50 is granted on June 16. The amount received as payment in full on June 23 is:
   - **a.** $700.
   - **b.** $686.
   - **c.** $685.
   - **d.** $650.

5. **(LO 2)** Which of the following accounts will normally appear in the ledger of a merchandising company that uses a perpetual inventory system?
   - **a.** Purchases.
   - **b.** Freight-In.
   - **c.** Cost of Goods Sold.
   - **d.** Purchase Discounts.

6. **(LO 3)** To record the sale of goods for cash in a perpetual inventory system:
   - **a.** only one journal entry is necessary to record cost of goods sold and reduction of inventory.
   - **b.** only one journal entry is necessary to record the receipt of cash and the sales revenue.
   - **c.** two journal entries are necessary: one to record the receipt of cash and sales revenue, and one to record the cost of goods sold and reduction of inventory.
   - **d.** two journal entries are necessary: one to record the receipt of cash and reduction of inventory, and one to record the cost of goods sold and sales revenue.

7. **(LO 4)** The steps in the accounting cycle for a merchandising company are the same as those in a service company **except**:
   - **a.** an additional adjusting journal entry for inventory may be needed in a merchandising company.
   - **b.** closing journal entries are not required for a merchandising company.
   - **c.** a post-closing trial balance is not required for a merchandising company.
   - **d.** a multiple-step income statement is required for a merchandising company.

8. **(LO 5)** The multiple-step income statement for a merchandising company shows each of the following features **except**:
   - **a.** gross profit.
   - **b.** cost of goods sold.
   - **c.** a sales section.
   - **d.** an investing activities section.

9. **(LO 5)** If net sales are $400,000, cost of goods sold is $310,000, and operating expenses are $60,000, the gross profit is:
   - **a.** $30,000.
   - **b.** $90,000.
   - **c.** $340,000.
   - **d.** $400,000.

10. **(LO 5)** A single-step income statement:
    - **a.** reports gross profit.
    - **b.** does not report cost of goods sold.
    - **c.** reports sales revenue and "Other revenues and gains" in the revenues section of the income statement.
    - **d.** reports operating income separately.

11. **(LO 5)** Which of the following appears on both a single-step and a multiple-step income statement?
    - **a.** Inventory.
    - **b.** Gross profit.
    - **c.** Income from operations.
    - **d.** Cost of goods sold.

*12. **(LO 6)** In a worksheet using a perpetual inventory system, Inventory is shown in the following columns:
   - **a.** adjusted trial balance debit and balance sheet debit.
   - **b.** income statement debit and balance sheet debit.
   - **c.** income statement credit and balance sheet debit.
   - **d.** income statement credit and adjusted trial balance debit.

*13. **(LO 7)** In determining cost of goods sold in a periodic system:
   - **a.** purchase discounts are deducted from net purchases.
   - **b.** freight-out is added to net purchases.
   - **c.** purchase returns and allowances are deducted from net purchases.
   - **d.** freight-in is added to net purchases.

*14. **(LO 7)** If beginning inventory is $60,000, cost of goods purchased is $380,000, and ending inventory is $50,000, cost of goods sold is:
   - **a.** $390,000.
   - **b.** $370,000.
   - **c.** $330,000.
   - **d.** $420,000.

*15. **(LO 7)** When goods are purchased for resale by a company using a periodic inventory system:
   - **a.** purchases on account are debited to Inventory.
   - **b.** purchases on account are debited to Purchases.
   - **c.** purchase returns are debited to Purchase Returns and Allowances.
   - **d.** freight costs are debited to Purchases.

Solutions

1. **c.** Gross profit will result if net sales are greater than cost of goods sold. The other choices are incorrect because (a) operating expenses and net income are not used in the computation of gross profit; (b) gross profit results when net sales are greater than cost of goods sold, not operating expenses; and (d) gross profit results when net sales, not operating expenses, are greater than cost of goods sold.

2. **a.** Under a perpetual inventory system, when a company purchases goods for resale, purchases on account are debited to the Inventory account, not (b) Purchases or (c) Purchase Returns and Allowances. Choice (d) is incorrect because freight costs are also debited to the Inventory account, not the Freight-Out account.

3. **c.** Both Sales Discounts and Sales Returns and Allowances normally have a debit balance. Choices (a) and (b) are both correct, but (c) is the better answer. Choice (d) is incorrect as both (a) and (b) are correct.

4. **b.** The full amount of $686 is paid within 10 days of the purchase ($750 – $50) – [($750 – $50) × 2%]. The other choices are incorrect because (a) does not consider the discount of $14; (c) the amount of the discount is based upon the amount after the return is granted ($700 × 2%), not the amount before the return of merchandise ($750 × 2%); and (d) does not constitute payment in full on June 23.

5. **c.** The Cost of Goods Sold account normally appears in the ledger of a merchandising company using a perpetual inventory system. The other choices are incorrect because (a) the Purchases account, (b) the Freight-In account, and (d) the Purchase Discounts account all appear in the ledger of a merchandising company that uses a periodic inventory system.

6. **c.** Two journal entries are necessary: one to record the receipt of cash and sales revenue, and one to record the cost of goods sold and reduction of inventory. The other choices are incorrect because (a) only considers the recognition of the expense and ignores the revenue, (b) only considers the recognition of revenue and leaves out the expense or cost of merchandise sold, and (d) the receipt of cash and sales revenue, not reduction of inventory, are paired together, and the cost of goods sold and reduction of inventory, not sales revenue, are paired together.

7. **a.** An additional adjusting journal entry for inventory may be needed in a merchandising company to adjust for a physical inventory count, but it is not needed for a service company. The other choices are incorrect because (b) closing journal entries and (c) a post-closing trial balance are required for both types of companies. Choice (d) is incorrect because while a multiple-step income statement is not required for a merchandising company, it is useful to distinguish income generated from operating the business versus income or loss from non-recurring, nonoperating items.

8. **d.** An investing activities section appears on the statement of cash flows, not on a multiple-step income statement. Choices (a) gross profit, (b) cost of goods sold, and (c) a sales section are all features of a multiple-step income statement.

9. **b.** Gross profit = Net sales ($400,000) – Cost of goods sold ($310,000) = $90,000, not (a) $30,000, (c) $340,000, or (d) $400,000.

10. **c.** Both sales revenue and "Other revenues and gains" are reported in the revenues section of a single-step income statement. The other choices are incorrect because (a) gross profit is not reported on a single-step income statement, (b) cost of goods sold is included in the expenses section of a single-step income statement, and (d) income from operations is not shown separately on a single-step income statement.

11. **d.** Cost of goods sold appears on both a single-step and a multiple-step income statement. The other choices are incorrect because (a) inventory does not appear on either a single-step or a multiple-step income statement and (b) gross profit and (c) income from operations appear on a multiple-step income statement but not on a single-step income statement.

12. **a.** In a worksheet using a perpetual inventory system, inventory is shown in the adjusted trial balance debit column and in the balance sheet debit column. The other choices are incorrect because the Inventory account is not shown in the income statement columns.

*13. **d.** In determining cost of goods sold in a periodic system, freight-in is added to net purchases. The other choices are incorrect because (a) purchase discounts are deducted from purchases, not net purchases; (b) freight-out is a cost of sales, not a cost of purchases; and (c) purchase returns and allowances are deducted from purchases, not net purchases.

*14. **a.** Beginning inventory ($60,000) + Cost of goods purchased ($380,000) – Ending inventory ($50,000) = Cost of goods sold ($390,000), not (b) $370,000, (c) $330,000, or (d) $420,000.

*15. **b.** Purchases for resale are debited to the Purchases account. The other choices are incorrect because (a) purchases on account are debited to Purchases, not Inventory; (c) Purchase Returns and Allowances are always credited; and (d) freight costs are debited to Freight-In, not Purchases.

Practice Brief Exercises

Compute the missing amounts in determining cost of goods sold.

1. **(LO 1)** Presented below are the components in determining cost of goods sold for (a) Frazier Company, (b) Todd Company, and (c) Abreu Enterprises. Determine the missing amounts.

	Beginning Inventory	Purchases	Cost of Goods Available for Sale	Ending Inventory	Cost of Goods Sold
a.	$120,000	$150,000	?	?	$160,000
b.	$ 50,000	?	$125,000	$45,000	?
c.	?	$220,000	$330,000	$61,000	?

Solution

1. **a.** Cost of goods available for sale = $120,000 + $150,000 = $270,000

Ending inventory = $270,000 – $160,000 = $110,000

b. Purchases = $125,000 – $50,000 = $75,000
Cost of goods sold = $125,000 – $45,000 = $80,000

c. Beginning inventory = $330,000 – $220,000 = $110,000
Cost of goods sold = $330,000 – $61,000 = $269,000

2. **(LO 2)** Prepare the journal entries to record the following transactions on Robertson Company's books using a perpetual inventory system.

Journalize purchase transactions.

a. On March 2, Melky Company sold $800,000 of merchandise to Robertson Company, terms 2/10, n/30.

b. On March 6, Robertson Company returned $100,000 of the merchandise purchased on March 2.

c. On March 12, Robertson Company paid the balance due to Melky Company.

Solution

2. **a.** Inventory	800,000	
Accounts Payable		800,000
b. Accounts Payable	100,000	
Inventory		100,000
c. Accounts Payable ($800,000 – $100,000)	700,000	
Inventory ($700,000 × 2%)		14,000
Cash ($700,000 – $14,000)		686,000

3. **(LO 4)** Cabrera Company has the following account balances: Sales Revenue $300,000, Sales Returns and Allowances $10,000, Cost of Goods Sold $174,000, and Inventory $50,000. Prepare the entries to record the closing of these items to Income Summary.

Prepare closing entries.

Solution

3. Sales Revenue	300,000	
Income Summary		300,000
Income Summary	184,000	
Cost of Goods Sold		174,000
Sales Returns and Allowances		10,000

4. **(LO 5)** Assume Yoan Company has the following reported amounts: Sales revenue $400,000, Sales discounts $10,000, Cost of goods sold $234,000, and Operating expenses $60,000. Compute the following: (a) net sales, (b) gross profit, (c) income from operations, and (d) gross profit rate. (Round to one decimal place.)

Compute net sales, gross profit, income from operations, and gross profit rate.

Solution

4. **a.** Net sales = $400,000 – $10,000 = $390,000

b. Gross profit = $390,000 – $234,000 = $156,000

c. Income from operations = $156,000 – $60,000 = $96,000

d. Gross profit rate = $156,000 ÷ $390,000 = 40%

Practice Exercises

1. **(LO 2, 3)** On June 10, Spinner Company purchased $10,000 of merchandise on account from Lawrence Company, FOB shipping point, terms 2/10, n/30. Spinner pays the freight costs of $600 on June 11. Damaged goods totaling $700 are returned to Lawrence for credit on June 12. The fair value of these goods is $300. On June 19, Spinner pays Lawrence in full, less the purchase discount. Both companies use a perpetual inventory system.

Prepare purchase and sales entries.

Instructions

a. Prepare separate entries for each transaction on the books of Spinner Company.

b. Prepare separate entries for each transaction for Lawrence Company. The merchandise purchased by Spinner on June 10 had cost Lawrence $6,400.

Solution

1. a.

June 10	Inventory	10,000	
	Accounts Payable		10,000
11	Inventory	600	
	Cash		600
12	Accounts Payable	700	
	Inventory		700
19	Accounts Payable ($10,000 – $700)	9,300	
	Inventory ($9,300 × 2%)		186
	Cash ($9,300 – $186)		9,114

b.

June 10	Accounts Receivable	10,000	
	Sales Revenue		10,000
	Cost of Goods Sold	6,400	
	Inventory		6,400
12	Sales Returns and Allowances	700	
	Accounts Receivable		700
	Inventory	300	
	Cost of Goods Sold		300
19	Cash ($9,300 – $186)	9,114	
	Sales Discounts ($9,300 × 2%)	186	
	Accounts Receivable ($10,000 – $700)		9,300

Prepare multiple-step and single-step income statements.

2. (LO 5) Financial Statement In its income statement for the year ended December 31, 2020, Sale Company reported the following condensed data.

Interest expense	$ 50,000	Net sales	$1,650,000
Operating expenses	590,000	Interest revenue	20,000
Cost of goods sold	902,000	Loss on disposal of equipment	7,000

Instructions

a. Prepare a multiple-step income statement.

b. Prepare a single-step income statement.

Solution

2. a.

Sale Company
Income Statement
For the Year Ended December 31, 2020

Net sales			$1,650,000
Cost of goods sold			902,000
Gross profit			748,000
Operating expenses			590,000
Income from operations			158,000
Other revenues and gains			
Interest revenue		$20,000	
Other expenses and losses			
Interest expense	$50,000		
Loss on disposal of equipment	7,000	57,000	(37,000)
Net income			$ 121,000

b.

Sale Company
Income Statement
For the Year Ended December 31, 2020

Revenues		
Net sales	$1,650,000	
Interest revenue	20,000	
Total revenues		$1,670,000
Expenses		
Cost of goods sold	902,000	
Operating expenses	590,000	
Interest expenses	50,000	
Loss on sale of equipment	7,000	
Total expenses		1,549,000
Net income		$ 121,000

Practice Problem

(LO 5) Financial Statement The adjusted trial balance columns of Falcetto Company's worksheet for the year ended December 31, 2020, are as follows.

Prepare a multiple-step income statement.

	Debit		Credit
Cash	14,500	Accumulated Depreciation—Equipment	18,000
Accounts Receivable	11,100	Notes Payable	25,000
Inventory	29,000	Accounts Payable	10,600
Prepaid Insurance	2,500	Owner's Capital	81,000
Equipment	95,000	Sales Revenue	536,800
Owner's Drawings	12,000	Interest Revenue	2,500
Sales Returns and Allowances	6,700		673,900
Sales Discounts	5,000		
Cost of Goods Sold	363,400		
Freight-Out	7,600		
Advertising Expense	12,000		
Salaries and Wages Expense	56,000		
Utilities Expense	18,000		
Rent Expense	24,000		
Depreciation Expense	9,000		
Insurance Expense	4,500		
Interest Expense	3,600		
	673,900		

Instructions

Prepare a multiple-step income statement for Falcetto Company.

Solution

Falcetto Company
Income Statement
For the Year Ended December 31, 2020

Sales		
Sales revenue		$536,800
Less: Sales returns and allowances	$ 6,700	
Sales discounts	5,000	11,700

Net sales		525,100
Cost of goods sold		363,400
Gross profit		161,700
Operating expenses		
Salaries and wages expense	56,000	
Rent expense	24,000	
Utilities expense	18,000	
Advertising expense	12,000	
Depreciation expense	9,000	
Freight-out	7,600	
Insurance expense	4,500	
Total operating expenses		131,100
Income from operations		30,600
Other revenues and gains		
Interest revenue	2,500	
Other expenses and losses		
Interest expense	3,600	1,100
Net income		$ 29,500

WileyPLUS

Brief Exercises, DO IT! Exercises, Exercises, Problems, and many additional resources are available for practice in WileyPLUS.

Note: All asterisked Questions, Exercises, and Problems relate to material in the appendices to the chapter.

Questions

1. (a) "The steps in the accounting cycle for a merchandising company are different from the accounting cycle for a service company." Do you agree or disagree? (b) Is the measurement of net income for a merchandising company conceptually the same as for a service company? Explain.

2. Why is the normal operating cycle for a merchandising company likely to be longer than for a service company?

3. What components of revenues and expenses are different between merchandising and service companies?

4. How does income measurement differ between a merchandising and a service company?

5. When is cost of goods sold determined in a perpetual inventory system?

6. Distinguish between FOB shipping point and FOB destination. Identify the freight terms that will result in a debit to Inventory by the buyer and a debit to Freight-Out by the seller.

7. Explain the meaning of the credit terms 2/10, n/30.

8. Goods costing $2,000 are purchased on account on July 15 with credit terms of 2/10, n/30. On July 18, a $200 credit memo is received from the supplier for damaged goods. Give the journal entry on July 24 to record payment of the balance due within the discount period using a perpetual inventory system.

9. Celina Harris believes revenues from credit sales may be recorded before they are collected in cash. Do you agree? Explain.

10. (a) What is the primary source document for recording (1) cash sales and (2) credit sales? (b) Using XXs for amounts, give the journal entry for each of the transactions in part (a).

11. A credit sale is made on July 10 for $900, terms 2/10, n/30. On July 12, $100 of goods are returned for credit. Give the journal entry on July 19 to record the receipt of the balance due within the discount period.

12. Explain why the Inventory account will usually require adjustment at year-end.

13. Prepare the closing entries for the Sales Revenue account, assuming a balance of $200,000 and the Cost of Goods Sold account with a $145,000 balance.

14. What merchandising account(s) will appear in the post-closing trial balance?

15. Cupery Co. has net sales of $105,000, cost of goods sold of $70,000, and operating expenses of $20,000. What is its gross profit and its gross profit rate?

16. Stefan Page Company reports net sales of $800,000, gross profit of $370,000, and net income of $240,000. What are its operating expenses?

17. Identify the distinguishing features of an income statement for a merchandising company.

18. Identify the sections of a multiple-step income statement that relate to (a) operating activities, and (b) nonoperating activities.

19. How does the single-step form of income statement differ from the multiple-step form?

20. Determine **Apple**'s gross profit rate for 2015 and 2014. Indicate whether it increased or decreased from 2014 to 2015.

*21. Indicate the columns of the worksheet in a perpetual system in which (a) inventory and (b) cost of goods sold will be shown.

*22. Identify the accounts that are added to or deducted from Purchases in a periodic system to determine the cost of goods purchased. For each account, indicate whether it is added or deducted.

*23. Goods costing $3,000 are purchased on account on July 15 with credit terms of 2/10, n/30. On July 18, a $200 credit was received from the supplier for damaged goods. Give the journal entry on July 24 to record payment of the balance due within the discount period, assuming a periodic inventory system.

Brief Exercises

BE5.1 (LO 1) Presented below are the components in determining cost of goods sold. Determine the missing amounts.

Compute missing amounts in determining cost of goods sold.

	Beginning Inventory	Purchases	Cost of Goods Available for Sale	Ending Inventory	Cost of Goods Sold
a.	$80,000	$100,000	?	?	$120,000
b.	$50,000	?	$115,000	$35,000	?
c.	?	$110,000	$160,000	$29,000	?

BE5.2 (LO 1) Presented below are the components in Veasy Company's income statement. Determine the missing amounts.

Compute missing amounts in determining net income.

	Sales Revenue	Cost of Goods Sold	Gross Profit	Operating Expenses	Net Income
a.	$ 75,000	?	$28,000	?	$ 9,800
b.	$108,000	$70,000	?	?	$29,500
c.	?	$83,900	$79,600	$39,500	?

BE5.3 (LO 2, 3) Cha Company buys merchandise on account from Wirtz Company. The selling price of the goods is $780, and the cost of the goods is $470. Both companies use perpetual inventory systems. Journalize the transaction on the books of both companies.

Journalize perpetual inventory entries.

BE5.4 (LO 3) Prepare the journal entries to record the following transactions on Novy Company's books using a perpetual inventory system.

Journalize sales transactions.

a. On March 2, Novy Company sold $900,000 of merchandise on account to Opps Company, terms 2/10, n/30. The cost of the merchandise sold was $590,000.

b. On March 6, Opps Company returned $90,000 of the merchandise purchased on March 2. The cost of the returned merchandise was $62,000.

c. On March 12, Novy Company received the balance due from Opps Company.

BE5.5 (LO 2) From the information in BE5.4, prepare the journal entries to record these transactions on Opps Company's books under a perpetual inventory system.

Journalize purchase transactions.

BE5.6 (LO 4) At year-end, the perpetual inventory records of Gutierrez Company showed merchandise inventory of $98,000. The company determined, however, that its actual inventory on hand was $96,100. Record the necessary adjusting entry.

Prepare adjusting entry for inventory.

BE5.7 (LO 4) Brueser Company has the following account balances: Sales Revenue $195,000, Sales Discounts $2,000, Cost of Goods Sold $117,000, and Inventory $40,000. Prepare the entries to record the closing of these items to Income Summary.

Prepare closing entries for accounts.

BE5.8 (LO 5) **Financial Statement** Nelson Company provides the following information for the month ended October 31, 2020: sales on credit $280,000, cash sales $95,000, sales discounts $5,000, and sales returns and allowances $11,000. Prepare the sales section of the income statement based on this information.

Prepare sales section of income statement.

Contrast presentation in multiple-step and single-step income statements.

BE5.9 (LO 5) Writing Financial Statement Explain where each of the following items would appear on (1) a multiple-step income statement, and on (2) a single-step income statement: (a) gain on sale of equipment, (b) interest expense, (c) casualty loss from vandalism, and (d) cost of goods sold.

Compute net sales, gross profit, income from operations, and gross profit rate.

BE5.10 (LO 5) Assume Kupfer Company has the following reported amounts: Sales revenue $510,000, Sales returns and allowances $15,000, Cost of goods sold $330,000, and Operating expenses $90,000. Compute the following: (a) net sales, (b) gross profit, (c) income from operations, and (d) gross profit rate. (Round to one decimal place.)

Identify worksheet columns for selected accounts.

***BE5.11 (LO 6)** Presented below is the format of the worksheet using the perpetual inventory system presented in Appendix 5A.

Trial Balance		Adjustments		Adjusted Trial Balance		Income Statement		Balance Sheet	
Dr.	Cr.	Dr.	Cr.	Dr.	Cr.	Dr.	Cr.	Dr.	Cr.

Indicate where the following items will appear on the worksheet: (a) Cash, (b) Inventory, (c) Sales revenue, and (d) Cost of goods sold.

Example:

Cash: Trial balance debit column; Adjusted trial balance debit column; and Balance sheet debit column.

Compute net purchases and cost of goods purchased.

***BE5.12 (LO 7)** Assume that Morgan Company uses a periodic inventory system and has these account balances: Purchases $450,000, Purchase Returns and Allowances $13,000, Purchase Discounts $9,000, and Freight-In $18,000. Determine net purchases and cost of goods purchased.

Compute cost of goods sold and gross profit.

***BE5.13 (LO 7)** Assume the same information as in BE5.12 and also that Morgan Company has beginning inventory of $60,000, ending inventory of $90,000, and net sales of $730,000. Determine the amounts to be reported for cost of goods sold and gross profit.

Journalize purchase transactions.

***BE5.14 (LO 7)** Prepare the journal entries to record these transactions on Shabani Company's books using a periodic inventory system.

a. On March 2, Shabani Company purchased $900,000 of merchandise on account from Ballas Company, terms 2/10, n/30.

b. On March 6, Shabani Company returned $110,000 of the merchandise purchased on March 2.

c. On March 12, Shabani Company paid the balance due to Ballas Company.

Prepare closing entries for merchandise accounts.

***BE5.15 (LO 7)** T. Corlett Company has the following merchandise account balances: Sales Revenue $180,000, Sales Discounts $2,000, Purchases $120,000, and Purchases Returns and Allowances $30,000. In addition, it has a beginning inventory of $40,000 and an ending inventory of $30,000. Prepare the entries to record the closing of these items to Income Summary using the periodic inventory system.

Identify worksheet columns for selected accounts

***BE5.16 (LO 7)** Presented below is the format of the worksheet using the periodic inventory system presented in Appendix 5B.

Trial Balance		Adjustments		Adjusted Trial Balance		Income Statement		Balance Sheet	
Dr.	Cr.	Dr.	Cr.	Dr.	Cr.	Dr.	Cr.	Dr.	Cr.

Indicate where the following items will appear on the worksheet: (a) Cash, (b) Beginning inventory, (c) Accounts payable, and (d) Ending inventory.

Example

Cash: Trial balance debit column; Adjustment trial balance debit column; and Balance sheet debit column.

DO IT! Exercises

Answer general questions about merchandisers.

DO IT! 5.1 (LO 1) Indicate whether the following statements are true or false. If false, indicate how to correct the statement.

1. A merchandising company reports gross profit but a service company does not.
2. Under a periodic inventory system, a company determines the cost of goods sold each time a sale occurs.

3. A service company is likely to use accounts receivable but a merchandising company is not likely to do so.
4. Under a periodic inventory system, the cost of goods on hand at the beginning of the accounting period plus the cost of goods purchased less the cost of goods on hand at the end of the accounting period equals cost of goods sold.

DO IT! 5.2 (LO 2) On October 5, Wang Company buys merchandise on account from Davis Company. The selling price of the goods is $4,800, and the cost to Davis Company is $3,100. On October 8, Wang returns defective goods with a selling price of $650 and a fair value of $100. Record the transactions on the books of Wang Company.

Record transactions of purchasing company.

DO IT! 5.3 (LO 3) Assume information similar to that in **DO IT! 5.2**. On October 5, Wang Company buys merchandise on account from Davis Company. The selling price of the goods is $4,800, and the cost to Davis Company is $3,100. On October 8, Wang returns defective goods with a selling price of $650 and a fair value of $100. Record the transactions on the books of Davis Company.

Record transactions of selling company.

DO IT! 5.4 (LO 4) The trial balance of Beads and Bangles at December 31 shows Inventory $21,000, Sales Revenue $156,000, Sales Returns and Allowances $4,000, Sales Discounts $3,000, Cost of Goods Sold $92,400, Interest Revenue $5,000, Freight-Out $1,800, Utilities Expense $7,700, and Salaries and Wages Expense $19,500. Prepare the closing entries for Beads and Bangles for these accounts.

Prepare closing entries for a merchandising company.

DO IT! 5.5 (LO 5) **Financial Statement** The following information is available for Berlin Corp. for the year ended -December 31, 2020:

Prepare a multiple-step income statement and comprehensive income statement.

Other revenues and gains	$ 12,700	Sales revenue	$592,000
Other expenses and losses	13,300	Operating expenses	186,000
Cost of goods sold	156,000	Sales returns and	
Other comprehensive income	5,400	allowances	40,000

Prepare a multiple-step income statement for Berlin Corp. and a comprehensive income statement.

Exercises

E5.1 (LO 1) Mr. McKenzie has prepared the following list of statements about service companies and merchandisers.

Answer general questions about merchandisers.

1. Measuring net income for a merchandiser is conceptually the same as for a service company.
2. For a merchandiser, sales less operating expenses is called gross profit.
3. For a merchandiser, the primary source of revenues is the sale of inventory.
4. Sales salaries and wages is an example of an operating expense.
5. The operating cycle of a merchandiser is the same as that of a service company.
6. In a perpetual inventory system, no detailed inventory records of goods on hand are maintained.
7. In a periodic inventory system, the cost of goods sold is determined only at the end of the accounting period.
8. A periodic inventory system provides better control over inventories than a perpetual system.

Instructions

Identify each statement as true or false. If false, indicate how to correct the statement.

E5.2 (LO 2) Information related to Kerber Co. is presented below.

Journalize purchase transactions.

1. On April 5, purchased merchandise on account from Wilkes Company for $23,000, terms 2/10, net/30, FOB shipping point.
2. On April 6, paid freight costs of $900 on merchandise purchased from Wilkes.
3. On April 7, purchased equipment on account for $26,000.
4. On April 8, returned damaged merchandise to Wilkes Company and was granted a $3,000 credit for returned merchandise.
5. On April 15, paid the amount due to Wilkes Company in full.

Instructions

a. Prepare the journal entries to record these transactions on the books of Kerber Co. under a perpetual inventory system.

b. Assume that Kerber Co. paid the balance due to Wilkes Company on May 4 instead of April 15. Prepare the journal entry to record this payment.

Journalize perpetual inventory entries.

E5.3 (LO 2, 3) On September 1, Nixa Office Supply had an inventory of 30 calculators at a cost of $18 each. The company uses a perpetual inventory system. During September, the following transactions occurred.

Sept. 6	Purchased 90 calculators at $22 each from York.
9	Paid freight of $90 on calculators purchased from York Co.
10	Returned 3 calculators to York Co. for $69 cash (including freight) because they did not meet specifications.
12	Sold 26 calculators costing $23 (including freight) for $31 each on account to Sura Book Store, terms n/30.
14	Granted credit of $31 to Sura Book Store for the return of one calculator that was not ordered.
20	Sold 30 calculators costing $23 for $32 each on account to Davis Card Shop, terms n/30.

Instructions

Journalize the September transactions.

Prepare purchase and sales entries.

E5.4 (LO 2, 3) On June 10, Diaz Company purchased $8,000 of merchandise on account from Taylor Company, FOB shipping point, terms 2/10, n/30. Diaz pays the freight costs of $400 on June 11. Damaged goods totaling $300 are returned to Taylor for credit on June 12. The fair value of these goods is $70. On June 19, Diaz pays Taylor Company in full, less the purchase discount. Both companies use a perpetual inventory system.

Instructions

a. Prepare separate entries for each transaction on the books of Diaz Company.

b. Prepare separate entries for each transaction for Taylor Company. The merchandise purchased by Diaz on June 10 had cost Taylor $4,800.

Journalize sales transactions.

E5.5 (LO 3) Presented below are transactions related to R. Humphrey Company.

1. On December 3, R. Humphrey Company sold $570,000 of merchandise on account to Frazier Co., terms 1/10, n/30, FOB destination. R. Humphrey paid $400 for freight charges. The cost of the merchandise sold was $350,000.
2. On December 8, Frazier Co. was granted an allowance of $20,000 for merchandise purchased on December 3.
3. On December 13, R. Humphrey Company received the balance due from Frazier Co.

Instructions

a. Prepare the journal entries to record these transactions on the books of R. Humphrey Company using a perpetual inventory system.

b. Assume that R. Humphrey Company received the balance due from Frazier Co. on January 2 of the following year instead of December 13. Prepare the journal entry to record the receipt of payment on January 2.

Prepare sales section and closing entries.

E5.6 (LO 4, 5) **Financial Statement** The adjusted trial balance of Sang Company shows the following data pertaining to sales at the end of its fiscal year October 31, 2020: Sales Revenue $820,000, Freight-Out $16,000, Sales Returns and Allowances $25,000, and Sales Discounts $13,000.

Instructions

a. Prepare the sales section of the income statement.

b. Prepare separate closing entries for (1) sales revenue, and (2) the contra accounts to sales revenue.

Prepare adjusting and closing entries.

E5.7 (LO 4) Tim Jarosz Company had the following account balances at year-end: Cost of Goods Sold $60,000, Inventory $15,000, Operating Expenses $29,000, Sales Revenue $115,000, Sales Discounts

$1,200, and Sales Returns and Allowances $1,700. A physical count of inventory determines that merchandise inventory on hand is $13,600.

Instructions

a. Prepare the adjusting entry necessary as a result of the physical count.

b. Prepare closing entries.

E5.8 (LO 4) Presented below is information related to Hoerl Co. for the month of January 2020.

Prepare adjusting and closing entries.

Ending inventory per perpetual records	$ 21,600	Insurance expense	$ 12,000
Ending inventory actually on hand	21,000	Rent expense	20,000
Cost of goods sold	218,000	Salaries and wages expense	55,000
Freight-out	7,000	Sales discounts	10,000
		Sales returns and allowances	13,000
		Sales revenue	380,000

Instructions

a. Prepare the necessary adjusting entry for inventory.

b. Prepare the necessary closing entries.

E5.9 (LO 5) Financial Statement Presented below is information for Kaila Company for the month of March 2020.

Prepare a multiple-step income statement and calculate profitability.

Cost of goods sold	$215,000	Rent expense	$ 30,000
Freight-out	7,000	Sales discounts	8,000
Insurance expense	6,000	Sales returns and allowances	13,000
Salaries and wages expense	58,000	Sales revenue	380,000

Instructions

a. Prepare a multiple-step income statement.

b. Compute the gross profit rate.

E5.10 (LO 5) Financial Statement In its income statement for the year ended December 31, 2020, Anhad Company reported the following condensed data.

Prepare income statements and a comprehensive income statement.

Excel

Operating expenses	$ 725,000	Interest revenue	$ 28,000
Cost of goods sold	1,289,000	Loss on disposal of plant assets	17,000
Interest expense	70,000	Net sales	2,200,000
		Other comprehensive loss	8,300

Instructions

a. Prepare a multiple-step income statement.

b. Prepare a single-step income statement.

c. Prepare a comprehensive income statement.

E5.11 (LO 2, 3) An inexperienced accountant for Stahr Company made the following errors in recording merchandising transactions.

Prepare correcting entries for sales and purchases.

1. A $210 refund to a customer for faulty merchandise was debited to Sales Revenue $210 and credited to Cash $210.
2. A $180 credit purchase of supplies was debited to Inventory $180 and credited to Cash $180.
3. A $215 sales discount was debited to Sales Revenue.
4. A cash payment of $20 for freight on merchandise purchases was debited to Freight-Out $200 and credited to Cash $200.

Instructions

Prepare separate correcting entries for each error, assuming that the incorrect entry is not reversed. (Omit explanations.)

E5.12 (LO 5) Financial Statement In 2020, Laquen Company had net sales of $900,000 and cost of goods sold of $522,000. Operating expenses were $225,000, and interest expense was $11,000. Laquen prepares a multiple-step income statement.

Compute various income measures.

Instructions

a. Compute Laquen's gross profit.

b. Compute the gross profit rate. Why is this rate computed by financial statement users?

c. What is Laquen's income from operations and net income?

d. If Laquen prepared a single-step income statement, what amount would it report for net income?

e. In what section of its classified balance sheet should Laquen report inventory?

Compute missing amounts and compute gross profit rate.

E5.13 (LO 5) Presented below is financial information for two different companies.

	Summer Company	Winter Company
Sales revenue	$92,000	(d)
Sales returns	(a)	$ 5,000
Net sales	87,000	102,000
Cost of goods sold	56,000	(e)
Gross profit	(b)	41,500
Operating expenses	15,000	(f)
Net income	(c)	18,000

Instructions

a. Determine the missing amounts.

b. Determine the gross profit rates. (Round to one decimal place.)

Compute missing amounts.

E5.14 (LO 5) Financial information is presented below for three different companies.

	Hardy Cosmetics	Yee Grocery	Wang Wholesalers
Sales revenue	$90,000	$ (e)	$122,000
Sales returns and allowances	(a)	5,000	12,000
Net sales	86,000	95,000	(i)
Cost of goods sold	56,000	(f)	(j)
Gross profit	(b)	38,000	24,000
Operating expenses	15,000	(g)	18,000
Income from operations	(c)	(h)	(k)
Other expenses and losses	4,000	7,000	(l)
Net income	(d)	11,000	5,000

Instructions

Determine the missing amounts.

Complete worksheet using a perpetual inventory system.

***E5.15 (LO 6)** The following are selected accounts for McPhan Company as reported in the worksheet using a perpetual inventory system at the end of May 2020.

Accounts	Adjusted Trial Balance		Income Statement		Balance Sheet	
	Dr.	Cr.	Dr.	Cr.	Dr.	Cr.
Cash	11,000					
Inventory	76,000					
Sales Revenue		480,000				
Sales Returns and Allowances	10,000					
Sales Discounts	9,000					
Cost of Goods Sold	300,000					

Instructions

Complete the worksheet by extending amounts reported in the adjusted trial balance to the appropriate columns in the worksheet. Do not total individual columns.

Prepare a worksheet using a perpetual inventory system.

***E5.16 (LO 6)** The trial balance columns of the worksheet using a perpetual inventory system for Balistreri Company at June 30, 2020, are as follows.

Balistreri Company
Worksheet
For the Month Ended June 30, 2020

Account Titles	Trial Balance Debit	Trial Balance Credit
Cash	1,920	
Accounts Receivable	2,440	
Inventory	11,640	
Accounts Payable		1,120
Owner's Capital		3,500
Sales Revenue		42,500
Cost of Goods Sold	20,560	
Operating Expenses	10,560	
	47,120	47,120

Other data:

Operating expenses incurred on account, but not yet recorded, total $1,500.

Instructions

Enter the trial balance on a worksheet and complete the worksheet.

***E5.17 (LO 7)** The trial balance of A. Wiencek Company at the end of its fiscal year, August 31, 2020, includes these accounts: Inventory $19,500; Purchases $149,000; Sales Revenue $190,000; Freight-In $5,000; Sales Returns and Allowances $3,000; Freight-Out $1,000; and Purchase Returns and Allowances $2,000. The ending inventory is $23,000.

Prepare cost of goods sold section.

Instructions

Prepare a cost of goods sold section for the year ending August 31 (periodic inventory).

***E5.18 (LO 7)** On January 1, 2020, Brooke Hanson Corporation had inventory of $50,000. At December 31, 2020, Brooke Hanson had the following account balances.

Compute various income statement items.

Freight-in	$ 4,000
Purchases	509,000
Purchase discounts	6,000
Purchase returns and allowances	2,000
Sales revenue	840,000
Sales discounts	5,000
Sales returns and allowances	10,000

At December 31, 2020, Brooke Hanson determines that its ending inventory is $60,000.

Instructions

a. Compute Brooke Hanson's 2020 gross profit.

b. Compute Brooke Hanson's 2020 operating expenses if net income is $130,000 and there are no nonoperating activities.

***E5.19 (LO 7)** Below is a series of cost of goods sold sections for companies B, F, L, and R.

Prepare cost of goods sold section.

	B	F	L	R
Beginning inventory	$ 180	$ 70	$1,000	$ (j)
Purchases	1,620	1,060	(g)	43,590
Purchase returns and allowances	40	(d)	290	(k)
Net purchases	(a)	1,030	6,210	41,090
Freight-in	110	(e)	(h)	2,240
Cost of goods purchased	(b)	1,280	7,940	(l)
Cost of goods available for sale	1,870	1,350	(i)	49,530
Ending inventory	250	(f)	1,450	6,230
Cost of goods sold	(c)	1,230	7,490	43,300

Instruction

Fill in the lettered blanks to complete the cost of goods sold sections.

Journalize purchase transactions.

***E5.20 (LO 7)** This information relates to Nandi Co.

1. On April 5, purchased merchandise on account from Dion Company for $25,000, terms 2/10, net/30, FOB shipping point.
2. On April 6, paid freight costs of $900 on merchandise purchased from Dion Company.
3. On April 7, purchased equipment on account for $30,000.
4. On April 8, returned some of April 5 merchandise, which cost $2,800, to Dion Company.
5. On April 15, paid the amount due to Dion Company in full.

Instructions

a. Prepare the journal entries to record these transactions on the books of Nandi Co. using a periodic inventory system.

b. Assume that Nandi Co. paid the balance due to Dion Company on May 4 instead of April 15. Prepare the journal entry to record this payment.

Journalize purchase transactions.

***E5.21 (LO 7)** Presented below is information related to Chung Co.

1. On April 5, purchased merchandise on account from Jose Company for $21,000, terms 2/10, net/30, FOB shipping point.
2. On April 6, paid freight costs of $800 on merchandise purchased from Jose.
3. On April 7, purchased equipment on account from Winker Mfg. Co. for $26,000.
4. On April 8, returned merchandise, which cost $4,000, to Jose Company.
5. On April 15, paid the amount due to Jose Company in full.

Instructions

a. Prepare the journal entries to record these transactions on the books of Chung Co. using a periodic inventory system.

b. Assume that Chung Co. paid the balance due to Jose Company on May 4 instead of April 15. Prepare the journal entry to record this payment.

Complete worksheet for selected accounts.

***E5.22 (LO 7)** Presented below are selected accounts for T. Swift Company as reported in the worksheet at the end of May 2020. Ending inventory is $75,000.

Accounts	Adjusted Trial Balance		Income Statement		Balance Sheet	
	Dr.	Cr.	Dr.	Cr.	Dr.	Cr.
Cash	9,000					
Inventory	80,000					
Purchases	240,000					
Purchase Returns and Allowances		30,000				
Sales Revenue		450,000				
Sales Returns and Allowances	10,000					
Sales Discounts	5,000					
Rent Expense	42,000					

Instructions

Complete the worksheet by extending amounts reported in the adjustment trial balance to the appropriate columns in the worksheet. The company uses the periodic inventory system.

Problems: Set A

Journalize purchase and sales transactions under a perpetual inventory system.

Excel

P5.1A (LO 2, 3) Kern's Book Warehouse distributes hardcover books to retail stores and extends credit terms of 2/10, n/30 to all of its customers. At the end of May, Kern's inventory consisted of books purchased for $1,800. During June, the following merchandising transactions occurred.

June 1 Purchased books on account for $1,600 from Binsfeld Publishers, FOB destination, terms 2/10, n/30. The appropriate party also made a cash payment of $50 for the freight on this date.
3 Sold books on account to Reading Rainbow for $2,500. The cost of the books sold was $1,440.
6 Received $100 credit for books returned to Binsfeld Publishers.
9 Paid Binsfeld Publishers in full, less discount.
15 Received payment in full from Reading Rainbow.
17 Sold books on account to Rapp Books for $1,800. The cost of the books sold was $1,080.
20 Purchased books on account for $1,800 from McGinn Publishers, FOB destination, terms 2/15, n/30. The appropriate party also made a cash payment of $60 for the freight on this date.
24 Received payment in full from Rapp Books.
26 Paid McGinn Publishers in full, less discount.
28 Sold books on account to Baeten Bookstore for $1,600. The cost of the books sold was $970.
30 Granted Baeten Bookstore $120 credit for books returned costing $72.

Kern's Book Warehouse's chart of accounts includes the following: No. 101 Cash, No. 112 Accounts Receivable, No. 120 Inventory, No. 201 Accounts Payable, No. 401 Sales Revenue, No. 412 Sales Returns and Allowances, No. 414 Sales Discounts, and No. 505 Cost of Goods Sold.

Instructions

Journalize the transactions for the month of June for Kern's Book Warehouse using a perpetual inventory system.

P5.2A (LO 2, 3, 5) **Financial Statement** Renner Hardware Store completed the following merchandising transactions in the month of May. At the beginning of May, the ledger of Renner showed Cash of $5,000 and Owner's Capital of $5,000.

Journalize, post, and prepare a partial income statement.

GLS

May 1 Purchased merchandise on account from Braun's Wholesale Supply $4,200, terms 2/10, n/30.
2 Sold merchandise on account $2,100, terms 1/10, n/30. The cost of the merchandise sold was $1,300.
5 Received credit from Braun's Wholesale Supply for merchandise returned $300.
9 Received collections in full, less discounts, from customers billed on sales of $2,100 on May 2.
10 Paid Braun's Wholesale Supply in full, less discount.
11 Purchased supplies for cash $400.
12 Purchased merchandise for cash $1,400.
15 Received refund for poor quality merchandise from supplier on cash purchase $150.
17 Purchased merchandise from Valley Distributors $1,300, FOB shipping point, terms 2/10, n/30.
19 Paid freight on May 17 purchase $130.
24 Sold merchandise for cash $3,200. The merchandise sold had a cost of $2,000.
25 Purchased merchandise on account from Lumley, Inc. $620, FOB destination, terms 2/10, n/30.
27 Paid Valley Distributors in full, less discount.
29 Made refunds to cash customers for defective merchandise $70. The returned merchandise had a fair value of $30.
31 Sold merchandise on account $1,000 terms n/30. The cost of the merchandise sold was $560.

Renner Hardware's chart of accounts includes the following: No. 101 Cash, No. 112 Accounts Receivable, No. 120 Inventory, No. 126 Supplies, No. 201 Accounts Payable, No. 301 Owner's Capital, No. 401 Sales Revenue, No. 412 Sales Returns and Allowances, No. 414 Sales Discounts, and No. 505 Cost of Goods Sold.

Instructions

a. Journalize the transactions using a perpetual inventory system.

b. Enter the beginning cash and capital balances and post the transactions. (Use J1 for the journal reference.)

c. Prepare an income statement through gross profit for the month of May 2020.

c. Gross profit $2,379

Prepare financial statements and adjusting and closing entries.

P5.3A (LO 4, 5) Financial Statement Big Box Store is located in midtown Madison. During the past several years, net income has been declining because of suburban shopping centers. At the end of the company's fiscal year on November 30, 2020, the following accounts appeared in two of its trial balances.

	Unadjusted	Adjusted		Unadjusted	Adjusted
Accounts Payable	$ 25,200	$ 25,200	Notes Payable	$ 37,000	$ 37,000
Accounts Receivable	30,500	30,500	Owner's Capital	101,700	101,700
Accumulated Depr.—Equip.	34,000	45,000	Owner's Drawings	10,000	10,000
Cash	26,000	26,000	Prepaid Insurance	10,500	3,500
Cost of Goods Sold	518,000	518,000	Property Tax Expense		2,500
Freight-Out	6,500	6,500	Property Taxes Payable		2,500
Equipment	146,000	146,000	Rent Expense	15,000	15,000
Depreciation Expense		11,000	Salaries and Wages Expense	96,000	96,000
Insurance Expense		7,000	Sales Revenue	720,000	720,000
Interest Expense	6,400	6,400	Sales Commissions Expense	6,500	11,000
Interest Revenue	2,000	2,000	Sales Commissions Payable		4,500
Inventory	32,000	32,000	Sales Returns and Allowances	8,000	8,000
			Utilities Expense	8,500	8,500

Instructions

a. Net income $32,100
Owner's capital $123,800
Total assets $193,000

a. Prepare a multiple-step income statement, an owner's equity statement, and a classified balance sheet. Notes payable are due in 2023.

b. Journalize the adjusting entries that were made.

c. Journalize the closing entries that are necessary.

Journalize, post, and prepare a trial balance.

GLS

P5.4A (LO 2, 3, 4) Financial Statement Yolanda Hagen, a former disc golf star, operates Yolanda's Discorama. At the beginning of the current season on April 1, the ledger of Yolanda's Discorama showed Cash $1,800, Inventory $2,500, and Owner's Capital $4,300. The following transactions were completed during April.

Apr.	5	Purchased golf discs, bags, and other inventory on account from Mumford Co. $1,200, FOB shipping point, terms 2/10, n/60.
	7	Paid freight on the Mumford purchase $50.
	9	Received credit from Mumford Co. for merchandise returned $100.
	10	Sold merchandise on account for $900, terms n/30. The merchandise sold had a cost of $540.
	12	Purchased disc golf shirts and other accessories on account from Saucer Sportswear $670, terms 1/10, n/30.
	14	Paid Mumford Co. in full, less discount.
	17	Received credit from Saucer Sportswear for merchandise returned $70.
	20	Made sales on account for $610, terms n/30. The cost of the merchandise sold was $370.
	21	Paid Saucer Sportswear in full, less discount.
	27	Granted an allowance to customers for clothing that was flawed $20.
	30	Received payments on account from customers $900.

The chart of accounts for the store includes the following: No. 101 Cash, No. 112 Accounts Receivable, No. 120 Inventory, No. 201 Accounts Payable, No. 301 Owner's Capital, No. 401 Sales Revenue, No. 412 Sales Returns and Allowances, and No. 505 Cost of Goods Sold.

Instructions

a. Journalize the April transactions using a perpetual inventory system.

b. Enter the beginning balances in the ledger accounts and post the April transactions. (Use J1 for the journal reference.)

c. Total debits $5,810

c. Prepare a trial balance on April 30, 2020.

Complete accounting cycle beginning with a worksheet.

Excel

P5.5A (LO 4, 5, 6) Financial Statement The trial balance of Gaolee Fashion Center contained the following accounts at November 30, the end of the company's fiscal year.

Gaolee Fashion Center
Trial Balance
November 30, 2020

	Debit	Credit
Cash	$ 20,700	
Accounts Receivable	30,700	
Inventory	44,700	
Supplies	6,200	
Equipment	133,000	
Accumulated Depreciation—Equipment		$ 28,000
Notes Payable		60,000
Accounts Payable		48,500
Owner's Capital		93,000
Owner's Drawings	12,000	
Sales Revenue		755,200
Sales Returns and Allowances	8,800	
Cost of Goods Sold	497,400	
Salaries and Wages Expense	140,000	
Advertising Expense	24,400	
Utilities Expense	14,000	
Maintenance and Repairs Expense	12,100	
Freight-Out	16,700	
Rent Expense	24,000	
Totals	$984,700	$984,700

Adjustment data:

1. Supplies on hand totaled $2,600.
2. Depreciation is $11,500 on the equipment.
3. Interest of $3,800 is accrued on notes payable at November 30.
4. Inventory actually on hand is $44,400.

Instructions

a. Enter the trial balance on a worksheet, and complete the worksheet.

b. Prepare a multiple-step income statement and an owner's equity statement for the year, and a classified balance sheet as of November 30, 2020. Notes payable of $20,000 are due in January 2021.

c. Journalize the adjusting entries.

d. Journalize the closing entries.

e. Prepare a post-closing trial balance.

a. Adj. trial balance $1,000,000
Net loss $1,400

b. Gross profit $248,700
Total assets $191,900

Determine cost of goods sold and gross profit under periodic approach.

P5.6A (LO 5, 7) Financial Statement At the end of Donaldson Department Store's fiscal year on November 30, 2020, these accounts appeared in its adjusted trial balance.

Freight-In	$ 7,500
Inventory	40,000
Purchases	585,000
Purchase Discounts	6,300
Purchase Returns and Allowances	2,700
Sales Revenue	1,000,000
Sales Returns and Allowances	20,000

Additional facts:

1. Merchandise inventory on November 30, 2020, is $52,600.
2. Donaldson Department Store uses a periodic system.

Instructions

Prepare an income statement through gross profit for the year ended November 30, 2020.

Gross profit $409,100

Calculate missing amounts and assess profitability.

P5.7A (LO 5, 7) Writing Kayla Inc. operates a retail operation that purchases and sells home entertainment products. The company purchases all merchandise inventory on credit and uses a periodic inventory system. The Accounts Payable account is used for recording inventory purchases only; all other current liabilities are accrued in separate accounts. You are provided with the following selected information for the fiscal years 2017 through 2020, inclusive.

	2017	2018	2019	2020
Income Statement Data				
Sales revenue		$55,000	$ (e)	$47,000
Cost of goods sold		(a)	14,800	14,300
Gross profit		38,300	35,200	(i)
Operating expenses		34,900	(f)	28,800
Net income		$ (b)	$ 2,500	$ (j)
Balance Sheet Data				
Inventory	$7,200	$ (c)	$ 8,100	$ (k)
Accounts payable	3,200	3,600	2,500	(l)
Additional Information				
Purchases of merchandise inventory on account		$14,200	$ (g)	$13,200
Cash payments to suppliers		(d)	(h)	13,600

c. $4,700
g. $18,200
i. $32,700

Instructions

a. Calculate the missing amounts.

b. Sales declined over the 3-year fiscal period, 2018–2020. Does that mean that profitability necessarily also declined? Explain, computing the gross profit rate and the profit margin (Net income ÷ Sales revenue) for each fiscal year to help support your answer. (Round to one decimal place.)

Journalize, post, and prepare trial balance and partial income statement using periodic approach.

GLS

P5.8A (LO 7) Financial Statement At the beginning of the current season on April 1, the ledger of Gage Pro Shop showed Cash $3,000, Inventory $4,000, and Owner's Capital $7,000. These transactions occurred during April 2020.

Apr.	5	Purchased golf bags, clubs, and balls on account from Tiger Co. $1,200, FOB shipping point, terms 2/10, n/60.
	7	Paid freight on Tiger Co. purchases $50.
	9	Received credit from Tiger Co. for merchandise returned $100.
	10	Sold merchandise on account to customers $600, terms n/30.
	12	Purchased golf shoes, sweaters, and other accessories on account from Classic Sportswear $450, terms 1/10, n/30.
	14	Paid Tiger Co. in full.
	17	Received credit from Classic Sportswear for merchandise returned $50.
	20	Made sales on account to customers $600, terms n/30.
	21	Paid Classic Sportswear in full.
	27	Granted credit to customers for clothing that had flaws $35.
	30	Received payments on account from customers $600.

The chart of accounts for the pro shop includes Cash, Accounts Receivable, Inventory, Accounts Payable, Owner's Capital, Sales Revenue, Sales Returns and Allowances, Purchases, Purchase Returns and Allowances, Purchase Discounts, and Freight-In.

Instructions

a. Journalize the April transactions using a periodic inventory system.

b. Using T-accounts, enter the beginning balances in the ledger accounts and post the April transactions.

c. Prepare a trial balance on April 30, 2020.

d. Prepare an income statement through gross profit, assuming merchandise inventory on hand at April 30 is $4,824.

c. Tot. trial balance $8,376
d. Gross profit $465

Continuing Case

Cookie Creations

© leungchopan/ Shutterstock

(*Note:* This is a continuation of the Cookie Creations case from Chapters 1 through 4.)

CC5 Because Natalie has had such a successful first few months, she is considering other opportunities to develop her business. One opportunity is the sale of fine European mixers. The owner of Kzinski Supply Company has approached Natalie to become the exclusive U.S. distributor of these fine mixers. The current cost of a mixer is approximately $525 (U.S.), and Natalie would sell each one for $1,050. Natalie comes to you for advice on how to account for these mixers.

Go to **WileyPLUS** *for complete case details and instructions.*

Ethics Case

EC5 Tiffany Lyons was just hired as the assistant treasurer of Key West Stores. The company is a specialty chain store with nine retail stores concentrated in one metropolitan area. Among other things, the payment of all invoices is centralized in one of the departments Tiffany will manage. Her primary responsibility is to maintain the company's high credit rating by paying all bills when due and to take advantage of all cash discounts.

Jay Barnes, the former assistant treasurer who has been promoted to treasurer, is training Tiffany in her new duties. He instructs Tiffany that she is to continue the practice of preparing all checks "net of discount" and dating the checks the last day of the discount period. "But," Jay continues, "we always hold the checks at least 4 days beyond the discount period before mailing them. That way, we get another 4 days of interest on our money. Most of our creditors need our business and don't complain. And, if they scream about our missing the discount period, we blame it on the mailroom or the post office. We've only lost one discount out of every hundred we take that way. I think everybody does it. By the way, welcome to our team!"

Instructions

a. What are the ethical considerations in this case?

b. Who are the stakeholders that are harmed or benefitted in this situation?

c. Should Tiffany continue the practice started by Jay? Does she have any choice?

Comprehensive Accounting Cycle Review

ACR5 **Financial Statement** On December 1, 2020, Rodriguez Distributing Company had the following account balances.

	Debit		Credit
Cash	$ 7,200	Accumulated Depreciation— Equipment	$ 2,200
Accounts Receivable	4,600	Accounts Payable	4,500
Inventory	12,000	Salaries and Wages Payable	1,000
Supplies	1,200	Owner's Capital	39,300
Equipment	22,000		
	$47,000		$47,000

During December, the company completed the following summary transactions.

Dec. 6 Paid $1,600 for salaries and wages due employees, of which $600 is for December and $1,000 is for November salaries and wages payable.

8 Received $2,200 cash from customers in payment of account (no discount allowed).

10 Sold merchandise for cash $6,300. The cost of the merchandise sold was $4,100.

13 Purchased merchandise on account from Boehm Co. $9,000, terms 2/10, n/30.

15 Purchased supplies for cash $2,000.

18 Sold merchandise on account $15,000, terms 3/10, n/30. The cost of the merchandise sold was $10,000.

20 Paid salaries and wages $1,800.

23 Paid Boehm Co. in full, less discount.

27 Received collections in full, less discounts, from customers billed on December 18.

Adjustment data:

1. Accrued salaries and wages payable $840.
2. Depreciation $200 per month.
3. Supplies on hand $1,500.

Instructions

a. Journalize the December transactions using a perpetual inventory system.

b. Enter the December 1 balances in the ledger T-accounts and post the December transactions. Use Cost of Goods Sold, Depreciation Expense, Salaries and Wages Expense, Sales Revenue, Sales Discounts, and Supplies Expense.

c. Journalize and post adjusting entries.

d. Prepare an adjusted trial balance.

e. Prepare an income statement and an owner's equity statement for December and a classified balance sheet at December 31.

d. Totals $68,340
e. Net income $1,610

Expand Your Critical Thinking

Financial Reporting Problem: Apple Inc.

CT5.1 The financial statements of **Apple Inc.** are presented in Appendix A at the end of this textbook. The complete annual report, including the notes to the financial statements, is available at the company's website.

Instructions

Answer the following questions using Apple's Consolidated Statement of Income.

a. What was the percentage change in (1) net sales and in (2) net income from 2013 to 2014 and from 2014 to 2015?

b. What was the company's gross profit rate in 2013, 2014, and 2015?

c. What was the company's percentage of net income to net sales in 2013, 2014, and 2015? Comment on any trend in this percentage.

Comparative Analysis Problem: PepsiCo, Inc. vs. The Coca-Cola Company

CT5.2 **PepsiCo, Inc.**'s financial statements are presented in Appendix B. Financial statements of **The Coca-Cola Company** are presented in Appendix C. The complete annual reports of PepsiCo and Coca-Cola, including the notes to the financial statements, are available at each company's respective website.

Instructions

a. Based on the information contained in these financial statements, determine each of the following for each company.

1. Gross profit for 2015.
2. Gross profit rate for 2015.
3. Operating income for 2015.
4. Percentage change in operating income from 2014 to 2015.

b. What conclusions concerning the relative profitability of the two companies can you draw from these data?

Comparative Analysis Problem: Amazon.com, Inc. vs. Wal-Mart Stores, Inc.

CT5.3 **Amazon.com, Inc.**'s financial statements are presented in Appendix D. Financial statements of **Wal-Mart Stores, Inc.** are presented in Appendix E. (Use Wal-Mart's January 31, 2016, financial statements for comparative purposes.) The complete annual reports of Amazon and Wal-Mart, including the notes to the financial statements, are available at each company's respective website.

Instructions

a. Based on the information contained in these financial statements, determine each of the following for each company. Use Amazon's net product sales to compute gross profit information.

1. Gross profit for 2015.
2. Gross profit rate for 2015.
3. Operating income for 2015.
4. Percentage change in operating income from 2014 to 2015.

b. What conclusions concerning the relative profitability of the two companies can you draw from these data?

Real-World Focus

CT5.4 No financial decision-maker should ever rely solely on the financial information reported in the annual report to make decisions. It is important to keep abreast of financial news. This activity demonstrates how to search for financial news on the Web.

Instructions

Search the Internet for an article on either **PepsiCo** or **Coca-Cola** that sounds interesting to you and then answer the following questions.

a. What was the source of the article (e.g., Reuters, Businesswire, PR Newswire)?

b. Assume that you are a personal financial planner and that one of your clients owns stock in the company. Write a brief memo to your client, summarizing the article and explaining the implications of the article for his or her investment.

Decision-Making Across the Organization

CT5.5 **Financial Statement** Three years ago, Amy Hessler and her brother-in-law Jacob Seelig opened Family Department Store. For the first two years, business was good, but the following condensed income results for 2019 were disappointing.

Family Department Store
Income Statement
For the Year Ended December 31, 2019

Net sales		$700,000
Cost of goods sold		553,000
Gross profit		147,000
Operating expenses		
Selling expenses	$100,000	
Administrative expenses	20,000	120,000
Net income		$ 27,000

Amy believes the problem lies in the relatively low gross profit rate (gross profit divided by net sales) of 21%. Jacob believes the problem is that operating expenses are too high.

Amy thinks the gross profit rate can be improved by making both of the following changes. She does not anticipate that these changes will have any effect on operating expenses.

1. Increase average selling prices by 17%. This increase is expected to lower sales volume so that total sales will increase only 6%.
2. Buy merchandise in larger quantities and take all purchase discounts. These changes to selling prices and purchasing practices are expected to increase the gross profit rate from 21% to 24%.

Jacob thinks expenses can be cut by making both of the following changes. He feels that these changes will not have any effect on net sales.

1. Cut sales salaries (selling expense) of $60,000 in half and give sales personnel a commission of 2% of net sales.
2. Reduce store deliveries to one day per week rather than twice a week. This change will reduce delivery expenses (selling expense) of $30,000 by 40%.

Amy and Jacob come to you for help in deciding the best way to improve net income.

Instructions

With the class divided into groups, answer the following.

a. Prepare a condensed income statement for 2020, assuming (1) Amy's changes are implemented and (2) Jacob's ideas are adopted.

b. What is your recommendation to Amy and Jacob?

c. Prepare a condensed income statement for 2020, assuming both sets of proposed changes are made.

Communication Activity

CT5.6 The following situation is in chronological order.

1. Parker decides to buy a surfboard.
2. He calls Surfing USA Co. to inquire about its surfboards.
3. Two days later, he requests Surfing USA Co. to make a surfboard.
4. Three days later, Surfing USA Co. sends him a purchase order to fill out.
5. He sends back the purchase order.
6. Surfing USA Co. receives the completed purchase order.
7. Surfing USA Co. completes the surfboard.
8. Parker picks up the surfboard.
9. Surfing USA Co. bills Parker.
10. Surfing USA Co. receives payment from Parker.

Instructions

In a memo to the president of Surfing USA Co., answer the following.

a. When should Surfing USA Co. record the sale?

b. Suppose that with his purchase order, Parker is required to make a down payment. Would that change your answer?

All About You

CT5.7 There are many situations in business where it is difficult to determine the proper period in which to record revenue. Suppose that after graduation with a degree in finance, you take a job as a manager at a consumer electronics store called Impact Electronics. The company has expanded rapidly in order to compete with **Best Buy**. Impact has also begun selling gift cards for its electronic products. The cards are available in any dollar amount and allow the holder of the card to purchase an item for up to 2 years from the time the card is purchased. If the card is not used during that 2 years, it expires.

Instructions

Answer the following questions.

At what point should the revenue from the gift cards be recognized? Should the revenue be recognized at the time the card is sold, or should it be recorded when the card is redeemed? Explain the reasoning to support your answers.

FASB Codification Activity

CT5.8 If your school has a subscription to the FASB Codification, log in and prepare responses to the following.

Instructions

a. Access the glossary ("Master Glossary") to answer the following:

1. What is the definition provided for inventory?
2. What is a customer?

b. What guidance does the Codification provide concerning reporting inventories above cost?

A Look at IFRS

LEARNING OBJECTIVE 8

Compare the accounting for merchandising under GAAP and IFRS.

The basic accounting entries for merchandising are the same under both GAAP and IFRS. The income statement is a required statement under both sets of standards. The basic format is similar although some differences do exist.

Key Points

Following are the key similarities and differences between GAAP and IFRS related to inventories.

Similarities

- Under both GAAP and IFRS, a company can choose to use either a perpetual or periodic inventory systems.
- The definition of inventories is basically the same under GAAP and IFRS.
- As indicated above, the basic accounting entries for merchandising are the same under both GAAP and IFRS.
- Both GAAP and IFRS require that income statement information be presented for multiple years. For example, IFRS requires that 2 years of income statement information be presented, whereas GAAP requires 3 years.

Differences

- Under GAAP companies generally classify income statement items by function. Classification by function leads to descriptions like administration, distribution (selling), and manufacturing. Under IFRS, companies must classify expenses either by nature or by function. Classification by nature leads to descriptions such as the following: salaries, depreciation expense, and utilities expense. If a company uses the functional-expense method on the income statement, disclosure by nature is required in the notes to the financial statements.
- Presentation of the income statement under GAAP follows either a single-step or multiple-step format. IFRS does not mention a single-step or multiple-step approach.
- Under IFRS revaluation of land, buildings, and intangible assets is permitted. The initial gains and losses resulting from this revaluation are reported as adjustments to equity, often referred to as **other comprehensive income**. The effect of this difference is that the use of IFRS results in more transactions affecting equity (other comprehensive income) but not net income.

Looking to the Future

The IASB and FASB are working on a project that would rework the structure of financial statements. Specifically, this project will address the issue of how to classify various items in the income statement. A main goal of this new approach is to provide information that better represents how businesses are run. In addition, this approach draws attention away from just one number—net income. It will adopt major groupings similar to those currently used by the statement of cash flows (operating, investing, and financing), so that numbers can be more readily traced across statements. For example, the amount of income that is generated by operations would be traceable to the assets and liabilities used to generate the income. Finally, this approach would also provide detail, beyond that currently seen in most statements (either GAAP or IFRS), by requiring that line items be presented both by function and by nature. The new financial statement format was heavily influenced by suggestions from financial statement analysts.

IFRS Practice

IFRS Self-Test Questions

1. Which of the following would **not** be included in the definition of inventory under IFRS?
   - **a.** Photocopy paper held for sale by an office supply store.
   - **b.** Stereo equipment held for sale by an electronics store.
   - **c.** Used office equipment held for sale by the human relations department of a plastics company.
   - **d.** All of the above would meet the definition.

2. Which of the following would **not** be a line item of a company reporting costs by nature?
   - **a.** Depreciation expense.
   - **b.** Salaries expense.
   - **c.** Interest expense.
   - **d.** Manufacturing expense.

3. Which of the following would **not** be a line item of a company reporting costs by function?
   - **a.** Administration.
   - **b.** Manufacturing.
   - **c.** Utilities expense.
   - **d.** Distribution.

4. Which of the following statements is **false**?
   - **a.** IFRS specifically requires use of a multiple-step income statement.
   - **b.** Under IFRS, companies can use either a perpetual or periodic system.
   - **c.** The proposed new format for financial statements was heavily influenced by the suggestions of financial statement analysts.
   - **d.** The new income statement format will try to de-emphasize the focus on the "net income" line item.

IFRS Exercises

IFRS5.1 Explain the difference between the "nature-of-expense" and "function-of-expense" classifications.

IFRS5.2 For each of the following income statement line items, state whether the item is a "by nature" expense item or a "by function" expense item.

________	Cost of goods sold	________	Utilities expense
________	Depreciation expense	________	Delivery expense
________	Salaries and wages expense	________	General and administrative expenses
________	Selling expenses		

IFRS5.3 Matilda Company reported the following amounts (in euros) in 2020: Net income, €150,000; Unrealized gain related to revaluation of buildings, €10,000; and Unrealized loss on non-trading securities, €(35,000). Determine Matilda's total comprehensive income for 2020.

International Financial Reporting Problem: Louis Vuitton

IFRS5.4 The financial statements of **Louis Vuitton** are presented in Appendix F. The complete annual report, including the notes to its financial statements, is available at the company's website.

Instructions

Use Louis Vuitton's annual report to answer the following questions.

a. Does Louis Vuitton use a multiple-step or a single-step income statement format? Explain how you made your determination.

b. Instead of "interest expense," what label does Louis Vuitton use for interest costs that it incurs?

c. Using the notes to the company's financial statements, determine the following:

   1. Composition of the inventory.

   2. Amount of inventory (gross) before impairment.

Answers to IFRS Self-Test Questions

1. c **2.** d **3.** c **4.** a

CHAPTER 6

James Porter/Workbook/Getty Images, Inc.

Inventories

Chapter Preview

In the previous chapter, we discussed the accounting for merchandise inventory using a perpetual inventory system. In this chapter, we explain the methods used to calculate the cost of inventory on hand at the balance sheet date and the cost of goods sold.

Feature Story

"Where Is That Spare Bulldozer Blade?"

Let's talk inventory—big, bulldozer-size inventory. **Caterpillar Inc.** is the world's largest manufacturer of construction and mining equipment, diesel and natural gas engines, and industrial gas turbines. It sells its products in over 200 countries, making it one of the most successful U.S. exporters. More than 70% of its productive assets are located domestically, and nearly 50% of its sales are foreign.

In the past, Caterpillar's profitability suffered, but today it is very successful. A big part of this turnaround can be attributed to effective management of its inventory. Imagine what it costs Caterpillar to have too many bulldozers sitting around in inventory—a situation the company definitely wants to avoid. Yet Caterpillar must also make sure it has enough inventory to meet demand.

At one time during a 7-year period, Caterpillar's sales increased by 100% while its inventory increased by only 50%. To achieve this dramatic reduction in the amount of resources tied up in inventory while continuing to meet customers' needs, Caterpillar used a two-pronged approach. First, it completed a factory modernization program, which greatly increased its production efficiency. The program reduced by 60% the amount of inventory the company processes at any one time. It also reduced by an incredible 75% the time it takes to manufacture a part.

Second, Caterpillar dramatically improved its parts distribution system. It ships more than 100,000 items daily from its

23 distribution centers strategically located around the world (10 million square feet of warehouse space—remember, we're talking bulldozers). The company can virtually guarantee that it can get any part to anywhere in the world within 24 hours.

These changes led to record exports, profits, and revenues for Caterpillar. It would seem that things couldn't be better. But industry analysts, as well as the company's managers, thought otherwise. In order to maintain Caterpillar's position as the industry leader, management began another major overhaul of inventory production and inventory management processes. The goal: to cut the number of repairs in half, increase productivity by 20%, and increase inventory turnover by 40%.

In short, Caterpillar's ability to manage its inventory has been a key reason for its past success and will very likely play a huge part in its future profitability as well.

Chapter Outline

LEARNING OBJECTIVES

LO 1 Discuss how to classify and determine inventory.	• Classifying inventory • Determining inventory quantities	**DO IT! 1** Rules of Ownership
LO 2 Apply inventory cost flow methods and discuss their financial effects.	• Specific identification • Cost flow assumptions • Financial statement and tax effects • Using inventory cost flow methods consistently	**DO IT! 2** Cost Flow Methods
LO 3 Indicate the effects of inventory errors on the financial statements.	• Income statement effects • Balance sheet effects	**DO IT! 3** Inventory Errors
LO 4 Explain the statement presentation and analysis of inventory.	• Presentation • Lower-of-cost-or-net realizable value • Analysis	**DO IT! 4** LCNRV and Inventory Turnover

Go to the Review and Practice section at the end of the chapter for a review of key concepts and practice applications with solutions.
Visit WileyPLUS with ORION for additional tutorials and practice opportunities.

Classifying and Determining Inventory

LEARNING OBJECTIVE 1

Discuss how to classify and determine inventory.

Two important steps in the reporting of inventory at the end of the accounting period are the classification of inventory based on its degree of completeness and the determination of inventory amounts.

Classifying Inventory

How a company classifies its inventory depends on whether the firm is a merchandiser or a manufacturer. In a **merchandising** company, such as those described in Chapter 5, inventory consists of many different items. For example, in a grocery store, canned goods, dairy products, meats, and produce are just a few of the inventory items on hand. These items have two common characteristics: (1) they are owned by the company, and (2) they are in a form ready for sale to customers in the ordinary course of business. Thus, merchandisers need only one inventory classification, **merchandise inventory**, to describe the many different items that make up the total inventory.

In a **manufacturing** company, some inventory may not yet be ready for sale. As a result, manufacturers usually classify inventory into three categories: finished goods, work in process, and raw materials (see **Helpful Hint**). **Finished goods inventory** is manufactured items that are completed and ready for sale. **Work in process** is that portion of manufactured inventory that has been placed into the production process but is not yet complete. **Raw materials** are the basic goods that will be used in production but have not yet been placed into production.

HELPFUL HINT

Regardless of the classification, companies report all inventories under Current Assets on the balance sheet.

For example, **Caterpillar** classifies earth-moving tractors completed and ready for sale as **finished goods**. It classifies the tractors on the assembly line in various stages of production as **work in process**. The steel, glass, tires, and other components that are on hand waiting to be used in the production of tractors are identified as **raw materials**. **Illustration 6.1** shows an adapted excerpt from Note 7 of Caterpillar's annual report.

ILLUSTRATION 6.1

Composition of Caterpillar's inventory

	December 31	
(millions of dollars)	**2016**	**2015**
Raw materials	$2,102	$2,467
Work-in-process	1,719	1,857
Finished goods	4,576	5,122
Supplies	217	254
Total inventories	**$8,614**	**$9,700**

By observing the levels and changes in the levels of these three inventory types, financial statement users can gain insight into management's production plans. For example, low levels of raw materials and high levels of finished goods suggest that management believes it has enough inventory on hand and production will be slowing down—perhaps in anticipation of a recession. Conversely, high levels of raw materials and low levels of finished goods probably signal that management is planning to step up production.

Many companies have significantly lowered inventory levels and costs using **just-in-time (JIT) inventory** methods. Under a just-in-time method, companies manufacture or purchase goods only when needed. **Dell** is famous for having developed a system for making computers in response to individual customer requests. Even though it makes each computer to meet each customer's particular specifications, Dell is able to assemble the computer and put it on a truck in less than 48 hours. The success of the JIT system depends on reliable suppliers. By integrating its information systems with those of its suppliers, Dell reduced its inventories to nearly zero. This is a huge advantage in an industry where products become obsolete nearly overnight.

The accounting concepts discussed in this chapter apply to the inventory classifications of both merchandising and manufacturing companies. Our focus here is on merchandise inventory. Additional issues specific to manufacturing companies are discussed as part of managerial accounting.

Accounting Across the Organization Ford

A Big Hiccup

JIT can save a company a lot of money, but it isn't without risk. An unexpected disruption in the supply chain can cost a company a lot of money. Japanese automakers experienced just such a disruption when a 6.8-magnitude earthquake caused major damage to the company that produces 50% of their piston rings. The rings themselves cost only $1.50, but you can't make a car without them. As a result, the automakers were forced to shut down production for a few days—a loss of tens of thousands of cars.

Similarly, a major snowstorm halted production at the Canadian plants of **Ford**. A Ford spokesperson said, "Because the plants run with just-in-time inventory, we don't have large stockpiles of parts sitting around. When you have a somewhat significant disruption, you can pretty quickly run out of parts."

Sources: Amy Chozick, "A Key Strategy of Japan's Car Makers Backfires," *Wall Street Journal* (July 20, 2007); and Kate Linebaugh, "Canada Military Evacuates Motorists Stranded by Snow," *Wall Street Journal* (December 15, 2010).

What steps might the companies take to avoid such a serious disruption in the future? (Go to WileyPLUS for this answer and additional questions.)

Determining Inventory Quantities

No matter whether they are using a periodic or perpetual inventory system, all companies need to determine inventory quantities at the end of the accounting period. If using a perpetual system, companies take a physical inventory for the following reasons:

1. To check the accuracy of their perpetual inventory records.
2. To determine the amount of inventory lost due to wasted raw materials, shoplifting, or employee theft.

Companies using a periodic inventory system take a physical inventory for **two different purposes**: to determine the inventory on hand at the balance sheet date, and to determine the cost of goods sold for the period.

Determining inventory quantities involves two steps: (1) taking a physical inventory of goods on hand and (2) determining the ownership of goods.

Taking a Physical Inventory

ETHICS NOTE

In a famous fraud, a salad oil company filled its storage tanks mostly with water. The oil rose to the top, so auditors thought the tanks were full of oil. The company also said it had more tanks than it really did: It repainted numbers on the tanks to confuse auditors.

Companies take a physical inventory at the end of the accounting period. Taking a physical inventory involves actually counting, weighing, or measuring each kind of inventory on hand (see **Ethics Note**). In many companies, taking an inventory is a formidable task. Retailers such as **Target**, **True Value Hardware**, or **Home Depot** have thousands of different inventory items. An inventory count is generally more accurate when goods are not being sold or received during the counting. Consequently, companies often "take inventory" when the business is closed or when business is slow. Many retailers close early on a chosen day in January—after the holiday sales and returns, when inventories are at their lowest level—to count inventory. **Wal-Mart Stores, Inc.**, for example, has a year-end of January 31.

Determining Ownership of Goods

One challenge in computing inventory quantities is determining what inventory a company owns. To determine ownership of goods, two questions must be answered: Do all of the goods included in the count belong to the company? Does the company own any goods that were not included in the count?

Ethics Insight Leslie Fay

© Greg Brookes/iStockphoto

Falsifying Inventory to Boost Income

Managers at women's apparel maker **Leslie Fay** were convicted of falsifying inventory records to boost net income in an attempt to increase management bonuses. In another case, executives at **Craig Consumer Electronics** were accused of defrauding lenders by manipulating inventory records. The indictment said the company classified "defective goods as new or refurbished" and claimed that it owned certain shipments "from overseas suppliers" when, in fact, Craig either did not own the shipments or the shipments did not exist.

What effect does an overstatement of inventory have on a company's financial statements? (Go to WileyPLUS for this answer and additional questions.)

Goods in Transit. A complication in determining ownership is **goods in transit** (on board a truck, train, ship, or plane) at the end of the period. The company may have purchased goods that have not yet been received, or it may have sold goods that have not yet been delivered. To arrive at an accurate count, the company must determine ownership of these goods.

Goods in transit should be included in the inventory of the company that has legal title to the goods. Legal title is determined by the terms of the sale, as shown in **Illustration 6.2** and described below.

ILLUSTRATION 6.2 **Terms of sale**

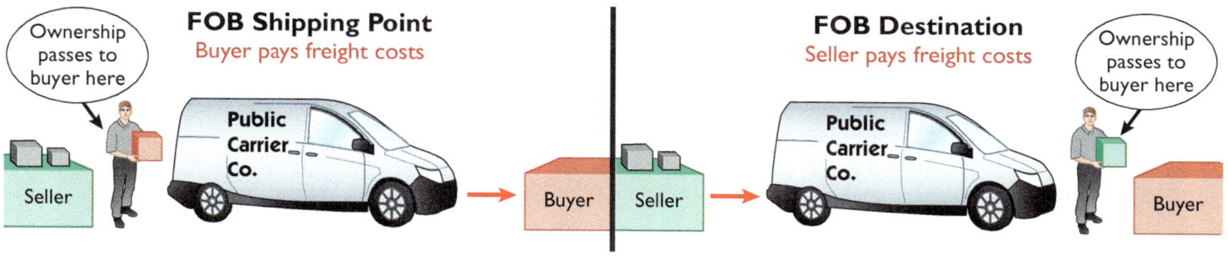

1. When the terms are **FOB (free on board) shipping point**, ownership of the goods passes to the buyer when the public carrier accepts the goods from the seller.
2. When the terms are **FOB destination**, ownership of the goods remains with the seller until the goods reach the buyer.

If goods in transit at the statement date are ignored, inventory quantities may be seriously miscounted. Assume, for example, that Hargrove Company has 20,000 units of inventory on hand on December 31. It also has the following goods in transit:

1. Sales of 1,500 units shipped December 31 FOB destination.
2. Purchases of 2,500 units shipped FOB shipping point by the seller on December 31.

Hargrove has legal title to both the 1,500 units sold and the 2,500 units purchased. If the company ignores the units in transit, it would understate inventory quantities by 4,000 units (1,500 + 2,500).

As we will see later in the chapter, inaccurate inventory counts affect not only the inventory amount shown on the balance sheet but also the cost of goods sold calculation on the income statement.

Consigned Goods. In some lines of business, it is common to hold the goods of other parties and try to sell the goods for them for a fee, but without taking ownership of the goods. These are called **consigned goods**.

For example, you might have a used car that you would like to sell. If you take the item to a dealer, the dealer might be willing to put the car on its lot and charge you a commission if it is sold. Under this agreement, the dealer **would not take ownership** of the car, which would still belong to you. Therefore, if an inventory count were taken, the car would not be included in the dealer's inventory because the dealer does not own it.

Many car, boat, and antique dealers sell goods on consignment to keep their inventory costs down and to avoid the risk of purchasing an item that they will not be able to sell. Today, even some manufacturers are making consignment agreements with their suppliers in order to keep their inventory levels low.

Anatomy of a Fraud

Ted Nickerson, CEO of clock manufacturer Dally Industries, had expensive tastes. To support this habit, Ted took out large loans, which he collateralized with his shares of Dally Industries stock. If the price of Dally's stock fell, he was required to provide the bank with more shares of stock. To achieve target net income figures and thus maintain the stock price, Ted coerced employees in the company to alter inventory figures. Inventory quantities were manipulated by changing the amounts on inventory control tags after the year-end physical inventory count. For example, if a tag said there were 20 units of a particular item, the tag was changed to 220. Similarly, the unit costs that were used to determine the value of ending inventory were increased from, for example, \$125 per unit to \$1,250. Both of these fraudulent changes had the effect of increasing the amount of reported ending inventory. This reduced cost of goods sold and increased net income.

Total take: \$245,000

The Missing Control

Independent internal verification. The company should have spot-checked its inventory records periodically, verifying that the number of units in the records agreed with the amount on hand and that the unit costs agreed with vendor price sheets.

Source: Adapted from Wells, *Fraud Casebook* (2007), pp. 502–509.

DO IT! 1 | Rules of Ownership

Hasbeen Company completed its inventory count. It arrived at a total inventory value of \$200,000. As a new member of Hasbeen's accounting department, you have been given the information listed below. Discuss how this information affects the reported cost of inventory.

1. Hasbeen included in the inventory goods held on consignment for Falls Co., costing \$15,000.
2. The company did not include in the count purchased goods of \$10,000 which were in transit (terms: FOB shipping point).
3. The company did not include in the count sold inventory with a cost of \$12,000 which was in transit (terms: FOB shipping point).

ACTION PLAN

- **Apply the rules of ownership to goods held on consignment.**
- **Apply the rules of ownership to goods in transit.**

Solution

The goods of \$15,000 held on consignment should be deducted from the inventory count. The goods of \$10,000 purchased FOB shipping point should be added to the inventory count. Sold goods of \$12,000 which were in transit FOB shipping point should not be included in the ending inventory. Thus, inventory should be carried at \$195,000 (\$200,000 – \$15,000 + \$10,000).

Related exercise material: **BE6.1, BE6.2, DO IT! 6.1, E6.1, E6.2, and E6.3.**

Inventory Methods and Financial Effects

LEARNING OBJECTIVE 2

Apply inventory cost flow methods and discuss their financial effects.

Inventory is accounted for at cost. Cost includes all expenditures necessary to acquire goods and place them in a condition ready for sale. For example, freight costs incurred to acquire inventory are added to the cost of inventory, but the cost of shipping goods to a customer is a selling expense.

After a company has determined the quantity of units of inventory, it applies unit costs to the quantities to compute the total cost of the inventory and the cost of goods sold. This process can be complicated if a company has purchased inventory items at different times and at different prices.

For example, assume that Crivitz TV Company purchases three identical 50-inch TVs on different dates at costs of $720, $750, and $800. During the year, Crivitz sold two TVs at $1,200 each. These facts are summarized in **Illustration 6.3**.

ILLUSTRATION 6.3

Data for inventory costing example

Purchases			
February 3	1 TV	at	$720
March 5	1 TV	at	$750
May 22	1 TV	at	$800
Sales			
June 1	2 TVs	for	$2,400 ($1,200 × 2)

Cost of goods sold will differ depending on which two TVs the company sold. For example, it might be $1,470 ($720 + $750), or $1,520 ($720 + $800), or $1,550 ($750 + $800). In this section, we discuss alternative costing methods available to Crivitz.

Specific Identification

If Crivitz can positively identify which particular units it sold and which are still in ending inventory, it can use the **specific identification method** of inventory costing. For example, if Crivitz sold the TVs it purchased on February 3 and May 22, then its cost of goods sold is $1,520 ($720 + $800), and its ending inventory is $750 (see **Illustration 6.4**). Using this method, companies can accurately determine ending inventory and cost of goods sold.

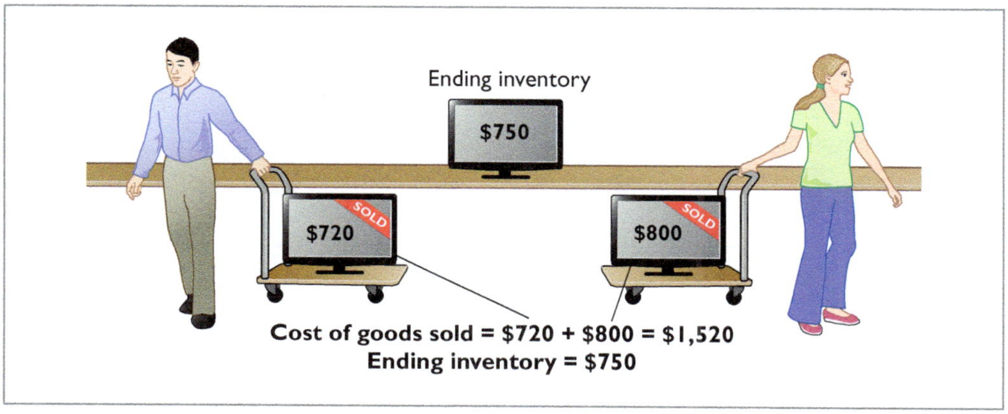

ILLUSTRATION 6.4

Specific identification method

ETHICS NOTE

A major disadvantage of the specific identification method is that management may be able to manipulate net income. For example, it can boost net income by selling units purchased at a low cost, or reduce net income by selling units purchased at a high cost.

Specific identification requires that companies keep records of the original cost of each individual inventory item. Historically, specific identification was possible only when a company sold a limited variety of high-unit-cost items that could be identified clearly from the time of purchase through the time of sale. Examples of such products are cars, pianos, or expensive antiques.

Today, bar coding, electronic product codes, and radio frequency identification make it theoretically possible to do specific identification with nearly any type of product. The reality is, however, that this practice is still relatively rare (see **Ethics Note**). Instead, rather than keep track of the cost of each particular item sold, most companies make assumptions, called **cost flow assumptions**, about which units were sold.

Cost Flow Assumptions

Because specific identification is often impractical, other cost flow methods are permitted. These differ from specific identification in that they **assume** flows of costs that may be unrelated to the physical flow of goods. There are three assumed cost flow methods:

1. First-in, first-out (FIFO)
2. Last-in, first-out (LIFO)
3. Average-cost

There is no accounting requirement that the cost flow assumption be consistent with the physical movement of the goods. Company management selects the appropriate cost flow method.

To demonstrate the three cost flow methods, we will use a **periodic** inventory system. We assume a periodic system because **very few companies use perpetual LIFO, FIFO, or average-cost** to cost their inventory and related cost of goods sold. Instead, companies that use perpetual systems often use an assumed cost (called a standard cost) to record cost of goods sold at the time of sale. Then, at the end of the period when they count their inventory, they **recalculate cost of goods sold using periodic FIFO, LIFO, or average-cost** as shown in this chapter and adjust cost of goods sold to this recalculated number.[1]

To illustrate the three inventory cost flow methods, we will use the data for Houston Electronics' Astro condensers, shown in **Illustration 6.5**.

ILLUSTRATION 6.5
Data for Houston Electronics

Houston Electronics
Astro Condensers

Date	Explanation	Units	Unit Cost	Total Cost
Jan. 1	Beginning inventory	100	$10	$ 1,000
Apr. 15	Purchase	200	11	2,200
Aug. 24	Purchase	300	12	3,600
Nov. 27	Purchase	400	13	5,200
	Total units available for sale	1,000		$12,000
	Units in ending inventory	450		
	Units sold	550		

The cost of goods sold formula in a periodic system is:

Beginning Inventory + **Cost of Goods Purchased** − **Ending Inventory** = **Cost of Goods Sold**

[1]Also, some companies use a perpetual system to keep track of units, but they do not make an entry for perpetual cost of goods sold. In addition, firms that employ LIFO tend to use **dollar-value LIFO**, a method discussed in upper-level courses. FIFO periodic and FIFO perpetual give the same result. Therefore, companies should not incur the additional cost to use FIFO perpetual. Few companies use perpetual average-cost because of the added cost of recordkeeping. Finally, for instructional purposes, we believe it is easier to demonstrate the cost flow assumptions under the periodic system, which makes it more pedagogically appropriate.

Houston Electronics had a total of 1,000 units available to sell during the period (beginning inventory plus purchases). The total cost of these 1,000 units is $12,000, referred to as **cost of goods available for sale**. A physical inventory taken at December 31 determined that there were 450 units in ending inventory. Therefore, Houston sold 550 units (1,000 – 450) during the period. To determine the cost of the 550 units that were sold (the cost of goods sold), we assign a cost to the ending inventory and subtract that value from the cost of goods available for sale. The value assigned to the ending inventory **depends on which cost flow method we use**. No matter which cost flow assumption we use, though, the sum of cost of goods sold plus the cost of the ending inventory must equal the cost of goods available for sale—in this case, $12,000.

First-In, First-Out (FIFO)

The **first-in, first-out (FIFO) method** assumes that the **earliest goods** purchased are the first to be sold. FIFO often parallels the actual physical flow of merchandise. That is, it generally is good business practice to sell the oldest units first. Under the FIFO method, therefore, the **costs** of the earliest goods purchased are the first to be recognized in determining cost of goods sold. (This does not necessarily mean that the oldest units **are** sold first, but that the costs of the oldest units are **recognized** first. In a bin of picture hangers at the hardware store, for example, no one really knows, nor would it matter, which hangers are sold first.) **Illustration 6.6** shows the allocation of the cost of goods available for sale at Houston Electronics under FIFO (see **Helpful Hint**).

ILLUSTRATION 6.6

Allocation of costs—FIFO method

COST OF GOODS AVAILABLE FOR SALE

Date	Explanation	Units	Unit Cost	Total Cost
Jan. 1	Beginning inventory	100	$10	$ 1,000
Apr. 15	Purchase	200	11	2,200
Aug. 24	Purchase	300	12	3,600
Nov. 27	Purchase	400	13	5,200
	Total	1,000		$12,000

STEP 1: ENDING INVENTORY

Date	Units	Unit Cost	Total Cost
Nov. 27	400	$13	$5,200
Aug. 24	50	12	600
Total	450		$5,800

STEP 2: COST OF GOODS SOLD

Cost of goods available for sale	$12,000
Less: Ending inventory	5,800
Cost of goods sold	$ 6,200

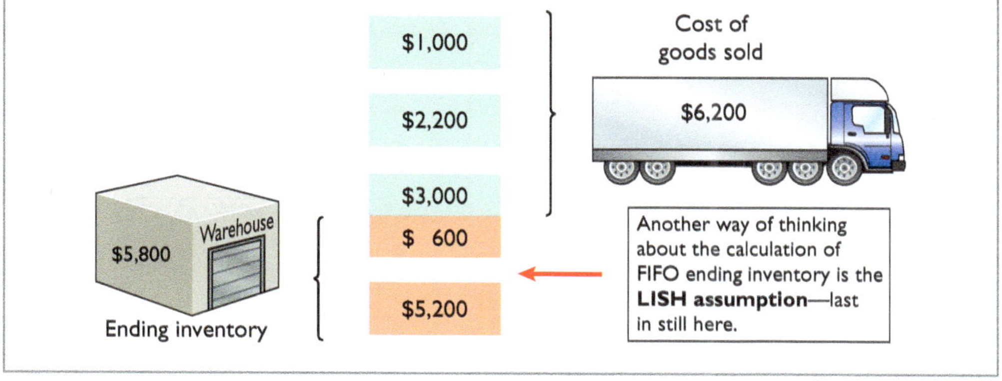

HELPFUL HINT

Note the sequencing of the allocation: (1) compute ending inventory, and (2) determine cost of goods sold.

Under FIFO, since it is assumed that the first goods purchased were the first goods sold, ending inventory is based on the prices of the most recent units purchased. That is, **under FIFO, companies obtain the cost of the ending inventory by taking the unit cost**

of the most recent purchase and working backward until all units of inventory have been costed. In this example, Houston Electronics prices the 450 units of ending inventory using the **most recent** prices. The last purchase was 400 units at $13 on November 27. The remaining 50 units are priced using the unit cost of the second most recent purchase, $12, on August 24. Next, Houston Electronics calculates cost of goods sold by subtracting the cost of the units **not sold** (ending inventory) from the cost of all goods available for sale.

Illustration 6.7 demonstrates that companies also can calculate cost of goods sold by pricing the 550 units sold using the prices of the first 550 units acquired. Note that of the 300 units purchased on August 24, only 250 units are assumed sold. This agrees with our calculation of the cost of ending inventory, where 50 of these units were assumed unsold and thus included in ending inventory.

ILLUSTRATION 6.7
Proof of cost of goods sold

Date	Units	Unit Cost	Total Cost
Jan. 1	100	$10	$1,000
Apr. 15	200	11	2,200
Aug. 24	250	12	3,000
Total	550		**$6,200**

Last-In, First-Out (LIFO)

The **last-in, first-out (LIFO) method** assumes that the **latest goods** purchased are the first to be sold. LIFO seldom coincides with the actual physical flow of inventory. (Exceptions include goods stored in piles, such as coal or hay, where goods are removed from the top of the pile as they are sold.) Under the LIFO method, the **costs** of the latest goods purchased are the first to be recognized in determining cost of goods sold. **Illustration 6.8** shows the allocation of the cost of goods available for sale at Houston Electronics under LIFO.

ILLUSTRATION 6.8
Allocation of costs—LIFO method

COST OF GOODS AVAILABLE FOR SALE

Date	Explanation	Units	Unit Cost	Total Cost
Jan. 1	Beginning inventory	100	$10	$ 1,000
Apr. 15	Purchase	200	11	2,200
Aug. 24	Purchase	300	12	3,600
Nov. 27	Purchase	400	13	5,200
	Total	1,000		**$12,000**

STEP 1: ENDING INVENTORY

Date	Units	Unit Cost	Total Cost
Jan. 1	100	$10	$1,000
Apr. 15	200	11	2,200
Aug. 24	150	12	1,800
Total	450		**$5,000**

STEP 2: COST OF GOODS SOLD

Cost of goods available for sale	$12,000
Less: Ending inventory	5,000
Cost of goods sold	**$ 7,000**

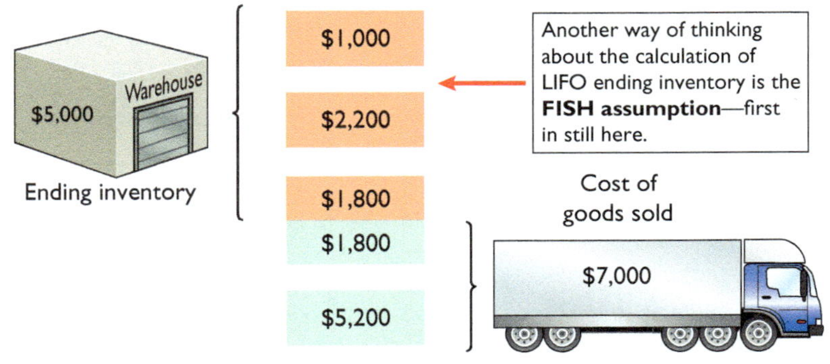

Under LIFO, since it is assumed that the first goods sold were those that were most recently purchased, ending inventory is based on the prices of the oldest units purchased. That is, **under LIFO, companies obtain the cost of the ending inventory by taking the unit cost of the earliest goods available for sale and working forward until all units of inventory have been costed**. In this example, Houston Electronics prices the 450 units of ending inventory using the **earliest** prices. The first purchase was 100 units at $10 in the January 1 beginning inventory. Then, 200 units were purchased at $11. The remaining 150 units needed are priced at $12 per unit (August 24 purchase). Next, Houston Electronics calculates cost of goods sold by subtracting the cost of the units **not sold** (ending inventory) from the cost of all goods available for sale.

Illustration 6.9 demonstrates that companies also can calculate cost of goods sold by pricing the 550 units sold using the prices of the last 550 units acquired. Note that of the 300 units purchased on August 24, only 150 units are assumed sold. This agrees with our calculation of the cost of ending inventory, where 150 of these units were assumed unsold and thus included in ending inventory.

ILLUSTRATION 6.9

Proof of cost of goods sold

Date	Units	Unit Cost	Total Cost
Nov. 27	400	$13	$5,200
Aug. 24	150	12	1,800
Total	550		$7,000

Under a periodic inventory system, which we are using here, **all goods purchased during the period are assumed to be available for the first sale, regardless of the date of purchase**.

Average-Cost

The **average-cost method** allocates the cost of goods available for sale on the basis of the **weighted-average unit cost** incurred. The average-cost method assumes that goods are similar in nature. **Illustration 6.10** presents the formula and a sample computation of the weighted-average unit cost.

ILLUSTRATION 6.10

Formula for weighted-average unit cost

Cost of Goods Available for Sale	÷	Total Units Available for Sale	=	Weighted-Average Unit Cost
$12,000	÷	1,000	=	$12

The company then applies the weighted-average unit cost to the units on hand to determine the cost of the ending inventory. **Illustration 6.11** shows the allocation of the cost of goods available for sale at Houston Electronics using average-cost.

ILLUSTRATION 6.11

Allocation of costs—average-cost method

COST OF GOODS AVAILABLE FOR SALE

Date	Explanation	Units	Unit Cost	Total Cost
Jan. 1	Beginning inventory	100	$10	$ 1,000
Apr. 15	Purchase	200	11	2,200
Aug. 24	Purchase	300	12	3,600
Nov. 27	Purchase	400	13	5,200
	Total	1,000		$12,000

ILLUSTRATION 6.11

(Continued)

STEP 1: ENDING INVENTORY					STEP 2: COST OF GOODS SOLD	
$12,000	÷	1,000	=	$12	Cost of goods available for sale	$12,000
		Unit		**Total**	Less: Ending inventory	5,400
Units		**Cost**		**Cost**	Cost of goods sold	$ 6,600
450		$12		$5,400		

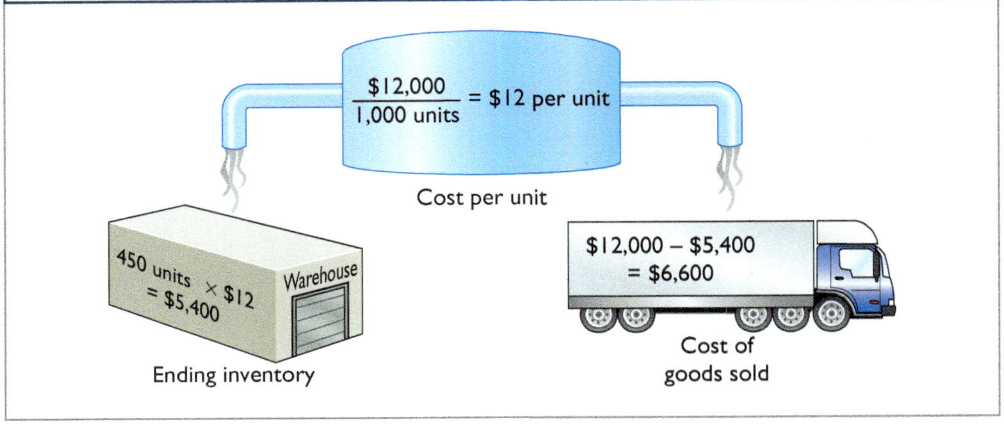

We can verify the cost of goods sold under this method by multiplying the units sold times the weighted-average unit cost (550 × $12 = $6,600). Note that this method does **not** use the average of the unit costs. That average is $11.50 ($10 + $11 + $12 + $13 = $46; $46 ÷ 4). The average-cost method instead uses the average **weighted by** the quantities purchased at each unit cost.

Financial Statement and Tax Effects of Cost Flow Methods

Each of the three assumed cost flow methods is acceptable for use. For example, **Reebok International Ltd.** and **Wendy's International** currently use the FIFO method of inventory costing. **Campbell Soup Company**, **Kroger**, and **Walgreen Drugs** use LIFO for part or all of their inventory. **Bristol-Myers Squibb**, **Starbucks**, and **Motorola** use the average-cost method. In fact, a company may also use more than one cost flow method at the same time. **Stanley Black & Decker Manufacturing Company**, for example, uses LIFO for domestic inventories and FIFO for foreign inventories. **Illustration 6.12** shows the use of the three cost flow methods in 500 large U.S. companies.

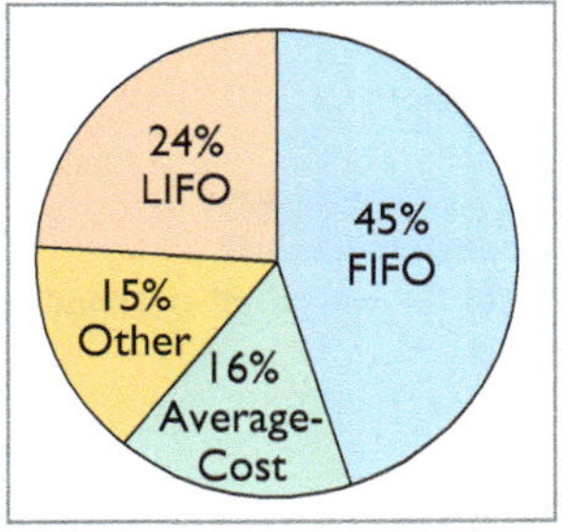

ILLUSTRATION 6.12

Use of cost flow methods in major U.S. companies

The reasons companies adopt different inventory cost flow methods are varied, but they usually involve one of three factors: (1) income statement effects, (2) balance sheet effects, or (3) tax effects.

Income Statement Effects

To understand why companies might choose a particular cost flow method, let's examine the effects of the different cost flow assumptions on the financial statements of Houston Electronics. The condensed income statements in **Illustration 6.13** assume that Houston sold its 550 units for $18,500, had operating expenses of $9,000, and is subject to an income tax rate of 30%.

Note the cost of goods available for sale ($12,000) is the same under each of the three inventory cost flow methods. However, the ending inventories and the costs of goods sold are different. This difference is due to the unit costs that the company allocated to cost of goods sold and to ending inventory. Each dollar of difference in ending inventory results in a corresponding dollar difference in income before income taxes. For Houston, an $800 difference exists between FIFO and LIFO cost of goods sold.

ILLUSTRATION 6.13

Comparative effects of cost flow methods

Houston Electronics
Condensed Income Statements

	FIFO	LIFO	Average-Cost
Sales revenue	$18,500	$18,500	$18,500
Beginning inventory	1,000	1,000	1,000
Purchases	11,000	11,000	11,000
Cost of goods available for sale	12,000	12,000	12,000
Ending inventory	**5,800**	**5,000**	**5,400**
Cost of goods sold	6,200	7,000	6,600
Gross profit	12,300	11,500	11,900
Operating expenses	9,000	9,000	9,000
Income before income taxes*	3,300	2,500	2,900
Income tax expense (30%)	990	750	870
Net income	**$ 2,310**	**$ 1,750**	**$ 2,030**

*We are assuming that Houston Electronics is a corporation, and corporations are required to pay income taxes.

In periods of changing prices, the cost flow assumption can have significant impacts both on income and on evaluations of income, such as the following.

1. In a period of inflation, FIFO produces a higher net income because lower unit costs of the first units purchased are matched against revenue.
2. In a period of inflation, LIFO produces a lower net income because higher unit costs of the last goods purchased are matched against revenue.
3. If prices are falling, the results from the use of FIFO and LIFO are reversed. FIFO will report the lowest net income and LIFO the highest.
4. Regardless of whether prices are rising or falling, average-cost produces net income between FIFO and LIFO.

As shown in the Houston example (Illustration 6.13), in a period of rising prices FIFO reports the highest net income ($2,310) and LIFO the lowest ($1,750); average-cost falls between these two amounts ($2,030).

To management, higher net income is an advantage. It causes external users to view the company more favorably. In addition, management bonuses, if based on net income, will be higher. Therefore, when prices are rising (which is usually the case), companies tend to prefer FIFO because it results in higher net income.

Others believe that LIFO presents a more realistic net income number. That is, LIFO matches the more recent costs against current revenues to provide a better measure of net income. During periods of inflation, many challenge the quality of non-LIFO earnings, noting that failing to match current costs against current revenues leads to an understatement of cost of goods sold and an overstatement of net income. As some indicate, net income computed using FIFO creates **"paper or phantom profits"**—that is, earnings that do not really exist.

Balance Sheet Effects

A major advantage of the FIFO method is that in a period of inflation, the costs allocated to ending inventory will approximate their current cost. For example, for Houston Electronics, 400 of the 450 units in the ending inventory are costed under FIFO at the higher November 27 unit cost of $13.

Conversely, a major shortcoming of the LIFO method is that in a period of inflation, the costs allocated to ending inventory may be significantly understated in terms of current cost. The understatement becomes greater over prolonged periods of inflation if the inventory includes goods purchased in one or more prior accounting periods. For example, **Caterpillar** has used LIFO for more than 50 years. Its balance sheet shows ending inventory of $9,700 million. But the inventory's actual current cost if FIFO had been used is $12,189 million.

Tax Effects

HELPFUL HINT

A tax rule, often referred to as the LIFO conformity rule, requires that if companies use LIFO for tax purposes they must also use it for financial reporting purposes. This means that if a company chooses the LIFO method to reduce its tax bills, it will also have to report lower net income in its financial statements.

We have seen that both inventory on the balance sheet and net income on the income statement are higher when companies use FIFO in a period of inflation. Yet, many companies have selected LIFO. Why? The reason is that LIFO results in the lowest income taxes (because of lower net income) during times of rising prices (see **Helpful Hint**). For example, at Houston Electronics, income taxes are $750 under LIFO, compared to $990 under FIFO. The tax savings of $240 makes more cash available for use in the business.

Using Inventory Cost Flow Methods Consistently

Whatever cost flow method a company chooses, it should use that method consistently from one accounting period to another. This approach is often referred to as the **consistency concept**, which means that a company uses the same accounting principles and methods from year to year. Consistent application enhances the comparability of financial statements over successive time periods. In contrast, using the FIFO method one year and the LIFO method the next year would make it difficult to compare the net incomes of the two years.

Although consistent application is preferred, it does not mean that a company may never change its inventory costing method. When a company adopts a different method, it should disclose in the financial statements the change and its effects on net income. **Illustration 6.14** shows a typical disclosure, using information from recent financial statements of **Quaker Oats** (now a unit of **PepsiCo**).

ILLUSTRATION 6.14

Disclosure of change in cost flow method

Real World

Quaker Oats
Notes to the Financial Statements

Note 1: Effective July 1, the Company adopted the LIFO cost flow assumption for valuing the majority of U.S. Grocery Products inventories. The Company believes that the use of the LIFO method better matches current costs with current revenues. The effect of this change on the current year was to decrease net income by $16.0 million.

International Insight **ExxonMobil Corporation**

Bloomberg/Getty Images

Is LIFO Fair?

ExxonMobil Corporation, like many U.S. companies, uses LIFO to value its inventory for financial reporting and tax purposes. In one year, this resulted in a cost of goods sold figure that was $5.6 billion higher than under FIFO. By increasing cost of goods sold, ExxonMobil reduces net income, which reduces taxes. Critics say that LIFO provides an unfair "tax dodge." As Congress looks for more sources of tax revenue, some lawmakers favor the elimination of LIFO. Supporters of LIFO argue that the method is conceptually sound because it matches current costs with current revenues. In addition, they point out that this matching provides protection against inflation.

International accounting standards do not allow the use of LIFO. Because of this, the net income of foreign oil companies such as **BP** and **Royal Dutch Shell** are not directly comparable to U.S. companies, which can make analysis difficult.

Source: David Reilly, "Big Oil's Accounting Methods Fuel Criticism," *Wall Street Journal* (August 8, 2006), p. C1.

What are the arguments for and against the use of LIFO? (Go to WileyPLUS for this answer and additional questions.)

DO IT! 2 | Cost Flow Methods

The accounting records of Shumway Ag Implements show the following data.

Beginning inventory	4,000 units at $ 3
Purchases	6,000 units at $ 4
Sales	7,000 units at $12

Determine the cost of goods sold during the period under a periodic inventory system using (a) the FIFO method, (b) the LIFO method, and (c) the average-cost method.

ACTION PLAN

- **Understand the periodic inventory system.**
- **Allocate costs between goods sold and goods on hand (ending inventory) for each cost flow method.**
- **Compute cost of goods sold for each method.**

Solution

Cost of goods available for sale = (4,000 × $3) + (6,000 × $4) = $36,000
Ending inventory = 10,000 − 7,000 = 3,000 units

a. FIFO: $36,000 − (3,000 × $4) = $24,000

b. LIFO: $36,000 − (3,000 × $3) = $27,000

c. Average cost per unit: [(4,000 @ $3) + (6,000 @ $4)] ÷ 10,000 = $3.60
Average-cost: $36,000 − (3,000 × $3.60) = $25,200

Related exercise material: **BE6.3, BE6.4, BE6.5, BE6.6, DO IT! 6.2, E6.4, E6.5, E6.6, E6.7, E6.8, and E6.9.**

Effects of Inventory Errors

LEARNING OBJECTIVE 3

Indicate the effects of inventory errors on the financial statements.

Unfortunately, errors occasionally occur in accounting for inventory. In some cases, errors are caused by failure to count or price the inventory correctly. In other cases, errors occur because companies do not properly recognize the transfer of legal title to goods that are in transit. When errors occur, they affect both the income statement and the balance sheet.

Income Statement Effects

The ending inventory of one period automatically becomes the beginning inventory of the next period. Thus, inventory errors affect the computation of cost of goods sold and net income in two periods.

The effects on cost of goods sold can be computed by first entering incorrect data in the formula in **Illustration 6.15** and then substituting the correct data.

Beginning Inventory	+	Cost of Goods Purchased	−	Ending Inventory	=	Cost of Goods Sold

ILLUSTRATION 6.15
Formula for cost of goods sold

If **beginning** inventory is understated, cost of goods sold will be understated. If **ending** inventory is understated, cost of goods sold will be overstated. **Illustration 6.16** shows the effects of inventory errors on the current year's income statement.

ILLUSTRATION 6.16

Effects of inventory errors on current year's income statement

When Inventory Error:	Cost of Goods Sold Is:	Net Income Is:
Understates beginning inventory	Understated	Overstated
Overstates beginning inventory	Overstated	Understated
Understates ending inventory	Overstated	Understated
Overstates ending inventory	Understated	Overstated

ETHICS NOTE

Inventory fraud increases during recessions. Such fraud includes pricing inventory at amounts in excess of its actual value, or claiming to have inventory when no inventory exists. Inventory fraud usually overstates ending inventory, thereby understating cost of goods sold and creating higher income.

An error in the ending inventory of the current period will have a **reverse effect on net income of the next accounting period**. **Illustration 6.17** shows this effect. Note that the understatement of ending inventory in 2019 results in an understatement of beginning inventory in 2020 and an overstatement of net income in 2020.

Over the two years, though, total net income is correct because the errors **offset each other**. Notice that total income using incorrect data is $35,000 ($22,000 + $13,000), which is the same as the total income of $35,000 ($25,000 + $10,000) using correct data. Also note in this example that an error in the beginning inventory does not result in a corresponding error in the ending inventory for that period. The correctness of the ending inventory depends entirely on the accuracy of taking and costing the inventory at the balance sheet date under the periodic inventory system (see **Ethics Note**).

ILLUSTRATION 6.17 **Effects of inventory errors on two years' income statements**

Sample Company
Condensed Income Statements

	2019				2020			
	Incorrect		Correct		Incorrect		Correct	
Sales revenue		$80,000		$80,000		$90,000		$90,000
Beginning inventory	$ 20,000		$20,000		**$12,000**		**$15,000**	
Cost of goods purchased	40,000		40,000		68,000		68,000	
Cost of goods available for sale	60,000		60,000		80,000		83,000	
Ending inventory	**12,000**		**15,000**		23,000		23,000	
Cost of goods sold		48,000		45,000		57,000		60,000
Gross profit		32,000		35,000		33,000		30,000
Operating expenses		10,000		10,000		20,000		20,000
Net income		$22,000		$25,000		$13,000		$10,000

$(3,000) Net income understated

$3,000 Net income overstated

The errors cancel. Thus, the combined total income for the 2-year period is correct.

Balance Sheet Effects

Companies can determine the effect of ending inventory errors on the balance sheet by using the basic accounting equation: Assets = Liabilities + Owner's Equity. Errors in the ending inventory have the effects shown in **Illustration 6.18**.

ILLUSTRATION 6.18

Effects of ending inventory errors on balance sheet

Ending Inventory Error	Assets	Liabilities	Owner's Equity
Overstated	Overstated	No effect	Overstated
Understated	Understated	No effect	Understated

The effect of an error in ending inventory on the subsequent period was shown in Illustration 6.17. Note that if the error is not corrected, the combined total net income for the two periods would be correct. Thus, total owner's equity reported on the balance sheet at the end of 2020 will also be correct.

DO IT! 3 | Inventory Errors

Visual Company overstated its 2019 ending inventory by $22,000. Determine the impact this error has on ending inventory, cost of goods sold, and owner's equity in 2019 and 2020.

ACTION PLAN

- **An ending inventory error in one period will have an equal and opposite effect on cost of goods sold and net income in the next period.**
- **After two years, the errors have offset each other.**

Solution

	2019	2020
Ending inventory	$22,000 overstated	No effect
Cost of goods sold	$22,000 understated	$22,000 overstated
Owner's equity	$22,000 overstated	No effect

Related exercise material: **BE6.7, DO IT! 6.3, E6.10, and E6.11.**

Inventory Statement Presentation and Analysis

LEARNING OBJECTIVE 4

Explain the statement presentation and analysis of inventory.

Presentation

As indicated in Chapter 5, inventory is classified in the balance sheet as a current asset immediately below receivables. In a multiple-step income statement, cost of goods sold is subtracted from net sales. There also should be disclosure of (1) the major inventory classifications, (2) the basis of accounting (cost, or lower-of-cost-or-net realizable value), and (3) the cost method (FIFO, LIFO, or average-cost).

Lower-of-Cost-or-Net Realizable Value

The value of inventory for companies selling high-technology or fashion goods can drop very quickly due to continual changes in technology or fashions. These circumstances sometimes call for inventory valuation methods other than those presented so far. For example, purchasing managers at **Ford** at one time decided to make a large purchase of palladium, a precious metal used in vehicle emission devices. They made this purchase because they feared a future shortage. The shortage did not materialize, and by the end of the year the price of palladium had plummeted. Ford's inventory was then worth $1 billion less than its original cost. Do you think Ford's inventory should have been stated at cost, in accordance with the historical cost principle, or at its lower net realizable value?

As you probably reasoned, this situation requires a departure from the cost basis of accounting. When the value of inventory is lower than its cost, companies must "write down" the inventory to its net realizable value. This is done by valuing the inventory at the **lower-of-cost-or-net realizable value (LCNRV)** in the period in which the price decline occurs. LCNRV is an example of the accounting concept of **conservatism**, which means that the best choice among accounting alternatives is the method that is least likely to overstate assets and net income.

Under the LCNRV basis, **net realizable value** refers to the net amount that a company excepts to realize (receive) from the sale of inventory. Specifically, net realizable value is the estimated selling price in the normal course of business, less estimated costs to complete and sell.

Companies apply LCNRV to the items in inventory after they have used one of the inventory costing methods (specific identification, FIFO, or average-cost) to determine cost.[2] To illustrate the application of LCNRV, assume that Ken Tuckie TV has the following lines of merchandise with costs and net realizable values as indicated. LCNRV produces the results shown in **Illustration 6.19**. Note that the amounts shown in the final column are the lower-of-cost-or-net realizable value amounts for each item.

ILLUSTRATION 6.19

Computation of lower-of-cost-or-net realizable value

	Units	Cost per Unit	Net Realizable Value per Unit	Lower-of-Cost-or-Net Realizable Value	
Flat-screen TVs	100	$600	$550	$ 55,000	($550 × 100)
Satellite radios	500	90	104	45,000	($90 × 500)
DVD recorders	850	50	48	40,800	($48 × 850)
DVDs	3,000	5	6	15,000	($5 × 3,000)
Total inventory				$155,800	

Analysis

The amount of inventory carried by a company has significant economic consequences. And inventory management is a double-edged sword that requires constant attention. On the one hand, management wants to have a great variety and quantity available so that customers have a wide selection and items are always in stock. But, such a policy may incur high carrying costs (e.g., investment, storage, insurance, obsolescence, and damage). On the other hand, low inventory levels lead to stock-outs and lost sales. Common ratios used to manage and evaluate inventory levels are inventory turnover and a related measure, days in inventory.

Inventory turnover measures the number of times on average the inventory is sold during the period. Its purpose is to measure the liquidity of the inventory. The inventory turnover is computed by dividing cost of goods sold by the average inventory during the period. Unless seasonal factors are significant, average inventory can be computed from the beginning and ending inventory balances. For example, **Wal-Mart** reported in its January 31, 2016, annual report a beginning inventory of $45,141 million, an ending inventory of $44,469 million, and cost of goods sold for the year ended January 31, 2016, of $360,984 million. The inventory turnover formula and computation for Wal-Mart are shown in **Illustration 6.20**.

ILLUSTRATION 6.20

Inventory turnover formula and computation for Wal-Mart

Cost of Goods Sold	÷	Average Inventory	=	Inventory Turnover
$360,984	÷	$\frac{\$44,469 + \$45,141}{2}$	=	8.1 times

A variant of the inventory turnover is **days in inventory**. This measures the average number of days inventory is held. It is calculated as 365 divided by the inventory turnover. For example, Wal-Mart's inventory turnover of 8.1 times divided into 365 is approximately 45.1 days. This is the approximate time that it takes a company to sell the inventory once it arrives at the store.

[2]Special rules apply to companies that use LIFO, which are discussed in more advanced courses.

There are typical levels of inventory in every industry. Companies that are able to keep their inventory at lower levels and higher turnovers and still satisfy customer needs are the most successful.

Accounting Across the Organization Sony

© Dmitry Kutlayev/iStockphoto

Too Many TVs or Too Few?

Financial analysts closely monitor the inventory management practices of companies. For example, some analysts following **Sony** expressed concern because the company built up its inventory of televisions in an attempt to sell 25 million liquid crystal display (LCD) TVs—a 60% increase over the prior year. A year earlier, Sony had cut its inventory levels so that its quarterly days in inventory was down to 38 days, compared to 61 days for the same quarter a year before that. But in the next year, as a result of its inventory build-up, days in inventory rose to 59 days. Management said that it didn't think that Sony's inventory levels were too high. However, analysts were concerned that the company would have to engage in very heavy discounting in order to sell off its inventory. Analysts noted that the losses from discounting can be "punishing."

Source: Daisuke Wakabayashi, "Sony Pledges to Corral Inventory," *Wall Street Journal* Online (November 2, 2010).

For Sony, what are the advantages and disadvantages of having a low days in inventory measure? (Go to WileyPLUS for this answer and additional questions.)

DO IT! 4 | LCNRV and Inventory Turnover

a. Tracy Company sells three different types of home heating stoves (gas, wood, and pellet). The cost and net realizable value of its inventory of stoves are as follows.

	Cost	Net Realizable Value
Gas	$ 84,000	$ 79,000
Wood	250,000	280,000
Pellet	112,000	101,000

Determine the value of the company's inventory under the lower-of-cost-or-net realizable value approach.

ACTION PLAN

- **Determine whether cost or net realizable value is lower for each inventory type.**
- **Sum the lowest value of each inventory type to determine the total value of inventory.**

Solution

The lowest value for each inventory type is gas $79,000, wood $250,000, and pellet $101,000. The total inventory value is the sum of these amounts, $430,000.

b. Early in 2020, Westmoreland Company switched to a just-in-time inventory system. Its sales revenue, cost of goods sold, and inventory amounts for 2019 and 2020 are shown below.

	2019	2020
Sales revenue	$2,000,000	$1,800,000
Cost of goods sold	1,000,000	910,000
Beginning inventory	290,000	210,000
Ending inventory	210,000	50,000

Determine the inventory turnover and days in inventory for 2019 and 2020. Discuss the changes in the amount of inventory, the inventory turnover and days in inventory, and the amount of sales across the two years.

ACTION PLAN

- **To find the inventory turnover, divide cost of goods sold by average inventory.**
- **To determine days in inventory, divide 365 days by the inventory turnover.**

Solution

	2019		2020	
Inventory turnover	$1,000,000 / (($290,000 + $210,000)/2)	= 4	$910,000 / (($210,000 + $50,000)/2)	= 7
Days in inventory	365 ÷ 4 = 91.3 days		365 ÷ 7 = 52.1 days	

The company experienced a very significant decline in its ending inventory as a result of the just-in-time inventory. This decline improved its inventory turnover and its days in inventory. However, its sales declined by 10%. It is possible that this decline was caused by the dramatic reduction in the amount of inventory that was on hand, which increased the likelihood of "stock-outs." To determine the optimal inventory level, management must weigh the benefits of reduced inventory against the potential lost sales caused by stock-outs.

Related exercise material: **BE6.8, BE6.9, DO IT! 6.4, E6.12, E6.13, E6.14, and E6.15.**

ACTION PLAN (CONT.)

- **Just-in-time inventory reduces the amount of inventory on hand, which reduces carrying costs. Reducing inventory levels by too much has potential negative implications for sales.**

Appendix 6A Inventory Methods and the Perpetual System

LEARNING OBJECTIVE *5

Apply the inventory cost flow methods to perpetual inventory records.

What inventory cost flow methods can companies employ if they use a perpetual inventory system? Simple—they can use any of the inventory cost flow methods described in the chapter. To illustrate the application of the three assumed cost flow methods (FIFO, LIFO, and average-cost), we will use the data shown in **Illustration 6A.1** and in this chapter for Houston Electronics' Astro condensers.

ILLUSTRATION 6A.1
Inventoriable units and costs

Houston Electronics
Astro Condensers

Date	Explanation	Units	Unit Cost	Total Cost	Balance in Units
1/1	Beginning inventory	100	$10	$ 1,000	100
4/15	Purchases	200	11	2,200	300
8/24	Purchases	300	12	3,600	600
9/10	Sale	550			50
11/27	Purchases	400	13	5,200	450
				$12,000	

First-In, First-Out (FIFO)

Under perpetual FIFO, the company charges to cost of goods sold the cost of the earliest goods on hand **prior to each sale**. Therefore, the cost of goods sold on September 10 consists of the units on hand January 1 and the units purchased April 15 and August 24. **Illustration 6A.2** shows the inventory under a FIFO method perpetual system.

ILLUSTRATION 6A.2
Perpetual system—FIFO

Date	Purchases		Cost of Goods Sold	Balance (in units and cost)	
January 1				(100 @ $10)	$1,000
April 15	(200 @ $11)	$2,200		(100 @ $10) (200 @ $11)	$3,200
August 24	(300 @ $12)	$3,600		(100 @ $10) (200 @ $11) (300 @ $12)	$6,800
September 10			(100 @ $10) (200 @ $11) (250 @ $12) $6,200	(50 @ $12)	$ 600
November 27	(400 @ $13)	$5,200		(50 @ $12) (400 @ $13)	$5,800

Cost of goods sold: $6,200
Ending inventory: $5,800

The ending inventory in this situation is $5,800, and the cost of goods sold is $6,200 [(100 @ $10) + (200 @ $11) + (250 @ $12)].

Compare Illustrations 6.6 and 6A.2. You can see that the results under FIFO in a perpetual system are the **same as in a periodic system**. In both cases, the ending inventory is $5,800 and cost of goods sold is $6,200. Regardless of the system, the first costs in are the costs assigned to cost of goods sold.

Last-In, First-Out (LIFO)

Under the LIFO method using a perpetual system, the company charges to cost of goods sold the cost of the most recent purchase prior to sale. Therefore, the cost of the goods sold on September 10 consists of all the units from the August 24 and April 15 purchases plus 50 of the units in beginning inventory. **Illustration 6A.3** shows the computation of the ending inventory under the LIFO method.

ILLUSTRATION 6A.3
Perpetual system—LIFO

Date	Purchases		Cost of Goods Sold	Balance (in units and cost)	
January 1				(100 @ $10)	$1,000
April 15	(200 @ $11)	$2,200		(100 @ $10) (200 @ $11)	$3,200
August 24	(300 @ $12)	$3,600		(100 @ $10) (200 @ $11) (300 @ $12)	$6,800
September 10			(300 @ $12) (200 @ $11) (50 @ $10) $6,300	(50 @ $10)	$ 500
November 27	(400 @ $13)	$5,200		(50 @ $10) (400 @ $13)	$5,700

Cost of goods sold: $6,300
Ending inventory: $5,700

The use of LIFO in a perpetual system will usually produce cost allocations that differ from those using LIFO in a periodic system. In a perpetual system, the latest units purchased **prior to each sale** are allocated to cost of goods sold. In contrast, in a periodic system, the latest units purchased **during the period** are allocated to cost of goods sold. Thus, when a purchase is made after the last sale, the LIFO periodic system will apply this purchase to the previous sale.

See Illustration 6.9, which shows the proof that the 400 units at $13 purchased on November 27 applied to the sale of 550 units on September 10.

Under the LIFO perpetual system in Illustration 6A.3, the 400 units at $13 purchased on November 27 are all applied to the ending inventory. The ending inventory in this LIFO perpetual illustration is $5,700, and cost of goods sold is $6,300, as compared to the LIFO periodic Illustration 6.8 where the ending inventory is $5,000 and cost of goods sold is $7,000.

Average-Cost

The average-cost method in a perpetual inventory system is called the **moving-average method**. Under this method, the company computes a new average **after each purchase**, by dividing the cost of goods available for sale by the units on hand. The average cost is then applied to (1) the units sold, to determine the cost of goods sold, and (2) the remaining units on hand, to determine the ending inventory amount. **Illustration 6A.4** shows the application of the moving-average cost method by Houston Electronics (computations of the moving-average unit cost are shown after Illustration 6A.4).

ILLUSTRATION 6A.4

Perpetual system—moving-average method

Date	Purchases	Cost of Goods Sold	Balance (in units and cost)	
January 1			(100 @ $10)	$1,000
April 15	(200 @ $11) $2,200		(300 @ $10.667)	$3,200
August 24	(300 @ $12) $3,600		(600 @ $11.333)	$6,800
September 10		(550 @ $11.333)	(50 @ $11.333)	$ 567
		$6,233		
November 27	(400 @ $13) $5,200		(450 @ $12.816)	$5,767

Cost of goods sold: $6,233

Ending inventory: $5,767

As indicated, Houston Electronics computes **a new average each time it makes a purchase**.

1. On April 15, after Houston buys 200 units for $2,200, a total of 300 units costing $3,200 ($1,000 + $2,200) are on hand. The average unit cost is $10.667 ($3,200 ÷ 300).
2. On August 24, after Houston buys 300 units for $3,600, a total of 600 units costing $6,800 ($1,000 + $2,200 + $3,600) are on hand. The average cost per unit is $11.333 ($6,800 ÷ 600).
3. On September 10, to compute cost of goods sold, Houston uses this unit cost of $11.333 until it makes another purchase, when the company computes a new unit cost. Accordingly, the unit cost of the 550 units sold on September 10 is $11.333, and the total cost of goods sold is $6,233.
4. On November 27, following the purchase of 400 units for $5,200, there are 450 units on hand costing $5,767 ($567 + $5,200) with a new average cost of $12.816 ($5,767 ÷ 450).

Compare this moving-average cost under the perpetual inventory system to Illustration 6.11, which shows the average-cost method under a periodic inventory system.

Appendix 6B Estimating Inventories

LEARNING OBJECTIVE *6

Describe the two methods of estimating inventories.

In the chapter, we assumed that a company would be able to physically count its inventory. What if it cannot? What if the inventory were destroyed by fire or flood, for example? In that case, the company would use an estimate.

Two circumstances explain why companies sometimes estimate inventories. First, a casualty such as fire, flood, or earthquake may make it impossible to take a physical inventory. Second, managers may want monthly or quarterly financial statements, but a physical inventory is taken only annually. The need for estimating inventories occurs primarily with a periodic inventory system because of the absence of perpetual inventory records.

There are two widely used methods of estimating inventories: (1) the gross profit method, and (2) the retail inventory method.

Gross Profit Method

The **gross profit method** estimates the cost of ending inventory by applying a gross profit rate to net sales. This method is relatively simple but effective. Accountants, auditors, and managers frequently use the gross profit method to test the reasonableness of the ending inventory amount. It will detect large errors.

To use this method, a company needs to know its net sales, cost of goods available for sale, and gross profit rate. The company then can estimate its gross profit for the period. **Illustration 6B.1** shows the formulas for using the gross profit method.

Step 1:	**Net Sales**	−	**Estimated Gross Profit**	=	**Estimated Cost of Goods Sold**
Step 2:	**Cost of Goods Available for Sale**	−	**Estimated Cost of Goods Sold**	=	**Estimated Cost of Ending Inventory**

ILLUSTRATION 6B.1
Gross profit method formulas

To illustrate, assume that Kishwaukee Company wishes to prepare an income statement for the month of January. Its records show net sales of $200,000, beginning inventory $40,000, and cost of goods purchased $120,000. In the preceding year, the company realized a 30% gross profit rate. It expects to earn the same rate this year. Given these facts and assumptions, Kishwaukee can compute the estimated cost of the ending inventory at January 31 under the gross profit method as shown in **Illustration 6B.2**.

Step 1:	
Net sales	$200,000
Less: Estimated gross profit (30% × $200,000)	60,000
Estimated cost of goods sold	**$140,000**
Step 2:	
Beginning inventory	$ 40,000
Cost of goods purchased	120,000
Cost of goods available for sale	160,000
Less: Estimated cost of goods sold	140,000
Estimated cost of ending inventory	**$ 20,000**

ILLUSTRATION 6B.2
Example of gross profit method

The gross profit method is based on the assumption that the gross profit rate will remain constant. But, it may not remain constant, due to a change in merchandising policies or in market conditions. In such cases, the company should adjust the rate to reflect current operating conditions. In some cases, companies can obtain a more accurate estimate by applying this method on a department or product-line basis.

Note that companies should not use the gross profit method to prepare financial statements at the end of the year. These statements should be based on a physical inventory count.

Retail Inventory Method

A retail store such as **Home Depot**, **Ace Hardware**, or **Walmart** has thousands of different types of merchandise at low unit costs. In such cases, it is difficult and time-consuming to apply unit costs to inventory quantities. An alternative is to use the **retail inventory method** to estimate the cost of inventory. Most retail companies can establish a relationship between cost and sales price. The company then applies the cost-to-retail percentage to the ending inventory at retail prices to determine inventory at cost.

Under the retail inventory method, a company's records must show both the cost and retail value of the goods available for sale. **Illustration 6B.3** presents the formulas for using the retail inventory method.

ILLUSTRATION 6B.3

Retail inventory method formulas

Step 1:	Goods Available for Sale at Retail	−	Net Sales	=	Ending Inventory at Retail
Step 2:	Goods Available for Sale at Cost	÷	Goods Available for Sale at Retail	=	Cost-to-Retail Ratio
Step 3:	Ending Inventory at Retail	×	Cost-to-Retail Ratio	=	Estimated Cost of Ending Inventory

We can demonstrate the logic of the retail method by using unit-cost data. Assume that Ortiz Inc. has marked 10 units purchased at $7 to sell for $10 per unit. Thus, the cost-to-retail ratio is 70% ($70 ÷ $100). If four units remain unsold, their retail value is $40 (4 × $10), and their cost is $28 ($40 × 70%). This amount agrees with the total cost of goods on hand on a per unit basis (4 × $7).

Illustration 6B.4 shows application of the retail method for Valley West. Note that it is not necessary to take a physical inventory to determine the estimated cost of goods on hand at any given time.

ILLUSTRATION 6B.4

Application of retail inventory method

	At Cost	At Retail
Beginning inventory	$14,000	$ 21,500
Goods purchased	61,000	78,500
Goods available for sale	$75,000	100,000
Less: Net sales		70,000
Step (1) Ending inventory at retail =		**$ 30,000**

Step (2) Cost-to-retail ratio = $75,000 ÷ $100,000 = 75%
Step (3) Estimated cost of ending inventory = $30,000 × 75% = $22,500

HELPFUL HINT

In determining inventory at retail, companies use selling prices of the units.

The retail inventory method also facilitates taking a physical inventory at the end of the year. Valley West can value the goods on hand at the prices marked on the merchandise, and then apply the cost-to-retail ratio to the goods on hand at retail to determine the ending inventory at cost (see **Helpful Hint**).

The major disadvantage of the retail method is that it is an averaging technique. Thus, it may produce an incorrect inventory valuation if the mix of the ending inventory is not representative of the mix in the goods available for sale. Assume, for example, that the cost-to-retail ratio of 75% for Valley West consists of equal proportions of inventory items that have cost-to-retail ratios of 70%, 75%, and 80%. If the ending inventory contains only items with a 70% ratio, an incorrect inventory cost will result. Companies can minimize this problem by applying the retail method on a department or product-line basis.

Review and Practice

Learning Objectives Review

1 Discuss how to classify and determine inventory.

Merchandisers need only one inventory classification, merchandise inventory, to describe the different items that make up total inventory. Manufacturers, on the other hand, usually classify inventory into three categories: finished goods, work in process, and raw materials. To determine inventory quantities, manufacturers (1) take a physical inventory of goods on hand and (2) determine the ownership of goods in transit or on consignment.

2 Apply inventory cost flow methods and discuss their financial effects.

The primary basis of accounting for inventories is cost. Cost of goods available for sale includes (a) cost of beginning inventory and (b) cost of goods purchased. The inventory cost flow methods are specific identification and three assumed cost flow methods—FIFO, LIFO, and average-cost.

When prices are rising, the first-in, first-out (FIFO) method results in lower cost of goods sold and higher net income than the other methods. The last-in, first-out (LIFO) method results in the lowest income taxes. The reverse is true when prices are falling. In the balance sheet, FIFO results in an ending inventory that is closest to current value. Inventory under LIFO is the farthest from current value.

3 Indicate the effects of inventory errors on the financial statements.

In the income statement of the current year: (a) If beginning inventory is understated, net income is overstated. The reverse occurs if beginning inventory is overstated. (b) If ending inventory is overstated, net income is overstated. If ending inventory is understated, net income is understated. In the following period, its effect on net income for that period is reversed, and total net income for the two years will be correct.

In the balance sheet: Ending inventory errors will have the same effect on total assets and total owner's equity and no effect on liabilities.

4 Explain the statement presentation and analysis of inventory.

Inventory is classified in the balance sheet as a current asset immediately below receivables. There also should be disclosure of (1) the major inventory classifications, (2) the basis of accounting, and (3) the cost method.

Companies use the lower-of-cost-or-net realizable value (LCNRV) basis when the net realizable value is less than cost. Under LCNRV, companies recognize the loss in the period in which the price decline occurs.

The inventory turnover is cost of goods sold divided by average inventory. To convert it to average days in inventory, divide 365 days by the inventory turnover.

*5 Apply the inventory cost flow methods to perpetual inventory records.

Under FIFO and a perpetual inventory system, companies charge to cost of goods sold the cost of the earliest goods on hand prior to each sale. Under LIFO and a perpetual system, companies charge to cost of goods sold the cost of the most recent purchase prior to sale. Under the moving-average (average-cost) method and a perpetual system, companies compute a new average cost after each purchase.

*6 Describe the two methods of estimating inventories.

The two methods of estimating inventories are the gross profit method and the retail inventory method. Under the gross profit method, companies apply a gross profit rate to net sales to determine estimated gross profit and cost of goods sold. They then subtract estimated cost of goods sold from cost of goods available for sale to determine the estimated cost of the ending inventory.

Under the retail inventory method, companies compute a cost-to-retail ratio by dividing the cost of goods available for sale by the retail value of the goods available for sale. They then apply this ratio to the ending inventory at retail to determine the estimated cost of the ending inventory.

Glossary Review

Average-cost method Inventory costing method that uses the weighted-average unit cost to allocate to ending inventory and cost of goods sold the cost of goods available for sale. (p. 6-11).

Consigned goods Goods held for sale by one party although ownership of the goods is retained by another party. (p. 6-6).

Consistency concept Dictates that a company use the same accounting principles and methods from year to year. (p. 6-14).

Days in inventory Measure of the average number of days inventory is held; calculated as 365 divided by inventory turnover. (p. 6-18).

Finished goods inventory Manufactured items that are completed and ready for sale. (p. 6-3).

First-in, first-out (FIFO) method Inventory costing method that assumes that the costs of the earliest goods purchased are the first to be recognized as cost of goods sold. (p. 6-9).

FOB (free on board) destination Freight terms indicating that ownership of the goods remains with the seller until the goods reach the buyer. (p. 6-5).

FOB (free on board) shipping point Freight terms indicating that ownership of the goods passes to the buyer when the public carrier accepts the goods from the seller. (p. 6-5).

***Gross profit method** A method for estimating the cost of the ending inventory by applying a gross profit rate to net sales and subtracting estimated cost of goods sold from cost of goods available for sale. (p. 6-23).

Inventory turnover A ratio that measures the number of times on average the inventory sold during the period; computed by dividing cost of goods sold by the average inventory during the period. (p. 6-18).

Just-in-time (JIT) inventory Inventory system in which companies manufacture or purchase goods only when needed for use. (p. 6-3).

Last-in, first-out (LIFO) method Inventory costing method that assumes the costs of the latest units purchased are the first to be allocated to cost of goods sold. (p. 6-10).

Lower-of-cost-or-net realizable value (LCNRV) basis A basis whereby inventory is stated at the lower of either its cost or its net realizable value. (p. 6-17).

***Moving-average method** A new average is computed after each purchase, by dividing the cost of goods available for sale by the units on hand. (p. 6-22).

Net realizable value Net amount that a company expects to realize (receive) from the sale of inventory. Specifically, it is the estimated selling price in the normal course of business, less estimated costs to complete and sell. (p. 6-18)

Raw materials Basic goods that will be used in production but have not yet been placed into production. (p. 6-3).

***Retail inventory method** A method for estimating the cost of the ending inventory by applying a cost-to-retail ratio to the ending inventory at retail. (p. 6-24).

Specific identification method An actual physical flow costing method in which items still in inventory are specifically costed to arrive at the total cost of the ending inventory. (p. 6-7).

Weighted-average unit cost Average cost that is weighted by the number of units purchased at each unit cost. (p. 6-11).

Work in process That portion of manufactured inventory that has been placed into the production process but is not yet complete. (p. 6-3).

Practice Multiple-Choice Questions

1. **(LO 1)** When is a physical inventory usually taken?
   - **a.** When the company has its greatest amount of inventory.
   - **b.** When a limited number of goods are being sold or received.
   - **c.** At the end of the company's fiscal year.
   - **d.** Both (b) and (c).

2. **(LO 1)** Which of the following should **not** be included in the physical inventory of a company?
   - **a.** Goods held on consignment from another company.
   - **b.** Goods shipped on consignment to another company.
   - **c.** Goods in transit from another company shipped FOB shipping point.
   - **d.** None of the above.

3. **(LO 1)** As a result of a thorough physical inventory, Railway Company determined that it had inventory worth $180,000 at December 31, 2020. This count did not take into consideration the following facts: Rogers Consignment store currently has goods worth $35,000 on its sales floor that belong to Railway but are being sold on consignment by Rogers. The selling price of these goods is $50,000. Railway purchased $13,000 of goods that were shipped on December 27, FOB destination, that will be received by Railway on January 3. Determine the correct amount of inventory that Railway should report.
   - **a.** $230,000.
   - **b.** $215,000.
   - **c.** $228,000.
   - **d.** $193,000.

4. **(LO 2)** Cost of goods available for sale consists of two elements: beginning inventory and
   - **a.** ending inventory.
   - **b.** cost of goods purchased.
   - **c.** cost of goods sold.
   - **d.** All of the answer choices are correct.

5. **(LO 2)** Poppins Company has the following:

	Units	Unit Cost
Inventory, Jan. 1	8,000	$11
Purchase, June 19	13,000	12
Purchase, Nov. 8	5,000	13

If 9,000 units are on hand at December 31, the cost of the ending inventory under FIFO is:
   - **a.** $99,000.
   - **b.** $108,000.
   - **c.** $113,000.
   - **d.** $117,000.

6. **(LO 2)** Using the data in Question 5, the cost of the ending inventory under LIFO is:
   - **a.** $113,000.
   - **b.** $108,000.
   - **c.** $99,000.
   - **d.** $100,000.

7. **(LO 2)** Hansel Electronics has the following:

	Units	Unit Cost
Inventory, Jan. 1	5,000	$ 8
Purchase, April 2	15,000	$10
Purchase, Aug. 28	20,000	$12

If Hansel has 7,000 units on hand at December 31, the cost of ending inventory under the average-cost method is:
   - **a.** $84,000.
   - **b.** $70,000.
   - **c.** $56,000.
   - **d.** $75,250.

8. **(LO 2)** In periods of rising prices, LIFO will produce:
   - **a.** higher net income than FIFO.
   - **b.** the same net income as FIFO.
   - **c.** lower net income than FIFO.
   - **d.** higher net income than average-cost.

9. **(LO 2)** Considerations that affect the selection of an inventory costing method do **not** include:
   - **a.** tax effects.
   - **b.** balance sheet effects.
   - **c.** income statement effects.
   - **d.** perpetual vs. periodic inventory system.

10. **(LO 3)** Falk Company's ending inventory is understated $4,000. The effects of this error on the current year's cost of goods sold and net income, respectively, are:
   - **a.** understated, overstated.
   - **b.** overstated, understated.

c. overstated, overstated.

d. understated, understated.

11. (LO 3) Pauline Company overstated its inventory by $15,000 at December 31, 2019. It did not correct the error in 2019 or 2020. As a result, Pauline's owner's equity was:

a. overstated at December 31, 2019, and understated at December 31, 2020.

b. overstated at December 31, 2019, and properly stated at December 31, 2020.

c. understated at December 31, 2019, and understated at December 31, 2020.

d. overstated at December 31, 2019, and overstated at December 31, 2020.

12. (LO 4) The lower-of-cost-or-net realizable value rule for inventory is an example of the application of:

a. the conservatism convention.

b. the historical cost principle.

c. the materiality concept.

d. the economics entity assumption.

13. (LO 4) Norton Company purchased 1,000 widgets and has 200 widgets in its ending inventory at a cost of $91 each and a net realizable value of $80 each. The ending inventory under lower-of-cost-or-net realizable value is:

a. $91,000. c. $18,200.

b. $80,000. d. $16,000.

14. (LO 4) Santana Company had beginning inventory of $80,000, ending inventory of $110,000, cost of goods sold of $285,000, and sales of $475,000. Santana's days in inventory is:

a. 73 days. c. 102.5 days.

b. 121.7 days. d. 84.5 days.

15. (LO 4) Which of these would cause the inventory turnover to increase the most?

a. Increasing the amount of inventory on hand.

b. Keeping the amount of inventory on hand constant but increasing sales.

c. Keeping the amount of inventory on hand constant but decreasing sales.

d. Decreasing the amount of inventory on hand and increasing sales.

*16. (LO 5) In a perpetual inventory system:

a. LIFO cost of goods sold will be the same as in a periodic inventory system.

b. average costs are a simple average of unit costs incurred.

c. a new average is computed under the average-cost method after each sale.

d. FIFO cost of goods sold will be the same as in a periodic inventory system.

*17. (LO 6) King Company has sales of $150,000 and cost of goods available for sale of $135,000. If the gross profit rate is 30%, the estimated cost of the ending inventory under the gross profit method is:

a. $15,000. c. $45,000.

b. $30,000. d. $75,000.

Solutions

1. **d.** A physical inventory is usually taken when a limited number of goods are being sold or received, and at the end of the company's fiscal year. Choice (a) is incorrect because a physical inventory count is usually taken when the company has the least, not greatest, amount of inventory. Choices (b) and (c) are correct, but (d) is the better answer.

2. **a.** Goods held on consignment should not be included because another company has title (ownership) to the goods. The other choices are incorrect because (b) goods shipped on consignment to another company and (c) goods in transit from another company shipped FOB shipping point should be included in a company's ending inventory. Choice (d) is incorrect because (a) is not included in the physical inventory.

3. **b.** The inventory held on consignment by Rogers should be included in Railway's inventory balance at cost ($35,000). The purchased goods of $13,000 should not be included in inventory until January 3 because the goods are shipped FOB destination. Therefore, the correct amount of inventory is $215,000 ($180,000 + $35,000), not (a) $230,000, (c) $228,000, or (d) $193,000.

4. **b.** Cost of goods available for sale consists of beginning inventory and cost of goods purchased, not (a) ending inventory or (c) cost of goods sold. Therefore, choice (d) All of the above is also incorrect.

5. **c.** Under FIFO, ending inventory will consist of 5,000 units from the Nov. 8 purchase and 4,000 units from the June 19 purchase. Therefore, ending inventory is (5,000 × $13) + (4,000 × $12) = $113,000, not (a) $99,000, (b) $108,000, or (d) $117,000.

6. **d.** Under LIFO, ending inventory will consist of 8,000 units from the inventory at Jan. 1 and 1,000 units from the June 19 purchase. Therefore, ending inventory is (8,000 × $11) + (1,000 × $12) = $100,000, not (a) $113,000, (b) $108,000, or (c) $99,000.

7. **d.** Under the average-cost method, total cost of goods available for sale needs to be calculated in order to determine average cost per unit. The total cost of goods available is $430,000 = (5,000 × $8) + (15,000 × $10) + (20,000 × $12). The average cost per unit = ($430,000/40,000 total units available for sale) = $10.75. Therefore, ending inventory is ($10.75 × 7,000) = $75,250, not (a) $84,000, (b) $70,000, or (c) $56,000.

8. **c.** In periods of rising prices, LIFO will produce lower net income than FIFO, not (a) higher than FIFO or (b) the same as FIFO. Choice (d) is incorrect because in periods of rising prices, LIFO will produce lower net income than average-cost. LIFO therefore charges the highest inventory cost against revenues in a period of rising prices.

9. **d.** Perpetual vs. periodic inventory system is not one of the factors that affect the selection of an inventory costing method. The other choices are incorrect because (a) tax effects, (b) balance sheet effects, and (c) income statement effects all affect the selection of an inventory costing method.

10. **b.** Because ending inventory is too low, cost of goods sold will be too high (overstated) and since cost of goods sold (an expense) is too high, net income will be too low (understated). Therefore, the other choices are incorrect.

11. b. Owner's equity is overstated by $15,000 at December 31, 2019, and is properly stated at December 31, 2020. An ending inventory error in one period will have an equal and opposite effect on cost of goods sold and net income in the next period; after two years, the errors have offset each other. The other choices are incorrect because owner's equity (a) is properly stated, not understated, at December 31, 2020; (c) is overstated, not understated, by $15,000 at December 31, 2019, and is properly stated, not understated, at December 31, 2020; and (d) is properly stated at December 31, 2020, not overstated.

12. a. Conservatism means to use the lowest value for assets and revenues when in doubt. The other choices are incorrect because (b) historical cost means that companies value assets at the original cost, (c) materiality means that an amount is large enough to affect a decision-maker, and (d) economic entity means to keep the company's transactions separate from the transactions of other entities.

13. d. Under the LCNRV basis, net realizable value is defined as the estimated selling price in the normal course of business, less estimated costs to complete and sell. Therefore, ending inventory would be valued at 200 widgets × $80 each = $16,000 not (a) $91,000, (b) $80,000, or (c) $18,200.

14. b. Santana's days in inventory = 365/Inventory turnover = 365/[$285,000/($80,000 + $110,000)/2)] = 121.7 days, not (a) 73 days, (c) 102.5 days, or (d) 84.5 days.

15. d. Decreasing the amount of inventory on hand will cause the denominator to decrease, causing inventory turnover to increase. Increasing sales will cause the numerator of the ratio to increase (higher sales means higher COGS), thus causing inventory turnover to increase even more. The other choices are incorrect because (a) increasing the amount of inventory on hand causes the denominator of the ratio to increase while the numerator stays the same, causing inventory turnover to decrease; (b) keeping the amount of inventory on hand constant but increasing sales will cause inventory turnover to increase because the numerator of the ratio will increase (higher sales means higher COGS) while the denominator stays the same, which will result in a lesser inventory increase than decreasing amount of inventory on hand and increasing sales; and (c) keeping the amount of inventory on hand constant but decreasing sales will cause inventory turnover to decrease because the numerator of the ratio will decrease (lower sales means lower COGS) while the denominator stays the same.

***16. d.** FIFO cost of goods sold is the same under both a periodic and a perpetual inventory system. The other choices are incorrect because (a) LIFO cost of goods sold is not the same under a periodic and a perpetual inventory system; (b) average costs are based on a moving average of unit costs, not an average of unit costs; and (c) a new average is computed under the average-cost method after each purchase, not sale.

***17. b.** COGS = Sales ($150,000) − Gross profit ($150,000 × 30%) = $105,000. Ending inventory = Cost of goods available for sale ($135,000) − COGS ($105,000) = $30,000, not (a) $15,000, (c) $45,000, or (d) $75,000.

Practice Brief Exercises

Compute ending inventory using FIFO and LIFO.

1. **(LO 2)** In its first month of operations, Moncada Company made three purchases of merchandise in the following sequence: (1) 200 units at $7, (2) 300 units at $8, and (3) 150 units at $9. Assuming there are 220 units on hand, compute the cost of the ending inventory under the (a) FIFO method and (b) LIFO method. Moncada uses a periodic inventory system.

Solution

1. **a.** The ending inventory under FIFO consists of (150 units at $9) + (70 units at $8) for a total allocation of $1,910 ($1,350 + $560).

   b. The ending inventory under LIFO consists of (200 units at $7) + (20 units at $8) for a total allocation of $1,560 ($1,400 + $160).

Determine correct income statement amounts.

2. **(LO 3)** **Financial Statement** Avisail Company reports net income of $80,000 in 2020. However, ending inventory was overstated $9,000. What is the correct net income for 2020? What effect, if any, will this error have on total assets as reported in the balance sheet at December 31, 2020?

Solution

2. The overstatement of ending inventory caused cost of goods sold to be understated $9,000 and net income to be overstated $9,000. The correct net income for 2020 is $71,000 ($80,000 − $9,000). Total assets in the balance sheet will be overstated by the amount that ending inventory is overstated, $9,000.

Compute inventory turnover and days in inventory.

3. **(LO 4)** At December 31, 2020, the following information was available for Garcia Company: ending inventory $30,000, beginning inventory $42,000, cost of goods sold $240,000, and sales revenue $400,000. Calculate inventory turnover and days in inventory for Garcia Company.

Solution

3. Inventory turnover: $\frac{\$240{,}000}{(\$30{,}000 + \$42{,}000)/2} = \frac{\$240{,}000}{\$36{,}000} = 6.67$

Days in inventory: $\frac{365}{6.67} = 54.7$ days

Practice Exercises

Determine the correct inventory amount.

1. **(LO 1)** Matt Clark, an auditor with Grant CPAs, is performing a review of Parson Company's inventory account. Parson did not have a good year and top management is under pressure to boost reported income. According to its records. the inventory balance at year-end was $600,000. However, the following information was not considered when determining that amount.

1. The physical count did not include goods purchased by Parson with a cost of $30,000 that were shipped FOB destination on December 28 and did not arrive at Parson's warehouse until January 3.
2. Included in the company's count were goods with a cost of $150,000 that the company is holding on consignment. The goods belong to Alvarez Corporation.
3. Included in the inventory account was $21,000 of office supplies that were stored in the warehouse and were to be used by the company's supervisors and managers during the coming year.
4. The company received an order on December 28 that was boxed and was sitting on the loading dock awaiting pick-up on December 31. The shipper picked up the goods on January 1 and delivered them on January 6. The shipping terms were FOB shipping point. The goods had a selling price of $29,000 and a cost of $19,000. The goods were not included in the count because they were sitting on the dock.
5. On December 29, Parson shipped goods with a selling price of $56,000 and a cost of $40,000 to Decco Corporation FOB shipping point. The goods arrived on January 3. Decco had only ordered goods with a selling price of $10,000 and a cost of $6,000. However, a Parson's sales manager had authorized the shipment and said that if Decco wanted to ship the goods back next week, it could.
6. Included in the count was $27,000 of goods that were parts for a machine that the company no longer made. Given the high-tech nature of Parson's products, it was unlikely that these obsolete parts had any other use. However, management would prefer to keep them on the books at cost, "since that is what we paid for them, after all."

Instructions

Prepare a schedule to determine the correct inventory amount. Provide explanations for each item above, saying why you did or did not make an adjustment for each item.

Solution

1. Ending inventory—as reported	$600,000
1. No effect—title does not pass to Parson until goods are received (Jan. 3).	0
2. Subtract from inventory: The goods belong to Alvarez Corporation. Parson is merely holding them for Alvarez.	(150,000)
3. Subtract from inventory: Office supplies should be carried in a separate account. They are not considered inventory held for resale.	(21,000)
4. Add to inventory: The goods belong to Parson until they are shipped (Jan. 1).	19,000
5. Add to inventory: Decco ordered goods with a cost of $6,000. Parson should record the corresponding sales revenue of $10,000. Parson's decision to ship extra "unordered" goods does not constitute a sale. The manager's statement that Decco could ship the goods back indicates that Parson knows this overshipment is not a legitimate sale. The manager acted unethically in an attempt to improve Parson's reported income by overshipping.	34,000
6. Subtract from inventory: GAAP require that inventory be valued at the lower-of-cost-or-net realizable value. Obsolete parts should be adjusted from cost to zero if they have no other use.	(27,000)
Correct inventory	$455,000

Determine effects of inventory errors.

2. **(LO 3)** Rhode Software reported cost of goods sold as follows.

	2019	2020
Beginning inventory	$ 27,000	$ 40,000
Cost of goods purchased	200,000	235,000
Cost of goods available for sale	227,000	275,000
Ending inventory	40,000	45,000
Cost of goods sold	$187,000	$230,000

Rhode made two errors: (1) 2019 ending inventory was overstated $4,000, and (2) 2020 ending inventory was understated $9,000.

Instructions

Compute the correct cost of goods sold for each year.

Solution

2.

	2019	2020
Beginning inventory	$ 27,000	$ 36,000
Cost of goods purchased	200,000	235,000
Cost of goods available for sale	227,000	271,000
Corrected ending inventory	(36,000)[a]	(54,000)[b]
Cost of goods sold	$191,000	$217,000

[a]$40,000 – $4,000 = $36,000; [b]$45,000 + $9,000 = $54,000

Determine LCNRV valuation.

3. **(LO 4)** Creve Couer Camera uses the lower-of-cost-or-net realizable value basis for its inventory. The following data are available at December 31.

	Units	Cost per Unit	Net Realizable Value per Unit
Cameras:			
Minolta	5	$160	$156
Canon	7	145	153
Light Meters:			
Vivitar	12	120	114
Kodak	10	130	142

Instructions

What amount should be reported on Creve Couer Camera's financial statements, assuming the lower-of-cost-or-net realizable value rule is applied?

Solution

3.

	Cost per Unit	Net Realizable Value per Unit	Lower-of-Cost or-Net Realizable Value	Units	Inventory at Lower-of-Cost-or-Net Realizable Value
Cameras:					
Minolta	$160	$156	$156	5	$ 780
Canon	145	153	145	7	1,015
Light Meters:					
Vivitar	120	114	114	12	1,368
Kodak	130	142	130	10	1,300
Total					$4,463

Practice Problems

Compute inventory and cost of goods sold using three cost flow methods in a periodic inventory system.

1. **(LO 2)** Englehart Company has the following inventory, purchases, and sales data for the month of March.

Inventory:	March 1	200 units @ $4.00	$ 800
Purchases:	March 10	500 units @ $4.50	2,250
	March 20	400 units @ $4.75	1,900
	March 30	300 units @ $5.00	1,500
Sales:	March 15	500 units	
	March 25	400 units	

The physical inventory count on March 31 shows 500 units on hand.

Instructions

Under a **periodic inventory system**, determine the cost of inventory on hand at March 31 and the cost of goods sold for March under (a) FIFO, (b) LIFO, and (c) average-cost. (For average-cost, carry cost per unit to three decimal places.)

Solution

1. The cost of goods available for sale is $6,450, as follows.

Inventory:		200 units @ $4.00	$ 800
Purchases:	March 10	500 units @ $4.50	2,250
	March 20	400 units @ $4.75	1,900
	March 30	300 units @ $5.00	1,500
Total goods available for sale			$6,450

a. **FIFO Method**

Ending inventory:

Date	Units	Unit Cost	Total Cost	
March 30	300	$5.00	$1,500	
March 20	200	4.75	950	$2,450

Cost of goods sold: $6,450 – $2,450 = $4,000

b. **LIFO Method**

Ending inventory:

Date	Units	Unit Cost	Total Cost	
March 1	200	$4.00	$ 800	
March 10	300	4.50	1,350	$2,150

Cost of goods sold: $6,450 – $2,150 = $4,300

c. **Average-Cost Method**

Average unit cost: $6,450 ÷ 1,400 = $4.607
Ending inventory: 500 × $4.607 = $2,303.50

Cost of goods sold: $6,450 – $2,303.50 = $4,146.50

Compute inventory and cost of goods sold using three cost flow methods in a perpetual inventory system.

*2. **(LO 5) Practice Problem 1** showed cost of goods sold computations under a periodic inventory system. Now let's assume that Englehart Company uses a perpetual inventory system. The company has the same inventory, purchases, and sales data for the month of March as shown earlier:

Inventory:	March 1	200 units @ $4.00	$ 800
Purchases:	March 10	500 units @ $4.50	2,250
	March 20	400 units @ $4.75	1,900
	March 30	300 units @ $5.00	1,500
Sales:	March 15	500 units	
	March 25	400 units	

The physical inventory count on March 31 shows 500 units on hand.

Instructions

Under a **perpetual inventory system,** determine the cost of inventory on hand at March 31 and the cost of goods sold for March under (a) FIFO, (b) LIFO, and (c) moving-average cost.

Solution

2. The cost of goods available for sale is $6,450, as follows.

Inventory:		200 units @ $4.00	$ 800
Purchases:	March 10	500 units @ $4.50	2,250
	March 20	400 units @ $4.75	1,900
	March 30	300 units @ $5.00	1,500
Total:			$6,450

Under a **perpetual inventory system,** the cost of goods sold under each cost flow method is as follows.

a. **FIFO Method**

Date	Purchases	Cost of Goods Sold	Balance
March 1			(200 @ $4.00) $ 800
March 10	(500 @ $4.50) $2,250		(200 @ $4.00) (500 @ $4.50) } $3,050
March 15		(200 @ $4.00) (300 @ $4.50) $2,150	(200 @ $4.50) $ 900
March 20	(400 @ $4.75) $1,900		(200 @ $4.50) (400 @ $4.75) } $2,800
March 25		(200 @ $4.50) (200 @ $4.75) $1,850	(200 @ $4.75) $ 950
March 30	(300 @ $5.00) $1,500		(200 @ $4.75) (300 @ $5.00) } $2,450

Ending inventory $2,450 Cost of goods sold: $2,150 + $1,850 = $4,000

b. **LIFO Method**

Date	Purchases	Cost of Goods Sold	Balance
March 1			(200 @ $4.00) $ 800
March 10	(500 @ $4.50) $2,250		(200 @ $4.00) (500 @ $4.50) } $3,050
March 15		(500 @ $4.50) $2,250	(200 @ $4.00) $ 800
March 20	(400 @ $4.75) $1,900		(200 @ $4.00) (400 @ $4.75) } $2,700
March 25		(400 @ $4.75) $1,900	(200 @ $4.00) $ 800
March 30	(300 @ $5.00) $1,500		(200 @ $4.00) (300 @ $5.00) } $2,300

Ending inventory $2,300 Cost of goods sold: $2,250 + $1,900 = $4,150

c. **Moving-Average Cost Method**

Date	Purchases	Cost of Goods Sold	Balance
March 1			(200 @ $ 4.00) $ 800
March 10	(500 @ $4.50) $2,250		(700 @ $4.357) $3,050
March 15		(500 @ $4.357) $2,179	(200 @ $4.357) $ 871
March 20	(400 @ $4.75) $1,900		(600 @ $4.618) $2,771
March 25		(400 @ $4.618) $1,847	(200 @ $4.618) $ 924
March 30	(300 @ $5.00) $1,500		(500 @ $4.848) $2,424

Ending inventory $2,424 Cost of goods sold: $2,179 + $1,847 = $4,026

WileyPLUS

Brief Exercises, DO IT! Exercises, Exercises, Problems, and many additional resources are available for practice in WileyPLUS.

Note: All asterisked Questions, Exercises, and Problems relate to material in the appendices to the chapter.

Questions

1. "The key to successful business operations is effective inventory management." Do you agree? Explain.

2. An item must possess two characteristics to be classified as inventory by a merchandiser. What are these two characteristics?

3. Your friend Ben Johnson has been hired to help take the physical inventory in Pearson Hardware Store. Explain to Ben what this job will entail.

4. **a.** Jovad Company ships merchandise to Martin Company on December 30. The merchandise reaches the buyer on January 6. Indicate the terms of sale that will result in the goods being included in (1) Jovad's December 31 inventory, and (2) Martin's December 31 inventory.

   b. Under what circumstances should Jovad Company include consigned goods in its inventory?

5. Topp Hat Shop received a shipment of hats for which it paid the wholesaler $2,970. The price of the hats was $3,000 but Topp was given a $30 cash discount and required to pay freight charges of $50. What amount will Topp record for inventory? Why?

6. Explain the difference between the terms FOB shipping point and FOB destination.

7. Leah Clement believes that the allocation of cost of goods available for sale should be based on the actual physical flow of the goods. Explain to Leah why this may be both impractical and inappropriate.

8. What is the major advantage and the major disadvantage of the specific identification method of inventory costing?

9. "The selection of an inventory cost flow method is a decision made by accountants." Do you agree? Explain. Once a method has been selected, what accounting requirement applies?

10. Which assumed inventory cost flow method:

    a. usually parallels the actual physical flow of merchandise?

    b. divides cost of goods available by total units available for sale to determine a unit cost?

    c. assumes that the latest units purchased are the first to be sold?

11. In a period of rising prices, the inventory reported in Bert Company's balance sheet is close to the current cost of the inventory, whereas Ernie Company's inventory is considerably below its current cost. Identify the inventory cost flow method being used by each company. Which company probably has been reporting the higher gross profit?

12. Oscar Company has been using the FIFO cost flow method during a prolonged period of inflation. During the same time period, Oscar has been paying out all of its net income as dividends. What adverse effects may result from this policy?

13. Kyle Adams is studying for the next accounting mid-term examination. What should Kyle know about (a) departing from the cost basis of accounting for inventories and (b) the meaning of "net realizable value" in the lower-of-cost-or-net realizable value method?

14. Hendrix Entertainment Center has 5 TVs on hand at the balance sheet date that cost $400 each. The net realizable value is $380 per unit. Under the lower-of-cost-or-net realizable value basis of accounting for inventories, what value should Hendrix report for the TVs on the balance sheet? Why?

15. Warnke Stores has 20 toasters on hand at the balance sheet date. Each costs $27. The net realizable value is $30 per unit. Under the lower-of-cost-or-net realizable value basis of accounting for inventories, what value should Warnke report for the toasters on the balance sheet? Why?

16. Sayaovang Company discovers in 2020 that its ending inventory at December 31, 2019, was $7,000 understated. What effect will this error have on (a) 2019 net income, (b) 2020 net income, and (c) the combined net income for the 2 years?

17. Dreher Company's balance sheet shows Inventory $162,800. What additional disclosures should be made?

18. Under what circumstances might inventory turnover be too high? That is, what possible negative consequences might occur?

19. What inventory cost flow does **Apple** use for its inventories? (*Hint:* You will need to examine the notes for Apple's financial statements.)

*20. "When perpetual inventory records are kept, the results under the FIFO and LIFO methods are the same as they would be in a periodic inventory system." Do you agree? Explain.

*21. How does the average-cost method of inventory costing differ between a perpetual inventory system and a periodic inventory system?

*22. When is it necessary to estimate inventories?

*23. Both the gross profit method and the retail inventory method are based on averages. For each method, indicate the average used, how it is determined, and how it is applied.

*24. Pawlowski Company has net sales of $400,000 and cost of goods available for sale of $300,000. If the gross profit rate is 35%, what is the estimated cost of the ending inventory? Show computations.

*25. Cinderella Shoe Shop had goods available for sale in 2020 with a retail price of $120,000. The cost of these goods was $84,000. If sales during the period were $80,000, what is the ending inventory at cost using the retail inventory method?

Brief Exercises

Identify items to be included in taking a physical inventory.

BE6.1 (LO 1) Peosta Company identifies the following items for possible inclusion in the taking of a physical inventory. Indicate whether each item should be included or excluded from the inventory taking.

a. Goods shipped on consignment by Peosta to another company.

b. Goods in transit from a supplier shipped FOB destination.

c. Goods held on consignment from another company.

Determine ending inventory amount.

BE6.2 (LO 1) Stallman Company took a physical inventory on December 31 and determined that goods costing $200,000 were on hand. Not included in the physical count were $25,000 of goods purchased from Pelzer Corporation, FOB shipping point, and $22,000 of goods sold to Alvarez Company for $30,000, FOB destination. Both the Pelzer purchase and the Alvarez sale were in transit at year-end. What amount should Stallman report as its December 31 inventory?

Compute ending inventory using FIFO and LIFO.

BE6.3 (LO 2) In its first month of operations, Weatherall Company made three purchases of merchandise in the following sequence: (1) 300 units at $6, (2) 400 units at $7, and (3) 200 units at $8. Assuming there are 380 units on hand, compute the cost of the ending inventory under the (a) FIFO method and (b) LIFO method. Weatherall uses a periodic inventory system.

Compute the ending inventory using average-cost.

BE6.4 (LO 2) Data for Weatherall Company are presented in BE6.3. Compute the cost of the ending inventory under the average-cost method, assuming there are 380 units on hand.

Explain the financial statement effect of inventory cost flow assumptions.

BE6.5 (LO 2) **Financial Statement** The management of Mastronardo Corp. is considering the effects of inventory-costing methods on its financial statements and its income tax expense. Assuming that the price the company pays for inventory is increasing, which method will:

a. Provide the highest net income?

b. Provide the highest ending inventory?

c. Result in the lowest income tax expense?

d. Result in the most stable earnings over a number of years?

Explain the financial statement effect of inventory cost flow assumptions.

BE6.6 (LO 2) **Financial Statement** In its first month of operation, Hoffman Company purchased 100 units of inventory for $6, then 200 units for $7, and finally 140 units for $8. At the end of the month, 180 units remained. Compute the amount of phantom profit that would result if the company used FIFO rather than LIFO. Explain why this amount is referred to as phantom profit. The company uses the periodic method.

Determine correct income statement amounts.

BE6.7 (LO 3) Larkin Company reports net income of $90,000 in 2020. However, ending inventory was understated $7,000. What is the correct net income for 2020? What effect, if any, will this error have on total assets as reported in the balance sheet at December 31, 2020?

Determine the LCNRV valuation using inventory categories.

BE6.8 (LO 4) Cruz Video Center accumulates the following cost and net realizable data at December 31.

Inventory Categories	Cost Data	Net Realizable Data
Cameras	$12,000	$12,300
Camcorders	9,500	9,700
Blu-ray players	14,000	12,900

Compute the lower-of-cost-or-net realizable value valuation for the company's total inventory.

Compute inventory turnover and days in inventory.

BE6.9 (LO 4) At December 31, 2020, the following information was available for E. Hetzel Company: ending inventory $40,000, beginning inventory $56,000, cost of goods sold $270,000, and sales revenue $380,000. Calculate inventory turnover and days in inventory for E. Hetzel Company.

Apply cost flow methods to perpetual inventory records.

***BE6.10 (LO 5)** Rosario Department Store uses a perpetual inventory system. Data for product E2-D2 include the following purchases.

Date	Number of Units	Unit Price
May 7	50	$10
July 28	30	13

On June 1, Rosario sold 26 units, and on August 27, 40 more units. Prepare the perpetual inventory schedule for the above transactions using (a) FIFO, (b) LIFO, and (c) moving-average cost. (Round average cost per unit to nearest cent.)

Apply the gross profit method.

***BE6.11 (LO 6)** At May 31, Brunet Company has net sales of $340,000 and cost of goods available for sale of $230,000. Compute the estimated cost of the ending inventory, assuming the gross profit rate is 35%.

Apply the retail inventory method.

***BE6.12 (LO 6)** On June 30, Joanna Fabrics has the following data pertaining to the retail inventory method. Goods available for sale: at cost $38,000; at retail $50,000; net sales $40,000; and ending inventory at retail $10,000. Compute the estimated cost of the ending inventory using the retail inventory method.

DO IT! Exercises

Apply rules of ownership to determine inventory cost.

DO IT! 6.1 (LO 1) Gresa Company just took its physical inventory. The count of inventory items on hand at the company's business locations resulted in a total inventory cost of $300,000. In reviewing the details of the count and related inventory transactions, you have discovered the following.

1. Gresa has sent inventory costing $26,000 on consignment to Alissa Company. All of this inventory was at Alissa's showrooms on December 31.
2. The company did not include in the count inventory (cost, $20,000) that was sold on December 28, terms FOB shipping point. The goods were in transit on December 31.
3. The company did not include in the count inventory (cost, $14,000) that was purchased with terms of FOB shipping point. The goods were in transit on December 31.

Compute the correct December 31 inventory.

Compute cost of goods sold under different cost flow methods.

DO IT! 6.2 (LO 2) The accounting records of Americo Electronics show the following data.

Beginning inventory	3,000 units at $5
Purchases	8,000 units at $7
Sales	9,400 units at $10

Determine cost of goods sold during the period under a periodic inventory system using (a) the FIFO method, (b) the LIFO method, and (c) the average-cost method. (Round unit cost to nearest tenth of a cent.)

Determine effect of inventory error.

DO IT! 6.3 (LO 3) Vanida Company understated its 2019 ending inventory by $27,000. Determine the impact this error has on ending inventory, cost of goods sold, and owner's equity in 2019 and 2020.

Compute inventory value under LCNRV.

DO IT! 6.4a (LO 4) Cody Company sells three different categories of tools (small, medium, and large). The cost and net realizable value of its inventory of tools are as follows.

	Cost	Net Realizable Value
Small	$ 64,000	$ 73,000
Medium	290,000	260,000
Large	152,000	171,000

Determine the value of the company's inventory under the lower-of-cost-or-net realizable value approach.

Compute inventory turnover and assess inventory level.

DO IT! 6.4b (LO 4) Early in 2020, Yeng Company switched to a just-in-time inventory system. Its sales revenue, cost of goods sold, and inventory amounts for 2019 and 2020 are shown below.

	2019	2020
Sales	$3,120,000	$3,713,000
Cost of goods sold	1,200,000	1,425,000
Beginning inventory	180,000	220,000
Ending inventory	220,000	100,000

Determine the inventory turnover and days in inventory for 2019 and 2020. Discuss the changes in the amount of inventory, the inventory turnover and days in inventory, and the amount of sales across the two years.

Exercises

Determine the correct inventory amount.

E6.1 (LO 1) Tri-State Bank and Trust is considering giving Wilfred Company a loan. Before doing so, management decides that further discussions with Wilfred's accountant may be desirable. One area of particular concern is the inventory account, which has a year-end balance of $297,000. Discussions with the accountant reveal the following.

1. Wilfred shipped goods costing $38,000 to Lilja Company, FOB shipping point, on December 28. The goods are not expected to arrive at Lilja until January 12. The goods were not included in the physical inventory because they were not in the warehouse.
2. The physical count of the inventory did not include goods costing $95,000 that were shipped to Wilfred FOB destination on December 27 and were still in transit at year-end.
3. Wilfred received goods costing $22,000 on January 2. The goods were shipped FOB shipping point on December 26 by Brent Co. The goods were not included in the physical count.
4. Wilfred shipped goods costing $35,000 to Jesse Co., FOB destination, on December 30. The goods were received at Jesse on January 8. They were not included in Wilfred's physical inventory.
5. Wilfred received goods costing $44,000 on January 2 that were shipped FOB destination on December 29. The shipment was a rush order that was supposed to arrive December 31. This purchase was included in the ending inventory of $297,000.

Instructions

Determine the correct inventory amount on December 31.

Determine the correct inventory amount.

E6.2 (LO 1) Kari Downs, an auditor with Wheeler CPAs, is performing a review of Depue Company's inventory account. Depue did not have a good year, and top management is under pressure to boost reported income. According to its records, the inventory balance at year-end was $740,000. However, the following information was not considered when determining that amount.

1. Included in the company's count were goods with a cost of $250,000 that the company is holding on consignment. The goods belong to Kroeger Corporation.
2. The physical count did not include goods purchased by Depue with a cost of $40,000 that were shipped FOB destination on December 28 and did not arrive at Depue warehouse until January 3.
3. Included in the inventory account was $14,000 of office supplies that were stored in the warehouse and were to be used by the company's supervisors and managers during the coming year.
4. The company received an order on December 29 that was boxed and sitting on the loading dock awaiting pick-up on December 31. The shipper picked up the goods on January 1 and delivered them on January 6. The shipping terms were FOB shipping point. The goods had a selling price of $40,000 and a cost of $28,000. The goods were not included in the count because they were sitting on the dock.
5. On December 29, Depue shipped goods with a selling price of $80,000 and a cost of $60,000 to Macchia Sales Corporation FOB shipping point. The goods arrived on January 3. Macchia had only ordered goods with a selling price of $10,000 and a cost of $8,000. However, a sales manager at Depue had authorized the shipment and said that if Machia wanted to ship the goods back next week, it could.
6. Included in the count was $40,000 of goods that were parts for a machine that the company no longer made. Given the high-tech nature of Depue's products, it was unlikely that these obsolete parts had any other use. However, management would prefer to keep them on the books at cost, "since that is what we paid for them, after all."

Instructions

Prepare a schedule to determine the correct inventory amount. Provide explanations for each item above, saying why you did or did not make an adjustment for each item.

Identify items in inventory.

E6.3 (LO 1) Gato Inc. had the following inventory situations to consider at January 31, its year-end.

a. Goods held on consignment for Steele Corp. since December 12.

b. Goods shipped on consignment to Logan Holdings Inc. on January 5.

c. Goods shipped to a customer, FOB destination, on January 29 that are still in transit.

d. Goods shipped to a customer, FOB shipping point, on January 29 that are still in transit.

e. Goods purchased FOB destination from a supplier on January 25 that are still in transit.

f. Goods purchased FOB shipping point from a supplier on January 25 that are still in transit.

g. Office supplies on hand at January 31.

Instructions

Identify which of the preceding items should be included in inventory. If the item should not be included in inventory, state in what account, if any, it should have been recorded.

E6.4 (LO 2) On December 1, Kiyak Electronics Ltd. has three DVD players left in stock. All are identical, all are priced to sell at $150. One of the three DVD players left in stock, with serial #1012, was purchased on June 1 at a cost of $100. Another, with serial #1045, was purchased on November 1 for $88. The last player, serial #1056, was purchased on November 30 for $80.

Calculate cost of goods sold using specific identification and FIFO.

Instructions

a. Calculate the cost of goods sold using the FIFO periodic inventory method assuming that two of the three players were sold by the end of December, Kiyak Electronics' year-end.

b. If Kiyak Electronics used the specific identification method instead of the FIFO method, how might it alter its earnings by "selectively choosing" which particular players to sell to the two customers? What would Kiyak's cost of goods sold be if the company wished to minimize earnings? Maximize earnings?

c. Which of the two inventory methods do you recommend that Kiyak use? Explain why.

E6.5 (LO 2) Elsa's Boards sells a snowboard, Xpert, that is popular with snowboard enthusiasts. Information relating to Elsa's purchases of Xpert snowboards during September is shown below. During the same month, 121 Xpert snowboards were sold. Elsa's uses a periodic inventory system.

Compute inventory and cost of goods sold using FIFO and LIFO.

Date	Explanation	Units	Unit Cost	Total Cost
Sept. 1	Inventory	26	$ 97	$ 2,522
Sept. 12	Purchases	45	102	4,590
Sept. 19	Purchases	20	104	2,080
Sept. 26	Purchases	50	105	5,250
	Totals	141		$14,442

Instructions

a. Compute the ending inventory at September 30 and cost of goods sold using the FIFO and LIFO methods. Prove the amount allocated to cost of goods sold under each method.

b. For both FIFO and LIFO, calculate the sum of ending inventory and cost of goods sold. What do you notice about the answers you found for each method?

E6.6 (LO 2) Ballas Co. uses a periodic inventory system. Its records show the following for the month of May, in which 68 units were sold.

Compute inventory and cost of goods sold using FIFO and LIFO.

		Units	Unit Cost	Total Cost
May 1	Inventory	30	$ 8	$240
15	Purchases	25	11	275
24	Purchases	35	12	420
	Totals	90		$935

Instructions

Compute the ending inventory at May 31 and cost of goods sold using the FIFO and LIFO methods. Prove the amount allocated to cost of goods sold under each method.

E6.7 (LO 2) Moath Company reports the following for the month of June.

Compute inventory and cost of goods sold using FIFO and LIFO.

		Units	Unit Cost	Total Cost
June 1	Inventory	200	$5	$1,000
12	Purchase	400	6	2,400
23	Purchase	300	7	2,100
30	Inventory	100		

Instructions

a. Compute the cost of the ending inventory and the cost of goods sold under (1) FIFO and (2) LIFO.

b. Which costing method gives the higher ending inventory? Why?

c. Which method results in the higher cost of goods sold? Why?

Compute inventory under FIFO, LIFO, and average-cost.

E6.8 (LO 2) Shawn Company had 100 units in beginning inventory at a total cost of $10,000. The company purchased 200 units at a total cost of $26,000. At the end of the year, Shawn had 75 units in ending inventory.

Instructions

a. Compute the cost of the ending inventory and the cost of goods sold under (1) FIFO, (2) LIFO, and (3) average-cost.

b. Which cost flow method would result in the highest net income?

c. Which cost flow method would result in inventories approximating current cost in the balance sheet?

d. Which cost flow method would result in Shawn paying the least taxes in the first year?

Compute inventory and cost of goods sold using average-cost.

E6.9 (LO 2) Inventory data for Moath Company are presented in E6.7.

Instructions

a. Compute the cost of the ending inventory and the cost of goods sold using the average-cost method.

b. Will the results in (a) be higher or lower than the results under (1) FIFO and (2) LIFO?

c. Why is the average unit cost not $6?

Determine effects of inventory errors.

E6.10 (LO 3) Elliott's Hardware reported cost of goods sold as follows.

	2019	2020
Beginning inventory	$ 20,000	$ 30,000
Cost of goods purchased	150,000	175,000
Cost of goods available for sale	170,000	205,000
Ending inventory	30,000	35,000
Cost of goods sold	$140,000	$170,000

Elliott's made two errors: (1) 2019 ending inventory was overstated $3,000, and (2) 2020 ending inventory was understated $5,000.

Instructions

Compute the correct cost of goods sold for each year.

Prepare correct income statements.

E6.11 (LO 3) **Financial Statement** **Writing** Smart Watch Company reported the following income statement data for a 2-year period.

	2019	2020
Sales revenue	$220,000	$250,000
Cost of goods sold		
Beginning inventory	32,000	44,000
Cost of goods purchased	173,000	202,000
Cost of goods available for sale	205,000	246,000
Ending inventory	44,000	52,000
Cost of goods sold	161,000	194,000
Gross profit	$ 59,000	$ 56,000

Smart uses a periodic inventory system. The inventories at January 1, 2019, and December 31, 2020, are correct. However, the ending inventory at December 31, 2019, was overstated $6,000.

Instructions

a. Prepare correct income statement data for the 2 years.

b. What is the cumulative effect of the inventory error on total gross profit for the 2 years?

c. Explain in a letter to the president of Smart Watch Company what has happened, i.e., the nature of the error and its effect on the financial statements.

Determine ending inventory under LCNRV.

E6.12 (LO 4) Freeze Frame Camera Shop uses the lower-of-cost-or-net realizable value basis for its inventory. The following data are available at December 31.

Item	Units	Unit Cost	Net Realizable Value
Cameras:			
Minolta	5	$170	$156
Canon	6	150	152
Light meters:			
Vivitar	10	125	115
Kodak	14	120	135

Instructions

Determine the amount of the ending inventory by applying the lower-of-cost-or-net realizable value basis.

E6.13 (LO 4) Charapata Company applied FIFO to its inventory and got the following results for its ending inventory.

Compute lower-of-cost-or-net realizable value.

Cameras	100 units at a cost per unit of $65
Blu-ray players	150 units at a cost per unit of $75
iPods	125 units at a cost per unit of $80

The net realizable value at year-end was cameras $71, Blu-ray players $67, and iPods $78.

Instructions

Determine the amount of ending inventory at lower-of-cost-or-net realizable value.

E6.14 (LO 4) This information is available for Abdullah's Photo Corporation for 2018, 2019, and 2020.

Compute inventory turnover, days in inventory, and gross profit rate.

	2018	2019	2020
Beginning inventory	$ 100,000	$ 300,000	$ 400,000
Ending inventory	300,000	400,000	480,000
Cost of goods sold	900,000	1,152,000	1,300,000
Sales revenue	1,200,000	1,600,000	1,900,000

Instructions

Calculate inventory turnover (round to two decimal places), days in inventory (round to one decimal place), and gross profit rate (from Chapter 5, round to nearest percentage) for Abdullah's Photo Corporation for 2018, 2019, and 2020. Comment on any trends.

E6.15 (LO 4) The cost of goods sold computations for Sooner Company and Later Company are shown below.

Compute inventory turnover and days in inventory.

	Sooner Company	Later Company
Beginning inventory	$ 45,000	$ 71,000
Cost of goods purchased	200,000	290,000
Cost of goods available for sale	245,000	361,000
Ending inventory	55,000	69,000
Cost of goods sold	$190,000	$292,000

Instructions

a. Compute inventory turnover (round to two decimal places) and days in inventory (round to nearest day) for each company.

b. Which company moves its inventory more quickly?

***E6.16 (LO 5)** Ehrhart Appliance uses a perpetual inventory system. For its flat-screen television sets, the January 1 inventory was 3 sets at $600 each. On January 10, Ehrhart purchased 6 units at $660 each. The company sold 2 units on January 8 and 5 units on January 15.

Apply cost flow methods to perpetual records.

Instructions

Compute the ending inventory under (a) FIFO, (b) LIFO, and (c) moving-average cost.

***E6.17 (LO 5)** Moath Company reports the following for the month of June.

Calculate inventory and cost of goods sold using three cost flow methods in a perpetual inventory system.

Date	Explanation	Units	Unit Cost	Total Cost
June 1	Inventory	200	$5	$1,000
12	Purchase	400	6	2,400
23	Purchase	300	7	2,100
30	Inventory	100		

Instructions

a. Calculate the cost of the ending inventory and the cost of goods sold for each cost flow assumption, using a perpetual inventory system. Assume a sale of 440 units occurred on June 15 for a selling price of $8 and a sale of 360 units on June 27 for $9.

b. How do the results differ from the answers to E6.7 and E6.9?

c. Why is the average unit cost not $6 [($5 + $6 + $7) ÷ 3 = $6]?

Apply cost flow methods to perpetual records.

***E6.18 (LO 5)** Information about Elsa's Boards is presented in E6.5. Additional data regarding Elsa's sales of Xpert snowboards are provided below. Assume that Elsa's uses a perpetual inventory system.

Date		Units	Unit Price	Total Revenue
Sept. 5	Sale	12	$199	$ 2,388
Sept. 16	Sale	50	199	9,950
Sept. 29	Sale	59	209	12,331
	Totals	121		$24,669

Instructions

a. Compute ending inventory at September 30 using FIFO, LIFO, and moving-average cost.

b. Compare ending inventory using a perpetual inventory system to ending inventory using a periodic inventory system (from E6.5).

c. Which inventory cost flow method (FIFO, LIFO) gives the same ending inventory value under both periodic and perpetual? Which method gives different ending inventory values?

Use the gross profit method to estimate inventory.

***E6.19 (LO 6)** Shereen Company reported the following information for November and December 2020.

	November	December
Cost of goods purchased	$536,000	$ 610,000
Inventory, beginning-of-month	130,000	120,000
Inventory, end-of-month	120,000	?
Sales revenue	840,000	1,000,000

Shereen's ending inventory at December 31 was destroyed in a fire.

Instructions

a. Compute the gross profit rate for November.

b. Using the gross profit rate for November, determine the estimated cost of inventory lost in the fire.

Determine merchandise lost using the gross profit method of estimating inventory.

***E6.20 (LO 6)** The inventory of Hang Company was destroyed by fire on March 1. From an examination of the accounting records, the following data for the first 2 months of the year are obtained: Sales Revenue $51,000, Sales Returns and Allowances $1,000, Purchases $31,200, Freight-In $1,200, and Purchase Returns and Allowances $1,400.

Instructions

Determine the merchandise lost by fire, assuming:

a. A beginning inventory of $20,000 and a gross profit rate of 30% on net sales.

b. A beginning inventory of $30,000 and a gross profit rate of 40% on net sales.

Determine ending inventory at cost using retail method.

Excel

***E6.21 (LO 6)** Kicks Shoe Store uses the retail inventory method for its two departments, Women's Shoes and Men's Shoes. The following information for each department is obtained.

Item	Women's Shoes	Men's Shoes
Beginning inventory at cost	$ 25,000	$ 45,000
Cost of goods purchased at cost	110,000	136,300
Net sales	178,000	185,000
Beginning inventory at retail	46,000	60,000
Cost of goods purchased at retail	179,000	185,000

Instructions

Compute the estimated cost of the ending inventory for each department under the retail inventory method.

Problems: Set A

Determine items and amounts to be recorded in inventory.

P6.1A (LO 1) Houghton Limited is trying to determine the value of its ending inventory as of February 28, 2020, the company's year-end. The following transactions occurred, and the accountant asked your help in determining whether they should be recorded or not.

a. On February 26, Houghton shipped goods costing $800 to a customer and charged the customer $1,000. The goods were shipped with terms FOB shipping point and the receiving report indicates that the customer received the goods on March 2.

b. On February 26, Crain Inc. shipped goods to Houghton under terms FOB shipping point. The invoice price was $450 plus $30 for freight. The receiving report indicates that the goods were received by Houghton on March 2.

c. Houghton had $720 of inventory isolated in the warehouse. The inventory is designated for a customer who has requested that the goods be shipped on March 10.

d. Also included in Houghton's warehouse is $700 of inventory that Korenic Producers shipped to Houghton on consignment.

e. On February 26, Houghton issued a purchase order to acquire goods costing $900. The goods were shipped with terms FOB destination on February 27. Houghton received the goods on March 2.

f. On February 26, Houghton shipped goods to a customer under terms FOB destination. The invoice price was $390; the cost of the items was $240. The receiving report indicates that the goods were received by the customer on March 2.

g. Houghton had damaged goods set aside in the warehouse because they are no longer saleable. These goods originally cost $400, and Houghton had expected to sell these items for $600.

Instructions

For each of the preceding transactions, specify whether the item in question should be included in ending inventory, and if so, at what amount. For each item that is not included in ending inventory, indicate who owns it and in what account, if any, it should have been recorded.

Determine cost of goods sold and ending inventory using FIFO, LIFO, and average-cost with analysis.

Excel

P6.2A (LO 2) Glee Distribution markets CDs of the performing artist Unique. At the beginning of October, Glee had in beginning inventory 2,000 of Unique's CDs with a unit cost of $7. During October, Glee made the following purchases of Unique's CDs.

Oct. 3	2,500 @ $8	Oct. 19	3,000 @ $10
Oct. 9	3,500 @ $9	Oct. 25	4,000 @ $11

During October, 10,900 units were sold. Glee uses a periodic inventory system.

Instructions

a. Determine the cost of goods available for sale.

b. Determine (1) the ending inventory and (2) the cost of goods sold under each of the assumed cost flow methods (FIFO, LIFO, and average-cost). Prove the accuracy of the cost of goods sold under the FIFO and LIFO methods.

c. Which cost flow method results in (1) the highest inventory amount for the balance sheet and (2) the highest cost of goods sold for the income statement?

b. (2) Cost of goods sold:

FIFO	$ 94,500
LIFO	$108,700
Average	$101,370

Determine cost of goods sold and ending inventory, using FIFO, LIFO, and average-cost with analysis.

P6.3A (LO 2) Financial Statement Sekhon Company had a beginning inventory on January 1 of 160 units of Product 4-18-15 at a cost of $20 per unit. During the year, the following purchases were made.

Mar. 15	400 units at $23	Sept. 4	330 units at $26
July 20	250 units at $24	Dec. 2	100 units at $29

1,000 units were sold. Sekhon Company uses a periodic inventory system.

Instructions

a. Determine the cost of goods available for sale.

b. Determine (1) the ending inventory, and (2) the cost of goods sold under each of the assumed cost flow methods (FIFO, LIFO, and average-cost). Prove the accuracy of the cost of goods sold under the FIFO and LIFO methods.

c. Which cost flow method results in (1) the highest inventory amount for the balance sheet, and (2) the highest cost of goods sold for the income statement?

b. (2) Cost of goods sold:

FIFO	$23,340
LIFO	$24,840
Average	$24,097

Compute ending inventory, prepare income statements, and answer questions using FIFO and LIFO.

P6.4A (LO 2) Financial Statement Writing The management of Gresa Inc. is reevaluating the appropriateness of using its present inventory cost flow method, which is average-cost. The company requests your help in determining the results of operations for 2020 if either the FIFO or the LIFO method had been used. For 2020, the accounting records show these data:

Inventories		Purchases and Sales	
Beginning (7,000 units)	$14,000	Total net sales (180,000 units)	$747,000
Ending (17,000 units)		Total cost of goods purchased (190,000 units)	466,000

Purchases were made quarterly as follows.

Quarter	Units	Unit Cost	Total Cost
1	50,000	$2.20	$110,000
2	40,000	2.35	94,000
3	40,000	2.50	100,000
4	60,000	2.70	162,000
	190,000		$466,000

Operating expenses were $130,000, and the company's income tax rate is 40%.

Instructions

a. Gross profit:
FIFO $312,900
LIFO $303,000

a. Prepare comparative condensed income statements for 2020 under FIFO and LIFO. (Show computations of ending inventory.)

b. Answer the following questions for management.

1. Which cost flow method (FIFO or LIFO) produces the more meaningful inventory amount for the balance sheet? Why?
2. Which cost flow method (FIFO or LIFO) produces the more meaningful net income? Why?
3. Which cost flow method (FIFO or LIFO) is more likely to approximate the actual physical flow of goods? Why?
4. How much more cash will be available for management under LIFO than under FIFO? Why?
5. Will gross profit under the average-cost method be higher or lower than FIFO? Than LIFO? (*Note:* It is not necessary to quantify your answer.)

Calculate ending inventory, cost of goods sold, gross profit, and gross profit rate under periodic method; compare results.

P6.5A (LO 2) You are provided with the following information for Koetteritz Inc. for the month ended June 30, 2020. Koetteritz uses the periodic method for inventory.

Date	Description	Quantity	Unit Cost or Selling Price
June 1	Beginning inventory	40	$40
June 4	Purchase	135	43
June 10	Sale	110	70
June 11	Sale return	15	70
June 18	Purchase	55	46
June 18	Purchase return	10	46
June 25	Sale	65	76
June 28	Purchase	35	50

Instructions

a. (iii) Gross profit:
LIFO $4,330
FIFO $4,830
Average $4,546.90

a. Calculate (i) ending inventory, (ii) cost of goods sold, (iii) gross profit, and (iv) gross profit rate under each of the following methods.

(1) LIFO. (2) FIFO. (3) Average-cost.

b. Compare results for the three cost flow assumptions.

Compare specific identification, FIFO, and LIFO under periodic method; use cost flow assumption to justify price increase.

P6.6A (LO 2) Financial Statement You are provided with the following information for Gobler Inc. Gobler Inc. uses the periodic method of accounting for its inventory transactions.

March 1 Beginning inventory 2,000 liters at a cost of 60¢ per liter.
March 3 Purchased 2,500 liters at a cost of 65¢ per liter.
March 5 Sold 2,300 liters for $1.05 per liter.
March 10 Purchased 4,000 liters at a cost of 72¢ per liter.
March 20 Purchased 2,500 liters at a cost of 80¢ per liter.
March 30 Sold 5,200 liters for $1.25 per liter.

Instructions

a. Prepare partial income statements for 2020 through gross profit, and calculate the value of ending inventory that would be reported on the balance sheet, under each of the following cost flow assumptions. (Round ending inventory and cost of goods sold to the nearest dollar.)

1. Specific identification method assuming:

(i) The March 5 sale consisted of 1,000 liters from the March 1 beginning inventory and 1,300 liters from the March 3 purchase; and

(ii) The March 30 sale consisted of the following number of units sold from beginning inventory and each purchase: 450 liters from March 1; 550 liters from March 3; 2,900 liters from March 10; 1,300 liters from March 20.

2. FIFO.

3. LIFO.

b. How can companies use a cost flow method to justify price increases? Which cost flow method would best support an argument to increase prices?

a. Gross profit:
1. Specific identification $3,715
2. FIFO $3,930
3. LIFO $3,385

P6.7A (LO 2) **Financial Statement** **Writing** The management of Danica Co. asks your help in determining the comparative effects of the FIFO and LIFO inventory cost flow methods. For 2020, the accounting records provide the following data.

Compute ending inventory, prepare income statements, and answer questions using FIFO and LIFO.

Inventory, January 1 (10,000 units)	$ 47,000
Cost of 100,000 units purchased	532,000
Selling price of 84,000 units sold	735,000
Operating expenses	140,000

Units purchased consisted of 35,000 units at $5.10 on May 10; 35,000 units at $5.30 on August 15; and 30,000 units at $5.60 on November 20. Income taxes are 30%.

Instructions

a. Prepare comparative condensed income statements for 2020 under FIFO and LIFO. (Show computations of ending inventory.)

b. Answer the following questions for management.

1. Which inventory cost flow method produces the most meaningful inventory amount for the balance sheet? Why?

2. Which inventory cost flow method produces the most meaningful net income? Why?

3. Which inventory cost flow method is most likely to approximate actual physical flow of the goods? Why?

4. How much additional cash will be available for management under LIFO than under FIFO? Why?

5. How much of the gross profit under FIFO is illusory in comparison with the gross profit under LIFO?

a. Net income
FIFO $113,120
LIFO $101,220

***P6.8A (LO 5)** Dempsey Inc. is a retailer operating in British Columbia. Dempsey uses the perpetual inventory method. All sales returns from customers result in the goods being returned to inventory; the inventory is not damaged. Assume that there are no credit transactions; all amounts are settled in cash. You are provided with the following information for Dempsey Inc. for the month of January 2020.

Calculate cost of goods sold and ending inventory under LIFO, FIFO, and moving-average cost under the perpetual system; compare gross profit under each assumption.

Date	Description	Quantity	Unit Cost or Selling Price
January 1	Beginning inventory	100	$15
January 5	Purchase	140	18
January 8	Sale	110	28
January 10	Sale return	10	28
January 15	Purchase	55	20
January 16	Purchase return	5	20
January 20	Sale	90	32
January 25	Purchase	20	22

Instructions

a. For each of the following cost flow assumptions, calculate (i) cost of goods sold, (ii) ending inventory, and (iii) gross profit.

1. LIFO.

2. FIFO.

3. Moving-average cost. (Round cost per unit to three decimal places.)

b. Compare results for the three cost flow assumptions.

a. (iii) Gross profit:
LIFO $2,160
FIFO $2,560
Average $2,421

Determine ending inventory under a perpetual inventory system.

***P6.9A (LO 5)** Wittmann Co. began operations on July 1. It uses a perpetual inventory system. During July, the company had the following purchases and sales.

	Purchases		
Date	Units	Unit Cost	Sales Units
July 1	5	$122	
July 6			3
July 11	7	$136	
July 14			5
July 21	8	$147	
July 27			5

Instructions

a. Ending inventory
FIFO $1,029
Avg. $996
LIFO $957

a. Determine the ending inventory under a perpetual inventory system using (1) FIFO, (2) moving-average cost, and (3) LIFO.

b. Which costing method produces the highest ending inventory valuation?

Compute gross profit rate and inventory loss using gross profit method.

Excel

***P6.10A (LO 6)** Bao Company lost all of its inventory in a fire on December 26, 2020. The accounting records showed the following gross profit data for November and December.

	November	December (to 12/26)
Net sales	$600,000	$700,000
Beginning inventory	32,000	36,000
Purchases	389,000	420,000
Purchase returns and allowances	13,300	14,900
Purchase discounts	8,500	9,500
Freight-in	8,800	9,900
Ending inventory	36,000	?

Bao is fully insured for fire losses but must prepare a report for the insurance company.

Instructions

a. Gross profit rate 38%

a. Compute the gross profit rate for November.

b. Using the gross profit rate for November, determine the estimated cost of the inventory lost in the fire.

Compute ending inventory using retail method.

***P6.11A (LO 6)** Rayre Books uses the retail inventory method to estimate its monthly ending inventories. The following information is available for two of its departments at October 31, 2020.

	Hardcovers		Paperbacks	
	Cost	Retail	Cost	Retail
Beginning inventory	$ 420,000	$ 640,000	$ 280,000	$ 360,000
Purchases	2,135,000	3,200,000	1,155,000	1,540,000
Freight-in	24,000		12,000	
Purchase discounts	44,000		22,000	
Net sales		3,100,000		1,570,000

At December 31, Rayre Books takes a physical inventory at retail. The actual retail values of the inventories in each department are Hardcovers $744,000 and Paperbacks $335,000.

Instructions

a. Hardcovers: End. Inv.
$488,400

a. Determine the estimated cost of the ending inventory for each department at **October 31**, 2020, using the retail inventory method.

b. Compute the ending inventory at cost for each department at **December 31**, assuming the cost-to-retail ratios for the year are 65% for Hardcovers and 75% for Paperbacks.

Continuing Case

Cookie Creations

© leungchopan/ Shutterstock

(*Note:* This is a continuation of the Cookie Creations case from Chapters 1 through 5.)

CC6 Natalie is busy establishing both divisions of her business (cookie classes and mixer sales) and completing her business degree. Her goals for the next 11 months are to sell one mixer per month and to give two to three classes per week.

The cost of the fine European mixers is expected to increase. Natalie has just negotiated new terms with Kzinski that include shipping costs in the negotiated purchase price (mixers will be shipped FOB destination). Natalie must choose a cost flow assumption for her mixer inventory.

Go to **WileyPLUS** *for complete case details and instructions.*

Ethics Case

EC6 R. J. Graziano Wholesale Corp. uses the LIFO method of inventory costing. In the current year, profit at R. J. Graziano is running unusually high. The corporate tax rate is also high this year, but it is scheduled to decline significantly next year. In an effort to lower the current year's net income and to take advantage of the changing income tax rate, the president of R. J. Graziano Wholesale instructs the plant accountant to recommend to the purchasing department a large purchase of inventory for delivery 3 days before the end of the year. The price of the inventory to be purchased has doubled during the year, and the purchase will represent a major portion of the ending inventory value.

Instructions

a. What is the effect of this transaction on this year's and next year's income statement and income tax expense? Why?

b. If R. J. Graziano Wholesale had been using the FIFO method of inventory costing, would the president give the same directive?

c. Should the plant accountant order the inventory purchase to lower income? What are the ethical implications of this order?

Comprehensive Accounting Cycle Review

ACR6 **Financial Statement** On December 1, 2020, Annalise Company had the account balances shown below.

	Debit		Credit
Cash	$ 4,800	Accumulated Depreciation—Equipment	$ 1,500
Accounts Receivable	3,900	Accounts Payable	3,000
Inventory	1,800*	Owner's Capital	27,000
Equipment	21,000		$31,500
	$31,500		

*(3,000 × $0.60)

The following transactions occurred during December.

Dec. 3 Purchased 4,000 units of inventory on account at a cost of $0.74 per unit.

5 Sold 4,400 units of inventory on account for $0.90 per unit. (Annalise sold 3,000 of the $0.60 units and 1,400 of the $0.74.)

7 Granted the December 5 customer $180 credit for 200 units of inventory returned costing $120. These units were returned to inventory.

17 Purchased 2,200 units of inventory for cash at $0.80 each.

22 Sold 2,100 units of inventory on account for $0.95 per unit. (Annalise sold 2,100 of the $0.74 units.)

Adjustment data:

1. Accrued salaries payable $400.
2. Depreciation $200 per month.

Instructions

a. Journalize the December transactions and adjusting entries, assuming Annalise uses the perpetual inventory method.

b. Enter the December 1 balances in the ledger T-accounts and post the December transactions. In addition to the accounts mentioned above, use the following additional accounts: Cost of Goods Sold, Depreciation Expense, Salaries and Wages Expense, Salaries and Wages Payable, Sales Revenue, and Sales Returns and Allowances.

c. Prepare an adjusted trial balance as of December 31, 2020.

d. Prepare an income statement for December 2020 and a classified balance sheet at December 31, 2020.

e. Compute ending inventory and cost of goods sold under FIFO, assuming Annalise Company uses the periodic inventory system.

f. Compute ending inventory and cost of goods sold under LIFO, assuming Annalise Company uses the periodic inventory system.

Expand Your Critical Thinking

Financial Reporting Problem: Apple Inc.

CT6.1 The notes that accompany a company's financial statements provide informative details that would clutter the amounts and descriptions presented in the statements. Refer to the financial statements of **Apple Inc.** in Appendix A as well as its annual report. The complete annual report, including the notes to the financial statements, is available at the company's website.

Instructions

Answer the following questions. Complete the requirements in millions of dollars, as shown in Apple's annual report.

a. What did Apple report for the amount of inventories in its consolidated balance sheet at September 27, 2014? At September 26, 2015?

b. Compute the dollar amount of change and the percentage change in inventories between 2014 and 2015. Compute inventory as a percentage of current assets at September 26, 2015.

c. How does Apple value its inventories? Which inventory cost flow method does Apple use? (See Notes to the Financial Statements.)

d. What is the cost of sales (cost of goods sold) reported by Apple for 2015, 2014, and 2013? Compute the percentage of cost of sales to net sales in 2015.

Comparative Analysis Problem: PepsiCo, Inc. vs. The Coca-Cola Company

CT6.2 PepsiCo's financial statements are presented in Appendix B. Financial statements of **The Coca-Cola Company** are presented in Appendix C. The complete annual reports of PepsiCo and Coca-Cola, including the notes to the financial statements, are available at each company's respective website.

Instructions

a. Based on the information contained in these financial statements, compute the following 2015 ratios for each company.

1. Inventory turnover.
2. Days in inventory.

b. What conclusions concerning the management of the inventory can you draw from these data?

Comparative Analysis Problem: Amazon.com, Inc. vs. Wal-Mart Stores, Inc.

CT6.3 Amazon.com, Inc.'s financial statements are presented in Appendix D. Financial statements of **Wal-Mart Stores, Inc.** are presented in Appendix E. The complete annual reports of Amazon and Wal-Mart, including the notes to the financial statements, are available at each company's respective website.

Instructions

a. Based on the information contained in these financial statements, compute the following 2015 ratios for each company.

  1. Inventory turnover.

  2. Days in inventory.

b. What conclusions concerning the management of the inventory can you draw from these data?

Real-World Focus

CT6.4 A company's annual report usually will identify the inventory method used. Knowing that, you can analyze the effects of the inventory method on the income statement and balance sheet.

Instructions

Answer the following questions based on **Cisco**'s current year's annual report (available on the company's website).

a. At Cisco's fiscal year-end, what was the inventory on the balance sheet?

b. How has this changed from the previous fiscal year-end?

c. How much of the inventory was finished goods?

Decision-Making Across the Organization

CT6.5 On April 10, 2020, fire damaged the office and warehouse of Corvet Company. Most of the accounting records were destroyed, but the following account balances were determined as of March 31, 2020: Inventory (January 1, 2020), $80,000; Sales Revenue (January 1–March 31, 2020), $180,000; Purchases (January 1–March 31, 2020), $94,000.

The company's fiscal year ends on December 31. It uses a periodic inventory system.

From an analysis of the April bank statement, you discover cancelled checks of $4,200 for cash purchases during the period April 1–10. Deposits during the same period totaled $18,500. Of that amount, 60% were collections on accounts receivable, and the balance was cash sales.

Correspondence with the company's principal suppliers revealed $12,400 of purchases on account from April 1 to April 10. Of that amount, $1,600 was for merchandise in transit on April 10 that was shipped FOB destination.

Correspondence with the company's principal customers produced acknowledgments of credit sales totaling $37,000 from April 1 to April 10. It was estimated that $5,600 of credit sales will never be acknowledged or recovered from customers.

Corvet Company reached an agreement with the insurance company that its fire-loss claim should be based on the average of the gross profit rates for the preceding 2 years. The financial statements for 2018 and 2019 showed the following data.

	2019	2018
Net sales	$600,000	$480,000
Cost of goods purchased	404,000	356,000
Beginning inventory	60,000	40,000
Ending inventory	80,000	60,000

Inventory with a cost of $17,000 was salvaged from the fire.

Instructions

With the class divided into groups, answer the following.

a. Determine the balances in (1) Sales Revenue and (2) Purchases at April 10.

***b.** Determine the average gross profit rate for the years 2018 and 2019. (*Hint:* Find the gross profit rate for each year and divide the sum by 2.)

***c.** Determine the inventory loss as a result of the fire, using the gross profit method.

Communication Activity

CT6.6 You are the controller of Small Toys Inc. Pamela Bames, the president, recently mentioned to you that she found an error in the 2019 financial statements which she believes has corrected itself. She determined, in discussions with the Purchasing Department, that 2019 ending inventory was overstated by $1 million. Pamela says that the 2020 ending inventory is correct. Thus, she assumes that 2020 income is correct. Pamela says to you, "What happened has happened—there's no point in worrying about it anymore."

Instructions

You conclude that Pamela is incorrect. Write a brief, tactful memo to Pamela, clarifying the situation.

All About You

CT6.7 Some of the largest business frauds ever perpetrated have involved the misstatement of inventory. Two classics were at **Leslie Fay** and **McKesson Corporation**.

Instructions

There is considerable information regarding inventory frauds available on the Internet. Search for information about one of the two cases mentioned above, or inventory fraud at any other company, and prepare a short explanation of the nature of the inventory fraud.

FASB Codification Activity

CT6.8 If your school has a subscription to the FASB Codification, log in and prepare responses to the following.

Instructions

a. The primary basis for accounting for inventories is cost. How is cost defined in the Codification?

b. What does the Codification state regarding the use of consistency in the selection or employment of a basis for inventory?

A Look at IFRS

LEARNING OBJECTIVE 7

Compare the accounting for inventories under GAAP and IFRS.

The major IFRS requirements related to accounting and reporting for inventories are the same as GAAP. The major difference is that IFRS prohibits the use of the LIFO cost flow assumption.

Key Points

Following are the key similarities and differences between GAAP and IFRS related to inventories.

Similarities

- IFRS and GAAP account for inventory acquisitions at historical cost and value inventory at the lower-of-cost-or-net realizable value subsequent to acquisition.
- Who owns the goods—goods in transit or consigned goods—as well as the costs to include in inventory are essentially accounted for the same under IFRS and GAAP.

Differences

- The requirements for accounting for and reporting inventories are more principles-based under IFRS. That is, GAAP provides more detailed guidelines in inventory accounting.
- A major difference between IFRS and GAAP relates to the LIFO cost flow assumption. GAAP permits the use of LIFO for inventory valuation. IFRS prohibits its use. FIFO and average-cost are the only two acceptable cost flow assumptions permitted under IFRS. Both sets of standards permit specific identification where appropriate.

Looking to the Future

One convergence issue that will be difficult to resolve relates to the use of the LIFO cost flow assumption. As indicated, IFRS specifically prohibits its use. Conversely, the LIFO cost flow assumption is widely used in the United States because of its favorable tax advantages. In addition, many argue that LIFO from a financial reporting point of view provides a better matching of current costs against revenue and, therefore, enables companies to compute a more realistic income.

IFRS Practice

IFRS Self-Test Questions

1. Which of the following should **not** be included in the inventory of a company using IFRS?

   a. Goods held on consignment from another company.

   b. Goods shipped on consignment to another company.

   c. Goods in transit from another company shipped FOB shipping point.

   d. All of the above are included in inventory.

2. Which method of inventory costing is prohibited under IFRS?

   a. Specific identification.

   b. LIFO.

   c. FIFO.

   d. Average-cost.

IFRS Exercises

IFRS6.1 Briefly describe some of the similarities and differences between GAAP and IFRS with respect to the accounting for inventories.

IFRS6.2 LaTour Inc. is based in France and prepares its financial statements (in euros) in accordance with IFRS. In 2020, it reported cost of goods sold of €578 million and average inventory of €154 million. Briefly discuss how analysis of LaTour's inventory turnover (and comparisons to a company using GAAP) might be affected by differences in inventory accounting between IFRS and GAAP.

International Financial Reporting Problem: Louis Vuitton

IFRS6.3 The financial statements of **Louis Vuitton** are presented in Appendix F. The complete annual report, including the notes to its financial statements, is available at the company's website.

Instructions

Using the notes to the company's financial statements, answer the following questions.

a. What cost flow assumption does the company use to value inventory other than wine?

b. What amount of goods purchased for retail and finished products did the company report at December 31, 2015?

Answers to IFRS Self-Test Questions

1. a **2.** b

CHAPTER 7

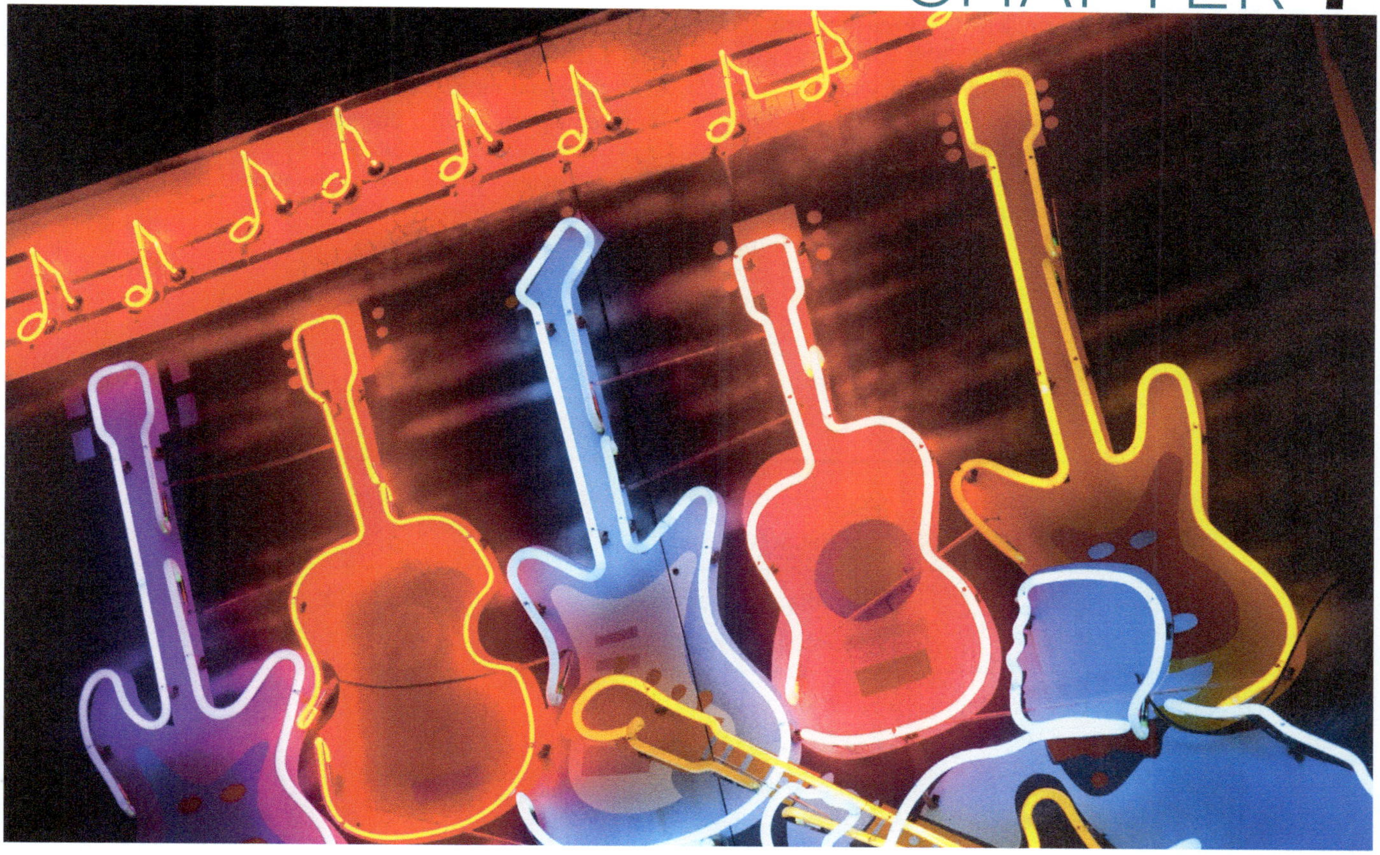

Terra Images/Age Fotostock America, Inc.

Accounting Information Systems

Chapter Preview

As the following Feature Story demonstrates, a reliable information system is a necessity for any company. Whether companies use pen, pencil, or computers in maintaining accounting records, certain principles and procedures apply. The purpose of this chapter is to explain and illustrate these features.

Feature Story

QuickBooks® Helps This Retailer Sell Guitars

Starting a small business requires many decisions. For example, you have to decide where to locate, how much space you need, how much inventory to have, how many employees to hire, and where to advertise. Small business owners are typically so concerned about the product and sales side of their business that they often do not give enough thought to something that is also critical to their success—how to keep track of financial results.

Small business owners today can choose either manual or computerized accounting systems. For example, Paul and Laura West were the owners of the first independent dealership of Carvin guitars and professional audio equipment. When they founded their company in Sacramento, California, they decided to purchase a computerized accounting system that would integrate many aspects of their retail operations. They wanted to use their accounting software to manage their inventory of guitars and amplifiers, enter sales, record and report financial data, and process credit card and debit card transactions. They evaluated a number of options and chose QuickBooks® by **Intuit Inc.**

QuickBooks®, like most other popular software packages, has programs designed for the needs of a specific type of business, which in this case is retailing. This QuickBooks® retailing package automatically collects sales information from its point-of-sale scanning devices. It also keeps track of inventory levels and automatically generates purchase orders for popular items when re-order points are reached. It even supports specialized advertising campaigns.

For example, QuickBooks® compiled a customer database from which the Wests sent out targeted direct mailings to potential customers. The computerized system also enabled data files to be emailed to the company's accountant. This kept down costs and made it easier and more efficient for the Wests to generate financial reports as needed. The Wests believed that the investment in the computerized system saved them time and money, and allowed them to spend more time on other aspects of their business.

Source: Intuit Inc., "QuickBooks® and ProAdvisor® Help Make Guitar Store a Hit," *Journal of Accountancy* (May 2006), p. 101.

Chapter Outline

LEARNING OBJECTIVES

LO 1 Explain the basic concepts of an accounting information system.	• Computerized accounting systems • Manual accounting systems	**DO IT! 1** Basic AIS Concepts
LO 2 Describe the nature and purpose of a subsidiary ledger.	• Subsidiary ledger example • Advantages of subsidiary ledgers	**DO IT! 2** Subsidiary Ledgers
LO 3 Record transactions in special journals.	• Sales journal • Cash receipts journal • Purchases journal • Cash payments journal • Effects of special journals • Cyber security	**DO IT! 3** Special Journals

Go to the Review and Practice section at the end of the chapter for a review of key concepts and practice applications with solutions.
Visit WileyPLUS with ORION for additional tutorials and practice opportunities.

Overview of Accounting Information Systems

LEARNING OBJECTIVE 1

Explain the basic concepts of an accounting information system.

The **accounting information system** collects and processes transaction data and communicates financial information to decision-makers. It includes each of the steps in the accounting cycle that you studied in earlier chapters. It also includes the documents that provide evidence of the transactions, and the records, trial balances, worksheets, and financial statements that result. An **accounting system** may be either manual or computerized. Most businesses use some sort of computerized accounting system, whether it is an off-the-shelf system for small businesses, like QuickBooks® or Sage 50, or a more complex custom-made system.

Efficient and effective accounting information systems are based on certain basic principles. These principles, as described in **Illustration 7.1**, are (1) cost-effectiveness, (2) usefulness, and (3) flexibility. If the accounting system is cost-effective, provides useful output, and has the flexibility to meet future needs, it can contribute to both individual and organizational goals.

ILLUSTRATION 7.1

Principles of an efficient and effective accounting information system

Cost-Effectiveness

The accounting system must be cost-effective. Benefits of information must outweigh the costs of providing it.

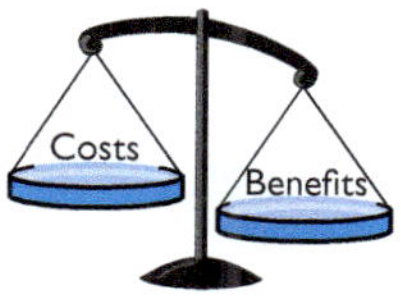

Useful Output

To be useful, information must be understandable, relevant, reliable, timely, and accurate. Designers of accounting systems must consider the needs and knowledge of various users.

Flexibility

The accounting system should accommodate a variety of users and changing information needs. The system should be sufficiently flexible to meet the resulting changes in the demands made upon it.

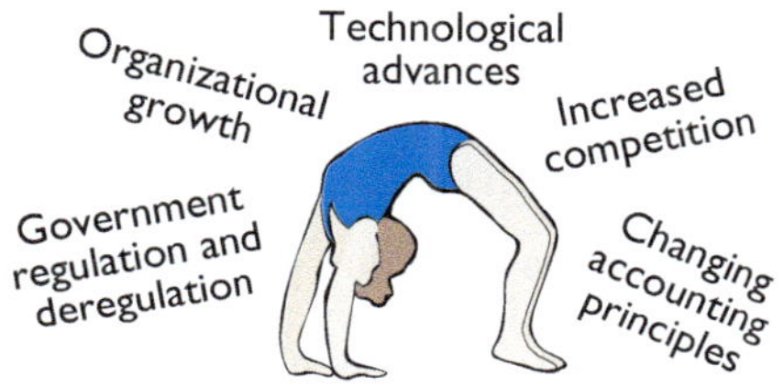

Computerized Accounting Systems

Many small businesses use a computerized general ledger accounting system. **General ledger accounting systems** are software programs that integrate the various accounting functions related to sales, purchases, receivables, payables, cash receipts and disbursements, and payroll. They also generate financial statements. Computerized systems have a number of advantages over manual systems. First, the company typically enters data only once in a computerized system. Second, because the computer does most steps automatically, it eliminates many errors resulting from human intervention in a manual system, such as errors in posting or preparation of financial statements. Computerized systems also provide up-to-the-minute information. More timely information often results in better business decisions. Many different general ledger software packages are available.

Choosing a Software Package

To identify the right software for your business, you must understand your company's operations. For example, consider its needs with regard to inventory, billing, payroll, and cash management. In addition, the company might have specific needs that are not supported by all software systems. For example, you might want to track employees' hours on individual jobs or to extract information for determining sales commissions. Choosing the right system is critical because installation of even a basic system is time-consuming, and learning a new system will require many hours of employee time.

Entry-Level Software

Software publishers tend to classify businesses into groups based on revenue and the number of employees. Companies with revenues of less than $5 million and up to 20 employees generally use **entry-level programs**. The two leading entry-level programs are **Intuit**'s QuickBooks® and **The Sage Group**'s Sage 50. These programs control more than 90% of the market. Each of these entry-level programs comes in many different industry-specific versions. For example, some are designed for very specific industry applications such as restaurants, retailing, construction, manufacturing, or nonprofit.

Quality entry-level packages typically involve more than recording transactions and preparing financial statements. Here are some common features and benefits:

- **Easy data access and report preparation.** Users can easily access information related to specific customers or suppliers. For example, you can view all transactions, invoices, payments, as well as contact information for a specific client.
- **Audit trail.** As a result of the Sarbanes-Oxley Act, companies are now far more concerned that their accounting system minimizes opportunities for fraud. Many programs provide an "audit trail" that enables the tracking of all transactions.
- **Internal controls.** Some systems have an internal accounting review that identifies suspicious transactions or likely mistakes such as wrong account numbers or duplicate transactions (see **Ethics Note**).
- **Customization.** This feature enables the company to create data fields specific to the needs of its business.
- **Network-compatibility.** Multiple users in the company can access the system at the same time.

ETHICS NOTE

Entire books and movies have used cyber attacks as a major theme. Most programmers would agree that ensuring cyber security is the most difficult and time-consuming phase of their jobs.

Enterprise Resource Planning Systems

Enterprise resource planning (ERP) systems are typically used by manufacturing companies with more than 500 employees and $500 million in sales. The best-known of these systems are **SAP AG**'s SAP ERP (the most widely used) and **Oracle**'s ERP. ERP systems go far beyond the functions of an entry-level general ledger package. They integrate all aspects of the organization, including accounting, sales, human resource management, and manufacturing. Because of the complexity of an ERP system, implementation can take three years and cost five times as much as the purchase price of the system. Purchase and implementation of ERP systems can cost from $250,000 to as much as $50 million for the largest multinational corporations.

Ethics Insight

© Sean Locke/iStockphoto

Curbing Fraudulent Activity with Software

The Sarbanes-Oxley Act (SOX) requires that companies demonstrate that they have adequate controls in place to detect significant fraudulent behavior by employees. The SOX requirements have created a huge market for software that can monitor and trace every recorded transaction and adjusting entry. This enables companies to pinpoint who used the accounting system and when they used it. These systems also require "electronic signatures" by employees for all significant transactions. Such signatures verify that employees have followed all required procedures, and that all actions are properly authorized. One firm that specializes in compliance software had 10 clients prior to SOX and 250 after SOX.

Note that small businesses have no standards like SOX and often do not have the resources to implement a fraud–prevention system. As a result, small businesses lose nearly $630 billion to fraud each year. To address this problem, more sophisticated software is being designed for small business fraud prevention.

Sources: W. M. Bulkeley and C. Forelle, "Anti-Crime Program: How Corporate Scandals Gave Tech Firms a New Business Line," *Wall Street Journal* (December 9, 2005), p. A1; and "New Software Fights Small Business Fraud," *FOX Business* (August 9, 2013).

Why might this software help reduce fraudulent activity by employees? (Go to WileyPLUS for this answer and additional questions.)

Manual Accounting Systems

In **manual accounting systems**, someone performs each of the steps in the accounting cycle by hand. For example, someone manually enters each accounting transaction in the journal and manually posts each to the ledger. Other manual computations must be made to obtain ledger account balances and to prepare a trial balance and financial statements. In the remainder of this chapter, we illustrate the use of a manual system.

You might be wondering, "Why cover manual accounting systems if the real world uses computerized systems?" First, small businesses still abound. Most of them begin operations with manual accounting systems and convert to computerized systems as the business grows. You may work in a small business or start your own someday, so it is useful to know how a manual system works. Second, to understand what computerized accounting systems do, you also need to understand manual accounting systems.

The manual accounting system represented in the first six chapters of this textbook is satisfactory in a company with a low volume of transactions. However, in most companies, it is necessary to add additional ledgers and journals to the accounting system to record transaction data efficiently.

DO IT! 1 | Basic AIS Concepts

Indicate whether the following statements are true or false. If false, indicate how to correct the statement.

1. An accounting information system collects and processes transaction data and communicates financial information to decision-makers.
2. A company typically enters data only once in a manual accounting system.
3. Enterprise resource planning (ERP) systems are typically used by companies with revenues of less than $5 million and up to 20 employees.

ACTION PLAN

- **Understand the principles of an effective accounting information system.**
- **Recognize the types of available general ledger software packages.**

Solution

1. True. **2.** False. A company typically enters data only once in a computerized accounting system. **3.** False. Enterprise resource planning (ERP) systems are typically used by manufacturing companies with more than 500 employees and $500 million in sales.

Related exercise material: **BE7.1, BE7.2, BE7.3, and DO IT! 7.1.**

Subsidiary Ledgers

LEARNING OBJECTIVE 2

Describe the nature and purpose of a subsidiary ledger.

Imagine a business that has several thousand charge (credit) customers and shows the transactions with these customers in only one general ledger account—Accounts Receivable. It would be nearly impossible to determine the balance owed by an individual customer at any specific time. Similarly, the amount payable to one creditor would be difficult to locate quickly from a single Accounts Payable account in the general ledger.

Instead, companies use subsidiary ledgers to keep track of individual balances. A **subsidiary ledger** is a group of accounts with a common characteristic (for example, all accounts receivable). It is an addition to and an expansion of the general ledger. The subsidiary ledger frees the general ledger from the details of individual balances.

Two common subsidiary ledgers are as follows.

1. The **accounts receivable** (or **customers'**) **subsidiary ledger**, which collects transaction data of individual customers.
2. The **accounts payable** (or **creditors'**) **subsidiary ledger**, which collects transaction data of individual creditors.

In each of these subsidiary ledgers, companies usually arrange individual accounts in alphabetical order.

A general ledger account summarizes the detailed data from a subsidiary ledger. For example, the detailed data from the accounts receivable subsidiary ledger are summarized in Accounts Receivable in the general ledger. The general ledger account that summarizes subsidiary ledger data is called a **control account**. **Illustration 7.2** presents an overview of the relationship of subsidiary ledgers to the general ledger. There, the general ledger control accounts and subsidiary ledger accounts are in green. Note that Cash and Owner's Capital in this illustration are not control accounts because there are no subsidiary ledger accounts related to these accounts.

ILLUSTRATION 7.2 **Relationship of general ledger and subsidiary ledgers**

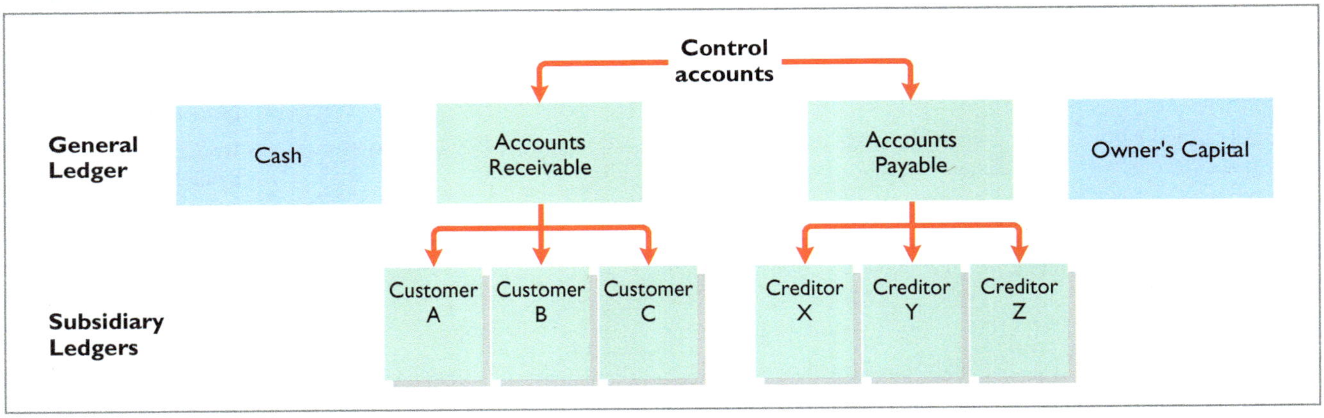

At the end of an accounting period, each general ledger control account balance must equal the composite balance of the individual accounts in the related subsidiary ledger. For example, the balance in Accounts Payable in Illustration 7.2 must equal the total of the subsidiary balances of Creditors X + Y + Z.

Subsidiary Ledger Example

Illustration 7.3 lists credit sales and collections on account for Pujols Company.

ILLUSTRATION 7.3
Sales and collection transactions

Credit Sales			Collections on Account		
Jan. 10	Aaron Co.	$ 6,000	Jan. 19	Aaron Co.	$4,000
12	Branden Inc.	3,000	21	Branden Inc.	3,000
20	Caron Co.	3,000	29	Caron Co.	1,000
		$12,000			$8,000

Illustration 7.4 provides an example of a control account and subsidiary ledger for Pujols Company. (Due to space considerations, the explanation column in these accounts is not

ILLUSTRATION 7.4 Relationship between general and subsidiary ledgers

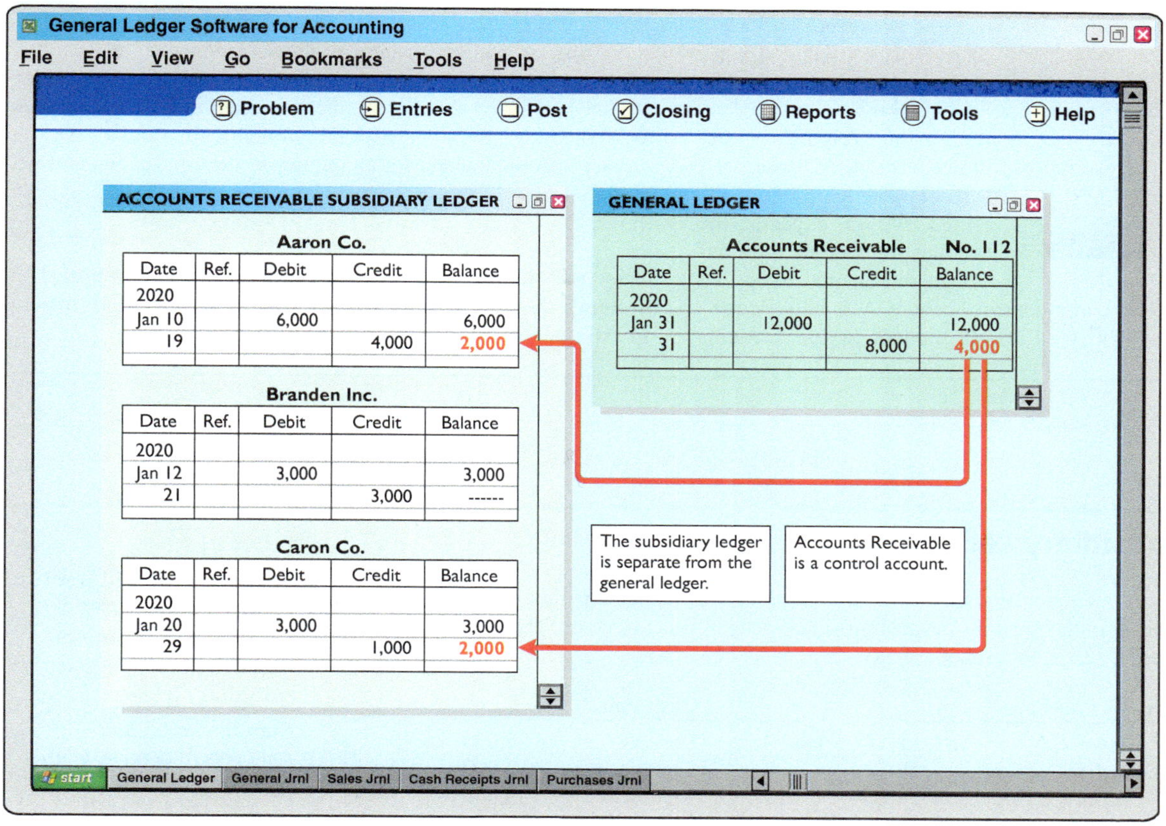

shown in this and subsequent illustrations.) Illustration 7.4 is based on the transactions listed in Illustration 7.3.

Pujols can reconcile the total debits ($12,000) and credits ($8,000) in Accounts Receivable in the general ledger to the detailed debits and credits in the subsidiary accounts. Also, the balance of $4,000 in the control account agrees with the total of the balances in the individual accounts (Aaron Co. $2,000 + Branden Inc. $0 + Caron Co. $2,000) in the subsidiary ledger.

As Illustration 7.4 shows, companies make monthly postings to the control accounts in the general ledger. This practice allows them to prepare monthly financial statements. Companies post to the individual accounts in the subsidiary ledger daily. Daily posting ensures that account information is current. This enables the company to monitor credit limits, bill customers, and answer inquiries from customers about their account balances.

Advantages of Subsidiary Ledgers

Subsidiary ledgers have several advantages:

1. **They show in a single account transactions affecting one customer or one creditor**, thus providing up-to-date information on specific account balances.
2. **They free the general ledger of excessive details.** As a result, a trial balance of the general ledger does not contain vast numbers of individual account balances.
3. **They help locate errors in individual accounts** by reducing the number of accounts in one ledger and by using control accounts.
4. **They make possible a division of labor** in posting. One employee can post to the general ledger while someone else posts to the subsidiary ledgers.

Accounting Across the Organization

© Niels Laan/iStockphoto

"I'm John Smith, a.k.a. 13695071642"

Rather than relying on customer or creditor names in a subsidiary ledger, a computerized system expands the account number of the control account in a prespecified manner. For example, if the control account Accounts Receivable was numbered 10010, the first account in the accounts receivable subsidiary ledger might be numbered 10010–0001. Most systems allow inquiries about specific accounts in the subsidiary ledger (by account number) or about the control account. With the latter, the system would automatically total all the subsidiary accounts whenever an inquiry to the control account was made.

Why use numbers to identify names in a computerized system? (Go to WileyPLUS for this answer and additional questions.)

DO IT! 2 | Subsidiary Ledgers

Presented below is information related to Sims Company for its first month of operations. Determine the balances that appear in the accounts payable subsidiary ledger. What Accounts Payable balance appears in the general ledger at the end of January?

Credit Purchases			Cash Paid		
Jan. 5	Devon Co.	$11,000	Jan. 9	Devon Co.	$7,000
11	Shelby Co.	7,000	14	Shelby Co.	2,000
22	Taylor Co.	14,000	27	Taylor Co.	9,000

ACTION PLAN

- **Subtract cash paid from credit purchases to determine the balances in the accounts payable subsidiary ledger.**
- **Sum the individual balances to determine the Accounts Payable balance.**

Solution

Subsidiary ledger balances:

Devon Co.: $4,000 ($11,000 – $7,000)

Shelby Co.: $5,000 ($7,000 – $2,000)

Taylor Co.: $5,000 ($14,000 – $9,000)

General ledger Accounts Payable balance: $14,000 ($4,000 + $5,000 + $5,000)

Related exercise material: **BE7.4, BE7.5, DO IT! 7.2, E7.1, E7.2, E7.3, E7.4, and E7.5.**

Special Journals

LEARNING OBJECTIVE 3

Record transactions in special journals.

So far, you have learned to journalize transactions in a two-column general journal and post each entry to the general ledger. This procedure is satisfactory in only very small companies. To expedite journalizing and posting, most companies use special journals **in addition to the general journal**.

Companies use **special journals** to record similar types of transactions. Examples are all sales of merchandise on account or all cash receipts. The types of transactions that occur frequently in a company determine what special journals the company uses. Most merchandising companies record daily transactions using the journals shown in **Illustration 7.5**.

ILLUSTRATION 7.5 **Use of special journals and the general journal**

Sales Journal	Cash Receipts Journal	Purchases Journal	Cash Payments Journal	General Journal
Used for: All sales of merchandise on account	Used for: All cash received (including cash sales)	Used for: All purchases of merchandise on account	Used for: All cash paid (including cash purchases)	Used for: Transactions that cannot be entered in a special journal, including correcting, adjusting, and closing entries

If a transaction cannot be recorded in a special journal, the company records it in the general journal. For example, if a company had special journals for only the four types of transactions listed above, it would record purchase returns and allowances that do not affect cash in the general journal. Similarly, **correcting, adjusting, and closing entries are recorded in the general journal**. In some situations, companies might use special journals other than those listed above. For example, when sales returns and allowances that do not affect cash are frequent, a company might use a special journal to record these transactions.

Special journals **permit greater division of labor** because several people can record entries in different journals at the same time. For example, one employee may journalize all cash receipts, and another may journalize all credit sales. Also, the use of special journals **reduces the time needed to complete the posting process**. With special journals, companies may post some accounts monthly instead of daily, as we will illustrate later in the chapter (see **Helpful Hint**). On the following pages, we discuss the four special journals shown in Illustration 7.5.

HELPFUL HINT

Postings are also made daily to individual ledger accounts in the inventory subsidiary ledger to maintain a perpetual inventory.

Sales Journal

In the **sales journal**, companies record **sales of merchandise on account**. Cash sales of merchandise go in the cash receipts journal. Credit sales of assets other than merchandise go in the general journal.

Journalizing Credit Sales

To demonstrate use of a sales journal, we will use data for Karns Wholesale Supply, which uses a **perpetual inventory system**. Under this system, each entry in the sales journal results in one entry **at selling price** and another entry **at cost**. The entry at selling price is a debit to Accounts Receivable (a control account) and a credit of equal amount to Sales Revenue. The entry at cost is a debit to Cost of Goods Sold and a credit of equal amount to Inventory (a control account). Using a sales journal with two amount columns, the company can show on only one line a sales transaction at both selling price and cost. **Illustration 7.6** shows this two-column sales journal of Karns Wholesale Supply, using assumed credit sales transactions (for sales invoices 101–107).

ILLUSTRATION 7.6 Journalizing the sales journal—perpetual inventory system

General Ledger Software for Accounting

File Edit View Go Bookmarks Tools Help

Problem Entries Post Closing Reports Tools Help

SALES JOURNAL S1

Date	Account Debited	Invoice No.	Ref.	Accts. Receivable Dr. Sales Revenue Cr.	Cost of Goods Sold Dr. Inventory Cr.
2020					
May 3	Abbot Sisters	101		10,600	6,360
7	Babson Co.	102		11,350	7,370
14	Carson Bros.	103		7,800	5,070
19	Deli Co.	104		9,300	6,510
21	Abbot Sisters	105		15,400	10,780
24	Deli Co.	106		21,210	15,900
27	Babson Co.	107		14,570	10,200
				90,230	62,190

start | General Ledger | General Jrnl | Sales Jrnl | Cash Receipts Jrnl | Purchases Jrnl

Note that, unlike the general journal, an explanation is not required for each entry in a special journal. Also, the use of prenumbered invoices ensures that all invoices are journalized and no invoices are duplicated. Finally, the reference (Ref.) column is not used in journalizing. It is used in posting the sales journal, as explained in the next section.

Posting the Sales Journal

Companies make daily postings from the sales journal **to the individual accounts receivable** in the subsidiary ledger. Posting **to the general ledger** is done **monthly**. **Illustration 7.7** shows both the daily and monthly postings.

A check mark (✓) is inserted in the reference column to indicate that the daily posting to the customer's account has been made. If the subsidiary ledger accounts were numbered, the account number would be entered in place of the check mark. At the end of the month, Karns posts the column totals of the sales journal to the general ledger. Here, the column totals are as follows: From the selling-price column, a debit of $90,230 to Accounts Receivable (account No. 112) and a credit of $90,230 to Sales Revenue (account No. 401); from the cost column, a debit of $62,190 to Cost of Goods Sold (account No. 505) and a credit of $62,190 to Inventory (account No. 120). Karns inserts the account numbers below the column totals to indicate that the postings have been made. In both the general ledger and subsidiary ledger accounts, the reference **S1** indicates that the posting came from page 1 of the sales journal.

Proving the Ledgers

The next step is to "prove" the ledgers. To do so, Karns must determine two things: (1) The total of the general ledger debit balances must equal the total of the general ledger credit balances. (2) The sum of the subsidiary ledger balances must equal the balance in the control account. **Illustration 7.8** shows the proof of the postings from the sales journal to the general and subsidiary ledgers.

Advantages of the Sales Journal

The use of a special journal to record sales on account has a number of advantages. First, the one-line entry for each sales transaction saves time. In the sales journal, it is not necessary to write out the four account titles for each transaction. Second, only totals, rather than individual entries, are posted to the general ledger. This saves posting time and reduces the possibilities

ILLUSTRATION 7.7 Posting the sales journal

General Ledger Software for Accounting

File Edit View Go Bookmarks Tools Help

Problem Entries Post Closing Reports Tools Help

SALES JOURNAL S1

Date	Account Debited	Invoice No.	Ref.	Accts. Receivable Dr. Sales Revenue Cr.	Cost of Goods Sold Dr. Inventory Cr.
2020					
May 3	Abbot Sisters	101	√	10,600	6,360
7	Babson Co.	102	√	11,350	7,370
14	Carson Bros.	103	√	7,800	5,070
19	Deli Co.	104	√	9,300	6,510
21	Abbot Sisters	105	√	15,400	10,780
24	Deli Co.	106	√	21,210	15,900
27	Babson Co.	107	√	14,570	10,200
				90,230	62,190
				(112) / (401)	(505) / (120)

At the end of the accounting period, the company posts totals to the general ledger.

The company posts individual amounts to the subsidiary ledger daily.

ACCOUNTS RECEIVABLE SUBSIDIARY LEDGER

Abbot Sisters

Date	Ref.	Debit	Credit	Balance
2020				
May 3	S1	10,600		10,600
21	S1	15,400		26,000

Babson Co.

Date	Ref.	Debit	Credit	Balance
2020				
May 7	S1	11,350		11,350
27	S1	14,570		25,920

Carson Bros.

Date	Ref.	Debit	Credit	Balance
2020				
May 14	S1	7,800		7,800

Deli Co.

Date	Ref.	Debit	Credit	Balance
2020				
May 19	S1	9,300		9,300
24	S1	21,210		30,510

GENERAL LEDGER

Accounts Receivable No. 112

Date	Ref.	Debit	Credit	Balance
2020				
May 31	S1	90,230		90,230

Inventory No. 120

Date	Ref.	Debit	Credit	Balance
2020				
May 31	S1		62,190	62,190[1]

Sales Revenue No. 401

Date	Ref.	Debit	Credit	Balance
2020				
May 31	S1		90,230	90,230

Cost of Goods Sold No. 505

Date	Ref.	Debit	Credit	Balance
2020				
May 31	S1	62,190		62,190

The subsidiary ledger is separate from the general ledger.

Accounts Receivable is a control account.

[1]The normal balance for Inventory is a debit. But because of the sequence in which we have posted the special journals, with the sales journal first, the credits to Inventory are posted before the debits. This posting sequence explains the credit balance in Inventory, which exists only until the other journals are posted.

start General Ledger General Jrnl Sales Jrnl Cash Receipts Jrnl Purchases Jrnl

of errors in posting. Finally, a division of labor results because one individual can take responsibility for the sales journal.

Cash Receipts Journal

In the **cash receipts journal**, companies record all receipts of cash. The most common types of cash receipts are cash sales of merchandise and collections of accounts receivable. Many

ILLUSTRATION 7.8

Proving the equality of the postings from the sales journal

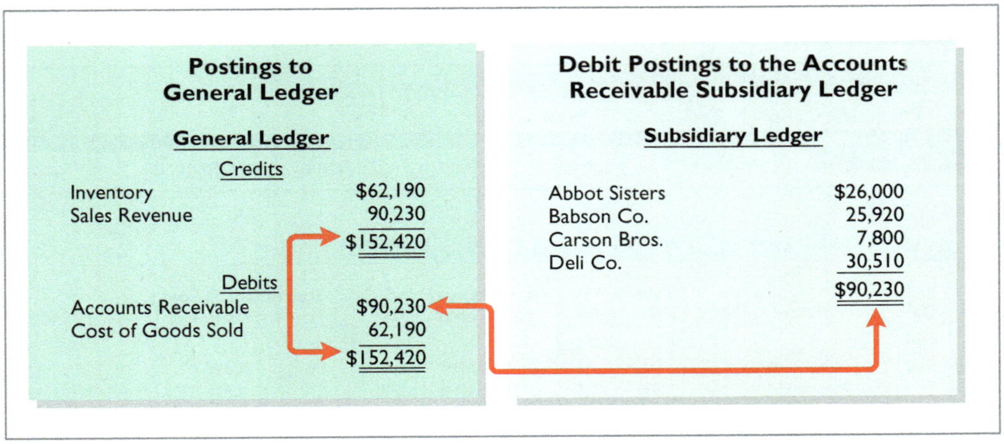

other possibilities exist, such as receipt of money from bank loans and cash proceeds from disposal of equipment. A one- or two-column cash receipts journal would not have space enough for all possible cash receipt transactions. Therefore, companies use a multiple-column cash receipts journal.

Generally, a cash receipts journal includes the following columns: debit columns for Cash and Sales Discounts, and credit columns for Accounts Receivable, Sales Revenue, and "Other Accounts." Companies use the Other Accounts category when the cash receipt does not involve a cash sale or a collection of accounts receivable. Under a perpetual inventory system, each sales entry also is accompanied by an entry that debits Cost of Goods Sold and credits Inventory for the cost of the merchandise sold. **Illustration 7.9** shows a six-column cash receipts journal.

Companies may use additional credit columns if these columns significantly reduce postings to a specific account. For example, a loan company such as **Household International** receives thousands of cash collections from customers. Using separate credit columns for Loans Receivable and Interest Revenue, rather than the Other Accounts credit column, would reduce postings.

Journalizing Cash Receipts Transactions

To illustrate the journalizing of cash receipts transactions, we will continue with the May transactions of Karns Wholesale Supply. Collections from customers relate to the entries recorded in the sales journal in Illustration 7.6. The entries in the cash receipts journal are based on the following cash receipts.

May	1	D. A. Karns makes an investment of $5,000 in the business.
	7	Cash sales of merchandise total $1,900 (cost, $1,240).
	10	Received a check for $10,388 from Abbot Sisters in payment of invoice No. 101 for $10,600 less a 2% discount.
	12	Cash sales of merchandise total $2,600 (cost, $1,690).
	17	Received a check for $11,123 from Babson Co. in payment of invoice No. 102 for $11,350 less a 2% discount.
	22	Received cash by signing a note for $6,000.
	23	Received a check for $7,644 from Carson Bros. in full for invoice No. 103 for $7,800 less a 2% discount.
	28	Received a check for $9,114 from Deli Co. in full for invoice No. 104 for $9,300 less a 2% discount.

The following discussion provides further information about the columns in the cash receipts journal.

Debit Columns:

1. **Cash.** Karns enters in this column the amount of cash actually received in each transaction. The column total indicates the total cash receipts for the month.

ILLUSTRATION 7.9 Journalizing and posting the cash receipts journal

General Ledger Software for Accounting

File Edit View Go Bookmarks Tools Help

Problem Entries Post Closing Reports Tools Help

CASH RECEIPTS JOURNAL CR1

Date	Account Credited	Ref.	Cash Dr.	Sales Discounts Dr.	Accounts Receivable Cr.	Sales Revenue Cr.	Other Accounts Cr.	Cost of Goods Sold Dr. Inventory Cr.
2020								
May 1	Owner's Capital	301	5,000				5,000	
7			1,900			1,900		1,240
10	Abbot Sisters	√	10,388	212	10,600			
12			2,600			2,600		1,690
17	Babson Co.	√	11,123	227	11,350			
22	Notes Payable	200	6,000				6,000	
23	Carson Bros.	√	7,644	156	7,800			
28	Deli Co.	√	9,114	186	9,300			
			53,769	781	39,050	4,500	11,000	2,930
			(101)	(414)	(112)	(401)	(x)	(505)/(120)

The company posts individual amounts to the subsidiary ledger daily.

At the end of the accounting period, the company posts totals to the general ledger.

ACCOUNTS RECEIVABLE SUBSIDIARY LEDGER

Abbot Sisters

Date	Ref.	Debit	Credit	Balance
2020				
May 3	S1	10,600		10,600
10	CR1		10,600	--------
21	S1	15,400		15,400

Babson Co.

Date	Ref.	Debit	Credit	Balance
2020				
May 7	S1	11,350		11,350
17	CR1		11,350	--------
27	S1	14,570		14,570

Carson Bros.

Date	Ref.	Debit	Credit	Balance
2020				
May 14	S1	7,800		7,800
23	CR1		7,800	-------

Deli Co.

Date	Ref.	Debit	Credit	Balance
2020				
May 19	S1	9,300		9,300
24	S1	21,210		30,510
28	CR1		9,300	21,210

The subsidiary ledger is separate from the general ledger.

Accounts Receivable is a control account.

GENERAL LEDGER

Cash **No. 101**

Date	Ref.	Debit	Credit	Balance
2020				
May 31	CR1	53,769		53,769

Accounts Receivable **No. 112**

Date	Ref.	Debit	Credit	Balance
2020				
May 31	S1	90,230		90,230
31	CR1		39,050	51,180

Inventory **No. 120**

Date	Ref.	Debit	Credit	Balance
2020				
May 31	S1		62,190	(62,190)
31	CR1		2,930	(65,120)

Notes Payable **No. 200**

Date	Ref.	Debit	Credit	Balance
2020				
May 22	CR1		6,000	6,000

Owner's Capital **No. 301**

Date	Ref.	Debit	Credit	Balance
2020				
May 1	CR1		5,000	5,000

Sales Revenue **No. 401**

Date	Ref.	Debit	Credit	Balance
2020				
May 31	S1		90,230	90,230
31	CR1		4,500	94,730

Sales Discounts **No. 414**

Date	Ref.	Debit	Credit	Balance
2020				
May 31	CR1	781		781

Cost of Goods Sold **No. 505**

Date	Ref.	Debit	Credit	Balance
2020				
May 31	S1	62,190		62,190
31	CR1	2,930		65,120

start General Ledger General Jrnl Sales Jrnl Cash Receipts Jrnl Purchases Jrnl

HELPFUL HINT

A *subsidiary ledger* account is credited when the entry involves a collection of accounts receivable. A *general ledger* account is credited when the account is not shown in a special column (and an amount must be entered in the Other Accounts column). Otherwise, no account is shown in the "Account Credited" column.

2. **Sales Discounts.** Karns includes a Sales Discounts column in its cash receipts journal. By doing so, it does not need to enter sales discount items in the general journal. As a result, the cash receipts journal shows on one line the collection of an account receivable within the discount period.

Credit Columns:

3. **Accounts Receivable.** Karns uses the Accounts Receivable column to record cash collections on account (see **Helpful Hint**). The amount entered here is the amount to be credited to the individual customer's account.
4. **Sales Revenue.** The Sales Revenue column records all cash sales of merchandise. Cash sales of other assets (plant assets, for example) are not reported in this column.
5. **Other Accounts.** Karns uses the Other Accounts column whenever the credit is other than to Accounts Receivable or Sales Revenue. For example, in the first entry, Karns enters $5,000 as a credit to Owner's Capital. This column is often referred to as the sundry accounts column.

Debit and Credit Column:

6. **Cost of Goods Sold and Inventory.** This column records debits to Cost of Goods Sold and credits to Inventory.

In a multi-column journal, generally only one line is needed for each entry. Debit and credit amounts for each line must be equal. When Karns journalizes the collection from Abbot Sisters on May 10, for example, three amounts are indicated. Note also that the Account Credited column identifies both general ledger and subsidiary ledger account titles. General ledger accounts are illustrated in the May 1 and May 22 entries. A subsidiary account is illustrated in the May 10 entry for the collection from Abbot Sisters.

When Karns has finished journalizing a multi-column journal, it totals the amount columns and compares the totals to prove the equality of debits and credits. **Illustration 7.10** shows the proof of the equality of Karns's cash receipts journal.

ILLUSTRATION 7.10

Proving the equality of the cash receipts journal

Debits		Credits	
Cash	$53,769	Accounts Receivable	$39,050
Sales Discounts	781	Sales Revenue	4,500
Cost of Goods Sold	2,930	Other Accounts	11,000
		Inventory	2,930
	$57,480		$57,480

Totaling the columns of a journal and proving the equality of the totals is called **footing** and **cross-footing** a journal.

Posting the Cash Receipts Journal

Posting a multi-column journal (Illustration 7.9) involves the following steps.

1. **At the end of the month,** the company posts all column totals, except for the Other Accounts total, to the account title(s) specified in the column heading (such as Cash or Accounts Receivable). The company then enters account numbers below the column totals to show that they have been posted. For example, Karns has posted Cash to account No. 101, Accounts Receivable to account No. 112, Inventory to account No. 120, Sales Revenue to account No. 401, Sales Discounts to account No. 414, and Cost of Goods Sold to account No. 505.
2. The company **separately posts the individual amounts comprising the Other Accounts total** to the general ledger accounts specified in the Account Credited column. See, for

example, the credit posting to Owner's Capital. The total amount of this column has not been posted. The symbol (X) is inserted below the total to this column to indicate that the amount has not been posted.

3. The individual amounts in a column, posted in total to a control account (Accounts Receivable, in this case), are posted **daily to the subsidiary ledger** account specified in the Account Credited column. See, for example, the credit posting of $10,600 to Abbot Sisters.

The symbol **CR**, used in both the subsidiary and general ledgers, identifies postings from the cash receipts journal.

Proving the Ledgers

After posting of the cash receipts journal is completed, Karns proves the ledgers. As shown in **Illustration 7.11**, the general ledger totals agree. Also, the sum of the subsidiary ledger balances equals the control account balance.

ILLUSTRATION 7.11

Proving the ledgers after posting the sales and the cash receipts journals

Schedule of Accounts Receivable
(from accounts receivable subsidiary ledger)

Abbot Sisters	$15,400
Babson Co.	14,570
Deli Co.	21,210
	$51,180

General Ledger

Debits

Cash	$ 53,769
Accounts Receivable	51,180
Sales Discounts	781
Cost of Goods Sold	65,120
	$170,850

Credits

Notes Payable	$ 6,000
Owner's Capital	5,000
Sales Revenue	94,730
Inventory	65,120
	$170,850

Purchases Journal

In the **purchases journal**, companies record all purchases of merchandise on account. Each entry in this journal results in a debit to Inventory and a credit to Accounts Payable (see **Helpful Hint**). For example, consider the following credit purchase transactions for Karns Wholesale Supply in **Illustration 7.12**.

HELPFUL HINT

A single-column purchases journal needs only to be footed to prove the equality of debits and credits.

ILLUSTRATION 7.12

Credit purchase transactions

Date	Supplier	Amount
5/6	Jasper Manufacturing Inc.	$11,000
5/10	Eaton and Howe Inc.	7,200
5/14	Fabor and Son	6,900
5/19	Jasper Manufacturing Inc.	17,500
5/26	Fabor and Son	8,700
5/29	Eaton and Howe Inc.	12,600

Illustration 7.13 shows the purchases journal for Karns Wholesale Supply. When using a one-column purchases journal (as in Illustration 7.13), a company cannot journalize other types of purchases on account or cash purchases in it. For example, if the company used the purchases journal in Illustration 7.13, Karns would have to record credit purchases of equipment or supplies in the general journal. Likewise, all cash purchases would be entered in the cash payments journal.

ILLUSTRATION 7.13 Journalizing and posting the purchases journal

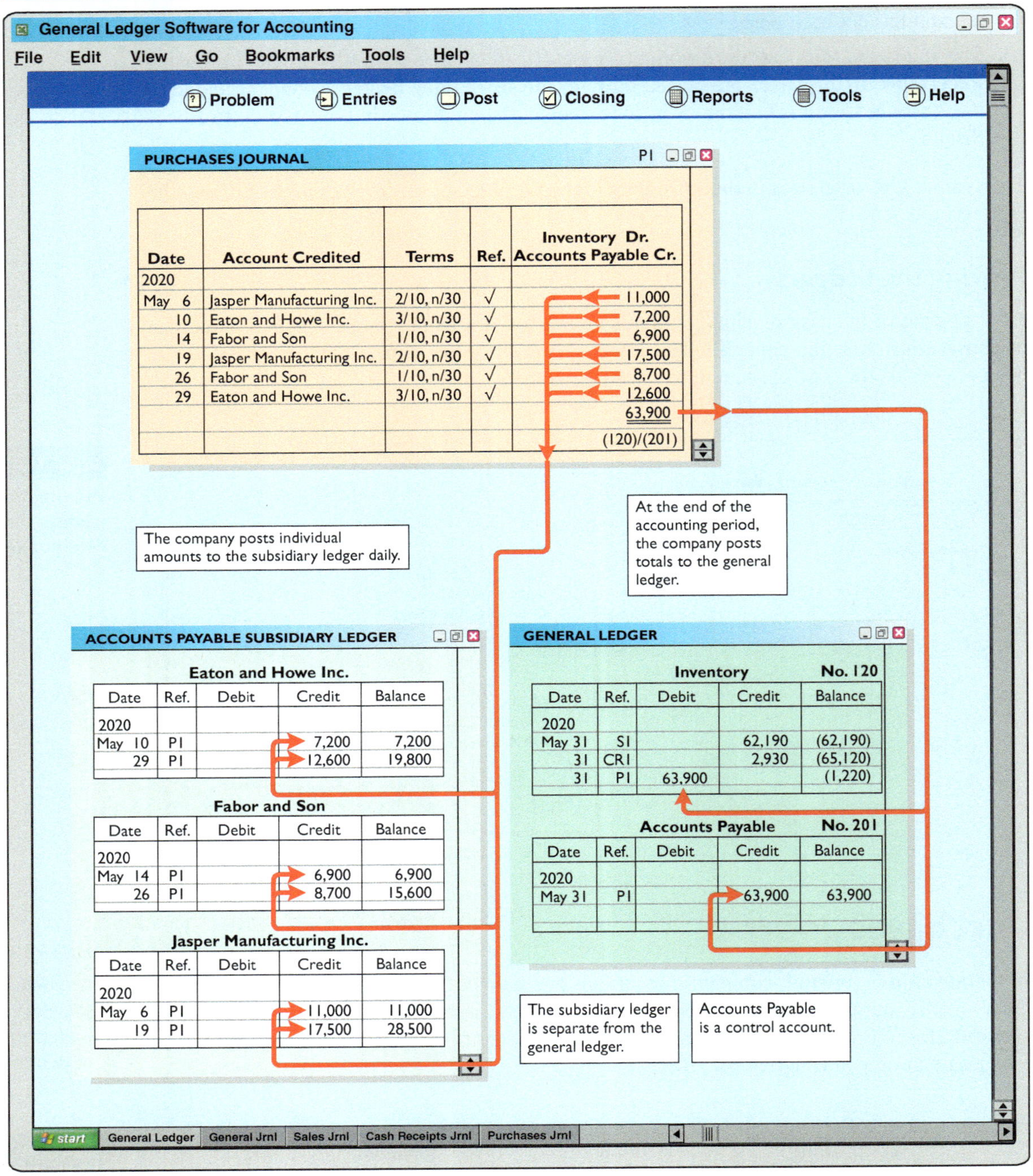

PURCHASES JOURNAL P1

Date	Account Credited	Terms	Ref.	Inventory Dr. Accounts Payable Cr.
2020				
May 6	Jasper Manufacturing Inc.	2/10, n/30	√	11,000
10	Eaton and Howe Inc.	3/10, n/30	√	7,200
14	Fabor and Son	1/10, n/30	√	6,900
19	Jasper Manufacturing Inc.	2/10, n/30	√	17,500
26	Fabor and Son	1/10, n/30	√	8,700
29	Eaton and Howe Inc.	3/10, n/30	√	12,600
				63,900
				(120)/(201)

ACCOUNTS PAYABLE SUBSIDIARY LEDGER

Eaton and Howe Inc.

Date	Ref.	Debit	Credit	Balance
2020				
May 10	P1		7,200	7,200
29	P1		12,600	19,800

Fabor and Son

Date	Ref.	Debit	Credit	Balance
2020				
May 14	P1		6,900	6,900
26	P1		8,700	15,600

Jasper Manufacturing Inc.

Date	Ref.	Debit	Credit	Balance
2020				
May 6	P1		11,000	11,000
19	P1		17,500	28,500

GENERAL LEDGER

Inventory — No. 120

Date	Ref.	Debit	Credit	Balance
2020				
May 31	S1		62,190	(62,190)
31	CR1		2,930	(65,120)
31	P1	63,900		(1,220)

Accounts Payable — No. 201

Date	Ref.	Debit	Credit	Balance
2020				
May 31	P1		63,900	63,900

Journalizing Credit Purchases of Merchandise

The journalizing procedure is similar to that for a sales journal. Companies make entries in the purchases journal from purchase invoices. In contrast to the sales journal, the purchases journal may not have an invoice number column because invoices received from different suppliers will not be in numerical sequence. To ensure that they record all purchase invoices, some companies consecutively number each invoice upon receipt and then use an internal document number column in the purchases journal. The entries for Karns Wholesale Supply are based on the assumed credit purchases listed in Illustration 7.12.

HELPFUL HINT

Postings to subsidiary ledger accounts are done daily because it is often necessary to know a current balance for the subsidiary accounts.

Posting the Purchases Journal

The procedures for posting the purchases journal are similar to those for the sales journal. In this case, Karns makes **daily** postings to the **accounts payable ledger** (see **Helpful Hint**).

It makes **monthly** postings to Inventory and Accounts Payable in the general ledger. In both ledgers, Karns uses **P1** in the reference column to show that the postings are from page 1 of the purchases journal.

Proof of the equality of the postings from the purchases journal to both ledgers is shown in **Illustration 7.14**.

ILLUSTRATION 7.14

Proving the equality of the purchases journal

Postings to General Ledger	
Inventory (debit)	$63,900
Accounts Payable (credit)	$63,900

Credit Postings to Accounts Payable Ledger	
Eaton and Howe Inc.	$19,800
Fabor and Son	15,600
Jasper Manufacturing Inc.	28,500
	$63,900

Expanding the Purchases Journal

Some companies expand the purchases journal to include all types of purchases on account, not just merchandise. Instead of one column for inventory and accounts payable, they use a multiple-column format. This format usually includes a credit column for Accounts Payable and debit columns for purchases of Inventory, Supplies, and Other Accounts. **Illustration 7.15** shows a multi-column purchases journal for Hanover Co. The posting procedures are similar to those shown earlier for posting the cash receipts journal. *For homework problems, assume the use of a single-column purchases journal unless instructed otherwise.*

ILLUSTRATION 7.15 **Multi-column purchases journal**

General Ledger Software for Accounting

File Edit View Go Bookmarks Tools Help

Problem Entries Post Closing Reports Tools Help

PURCHASES JOURNAL P1

Date	Account Credited	Ref.	Accounts Payable Cr.	Inventory Dr.	Supplies Dr.	Other Accounts Dr. Account	Ref.	Amount
2020								
June 1	Signe Audio	√	2,000		2,000			
3	Wight Co.	√	1,500	1,500				
5	Orange Tree Co.	√	2,600			Equipment	157	2,600
30	Sue's Business Forms	√	800		800			
			56,600	43,000	8,700			4,900

start General Ledger General Jrnl Sales Jrnl Cash Receipts Jrnl Purchases Jrnl

Cash Payments Journal

In a **cash payments (cash disbursements) journal**, companies record all disbursements of cash. Entries are made from prenumbered checks. Because companies make cash payments for various purposes, the cash payments journal has multiple columns. **Illustration 7.16** shows a four-column journal.

ILLUSTRATION 7.16 Journalizing and posting the cash payments journal

General Ledger Software for Accounting

File Edit View Go Bookmarks Tools Help

Problem | Entries | Post | Closing | Reports | Tools | Help

CASH PAYMENTS JOURNAL CP1

Date	Ck. No.	Account Debited	Ref.	Other Accounts Dr.	Accounts Payable Dr.	Inventory Cr.	Cash Cr.
2020							
May 1	101	Prepaid Insurance	130	1,200			1,200
3	102	Inventory	120	100			100
8	103	Inventory	120	4,400			4,400
10	104	Jasper Manuf. Inc.	√		11,000	220	10,780
19	105	Eaton & Howe Inc.	√		7,200	216	6,984
23	106	Fabor and Son	√		6,900	69	6,831
28	107	Jasper Manuf. Inc.	√		17,500	350	17,150
30	108	Owner's Drawings	306	500			500
				6,200	42,600	855	47,945
				(x)	(201)	(120)	(101)

The company posts individual amounts to the subsidiary ledger daily.

At the end of the accounting period, the company posts totals to the general ledger.

ACCOUNTS PAYABLE SUBSIDIARY LEDGER

Eaton and Howe Inc.

Date	Ref.	Debit	Credit	Balance
2020				
May 10	P1		7,200	7,200
19	CP1	7,200		-------
29	P1		12,600	12,600

Fabor and Son

Date	Ref.	Debit	Credit	Balance
2020				
May 14	P1		6,900	6,900
23	CP1	6,900		-------
26	P1		8,700	8,700

Jasper Manufacturing Inc.

Date	Ref.	Debit	Credit	Balance
2020				
May 6	P1		11,000	11,000
10	CP1	11,000		--------
19	P1		17,500	17,500
28	CP1	17,500		--------

The subsidiary ledger is separate from the general ledger.

Accounts Payable is a control account.

GENERAL LEDGER

Cash No. 101

Date	Ref.	Debit	Credit	Balance
2020				
May 31	CR1	53,769		53,769
31	CP1		47,945	5,824

Inventory No. 120

Date	Ref.	Debit	Credit	Balance
2020				
May 3	CP1	100		100
8	CP1	4,400		4,500
31	S1		62,190	57,690
31	CR1		2,930	60,620
31	P1	63,900		3,280
31	CP1		855	2,425

Prepaid Insurance No. 130

Date	Ref.	Debit	Credit	Balance
2020				
May 1	CP1	1,200		1,200

Accounts Payable No. 201

Date	Ref.	Debit	Credit	Balance
2020				
May 31	P1		63,900	63,900
31	CP1	42,600		21,300

Owner's Drawings No. 306

Date	Ref.	Debit	Credit	Balance
2020				
May 30	CP1	500		500

start | General Ledger | General Jrnl | Sales Jrnl | Cash Receipts Jrnl | Purchases Jrnl

Journalizing Cash Payments Transactions

The procedures for journalizing transactions in this journal are similar to those for the cash receipts journal. Karns records each transaction on one line, and for each line there must be equal debit and credit amounts. The entries in the cash payments journal in Illustration 7.16 are based on the following transactions for Karns Wholesale Supply.

May 1 Issued check No. 101 for $1,200 for the annual premium on a fire insurance policy.
3 Issued check No. 102 for $100 in payment of freight when terms were FOB shipping point.
8 Issued check No. 103 for $4,400 for the purchase of merchandise.
10 Sent check No. 104 for $10,780 to Jasper Manufacturing Inc. in payment of May 6 invoice for $11,000 less a 2% discount.
19 Mailed check No. 105 for $6,984 to Eaton and Howe Inc. in payment of May 10 invoice for $7,200 less a 3% discount.
23 Sent check No. 106 for $6,831 to Fabor and Son in payment of May 14 invoice for $6,900 less a 1% discount.
28 Sent check No. 107 for $17,150 to Jasper Manufacturing Inc. in payment of May 19 invoice for $17,500 less a 2% discount.
30 Issued check No. 108 for $500 to D. A. Karns as a cash withdrawal for personal use.

Note that whenever Karns enters an amount in the Other Accounts column, it must identify a specific general ledger account in the Account Debited column. The entries for checks No. 101, 102, 103, and 108 illustrate this situation. Similarly, Karns must identify a subsidiary account in the Account Debited column whenever it enters an amount in the Accounts Payable column. See, for example, the entry for check No. 104.

After Karns journalizes the cash payments journal, it totals the columns. The totals are then balanced to prove the equality of debits and credits.

Posting the Cash Payments Journal

The procedures for posting the cash payments journal are similar to those for the cash receipts journal. Karns posts the amounts recorded in the Accounts Payable column individually to the subsidiary ledger and in total to the control account. It posts Inventory and Cash only in total at the end of the month. Transactions in the Other Accounts column are posted individually to the appropriate account(s) affected. The company does not post totals for the Other Accounts column.

Illustration 7.16 shows the posting of the cash payments journal. Note that Karns uses the symbol **CP** as the posting reference. After postings are completed, the company proves the equality of the debit and credit balances in the general ledger. In addition, the control account balances should agree with the subsidiary ledger total balance. **Illustration 7.17** shows the agreement of these balances.

Schedule of Accounts Payable
(from accounts payable subsidiary ledger)

Eaton and Howe Inc.	$12,600
Fabor and Son	8,700
	$21,300

General Ledger

Debits	
Cash	$ 5,824
Accounts Receivable	51,180
Inventory	2,425
Prepaid Insurance	1,200
Owner's Drawings	500
Sales Discounts	781
Cost of Goods Sold	65,120
	$127,030

Credits	
Notes Payable	$ 6,000
Accounts Payable	21,300
Owner's Capital	5,000
Sales Revenue	94,730
	$127,030

ILLUSTRATION 7.17
Proving the ledgers after postings from the sales, cash receipts, purchases, and cash payments journals

Effects of Special Journals on the General Journal

Special journals for sales, purchases, and cash substantially reduce the number of entries that companies make in the general journal. **Only transactions that cannot be entered in a special journal are recorded in the general journal.** For example, a company may use the general journal to record such transactions as granting of credit to a customer for a sales return or allowance, granting of credit from a supplier for purchases returned, acceptance of a note receivable from a customer, and purchase of equipment by issuing a note payable. Also, **correcting, adjusting, and closing entries are made in the general journal**.

The general journal has columns for date, account title and explanation, reference, and debit and credit amounts. When control and subsidiary accounts are not involved, the procedures for journalizing and posting of transactions are the same as those described in earlier chapters. When control and subsidiary accounts are involved, companies make two changes from the earlier procedures:

1. In **journalizing**, they identify both the control and the subsidiary accounts.
2. In **posting**, there must be a **dual posting**: once to the control account and once to the subsidiary account.

To illustrate, assume that on May 31, Karns Wholesale Supply returns $500 of merchandise for credit to Fabor and Son. **Illustration 7.18** shows the entry in the general journal and the posting of the entry.

ILLUSTRATION 7.18 Journalizing and posting the general journal

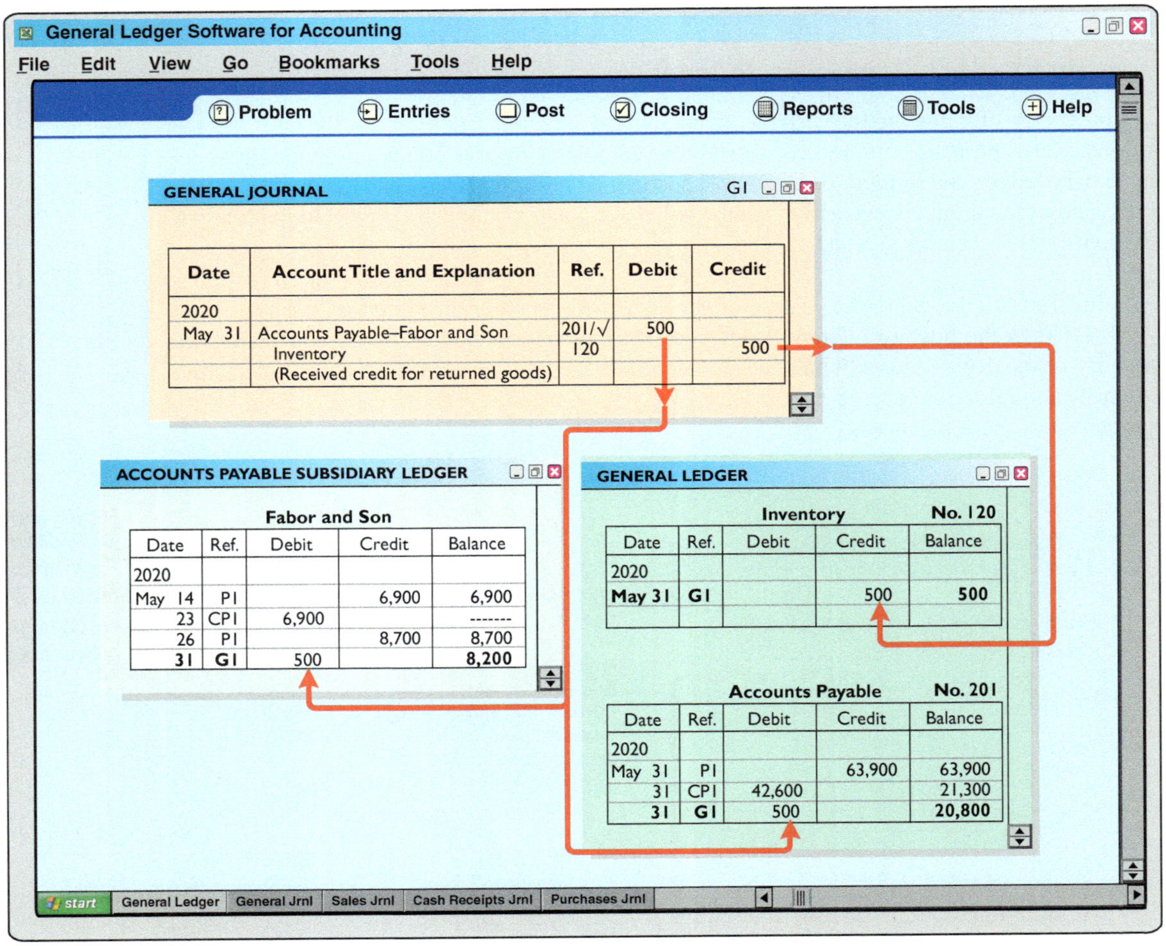

Date	Account Title and Explanation	Ref.	Debit	Credit
2020				
May 31	Accounts Payable–Fabor and Son	201/√	500	
	Inventory	120		500
	(Received credit for returned goods)			

Fabor and Son

Date	Ref.	Debit	Credit	Balance
2020				
May 14	P1		6,900	6,900
23	CP1	6,900		-------
26	P1		8,700	8,700
31	**G1**	500		**8,200**

Inventory No. 120

Date	Ref.	Debit	Credit	Balance
2020				
May 31	**G1**		500	**500**

Accounts Payable No. 201

Date	Ref.	Debit	Credit	Balance
2020				
May 31	P1		63,900	63,900
31	CP1	42,600		21,300
31	**G1**	500		**20,800**

Note that the general journal indicates two accounts (Accounts Payable, and Fabor and Son) for the debit, and two postings ("201/✓") in the reference column. One debit is posted to the control account and another debit is posted to the creditor's account in the subsidiary ledger. If Karns receives cash instead of credit on this return, then it would record the transaction in the cash receipts journal.

Cyber Security: A Final Comment

Have you ever been hacked? With the increasing use of cell phones, tablets, and other social media outlets, a real risk exists that your confidential information may be stolen and used illegally. Companies, individuals, and even nations have all been victims of **cybercrime**—a crime that involves the Internet, a computer system, or computer technology.

For companies, cybercrime is clearly a major threat as the hacking of employees' or customers' records related to cybercrime can cost millions of dollars. Unfortunately, the numbers of security breaches are increasing. A security breach at **Target**, for example, cost the company a minimum of $20 million, the CEO lost his job, and sales plummeted.

Here are three reasons for the rise in the successful hacks of corporate computer records.

1. Companies and their employees continue to increase their activity on the Internet, primarily due to the use of mobile devices and cloud computing.
2. Companies today collect and store unprecedented amounts of personal data on customers and employees.
3. Companies often take measures to protect themselves from cyber security attacks but then fail to check if employees are carrying out the proper security guidelines.

Note that cyber security risks extend far beyond company operations and compliance. Many hackers target highly sensitive intellectual information or other strategic assets. **Illustration 7.19** highlights the type of hackers and their motives, targets and impacts.

ILLUSTRATION 7.19 **Profiles of hackers**

Malicious Actors	Motives	Targets	Impacts
Nation-state	• Economic, political, and/ or military advantage	• Trade secrets • Sensitive business information • Emerging technologies • Critical infrastructure	• Loss of competitive advantage • Disruption to critical infrastructure
Organized crime	• Immediate financial gain • Collect information for future financial gains	• Financial/payment systems • Personally identifiable information • Payment card information • Protected health information	• Costly regulatory inquiries and penalties • Consumer and shareholder lawsuits • Loss of consumer confidence
Hacktivists	• Influence political and/or social change • Pressure businesses to change their practices	• Corporate secrets • Sensitive business information • Information related to key executives, employees, customers, and business partners	• Disruption of business activities • Harm to brand and reputation • Loss of consumer confidence
Insiders	• Personal advantage, monetary gain • Professional revenge • Patriotism	• Sales, deals, market strategies • Corporate secrets, intellectual property • Business operations • Personnel information	• Trade secret disclosure • Operational disruption • Harm to brand and reputation • National security impact

Source: PriceWaterhouseCoopers, "Answering Your Cybersecurity Questions" (January 2014).

Companies now recognize that cyber security systems that protect confidential data must be implemented. It follows that companies (and nations and individuals) must continually verify that their cyber security defenses are sound and uncompromised.

DO IT! 3 | Special Journals

Swisher Company had the following transactions during March.

1. Collected cash on account from Oakland Company.
2. Purchased equipment by signing a note payable.
3. Sold merchandise on account.
4. Purchased merchandise on account.
5. Paid $2,400 for a 2-year insurance policy.

Identify the journal in which each of the transactions above is recorded. The company uses the special journals described in the chapter plus a general journal.

ACTION PLAN

- **Determine if the transaction involves the receipt of cash (cash receipts journal) or the payment of cash (cash payments journal).**
- **Determine if the transaction is a sale of merchandise on account (sales journal) or a purchase of merchandise on account (purchases journal).**
- **All other transactions are recorded in the general journal.**

Solution

1. Collected cash on account from Oakland Company.	Cash receipts journal
2. Purchased equipment by signing a note payable.	General journal
3. Sold merchandise on account.	Sales journal
4. Purchased merchandise on account.	Purchases journal
5. Paid $2,400 for a 2-year insurance policy.	Cash payments journal

Related exercise material: **BE7.6, BE7.7, BE7.8, BE7.9, BE7.10, DO IT! 7.3, E7.6, E7.7, E7.8, and E7.10.**

Review and Practice

Learning Objectives Review

1 Explain the basic concepts of an accounting information system.

The basic principles in developing an accounting information system are cost-effectiveness, useful output, and flexibility. Most companies use a computerized accounting system. Smaller companies use entry-level software such as QuickBooks® or Sage 50. Larger companies use custom-made software packages, which often integrate all aspects of the organization.

2 Describe the nature and purpose of a subsidiary ledger.

A subsidiary ledger is a group of accounts with a common characteristic. It facilitates the recording process by freeing the general ledger from details of individual balances.

3 Record transactions in special journals.

Companies use special journals to group similar types of transactions. In a special journal, generally only one line is used to record a complete transaction.

Glossary Review

Accounting information system A system that collects and processes transaction data and communicates financial information to decision-makers. (p. 7-2).

Accounts payable (creditors') subsidiary ledger A subsidiary ledger that collects transaction data of individual creditors. (p. 7-6).

Accounts receivable (customers') subsidiary ledger A subsidiary ledger that collects transaction data of individual customers. (p. 7-6).

Cash payments (cash disbursements) journal A special journal that records all disbursements of cash. (p. 7-17).

Cash receipts journal A special journal that records all cash received. (p. 7-11).

Control account An account in the general ledger that summarizes subsidiary ledger data. (p. 7-6).

Cybercrime A crime that involves the Internet, a computer system, or computer technology. (p. 7-21).

Manual accounting system A system in which someone performs each of the steps in the accounting cycle by hand. (p. 7-5).

Purchases journal A special journal that records all purchases of merchandise on account. (p. 7-15).

Sales journal A special journal that records all sales of merchandise on account. (p. 7-9).

Special journals Journals that record similar types of transactions, such as all credit sales. (p. 7-8).

Subsidiary ledger A group of accounts with a common characteristic. (p. 7-5).

Practice Multiple-Choice Questions

1. **(LO 1)** The basic principles of an accounting information system include all of the following **except**:
   a. cost-effectiveness. c. useful output.
   b. flexibility. d. periodicity.

2. **(LO 1)** Which of the following is **not** an advantage of computerized accounting systems?
   a. Data is entered only once in computerized accounting systems.
   b. Computerized accounting systems provide up-to-date information.
   c. Computerized accounting systems eliminate entering of transaction information.
   d. Computerized accounting systems eliminate many errors resulting from human intervention.

3. **(LO 2)** Which of the following is **incorrect** concerning subsidiary ledgers?
   a. The purchases ledger is a common subsidiary ledger for creditor accounts.
   b. The accounts receivable ledger is a subsidiary ledger.
   c. A subsidiary ledger is a group of accounts with a common characteristic.
   d. An advantage of the subsidiary ledger is that it permits a division of labor in posting.

4. **(LO 2)** Two common subsidiary ledgers are:
   a. accounts receivable and cash receipts.
   b. accounts payable and cash payments.
   c. accounts receivable and accounts payable.
   d. sales and cost of goods sold.

5. **(LO 2)** At the beginning of the month, the accounts receivable subsidiary ledger showed balances for Apple Company $5,000 and Berry Company $7,000. During the month, credit sales were made to Apple $6,000, Berry $4,500, and Cantaloupe $8,500. Cash was collected on account from Berry $11,500 and Cantaloupe $3,000. At the end of the month, the control account Accounts Receivable in the general ledger should have a balance of:
   a. $11,000. c. $16,500.
   b. $12,000. d. $31,000.

6. **(LO 3)** A sales journal will be used for:

	Credit Sales	Cash Sales	Sales Discounts
a.	no	yes	yes
b.	yes	no	yes
c.	yes	no	no
d.	yes	yes	no

7. **(LO 3)** A purchase of equipment on account is recorded in the:
   a. cash receipts journal. c. cash payments journal.
   b. purchases journal. d. general journal.

8. **(LO 3)** A purchase of equipment using cash is recorded in the:
   a. cash receipts journal. c. cash payments journal.
   b. purchases journal. d. general journal.

9. **(LO 3)** Which of the following statements is **correct**?
   a. The sales discount column is included in the cash receipts journal.
   b. The purchases journal records all purchases of merchandise whether for cash or on account.
   c. The cash receipts journal records sales on account.
   d. Merchandise returned by the buyer is recorded by the seller in the purchases journal.

10. **(LO 3)** Dotel Company's cash receipts journal includes an Accounts Receivable column and an Other Accounts column. At the end of the month, these columns are posted to the general ledger as:

	Accounts Receivable	Other Accounts
a.	a column total	a column total
b.	individual amounts	a column total
c.	individual amounts	individual amounts
d.	a column total	individual amounts

11. **(LO 3)** Which of the following is **incorrect** concerning the posting of the cash receipts journal?
    a. The total of the Other Accounts column is not posted.
    b. All column totals except the total for the Other Accounts column are posted once at the end of the month to the account title(s) specified in the column heading.
    c. The totals of all columns are posted daily to the accounts specified in the column heading.
    d. The individual amounts in a column posted in total to a control account are posted daily to the subsidiary ledger account specified in the Account Credited column.

12. **(LO 3)** Postings from the purchases journal to the subsidiary ledger are generally made:
    a. yearly. c. weekly.
    b. monthly. d. daily.

13. **(LO 3)** Which statement is **incorrect** regarding the general journal?
    a. Only transactions that cannot be entered in a special journal are recorded in the general journal.

b. Dual postings are always required in the general journal.

c. The general journal may be used to record acceptance of a note receivable in payment of an account receivable.

d. Correcting, adjusting, and closing entries are made in the general journal.

14. (LO 3) When companies use special journals:

a. they record all purchase transactions in the purchases journal.

b. they record all cash received, except from cash sales, in the cash receipts journal.

c. they record all cash disbursements in the cash payments journal.

d. a general journal is not necessary.

15. (LO 3) If a customer returns goods for credit, the selling company normally makes an entry in the:

a. cash payments journal. **c.** general journal.

b. sales journal. **d.** cash receipts journal.

Solutions

1. d. Periodicity is not one of the basic principles of accounting information systems. The other choices are true statements.

2. c. Computerized accounting systems do not eliminate the entering of transaction information. The other choices are advantages of computerized accounting systems.

3. a. The accounts payable ledger, not the purchases ledger, is a common subsidiary ledger for creditor accounts. The other choices are true statements.

4. c. Accounts receivable and accounts payable are two common subsidiary ledgers. The other choices are incorrect because (a) cash receipts, (b) cash payments, and (d) sales revenue and cost of goods sold are not subsidiary ledgers.

5. c. The accounts receivable subsidiary ledger balances are the following: Apple Company $11,000 (beginning balance $5,000 + credit sales $6,000), Berry Company $0 (beginning balance $7,000 + credit sales $4,500 – cash collected on account $11,500), and Cantaloupe $5,500 (credit sales $8,500 – cash collected on account $3,000). The Accounts Receivable control account in the general ledger therefore has a balance of $16,500 ($11,000 + $0 + $5,500), not (a) $11,000, (b) $12,000, or (d) $31,000.

6. c. The sales journal is used for credit sales. The cash receipts journal is used for cash sales and sales discounts. Therefore, choices (a), (b), and (d) are incorrect.

7. d. Unless the company uses a multi-column purchases journal, the general journal is used to record the purchase of equipment **on account**. The other choices are incorrect because (a) the cash receipts journal would be used only if cash is received, (b) a one-column purchases journal cannot be used to record a purchase of equipment on account, and (c) the cash payments journal would be used only if this is a cash purchase.

8. c. The cash payments journal includes all cash paid, including all **cash** purchases. The other choices are incorrect because (a) the cash receipts journal includes all cash received, including cash sales, not cash purchases; (b) the purchases journal includes only purchases of inventory on account, not cash purchases; and (d) the general journal is only used if a transaction cannot be entered in a special journal. In this case, this transaction can be entered into the cash payments journal.

9. a. The sales discount column is included in the cash receipts journal. The other choices are incorrect because (b) the purchases journal only records purchases of inventory on account, not for cash; (c) the sales journal, not the cash receipts journal, records sales on account; and (d) when merchandise is returned by a buyer, the seller records this sales return in the general journal.

10. d. The Accounts Receivable column would be posted to the general ledger as a column total, and the Other Accounts column would be posted as individual amounts. Therefore, the other choices are incorrect.

11. c. The totals of all columns are not posted daily to the accounts specified in the column heading. Instead, all column totals except the total for the Other Accounts column (which is never posted) are posted once at the end of the month to the account title(s) specified in the column heading. The other choices are true statements.

12. d. Postings from the purchases journal to the subsidiary ledger are usually made daily, not (a) yearly, (b) monthly, or (c) weekly.

13. b. Dual postings are not always required in the general journal. Only when control and subsidiary accounts are involved are companies required to dual post: once to the control account and once to the subsidiary account. The other choices are true statements.

14. c. When special journals are used, companies record all cash disbursements in the cash payments journal. The other choices are incorrect because when special journals are used, (a) companies record only purchases of inventory on account in the purchases journal; (b) companies record all cash receipts, including cash sales, in the cash receipts journal; and (d) a general journal is still needed.

15. c. When a customer returns goods for **credit** (i.e., no cash is involved), the selling company records the transaction in the general journal, not the (a) cash payments journal, (b) sales journal, or (d) cash receipts journal.

Practice Brief Exercises

Identify subsidiary ledger balances.

1. (LO 2) The following information is related to Garcia Company for its first month of operations. Identify the balances that appear in the accounts receivable subsidiary ledger and the accounts receivable balance that appears in the general ledger at the end of January.

Credit Sales			Cash Collections		
Jan. 7	Rodan Co.	$11,000	Jan. 17	Rodan Co.	$6,000
15	Lawry Co.	7,000	24	Lawry Co.	5,000
23	Anderson Co.	10,000	29	Anderson Co.	8,000

Solution

1.

Accounts Receivable Subsidiary Ledger

Rodan Co.

Date	Ref.	Debit	Credit	Balance
Jan. 7		11,000		11,000
17			6,000	5,000

Lawry Co.

Date	Ref.	Debit	Credit	Balance
Jan. 15		7,000		7,000
24			5,000	2,000

Anderson Co.

Date	Ref.	Debit	Credit	Balance
Jan. 23		10,000		10,000
29			8,000	2,000

General Ledger

Accounts Receivable

Date	Ref.	Debit	Credit	Balance
Jan. 31		28,000		28,000
31			19,000	9,000

2. **(LO 2)** Presented below is information related to Garcia Company for its first month of operations. Identify the balances that appear in the accounts payable subsidiary ledger and the accounts payable balance that appears in the general ledger at the end of January.

Identify subsidiary ledger balances.

Credit Purchases

Jan. 4	Jones Co.	$22,000
12	Holland Co.	14,000
19	Geovany Co.	20,000

Cash Payments

Jan. 13	Jones Co.	$13,000
20	Holland Co.	11,000
25	Geovany Co.	17,000

Solution

2.

Accounts Payable Subsidiary Ledger

Jones Co.

Date	Ref.	Debit	Credit	Balance
Jan. 4			22,000	22,000
13		13,000		9,000

Holland Co.

Date	Ref.	Debit	Credit	Balance
Jan. 12			14,000	14,000
20		11,000		3,000

Geovany Co.

Date	Ref.	Debit	Credit	Balance
Jan. 19			20,000	20,000
25		17,000		3,000

General Ledger

Accounts Payable

Date	Ref.	Debit	Credit	Balance
Jan. 31			56,000	56,000
31		41,000		15,000

3. **(LO 3)** Soto Company has the following selected transactions during March.

Journalize transactions in general journal.

Mar. 2	Purchased equipment costing $9,400 from Jennings Company on account.
5	Received credit of $630 from May Company for merchandise damaged in shipment to Soto.
7	Issued credit of $500 to Morneau Company for merchandise the customer returned. The returned merchandise had a cost of $300.

Soto Company uses a one-column purchases journal, a sales journal, the columnar cash journals used in the text, and a general journal. Journalize the transactions in the general journal.

Solution

3.

Date	Account	Debit	Credit
Mar. 2	Equipment	9,400	
	Accounts Payable		9,400
5	Accounts Payable	630	
	Inventory		630
7	Sales Returns and Allowances	500	
	Accounts Receivable		500
	Inventory	300	
	Cost of Goods Sold		300

Practice Exercises

Post various journals to control and subsidiary accounts.

1. (LO 2, 3) On June 1, the balance of the Accounts Receivable control account in the general ledger of Rath Company was $13,620. The customers' subsidiary ledger contained account balances as follows: Wilson $2,000, Sanchez $3,140, Roberts $2,560, and Marks $5,920. At the end of June, the various journals contained the following information.

Sales journal: Sales to Roberts $900, to Wilson $1,400, to Hardy $1,500, and to Marks $1,200.
Cash receipts journal: Cash received from Roberts $1,610, from Marks $2,600, from Hardy $580, from Sanchez $2,100, and from Wilson $1,540.
General journal: An allowance is granted to Marks $325.

Instructions

a. Set up control and subsidiary accounts and enter the beginning balances. Do not construct the journals.

b. Post the various journals. Post the items as individual items or as totals, whichever would be the appropriate procedure. (No sales discounts given.)

c. Prepare a schedule of accounts receivable and prove the agreement of the control account with the subsidiary ledger at June 30, 2020.

Solution

1. **a.** and **b.**

GENERAL LEDGER

Accounts Receivable

Date	Explanation	Ref.	Debit	Credit	Balance
June 1	Balance	✓			13,620
		S	5,000		18,620
		CR		8,430	10,190
		G		325	9,865

ACCOUNTS RECEIVABLE SUBSIDIARY LEDGER

Hardy

Date	Explanation	Ref.	Debit	Credit	Balance
June 1					0
		S	1,500		1,500
		CR		580	920

Marks

Date	Explanation	Ref.	Debit	Credit	Balance
June 1	Balance	✓			5,920
		S	1,200		7,120
		CR		2,600	4,520
		G		325	4,195

Roberts

Date	Explanation	Ref.	Debit	Credit	Balance
June 1	Balance	✓			2,560
		S	900		3,460
		CR		1,610	1,850

Sanchez

Date	Explanation	Ref.	Debit	Credit	Balance
June 1	Balance	✓			3,140
		CR		2,100	1,040

Wilson

Date	Explanation	Ref.	Debit	Credit	Balance
June 1	Balance	✓			2,000
		S	1,400		3,400
		CR		1,540	1,860

c.

Rath Company
Schedule of Accounts Receivable
As of June 30, 2020

Hardy	$ 920
Marks	4,195
Roberts	1,850
Sanchez	1,040
Wilson	1,860
Total	$9,865
Accounts Receivable	$9,865

Indicate use of special journals.

2. **(LO 3)** Below are some typical transactions incurred by Brimmer Company.

1. Received credit for merchandise purchased on credit.
2. Payment of employee wages.
3. Sales discount taken on goods sold.
4. Income summary closed to owner's capital.
5. Purchase of office supplies for cash.
6. Depreciation on building.
7. Purchase of merchandise on account.
8. Return of merchandise sold for credit.
9. Payment of creditors on account.
10. Collection on account from customers.
11. Sale of merchandise on account.
12. Sale of land for cash.
13. Sale of merchandise for cash.

Instructions

For each transaction, indicate whether it would normally be recorded in a cash receipts journal, cash payments journal, sales journal, single-column purchases journal, or general journal.

Solution

2.
1. General journal
2. Cash payments journal
3. Cash receipts journal
4. General journal
5. Cash payments journal
6. General journal
7. Purchases journal
8. General journal
9. Cash payments journal
10. Cash receipts journal
11. Sales journal
12. Cash receipts journal
13. Cash receipts journal

Practice Problem

Journalize transactions in cash receipts journal and explain posting procedure.

(LO 3) Cassandra Wilson Company uses a six-column cash receipts journal with the following columns.

Cash (Dr.)
Sales Discounts (Dr.)
Accounts Receivable (Cr.)
Sales Revenue (Cr.)
Other Accounts (Cr.)
Cost of Goods Sold (Dr.) and Inventory (Cr.)

Cash receipts transactions for the month of July 2020 are as follows.

July 3 Cash sales total $5,800 (cost, $3,480).

5 Received a check for $6,370 from Jeltz Company in payment of an invoice dated June 26 for $6,500, terms 2/10, n/30.

9 Cassandra Wilson, the proprietor, made an additional investment of $5,000 in cash in the business.
10 Cash sales total $12,519 (cost, $7,511).
12 Received a check for $7,275 from R. Eliot & Co. in payment of a $7,500 invoice dated July 3, terms 3/10, n/30.
15 Received an advance of $700 cash for future services.
20 Cash sales total $15,472 (cost, $9,283).
22 Received a check for $5,880 from Beck Company in payment of $6,000 invoice dated July 13, terms 2/10, n/30.
29 Cash sales total $17,660 (cost, $10,596).
31 Received cash of $200 for interest earned for July.

Instructions

a. Journalize the transactions in the cash receipts journal.

b. Contrast the posting of the Accounts Receivable and Other Accounts columns.

Solution

a.

CASSANDRA WILSON COMPANY
Cash Receipts Journal

CR1

Date	Account Credited	Ref.	Cash Dr.	Sales Discounts Dr.	Accounts Receivable Cr.	Sales Revenue Cr.	Other Accounts Cr.	Cost of Goods Sold Dr. Inventory Cr.
2020								
7/3			5,800			5,800		3,480
5	Jeltz Company		6,370	130	6,500			
9	Owner's Capital		5,000				5,000	
10			12,519			12,519		7,511
12	R. Eliot & Co.		7,275	225	7,500			
15	Unearned Service Revenue		700				700	
20			15,472			15,472		9,283
22	Beck Company		5,880	120	6,000			
29			17,660			17,660		10,596
31	Interest Revenue		200				200	
			76,876	475	20,000	51,451	5,900	30,870

b. The Accounts Receivable column total is posted as a credit to Accounts Receivable. The individual amounts are credited to the customers' accounts identified in the Account Credited column, which are maintained in the accounts receivable subsidiary ledger. The amounts in the Other Accounts column are posted individually. They are credited to the account titles identified in the Account Credited column.

WileyPLUS

Brief Exercises, DO IT! Exercises, Exercises, Problems, and many additional resources are available for practice in WileyPLUS.

Questions

1. (a) What is an accounting information system? (b) "An accounting information system applies only to a manual system." Do you agree? Explain.

2. Certain principles should be followed in the development of an accounting information system. Identify and explain each of the principles.

3. What are common features of computerized accounting packages beyond recording transactions and preparing financial statements?

4. How does an enterprise resource planning (ERP) system differ from an entry-level computerized accounting system?

5. What are the advantages of using subsidiary ledgers?

6. (a) When do companies normally post to (1) the subsidiary accounts and (2) the general ledger control accounts? (b) Describe the relationship between a control account and a subsidiary ledger.

7. Identify and explain the four special journals discussed in the chapter. List an advantage of using each of these journals rather than using only a general journal.

8. Kensington Company uses special journals. It recorded in a sales journal a sale made on account to R. Stiner for $435. A few days later, R. Stiner returns $70 worth of merchandise for credit. Where should Kensington Company record the sales return? Why?

9. A $500 purchase of merchandise on account from Lore Company was properly recorded in the purchases journal. When posted, however, the amount recorded in the subsidiary ledger was $50. How might this error be discovered?

10. Why would special journals used in different businesses not be identical in format? What type of business would maintain a cash receipts journal but not include a column for accounts receivable?

11. The cash and the accounts receivable columns in the cash receipts journal were mistakenly over-added by $4,000 at the end of the month. (a) Will the customers' ledger agree with the Accounts Receivable control account? (b) Assuming no other errors, will the trial balance totals be equal?

12. One column total of a special journal is posted at month-end to only two general ledger accounts. One of these two accounts is Accounts Receivable. What is the name of this special journal? What is the other general ledger account to which that same month-end total is posted?

13. In what journal would the following transactions be recorded? (Assume that a two-column sales journal and a single-column purchases journal are used.)

a. Recording of depreciation expense for the year.

b. Credit given to a customer for merchandise purchased on credit and returned.

c. Sales of merchandise for cash.

d. Sales of merchandise on account.

e. Collection of cash on account from a customer.

f. Purchase of office supplies on account.

14. In what journal would the following transactions be recorded? (Assume that a two-column sales journal and a single-column purchases journal are used.)

a. Cash received from signing a note payable.

b. Investment of cash by the owner of the business.

c. Closing of the expense accounts at the end of the year.

d. Purchase of merchandise on account.

e. Credit received for merchandise purchased and returned to supplier.

f. Payment of cash on account due a supplier.

15. What transactions might be included in a multiple-column purchases journal that would not be included in a single-column purchases journal?

16. Give an example of a transaction in the general journal that causes an entry to be posted twice (i.e., to two accounts), one in the general ledger, the other in the subsidiary ledger. Does this affect the debit/credit equality of the general ledger?

17. Give some examples of appropriate general journal transactions for an organization using special journals.

Brief Exercises

BE7.1 (LO 1) Indicate whether each of the following statements is true or false.

Explain basic concepts of an accounting information system.

1. When designing an accounting system, we need to think about the needs and knowledge of both the top managers and various other users.
2. When the environment changes as a result of technological advances, increased competition, or government regulation, an accounting system does not have to be sufficiently flexible to meet the changes in order to save money.
3. In developing an accounting system, cost is relevant. The benefits obtained from the information disseminated must outweigh the cost of providing it.

BE7.2 (LO 1) Here is a list of words or phrases related to computerized accounting systems.

Explain basic concepts of an accounting information system.

1. Entry-level software.
2. Enterprise resource planning systems.
3. Network-compatible.
4. Audit trail.
5. Internal control.

Instructions

Match each word or phrase with the best description of it.

________ **a.** Allows multiple users to access the system at the same time.
________ **b.** Enables the tracking of all transactions.
________ **c.** Identifies suspicious transactions or likely mistakes such as wrong account numbers or duplicate transactions.
________ **d.** Large-scale computer systems that integrate all aspects of the organization including accounting, sales, human resource management, and manufacturing.
________ **e.** System for companies with revenues of less than $5 million and up to 20 employees.

Explain basic concepts of an accounting information system.

BE7.3 (LO 1) Benji Borke has prepared the following list of statements about accounting information systems.

1. The accounting information system includes each of the steps of the accounting cycle, the documents that provide evidence of transactions that have occurred, and the accounting records.
2. The benefits obtained from information provided by the accounting information system need not outweigh the cost of providing that information.
3. Designers of accounting systems must consider the needs and knowledge of various users.
4. If an accounting information system is cost-effective and provides useful output, it does not need to be flexible.

Instructions

Identify each statement as true or false. If false, indicate how to correct the statement.

Identify subsidiary ledger balances.

BE7.4 (LO 2) Presented below is information related to Gantner Company for its first month of operations. Identify the balances that appear in the accounts receivable subsidiary ledger and the accounts receivable balance that appears in the general ledger at the end of January.

Credit Sales			Cash Collections		
Jan. 7	Austin Co.	$10,000	Jan. 17	Austin Co.	$7,000
15	Diaz Co.	8,000	24	Diaz Co.	4,000
23	Noble Co.	9,000	29	Noble Co.	9,000

Identify subsidiary ledger accounts.

BE7.5 (LO 2) Identify in what ledger (general or subsidiary) each of the following accounts is shown.

a. Rent Expense.
b. Accounts Receivable—Cabrera.
c. Notes Payable.
d. Accounts Payable—Pacheco.

Identify special journals.

BE7.6 (LO 3) Identify the journal in which each of the following transactions is recorded.

a. Cash sales.
b. Owner withdrawal of cash.
c. Cash purchase of land.
d. Credit sales.
e. Purchase of merchandise on account.
f. Receipt of cash for services performed.

Identify entries to cash receipts journal.

BE7.7 (LO 3) Indicate whether each of the following debits and credits is included in the cash receipts journal. (Use "Yes" or "No" to answer this question.)

a. Debit to Sales Revenue.
b. Credit to Inventory.
c. Credit to Accounts Receivable.
d. Debit to Accounts Payable.

Identify transactions for special journals.

BE7.8 (LO 3) Villar Co. uses special journals and a general journal. Identify the journal in which each of the following transactions is recorded.

a. Purchased equipment on account.
b. Purchased merchandise on account.
c. Paid utility expense in cash.
d. Sold merchandise on account.

Identify transactions for special journals.

BE7.9 (LO 3) Identify the special journal(s) in which the following column headings appear.

a. Sales Discounts Dr.
b. Accounts Receivable Cr.
c. Cash Dr.
d. Sales Revenue Cr.
e. Inventory Dr.

Indicate postings for cash receipts journal.

BE7.10 (LO 3) Rauch Computer Components Inc. uses a multi-column cash receipts journal. Indicate which column(s) is/are posted only in total, only daily, or both in total and daily.

a. Accounts Receivable.
b. Sales Discounts.
c. Cash.
d. Other Accounts.

DO IT! Exercises

DO IT! 7.1 (LO 1) Indicate whether the following statements are true or false. If false, indicate how to correct the statement.

Explain basic concepts of an accounting information system.

1. A computerized accounting system must be customized to meet a company's needs.
2. Companies with revenues of less than $5 million and up to 20 employees generally use entry-level programs rather than ERP systems.
3. A manual accounting system provides more timely financial information than a computerized system.

DO IT! 7.2 (LO 2) Presented below is information related to Rizzo Company for its first month of operations. Determine the balances that appear in the accounts payable subsidiary ledger. What Accounts Payable balance appears in the general ledger at the end of January?

Determine subsidiary and general ledger balances.

Credit Purchases			Cash Paid		
Jan. 6	Gorst Company	$11,000	Jan. 11	Gorst Company	$ 6,500
Jan. 10	Tian Company	12,000	Jan. 16	Tian Company	12,000
Jan. 23	Maddox Company	10,000	Jan. 29	Maddox Company	7,700

DO IT! 7.3 (LO 3) Hinske Company had the following transactions during April.

Identify special journals.

1. Sold merchandise on account.
2. Purchased merchandise on account.
3. Collected cash from a sale to Renfro Company.
4. Recorded accrued interest on a note payable.
5. Paid $2,000 for supplies.

Identify the journal in which each of the transactions above is recorded.

Exercises

E7.1 (LO 2, 3) Nex Company uses both special journals and a general journal as described in this chapter. On June 30, after all monthly postings had been completed, the Accounts Receivable control account in the general ledger had a debit balance of $340,000; the Accounts Payable control account had a credit balance of $77,000.

Determine control account balances, and explain posting of special journals.

The July transactions recorded in the special journals are summarized below. No entries affecting accounts receivable and accounts payable were recorded in the general journal for July.

Sales journal	Total sales $161,400
Purchases journal	Total purchases $66,400
Cash receipts journal	Accounts receivable column total $131,000
Cash payments journal	Accounts payable column total $47,500

Instructions

a. What is the balance of the Accounts Receivable control account after the monthly postings on July 31?

b. What is the balance of the Accounts Payable control account after the monthly postings on July 31?

c. To what account(s) is the column total of $161,400 in the sales journal posted?

d. To what account(s) is the accounts receivable column total of $131,000 in the cash receipts journal posted?

E7.2 (LO 2) Writing Presented below is the subsidiary accounts receivable account of Jill Longley.

Explain postings to subsidiary ledger.

Date	Ref.	Debit	Credit	Balance
2020				
Sept. 2	S31	61,000		61,000
9	G4		14,000	47,000
27	CR8		47,000	—

Instructions

Write a memo to Sara Fogelman, chief financial officer, that explains each transaction.

Post various journals to control and subsidiary accounts.

E7.3 (LO 2, 3) On September 1, the balance of the Accounts Receivable control account in the general ledger of Montgomery Company was $10,960. The customers' subsidiary ledger contained account balances as follows: Hurley $1,440, Andino $2,640, Fowler $2,060, and Sogard $4,820. At the end of September, the various journals contained the following information.

Sales journal: Sales to Sogard $800, to Hurley $1,260, to Giambi $1,330, and to Fowler $1,600.
Cash receipts journal: Cash received from Fowler $1,310, from Sogard $3,300, from Giambi $380, from Andino $1,800, and from Hurley $1,240.
General journal: An allowance is granted to Sogard $220.

Instructions

a. Set up control and subsidiary accounts and enter the beginning balances. Do not construct the journals.

b. Post the various journals. Post the items as individual items or as totals, whichever would be the appropriate procedure. (No sales discounts given.)

c. Prepare a schedule of accounts receivable and prove the agreement of the controlling account with the subsidiary ledger at September 30, 2020.

Determine control and subsidiary ledger balances for accounts receivable.

E7.4 (LO 2) Kieschnick Company has a balance in its Accounts Receivable control account of $10,000 on January 1, 2020. The subsidiary ledger contains three accounts: Bixler Company, balance $4,000; Cuddyer Company, balance $2,500; and Freeze Company. During January, the following receivable-related transactions occurred.

	Credit Sales	Collections	Returns
Bixler Company	$9,000	$8,000	$ -0-
Cuddyer Company	7,000	2,500	3,000
Freeze Company	8,500	9,000	-0-

Instructions

a. What is the January 1 balance in the Freeze Company subsidiary account?

b. What is the January 31 balance in the control account?

c. Compute the balances in the subsidiary accounts at the end of the month.

d. Which January transaction would not be recorded in a special journal?

Determine control and subsidiary ledger balances for accounts payable.

E7.5 (LO 2) Pennington Company has a balance in its Accounts Payable control account of $9,250 on January 1, 2020. The subsidiary ledger contains three accounts: Hale Company, balance $3,000; Janish Company, balance $1,875; and Valdez Company. During January, the following payable-related transactions occurred.

	Purchases	Payments	Returns
Hale Company	$6,750	$6,000	$ -0-
Janish Company	5,250	1,875	2,250
Valdez Company	6,375	6,750	-0-

Instructions

a. What is the January 1 balance in the Valdez Company subsidiary account?

b. What is the January 31 balance in the control account?

c. Compute the balances in the subsidiary accounts at the end of the month.

d. Which January transaction would not be recorded in a special journal?

Record transactions in sales and purchases journal.

E7.6 (LO 3) Gomes Company uses special journals and a general journal. The following transactions occurred during September 2020.

Sept.	2	Sold merchandise on account to H. Drew, invoice no. 101, $620, terms n/30. The cost of the merchandise sold was $420.
	10	Purchased merchandise on account from A. Pagan $650, terms 2/10, n/30.
	12	Purchased office equipment on account from R. Cairo $6,500.
	21	Sold merchandise on account to G. Holliday, invoice no. 102 for $800, terms 2/10, n/30. The cost of the merchandise sold was $480.

25 Purchased merchandise on account from D. Downs $860, terms n/30.
27 Sold merchandise to S. Miller for $700 cash. The cost of the merchandise sold was $400.

Instructions

a. Prepare a sales journal (see Illustration 7.7) and a single-column purchases journal (see Illustration 7.13). (Use page 1 for each journal.)

b. Record the transaction(s) for September that should be journalized in the sales journal and the purchases journal.

E7.7 (LO 3) R. Santiago Co. uses special journals and a general journal. The following transactions occurred during May 2020.

Record transactions in cash receipts and cash payments journal.

May 1 R. Santiago invested $40,000 cash in the business.
2 Sold merchandise to Lawrie Co. for $6,300 cash. The cost of the merchandise sold was $4,200.
3 Purchased merchandise for $7,700 from J. Moskos using check no. 101.
14 Paid salary to H. Rivera $700 by issuing check no. 102.
16 Sold merchandise on account to K. Stanton for $900, terms n/30. The cost of the merchandise sold was $630.
22 A check of $9,000 is received from M. Mangini in full for invoice 101; no discount given.

Instructions

a. Prepare a multiple-column cash receipts journal (see Illustration 7.9) and a multiple-column cash payments journal (see Illustration 7.16). (Use page 1 for each journal.)

b. Record the transaction(s) for May that should be journalized in the cash receipts journal and cash payments journal.

E7.8 (LO 3) Francisco Company uses the columnar cash journals illustrated in the textbook. In April, the following selected cash transactions occurred.

Explain journalizing in cash journals.

1. Made a refund to a customer as an allowance for damaged goods.
2. Received collection from customer within the 3% discount period.
3. Purchased merchandise for cash.
4. Paid a creditor within the 3% discount period.
5. Received collection from customer after the 3% discount period had expired.
6. Paid freight on merchandise purchased.
7. Paid cash for office equipment.
8. Received cash refund from supplier for merchandise returned.
9. Withdrew cash for personal use of owner.
10. Made cash sales.

Instructions

Indicate (a) the journal, and (b) the columns in the journal that should be used in recording each transaction.

E7.9 (LO 3) Writing Hasselback Company has the following selected transactions during March.

Journalize transactions in general journal and explain postings.

Mar. 2 Purchased equipment costing $7,400 from Bole Company on account.
5 Received credit of $410 from Carwell Company for merchandise damaged in shipment to Hasselback.
7 Issued credit of $400 to Dempsey Company for merchandise the customer returned. The returned merchandise had a cost of $260.

Hasselback Company uses a one-column purchases journal, a sales journal, the columnar cash journals used in the text, and a general journal.

Instructions

a. Journalize the transactions in the general journal.

b. In a brief memo to the president of Hasselback Company, explain the postings to the control and subsidiary accounts from each type of journal.

E7.10 (LO 3) The following are some typical transactions incurred by Ricketts Company.

Indicate journalizing in special journals.

1. Payment of creditors on account.
2. Return of merchandise sold for credit.

3. Collection on account from customers.
4. Sale of land for cash.
5. Sale of merchandise on account.
6. Sale of merchandise for cash.
7. Received credit for merchandise purchased on credit.
8. Sales discount taken on goods sold.
9. Payment of employee wages.
10. Income summary closed to owner's capital.
11. Depreciation on building.
12. Purchase of office supplies for cash.
13. Purchase of merchandise on account.

Instructions

For each transaction, indicate whether it would normally be recorded in a cash receipts journal, cash payments journal, sales journal, single-column purchases journal, or general journal.

Explain posting to control account and subsidiary ledger.

E7.11 (LO 2, 3) The general ledger of Hensley Company contained the following Accounts Payable control account (in T-account form). Also shown is the related subsidiary ledger.

GENERAL LEDGER

Accounts Payable

Feb. 15	General journal	1,400	Feb. 1	Balance	26,025
28	?	?	5	General journal	265
			11	General journal	550
			28	Purchases	13,400
			Feb. 28	Balance	10,500

ACCOUNTS PAYABLE LEDGER

Benton

	Feb. 28	Bal. 4,600

Dooley

	Feb. 28	Bal. 2,300

Parks

	Feb. 28	Bal. ?

Instructions

a. Indicate the missing posting reference and amount in the control account, and the missing ending balance in the subsidiary ledger.

b. Indicate the amounts in the control account that were dual-posted (i.e., posted to the control account and the subsidiary accounts).

Prepare purchases and general journals.

E7.12 (LO 2, 3) Selected accounts from the ledgers of Youngblood Company at July 31 showed the following.

GENERAL LEDGER

Equipment — No. 157

Date	Explanation	Ref.	Debit	Credit	Balance
July 1		G1	3,900		3,900

Accounts Payable — No. 201

Date	Explanation	Ref.	Debit	Credit	Balance
July 1		G1		3,900	3,900
15		G1		400	4,300
18		G1	100		4,200
25		G1	200		4,000
31		P1		9,300	13,300

Inventory — No. 120

Date	Explanation	Ref.	Debit	Credit	Balance
July 15		G1	400		400
18		G1		100	300
25		G1		200	100
31		P1	9,300		9,400

ACCOUNTS PAYABLE LEDGER

Flaherty Equipment Co.

Date	Explanation	Ref.	Debit	Credit	Balance
July 1		G1		3,900	3,900

Weller Co.

Date	Explanation	Ref.	Debit	Credit	Balance
July 14		P1		1,100	1,100
25		G1	200		900

Marsh Co.

Date	Explanation	Ref.	Debit	Credit	Balance
July 3		P1		2,400	2,400
20		P1		1,700	4,100

Yates Co.

Date	Explanation	Ref.	Debit	Credit	Balance
July 12		P1		500	500
21		P1		600	1,100

Lange Corp

Date	Explanation	Ref.	Debit	Credit	Balance
July 17		P1		1,400	1,400
18		G1	100		1,300
29		P1		1,600	2,900

Bernardo Inc.

Date	Explanation	Ref.	Debit	Credit	Balance
July 15		G1		400	400

Instructions

From the data prepare:

a. The single-column purchases journal for July.

b. The general journal entries for July.

Determine correct posting amount to control account.

E7.13 (LO 2, 3) Tresh Products uses both special journals and a general journal as described in this chapter. Tresh also posts customers' accounts in the accounts receivable subsidiary ledger. The postings for the most recent month are included in the subsidiary T-accounts below.

Estes

Bal.	340	250
	200	

Gehrke

Bal.	150	150
	290	

Truong

Bal.	-0-	145
	145	

Weiser

Bal.	120	120
	190	
	150	

Instructions

Determine the correct amount of the end-of-month posting from the sales journal to the Accounts Receivable control account.

Compute balances in various accounts.

E7.14 (LO 3) Selected account balances for Hulse Company at January 1, 2020, are presented below.

Accounts Payable	$14,000
Accounts Receivable	22,000
Cash	17,000
Inventory	13,500

Hulse's sales journal for January shows a total of $110,000 in the selling-price column, and its one-column purchases journal for January shows a total of $77,000.

The column totals in Hulse's cash receipts journal are Cash Dr. $61,000, Sales Discounts Dr. $1,100, Accounts Receivable Cr. $45,000, Sales Revenue Cr. $6,000, and Other Accounts Cr. $11,100.

The column totals in Hulse's cash payments journal for January are Cash Cr. $55,000, Inventory Cr. $1,000, Accounts Payable Dr. $46,000, and Other Accounts Dr. $10,000. Hulse's total cost of goods sold for January is $63,600.

Accounts Payable, Accounts Receivable, Cash, Inventory, and Sales Revenue are not involved in the Other Accounts column in either the cash receipts or cash payments journal, and are not involved in any general journal entries.

Instructions

Compute the January 31 balance for Hulse in the following accounts.

a. Accounts Payable.

b. Accounts Receivable.

c. Cash.

d. Inventory.

e. Sales Revenue.

Problems: Set A

Journalize transactions in cash receipts journal; post to control account and subsidiary ledger.

GLS

P7.1A (LO 2, 3) Kozma Company's chart of accounts includes the following selected accounts.

101	Cash	401	Sales Revenue
112	Accounts Receivable	414	Sales Discounts
120	Inventory	505	Cost of Goods Sold
301	Owner's Capital		

On April 1, the accounts receivable ledger of Kozma Company showed the following balances: Morrow $1,550, Rose $1,200, Jennings Co. $2,900, and Dent $2,200. The April transactions involving the receipt of cash were as follows.

Apr.	1	The owner, T. Kozma, invested additional cash in the business $7,200.
	4	Received check for payment of account from Dent less 2% cash discount.
	5	Received check for $920 in payment of invoice no. 307 from Jennings Co.
	8	Made cash sales of merchandise totaling $7,245. The cost of the merchandise sold was $4,347.
	10	Received check for $600 in payment of invoice no. 309 from Morrow.
	11	Received cash refund from a supplier for damaged merchandise $740.
	23	Received check for $1,000 in payment of invoice no. 310 from Jennings Co.
	29	Received check for payment of account from Rose (no cash discount allowed).

Instructions

a. Balancing totals $25,452

a. Journalize the transactions above in a six-column cash receipts journal with columns for Cash Dr., Sales Discounts Dr., Accounts Receivable Cr., Sales Revenue Cr., Other Accounts Cr., and Cost of Goods Sold Dr./Inventory Cr. Foot and cross-foot the journal.

b. Insert the beginning balances in the Accounts Receivable control and subsidiary accounts, and post the April transactions to these accounts.

c. Accounts Receivable $1,930

c. Prove the agreement of the control account and subsidiary account balances.

Journalize transactions in cash payments journal; post to control account and subsidiary ledgers.

GLS

P7.2A (LO 2, 3) Reineke Company's chart of accounts includes the following selected accounts.

101	Cash	201	Accounts Payable
120	Inventory	306	Owner's Drawings
130	Prepaid Insurance	505	Cost of Goods Sold
157	Equipment		

On October 1, the accounts payable ledger of Reineke Company showed the following balances: Uggla Company $2,700, Orr Co. $2,500, Rosenthal Co. $1,800, and Clevenger Company $3,700. The October transactions involving the payment of cash were as follows.

Oct.	1	Purchased merchandise, check no. 63, $300.
	3	Purchased equipment, check no. 64, $800.
	5	Paid Uggla Company balance due of $2,700, less 2% discount, check no. 65, $2,646.
	10	Purchased merchandise, check no. 66, $2,550.
	15	Paid Rosenthal Co. balance due of $1,800, check no. 67.
	16	C. Reineke, the owner, pays his personal insurance premium of $400, check no. 68.
	19	Paid Orr Co. in full for invoice no. 610, $2,000 less 2% cash discount, check no. 69, $1,960.
	29	Paid Clevenger Company in full for invoice no. 264, $2,500, check no. 70.

Instructions

a. Balancing totals $13,050

a. Journalize the transactions above in a four-column cash payments journal with columns for Other Accounts Dr., Accounts Payable Dr., Inventory Cr., and Cash Cr. Foot and cross-foot the journal.

b. Insert the beginning balances in the Accounts Payable control and subsidiary accounts, and post the October transactions to these accounts.

c. Accounts Payable $1,700

c. Prove the agreement of the control account and the subsidiary account balances.

Journalize transactions in multi-column purchases journal and sales journal; post to the general and subsidiary ledgers.

GLS

P7.3A (LO 2, 3) The chart of accounts of LR Company includes the following selected accounts.

112	Accounts Receivable	401	Sales Revenue
120	Inventory	412	Sales Returns and Allowances
126	Supplies	505	Cost of Goods Sold
157	Equipment	610	Advertising Expense
201	Accounts Payable		

In July, the following transactions were completed. All purchases and sales were on account. The cost of all merchandise sold was 70% of the sales price.

July 1 Purchased merchandise from Eby Company $8,000.
2 Received freight bill from Shaw Shipping on Eby purchase $400.
3 Made sales to Fort Company $1,300 and to Hefner Bros. $1,500.
5 Purchased merchandise from Getz Company $3,200.
8 Received credit on merchandise returned to Getz Company $300.
13 Purchased store supplies from Dayne Supply $720.
15 Purchased merchandise from Eby Company $3,600 and from Bosco Company $4,300.
16 Made sales to Aybar Company $3,450 and to Hefner Bros. $1,870.
18 Received bill for advertising from Welton Advertisements $600.
21 Sales were made to Fort Company $310 and to Duncan Company $2,800.
22 Granted allowance to Fort Company for merchandise damaged in shipment $40.
24 Purchased merchandise from Getz Company $3,000.
26 Purchased equipment from Dayne Supply $900.
28 Received freight bill from Shaw Shipping on Getz purchase of July 24, $380.
30 Sales were made to Aybar Company $5,600.

Instructions

a. Journalize the transactions above in a purchases journal, a sales journal, and a general journal. The purchases journal should have the following column headings: Date, Account Credited (Debited), Ref., Accounts Payable Cr., Inventory Dr., and Other Accounts Dr.

b. Post to both the general and subsidiary ledger accounts. (Assume that all accounts have zero beginning balances.)

c. Prove the agreement of the control and subsidiary accounts.

a. Purchases journal—Accounts Payable $25,100
Sales journal—Sales Revenue $16,830

c. Accounts Receivable $16,790
Accounts Payable $24,800

P7.4A (LO 2, 3) Selected accounts from the chart of accounts of Mercer Company are shown below.

Journalize transactions in special journals.

GLS

101	Cash	401	Sales Revenue
112	Accounts Receivable	412	Sales Returns and Allowances
120	Inventory	414	Sales Discounts
126	Supplies	505	Cost of Goods Sold
157	Equipment	726	Salaries and Wages Expense
201	Accounts Payable		

The cost of all merchandise sold was 60% of the sales price. During January, Mercer completed the following transactions.

Jan. 3 Purchased merchandise on account from Gallagher Co. $9,000.
4 Purchased supplies for cash $80.
4 Sold merchandise on account to Wheeler $5,250, invoice no. 371, terms 1/10, n/30.
5 Returned $300 worth of damaged goods purchased on account from Gallagher Co. on January 3.
6 Made cash sales for the week totaling $3,150.
8 Purchased merchandise on account from Phegley Co. $4,500.
9 Sold merchandise on account to Linton Corp. $5,400, invoice no. 372, terms 1/10, n/30.
11 Purchased merchandise on account from Cora Co. $3,700.
13 Paid in full Gallagher Co. on account less a 2% discount.
13 Made cash sales for the week totaling $6,260.
15 Received payment from Linton Corp. for invoice no. 372.
15 Paid semi-monthly salaries of $14,300 to employees.
17 Received payment from Wheeler for invoice no. 371.
17 Sold merchandise on account to Delaney Co. $1,200, invoice no. 373, terms 1/10, n/30.
19 Purchased equipment on account from Dozier Corp. $5,500.
20 Cash sales for the week totaled $3,200.
20 Paid in full Phegley Co. on account less a 2% discount.
23 Purchased merchandise on account from Gallagher Co. $7,800.
24 Purchased merchandise on account from Atchison Corp. $5,100.
27 Made cash sales for the week totaling $4,230.
30 Received payment from Delaney Co. for invoice no. 373.
31 Paid semi-monthly salaries of $13,200 to employees.
31 Sold merchandise on account to Wheeler $9,330, invoice no. 374, terms 1/10, n/30.

Mercer Company uses the following journals.

1. Sales journal.
2. Single-column purchases journal.
3. Cash receipts journal with columns for Cash Dr., Sales Discounts Dr., Accounts Receivable Cr., Sales Revenue Cr., Other Accounts Cr., and Cost of Goods Sold Dr./Inventory Cr.

4. Cash payments journal with columns for Other Accounts Dr., Accounts Payable Dr., Inventory Cr., and Cash Cr.
5. General journal.

Instructions

a. Sales journal $21,180
Purchases journal $30,100
Cash receipts journal balancing total $38,794
Cash payments journal balancing total $40,780

Using the selected accounts provided:

a. Record the January transactions in the appropriate journal noted.

b. Foot and cross-foot all special journals.

c. Show how postings would be made by placing ledger account numbers and checkmarks as needed in the journals. (Actual posting to ledger accounts is not required.)

Journalize in sales and cash receipts journals; post; prepare a trial balance; prove control to subsidiary; prepare adjusting entries; prepare an adjusted trial balance.

GLS

P7.5A (LO 2, 3) Presented below are the purchases and cash payments journals for Fornelli Co. for its first month of operations.

PURCHASES JOURNAL **P1**

Date	Account Credited	Ref.	Inventory Dr. Accounts Payable Cr.
July 4	N. Alvarado		6,800
5	F. Rees		8,100
11	J. Gallup		5,920
13	C. Werly		15,300
20	M. Mangus		7,900
			44,020

CASH PAYMENTS JOURNAL **CP1**

Date	Account Debited	Ref.	Other Accounts Dr.	Accounts Payable Dr.	Inventory Cr.	Cash Cr.
July 4	Supplies		600			600
10	F. Rees			8,100	81	8,019
11	Prepaid Rent		6,000			6,000
15	N. Alvarado			6,800		6,800
19	Owner's Drawings		2,500			2,500
21	C. Werly			15,300	153	15,147
			9,100	30,200	234	39,066

In addition, the following transactions have not been journalized for July. The cost of all merchandise sold was 65% of the sales price.

July	1	The founder, N. Fornelli, invests $80,000 in cash.
	6	Sell merchandise on account to Dow Co. $6,200 terms 1/10, n/30.
	7	Make cash sales totaling $8,000.
	8	Sell merchandise on account to S. Goebel $4,600, terms 1/10, n/30.
	10	Sell merchandise on account to W. Leiss $4,900, terms 1/10, n/30.
	13	Receive payment in full from S. Goebel.
	16	Receive payment in full from W. Leiss.
	20	Receive payment in full from Dow Co.
	21	Sell merchandise on account to H. Kenney $5,000, terms 1/10, n/30.
	29	Returned damaged goods to N. Alvarado and received cash refund of $420.

Instructions

a. Open the following accounts in the general ledger.

101	Cash	306	Owner's Drawings
112	Accounts Receivable	401	Sales Revenue
120	Inventory	414	Sales Discounts
126	Supplies	505	Cost of Goods Sold
131	Prepaid Rent	631	Supplies Expense
201	Accounts Payable	729	Rent Expense
301	Owner's Capital		

b. Sales journal total $20,700
Cash receipts journal balancing total $109,320

b. Journalize the transactions that have not been journalized in the sales journal and the cash receipts journal (see Illustration 7.9).

c. Post to the accounts receivable and accounts payable subsidiary ledgers. Follow the sequence of transactions as shown in the problem.

d. Post the individual entries and totals to the general ledger.

e. Prepare a trial balance at July 31, 2020.

f. Determine whether the subsidiary ledgers agree with the control accounts in the general ledger.

g. The following adjustments at the end of July are necessary.

1. A count of supplies indicates that $140 is still on hand.
2. Recognize rent expense for July, $500.

Prepare the necessary entries in the general journal. Post the entries to the general ledger.

h. Prepare an adjusted trial balance at July 31, 2020.

e. Totals $122,520

f. Accounts Receivable $5,000
Accounts Payable $13,820

h. Totals $122,520

P7.6A (LO 2, 3) The post-closing trial balance for Horner Co. is shown below.

Journalize in special journals; post; prepare a trial balance.

GLS

Horner Co.
Post-Closing Trial Balance
December 31, 2020

	Debit	Credit
Cash	$ 41,500	
Accounts Receivable	15,000	
Notes Receivable	45,000	
Inventory	23,000	
Equipment	6,450	
Accumulated Depreciation—Equipment		$ 1,500
Accounts Payable		43,000
Owner's Capital		86,450
	$130,950	$130,950

The subsidiary ledgers contain the following information: (1) accounts receivable—B. Hannigan $2,500, I. Kirk $7,500, and T. Hodges $5,000; (2) accounts payable—T. Igawa $12,000, D. Danford $18,000, and K. Thayer $13,000. The cost of all merchandise sold was 60% of the sales price.

The transactions for January 2021 are as follows.

Jan. 3 Sell merchandise to M. Ziesmer $8,000, terms 2/10, n/30.
5 Purchase merchandise from E. Pheatt $2,000, terms 2/10, n/30.
7 Receive a check from T. Hodges $3,500.
11 Pay freight on merchandise purchased $300.
12 Pay rent of $1,000 for January.
13 Receive payment in full from M. Ziesmer.
14 Post all entries to the subsidiary ledgers. Issued credit of $300 to B. Hannigan for returned merchandise.
15 Send K. Thayer a check for $12,870 in full payment of account, discount $130.
17 Purchase merchandise from G. Roland $1,600, terms 2/10, n/30.
18 Pay sales salaries of $2,800 and office salaries $2,000.
20 Give D. Danford a 60-day note for $18,000 in full payment of account payable.
23 Total cash sales amount to $9,100.
24 Post all entries to the subsidiary ledgers. Sell merchandise on account to I. Kirk $7,400, terms 1/10, n/30.
27 Send E. Pheatt a check for $950.
29 Receive payment on a note of $40,000 from B. Stout.
30 Post all entries to the subsidiary ledgers. Return merchandise of $300 to G. Roland for credit.

Instructions

a. Open general and subsidiary ledger accounts for the following.

101	Cash	301	Owner's Capital
112	Accounts Receivable	401	Sales Revenue
115	Notes Receivable	412	Sales Returns and Allowances
120	Inventory	414	Sales Discounts
157	Equipment	505	Cost of Goods Sold
158	Accumulated Depreciation—Equipment	726	Salaries and Wages Expense
200	Notes Payable	729	Rent Expense
201	Accounts Payable		

b. Sales journal $15,400
Purchases journal $3,600
Cash receipts journal (balancing) $66,060
Cash payments journal (balancing) $20,050

d. Totals $144,800

e. Accounts Receivable $18,600
Accounts Payable $14,350

b. Record the January transactions in a sales journal, a single-column purchases journal, a cash receipts journal (see Illustration 7.9), a cash payments journal (see Illustration 7.16), and a general journal.

c. Post the appropriate amounts to the general ledger.

d. Prepare a trial balance at January 31, 2021.

e. Determine whether the subsidiary ledgers agree with controlling accounts in the general ledger.

Ethics Case

EC7 Wiemers Products Company operates three divisions, each with its own manufacturing plant and marketing/sales force. The corporate headquarters and central accounting office are in Wiemers, and the plants are in Freeport, Rockport, and Bayport, all within 50 miles of Wiemers. Corporate management treats each division as an independent profit center and encourages competition among them. They each have similar but different product lines. As a competitive incentive, bonuses are awarded each year to the employees of the fastest-growing and most-profitable division.

Indy Grover is the manager of Wiemers's centralized computerized accounting operation that enters the sales transactions and maintains the accounts receivable for all three divisions. Indy came up in the accounting ranks from the Bayport division where his wife, several relatives, and many friends still work.

As sales documents are entered into the computer, the originating division is identified by code. Most sales documents (95%) are coded, but some (5%) are not coded or are coded incorrectly. As the manager, Indy has instructed the data-entry personnel to assign the Bayport code to all uncoded and incorrectly coded sales documents. This is done, he says, "in order to expedite processing and to keep the computer files current since they are updated daily." All receivables and cash collections for all three divisions are handled by Wiemers as one subsidiary accounts receivable ledger.

Instructions

a. Who are the stakeholders in this situation?

b. What are the ethical issues in this case?

c. How might the system be improved to prevent this situation?

Comprehensive Accounting Cycle Review

ACR7.1 (Perpetual Method) Jeter Co. uses a perpetual inventory system and both an accounts receivable and an accounts payable subsidiary ledger. Balances related to both the general ledger and the subsidiary ledgers for Jeter are indicated in the working papers presented below. Also following are a series of transactions for Jeter Co. for the month of January. Credit sales terms are 2/10, n/30. The cost of all merchandise sold was 60% of the sales price.

GENERAL LEDGER

Account Number	Account Title	January 1 Opening Balance
101	Cash	$35,750
112	Accounts Receivable	13,000
115	Notes Receivable	39,000
120	Inventory	18,000
126	Supplies	1,000
130	Prepaid Insurance	2,000
157	Equipment	6,450
158	Accumulated Depreciation—Equip.	1,500
201	Accounts Payable	35,000
301	Owner's Capital	78,700

Schedule of Accounts Receivable
(from accounts receivable subsidiary ledger)

Customer	January 1 Opening Balance
R. Beltre	$1,500
B. Santos	7,500
S. Mahay	4,000

Schedule of Accounts Payable
(from accounts payable subsidiary ledger)

Creditor	January 1 Opening Balance
S. Meek	$ 9,000
R. Moses	15,000
D. Saito	11,000

Jan. 3 Sell merchandise on account to B. Corpas $3,600, invoice no. 510, and to J. Revere $1,800, invoice no. 511.
5 Purchase merchandise from S. Gamel $5,000 and D. Posey $2,200, terms n/30.
7 Receive checks from S. Mahay $4,000 and B. Santos $2,000 after discount period has lapsed.
8 Pay freight on merchandise purchased $235.
9 Send checks to S. Meek for $9,000 less 2% cash discount, and to D. Saito for $11,000 less 1% cash discount.
9 Issue credit of $300 to J. Revere for merchandise returned.
10 Daily cash sales from January 1 to January 10 total $15,500. Make one journal entry for these sales.
11 Sell merchandise on account to R. Beltre $1,600, invoice no. 512, and to S. Mahay $900, invoice no. 513.
12 Pay rent of $1,000 for January.
13 Receive payment in full from B. Corpas and J. Revere less cash discounts.
15 Withdraw $800 cash by M. Jeter for personal use.
15 Post all entries to the subsidiary ledgers.
16 Purchase merchandise from D. Saito $15,000, terms 1/10, n/30; S. Meek $14,200, terms 2/10, n/30; and S. Gamel $1,500, terms n/30.
17 Pay $400 cash for office supplies.
18 Return $200 of merchandise to S. Meek and receive credit.
20 Daily cash sales from January 11 to January 20 total $20,100. Make one journal entry for these sales.
21 Issue $15,000 note, maturing in 90 days, to R. Moses in payment of balance due.
21 Receive payment in full from S. Mahay less cash discount.
22 Sell merchandise on account to B. Corpas $2,700, invoice no. 514, and to R. Beltre $2,300, invoice no. 515.
22 Post all entries to the subsidiary ledgers.
23 Send checks to D. Saito and S. Meek for full payment less cash discounts.
25 Sell merchandise on account to B. Santos $3,500, invoice no. 516, and to J. Revere $6,100, invoice no. 517.
27 Purchase merchandise from D. Saito $14,500, terms 1/10, n/30; D. Posey $3,200, terms n/30; and S. Gamel $5,400, terms n/30.
27 Post all entries to the subsidiary ledgers.
28 Pay $200 cash for office supplies.
31 Daily cash sales from January 21 to January 31 total $21,300. Make one journal entry for these sales.
31 Pay sales salaries $4,300 and office salaries $3,800.

Instructions

a. Record the January transactions in a sales journal, a single-column purchases journal, a cash receipts journal as shown in Illustration 7.9, a cash payments journal as shown in Illustration 7.16, and a two-column general journal.

b. Post the journals to the general ledger.

c. Prepare a trial balance at January 31, 2020, in the trial balance columns of the worksheet. Complete the worksheet using the following additional information.

1. Office supplies at January 31 total $900.
2. Insurance coverage expires on October 31, 2020.
3. Annual depreciation on the equipment is $1,500.
4. Interest of $50 has accrued on the note payable.

d. Prepare a multiple-step income statement and an owner's equity statement for January and a classified balance sheet at the end of January.

e. Prepare and post adjusting and closing entries.

f. Prepare a post-closing trial balance, and determine whether the subsidiary ledgers agree with the control accounts in the general ledger.

ACR7.2 **(Periodic Inventory)** McBride Company has the following opening account balances in its general and subsidiary ledgers on January 1 and uses the periodic inventory system. All accounts have normal debit and credit balances.

GENERAL LEDGER

Account Number	Account Title	January 1 Opening Balance
101	Cash	$33,750
112	Accounts Receivable	13,000
115	Notes Receivable	39,000
120	Inventory	20,000
126	Supplies	1,000
130	Prepaid Insurance	2,000
157	Equipment	6,450
158	Accumulated Depreciation—Equip.	1,500
201	Accounts Payable	35,000
301	Owner's Capital	78,700

Schedule of Accounts Receivable
(from accounts receivable subsidiary ledger)

Customer	January 1 Opening Balance
R. Kotsay	$1,500
B. Boxberger	7,500
S. Andrus	4,000

Schedule of Accounts Payable
(from accounts payable subsidiary ledger)

Creditor	January 1 Opening Balance
S. Otero	$ 9,000
R. Rasmus	15,000
D. Baroni	11,000

In addition, the following transactions have not been journalized for January 2020.

Jan. 3 Sell merchandise on account to B. Berg $3,600, invoice no. 510, and J. Lutz $1,800, invoice no. 511.
5 Purchase merchandise on account from S. Colt $5,000 and D. Kahn $2,700.
7 Receive checks for $4,000 from S. Andrus and $2,000 from B. Boxberger.
8 Pay freight on merchandise purchased $180.
9 Send checks to S. Otero for $9,000 and D. Baroni for $11,000.
9 Issue credit of $300 to J. Lutz for merchandise returned.
10 Cash sales from January 1 to January 10 total $15,500. Make one journal entry for these sales.
11 Sell merchandise on account to R. Kotsay for $2,900, invoice no. 512, and to S. Andrus $900, invoice no. 513.
Post all entries to the subsidiary ledgers.
12 Pay rent of $1,000 for January.
13 Receive payment in full from B. Berg and J. Lutz.
15 Withdraw $800 cash by I. McBride for personal use.
16 Purchase merchandise on account from D. Baroni for $12,000, from S. Otero for $13,900, and from S. Colt for $1,500.
17 Pay $400 cash for supplies.
18 Return $200 of merchandise to S. Otero and receive credit.
20 Cash sales from January 11 to January 20 total $17,500. Make one journal entry for these sales.
21 Issue $15,000 note to R. Rasmus in payment of balance due.
21 Receive payment in full from S. Andrus.
Post all entries to the subsidiary ledgers.
22 Sell merchandise on account to B. Berg for $3,700, invoice no. 514, and to R. Kotsay for $800, invoice no. 515.
23 Send checks to D. Baroni and S. Otero in full payment.
25 Sell merchandise on account to B. Boxberger for $3,500, invoice no. 516, and to J. Lutz for $6,100, invoice no. 517.
27 Purchase merchandise on account from D. Baroni for $12,500, from D. Kahn for $1,200, and from S. Colt for $2,800.
28 Pay $200 cash for office supplies.
31 Cash sales from January 21 to January 31 total $22,920. Make one journal entry for these sales.
31 Pay sales salaries of $4,300 and office salaries of $3,600.

Instructions

a. Record the January transactions in the appropriate journal—sales, purchases, cash receipts, cash payments, and general.

b. Post the journals to the general and subsidiary ledgers. Add and number new accounts in an orderly fashion as needed.

c. Prepare a trial balance at January 31, 2020, using a worksheet. Complete the worksheet using the following additional information.

   1. Supplies at January 31 total $700.
   2. Insurance coverage expires on October 31, 2020.
   3. Annual depreciation on the equipment is $1,500.
   4. Interest of $30 has accrued on the note payable.
   5. Inventory at January 31 is $15,000.

d. Prepare a multiple-step income statement and an owner's equity statement for January and a classified balance sheet at the end of January.

e. Prepare and post the adjusting and closing entries.

f. Prepare a post-closing trial balance, and determine whether the subsidiary ledgers agree with the control accounts in the general ledger.

Expand Your Critical Thinking

Real-World Focus

CT7.1 **Sage 50** provides some of the leading accounting software packages. Information related to its products is found at its website.

Instructions

Review the features related to its products and then be ready to discuss them with the class.

Decision-Making Across the Organization

CT7.2 Ermler & Trump is a wholesaler of small appliances and parts. Ermler & Trump is operated by two owners, Jack Ermler and Andrea Trump. In addition, the company has one employee, a repair specialist, who is on a fixed salary. Revenues are earned through the sale of appliances to retailers (approximately 75% of total revenues), appliance parts to do-it-yourselfers (10%), and the repair of appliances brought to the store (15%). Appliance sales are made on both a credit and cash basis. Customers are billed on prenumbered sales invoices. Credit terms are always net/30 days. All parts sales and repair work are cash only.

Merchandise is purchased on account from the manufacturers of both the appliances and the parts. Practically all suppliers offer cash discounts for prompt payments, and it is company policy to take all discounts. Most cash payments are made by check. Checks are most frequently issued to suppliers, to trucking companies for freight on merchandise purchases, and to newspapers, radio, and TV stations for advertising. All advertising bills are paid as received. Jack and Andrea each make a monthly drawing in cash for personal living expenses. The salaried repairman is paid twice monthly. Ermler & Trump currently has a manual accounting system.

Instructions

With the class divided into groups, answer the following.

a. Identify the special journals that Ermler & Trump should have in its manual accounting system. List the column headings appropriate for each of the special journals.

b. What control and subsidiary accounts should be included in Ermler & Trump's manual accounting system? Why?

Communication Activity

CT7.3 Jill Locey, a classmate, has a part-time bookkeeping job. She is concerned about the inefficiencies in journalizing and posting transactions. Ben Newell is the owner of the company where Jill works. In response to numerous complaints from Jill and others, Ben hired two additional bookkeepers a month ago. However, the inefficiencies have continued at an even higher rate. The accounting information system for the company has only a general journal and a general ledger. Ben refuses to install a computerized accounting system.

Instructions

Now that Jill is an expert in manual accounting information systems, she decides to send a letter to Ben Newell explaining (1) why the additional personnel did not help and (2) what changes should be made to improve the efficiency of the accounting department. Write the letter that you think Jill should send.

All About You

CT7.4 In this chapter, you learned about a basic manual accounting information system. Computerized accounting systems range from the very basic and inexpensive to the very elaborate and expensive. However, even the most sophisticated systems are based on the fundamental structures and relationships that you learned in this chapter.

Instructions

Go to WileyPLUS and review the demonstration that is provided for the general ledger software package that is used with this textbook. Prepare a brief explanation of how the general ledger system works—that is, how it is used and what information it provides.

A Look at IFRS

LEARNING OBJECTIVE 4

Compare accounting information systems under GAAP and IFRS.

As discussed in Chapter 1, IFRS is growing in acceptance around the world. For example, recent statistics indicate a substantial number of the Global Fortune 500 companies use IFRS. And the chairman of the IASB predicts that IFRS adoption will grow from its current level of 115 countries to nearly 150 countries in the near future.

When countries accept IFRS for use as accepted accounting policies, companies need guidance to ensure that their first IFRS financial statements contain high-quality information. Specifically, *IFRS 1* requires that information in a company's first IFRS statements (1) be transparent, (2) provide a suitable starting point, and (3) have a cost that does not exceed the benefits.

Key Points

Following are the key similarities and differences between GAAP and IFRS related to accounting information systems.

Similarities

- The basic concepts related to an accounting information system are the same under GAAP and IFRS.
- The use of subsidiary ledgers and control accounts, as well as the system used for recording transactions, are the same under GAAP and IFRS.

Differences

- Many companies will be going through a substantial conversion process to switch from their current reporting standards to IFRS.
- Upon first-time adoption of IFRS, a company must present at least one year of comparative information under IFRS.

Looking to the Future

The basic recording process shown in this textbook is followed by companies around the globe. It is unlikely to change in the future. The definitional structure of assets, liabilities, equity, revenues, and expenses may change over time as the IASB and FASB evaluate their overall conceptual framework for establishing accounting standards. In addition, high-quality international accounting requires both high-quality accounting standards and high-quality auditing. Similar to the convergence of GAAP and IFRS, there is a movement to improve international auditing standards.

CHAPTER 8

© James Pauls/iStockphoto

Fraud, Internal Control, and Cash

Chapter Preview

As the following Feature Story about recording cash sales at **Barriques** indicates, control of cash is important to ensure that fraud does not occur. Companies also need controls to safeguard other types of assets. For example, Barriques undoubtedly has controls to prevent the theft of food and supplies, and controls to prevent the theft of tableware and dishes from its kitchen.

In this chapter, we explain the essential features of an internal control system and how it prevents fraud. We also describe how those controls apply to a specific asset—cash. The applications include some controls with which you may be already familiar, such as the use of a bank.

Feature Story

Minding the Money in Madison

For many years, **Barriques** in Madison, Wisconsin, has been named the city's favorite coffeehouse. Barriques not only does a booming business in coffee but also has wonderful baked goods, delicious sandwiches, and a fine selection of wines.

"Our customer base ranges from college students to neighborhood residents as well as visitors to our capital city," says bookkeeper Kerry Stoppleworth, who joined the company shortly after it was founded in 1998. "We are unique because we have customers who come in early on their way to work for a cup of coffee and then will stop back after work to pick up a bottle of wine for dinner. We stay very busy throughout all three parts of the day."

Like most businesses where purchases are low-cost and high-volume, cash control has to be simple. "We use a computerized point-of-sale (POS) system to keep track of our inventory and allow us to efficiently ring through an order for a customer," explains Stoppleworth. "You can either scan a barcode for an item or enter in a code for items that don't have a barcode such as cups of coffee or bakery items." The POS system also automatically tracks sales by department and maintains an electronic journal of all the sales transactions that occur during the day.

"There are two POS stations at each store, and throughout the day any of the staff may operate them," says Stoppleworth. At the end of the day, each POS station is reconciled separately. The staff counts the cash in the drawer and enters this amount into the closing totals in the POS system. The POS system then compares the cash and credit amounts, less the cash being carried forward to the next day (the float), to the shift total in the electronic journal. If there are discrepancies, a recount is done and the journal is reviewed transaction by transaction to identify the problem. The staff then creates a deposit ticket for the cash less the float and puts this in a drop safe with the electronic journal summary report for the manager to review and take to the bank the next day. Ultimately, the bookkeeper reviews all of these documents as well as the deposit receipt that the bank produces to make sure they are all in agreement.

As Stoppleworth concludes, "We keep the closing process and accounting simple so that our staff can concentrate on taking care of our customers and making great coffee and food."

Chapter Outline

LEARNING OBJECTIVES

LO 1 Define fraud and the principles of internal control.	• Fraud • The Sarbanes-Oxley Act • Internal control • Principles of internal control activities • Limitations of internal control	**DO IT! 1** Control Activities
LO 2 Apply internal control principles to cash.	• Cash receipts controls • Cash disbursements controls • Petty cash fund	**DO IT! 2a** Control over Cash Receipts **DO IT! 2b** Petty Cash Fund
LO 3 Identify the control features of a bank account.	• Making bank deposits • Writing checks • EFT system • Bank statements • Reconciling the bank account	**DO IT! 3** Bank Reconciliation
LO 4 Explain the reporting of cash.	• Cash equivalents • Restricted cash	**DO IT! 4** Reporting Cash

Go to the Review and Practice section at the end of the chapter for a review of key concepts and practice applications with solutions.
Visit WileyPLUS with ORION for additional tutorials and practice opportunities.

Fraud and Internal Control

LEARNING OBJECTIVE 1

Define fraud and the principles of internal control.

The Feature Story describes many of the internal control procedures used by **Barriques**. These procedures are necessary to discourage employees from fraudulent activities.

Fraud

A **fraud** is a dishonest act by an employee that results in personal benefit to the employee at a cost to the employer. Examples of fraud reported in the financial press include the following.

- A bookkeeper in a small company diverted $750,000 of bill payments to a personal bank account over a three-year period.
- A shipping clerk with 28 years of service shipped $125,000 of merchandise to himself.
- A computer operator embezzled $21 million from **Wells Fargo Bank** over a two-year period.
- A church treasurer "borrowed" $150,000 of church funds to finance a friend's business dealings.

Why does fraud occur? The three main factors that contribute to fraudulent activity are depicted by the **fraud triangle** in **Illustration 8.1**.

The most important element of the fraud triangle is **opportunity**. For an employee to commit fraud, the workplace environment must provide opportunities that an employee can take advantage of. Opportunities occur when the workplace lacks sufficient controls to deter and detect fraud. For example, inadequate monitoring of employee actions can create opportunities for theft and can embolden employees because they believe they will not be caught.

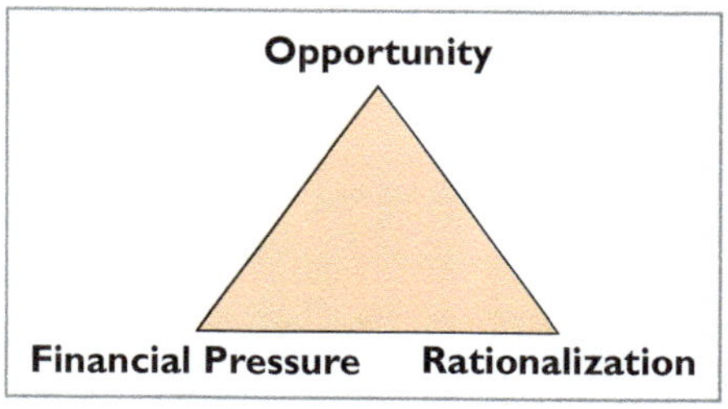

ILLUSTRATION 8.1 Fraud triangle

A second factor that contributes to fraud is **financial pressure**. Employees sometimes commit fraud because of personal financial problems caused by too much debt. Or, they might commit fraud because they want to lead a lifestyle that they cannot afford on their current salary.

The third factor that contributes to fraud is **rationalization**. In order to justify their fraud, employees rationalize their dishonest actions. For example, employees sometimes justify fraud because they believe they are underpaid while the employer is making lots of money. Employees feel justified in stealing because they believe they deserve to be paid more.

The Sarbanes-Oxley Act

What can be done to prevent or to detect fraud? After numerous corporate scandals came to light in the early 2000s, Congress addressed this issue by passing the **Sarbanes-Oxley Act (SOX)**. Under SOX, all publicly traded U.S. corporations are required to maintain an adequate system of internal control. Corporate executives and boards of directors must ensure that these controls are reliable and effective. In addition, independent outside auditors must attest to the adequacy of the internal control system. Companies that fail to comply are subject to fines, and company officers can be imprisoned. SOX also created the Public Company Accounting Oversight Board (PCAOB) to establish auditing standards and regulate auditor activity.

One poll found that 60% of investors believe that SOX helps safeguard their stock investments. Many say they would be unlikely to invest in a company that fails to follow SOX requirements. Although some corporate executives have criticized the time and expense involved in following SOX requirements, SOX appears to be working well. For example, the chief accounting officer of **Eli Lily** noted that SOX triggered a comprehensive review of how the company documents its controls. This review uncovered redundancies and pointed out controls that needed to be added. In short, it added up to time and money well spent.

Internal Control

Internal control is a process designed to provide reasonable assurance regarding the achievement of company objectives related to operations, reporting, and compliance. In more detail, the purposes of internal control are to safeguard assets, enhance the reliability of accounting records, increase efficiency of operations, and ensure compliance with laws and regulations. Internal control systems have five primary components as listed below.[1]

- **A control environment.** It is the responsibility of top management to make it clear that the organization values integrity and that unethical activity will not be tolerated. This component is often referred to as the "tone at the top."
- **Risk assessment.** Companies must identify and analyze the various factors that create risk for the business and must determine how to manage these risks.
- **Control activities.** To reduce the occurrence of fraud, management must design policies and procedures to address the specific risks faced by the company.
- **Information and communication.** The internal control system must capture and communicate all pertinent information both down and up the organization, as well as communicate information to appropriate external parties.
- **Monitoring.** Internal control systems must be monitored periodically for their adequacy. Significant deficiencies need to be reported to top management and/or the board of directors.

People, Planet, and Profit Insight

© Karl Dolenc/iStockphoto

And the Controls Are . . .

Internal controls are important for an effective financial reporting system. The same is true for sustainability reporting. An effective system of internal controls for sustainability reporting will help in the following ways: (1) prevent the unauthorized use of data; (2) provide reasonable assurance that the information is accurate, valid, and complete; and (3) report information that is consistent with overall sustainability accounting policies. With these types of controls, users will have the confidence that they can use the sustainability information effectively.

Some regulators are calling for even more assurance through audits of this information. Companies that potentially can cause environmental damage through greenhouse gases, as well as companies in the mining and extractive industries, are subject to reporting requirements. And, as demand for more information in the sustainability area expands, the need for audits of this information will grow.

Why is sustainability information important to investors? (Go to WileyPLUS for this answer and additional questions.)

Principles of Internal Control Activities

Each of the five components of an internal control system is important. Here, we will focus on one component, the control activities. The reason? These activities are the backbone of the company's efforts to address the risks it faces, such as fraud. The specific control activities used by a company will vary, depending on management's assessment of the risks faced. This assessment is heavily influenced by the size and nature of the company.

[1]The Committee of Sponsoring Organizations of the Treadway Commission, "Internal Control—Integrated Framework," *www.coso.org/documents/990025P_executive_summary_final_May20_e.pdf*; and Stephan J. McNally, "The 2013 COSO Framework and SOX Compliance," *Strategic Finance* (June 2013).

The six principles of control activities are as follows.

- Establishment of responsibility
- Segregation of duties
- Documentation procedures
- Physical controls
- Independent internal verification
- Human resource controls

We explain these principles in the following sections. You should recognize that they apply to most companies and are relevant to both manual and computerized accounting systems.

Establishment of Responsibility

An essential principle of internal control is to assign responsibility to specific employees. **Control is most effective when only one person is responsible for a given task.**

To illustrate, assume that the cash on hand at the end of the day in a **Safeway** supermarket is $10 short of the cash entered in the cash register. If only one person has operated the register, the shift manager can quickly determine responsibility for the shortage. If two or more individuals have worked the register, it may be impossible to determine who is responsible for the error.

Many retailers solve this problem by having registers with multiple drawers. This makes it possible for more than one person to operate a register but still allows identification of a particular employee with a specific drawer. Only the signed-in cashier has access to his or her drawer.

Establishing responsibility often requires limiting access only to authorized personnel, and then identifying those personnel. For example, the automated systems used by many companies have mechanisms such as identifying passcodes that keep track of who made a journal entry, who entered a sale, or who went into an inventory storeroom at a particular time. Use of identifying passcodes enables the company to establish responsibility by identifying the particular employee who carried out the activity.

Transfer of cash drawers

Anatomy of a Fraud

Maureen Frugali was a training supervisor for claims processing at Colossal Healthcare. As a standard part of the claims-processing training program, Maureen created fictitious claims for use by trainees. These fictitious claims were then sent to the accounts payable department. After the training claims had been processed, she was to notify Accounts Payable of all fictitious claims, so that they would not be paid. However, she did not inform Accounts Payable about every fictitious claim. She created some fictitious claims for entities that she controlled (that is, she would receive the payment), and she let Accounts Payable pay her.

Total take: $11 million

The Missing Control

Establishment of responsibility. The healthcare company did not adequately restrict the responsibility for authorizing and approving claims transactions. The training supervisor should not have been authorized to create claims in the company's "live" system.

Source: Adapted from Wells, *Fraud Casebook* (2007), pp. 61–70.

Segregation of Duties

Segregation of duties is indispensable in an internal control system. There are two common applications of this principle:

1. Different individuals should be responsible for related activities.
2. The responsibility for recordkeeping for an asset should be separate from the physical custody of that asset.

The rationale for segregation of duties is this: **The work of one employee should, without a duplication of effort, provide a reliable basis for evaluating the work of another employee.** For example, the personnel that design and program computerized systems should not be assigned duties related to day-to-day use of the system. Otherwise, they could design the system to benefit them personally and conceal the fraud through day-to-day use.

Segregation of Related Activities. **Making one individual responsible for related activities increases the potential for errors and irregularities.**

Purchasing Activities. Companies should, for example, assign related **purchasing activities** to different individuals. Related purchasing activities include ordering merchandise, approving orders, receiving goods, authorizing payment, and paying for goods or services. Various frauds are possible when one person handles related purchasing activities:

- If a purchasing agent is allowed to order goods without obtaining supervisory approval, the likelihood of the purchasing agent receiving kickbacks from suppliers increases.
- If an employee who orders goods also handles the invoice and receipt of the goods, as well as payment authorization, he or she might authorize payment for a fictitious invoice.

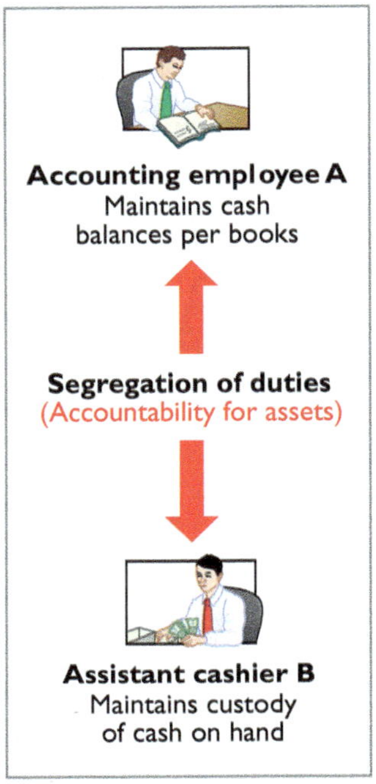

These abuses are less likely to occur when companies divide the purchasing tasks.

Sales Activities. Similarly, companies should assign related **sales activities** to different individuals. Related selling activities include making a sale, shipping (or delivering) the goods to the customer, billing the customer, and receiving payment. Various frauds are possible when one person handles related sales activities:

- If a salesperson can make a sale without obtaining supervisory approval, he or she might make sales at unauthorized prices to increase sales commissions.
- A shipping clerk who also has access to accounting records could ship goods to himself.
- A billing clerk who handles billing and receipt could understate the amount billed for sales made to friends and relatives.

These abuses are less likely to occur when companies divide the sales tasks. The salespeople make the sale, the shipping department ships the goods on the basis of the sales order, and the billing department prepares the sales invoice after comparing the sales order with the report of goods shipped.

Anatomy of a Fraud

Lawrence Fairbanks, the assistant vice-chancellor of communications at Aesop University, was allowed to make purchases of under $2,500 for his department without external approval. Unfortunately, he also sometimes bought items for himself, such as expensive antiques and other collectibles. How did he do it? He replaced the vendor invoices he received with fake vendor invoices that he created. The fake invoices had descriptions that were more consistent with the communications department's purchases. He submitted these fake invoices to the accounting department as the basis for their journal entries and to the accounts payable department as the basis for payment.

Total take: $475,000

The Missing Control

Segregation of duties. The university had not properly segregated related purchasing activities. Lawrence was ordering items, receiving the items, and receiving the invoice. By receiving the invoice, he had control over the documents that were used to account for the purchase and thus was able to substitute a fake invoice.

Source: Adapted from Wells, *Fraud Casebook* (2007), pp. 3–15.

Segregation of Recordkeeping from Physical Custody. The accountant should have neither physical custody of the asset nor access to it. Likewise, the custodian of the asset should not maintain or have access to the accounting records. **The custodian of the asset is not likely to convert the asset to personal use when one employee maintains the record of the asset, and a different employee has physical custody of the asset.** The separation of accounting responsibility from the custody of assets is especially important for cash and inventories because these assets are very vulnerable to fraud.

Anatomy of a Fraud

Angela Bauer was an accounts payable clerk for Aggasiz Construction Company. Angela prepared and issued checks to vendors and reconciled bank statements. She perpetrated a fraud in this way: She wrote checks for costs that the company had not actually incurred (e.g., fake taxes). A supervisor then approved and signed the checks. Before issuing the check, though, Angela would "white-out" the payee line on the check and change it to personal accounts that she controlled. She was able to conceal the theft because she also reconciled the bank account. That is, nobody else ever saw that the checks had been altered.

Total take: $570,000

The Missing Control

Segregation of duties. Aggasiz Construction Company did not properly segregate recordkeeping from physical custody. Angela had physical custody of the checks, which essentially was control of the cash. She also had recordkeeping responsibility because she prepared the bank reconciliation.

Source: Adapted from Wells, *Fraud Casebook* (2007), pp. 100–107.

Documentation Procedures

Documents provide evidence that transactions and events have occurred. For example, point-of-sale terminals are networked with a company's computing and accounting records, which results in direct documentation.

Similarly, a shipping document indicates that the goods have been shipped, and a sales invoice indicates that the company has billed the customer for the goods. By requiring signatures (or initials) on the documents, the company can identify the individual(s) responsible for the transaction or event. Companies should document transactions when they occur.

Companies should establish procedures for documents. First, whenever possible, companies should use **prenumbered documents, and all documents should be accounted for**. Prenumbering helps to prevent a transaction from being recorded more than once, or conversely, from not being recorded at all. Second, the control system should require that employees **promptly forward source documents for accounting entries to the accounting department. This control measure helps to ensure timely recording of the transaction** and contributes directly to the accuracy and reliability of the accounting records.

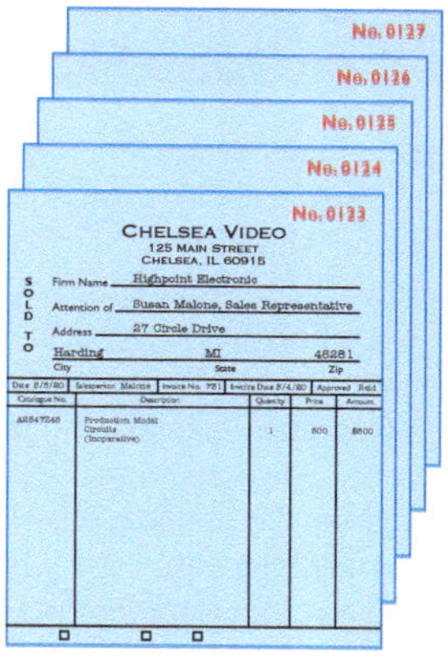

Prenumbered invoices

Anatomy of a Fraud

To support their reimbursement requests for travel costs incurred, employees at Mod Fashions Corporation's design center were required to submit receipts. The receipts could include the detailed bill provided for a meal, the credit card receipt provided when the credit card payment is made, or a copy of the employee's monthly credit card bill that listed the item. A number of the designers who frequently traveled together came up with a fraud scheme: They submitted claims for the same expenses. For example, if they had a meal together that cost $200, one person submitted the detailed meal bill, another submitted the credit card receipt, and a third submitted a monthly credit card bill showing the meal as a line item. Thus, all three received a $200 reimbursement.

Total take: $75,000

The Missing Control

Documentation procedures. Mod Fashions should require the original, detailed receipt. It should not accept photocopies, and it should not accept credit card statements. In addition, documentation procedures could be further improved by requiring the use of a corporate credit card (rather than a personal credit card) for all business expenses.

Source: Adapted from Wells, *Fraud Casebook* (2007), pp. 79–90.

Physical Controls

Use of physical controls is essential. **Physical controls** relate to the safeguarding of assets and enhance the accuracy and reliability of the accounting records. **Illustration 8.2** shows examples of these controls.

ILLUSTRATION 8.2 **Physical controls**

Physical Controls

Safes, vaults, and safety deposit boxes for cash and business papers	Locked warehouses and storage cabinets for inventories and records	Computer facilities with passkey access or fingerprint or eyeball scans	Alarms to prevent break-ins	Television monitors and garment sensors to deter theft	Time clocks for recording time worked

Anatomy of a Fraud

At Centerstone Health, a large insurance company, the mailroom each day received insurance applications from prospective customers. Mailroom employees scanned the applications into electronic documents before the applications were processed. Once the applications were scanned, they could be accessed online by authorized employees.

Insurance agents at Centerstone Health earn commissions based upon successful applications. The sales agent's name is listed on the application. However, roughly 15% of the applications are from customers who did not work with a sales agent. Two friends—Alex, an employee in recordkeeping, and Parviz, a sales agent—thought up a way to perpetrate a fraud. Alex identified scanned applications that did not list a sales agent. After business hours, he entered the mailroom and found the hard-copy applications that did not show a sales agent. He wrote in Parviz's name as the sales agent and then rescanned the application for processing. Parviz received the commission, which the friends then split.

Total take: $240,000

The Missing Control

Physical controls. Centerstone Health lacked two basic physical controls that could have prevented this fraud. First, the mailroom should have been locked during nonbusiness hours, and access during business hours should have been tightly controlled. Second, the scanned applications supposedly could be accessed only by authorized employees using their passwords. However, the password for each employee was the same as the employee's user ID. Since employee user-ID numbers were available to all other employees, all employees knew each other's passwords. Thus, Alex could enter the system using another employee's password and access the scanned applications.

Source: Adapted from Wells, *Fraud Casebook* (2007), pp. 316–326.

Independent Internal Verification

Most internal control systems provide for **independent internal verification**. This principle involves the review of data prepared by employees. To obtain maximum benefit from independent internal verification:

1. Companies should verify records periodically or on a surprise basis.
2. An employee who is independent of the personnel responsible for the information should make the verification.
3. Discrepancies and exceptions should be reported to a management level that can take appropriate corrective action.

Independent internal verification is especially useful in comparing recorded accountability with existing assets. The reconciliation of the electronic journal with the cash in the point-of-sale terminal at **Barriques** is an example of this internal control principle. Other common examples are the reconciliation of a company's cash balance per books with the cash balance per bank, and the verification of the perpetual inventory records through a count of physical inventory. **Illustration 8.3** shows the relationship between this principle and the segregation of duties principle.

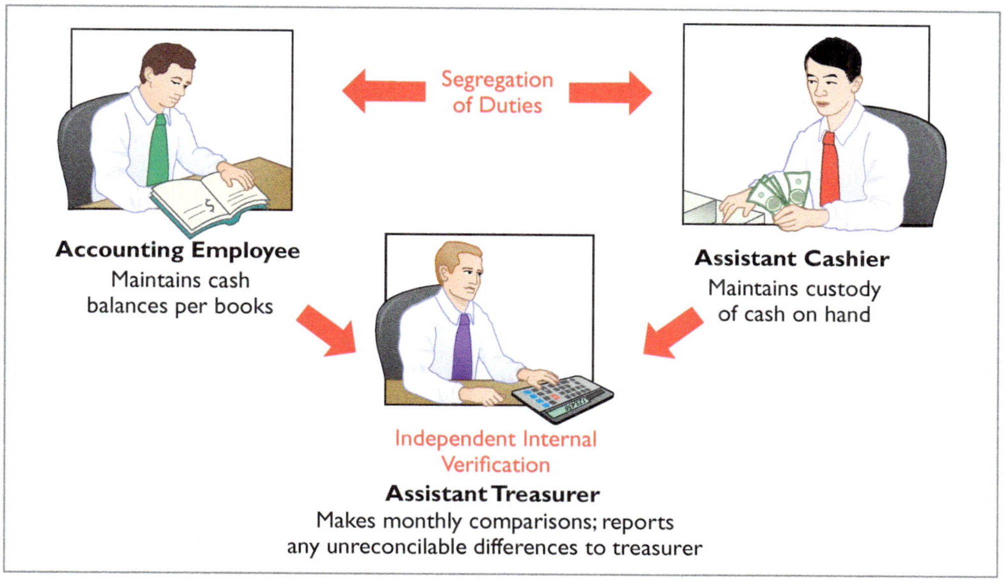

ILLUSTRATION 8.3

Comparison of segregation of duties principle with independent internal verification principle

Anatomy of a Fraud

Bobbi Jean Donnelly, the office manager for Mod Fashions Corporation's design center, was responsible for preparing the design center budget and reviewing expense reports submitted by design center employees. Her desire to upgrade her wardrobe got the better of her, and she enacted a fraud that involved filing expense-reimbursement requests for her own personal clothing purchases. Bobbi Jean was able to conceal the fraud because she was responsible for reviewing all expense reports, including her own. In addition, she sometimes was given ultimate responsibility for signing off on the expense reports when her boss was "too busy." Also, because she controlled the budget, when she submitted her expenses, she coded them to budget items that she knew were running under budget, so that they would not catch anyone's attention.

Total take: $275,000

The Missing Control

Independent internal verification. Bobbi Jean's boss should have verified her expense reports. When asked what he thought her expenses for a year were, the boss said about $10,000. At $115,000 per year, her actual expenses were more than 10 times what would have been expected. However, because he was "too busy" to verify her expense reports or to review the budget, he never noticed.

Source: Adapted from Wells, *Fraud Casebook* (2007), pp. 79–90.

Large companies often assign independent internal verification to internal auditors. **Internal auditors** are company employees who continuously evaluate the effectiveness of the company's internal control systems. They review the activities of departments and individuals to determine whether prescribed internal controls are being followed. They also recommend improvements when needed. For example, **WorldCom** was at one time the second largest U.S. telecommunications company. The fraud that caused its bankruptcy (the largest ever when it occurred) involved billions of dollars. It was uncovered by an internal auditor.

Human Resource Controls

Human resource control activities include the following.

1. **Bond employees who handle cash.** **Bonding** involves obtaining insurance protection against theft by employees. It contributes to the safeguarding of cash in two ways. First, the insurance company carefully screens all individuals before adding them to the policy and may reject risky applicants. Second, bonded employees know that the insurance company will vigorously prosecute all offenders.
2. **Rotate employees' duties and require employees to take vacations.** These measures deter employees from attempting thefts since they will not be able to permanently conceal their improper actions. Many banks, for example, have discovered employee thefts when the employee was on vacation or assigned to a new position.

3. **Conduct thorough background checks.** Many believe that the most important and inexpensive measure any business can take to reduce employee theft and fraud is for the human resource department to conduct thorough background checks. Two tips: (1) Check to see whether job applicants actually graduated from the schools they list. (2) Never use telephone numbers for previous employers provided by the applicant. Always look them up yourself.

Anatomy of a Fraud

Ellen Lowry was the desk manager and Josephine Rodriguez was the head of housekeeping at the Excelsior Inn, a luxury hotel. The two best friends were so dedicated to their jobs that they never took vacations, and they frequently filled in for other employees. In fact, Ms. Rodriguez, whose job as head of housekeeping did not include cleaning rooms, often cleaned rooms herself, "just to help the staff keep up." These two "dedicated" employees, working as a team, found a way to earn a little more cash. Ellen, the desk manager, provided significant discounts to guests who paid with cash. She kept the cash and did not register the guests in the hotel's computerized system. Instead, she took the room out of circulation "due to routine maintenance." Because the room did not show up as being used, it did not receive a normal housekeeping assignment. Instead, Josephine, the head of housekeeping, cleaned the rooms during the guests' stay.

Total take: $95,000

The Missing Control

Human resource controls. Ellen, the desk manager, had been fired by a previous employer after being accused of fraud. If the Excelsior Inn had conducted a thorough background check, it would not have hired her. The hotel fraud was detected when Ellen missed work for a few days due to illness. A system of mandatory vacations and rotating days off would have increased the chances of detecting the fraud before it became so large.

Source: Adapted from Wells, *Fraud Casebook* (2007), pp. 145–155.

Accounting Across the Organization

Stockbyte/Getty Images, Inc.

SOX Boosts the Role of Human Resources

Under SOX, a company needs to keep track of employees' degrees and certifications to ensure that employees continue to meet the specified requirements of a job. Also, to ensure proper employee supervision and proper separation of duties, companies must develop and monitor an organizational chart. When one corporation went through this exercise, it found that out of 17,000 employees, there were 400 people who did not report to anyone. The corporation also had 35 people who reported to each other. In addition, if an employee complains of an unfair firing and mentions financial issues at the company, the human resource department must refer the case to the company audit committee and possibly to its legal counsel.

Why would unsupervised employees or employees who report to each other represent potential internal control threats? (Go to WileyPLUS for this answer and additional questions.)

Limitations of Internal Control

HELPFUL HINT

Controls may vary with the risk level of the activity. For example, management may consider cash to be high risk and maintaining inventories in the stockroom as low risk. Thus, management would have stricter controls for cash.

Companies generally design their systems of internal control to provide **reasonable assurance** of proper safeguarding of assets and reliability of the accounting records. The concept of reasonable assurance rests on the premise that the costs of establishing control procedures should not exceed their expected benefit (see **Helpful Hint**).

To illustrate, consider shoplifting losses in retail stores. Stores could eliminate such losses by having a security guard stop and search customers as they leave the store. But store managers have concluded that the negative effects of such a procedure cannot be justified. Instead, they have attempted to control shoplifting losses by less costly procedures. They post signs saying, "We reserve the right to inspect all packages" and "All shoplifters will be prosecuted."

They use hidden cameras and store detectives to monitor customer activity, and they install sensor equipment at exits.

The **human element** is an important factor in every system of internal control. A good system can become ineffective as a result of employee fatigue, carelessness, or indifference. For example, a receiving clerk may not bother to count goods received and may just "fudge" the counts. Occasionally, two or more individuals may work together to get around prescribed controls. Such **collusion** can significantly reduce the effectiveness of a system, eliminating the protection offered by segregation of duties. No system of internal control is perfect.

The **size of the business** also may impose limitations on internal control. Small companies often find it difficult to segregate duties or to provide for independent internal verification. A study by the Association of Certified Fraud Examiners (*2014 Report to the Nation on Occupational Fraud and Abuse*) indicates that businesses with fewer than 100 employees are most at risk for employee theft. In fact, 29% of frauds occurred at companies with fewer than 100 employees. The median loss at small companies was $154,000, which was nearly as high as the median fraud at companies with more than 10,000 employees ($160,000). A $154,000 loss can threaten the very existence of a small company.

DO IT! 1 | Control Activities

Identify which control activity is violated in each of the following situations, and explain how the situation creates an opportunity for a fraud.

1. The person with primary responsibility for reconciling the bank account and making all bank deposits is also the company's accountant.
2. Wellstone Company's treasurer received an award for distinguished service because he had not taken a vacation in 30 years.
3. In order to save money spent on order slips and to reduce time spent keeping track of order slips, a local bar/restaurant does not buy prenumbered order slips.

ACTION PLAN

- **Familiarize yourself with each of the control activities.**
- **Understand the nature of the frauds that each control activity is intended to address.**

Solution

1. Violates the control activity of segregation of duties. Recordkeeping should be separate from physical custody. As a consequence, the employee could embezzle cash and make journal entries to hide the theft.
2. Violates the control activity of human resource controls. Key employees must take vacations. Otherwise, the treasurer, who manages the company's cash, might embezzle cash and use his position to conceal the theft.
3. Violates the control activity of documentation procedures. If prenumbered documents are not used, then it is virtually impossible to account for the documents. As a consequence, an employee could write up a dinner sale, receive the cash from the customer, and then throw away the order slip and keep the cash.

Related exercise material: **BE8.1, BE8.2, BE8.3, BE8.4, DO IT! 8.1, E8.1, E8.2, E8.3, E8.5, and E8.6.**

Cash Controls

LEARNING OBJECTIVE 2

Apply internal control principles to cash.

Cash is the one asset that is readily convertible into any other type of asset. It also is easily concealed and transported, and is highly desired. Because of these characteristics, **cash is the asset most susceptible to fraudulent activities**. In addition, because of the large volume of cash transactions, numerous errors may occur in executing and recording them. To safeguard cash and to ensure the accuracy of the accounting records for cash, effective internal control over cash is critical.

Cash Receipts Controls

Illustration 8.4 shows how the internal control principles explained earlier apply to cash receipts transactions. As you might expect, companies vary considerably in how they apply these principles. To illustrate internal control over cash receipts, we will examine control activities for a retail store with both over-the-counter and mail receipts.

ILLUSTRATION 8.4 **Application of internal control principles to cash receipts**

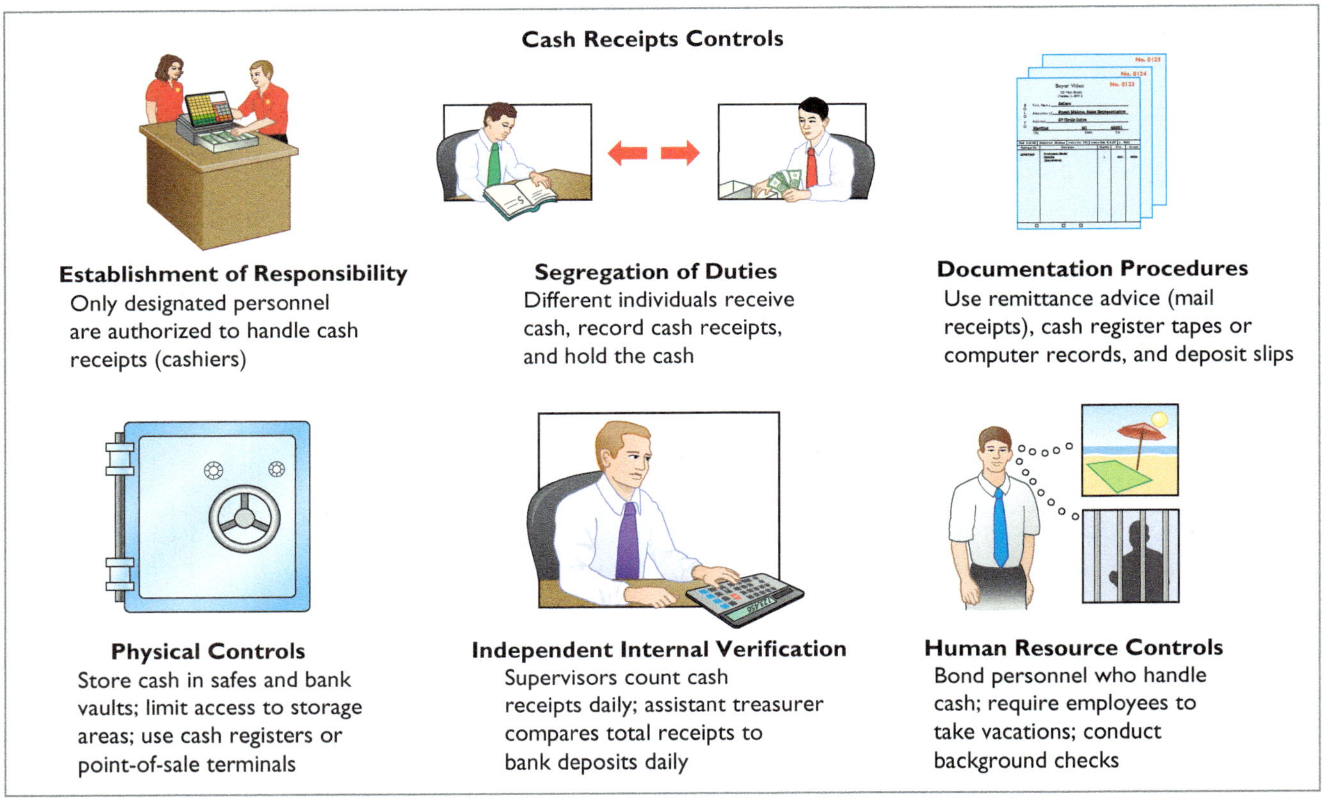

Over-the-Counter Receipts

In retail businesses, control of over-the-counter receipts centers on cash registers that are visible to customers. A cash sale is entered in a cash register (or point-of-sale terminal), with the amount clearly visible to the customer. This activity prevents the sales clerk from entering a lower amount and pocketing the difference. The customer receives an itemized cash register receipt and is expected to count the change received. (One weakness at **Barriques** in the Feature Story is that customers are only given a receipt if requested.) The cash register's tape is locked in the register until a supervisor removes it. This tape accumulates the daily transactions and totals.

At the end of the clerk's shift, the clerk counts the cash and sends the cash and the count to the cashier. The cashier counts the cash, prepares a deposit slip, and deposits the cash at the bank. The cashier also sends a duplicate of the deposit slip to the accounting department to indicate cash received. The supervisor removes the cash register tape and sends it to the accounting department as the basis for a journal entry to record the cash received.

(For point-of-sale systems, the accounting department receives information on daily transactions and totals through the computer network.) **Illustration 8.5** summarizes this process (see **Helpful Hint**).

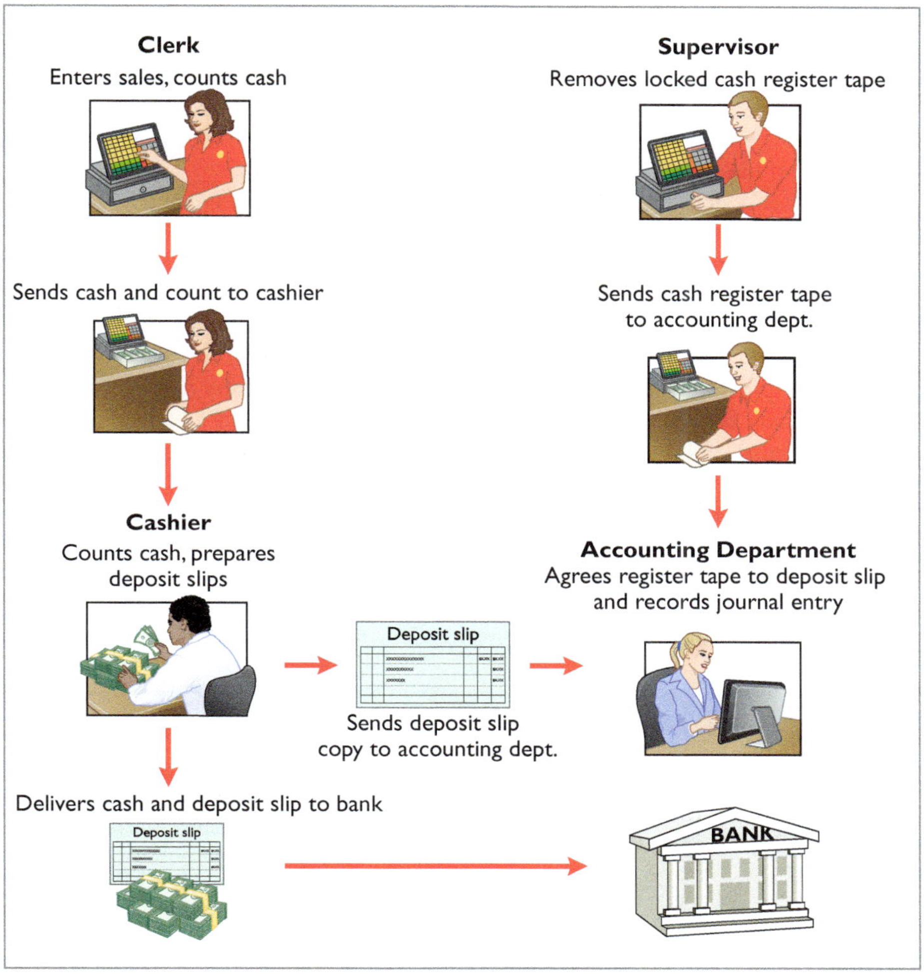

ILLUSTRATION 8.5

Control of over-the-counter receipts

HELPFUL HINT

Flowcharts such as this one enhance the understanding of the flow of documents, the processing steps, and the internal control procedures.

This system for handling cash receipts uses an important internal control principle—segregation of recordkeeping from physical custody. The supervisor has access to the cash register tape but **not** to the cash. The clerk and the cashier have access to the cash but **not** to the register tape. In addition, the cash register tape provides documentation and enables independent internal verification. Use of these three principles of internal control (segregation of recordkeeping from physical custody, documentation, and independent internal verification) provides an effective system of internal control. Any attempt at fraudulent activity should be detected unless there is collusion among the employees.

In some instances, the amount deposited at the bank will not agree with the cash recorded in the accounting records based on the cash register tape. These differences often result because the clerk hands incorrect change back to the retail customer. In this case, the difference between the actual cash and the amount reported on the cash register tape is reported in a Cash Over and Short account. For example, suppose that the cash register tape indicated sales of $6,956.20 but the amount of cash was only $6,946.10. A cash shortfall of $10.10 exists. To account for this cash shortfall and related cash, the company makes the following entry.

Cash	6,946.10	
Cash Over and Short	10.10	
Sales Revenue		6,956.20
(To record cash shortfall)		

A	=	L	+	OE
+6,946.10				
				−10.10
				+6,956.20

Cash Flows
+6,946.10

Cash Over and Short is an income statement item. It is reported as miscellaneous expense when there is a cash shortfall, and as miscellaneous revenue when there is an overage. Clearly, the amount should be small. Any material amounts in this account should be investigated.

Mail Receipts

All mail receipts should be opened in the presence of at least two mail clerks. These receipts are generally in the form of checks. A mail clerk should endorse each check "For Deposit Only." This restrictive endorsement reduces the likelihood that someone could divert the check to personal use. Banks will not give an individual cash when presented with a check that has this type of endorsement.

The mail clerks prepare, in triplicate, a list of the checks received each day. This list shows the name of the check issuer, the purpose of the payment, and the amount of the check. Each mail clerk signs the list to establish responsibility for the data. The original copy of the list, along with the checks, is then sent to the cashier's department. A copy of the list is sent to the accounting department for recording in the accounting records. The clerks also keep a copy.

This process provides excellent internal control for the company. By employing two clerks, the chance of fraud is reduced. Each clerk knows he or she is being observed by the other clerk(s). To engage in fraud, they would have to collude. The customers who submit payments also provide control because they will contact the company with a complaint if they are not properly credited for payment. Because the cashier has access to cash but not the records, and the accounting department has access to records but not cash, neither can engage in undetected fraud.

DO IT! 2a | Control over Cash Receipts

L. R. Cortez is concerned about the control over cash receipts in his fast-food restaurant, Big Cheese. The restaurant has two cash registers. At no time do more than two employees take customer orders and enter sales. Work shifts for employees range from 4 to 8 hours. Cortez asks your help in installing a good system of internal control over cash receipts.

ACTION PLAN

- **Differentiate among the internal control principles of (1) establishing responsibility, (2) using physical controls, and (3) independent internal verification.**
- **Design an effective system of internal control over cash receipts.**

Solution

Cortez should assign a separate cash register drawer to each employee at the start of each work shift, with register totals set at zero. Each employee should have access to only the assigned register drawer to enter all sales. Each customer should be given a receipt. At the end of the shift, the employee should do a cash count. A separate employee should compare the cash count with the register tape (or point-of-sale records) to be sure they agree. In addition, Cortez should install an automated point-of-sale system that would enable the company to compare orders entered in the register to orders processed by the kitchen.

Related exercise material: **BE8.5, BE8.6, BE8.7, BE8.8, DO IT! 8.2a, E8.2, and E8.3.**

Cash Disbursements Controls

Companies disburse cash for a variety of reasons, such as to pay expenses and liabilities or to purchase assets. **Generally, internal control over cash disbursements is more effective when companies pay by check or electronic funds transfer (EFT) rather than by cash.** One exception is **payments for incidental amounts that are paid out of petty cash.**[2]

[2]We explain the operation of a petty cash fund in the next section.

Companies generally issue checks only after following specified control procedures. **Illustration 8.6** shows how principles of internal control apply to cash disbursements.

ILLUSTRATION 8.6 **Application of internal control principles to cash disbursements**

Cash Disbursements Controls

Establishment of Responsibility
Only designated personnel are authorized to sign checks (treasurer) and approve vendors

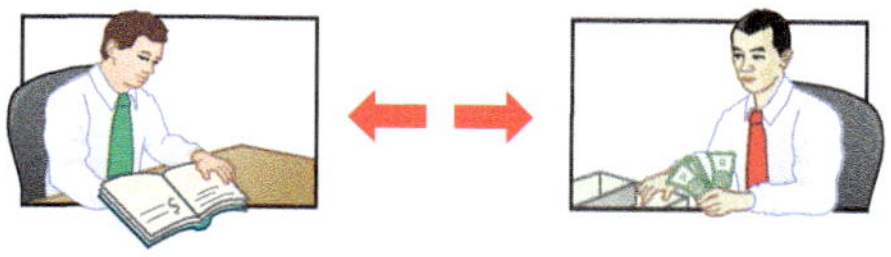

Segregation of Duties
Different individuals approve and make payments; check-signers do not record disbursements

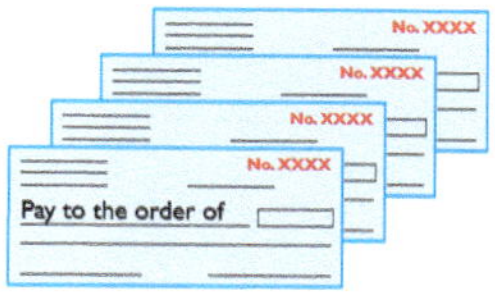

Documentation Procedures
Use prenumbered checks and account for them in sequence; each check must have an approved invoice; require employees to use corporate credit cards for reimbursable expenses; stamp invoices "paid"

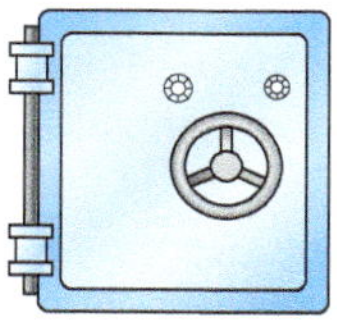

Physical Controls
Store blank checks in safes, with limited access; print check amounts by machine in indelible ink

Independent Internal Verification
Compare checks to invoices; reconcile bank statement monthly

Human Resource Controls
Bond personnel who handle cash; require employees to take vacations; conduct background checks

Voucher System Controls

Most medium and large companies use vouchers as part of their internal control over cash disbursements. A **voucher system** is a network of approvals by authorized individuals, acting independently, to ensure that all disbursements by check are proper.

The system begins with the authorization to incur a cost or expense. It ends with the issuance of a check for the liability incurred. A **voucher** is an authorization form prepared for each expenditure. Companies require vouchers for all types of cash disbursements except those from petty cash.

The starting point in preparing a voucher is to fill in the appropriate information about the liability on the face of the voucher. The vendor's invoice provides most of the needed information. Then, an employee in accounts payable records the voucher (in a journal called a **voucher register**) and files it according to the date on which it is to be paid. The company issues and sends a check on that date, and stamps the voucher "paid." The paid voucher is sent to the accounting department for recording (in a journal called the **check register**). A voucher system involves two journal entries, one to record the liability when the voucher is issued and a second to pay the liability that relates to the voucher.

The use of a voucher system, whether done manually or electronically, improves internal control over cash disbursements. First, the authorization process inherent in a voucher system establishes responsibility. Each individual has responsibility to review the underlying documentation to ensure that it is correct. In addition, the voucher system keeps track of the documents that back up each transaction. By keeping these documents in one place, a supervisor can independently verify the authenticity of each transaction. Consider, for example, the case of Aesop University presented in the "Anatomy of a Fraud" box earlier in the chapter. Aesop did not use a voucher system for transactions under $2,500. As a consequence, there was no independent verification of the documents, which enabled the employee to submit fake invoices to hide his unauthorized purchases.

Petty Cash Fund

As you just learned, better internal control over cash disbursements is possible when companies make payments by check. However, using checks to pay small amounts is both impractical and a nuisance. For instance, a company would not want to write checks to pay for postage due, working lunches, or taxi fares. A common way of handling such payments, while maintaining satisfactory control, is to use a **petty cash fund** to pay relatively small amounts (see **Ethics Note**). The operation of a petty cash fund, often called an **imprest system**, involves (1) establishing the fund, (2) making payments from the fund, and (3) replenishing the fund.[3]

ETHICS NOTE

Petty cash funds are authorized and legitimate. In contrast, "slush" funds are unauthorized and hidden (under the table).

Establishing the Petty Cash Fund

Two essential steps in establishing a petty cash fund are (1) appointing a petty cash custodian who will be responsible for the fund, and (2) determining the size of the fund. Ordinarily, a company expects the amount in the fund to cover anticipated disbursements for a three- to four-week period.

To establish the fund, a company issues a check payable to the petty cash custodian for the stipulated amount. For example, if Laird Company decides to establish a $100 fund on March 1, the general journal entry is as follows.

A	= L	+ OE
+100		
−100		

Cash Flows
no effect

Mar. 1	Petty Cash	100	
	Cash		100
	(To establish a petty cash fund)		

The fund custodian cashes the check and places the proceeds in a locked petty cash box or drawer. Most petty cash funds are established on a fixed-amount basis. The company will make no additional entries to the Petty Cash account unless management changes the stipulated amount of the fund. For example, if Laird decides on July 1 to increase the size of the fund to $250, it would debit Petty Cash $150 and credit Cash $150.

Making Payments from the Petty Cash Fund

The petty cash custodian has the authority to make payments from the fund that conform to prescribed management policies. Usually, management limits the size of expenditures that come from petty cash. Likewise, it may not permit use of the fund for certain types of transactions (such as making short-term loans to employees).

HELPFUL HINT

The petty cash receipt satisfies two internal control principles: (1) establishment of responsibility (signature of custodian), and (2) documentation procedures.

Each payment from the fund must be documented on a prenumbered petty cash receipt (or petty cash voucher), as shown in **Illustration 8.7** (see **Helpful Hint**). The signatures of both the fund custodian and the person receiving payment are required on the receipt. If other supporting documents such as a freight bill or invoice are available, they should be attached to the petty cash receipt.

---

[3]The term "imprest" means an advance of money for a designated purpose.

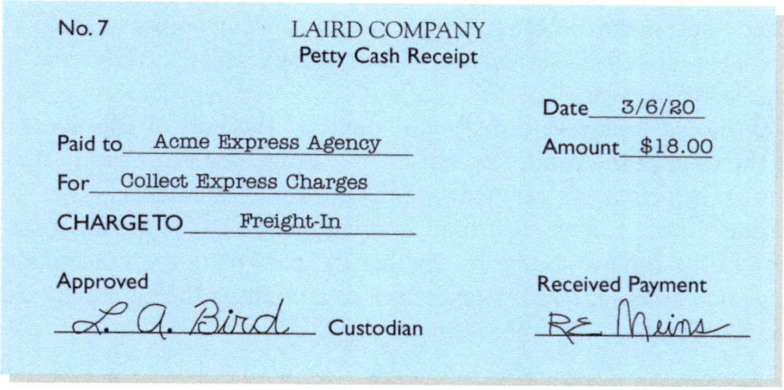
No. 7 LAIRD COMPANY
Petty Cash Receipt

Date 3/6/20

Paid to Acme Express Agency Amount $18.00

For Collect Express Charges

CHARGE TO Freight-In

Approved Received Payment

L. A. Bird Custodian R. E. Meins

ILLUSTRATION 8.7
Petty cash receipt

The petty cash custodian keeps the receipts in the petty cash box until the fund is replenished. The sum of the petty cash receipts and the money in the fund should equal the established total at all times. Management can (and should) make surprise counts at any time (or use an independent person, such as an internal auditor) to determine the correctness of the fund.

The company does not make an accounting entry to record a payment when it is made from petty cash. It is considered both inexpedient and unnecessary to do so. Instead, the company recognizes the accounting effects of each payment when it replenishes the fund.

Replenishing the Petty Cash Fund

When the money in the petty cash fund reaches a minimum level, the company replenishes the fund (see **Helpful Hint**). The petty cash custodian initiates a request for reimbursement. The individual prepares a schedule (or summary) of the payments that have been made and sends the schedule, supported by petty cash receipts and other documentation, to the treasurer's office. The treasurer's office examines the receipts and supporting documents to verify that proper payments from the fund were made. The treasurer then approves the request and issues a check to restore the fund to its established amount. At the same time, all supporting documentation is stamped "paid" so that it cannot be submitted again for payment.

HELPFUL HINT
Replenishing the petty cash fund involves three internal control procedures:
1. **segregation of duties,**
2. **documentation procedures, and**
3. **independent internal verification.**

To illustrate, assume that on March 15 Laird's petty cash custodian requests a check for $87. The fund contains $13 cash and petty cash receipts for postage $44, freight-out $38, and miscellaneous expenses $5. The general journal entry to record the check is as follows.

Mar. 15	Postage Expense	44	
	Freight-Out	38	
	Miscellaneous Expense	5	
	Cash		87
	(To replenish petty cash fund)		

A = L + OE
−44 Exp.
−38 Exp.
−87 −5 Exp.

Cash Flows
−87

Note that the reimbursement entry does not affect the Petty Cash account. Replenishment changes the composition of the fund by replacing the petty cash receipts with cash. It does not change the balance in the fund.

Occasionally, in replenishing a petty cash fund, the company may need to recognize a cash shortage or overage (see **Helpful Hint**). This results when the total of the cash plus receipts in the petty cash box does not equal the established amount of the petty cash fund. To illustrate, assume that Laird's petty cash custodian has only $12 in cash in the fund plus the receipts as listed. The request for reimbursement would therefore be for $88, and Laird would make the following entry.

HELPFUL HINT
Cash over and short situations result from mathematical errors or from failure to keep accurate records.

Mar. 15	Postage Expense	44	
	Freight-Out	38	
	Miscellaneous Expense	5	
	Cash Over and Short	1	
	Cash		88
	(To replenish petty cash fund)		

A = L + OE
−44 Exp
−38 Exp
−5 Exp
−1 Exp
−88

Cash Flows
−88

Conversely, if the custodian has $14 in cash, the reimbursement request would be for $86. The company would credit Cash Over and Short for $1 (overage). A company reports a debit balance in Cash Over and Short in the income statement as miscellaneous expense. It reports a credit balance in the account as miscellaneous revenue. The company closes Cash Over and Short to Income Summary at the end of the year.

Companies should replenish a petty cash fund **at the end of the accounting period, regardless of the cash in the fund**. Replenishment at this time is necessary in order to recognize the effects of the petty cash payments on the financial statements.

Internal control over a petty cash fund is strengthened by (1) having a supervisor make surprise counts of the fund to ascertain whether the paid petty cash receipts and fund cash equal the designated amount, and (2) cancelling or mutilating the paid petty cash receipts so they cannot be resubmitted for reimbursement.

Ethics Insight

© Chris Fernig/iStockphoto

How Employees Steal

Occupational fraud is using your own occupation for personal gain through the misuse or misapplication of the company's resources or assets. This type of fraud is one of three types:

1. **Asset misappropriation**, such as theft of cash on hand, fraudulent disbursements, false refunds, ghost employees, personal purchases, and fictitious employees. This fraud is the most common but the least costly.
2. **Corruption**, such as bribery, illegal gratuities, and economic extortion. This fraud generally falls in the middle between asset misappropriation and financial statement fraud as regards frequency and cost.
3. **Financial statement fraud**, such as fictitious revenues, concealed liabilities and expenses, improper disclosures, and improper asset values. This fraud occurs less frequently than other types of fraud but it is the most costly.

The graph below shows the frequency and the median loss for each type of occupational fraud. (Note that the sum of percentages exceeds 100% because some cases of fraud involved more than one type.)

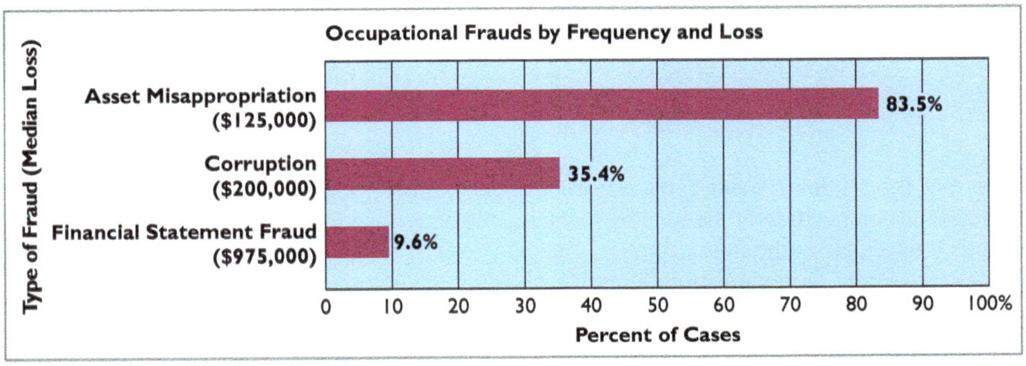

Source: *2016 Report to the Nations on Occupational Fraud and Abuse*, Association of Certified Fraud Examiners, pp. 10–12.

How can companies reduce the likelihood of occupational fraud? (Go to WileyPLUS for this answer and additional questions.)

DO IT! 2b | Petty Cash Fund

Bateer Company established a $50 petty cash fund on July 1. On July 30, the fund had $12 cash remaining and petty cash receipts for postage $14, office supplies $10, and delivery expense $15. Prepare journal entries to establish the fund on July 1 and to replenish the fund on July 30.

Solution

July 1	Petty Cash	50	
	Cash		50
	(To establish petty cash fund)		
30	Postage Expense	14	
	Supplies	10	
	Delivery Expense	15	
	Cash Over and Short		1
	Cash ($50 – $12)		38
	(To replenish petty cash)		

Related exercise material: **BE8.9, DO IT! 8.2b, E8.7 and E8.8.**

ACTION PLAN

- **To establish the fund, set up a separate general ledger account.**
- **Determine how much cash is needed to replenish the fund: subtract the cash remaining from the petty cash fund balance.**
- **Total the petty cash receipts. Determine any cash over or short—the difference between the cash needed to replenish the fund and the total of the petty cash receipts.**
- **Record the expenses incurred according to the petty cash receipts when replenishing the fund.**

Control Features of a Bank Account

LEARNING OBJECTIVE 3

Identify the control features of a bank account.

The use of a bank contributes significantly to good internal control over cash. A company safeguards its cash by using a bank as a depository and clearinghouse for checks received and checks written. The use of a bank checking account minimizes the amount of currency that must be kept on hand. It also facilitates control of cash because a double record is maintained of all bank transactions—one by the business and the other by the bank. The asset account Cash maintained by the company is the "flipside" of the bank's liability account for that company. A **bank reconciliation** is the process of comparing the bank's balance with the company's balance, and explaining the differences to make them agree.

Many companies have more than one bank account. For efficiency of operations and better control, national retailers like **Wal-Mart** and **Target** often have regional bank accounts. Similarly, a company such as **ExxonMobil** with more than 100,000 employees may have a payroll bank account as well as one or more general bank accounts. In addition, a company may maintain several bank accounts in order to have more than one source for short-term loans.

Making Bank Deposits

An authorized employee, such as the head cashier, should make a company's bank deposits. Each deposit must be documented by a deposit slip (ticket), as shown in **Illustration 8.8**.

Deposit slips are prepared in duplicate. The bank retains the original; the depositor keeps the duplicate, machine-stamped by the bank to establish its authenticity.

ILLUSTRATION 8.8
Deposit slip

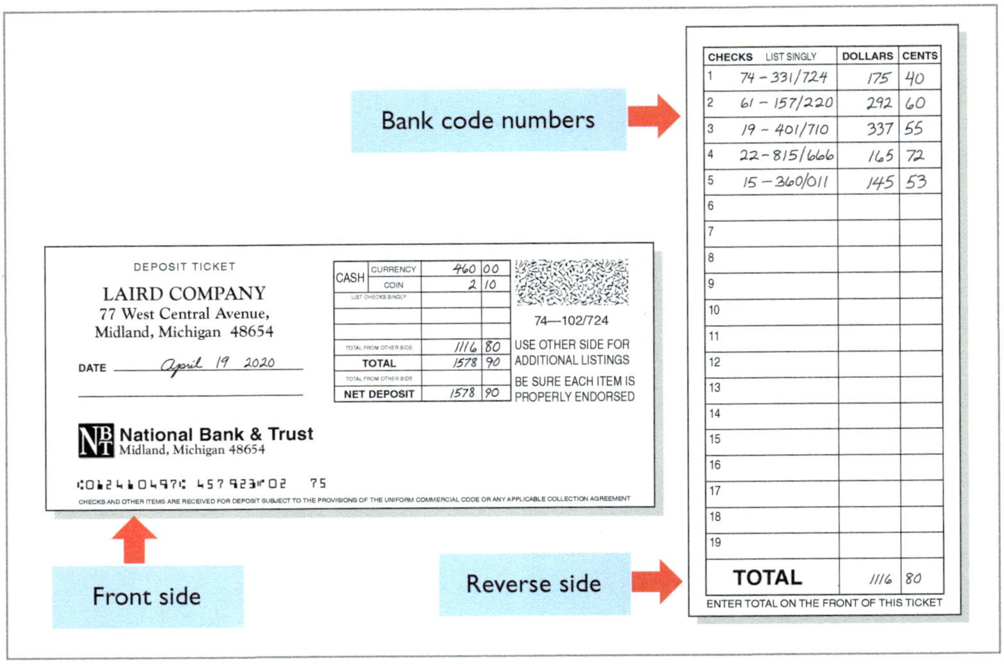

Writing Checks

A **check** is a written order signed by the depositor directing the bank to pay a specified sum of money to a designated recipient. There are three parties to a check: (1) the **maker** (or drawer) who issues the check, (2) the **bank** (or payer) on which the check is drawn, and (3) the **payee** to whom the check is payable. A check is a **negotiable instrument** that one party can transfer to another party by endorsement. Each check should be accompanied by an explanation of its purpose. In many companies, a remittance advice attached to the check, as shown in **Illustration 8.9**, explains the check's purpose.

ILLUSTRATION 8.9
Check with remittance advice

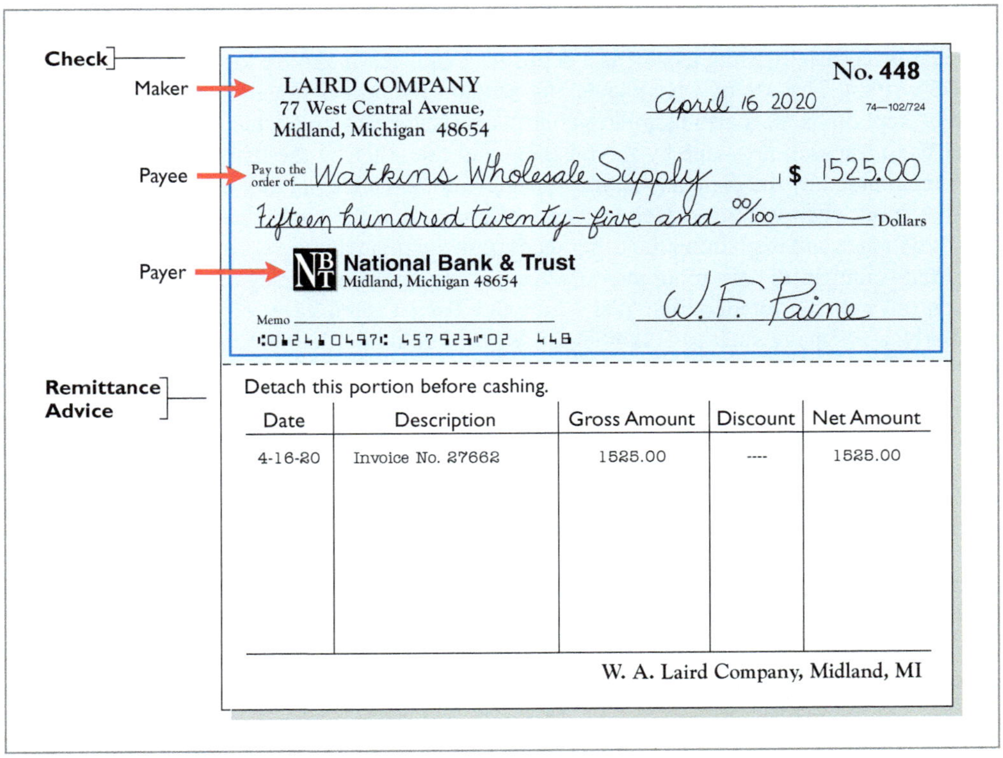

Electronic Funds Transfer (EFT) System

It is not surprising that companies and banks have developed approaches to transfer funds among parties without the use of paper (deposit tickets, checks, etc.). Such procedures, called **electronic funds transfers (EFT)**, are disbursement systems that use wire, telephone, or computers to transfer cash balances from one location to another. Use of EFT is quite common. For example, many employees receive no formal payroll checks from their employers. Instead, employers send electronic payroll data to the appropriate banks. Also, companies now frequently make regular payments such as those for utilities, rent, and insurance by EFT.

EFT transactions normally result in better internal control since no cash or checks are handled by company employees. This does not mean that opportunities for fraud are eliminated. In fact, the same basic principles related to internal control apply to EFT transfers. For example, without proper segregation of duties and authorizations, an employee might be able to redirect electronic payments into a personal bank account and conceal the theft with fraudulent accounting entries.

Bank Statements

Each month, the company receives from the bank a **bank statement** showing its bank transactions and balances.[4] For example, the statement for Laird Company in **Illustration 8.10** shows the following: (1) checks paid and other debits (such as debit card transactions or electronic

ILLUSTRATION 8.10
Bank statement

National Bank & Trust
Midland, Michigan 48654 Member FDIC

ACCOUNT STATEMENT
LAIRD COMPANY
77 WEST CENTRAL AVENUE
MIDLAND, MICHIGAN 48654

Statement Date/Credit Line Closing Date: April 30, 2020

457923
ACCOUNT NUMBER

Balance Last Statement	Deposits and Credits		Checks and Debits		Balance This Statement
	No.	Total Amount	No.	Total Amount	
13,256.90	20	34,805.10	26	32,154.55	15,907.45

Amounts Deducted from Account (debits)			Amounts Added to Account (credits)		Daily Balance	
Date	No.	Amount	Date	Amount	Date	Amount
4-2	435	644.95	4-2	4,276.85	4-2	16,888.80
4-3	EFT	1,000.00	4-3	2,137.50	4-3	18,249.65
4-5	436	2,260.00	4-5	1,350.47	4-4	17,063.86
4-4	437	1,185.79	4-7	982.46	4-5	15,154.33
4-3	438	776.65	4-8	1,320.28	4-7	14,648.89
4-8	439	1,781.70	4-9 EFT	1,035.00	4-8	11,767.47
4-7	440	1,487.90	4-11	2,720.00	4-9	12,802.47
4-7	EFT	320.00	4-12	757.41	4-11	13,936.87
4-8	441	2,100.00	4-13	1,218.56	4-12	13,468.28
4-11	442	1,585.60				
4-12	443	1,226.00				
4-29	NSF	425.60	4-27	1,545.57	4-27	13,005.45
4-29	459	1,080.30	4-29	2,929.45	4-29	14,429.00
4-30	DM	120.00	4-30	2,128.60	4-30	15,907.45
4-30	DM	30.00				
4-30	461	500.15				

Symbols: **CM** Credit Memo **EC** Error Correction **NSF** Not Sufficient Funds **EFT** Electronic Funds Transfer
DM Debit Memo **INT** Interest Earned **SC** Service Charge

[4]Our presentation assumes that a company makes all adjustments at the end of the month. In practice, a company may also make journal entries during the month as it reviews information from the bank regarding its account.

HELPFUL HINT

Essentially, the bank statement is a copy of the bank's records sent to the customer or made available online for review.

funds transfers for bill payments) that reduce the balance in the depositor's account, (2) deposits (by direct deposit, automated teller machine, or electronic funds transfer) and other credits that increase the balance in the depositor's account, and (3) the account balance after each day's transactions (see **Helpful Hint**).

Remember that **bank statements are prepared from the *bank's* perspective**. For example, **every deposit the bank receives is an increase in the bank's liabilities (an account payable to the depositor)**. Therefore, in Illustration 8.10, National Bank and Trust **credits** to Laird Company every deposit it received from Laird. The reverse occurs when the bank "pays" a check issued by Laird Company on its checking account balance: Payment reduces the bank's liability and is therefore **debited** to Laird's account with the bank.

The bank statement lists in numerical sequence all paid checks along with the date the check was paid and its amount. Upon paying a check, the bank stamps the check "paid"; a paid check is sometimes referred to as a **canceled** check. In addition, the bank includes with the bank statement memoranda explaining other debits and credits it made to the depositor's account.

A check that is not paid by a bank because of insufficient funds in a bank account is called an **NSF check** (not sufficient funds). The bank uses a debit memorandum when a previously deposited customer's check "bounces" because of insufficient funds. In such a case, the customer's bank marks the check NSF (not sufficient funds) and returns it to the depositor's bank. The bank then debits (decreases) the depositor's account, as shown by the symbol NSF in Illustration 8.10, and sends the NSF check and debit memorandum to the depositor as notification of the charge. The NSF check creates an account receivable for the depositor and reduces cash in the bank account.

Reconciling the Bank Account

Because the bank and the company maintain independent records of the company's checking account, you might assume that the respective balances will always agree. In fact, the two balances are seldom the same at any given time, and both balances differ from the "correct or true" balance. Therefore, it is necessary to make the balance per books and the balance per bank agree with the correct or true amount—a process called **reconciling the bank account**. The need for reconciliation has two causes:

1. **Time lags** that prevent one of the parties from recording the transaction in the same period.
2. **Errors** by either party in recording transactions.

Time lags occur frequently. For example, several days may elapse between the time a company pays by check and the date the bank pays the check. Similarly, when a company uses the bank's night depository to make its deposits, there will be a difference of one day between the time the company records the receipts and the time the bank does so. A time lag also occurs whenever the bank mails a debit or credit memorandum to the company.

You might think that if a company never writes checks (for example, if a small company uses only a debit card or electronic funds transfers), it does not need to reconcile its account. However, **the possibility of errors or fraud still necessitates periodic reconciliation**. The incidence of errors or fraud depends on the effectiveness of the internal controls maintained by the company and the bank. Bank errors are infrequent. However, either party could accidentally record a $450 check as $45 or $540. In addition, the bank might mistakenly charge a check drawn by C. D. Berg to the account of C. D. Burg.

Reconciliation Procedure

In reconciling the bank account, it is customary to reconcile the balance per books and balance per bank to their adjusted (correct or true) cash balances. **To obtain maximum benefit from a bank reconciliation, an employee who has no other responsibilities related to cash should prepare the reconciliation.** When companies do not follow the internal control principle of independent internal verification in preparing the reconciliation, cash embezzlements may escape unnoticed. For example, in the "Anatomy of a Fraud" box about Angela Bauer, a bank reconciliation might have exposed her embezzlement.

Illustration 8.11 shows the reconciliation process. The starting point in preparing the reconciliation is to enter the balance per bank statement and balance per books on a schedule (see **Helpful Hint**). The following steps should reveal all the reconciling items that cause the difference between the two balances.

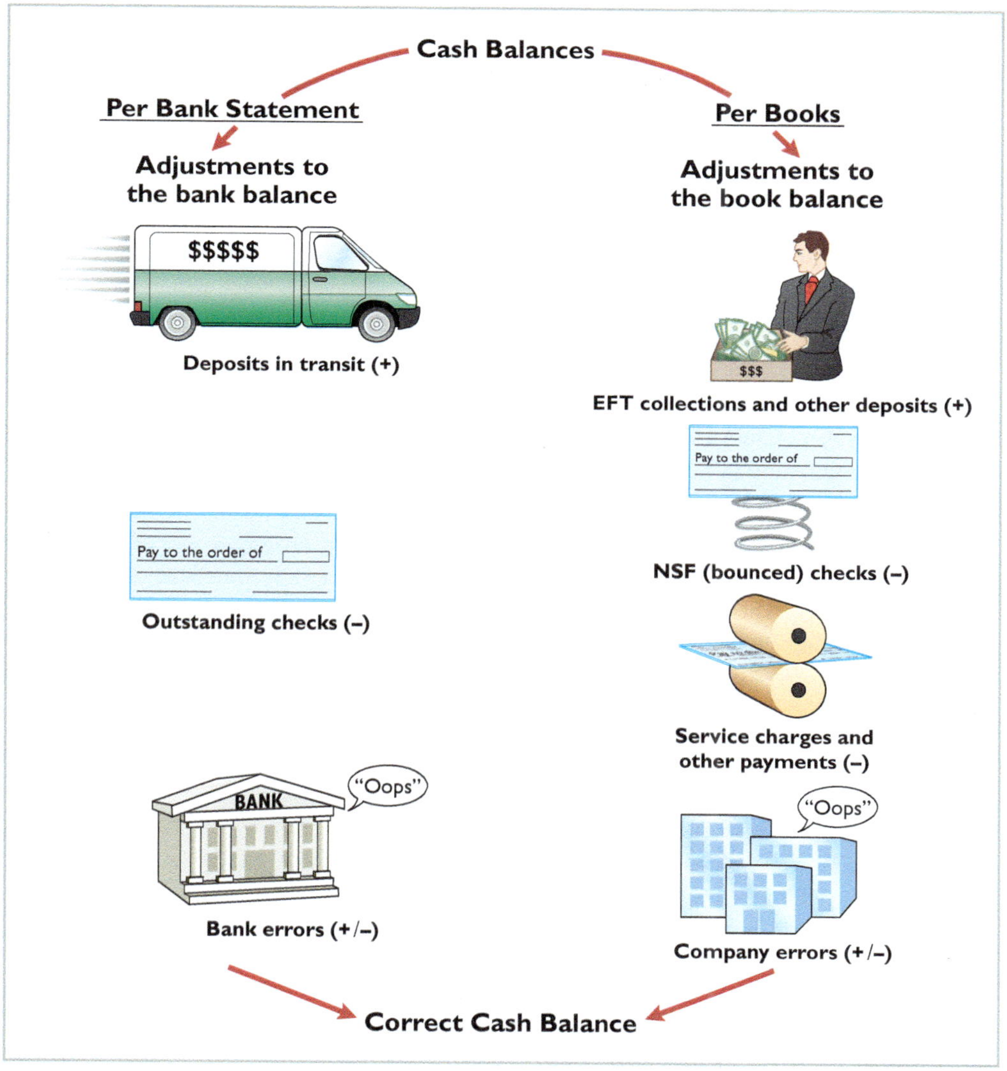

ILLUSTRATION 8.11
Bank reconciliation adjustments

HELPFUL HINT
Deposits in transit and outstanding checks are reconciling items because of time lags.

Reconciling Items per Bank. On the bank side of the reconciliation, the items to reconcile are deposits in transit (amounts added), outstanding checks (amounts deducted), and bank errors (if any). By adjusting the bank balance for these items, a company brings that balance up to date.

Step 1. Deposits in transit (+). Compare the individual deposits on the bank statement with the deposits in transit from the preceding bank reconciliation and with the deposits per company records or copies of duplicate deposit slips. Deposits recorded by the depositor that have not been recorded by the bank represent **deposits in transit**. Add these deposits to the balance per bank.

Step 2. Outstanding checks (–). Compare the paid checks shown on the bank statement or the paid checks returned with the bank statement with (a) checks outstanding from the preceding bank reconciliation, and (b) checks issued by the company recorded as cash payments. Issued checks recorded by the company that have not been paid by the bank represent **outstanding checks**. Deduct outstanding checks from the balance per bank.

Step 3. Bank errors (+/–). Note any errors made by the bank that were discovered in the previous steps. For example, if the bank processed a deposit of $1,693 as $1,639 in error, the difference of $54 ($1,693 – $1,639) is added to the balance per bank on the bank reconciliation. All errors made by the bank are reconciling items in determining the adjusted cash balance per the bank.

Reconciling Items Per Books. Reconciling items on the book side relate to amounts not yet recorded on the company's books and include adjustments from deposits and other amounts added, payments and other amounts deducted, and company errors (if any).

Step 1. **Other deposits (+).** Compare the other deposits on the bank statement with the company records. Any unrecorded amounts should be added to the balance per books. For example, if the bank statement shows electronic funds transfers from customers paying their accounts online, these amounts should be added to the balance per books on the bank reconciliation to update the company's records unless they had previously been recorded by the company.

Step 2. **Other payments (−).** Similarly, any unrecorded other payments should be deducted from the balance per books. For example, if the bank statement shows service charges (such as debit and credit card fees and other bank service charges), this amount is deducted from the balance per books on the bank reconciliation to make the company's records agree with the bank's records. **Normally, the company will already have recorded electronic payments.** However, if this has not been the case then these payments must be deducted from the balance per books on the bank reconciliation to make the company's records agree with the bank's records.

Step 3. **Book errors (+/−).** Note any errors made by the depositor that have been discovered in the previous steps. For example, say a company wrote check No. 443 to a supplier in the amount of $1,226 on April 12, but the accounting clerk recorded the check amount as $1,262. The error of $36 ($1,262 – $1,226) is added to the balance per books because the company reduced the balance per books by $36 too much when it recorded the check as $1,262 instead of $1,226. Only errors made by the company, not the bank, are included as reconciling items in determining the adjusted cash balance per books.

Bank Reconciliation Illustrated

HELPFUL HINT

Note in the bank statement in Illustration 8.10 that the bank has paid checks No. 459 and 461, but check No. 460 is not listed. Thus, this check is outstanding. If a complete bank statement were provided, checks No. 453 and 457 also would not be listed. Laird obtains the amounts for these three checks from its cash payments records.

Illustration 8.10 presented the bank statement for Laird Company which the company accessed online (see **Helpful Hint**). It shows a balance per bank of $15,907.45 on April 30, 2020. On this date the balance of cash per books is $11,709.45.

From the foregoing steps, Laird determines the following reconciling items for the bank.

Step 1. **Deposits in transit (+):** April 30 deposit (received by bank on May 1).	$2,201.40
Step 2. **Outstanding checks (−):** No. 453, $3,000.00; No. 457, $1,401.30; No. 460, $1,502.70.	5,904.00
Step 3. **Bank errors (+/−):** None.	

Reconciling items per books are as follows:

Step 1. **Other deposits (+):** Unrecorded electronic receipt from customer on account on April 9 determined from the bank statement.	$1,035.00
Step 2. **Other payments (−):** The electronic payments on April 3 and 7 were previously recorded by the company when they were initiated. Unrecorded charges determined from the bank statement are as follows:	
Returned NSF check on April 29	425.60
Debit and credit card fees on April 30	120.00
Bank service charges on April 30	30.00
Step 3. **Company errors (+):** Check No. 443 was correctly written by Laird for $1,226 and was correctly paid by the bank on April 12. However, it was recorded as $1,262 on Laird's books.	36.00

Illustration 8.12 shows Laird's bank reconciliation (see **Alternative Terminology**).

ILLUSTRATION 8.12
Bank reconciliation

Laird Company Bank Reconciliation April 30, 2020		
Cash balance per bank statement		$15,907.45
Add: Deposits in transit		2,201.40
		18,108.85
Less: Outstanding checks		
No. 453	$3,000.00	
No. 457	1,401.30	
No. 460	1,502.70	5,904.00
Adjusted cash balance per bank		**$12,204.85**
Cash balance per books		$11,709.45
Add: Electronic funds transfer received	$1,035.00	
Error in recording check No. 443	36.00	1,071.00
		12,780.45
Less: NSF check	425.60	
Debit and credit card fees	120.00	
Bank service charge	30.00	575.60
Adjusted cash balance per books		**$12,204.85**

ALTERNATIVE TERMINOLOGY

The terms *adjusted cash balance*, *true cash balance*, and *correct cash balance* are used interchangeably.

Entries from Bank Reconciliation

The depositor (that is, the company) next must record each reconciling item used to determine the **adjusted cash balance per books**. If the company does not journalize and post these items, the Cash account will not show the correct balance. The adjusting entries for the Laird Company bank reconciliation on April 30 are as follows (see **Helpful Hint**).

HELPFUL HINT

These entries are adjusting entries. In prior chapters, we considered Cash an account that did not require adjustment because we had not yet explained a bank reconciliation.

Collection of Electronic Funds Transfer. A payment of an account by a customer is recorded in the same way, whether the cash is received through the mail or electronically. The entry is as follows.

Apr. 30	Cash	1,035	
	Accounts Receivable		1,035
	(To record receipt of electronic funds transfer)		

A = L + OE
+1,035
−1,035

Cash Flows
+1,035

Book Error. An examination of the cash disbursements journal shows that check No. 443 was a payment on account to Andrea Company, a supplier. The correcting entry is as follows.

Apr. 30	Cash	36	
	Accounts Payable		36
	(To correct error in recording check No. 443)		

A = L + OE
+36 (A)
+36 (L)

Cash Flows
+36

NSF Check. As indicated earlier, an NSF check becomes an accounts receivable to the depositor. The entry is as follows.

Apr. 30	Accounts Receivable	425.60	
	Cash		425.60
	(To record NSF check)		

A = L + OE
+425.60
−425.60

Cash Flows
−425.60

Bank Charge Expense. Fees for processing debit and credit card transactions are normally debited to the Bank Charge Expense account, as are bank service charges. We have chosen to combine and record these in one journal entry, as shown below, although they also could be journalized separately.

Apr. 30	Bank Charge Expense	150	
	Cash		150
	(To record charges for debit and credit card fees of $120 and bank service charges of $30)		

A = L + OE
−150 Exp (OE)
−150 (A)

Cash Flows
−150

After Laird posts the entries, the Cash account will appear as in **Illustration 8.13**. The adjusted cash balance in the ledger should agree with the adjusted cash balance per books in the bank reconciliation in Illustration 8.12.

ILLUSTRATION 8.13

Adjusted balance in Cash account

Cash			
Apr. 30 Bal.	11,709.45	Apr. 30	425.60
30	1,035.00	30	150.00
30	36.00		
Apr. 30 Bal.	**12,204.85**		

What entries does the bank make? If the company discovers any bank errors in preparing the reconciliation, it should notify the bank so the bank can make the necessary corrections on its records. The bank does not make any entries for deposits in transit or outstanding checks. Only when these items reach the bank will the bank record these items.

Investor Insight

Mary Altaffer/©AP/Wide World Photos

Madoff's Ponzi Scheme

No recent fraud has generated more interest and rage than the one perpetrated by Bernard Madoff. Madoff was an elite New York investment fund manager who was highly regarded by securities regulators. Investors flocked to him because he delivered very steady returns of between 10% and 15%, no matter whether the market was going up or going down. However, for many years, Madoff did not actually invest the cash that people gave to him. Instead, he was running a Ponzi scheme: He paid returns to existing investors using cash received from new investors. As long as the size of his investment fund continued to grow from new investments at a rate that exceeded the amounts that he needed to pay out in returns, Madoff was able to operate his fraud smoothly.

To conceal his misdeeds, Madoff fabricated false investment statements that were provided to investors. In addition, Madoff hired an auditor that never verified the accuracy of the investment records but automatically issued unqualified opinions each year. A competing fund manager warned the SEC a number of times over a nearly 10-year period that he thought Madoff was engaged in fraud. The SEC never aggressively investigated the allegations. Investors, many of which were charitable organizations, lost more than $18 billion. Madoff was sentenced to a jail term of 150 years.

How was Madoff able to conceal such a giant fraud? (Go to WileyPLUS for this answer and additional questions.)

DO IT! 3 | Bank Reconciliation

Sally Kist owns Linen Kist Fabrics. Sally asks you to explain how she should treat the following reconciling items when reconciling the company's bank account: (1) a debit memorandum for an NSF check, (2) a credit memorandum received by the bank for an electronic funds transfer from one of the company's customers, (3) outstanding checks, and (4) a deposit in transit.

ACTION PLAN

- **Understand the purpose of a bank reconciliation.**
- **Identify time lags and explain how they cause reconciling items.**

Solution

Sally should treat the reconciling items as follows.

1. NSF check: Deduct from balance per books.
2. Electronic funds transfer received by bank: Add to balance per books.
3. Outstanding checks: Deduct from balance per bank.
4. Deposit in transit: Add to balance per bank.

Related exercise material: **BE8.10, BE8.11, BE8.12, BE8.13, BE8.14, BE8.15, DO IT! 8.3, E8.9, E8.10, E8.11, E8.12, and E8.13.**

Reporting Cash

LEARNING OBJECTIVE 4

Explain the reporting of cash.

Cash consists of coins, currency (paper money), checks, money orders, and money on hand or on deposit in a bank or similar depository. Companies report cash in two different statements: the balance sheet and the statement of cash flows. The balance sheet reports the amount of cash available at a given point in time. The statement of cash flows shows the sources and uses of cash during a period of time. The statement of cash flows was introduced in Chapter 1 and will be discussed in much detail in Chapter 17. In this section, we discuss some important points regarding the presentation of cash in the balance sheet.

When presented in a balance sheet, cash on hand, cash in banks, and petty cash are often combined and reported simply as **Cash**. Because it is the most liquid asset owned by the company, cash is listed first in the current assets section of the balance sheet.

Cash Equivalents

Many companies use the designation "Cash and cash equivalents" in reporting cash. (See **Illustration 8.14** for an example.) **Cash equivalents** are short-term, highly liquid investments that are both:

1. Readily convertible to known amounts of cash, and
2. So near their maturity that their market value is relatively insensitive to changes in interest rates. (Generally, only investments with original maturities of three months or less qualify under this definition.)

Real World

Delta Air Lines, Inc.
Balance Sheet
(partial, in millions)

Assets	
Current assets	
Cash and cash equivalents	**$2,844**
Short-term investments	959
Restricted cash	**122**

ILLUSTRATION 8.14
Balance sheet presentation of cash

Examples of cash equivalents are Treasury bills, commercial paper (short-term corporate notes), and money market funds. All typically are purchased with cash that is in excess of immediate needs (see **Ethics Note**).

Occasionally, a company will have a net negative balance in its bank account. In this case, the company should report the negative balance among current liabilities. For example, farm equipment manufacturer **Ag-Chem** at one time reported "Checks outstanding in excess of cash balances" of $2,145,000 among its current liabilities.

ETHICS NOTE

Recently, some companies were forced to restate their financial statements because they had too broadly interpreted which types of investments could be treated as cash equivalents. By reporting these items as cash equivalents, the companies made themselves look more liquid.

Restricted Cash

A company may have **restricted cash**, cash that is not available for general use but rather is restricted for a special purpose. For example, landfill companies are often required to maintain a fund of restricted cash to ensure they will have adequate resources to cover closing and clean-up costs at the end of a landfill site's useful life. **McKesson Corp.** recently reported restricted cash of $962 million to be paid out as the result of investor lawsuits.

Cash restricted in use should be reported separately on the balance sheet as restricted cash. If the company expects to use the restricted cash within the next year, it reports the amount as a current asset. When this is not the case, it reports the restricted funds as a noncurrent asset.

Illustration 8.14 shows restricted cash reported in the financial statements of **Delta Air Lines**. The company is required to maintain restricted cash as collateral to support insurance obligations related to workers' compensation claims. Delta does not have access to these funds for general use, and so it must report them separately, rather than as part of cash and cash equivalents.

DO IT! 4 | Reporting Cash

Indicate whether each of the following statements is true or false. If false, indicate how to correct the statement.

1. Cash and cash equivalents are comprised of coins, currency (paper money), money orders, and NSF checks.
2. Restricted cash is classified as either a current asset or noncurrent asset, depending on the circumstances.
3. A company may have a negative balance in its bank account. In this case, it should offset this negative balance against cash and cash equivalents on the balance sheet.
4. Because cash and cash equivalents often includes short-term investments, accounts receivable should be reported as the first item on the balance sheet.

ACTION PLAN

- **Understand how companies present cash and restricted cash on the balance sheet.**
- **Review the designations of cash equivalents and restricted cash, and how companies typically handle them.**

Solution

1. False. NSF checks should be reported as receivables, not cash and cash equivalents. **2.** True. **3.** False. Companies that have a negative balance in their bank accounts should report the negative balance as a current liability. **4.** False. Cash equivalents are readily convertible to known amounts of cash, and so near maturity (less than 3 months) that they are considered more liquid than accounts receivable and therefore are reported before accounts receivable on the balance sheet.

Related exercise material: **BE8.16, DO IT! 8.4, E8.14, and E8.15.**

Review and Practice

Learning Objectives Review

1 Define fraud and the principles of internal control.

A fraud is a dishonest act by an employee that results in personal benefit to the employee at a cost to the employer. The fraud triangle refers to the three factors that contribute to fraudulent activity by employees: opportunity, financial pressure, and rationalization. Internal control consists of all the related methods and measures adopted within an organization to safeguard its assets, enhance the reliability of its accounting records, increase efficiency of operations, and ensure compliance with laws and regulations.

The principles of internal control are establishment of responsibility, segregation of duties, documentation procedures, physical controls, independent internal verification, and human resource controls such as bonding and requiring employees to take vacations.

2 Apply internal control principles to cash.

Internal controls over cash receipts include (a) designating specific personnel to handle cash; (b) assigning different individuals to receive cash, record cash, and maintain custody of cash; (c) using remittance advices for mail receipts, cash register tapes for over-the-counter receipts, and deposit slips for bank deposits; (d) using company safes and bank vaults to store cash with access limited to authorized personnel, and using cash registers or point-of-sale terminals in executing over-the-counter receipts; (e) making independent daily counts of register receipts and daily comparison of total receipts with total deposits; and (f) bonding personnel that handle cash and requiring them to take vacations.

Internal controls over cash disbursements include (a) having specific individuals such as the treasurer authorized to sign checks and approve vendors; (b) assigning different individuals to approve items for payment, make the payment, and record the payment; (c) using prenumbered checks and accounting for all checks, with each check supported by an approved invoice; (d) storing blank checks in a safe or vault with access restricted to authorized personnel, and using a check-writing machine to imprint amounts on checks; (e) comparing each check with the approved invoice before issuing the check, and making monthly reconciliations of bank and book balances; and (f) bonding personnel who handle cash, requiring employees to take vacations, and conducting background checks.

Companies operate a petty cash fund to pay relatively small amounts of cash. They must establish the fund, make payments from the fund, and replenish the fund when the cash in the fund reaches a minimum level.

3 Identify the control features of a bank account.

A bank account contributes to good internal control by providing physical controls for the storage of cash. It minimizes the amount of currency that a company must keep on hand, and it creates a double record of a depositor's bank transactions. It is customary to reconcile the balance per books and balance per bank to their adjusted balances. The steps in the reconciling process are to determine deposits in transit and electronic funds transfers received by bank, outstanding checks, errors by the depositor or the bank, and unrecorded bank memoranda.

4 Explain the reporting of cash.

Companies list cash first in the current assets section of the balance sheet. In some cases, they report cash together with cash equivalents. Cash restricted for a special purpose is reported separately as a current asset or as a noncurrent asset, depending on when the cash is expected to be used.

Glossary Review

Bank reconciliation The process of comparing the bank's balance of an account with the company's balance and explaining any differences to make them agree. (p. 8-19).

Bank statement A monthly statement from the bank that shows the depositor's bank transactions and balances. (p. 8-21).

Bonding Obtaining insurance protection against theft by employees. (p. 8-9).

Cash Resources that consist of coins, currency, checks, money orders, and money on hand or on deposit in a bank or similar depository. (p. 8-27).

Cash equivalents Short-term, highly liquid investments that can be converted to a specific amount of cash. (p. 8-27).

Check A written order signed by a bank depositor, directing the bank to pay a specified sum of money to a designated recipient. (p. 8-20).

Deposits in transit Deposits recorded by the depositor but not yet recorded by the bank. (p. 8-23).

Electronic funds transfer (EFT) A disbursement system that uses wire, telephone, or computers to transfer funds from one location to another. (p. 8-21).

Fraud A dishonest act by an employee that results in personal benefit to the employee at a cost to the employer. (p. 8-3).

Fraud triangle The three factors that contribute to fraudulent activity by employees: opportunity, financial pressure, and rationalization. (p. 8-3).

Internal auditors Company employees who continuously evaluate the effectiveness of the company's internal control system. (p. 8-9).

Internal control A process designed to provide reasonable assurance regarding the achievement of company objectives related to operations, reporting, and compliance. (p. 8-4).

NSF check A check that is not paid by a bank because of insufficient funds in a customer's bank account. (p. 8-22).

Outstanding checks Checks issued and recorded by a company but not yet paid by the bank. (p. 8-23).

Petty cash fund A cash fund used to pay relatively small amounts. (p. 8-16).

Restricted cash Cash that must be used for a special purpose. (p. 8-27).

Sarbanes-Oxley Act (SOX) Regulations passed by Congress to try to reduce unethical corporate behavior. (p. 8-3).

Voucher An authorization form prepared for each payment in a voucher system. (p. 8-15).

Voucher system A network of approvals by authorized individuals acting independently to ensure that all disbursements by check are proper. (p. 8-15).

Practice Multiple-Choice Questions

1. **(LO 1)** Which of the following is **not** an element of the fraud triangle?
   - **a.** Rationalization.
   - **b.** Financial pressure.
   - **c.** Segregation of duties.
   - **d.** Opportunity.

2. **(LO 1)** An organization uses internal control to enhance the accuracy and reliability of accounting records and to:
   - **a.** safeguard assets.
   - **b.** prevent fraud.
   - **c.** produce correct financial statements.
   - **d.** deter employee dishonesty.

3. **(LO 1)** Which of the following was **not** a result of the Sarbanes-Oxley Act?

   a. Companies must file financial statements with the Internal Revenue Service.

   b. All publicly traded companies must maintain adequate internal controls.

   c. The Public Company Accounting Oversight Board was created to establish auditing standards and regulate auditor activity.

   d. Corporate executives and board of directors must ensure that controls are reliable and effective, and they can be fined or imprisoned for failure to do so.

4. **(LO 1)** The principles of internal control do **not** include:

   a. establishment of responsibility.

   b. documentation procedures.

   c. management responsibility.

   d. independent internal verification.

5. **(LO 1)** Physical controls do **not** include:

   a. safes and vaults to store cash.

   b. independent bank reconciliations.

   c. locked warehouses for inventories.

   d. bank safety deposit boxes for important papers.

6. **(LO 1)** Which of the following control activities is **not** relevant when a company uses a computerized (rather than manual) accounting system?

   a. Establishment of responsibility.

   b. Segregation of duties.

   c. Independent internal verification.

   d. All of these control activities are relevant to a computerized system.

7. **(LO 2)** Permitting only designated personnel to handle cash receipts is an application of the principle of:

   a. segregation of duties.

   b. establishment of responsibility.

   c. independent internal verification.

   d. human resource controls.

8. **(LO 2)** The use of prenumbered checks in disbursing cash is an application of the principle of:

   a. establishment of responsibility.

   b. segregation of duties.

   c. physical controls.

   d. documentation procedures.

9. **(LO 2)** A company writes a check to replenish a $100 petty cash fund when the fund contains receipts of $94 and $4 in cash. In recording the check, the company should:

   a. debit Cash Over and Short for $2.

   b. debit Petty Cash for $94.

   c. credit Cash for $94.

   d. credit Petty Cash for $2.

10. **(LO 3)** The control features of a bank account do **not** include:

   a. having bank auditors verify the correctness of the bank balance per books.

   b. minimizing the amount of cash that must be kept on hand.

   c. providing a double record of all bank transactions.

   d. safeguarding cash by using a bank as a depository.

11. **(LO 3)** In a bank reconciliation, deposits in transit are:

   a. deducted from the book balance.

   b. added to the book balance.

   c. added to the bank balance.

   d. deducted from the bank balance.

12. **(LO 3)** The reconciling item in a bank reconciliation that will result in an adjusting entry by the depositor is:

   a. outstanding checks. **c.** a bank error.

   b. deposit in transit. **d.** bank service charges.

13. **(LO 4)** Which of the following items in a cash drawer at November 30 is **not** cash?

   a. Money orders.

   b. Coins and currency.

   c. An NSF check.

   d. A customer check dated November 28.

14. **(LO 4)** Which of the following statements correctly describes the reporting of cash?

   a. Cash cannot be combined with cash equivalents.

   b. Restricted cash funds may be combined with cash.

   c. Cash is listed first in the current assets section.

   d. Restricted cash funds cannot be reported as a current asset.

Solutions

1. **c.** Segregation of duties is not an element of the fraud triangle. The other choices are fraud triangle elements.

2. **a.** Safeguarding assets is one of the purposes of using internal control. The other choices are incorrect because while internal control can help to (b) prevent fraud, (c) produce correct financial statements, and (d) deter employee dishonesty, these are not the main purposes of using it.

3. **a.** Filing financial statements with the IRS is not a result of the Sarbanes-Oxley Act (SOX); SOX focuses on the prevention or detection of fraud. The other choices are results of SOX.

4. **c.** Management responsibility is not one of the principles of internal control. The other choices are true statements.

5. **b.** Independent bank reconciliations are not a physical control. The other choices are true statements.

6. **d.** Establishment of responsibility, segregation of duties and independent internal verification are all relevant to a computerized system.

7. **b.** Permitting only designated personnel to handle cash receipts is an application of the principle of establishment of responsibility, not (a) segregation of duties, (c) independent internal verification, or (d) human resource controls.

8. **d.** The use of prenumbered checks in disbursing cash is an application of the principle of documentation procedures, not (a) establishment of responsibility, (b) segregation of duties, or (c) physical controls.

9. **a.** When this check is recorded, the company should debit Cash Over and Short for the shortage of $2 (total of the receipts plus cash in the drawer ($98) versus $100), not (b) debit Petty Cash for $94, (c) credit Cash for $94, or (d) credit Petty Cash for $2.

10. **a.** Having bank auditors verify the correctness of the bank balance per books is not one of the control features of a bank account. The other choices are true statements.

11. **c.** Deposits in transit are added to the bank balance on a bank reconciliation, not (a) deducted from the book balance, (b) added to the book balance, or (d) deducted from the bank balance.

12. **d.** Because the depositor does not know the amount of the bank service charges until the bank statements is received, an adjusting entry must be made when the statement is received. The other choices are incorrect because (a) outstanding checks do not require an adjusting entry by the depositor because the checks have already been recorded in the depositor's books, (b) deposits in transit do not require an adjusting entry by the depositor because the deposits have already been recorded in the depositor's books, and (c) bank errors do not require an adjusting entry by the depositor, but the depositor does need to inform the bank of the error so it can be corrected.

13. **c.** An NSF check should not be considered cash. The other choices are true statements.

14. **c.** Cash is listed first in the current assets section. The other choices are incorrect because (a) cash and cash equivalents can be appropriately combined when reporting cash on the balance sheet, (b) restricted cash is not to be combined with cash when reporting cash on the balance sheet, and (d) restricted funds can be reported as current assets if they will be used within one year.

Practice Brief Exercises

1. **(LO 2)** On May 31, Tyler's petty cash fund of $200 is replenished when the fund contains $7 in cash and receipts for postage $105, freight-out $49, and miscellaneous expense $40. Prepare the journal entry to record the replenishment of the petty cash fund.

Prepare entry to replenish a petty cash fund.

Solution

1. Mar. 20	Postage Expense	105	
	Freight-Out	49	
	Miscellaneous Expense	40	
	Cash		193
	Cash Over and Short		1

2. **(LO 3)** At August 31, Saladino Company has the following bank information: cash balance per bank $5,200, outstanding checks $1,462, deposits in transit $1,211, and a bank debit memo $110. Determine the adjusted cash balance per bank at July 31.

Prepare partial bank reconciliation.

Solution

2.

Cash balance per bank	$5,200
Add: Deposits in transit	1,211
	6,411
Less: Outstanding checks	1,462
Adjusted cash balance per bank	$4,949

3. **(LO 4)** **Financial Statement** Zian Company has the following cash balances: Cash in Bank $18,762, Payroll Bank Account $8,000, Petty Cash $150, and Plant Expansion Fund Cash $30,000 to be used 2 years from now. Explain how each balance should be reported on the balance sheet.

Explain the statement presentation of cash balances.

Solution

3. Zian Company should report Cash in Bank, Payroll Bank Account, and Petty Cash as current assets (usually combined as one Cash amount). Plant Expansion Fund Cash should be reported as a noncurrent asset, assuming the fund is not expected to be used during the next year.

Practice Exercises

1. **(LO 1, 2)** Listed below are five procedures followed by Viel Company.

Indicate good or weak internal control procedures.

1. Total cash receipts are compared to bank deposits daily by Vonda Marshall, who receives cash over the counter.

2. Employees write down hours worked and turn in the sheet to the cashier's office.
3. As a cost-saving measure, employees do not take vacations.
4. Only the sales manager can approve credit sales.
5. Three different employees are assigned one task each related to inventory: ship goods to customers, bill customers, and receive payment from customers.

Instructions

Indicate whether each procedure is an example of good internal control or of weak internal control. If it is an example of good internal control, indicate which internal control principle is being followed. If it is an example of weak internal control, indicate which internal control principles is violated. Use the table below.

Procedure	IC Good or Weak?	Related Internal Control Principle
1.		
2.		
3.		
4.		
5.		

Solution

1.

Procedure	IC Good or Weak?	Related Internal Control Principle
1.	Weak	Independent internal verification
2.	Weak	Physical controls
3.	Weak	Human resource controls
4.	Good	Establishment of responsibility
5.	Good	Segregation of duties

Prepare bank reconciliation and adjusting entries.

2. **(LO 3)** The information below relates to the Cash account in the ledger of Hillfarms Company.

Balance June 1—$9,947; Cash deposited—$37,120.
Balance June 30—$10,094; Checks written—$36,973.

The June bank statement shows a balance of $9,525 on June 30 and the following memoranda.

Credits		Debits	
Collection of electronic funds transfer	$884	NSF check: R. Doll	$245
Interest earned on checking accounts	$26	Safety deposit box rent	$35

At June 30, deposits in transit were $2,581, and outstanding checks totaled $1,382.

Instructions

a. Prepare the bank reconciliation at June 30.

b. Prepare the adjusting entries at June 30, assuming the NSF check was from a customer on account.

Solution

2. **a.**

Hillfarms Company
Bank Reconciliation
June 30

Cash balance per bank statement	$ 9,525
Add: Deposits in transit	2,581
	12,106
Less: Outstanding checks	1,382
Adjusted cash balance per bank	$10,724

Cash balance per books		$10,094
Add: Electronic funds transfer received	$884	
Interest earned	26	910
		11,004
Less: NSF check	245	
Safety deposit box rent	35	280
Adjusted cash balance per books		$10,724

b.

June 30	Cash	884	
	Accounts Receivable		884
30	Cash	26	
	Interest Revenue		26
30	Bank Charge Expense	35	
	Cash		35
30	Accounts Receivable (R. Doll)	245	
	Cash		245

Practice Problem

Prepare bank reconciliation and journalize entries.

(LO 3) Poorten Company's bank statement for May 2020 shows the following data.

Balance 5/1	$12,650	Balance 5/31	$14,280
Debit memorandum:		Credit memorandum:	
NSF check	$175	Collection of electronic funds transfer	$505

The cash balance per books at May 31 is $13,319. Your review of the data reveals the following.

1. The NSF check was from Copple Co., a customer.
2. Outstanding checks at May 31 total $2,410.
3. Deposits in transit at May 31 total $1,752.
4. A Poorten Company check for $352, dated May 10, cleared the bank on May 25. The company recorded this check, which was a payment on account, for $325.

Instructions

a. Prepare a bank reconciliation at May 31.

b. Journalize the entries required by the reconciliation.

Solution

a.

Poorten Company
Bank Reconciliation
May 31, 2020

Cash balance per bank statement		$14,280
Add: Deposits in transit		1,752
		16,032
Less: Outstanding checks		2,410
Adjusted cash balance per bank		$13,622
Cash balance per books		$13,319
Add: Electronic funds transfer received		505
		13,824
Less: NSF check	$175	
Error in recording check ($352 – $325)	27	202
Adjusted cash balance per books		$13,622

b.

May 31	Cash	505	
	Accounts Receivable		505
	(To record receipt of electronic funds transfer)		
31	Accounts Receivable	175	
	Cash		175
	(To record NSF check)		
31	Accounts Payable	27	
	Cash		27
	(To correct error in recording check)		

WileyPLUS

Brief Exercises, DO IT! Exercises, Exercises, Problems, and many additional resources are available for practice in WileyPLUS.

Questions

1. A local bank reported that it lost $150,000 as the result of an employee fraud. Edward Jasso is not clear on what is meant by an "employee fraud." Explain the meaning of fraud to Edward and give an example of frauds that might occur at a bank.

2. Fraud experts often say that there are three primary factors that contribute to employee fraud. Identify the three factors and explain what is meant by each.

3. Identify the five components of a good internal control system.

4. "Internal control is concerned only with enhancing the accuracy of the accounting records." Do you agree? Explain.

5. Discuss how the Sarbanes-Oxley Act has increased the importance of internal control to top managers of a company.

6. What principles of internal control apply to most organizations?

7. In the corner grocery store, all sales clerks make change out of one cash register drawer. Is this a violation of internal control? Why?

8. Liz Kelso is reviewing the principle of segregation of duties. What are the two common applications of this principle?

9. How do documentation procedures contribute to good internal control?

10. What internal control objectives are met by physical controls?

11. (a) Explain the control principle of independent internal verification. (b) What practices are important in applying this principle?

12. As the company accountant, the management of Nickle Company asks you to explain (a) the concept of reasonable assurance in internal control and (b) the importance of the human factor in internal control.

13. What principle(s) of internal control is (are) involved in making daily cash counts of over-the-counter receipts?

14. Assume that **Kohl's** installed new electronic cash registers in its department stores. How do cash registers improve internal control over cash receipts?

15. At Kellum Wholesale Company, two mail clerks open all mail receipts. How does this strengthen internal control?

16. "To have maximum effective internal control over cash disbursements, all payments should be made by check." Is this true? Explain.

17. Ken Deangelo Company's internal controls over cash disbursements provide for the treasurer to sign checks imprinted by a check-writing machine in indelible ink after comparing the check with the approved invoice. Identify the internal control principles that are present in these controls.

18. Explain how these principles apply to cash disbursements: (a) physical controls and (b) human resource controls.

19. (a) What is a voucher system? (b) What principles of internal control apply to a voucher system?

20. What is the essential feature of an electronic funds transfer (EFT) procedure?

21. (a) Identify the three activities that pertain to a petty cash fund and indicate an internal control principle that is applicable to each activity. (b) When are journal entries required in the operation of a petty cash fund?

22. "The use of a bank contributes significantly to good internal control over cash." Is this true? Why or why not?

23. Anna Korte is confused about the lack of agreement between the cash balance per books and the balance per bank. Explain the causes for the lack of agreement to Anna, and give an example of each cause.

24. Heather Kemp asks your help concerning an NSF check. Explain to Heather (a) what an NSF check is, (b) how it is treated in a bank reconciliation, and (c) whether it will require an adjusting entry.

25. (a) "Cash equivalents are the same as cash." Do you agree? Explain. (b) How should restricted cash funds be reported on the balance sheet?

26. Riverside Fertilizer Co. owns the following assets at the balance sheet date.

Cash in bank savings account	$ 8,000
Cash on hand	850
Cash refund due from the IRS	1,000
Checking account balance	14,000
Postdated checks	500

What amount should Riverside report as cash in the balance sheet?

27. At what amount does **Apple** report cash and cash equivalents in its 2015 consolidated balance sheet?

Brief Exercises

BE8.1 (LO 1) Match each situation with the fraud triangle factor—opportunity, financial pressure, or rationalization—that best describes it.

Identify fraud triangle concepts.

a. An employee's monthly credit card payments are nearly 75% of his or her monthly earnings.

b. An employee earns minimum wage at a firm that has reported record earnings for each of the last five years.

c. An employee has an expensive gambling habit.

d. An employee has check-writing and signing responsibilities for a small company, as well as reconciling the bank account.

BE8.2 (LO 1) Shelly Eckert has prepared the following list of statements about internal control.

Indicate internal control concepts.

a. One of the objectives of internal control is to safeguard assets from employee theft, robbery, and unauthorized use.

b. One of the objectives of internal control is to enhance the accuracy and reliability of the accounting records.

c. No laws require U.S. corporations to maintain an adequate system of internal control.

Identify each statement as true or false. If false, indicate how to correct the statement.

BE8.3 (LO 1) Jessica Mahan is the new owner of Penny Parking. She has heard about internal control but is not clear about its importance for her business. Explain to Jessica the four purposes of internal control and give her one application of each purpose for Penny Parking.

Explain the importance of internal control.

BE8.4 (LO 1) The internal control procedures in Valentine Company result in the following provisions. Identify the principles of internal control that are being followed in each case.

Identify internal control principles.

a. Employees who have physical custody of assets do not have access to the accounting records.

b. Each month, the assets on hand are compared to the accounting records by an internal auditor.

c. A prenumbered shipping document is prepared for each shipment of goods to customers.

BE8.5 (LO 2) Rosenquist Company has the following internal control procedures over cash receipts. Identify the internal control principle that is applicable to each procedure.

Identify the internal control principles applicable to cash receipts.

a. All over-the-counter receipts are entered in cash registers.

b. All cashiers are bonded.

c. Daily cash counts are made by cashier department supervisors.

d. The duties of receiving cash, recording cash, and custody of cash are assigned to different individuals.

e. Only cashiers may operate cash registers.

BE8.6 (LO 2) The cash register tape for Bluestem Industries reported sales of $6,871.50. Record the journal entry that would be necessary for each of the following situations. (a) Cash to be accounted for exceeds cash on hand by $50.75. (b) Cash on hand exceeds cash to be accounted for by $28.32.

Make journal entries for cash overage and shortfall.

BE8.7 (LO 2) While examining cash receipts information, the accounting department determined the following information: opening cash balance $160, cash on hand $1,125.74, and cash sales per register tape $980.83. Prepare the required journal entry based upon the cash count sheet.

Make journal entry using cash count sheet.

BE8.8 (LO 2) Pennington Company has the following internal control procedures over cash disbursements. Identify the internal control principle that is applicable to each procedure.

Identify the internal control principles applicable to cash disbursements.

a. Company checks are prenumbered.

b. The bank statement is reconciled monthly by an internal auditor.

c. Blank checks are stored in a safe in the treasurer's office.

d. Only the treasurer or assistant treasurer may sign checks.

e. Check-signers are not allowed to record cash disbursement transactions.

Prepare entry to replenish a petty cash fund.

BE8.9 (LO 2) On March 20, Dody's petty cash fund of $100 is replenished when the fund contains $9 in cash and receipts for postage $52, freight-out $26, and travel expense $10. Prepare the journal entry to record the replenishment of the petty cash fund.

Identify the control features of a bank account.

BE8.10 (LO 3) Lance Bachman is uncertain about the control features of a bank account. Explain the control benefits of (a) a check and (b) a bank statement.

Indicate location of reconciling items in a bank reconciliation.

BE8.11 (LO 3) The following reconciling items are applicable to the bank reconciliation for Ellington Company. Indicate how each item should be shown on a bank reconciliation: (a) outstanding checks, (b) bank debit memorandum for service charge, (c) bank credit memorandum for collecting a note for the depositor, and (d) deposits in transit.

Identify reconciling items that require adjusting entries.

BE8.12 (LO 3) Using the data in BE8.11, indicate (a) the items that will result in an adjustment to the depositor's records and (b) why the other items do not require adjustment.

Prepare partial bank reconciliation.

BE8.13 (LO 3) At July 31, Ramirez Company has the following bank information: cash balance per bank $7,420, outstanding checks $762, deposits in transit $1,620, and a bank service charge $20. Determine the adjusted cash balance per bank at July 31.

Prepare partial bank reconciliation.

BE8.14 (LO 3) At August 31, Pratt Company has a cash balance per books of $9,500 and the following additional data from the bank statement: charge for printing Pratt Company checks $35, interest earned on checking account balance $40, and outstanding checks $800. Determine the adjusted cash balance per books at August 31.

Compute outstanding checks.

BE8.15 (LO 3) In the month of November, Fiesta Company Inc. wrote checks in the amount of $9,750. In December, checks in the amount of $11,762 were written. In November, $8,800 of these checks were presented to the bank for payment, and $10,889 in December. What is the amount of outstanding checks at the end of November? At the end of December?

Explain the statement presentation of cash balances.

BE8.16 (LO 4) **Financial Statement** Zhang Company has the following cash balances: Cash in Bank $15,742, Payroll Bank Account $6,000, and Plant Expansion Fund Cash $25,000 to be used two years from now. Explain how each balance should be reported on the balance sheet.

DO IT! Exercises

Identify violations of control activities.

DO IT! 8.1 (LO 1) Identify which control activity is violated in each of the following situations, and explain how the situation creates an opportunity for fraud or inappropriate accounting practices.

1. Once a month, the sales department sends sales invoices to the accounting department to be recorded.
2. Leah Hutcherson orders merchandise for Rice Lake Company; she also receives merchandise and authorizes payment for merchandise.
3. Several clerks at Great Foods use the same cash register drawer.

Design system of internal control over cash receipts.

DO IT! 8.2a (LO 2) Gary Stanten is concerned with control over mail receipts at Gary's Sporting Goods. All mail receipts are opened by Al Krane. Al sends the checks to the accounting department, where they are stamped "For Deposit Only." The accounting department records and deposits the mail receipts weekly. Gary asks for your help in installing a good system of internal control over mail receipts.

Make journal entries for petty cash fund.

DO IT! 8.2b (LO 2) Wilkinson Company established a $100 petty cash fund on August 1. On August 31, the fund had $7 cash remaining and petty cash receipts for postage $31, office supplies $42, and miscellaneous expense $16. Prepare journal entries to establish the fund on August 1 and replenish the fund on August 31.

Explain treatment of items in bank reconciliation.

DO IT! 8.3 (LO 3) Roger Richman owns Richman Blankets. He asks you to explain how he should treat the following reconciling items when reconciling the company's bank account.

1. Outstanding checks.
2. A deposit in transit.

3. The bank charged to the company account a check written by another company.
4. A debit memorandum for a bank service charge.

DO IT! 8.4 (LO 4) Indicate whether each of the following statements is true or false.

Analyze statements about the reporting of cash.

1. A company has the following assets at the end of the year: cash on hand $40,000, cash refund due from customer $30,000, and checking account balance $22,000. Cash and cash equivalents is therefore $62,000.
2. A company that has received NSF checks should report these checks as a current liability on the balance sheet.
3. Restricted cash that is a current asset is reported as part of cash and cash equivalents.
4. A company has cash in the bank of $50,000, petty cash of $400, and stock investments of $100,000. Total cash and cash equivalents is therefore $50,400.

Exercises

E8.1 (LO 1) Eve Herschel is the owner of Herschel's Pizza. Herschel's is operated strictly on a carryout basis. Customers pick up their orders at a counter where a clerk exchanges the pizza for cash. While at the counter, the customer can see other employees making the pizzas and the large ovens in which the pizzas are baked.

Identify the principles of internal control.

Instructions

Identify the six principles of internal control and give an example of each principle that you might observe when picking up your pizza. (*Note:* It may not be possible to observe all the principles.)

E8.2 (LO 1, 2) The following control procedures are used at Torres Company for over-the-counter cash receipts.

Identify internal control weaknesses over cash receipts and suggest improvements.

1. To minimize the risk of robbery, cash in excess of $100 is stored in an unlocked briefcase in the stock room until it is deposited in the bank.
2. All over-the-counter receipts are processed by three clerks who use a cash register with a single cash drawer.
3. The company accountant makes the bank deposit and then records the day's receipts.
4. At the end of each day, the total receipts are counted by the cashier on duty and reconciled to the cash register total.
5. Cashiers are experienced; they are not bonded.

Instructions

a. For each procedure, explain the weakness in internal control, and identify the control principle that is violated.

b. For each weakness, suggest a change in procedure that will result in good internal control.

E8.3 (LO 1, 2) The following control procedures are used in Mendy Lang's Boutique Shoppe for cash disbursements.

Identify internal control weaknesses over cash disbursements and suggest improvements.

1. The company accountant prepares the bank reconciliation and reports any discrepancies to the owner.
2. The store manager personally approves all payments before signing and issuing checks.
3. Each week, 100 company checks are left in an unmarked envelope on a shelf behind the cash register.
4. After payment, bills are filed in a paid invoice folder.
5. The company checks are unnumbered.

Instructions

a. For each procedure, explain the weakness in internal control, and identify the internal control principle that is violated.

b. For each weakness, suggest a change in the procedure that will result in good internal control.

Identify internal control weaknesses for cash disbursements and suggest improvements.

E8.4 (LO 2) **Writing** At Danner Company, checks are not prenumbered because both the purchasing agent and the treasurer are authorized to issue checks. Each signer has access to unissued checks kept in an unlocked file cabinet. The purchasing agent pays all bills pertaining to goods purchased for resale. Prior to payment, the purchasing agent determines that the goods have been received and verifies the mathematical accuracy of the vendor's invoice. After payment, the invoice is filed by the vendor name, and the purchasing agent records the payment. The treasurer pays all other bills following approval by authorized employees. After payment, the treasurer stamps all bills PAID, files them by payment date, and records the checks in the cash disbursements journal. Danner Company maintains one checking account that is reconciled by the treasurer.

Instructions

a. List the weaknesses in internal control over cash disbursements.

b. Write a memo to the company treasurer indicating your recommendations for improvement.

Indicate whether procedure is good or weak internal control.

E8.5 (LO 1, 2) Listed below are five procedures followed by Eikenberry Company.

1. Several individuals operate the cash register using the same register drawer.
2. A monthly bank reconciliation is prepared by someone who has no other cash responsibilities.
3. Joe Cockrell writes checks and also records cash payment entries.
4. One individual orders inventory, while a different individual authorizes payments.
5. Unnumbered sales invoices from credit sales are forwarded to the accounting department every four weeks for recording.

Instructions

Indicate whether each procedure is an example of good internal control or of weak internal control. If it is an example of good internal control, indicate which internal control principle is being followed. If it is an example of weak internal control, indicate which internal control principle is violated. Use the table below.

Procedure	IC Good or Weak?	Related Internal Control Principle
1.		
2.		
3.		
4.		
5.		

Indicate whether procedure is good or weak internal control.

E8.6 (LO 1, 2) Listed below are five procedures followed by Gilmore Company.

1. Employees are required to take vacations.
2. Any member of the sales department can approve credit sales.
3. Paul Jaggard ships goods to customers, bills customers, and receives payment from customers.
4. Total cash receipts are compared to bank deposits daily by someone who has no other cash responsibilities.
5. Time clocks are used for recording time worked by employees.

Instructions

Indicate whether each procedure is an example of good internal control or of weak internal control. If it is an example of good internal control, indicate which internal control principle is being followed. If it is an example of weak internal control, indicate which internal control principle is violated. Use the table below.

Procedure	IC Good or Weak?	Related Internal Control Principle
1.		
2.		
3.		
4.		
5.		

Prepare journal entries for a petty cash fund.

E8.7 (LO 2) Setterstrom Company established a petty cash fund on May 1, cashing a check for $100. The company reimbursed the fund on June 1 and July 1 with the following results.

June 1: Cash in fund $1.75. Receipts: delivery expense $31.25, postage expense $39.00, and miscellaneous expense $25.00.

July 1: Cash in fund $3.25. Receipts: delivery expense $21.00, entertainment expense $51.00, and miscellaneous expense $24.75.

On July 10, Setterstrom increased the fund from $100 to $130.

Instructions

Prepare journal entries for Setterstrom Company for May 1, June 1, July 1, and July 10.

E8.8 (LO 2) Horvath Company uses an imprest petty cash system. The fund was established on March 1 with a balance of $100. During March, the following petty cash receipts were found in the petty cash box.

Prepare journal entries for a petty cash fund.

Date	Receipt No.	For	Amount
3/5	1	Stamp Inventory	$39
7	2	Freight-Out	21
9	3	Miscellaneous Expense	6
11	4	Travel Expense	24
14	5	Miscellaneous Expense	5

The fund was replenished on March 15 when the fund contained $2 in cash. On March 20, the amount in the fund was increased to $175.

Instructions

Journalize the entries in March that pertain to the operation of the petty cash fund.

E8.9 (LO 3) Don Wyatt is unable to reconcile the bank balance at January 31. Don's reconciliation is as follows.

Prepare bank reconciliation and adjusting entries.

Cash balance per bank	$3,560.20
Add: NSF check	490.00
Less: Bank service charge	25.00
Adjusted balance per bank	$4,025.20
Cash balance per books	$3,875.20
Less: Deposits in transit	530.00
Add: Outstanding checks	730.00
Adjusted balance per books	$4,075.20

Instructions

a. Prepare a correct bank reconciliation.

b. Journalize the entries required by the reconciliation.

E8.10 (LO 3) On April 30, the bank reconciliation of Westbrook Company shows three outstanding checks: no. 254, $650; no. 255, $620; and no. 257, $410. The May bank statement and the May cash payments journal show the following.

Determine outstanding checks.

Bank Statement			Cash Payments Journal		
Checks Paid			Checks Issued		
Date	Check No.	Amount	Date	Check No.	Amount
5/4	254	$650	5/2	258	$159
5/2	257	410	5/5	259	275
5/17	258	159	5/10	260	890
5/12	259	275	5/15	261	500
5/20	261	500	5/22	262	750
5/29	263	480	5/24	263	480
5/30	262	750	5/29	264	560

Instructions

Using Step 2 in the reconciliation procedure, list the outstanding checks at May 31.

E8.11 (LO 3) The following information pertains to Crane Video Company.

Prepare bank reconciliation and adjusting entries.

Excel

1. Cash balance per bank, July 31, $7,263.

2. July bank service charge not recorded by the depositor $28.

3. Cash balance per books, July 31, $7,284.

4. Deposits in transit, July 31, $1,300.
5. Bank collected $700 note for Crane in July, plus interest $36, less fee $20. The collection has not been recorded by Crane, and no interest has been accrued.
6. Outstanding checks, July 31, $591.

Instructions

a. Prepare a bank reconciliation at July 31.
b. Journalize the adjusting entries at July 31 on the books of Crane Video Company.

Prepare bank reconciliation and adjusting entries.

Excel

E8.12 (LO 3) The information below relates to the Cash account in the ledger of Minton Company.

Balance September 1—$17,150; Cash deposited—$64,000.
Balance September 30—$17,404; Checks written—$63,746.

The September bank statement shows a balance of $16,422 on September 30 and the following memoranda.

Credits		Debits	
Collection of $2,500 note plus interest $30	$2,530	NSF check: Richard Nance	$425
Interest earned on checking account	$45	Safety deposit box rent	$65

At September 30, deposits in transit were $5,450, and outstanding checks totaled $2,383.

Instructions

a. Prepare the bank reconciliation at September 30.
b. Prepare the adjusting entries at September 30, assuming (1) the NSF check was from a customer on account, and (2) no interest had been accrued on the note.

Compute deposits in transit and outstanding checks for two bank reconciliations.

E8.13 (LO 3) The cash records of Dawes Company show the following four situations.

For July:

1. The June 30 bank reconciliation indicated that deposits in transit total $920. During July, the general ledger account Cash shows deposits of $15,750, but the bank statement indicates that only $15,600 in deposits were received during the month.
2. The June 30 bank reconciliation also reported outstanding checks of $680. During the month of July, Dawes Company's books show that $17,200 of checks were issued. The bank statement showed that $16,400 of checks cleared the bank in July.

For September:

3. In September, deposits per the bank statement totaled $26,700, deposits per books were $26,400, and deposits in transit at September 30 were $2,100.
4. In September, cash disbursements per books were $23,700, checks clearing the bank were $25,000, and outstanding checks at September 30 were $2,100.

There were no bank debit or credit memoranda. No errors were made by either the bank or Dawes Company.

Instructions

Answer the following questions.

a. In situation (1), what were the deposits in transit at July 31?
b. In situation (2), what were the outstanding checks at July 31?
c. In situation (3), what were the deposits in transit at August 31?
d. In situation (4), what were the outstanding checks at August 31?

Show presentation of cash in financial statements.

E8.14 (LO 4) **Financial Statement** Wynn Company has recorded the following items in its financial records.

Cash in bank	$ 42,000
Cash in plant expansion fund	100,000
Cash on hand	12,000
Highly liquid investments	34,000
Petty cash	500
Receivables from customers	89,000
Stock investments	61,000

The highly liquid investments had maturities of 3 months or less when they were purchased. The stock investments will be sold in the next 6 to 12 months. The plant expansion project will begin in 3 years.

Instructions

a. What amount should Wynn report as "Cash and cash equivalents" on its balance sheet?

b. Where should the items not included in part (a) be reported on the balance sheet?

Identify reporting of cash.

E8.15 (LO 4) A new accountant at Wyne Inc. is trying to identify which of the amounts shown below should be reported as the current asset "Cash and cash equivalents" in the year-end balance sheet, as of April 30, 2020.

1. $60 of currency and coin in a locked box used for incidental cash transactions.
2. A $10,000 U.S. Treasury bill, due May 31, 2020.
3. $260 of April-dated checks that Wyne has received from customers but not yet deposited.
4. An $85 check received from a customer in payment of its April account, but postdated to May 1.
5. $2,500 in the company's checking account.
6. $4,800 in its savings account.
7. $75 of prepaid postage in its postage meter.
8. A $25 IOU from the company receptionist.

Instructions

a. What balance should Wyne report as its "Cash and cash equivalents" balance at April 30, 2020?

b. In what account(s) and in what financial statement(s) should the items not included in "Cash and cash equivalents" be reported?

Problems: Set A

Identify internal control principles over cash disbursements.

P8.1A (LO 1, 2) Bolz Office Supply Company recently changed its system of internal control over cash disbursements. The system includes the following features.

Instead of being unnumbered and manually prepared, all checks must now be prenumbered and prepared by using the new accounts payable software purchased by the company. Before a check can be issued, each invoice must have the approval of Kathy Moon, the purchasing agent, and Robin Self, the receiving department supervisor. Checks must be signed by either Jennifer Edwards, the treasurer, or Rich Woodruff, the assistant treasurer. Before signing a check, the signer is expected to compare the amount of the check with the amount on the invoice.

After signing a check, the signer stamps the invoice PAID and inserts within the stamp, the date, check number, and amount of the check. The "paid" invoice is then sent to the accounting department for recording.

Blank checks are stored in a safe in the treasurer's office. The combination to the safe is known only by the treasurer and assistant treasurer. Each month, the bank statement is reconciled with the bank balance per books by the assistant chief accountant. All employees who handle or account for cash are bonded.

Instructions

Identify the internal control principles and their application to cash disbursements of Bolz Office Supply Company.

Identify internal control weaknesses in cash receipts and cash disbursements.

P8.2A (LO 1, 2) Rondelli Middle School wants to raise money for a new sound system for its auditorium. The primary fund-raising event is a dance at which the famous disc jockey D.J. Sound will play classic and not-so-classic dance tunes. Matt Ballester, the music and theater instructor, has been given the responsibility for coordinating the fund-raising efforts. This is Matt's first experience with fund-raising. He decides to put the eighth-grade choir in charge of the event; he will be a relatively passive observer.

Matt had 500 unnumbered tickets printed for the dance. He left the tickets in a box on his desk and told the choir students to take as many tickets as they thought they could sell for $5 each. In order to ensure that no extra tickets would be floating around, he told them to dispose of any unsold tickets. When the students received payment for the tickets, they were to bring the cash back to Matt and he would put it in a locked box in his desk drawer.

Some of the students were responsible for decorating the gymnasium for the dance. Matt gave each of them a key to the money box and told them that if they took money out to purchase materials, they should put a note in the box saying how much they took and what it was used for. After 2 weeks the money box appeared to be getting full, so Matt asked Jeff Kenney to count the money, prepare a deposit slip, and deposit the money in a bank account Matt had opened.

The day of the dance, Matt wrote a check from the account to pay the DJ. D.J. Sound, however, said that he accepted only cash and did not give receipts. So Matt took $200 out of the cash box and gave it to D.J. At the dance, Matt had Sam Copper working at the entrance to the gymnasium, collecting tickets from students, and selling tickets to those who had not prepurchased them. Matt estimated that 400 students attended the dance.

The following day, Matt closed out the bank account, which had $250 in it, and gave that amount plus the $180 in the cash box to Principal Finke. Principal Finke seemed surprised that, after generating roughly $2,000 in sales, the dance netted only $430 in cash. Matt did not know how to respond.

Instructions

Identify as many internal control weaknesses as you can in this scenario, and suggest how each could be addressed.

Journalize and post petty cash fund transactions.

P8.3A (LO 2) Kael Company maintains a petty cash fund for small expenditures. These transactions occurred during the month of August.

Aug.	1	Established the petty cash fund by writing a check payable to the petty cash custodian for $200.
	15	Replenished the petty cash fund by writing a check for $175. On this date, the fund consisted of $25 in cash and these petty cash receipts: freight-out $74.40, entertainment expense $36, postage expense $33.70, and miscellaneous expense $27.50.
	16	Increased the amount of the petty cash fund to $400 by writing a check for $200.
	31	Replenished the petty cash fund by writing a check for $283. On this date, the fund consisted of $117 in cash and these petty cash receipts: postage expense $145, entertainment expense $90.60, and freight-out $46.40.

Instructions

a. Journalize the petty cash transactions.

b. Post to the Petty Cash account.

c. What internal control features exist in a petty cash fund?

Prepare a bank reconciliation and adjusting entries.

P8.4A (LO 3) On July 31, 2020, Keeds Company had a cash balance per books of $6,140. The statement from Dakota State Bank on that date showed a balance of $7,690.80. A comparison of the bank statement with the Cash account revealed the following facts.

1. The bank service charge for July was $25.
2. The bank collected $1,520 for Keeds Company through electronic funds transfer.
3. The July 31 receipts of $1,193.30 were not included in the bank deposits for July. These receipts were deposited by the company in a night deposit vault on July 31.
4. Company check No. 2480 issued to L. Taylor, a creditor, for $384 that cleared the bank in July was incorrectly entered as a cash payment on July 10 for $348.
5. Checks outstanding on July 31 totaled $1,860.10.
6. On July 31, the bank statement showed an NSF charge of $575 for a check received by the company from W. Krueger, a customer, on account.

Instructions

a. Adjusted cash bal. $7,024.00

a. Prepare the bank reconciliation as of July 31.

b. Prepare the necessary adjusting entries at July 31.

P8.5A (LO 3) The bank portion of the bank reconciliation for Langer Company at November 30, 2020, was as follows.

Prepare a bank reconciliation and adjusting entries from detailed data.

Langer Company
Bank Reconciliation
November 30, 2020

Cash balance per bank			$14,367.90
Add: Deposits in transit			2,530.20
			16,898.10
Less: Outstanding checks			
	Check Number	Check Amount	
	3451	$2,260.40	
	3470	720.10	
	3471	844.50	
	3472	1,426.80	
	3474	1,050.00	6,301.80
Adjusted cash balance per bank			$10,596.30

The adjusted cash balance per bank agreed with the cash balance per books at November 30.
The December bank statement showed the following checks and deposits.

Bank Statement

Checks			Deposits	
Date	**Number**	**Amount**	**Date**	**Amount**
12-1	3451	$ 2,260.40	12-1	$ 2,530.20
12-2	3471	844.50	12-4	1,211.60
12-7	3472	1,426.80	12-8	2,365.10
12-4	3475	1,640.70	12-16	2,672.70
12-8	3476	1,300.00	12-21	2,945.00
12-10	3477	2,130.00	12-26	2,567.30
12-15	3479	3,080.00	12-29	2,836.00
12-27	3480	600.00	12-30	1,025.00
12-30	3482	475.50	Total	$18,152.90
12-29	3483	1,140.00		
12-31	3485	540.80		
	Total	$15,438.70		

The cash records per books for December showed the following.

Cash Payments Journal

Date	Number	Amount	Date	Number	Amount
12-1	3475	$1,640.70	12-20	3482	$ 475.50
12-2	3476	1,300.00	12-22	3483	1,140.00
12-2	3477	2,130.00	12-23	3484	798.00
12-4	3478	621.30	12-24	3485	450.80
12-8	3479	3,080.00	12-30	3486	889.50
12-10	3480	600.00	Total		$13,933.20
12-17	3481	807.40			

Cash Receipts Journal

Date	Amount
12-3	$ 1,211.60
12-7	2,365.10
12-15	2,672.70
12-20	2,954.00
12-25	2,567.30
12-28	2,836.00
12-30	1,025.00
12-31	1,690.40
Total	$17,322.10

The bank statement contained two memoranda:

1. A credit of $2,242 for the collection of Langer Company of an electronic funds transfer.
2. A debit for the printing of additional company checks $85.

At December 31, the cash balance per books was $13,985.20, and the cash balance per the bank statement was $19,239.10. The bank did not make any errors, but **Langer Company made two errors.**

a. Adjusted balance per books $16,043.20

Instructions

a. Using the steps in the reconciliation procedure described in the chapter, prepare a bank reconciliation at December 31, 2020.

b. Prepare the adjusting entries based on the reconciliation. (*Hint:* The correction of any errors pertaining to recording checks should be made to Accounts Payable. The correction of any errors relating to recording cash receipts should be made to Accounts Receivable.)

Prepare a bank reconciliation and adjusting entries.

P8.6A (LO 3) Timmins Company of Emporia, Kansas, spreads herbicides and applies liquid fertilizer for local farmers. On May 31, 2020, the company's Cash account per its general ledger showed a balance of $6,738.90.

The bank statement from Emporia State Bank on that date showed the following balance.

Emporia State Bank

Checks and Debits	Deposits and Credits	Daily Balance
XXX	XXX	5-31 6,968.00

A comparison of the details on the bank statement with the details in the Cash account revealed the following facts.

1. The statement included a debit memo of $40 for the printing of additional company checks.
2. Cash sales of $883.15 on May 12 were deposited in the bank. The cash receipts entry and the deposit slip were incorrectly made for $933.15. The bank credited Timmins Company for the correct amount.
3. Outstanding checks at May 31 totaled $276.25, and deposits in transit were $1,880.15.
4. On May 18, the company issued check No. 1181 for $685 to H. Moses, on account. The check, which cleared the bank in May, was incorrectly journalized and posted by Timmins Company for $658.
5. $2,690 was collected by the bank for Timmins Company on May 31 through electronic funds transfer.
6. Included with the canceled checks was a check issued by Tomins Company to C. Pernod for $360 that was incorrectly charged to Timmins Company by the bank.
7. On May 31, the bank statement showed an NSF charge of $380 for a check issued by Sara Ballard, a customer, to Timmins Company on account.

Instructions

a. Adjusted cash bal. $8,931.90

a. Prepare the bank reconciliation at May 31, 2020.

b. Prepare the necessary adjusting entries for Timmins Company at May 31, 2020.

Prepare a comprehensive bank reconciliation with theft and internal control deficiencies.

P8.7A (LO 1, 2, 3) Daisey Company is a very profitable small business. It has not, however, given much consideration to internal control. For example, in an attempt to keep clerical and office expenses to a minimum, the company has combined the jobs of cashier and bookkeeper. As a result, Bret Turrin handles all cash receipts, keeps the accounting records, and prepares the monthly bank reconciliations.

The balance per the bank statement on October 31, 2020, was $18,380. Outstanding checks were No. 62 for $140.75, No. 183 for $180, No. 284 for $253.25, No. 862 for $190.71, No. 863 for $226.80, and No. 864 for $165.28. Included with the statement was a credit memorandum of $185 indicating the collection of a note receivable for Daisey Company by the bank on October 25. This memorandum has not been recorded by Daisey.

The company's ledger showed one Cash account with a balance of $21,877.72. The balance included undeposited cash on hand. Because of the lack of internal controls, Bret took for personal use all of the undeposited receipts in excess of $3,795.51. He then prepared the following bank reconciliation in an effort to conceal his theft of cash.

Cash balance per books, October 31		$21,877.72
Add: Outstanding checks		
No. 862	$190.71	
No. 863	226.80	
No. 864	165.28	482.79
		22,360.51
Less: Undeposited receipts		3,795.51
Unadjusted balance per bank, October 31		18,565.00
Less: Bank credit memorandum		185.00
Cash balance per bank statement, October 31		$18,380.00

Instructions

a. Prepare a correct bank reconciliation. (*Hint:* Deduct the amount of the theft from the adjusted balance per books.)

a. Adjusted cash bal. $21,018.72

b. Indicate the three ways that Bret attempted to conceal the theft and the dollar amount involved in each method.

c. What principles of internal control were violated in this case?

Continuing Case

Cookie Creations

(*Note:* This is a continuation of the Cookie Creations case from Chapters 1 through 6.)

© leungchopan/
Shutterstock

CC8 Part 1 Natalie is struggling to keep up with the recording of her accounting transactions. She is spending a lot of time marketing and selling mixers and giving her cookie classes. Her friend John is an accounting student who runs his own accounting service. He has asked Natalie if she would like to have him do her accounting. John and Natalie meet and discuss her business.

Part 2 Natalie decides that she cannot afford to hire John to do her accounting. One way that she can ensure that her cash account does not have any errors and is accurate and up-to-date is to prepare a bank reconciliation at the end of each month. Natalie would like you to help her.

Go to **WileyPLUS** *for complete case details and instructions.*

Ethics Case

EC8 You are the assistant controller in charge of general ledger accounting at Linbarger Bottling Company. Your company has a large loan from an insurance company. The loan agreement requires that the company's cash account balance be maintained at $200,000 or more, as reported monthly.

At June 30, the cash balance is $80,000, which you report to Lisa Infante, the financial vice president. Lisa excitedly instructs you to keep the cash receipts book open for one additional day for purposes of the June 30 report to the insurance company. Lisa says, "If we don't get that cash balance over $200,000, we'll default on our loan agreement. They could close us down, put us all out of our jobs!" Lisa continues, "I talked to Oconto Distributors (one of Linbarger's largest customers) this morning. They said they sent us a check for $150,000 yesterday. We should receive it tomorrow. If we include just that one check in our cash balance, we'll be in the clear. It's in the mail!"

Instructions

a. Who will suffer negative effects if you do not comply with Lisa Infante's instructions? Who will suffer if you do comply?

b. What are the ethical considerations in this case?

c. What alternatives do you have?

Comprehensive Accounting Cycle Review

ACR8 On December 1, 2020, Fullerton Company had the following account balances.

	Debit		Credit
Cash	$18,200	Accumulated Depreciation—Equipment	$ 3,000
Notes Receivable	2,200	Accounts Payable	6,100
Accounts Receivable	7,500	Owner's Capital	64,400
Inventory	16,000		$73,500
Prepaid Insurance	1,600		
Equipment	28,000		
	$73,500		

During December, the company completed the following transactions.

Dec. 7 Received $3,600 cash from customers in payment of account (no discount allowed).
12 Purchased merchandise on account from Vance Co. $12,000, terms 1/10, n/30.
17 Sold merchandise on account $16,000, terms 2/10, n/30. The cost of the merchandise sold was $10,000.
19 Paid salaries $2,200.
22 Paid Vance Co. in full, less discount.
26 Received collections in full, less discounts, from customers billed on December 17.
31 Received $2,700 cash from customers in payment of account (no discount allowed).

Adjustment data:

1. Depreciation $200 per month.
2. Insurance expired $400.

Instructions

a. Journalize the December transactions. (Assume a perpetual inventory system.)

b. Enter the December 1 balances in the ledger T-accounts and post the December transactions. Use Cost of Goods Sold, Depreciation Expense, Insurance Expense, Salaries and Wages Expense, Sales Revenue, and Sales Discounts.

c. The statement from Jackson County Bank on December 31 showed a balance of $26,130. A comparison of the bank statement with the Cash account revealed the following facts.

1. The bank collected a note receivable of $2,200 for Fullerton Company on December 15.
2. The December 31 receipts were deposited in a night deposit vault on December 31. These deposits were recorded by the bank in January.
3. Checks outstanding on December 31 totaled $1,210.
4. On December 31, the bank statement showed an NSF charge of $680 for a check received by the company from L. Bryan, a customer, on account.

Prepare a bank reconciliation as of December 31 based on the available information. (*Hint:* The cash balance per books is $26,100. This can be proven by finding the balance in the Cash account from parts (a) and (b).)

d. Journalize the adjusting entries resulting from the bank reconciliation and adjustment data.

e. Post the adjusting entries to the ledger T-accounts.

f. Prepare an adjusted trial balance.

g. Prepare an income statement for December and a classified balance sheet at December 31.

Expand Your Critical Thinking

Financial Reporting Problem: Apple Inc.

CT8.1 The financial statements of **Apple Inc.** are presented in Appendix A at the end of this textbook. The complete annual report, including the notes to the financial statements, is available at the company's website.

Instructions

a. What comments, if any, are made about cash in the "Report of the Independent Registered Public Accounting Firm"?

b. What data about cash and cash equivalents are shown in the consolidated balance sheet?

c. In its notes to Consolidated Financial Statements, how does Apple define cash equivalents?

d. In "Management's Annual Report on Internal Control over Financial Reporting," what does Apple's management say about internal control?

Comparative Analysis Problem: PepsiCo, Inc. vs. The Coca-Cola Company

CT8.2 **PepsiCo**'s financial statements are presented in Appendix B. Financial statements of **The Coca-Cola Company** are presented in Appendix C. The complete annual reports of PepsiCo and Coca-Cola, including the notes to the financial statements, are available at each company's respective website.

Instructions

a. Based on the information contained in these financial statements, determine each of the following for each company:

1. Cash and cash equivalents balance at December 26, 2015, for PepsiCo and at December 31, 2015, for Coca-Cola.
2. Increase (decrease) in cash and cash equivalents from 2014 to 2015.
3. Cash provided by operating activities during the year ended December 2015 (from statement of cash flows).

b. What conclusions concerning the management of cash can be drawn from these data?

Comparative Analysis Problem: Amazon.com, Inc. vs. Wal-Mart Stores, Inc.

CT8.3 **Amazon.com, Inc.**'s financial statements are presented in Appendix D. Financial statements of **Wal-Mart Stores, Inc.** are presented in Appendix E. The complete annual reports of Amazon and Wal-Mart, including the notes to the financial statements, are available at each company's respective website.

Instructions

a. Based on the information contained in these financial statements, determine each of the following for each company:

1. Cash and cash equivalents balance at December 31, 2015, for Amazon and at January 31, 2016, for Wal-Mart.
2. Increase (decrease) in cash and cash equivalents from 2014 to 2015.
3. Net cash provided by operating activities during the year ended December 31, 2015, for Amazon and January 31, 2016, for Wal-Mart from statement of cash flows.

b. What conclusions concerning the management of cash can be drawn from these data?

Real-World Focus

CT8.4 All organizations should have systems of internal control to combat fraud.

Instructions

Go to the **Association of Certified Fraud Examiner (ACFE)** website, search "Report to the Nations on Occupational Fraud and Abuse," click **Costs**, and then answer the following questions.

a. What is the percent of annual revenues lost to fraud?

b. What is the median loss for the United States due to occupational fraud?

c. What happens when organizations lack anti-fraud controls?

Decision-Making Across the Organization

CT8.5 The board of trustees of a local church is concerned about the internal accounting controls for the offering collections made at weekly services. The trustees ask you to serve on a three-person audit team with the internal auditor of a local college and a CPA who has just joined the church.

At a meeting of the audit team and the board of trustees you learn the following.

1. The church's board of trustees has delegated responsibility for the financial management and audit of the financial records to the finance committee. This group prepares the annual budget and approves major disbursements. It is not involved in collections or recordkeeping. No audit has been made in recent years because the same trusted employee has kept church records and served as financial secretary for 15 years. The church does not carry any fidelity insurance.
2. The collection at the weekly service is taken by a team of ushers who volunteer to serve one month. The ushers take the collection plates to a basement office at the rear of the church. They hand their plates to the head usher and return to the church service. After all plates have been turned in, the head usher counts the cash received. The head usher then places the cash in the church safe along with a notation of the amount counted. The head usher volunteers to serve for 3 months.
3. The next morning the financial secretary opens the safe and recounts the collection. The secretary withholds \$150–\$200 in cash, depending on the cash expenditures expected for the week, and deposits the remainder of the collections in the bank. To facilitate the deposit, church members who contribute by check are asked to make their checks payable to "Cash."

4. Each month, the financial secretary reconciles the bank statement and submits a copy of the reconciliation to the board of trustees. The reconciliations have rarely contained any bank errors and have never shown any errors per books.

Instructions

With the class divided into groups, answer the following.

a. Indicate the weaknesses in internal accounting control over the handling of collections.

b. List the improvements in internal control procedures that you plan to make at the next meeting of the audit team for (1) the ushers, (2) the head usher, (3) the financial secretary, and (4) the finance committee.

c. What church policies should be changed to improve internal control?

Communication Activity

CT8.6 As a new auditor for the CPA firm of Eaton, Quayle, and Hale, you have been assigned to review the internal controls over mail cash receipts of Pritchard Company. Your review reveals the following. Checks are promptly endorsed "For Deposit Only," but no list of the checks is prepared by the person opening the mail. The mail is opened either by the cashier or by the employee who maintains the accounts receivable records. Mail receipts are deposited in the bank weekly by the cashier.

Instructions

Write a letter to Danny Peak, owner of Pritchard Company, explaining the weaknesses in internal control and your recommendations for improving the system.

All About You

CT8.7 The print and electronic media are full of stories about potential security risks that may arise from your computer or smartphone. It is important to keep in mind, however, that there are also many other ways that your identity can be stolen. The federal government provides many resources to help protect you from identity thieves.

Instructions

Search the Internet for and then go to the federal government website on identity theft, and then identify five signs of identity theft.

FASB Codification Activity

CT8.8 If your school has a subscription to the FASB Codification, log in and prepare responses to the following.

a. How is cash defined in the Codification?

b. How are cash equivalents defined in the Codification?

c. What are the disclosure requirements related to cash and cash equivalents?

A Look at IFRS

LEARNING OBJECTIVE 5

Compare the accounting for fraud, internal control, and cash under GAAP and IFRS.

Fraud can occur anywhere. Because the three main factors that contribute to fraud are universal in nature, the principles of internal control activities are used globally by companies. While Sarbanes-Oxley

(SOX) does not apply to international companies, most large international companies have internal controls similar to those indicated in the chapter. IFRS and GAAP are also very similar in accounting for cash. *IAS No. 1 (revised),* "Presentation of Financial Statements," is the only standard that discusses issues specifically related to cash.

Key Points

Following are the key similarities and differences between GAAP and IFRS related to fraud, internal control, and cash.

Similarities

- The fraud triangle discussed in this chapter is applicable to all international companies. Some of the major frauds on an international basis are **Parmalat** (Italy), **Royal Ahold** (the Netherlands), and **Satyam Computer Services** (India).
- Rising economic crime poses a growing threat to companies, with nearly one-third of all organizations worldwide being victims of fraud in a recent 12-month period.
- Accounting scandals both in the United States and internationally have re-ignited the debate over the relative merits of GAAP, which takes a "rules-based" approach to accounting, versus IFRS, which takes a "principles-based" approach. The FASB announced that it intends to introduce more principles-based standards.
- On a lighter note, at one time the Ig Nobel Prize in Economics went to the CEOs of those companies involved in the corporate accounting scandals of that year for "adapting the mathematical concept of imaginary numbers for use in the business world." A parody of the Nobel Prizes, the Ig Nobel Prizes (read Ignoble, as not noble) are given each year in early October for 10 achievements that "first make people laugh, and then make them think." Organized by the scientific humor magazine *Annals of Improbable Research* (*AIR*), they are presented by a group that includes genuine Nobel laureates at a ceremony at Harvard University's Sanders Theater.
- Internal controls are a system of checks and balances designed to prevent and detect fraud and errors. While most companies have these systems in place, many have never completely documented them, nor had an independent auditor attest to their effectiveness. Both of these actions are required under SOX.
- Companies find that internal control review is a costly process but badly needed. One study estimates the cost of SOX compliance for U.S. companies at over $35 billion, with audit fees doubling in the first year of compliance. At the same time, examination of internal controls indicates lingering problems in the way companies operate. One study of first compliance with the internal-control testing provisions documented material weaknesses for about 13% of companies reporting in a two-year period (*PricewaterhouseCoopers' Global Economic Crime Survey*, 2005).
- The accounting and internal control procedures related to cash are essentially the same under both IFRS and this textbook. In addition, the definition used for cash equivalents is the same.
- Most companies report cash and cash equivalents together under IFRS, as shown in this textbook. In addition, IFRS follows the same accounting policies related to the reporting of restricted cash.

Differences

- The SOX internal control standards apply only to companies listed on U.S. exchanges. There is continuing debate over whether foreign issuers should have to comply with this extra layer of regulation.

Looking to the Future

Ethics has become a very important aspect of reporting. Different cultures have different perspectives on bribery and other questionable activities, and consequently penalties for engaging in such activities vary considerably across countries.

High-quality international accounting requires both high-quality accounting standards and high-quality auditing. Similar to the convergence of GAAP and IFRS, there is movement to improve international auditing standards. The International Auditing and Assurance Standards Board (IAASB) functions as an independent standard-setting body. It works to establish high-quality auditing and assurance and quality-control standards throughout the world. Whether the IAASB adopts internal control provisions similar to those in SOX remains to be seen. You can follow developments in the international audit arena at the IAASB website.

IFRS Practice

IFRS Self-Test Questions

1. Non-U.S companies that follow IFRS:
   - **a.** do not normally use the principles of internal control activities described in this textbook.
   - **b.** often offset cash with accounts payable on the balance sheet.
   - **c.** are not required to follow SOX.
   - **d.** None of the above.
2. The Sarbanes-Oxley Act applies to:
   - **a.** all U.S. companies listed on U.S. exchanges.
   - **b.** all companies that list stock on any stock exchange in any country.
   - **c.** all European companies listed on European exchanges.
   - **d.** Both (a) and (c).
3. High-quality international accounting requires both high-quality accounting standards and:
   - **a.** a reconsideration of SOX to make it less onerous.
   - **b.** high-quality auditing standards.
   - **c.** government intervention to ensure that the public interest is protected.
   - **d.** the development of new principles of internal control activities.

IFRS Exercise

IFRS8.1 Some people argue that the internal control requirements of the Sarbanes-Oxley Act (SOX) put U.S. companies at a competitive disadvantage to companies outside the United States. Discuss the competitive implications (both pros and cons) of SOX.

International Financial Reporting Problem: Louis Vuitton

IFRS8.2 The financial statements of **Louis Vuitton** are presented in Appendix F. The complete annual report, including the notes to its financial statements, is available at the company's website.

Instructions

Using the notes to the company's financial statements, what are Louis Vuitton's accounting policies related to cash and cash equivalents?

Answers to IFRS Self-Test Questions

1. c **2.** a **3.** b

CHAPTER 9

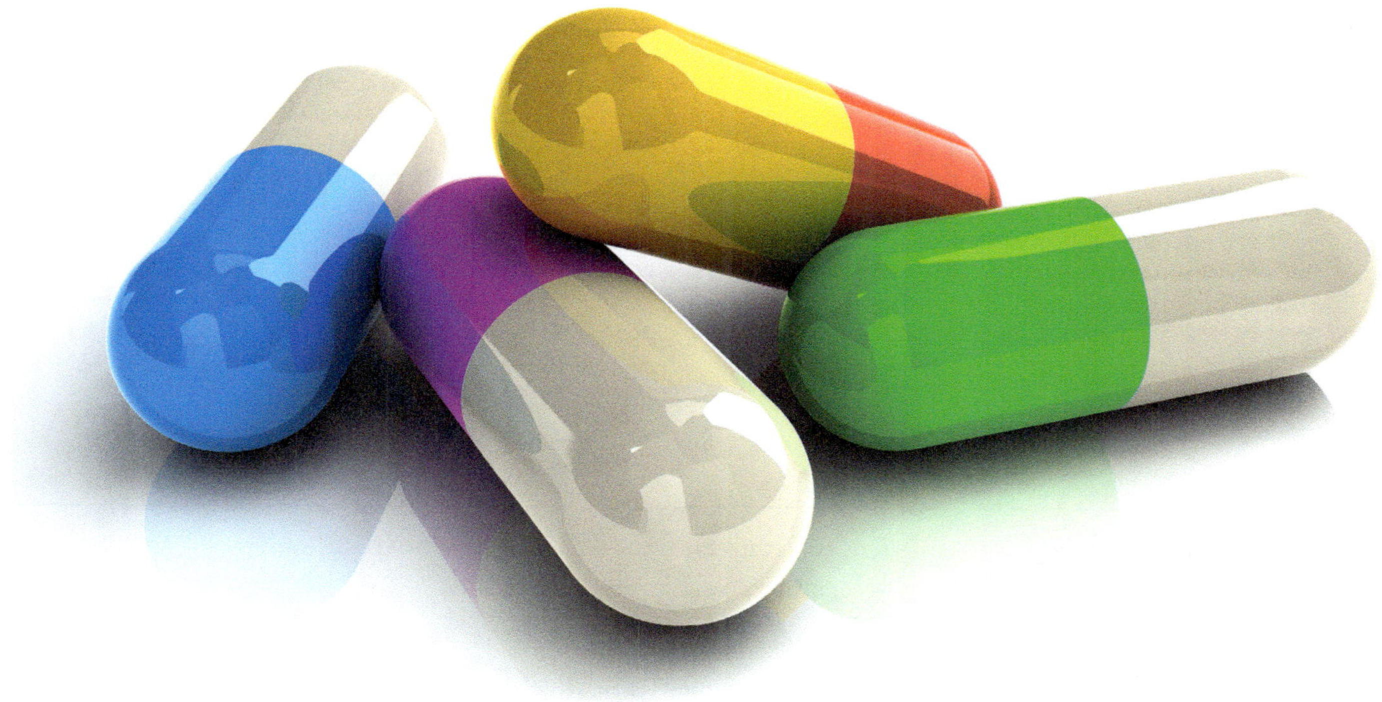

© Cogal/iStockphoto

Accounting for Receivables

Chapter Preview

As indicated in the following Feature Story, receivables are a significant asset for many pharmaceutical companies. Because a large portion of sales in the United States are credit sales, receivables are important to companies in other industries as well. As a consequence, companies must pay close attention to their receivables and manage them carefully. In this chapter, you will learn what journal entries companies make when they sell products, when they collect cash from those sales, and when they write off accounts they cannot collect.

Feature Story

A Dose of Careful Management Keeps Receivables Healthy

"Sometimes you have to know when to be very tough, and sometimes you can give them a bit of a break," said Vivi Su. She wasn't talking about her children but about the customers of a subsidiary of former pharmaceutical company **Whitehall-Robins**, where she worked as supervisor of credit and collections.

For example, while the company's regular terms were 1/15, n/30 (1% discount if paid within 15 days), a customer might have asked for and received a few days of grace and still got the discount. Or a customer might have placed orders above its credit limit, in which case, depending on its payment history and the circumstances, Ms. Su might have authorized shipment of the goods anyway.

"It's not about drawing a line in the sand, and that's all," she explained. "You want a good relationship with your customers—but you also need to bring in the money."

"The money," in Whitehall-Robins' case, amounted to some $170 million in sales a year. Nearly all of it came in through the credit accounts Ms. Su managed. The process started with the decision to grant a customer an account in the first place. The sales rep gave the customer a credit application. "My department reviews this application very carefully; a customer needs to supply three good references, and we also run a check with a credit firm like **Equifax**. If we accept them, then based on their size and history, we assign a credit limit," Ms. Su explained.

Once accounts were established, "I get an aging report every single day," said Ms. Su. "The rule of thumb is that we should always have at least 85% of receivables current—meaning they were billed less than 30 days ago," she continued. "But we try to do even better than that—I like to see 90%."

At 15 days overdue, Whitehall-Robins phoned the client. After 45 days, Ms. Su noted, "I send a letter. Then a second notice is sent in writing. After the third and final notice, the client has 10 days to pay, and then I hand it over to a collection agency, and it's out of my hands."

Ms. Su's boss, Terry Norton, recorded an estimate for bad debts every year, based on a percentage of receivables. The percentage depended on the current aging history. He also calculated and monitored the company's accounts receivable turnover, which the company reported in its financial statements.

Ms. Su knew that she and Mr. Norton were crucial to the profitability of Whitehall-Robins. "Receivables are generally the second-largest asset of any company (after its capital assets)," she pointed out. "So it's no wonder we keep a very close eye on them."

Chapter Outline

LEARNING OBJECTIVES

LO 1 Explain how companies recognize accounts receivable.	• Types of receivables • Recognizing accounts receivable	**DO IT! 1** Recognizing Accounts Receivable
LO 2 Describe how companies value accounts receivable and record their disposition.	• Valuing accounts receivable • Disposing of accounts receivable	**DO IT! 2a** Bad Debt Expense **2b** Factoring
LO 3 Explain how companies recognize, value, and dispose of notes receivable.	• Determining the maturity date • Computing interest • Recognizing notes receivable • Valuing notes receivable • Disposing of notes receivable	**DO IT! 3** Recognizing Notes Receivable
LO 4 Describe the statement presentation and analysis of receivables.	• Presentation • Analysis	**DO IT! 4** Analysis of Receivables

Go to the Review and Practice section at the end of the chapter for a review of key concepts and practice applications with solutions.
Visit WileyPLUS with ORION for additional tutorials and practice opportunities.

Recognition of Accounts Receivable

LEARNING OBJECTIVE 1

Explain how companies recognize accounts receivable.

The term **receivables** refers to amounts due from individuals and companies. Receivables are claims that are expected to be collected in cash. The management of receivables is a very important activity for any company that sells goods or services on credit.

Receivables are important because they represent one of a company's most liquid assets. For many companies, receivables are also one of the largest assets. For example, receivables represent 13.7% of the current assets of pharmaceutical giant **Rite Aid**. **Illustration 9.1** lists receivables as a percentage of total assets for five other well-known companies in a recent year.

Company	Receivables as a Percentage of Total Assets
Ford Motor Company	43.2%
General Electric	41.5
Minnesota Mining and Manufacturing Company (3M)	12.7
DuPont Co.	11.7
Intel Corporation	3.9

ILLUSTRATION 9.1

Receivables as a percentage of assets

Types of Receivables

The relative significance of a company's receivables as a percentage of its assets depends on various factors: its industry, the time of year, whether it extends long-term financing, and its credit policies. To reflect important differences among receivables, they are frequently classified as (1) accounts receivable, (2) notes receivable, and (3) other receivables.

Accounts receivable are amounts customers owe on account. They result from the sale of goods and services. Companies generally expect to collect accounts receivable within 30 to 60 days. They are usually the most significant type of claim held by a company.

Notes receivable are a written promise (as evidenced by a formal instrument) for amounts to be received. The note normally requires the collection of interest and extends for time periods of 60–90 days or longer. Notes and accounts receivable that result from sales transactions are often called **trade receivables**.

Other receivables include nontrade receivables such as interest receivable, loans to company officers, advances to employees, and income taxes refundable (see **Ethics Note**). These do not generally result from the operations of the business. Therefore, they are generally classified and reported as separate items in the balance sheet.

ETHICS NOTE

Companies report receivables from employees separately in the financial statements. The reason: Sometimes these receivables are not the result of an "arm's-length" transaction.

Recognizing Accounts Receivable

Recognizing accounts receivable is relatively straightforward. A service organization records a receivable when it performs service on account. A merchandiser records accounts receivable at the point of sale of merchandise on account. When a merchandiser sells goods, it increases (debits) Accounts Receivable and increases (credits) Sales Revenue.

The seller may offer terms that encourage early payment by providing a discount. Sales returns also reduce receivables. The buyer might find some of the goods unacceptable and choose to return the unwanted goods.

To review, assume that Jordache Co. on July 1, 2020, sells merchandise on account to Polo Company for $1,000, terms 2/10, n/30. On July 5, Polo returns merchandise with a sales price of $100 to Jordache Co. On July 11, Jordache receives payment from Polo Company for the balance due. The journal entries to record these transactions on the books of Jordache Co. are as follows (see **Helpful Hint**). **(Cost of goods sold entries are omitted.)**

HELPFUL HINT

These entries are the same as those described in Chapter 5. For simplicity, we have omitted inventory and cost of goods sold from this set of journal entries and from end-of-chapter material.

July 1	Accounts Receivable	1,000	
	Sales Revenue		1,000
	(To record sales on account)		
July 5	Sales Returns and Allowances	100	
	Accounts Receivable		100
	(To record merchandise returned)		
July 11	Cash ($900 – $18)	882	
	Sales Discounts ($900 × .02)	18	
	Accounts Receivable		900
	(To record collection of accounts receivable)		

Some retailers issue their own credit cards. When you use a retailer's credit card (**JCPenney**, for example), the retailer charges interest on the balance due if not paid within a specified period (usually 25–30 days).

To illustrate, assume that you use your JCPenney Company credit card to purchase clothing with a sales price of $300 on June 1, 2020. JCPenney will increase (debit) Accounts Receivable for $300 and increase (credit) Sales Revenue for $300 (cost of goods sold entry omitted) as follows.

A	=	L	+	OE
+300				+300 Rev

Cash Flows
no effect

June 1	Accounts Receivable	300	
	Sales Revenue		300
	(To record sale of merchandise)		

Assuming that you owe $300 at the end of the month and JCPenney charges 1.5% per month on the balance due, the adjusting entry that JCPenney makes to record interest revenue of $4.50 ($300 × 1.5%) on June 30 is as follows.

A	=	L	+	OE
+4.50				+4.50 Rev

Cash Flows
no effect

June 30	Accounts Receivable	4.50	
	Interest Revenue		4.50
	(To record interest on amount due)		

Interest revenue is often substantial for many retailers.

Anatomy of a Fraud

Tasanee was the accounts receivable clerk for a large nonprofit foundation that provided performance and exhibition space for the performing and visual arts. Her responsibilities included activities normally assigned to an accounts receivable clerk, such as recording revenues from various sources (donations, facility rental fees, ticket revenue, and bar receipts). However, she was also responsible for handling all cash and checks from the time they were received until the time she deposited them, as well as preparing the bank reconciliation. Tasanee took advantage of her situation by falsifying bank deposits and bank reconciliations so that she could steal cash from the bar receipts. Since nobody else logged the donations or matched the donation receipts to pledges prior to Tasanee receiving them, she was able to offset the cash that was stolen against donations that she received but didn't record. Her crime was made easier by the fact that her boss, the company's controller, only did a very superficial review of the bank reconciliation and thus didn't notice that some numbers had been cut out from other documents and taped onto the bank reconciliation.

Total take: $1.5 million

The Missing Controls

Segregation of duties. The foundation should not have allowed an accounts receivable clerk, whose job was to record receivables, to also handle cash, record cash, make deposits, and especially prepare the bank reconciliation.

Independent internal verification. The controller was supposed to perform a thorough review of the bank reconciliation. Because he did not, he was terminated from his position.

Source: Adapted from Wells, *Fraud Casebook* (2007), pp. 183–194.

DO IT! 1 | Recognizing Accounts Receivable

On May 1, Wilton sold merchandise on account to Bates for $50,000, terms 3/15, net 45. On May 4, Bates returns merchandise with a sales price of $2,000. On May 16, Wilton receives payment from Bates for the balance due. Prepare journal entries to record the May transactions on Wilton's books. (You may ignore cost of goods sold entries and explanations.)

ACTION PLAN

- **Prepare entry to record the receivable and related return.**
- **Compute the sales discount and related entry.**

Solution

May 1	Accounts Receivable	50,000	
	Sales Revenue		50,000
May 4	Sales Returns and Allowances	2,000	
	Accounts Receivable		2,000
May 16	Cash ($48,000 – $1,440)	46,560	
	Sales Discounts ($48,000 × .03)	1,440	
	Accounts Receivable		48,000

Related exercise material: **BE9.1, BE9.2, DO IT! 9.1, E9.1, E9.2, and E9.3.**

Valuation and Disposition of Accounts Receivable

LEARNING OBJECTIVE 2

Describe how companies value accounts receivable and record their disposition.

Valuing Accounts Receivable

Once companies record receivables in the accounts, the next question is: How should they report receivables in the financial statements? Companies report accounts receivable on the balance sheet as an asset. But determining the **amount** to report is sometimes difficult because some receivables will become uncollectible.

Each customer must satisfy the credit requirements of the seller before the credit sale is approved. Inevitably, though, some accounts receivable become uncollectible. For example, a customer may not be able to pay because of a decline in its sales revenue due to a downturn in the economy. Similarly, individuals may be laid off from their jobs or faced with unexpected hospital bills. Companies record credit losses as **Bad Debt Expense** (or Uncollectible Accounts Expense) (see **Alternative Terminology**). Such losses are a normal and necessary risk of doing business on a credit basis.

ALTERNATIVE TERMINOLOGY

You will sometimes see *Bad Debt Expense* called *Uncollectible Accounts Expense*.

When U.S. home prices fell, home foreclosures rose, and the economy slowed as a result of the financial crises of 2008, lenders experienced huge increases in their bad debt expense. For example, during one quarter **Wachovia** (a large U.S. bank now owned by **Wells Fargo**) increased bad debt expense from $108 million to $408 million. Similarly, **American Express** increased its bad debt expense by 70%.

Two methods are used in accounting for uncollectible accounts: (1) the direct write-off method and (2) the allowance method. The following sections explain these methods.

Direct Write-Off Method For Uncollectible Accounts

Under the **direct write-off method**, when a company determines a particular account to be uncollectible, it charges the loss to Bad Debt Expense. Assume, for example, that Warden Co. writes off as uncollectible M. E. Doran's $200 balance on December 12. Warden's entry is as follows.

Dec. 12	Bad Debt Expense	200	
	Accounts Receivable		200
	(To record write-off of M. E. Doran account)		

A	=	L	+	OE
				−200 Exp
−200				

Cash Flows
no effect

Under this method, Bad Debt Expense will show only **actual losses** from uncollectibles. The company will report accounts receivable at its gross amount.

Use of the direct write-off method can reduce the relevance of both the income statement and the balance sheet. Consider the following example. In 2020, Quick Buck Computer Company decided it could increase its revenues by offering computers to college students without requiring any money down and with no credit-approval process. On campuses across the country, it sold one million computers with a selling price of $800 each. This increased Quick Buck's revenues and receivables by $800 million. The promotion was a huge success! The 2020 balance sheet and income statement looked great. Unfortunately, during 2021, nearly 40% of the customers defaulted on their loans. This made the 2021 income statement and balance sheet look terrible. **Illustration 9.2** shows the effect of these events on the financial statements if the direct write-off method is used.

Under the direct write-off method, companies often record bad debt expense in a period different from the period in which they record the revenue. The method does not attempt to match bad debt expense to sales revenue in the income statement. Nor does the direct write-off method show accounts receivable in the balance sheet at the amount the company actually expects to receive. **Consequently, unless bad debt losses are insignificant, the direct write-off method is not acceptable for financial reporting purposes.**

ILLUSTRATION 9.2

Effects of direct write-off method

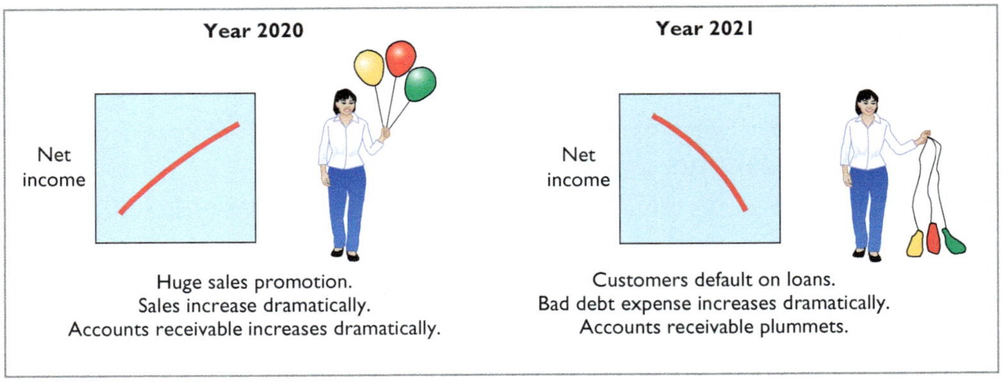

Allowance Method For Uncollectible Accounts

The **allowance method** of accounting for bad debts involves estimating uncollectible accounts at the end of each period. This provides better matching of expenses with revenues on the income statement. It also ensures that companies state receivables on the balance sheet at their cash (net) realizable value. **Cash (net) realizable value** is the net amount the company expects to receive in cash. It excludes amounts that the company estimates it will not collect. Thus, this method reduces receivables in the balance sheet by the amount of estimated uncollectible receivables.

Companies must use the allowance method for financial reporting purposes when bad debts are material in amount (see **Helpful Hint**). This method has three essential features:

HELPFUL HINT

In this context, *material* means significant or important to financial statement users.

1. Companies **estimate** uncollectible accounts receivable. They match this estimated expense **against revenues** in the same accounting period in which they record the revenues.
2. Companies debit estimated uncollectibles to Bad Debt Expense and credit them to Allowance for Doubtful Accounts through an adjusting entry at the end of each period. Allowance for Doubtful Accounts is a contra account to Accounts Receivable.
3. When companies write off a specific account, they debit actual uncollectibles to Allowance for Doubtful Accounts and credit that amount to Accounts Receivable.

Recording Estimated Uncollectibles. To illustrate the allowance method, assume that Hampson Furniture has credit sales of $1,200,000 in 2020. Of this amount, $200,000 of receivables remains uncollected at December 31. The credit manager estimates that $12,000 of these receivables will be uncollectible. The adjusting entry to record the estimated uncollectibles increases (debits) Bad Debt Expense and increases (credits) Allowance for Doubtful Accounts, as follows.

A	=	L	+	OE
				−12,000 Exp
−12,000				

Cash Flows
no effect

Dec. 31	Bad Debt Expense	12,000	
	Allowance for Doubtful Accounts		12,000
	(To record estimate of uncollectible accounts)		

Hampson reports Bad Debt Expense in the income statement as an operating expense. Thus, the estimated uncollectibles are matched with sales in 2020. Hampson records the expense in the same year it made the sales.

Allowance for Doubtful Accounts shows the estimated amount of claims on customers that the company expects will become uncollectible in the future. Companies use a contra account instead of a direct credit to Accounts Receivable because they do not know which customers will not pay. The credit balance in the allowance account will absorb the specific write-offs when they occur. As **Illustration 9.3** shows, the company deducts the allowance account from accounts receivable in the current assets section of the balance sheet.

HELPFUL HINT

Cash realizable value is sometimes referred to as *accounts receivable (net)*.

The amount of $188,000 in Illustration 9.3 represents the expected **cash realizable value** of the accounts receivable at the statement date (see **Helpful Hint**). **Companies do not close Allowance for Doubtful Accounts at the end of the fiscal year.**

Hampson Furniture
Balance Sheet (partial)

Current assets		
Cash		$ 14,800
Accounts receivable	**$200,000**	
Less: Allowance for doubtful accounts	**12,000**	**188,000**
Inventory		310,000
Supplies		25,000
Total current assets		$537,800

ILLUSTRATION 9.3
Presentation of allowance for doubtful accounts

Recording the Write-Off of an Uncollectible Account.

As described in the Feature Story, companies use various methods of collecting past-due accounts, such as letters, calls, and legal action. When they have exhausted all means of collecting a past-due account and collection appears impossible, the company writes off the account. In the credit card industry, for example, it is standard practice to write off accounts that are 210 days past due. To prevent premature or unauthorized write-offs, authorized management personnel should formally approve each write-off. **To maintain segregation of duties, the employee authorized to write off accounts should not have daily responsibilities related to cash or receivables.**

To illustrate a receivables write-off, assume that the financial vice president of Hampson Furniture authorizes a write-off of the $500 balance owed by R. A. Ware on March 1, 2021. The entry to record the write-off is as follows.

Mar. 1	Allowance for Doubtful Accounts	500	
	Accounts Receivable		500
	(Write-off of R. A. Ware account)		

A	=	L	+	OE
+500				
−500				

Cash Flows
no effect

The company does not increase bad debt expense when the write-off occurs. **Under the allowance method, companies debit every bad debt write-off to the allowance account rather than to Bad Debt Expense.** A debit to Bad Debt Expense would be incorrect because the company has already recognized the expense when it made the adjusting entry for estimated bad debts. Instead, the entry to record the write-off of an uncollectible account reduces both Accounts Receivable and Allowance for Doubtful Accounts. After posting, the general ledger accounts appear as shown in **Illustration 9.4**.

Accounts Receivable

Debit			Credit	
Jan. 1	Bal.	200,000	Mar. 1	**500**
Mar. 1	Bal.	199,500		

Allowance for Doubtful Accounts

Debit		Credit		
Mar. 1	**500**	Jan. 1	Bal.	12,000
		Mar. 1	Bal.	11,500

ILLUSTRATION 9.4
General ledger balances after write-off

A write-off affects **only balance sheet accounts**—not income statement accounts. The write-off of the account reduces both Accounts Receivable and Allowance for Doubtful Accounts. Cash realizable value in the balance sheet, therefore, remains the same, as **Illustration 9.5** shows.

	Before Write-Off	After Write-Off
Accounts receivable	$200,000	$199,500
Allowance for doubtful accounts	12,000	11,500
Cash realizable value	**$188,000**	**$188,000**

ILLUSTRATION 9.5
Cash realizable value comparison

Recovery of an Uncollectible Account.

Occasionally, a company collects from a customer after it has written off the account as uncollectible. The company makes two entries to record the recovery of a bad debt. (1) It reverses the entry made in writing off the account. This reinstates the customer's account. (2) It journalizes the collection in the usual manner.

To illustrate, assume that on July 1, R. A. Ware pays the $500 amount that Hampson had written off on March 1. Hampson makes the following entries.

A	=	L	+	OE
+500				
−500				

Cash Flows
no effect

(1)

July 1	Accounts Receivable	500	
	Allowance for Doubtful Accounts		500
	(To reverse write-off of R. A. Ware account)		

A	=	L	+	OE
+500				
−500				

Cash Flows
+500

(2)

July 1	Cash	500	
	Accounts Receivable		500
	(To record collection from R. A. Ware)		

Note that the recovery of a bad debt, like the write-off of a bad debt, affects **only balance sheet accounts**. The net effect of the two entries above is a debit to Cash and a credit to Allowance for Doubtful Accounts for $500. Accounts Receivable and Allowance for Doubtful Accounts both increase in entry (1) for two reasons. First, the company made an error in judgment when it wrote off the account receivable. Second, after R. A. Ware did pay, Accounts Receivable in the general ledger and Ware's account in the subsidiary ledger should show the collection for possible future credit purposes.

Estimating the Allowance. For Hampson Furniture in Illustration 9.3, the amount of the expected uncollectibles was given. However, in "real life," companies must estimate the amount of expected uncollectible accounts if they use the allowance method. **Illustration 9.6** shows an excerpt from the notes to **Nike**'s financial statements discussing its use of the allowance method.

ILLUSTRATION 9.6

Nike's allowance method disclosure

Real World

Nike, Inc.
Notes to the Financial Statements

Allowance for Uncollectible Accounts Receivable

We make ongoing estimates relating to the ability to collect our accounts receivable and maintain an allowance for estimated losses resulting from the inability of our customers to make required payments. In determining the amount of the allowance, we consider our historical level of credit losses and make judgments about the creditworthiness of significant customers based on ongoing credit evaluations. Since we cannot predict future changes in the financial stability of our customers, actual future losses from uncollectible accounts may differ from our estimates.

HELPFUL HINT

Where appropriate, the percentage-of-receivables basis may use only a single percentage rate.

Allowance for Doubtful Accounts

	Dec. 31 Unadj. Bal.	1,500
	Dec. 31 Adj.	8,500
	Dec. 31 Bal.	10,000

Frequently, companies estimate the allowance as a percentage of the outstanding receivables. Under the **percentage-of-receivables basis**, management establishes a percentage relationship between the amount of receivables and expected losses from uncollectible accounts (see **Helpful Hint**). For example, suppose Steffen Company has an ending balance in Accounts Receivable of $200,000 and an unadjusted credit balance in Allowance for Doubtful Accounts of $1,500. It estimates that 5% of its accounts receivable will eventually be uncollectible. It should report a balance in Allowance for Doubtful Accounts of $10,000 (.05 × $200,000). To increase the balance in Allowance for Doubtful Accounts from $1,500 to $10,000, the company debits (increases) Bad Debt Expense and credits (increases) Allowance for Doubtful Accounts by $8,500 ($10,000 – $1,500).

To more accurately estimate the ending balance in the allowance account, a company often prepares a schedule, called **aging the accounts receivable**. This schedule classifies customer balances by the length of time they have been unpaid.

After the company arranges the accounts by age, it determines the expected bad debt losses by applying percentages, based on past experience, to the totals of each category. The longer a receivable is past due, the less likely it is to be collected. As a result, the estimated percentage of uncollectible debts increases as the number of days past due increases (see **Helpful Hint**). **Illustration 9.7** shows an aging schedule for Dart Company. Note the increasing uncollectible percentages from 2% to 40%.

ILLUSTRATION 9.7

Aging schedule

Worksheet

Customer	Total	Not Yet Due	Number of Days Past Due: 1–30	31–60	61–90	Over 90
T. E. Adert	$ 600		$ 300		$ 200	$ 100
R. C. Bortz	300	$ 300				
B. A. Carl	450		200	$ 250		
O. L. Diker	700	500			200	
T. O. Ebbet	600			300		300
Others	36,950	26,200	5,200	2,450	1,600	1,500
	$39,600	$27,000	$5,700	$3,000	$2,000	$1,900
Estimated percentage uncollectible		2%	4%	10%	20%	40%
Total estimated uncollectible accounts	$ 2,228	$ 540	$ 228	$ 300	$ 400	$ 760

HELPFUL HINT

The older categories have higher percentages because the longer an account is past due, the less likely it is to be collected.

Total estimated uncollectible accounts for Dart Company ($2,228) represent the existing customer claims expected to become uncollectible in the future. Thus, this amount represents the **required balance** in Allowance for Doubtful Accounts at the balance sheet date. Accordingly, **the amount of bad debt expense that should be recorded in the adjusting entry is the difference between the required balance and the existing balance in the allowance account**. The existing, unadjusted balance in Allowance for Doubtful Accounts is the net result of the beginning balance (a normal credit balance) less the write-offs of specific accounts during the year (debits to the allowance account).

For example, if the unadjusted trial balance shows Allowance for Doubtful Accounts with a credit balance of $528, then an adjusting entry for $1,700 ($2,228 – $528) is necessary:

Dec. 31	Bad Debt Expense	1,700	
	Allowance for Doubtful Accounts		1,700
	(To adjust allowance account to total estimated uncollectibles)		

A = L + OE

−1,700 | | −1,700 Exp

Cash Flows

no effect

After Dart posts the adjusting entry, its accounts appear as shown in **Illustration 9.8**.

ILLUSTRATION 9.8

Bad debt accounts after posting

Bad Debt Expense

Debit	Credit
Dec. 31 Adj. **1,700**	

Allowance for Doubtful Accounts

Debit	Credit
	Dec. 31 Unadj. Bal. 528
	Dec. 31 Adj. **1,700**
	Dec. 31 Bal. 2,228

An important aspect of accounts receivable management is simply maintaining a close watch on the accounts. Studies have shown that accounts more than 60 days past due lose approximately 50% of their value if no payment activity occurs within the next 30 days. For each additional 30 days that pass, the collectible value halves once again.

Occasionally, the allowance account will have a **debit balance** prior to adjustment. This occurs because the debits to the allowance account from write-offs during the year **exceeded** the beginning balance in the account which was based on previous estimates for bad debts. In such a case, the company **adds the debit balance to the required balance** when it makes the adjusting entry. Thus, if there was a $500 **debit** balance in the allowance account before

A	=	L	+	OE
				−2,728 Exp
−2,728				

Cash Flows
no effect

adjustment, the adjusting entry would be for $2,728 ($2,228 + $500) to arrive at a credit balance of $2,228 as shown below.

Dec. 31	Bad Debt Expense	2,728	
	Allowance for Doubtful Accounts		2,728
	(To adjust allowance account to total estimated uncollectibles)		

After Dart posts the adjusting entry, its accounts appear as shown in **Illustration 9.9**.

ILLUSTRATION 9.9
Bad debt accounts after posting

Bad Debt Expense

Debit	Credit
Dec. 31 Adj. **2,728**	

Allowance for Doubtful Accounts

Debit	Credit
Dec. 31 Unadj. Bal. 500	Dec. 31 Adj. **2,728**
	Dec. 31 Bal. 2,228

The percentage-of-receivables basis provides an estimate of the cash realizable value of the receivables. It also provides a reasonable matching of expenses to revenue.

The note regarding accounts receivable shown in **Illustration 9.10** comes from the annual report of the shoe company **Skechers USA**.

ILLUSTRATION 9.10
Skechers USA's note disclosure of accounts receivable

Real World

Skechers USA
Notes to the Financial Statements

The likelihood of a material loss on an uncollectible account would be mainly dependent on deterioration in the overall economic conditions in a particular country or region. Reserves are fully provided for all probable losses of this nature. For receivables that are not specifically identified as high risk, we provide a reserve based upon our historical loss rate as a percentage of sales. Gross trade accounts receivable were $293.1 million and $241.9 million, and the allowance for bad debts, returns, sales allowances and customer chargebacks were $21.0 million and $15.9 million, at December 31, 2014 and 2013, respectively. Our credit losses charged to expense for the years ended December 31, 2014, 2013 and 2012 were $11.8 million, $2.6 million and $1.5 million, respectively. In addition, we recorded sales return and allowance expense (recoveries) for the years ended December 31, 2014, 2013 and 2012 of $2.3 million, $0.2 million and $(0.4) million, respectively.

Ethics Insight

© Christy Thompson/Shutterstock

Cookie Jar Allowances

There are many pressures on companies to achieve earnings targets. For managers, poor earnings can lead to dismissal or lack of promotion. It is not surprising then that management may be tempted to look for ways to boost their earnings number.

One way a company can achieve greater earnings is to lower its estimate of what is needed in its Allowance for Doubtful Accounts (sometimes referred to as "tapping the cookie jar"). For example, suppose a company has an Allowance for Doubtful Accounts of $10 million and decides to reduce this balance to $9 million. As a result of this change, Bad Debt Expense decreases by $1 million and earnings increase by $1 million.

Large banks such as **JP Morgan Chase**, **Wells Fargo**, and **Bank of America** recently decreased their Allowance for Doubtful Accounts by over $4 billion. These reductions came at a time when these big banks were still suffering from lower mortgage lending and trading activity, both of which lead to lower earnings. They justified these reductions in the allowance balances by noting that credit quality and economic conditions had improved. This may be so, but it sure is great to have a cookie jar that might be tapped when a boost in earnings is needed.

How might investors determine that a company is managing its earnings? (Go to WileyPLUS for this answer and additional questions.)

DO IT! 2a | Bad Debt Expense

Brule Corporation has been in business for 5 years. The unadjusted trial balance at the end of the current year shows Accounts Receivable $30,000, Sales Revenue $180,000, and Allowance for Doubtful Accounts with a debit balance of $2,000. Brule estimates bad debts to be 10% of accounts receivable. Prepare the entry necessary to adjust Allowance for Doubtful Accounts.

Solution

Brule should make the following entry to bring the debit balance in Allowance for Doubtful Accounts up to a normal, credit balance of $3,000 (10% × $30,000):

Bad Debt Expense [(10% × $30,000) + $2,000]	5,000	
Allowance for Doubtful Accounts		5,000
(To record estimate of uncollectible accounts)		

Related exercise material: **BE9.3, BE9.6, DO IT! 9.2a, E9.4, E9.5, E9.6, E9.7, and E9.8.**

ACTION PLAN

- **Estimate the amount the company does not expect to collect.**
- **Consider the existing balance in the allowance account when using the percentage-of-receivables basis.**
- **Report receivables at their cash (net) realizable value—that is, the amount the company expects to collect in cash.**

Disposing of Accounts Receivable

In the normal course of events, companies collect accounts receivable in cash and remove the receivables from the books. However, as credit sales and receivables have grown in significance, the "normal course of events" has changed. Companies now frequently sell their receivables to another company for cash, thereby shortening the cash-to-cash operating cycle.

Companies sell receivables for two major reasons. First, **they may be the only reasonable source of cash**. When money is tight, companies may not be able to borrow money in the usual credit markets. Or if money is available, the cost of borrowing may be prohibitive.

A second reason for selling receivables is that **billing and collection are often time-consuming and costly**. It is often easier for a retailer to sell the receivables to another party with expertise in billing and collection matters. Credit card companies such as **MasterCard**, **Visa**, and **Discover** specialize in billing and collecting accounts receivable.

Sale of Receivables to a Factor

A common sale of receivables is a sale to a factor. A **factor** is a finance company or bank that buys receivables from businesses and then collects the payments directly from the customers. Factoring is a multibillion dollar business.

Factoring arrangements vary widely. Typically, the factor charges a commission to the company that is selling the receivables. This fee often ranges from 1–3% of the amount of receivables purchased. To illustrate, assume that Hendredon Furniture factors $600,000 of receivables to Federal Factors. Federal Factors assesses a service charge of 2% of the amount of receivables sold. The journal entry to record the sale by Hendredon Furniture on April 2, 2020, is as follows.

Apr. 2	Cash	588,000	
	Service Charge Expense (2% × $600,000)	12,000	
	Accounts Receivable		600,000
	(To record the sale of accounts receivable)		

A	=	L	+	OE
+588,000				
				−12,000 Exp
−600,000				

Cash Flows
+588,000

If Hendredon often sells its receivables, it records the service charge expense as an operating expense. If the company infrequently sells receivables, it may report this amount in the "Other expenses and losses" section of the income statement.

National Credit Card Sales

ETHICS NOTE

In exchange for lower interest rates, some companies have eliminated the 25-day grace period before finance charges kick in. Be sure you read the fine print in any credit agreement you sign.

Over one billion credit cards are in use in the United States—more than three credit cards for every man, woman, and child in this country. Visa, MasterCard, and American Express are the national credit cards that most individuals use. Three parties are involved when national credit cards are used in retail sales: (1) the credit card issuer, who is independent of the retailer; (2) the retailer; and (3) the customer. **A retailer's acceptance of a national credit card is another form of selling (factoring) the receivable.**

Illustration 9.11 shows the major advantages of national credit cards to the retailer. In exchange for these advantages, the retailer pays the credit card issuer a fee of 2–4% of the invoice price for its services (see Ethics Note).

ILLUSTRATION 9.11

Advantages of credit cards to the retailer

Accounting for Credit Card Sales. The retailer generally considers sales from the use of national credit card sales as **cash sales**. The retailer must pay to the bank that issues the card a fee for processing the transactions. The retailer records the credit card slips in a similar manner as checks deposited from a cash sale.

To illustrate, Anita Ferreri purchases $1,000 of compact discs for her restaurant from Karen Kerr Music Co., using her Visa First Bank Card. First Bank charges a service fee of 3%. The entry to record this transaction by Karen Kerr Music on March 22, 2020, is as follows.

A	=	L	+	OE
+970				
				−30 Exp
				+1,000 Rev

Cash Flows
+970

Mar. 22	Cash	970	
	Service Charge Expense	30	
	Sales Revenue		1,000
	(To record Visa credit card sales)		

Accounting Across the Organization Nordstrom

© Michael Braun/iStockphoto

How Does a Credit Card Work?

Most of you know how to use a credit card, but do you know what happens in the transaction and how the transaction is processed? Suppose that you use a **Visa** card to purchase some new ties at **Nordstrom**. The customer swipes the credit card (or inserts it if it is a chip card), which allows the information to be read. The salesperson enters the amount of the purchase. The machine contacts the Visa computer, which routes the call back to the bank that issued your Visa card. The issuing bank verifies that the account exists, that the card is not stolen, and that you have not exceeded your credit limit. At this point, the slip is printed, which you sign.

Visa acts as the clearing agent for the transaction. It transfers funds from the issuing bank to Nordstrom's bank account. Generally this transfer of funds, from sale to the receipt of funds in the merchant's account, takes two to three days.

In the meantime, Visa puts a pending charge on your account for the amount of the tie purchase; that amount counts immediately against your available credit limit. At the end of the billing period, Visa sends you an invoice (your credit card bill) which shows the various charges you made, and the amounts that Visa expended on your behalf, for the month. You then must "pay the piper" for your stylish new ties.

Assume that Nordstrom prepares a bank reconciliation at the end of each month. If some credit card sales have not been processed by the bank, how should Nordstrom treat these transactions on its bank reconciliation? (Go to WileyPLUS for this answer and additional questions.)

DO IT! 2b | Factoring

Peter M. Kell Wholesalers Co. needs to raise $120,000 in cash to safely cover next Friday's employee payroll. Kell has reached its debt ceiling. Kell's present balance of outstanding receivables totals $750,000. Kell decides to factor $125,000 of its receivables on September 7, 2020, to alleviate this cash crunch. Record the entry that Kell would make when it raises the needed cash. (Assume a 1% service charge.)

ACTION PLAN

- **Consider sale of receivables to a factor.**
- **Weigh cost of factoring against benefit of having cash in hand.**

Solution

Assuming that Kell Co. factors $125,000 of its accounts receivable at a 1% service charge, it would make this entry:

Sept. 7	Cash	123,750	
	Service Charge Expense (1% × $125,000)	1,250	
	Accounts Receivable		125,000
	(To record sale of receivables to factor)		

Related exercise material: **BE9.7, DO IT! 9.2b, E9.9, E9.10, and E9.11.**

Notes Receivable

LEARNING OBJECTIVE 3

Explain how companies recognize, value, and dispose of notes receivable.

Companies may also grant credit in exchange for a formal credit instrument known as a promissory note. A **promissory note** is a written promise to pay a specified amount of money on demand or at a definite time. Promissory notes may be used (1) when individuals and companies lend or borrow money, (2) when the amount of the transaction and the credit period exceed normal limits, or (3) in settlement of accounts receivable.

In a promissory note, the party making the promise to pay is called the **maker**. The party to whom payment is to be made is called the **payee**. The note may specifically identify the payee by name or may designate the payee simply as the bearer of the note.

In the note shown in **Illustration 9.12**, Calhoun Company is the maker and Wilma Company is the payee. To Wilma Company, the promissory note is a note receivable. To Calhoun Company, it is a note payable (see **Helpful Hint**).

ILLUSTRATION 9.12

Promissory note

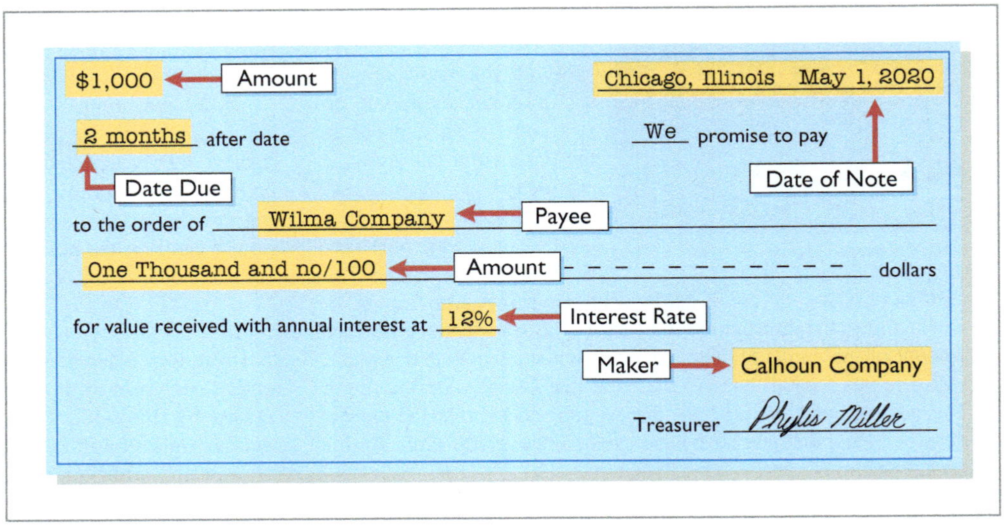

HELPFUL HINT

For this note, the maker, Calhoun Company, debits Cash and credits Notes Payable. The payee, Wilma Company, debits Notes Receivable and credits Cash.

Notes receivable give the holder a stronger legal claim to assets than do accounts receivable. Like accounts receivable, notes receivable can be readily sold to another party. Promissory notes are negotiable instruments (as are checks), which means that they can be transferred to another party by endorsement.

Companies frequently accept notes receivable from customers who need to extend the payment of an outstanding account receivable. They often require such notes from high-risk customers. In some industries (such as the pleasure and sport boat industry), all credit sales are supported by notes. The majority of notes, however, originate from lending transactions.

The basic issues in accounting for notes receivable are the same as those for accounts receivable. On the following pages, we look at these issues. Before we do, however, we need to consider two issues that do not apply to accounts receivable: determining the maturity date and computing interest.

Determining the Maturity Date

Illustration 9.13 shows three ways of stating the maturity date of a promissory note.

ILLUSTRATION 9.13

Maturity date of different notes

When the life of a note is expressed in terms of months, you find the date when it matures by counting the months from the date of issue. For example, the maturity date of a three-month note dated May 1 is August 1. A note drawn on the last day of a month matures on the last day of a subsequent month. That is, a July 31 note due in two months matures on September 30.

When the due date is stated in terms of days, you need to count the exact number of days to determine the maturity date. In counting, **omit the date the note is issued but include the due date**. For example, the maturity date of a 60-day note dated July 17 is September 15, computed as shown in **Illustration 9.14**.

Term of note		60 days
July (31–17)	14	
August	31	45
Maturity date: September		**15**

ILLUSTRATION 9.14
Computation of maturity date

Computing Interest

Illustration 9.15 gives the basic formula for computing interest on an interest-bearing note.

Face Value of Note	×	**Annual Interest Rate**	×	**Time in Terms of One Year**	=	**Interest**

ILLUSTRATION 9.15
Formula for computing interest

The interest rate specified in a note is an **annual** rate of interest (see **Helpful Hint**). The time factor in the formula in Illustration 9.15 expresses the fraction of a year that the note is outstanding. When the maturity date is stated in days, the time factor is often the number of days divided by 360. Remember that when counting days, omit the date that the note is issued but include the due date. When the due date is stated in months, the time factor is the number of months divided by 12. **Illustration 9.16** shows computation of interest for various time periods.

HELPFUL HINT
The interest rate specified is the *annual* rate.

Terms of Note	Interest Computation							
	Face	×	Rate	×	Time	=	Interest
$ 730, 12%, 120 days	$ 730	×	12%	×	**120/360**	=	$ 29.20
$1,000, 9%, 6 months	$1,000	×	9%	×	**6/12**	=	$ 45.00
$2,000, 6%, 1 year	$2,000	×	6%	×	**1/1**	=	$120.00

ILLUSTRATION 9.16
Computation of interest

There are different ways to calculate interest. For example, the computation in Illustration 9.16 assumes 360 days for the length of the year. Most financial institutions use 365 days to compute interest. *For homework problems, assume 360 days to simplify computations.*

Recognizing Notes Receivable

To illustrate the basic entry for notes receivable, we will use Calhoun Company's $1,000, two-month, 12% promissory note dated May 1. Assuming that Calhoun Company wrote the note to settle an open account, Wilma Company makes the following entry for the receipt of the note.

A	=	L	+	OE
+1,000				
−1,000				

Cash Flows
no effect

May 1	Notes Receivable	1,000	
	Accounts Receivable		1,000
	(To record acceptance of Calhoun Company note)		

The company records the note receivable at its **face value**, the value shown on the face of the note. No interest revenue is reported when the note is accepted because the revenue recognition principle does not recognize revenue until the performance obligation is satisfied. Interest is earned (accrued) as time passes.

If a company issues cash in exchange for a note, the entry is a debit to Notes Receivable and a credit to Cash in the amount of the loan.

Valuing Notes Receivable

Valuing short-term notes receivable is the same as valuing accounts receivable. Like accounts receivable, companies report short-term notes receivable at their **cash (net) realizable value**. The notes receivable allowance account is Allowance for Doubtful Accounts. The estimations involved in determining cash realizable value and in recording bad debt expense and the related allowance are done similarly to accounts receivable.

Disposing of Notes Receivable

Notes may be held to their maturity date, at which time the face value plus accrued interest is due. In some situations, the maker of the note defaults, and the payee must make an appropriate adjustment. In other situations, similar to accounts receivable, the holder of the note speeds up the conversion to cash by selling the receivables (as described earlier in this chapter).

Honor of Notes Receivable

A note is **honored** when its maker pays in full at its maturity date. For each interest-bearing note, the **amount due at maturity** is the face value of the note plus interest for the length of time specified on the note.

To illustrate, assume that Wolder Co. lends Higley Co. $10,000 on June 1, accepting a five-month, 9% interest note. In this situation, interest is $375 ($10,000 × 9% × $\frac{5}{12}$). The amount due, **the maturity value**, is $10,375 ($10,000 + $375). To obtain payment, Wolder (the payee) must present the note either to Higley Co. (the maker) or to the maker's agent, such as a bank. If Wolder presents the note to Higley Co. on November 1, the maturity date, Wolder's entry to record the collection is as follows.

A	=	L	+	OE
+10,375				
−10,000				
				+375 Rev

Cash Flows
+10,375

Nov. 1	Cash	10,375	
	Notes Receivable		10,000
	Interest Revenue ($10,000 × 9% × $\frac{5}{12}$)		375
	(To record collection of Higley note and interest)		

Accrual of Interest Receivable

Suppose instead that Wolder Co. prepares financial statements as of September 30. The timeline in **Illustration 9.17** presents this situation.

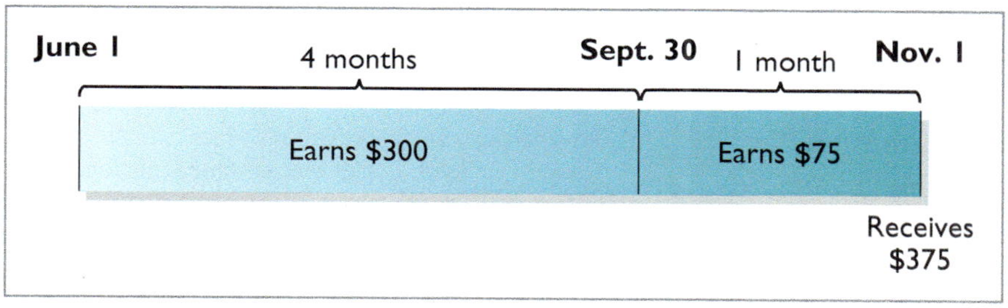

ILLUSTRATION 9.17
Timeline of interest earned

To reflect interest earned but not yet received, Wolder must accrue interest on September 30. In this case, the adjusting entry by Wolder is for four months of interest, or $300, as shown below.

Sept. 30	Interest Receivable ($10,000 × 9% × $\frac{4}{12}$)	300	
	Interest Revenue		300
	(To accrue 4 months' interest on Higley note)		

A	=	L	+	OE
+300				+300 Rev

Cash Flows
no effect

At the note's maturity on November 1, Wolder receives $10,375. This amount represents repayment of the $10,000 note as well as five months of interest, or $375, as shown below. The $375 is comprised of the $300 Interest Receivable accrued on September 30 plus $75 earned during October. Wolder's entry to record the honoring of the Higley note on November 1 is as follows.

Nov. 1	Cash [$10,000 + ($10,000 × 9% × $\frac{5}{12}$)]	10,375	
	Notes Receivable		10,000
	Interest Receivable		300
	Interest Revenue ($10,000 × 9% × $\frac{1}{12}$)]		75
	(To record collection of Higley note and interest)		

A	=	L	+	OE
+10,375				
−10,000				
−300				+75 Rev

Cash Flows
+10,375

In this case, Wolder credits Interest Receivable because the receivable was established in the adjusting entry on September 30.

Dishonor of Notes Receivable

A **dishonored (defaulted) note** is a note that is not paid in full at maturity. A dishonored note receivable is no longer negotiable. However, the payee still has a claim against the maker of the note for both the note and the interest. Therefore, the note holder usually transfers the Notes Receivable account to an Accounts Receivable account.

To illustrate, assume that Higley Co. on November 1 indicates that it cannot pay at the present time. The entry to record the dishonor of the note depends on whether Wolder Co. expects eventual collection. If it does expect eventual collection, Wolder Co. debits the amount due (face value and interest) on the note to Accounts Receivable. It would make the following entry at the time the note is dishonored (assuming no previous accrual of interest).

Nov. 1	Accounts Receivable	10,375	
	Notes Receivable		10,000
	Interest Revenue		375
	(To record the dishonor of Higley note)		

A	=	L	+	OE
+10,375				
−10,000				+375 Rev

Cash Flows
no effect

If instead on November 1 there is no hope of collection, the note holder would write off the face value of the note by debiting Allowance for Doubtful Accounts. No interest revenue would be recorded because collection will not occur.

Accounting Across the Organization Countrywide Financial Corporation

© Andy Dean/iStockphoto

Bad Information Can Lead to Bad Loans

Many factors have contributed to the financial crisis of 2008. One significant factor that resulted in many bad loans was a failure by lenders to investigate loan customers sufficiently. For example, **Countrywide Financial Corporation** wrote many loans under its "Fast and Easy" loan program. That program allowed borrowers to provide little or no documentation for their income or their assets. Other lenders had similar programs, which earned the nickname "liars' loans." One study found that in these situations, 60% of applicants overstated their incomes by more than 50% in order to qualify for a loan. Critics of the banking industry say that because loan officers were compensated for loan volume and because banks were selling the loans to investors rather than holding them, the lenders had little incentive to investigate the borrowers' creditworthiness.

Sources: Glenn R. Simpson and James R. Hagerty, "Countrywide Loss Focuses Attention on Underwriting," *Wall Street Journal* (April 30, 2008), p. B1; and Michael Corkery, "Fraud Seen as Driver in Wave of Foreclosures," *Wall Street Journal* (December 21, 2007), p. A1.

What steps should the banks have taken to ensure the accuracy of financial information provided on loan applications? (Go to WileyPLUS for this answer and additional questions.)

DO IT! 3 | Recognizing Notes Receivable

Gambit Stores accepts from Leonard Co. a $3,400, 90-day, 6% note dated May 10 in settlement of Leonard's overdue account. (a) What is the maturity date of the note? (b) What is the interest payable at the maturity date? (c) What entry does Gambit make at the maturity date, assuming Leonard pays the note and interest in full at that time?

ACTION PLAN

- **Count the exact number of days to determine the maturity date. Omit the date the note is issued, but include the due date.**
- **Compute the accrued interest.**
- **Prepare the entry for payment of the note and the interest.**

Solution

a. The maturity date is August 8, computed as follows.

Term of note:		90 days
May (31–10)	21	
June	30	
July	31	82
Maturity date: August		8

b. The interest payable at the maturity date is $51, computed as follows.

Face	×	Rate	×	Time	=	Interest
$3,400	×	6%	×	90/360	=	$51

c. Gambit Stores records this entry at the maturity date:

Cash	3,451	
Notes Receivable		3,400
Interest Revenue		51
(To record collection of Leonard note and interest)		

Related exercise material: **BE9.8, BE9.9, BE9.10, DO IT! 9.3, E9.12, E9.13, and E9.14.**

Presentation and Analysis

LEARNING OBJECTIVE 4

Describe the statement presentation and analysis of receivables.

If a company has significant receivables, analysts carefully review the company's financial statement disclosures to evaluate how well the company is managing its receivables.

Presentation

Companies should identify in the balance sheet or in the notes to the financial statements each of the major types of receivables. Short-term receivables appear in the current assets section of the balance sheet. Short-term investments appear before short-term receivables because these investments are more liquid (nearer to cash). Companies report both the gross amount of receivables and the allowance for doubtful accounts.

In the income statement, companies report bad debt expense and service charge expense as operating expenses. Interest revenue appears under "Other revenues and gains" in the non-operating activities section of the income statement.

Presented below are examples of different types of information provided to help users understand the issues related to receivables. **Illustration 9.18**, for example, shows the composition of **Deere & Company**'s net receivables. Given that receivables represent 60% of the total assets of this heavy equipment manufacturer, investors are interested in the types of receivables and their significance.

ILLUSTRATION 9.18

Balance sheet presentation of receivables

Real World

Deere & Company
Balance Sheet (partial)
(in millions)

Receivables	
Receivables from unconsolidated subsidiaries	$ 30
Trade accounts and notes receivable	3,278
Financing receivables	27,583
Restricted financing receivables	4,616
Other receivables	1,500
Total receivables	37,007
Less: Allowance for doubtful trade receivables	175
Net receivables	$36,832

Illustration 9.19 contains an excerpt from the notes to the financial statements of **Skechers**, discussing how it monitors receivables.

ILLUSTRATION 9.19

Note on monitoring Skechers' receivables

Real World

Skechers USA
Notes to the Financial Statements

To minimize the likelihood of uncollectibility, customers' credit-worthiness is reviewed periodically based on external credit reporting services, financial statements issued by the customer and our experience with the account, and it is adjusted accordingly. When a customer's account becomes significantly past due, we generally place a hold on the account and discontinue further shipments to that customer, minimizing further risk of loss.

If a company has significant concentrations of credit risk, it must discuss this risk in the notes to its financial statements. A **concentration of credit risk** is a threat of nonpayment from a single large customer or class of customers that could adversely affect the financial health of the company. **Illustration 9.20** shows an excerpt from the credit risk note from Skechers' 2015 annual report. The company reports that its five largest customers account for 14.6% of its net sales.

ILLUSTRATION 9.20

Excerpt from Skechers' note on concentration of credit risk

Real World

Skechers USA

Notes to the Financial Statements

During 2015, 2014 and 2013, no customer accounted for 10.0% or more of net sales. As of December 31, 2015, one customer accounted for 10.6% of gross trade receivables. No other customer accounted for more than 10% of net trade receivables at December 31, 2015 or 2014. During 2015, 2014 and 2013, net sales to the five largest customers were approximately 14.6%, 15.7% and 18.1%, respectively.

This note to Skechers' financial statements indicates it has a relatively high concentration of credit risk. A default by any of these large customers could have a significant negative impact on its financial performance.

Analysis

Investors and corporate managers compute financial ratios to evaluate the liquidity of a company's accounts receivable. They use the **accounts receivable turnover** to assess the liquidity of the receivables. This ratio measures the number of times, on average, the company collects accounts receivable during the period. It is computed by dividing net credit sales (net sales less cash sales) by the average net accounts receivable during the year. Unless seasonal factors are significant, average net accounts receivable outstanding can be computed from the beginning and ending balances of net accounts receivable.

For example, **Cisco Systems** had net sales of $37,750 million in a recent year. It had a beginning accounts receivable (net) balance of $5,157 million and an ending accounts receivable (net) balance of $5,344 million. Assuming that Cisco's sales were all on credit, its accounts receivable turnover is computed as shown in **Illustration 9.21**.

ILLUSTRATION 9.21

Accounts receivable turnover and computation

Net Credit Sales	÷	Average Net Accounts Receivable	=	Accounts Receivable Turnover
$37,750	÷	$\frac{\$5,157 + \$5,344}{2}$	=	7.2 times

The result indicates an accounts receivable turnover of 7.2 times per year. The higher the turnover, the more liquid the company's receivables.

A variant of the accounts receivable turnover that makes the liquidity even more evident is its conversion into an **average collection period** in terms of days. This is done by dividing the accounts receivable turnover into 365 days. For example, Cisco's turnover of 7.2 times is divided into 365 days, as shown in **Illustration 9.22**, to obtain approximately 51 days. This means that it takes Cisco 51 days to collect its accounts receivable.

ILLUSTRATION 9.22

Average collection period for receivables formula and computation

Days in Year	÷	Accounts Receivable Turnover	=	Average Collection Period in Days
365 days	÷	7.2 times	=	51 days

Companies frequently use the average collection period to assess the effectiveness of a company's credit and collection policies. The general rule is that the collection period should not greatly exceed the credit term period (that is, the time allowed for payment).

DO IT! 4 | Analysis of Receivables

In 2020, Phil Mickelson Company has net credit sales of $923,795 for the year. It had a beginning accounts receivable (net) balance of $38,275 and an ending accounts receivable (net) balance of $35,988. Compute Phil Mickelson Company's (a) accounts receivable turnover and (b) average collection period in days.

Solution

a.	Net credit sales	÷	Average net accounts receivable	=	Accounts receivable turnover
	$923,795	÷	$\frac{\$38,275 + \$35,988}{2}$	=	24.9 times
b.	Days in year	÷	Accounts receivable turnover	=	Average collection period in days
	365	÷	24.9 times	=	14.7 days

Related exercise material: **BE9.12, DO IT! 9.4, and E9.17.**

ACTION PLAN

- **Review the formula to compute the accounts receivable turnover.**
- **Make sure that both the beginning and ending accounts receivable balances are considered in the computation.**
- **Review the formula to compute the average collection period in days.**

Review and Practice

Learning Objectives Review

1 Explain how companies recognize accounts receivable.

Receivables are frequently classified as (1) accounts, (2) notes, and (3) other. Accounts receivable are amounts customers owe on account. Notes receivable are claims for which lenders issue formal instruments of credit as proof of the debt. Other receivables include nontrade receivables such as interest receivable, loans to company officers, advances to employees, and income taxes refundable.

Companies record accounts receivable when they perform a service on account or at the point of sale of merchandise on account. Accounts receivable are reduced by sales returns and allowances. Cash discounts reduce the amount received on accounts receivable. When interest is charged on a past due receivable, the company adds this interest to the accounts receivable balance and recognizes it as interest revenue.

2 Describe how companies value accounts receivable and record their disposition.

There are two methods of accounting for uncollectible accounts: the allowance method and the direct write-off method. Companies use the percentage-of-receivables basis to estimate uncollectible accounts using the allowance method. The percentage-of-receivables basis emphasizes the cash realizable value of the accounts receivable. An aging schedule is often used with this basis.

When a company collects an account receivable, it credits Accounts Receivable. When a company sells (factors) an account receivable, a service charge expense reduces the amount received.

3 Explain how companies recognize, value, and dispose of notes receivable.

For a note stated in months, the maturity date is found by counting the months from the date of issue. For a note stated in days, the number of days is counted, omitting the issue date and counting the due date. The formula for computing interest is Face value × Interest rate × Time.

Companies record notes receivable at face value. In some cases, it is necessary to accrue interest prior to maturity. In this case, companies debit Interest Receivable and credit Interest Revenue.

Notes can be held to maturity. At that time the face value plus accrued interest is due, and the note is removed from the accounts. In many cases, the holder of the note speeds up the conversion by selling the receivable to another party (a factor). In some situations, the maker of the note dishonors the note (defaults), in which case the company transfers the note and accrued interest to an account receivable or writes off the note.

4 Describe the statement presentation and analysis of receivables.

As with accounts receivable, companies report notes receivable at their cash (net) realizable value. The notes receivable allowance account is Allowance for Doubtful Accounts. The computation and estimations involved in valuing notes receivable at cash realizable value, and in recording the proper amount of bad debt expense and the related allowance, are similar to those for accounts receivable.

Companies should identify in the balance sheet or in the notes to the financial statements each major type of receivable. Short-term receivables are considered current assets. Companies report the gross amount of receivables and the allowance for doubtful accounts. They report bad debt and service charge expenses in the multiple-step income statement as operating (selling) expenses. Interest revenue appears under other revenues and gains in the nonoperating activities section of the statement. Managers and investors evaluate accounts receivable for liquidity by computing a turnover ratio and an average collection period.

Glossary Review

Accounts receivable Amounts owed by customers on account. (p. 9-3).

Accounts receivable turnover A measure of the liquidity of accounts receivable; computed by dividing net credit sales by average net accounts receivable. (p. 9-20).

Aging the accounts receivable The analysis of customer balances by the length of time they have been unpaid. (p. 9-8).

Allowance method A method of accounting for bad debts that involves estimating uncollectible accounts at the end of each period. (p. 9-6).

Average collection period The average amount of time that a receivable is outstanding; calculated by dividing 365 days by the accounts receivable turnover. (p. 9-20).

Bad Debt Expense An expense account to record uncollectible receivables. (p. 9-5).

Cash (net) realizable value The net amount a company expects to receive in cash. (p. 9-6).

Direct write-off method A method of accounting for bad debts that involves expensing accounts at the time they are determined to be uncollectible. (p. 9-5).

Dishonored (defaulted) note A note that is not paid in full at maturity. (p. 9-17).

Factor A finance company or bank that buys receivables from businesses and then collects the payments directly from the customers. (p. 9-11).

Maker The party in a promissory note who is making the promise to pay. (p. 9-13).

Notes receivable Written promise (as evidenced by a formal instrument) for amounts to be received. (p. 9-3).

Other receivables Various forms of nontrade receivables, such as interest receivable and income taxes refundable. (p. 9-3).

Payee The party to whom payment of a promissory note is to be made. (p. 9-13).

Percentage-of-receivables basis Management estimates what percentage of receivables will result in losses from uncollectible accounts. (p. 9-8).

Promissory note A written promise to pay a specified amount of money on demand or at a definite time. (p. 9-13).

Receivables Amounts due from individuals and other companies. (p. 9-2).

Trade receivables Notes and accounts receivable that result from sales transactions. (p. 9-3).

Practice Multiple-Choice Questions

1. **(LO 1)** Receivables are frequently classified as:
   - **a.** accounts receivable, company receivables, and other receivables.
   - **b.** accounts receivable, notes receivable, and employee receivables.
   - **c.** accounts receivable and general receivables.
   - **d.** accounts receivable, notes receivable, and other receivables.

2. **(LO 1)** Buehler Company on June 15 sells merchandise on account to Chaz Co. for $1,000, terms 2/10, n/30. On June 20, Chaz Co. returns merchandise worth $300 to Buehler Company. On June 24, payment is received from Chaz Co. for the balance due. What is the amount of cash received?
   - **a.** $700.
   - **b.** $680.
   - **c.** $686.
   - **d.** None of the above.

3. **(LO 2)** Hughes Company has a credit balance of $5,000 in its Allowance for Doubtful Accounts before any adjustments are made at the end of the year. Based on review and aging of its accounts receivable at the end of the year, Hughes estimates that $60,000 of its receivables are uncollectible. The amount of bad debt expense which should be reported for the year is:
   - **a.** $5,000.
   - **b.** $55,000.
   - **c.** $60,000.
   - **d.** $65,000.

4. **(LO 2)** Use the same information as in Question 3, except that Hughes has a debit balance of $5,000 in its Allowance for Doubtful Accounts before any adjustments are made at the end of the year. In this situation, the amount of bad debt expense that should be reported for the year is:
   - **a.** $5,000.
   - **b.** $55,000.
   - **c.** $60,000.
   - **d.** $65,000.

5. **(LO 2)** Accounts receivable at the end of the month are $800,000. Bad debts are expected to be 1.5% of accounts receivable. If Allowance for Doubtful Accounts has a credit balance of $1,000 before adjustment, what is the balance after adjustment?
   - **a.** $7,000.
   - **b.** $11,000.
   - **c.** $12,000.
   - **d.** $13,000.

6. (LO 2) At December 31, 2020, Roso Carlson Company had accounts receivable of $750,000. On January 1, 2020, Allowance for Doubtful Accounts had a credit balance of $18,000. During 2020, $30,000 of uncollectible accounts receivable were written off. Past experience indicates that 3% of accounts receivable become uncollectible. What should be the bad debt expense for 2020?

a. $10,500. **c.** $30,000.
b. $22,500. **d.** $34,500.

7. (LO 2) An analysis and aging of the accounts receivable of Prince Company at December 31 reveals the following data.

Accounts receivable	$800,000
Allowance for doubtful accounts per books before adjustment	50,000
Amounts expected to become uncollectible	65,000

The cash realizable value of the accounts receivable at December 31, after adjustment, is:

a. $685,000. **c.** $800,000.
b. $750,000. **d.** $735,000.

8. (LO 2) Which of the following statements about Visa credit card sales is **incorrect**?

a. The credit card issuer makes the credit investigation of the customer.

b. The retailer is not involved in the collection process.

c. Two parties are involved.

d. The retailer receives cash more quickly than it would from individual customers on account.

9. (LO 2) Blinka Retailers accepted $50,000 of Citibank Visa credit card charges for merchandise sold on July 1. Citibank charges 4% for its credit card use. The entry to record this transaction by Blinka Retailers will include a credit to Sales Revenue of $50,000 and a debit(s) to:

a. Cash	$48,000
and Service Charge Expense	$2,000
b. Accounts Receivable	$48,000
and Service Charge Expense	$2,000
c. Cash	$50,000
d. Accounts Receivable	$50,000

10. (LO 3) One of the following statements about promissory notes is incorrect. The **incorrect** statement is:

a. The party making the promise to pay is called the maker.

b. The party to whom payment is to be made is called the payee.

c. A promissory note is not a negotiable instrument.

d. A promissory note is often required from high-risk customers.

11. (LO 3) Foti Co. accepts a $1,000, 3-month, 6% promissory note in settlement of an account with Bartelt Co. The entry to record this transaction is as follows.

a. Notes Receivable	1,015	
Accounts Receivable		1,015
b. Notes Receivable	1,000	
Accounts Receivable		1,000
c. Notes Receivable	1,000	
Sales Revenue		1,000
d. Notes Receivable	1,030	
Accounts Receivable		1,030

12. (LO 3) Ginter Co. holds Kolar Inc.'s $10,000, 120-day, 9% note. The entry made by Ginter Co. when the note is collected, assuming no interest has been previously accrued, is:

a. Cash	10,300	
Notes Receivable		10,300
b. Cash	10,000	
Notes Receivable		10,000
c. Accounts Receivable	10,300	
Notes Receivable		10,000
Interest Revenue		300
d. Cash	10,300	
Notes Receivable		10,000
Interest Revenue		300

13. (LO 4) Accounts and notes receivable are reported in the current assets section of the balance sheet at:

a. cash (net) realizable value.

b. net book value.

c. lower-of-cost-or-net realizable value.

d. invoice cost.

14. (LO 4) Oliveras Company had net credit sales during the year of $800,000 and cost of goods sold of $500,000. The balance in accounts receivable at the beginning of the year was $100,000, and the end of the year it was $150,000. What were the accounts receivable turnover and the average collection period in days?

a. 4.0 and 91.3 days.

b. 5.3 and 68.9 days.

c. 6.4 and 57 days.

d. 8.0 and 45.6 days.

Solutions

1. **d.** Receivables are frequently classified as accounts receivable, notes receivable, and other receivables. The other choices are incorrect because receivables are not frequently classified as (a) company receivables, (b), employee receivables, or (c) general receivables.

2. **c.** Because payment is received within 10 days of the purchase, the cash received is $686 {[$1,000 – $300] – [($1,000 – $300) × 2%]}. The other choices are incorrect because (a) $700 does not consider the 2% discount; (b) the amount of the discount is based upon the amount after the return is granted ($700 × 2%), not the amount before the return of merchandise ($1,000 × 2%); and (d) there is a correct answer.

3. **b.** By crediting Allowance for Doubtful Accounts for $55,000, the new balance will be the required balance of $60,000. This adjusting entry debits Bad Debt Expense for $55,000 and credits Allowance for Doubtful Accounts for $55,000, not (a) $5,000, (c) $60,000, or (d) $65,000.

4. **d.** By crediting Allowance for Doubtful Accounts for $65,000, the new balance will be the required balance of $60,000. This adjusting entry debits Bad Debt Expense for $65,000 and credits

Allowance for Doubtful Accounts for $65,000, not (a) $5,000, (b) $55,000, or (c) $60,000.

5. **b.** Accounts receivable times the percentage expected to default equals $12,000 ($800,000 × 1.5%). Because the balance in Allowance for Doubtful Accounts is presently $1,000, the adjusting entry debits Bad Debt Expense for $11,000 ($12,000 – $1,000) and credits Allowance for Doubtful Accounts for $11,000, not (a) $7,000, (c) $12,000, or (d) $13,000.

6. **d.** The accounts written off during the year will result in a debit balance in Allowance for Doubtful Accounts of $12,000 ($30,000 – $18,000) at the end of the year. As indicated, 3% of accounts receivable are uncollectible, or $22,500 ($750,000 × 3%). Given a debit balance of $12,000 in Allowance for Doubtful Accounts at the end of the year, the adjusting entry at the end of the year is a debit to Bad Debt Expense of $34,500 ($22,500 + $12,000) and a credit to Allowance for Doubtful Accounts of $34,500 not (a) $10,500, (b) $22,500, or (c) $30,000.

7. **d.** Accounts Receivable less the expected uncollectible amount equals the cash realizable value of $735,000 ($800,000 – $65,000), not (a) $685,000, (b) $750,000, or (c) $800,000.

8. **c.** There are three parties, not two, involved in Visa credit card sales: the credit card company, the retailer, and the customer. The other choices are true statements.

9. **a.** Credit card sales are considered cash sales. Cash is debited $48,000 for the net amount received ($50,000 – $2,000 for credit card use fee), and Service Charge Expense is debited $2,000 for the 4% credit card use fee ($50,000 × 4%). The other choices are therefore incorrect.

10. **c.** A promissory note is a negotiable instrument. The other choices are true statements.

11. **b.** Notes Receivable is recorded at face value ($1,000). No interest on the note is recorded until it is earned. Accounts Receivable is credited because no new sales have been made. The other choices are therefore incorrect.

12. **d.** Cash is debited for its maturity value [$10,000 + interest earned ($10,000 × 1/3 × 9%)], Notes Receivable credited for its face value, and Interest Revenue credited for the amount of interest earned. The other choices are therefore incorrect.

13. **a.** Accounts Receivable is reported in the current assets section of the balance sheet at the gross amount less the allowance for doubtful accounts, not at (b) net book value, (c) lower-of-cost-or-net realizable value, or (d) invoice cost.

14. **c.** The accounts receivable turnover is 6.4 [$800,000/($100,000 + $150,000)/2]. The average collection period in days is 57 days (365/6.4). The other choices are therefore incorrect.

Practice Brief Exercises

Record basic accounts receivable transactions.

1. **(LO 1)** Record the following transactions on the books of Gonzalez Co.

a. On August 1, Gonzalez Co. sold merchandise on account to Miguel Inc. for $15,500, terms 1/10, n/30.

b. On August 8, Miguel Inc. returned merchandise worth $3,100 to Gonzalez Co.

c. On August 11, Miguel Inc. paid for the merchandise.

Solution

1. **a.** Accounts Receivable	15,500	
Sales Revenue		15,500
b. Sales Returns and Allowances	3,100	
Accounts Receivable		3,100
c. Cash ($12,400 – $124)	12,276	
Sales Discounts ($12,400 × 1%)	124	
Accounts Receivable ($15,500 – $3,100)		12,400

Prepare entry using percentage-of-receivables method.

2. **(LO 2)** Sanchez Co. uses the percentage-of-receivables basis in 2020 to record bad debt expense. It estimates that 3% of accounts receivable will become uncollectible. Sales revenues are $900,000 for 2020, and sales returns and allowances are $50,000 at December 31, 2020. Accounts receivable has a balance of $139,000, and the allowance for doubtful accounts has a credit balance of $3,000. Prepare the adjusting entry to record bad debt expense in 2020.

Solution

2. Bad Debt Expense [($139,000 × 3%) – $3,000]	1,170	
Allowance for Doubtful Accounts		1,170

Prepare entry for notes receivable exchanged for account receivable.

3. **(LO 3)** On January 20, 2020, Carlos Co. sold merchandise on account to Carson Co. for $20,000, n/30. On February 19, Carson Co. gave Carlos Co. an 8% promissory note in settlement of this account. Prepare the journal entry to record the sale and the settlement of the account receivable.

Solution

Jan. 20	Accounts Receivable	20,000	
	Sales Revenue		20,000
Feb. 19	Notes Receivable	20,000	
	Accounts Receivable		20,000

Practice Exercises

Journalize entries to record allowance for doubtful accounts using two different bases.

1. **(LO 2)** The ledger of Nuro Company at the end of the current year shows Accounts Receivable $180,000, Sales Revenue $1,800,000, and Sales Returns and Allowances $60,000.

Instructions

a. If Nuro uses the direct write-off method to account for uncollectible accounts, journalize the adjusting entry at December 31, assuming Nuro determines that $2,900 of the Accounts Receivable balance is uncollectible.

b. If Allowance for Doubtful Accounts has a credit balance of $4,300 in the trial balance, journalize the adjusting entry at December 31, assuming bad debts are expected to be 10% of accounts receivable.

c. If Allowance for Doubtful Accounts has a debit balance of $410 in the trial balance, journalize the adjusting entry at December 31, assuming bad debts are expected to be 6% of accounts receivable.

Solution

1. a.	Dec. 31	Bad Debt Expense	2,900	
		Accounts Receivable		2,900
b.	Dec. 31	Bad Debt Expense	13,700	
		Allowance for Doubtful Accounts [($180,000 × 10%) – $4,300]		13,700
c.	Dec. 31	Bad Debt Expense	11,210	
		Allowance for Doubtful Accounts [($180,000 × 6%) + $410]		11,210

Journalize entries for notes receivable transactions.

2. **(LO 3)** Sargeant Supply Co. has the following transactions related to notes receivable during the last 2 months of 2020.

Nov. 1	Loaned $20,000 cash to Mary Hawkins on a 1-year, 12% note.
Dec. 11	Sold goods to Eminem, Inc., receiving a $9,000, 90-day, 8% note.
16	Received a $8,000, 6-month, 9% note in exchange for Rick DeLong's outstanding accounts receivable.
31	Accrued interest revenue on all notes receivable.

Instructions

a. Journalize the transactions for Sargeant Supply Co.

b. Record the collection of the Hawkins note at its maturity in 2021.

Solution

2. a.

2020

Nov. 1	Notes Receivable	20,000	
	Cash		20,000

Dec. 11	Notes Receivable	9,000	
	Sales Revenue		9,000
16	Notes Receivable	8,000	
	Accounts Receivable		8,000
31	Interest Receivable	470	
	Interest Revenue*		470

*Calculation of interest revenue:

Hawkins' note:	$20,000 × 12% × 2/12 =	$400
Eminem's note:	9,000 × 8% × 20/360 =	40
DeLong's note:	8,000 × 9% × 15/360 =	30
Total accrued interest		$470

b. **2021**

Nov. 1	Cash	22,400	
	Interest Receivable		400
	Interest Revenue**		2,000
	Notes Receivable		20,000

**($20,000 × 12% × 10/12)

Practice Problem

Prepare entries for various receivables transactions.

(LO 1, 2, 3) The following selected transactions relate to Dylan Company.

Mar.	1	Sold $20,000 of merchandise to Potter Company, terms 2/10, n/30.
	11	Received payment in full from Potter Company for balance due on existing accounts receivable.
	12	Accepted Juno Company's $20,000, 6-month, 12% note for balance due.
	13	Made Dylan Company credit card sales for $13,200.
	15	Made Visa credit card sales totaling $6,700. A 3% service fee is charged by Visa.
Apr.	11	Sold accounts receivable of $8,000 to Harcot Factor. Harcot Factor assesses a service charge of 2% of the amount of receivables sold.
	13	Received collections of $8,200 on Dylan Company credit card sales and added finance charges of 1.5% to the remaining balances.
May	10	Dylan uses the percentage-of-receivables basis to estimate bad debts.
June	30	Accounts receivable total $2,000,000. The bad debt percentage is 1% of accounts receivable. At June 30, the balance in the allowance account is $3,500 before adjustment.
July	16	One of the accounts receivable written off in May was from J. Simon, who pays the amount due, $4,000, in full.

Instructions

Prepare the journal entries for the transactions. (Ignore entries for cost of goods sold.)

Solution

Mar. 1	Accounts Receivable	20,000	
	Sales Revenue		20,000
	(To record sales on account)		
11	Cash	19,600	
	Sales Discounts (2% × $20,000)	400	
	Accounts Receivable		20,000
	(To record collection of accounts receivable)		
12	Notes Receivable	20,000	
	Accounts Receivable		20,000
	(To record acceptance of Juno Company note)		
13	Accounts Receivable	13,200	
	Sales Revenue		13,200
	(To record company credit card sales)		

Date	Account Titles and Explanation	Debit	Credit
15	Cash	6,499	
	Service Charge Expense (3% × $6,700)	201	
	Sales Revenue		6,700
	(To record credit card sales)		
Apr. 11	Cash	7,840	
	Service Charge Expense (2% × $8,000)	160	
	Accounts Receivable		8,000
	(To record sale of receivables to factor)		
13	Cash	8,200	
	Accounts Receivable		8,200
	(To record collection of accounts receivable)		
	Accounts Receivable [($13,200 – $8,200) × 1.5%]	75	
	Interest Revenue		75
	(To record interest on amount due)		
May 10	Allowance for Doubtful Accounts	16,000	
	Accounts Receivable		16,000
	(To record write-off of accounts receivable)		
June 30	Bad Debt Expense [($2,000,000 × 1%) – $3,500]	16,500	
	Allowance for Doubtful Accounts		16,500
	(To record estimate of uncollectible accounts)		
July 16	Accounts Receivable	4,000	
	Allowance for Doubtful Accounts		4,000
	(To reverse write-off of accounts receivable)		
	Cash	4,000	
	Accounts Receivable		4,000
	(To record collection of accounts receivable)		

WileyPLUS

Brief Exercises, Exercises, DO IT! Exercises, Problems, and many additional resources are available for practice in WileyPLUS.

Questions

1. What is the difference between an account receivable and a note receivable?

2. What are some common types of receivables other than accounts receivable and notes receivable?

3. **Texaco Oil Company** issues its own credit cards. Assume that Texaco charges you $40 interest on an unpaid balance. Prepare the journal entry that Texaco makes to record this revenue.

4. What are the essential features of the allowance method of accounting for bad debts?

5. Roger Holloway cannot understand why cash realizable value does not decrease when an uncollectible account is written off under the allowance method. Clarify this point for Roger.

6. What types of receivables does **Apple** report on its balance sheet? Does it use the allowance method or the direct write-off method to account for uncollectibles?

7. Borke Company has a credit balance of $3,000 in Allowance for Doubtful Accounts before adjustment. The total estimated uncollectibles under the percentage-of-receivables basis is $5,800. Prepare the adjusting entry to record bad debt expense.

8. How are bad debts accounted for under the direct write-off method? What are the disadvantages of this method?

9. Regina Golden, the vice president of sales for Tropical Pools and Spas, wants the company's credit department to be less restrictive in granting credit. "How can we sell anything when you guys won't approve anybody?" she asks. Discuss the pros and cons of easy credit. What are the accounting implications?

10. **JCPenney Company** accepts both its own credit cards and national credit cards. What are the advantages of accepting both types of cards?

11. An article recently appeared in the *Wall Street Journal* indicating that companies are selling their receivables at a record rate. Why are companies selling their receivables?

12. Westside Textiles decides to sell $800,000 of its accounts receivable to First Factors Inc. First Factors assesses a service charge of 3% of the amount of receivables sold. Prepare the journal entry that Westside Textiles makes to record this sale.

13. Your roommate is uncertain about the advantages of a promissory note. Compare the advantages of a note receivable with those of an account receivable.

14. How may the maturity date of a promissory note be stated?

15. Indicate the maturity date of each of the following promissory notes:

Date of Note	Terms
a. March 13	one year after date of note
b. May 4	3 months after date
c. June 20	30 days after date
d. July 1	60 days after date

16. Compute the missing amounts for each of the following notes.

	Principal	Annual Interest Rate	Time	Total Interest
a.	?	9%	120 days	$ 450
b.	$30,000	10%	3 years	?
c.	$60,000	?	5 months	$1,500
d.	$45,000	8%	?	$1,200

17. Jana Company dishonors a note at maturity. What are the options available to the lender?

18. **General Motors Corporation** has accounts receivable and notes receivable. How should the receivables be reported on the balance sheet?

19. The accounts receivable turnover is 8.14, and average net receivables during the period are $400,000. What is the amount of net credit sales for the period?

20. What percentage does **Apple**'s 2015 allowance for doubtful accounts represent as a percentage of its gross receivables?

Brief Exercises

Identify different types of receivables.

BE9.1 (LO 1) Presented below are three receivables transactions. Indicate whether these receivables are reported as accounts receivable, notes receivable, or other receivables on a balance sheet.

a. Sold merchandise on account for $64,000 to a customer.

b. Received a promissory note of $57,000 for services performed.

c. Advanced $10,000 to an employee.

Record basic accounts receivable transactions.

BE9.2 (LO 1) Record the following transactions on the books of RAS Co.

a. On July 1, RAS Co. sold merchandise on account to Waegelein Inc. for $17,200, terms 2/10, n/30.

b. On July 8, Waegelein Inc. returned merchandise worth $3,800 to RAS Co.

c. On July 11, Waegelein Inc. paid for the merchandise.

Prepare entry for allowance method and partial balance sheet.

BE9.3 (LO 2, 4) **Financial Statement** During its first year of operations, Gavin Company had credit sales of $3,000,000; $600,000 remained uncollected at year-end. The credit manager estimates that $31,000 of these receivables will become uncollectible.

a. Prepare the journal entry to record the estimated uncollectibles.

b. Prepare the current assets section of the balance sheet for Gavin Company. Assume that in addition to the receivables it has cash of $90,000, inventory of $130,000, and prepaid insurance of $7,500.

Prepare entry for write-off; determine cash realizable value.

BE9.4 (LO 2) At the end of 2020, Carpenter Co. has accounts receivable of $700,000 and an allowance for doubtful accounts of $54,000. On January 24, 2021, the company learns that its receivable from Megan Gray is not collectible, and management authorizes a write-off of $6,200.

a. Prepare the journal entry to record the write-off.

b. What is the cash realizable value of the accounts receivable (1) before the write-off and (2) after the write-off?

Prepare entries for collection of bad debt write-off.

BE9.5 (LO 2) Assume the same information as BE9.4. On March 4, 2021, Carpenter Co. receives payment of $6,200 in full from Megan Gray. Prepare the journal entries to record this transaction.

Prepare entry using percentage-of-receivables method.

BE9.6 (LO 2) Kingston Co. uses the percentage-of-receivables basis to record bad debt expense. It estimates that 1% of accounts receivable will become uncollectible. Accounts receivable are $420,000 at the end of the year, and the allowance for doubtful accounts has a credit balance of $1,500.

a. Prepare the adjusting journal entry to record bad debt expense for the year.

b. If the allowance for doubtful accounts had a debit balance of $800 instead of a credit balance of $1,500, determine the amount to be reported for bad debt expense.

Prepare entries to dispose of accounts receivable.

BE9.7 (LO 2) Presented below are two independent transactions.

a. Tony's Restaurant accepted a Visa card in payment of a $175 lunch bill. The bank charges a 4% fee. What entry should Tony's make?

b. Larkin Company sold its accounts receivable of $60,000. What entry should Larkin make, given a service charge of 3% on the amount of receivables sold?

Compute interest and determine maturity dates on notes.

BE9.8 (LO 3) Compute interest and find the maturity date for the following notes.

	Date of Note	Principal	Interest Rate (%)	Terms
a.	June 10	$80,000	6%	60 days
b.	July 14	$64,000	7%	90 days
c.	April 27	$12,000	8%	75 days

Determine maturity dates and compute interest and rates on notes.

BE9.9 (LO 3) Presented below are data on three promissory notes. Determine the missing amounts.

	Date of Note	Terms	Maturity Date	Principal	Annual Interest Rate	Total Interest
a.	April 1	60 days	?	$600,000	6%	?
b.	July 2	30 days	?	90,000	?	$600
c.	March 7	6 months	?	120,000	10%	?

Prepare entry for notes receivable exchanged for account receivable.

BE9.10 (LO 3) On January 10, 2020, Perez Co. sold merchandise on account to Robertsen Co. for $15,600, n/30. On February 9, Robertsen Co. gave Perez Co. a 10% promissory note in settlement of this account. Prepare the journal entry to record the sale and the settlement of the account receivable. (Omit cost of goods sold entries.)

Prepare entry for estimated uncollectibles and classifications, and compute ratios.

BE9.11 (LO 2, 4) **Financial Statement** During its first year of operations, Fertig Company had credit sales of $3,000,000, of which $400,000 remained uncollected at year-end. The credit manager estimates that $18,000 of these receivables will become uncollectible.

a. Prepare the journal entry to record the estimated uncollectibles. (Assume an unadjusted balance of zero in Allowance for Doubtful Accounts.)

b. Prepare the current assets section of the balance sheet for Fertig Company, assuming that in addition to the receivables it has cash of $90,000, merchandise inventory of $180,000, and supplies of $13,000.

c. Calculate the accounts receivable turnover and average collection period. Assume that average net accounts receivable were $300,000. Explain what these measures tell us.

Compute ratios to analyze receivables.

BE9.12 (LO 4) The financial statements of **Minnesota Mining and Manufacturing Company (3M)** report net sales of $20.0 billion. Accounts receivable (net) are $2.7 billion at the beginning of the year and $2.8 billion at the end of the year. Compute 3M's accounts receivable turnover. Compute 3M's average collection period for accounts receivable in days.

DO IT! Exercises

Prepare entries to recognize accounts receivable.

DO IT! 9.1 (LO 1) On March 1, Lincoln sold merchandise on account to Amelia Company for $28,000, terms 1/10, net 45. On March 6, Amelia returns merchandise with a sales price of $1,000. On March 11, Lincoln receives payment from Amelia for the balance due. Prepare journal entries to record the March transactions on Lincoln's books. (You may ignore cost of goods sold entries and explanations.)

Prepare entry for uncollectible accounts.

DO IT! 9.2a (LO 2) Gonzalez Company has been in business several years. At the end of the current year, the ledger shows the following:

Accounts Receivable	$ 310,000 Dr.
Sales Revenue	2,200,000 Cr.
Allowance for Doubtful Accounts	6,100 Cr.

Bad debts are estimated to be 5% of accounts receivable. Prepare the entry to adjust Allowance for Doubtful Accounts.

Prepare entry for factored accounts.

DO IT! 9.2b (LO 2) Neumann Distributors is a growing company whose ability to raise capital has not been growing as quickly as its expanding assets and sales. Neumann's local banker has indicated that the company cannot increase its borrowing for the foreseeable future. Neumann's suppliers are demanding payment for goods acquired within 30 days of the invoice date, but Neumann's customers are slow in paying for their purchases (60–90 days). As a result, Neumann has a cash flow problem.

Neumann needs $160,000 to cover next Friday's payroll. Its balance of outstanding accounts receivable totals $800,000. To alleviate this cash crunch, the company sells $170,000 of its receivables. Record the entry that Neumann would make. (Assume a 2% service charge.)

Compute maturity date and interest on note.

DO IT! 9.3 (LO 3) Gentry Wholesalers accepts from Benton Stores a $6,200, 4-month, 9% note dated May 31 in settlement of Benton's overdue account. (a) What is the maturity date of the note? (b) What is the interest payable at the maturity date?

Compute ratios for receivables.

DO IT! 9.4 (LO 4) In 2020, Wainwright Company has net credit sales of $1,300,000 for the year. It had a beginning accounts receivable (net) balance of $101,000 and an ending accounts receivable (net) balance of $107,000. Compute Wainwright Company's (a) accounts receivable turnover and (b) average collection period in days.

Exercises

Prepare entries for recognizing accounts receivable.

E9.1 (LO 1) On January 6, Jacob Co. sells merchandise on account to Harley Inc. for $9,200, terms 1/10, n/30. On January 16, Harley pays the amount due.

Instructions

Prepare the entries on Jacob Co.'s books to record the sale and related collection. (Omit cost of goods sold entries.)

Journalize entries related to accounts receivable.

E9.2 (LO 1) Presented below are selected transactions of Molina Company. Molina sells in large quantities to other companies and also sells its product in a small retail outlet.

March	1	Sold merchandise on account to Dodson Company for $5,000, terms 2/10, n/30.
	3	Dodson Company returned merchandise worth $500 to Molina.
	9	Molina collected the amount due from Dodson Company from the March 1 sale.
	15	Molina sold merchandise for $400 in its retail outlet. The customer used his Molina credit card.
	31	Molina added 1.5% monthly interest to the customer's credit card balance.

Instructions

Prepare journal entries for the transactions above. (Ignore cost of goods sold entries and explanations.)

Journalize entries for recognizing accounts receivable.

E9.3 (LO 1) Presented below are two independent situations.

Instructions

a. On January 6, Brumbaugh Co. sells merchandise on account to Pryor Inc. for $7,000, terms 2/10, n/30. On January 16, Pryor Inc. pays the amount due. Prepare the entries on Brumbaugh's books to record the sale and related collection. (Omit cost of goods sold entries.)

b. On January 10, Andrew Farley uses his Paltrow Co. credit card to purchase merchandise from Paltrow Co. for $9,000. On February 10, Farley is billed for the amount due of $9,000. On February 12, Farley pays $5,000 on the balance due. On March 10, Farley is billed for the amount due, including interest at 1% per month on the unpaid balance as of February 12. Prepare the entries on Paltrow Co.'s books related to the transactions that occurred on January 10, February 12, and March 10. (Omit cost of goods sold entries.)

Journalize receivables transactions.

E9.4 (LO 1, 2) At the beginning of the current period, Rose Corp. had balances in Accounts Receivable of $200,000 and in Allowance for Doubtful Accounts of $9,000 (credit). During the period, it had net credit sales of $800,000 and collections of $763,000. It wrote off as uncollectible accounts receivable of $7,300. However, a $3,100 account previously written off as uncollectible was recovered before the end of the current period. Uncollectible accounts are estimated to total $25,000 at the end of the period. (Omit cost of goods sold entries.)

Instructions

a. Prepare the entries to record sales and collections during the period.

b. Prepare the entry to record the write-off of uncollectible accounts during the period.

c. Prepare the entries to record the recovery of the uncollectible account during the period.

d. Prepare the entry to record bad debt expense for the period.

e. Determine the ending balances in Accounts Receivable and Allowance for Doubtful Accounts.

f. What is the net realizable value of the receivables at the end of the period?

Journalize entries to record allowance for doubtful accounts using two different bases.

E9.5 (LO 2) The ledger of Costello Company at the end of the current year shows Accounts Receivable $110,000, Sales Revenue $840,000, and Sales Returns and Allowances $20,000.

Instructions

a. If Costello uses the direct write-off method to account for uncollectible accounts, journalize the adjusting entry at December 31, assuming Costello determines that L. Dole's $1,400 balance is uncollectible.

b. If Allowance for Doubtful Accounts has a credit balance of $2,100 in the trial balance, journalize the adjusting entry at December 31, assuming bad debts are expected to be 10% of accounts receivable.

c. If Allowance for Doubtful Accounts has a debit balance of $200 in the trial balance, journalize the adjusting entry at December 31, assuming bad debts are expected to be 6% of accounts receivable.

Determine bad debt expense, and prepare the adjusting entry.

E9.6 (LO 2) Godfreid Company has accounts receivable of $95,400 at March 31, 2020. Credit terms are 2/10, n/30. At March 31, 2020, there is a $2,100 credit balance in Allowance for Doubtful Accounts prior to adjustment. The company uses the percentage-of-receivables basis for estimating uncollectible accounts. The company's estimates of bad debts are as shown below.

	Balance, March 31		
Age of Accounts	**2020**	**2019**	**Estimated Percentage Uncollectible**
Current	$65,000	$75,000	2%
1–30 days past due	12,900	8,000	5
31–90 days past due	10,100	2,400	30
Over 90 days past due	7,400	1,100	50
	$95,400	$86,500	

Instructions

a. Determine the total estimated uncollectibles.

b. Prepare the adjusting entry at March 31, 2020, to record bad debt expense.

c. Discuss the implications of the changes in the aging schedule from 2019 to 2020.

Journalize write-off and recovery.

E9.7 (LO 2) At December 31, 2019, Blanda Company had a credit balance of $15,000 in Allowance for Doubtful Accounts. During 2020, Blanda wrote off accounts totaling $11,000. One of those accounts ($1,800) was later collected. At December 31, 2020, an aging schedule indicated that the balance in Allowance for Doubtful Accounts should be $19,000.

Instructions

Prepare journal entries to record the 2020 transactions of Blanda Company.

Journalize percentage-of-receivables basis, write-off, recovery.

E9.8 (LO 2) On December 31, 2020, Ling Co. estimated that 2% of its net accounts receivable of $450,000 will become uncollectible. The company recorded this amount as an addition to Allowance for Doubtful Accounts. The allowance account had a zero balance before adjustment at December 31, 2020. On May 11, 2021, Ling Co. determined that the Jeff Shoemaker account was uncollectible and wrote off $1,100. On June 12, 2021, Shoemaker paid the amount previously written off.

Instructions

Prepare the journal entries on December 31, 2020, May 11, 2021, and June 12, 2021.

Journalize entries for the sale of accounts receivable.

E9.9 (LO 2) Presented below are two independent situations.

Instructions

a. On March 3, Kitselman Appliances sells $650,000 of its receivables to Ervay Factors Inc. Ervay Factors assesses a finance charge of 3% of the amount of receivables sold. Prepare the entry on Kitselman Appliances' books to record the sale of the receivables.

b. On May 10, Fillmore Company sold merchandise for $3,000 and accepted the customer's America Bank MasterCard. America Bank charges a 4% service charge for credit card sales. Prepare the entry on Fillmore Company's books to record the sale of merchandise.

Journalize entries for credit card sales.

E9.10 (LO 2) Presented below are two independent situations.

Instructions

a. On April 2, Jennifer Elston uses her **JCPenney Company** credit card to purchase merchandise from a JCPenney store for $1,500. On May 1, Elston is billed for the $1,500 amount due. Elston pays $500 on the balance due on May 3. Elston receives a bill dated June 1 for the amount due, including interest at 1.0% per month on the unpaid balance as of May 3. Prepare the entries on JCPenney Co.'s books related to the transactions that occurred on April 2, May 3, and June 1.

b. On July 4, Spangler's Restaurant accepts a Visa card for a $200 dinner bill. Visa charges a 2% service fee. Prepare the entry on Spangler's books related to this transaction.

Journalize credit card sales.

E9.11 (LO 2) Colaw Stores accepts both its own and national credit cards. During the year, the following selected summary transactions occurred.

Jan. 15	Made Colaw credit card sales totaling $18,000. (There were no balances prior to January 15.)
20	Made Visa credit card sales (service charge fee 2%) totaling $4,500.
Feb. 10	Collected $10,000 on Colaw credit card sales.
15	Added finance charges of 1.5% to Colaw credit card account balances.

Instructions

Journalize the transactions for Colaw Stores.

Journalize entries for notes receivable transactions.

E9.12 (LO 3) Elburn Supply Co. has the following transactions related to notes receivable during the last 2 months of 2020. The company does not make entries to accrue interest except at December 31.

Nov. 1	Loaned $30,000 cash to Manny Lopez on a 12 month, 10% note.
Dec. 11	Sold goods to Ralph Kremer, Inc., receiving a $6,750, 90-day, 8% note.
16	Received a $4,000, 180 day, 9% note in exchange for Joe Fernetti's outstanding accounts receivable.
31	Accrued interest revenue on all notes receivable.

Instructions

a. Journalize the transactions for Elburn Supply Co. (Ignore entries for cost of goods sold.)

b. Record the collection of the Lopez note at its maturity in 2021.

Journalize entries for notes receivable.

E9.13 (LO 3) Record the following transactions for Redeker Co. in the general journal.

2020	
May 1	Received a $9,000, 12-month, 10% note in exchange for Mark Chamber's outstanding accounts receivable.
Dec. 31	Accrued interest on the Chamber note.
Dec. 31	Closed the interest revenue account.
2021	
May 1	Received principal plus interest on the Chamber note. (No interest has been accrued in 2021.)

Prepare entries for note receivable transactions.

E9.14 (LO 3) Vandiver Company had the following select transactions.

Apr. 1, 2020	Accepted Goodwin Company's 12-month, 6% note in settlement of a $30,000 account receivable.
July 1, 2020	Loaned $25,000 cash to Thomas Slocombe on a 9-month, 10% note.
Dec. 31, 2020	Accrued interest on all notes receivable.
Apr. 1, 2021	Received principal plus interest on the Goodwin note.
Apr. 1, 2021	Thomas Slocombe dishonored its note; Vandiver expects it will eventually collect.

Instructions

Prepare journal entries to record the transactions. Vandiver prepares adjusting entries once a year on December 31.

E9.15 (LO 3) On May 2, McLain Company lends $9,000 to Chang, Inc., issuing a 6-month, 7% note. At the maturity date, November 2, Chang indicates that it cannot pay.

Journalize entries for dishonor of notes receivable.

Instructions

a. Prepare the entry to record the issuance of the note.

b. Prepare the entry to record the dishonor of the note, assuming that McLain Company expects collection will occur.

c. Prepare the entry to record the dishonor of the note, assuming that McLain Company does not expect collection in the future.

E9.16 (LO 4) Eileen Corp. had the following balances in receivable accounts at October 31, 2020 (in thousands): Allowance for Doubtful Accounts $52, Accounts Receivable $2,910, Other Receivables $189, and Notes Receivable $1,353.

Prepare a balance sheet presentation of receivables.

Instructions

Prepare the balance sheet presentation of Eileen Corp.'s receivables in good form.

E9.17 (LO 4) Kerwick Company had accounts receivable of $100,000 on January 1, 2020. The only transactions that affected accounts receivable during 2020 were net credit sales of $1,000,000, cash collections of $920,000, and accounts written off of $30,000.

Compute accounts receivable turnover and average collection period.

Instructions

a. Compute the ending balance of accounts receivable.

b. Compute the accounts receivable turnover for 2020.

c. Compute the average collection period in days.

Problems: Set A

P9.1A (LO 1, 2, 4) At December 31, 2019, House Co. reported the following information on its balance sheet.

Prepare journal entries related to bad debt expense.

Accounts receivable	$960,000
Less: Allowance for doubtful accounts	80,000

During 2020, the company had the following transactions related to receivables.

1.	Sales on account	$3,700,000
2.	Sales returns and allowances	50,000
3.	Collections of accounts receivable	2,810,000
4.	Write-offs of accounts receivable deemed uncollectible	90,000
5.	Recovery of bad debts previously written off as uncollectible	29,000

Instructions

a. Prepare the journal entries to record each of these five transactions. Assume that no cash discounts were taken on the collections of accounts receivable.

b. Enter the January 1, 2020, balances in Accounts Receivable and Allowance for Doubtful Accounts, post the entries to the two accounts (use T-accounts), and determine the balances.

c. Prepare the journal entry to record bad debt expense for 2020, assuming that an aging of accounts receivable indicates that expected bad debts are $115,000.

d. Compute the accounts receivable turnover for 2020 assuming the expected bad debt information provided in (c).

b. Accounts receivable $1,710,000
ADA $19,000
c. Bad debt expense $96,000

Compute bad debt amounts.

P9.2A (LO 2) Writing Information related to Mingenback Company for 2020 is summarized below.

Total credit sales	$2,500,000
Accounts receivable at December 31	875,000
Bad debts written off	33,000

Instructions

a. What amount of bad debt expense will Mingenback Company report if it uses the direct write-off method of accounting for bad debts?

b. Assume that Mingenback Company estimates its bad debt expense based on 6% of accounts receivable. What amount of bad debt expense will Mingenback record if it has an Allowance for Doubtful Accounts credit balance of $3,000?

c. Assume the same facts as in (b), except that there is a $3,000 debit balance in Allowance for Doubtful Accounts. What amount of bad debt expense will Mingenback record?

d. What is the weakness of the direct write-off method of reporting bad debt expense?

Journalize entries to record transactions related to bad debts.

P9.3A (LO 2) Presented below is an aging schedule for Halleran Company.

Worksheet

Customer	Total	Not Yet Due	Number of Days Past Due: 1–30	31–60	61–90	Over 90
Anders	$ 22,000		$10,000	$12,000		
Blake	40,000	$ 40,000				
Coulson	57,000	16,000	6,000		$35,000	
Deleon	34,000					$34,000
Others	132,000	96,000	16,000	14,000		6,000
	$285,000	$152,000	$32,000	$26,000	$35,000	$40,000
Estimated Percentage Uncollectible		3%	6%	13%	25%	50%
Total Estimated Bad Debts	$ 38,610	$ 4,560	$ 1,920	$ 3,380	$ 8,750	$20,000

At December 31, 2020, the unadjusted balance in Allowance for Doubtful Accounts is a credit of $12,000.

Instructions

a. Bad debt expense $26,610

a. Journalize and post the adjusting entry for bad debts at December 31, 2020.

b. Journalize and post to the allowance account the following events and transactions in the year 2021.

1. On March 31, a $1,000 customer balance originating in 2020 is judged uncollectible.
2. On May 31, a check for $1,000 is received from the customer whose account was written off as uncollectible on March 31.

c. Bad debt expense $32,400

c. Journalize the adjusting entry for bad debts on December 31, 2021, assuming that the unadjusted balance in Allowance for Doubtful Accounts is a debit of $800 and the aging schedule indicates that total estimated bad debts will be $31,600.

Journalize transactions related to bad debts.

P9.4A (LO 2) Writing Rigney Inc. uses the allowance method to estimate uncollectible accounts receivable. The company produced the following aging of the accounts receivable at year-end.

Worksheet

	Total	Number of Days Outstanding: 0–30	31–60	61–90	91–120	Over 120
Accounts receivable	200,000	77,000	46,000	39,000	23,000	15,000
% uncollectible		1%	4%	5%	8%	20%
Estimated bad debts						

Instructions

a. Tot. est. bad debts $9,400

a. Calculate the total estimated bad debts based on the information provided.

b. Prepare the year-end adjusting journal entry to record the bad debts using the aged uncollectible accounts receivable determined in (a). Assume the current balance in Allowance for Doubtful Accounts is a $8,000 debit.

c. Of the above accounts, $5,000 is determined to be specifically uncollectible. Prepare the journal entry to write off the uncollectible account.

d. The company collects $5,000 subsequently on a specific account that had previously been determined to be uncollectible in (c). Prepare the journal entry(ies) necessary to restore the account and record the cash collection.

e. Comment on how your answers to (a)–(d) would change if Rigney Inc. used 4% of **total** accounts receivable rather than aging the accounts receivable. What are the advantages to the company of aging the accounts receivable rather than applying a percentage to total accounts receivable?

Journalize entries to record transactions related to bad debts.

P9.5A (LO 2) Writing At December 31, 2020, the trial balance of Darby Company contained the following amounts before adjustment.

	Debit	Credit
Accounts Receivable	$385,000	
Allowance for Doubtful Accounts		$ 1,000
Sales Revenue		970,000

Instructions

a. Based on the information given, which method of accounting for bad debts is Darby Company using—the direct write-off method or the allowance method? How can you tell?

b. Prepare the adjusting entry at December 31, 2020, for bad debt expense, assuming an aging schedule indicates that $11,750 of accounts receivable will be uncollectible.

b. $10,750

c. Repeat part (b) assuming that instead of a credit balance there is a $1,000 debit balance in Allowance for Doubtful Accounts.

d. During the next month, January 2021, a $3,000 account receivable is written off as uncollectible. Prepare the journal entry to record the write-off.

e. Repeat part (d) assuming that Darby uses the direct write-off method instead of the allowance method in accounting for uncollectible accounts receivable.

f. What type of account is Allowance for Doubtful Accounts? How does it affect how accounts receivable is reported on the balance sheet at the end of the accounting period?

Prepare entries for various credit card and notes receivable transactions.

GLS

P9.6A (LO 1, 2, 3, 4) Financial Statement Milton Company closes its books on its July 31 year-end. The company does not make entries to accrue for interest except at its year-end. On June 30, the Notes Receivable account balance is $23,800. Notes Receivable includes the following.

Date	Maker	Face Value	Term	Maturity Date	Interest Rate
April 21	Coote Inc.	$ 6,000	90 days	July 20	8%
May 25	Brady Co.	7,800	60 days	July 24	10%
June 30	BMG Corp.	10,000	6 months	December 31	6%

During July, the following transactions were completed.

July 5	Made sales of $4,500 on Milton credit cards.
14	Made sales of $600 on Visa credit cards. The credit card service charge is 3%.
20	Received payment in full from Coote Inc. on the amount due.
24	Received payment in full from Brady Co. on the amount due.

Instructions

a. Journalize the July transactions and the July 31 adjusting entry for accrued interest receivable. (Interest is computed using 360 days; omit cost of goods sold entries.)

b. A/R bal. $4,500

b. Enter the balances at July 1 in the receivable accounts and post the entries to all of the receivable accounts. (Use T-accounts.)

c. Tot. receivables $14,550

c. Show the balance sheet presentation of the receivable accounts at July 31.

Prepare entries for various receivable transactions.

P9.7A (LO 1, 2, 3) On January 1, 2020, Harter Company had Accounts Receivable $139,000, Notes Receivable $25,000, and Allowance for Doubtful Accounts $13,200. The note receivable is from Willingham Company. It is a 4-month, 9% note dated December 31, 2019. Harter Company prepares financial statements annually at December 31. During the year, the following selected transactions occurred.

Jan.	5	Sold $20,000 of merchandise to Sheldon Company, terms n/15.
	20	Accepted Sheldon Company's $20,000, 3-month, 8% note for balance due.
Feb.	18	Sold $8,000 of merchandise to Patwary Company and accepted Patwary's $8,000, 6-month, 9% note for the amount due.
Apr.	20	Collected Sheldon Company note in full.
	30	Received payment in full from Willingham Company on the amount due.
May	25	Accepted Potter Inc.'s $6,000, 3-month, 7% note in settlement of a past-due balance on account.
Aug.	18	Received payment in full from Patwary Company on note due.
	25	The Potter Inc. note was dishonored. Potter Inc. is not bankrupt; future payment is anticipated.
Sept.	1	Sold $12,000 of merchandise to Stanbrough Company and accepted a $12,000, 6-month, 10% note for the amount due.

Instructions

Journalize the transactions. (Omit cost of goods sold entries.)

Calculate and interpret various ratios.

P9.8A (LO 4) Suppose the amounts presented here are basic financial information (in millions) from the 2020 annual reports of **Nike** and **adidas**.

	Nike	adidas
Sales revenue	$19,176.1	$10,381
Allowance for doubtful accounts, beginning	78.4	119
Allowance for doubtful accounts, ending	110.8	124
Accounts receivable balance (gross), beginning	2,873.7	1,743
Accounts receivable balance (gross), ending	2,994.7	1,553

Instructions

Calculate the accounts receivable turnover and average collection period for both companies. Comment on the difference in their collection experiences.

Prepare financial statements.

P9.9A (LO 4) **Financial Statement** The adjusted trial balance of Gibson Company for the year ended December 31, 2020, is as follows:

	Debit	Credit
Cash	$ 6,400	
Accounts Receivable	2,700	
Notes Receivable	6,300	
Inventory	10,000	
Equipment	7,500	
Allowance for Doubtful Accounts		$ 300
Accumulated Depreciation—Equipment		1,000
Notes Payable		1,100
Accounts Payable		600
Common Stock		17,000
Retained Earnings		11,000
Dividends	1,000	
Sales Revenue		13,000
Interest Revenue		100
Cost of Goods Sold	8,000	
Salary and Wages Expense	1,400	
Rent Expense	700	
Bad Debt Expense	60	
Service Charge Expense	40	
	$44,100	$44,100

Instructions

Prepare a multiple-step income statement, retained earnings statement, and a classified balance sheet. The notes payable is due on January 10, 2021.

Retained earnings $12,900

Continuing Case

Cookie Creations

(*Note:* This is a continuation of the Cookie Creations case from Chapters 1 through 8.)

© leungchopan/
Shutterstock

CC9 One of Natalie's friends, Curtis Lesperance, runs a coffee shop where he sells specialty coffees and prepares and sells muffins and cookies. He is eager to buy one of Natalie's fine European mixers, which would enable him to make larger batches of muffins and cookies. However, Curtis cannot afford to pay for the mixer for at least 30 days. He asks Natalie if she would be willing to sell him the mixer on credit. Natalie comes to you for advice.

Go to **WileyPLUS** *for complete case details and instructions.*

Ethics Case

EC9 The controller of Diaz Co. believes that the yearly allowance for doubtful accounts for Diaz Co. should be 2% of its accounts receivable balance at the end of the year. The president of Diaz Co., nervous that the owners might expect the company to sustain its 10% growth rate, suggests that the controller increase the allowance for doubtful accounts to 4%. The president thinks that the lower net income, which reflects a lower growth rate, will be a more sustainable rate for Diaz Co.

Instructions

a. Who are the stakeholders in this case?

b. Does the president's request pose an ethical dilemma for the controller?

c. Should the controller be concerned with Diaz Co.'s growth rate? Explain your answer.

Comprehensive Accounting Cycle Review

ACR9 **Financial Statement** Winter Company's balance sheet at December 31, 2019, is presented below.

Winter Company
Balance Sheet
December 31, 2019

Cash	$13,100	Accounts payable	$ 8,750
Accounts receivable	19,780	Owner's capital	32,730
Allowance for doubtful accounts	(800)		$41,480
Inventory	9,400		
	$41,480		

During January 2020, the following transactions occurred. Winter uses the perpetual inventory method.

Jan. 1 Winter accepted a 4-month, 8% note from Merando Company in payment of Merando's $1,200 account.

3 Winter wrote off as uncollectible the accounts of Inwood Corporation ($450) and Goza Company ($280).

8 Winter purchased $17,200 of inventory on account.

11 Winter sold for $28,000 on account inventory that cost $19,600.

15 Winter sold inventory that cost $700 to Mark Lauber for $1,000. Lauber charged this amount on his Visa First Bank card. The service fee charged Winter by First Bank is 3%.

17 Winter collected $22,900 from customers on account.

21 Winter paid $14,300 on accounts payable.
24 Winter received payment in full ($280) from Goza Company on the account written off on January 3.
27 Winter purchased supplies for $1,400 cash.
31 Winter paid other operating expenses, $3,718.

Adjustment data:

1. Interest is recorded for the month on the note from January 1.
2. Bad debts are expected to be 6% of the January 31, 2020, accounts receivable.
3. A count of supplies on January 31, 2020, reveals that $560 remains unused.

Instructions

(You may want to set up T-accounts to determine ending balances.)

a. Prepare journal entries for the transactions listed above and adjusting entries. (Include entries for cost of goods sold using the perpetual system.)

b. Totals $74,765

b. Prepare an adjusted trial balance at January 31, 2020.

c. Tot. assets $47,473

c. Prepare an income statement and an owner's equity statement for the month ending January 31, 2020, and a classified balance sheet as of January 31, 2020.

Expand Your Critical Thinking

Financial Reporting Problem: RLF Company

CT9.1 RLF Company sells office equipment and supplies to many organizations in the city and surrounding area on contract terms of 2/10, n/30. In the past, over 75% of the credit customers have taken advantage of the discount by paying within 10 days of the invoice date.

The number of customers taking the full 30 days to pay has increased within the last year. Current indications are that less than 60% of the customers are now taking the discount. Bad debts as a percentage of gross credit sales have risen from the 2.5% provided in past years to about 4.5% in the current year.

The company's Finance Committee has requested more information on the collections of accounts receivable. The controller responded to this request with the report reproduced below.

RLF Company
Accounts Receivable Collections
May 31, 2020

The fact that some credit accounts will prove uncollectible is normal. Annual bad debt write-offs have been 2.5% of gross credit sales over the past 5 years. During the last fiscal year, this percentage increased to slightly less than 4.5%. The current Accounts Receivable balance is $1,400,000. The condition of this balance in terms of age and probability of collection is as follows.

Proportion of Total	Age Categories	Probability of Collection
60%	not yet due	98%
22%	less than 30 days past due	96%
9%	30 to 60 days past due	94%
5%	61 to 120 days past due	91%
$2^1/_2$%	121 to 180 days past due	75%
$1^1/_2$%	over 180 days past due	30%

Allowance for Doubtful Accounts had a credit balance of $29,500 on June 1, 2019. RLF has provided for a monthly bad debt expense accrual during the current fiscal year based on the assumption that 4.5% of gross credit sales will be uncollectible. Total gross credit sales for the 2019–2020 fiscal year amounted to $2,900,000. Write-offs of bad accounts during the year totaled $102,000.

Instructions

a. Prepare an accounts receivable aging schedule for RLF Company using the age categories identified in the controller's report to the Finance Committee showing the following.

1. The amount of accounts receivable outstanding for each age category and in total.

2. The estimated amount that is uncollectible for each category and in total.

b. Compute the amount of the year-end adjustment necessary to bring Allowance for Doubtful Accounts to the balance indicated by the age analysis. Then prepare the necessary journal entry to adjust the accounting records.

c. In a recessionary environment with tight credit and high interest rates:

1. Identify steps RLF Company might consider to improve the accounts receivable situation.

2. Then evaluate each step identified in terms of the risks and costs involved.

Comparative Analysis Problem: PepsiCo, Inc. vs. The Coca-Cola Company

CT9.2 **PepsiCo, Inc.**'s financial statements are presented in Appendix B. Financial statements of **The Coca-Cola Company** are presented in Appendix C. The complete annual reports of PepsiCo and Coca-Cola, including the notes to the financial statements, are available at each company's respective website.

Instructions

a. Based on the information in these financial statements, compute the following 2015 ratios for each company. (Assume all sales are credit sales and that PepsiCo's receivables on its balance sheet are all trade receivables.)

1. Accounts receivable turnover.

2. Average collection period for receivables.

b. What conclusions about managing accounts receivable can you draw from these data?

Comparative Analysis Problem: Amazon.com, Inc. vs. Wal-Mart Stores, Inc.

CT9.3 **Amazon.com, Inc.**'s financial statements are presented in Appendix D. Financial statements of **Wal-Mart Stores, Inc.** are presented in Appendix E. The complete annual reports of Amazon and Wal-Mart, including the notes to the financial statements, are available at each company's respective website.

Instructions

a. Based on the information in these financial statements, compute the following ratios for each company (for the most recent year shown). (Assume all sales are credit sales.)

1. Accounts receivable turnover.

2. Average collection period for receivables.

b. What conclusions about managing accounts receivable can you draw from these data?

Real-World Focus

CT9.4 **Purpose:** To learn more about factoring.

Instructions

Search the Internet under "commercial capital factoring" and then go to the corresponding **Commercial Capital LLC** website. Click on **Invoice Factoring** and answer the following questions.

a. What are some of the benefits of factoring?

b. What is the range of the percentages of the typical discount rate?

c. If a company factors its receivables, what percentage of the value of the receivables can it expect to receive from the factor in the form of cash, and how quickly will it receive the cash?

Decision-Making Across the Organization

CT9.5 Carol and Sam Foyle own Campus Fashions. From its inception Campus Fashions has sold merchandise on either a cash or credit basis, but no credit cards have been accepted. During the past several months, the Foyles have begun to question their sales policies. First, they have lost some sales because of refusing to accept credit cards. Second, representatives of two metropolitan banks have been persuasive in almost convincing them to accept their national credit cards. One bank, City National Bank, has stated that its credit card fee is 4%.

The Foyles decide that they should determine the cost of carrying their own credit sales. From the accounting records of the past 3 years, they accumulate the following data.

	2021	2020	2019
Net credit sales	$500,000	$550,000	$400,000
Collection agency fees for slow-paying customers	2,450	2,500	2,300
Salary of part-time accounts receivable clerk	4,100	4,100	4,100

Uncollectible account expense is 1.6% of net credit sales, billing and mailing costs 0.5%, and credit investigation fee on new customers is 0.15%.

Carol and Sam also determine that the average accounts receivable balance outstanding during the year is 5% of net credit sales. The Foyles estimate that they could earn an average of 8% annually on cash invested in other business opportunities.

Instructions

With the class divided into groups, answer the following.

a. Prepare a table showing, for each year, total credit and collection expenses in dollars and as a percentage of net credit sales.

b. Determine the net credit and collection expense in dollars and as a percentage of sales after considering the revenue not earned from other investment opportunities.

c. Discuss both the financial and nonfinancial factors that are relevant to the decision.

Communication Activity

CT9.6 Jill Epp, a friend of yours, overheard a discussion at work about changes her employer wants to make in accounting for uncollectible accounts. Jill knows little about accounting, and she asks you to help make sense of what she heard. Specifically, she asks you to explain the differences between the percentage-of-receivables and the direct write-off methods for uncollectible accounts.

Instructions

In a letter of one page (or less), explain to Jill the two methods of accounting for uncollectibles. Be sure to discuss differences among these methods.

All About You

CT9.7 Credit card usage in the United States is substantial. Many startup companies use credit cards as a way to help meet short-term financial needs. The most common forms of debt for startups are use of credit cards and loans from relatives.

Suppose that you start up Brothers Sandwich Shop. You invested your savings of $20,000 and borrowed $70,000 from your relatives. Although sales in the first few months are good, you see that you may not have sufficient cash to pay expenses and maintain your inventory at acceptable levels, at least in the short term. You decide you may need to use one or more credit cards to fund the possible cash shortfall.

Instructions

a. Go to the Internet and find two sources that provide insight into how to compare credit card terms.

b. Develop a list, in descending order of importance, as to what features are most important to you in selecting a credit card for your business.

c. Examine the features of your present credit card. (If you do not have a credit card, select a likely one online for this exercise.) Given your analysis above, what are the three major disadvantages of your present credit card?

FASB Codification Activity

CT9.8 If your school has a subscription to the FASB Codification, log in and prepare responses to the following.

a. How are receivables defined in the Codification?

b. What are the conditions under which losses from uncollectible receivables (Bad Debt Expense) should be reported?

A Look at IFRS

LEARNING OBJECTIVE 5

Compare the accounting for receivables under GAAP and IFRS.

The basic accounting and reporting issues related to the recognition, measurement, and disposition of receivables are essentially the same between IFRS and GAAP.

Key Points

Following are the key similarities and differences between GAAP and IFRS as related to the accounting for receivables.

Similarities

- The recording of receivables, recognition of sales returns and allowances and sales discounts, and the allowance method to record bad debts are the same between IFRS and GAAP.
- Both IFRS and GAAP often use the term impairment to indicate that a receivable or a percentage of receivables may not be collected.
- The FASB and IASB have worked to implement fair value measurement (the amount they currently could be sold for) for financial instruments, such as receivables. Both Boards have faced bitter opposition from various factions.

Differences

- Although IFRS implies that receivables with different characteristics should be reported separately, there is no standard that mandates this segregation.
- IFRS and GAAP differ in the criteria used to determine how to record a factoring transaction. IFRS uses a combination approach focused on risks and rewards and loss of control. GAAP uses loss of control as the primary criterion. In addition, IFRS permits partial derecognition of receivables; GAAP does not.

Looking to the Future

The question of recording fair values for financial instruments will continue to be an important issue to resolve as the Boards work toward convergence. Both the IASB and the FASB have indicated that they believe that financial statements would be more transparent and understandable if companies recorded and reported all financial instruments at fair value. That said, in *IFRS 9*, which was issued in 2009, the IASB created a split model, where some financial instruments are recorded at fair value, but other financial assets, such as loans and receivables, can be accounted for at amortized cost if certain criteria are met. Critics say that this can result in two companies with identical securities accounting for those securities in different ways. A proposal by the FASB would require that practically all equity instruments be reported at fair value, and that debt instruments may or may not be reported at fair value depending on whether certain criteria are met.

IFRS Practice

IFRS Self-Test Questions

1. Which of the following statements is **false**?
   a. Receivables include equity securities purchased by the company.
   b. Receivables include credit card receivables.
   c. Receivables include amounts owed by employees as a result of company loans to employees.
   d. Receivables include amounts resulting from transactions with customers.
2. In recording a factoring transaction:
   a. IFRS focuses on loss of control.
   b. GAAP focuses on loss of control and risks and rewards.
   c. IFRS and GAAP allow partial derecognition.
   d. IFRS allows partial derecognition.
3. Under IFRS:
   a. the entry to record estimated uncollected accounts is the same as GAAP.
   b. it is always acceptable to use the direct write-off method.
   c. all financial instruments are recorded at fair value.
   d. None of the above.

International Financial Reporting Problem: Louis Vuitton

IFRS9.1 The financial statements of **Louis Vuitton** are presented in Appendix F. The complete annual report, including the notes to its financial statements, is available at the company's website.

Instructions

Use the company's annual report to answer the following questions.

a. What is the accounting policy related to accounting for trade accounts receivable?

b. According to the notes to the financial statements, what accounted for the difference between gross trade accounts receivable and net accounts receivable?

c. According to the notes to the financial statements, what was the major reason why the balance in receivables increased relative to the previous year?

d. Using information in the notes to the financial statements, determine what percentage the provision for impairment of receivables was as a percentage of total trade receivables for 2015 and 2014. How did the ratio change from 2014 to 2015, and what does this suggest about the company's receivables?

Answers to IFRS Self-Test Questions

1. a **2.** d **3.** a

CHAPTER 18

Justin Sullivan/Getty Images, Inc.

Financial Analysis: The Big Picture

Chapter Preview

We can all learn an important lesson from Warren Buffett: Study companies carefully if you wish to invest. Do not get caught up in fads but instead find companies that are financially healthy. Using some of the basic decision tools presented in this textbook, you can perform a rudimentary analysis on any company and draw basic conclusions about its financial health. Although it would not be wise for you to bet your life savings on a company's stock relying solely on your current level of knowledge, we strongly encourage you to practice your new skills wherever possible. Only with practice will you improve your ability to interpret financial numbers.

Before we unleash you on the world of high finance, we present a few more important concepts and techniques as well as one more comprehensive review of corporate financial statements. We use all of the decision tools presented in this textbook to analyze a single company, with comparisons to a competitor and industry averages.

Feature Story

It Pays to Be Patient

A recent issue of *Forbes* magazine listed Warren Buffett as the second richest person in the world. His estimated wealth was $69 billion, give or take a few million. How much is $69 billion? If you invested $69 billion in an investment earning just 4%, you could spend $7.6 million per day—every day—forever.

So, how does Buffett spend his money? Basically, he doesn't! He still lives in the same house that he purchased in Omaha, Nebraska, in 1958 for $31,500. He still drives his own car (a Cadillac DTS). And, in case you were thinking that his kids are riding the road to Easy Street, think again. Buffett has committed to donate virtually all of his money to charity before he dies.

How did Buffett amass this wealth? Through careful investing. Buffett epitomizes a "value investor." He applies the basic techniques he learned in the 1950s from the great value investor Benjamin Graham. He looks for companies that have good long-term potential but are currently underpriced. He invests in companies that have low exposure to debt and that reinvest their earnings for future growth. He does not get caught up in fads or the latest trends.

For example, Buffett sat out on the dot-com mania in the 1990s. When other investors put lots of money into fledgling high-tech firms, Buffett didn't bite because he did not find dot-com companies that met his criteria. He didn't get to enjoy the stock price boom on the way up, but on the other hand, he didn't have to ride the price back down to Earth. When the dot-com bubble burst, everyone else was suffering from investment shock. Buffett swooped in and scooped up deals on companies that he had been following for years.

In 2012, the stock market had again reached near record highs. Buffett's returns had been significantly lagging the market. Only 26% of his investments at that time were in stock, and he was sitting on $38 billion in cash. One commentator noted that "if the past is any guide, just when Buffett seems to look most like a loser, the party is about to end."

If you think you want to follow Buffett's example and transform your humble nest egg into a mountain of cash, be warned. His techniques have been widely circulated and emulated, but never practiced with the same degree of success. You should probably start by honing your financial analysis skills. A good way for you to begin your career as a successful investor is to master the fundamentals of financial analysis discussed in this chapter.

Source: Jason Zweig, "Buffett Is Out of Step," *Wall Street Journal* (May 7, 2012).

Chapter Outline

LEARNING OBJECTIVES

LO 1 Apply the concepts of sustainable income and quality of earnings.	• Sustainable income • Quality of earnings	**DO IT! 1** Unusual Items
LO 2 Apply horizontal analysis and vertical analysis.	• Horizontal analysis • Vertical analysis	**DO IT! 2** Horizontal Analysis
LO 3 Analyze a company's performance using ratio analysis.	• Liquidity ratios • Solvency ratios • Profitability ratios • Comprehensive example	**DO IT! 3** Ratio Analysis

Go to the Review and Practice section at the end of the chapter for a review of key concepts and practice applications with solutions.
Visit WileyPLUS with Orion for additional tutorials and practice opportunities.

Sustainable Income and Quality of Earnings

LEARNING OBJECTIVE 1

Apply the concepts of sustainable income and quality of earnings.

Sustainable Income

The value of a company like **Google** is a function of the amount, timing, and uncertainty of its future cash flows. Google's current and past income statements are particularly useful in helping analysts predict these future cash flows. In using this approach, analysts must make sure that Google's past income numbers reflect its **sustainable income**, that is, do not include unusual (out-of-the-ordinary) revenues, expenses, gains, and losses. **Sustainable income** is, therefore, the most likely level of income to be obtained by a company in the future. Sustainable income differs from actual net income by the amount of unusual revenues, expenses, gains, and losses included in the current year's income. Analysts are interested in sustainable income because it helps them derive an estimate of future earnings without the "noise" of unusual items.

Fortunately, an income statement provides information on sustainable income by separating operating transactions from nonoperating transactions. This statement also highlights intermediate components of income such as income from operations, income before income taxes, and income from continuing operations. In addition, information on unusual items such as gains or losses on discontinued items and components of other comprehensive income are disclosed.

Illustration 18.1 presents a statement of comprehensive income for Cruz Company for the year 2020. A statement of comprehensive income includes not only net income but a broader measure of income called comprehensive income. The two major unusual items in this statement are discontinued operations and other comprehensive income (highlighted in red). When estimating future cash flows, analysts must consider the implications of each of these components.

ILLUSTRATION 18.1

Statement of comprehensive income

Cruz Company Statement of Comprehensive Income For the Year Ended 2020	
Sales revenue	$900,000
Cost of goods sold	650,000
Gross profit	250,000
Operating expenses	100,000
Income from operations	150,000
Other revenues (expenses) and gains (losses)	20,000
Income before income taxes	170,000
Income tax expense	24,000
Income from continuing operations	146,000
Discontinued operations (net of tax)	**30,000**
Net income	176,000
Other comprehensive income items (net of tax)	**10,000**
Comprehensive income	$186,000

In looking at Illustration 18.1, note that Cruz Company's two major types of unusual items, discontinued operations and other comprehensive income, are reported net of tax. That is, Cruz first calculates income tax expense before income from continuing operations. Then, it calculates income tax expense related to the discontinued operations and other comprehensive income, and displays each item separately, net of tax. The general concept is, "Let the tax follow the income or loss." We discuss discontinued operations and other comprehensive income in more detail next.

Discontinued Operations

Discontinued operations refers to the disposal of a **significant component** of a business, such as the elimination of a major class of customers or an entire activity. For example, to downsize its operations, **General Dynamics Corp.** sold its missile business to **Hughes Aircraft Co.** for $450 million. In the net income section of its statement of comprehensive income, General Dynamics reported the sale in a separate section entitled "Discontinued operations."

Following the disposal of a significant component, the company should report on its statement both income from continuing operations and income (or loss) from discontinued operations. **The income (loss) from discontinued operations consists of two parts: the income (loss) from operations** and **the gain (loss) on disposal of the component.**

To illustrate, assume that during 2020 Acro Energy Inc. has income before income taxes of $800,000. During 2020, Acro discontinued and sold its unprofitable chemical division. The loss in 2020 from chemical operations (net of $60,000 taxes) was $140,000. The loss on disposal of the chemical division (net of $30,000 taxes) was $70,000. Assuming a 30% tax rate on income, **Illustration 18.2** shows Acro's statement of comprehensive income presentation (see **Helpful Hint**).

ILLUSTRATION 18.2

Statement presentation of discontinued operations

HELPFUL HINT

Observe the dual disclosures: (1) the results of operation of the discontinued division must be separated from the results of continuing operations, and (2) the company must also report the disposal of the division.

Acro Energy Inc.
Statement of Comprehensive Income (partial)
For the Year Ended December 31, 2020

Income before income taxes		$800,000
Income tax expense		240,000
Income from continuing operations		560,000
Discontinued operations		
Loss from operation of chemical division, net of $60,000 income tax savings	**$140,000**	
Loss from disposal of chemical division, net of $30,000 income tax savings	**70,000**	**210,000**
Net income		$350,000

Note that the statement uses the caption "Income from continuing operations" and adds a new section "Discontinued operations." **The new section reports both the operating loss and the loss on disposal net of applicable income taxes.** This presentation clearly indicates the separate effects of continuing operations and discontinued operations on net income.

Investor Insight

© Andrey Armyagov/iStockphoto

What Does "Non-Recurring" Really Mean?

Many companies incur restructuring charges as they attempt to reduce costs. They often label these items in the income statement as "non-recurring" charges, to suggest that they are isolated events, unlikely to occur in future periods. The question for analysts is, are these costs really one-time, "non-recurring events" or do they reflect problems that the company will be facing for many periods in the future? If they are one-time events, then they can be largely ignored when trying to predict future earnings.

But, some companies report "one-time" restructuring charges over and over again. For example, **Procter & Gamble** reported a restructuring charge in 12 consecutive quarters, and **Motorola** had "special" charges in 14 consecutive quarters. On the other hand, other companies have a restructuring charge only once in a 5- or 10-year period. There appears to be no substitute for careful analysis of the numbers that comprise net income.

If a company takes a large restructuring charge, what is the effect on the company's current income statement versus future ones? (Go to WileyPLUS for this answer and additional questions.)

Comprehensive Income

Most revenues, expenses, gains, and losses are included in net income. However, as discussed in earlier chapters, certain gains and losses that bypass net income are reported as part of a more inclusive earnings measure called comprehensive income. **Comprehensive income** is the sum of net income and other comprehensive income items.[1]

Illustration of Comprehensive Income. Accounting standards require that companies adjust most investments in stocks and bonds up or down to their market price at the end of each accounting period. For example, assume that during 2020, its first year of operations, Stassi Corporation purchased **IBM** bonds for $10,500 as an investment, which it intends to sell sometime in the future. At the end of 2020, Stassi was still holding the investment, but the bonds' market price was now $8,000. In this case, Stassi is required to reduce the recorded value of its IBM investment by $2,500. The $2,500 difference is an unrealized loss.

Should Stassi include this $2,500 unrealized loss in net income? It depends on whether Stassi classifies the IBM bonds as a trading security or an available-for-sale security. A **trading security** is bought and held primarily for sale in the near term to generate income on short-term price differences. Companies report unrealized losses on trading securities in the "Other expenses and losses" section of the income statement. The rationale: It is likely that the company will realize the unrealized loss (or an unrealized gain), so the company should report the loss (gain) as part of net income.

If Stassi did not purchase the investment for trading purposes, it is classified as available-for-sale. **Available-for-sale securities** are held with the intent of selling them sometime in the future. Companies do not include unrealized gains or losses on available-for-sale securities in net income. Instead, they report them as part of "Other comprehensive income." Other comprehensive income is not included in net income.

Format. One format for reporting other comprehensive income is to report a separate comprehensive income statement. For example, assuming that Stassi Corporation has a net income of $300,000 and a 20% tax rate, the unrealized loss would be reported below net income, net of tax, as shown in **Illustration 18.3**.

ILLUSTRATION 18.3

Lower portion of combined statement of income and comprehensive income

Stassi Corporation
Comprehensive Income Statement
For the Year Ended December 31, 2020

Net income	$300,000
Other comprehensive income	
Unrealized loss on available-for-sale securities, net of $500 tax savings	2,000
Comprehensive income	$298,000

Companies report the cumulative amount of other comprehensive income from all years as a separate component of stockholders' equity. To illustrate, assume Stassi has common stock of $3,000,000, retained earnings of $300,000, and accumulated other comprehensive loss of $2,000. (To simplify, we are assuming that this is Stassi's first year of operations. Since it has only operated for one year, the cumulative amount of other comprehensive income is this year's loss of $2,000.) **Illustration 18.4** shows the balance sheet presentation of the accumulated other comprehensive loss.

[1]The FASB's Conceptual Framework describes comprehensive income as including all changes in stockholders' equity during a period except those changes resulting from investments by stockholders and distributions to stockholders.

ILLUSTRATION 18.4

Unrealized loss in stockholders' equity section

Stassi Corporation
Balance Sheet (partial)

Stockholders' equity	
Common stock	$3,000,000
Retained earnings	300,000
Total paid-in capital and retained earnings	3,300,000
Accumulated other comprehensive loss	**(2,000)**
Total stockholders' equity	$3,298,000

Note that the presentation of the accumulated other comprehensive loss is similar to the presentation of the cost of treasury stock in the stockholders' equity section. (An unrealized gain would be added in this section of the balance sheet.)

Complete Statement of Comprehensive Income. As seen in Illustration 18.1, as an alternative to preparing a separate comprehensive income statement, many companies report net income and other comprehensive income in a combined statement of comprehensive income. (*For your homework in this chapter, use this combined format.*) The statement of comprehensive income for Pace Corporation in **Illustration 18.5** presents the types of items found on this statement, such as net sales, cost of goods sold, operating expenses, and income taxes. In addition, it shows how companies report discontinued operations and other comprehensive income (highlighted in red).

ILLUSTRATION 18.5

Complete statement of comprehensive income

Pace Corporation
Statement of Comprehensive Income
For the Year Ended December 31, 2020

Net sales		$440,000
Cost of goods sold		260,000
Gross profit		180,000
Operating expenses		110,000
Income from operations		70,000
Other revenues and gains		5,600
Other expenses and losses		9,600
Income before income taxes		66,000
Income tax expense ($66,000 × 30%)		19,800
Income from continuing operations		46,200
Discontinued operations		
Loss from operation of plastics division, net of income tax savings $18,000 ($60,000 × 30%)	**$42,000**	
Gain on disposal of plastics division, net of $15,000 income taxes ($50,000 × 30%)	**35,000**	**7,000**
Net income		**39,200**
Other comprehensive income		
Unrealized gain on available-for-sale securities, net of income taxes ($15,000 × 30%)		**10,500**
Comprehensive income		**$ 49,700**

Changes in Accounting Principle

For ease of comparison, users of financial statements expect companies to prepare their statements on a basis **consistent** with the preceding period. A **change in accounting principle** occurs when the principle used in the current year is different from the one used in the preceding year. An example is a change in inventory costing methods (such as FIFO to average-cost). Accounting rules permit a change when management can show that the new principle is preferable to the old principle.

Companies report most changes in accounting principle retroactively.[2] That is, they report both the current period and previous periods using the new principle. As a result, the same principle applies in all periods. This treatment improves the ability to compare results across years.

Investor Insight United Parcel Service (UPS)

Larry MacDougal/AP/Wide World Photos

More Frequent Ups and Downs

In the past, U.S. companies used a method to account for their pension plans that smoothed out the gains and losses on their pension portfolios by spreading gains and losses over multiple years. Many felt that this approach was beneficial because it reduced the volatility of reported net income. However, recently some companies have opted to adopt a method that comes closer to recognizing gains and losses in the period in which they occur. Some of the companies that have adopted this approach are **United Parcel Service (UPS)**, **Honeywell International**, **IBM**, **AT&T**, and **Verizon Communications**. The CFO at UPS said he favored the new approach because "events that occurred in prior years will no longer distort current-year results. It will result in better transparency by eliminating the noise of past plan performance." When UPS switched, it resulted in a charge of $827 million from the change in accounting principle.

Source: Bob Sechler and Doug Cameron, "UPS Alters Pension-Plan Accounting," *Wall Street Journal* (January 30, 2012).

When predicting future earnings, how should analysts treat the one-time charge that results from a switch to the different approach for accounting for pension plans? (Go to WileyPLUS for this answer and additional questions.)

Quality of Earnings

The quality of a company's earnings is of extreme importance to analysts. A company that has a high **quality of earnings** provides full and transparent information that will not confuse or mislead users of the financial statements.

Recent accounting scandals suggest that some companies are spending too much time managing their income and not enough time managing their business. Here are some of the factors affecting quality of earnings.

Alternative Accounting Methods

Variations among companies in the application of generally accepted accounting principles may hamper comparability and reduce quality of earnings. For example, suppose one company uses the FIFO method of inventory costing, while another company in the same industry uses LIFO. If inventory is a significant asset to both companies, it is unlikely that their current ratios are comparable. For example, if **General Motors Corporation** used FIFO instead of LIFO for inventory valuation, its inventories in a recent year would have been 26% higher, which significantly affects the current ratio (and other ratios as well).

In addition to differences in inventory costing methods, differences also exist in reporting such items as depreciation and amortization. Although these differences in accounting methods might be detectable from reading the notes to the financial statements, adjusting the financial data to compensate for the different methods is often difficult, if not impossible.

[2]An exception to the general rule is a change in depreciation methods. The effects of this change are reported in current and future periods. Discussion of this approach is left for more advanced courses.

Pro Forma Income

Companies whose stock is publicly traded are required to present their income statement following generally accepted accounting principles (GAAP). In recent years, many companies have been also reporting a second measure of income, called pro forma income. **Pro forma income** usually excludes items that the company thinks are unusual or non-recurring. For example, in a recent year, **Cisco Systems** (a high-tech company) reported a quarterly net loss under GAAP of $2.7 billion. Cisco reported pro forma income for the same quarter as a profit of $230 million. This large difference in profits between GAAP income numbers and pro forma income is not unusual. For example, during one nine-month period, the 100 largest companies on the Nasdaq stock exchange reported a total pro forma income of $19.1 billion but a total loss as measured by GAAP of $82.3 billion—a difference of about $100 billion!

To compute pro forma income, companies generally exclude any items they deem inappropriate for measuring their performance. Many analysts and investors are critical of the practice of using pro forma income because these numbers often make companies look better than they really are. As the financial press noted, pro forma numbers might be called "earnings before bad stuff." Companies, on the other hand, argue that pro forma numbers more clearly indicate sustainable income because they exclude unusual and non-recurring expenses. "Cisco's technique gives readers of financial statements a clear picture of Cisco's normal business activities," the company said in a statement issued in response to questions about its pro forma income accounting.

Recently, the SEC provided some guidance on how companies should present pro forma information. Stay tuned: Everyone seems to agree that pro forma numbers can be useful if they provide insights into determining a company's sustainable income. However, many companies have abused the flexibility that pro forma numbers allow and have used the measure as a way to put their companies in a more favorable light.

Improper Recognition

Because some managers feel pressure from Wall Street to continually increase earnings, they manipulate earnings numbers to meet these expectations. The most common abuse is the improper recognition of revenue. One practice that some companies use is called **channel stuffing**. Offering deep discounts, companies encourage customers to buy early (stuff the channel) rather than later. This boosts the seller's earnings in the current period, but it often leads to a disaster in subsequent periods because customers have no need for additional goods. To illustrate, **Bristol-Myers Squibb** at one time indicated that it used sales incentives to encourage wholesalers to buy more drugs than they needed. As a result, the company had to issue revised financial statements showing corrected revenues and income.

Another practice is the improper capitalization of operating expenses. **WorldCom** capitalized over $7 billion of operating expenses in order to report positive net income. In other situations, companies fail to report all their liabilities. **Enron** promised to make payments on certain contracts if financial difficulty developed, but these guarantees were not reported as liabilities. In addition, disclosure was so lacking in transparency that it was impossible to understand what was happening at the company.

DO IT! 1 | Unusual Items

In its proposed 2020 income statement, AIR Corporation reports income before income taxes $400,000, unrealized gain on available-for-sale securities $100,000, income taxes $120,000 (not including unusual items), loss from operation of discontinued flower division $50,000, and loss on disposal of discontinued flower division $90,000. The income tax rate is 30%. Prepare a correct statement of comprehensive income, beginning with "Income before income taxes."

ACTION PLAN

- **Show discontinued operations and other comprehensive income net of tax.**

Solution

AIR Corporation Statement of Comprehensive Income (partial) For the Year Ended December 31, 2020		
Income before income taxes		$400,000
Income tax expense		120,000
Income from continuing operations		280,000
Discontinued operations		
Loss from operation of flower division, net of $15,000 income tax savings	$35,000	
Loss on disposal of flower division, net of $27,000 income tax savings	63,000	98,000
Net income		182,000
Other comprehensive income		
Unrealized gain on available-for-sale securities, net of $30,000 income taxes		70,000
Comprehensive income		$252,000

Related exercise material: **BE18.1, BE18.2, DO IT! 18.1, E18.1, and E18.2.**

Horizontal Analysis and Vertical Analysis

LEARNING OBJECTIVE 2

Apply horizontal analysis and vertical analysis.

As indicated, in assessing the financial performance of a company, investors are interested in the core or sustainable earnings of a company. In addition, investors are interested in making comparisons from period to period. Throughout this textbook, we have relied on three types of comparisons to improve the decision-usefulness of financial information:

1. **Intracompany basis.** Comparisons within a company are often useful to detect changes in financial relationships and significant trends. For example, a comparison of **Kellogg**'s current year's cash amount with the prior year's cash amount shows either an increase or a decrease. Likewise, a comparison of Kellogg's year-end cash amount with the amount of its total assets at year-end shows the proportion of total assets in the form of cash.
2. **Intercompany basis.** Comparisons with other companies provide insight into a company's competitive position. For example, investors can compare Kellogg's total sales for the year with the total sales of its competitors in the breakfast cereal area, such as **General Mills**.
3. **Industry averages.** Comparisons with industry averages provide information about a company's relative position within the industry. For example, financial statement readers can compare Kellogg's financial data with the averages for its industry compiled by financial rating organizations such as **Dun & Bradstreet**, **Moody's**, and **Standard & Poor's**, or with information provided on the Internet by organizations such as **Yahoo!** on its financial site.

We use three basic tools in financial statement analysis to highlight the significance of financial statement data:

1. Horizontal analysis
2. Vertical analysis
3. Ratio analysis

In previous chapters, we relied primarily on ratio analysis, supplemented with some basic horizontal and vertical analysis. In the remainder of this section, we introduce more formal forms of horizontal and vertical analysis. In the next section, we review ratio analysis in some detail.

Horizontal Analysis

Horizontal analysis, also known as trend analysis, is a technique for evaluating a series of financial statement data over a period of time. Its purpose is to determine the increase or decrease that has taken place, expressed as either an amount or a percentage. For example, here are recent net sales figures (in thousands) of Chicago Cereal Company:

2020	2019	2018	2017	2016
$11,776	$10,907	$10,177	$9,614	$8,812

If we assume that 2016 is the base year, we can measure all percentage increases or decreases relative to this base-period amount with the formula shown in Illustration 18.6.

ILLUSTRATION 18.6
Horizontal analysis—computation of changes since base period

$$\text{Change Since Base Period} = \frac{\text{Current-Year Amount} - \text{Base-Year Amount}}{\text{Base-Year Amount}}$$

For example, we can determine that net sales for Chicago Cereal increased approximately 9.1% [($9,614 − $8,812) ÷ $8,812] from 2016 to 2017. Similarly, we can also determine that net sales increased by 33.6% [($11,776 − $8,812) ÷ $8,812] from 2016 to 2020.

Alternatively, we can express current-year sales as a percentage of the base period. To do so, we would divide the current-year amount by the base-year amount, as shown in Illustration 18.7.

ILLUSTRATION 18.7
Horizontal analysis—computation of current year in relation to base year

$$\text{Current Results in Relation to Base Period} = \frac{\text{Current-Year Amount}}{\text{Base-Year Amount}}$$

Current-period sales expressed as a percentage of the base period for each of the five years, using 2016 as the base period, are shown in Illustration 18.8.

ILLUSTRATION 18.8
Horizontal analysis of net sales

Chicago Cereal Company
Net Sales (in thousands)
Base Period 2016

2020	2019	2018	2017	2016
$11,776	$10,907	$10,177	$9,614	$8,812
133.6%	123.8%	115.5%	109.1%	100%

The large increase in net sales during 2017 would raise questions regarding possible reasons for such a significant change. Chicago Cereal's 2017 notes to the financial statements explain that the company completed an acquisition of Elf Foods Company during 2017. This major acquisition would help explain the increase in sales highlighted by horizontal analysis.

To further illustrate horizontal analysis, we use the financial statements of Chicago Cereal Company. Its two-year condensed balance sheets for 2020 and 2019, showing dollar and percentage changes, are presented in **Illustration 18.9** (see **Helpful Hint**).

ILLUSTRATION 18.9

Horizontal analysis of balance sheets

Chicago Cereal Company
Condensed Balance Sheets
December 31 (in thousands)

			Increase (Decrease) during 2020	
Assets	**2020**	**2019**	**Amount**	**Percent**
Current assets	$ 2,717	$ 2,427	$ 290	11.9
Property assets (net)	2,990	2,816	174	6.2
Other assets	5,690	5,471	219	4.0
Total assets	$11,397	$10,714	$ 683	6.4
Liabilities and Stockholders' Equity				
Current liabilities	$ 4,044	$ 4,020	$ 24	0.6
Long-term liabilities	4,827	4,625	202	4.4
Total liabilities	8,871	8,645	226	2.6
Stockholders' equity				
Common stock	493	397	96	24.2
Retained earnings	3,390	2,584	806	31.2
Treasury stock (cost)	(1,357)	(912)	(445)	48.8
Total stockholders' equity	2,526	2,069	457	22.1
Total liabilities and stockholders' equity	$11,397	$10,714	$ 683	6.4

HELPFUL HINT

When using horizontal analysis, be sure to examine both dollar amount changes and percentage changes. It is not necessarily bad if a company's earnings are growing at a declining rate. The amount of increase may be the same as or more than the base year, but the percentage change may be less because the base is greater each year.

The comparative balance sheets show that a number of changes occurred in Chicago Cereal's financial position from 2019 to 2020. In the assets section, current assets increased $290,000, or 11.9% ($290 ÷ $2,427), and property assets (net) increased $174,000, or 6.2%. Other assets increased $219,000, or 4.0%. In the liabilities section, current liabilities increased $24,000, or 0.6%, while long-term liabilities increased $202,000, or 4.4%. In the stockholders' equity section, we find that retained earnings increased $806,000, or 31.2%.

Illustration 18.10 presents two-year comparative income statements of Chicago Cereal Company for 2020 and 2019, showing dollar and percentage changes (see **Helpful Hint**).

ILLUSTRATION 18.10

Horizontal analysis of income statements

Chicago Cereal Company
Condensed Income Statements
For the Years Ended December 31 (in thousands)

			Increase (Decrease) during 2020	
	2020	**2019**	**Amount**	**Percent**
Net sales	$11,776	$10,907	$869	8.0
Cost of goods sold	6,597	6,082	515	8.5
Gross profit	5,179	4,825	354	7.3
Selling and administrative expenses	3,311	3,059	252	8.2
Income from operations	1,868	1,766	102	5.8
Interest expense	321	294	27	9.2
Income before income taxes	1,547	1,472	75	5.1
Income tax expense	444	468	(24)	(5.1)
Net income	$ 1,103	$ 1,004	$ 99	9.9

HELPFUL HINT

Note that, in a horizontal analysis, while the amount column is additive (the total is $99,000), the percentage column is not additive (9.9% is not a total).

Horizontal analysis of the income statements shows the following changes. Net sales increased $869,000, or 8.0% ($869 ÷ $10,907). Cost of goods sold increased $515,000, or 8.5% ($515 ÷ $6,082). Selling and administrative expenses increased $252,000, or 8.2% ($252 ÷ $3,059). Overall, gross profit increased 7.3% and net income increased 9.9%. The increase in net income can be attributed to the increase in net sales and a decrease in income tax expense.

The measurement of changes from period to period in percentages is relatively straightforward and quite useful. However, complications can result in making the computations. If an item has no value in a base year or preceding year and a value in the next year, no percentage change can be computed.

Vertical Analysis

Vertical analysis, also called common-size analysis, is a technique for evaluating financial statement data that expresses each item in a financial statement as a **percentage of a base amount**. For example, on a balance sheet we might express current assets as 22% of total assets (total assets being the base amount). Or, on an income statement we might express selling expenses as 16% of net sales (net sales being the base amount).

Presented in **Illustration 18.11** are the comparative balance sheets of Chicago Cereal for 2020 and 2019, analyzed vertically. The base for the asset items is **total assets**, and the base for the liability and stockholders' equity items is **total liabilities and stockholders' equity**.

ILLUSTRATION 18.11

Vertical analysis of balance sheets

Chicago Cereal Company
Condensed Balance Sheets
December 31 (in thousands)

	2020		2019	
Assets	**Amount**	**Percent***	**Amount**	**Percent***
Current assets	$ 2,717	23.8	$ 2,427	22.6
Property assets (net)	2,990	26.2	2,816	26.3
Other assets	5,690	50.0	5,471	51.1
Total assets	$11,397	100.0	$10,714	100.0
Liabilities and Stockholders' Equity				
Current liabilities	$ 4,044	35.5	$ 4,020	37.5
Long-term liabilities	4,827	42.4	4,625	43.2
Total liabilities	8,871	77.9	8,645	80.7
Stockholders' equity				
Common stock	493	4.3	397	3.7
Retained earnings	3,390	29.7	2,584	24.1
Treasury stock (cost)	(1,357)	(11.9)	(912)	(8.5)
Total stockholders' equity	2,526	22.1	2,069	19.3
Total liabilities and stockholders' equity	$11,397	100.0	$10,714	100.0

*Numbers have been rounded to total 100%.

In addition to showing the relative size of each category on the balance sheets, vertical analysis can show the percentage change in the individual asset, liability, and stockholders' equity items. In this case, current assets increased $290,000 from 2019 to 2020, and they increased from 22.6% to 23.8% of total assets. Property assets (net) decreased from 26.3% to 26.2% of total assets. Other assets decreased from 51.1% to 50.0% of total assets. Also, retained earnings increased by $806,000 from 2019 to 2020, and total stockholders' equity increased from 19.3% to 22.1% of total liabilities and stockholders' equity. This switch to a higher percentage of equity financing has two causes. First, while total liabilities increased by $226,000, the percentage of liabilities declined from 80.7% to 77.9% of total liabilities and stockholders' equity. Second, retained earnings increased by $806,000, from 24.1% to 29.7%

of total liabilities and stockholders' equity. Thus, the company shifted toward equity financing by relying less on debt and by increasing the amount of retained earnings.

Vertical analysis of the comparative income statements of Chicago Cereal, shown in **Illustration 18.12**, reveals that cost of goods sold **as a percentage of net sales** increased from 55.8% to 56.0%, and selling and administrative expenses increased from 28.0% to 28.1%. Net income as a percentage of net sales increased from 9.2% to 9.4%. Chicago Cereal's increase in net income as a percentage of sales is due primarily to the decrease in income tax expense as a percentage of sales.

ILLUSTRATION 18.12

Vertical analysis of income statements

Chicago Cereal Company
Condensed Income Statements
For the Years Ended December 31 (in thousands)

	2020		2019	
	Amount	**Percent***	**Amount**	**Percent***
Net sales	$11,776	100.0	$10,907	100.0
Cost of goods sold	6,597	56.0	6,082	55.8
Gross profit	5,179	44.0	4,825	44.2
Selling and administrative expenses	3,311	28.1	3,059	28.0
Income from operations	1,868	15.9	1,766	16.2
Interest expense	321	2.7	294	2.7
Income before income taxes	1,547	13.2	1,472	13.5
Income tax expense	444	3.8	468	4.3
Net income	$ 1,103	9.4	$ 1,004	9.2

*Numbers have been rounded to total 100%.

Vertical analysis also enables you to compare companies of different sizes. For example, one of Chicago Cereal's competitors is Giant Mills. Giant Mills' sales are 1,000 times larger than those of Chicago Cereal. Vertical analysis enables us to meaningfully compare the condensed income statements of Chicago Cereal and Giant Mills, as shown in **Illustration 18.13**.

ILLUSTRATION 18.13

Intercompany comparison by vertical analysis

Condensed Income Statements
For the Year Ended December 31, 2020

	Chicago Cereal (in thousands)		Giant Mills, Inc. (in millions)	
	Amount	**Percent***	**Amount**	**Percent***
Net sales	$11,776	100.0	$17,910	100.0
Cost of goods sold	6,597	56.0	11,540	64.4
Gross profit	5,179	44.0	6,370	35.6
Selling and administrative expenses	3,311	28.1	3,474	19.4
Non-recurring charges and (gains)	0	—	(62)	(0.3)
Income from operations	1,868	15.9	2,958	16.5
Other expenses and revenues (including income taxes)	765	6.5	1,134	6.3
Net income	$ 1,103	9.4	$ 1,824	10.2

*Numbers have been rounded to total 100%.

Although Chicago Cereal's net sales are much less than those of Giant Mills, vertical analysis eliminates the impact of this size difference for our analysis. Chicago Cereal has a higher gross profit percentage 44.0%, compared to 35.6% for Giant Mills. But, Chicago Cereal's selling and administrative expenses are 28.1% of net sales, while those of Giant Mills are 19.4% of net sales. Looking at net income, we see that Giant Mills' percentage is higher. Chicago Cereal's net income as a percentage of net sales is 9.4%, compared to 10.2% for Giant Mills.

Anatomy of a Fraud

Sometimes relationships between numbers can be used to detect fraud. Financial ratios that appear abnormal or statistical abnormalities in the numbers themselves can reveal fraud. For example, the fact that **WorldCom**'s line costs, as a percentage of either total expenses or revenues, differed very significantly from its competitors should have alerted people to the possibility of fraud. Or, consider the case of a bank manager, who cooperated with a group of his friends to defraud the bank's credit card department. The manager's friends would apply for credit cards and then run up balances of slightly less than $5,000. The bank had a policy of allowing bank personnel to write-off balances of less than $5,000 without seeking supervisor approval. The fraud was detected by applying statistical analysis based on Benford's Law. Benford's Law states that in a random collection of numbers, the frequency of lower digits (e.g., 1, 2, or 3) should be much higher than higher digits (e.g., 7, 8, or 9). In this case, bank auditors analyzed the first two digits of amounts written off. There was a spike at 48 and 49, which was not consistent with what would be expected if the numbers were random.

Total take: Thousands of dollars

The Missing Control

Independent internal verification. While it might be efficient to allow employees to write off accounts below a certain level, it is important that these write-offs be reviewed and verified periodically. Such a review would likely call attention to an employee with large amounts of write-offs, or in this case, write-offs that were frequently very close to the approval threshold.

Source: Mark J. Nigrini, "I've Got Your Number," *Journal of Accountancy Online* (May 1999).

DO IT! 2 | Horizontal Analysis

Summary financial information for Rosepatch Company is as follows.

	December 31, 2020	December 31, 2019
Current assets	$234,000	$180,000
Plant assets (net)	756,000	420,000
Total assets	$990,000	$600,000

Compute the amount and percentage changes in 2020 using horizontal analysis, assuming 2019 is the base year.

ACTION PLAN

- **Find the percentage change by dividing the amount of the increase by the 2019 amount (base year).**

Solution

	Increase in 2020	
	Amount	**Percent**
Current assets	$ 54,000	30% [($234,000 – $180,000) ÷ $180,000]
Plant assets (net)	336,000	80% [($756,000 – $420,000) ÷ $420,000]
Total assets	$390,000	65% [($990,000 – $600,000) ÷ $600,000]

Related exercise material: **BE18.4, BE18.6, BE18.7, BE18.9, DO IT! 18.2, E18.3, E18.5, and E18.6.**

Ratio Analysis

LEARNING OBJECTIVE 3

Analyze a company's performance using ratio analysis.

Ratio analysis expresses the relationship among selected items of financial statement data. A **ratio** expresses the mathematical relationship between one quantity and another. The relationship is expressed in terms of either a percentage, a rate, or a simple proportion. To illustrate, in a recent year, **Nike, Inc.** had current assets of $13,626 million and current liabilities of $3,926 million. We can find the relationship between these two measures by dividing current assets by current liabilities. The alternative means of expression are as follows.

Percentage: Current assets are 347% of current liabilities.
Rate: Current assets are 3.47 times current liabilities.
Proportion: The relationship of current assets to liabilities is 3.47:1.

To analyze the primary financial statements, we can use ratios to evaluate liquidity, profitability, and solvency. **Illustration 18.14** describes these classifications.

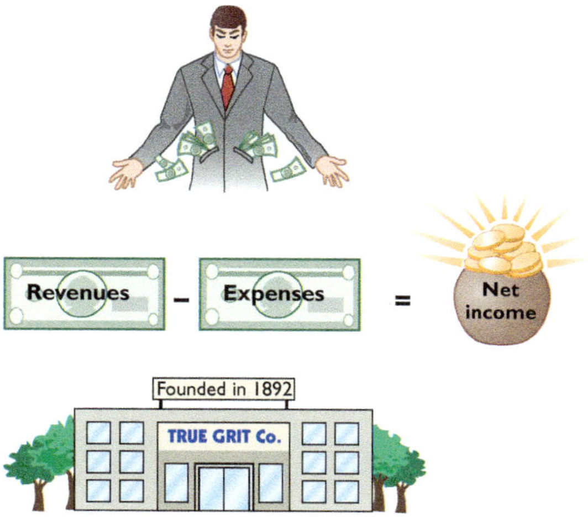

Liquidity Ratios

Measure short-term ability of the company to pay its maturing obligations and to meet unexpected needs for cash

Profitability Ratios

Measure the income or operating success of a company for a given period of time

Solvency Ratios

Measure the ability of the company to survive over a long period of time

ILLUSTRATION 18.14
Financial ratio classifications

Ratios can provide clues to underlying conditions that may not be apparent from individual financial statement components. However, a single ratio by itself is not very meaningful. Thus, in the discussion of ratios we will use the following types of comparisons.

1. **Intracompany comparisons** for two years for Chicago Cereal.
2. **Industry average comparisons** based on median ratios for the industry.
3. **Intercompany comparisons** based on Giant Mills as Chicago Cereal's principal competitor.

Liquidity Ratios

Liquidity ratios (**Illustration 18.15**) measure the short-term ability of the company to pay its maturing obligations and to meet unexpected needs for cash. Short-term creditors such as bankers and suppliers are particularly interested in assessing liquidity.

Liquidity Ratios	
Working capital	Current assets – Current liabilities
Current ratio	$\frac{\text{Current assets}}{\text{Current liabilities}}$
Inventory turnover	$\frac{\text{Cost of goods sold}}{\text{Average inventory}}$
Days in inventory	$\frac{\text{365 days}}{\text{Inventory turnover}}$
Accounts receivable turnover	$\frac{\text{Net credit sales}}{\text{Average net accounts receivable}}$
Average collection period	$\frac{\text{365 days}}{\text{Accounts receivable turnover}}$

ILLUSTRATION 18.15
Summary of liquidity ratios

Investor Insight

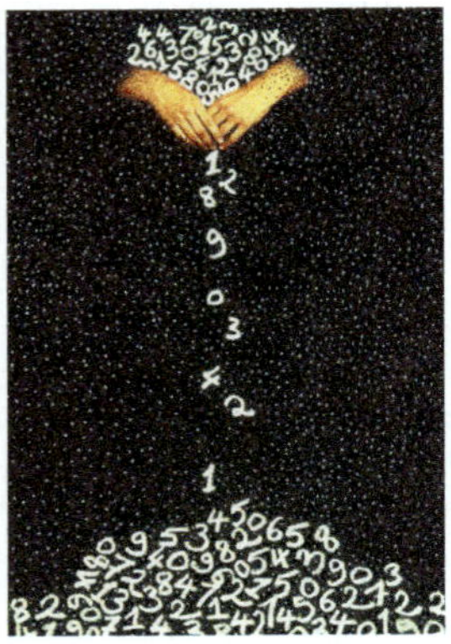

Nova Stock/SuperStock

How to Manage the Current Ratio

The apparent simplicity of the current ratio can have real-world limitations because adding equal amounts to both the numerator and the denominator causes the ratio to decrease.

Assume, for example, that a company has $2,000,000 of current assets and $1,000,000 of current liabilities. Its current ratio is 2:1. If it purchases $1,000,000 of inventory on account, it will have $3,000,000 of current assets and $2,000,000 of current liabilities. Its current ratio decreases to 1.5:1. If, instead, the company pays off $500,000 of its current liabilities, it will have $1,500,000 of current assets and $500,000 of current liabilities. Its current ratio increases to 3:1. Thus, any trend analysis should be done with care because the ratio is susceptible to quick changes and is easily influenced by management.

How might management influence a company's current ratio? (Go to WileyPLUS for this answer and additional questions.)

Solvency Ratios

Solvency ratios (**Illustration 18.16**) measure the ability of the company to survive over a long period of time. Long-term creditors and stockholders are interested in a company's long-run solvency, particularly its ability to pay interest as it comes due and to repay the balance of debt at its maturity.

ILLUSTRATION 18.16

Summary of solvency ratios

Solvency Ratios	
Debt to assets ratio	$\dfrac{\text{Total liabilities}}{\text{Total assets}}$
Times interest earned	$\dfrac{\text{Net income + Interest expense + Income tax expense}}{\text{Interest expense}}$
Free cash flow	Net cash provided by operating activities − Capital expenditures − Cash dividends

Profitability Ratios

Profitability ratios (**Illustration 18.17**) measure the income or operating success of a company for a given period of time. A company's income, or lack of it, affects its ability to obtain debt

ILLUSTRATION 18.17

Summary of profitability ratios

Profitability Ratios	
Earnings per share	$\dfrac{\text{Net income − Preferred dividends}}{\text{Weighted-average common shares outstanding}}$
Price-earnings ratio	$\dfrac{\text{Market price per share}}{\text{Earnings per share}}$
Gross profit rate	$\dfrac{\text{Gross profit}}{\text{Net sales}}$
Profit margin	$\dfrac{\text{Net income}}{\text{Net sales}}$
Return on assets	$\dfrac{\text{Net income}}{\text{Average total assets}}$
Asset turnover	$\dfrac{\text{Net sales}}{\text{Average total assets}}$
Payout ratio	$\dfrac{\text{Cash dividends declared on common stock}}{\text{Net income}}$
Return on common stockholders' equity	$\dfrac{\text{Net income − Preferred dividends}}{\text{Average common stockholders' equity}}$

and equity financing, its liquidity position, and its ability to grow. As a consequence, creditors and investors alike are interested in evaluating profitability. Profitability is frequently used as the ultimate test of management's operating effectiveness.

Investor Insight

© Ferran Traite Soler/iStockphoto

High Ratings Can Bring Low Returns

Moody's, **Standard & Poor's**, and **Fitch** are three big firms that perform financial analysis on publicly traded companies and then publish ratings of the companies' creditworthiness. Investors and lenders rely heavily on these ratings in making investment and lending decisions. Some people feel that the collapse of the financial markets was worsened by inadequate research reports and ratings provided by the financial rating agencies. Critics contend that the rating agencies were reluctant to give large companies low ratings because they feared that by offending them they would lose out on business opportunities. For example, the rating agencies gave many so-called mortgage-backed securities ratings that suggested that they were low risk. Later, many of these very securities became completely worthless. Steps have been taken to reduce the conflicts of interest that lead to these faulty ratings.

Source: Aaron Lucchetti and Judith Burns, "Moody's CEO Warned Profit Push Posed a Risk to Quality of Ratings," *Wall Street Journal Online* (October 23, 2008).

Why are credit rating agencies important to the financial markets? (Go to WileyPLUS for this answer and additional questions.)

Comprehensive Example of Ratio Analysis

In this section, we provide a comprehensive review of ratios used for evaluating the financial health and performance of a company. We use the financial information in **Illustrations 18.18** through **18.21** to calculate Chicago Cereal Company's 2020 ratios. You can use these data to review the computations.

ILLUSTRATION 18.18
Chicago Cereal Company's balance sheets

Chicago Cereal Company
Balance Sheets
December 31 (in thousands)

Assets	**2020**	**2019**
Current assets		
Cash	$ 524	$ 411
Accounts receivable	1,026	945
Inventory	924	824
Prepaid expenses and other current assets	243	247
Total current assets	2,717	2,427
Property assets (net)	2,990	2,816
Intangibles and other assets	5,690	5,471
Total assets	$11,397	$10,714
Liabilities and Stockholders' Equity		
Current liabilities	$ 4,044	$ 4,020
Long-term liabilities	4,827	4,625
Stockholders' equity—common	2,526	2,069
Total liabilities and stockholders' equity	$11,397	$10,714

ILLUSTRATION 18.19

Chicago Cereal Company's income statements

Chicago Cereal Company
Condensed Income Statements
For the Years Ended December 31 (in thousands)

	2020	2019
Net sales	$11,776	$10,907
Cost of goods sold	6,597	6,082
Gross profit	5,179	4,825
Selling and administrative expenses	3,311	3,059
Income from operations	1,868	1,766
Interest expense	321	294
Income before income taxes	1,547	1,472
Income tax expense	444	468
Net income	$ 1,103	$ 1,004

ILLUSTRATION 18.20

Chicago Cereal Company's statements of cash flows

Chicago Cereal Company
Condensed Statements of Cash Flows
For the Years Ended December 31 (in thousands)

	2020	2019
Cash flows from operating activities		
Cash receipts from operating activities	$11,695	$10,841
Cash payments for operating activities	10,192	9,431
Net cash provided by operating activities	1,503	1,410
Cash flows from investing activities		
Purchases of property, plant, and equipment	(472)	(453)
Other investing activities	(129)	8
Net cash used in investing activities	(601)	(445)
Cash flows from financing activities		
Issuance of common stock	163	218
Issuance of debt	2,179	721
Reductions of debt	(2,011)	(650)
Payment of dividends	(475)	(450)
Repurchase of common stock and other items	(645)	(612)
Net cash provided (used) by financing activities	(789)	(773)
Increase (decrease) in cash and cash equivalents	113	192
Cash and cash equivalents at beginning of year	411	219
Cash and cash equivalents at end of year	$ 524	$ 411

ILLUSTRATION 18.21

Additional information for Chicago Cereal Company

Additional information:

	2020	2019
Weighted-average number of shares (thousands)	418.7	418.5
Stock price at year-end	$52.92	$50.06

As indicated in the chapter, we can classify ratios into three types for analysis of the primary financial statements:

1. **Liquidity ratios.** Measures of the short-term ability of the company to pay its maturing obligations and to meet unexpected needs for cash.

2. **Solvency ratios.** Measures of the ability of the company to survive over a long period of time.
3. **Profitability ratios.** Measures of the income or operating success of a company for a given period of time.

As a tool of analysis, ratios can provide clues to underlying conditions that may not be apparent from an inspection of the individual components of a particular ratio. But, a single ratio by itself is not very meaningful. Accordingly, in this discussion we use the following three comparisons.

1. **Intracompany comparisons** covering two years for Chicago Cereal (using comparative financial information from Illustrations 18.18 through 18.21).
2. **Intercompany comparisons** using Giant Mills as one of Chicago Cereal's competitors.
3. **Industry average comparisons** based on **MSN.com** median ratios for manufacturers of flour and other grain mill products and comparisons with other sources. For some of the ratios that we use, industry comparisons are not available (denoted "na").

Liquidity Ratios

Liquidity ratios measure the short-term ability of the company to pay its maturing obligations and to meet unexpected needs for cash. Short-term creditors such as bankers and suppliers are particularly interested in assessing liquidity. The measures used to determine the company's short-term debt-paying ability are the current ratio, the accounts receivable turnover, the average collection period, the inventory turnover, and days in inventory.

1. **Current ratio.** The **current ratio** expresses the relationship of current assets to current liabilities, computed by dividing current assets by current liabilities. It is widely used for evaluating a company's liquidity and short-term debt-paying ability. The 2020 and 2019 current ratios for Chicago Cereal and comparative data are shown in **Illustration 18.22**.

ILLUSTRATION 18.22 **Current ratio**

Ratio	Formula		Chicago Cereal 2020	Chicago Cereal 2019	Giant Mills 2020	Industry Average
Current ratio	$\frac{\text{Current assets}}{\text{Current liabilities}}$	$\frac{\$2,717}{\$4,044} =$	.67	.60	.67	1.06

What do the measures tell us? Chicago Cereal's 2020 current ratio of .67 means that for every dollar of current liabilities, it has $0.67 of current assets. We sometimes state such ratios as .67:1 to reinforce this interpretation. Its current ratio—and therefore its liquidity—increased significantly in 2020. It is well below the industry average but the same as that of Giant Mills.

2. **Accounts receivable turnover.** Analysts can measure liquidity by how quickly a company converts certain assets to cash. A low value for the current ratio can sometimes be compensated for if some of the company's current assets are highly liquid.

   How liquid, for example, are the receivables? The ratio used to assess the liquidity of the receivables is the **accounts receivable turnover**, which measures the number of times, on average, a company collects receivables during the period. The accounts receivable turnover is computed by dividing net credit sales (net sales less cash sales) by average net accounts receivable during the year. The accounts receivable turnover for Chicago Cereal is shown in **Illustration 18.23**.

ILLUSTRATION 18.23 **Accounts receivable turnover**

Ratio	Formula	Chicago Cereal			Giant Mills	Industry Average
			2020	2019	2020	
Accounts receivable turnover	$\frac{\text{Net credit sales}}{\text{Average net accounts receivable}}$	$\frac{\$11,776}{(\$1,026 + \$945) \div 2} =$	11.9	12.0	12.2	11.2

In computing the rate, we assumed that all Chicago Cereal's sales are credit sales. Its accounts receivable turnover declined slightly in 2020. The turnover of 11.9 times is higher than the industry average of 11.2 times, and slightly lower than Giant Mills' turnover of 12.2 times.

3. **Average collection period.** A popular variant of the accounts receivable turnover converts it into an **average collection period** in days. This is done by dividing the accounts receivable turnover into 365 days. The average collection period for Chicago Cereal is shown in **Illustration 18.24**.

ILLUSTRATION 18.24 **Average collection period**

Ratio	Formula	Chicago Cereal			Giant Mills	Industry Average
			2020	2019	2020	
Average collection period	$\frac{\text{365 days}}{\text{Accounts receivable turnover}}$	$\frac{365}{11.9} =$	30.7	30.4	29.9	32.6

Chicago Cereal's 2020 accounts receivable turnover of 11.9 times is divided into 365 days to obtain approximately 31 days. This means that the average collection period for receivables is about 31 days. Its average collection period is slightly longer than that of Giant Mills and shorter than that of the industry.

Analysts frequently use the average collection period to assess the effectiveness of a company's credit and collection policies. The general rule is that the collection period should not greatly exceed the credit term period (i.e., the time allowed for payment).

4. **Inventory turnover.** The **inventory turnover** measures the number of times average inventory was sold during the period. Its purpose is to measure the liquidity of the inventory. A high measure indicates that inventory is being sold and replenished frequently. The inventory turnover is computed by dividing the cost of goods sold by the average inventory during the period. Unless seasonal factors are significant, average inventory can be computed from the beginning and ending inventory balances. Chicago Cereal's inventory turnover is shown in **Illustration 18.25**.

ILLUSTRATION 18.25 **Inventory turnover**

Ratio	Formula	Chicago Cereal			Giant Mills	Industry Average
			2020	2019	2020	
Inventory turnover	$\frac{\text{Cost of goods sold}}{\text{Average inventory}}$	$\frac{\$6,597}{(\$924 + \$824) \div 2} =$	7.5	7.9	7.4	6.7

Chicago Cereal's inventory turnover decreased slightly in 2020. The turnover of 7.5 times is higher than the industry average of 6.7 times and similar to that of Giant Mills. Generally, the faster the inventory turnover, the less cash is tied up in inventory and the less the chance of inventory becoming obsolete. Of course, a downside of high inventory turnover is that it sometimes results in lost sales because if a company keeps less inventory on hand, it is more likely to run out of inventory when it is needed.

5. **Days in inventory.** A variant of the inventory turnover is the **days in inventory**, which measures the average number of days inventory is held. The days in inventory for Chicago Cereal is shown in **Illustration 18.26**.

ILLUSTRATION 18.26
Days in inventory

Ratio	Formula	Chicago Cereal			Giant Mills	Industry
			2020	2019	2020	Average
Days in inventory	$\frac{\text{365 days}}{\text{Inventory turnover}}$	$\frac{365}{7.5}$ =	48.7	46.2	49.3	54.5

Chicago Cereal's 2020 inventory turnover of 7.5 divided into 365 is approximately 49 days. An average selling time of 49 days is faster than the industry average and similar to that of Giant Mills. Some of this difference might be explained by differences in product lines across the two companies, although in many ways the types of products of these two companies are quite similar.

Inventory turnovers vary considerably among industries. For example, grocery store chains have a turnover of 10 times and an average selling period of 37 days. In contrast, jewelry stores have an average turnover of 1.3 times and an average selling period of 281 days. Within a company, there may even be significant differences in inventory turnover among different types of products. Thus, in a grocery store the turnover of perishable items such as produce, meats, and dairy products is faster than the turnover of soaps and detergents.

To conclude, nearly all of these liquidity measures suggest that Chicago Cereal's liquidity changed little during 2020. Its liquidity appears acceptable when compared to the industry as a whole and when compared to Giant Mills.

Solvency Ratios

Solvency ratios measure the ability of the company to survive over a long period of time. Long-term creditors and stockholders are interested in a company's long-run solvency, particularly its ability to pay interest as it comes due and to repay the face value of debt at maturity. The debt to assets ratio and times interest earned provide information about debt-paying ability. In addition, free cash flow provides information about the company's solvency and its ability to pay additional dividends or invest in new projects.

6. **Debt to assets ratio.** The **debt to assets ratio** measures the percentage of total financing provided by creditors. It is computed by dividing total liabilities (both current and long-term debt) by total assets. This ratio indicates the degree of financial leveraging. It also provides some indication of the company's ability to withstand losses without impairing the interests of its creditors. The higher the percentage of debt to assets, the greater the risk that the company may be unable to meet its maturing obligations. Thus, from the creditors' point of view, a low ratio of debt to assets is desirable. Chicago Cereal's debt to assets ratio is shown in **Illustration 18.27**.

ILLUSTRATION 18.27
Debt to assets ratio

Ratio	Formula	Chicago Cereal			Giant Mills	Industry
			2020	2019	2020	Average
Debt to assets ratio	$\frac{\text{Total liabilities}}{\text{Total assets}}$	$\frac{\$8,871}{\$11,397}$ =	78%	81%	55%	55%

Chicago Cereal's 2020 ratio of 78% means that creditors have provided financing sufficient to cover 78% of the company's total assets. Alternatively, it says that it would have to liquidate 78% of its assets at their book value in order to pay off all of its debts. Its ratio is above the industry average of 55%, as well as that of Giant Mills. This suggests that it is less solvent than the industry average and Giant Mills. Chicago Cereal's solvency improved slightly during the year.

The adequacy of this ratio is often judged in light of the company's earnings. Generally, companies with relatively stable earnings, such as public utilities, have higher debt to assets ratios than cyclical companies with widely fluctuating earnings, such as many high-tech companies.

Another ratio with a similar meaning is the **debt to equity ratio**. It shows the relative use of borrowed funds (total liabilities) compared with resources invested by the owners. Because this ratio can be computed in several ways, be careful when making comparisons with it. Debt may be defined to include only the noncurrent portion of liabilities, and intangible assets may be excluded from stockholders' equity (which would equal tangible net worth). If debt and assets are defined as above (all liabilities and all assets), then when the debt to assets ratio equals 50%, the debt to equity ratio is 1:1.

7. **Times interest earned.** The **times interest earned** (also called interest coverage) indicates the company's ability to meet interest payments as they come due. It is computed by dividing the sum of net income, interest expense, and income tax expense by interest expense. Note that this ratio uses income before interest expense and income taxes because this amount represents what is available to cover interest. Chicago Cereal's times interest earned is shown in **Illustration 18.28**.

ILLUSTRATION 18.28 Times interest earned

Ratio	Formula	Chicago Cereal			Giant Mills	Industry
			2020	2019	2020	Average
Times interest earned	(Net Income + Interest expense + Income tax expense) / Interest expense	($1,103 + $321 + $444) / $321 =	5.8	6.0	9.9	5.5

For Chicago Cereal, the 2020 interest coverage was 5.8 times, which indicates that income before interest and taxes was 5.8 times the amount needed for interest expense. This is less than the rate for Giant Mills, but it slightly exceeds the rate for the industry. The debt to assets ratio decreased for Chicago Cereal during 2020, and its times interest earned held relatively constant.

8. **Free cash flow.** One indication of a company's solvency, as well as of its ability to pay dividends or expand operations, is the amount of excess cash it generated after investing in capital expenditures and paying dividends. This amount is referred to as **free cash flow**. For example, if you generate $100,000 of net cash provided by operating activities but you spend $30,000 on capital expenditures and pay $10,000 in dividends, you have $60,000 ($100,000 – $30,000 – $10,000) to use either to expand operations, pay additional dividends, or pay down debt. Chicago Cereal's free cash flow is shown in **Illustration 18.29**.

ILLUSTRATION 18.29 Free cash flow

Ratio	Formula	Chicago Cereal			Giant Mills	Industry
			2020	2019	2020	Average
Free cash flow	Net cash provided by operating activities – Capital expenditures – Cash dividends	$1,503 – $472 – $475 =	$556	$507	$895	na
			(in thousands)		(in millions)	

Chicago Cereal's free cash flow increased slightly from 2019 to 2020. During both years, the net cash provided by operating activities was more than enough to allow it to acquire additional productive assets and maintain dividend payments. It could have used the remaining cash to reduce debt if necessary. Given that Chicago Cereal is much smaller than Giant Mills, we would expect its free cash flow to be substantially smaller, which it is.

Profitability Ratios

Profitability ratios measure the income or operating success of a company for a given period of time. A company's income, or the lack of it, affects its ability to obtain debt and equity financing, its liquidity position, and its ability to grow. As a consequence, creditors and investors alike are interested in evaluating profitability. Analysts frequently use profitability as the ultimate test of management's operating effectiveness.

The relationships among measures of profitability are very important. Understanding them can help management determine where to focus its efforts to improve profitability. **Illustration 18.30** diagrams these relationships. Our discussion of Chicago Cereal's profitability is structured around this diagram.

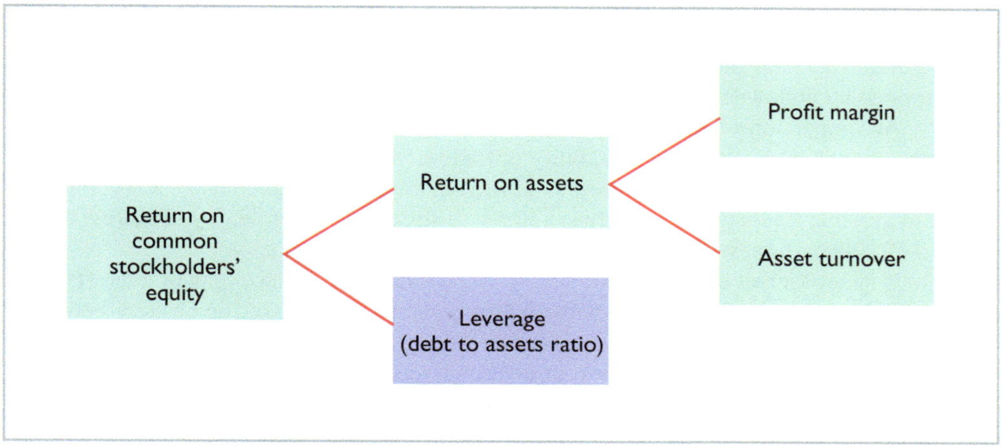

ILLUSTRATION 18.30 **Relationships among profitability measures**

9. **Return on common stockholders' equity (ROE).** A widely used measure of profitability from the common stockholder's viewpoint is the **return on common stockholders' equity (ROE)**. This ratio shows how many dollars of net income the company earned for each dollar invested by the owners. It is computed by dividing net income minus any preferred dividends—that is, income available to common stockholders—by average common stockholders' equity. The return on common stockholders' equity for Chicago Cereal is shown in **Illustration 18.31**.

ILLUSTRATION 18.31 **Return on common stockholders' equity**

Ratio	Formula	Chicago Cereal			Giant Mills 2020	Industry Average
			2020	2019		
Return on common stockholders' equity	(Net Income − Preferred dividends) / Average common stockholders' equity	$\frac{\$1,103 - \$0}{(\$2,526 + \$2,069) \div 2}$ =	48%	46%	25%	19%

Chicago Cereal's 2020 return on common stockholders' equity is unusually high at 48%. The industry average is 19% and Giant Mills' return is 25%. In the subsequent sections, we investigate the causes of this high return.

10. **Return on assets.** The return on common stockholders' equity is affected by two factors: the **return on assets** and the degree of leverage. The return on assets measures the overall profitability of assets in terms of the income earned on each dollar invested in assets. It is computed by dividing net income by average total assets. Chicago Cereal's return on assets is shown in **Illustration 18.32**.

ILLUSTRATION 18.32 **Return on assets**

Ratio	Formula		Chicago Cereal 2020	Chicago Cereal 2019	Giant Mills 2020	Industry Average
Return on assets	$\frac{\text{Net income}}{\text{Average total assets}}$	$\frac{\$1{,}103}{(\$11{,}397 + \$10{,}714) \div 2} =$	10.0%	9.4%	6.2%	5.3%

Chicago Cereal had a 10.0% return on assets in 2020. This rate is significantly higher than that of Giant Mills and the industry average.

Note that its rate of return on common stockholders' equity (48%) is substantially higher than its rate of return on assets (10%). The reason is that it has made effective use of **leverage**. **Leveraging** or **trading on the equity** at a gain means that the company has borrowed money at a lower rate of interest than the rate of return it earns on the assets it purchased with the borrowed funds. Leverage enables management to use money supplied by nonowners to increase the return to owners.

A comparison of the rate of return on assets with the rate of interest paid for borrowed money indicates the profitability of trading on the equity. If you borrow money at 8% and your rate of return on assets is 11%, you are trading on the equity at a gain. Note, however, that trading on the equity is a two-way street. For example, if you borrow money at 11% and earn only 8% on it, you are trading on the equity at a loss.

Chicago Cereal earns more on its borrowed funds than it has to pay in interest. Thus, the return to stockholders exceeds the return on assets because of the positive benefit of leverage. Recall from our earlier discussion that Chicago Cereal's percentage of debt financing, as measured by the ratio of debt to assets (or debt to equity), was higher than Giant Mills' and the industry average. It appears that Chicago Cereal's high return on common stockholders' equity is due in part to its use of leverage.

11. **Profit margin.** The return on assets is affected by two factors, the first of which is the profit margin. The **profit margin**, or rate of return on sales, is a measure of the percentage of each dollar of sales that results in net income. It is computed by dividing net income by net sales for the period. Chicago Cereal's profit margin is shown in **Illustration 18.33**.

ILLUSTRATION 18.33
Profit margin

Ratio	Formula		Chicago Cereal 2020	Chicago Cereal 2019	Giant Mills 2020	Industry Average
Profit margin	$\frac{\text{Net income}}{\text{Net sales}}$	$\frac{\$1{,}103}{\$11{,}776} =$	9.4%	9.2%	8.2%	6.1%

Chicago Cereal experienced a slight increase in its profit margin from 2019 to 2020 of 9.2% to 9.4%. Its profit margin was higher than the industry average and that of Giant Mills.

High-volume (high inventory turnover) businesses such as grocery stores and pharmacy chains generally have low profit margins. Low-volume businesses such as jewelry stores and airplane manufacturers have high profit margins.

12. **Asset turnover.** The other factor that affects the return on assets is the asset turnover. The **asset turnover** measures how efficiently a company uses its assets to generate sales. It is determined by dividing net sales by average total assets for the period. The resulting number shows the dollars of sales produced by each dollar invested in assets. **Illustration 18.34** shows the asset turnover for Chicago Cereal.

ILLUSTRATION 18.34
Asset turnover

Ratio	Formula		Chicago Cereal 2020	Chicago Cereal 2019	Giant Mills 2020	Industry Average
Asset turnover	Net sales ÷ Average total assets	\$11,776 ÷ ((\$11,397 + \$10,714) ÷ 2) =	1.07	1.02	.76	.87

The asset turnover shows that in 2020, Chicago Cereal generated sales of \$1.07 for each dollar it had invested in assets. The ratio rose from 2019 to 2020. Its asset turnover is above the industry average and that of Giant Mills.

Asset turnovers vary considerably among industries. The average asset turnover for utility companies is .45, for example, while the grocery store industry has an average asset turnover of 3.49.

In summary, Chicago Cereal's return on assets increased from 9.4% in 2019 to 10.0% in 2020. Underlying this increase was an increased profitability on each dollar of sales (as measured by the profit margin) and a rise in the sales-generating efficiency of its assets (as measured by the asset turnover). We can analyze the combined effects of profit margin and asset turnover on return on assets for Chicago Cereal as shown in **Illustration 18.35**.

ILLUSTRATION 18.35 **Composition of return on assets**

Ratios:	Profit Margin	×	Asset Turnover	=	Return on Assets
	Net Income ÷ Net Sales	×	Net Sales ÷ Average Total Assets	=	Net Income ÷ Average Total Assets
Chicago Cereal					
2020	9.4%	×	1.07 times	=	10.1%*
2019	9.2%	×	1.02 times	=	9.4%

*Difference from value in Illustration 18.32 due to rounding.

13. **Gross profit rate.** One factor that strongly influences the profit margin is the gross profit rate. The **gross profit rate** is determined by dividing gross profit (net sales less cost of goods sold) by net sales. This rate indicates a company's ability to maintain an adequate selling price above its cost of goods sold.

    As an industry becomes more competitive, this ratio declines. For example, in the early years of the personal computer industry, gross profit rates were quite high. Today, because of increased competition and a belief that most brands of personal computers are similar in quality, gross profit rates have become thin. Analysts should closely monitor gross profit rates over time. **Illustration 18.36** shows Chicago Cereal's gross profit rate.

ILLUSTRATION 18.36
Gross profit rate

Ratio	Formula		Chicago Cereal 2020	Chicago Cereal 2019	Giant Mills 2020	Industry Average
Gross profit rate	Gross profit ÷ Net sales	\$5,179 ÷ \$11,776 =	44%	44%	34%	30%

Chicago Cereal's gross profit rate remained constant from 2019 to 2020.

14. **Earnings per share (EPS).** Stockholders usually think in terms of the number of shares they own or plan to buy or sell. Expressing net income earned on a per share basis provides a useful perspective for determining profitability. **Earnings per share** is a measure of the net income earned on each share of common stock. It is computed by dividing net income by the average number of common shares outstanding during the year.

The terms "net income per share" or "earnings per share" refer to the amount of net income applicable to each share of **common stock**. Therefore, when we compute earnings per share, if there are preferred dividends declared for the period, we must deduct them from net income to arrive at income available to the common stockholders. Chicago Cereal's earnings per share is shown in **Illustration 18.37**.

ILLUSTRATION 18.37

Earnings per share

Ratio	**Formula**		**Chicago Cereal 2020**	**Chicago Cereal 2019**	**Giant Mills 2020**	**Industry Average**
Earnings per share (EPS)	$\frac{\text{Net income} - \text{Preferred dividends}}{\text{Weighted-average common shares outstanding}}$	$\frac{\$1{,}103 - \$0}{418.7} =$	$2.63	$2.40	$2.90	na

Note that no industry average is presented in Illustration 18.37. Industry data for earnings per share are not reported, and in fact the Chicago Cereal and Giant Mills ratios should not be compared. Such comparisons are not meaningful because of the wide variations in the number of shares of outstanding stock among companies. Chicago Cereal's earnings per share increased 23 cents per share in 2020. This represents a 9.6% increase from the 2019 EPS of $2.40.

15. **Price-earnings ratio.** The **price-earnings ratio** is an oft-quoted statistic that measures the ratio of the market price of each share of common stock to the earnings per share. The price-earnings (P-E) ratio reflects investors' assessments of a company's future earnings. It is computed by dividing the market price per share of the stock by earnings per share. Chicago Cereal's price-earnings ratio is shown in **Illustration 18.38**.

ILLUSTRATION 18.38

Price-earnings ratio

Ratio	**Formula**		**Chicago Cereal 2020**	**Chicago Cereal 2019**	**Giant Mills 2020**	**Industry Average**
Price-earnings ratio	$\frac{\text{Market price per share}}{\text{Earnings per share}}$	$\frac{\$52.92}{\$2.63} =$	20.1	20.9	24.3	35.8

At the end of 2020 and 2019, the market price of Chicago Cereal's stock was $52.92 and $50.06, respectively.

In 2020, each share of Chicago Cereal's stock sold for 20.1 times the amount that was earned on each share. Chicago Cereal's price-earnings ratio is lower than Giant Mills' ratio of 24.3 and lower than the industry average of 35.8 times. Its lower P-E ratio suggests that the market is less optimistic about Chicago Cereal than about Giant Mills. However, it might also signal that Chicago Cereal's stock is underpriced.

16. **Payout ratio.** The **payout ratio** measures the percentage of earnings distributed in the form of cash dividends. It is computed by dividing cash dividends declared on common stock by net income. Companies that have high growth rates are characterized by low payout ratios because they reinvest most of their net income in the business. The payout ratio for Chicago Cereal is shown in **Illustration 18.39**.

The 2020 and 2019 payout ratios for Chicago Cereal are slightly lower than that of Giant Mills (54%) but higher than the industry average (37%).

Management has some control over the amount of dividends paid each year, and companies are generally reluctant to reduce a dividend below the amount paid in a previous year. Therefore, the payout ratio will actually increase if a company's net income

Ratio	Formula	Chicago Cereal	2020	2019	Giant Mills 2020	Industry Average
Payout ratio	$\frac{\text{Cash dividends declared on common stock}}{\text{Net income}}$	$\frac{\$475}{\$1,103}$ =	43%	45%	54%	37%

ILLUSTRATION 18.39
Payout ratio

declines but the company keeps its total dividend payment the same. Of course, unless the company returns to its previous level of profitability, maintaining this higher dividend payout ratio is probably not possible over the long run.

Before drawing any conclusions regarding Chicago Cereal's dividend payout ratio, we should calculate this ratio over a longer period of time to evaluate any trends and also try to find out whether management's philosophy regarding dividends has changed recently. The "Selected Financial Data" section of Chicago Cereal's Management Discussion and Analysis shows that over a 5-year period, earnings per share rose 45%, while dividends per share grew only 19%.

In terms of the types of financial information available and the ratios used by various industries, what can be practically covered in this textbook gives you only the "Titanic approach." That is, you are seeing only the tip of the iceberg compared to the vast databases and types of ratio analysis that are available on computers. The availability of information is not a problem. The real trick is to be discriminating enough to perform relevant analysis and select pertinent comparative data.

DO IT! 3 | Ratio Analysis

The condensed financial statements of John Cully Company, for the years ended June 30, 2020 and 2019, are presented as follows.

John Cully Company
Balance Sheets
June 30

	(in thousands) 2020	2019
Assets		
Current assets		
Cash and cash equivalents	$ 553.3	$ 611.6
Accounts receivable (net)	776.6	664.9
Inventory	768.3	653.5
Prepaid expenses and other current assets	204.4	269.2
Total current assets	2,302.6	2,199.2
Investments	12.3	12.6
Property, plant, and equipment (net)	694.2	647.0
Intangibles and other assets	876.7	849.3
Total assets	$3,885.8	$3,708.1
Liabilities and Stockholders' Equity		
Current liabilities	$1,497.7	$1,322.0
Long-term liabilities	679.5	637.1
Stockholders' equity—common	1,708.6	1,749.0
Total liabilities and stockholders' equity	$3,885.8	$3,708.1

ACTION PLAN

- **Remember that the current ratio includes all current assets.**
- **Use average balances for turnover ratios like inventory, accounts receivable, and return on assets.**

John Cully Company
Income Statements
For the Years Ended June 30

	(in thousands)	
	2020	2019
Sales revenue	$6,336.3	$5,790.4
Costs and expenses		
Cost of goods sold	1,617.4	1,476.3
Selling and administrative expenses	4,007.6	3,679.0
Interest expense	13.9	27.1
Total costs and expenses	5,638.9	5,182.4
Income before income taxes	697.4	608.0
Income tax expense	291.3	232.6
Net income	$ 406.1	$ 375.4

Compute the following ratios for 2020 and 2019.

a. Current ratio.

b. Inventory turnover. (Inventory on 6/30/18 was $599.0.)

c. Profit margin.

d. Return on assets. (Assets on 6/30/18 were $3,349.9.)

e. Return on common stockholders' equity. (Stockholders' equity on 6/30/18 was $1,795.9.)

f. Debt to assets ratio.

g. Times interest earned.

Solution

	2020	2019
a. Current ratio:		
$2,302.6 ÷ $1,497.7 =	1.5:1	
$2,199.2 ÷ $1,322.0 =		1.7:1
b. Inventory turnover:		
$1,617.4 ÷ [($768.3 + $653.5) ÷ 2] =	2.3 times	
$1,476.3 ÷ [($653.5 + $599.0) ÷ 2] =		2.4 times
c. Profit margin:		
$406.1 ÷ $6,336.3 =	6.4%	
$375.4 ÷ $5,790.4 =		6.5%
d. Return on assets:		
$406.1 ÷ [($3,885.8 + $3,708.1) ÷ 2] =	10.7%	
$375.4 ÷ [($3,708.1 + $3,349.9) ÷ 2] =		10.6%
e. Return on common stockholders' equity:		
($406.1 – $0) ÷ [($1,708.6 + $1,749.0) ÷ 2] =	23.5%	
($375.4 – $0) ÷ [($1,749.0 + $1,795.9) ÷ 2] =		21.2%
f. Debt to assets ratio:		
($1,497.7 + $679.5) ÷ $3,885.8 =	56.0%	
($1,322.0 + $637.1) ÷ $3,708.1 =		52.8%
g. Times interest earned:		
($406.1 + $13.9 + $291.3) ÷ $13.9 =	51.2 times	
($375.4 + $27.1 + $232.6) ÷ $27.1 =		23.4 times

Related exercise material: **BE18.10, BE18.11, BE18.12, BE18.13, BE18.14, BE18.15, DO IT! 18.3, E18.7, E18.8, E18.9, E18.10, E18.11, E18.12, and E18.13.**

Review and Practice

Learning Objectives Review

1 Apply the concepts of sustainable income and quality of earnings.

Sustainable income analysis is useful in evaluating a company's performance. Sustainable income is the most likely level of income to be obtained by the company in the future. Discontinued operations and other comprehensive income are presented separately to highlight their unusual nature. Items below income from continuing operations must be presented net of tax.

A high quality of earnings provides full and transparent information that will not confuse or mislead users of the financial statements. Issues related to quality of earnings are (1) alternative accounting methods, (2) pro forma income, and (3) improper recognition.

2 Apply horizontal analysis and vertical analysis.

Horizontal analysis is a technique for evaluating a series of data over a period of time to determine the increase or decrease that has taken place, expressed as either a dollar amount or a percentage.

Vertical analysis is a technique that expresses each item in a financial statement as a percentage of a relevant total or a base amount.

3 Analyze a company's performance using ratio analysis.

Financial ratios as provided in Illustration 18.15 (liquidity), Illustration 18.16 (solvency), and Illustration 18.17 (profitability) are used to provide clues to the underlying conditions of a company. Analysis is enhanced by intracompany, intercompany, and industry comparisons of these three classes of ratios.

Glossary Review

Accounts receivable turnover A measure of the liquidity of receivables; computed as net credit sales divided by average net accounts receivable. (p. 18-19).

Asset turnover A measure of how efficiently a company uses its assets to generate sales; computed as net sales divided by average total assets. (p. 18-24).

Available-for-sale securities Securities that are held with the intent of selling them sometime in the future. (p. 18-5).

Average collection period The average number of days that receivables are outstanding; calculated as accounts receivable turnover divided into 365 days. (p. 18-20).

Change in accounting principle Use of an accounting principle in the current year different from the one used in the preceding year. (p. 18-6).

Comprehensive income The sum of net income and other comprehensive income items. (p. 18-5).

Current ratio A measure used to evaluate a company's liquidity and short-term debt-paying ability; calculated as current assets divided by current liabilities. (p. 18-19).

Days in inventory A measure of the average number of days inventory is held; computed as inventory turnover divided into 365 days. (p. 18-21).

Debt to assets ratio A measure of the percentage of total financing provided by creditors; computed as total liabilities divided by total assets. (p. 18-21).

Discontinued operations The disposal of a significant component of a business. (p. 18-4).

Earnings per share The net income earned by each share of common stock; computed as net income less preferred dividends divided by the weighted-average common shares outstanding. (p. 18-25).

Free cash flow A measure of solvency. Cash remaining from operating activities after adjusting for capital expenditures and dividends paid. (p. 18-22).

Gross profit rate Gross profit expressed as a percentage of sales; computed as gross profit divided by net sales. (p. 18-25).

Horizontal analysis A technique for evaluating a series of financial statement data over a period of time to determine the increase (decrease) that has taken place, expressed as either a dollar amount or a percentage. (p. 18-10).

Inventory turnover A measure of the liquidity of inventory. Measures the number of times average inventory was sold during the period; computed as cost of goods sold divided by average inventory. (p. 18-20).

Leveraging Borrowing money at a lower rate of interest than can be earned by using the borrowed money; also referred to as *trading on the equity*. (p. 18-24).

Liquidity ratios Measures of the short-term ability of the company to pay its maturing obligations and to meet unexpected needs for cash. (p. 18-15).

Payout ratio A measure of the percentage of earnings distributed in the form of cash dividends; calculated as cash dividends declared on common stock divided by net income. (p. 18-26).

Price-earnings (P-E) ratio A comparison of the market price of each share of common stock to the earnings per share; computed as the market price per share of the stock divided by earnings per share. (p. 18-26).

Profitability ratios Measures of the income or operating success of a company for a given period of time. (p. 18-16).

Profit margin A measure of the net income generated by each dollar of sales; computed as net income divided by net sales. (p. 18-24).

Pro forma income A measure of income that usually excludes items that a company thinks are unusual or non-recurring. (p. 18-8).

Quality of earnings Indicates the level of full and transparent information that is provided to users of the financial statements. (p. 18-7).

Ratio An expression of the mathematical relationship between one quantity and another. The relationship may be expressed either as a percentage, a rate, or a simple proportion. (p. 18-14).

Ratio analysis A technique for evaluating financial statements that expresses the relationship between selected financial statement data. (p. 18-14).

Return on assets A profitability measure that indicates the amount of net income generated by each dollar of assets; calculated as net income divided by average total assets. (p. 18-24).

Return on common stockholders' equity (ROE) A measure of the dollars of net income earned for each dollar invested by the owners; computed as income available to common stockholders divided by average common stockholders' equity. (p. 18-23).

Solvency ratios Measures of the ability of a company to survive over a long period of time, particularly to pay interest as it comes due and to repay the balance of debt at its maturity. (p. 18-16).

Sustainable income The most likely level of income to be obtained by a company in the future. (p. 18-3).

Times interest earned A measure of a company's solvency and ability to meet interest payments as they come due; calculated as the sum of net income, interest expense, and income tax expense divided by interest expense. (p. 18-22).

Trading on the equity *See leveraging*. (p. 18-24).

Trading securities Securities bought and held primarily for sale in the near term to generate income on short-term price differences. (p. 18-5).

Vertical analysis A technique for evaluating financial statement data that expresses each item in a financial statement as a percentage of a base amount. (p. 18-12).

Practice Multiple-Choice Questions

1. **(LO 1)** In reporting discontinued operations, the income statement should show in a special section:
   - **a.** gains on the disposal of the discontinued component.
   - **b.** losses on the disposal of the discontinued component.
   - **c.** Neither (a) nor (b).
   - **d.** Both (a) and (b).

2. **(LO 1)** Cool Stools Corporation has income before taxes of $400,000 and a loss on discontinued operations of $100,000. If the income tax rate is 25% on all items, the statement of comprehensive income should show income from continuing operations and discontinued operations, respectively, of
   - **a.** $325,000 and $100,000.
   - **b.** $325,000 and $75,000.
   - **c.** $300,000 and $100,000.
   - **d.** $300,000 and $75,000.

3. **(LO 1)** Which of the following would be considered an "Other comprehensive income" item?
   - **a.** Gain on disposal of discontinued operations.
   - **b.** Unrealized loss on available-for-sale securities.
   - **c.** Loss related to flood.
   - **d.** Net income.

4. **(LO 1)** Which situation below might indicate a company has a low quality of earnings?
   - **a.** The same accounting principles are used each year.
   - **b.** Revenue is recognized when the performance obligation is satisfied.
   - **c.** Maintenance costs are capitalized and then depreciated.
   - **d.** The company's P-E ratio is high relative to competitors.

5. **(LO 2)** In horizontal analysis, each item is expressed as a percentage of the:
   - **a.** net income amount.
   - **b.** stockholders' equity amount.
   - **c.** total assets amount.
   - **d.** base-year amount.

6. **(LO 2)** Adams Corporation reported net sales of $300,000, $330,000, and $360,000 in the years 2018, 2019, and 2020, respectively. If 2018 is the base year, what percentage do 2020 sales represent of the base?
   - **a.** 77%.
   - **b.** 108%.
   - **c.** 120%.
   - **d.** 130%.

7. **(LO 2)** The following schedule is a display of what type of analysis?

	Amount	Percent
Current assets	$200,000	25%
Property, plant, and equipment	600,000	75%
Total assets	$800,000	

   - **a.** Horizontal analysis.
   - **b.** Differential analysis.
   - **c.** Vertical analysis.
   - **d.** Ratio analysis.

8. **(LO 2)** In vertical analysis, the base amount for depreciation expense is generally:
   - **a.** net sales.
   - **b.** depreciation expense in a previous year.
   - **c.** gross profit.
   - **d.** fixed assets.

9. **(LO 3)** Which measure is an evaluation of a company's ability to pay current liabilities?
   - **a.** Accounts receivable turnover.
   - **b.** Current ratio.
   - **c.** Both (a) and (b).
   - **d.** None of the above.

10. **(LO 3)** Which measure is useful in evaluating the efficiency in managing inventories?
    - **a.** Inventory turnover.
    - **b.** Days in inventory.
    - **c.** Both (a) and (b).
    - **d.** None of the above.

11. **(LO 3)** Which of these is **not** a liquidity ratio?
    - **a.** Current ratio.
    - **b.** Asset turnover.
    - **c.** Inventory turnover.
    - **d.** Accounts receivable turnover.

12. **(LO 3)** Plano Corporation reported net income $24,000, net sales $400,000, and average assets $600,000 for 2020. What is the 2020 profit margin?

a. 6%.
b. 12%.
c. 40%.
d. 200%.

Use the following financial statement information as of the end of each year to answer Questions 13–17.

	2020	2019
Inventory	$ 54,000	$ 48,000
Current assets	81,000	106,000
Total assets	382,000	326,000
Current liabilities	27,000	36,000
Total liabilities	102,000	88,000
Common stockholders' equity	240,000	198,000
Net sales	784,000	697,000
Cost of goods sold	306,000	277,000
Net income	134,000	90,000
Income tax expense	22,000	18,000
Interest expense	12,000	12,000
Dividends paid to preferred stockholders	4,000	4,000
Dividends paid to common stockholders	15,000	10,000

13. **(LO 3)** Compute the days in inventory for 2020.

a. 64.4 days.
b. 60.8 days.
c. 6 days.
d. 24 days.

14. **(LO 3)** Compute the current ratio for 2020.

a. 1.26:1.
b. 3.0:1.
c. 0.80:1.
d. 3.75:1.

15. **(LO 3)** Compute the profit margin for 2020.

a. 17.1%.
b. 18.1%.
c. 37.9%.
d. 5.9%.

16. **(LO 3)** Compute the return on common stockholders' equity for 2020.

a. 54.2%.
b. 52.5%.
c. 61.2%.
d. 59.4%.

17. **(LO 3)** Compute the times interest earned for 2020.

a. 11.2 times.
b. 65.3 times.
c. 14.0 times.
d. 13.0 times.

Solutions

1. **d.** Gains and losses from the operations of a discontinued segment and gains and losses on the disposal of the discontinued segment are shown in a separate section immediately after continuing operations in the income statement. Choices (a) and (b) are correct, but (d) is the better answer. Choice (c) is wrong as both (a) and (b) are correct.

2. **d.** Income tax expense = 25% × $400,000 = $100,000; therefore, income from continuing operations = $400,000 − $100,000 = $300,000. The loss on discontinued operations is shown net of tax, $100,000 × 75% = $75,000. The other choices are therefore incorrect.

3. **b.** Unrealized gains and losses on available-for-sale securities are part of other comprehensive income. The other choices are incorrect because (a) a gain on the disposal of discontinued operations is reported as an unusual item, (c) loss related to a flood is reported among other expenses and losses, and (d) net income is a separate line item.

4. **c.** Capitalizing and then depreciating maintenance costs suggests that a company is trying to avoid expensing certain costs by deferring them to future accounting periods to increase current-period income. The other choices are incorrect because (a) using the same accounting principles each year and (b) recognizing revenue when the performance obligation is satisfied is in accordance with GAAP. Choice (d) is incorrect because a high P-E ratio does not suggest that a firm has low quality of earnings.

5. **d.** Horizontal analysis converts each succeeding year's balance to a percentage of the base year amount, not (a) net income amount, (b) stockholders' equity amount, or (c) total assets amount.

6. **c.** The trend percentage for 2020 is 120% ($360,000/$300,000), not (a) 77%, (b) 108%, or (d) 130%.

7. **c.** The data in the schedule is a display of vertical analysis because the individual asset items are expressed as a percentage of total assets. The other choices are therefore incorrect. Horizontal analysis is a technique for evaluating a series of data over a period of time.

8. **a.** In vertical analysis, net sales is used as the base amount for income statement items, not (b) depreciation expense in a previous year, (c) gross profit, or (d) fixed assets.

9. **c.** Both the accounts receivable turnover and the current ratio measure a firm's ability to pay current liabilities. Choices (a) and (b) are correct but (c) is the better answer. Choice (d) is incorrect because both (a) and (b) are correct.

10. **c.** Both inventory turnover and days in inventory measure a firm's efficiency in managing inventories. Choices (a) and (b) are correct but (c) is the better answer. Choice (d) is incorrect because both (a) and (b) are correct.

11. **b.** Asset turnover is a measure of profitability. The other choices are incorrect because the (a) current ratio, (c) inventory turnover, and (d) accounts receivable turnover are all measures of a firm's liquidity.

12. **a.** Profit margin = Net income ($24,000) ÷ Net sales ($400,000) = 6%, not (b) 12%, (c) 40%, or (d) 200%.

13. **b.** Inventory turnover = Cost of goods sold/Average inventory {$306,000/[($54,000 + $48,000)/2]} = 6 times. Thus, days in inventory = 60.8 (365/6), not (a) 64.4, (c) 6, or (d) 24 days.

14. **b.** Current ratio = Current assets/Current liabilities ($81,000/$27,000) = 3.0:1, not (a) 1.26:1, (c) 0.80:1, or (d) 3.75:1.

15. **a.** Profit margin = Net income/Net sales ($134,000/$784,000) = 17.1%, not (b) 18.1%, (c) 37.9%, or (d) 5.9%.

16. **d.** Return on common stockholders' equity = Net income ($134,000) − Dividends to preferred stockholders ($4,000)/Average common stockholders' equity [($240,000 + $198,000)/2] = 59.4%, not (a) 54.2%, (b) 52.5%, or (c) 61.2%.

17. **c.** Times interest earned = Net income + Interest expense + Income tax expense divided by Interest expense [($134,000 + $12,000 + $22,000)/$12,000] = 14.0 times, not (a) 11.2, (b) 65.3, or (d) 13.0 times.

Practice Brief Exercises

Prepare a discontinued operations section.

1. **(LO 1)** **Financial Statement** On September 30, Reynaldo Corporation discontinued its operations in Africa. During the year, the operating gain was $100,000 before taxes. On September 1, Reynaldo disposed of its African facilities at a pretax loss of $350.000. The applicable tax rate is 30%. Show the discontinued operations section of the statement of comprehensive income.

Solution

1.

Reynaldo Corporation
Partial Income Statement

Gain from operations of discontinued division, net of $30,000 income taxes ($100,000 × 30%)	$ 30,000	
Loss from disposal of discontinued division, net of $105,000 income tax saving ($350,000 × 30%)	(245,000)	$(215,000)

Prepare horizontal analysis.

2. **(LO 2)** Using the following data from the comparative balance sheet of Alfredo Company, perform horizontal analysis.

	December 31, 2020	December 31, 2019
Accounts payable	$ 300,000	$ 200,000
Common stock	700,000	600,000
Total liabilities and equity	2,000,000	1,800,000

Solution

2.

			Increase or (Decrease)	
	December 31, 2020	December 31, 2019	Amount	Percent*
Accounts payable	$ 300,000	$ 200,000	$100,000	50%
Common stock	700,000	600,000	100,000	17
Total liabilities and stockholders' equity	2,000,000	1,800,000	200,000	11

*100/200 = 50%; 100/600 = 16.7%; 200/1,800 = 11.1%

Calculate ratios.

3. **(LO 2)** Gonzalez Company has beginning inventory of $400,000, cost of goods sold of $2,200,000, and days in inventory of 73. What is Gonzalez' inventory turnover and ending inventory?

Solution

3. Days in inventory = 365/Inventory turnover
73 = 365/Inventory turnover.
Inventory turnover = 5 (365/73)

Inventory turnover = Cost of goods sold/Average inventory
5 = $2,200,000/Average inventory
Average inventory = $2,200,000/5 = $440,000.

Since beginning inventory is $400,000, ending inventory must be $480,000: ($400,000 + $480,000)/2 = $440,000.

Practice Exercises

Prepare horizontal and vertical analysis.

1. **(LO 2)** The comparative condensed balance sheets of Roadway Corporation are presented below.

Roadway Corporation
Condensed Balance Sheets
December 31

Assets	2020	2019
Current assets	$ 76,000	$ 80,000
Property, plant, and equipment (net)	99,000	90,000
Intangibles	25,000	40,000
Total assets	$200,000	$210,000

Liabilities and Stockholders' Equity	**2020**	**2019**
Current liabilities	$ 40,800	$ 48,000
Long-term liabilities	143,000	150,000
Stockholders' equity	16,200	12,000
Total liabilities and stockholders' equity	$200,000	$210,000

Instructions

a. Prepare a horizontal analysis of the balance sheet data for Roadway Corporation using 2019 as a base.

b. Prepare a vertical analysis of the balance sheet data for Roadway Corporation in columnar form for 2020.

Solution

1. **a.**

Roadway Corporation
Condensed Balance Sheets
December 31

	2020	**2019**	**Increase (Decrease)**	**Percent Change from 2019**
Assets				
Current assets	$ 76,000	$ 80,000	$ (4,000)	(5.0%)
Property, plant, and equipment (net)	99,000	90,000	9,000	10.0%
Intangibles	25,000	40,000	(15,000)	(37.5%)
Total assets	$200,000	$210,000	$(10,000)	(4.8%)
Liabilities and Stockholders' Equity				
Current liabilities	$ 40,800	$ 48,000	$ (7,200)	(15.0%)
Long-term liabilities	143,000	150,000	(7,000)	(4.7%)
Stockholders' equity	16,200	12,000	4,200	35.0%
Total liabilities and stockholders' equity	$200,000	$210,000	$(10,000)	(4.8%)

b.

Roadway Corporation
Condensed Balance Sheet
December 31, 2020

	Amount	**Percent**
Assets		
Current assets	$ 76,000	38.0%
Property, plant, and equipment (net)	99,000	49.5%
Intangibles	25,000	12.5%
Total assets	$200,000	100.0%
Liabilities and Stockholders' Equity		
Current liabilities	$ 40,800	20.4%
Long-term liabilities	143,000	71.5%
Stockholders' equity	16,200	8.1%
Total liabilities and stockholders' equity	$200,000	100.0%

Compute ratios.

2. **(LO 3)** Rondo Corporation's comparative balance sheets are presented below.

Rondo Corporation
Balance Sheets
December 31

	2020	2019
Cash	$ 5,300	$ 3,700
Accounts receivable	21,200	23,400
Inventory	9,000	7,000
Land	20,000	26,000
Buildings	70,000	70,000
Accumulated depreciation—buildings	(15,000)	(10,000)
Total	$110,500	$120,100
Accounts payable	$ 10,370	$ 31,100
Common stock	75,000	69,000
Retained earnings	25,130	20,000
Total	$110,500	$120,100

Rondo's 2020 income statement included net sales of $120,000, cost of goods sold of $70,000, and net income of $14,000.

Instructions

Compute the following ratios for 2020.

a. Current ratio.
b. Accounts receivable turnover.
c. Inventory turnover.
d. Profit margin.
e. Asset turnover.
f. Return on assets.
g. Return on common stockholders' equity.
h. Debt to assets ratio.

Solution

2. **a.** ($5,300 + $21,200 + $9,000)/$10,370 = 3.42 times
b. $120,000/[($21,200 + $23,400)/2] = 5.38 times
c. $70,000/[($9,000 + $7,000)/2] = 8.8 times
d. $14,000/$120,000 = 11.7%
e. $120,000/[($110,500 + $120,100)/2] = 1.04 times
f. $14,000/[($110,500 + $120,100)/2] = 12.1%
g. $14,000/{[($75,000 + $25,130) + ($69,000 + $20,000)]/2} = 14.8%
h. $10,370/$110,500 = 9.4%

Practice Problem

Prepare a statement of comprehensive income.

(LO 1) **Financial Statement** The events and transactions of Dever Corporation for the year ending December 31, 2020, resulted in the following data.

Cost of goods sold	$2,600,000
Net sales	4,400,000
Other expenses and losses	9,600
Other revenues and gains	5,600
Selling and administrative expenses	1,100,000
Income from operations of plastics division	70,000
Gain from disposal of plastics division	500,000
Unrealized loss on available-for-sale securities	60,000

Analysis reveals the following:

1. All items are before the applicable income tax rate of 30%.
2. The plastics division was sold on July 1.
3. All operating data for the plastics division have been segregated.

Instructions

Prepare a statement of comprehensive income for the year.

Solution

Dever Corporation
Statement of Comprehensive Income
For the Year Ended December 31, 2020

Net sales		$4,400,000
Cost of goods sold		2,600,000
Gross profit		1,800,000
Selling and administrative expenses		1,100,000
Income from operations		700,000
Other revenues and gains		5,600
Other expenses and losses		9,600
Income before income taxes		696,000
Income tax expense ($696,000 × 30%)		208,800
Income from continuing operations		487,200
Discontinued operations		
Income from operation of plastics division, net of $21,000 income taxes ($70,000 × 30%)	49,000	
Gain from disposal of plastics division, net of $150,000 income taxes ($500,000 × 30%)	350,000	399,000
Net income		886,200
Unrealized loss on available-for-sale securities, net of $18,000 income tax savings ($60,000 × 30%)		42,000
Comprehensive income		$ 844,200

WileyPLUS

Brief Exercises, DO IT! Exercises, Exercises, Problems, and many additional resources are available for practice in WileyPLUS.

Questions

1. Explain sustainable income. What relationship does this concept have to the treatment of discontinued operations on the income statement?

2. Hogan Inc. reported 2019 earnings per share of $3.26 and had no discontinued operations. In 2020, earnings per share on income from continuing operations was $2.99, and earnings per share on net income was $3.49. Do you consider this trend to be favorable? Why or why not?

3. Moosier Inc. has been in operation for 3 years and uses the FIFO method of pricing inventory. During the fourth year, Moosier changes to the average-cost method for all its inventory. How will Moosier report this change?

4. What amount did **Apple** report as "Other comprehensive income (loss)" in its consolidated statement of comprehensive income ending September 26, 2015? By what percentage did Apple's "Comprehensive income" differ from its "Net income"?

5. Identify and explain factors that affect quality of earnings.

6. Explain how the choice of one of the following accounting methods over the other raises or lowers a company's net income during a period of continuing inflation.

   a. Use of FIFO instead of LIFO for inventory costing.

   b. Use of a 6-year life for machinery instead of a 9-year life.

   c. Use of straight-line depreciation instead of declining-balance depreciation.

7. Two popular methods of financial statement analysis are horizontal analysis and vertical analysis. Explain the difference between these two methods.

8. **a.** If Erin Company had net income of $300,000 in 2019 and it experienced a 24.5% increase in net income for 2020, what is its net income for 2020?

   b. If 6 cents of every dollar of Erin's revenue is net income in 2019, what is the dollar amount of 2019 revenue?

9. **a.** Gina Jaimes believes that the analysis of financial statements is directed at two characteristics of a company: liquidity and profitability. Is Gina correct? Explain.

   b. Are short-term creditors, long-term creditors, and stockholders interested in primarily the same characteristics of a company? Explain.

10. **a.** Distinguish among the following bases of comparison: intracompany, intercompany, and industry averages.

    b. Give the principal value of using each of the three bases of comparison.

11. Name the major ratios useful in assessing (a) liquidity and (b) solvency.

12. Vern Thoms is puzzled. His company had a profit margin of 10% in 2020. He feels that this is an indication that the company is doing well. Tina Amos, his accountant, says that more information is needed to determine the company's financial well-being. Who is correct? Why?

13. What does each type of ratio measure?

    a. Liquidity ratios.

    b. Solvency ratios.

    c. Profitability ratios.

14. What is the difference between the current ratio and working capital?

15. Handi Mart, a retail store, has an accounts receivable turnover of 4.5 times. The industry average is 12.5 times. Does Handi Mart have a collection problem with its receivables?

16. Which ratios should be used to help answer each of these questions?

    a. How efficient is a company in using its assets to produce sales?

    b. How near to sale is the inventory on hand?

    c. How many dollars of net income were earned for each dollar invested by the owners?

    d. How able is a company to meet interest charges as they fall due?

17. At year-end, the price-earnings ratio of **General Motors** was 11.3, and the price-earnings ratio of **Microsoft** was 28.14. Which company did the stock market favor? Explain.

18. What is the formula for computing the payout ratio? Do you expect this ratio to be high or low for a growth company?

19. Holding all other factors constant, indicate whether each of the following changes generally signals good or bad news about a company.

    a. Increase in profit margin.

    b. Decrease in inventory turnover.

    c. Increase in current ratio.

    d. Decrease in earnings per share.

    e. Increase in price-earnings ratio.

    f. Increase in debt to assets ratio.

    g. Decrease in times interest earned.

20. The return on assets for Ayala Corporation is 7.6%. During the same year, Ayala's return on common stockholders' equity is 12.8%. What is the explanation for the difference in the two rates?

21. Which two ratios do you think should be of greatest interest in each of the following cases?

    a. A pension fund considering the purchase of 20-year bonds.

    b. A bank contemplating a short-term loan to a customer.

    c. A common stockholder.

22. Keanu Inc. has net income of $200,000, average shares of common stock outstanding of 40,000, and preferred dividends for the period of $20,000. What is Keanu's earnings per share of common stock? Fred Tyme, the president of Keanu, believes that the computed EPS of the company is high. Comment.

Brief Exercises

Prepare a discontinued operations section.

BE18.1 (LO 1) Financial Statement On June 30, Flores Corporation discontinued its operations in Mexico. On September 1, Flores disposed of the Mexico facility at a pretax loss of $640,000. The applicable tax rate is 25%. Show the discontinued operations section of Flores's statement of comprehensive income.

Prepare statement of comprehensive income including unusual items.

BE18.2 (LO 1) Financial Statement An inexperienced accountant for Silva Corporation showed the following in the income statement: income before income taxes $450,000 and unrealized gain on available-for-sale securities (before taxes) $70,000. The unrealized gain on available-for-sale securities and income before income taxes are both subject to a 25% tax rate. Prepare a correct statement of comprehensive income.

Indicate how a change in accounting principle is reported.

BE18.3 (LO 1) On January 1, 2020, Bryce Inc. changed from the LIFO method of inventory pricing to the FIFO method. Explain how this change in accounting principle should be treated in the company's financial statements.

Prepare horizontal analysis.

BE18.4 (LO 2) Using these data from the comparative balance sheet of Rollaird Company, perform horizontal analysis.

	December 31, 2020	December 31, 2019
Accounts receivable	$ 460,000	$ 400,000
Inventory	780,000	650,000
Total assets	3,164,000	2,800,000

BE18.5 (LO 2) Using the data presented in BE18.4 for Rollaird Company, perform vertical analysis.

Prepare vertical analysis.

BE18.6 (LO 2) Net income was $500,000 in 2018, $485,000 in 2019, and $518,400 in 2020. What is the percentage of change from (a) 2018 to 2019, and (b) from 2019 to 2020? Is the change an increase or a decrease?

Calculate percentage of change.

BE18.7 (LO 2) If Coho Company had net income of $382,800 in 2020 and it experienced a 16% increase in net income over 2019, what was its 2019 net income?

Calculate net income.

BE18.8 (LO 2) Vertical analysis (common-size) percentages for Palau Company's sales revenue, cost of goods sold, and expenses are as follows.

Analyze change in net income.

Vertical Analysis	2020	2019	2018
Sales revenue	100.0%	100.0%	100.0%
Cost of goods sold	60.5	62.9	64.8
Expenses	26.0	26.6	27.5

Did Palau's net income as a percent of sales increase, decrease, or remain unchanged over the 3-year period? Provide numerical support for your answer.

BE18.9 (LO 2) **Writing** Horizontal analysis (trend analysis) percentages for Phoenix Company's sales revenue, cost of goods sold, and expenses are listed here.

Analyze change in net income.

Horizontal Analysis	2020	2019	2018
Sales revenue	96.2%	104.8%	100.0%
Cost of goods sold	101.0	98.0	100.0
Expenses	105.6	95.4	100.0

Explain whether Phoenix's net income increased, decreased, or remained unchanged over the 3-year period.

BE18.10 (LO 3) **Writing** Suppose these selected condensed data are taken from recent balance sheets of **Bob Evans Farms** (in thousands).

Calculate current ratio.

	2020	2019
Cash	$ 13,606	$ 7,669
Accounts receivable	23,045	19,951
Inventory	31,087	31,345
Other current assets	12,522	11,909
Total current assets	$ 80,260	$ 70,874
Total current liabilities	$245,805	$326,203

Compute the current ratio for each year and comment on your results.

BE18.11 (LO 3) **Writing** The following data are taken from the financial statements of Colby Company.

Evaluate collection of accounts receivable.

	2020	2019
Accounts receivable (net), end of year	$ 550,000	$ 540,000
Net sales on account	4,300,000	4,000,000
Terms for all sales are 1/10, n/45		

a. Compute for each year (1) the accounts receivable turnover and (2) the average collection period. At the end of 2018, accounts receivable was $520,000.

b. What conclusions about the management of accounts receivable can be drawn from these data?

BE18.12 (LO 3) **Writing** The following data were taken from the income statements of Mydorf Company.

Evaluate management of inventory.

	2020	2019
Sales revenue	$6,420,000	$6,240,000
Beginning inventory	960,000	840,000
Purchases	4,840,000	4,661,000
Ending inventory	1,020,000	960,000

a. Compute for each year (1) the inventory turnover and (2) days in inventory.

b. What conclusions concerning the management of the inventory can be drawn from these data?

BE18.13 (LO 3) **Writing** **Staples, Inc.** is one of the largest suppliers of office products in the United States. Suppose it had net income of $738.7 million and sales of $24,275.5 million in 2020. Its total assets were $13,073.1 million at the beginning of the year and $13,717.3 million at the end of the year.

Calculate profitability ratios.

What is Staples, Inc.'s (a) asset turnover and (b) profit margin? (Round to two decimals.) Provide a brief interpretation of your results.

Calculate profitability ratios.

BE18.14 (LO 3) Hollie Company has stockholders' equity of $400,000 and net income of $72,000. It has a payout ratio of 18% and a return on assets of 20%. How much did Hollie pay in cash dividends, and what were its average total assets?

Calculate and analyze free cash flow.

BE18.15 (LO 3) **Writing** Selected data taken from a recent year's financial statements of trading card company **Topps Company, Inc.** are as follows (in millions).

Net sales	$326.7
Current liabilities, beginning of year	41.1
Current liabilities, end of year	62.4
Net cash provided by operating activities	10.4
Total liabilities, beginning of year	65.2
Total liabilities, end of year	73.2
Capital expenditures	3.7
Cash dividends	6.2

Compute the free cash flow. Provide a brief interpretation of your results.

DO IT! Exercises

Prepare statement of comprehensive income including unusual items.

DO IT! 18.1 (LO 1) **Financial Statement** In its proposed 2020 income statement, Hrabik Corporation reports income before income taxes $500,000, income taxes $100,000 (not including unusual items), loss on operation of discontinued music division $60,000, gain on disposal of discontinued music division $40,000, and unrealized loss on available-for-sale securities $150,000. The income tax rate is 20%. Prepare a correct statement of comprehensive income, beginning with income before income taxes.

Prepare horizontal analysis.

DO IT! 18.2 (LO 2) Summary financial information for Gandaulf Company is as follows.

	Dec. 31, 2020	Dec. 31, 2019
Current assets	$ 200,000	$ 220,000
Plant assets	1,040,000	780,000
Total assets	$1,240,000	$1,000,000

Compute the amount and percentage changes in 2020 using horizontal analysis, assuming 2019 is the base year.

Compute ratios.

DO IT! 18.3 (LO 3) The condensed financial statements of Murawski Company for the years 2019 and 2020 are presented as follows. (Amounts in thousands.)

Murawski Company
Balance Sheets
December 31

	2020	2019
Current assets		
Cash and cash equivalents	$ 330	$ 360
Accounts receivable (net)	470	400
Inventory	460	390
Prepaid expenses	120	160
Total current assets	1,380	1,310
Investments	10	10
Property, plant, and equipment	420	380
Intangibles and other assets	530	510
Total assets	$2,340	$2,210
Current liabilities	$ 900	$ 790
Long-term liabilities	410	380
Stockholders' equity—common	1,030	1,040
Total liabilities and stockholders' equity	$2,340	$2,210

Murawski Company Income Statements For the Years Ended December 31		
	2020	**2019**
Sales revenue	$3,800	$3,460
Costs and expenses		
Cost of goods sold	955	890
Selling & administrative expenses	2,400	2,330
Interest expense	25	20
Total costs and expenses	3,380	3,240
Income before income taxes	420	220
Income tax expense	126	66
Net income	$ 294	$ 154

Compute the following ratios for 2020 and 2019.

a. Current ratio.

b. Inventory turnover. (Inventory on 12/31/18 was $340.)

c. Profit margin.

d. Return on assets. (Assets on 12/31/18 were $1,900.)

e. Return on common stockholders' equity. (Stockholders' equity on 12/31/18 was $900.)

f. Debt to assets ratio.

g. Times interest earned.

Exercises

E18.1 (LO 1) **Financial Statement** **Writing** For its fiscal year ending October 31, 2020, Haas Corporation reports the following partial data shown below.

Prepare a correct statement of comprehensive income.

Income before income taxes	$540,000
Income tax expense (20% × $420,000)	84,000
Income from continuing operations	456,000
Loss on discontinued operations	120,000
Net income	$336,000

The loss on discontinued operations was comprised of a $50,000 loss from operations and a $70,000 loss from disposal. The income tax rate is 20% on all items.

Instructions

a. Prepare a correct statement of comprehensive income beginning with income before income taxes.

b. Explain in memo form why the income statement data are misleading.

E18.2 (LO 1) **Financial Statement** Trayer Corporation has income from continuing operations of $290,000 for the year ended December 31, 2020. It also has the following items (before considering income taxes).

Prepare statement of comprehensive income.

1. An unrealized loss of $80,000 on available-for-sale securities.
2. A gain of $30,000 on the discontinuance of a division (comprised of a $10,000 loss from operations and a $40,000 gain on disposal).

Assume all items are subject to income taxes at a 20% tax rate.

Instructions

Prepare a statement of comprehensive income, beginning with income from continuing operations.

Prepare horizontal analysis.

Excel

E18.3 (LO 2) Here is financial information for Glitter Inc.

	December 31, 2020	December 31, 2019
Current assets	$106,000	$ 90,000
Plant assets (net)	400,000	350,000
Current liabilities	99,000	65,000
Long-term liabilities	122,000	90,000
Common stock, $1 par	130,000	115,000
Retained earnings	155,000	170,000

Instructions

Prepare a schedule showing a horizontal analysis for 2020, using 2019 as the base year.

Prepare vertical analysis.

Excel

E18.4 (LO 2) Operating data for Joshua Corporation are presented below.

	2020	2019
Sales revenue	$800,000	$600,000
Cost of goods sold	520,000	408,000
Selling expenses	120,000	72,000
Administrative expenses	60,000	48,000
Income tax expense	30,000	24,000
Net income	70,000	48,000

Instructions

Prepare a schedule showing a vertical analysis for 2020 and 2019.

Prepare horizontal and vertical analyses.

E18.5 (LO 2) Suppose the comparative balance sheets of **Nike, Inc.** are presented here.

Nike, Inc.
Comparative Balance Sheets
May 31
($ in millions)

Assets	**2020**	**2019**
Current assets	$ 9,734	$ 8,839
Property, plant, and equipment (net)	1,958	1,891
Other assets	1,558	1,713
Total assets	$13,250	$12,443
Liabilities and Stockholders' Equity		
Current liabilities	$ 3,277	$ 3,322
Long-term liabilities	1,280	1,296
Stockholders' equity	8,693	7,825
Total liabilities and stockholders' equity	$13,250	$12,443

Instructions

a. Prepare a horizontal analysis of the balance sheet data for Nike, using 2019 as a base. (Show the amount of increase or decrease as well.)

b. Prepare a vertical analysis of the balance sheet data for Nike for 2020.

Prepare horizontal and vertical analyses.

E18.6 (LO 2) Here are the comparative income statements of Delaney Corporation.

Delaney Corporation
Comparative Income Statements
For the Years Ended December 31

	2020	2019
Net sales	$598,000	$500,000
Cost of goods sold	477,000	420,000
Gross profit	121,000	80,000
Operating expenses	80,000	44,000
Net income	$ 41,000	$ 36,000

Instructions

a. Prepare a horizontal analysis of the income statement data for Delaney Corporation, using 2019 as a base. (Show the amounts of increase or decrease.)

b. Prepare a vertical analysis of the income statement data for Delaney Corporation for both years.

E18.7 (LO 3) Nordstrom, Inc. operates department stores in numerous states. Suppose selected financial statement data (in millions) for 2020 are presented below.

Compute liquidity ratios.

	End of Year	Beginning of Year
Cash and cash equivalents	$ 795	$ 72
Accounts receivable (net)	2,035	1,942
Inventory	898	900
Other current assets	326	303
Total current assets	$4,054	$3,217
Total current liabilities	$2,014	$1,601

For the year, net credit sales were $8,258 million, cost of goods sold was $5,328 million, and net cash provided by operating activities was $1,251 million.

Instructions

Compute the current ratio, accounts receivable turnover, average collection period, inventory turnover, and days in inventory at the end of the current year.

E18.8 (LO 3) Gwynn Incorporated had the following transactions involving current assets and current liabilities during February 2020.

Perform current ratio analysis.

Feb.	3	Collected accounts receivable of $15,000.
	7	Purchased equipment for $23,000 cash.
	11	Paid $3,000 for a 1-year insurance policy.
	14	Paid accounts payable of $12,000.
	18	Declared cash dividends, $4,000.

Additional information:

As of February 1, 2020, current assets were $120,000 and current liabilities were $40,000.

Instructions

Compute the current ratio as of the beginning of the month and after each transaction.

E18.9 (LO 3) Lendell Company has these comparative balance sheet data:

Compute selected ratios.

Lendell Company
Balance Sheets
December 31

	2020	2019
Cash	$ 15,000	$ 30,000
Accounts receivable (net)	70,000	60,000
Inventory	60,000	50,000
Plant assets (net)	200,000	180,000
	$345,000	$320,000
Accounts payable	$ 50,000	$ 60,000
Mortgage payable (15%)	100,000	100,000
Common stock, $10 par	140,000	120,000
Retained earnings	55,000	40,000
	$345,000	$320,000

Additional information for 2020:

1. Net income was $25,000.
2. Sales on account were $375,000. Sales returns and allowances amounted to $25,000.
3. Cost of goods sold was $198,000.

4. Net cash provided by operating activities was $48,000.
5. Capital expenditures were $25,000, and cash dividends were $10,000.

Instructions

Compute the following ratios at December 31, 2020.

a. Current ratio.
b. Accounts receivable turnover.
c. Average collection period.
d. Inventory turnover.
e. Days in inventory.
f. Free cash flow.

Compute selected ratios.

E18.10 (LO 3) Suppose selected comparative statement data for the giant bookseller **Barnes & Noble** are presented here. All balance sheet data are as of the end of the fiscal year (in millions).

	2020	2019
Net sales	$5,121.8	$5,286.7
Cost of goods sold	3,540.6	3,679.8
Net income	75.9	135.8
Accounts receivable	81.0	107.1
Inventory	1,203.5	1,358.2
Total assets	2,993.9	3,249.8
Total common stockholders' equity	921.6	1,074.7

Instructions

Compute the following ratios for 2020.

a. Profit margin.
b. Asset turnover.
c. Return on assets.
d. Return on common stockholders' equity.
e. Gross profit rate.

Compute selected ratios.

E18.11 (LO 3) Here is the income statement for Myers, Inc.

Myers, Inc.
Income Statement
For the Year Ended December 31, 2020

Sales revenue	$400,000
Cost of goods sold	230,000
Gross profit	170,000
Expenses (including $16,000 interest and $24,000 income taxes)	98,000
Net income	$ 72,000

Additional information:

1. Common stock outstanding January 1, 2020, was 32,000 shares, and 40,000 shares were outstanding at December 31, 2020.
2. The market price of Myers stock was $14 at December 31, 2020.
3. Cash dividends of $21,000 were paid, $5,000 of which were to preferred stockholders.

Instructions

Compute the following measures for 2020.

a. Earnings per share.
b. Price-earnings ratio.
c. Payout ratio.
d. Times interest earned.

Compute amounts from ratios.

E18.12 (LO 3) Panza Corporation experienced a fire on December 31, 2020, in which its financial records were partially destroyed. It has been able to salvage some of the records and has ascertained the following balances.

	December 31, 2020	December 31, 2019
Cash	$ 30,000	$ 10,000
Accounts receivable (net)	72,500	126,000
Inventory	200,000	180,000
Accounts payable	50,000	90,000
Notes payable	30,000	60,000
Common stock, $100 par	400,000	400,000
Retained earnings	113,500	101,000

Additional information:

1. The inventory turnover is 3.8 times.
2. The return on common stockholders' equity is 22%. The company had no additional paid-in capital.
3. The accounts receivable turnover is 11.2 times.
4. The return on assets is 18%.
5. Total assets at December 31, 2019, were $605,000.

Instructions

Compute the following for Panza Corporation.

a. Cost of goods sold for 2020.

b. Net credit sales for 2020.

c. Net income for 2020.

d. Total assets at December 31, 2020.

E18.13 (LO 3) The condensed financial statements of Ness Company for the years 2019 and 2020 are presented below.

Compute ratios.

Ness Company
Balance Sheets
December 31 (in thousands)

	2020	2019
Current assets		
Cash and cash equivalents	$ 330	$ 360
Accounts receivable (net)	470	400
Inventory	460	390
Prepaid expenses	130	160
Total current assets	1,390	1,310
Property, plant, and equipment (net)	410	380
Investments	10	10
Intangibles and other assets	530	510
Total assets	$2,340	$2,210
Current liabilities	$ 820	$ 790
Long-term liabilities	480	380
Stockholders' equity—common	1,040	1,040
Total liabilities and stockholders' equity	$2,340	$2,210

Ness Company
Income Statements
For the Years Ended December 31 (in thousands)

	2020	2019
Sales revenue	$3,800	$3,460
Costs and expenses		
Cost of goods sold	970	890
Selling & administrative expenses	2,400	2,330
Interest expense	10	20
Total costs and expenses	3,380	3,240
Income before income taxes	420	220
Income tax expense	168	88
Net income	$ 252	$ 132

Compute the following ratios for 2020 and 2019.

a. Current ratio.

b. Inventory turnover. (Inventory on December 31, 2018, was $340.)

c. Profit margin.

d. Return on assets. (Assets on December 31, 2018, were $1,900.)

e. Return on common stockholders' equity. (Equity on December 31, 2018, was $900.)

f. Debt to assets ratio.

g. Times interest earned.

Problems: Set A

Prepare vertical analysis and comment on profitability.

P18.1A (LO 2, 3) Writing Here are comparative statement data for Duke Company and Lord Company, two competitors. All balance sheet data are as of December 31, 2020, and December 31, 2019.

	Duke Company		Lord Company	
	2020	**2019**	**2020**	**2019**
Net sales	$1,849,000		$546,000	
Cost of goods sold	1,063,200		289,000	
Operating expenses	240,000		82,000	
Interest expense	6,800		3,600	
Income tax expense	62,000		28,000	
Current assets	325,975	$312,410	83,336	$ 79,467
Plant assets (net)	526,800	500,000	139,728	125,812
Current liabilities	66,325	75,815	35,348	30,281
Long-term liabilities	113,990	90,000	29,620	25,000
Common stock, $10 par	500,000	500,000	120,000	120,000
Retained earnings	172,460	146,595	38,096	29,998

Instructions

a. Prepare a vertical analysis of the 2020 income statement data for Duke Company and Lord Company.

b. Comment on the relative profitability of the companies by computing the 2020 return on assets and the return on common stockholders' equity for both companies.

Compute ratios from balance sheets and income statements.

P18.2A (LO 3) The comparative statements of Wahlberg Company are presented here.

Wahlberg Company
Income Statements
For the Years Ended December 31

	2020	**2019**
Net sales	$1,890,540	$1,750,500
Cost of goods sold	1,058,540	1,006,000
Gross profit	832,000	744,500
Selling and administrative expenses	500,000	479,000
Income from operations	332,000	265,500
Other expenses and losses		
Interest expense	22,000	20,000
Income before income taxes	310,000	245,500
Income tax expense	92,000	73,000
Net income	$ 218,000	$ 172,500

Wahlberg Company
Balance Sheets
December 31

Assets	**2020**	**2019**
Current assets		
Cash	$ 60,100	$ 64,200
Debt investments (short-term)	74,000	50,000
Accounts receivable	117,800	102,800
Inventory	126,000	115,500
Total current assets	377,900	332,500
Plant assets (net)	649,000	520,300
Total assets	$1,026,900	$852,800
Liabilities and Stockholders' Equity		
Current liabilities		
Accounts payable	$ 160,000	$145,400
Income taxes payable	43,500	42,000
Total current liabilities	203,500	187,400
Bonds payable	220,000	200,000
Total liabilities	423,500	387,400
Stockholders' equity		
Common stock ($5 par)	290,000	300,000
Retained earnings	313,400	165,400
Total stockholders' equity	603,400	465,400
Total liabilities and stockholders' equity	$1,026,900	$852,800

All sales were on account. Net cash provided by operating activities for 2020 was $220,000. Capital expenditures were $136,000, and cash dividends were $70,000.

Instructions

Compute the following ratios for 2020.

a. Earnings per share.
b. Return on common stockholders' equity.
c. Return on assets.
d. Current ratio.
e. Accounts receivable turnover.
f. Average collection period.
g. Inventory turnover.
h. Days in inventory.
i. Times interest earned.
j. Asset turnover.
k. Debt to assets ratio.
l. Free cash flow.

P18.3A (LO 3) Writing Condensed balance sheet and income statement data for Jergan Corporation are presented here.

Perform ratio analysis, and discuss changes in financial position and operating results.

Excel

Jergan Corporation
Balance Sheets
December 31

	2020	**2019**	**2018**
Cash	$ 30,000	$ 20,000	$ 18,000
Accounts receivable (net)	50,000	45,000	48,000
Other current assets	90,000	95,000	64,000
Investments	55,000	70,000	45,000
Plant and equipment (net)	500,000	370,000	358,000
	$725,000	$600,000	$533,000
Current liabilities	$ 85,000	$ 80,000	$ 70,000
Long-term debt	145,000	85,000	50,000
Common stock, $10 par	320,000	310,000	300,000
Retained earnings	175,000	125,000	113,000
	$725,000	$600,000	$533,000

Jergan Corporation
Income Statements
For the Years Ended December 31

	2020	2019
Sales revenue	$740,000	$600,000
Less: Sales returns and allowances	40,000	30,000
Net sales	700,000	570,000
Cost of goods sold	425,000	350,000
Gross profit	275,000	220,000
Operating expenses (including income taxes)	180,000	150,000
Net income	$ 95,000	$ 70,000

Additional information:

1. The market price of Jergan's common stock was $7.00, $7.50, and $8.50 for 2018, 2019, and 2020, respectively.
2. You must compute dividends paid. All dividends were paid in cash.

Instructions

a. Compute the following ratios for 2019 and 2020.

1. Profit margin.
2. Gross profit rate.
3. Asset turnover.
4. Earnings per share.
5. Price-earnings ratio.
6. Payout ratio.
7. Debt to assets ratio.

b. Based on the ratios calculated, discuss briefly the improvement or lack thereof in the financial position and operating results from 2019 to 2020 of Jergan Corporation.

Compute ratios; comment on overall liquidity and profitability.

P18.4A (LO 3) The following financial information is for Priscoll Company.

Priscoll Company
Balance Sheets
December 31

Assets	2020	2019
Cash	$ 70,000	$ 65,000
Debt investments (short-term)	55,000	40,000
Accounts receivable	104,000	90,000
Inventory	230,000	165,000
Prepaid expenses	25,000	23,000
Land	130,000	130,000
Building and equipment (net)	260,000	185,000
Total assets	$874,000	$698,000
Liabilities and Stockholders' Equity		
Notes payable (short-term)	$170,000	$120,000
Accounts payable	65,000	52,000
Accrued liabilities	40,000	40,000
Bonds payable, due 2023	250,000	170,000
Common stock, $10 par	200,000	200,000
Retained earnings	149,000	116,000
Total liabilities and stockholders' equity	$874,000	$698,000

Priscoll Company
Income Statements
For the Years Ended December 31

	2020	2019
Sales revenue	$882,000	$790,000
Cost of goods sold	640,000	575,000
Gross profit	242,000	215,000
Operating expenses	190,000	167,000
Net income	$ 52,000	$ 48,000

Additional information:

1. Inventory at the beginning of 2019 was $115,000.
2. Accounts receivable (net) at the beginning of 2019 were $86,000.
3. Total assets at the beginning of 2019 were $660,000.
4. No common stock transactions occurred during 2019 or 2020.
5. All sales were on account.

Instructions

a. Indicate, by using ratios, the change in liquidity and profitability of Priscoll Company from 2019 to 2020. (*Note:* Not all profitability ratios can be computed nor can cash-basis ratios be computed.)

b. The following are three independent situations and a ratio that may be affected. For each situation, compute the affected ratio (1) as of December 31, 2020, and (2) as of December 31, 2021, after giving effect to the situation.

Situation	Ratio
1. 18,000 shares of common stock were sold at par on July 1, 2021. Net income for 2021 was $54,000.	Return on common stockholders' equity
2. All of the notes payable were paid in 2021. All other liabilities remained at their December 31, 2020, levels. At December 31, 2021, total assets were $900,000.	Debt to assets ratio
3. The market price of common stock was $9 and $12 on December 31, 2020 and 2021, respectively. Net income for 2021 was $54,000.	Price-earnings ratio

P18.5A **(LO 3)** **Writing** Suppose selected financial data of **Target** and **Wal-Mart** for 2020 are presented here (in millions).

Compute selected ratios, and compare liquidity, profitability, and solvency for two companies.

	Target Corporation	Wal-Mart Stores, Inc.
	Income Statement Data for Year	
Net sales	$65,357	$408,214
Cost of goods sold	45,583	304,657
Selling and administrative expenses	15,101	79,607
Interest expense	707	2,065
Other income (expense)	(94)	(411)
Income tax expense	1,384	7,139
Net income	$ 2,488	$ 14,335
	Balance Sheet Data (End of Year)	
Current assets	$18,424	$ 48,331
Noncurrent assets	26,109	122,375
Total assets	$44,533	$170,706
Current liabilities	$11,327	$ 55,561
Long-term debt	17,859	44,089
Total stockholders' equity	15,347	71,056
Total liabilities and stockholders' equity	$44,533	$170,706
	Beginning-of-Year Balances	
Total assets	$44,106	$163,429
Total stockholders' equity	13,712	65,682
Current liabilities	10,512	55,390
Total liabilities	30,394	97,747

	Target Corporation	Wal-Mart Stores, Inc.
	Other Data	
Average net accounts receivable	$ 7,525	$ 4,025
Average inventory	6,942	33,836
Net cash provided by operating activities	5,881	26,249
Capital expenditures	1,729	12,184
Dividends	496	4,217

Instructions

a. For each company, compute the following ratios.

1. Current ratio.
2. Accounts receivable turnover.
3. Average collection period.
4. Inventory turnover.
5. Days in inventory.
6. Profit margin.
7. Asset turnover.
8. Return on assets.
9. Return on common stockholders' equity.
10. Debt to assets ratio.
11. Times interest earned.
12. Free cash flow.

b. Compare the liquidity, solvency, and profitability of the two companies.

Continuing Case

© leungchopan/ Shutterstock

Cookie Creations

(*Note:* This is a continuation of the Cookie Creations case from Chapters 1 through 17.)

CC18 Natalie and Curtis have comparative balance sheets and income statements for Cookie & Coffee Creations Inc. They have been told that they can use these financial statements to prepare horizontal and vertical analyses, to calculate financial ratios, to analyze how their business is doing, and to make some decisions they have been considering.

Go to **WileyPLUS** *for complete case details and instructions.*

Ethics Case

EC18 René Kelly, president of RL Industries, wishes to issue a press release to bolster her company's image and maybe even its stock price, which has been gradually falling. As controller, you have been asked to provide a list of 20 financial ratios and other operating statistics for RL Industries' first-quarter financials and operations.

Two days after you provide the data requested, Erin Lourdes, the public relations director of RL, asks you to prove the accuracy of the financial and operating data contained in the press release written by the president and edited by Erin. In the news release, the president highlights the sales increase of 25% over last year's first quarter and the positive change in the current ratio from 1.5:1 last year to 3:1 this year. She also emphasizes that production was up 50% over the prior year's first quarter.

You note that the release contains only positive or improved ratios and none of the negative or deteriorated ratios. For instance, no mention is made that the debt to assets ratio has increased from 35% to 55%, that inventories are up 89%, and that although the current ratio improved, the accounts receivable turnover fell from 12 to 9. Nor is there any mention that the reported profit for the quarter would have been a loss had not the estimated lives of RL plant and machinery been increased by 30%. Erin emphasized, "The Pres wants this release by early this afternoon."

Instructions

a. Who are the stakeholders in this situation?

b. Is there anything unethical in the president's actions?

c. Should you as controller remain silent? Does Erin have any responsibility?

Expand Your Critical Thinking

Financial Reporting Problem: Apple Inc.

CT18.1 Your parents are considering investing in **Apple Inc.** common stock. They ask you, as an accounting expert, to make an analysis of the company for them. Apple's financial statements are presented in Appendix A. The complete annual report, including the notes to the financial statements, is available at the company's website.

Instructions

(Follow the approach in the chapter for rounding numbers.)

a. Make a 3-year trend analysis, using 2013 as the base year, of (1) net sales and (2) net income. Comment on the significance of the trend results.

b. Compute for 2015 and 2014 the (1) profit margin, (2) asset turnover, (3) return on assets, and (4) return on common stockholders' equity. How would you evaluate Apple's profitability? Total assets at September 28, 2013, were $207,000 and total stockholders' equity at September 28, 2013, was $123,549.

c. Compute for 2015 and 2014 the (1) debt to assets ratio and (2) times interest earned. How would you evaluate Apple's long-term solvency?

d. What information outside the annual report may also be useful to your parents in making a decision about Apple?

Comparative Analysis Problem: PepsiCo, Inc. vs. The Coca-Cola Company

CT18.2 **PepsiCo**'s financial statements are presented in Appendix B. Financial statements of **The Coca-Cola Company** are presented in Appendix C. The complete annual reports of PepsiCo and Coca-Cola, including the notes to the financial statements, are available at each company's respective website.

Instructions

a. Based on the information contained in these financial statements, determine each of the following for each company.

1. The percentage increase (decrease) in (i) net sales and (ii) net income from 2014 to 2015.
2. The percentage increase in (i) total assets and (ii) total common stockholders' (shareholders') equity from 2014 to 2015.
3. The basic earnings per share and price-earnings ratio for 2015. (For both PepsiCo and Coca-Cola, use the basic earnings per share.) Coca-Cola's common stock had a market price of $42.63 at the end of fiscal-year 2015, and PepsiCo's common stock had a market price of $103.41.

b. What conclusions concerning the two companies can be drawn from these data?

Comparative Analysis Problem: Amazon.com, Inc. vs. Wal-Mart Stores, Inc.

CT18.3 **Amazon.com, Inc.**'s financial statements are presented in Appendix D. Financial statements of **Wal-Mart Stores, Inc.** are presented in Appendix E. The complete annual reports of Amazon and Wal-Mart, including the notes to the financial statements, are available at each company's respective website.

Instructions

a. Based on the information contained in these financial statements, determine each of the following for each company.

1. The percentage increase (decrease) in (i) net sales and (ii) net income from 2014 to 2015.
2. The percentage increase in (i) total assets and (ii) total common stockholders' (shareholders') equity from 2014 to 2015.
3. The basic earnings per share and price-earnings ratio for 2015. (For both Amazon and Wal-Mart, use the basic earnings per share.) Amazon's common stock had a market price of $398.79 at the end of fiscal-year 2015, and Wal-Mart's common stock had a market price of $74.68.

b. What conclusions concerning the two companies can be drawn from these data?

Decision-Making Across the Organization

CT18.4 You are a loan officer for White Sands Bank of Taos. Paul Jason, president of P. Jason Corporation, has just left your office. He is interested in an 8-year loan to expand the company's operations. The borrowed funds would be used to purchase new equipment. As evidence of the company's debt-worthiness, Jason provided you with the following facts.

	2020	2019
Current ratio	3.1	2.1
Asset turnover	2.8	2.2
Net income	Up 32%	Down 8%
Earnings per share	\$3.30	\$2.50

Jason is a very insistent (some would say pushy) man. When you told him that you would need additional information before making your decision, he acted offended and said, "What more could you possibly want to know?" You responded that, at a minimum, you would need complete, audited financial statements.

Instructions

With the class divided into groups, answer the following.

a. Explain why you would want the financial statements to be audited.

b. Discuss the implications of the ratios provided for the lending decision you are to make. That is, does the information paint a favorable picture? Are these ratios relevant to the decision?

c. List three other ratios that you would want to calculate for this company, and explain why you would use each.

Real-World Focus

CT18.5 ***Purpose:*** To employ comparative data and industry data to evaluate a company's performance and financial position.

Instructions

Identify two competing companies and then go to the Money homepage of the **MSN** website. Under the "Fundamentals" heading, use the Growth, Profitability, Financial health, Price ratios, and Management effectiveness tabs to answer the following questions.

a. Evaluate the company's liquidity relative to the industry averages and to the competitor that you chose.

b. Evaluate the company's solvency relative to the industry averages and to the competitor that you chose.

c. Evaluate the company's profitability relative to the industry averages and to the competitor that you chose.

CT18.6 The April 25, 2012, edition of the *Wall Street Journal* contains an article by Spencer Jakab entitled "Amazon's Valuation Is Hard to Justify."

Instructions

Read the article and answer the following questions.

a. Explain what is meant by the statement that "On a split-adjusted basis, today's share price is the equivalent of \$1,166."

b. The article says that **Amazon.com** nearly doubled its capital spending on items such as fulfillment centers (sophisticated warehouses where it finds, packages, and ships goods to customers). Discuss the implications that this spending would have on the company's return on assets in the short-term and in the long-term.

c. How does Amazon's P-E ratio compare to that of **Apple**, **Netflix**, and **Wal-Mart**? What does this suggest about investors' expectations about Amazon's future earnings?

d. What factor does the article cite as a possible hurdle that might reduce Amazon's ability to raise its operating margin back to previous levels?

Communication Activity

CT18.7 Larry Dundee is the chief executive officer of Palmer Electronics. Dundee is an expert engineer but a novice in accounting. Dundee asks you, as an accounting student, to explain (a) the bases for comparison in analyzing Palmer's financial statements and (b) the factors affecting quality of earnings.

Instructions

Write a memo to Larry Dundee that explains the basis for comparison and the factors affecting quality of earnings.

All About You

CT18.8 In this chapter, you learned how to use many tools for performing a financial analysis of a company. When making personal investments, however, it is most likely that you won't be buying stocks and bonds in individual companies. Instead, when most people want to invest in stock, they buy mutual funds. By investing in a mutual fund, you reduce your risk because the fund diversifies by buying the stock of a variety of different companies, bonds, and other investments, depending on the stated goals of the fund.

Before you invest in a fund, you will need to decide what type of fund you want. For example, do you want a fund that has the potential of high growth (but also high risk), or are you looking for lower risk and a steady stream of income? Do you want a fund that invests only in U.S. companies, or do you want one that invests globally? Many resources are available to help you with these types of decisions.

Instructions

Search the Internet for "investment allocation questionnaire" and then complete one from a reputable some. Which type of investment fund is appropriate for you and why?

FASB Codification Activity

CT18.9 If your school has a subscription to the FASB Codification, log in and prepare responses to the following. Use the Master Glossary for determining the proper definitions.

a. Discontinued operations.

b. Comprehensive income.

A Look at IFRS

LEARNING OBJECTIVE 4

Compare financial statement analysis and income statement presentation under GAAP and IFRS.

The tools of financial statement analysis are the same throughout the world. Techniques such as vertical and horizontal analysis, for example, are tools used by analysts regardless of whether GAAP- or IFRS-related financial statements are being evaluated. In addition, the ratios provided in the textbook are the same ones that are used internationally.

The beginning of this chapter relates to the income statement. As in GAAP, the income statement is a required statement under IFRS. In addition, the content and presentation of an IFRS income statement is similar to the one used for GAAP. *IAS 1* (revised), "Presentation of Financial Statements," provides general guidelines for the reporting of income statement information. In general, the differences in the presentation of financial statement information are relatively minor.

Key Points

Following are the key similarities between GAAP and IFRS as related to financial statement analysis and income statement presentation. There are no significant differences between the two standards.

- The tools of financial statement analysis covered in this chapter are universal and therefore no significant differences exist in the analysis methods used.
- The basic objectives of the income statement are the same under both GAAP and IFRS. As indicated in the textbook, a very important objective is to ensure that users of the income statement can evaluate the sustainable income of the company. Thus, both the IASB and the FASB are interested in distinguishing normal levels of income from unusual items in order to better predict a company's future profitability.
- The basic accounting for discontinued operations is the same under IFRS and GAAP.

- The accounting for changes in accounting principles and changes in accounting estimates are the same for both GAAP and IFRS.
- Both GAAP and IFRS follow the same approach in reporting comprehensive income.

Looking to the Future

The FASB and the IASB are working on a project that would rework the structure of financial statements. Recently, the IASB decided to require a statement of comprehensive income, similar to what was required under GAAP. In addition, another part of this project addresses the issue of how to classify various items in the income statement. A main goal of this new approach is to provide information that better represents how businesses are run. In addition, the approach draws attention away from one number—net income.

IFRS Practice

IFRS Self-Test Questions

1. The basic tools of financial analysis are the same under both GAAP and IFRS **except** that:

   a. horizontal analysis cannot be done because the format of the statements is sometimes different.

   b. analysis is different because vertical analysis cannot be done under IFRS.

   c. the current ratio cannot be computed because current liabilities are often reported before current assets in IFRS statements of position.

   d. None of the above.

2. Presentation of comprehensive income must be reported under IFRS in:

   a. the statement of stockholders' equity.

   b. the income statement ending with net income.

   c. the notes to the financial statements.

   d. a statement of comprehensive income.

3. In preparing its income statement for 2020, Parmalane assembles the following information.

Sales revenue	$500,000
Cost of goods sold	300,000
Operating expenses	40,000
Loss on discontinued operations	20,000

Ignoring income taxes, what is Parmalane's income from continuing operations for 2020 under IFRS?

   a. $260,000.

   b. $250,000.

   c. $240,000.

   d. $160,000.

International Financial Reporting Problem: Louis Vuitton

IFRS18.1 The financial statements of **Louis Vuitton** are presented in Appendix F. The complete annual report, including the notes to its financial statements, is available at the company's website.

Instructions

Use the company's **2015 annual report** to answer the following questions.

a. What was the company's profit margin for 2015? Has it increased or decreased from 2014?

b. What was the company's operating profit for 2015?

c. The company reported comprehensive income of €4,148 million in 2015. What are the other comprehensive gains and losses recorded in 2015?

Answers to IFRS Self-Test Questions

1. d **2.** d **3.** d

CHECKLIST OF KEY FIGURES
for Exercises in
Weygandt, Kimmel, & Kieso
ACCOUNTING PRINCIPLES, 13th Edition, Volume I
Chapters 1-12

Exer. No.	Check Figures
1-8	(b) Increase in owner's equity $15,740. (c) Net income, $2,740.
1-9	Total assets $17,640.
1-10	(a) Net income $62,000. (b) Net loss $24,000. (c) Net income $43,000.
1-11	(a) $25,000; (c) $49,000. (b) $7,000; (d) $15,000.
1-12	Net income $18,100. Capital, Dec. 31 $54,100.
1-13	Total assets $75,500.
1-14	(a) Net income $45,000. (b) Total assets $156,000.
1-15	Net income $135,500.
1-16	Capital, Dec. 31 $68,000.
2-11	(b) Trial balance totals $12,000.
2-12	(b) Trial balance totals $19,200.
2-13	(b) Trial balance totals $11,990.
2-14	(b) Cash ending balance $2,100.
2-16	Trial balance totals $74,819.
3-3	(b) Net income $35,000.
3-10	Net income $1,250.
3-11	(a) $800. (b) $4,800; Aug. 1, 2019. (c) $1,820.
3-14	Net Income $55,000.
3-18	Net income $11,400. Total assets $34,300.
3-19	(b) Cash received $145,000.
3-21	(c) Insurance expense $160; Supplies expense $1,050; Service revenue $2,100.
4-1	Balance sheet column totals $5,260.
4-2	Balance sheet column totals $46,820.
4-3	Net income $3,283; Total assets $38,270.
4-4	(c) Post-closing trial balance $43,170.
4-6	(a) Accounts Receivable $25,000.
4-7	(b) Post-closing trial balance $8,096.
4-8	(c) Post-closing trial balance $34,520.
4-9	(a) Net loss ($8,100). (b) Total assets $27,120.
4-11	(b) Net income $5,000.
4-14	(a) Current assets $37,240; Current liabilities $46,100.
4-16	Current assets $9,960; Current liabilities $1,714.
4-17	(a) Net loss ($3,800). (b) Total assets $52,380.
4-19	(e) Interest expense balance $800.
5-2	(a) Cash in full $19,600. (b) Cash paid $20,000.
5-4	(a) Cash in full $7,546.
5-5	(a) Sales discounts $5,500. (b) Cash received $550,000.
5-6	(a) Net sales $782,000.
5-7	(b) Cost of goods sold $61,400.
5-8	(b) Cost of goods sold $218,600.
5-9	(a) Net income $43,000.
5-10	(a) Income from operations $186,000. (b)Total revenues $2,228,000.
5-12	(c) Income from operations $153,000; Net income $142,000.
5-13	(b) $31,000. (d) $107,000. (f) $23,500.
5-14	(b) $30,000; (d) $11,000; (f) $57,000.
5-16	Net Income $9,880.
5-17	Cost of goods sold $148,500.
5-18	(a) Gross profit $330,000.
5-19	(b) $1,690; (d) $30; (f) $120; (h) $1,730; (j) $6,200; (l) $43,330.
5-20	(a) 5. Cash paid $21,756.
5-21	(a) 5. Cash paid $16,660.
6-1	Inventory $310,000.
6-2	Inventory $516,000.
6-4	(a) $188. (b) Minimize $188; Maximize $168.
6-5	(a) FIFO $2,100; LIFO $1,940.
6-6	FIFO inventory $264; LIFO inventory $176.
6-7	(a) FIFO inventory $700; LIFO inventory $500.

6-8 (a) 1. Ending inventory $9,750.
3. Ending inventory $9,000.
6-9 (a) Inventory $611; Cost of goods sold $4,889.
6-10 2019 $143,000; 2020 $162,000.
6-11 (a) 2019 $53,000; 2020 $62,000.
(b) $0.
6-12 End. inventory $4,510.
6-13 Ending inventory $26,300.
6-14 2019: Inventory turnover 3.29; Days in inventory 110.9; Gross profit rate 28%.
6-15 (a) Sooner 3.80; 96 days.
6-16 FIFO $1,320; LIFO $1,260; Average $1,303.
6-17 (a) Cost of goods sold:
FIFO $4,800; LIFO $5,000; Average $4,846.
6-18 (a) FIFO $2,100; LIFO $2,017; Average $2,085.
6-19 (a) Gross profit $294,000.
(b) Ending inventory $80,000.
6-20 (a) $16,000; (b) $31,000.
6-21 Women $28,200; Men $44,400.

7-1 (a) $370,400; (b) $95,900.
7-3 (c) $7,700.
7-4 (b) $12,000.
7-5 (b) $10,750.
7-6 (b) Sales journal total $1,420;
Purchases journal total $1,510.
7-7 (b) Cash rec. journal - cash $55,300; Cash pay. journal - cash $8,400.
7-11 (a) CP journal $28,340;
Dooley balance 2,300.
(b) $1,400, $265, $550.
7-12 (a) Purchases journal total $9,300.
7-13 EOM posting $975.
7-14 (a) $45,000; (d) $25,900.

8-7 Cash Over and Short $3.00.
8-8 Cash Over and Short $3.
8-9 (a) Adj. cash bal. $3,360.20.
8-10 Total $2,070.
8-11 (a) Adj. cash bal. per books $7,972.
8-12 (a) Adj. cash bal. per bank $19,489.
8-13 (a) $1,070; (b) $1,480.
(c) $2,400; (d) $3,400.
8-14 (a) Total $88,500.

9-2 Sales discounts $90.
9-3 (a) Sales discount $140.
(b) Interest $40.
9-6 (a) $8,675; (b) $6,575.
9-7 Bad debt expense $13,200.
9-8 Bad debt expense $9,000.
9-9 Service charge expense
(a) $19,500;
(b) $120.
9-10 (a) Interest revenue $10.
(b) Service charge expense $4.
9-11 (a) Service charge expense $90;
Interest revenue $120.
9-12 (a) Interest $545.
9-13 Interest receivable $600.
9-14 Total 2020 interest revenue $3,675.
9-15 (b) Interest revenue $315.
9-17 (b) 8.

10-3 (a) $88,000.
10-5 (a) $1.40 per mile.
(b) 2020 depreciation expense $36,400.
10-6 (a) $6,900; (b) $23,460.
(c) $15,000; $54,000.
10-7 (a) (3) 2021 depreciation $6,375.
10-8 (a) Building $15,000;
Warehouse $5,000.
10-9 June 30 Gain $500;
Dec. 31 Loss $8,000.
10-10 (a) Gain on disposal $2,000.
(d) Loss on disposal $9,000.
10-11 (a) Depletion $80,000.
10-12 Amort. Exp. $10,000.
10-13 Amort. Exp. $109,000;
10-14 2.5 times.
10-15 (a) Cost of new trucks $55,000;
Loss $4,000.
(b) Cost of new machine $14,000.
10-16 (a) Loss on disposal $4,000.
(b) Cost of new truck $3,000.

11-1 Total interest expense--2020 $2,600.
11-2 (d) $3,600.
11-3 2. Sales Taxes Payable $1,680.
11-4 (b) Subscription Revenue $25,000.
(c) Subscription Revenue $75,000.
11-5 (b) Warranty Expense $12,900.
(c) Warranty Liab. $7,500 dr.
11-7 (a) Total current liab. $163,000.
11-8 (a) 2020 Current ratio 2.20:1;
2020 Working capital $5,898.
(b) Current ratio 2.26:1.
11-9 (a) (1) $688; (2) $52.63; (3) $29;

(4) $13.76; (5) $567.61.

11-10 Seligman $344.25; Marshall $344.25.

11-11 (a) Net pay $1,547.18.
(b) Payroll tax expense $260.38.

11-12 (a) (1) $900; (2) $10,000; (3) $400; (4) $2,405; (5) $10,000.

11-13 (a) FICA $60,065; SUTA $5,400; FUTA $800.
(b) Payroll tax exp. $66,265.

11-14 Vacation ben. exp. $2,800; Pension expense $4,000.

11-15 1. Vacation ben. exp. $14,000.

12-2 (b) $222,000.

12-3 Vopat, Capital $46,500.

12-4 (a) (1) McGill $30,600.
(2) McGill $22,200.

12-5 (c) Coburn, Capital $41,000.
(d) Webb, Capital $105,000.

12-6 (a) Dody, Capital $33,000.
(b) Total owners' equity $65,000.

12-7 Nick, Capital $83,000; Frank, Capital $69,000.

12-8 Cash: Floyd $48,000, DeWitt $22,000.

12-9 (a) Gain on realization $5,000.
(d) DeWitt $22,000.

12-10 (a) (2) Utech, Capital $15,000.
(b) (2) Vogel, Capital $12,000.

12-11 (a) Jernigan, Capital $17,000.
(b) Jernigan, Capital $13,000.
(c) Jernigan, Capital $7,000.

12-12 (a) Bonus: Pagon $9,000, Tabor $6,000.
(b) Bonus: Wolford $13,000.

12-13 1. Essex, Capital $15,000.
2. Gilmore, Capital $30,000.
3. Essex, Capital $30,000.

12-14 1. Bonus: Rice $4,000.
2. Bonus: Higgins $5,000. Mayo $3,000.

12-15 (a) Bonus: Foss $8,000, Espinosa $3,200.
(b) Bonus: Foss $10,000.

CHECKLIST OF KEY FIGURES
for Exercises in
Weygandt, Kimmel, & Kieso
ACCOUNTING PRINCIPLES, 13th Edition,
Volume II, Chapters 13 - 27

Exer. No.	Check Figures
13-3	(a) Total paid-in cap. in excess of par $80,000. (b) Total paid-in cap. in excess of stated value $520,000.
13-4	(a) Paid-in cap. in excess of par $42,000
13-5	Mar. 2 Organ. expense $30,000.
13-6	1. Land $110,000; 2. Land $220,000.
13-7	(a) Paid-in cap. from treasury stock $12,000 (net). (b) Ret. Earnings $4,000(Dr.).
13-9	(b) Preferred stock $1,600,000; Paid-in cap. in excess of par-pref. $144,000.
13-10	Total paid-in cap. in excess of par $130,000.
13-11	Total stock. equity $4,294,000.
13-12	(a) 590,000; (c) $50.
13-13	Total stock. equity $11,682.
13-15	Total stock. equity $2, 719,000.
14-1	(a) Total dividends declared $266,400.
14-2	(a) 2021 pref. dividends $6,000. (b) 2021 pref. dividends $7,000.
14-3	(a) Debit to Stock Div. $378,000. (b) $720,000.
14-4	Outstanding shares: after stock div. 52,500; after stock split 100,000.
14-5	(b) Com. stock $440,000; Ret. Earnings $35,000.
14-8	Ending balance $710,000.
14-9	Ending balance $345,000.
14-10	2020 return on com. S. E. 18.3%.
14-11	2020 payout ratio 23.5%.
14-12	(a) Net income $129,500.
14-13	(a) Net income $55,650.
14-14	Net income $490,000.
14-15	2020 EPS $2.70.
14-16	2020 EPS $1.20.
14-17	(a) $2.25; (b) $2.50.
14-18	(a) Tot. stock. equity $11,626.
14-19	(a) Book value/sh. $13.50.
15-2	(b) Interest accrued $50,000.
15-3	(b) Interest expense $32,000.
15-4	(b) Interest expense $36,000.
15-5	(c) Gain on bond redemption $49,000.
15-6	(a) (2) Total cost of borrow. $215,000.
15-7	(b) Loss $18,000. (c) Interest expense $70,000.
15-8	1. Loss $15,100; 2. Gain $4,000.
15-9	First install. interest $20,000; Second install. interest $22,000.
15-10	(a) Second install. interest $22,720. (b) Current liab. $17,280.
15-11	Total long-term liab. $301,500.
15-12	EPS-stock $2.67, bonds $3.09.
15-13	(c) 13.5 times.
15-15	(b) Amortization $900.
15-16	(b) Amortization $7,000.
15-17	(b) Amortization $858.
15-18	(b) Amortization $2,122.
16-2	2. Accrued interest $3,600. 4. Gain on sale $3,000.
16-3	Loss on sale $1,500.
16-4	Total dividend revenue $900.
16-5	Gain on sale $1,600.
16-6	Loss on sale $300.
16-7	(b) Stock investments $215,000.
16-8	(a) Dividend revenue $6,000. (b) Revenue from investment $32,000.
16-10	(a) Unrealized gain or loss $2,000.
16-11	(a) Unrealized gain or loss $2,000.
16-12	(a) Trading-unrealized gain $6,000; Avail.-for-sale-unrealized gain or loss $4,000.
17-4	Net cash provided $311,000.
17-5	Net cash provided $168,000.
17-6	Net cash provided by operating activities $427,900.
17-7	Net cash provided by operating activities $112,000.
17-8	(a) Net cash provided by operating activities $12,200.
17-9	Net cash provided $129,000.
17-10	(a) Net cash provided by operating activities $29,600.
17-11	Net cash provided by operating activities $77,000.
17-12	(a) Suppliers $4,733.9; (b) Operating expenses $9,365.9.
17-13	Net cash provided $30,000.

17-14 Rent $51,100; Receipts from customers $184,000.
17-15 Total reconciling items $486,000.

18-1 Net income $336,000
18-2 Net income $314,000
18-3 Total assets 15.0% increase.
18-4 Net income: 2019, 8.0%; 2020, 8.8%.
18-5 (a) Total assets increase 6.5%.
(b) Current assets 73.5%.
18-6 (a) Net income decrease 13.9%.
(b) Net income 2020 6.8%.
18-7 (a) Current 2.01:1; Inventory 5.9.
18-8 Feb. 7, 2.43:1.
Feb. 18, 2.66:1.
18-9 (b) 5.4 times (d) 3.6 times.
18-10 (a) 1.5%; (c) 2.4%.
18-11 (a) $1.86; (c) 22.2%.
18-12 (a) $722,000; (c) $111,595.
18-13 (b) 2.28; (d) 11.1%.

19-2 (a) DM 5, 10.
(b) DL 1, 6.
19-4 (a) $170,350; (c) $69,140.
19-5 (a) 3, 7; (c) 1, 2, 4, 9, 10.
19-7 (a) $41,100.
19-8 (a) CGM $323,500.
19-9 Total manfg. costs $411,000.
19-10 (a) $92,150; (c) $36,225; (e) $252,500; (g) $21,700; (i) $267,000.
19-11 (b) $17,000; (d) $60,000; (f) $245,000; (h) $63,000.
19-12 (a) $72,500; (b) $22,100.
19-13 (a) $21,100.
19-14 (a) CGM $537,300.
19-15 (a) 1, 2, 3, 5, 6, 7, 9, 10, 13, 14, 15, 16.
(b) 4, 8, 10, 11, 12.
19-16 (a) $114,800; (b) $28,100.
19-17 (a) RM $5,250; FG $18,630; CGS $43,470.

20-1 (a) Total labor $90,000.
(b) Work in process $76,500.
20-2 (b) Job 430 $9,800; Job 431 $16,560.
20-3 (a) 1. $15,200; 2. 70%, 80%.
20-4 (a) $53,150; (c) $9,200; (e) $342,000; (g) $345,700.
20-5 (a) $2.40/mh; (b) $10,000 underapp.
20-6 (a) (2) 125%; (3) Total cost $7,760.
20-7 7. $81,000.
20-8 Completed jobs $240,930.
20-9 (a) Cost of goods manfg. $151,200.
(b) Gross profit $60,700.
20-10 (a) $9,300, $18,600, $9,500.
(b) $1,200, $9,600, $19,200.
20-11 (b) $32,120.
20-12 (a) $9,600 (Waters).
20-13 (b) $972,000.

21-3 (a) 300; (c) $3.60; (e) $1,440.
21-4 6. $61,200.
21-5 (b) Jan. 13,000 M; 12,200 CC.
May 21,000 M; 19,600 CC.
21-6 (a) 15,000 M; 13,800 CC.
(b) T/O $66,000; WIP $13,500.
21-7 Unit costs: M $3.30; CC $7.50.
T/O $75,600; WIP $14,400.
21-8 (a) 18,000 M; 17,400 CC.
(c) T/O $1,275,000; WIP $60,000.
21-9 (b) M $2.00; CC $5.00.
(c) T/O $210,000; WIP $24,000.
21-10 (b) M $0.55; CC $2.00.
(c) T/O $408,000; WIP $42,000.
21-11 (a) M 44,500; CC 40,000.
(c) T/O $594,475; WIP 27,325.
21-13 M $3.00; CC $2.50.
T/O $302,500; WIP $38,500.
21-14 (b) DM 990; CC 920.
21-15 (a) M 1,100; CC 980.
21-16 (b) M $4.50; CC $23.00.
21-17 (b) M $3.75; CC $2.75.
21-18 (c) T/O $196,400: WIP $10,800.
21-19 (b) $6.00; (d) Tot. cost $5,080.
21-20 M $3.00; CC $1.80; Tot. Costs T/O $243,675

22-3 (a) $600 + $7 per mach. hour.
22-5 (a) Var. cost/MH $.44.
22-6 (b) Var. cost/unit $10.
22-8 (a) $36; (b) $6,000.
22-9 (a) $18; (b) $27,000.
22-10 (a) $48; (b) $52,560.
22-11 (a) 1. $24,000; 2. 1,000.
22-12 (a) $3.40; 32%; (b) $22,400.
22-13 (a) Net inc. $18,000.
22-14 (a) 13,000; (c) $154.
22-15 1. $110,000.
22-16 (a) 1. 400,000; 2. $1,600,000.
(c) 1. $400,000; 2. 20%.
22-17 (b) $48,750; (d) Tot. CM $40,000.
22-18 (c) Tot. costs $3,785.47.

23-2 (a) NI increase $3,000.
23-3 (a) NI increase $4,200.
23-4 NI increase $250,000.
23-5 (a) Make $420,000; Buy $433,500.
(c) Cost saving $6,500.
23-6 I.NI increase $25,000.
23-7 (a) NI decrease $(45)
23-8 (a) NI decrease $(11.50)
23-9 Process further; increases NI $5/unit.
23-10 (b) NI $60,000.
23-11 Incr. prof. – Sulu $95,000
23-12 (b) Inc. prof. – D $6,000
23-13 (b) NI increase $15,000.
23-14 Yes; NI $6,000 higher.
23-15 No; NI $9,000 lower.
23-16 (b) NI Tingler $7,500.
23-17 NI (C & E) $449,500.

24-2 For 6 months: Total units 69,000; Total sales $1,305,000.
24-3 Total rev. – Q 1: $619,000; Q 3: $505,000.
24-4 Required prod. units: HD-240, 30,500 units.
24-5 Total cost of dir. mat. purchases: Jan. $57,600; March $28,800.
24-6 (a) Required prod. units 11,500.
(b) Total cost of dir. mat. purchases $147,360.
24-7 Total costs of materials $20,580.
24-8 (b) Total cost of dir. mat. purchases $88,960.
24-9 Total dir. labor cost $2,835,000.
24-10 Total dir. labor cost $544,800.
24-11 Total overhead $443,000.
24-12 Total sell. and admin. expenses $138,000.
24-13 (b) Net income $280,000.
24-14 End. cash balances: January $27,500, February $20,000.
24-15 Borrowings $14,000.
24-16 (a) Borrowings $7,000.
24-17 (a) Total collections $219,900.
24-18 (a) (1) Total collections $336,000.
(2) Total payments $43,400.
24-19 Borrowings $13,000.
24-20 (a) Merchandise purchases: June $397,500.
(b) Gross profit $125,000.

25-3 Total costs: 7,000 DLH, $20,700; 8,000 DLH, $22,800.
25-4 (a) Budget $24,900; Actual $23,800.
(b) Budget $23,850; Actual $23,800.
25-5 Total expenses: Sales $170,000, $68,500; Sales $180,000, $70,000.
25-6 (a) Budget $68,500, Actual $69,450.
(b) Budget $70,000, Actual $69,450.
25-7 (a) Total costs; 100,000 units, $1,540,000.
25-8 (a) Total costs; 600 hrs., $22,000.
(d) Cost/Client $46.
25-9 (a) Difference $1,450 F; (b) No.
25-10 (a) Budget $92,000, Actual 93,000.
(b) Budget $77,000, Actual 77,700.
25-11 (a) Difference $550 F.
25-12 (a) Fabricating $50,000 + $2.00;
Assembling $40,000 + $1.60.
(b) Fabricating $156,000;
Assembling $115,200.
25-13 (a) $1,700 U; (b) $5,700 U; (c) $9,400 U.
25-14 (a) Difference $4,125 U.
25-15 (a) 1. $170,000; 3. $130,000; 5. $85,000.
(b) $5,000 U.
25-16 (a) Difference $30,000 F.
25-17 (a) 9%; (b) 1. 11.1%, 2. 12%, 3. 9.4%.
25-18 (a) ROI – Actual 13.0%
25-19 Planes: Contl. mar. $3,000,000; Serv. rev.
$10,000,000.

26-1 (b) Standard cost $28.60.
26-2 Standard cost $5.78.
26-3 Standard cost $78.55.
26-4 (b) Standard rate $16.20.
26-5 (a) P $8,700 F; Q $4,000 U.
(b) P $4,200 U; Q $1,000 F.
26-6 (b) P $6,090 U; Q $7,200 U.
(c) P $4,060 F; Q $4,900 F.
26-7 MP $285 U; MQ $150 U;
LP $280 F; LQ $120 U.
26-8 (a) MP $2,440 F; MQ $2,600 U;
LP $2,075 U; LQ $1,875 F.
26-9 (a) 20,500.
(c) $3.98
26-10 TQ $440 U; TP $398 U.
26-11 TV $3,000 U.
26-12 (a) F $6.
(b) $807,500.
26-13 (a) MP $1,800 F; MQ $1,500 U.
26-14 (a) TP $75 F.
26-15 Quan. purch. 27,500.
26-16 NI $13,500.
26-20 MPV $1,800 U; MQV $2,200 U;
LPV $7,650 F; LQV $550 F;

Overhead applied $84,700.

26-21	(a) $136,000; (b) $139,000 (c) $143,500; (d) $145,900; (e) $163,800.
26-22	MP $285 U; MQ $150 U; LP $280 F; LQ $120 U.
26-23	(a) T $3.30; F $1.20. (b) T $2,040 U; CV $1,680 U.
26-24	(a) 1. Total over. $31,800; 5. VV $600 U.
26-25	(a) TV $1,500 U; CV $1,900 U.

27-1	(a) $4,560 NPV.
27-2	(a) AA 2.50; BB 2.2; CC 1.75. (b) AA $(34), BB $2,019, CC $7,003.
27-3	$2,285,000 net invest.
27-4	$7,522 NPV – Mach. A.
27-6	(a) 4.1 years.
27-7	(a) 22A 10%, 23A 2%, 24A 9%
27.8	15% ARR.
27-9	(a) 7 years.
27-10	(a) 1. 3.8 years; 2. 12.63%.
27.11	(b) 26.67% ARR.
27.12	(a) A $(5,518).

G-9	$567,153.
G-10	$282,334.50.
G-13	$424,925.
G-16	$2,208,698.
G-20	8%.
G-23	76,118.70.
G-27	(a) $85,186.34.

Specimen Financial Statements: Apple Inc.

Once each year, a corporation communicates to its stockholders and other interested parties by issuing a complete set of audited financial statements. The **annual report**, as this communication is called, summarizes the financial results of the company's operations for the year and its plans for the future. Many annual reports are attractive, multicolored, glossy public relations pieces, containing pictures of corporate officers and directors as well as photos and descriptions of new products and new buildings. Yet the basic function of every annual report is to report financial information, almost all of which is a product of the corporation's accounting system.

The content and organization of corporate annual reports have become fairly standardized. Excluding the public relations part of the report (pictures, products, etc.), the following are the traditional financial portions of the annual report:

- Financial Highlights
- Letter to the Stockholders
- Management's Discussion and Analysis
- Financial Statements
- Notes to the Financial Statements
- Management's Responsibility for Financial Reporting
- Management's Report on Internal Control over Financial Reporting
- Report of Independent Registered Public Accounting Firm
- Selected Financial Data

The official SEC filing of the annual report is called a **Form 10-K**, which often omits the public relations pieces found in most standard annual reports. On the following pages, we present **Apple Inc.**'s financial statements taken from the company's 2015 Form 10-K. The complete Form 10-K, including notes to the financial statements, is available at the company's website.

CONSOLIDATED STATEMENTS OF OPERATIONS

(In millions, except number of shares which are reflected in thousands and per share amounts)

	Years ended		
	September 26, 2015	September 27, 2014	September 28, 2013
Net sales	$ 233,715	$ 182,795	$ 170,910
Cost of sales	140,089	112,258	106,606
Gross margin	93,626	70,537	64,304
Operating expenses:			
Research and development	8,067	6,041	4,475
Selling, general and administrative	14,329	11,993	10,830
Total operating expenses	22,396	18,034	15,305
Operating income	71,230	52,503	48,999
Other income/(expense), net	1,285	980	1,156
Income before provision for income taxes	72,515	53,483	50,155
Provision for income taxes	19,121	13,973	13,118
Net income	$ 53,394	$ 39,510	$ 37,037
Earnings per share:			
Basic	$ 9.28	$ 6.49	$ 5.72
Diluted	$ 9.22	$ 6.45	$ 5.68
Shares used in computing earnings per share:			
Basic	5,753,421	6,085,572	6,477,320
Diluted	5,793,069	6,122,663	6,521,634
Cash dividends declared per share	$ 1.98	$ 1.82	$ 1.64

See accompanying Notes to Consolidated Financial Statements.

CONSOLIDATED STATEMENTS OF COMPREHENSIVE INCOME
(In millions)

	Years ended		
	September 26, 2015	September 27, 2014	September 28, 2013
Net income	$ 53,394	$ 39,510	$ 37,037
Other comprehensive income/(loss):			
Change in foreign currency translation, net of tax effects of $201, $50 and $35, respectively	(411)	(137)	(112)
Change in unrealized gains/losses on derivative instruments:			
Change in fair value of derivatives, net of tax benefit/(expense) of $(441), $(297) and $(351), respectively	2,905	1,390	522
Adjustment for net (gains)/losses realized and included in net income, net of tax expense/(benefit) of $630, $(36) and $255, respectively	(3,497)	149	(458)
Total change in unrealized gains/losses on derivative instruments, net of tax	(592)	1,539	64
Change in unrealized gains/losses on marketable securities:			
Change in fair value of marketable securities, net of tax benefit/(expense) of $264, $(153) and $458, respectively	(483)	285	(791)
Adjustment for net (gains)/losses realized and included in net income, net of tax expense/(benefit) of $(32), $71 and $82, respectively	59	(134)	(131)
Total change in unrealized gains/losses on marketable securities, net of tax	(424)	151	(922)
Total other comprehensive income/(loss)	(1,427)	1,553	(970)
Total comprehensive income	$ 51,967	$ 41,063	$ 36,067

See accompanying Notes to Consolidated Financial Statements.

CONSOLIDATED BALANCE SHEETS

(In millions, except number of shares which are reflected in thousands and par value)

	September 26, 2015	September 27, 2014
ASSETS:		
Current assets:		
Cash and cash equivalents	$ 21,120	$ 13,844
Short-term marketable securities	20,481	11,233
Accounts receivable, less allowances of $82 and $86, respectively	16,849	17,460
Inventories	2,349	2,111
Deferred tax assets	5,546	4,318
Vendor non-trade receivables	13,494	9,759
Other current assets	9,539	9,806
Total current assets	89,378	68,531
Long-term marketable securities	164,065	130,162
Property, plant and equipment, net	22,471	20,624
Goodwill	5,116	4,616
Acquired intangible assets, net	3,893	4,142
Other assets	5,556	3,764
Total assets	$ 290,479	$ 231,839
LIABILITIES AND SHAREHOLDERS' EQUITY:		
Current liabilities:		
Accounts payable	$ 35,490	$ 30,196
Accrued expenses	25,181	18,453
Deferred revenue	8,940	8,491
Commercial paper	8,499	6,308
Current portion of long-term debt	2,500	0
Total current liabilities	80,610	63,448
Deferred revenue, non-current	3,624	3,031
Long-term debt	53,463	28,987
Other non-current liabilities	33,427	24,826
Total liabilities	171,124	120,292
Commitments and contingencies		
Shareholders' equity:		
Common stock and additional paid-in capital, $0.00001 par value: 12,600,000 shares authorized; 5,578,753 and 5,866,161 shares issued and outstanding, respectively	27,416	23,313
Retained earnings	92,284	87,152
Accumulated other comprehensive income	(345)	1,082
Total shareholders' equity	119,355	111,547
Total liabilities and shareholders' equity	$ 290,479	$ 231,839

See accompanying Notes to Consolidated Financial Statements.

CONSOLIDATED STATEMENTS OF SHAREHOLDERS' EQUITY

(In millions, except number of shares which are reflected in thousands)

	Common Stock and Additional Paid-In Capital		Retained Earnings	Accumulated Other Comprehensive Income/(Loss)	Total Shareholders' Equity
	Shares	Amount			
Balances as of September 29, 2012	6,574,458	$ 16,422	$ 101,289	$ 499	$ 118,210
Net income	0	0	37,037	0	37,037
Other comprehensive income/(loss)	0	0	0	(970)	(970)
Dividends and dividend equivalents declared	0	0	(10,676)	0	(10,676)
Repurchase of common stock	(328,837)	0	(22,950)	0	(22,950)
Share-based compensation	0	2,253	0	0	2,253
Common stock issued, net of shares withheld for employee taxes	48,873	(143)	(444)	0	(587)
Tax benefit from equity awards, including transfer pricing adjustments	0	1,232	0	0	1,232
Balances as of September 28, 2013	6,294,494	19,764	104,256	(471)	123,549
Net income	0	0	39,510	0	39,510
Other comprehensive income/(loss)	0	0	0	1,553	1,553
Dividends and dividend equivalents declared	0	0	(11,215)	0	(11,215)
Repurchase of common stock	(488,677)	0	(45,000)	0	(45,000)
Share-based compensation	0	2,863	0	0	2,863
Common stock issued, net of shares withheld for employee taxes	60,344	(49)	(399)	0	(448)
Tax benefit from equity awards, including transfer pricing adjustments	0	735	0	0	735
Balances as of September 27, 2014	5,866,161	23,313	87,152	1,082	111,547
Net income	0	0	53,394	0	53,394
Other comprehensive income/(loss)	0	0	0	(1,427)	(1,427)
Dividends and dividend equivalents declared	0	0	(11,627)	0	(11,627)
Repurchase of common stock	(325,032)	0	(36,026)	0	(36,026)
Share-based compensation	0	3,586	0	0	3,586
Common stock issued, net of shares withheld for employee taxes	37,624	(231)	(609)	0	(840)
Tax benefit from equity awards, including transfer pricing adjustments	0	748	0	0	748
Balances as of September 26, 2015	5,578,753	$ 27,416	$ 92,284	$ (345)	$ 119,355

See accompanying Notes to Consolidated Financial Statements.

CONSOLIDATED STATEMENTS OF CASH FLOWS
(In millions)

	Years ended September 26, 2015	Years ended September 27, 2014	Years ended September 28, 2013
Cash and cash equivalents, beginning of the year	$ 13,844	$ 14,259	$ 10,746
Operating activities:			
Net income	53,394	39,510	37,037
Adjustments to reconcile net income to cash generated by operating activities:			
Depreciation and amortization	11,257	7,946	6,757
Share-based compensation expense	3,586	2,863	2,253
Deferred income tax expense	1,382	2,347	1,141
Changes in operating assets and liabilities:			
Accounts receivable, net	611	(4,232)	(2,172)
Inventories	(238)	(76)	(973)
Vendor non-trade receivables	(3,735)	(2,220)	223
Other current and non-current assets	(179)	167	1,080
Accounts payable	5,400	5,938	2,340
Deferred revenue	1,042	1,460	1,459
Other current and non-current liabilities	8,746	6,010	4,521
Cash generated by operating activities	81,266	59,713	53,666
Investing activities:			
Purchases of marketable securities	(166,402)	(217,128)	(148,489)
Proceeds from maturities of marketable securities	14,538	18,810	20,317
Proceeds from sales of marketable securities	107,447	189,301	104,130
Payments made in connection with business acquisitions, net	(343)	(3,765)	(496)
Payments for acquisition of property, plant and equipment	(11,247)	(9,571)	(8,165)
Payments for acquisition of intangible assets	(241)	(242)	(911)
Other	(26)	16	(160)
Cash used in investing activities	(56,274)	(22,579)	(33,774)
Financing activities:			
Proceeds from issuance of common stock	543	730	530
Excess tax benefits from equity awards	749	739	701
Taxes paid related to net share settlement of equity awards	(1,499)	(1,158)	(1,082)
Dividends and dividend equivalents paid	(11,561)	(11,126)	(10,564)
Repurchase of common stock	(35,253)	(45,000)	(22,860)
Proceeds from issuance of term debt, net	27,114	11,960	16,896
Change in commercial paper, net	2,191	6,306	0
Cash used in financing activities	(17,716)	(37,549)	(16,379)
Increase/(decrease) in cash and cash equivalents	7,276	(415)	3,513
Cash and cash equivalents, end of the year	$ 21,120	$ 13,844	$ 14,259
Supplemental cash flow disclosure:			
Cash paid for income taxes, net	$ 13,252	$ 10,026	$ 9,128
Cash paid for interest	$ 514	$ 339	$ 0

See accompanying Notes to Consolidated Financial Statements.

Specimen Financial Statements: PepsiCo, Inc.

PepsiCo, Inc. is a world leader in convenient snacks, foods, and beverages. The following are PepsiCo's financial statements as presented in its 2015 annual report. The complete annual report, including notes to the financial statements, is available at the company's website.

Consolidated Statement of Income
PepsiCo, Inc. and Subsidiaries
Fiscal years ended December 26, 2015, December 27, 2014 and December 28, 2013
(in millions except per share amounts)

	2015	2014	2013
Net Revenue	$ 63,056	$ 66,683	$ 66,415
Cost of sales	28,384	30,884	31,243
Gross profit	34,672	35,799	35,172
Selling, general and administrative expenses	24,885	26,126	25,357
Venezuela impairment charges	1,359	—	—
Amortization of intangible assets	75	92	110
Operating Profit	8,353	9,581	9,705
Interest expense	(970)	(909)	(911)
Interest income and other	59	85	97
Income before income taxes	7,442	8,757	8,891
Provision for income taxes	1,941	2,199	2,104
Net income	5,501	6,558	6,787
Less: Net income attributable to noncontrolling interests	49	45	47
Net Income Attributable to PepsiCo	$ 5,452	$ 6,513	$ 6,740
Net Income Attributable to PepsiCo per Common Share			
Basic	$ 3.71	$ 4.31	$ 4.37
Diluted	$ 3.67	$ 4.27	$ 4.32
Weighted-average common shares outstanding			
Basic	1,469	1,509	1,541
Diluted	1,485	1,527	1,560
Cash dividends declared per common share	$ 2.7625	$ 2.5325	$ 2.24

See accompanying notes to the consolidated financial statements.

Consolidated Statement of Comprehensive Income

PepsiCo, Inc. and Subsidiaries

Fiscal years ended December 26, 2015, December 27, 2014 and December 28, 2013

(in millions)

	2015		
	Pre-tax amounts	**Tax amounts**	**After-tax amounts**
Net income			$ 5,501
Other Comprehensive Loss			
Currency translation:			
Currency translation adjustment	$ (2,938)	$ —	(2,938)
Reclassification associated with Venezuelan entities	111	—	111
Cash flow hedges:			
Reclassification of net losses to net income	97	(47)	50
Net derivative losses	(95)	48	(47)
Pension and retiree medical:			
Reclassification of net losses to net income	246	(74)	172
Reclassification associated with Venezuelan entities	20	(4)	16
Remeasurement of net liabilities and translation	(88)	71	(17)
Unrealized gains on securities	3	(2)	1
Total Other Comprehensive Loss	$ (2,644)	$ (8)	(2,652)
Comprehensive income			2,849
Comprehensive income attributable to noncontrolling interests			(47)
Comprehensive Income Attributable to PepsiCo			$ 2,802

	2014		
	Pre-tax amounts	Tax amounts	After-tax amounts
Net income			$ 6,558
Other Comprehensive Loss			
Currency translation adjustment	$ (5,010)	$ —	(5,010)
Cash flow hedges:			
Reclassification of net losses to net income	249	(95)	154
Net derivative losses	(88)	44	(44)
Pension and retiree medical:			
Reclassification of net losses to net income	369	(122)	247
Remeasurement of net liabilities and translation	(1,323)	437	(886)
Unrealized losses on securities	(11)	5	(6)
Other	1	—	1
Total Other Comprehensive Loss	$ (5,813)	$ 269	(5,544)
Comprehensive income			1,014
Comprehensive income attributable to noncontrolling interests			(43)
Comprehensive Income Attributable to PepsiCo			$ 971

	2013		
	Pre-tax amounts	Tax amounts	After-tax amounts
Net income			$ 6,787
Other Comprehensive Income			
Currency translation adjustment	$ (1,303)	$ —	(1,303)
Cash flow hedges:			
Reclassification of net losses to net income	45	(17)	28
Net derivative losses	(20)	10	(10)
Pension and retiree medical:			
Reclassification of net losses to net income	353	(123)	230
Remeasurement of net liabilities and translation	2,164	(764)	1,400
Unrealized gains on securities	57	(28)	29
Other	—	(16)	(16)
Total Other Comprehensive Income	$ 1,296	$ (938)	358
Comprehensive income			7,145
Comprehensive income attributable to noncontrolling interests			(45)
Comprehensive Income Attributable to PepsiCo			$ 7,100

See accompanying notes to the consolidated financial statements.

Consolidated Statement of Cash Flows

PepsiCo, Inc. and Subsidiaries
Fiscal years ended December 26, 2015, December 27, 2014 and December 28, 2013
(in millions)

	2015	2014	2013
Operating Activities			
Net income	$ **5,501**	$ 6,558	$ 6,787
Depreciation and amortization	**2,416**	2,625	2,663
Share-based compensation expense	**295**	297	303
Merger and integration charges	—	—	10
Cash payments for merger and integration charges	—	—	(25)
Restructuring and impairment charges	**230**	418	163
Cash payments for restructuring charges	**(208)**	(266)	(133)
Charge related to the transaction with Tingyi	**73**	—	—
Cash payments for restructuring and other charges related to the transaction with Tingyi	—	—	(26)
Venezuela impairment charges	**1,359**	—	—
Venezuela remeasurement charges	—	105	111
Excess tax benefits from share-based payment arrangements	**(133)**	(114)	(117)
Pension and retiree medical plan expenses	**467**	667	663
Pension and retiree medical plan contributions	**(205)**	(655)	(262)
Deferred income taxes and other tax charges and credits	**78**	(19)	(1,058)
Change in assets and liabilities:			
Accounts and notes receivable	**(461)**	(343)	(88)
Inventories	**(244)**	(111)	4
Prepaid expenses and other current assets	**(50)**	80	(51)
Accounts payable and other current liabilities	**1,692**	1,162	1,007
Income taxes payable	**55**	371	86
Other, net	**(285)**	(269)	(349)
Net Cash Provided by Operating Activities	**10,580**	10,506	9,688
Investing Activities			
Capital spending	**(2,758)**	(2,859)	(2,795)
Sales of property, plant and equipment	**86**	115	109
Acquisitions and investments in noncontrolled affiliates	**(86)**	(88)	(109)
Reduction of cash due to Venezuela deconsolidation	**(568)**	—	—
Divestitures	**76**	203	130
Short-term investments, by original maturity			
More than three months - purchases	**(4,428)**	(6,305)	—
More than three months - maturities	**4,111**	3,891	—
Three months or less, net	**3**	116	61
Other investing, net	**(5)**	(10)	(21)
Net Cash Used for Investing Activities	**(3,569)**	(4,937)	(2,625)
Financing Activities			
Proceeds from issuances of long-term debt	$ **8,702**	$ 3,855	$ 4,195
Payments of long-term debt	**(4,095)**	(2,189)	(3,894)
Short-term borrowings, by original maturity			
More than three months - proceeds	**15**	50	23
More than three months - payments	**(43)**	(10)	(492)
Three months or less, net	**53**	(2,037)	1,634
Cash dividends paid	**(4,040)**	(3,730)	(3,434)
Share repurchases - common	**(5,000)**	(5,012)	(3,001)
Share repurchases - preferred	**(5)**	(10)	(7)
Proceeds from exercises of stock options	**504**	755	1,123
Excess tax benefits from share-based payment arrangements	**133**	114	117
Acquisition of noncontrolling interests	—	—	(20)
Other financing	**(52)**	(50)	(33)
Net Cash Used for Financing Activities	**(3,828)**	(8,264)	(3,789)
Effect of exchange rate changes on cash and cash equivalents	**(221)**	(546)	(196)
Net Increase/(Decrease) in Cash and Cash Equivalents	**2,962**	(3,241)	3,078
Cash and Cash Equivalents, Beginning of Year	**6,134**	9,375	6,297
Cash and Cash Equivalents, End of Year	$ **9,096**	$ 6,134	$ 9,375

See accompanying notes to the consolidated financial statements.

Consolidated Balance Sheet
PepsiCo, Inc. and Subsidiaries
December 26, 2015 and December 27, 2014
(in millions except per share amounts)

	2015	2014
ASSETS		
Current Assets		
Cash and cash equivalents	$ 9,096	$ 6,134
Short-term investments	2,913	2,592
Accounts and notes receivable, net	6,437	6,651
Inventories	2,720	3,143
Prepaid expenses and other current assets	1,865	2,143
Total Current Assets	23,031	20,663
Property, Plant and Equipment, net	16,317	17,244
Amortizable Intangible Assets, net	1,270	1,449
Goodwill	14,177	14,965
Other nonamortizable intangible assets	11,811	12,639
Nonamortizable Intangible Assets	25,988	27,604
Investments in Noncontrolled Affiliates	2,311	2,689
Other Assets	750	860
Total Assets	$ 69,667	$ 70,509
LIABILITIES AND EQUITY		
Current Liabilities		
Short-term obligations	$ 4,071	$ 5,076
Accounts payable and other current liabilities	13,507	13,016
Total Current Liabilities	17,578	18,092
Long-Term Debt Obligations	29,213	23,821
Other Liabilities	5,887	5,744
Deferred Income Taxes	4,959	5,304
Total Liabilities	57,637	52,961
Commitments and contingencies		
Preferred Stock, no par value	41	41
Repurchased Preferred Stock	(186)	(181)
PepsiCo Common Shareholders' Equity		
Common stock, par value $1^2/_3$¢ per share (authorized 3,600 shares, issued, net of repurchased common stock at par value: 1,448 and 1,488 shares, respectively)	24	25
Capital in excess of par value	4,076	4,115
Retained earnings	50,472	49,092
Accumulated other comprehensive loss	(13,319)	(10,669)
Repurchased common stock, in excess of par value (418 and 378 shares, respectively)	(29,185)	(24,985)
Total PepsiCo Common Shareholders' Equity	12,068	17,578
Noncontrolling interests	107	110
Total Equity	12,030	17,548
Total Liabilities and Equity	$ 69,667	$ 70,509

See accompanying notes to the consolidated financial statements.

Consolidated Statement of Equity

PepsiCo, Inc. and Subsidiaries
Fiscal years ended December 26, 2015, December 27, 2014 and December 28, 2013
(in millions)

	2015		2014		2013	
	Shares	Amount	Shares	Amount	Shares	Amount
Preferred Stock	0.8	$ 41	0.8	$ 41	0.8	$ 41
Repurchased Preferred Stock						
Balance, beginning of year	(0.7)	(181)	(0.6)	(171)	(0.6)	(164)
Redemptions	—	(5)	(0.1)	(10)	—	(7)
Balance, end of year	(0.7)	(186)	(0.7)	(181)	(0.6)	(171)
Common Stock						
Balance, beginning of year	1,488	25	1,529	25	1,544	26
Repurchased common stock	(40)	(1)	(41)	—	(15)	(1)
Balance, end of year	1,448	24	1,488	25	1,529	25
Capital in Excess of Par Value						
Balance, beginning of year		4,115		4,095		4,178
Share-based compensation expense		299		294		303
Stock option exercises, RSUs, PSUs and PEPunits converted [(a)]		(182)		(200)		(287)
Withholding tax on RSUs, PSUs and PEPunits converted		(151)		(91)		(87)
Other		(5)		17		(12)
Balance, end of year		4,076		4,115		4,095
Retained Earnings						
Balance, beginning of year		49,092		46,420		43,158
Net income attributable to PepsiCo		5,452		6,513		6,740
Cash dividends declared - common		(4,071)		(3,840)		(3,477)
Cash dividends declared - preferred		(1)		(1)		(1)
Balance, end of year		50,472		49,092		46,420
Accumulated Other Comprehensive Loss						
Balance, beginning of year		(10,669)		(5,127)		(5,487)
Other comprehensive (loss)/income attributable to PepsiCo		(2,650)		(5,542)		360
Balance, end of year		(13,319)		(10,669)		(5,127)
Repurchased Common Stock						
Balance, beginning of year	(378)	(24,985)	(337)	(21,004)	(322)	(19,458)
Share repurchases	(52)	(4,999)	(57)	(5,012)	(37)	(3,000)
Stock option exercises, RSUs, PSUs and PEPunits converted	12	794	15	1,030	22	1,451
Other	—	5	1	1	—	3
Balance, end of year	(418)	(29,185)	(378)	(24,985)	(337)	(21,004)
Total PepsiCo Common Shareholders' Equity		12,068		17,578		24,409
Noncontrolling Interests						
Balance, beginning of year		110		110		105
Net income attributable to noncontrolling interests		49		45		47
Distributions to noncontrolling interests		(48)		(41)		(34)
Currency translation adjustment		(2)		(2)		(2)
Acquisitions and divestitures		—		—		(6)
Other, net		(2)		(2)		—
Balance, end of year		107		110		110
Total Equity		$ 12,030		$ 17,548		$ 24,389

(a) Includes total tax benefits of $107 million in 2015, $74 million in 2014 and $45 million in 2013.

See accompanying notes to the consolidated financial statements.

Specimen Financial Statements: The Coca-Cola Company

The Coca-Cola Company is a global leader in the beverage industry. It offers hundreds of brands, including soft drinks, fruit juices, sports drinks and other beverages in more than 200 countries. The following are Coca-Cola's financial statements as presented in its 2015 annual report. The complete annual report, including notes to the financial statements, is available at the company's website.

THE COCA-COLA COMPANY AND SUBSIDIARIES

CONSOLIDATED STATEMENTS OF INCOME

Year Ended December 31,	**2015**	2014	2013
(In millions except per share data)			
NET OPERATING REVENUES	**$ 44,294**	$ 45,998	$ 46,854
Cost of goods sold	**17,482**	17,889	18,421
GROSS PROFIT	**26,812**	28,109	28,433
Selling, general and administrative expenses	**16,427**	17,218	17,310
Other operating charges	**1,657**	1,183	895
OPERATING INCOME	**8,728**	9,708	10,228
Interest income	**613**	594	534
Interest expense	**856**	483	463
Equity income (loss) — net	**489**	769	602
Other income (loss) — net	**631**	(1,263)	576
INCOME BEFORE INCOME TAXES	**9,605**	9,325	11,477
Income taxes	**2,239**	2,201	2,851
CONSOLIDATED NET INCOME	**7,366**	7,124	8,626
Less: Net income attributable to noncontrolling interests	**15**	26	42
NET INCOME ATTRIBUTABLE TO SHAREOWNERS OF THE COCA-COLA COMPANY	**$ 7,351**	$ 7,098	$ 8,584
BASIC NET INCOME PER SHARE[1]	**$ 1.69**	$ 1.62	$ 1.94
DILUTED NET INCOME PER SHARE[1]	**$ 1.67**	$ 1.60	$ 1.90
AVERAGE SHARES OUTSTANDING	**4,352**	4,387	4,434
Effect of dilutive securities	**53**	63	75
AVERAGE SHARES OUTSTANDING ASSUMING DILUTION	**4,405**	4,450	4,509

[1] Calculated based on net income attributable to shareowners of The Coca-Cola Company.

Refer to Notes to Consolidated Financial Statements.

THE COCA-COLA COMPANY AND SUBSIDIARIES

CONSOLIDATED STATEMENTS OF COMPREHENSIVE INCOME

Year Ended December 31,	**2015**	2014	2013
(In millions)			
CONSOLIDATED NET INCOME	**$ 7,366**	$ 7,124	$ 8,626
Other comprehensive income:			
Net foreign currency translation adjustment	**(3,959)**	(2,382)	(1,187)
Net gain (loss) on derivatives	**142**	357	151
Net unrealized gain (loss) on available-for-sale securities	**(684)**	714	(80)
Net change in pension and other benefit liabilities	**86**	(1,039)	1,066
TOTAL COMPREHENSIVE INCOME	**2,951**	4,774	8,576
Less: Comprehensive income (loss) attributable to noncontrolling interests	**(3)**	21	39
TOTAL COMPREHENSIVE INCOME ATTRIBUTABLE TO SHAREOWNERS OF THE COCA-COLA COMPANY	**$ 2,954**	$ 4,753	$ 8,537

Refer to Notes to Consolidated Financial Statements.

THE COCA-COLA COMPANY AND SUBSIDIARIES

CONSOLIDATED BALANCE SHEETS

December 31,	**2015**	2014
(In millions except par value)		
ASSETS		
CURRENT ASSETS		
Cash and cash equivalents	**$ 7,309**	$ 8,958
Short-term investments	**8,322**	9,052
TOTAL CASH, CASH EQUIVALENTS AND SHORT-TERM INVESTMENTS	**15,631**	18,010
Marketable securities	**4,269**	3,665
Trade accounts receivable, less allowances of $352 and $331, respectively	**3,941**	4,466
Inventories	**2,902**	3,100
Prepaid expenses and other assets	**2,752**	3,066
Assets held for sale	**3,900**	679
TOTAL CURRENT ASSETS	**33,395**	32,986
EQUITY METHOD INVESTMENTS	**12,318**	9,947
OTHER INVESTMENTS	**3,470**	3,678
OTHER ASSETS	**4,207**	4,407
PROPERTY, PLANT AND EQUIPMENT — net	**12,571**	14,633
TRADEMARKS WITH INDEFINITE LIVES	**5,989**	6,533
BOTTLERS' FRANCHISE RIGHTS WITH INDEFINITE LIVES	**6,000**	6,689
GOODWILL	**11,289**	12,100
OTHER INTANGIBLE ASSETS	**854**	1,050
TOTAL ASSETS	**$ 90,093**	$ 92,023
LIABILITIES AND EQUITY		
CURRENT LIABILITIES		
Accounts payable and accrued expenses	**$ 9,660**	$ 9,234
Loans and notes payable	**13,129**	19,130
Current maturities of long-term debt	**2,677**	3,552
Accrued income taxes	**331**	400
Liabilities held for sale	**1,133**	58
TOTAL CURRENT LIABILITIES	**26,930**	32,374
LONG-TERM DEBT	**28,407**	19,063
OTHER LIABILITIES	**4,301**	4,389
DEFERRED INCOME TAXES	**4,691**	5,636
THE COCA-COLA COMPANY SHAREOWNERS' EQUITY		
Common stock, $0.25 par value; Authorized — 11,200 shares; Issued — 7,040 and 7,040 shares, respectively	**1,760**	1,760
Capital surplus	**14,016**	13,154
Reinvested earnings	**65,018**	63,408
Accumulated other comprehensive income (loss)	**(10,174)**	(5,777)
Treasury stock, at cost — 2,716 and 2,674 shares, respectively	**(45,066)**	(42,225)
EQUITY ATTRIBUTABLE TO SHAREOWNERS OF THE COCA-COLA COMPANY	**25,554**	30,320
EQUITY ATTRIBUTABLE TO NONCONTROLLING INTERESTS	**210**	241
TOTAL EQUITY	**25,764**	30,561
TOTAL LIABILITIES AND EQUITY	**$ 90,093**	$ 92,023

Refer to Notes to Consolidated Financial Statements.

THE COCA-COLA COMPANY AND SUBSIDIARIES

CONSOLIDATED STATEMENTS OF CASH FLOWS

Year Ended December 31,	**2015**	2014	2013
(In millions)			
OPERATING ACTIVITIES			
Consolidated net income	**$ 7,366**	$ 7,124	$ 8,626
Depreciation and amortization	**1,970**	1,976	1,977
Stock-based compensation expense	**236**	209	227
Deferred income taxes	**73**	(40)	648
Equity (income) loss — net of dividends	**(122)**	(371)	(201)
Foreign currency adjustments	**(137)**	415	168
Significant (gains) losses on sales of assets — net	**(374)**	831	(670)
Other operating charges	**929**	761	465
Other items	**744**	149	234
Net change in operating assets and liabilities	**(157)**	(439)	(932)
Net cash provided by operating activities	**10,528**	10,615	10,542
INVESTING ACTIVITIES			
Purchases of investments	**(15,831)**	(17,800)	(14,782)
Proceeds from disposals of investments	**14,079**	12,986	12,791
Acquisitions of businesses, equity method investments and nonmarketable securities	**(2,491)**	(389)	(353)
Proceeds from disposals of businesses, equity method investments and nonmarketable securities	**565**	148	872
Purchases of property, plant and equipment	**(2,553)**	(2,406)	(2,550)
Proceeds from disposals of property, plant and equipment	**85**	223	111
Other investing activities	**(40)**	(268)	(303)
Net cash provided by (used in) investing activities	**(6,186)**	(7,506)	(4,214)
FINANCING ACTIVITIES			
Issuances of debt	**40,434**	41,674	43,425
Payments of debt	**(37,738)**	(36,962)	(38,714)
Issuances of stock	**1,245**	1,532	1,328
Purchases of stock for treasury	**(3,564)**	(4,162)	(4,832)
Dividends	**(5,741)**	(5,350)	(4,969)
Other financing activities	**251**	(363)	17
Net cash provided by (used in) financing activities	**(5,113)**	(3,631)	(3,745)
EFFECT OF EXCHANGE RATE CHANGES ON CASH AND CASH EQUIVALENTS	**(878)**	(934)	(611)
CASH AND CASH EQUIVALENTS			
Net increase (decrease) during the year	**(1,649)**	(1,456)	1,972
Balance at beginning of year	**8,958**	10,414	8,442
Balance at end of year	**$ 7,309**	$ 8,958	$ 10,414

Refer to Notes to Consolidated Financial Statements.

THE COCA-COLA COMPANY AND SUBSIDIARIES

CONSOLIDATED STATEMENTS OF SHAREOWNERS' EQUITY

Year Ended December 31,	2015	2014	2013
(In millions except per share data)			
EQUITY ATTRIBUTABLE TO SHAREOWNERS OF THE COCA-COLA COMPANY			
NUMBER OF COMMON SHARES OUTSTANDING			
Balance at beginning of year	**4,366**	4,402	4,469
Purchases of treasury stock	**(86)**	(98)	(121)
Treasury stock issued to employees related to stock compensation plans	**44**	62	54
Balance at end of year	**4,324**	4,366	4,402
COMMON STOCK	**$ 1,760**	$ 1,760	$ 1,760
CAPITAL SURPLUS			
Balance at beginning of year	**13,154**	12,276	11,379
Stock issued to employees related to stock compensation plans	**532**	526	569
Tax benefit (charge) from stock compensation plans	**94**	169	144
Stock-based compensation	**236**	209	227
Other activities	**—**	(26)	(43)
Balance at end of year	**14,016**	13,154	12,276
REINVESTED EARNINGS			
Balance at beginning of year	**63,408**	61,660	58,045
Net income attributable to shareowners of The Coca-Cola Company	**7,351**	7,098	8,584
Dividends (per share — $1.32, $1.22 and $1.12 in 2015, 2014 and 2013, respectively)	**(5,741)**	(5,350)	(4,969)
Balance at end of year	**65,018**	63,408	61,660
ACCUMULATED OTHER COMPREHENSIVE INCOME (LOSS)			
Balance at beginning of year	**(5,777)**	(3,432)	(3,385)
Net other comprehensive income (loss)	**(4,397)**	(2,345)	(47)
Balance at end of year	**(10,174)**	(5,777)	(3,432)
TREASURY STOCK			
Balance at beginning of year	**(42,225)**	(39,091)	(35,009)
Stock issued to employees related to stock compensation plans	**696**	891	745
Purchases of treasury stock	**(3,537)**	(4,025)	(4,827)
Balance at end of year	**(45,066)**	(42,225)	(39,091)
TOTAL EQUITY ATTRIBUTABLE TO SHAREOWNERS OF THE COCA-COLA COMPANY	**$ 25,554**	$ 30,320	$ 33,173
EQUITY ATTRIBUTABLE TO NONCONTROLLING INTERESTS			
Balance at beginning of year	**$ 241**	$ 267	$ 378
Net income attributable to noncontrolling interests	**15**	26	42
Net foreign currency translation adjustment	**(18)**	(5)	(3)
Dividends paid to noncontrolling interests	**(31)**	(25)	(58)
Acquisition of interests held by noncontrolling owners	**—**	—	(34)
Contributions by noncontrolling interests	**—**	—	6
Business combinations	**(3)**	(22)	25
Deconsolidation of certain entities	**—**	—	(89)
Other activities	**6**	—	—
TOTAL EQUITY ATTRIBUTABLE TO NONCONTROLLING INTERESTS	**$ 210**	$ 241	$ 267

Refer to Notes to Consolidated Financial Statements.

Specimen Financial Statements: Amazon.com, Inc.

Amazon.com, Inc. is the world's largest online retailer. It also produces consumer electronics—notably the Kindle e-book reader and the Kindle Fire Tablet computer—and is a major provider of cloud computing services. The following are Amazon's financial statements as presented in the company's 2015 annual report. The complete annual report, including notes to the financial statements, is available at the company's website.

AMAZON.COM, INC.
CONSOLIDATED STATEMENTS OF CASH FLOWS
(in millions)

	Year Ended December 31,		
	2015	2014	2013
CASH AND CASH EQUIVALENTS, BEGINNING OF PERIOD	$ 14,557	$ 8,658	$ 8,084
OPERATING ACTIVITIES:			
Net income (loss)	596	(241)	274
Adjustments to reconcile net income (loss) to net cash from operating activities:			
Depreciation of property and equipment, including internal-use software and website development, and other amortization, including capitalized content costs	6,281	4,746	3,253
Stock-based compensation	2,119	1,497	1,134
Other operating expense (income), net	155	129	114
Losses (gains) on sales of marketable securities, net	5	(3)	1
Other expense (income), net	245	62	166
Deferred income taxes	81	(316)	(156)
Excess tax benefits from stock-based compensation	(119)	(6)	(78)
Changes in operating assets and liabilities:			
Inventories	(2,187)	(1,193)	(1,410)
Accounts receivable, net and other	(1,755)	(1,039)	(846)
Accounts payable	4,294	1,759	1,888
Accrued expenses and other	913	706	736
Additions to unearned revenue	7,401	4,433	2,691
Amortization of previously unearned revenue	(6,109)	(3,692)	(2,292)
Net cash provided by (used in) operating activities	11,920	6,842	5,475
INVESTING ACTIVITIES:			
Purchases of property and equipment, including internal-use software and website development, net	(4,589)	(4,893)	(3,444)
Acquisitions, net of cash acquired, and other	(795)	(979)	(312)
Sales and maturities of marketable securities	3,025	3,349	2,306
Purchases of marketable securities	(4,091)	(2,542)	(2,826)
Net cash provided by (used in) investing activities	(6,450)	(5,065)	(4,276)

(continued next page)

AMAZON.COM, INC.

CONSOLIDATED STATEMENTS OF CASH FLOWS
(in millions)

	Year Ended December 31, 2015	2014	2013
(continued)			
FINANCING ACTIVITIES:			
Excess tax benefits from stock-based compensation	119	6	78
Proceeds from long-term debt and other	353	6,359	394
Repayments of long-term debt and other	(1,652)	(513)	(231)
Principal repayments of capital lease obligations	(2,462)	(1,285)	(775)
Principal repayments of finance lease obligations	(121)	(135)	(5)
Net cash provided by (used in) financing activities	(3,763)	4,432	(539)
Foreign-currency effect on cash and cash equivalents	(374)	(310)	(86)
Net increase (decrease) in cash and cash equivalents	1,333	5,899	574
CASH AND CASH EQUIVALENTS, END OF PERIOD	$ 15,890	$ 14,557	$ 8,658
SUPPLEMENTAL CASH FLOW INFORMATION:			
Cash paid for interest on long-term debt	$ 325	$ 91	$ 97
Cash paid for interest on capital and finance lease obligations	153	86	41
Cash paid for income taxes (net of refunds)	273	177	169
Property and equipment acquired under capital leases	4,717	4,008	1,867
Property and equipment acquired under build-to-suit leases	544	920	877

See accompanying notes to consolidated financial statements.

AMAZON.COM, INC.

CONSOLIDATED STATEMENTS OF OPERATIONS
(in millions, except per share data)

	Year Ended December 31, 2015	2014	2013
Net product sales	$ 79,268	$ 70,080	$ 60,903
Net service sales	27,738	18,908	13,549
Total net sales	107,006	88,988	74,452
Operating expenses (1):			
Cost of sales	71,651	62,752	54,181
Fulfillment	13,410	10,766	8,585
Marketing	5,254	4,332	3,133
Technology and content	12,540	9,275	6,565
General and administrative	1,747	1,552	1,129
Other operating expense (income), net	171	133	114
Total operating expenses	104,773	88,810	73,707
Income from operations	2,233	178	745
Interest income	50	39	38
Interest expense	(459)	(210)	(141)
Other income (expense), net	(256)	(118)	(136)
Total non-operating income (expense)	(665)	(289)	(239)
Income (loss) before income taxes	1,568	(111)	506
Provision for income taxes	(950)	(167)	(161)
Equity-method investment activity, net of tax	(22)	37	(71)
Net income (loss)	$ 596	$ (241)	$ 274
Basic earnings per share	$ 1.28	$ (0.52)	$ 0.60
Diluted earnings per share	$ 1.25	$ (0.52)	$ 0.59
Weighted-average shares used in computation of earnings per share:			
Basic	467	462	457
Diluted	477	462	465

(1) Includes stock-based compensation as follows:

	2015	2014	2013
Fulfillment	$ 482	$ 375	$ 294
Marketing	190	125	88
Technology and content	1,224	804	603
General and administrative	223	193	149

See accompanying notes to consolidated financial statements.

AMAZON.COM, INC.

CONSOLIDATED STATEMENTS OF COMPREHENSIVE INCOME (LOSS)
(in millions)

	Year Ended December 31,		
	2015	2014	2013
Net income (loss)	$ 596	$ (241)	$ 274
Other comprehensive income (loss):			
Foreign currency translation adjustments, net of tax of $10, $(3), and $(20)	(210)	(325)	63
Net change in unrealized gains (losses) on available-for-sale securities:			
Unrealized gains (losses), net of tax of $(5), $1, and $3	(7)	2	(10)
Reclassification adjustment for losses (gains) included in "Other income (expense), net," net of tax of $0, $(1), and $(1)	5	(3)	1
Net unrealized gains (losses) on available-for-sale securities	(2)	(1)	(9)
Total other comprehensive income (loss)	(212)	(326)	54
Comprehensive income (loss)	$ 384	$ (567)	$ 328

See accompanying notes to consolidated financial statements.

AMAZON.COM, INC.

CONSOLIDATED BALANCE SHEETS
(in millions, except per share data)

	December 31, 2015	December 31, 2014
ASSETS		
Current assets:		
Cash and cash equivalents	$ 15,890	$ 14,557
Marketable securities	3,918	2,859
Inventories	10,243	8,299
Accounts receivable, net and other	6,423	5,612
Total current assets	36,474	31,327
Property and equipment, net	21,838	16,967
Goodwill	3,759	3,319
Other assets	3,373	2,892
Total assets	$ 65,444	$ 54,505
LIABILITIES AND STOCKHOLDERS' EQUITY		
Current liabilities:		
Accounts payable	$ 20,397	$ 16,459
Accrued expenses and other	10,384	9,807
Unearned revenue	3,118	1,823
Total current liabilities	33,899	28,089
Long-term debt	8,235	8,265
Other long-term liabilities	9,926	7,410
Commitments and contingencies (Note 7)		
Stockholders' equity:		
Preferred stock, $0.01 par value:		
Authorized shares — 500		
Issued and outstanding shares — none	—	—
Common stock, $0.01 par value:		
Authorized shares — 5,000		
Issued shares — 494 and 488		
Outstanding shares — 471 and 465	5	5
Treasury stock, at cost	(1,837)	(1,837)
Additional paid-in capital	13,394	11,135
Accumulated other comprehensive loss	(723)	(511)
Retained earnings	2,545	1,949
Total stockholders' equity	13,384	10,741
Total liabilities and stockholders' equity	$ 65,444	$ 54,505

See accompanying notes to consolidated financial statements.

AMAZON.COM, INC.

CONSOLIDATED STATEMENTS OF STOCKHOLDERS' EQUITY
(in millions)

	Common Stock						
	Shares	Amount	Treasury Stock	Additional Paid-In Capital	Accumulated Other Comprehensive Income (Loss)	Retained Earnings	Total Stockholders' Equity
Balance as of January 1, 2013	454	$ 5	$ (1,837)	$ 8,347	$ (239)	$ 1,916	$ 8,192
Net income	—	—	—	—	—	274	274
Other comprehensive income (loss)	—	—	—	—	54	—	54
Exercise of common stock options	5	—	—	4	—	—	4
Excess tax benefits from stock-based compensation	—	—	—	73	—	—	73
Stock-based compensation and issuance of employee benefit plan stock	—	—	—	1,149	—	—	1,149
Balance as of December 31, 2013	459	5	(1,837)	9,573	(185)	2,190	9,746
Net loss	—	—	—	—	—	(241)	(241)
Other comprehensive income (loss)	—	—	—	—	(326)	—	(326)
Exercise of common stock options	6	—	—	2	—	—	2
Excess tax benefits from stock-based compensation	—	—	—	6	—	—	6
Stock-based compensation and issuance of employee benefit plan stock	—	—	—	1,510	—	—	1,510
Issuance of common stock for acquisition activity	—	—	—	44	—	—	44
Balance as of December 31, 2014	465	5	(1,837)	11,135	(511)	1,949	10,741
Net income	—	—	—	—	—	596	596
Other comprehensive income (loss)	—	—	—	—	(212)	—	(212)
Exercise of common stock options	6	—	—	4	—	—	4
Excess tax benefits from stock-based compensation	—	—	—	119	—	—	119
Stock-based compensation and issuance of employee benefit plan stock	—	—	—	2,131	—	—	2,131
Issuance of common stock for acquisition activity	—	—	—	5	—	—	5
Balance as of December 31, 2015	471	$ 5	$ (1,837)	$ 13,394	$ (723)	$ 2,545	$ 13,384

See accompanying notes to consolidated financial statements.

Specimen Financial Statements: Wal-Mart Stores, Inc.

The following are **Wal-Mart Stores, Inc.**'s financial statements as presented in the company's 2016 annual report. The complete annual report, including notes to the financial statements, is available at the company's website.

Consolidated Statements of Income

(Amounts in millions, except per share data)	Fiscal Years Ended January 31, 2016	2015	2014
Revenues:			
Net sales	**$478,614**	$482,229	$473,076
Membership and other income	**3,516**	3,422	3,218
Total revenues	**482,130**	485,651	476,294
Costs and expenses:			
Cost of sales	**360,984**	365,086	358,069
Operating, selling, general and administrative expenses	**97,041**	93,418	91,353
Operating income	**24,105**	27,147	26,872
Interest:			
Debt	**2,027**	2,161	2,072
Capital lease and financing obligations	**521**	300	263
Interest income	**(81)**	(113)	(119)
Interest, net	**2,467**	2,348	2,216
Income from continuing operations before income taxes	**21,638**	24,799	24,656
Provision for income taxes:			
Current	**7,584**	8,504	8,619
Deferred	**(1,026)**	(519)	(514)
Total provision for income taxes	**6,558**	7,985	8,105
Income from continuing operations	**15,080**	16,814	16,551
Income from discontinued operations, net of income taxes	**—**	285	144
Consolidated net income	**15,080**	17,099	16,695
Consolidated net income attributable to noncontrolling interest	**(386)**	(736)	(673)
Consolidated net income attributable to Walmart	**$ 14,694**	$ 16,363	$ 16,022
Basic net income per common share:			
Basic income per common share from continuing operations attributable to Walmart	**$ 4.58**	$ 5.01	$ 4.87
Basic income per common share from discontinued operations attributable to Walmart	**—**	0.06	0.03
Basic net income per common share attributable to Walmart	**$ 4.58**	$ 5.07	$ 4.90
Diluted net income per common share:			
Diluted income per common share from continuing operations attributable to Walmart	**$ 4.57**	$ 4.99	$ 4.85
Diluted income per common share from discontinued operations attributable to Walmart	**—**	0.06	0.03
Diluted net income per common share attributable to Walmart	**$ 4.57**	$ 5.05	$ 4.88
Weighted-average common shares outstanding:			
Basic	**3,207**	3,230	3,269
Diluted	**3,217**	3,243	3,283
Dividends declared per common share	**$ 1.96**	$ 1.92	$ 1.88

See accompanying notes.

Consolidated Statements of Comprehensive Income

	Fiscal Years Ended January 31,		
(Amounts in millions)	**2016**	2015	2014
Consolidated net income	**$15,080**	$17,099	$16,695
Less consolidated net income attributable to nonredeemable noncontrolling interest	**(386)**	(736)	(606)
Less consolidated net income attributable to redeemable noncontrolling interest	—	—	(67)
Consolidated net income attributable to Walmart	**14,694**	16,363	16,022
Other comprehensive income (loss), net of income taxes			
Currency translation and other	**(5,220)**	(4,558)	(3,221)
Net investment hedges	**366**	379	75
Cash flow hedges	**(202)**	(470)	207
Minimum pension liability	**86**	(69)	153
Other comprehensive income (loss), net of income taxes	**(4,970)**	(4,718)	(2,786)
Less other comprehensive income (loss) attributable to nonredeemable noncontrolling interest	**541**	546	311
Less other comprehensive income (loss) attributable to redeemable noncontrolling interest	—	—	66
Other comprehensive income (loss) attributable to Walmart	**(4,429)**	(4,172)	(2,409)
Comprehensive income, net of income taxes	**10,110**	12,381	13,909
Less comprehensive income (loss) attributable to nonredeemable noncontrolling interest	**155**	(190)	(295)
Less comprehensive income (loss) attributable to redeemable noncontrolling interest	—	—	(1)
Comprehensive income attributable to Walmart	**$10,265**	$12,191	$13,613

See accompanying notes.

Consolidated Balance Sheets

(Amounts in millions)	Fiscal Years Ended January 31, 2016	2015
ASSETS		
Current assets:		
Cash and cash equivalents	**$ 8,705**	$ 9,135
Receivables, net	**5,624**	6,778
Inventories	**44,469**	45,141
Prepaid expenses and other	**1,441**	2,224
Total current assets	**60,239**	63,278
Property and equipment:		
Property and equipment	**176,958**	177,395
Less accumulated depreciation	**(66,787)**	(63,115)
Property and equipment, net	**110,171**	114,280
Property under capital lease and financing obligations:		
Property under capital lease and financing obligations	**11,096**	5,239
Less accumulated amortization	**(4,751)**	(2,864)
Property under capital lease and financing obligations, net	**6,345**	2,375
Goodwill	**16,695**	18,102
Other assets and deferred charges	**6,131**	5,455
Total assets	**$199,581**	$203,490
LIABILITIES AND EQUITY		
Current liabilities:		
Short-term borrowings	**$ 2,708**	$ 1,592
Accounts payable	**38,487**	38,410
Accrued liabilities	**19,607**	19,152
Accrued income taxes	**521**	1,021
Long-term debt due within one year	**2,745**	4,791
Capital lease and financing obligations due within one year	**551**	287
Total current liabilities	**64,619**	65,253
Long-term debt	**38,214**	40,889
Long-term capital lease and financing obligations	**5,816**	2,606
Deferred income taxes and other	**7,321**	8,805
Commitments and contingencies		
Equity:		
Common stock	**317**	323
Capital in excess of par value	**1,805**	2,462
Retained earnings	**90,021**	85,777
Accumulated other comprehensive income (loss)	**(11,597)**	(7,168)
Total Walmart shareholders' equity	**80,546**	81,394
Nonredeemable noncontrolling interest	**3,065**	4,543
Total equity	**83,611**	85,937
Total liabilities and equity	**$199,581**	$203,490

See accompanying notes.

Consolidated Statements of Shareholders' Equity and Redeemable Noncontrolling Interest

(Amounts in millions)	Common Stock Shares	Common Stock Amount	Capital in Excess of Par Value	Retained Earnings	Accumulated Other Comprehensive Income (Loss)	Total Walmart Shareholders' Equity	Nonredeemable Noncontrolling Interest	Total Equity	Redeemable Noncontrolling Interest
Balances as of February 1, 2013	3,314	$332	$ 3,620	$ 72,978	$ (587)	$ 76,343	$ 5,395	$ 81,738	$ 519
Consolidated net income	—	—	—	16,022	—	16,022	595	16,617	78
Other comprehensive income, net of income taxes	—	—	—	—	(2,409)	(2,409)	(311)	(2,720)	(66)
Cash dividends declared ($1.88 per share)	—	—	—	(6,139)	—	(6,139)	—	(6,139)	—
Purchase of Company stock	(87)	(9)	(294)	(6,254)	—	(6,557)	—	(6,557)	—
Redemption value adjustment of redeemable noncontrolling interest	—	—	(1,019)	—	—	(1,019)	—	(1,019)	1,019
Other	6	—	55	(41)	—	14	(595)	(581)	(59)
Balances as of January 31, 2014	3,233	323	2,362	76,566	(2,996)	76,255	5,084	81,339	1,491
Consolidated net income	—	—	—	16,363	—	16,363	736	17,099	—
Other comprehensive loss, net of income taxes	—	—	—	—	(4,172)	(4,172)	(546)	(4,718)	—
Cash dividends declared ($1.92 per share)	—	—	—	(6,185)	—	(6,185)	—	(6,185)	—
Purchase of Company stock	(13)	(1)	(29)	(950)	—	(980)	—	(980)	—
Purchase of redeemable noncontrolling interest	—	—	—	—	—	—	—	—	(1,491)
Other	8	1	129	(17)	—	113	(731)	(618)	—
Balances as of January 31, 2015	**3,228**	**323**	**2,462**	**85,777**	**(7,168)**	**81,394**	**4,543**	**85,937**	—
Consolidated net income	—	—	—	**14,694**	—	**14,694**	**386**	**15,080**	—
Other comprehensive income, net of income taxes	—	—	—	—	**(4,429)**	**(4,429)**	**(541)**	**(4,970)**	—
Cash dividends declared ($1.96 per share)	—	—	—	**(6,294)**	—	**(6,294)**	—	**(6,294)**	—
Purchase of Company stock	**(65)**	**(6)**	**(102)**	**(4,148)**	—	**(4,256)**	—	**(4,256)**	—
Cash dividend declared to noncontrolling interest	—	—	—	—	—	—	**(691)**	**(691)**	—
Other	**(1)**	—	**(555)**	**(8)**	—	**(563)**	**(632)**	**(1,195)**	—
Balances as of January 31, 2016	**3,162**	**$317**	**$1,805**	**$90,021**	**$(11,597)**	**$80,546**	**$3,065**	**$83,611**	**$ —**

See accompanying notes.

Consolidated Statements of Cash Flows

	Fiscal Years Ended January 31,		
(Amounts in millions)	**2016**	2015	2014
Cash flows from operating activities:			
Consolidated net income	**$ 15,080**	$ 17,099	$ 16,695
Income from discontinued operations, net of income taxes	**—**	(285)	(144)
Income from continuing operations	**15,080**	16,814	16,551
Adjustments to reconcile income from continuing operations to net cash provided by operating activities:			
Depreciation and amortization	**9,454**	9,173	8,870
Deferred income taxes	**(672)**	(503)	(279)
Other operating activities	**1,410**	785	938
Changes in certain assets and liabilities, net of effects of acquisitions:			
Receivables, net	**(19)**	(569)	(566)
Inventories	**(703)**	(1,229)	(1,667)
Accounts payable	**2,008**	2,678	531
Accrued liabilities	**1,303**	1,249	103
Accrued income taxes	**(472)**	166	(1,224)
Net cash provided by operating activities	**27,389**	28,564	23,257
Cash flows from investing activities:			
Payments for property and equipment	**(11,477)**	(12,174)	(13,115)
Proceeds from disposal of property and equipment	**635**	570	727
Proceeds from disposal of certain operations	**246**	671	—
Other investing activities	**(79)**	(192)	(138)
Net cash used in investing activities	**(10,675)**	(11,125)	(12,526)
Cash flows from financing activities:			
Net change in short-term borrowings	**1,235**	(6,288)	911
Proceeds from issuance of long-term debt	**39**	5,174	7,072
Payments of long-term debt	**(4,432)**	(3,904)	(4,968)
Dividends paid	**(6,294)**	(6,185)	(6,139)
Purchase of Company stock	**(4,112)**	(1,015)	(6,683)
Dividends paid to noncontrolling interest	**(719)**	(600)	(426)
Purchase of noncontrolling interest	**(1,326)**	(1,844)	(296)
Other financing activities	**(513)**	(409)	(260)
Net cash used in financing activities	**(16,122)**	(15,071)	(10,789)
Effect of exchange rates on cash and cash equivalents	**(1,022)**	(514)	(442)
Net increase (decrease) in cash and cash equivalents	**(430)**	1,854	(500)
Cash and cash equivalents at beginning of year	**9,135**	7,281	7,781
Cash and cash equivalents at end of period	**$ 8,705**	$ 9,135	$ 7,281
Supplemental disclosure of cash flow information:			
Income taxes paid	**8,111**	8,169	8,641
Interest paid	**2,540**	2,433	2,362

See accompanying notes.

Specimen Financial Statements: Louis Vuitton

Louis Vuitton is a French company and is one of the leading international fashion houses in the world. Louis Vuitton has been named the world's most valuable luxury brand. Note that its financial statements are IFRS-based and are presented in euros (€). The complete financial statements are available at the company's website.

CONSOLIDATED INCOME STATEMENT

(EUR millions, except for earnings per share)	Notes	2015	2014	2013
Revenue	23-24	**35,664**	30,638	29,016
Cost of sales		(12,553)	(10,801)	(9,997)
Gross margin		**23,111**	19,837	19,019
Marketing and selling expenses		(13,830)	(11,744)	(10,767)
General and administrative expenses		(2,663)	(2,373)	(2,212)
Income (loss) from joint ventures and associates	7	(13)	(5)	(23)
Profit from recurring operations	23-24	**6,605**	5,715	6,017
Other operating income and expenses	25	(221)	(284)	(119)
Operating profit		**6,384**	5,431	5,898
Cost of net financial debt		(78)	(115)	(101)
Other financial income and expenses		(336)	3,062	(97)
Net financial income (expense)	26	**(414)**	2,947	(198)
Income taxes	27	(1,969)	(2,273)	(1,753)
Net profit before minority interests		**4,001**	6,105	3,947
Minority interests	17	(428)	(457)	(511)
Net profit, Group share		**3,573**	5,648	3,436
Basic Group share of net earnings per share *(EUR)*	28	**7.11**	11.27	6.87
Number of shares on which the calculation is based		502,395,491	501,309,369	500,283,414
Diluted Group share of net earnings per share *(EUR)*	28	**7.08**	11.21	6.83
Number of shares on which the calculation is based		504,894,946	503,861,733	503,217,497

CONSOLIDATED STATEMENT OF COMPREHENSIVE GAINS AND LOSSES

(EUR millions)	2015	2014	2013
Net profit before minority interests	4,001	6,105	3,947
Translation adjustments	631	534	(346)
Tax impact	135	104	(48)
	766	**638**	**(394)**
Change in value of available for sale financial assets	(32)	494	963
Amounts transferred to income statement	(91)	(3,326)	(16)
Tax impact	20	184	(35)
	(103)	**(2,648)**	**912**
Change in value of hedges of future foreign currency cash flows	(63)	(30)	304
Amounts transferred to income statement	33	(163)	(265)
Tax impact	3	57	(17)
	(27)	**(136)**	**22**
Gains and losses recognized in equity, transferable to income statement	**636**	**(2,146)**	**540**
Change in value of vineyard land	64	(17)	369
Amounts transferred to consolidated reserves	-	(10)	-
Tax impact	(21)	9	(127)
	43	**(18)**	**242**
Employee benefit commitments: change in value resulting from actuarial gains and losses	42	(161)	80
Tax impact	(16)	52	(22)
	26	**(109)**	**58**
Gains and losses recognized in equity, not transferable to income statement	**69**	**(127)**	**300**
Comprehensive income	**4,706**	**3,832**	**4,787**
Minority interests	(558)	(565)	(532)
Comprehensive income, Group share	**4,148**	**3,267**	**4,255**

CONSOLIDATED BALANCE SHEET

ASSETS *(EUR millions)*	Notes	2015	2014	2013
Brands and other intangible assets	3	13,572	13,031	12,596
Goodwill	4	10,122	8,810	9,058
Property, plant and equipment	6	11,157	10,387	9,621
Investments in joint ventures and associates	7	729	519	480
Non-current available for sale financial assets	8	574	580	7,080
Other non-current assets	9	552	489	457
Deferred tax	27	1,945	1,436	913
Non-current assets		**38,651**	**35,252**	**40,205**
Inventories and work in progress	10	10,096	9,475	8,492
Trade accounts receivable	11	2,521	2,274	2,174
Income taxes		384	354	223
Other current assets	12	2,355	1,916	1,856
Cash and cash equivalents	14	3,594	4,091	3,226
Current assets		**18,950**	**18,110**	**15,971**
Total assets		**57,601**	**53,362**	**56,176**

LIABILITIES AND EQUITY *(EUR millions)*	Notes	2015	2014	2013
Share capital	15.1	152	152	152
Share premium account	15.1	2,579	2,655	3,849
Treasury shares and LVMH share-settled derivatives	15.2	(240)	(374)	(451)
Cumulative translation adjustment	15.4	1,137	492	(8)
Revaluation reserves		949	1,019	3,900
Other reserves		16,189	12,171	16,001
Net profit, Group share		3,573	5,648	3,436
Equity, Group share		24,339	21,763	26,879
Minority interests	17	1,460	1,240	1,028
Total equity		**25,799**	**23,003**	**27,907**
Long-term borrowings	18	4,511	5,054	4,149
Non-current provisions	19	1,950	2,291	1,797
Deferred tax	27	4,685	4,392	4,280
Other non-current liabilities	20	7,957	6,447	6,404
Non-current liabilities		**19,103**	**18,184**	**16,630**
Short-term borrowings	18	3,769	4,189	4,674
Trade accounts payable	21.1	3,960	3,606	3,297
Income taxes		640	549	357
Current provisions	19	421	332	324
Other current liabilities	21.2	3,909	3,499	2,987
Current liabilities		**12,699**	**12,175**	**11,639**
Total liabilities and equity		**57,601**	**53,362**	**56,176**

CONSOLIDATED STATEMENT OF CHANGES IN EQUITY

(EUR millions)	Number of shares	Share capital	Share premium account	Treasury shares and LVMH-share settled derivatives	Cumulative translation adjustment	Revaluation reserves				Net profit and other reserves	Total equity		
						Available for sale financial assets	Hedges of future foreign currency cash flows	Vineyard land	Employee benefit commit-ments		Group share	Minority interests	Total
Notes		15.1		15.2	15.4							17	
As of December 31, 2012	508,163,349	152	3,848	(414)	342	1,943	118	758	(88)	17,765	24,424	1,084	25,508
Gains and losses recognized in equity					(350)	912	18	188	51	-	819	21	840
Net profit										3,436	3,436	511	3,947
Comprehensive income		-	-	-	(350)	912	18	188	51	3,436	4,255	532	4,787
Stock option plan and similar expenses										31	31	3	34
(Acquisition)/disposal of treasury shares and LVMH share-settled derivatives				(103)						(7)	(110)	-	(110)
Exercise of LVMH share subscription options	1,025,418		67								67	-	67
Retirement of LVMH shares	(1,395,106)		(66)	66							-	-	-
Capital increase in subsidiaries											-	8	8
Interim and final dividends paid										(1,500)	(1,500)	(228)	(1,728)
Acquisition of a controlling interest in Loro Piana											-	235	235
Changes in control of consolidated entities										1	1	(1)	-
Acquisition and disposal of minority interests' shares										(73)	(73)	(76)	(149)
Purchase commitments for minority interests' shares										(216)	(216)	(529)	(745)
As of December 31, 2013	507,793,661	152	3,849	(451)	(8)	2,855	136	946	(37)	19,437	26,879	1,028	27,907
Gains and losses recognized in equity					500	(2,648)	(122)	(15)	(96)	-	(2,381)	108	(2,273)
Net profit										5,648	5,648	457	6,105
Comprehensive income		-	-	-	500	(2,648)	(122)	(15)	(96)	5,648	3,267	565	3,832
Stock option plan and similar expenses										37	37	2	39
(Acquisition)/disposal of treasury shares and LVMH share-settled derivatives				27						(17)	10	-	10
Exercise of LVMH share subscription options	980,323		59								59	-	59
Retirement of LVMH shares	(1,062,271)		(50)	50							-	-	-
Capital increase in subsidiaries											-	3	3
Interim and final dividends paid										(1,579)	(1,579)	(328)	(1,907)
Distribution in kind of Hermès shares. See Note 8.			(1,203)							(5,652)	(6,855)	-	(6,855)
Changes in control of consolidated entities										(5)	(5)	11	6
Acquisition and disposal of minority interests' shares										(2)	(2)	32	30
Purchase commitments for minority interests' shares										(48)	(48)	(73)	(121)
As of December 31, 2014	507,711,713	152	2,655	(374)	492	207	14	931	(133)	17,819	21,763	1,240	23,003
Gains and losses recognized in equity					645	(103)	(25)	33	25	-	575	130	705
Net profit										3,573	3,573	428	4,001
Comprehensive income		-	-	-	645	(103)	(25)	33	25	3,573	4,148	558	4,706
Stock option plan and similar expenses										35	35	2	37
(Acquisition)/disposal of treasury shares and LVMH share-settled derivatives				23						(13)	10	-	10
Exercise of LVMH share subscription options	552,137		35								35	-	35
Retirement of LVMH shares	(1,124,740)		(111)	111							-	-	-
Capital increase in subsidiaries										-	-	89	89
Interim and final dividends paid										(1,659)	(1,659)	(229)	(1,888)
Changes in control of consolidated entities										(9)	(9)	1	(8)
Acquisition and disposal of minority interests' shares										5	5	(3)	2
Purchase commitments for minority interests' shares										11	11	(198)	(187)
As of December 31, 2015	507,139,110	152	2,579	(240)	1,137	104	(11)	964	(108)	19,762	24,339	1,460	25,799

CONSOLIDATED CASH FLOW STATEMENT

(EUR millions)	Notes	2015	2014	2013
I. OPERATING ACTIVITIES AND OPERATING INVESTMENTS				
Operating profit		6,384	5,431	5,898
Income/(loss) and dividends from joint ventures and associates	7	27	26	49
Net increase in depreciation, amortization and provisions		2,081	1,895	1,435
Other computed expenses		(456)	(188)	(29)
Other adjustments		(91)	(84)	(76)
Cash from operations before changes in working capital		**7,945**	**7,080**	**7,277**
Cost of net financial debt: interest paid		(75)	(116)	(111)
Income taxes paid		(1,807)	(1,639)	(1,832)
Net cash from operating activities before changes in working capital		**6,063**	**5,325**	**5,334**
Change in working capital	14.1	(429)	(718)	(620)
Net cash from operating activities		**5,634**	**4,607**	**4,714**
Operating investments	14.2	(1,955)	(1,775)	(1,657)
Net cash from operating activities and operating investments (free cash flow)		**3,679**	**2,832**	**3,057**
II. FINANCIAL INVESTMENTS				
Purchase of non-current available for sale financial assets	8	(78)	(57)	(197)
Proceeds from sale of non-current available for sale financial assets	8	68	160	38
Dividends received	8	4	69	71
Income taxes paid related to financial investments		(265)	(237)	(11)
Impact of purchase and sale of consolidated investments	2.4	(240)	(167)	(2,161)
Net cash from (used in) financial investments		**(511)**	**(232)**	**(2,260)**
III. TRANSACTIONS RELATING TO EQUITY				
Capital increases of LVMH SE	15.1	35	59	66
Capital increases of subsidiaries subscribed by minority interests	17	81	3	7
Acquisition and disposals of treasury shares and LVMH share-settled derivatives	15.2	1	1	(113)
Interim and final dividends paid by LVMH SE [a]	15.3	(1,671)	(1,619)	(1,501)
Income taxes paid related to interim and final dividends paid		(304)	(79)	(137)
Interim and final dividends paid to minority interests in consolidated subsidiaries	17	(228)	(336)	(220)
Purchase and proceeds from sale of minority interests	2.4	(4)	10	(150)
Net cash from (used in) transactions relating to equity		**(2,090)**	**(1,961)**	**(2,048)**
Change in cash before financing activities		**1,078**	**639**	**(1,251)**
IV. FINANCING ACTIVITIES				
Proceeds from borrowings		1,008	2,407	3,095
Repayment of borrowings		(2,443)	(2,100)	(1,057)
Purchase and proceeds from sale of current available for sale financial assets	13	(3)	(106)	101
Net cash from (used in) financing activities		**(1,438)**	**201**	**2,139**
V. EFFECT OF EXCHANGE RATE CHANGES		(33)	27	47
NET INCREASE (DECREASE) IN CASH AND CASH EQUIVALENTS (I+II+III+IV+V)		(393)	867	935
CASH AND CASH EQUIVALENTS AT BEGINNING OF PERIOD	14	3,783	2,916	1,981
CASH AND CASH EQUIVALENTS AT END OF PERIOD	14	3,390	3,783	2,916
TOTAL INCOME TAXES PAID		(2,376)	(1,955)	(1,980)
Transactions included in the table above, generating no change in cash:				
- acquisition of assets by means of finance leases		4	5	7

(a) The distribution in kind of Hermès shares had no impact on cash, apart from related income tax effects. See Note 8.

Time Value of Money

Appendix Preview

Would you rather receive $1,000 today or a year from now? You should prefer to receive the $1,000 today because you can invest the $1,000 and then earn interest on it. As a result, you will have more than $1,000 a year from now. What this example illustrates is the concept of the **time value of money**. Everyone prefers to receive money today rather than in the future because of the interest factor.

Appendix Outline

LEARNING OBJECTIVES

1 Compute interest and future values.	• Nature of interest • Future value of a single amount • Future value of an annuity
2 Compute present values.	• Present value variables • Present value of a single amount • Present value of an annuity • Time periods and discounting • Present value of a long-term note or bond
3 Compute the present value in capital budgeting situations.	• Using alternative discount rates
4 Use a financial calculator to solve time value of money problems.	• Present value of a single sum • Present value of an annuity • Future value of a single sum • Future value of an annuity • Internal rate of return • Useful financial calculator applications

Interest and Future Values

LEARNING OBJECTIVE 1

Compute interest and future values.

Nature of Interest

Interest is payment for the use of another person's money. It is the difference between the amount borrowed or invested (called the **principal**) and the amount repaid or collected. The amount of interest to be paid or collected is usually stated as a rate over a specific period of time. The rate of interest is generally stated as an annual rate.

The amount of interest involved in any financing transaction is based on three elements:

1. **Principal (p):** The original amount borrowed or invested.
2. **Interest Rate (i):** An annual percentage of the principal.
3. **Time (n):** The number of periods that the principal is borrowed or invested.

Simple Interest

Simple interest is computed on the principal amount only. It is the return on the principal for one period (we use an annual interest rate unless stated otherwise). Simple interest is usually expressed as shown in **Illustration G.1**.

ILLUSTRATION G.1
Interest computation

$$\text{Interest} = \underset{p}{\text{Principal}} \times \underset{i}{\text{Rate}} \times \underset{n}{\text{Time}}$$

For example, if you borrowed $5,000 for 2 years at a simple interest rate of 12% annually, you would pay $1,200 in total interest, computed as follows.

$$\begin{aligned} \text{Interest} &= p \times i \times n \\ &= \$5{,}000 \times .12 \times 2 \\ &= \$1{,}200 \end{aligned}$$

Compound Interest

Compound interest is computed on principal **and** on any interest earned that has not been paid or withdrawn. It is the return on (or growth of) the principal for two or more time periods. Compounding computes interest not only on the principal but also on the interest earned to date on that principal, assuming the interest is left on deposit.

To illustrate the difference between simple and compound interest, assume that you deposit $1,000 in Bank Two, where it will earn simple interest of 9% per year, and you deposit another $1,000 in Citizens Bank, where it will earn compound interest of 9% per year compounded annually. Also assume that in both cases you will not withdraw any cash until three years from the date of deposit. **Illustration G.2** shows the computation of interest to be received and the accumulated year-end balances.

ILLUSTRATION G.2 **Simple versus compound interest**

Bank Two

Simple Interest Calculation	Simple Interest	Accumulated Year-End Balance
Year 1 $1,000.00 × 9%	$ 90.00	$1,090.00
Year 2 $1,000.00 × 9%	90.00	$1,180.00
Year 3 $1,000.00 × 9%	90.00	$1,270.00
	$ 270.00	

Citizens Bank

Compound Interest Calculation	Compound Interest	Accumulated Year-End Balance
Year 1 $1,000.00 × 9%	$ 90.00	$1,090.00
Year 2 $1,090.00 × 9%	98.10	$1,188.10
Year 3 $1,188.10 × 9%	106.93	$1,295.03
	$ 295.03	

$25.03 Difference

Note in Illustration G.2 that simple interest uses the initial principal of $1,000 to compute the interest in all three years. Compound interest uses the accumulated balance (principal plus interest to date) at each year-end to compute interest in the succeeding year—which explains why your compound interest account is larger.

Obviously, if you had a choice between investing your money at simple interest or at compound interest, you would choose compound interest, all other things—especially risk—being equal. In the example, compounding provides $25.03 of additional interest income. For practical purposes, compounding assumes that unpaid interest earned becomes a part of the principal, and the accumulated balance at the end of each year becomes the new principal on which interest is earned during the next year.

Most business situations use compound interest. Simple interest is generally applicable only to short-term situations of one year or less.

Future Value of a Single Amount

The **future value of a single amount** is the value at a future date of a given amount invested, assuming compound interest. For example, in Illustration G.2, $1,295.03 is the future value of the $1,000 investment earning 9% for three years. The $1,295.03 is determined more easily by using the formula shown in **Illustration G.3**.

$$FV = p \times (1 + i)^n$$

ILLUSTRATION G.3
Formula for future value

where:

FV = future value of a single amount
p = principal (or present value; the value today)
i = interest rate for one period
n = number of periods

The $1,295.03 is computed as follows.

$$\begin{aligned} FV &= p \times (1 + i)^n \\ &= \$1{,}000 \times (1 + .09)^3 \\ &= \$1{,}000 \times 1.29503 \\ &= \$1{,}295.03 \end{aligned}$$

The 1.29503 is computed by multiplying (1.09 × 1.09 × 1.09). The amounts in this example can be depicted in the time diagram shown in **Illustration G.4**.

ILLUSTRATION G.4 **Time diagram**

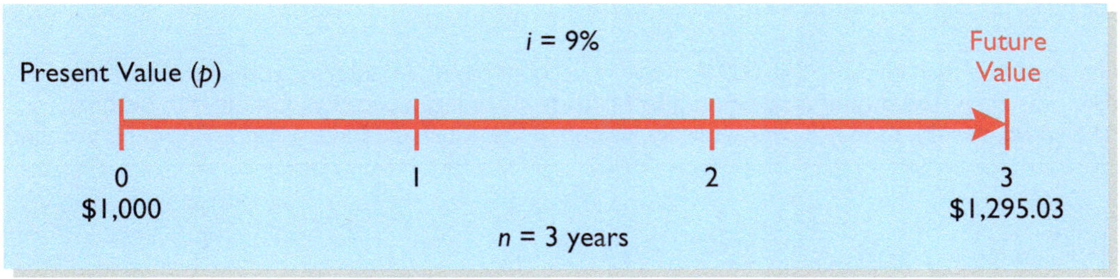

Another method used to compute the future value of a single amount involves a compound interest table. This table shows the future value of 1 for n periods. **Table 1** is such a table.

In Table 1, n is the number of compounding periods, the percentages are the periodic interest rates, and the 5-digit decimal numbers in the respective columns are the future value of 1 factors. To use Table 1, you multiply the principal amount by the future value factor for the specified number of periods and interest rate. For example, the future value factor for two periods at 9% is 1.18810. Multiplying this factor by $1,000 equals $1,188.10—which is the

TABLE 1 **Future Value of 1**

(n) Periods	4%	5%	6%	7%	8%	9%	10%	11%	12%	15%
0	1.00000	1.00000	1.00000	1.00000	1.00000	1.00000	1.00000	1.00000	1.00000	1.00000
1	1.04000	1.05000	1.06000	1.07000	1.08000	1.09000	1.10000	1.11000	1.12000	1.15000
2	1.08160	1.10250	1.12360	1.14490	1.16640	1.18810	1.21000	1.23210	1.25440	1.32250
3	1.12486	1.15763	1.19102	1.22504	1.25971	1.29503	1.33100	1.36763	1.40493	1.52088
4	1.16986	1.21551	1.26248	1.31080	1.36049	1.41158	1.46410	1.51807	1.57352	1.74901
5	1.21665	1.27628	1.33823	1.40255	1.46933	1.53862	1.61051	1.68506	1.76234	2.01136
6	1.26532	1.34010	1.41852	1.50073	1.58687	1.67710	1.77156	1.87041	1.97382	2.31306
7	1.31593	1.40710	1.50363	1.60578	1.71382	1.82804	1.94872	2.07616	2.21068	2.66002
8	1.36857	1.47746	1.59385	1.71819	1.85093	1.99256	2.14359	2.30454	2.47596	3.05902
9	1.42331	1.55133	1.68948	1.83846	1.99900	2.17189	2.35795	2.55803	2.77308	3.51788
10	1.48024	1.62889	1.79085	1.96715	2.15892	2.36736	2.59374	2.83942	3.10585	4.04556
11	1.53945	1.71034	1.89830	2.10485	2.33164	2.58043	2.85312	3.15176	3.47855	4.65239
12	1.60103	1.79586	2.01220	2.25219	2.51817	2.81267	3.13843	3.49845	3.89598	5.35025
13	1.66507	1.88565	2.13293	2.40985	2.71962	3.06581	3.45227	3.88328	4.36349	6.15279
14	1.73168	1.97993	2.26090	2.57853	2.93719	3.34173	3.79750	4.31044	4.88711	7.07571
15	1.80094	2.07893	2.39656	2.75903	3.17217	3.64248	4.17725	4.78459	5.47357	8.13706
16	1.87298	2.18287	2.54035	2.95216	3.42594	3.97031	4.59497	5.31089	6.13039	9.35762
17	1.94790	2.29202	2.69277	3.15882	3.70002	4.32763	5.05447	5.89509	6.86604	10.76126
18	2.02582	2.40662	2.85434	3.37993	3.99602	4.71712	5.55992	6.54355	7.68997	12.37545
19	2.10685	2.52695	3.02560	3.61653	4.31570	5.14166	6.11591	7.26334	8.61276	14.23177
20	2.19112	2.65330	3.20714	3.86968	4.66096	5.60441	6.72750	8.06231	9.64629	16.36654

accumulated balance at the end of year 2 in the Citizens Bank example in Illustration G.2. The \$1,295.03 accumulated balance at the end of the third year is calculated from Table 1 by multiplying the future value factor for three periods (1.29503) by the \$1,000.

The demonstration problem in **Illustration G.5** shows how to use Table 1.

ILLUSTRATION G.5 **Demonstration problem—Using Table 1 for *FV* of 1**

John and Mary Rich invested \$20,000 in a savings account paying 6% interest at the time their son, Mike, was born. The money is to be used by Mike for his college education. On his 18th birthday, Mike withdraws the money from his savings account. How much did Mike withdraw from his account?

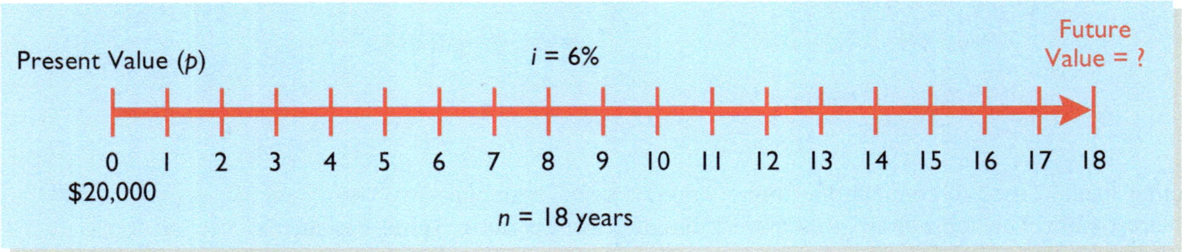

Answer: The future value factor from Table 1 is 2.85434 (18 periods at 6%). The future value of \$20,000 earning 6% per year for 18 years is **\$57,086.80** (\$20,000 × 2.85434).

Future Value of an Annuity

The preceding discussion involved the accumulation of only a single principal sum. Individuals and businesses frequently encounter situations in which a **series** of equal dollar amounts are to be paid or received at evenly spaced time intervals (periodically), such as loans or lease (rental) contracts. A series of payments or receipts of equal dollar amounts is referred to as an **annuity**.

The **future value of an annuity** is the sum of all the payments (receipts) plus the accumulated compound interest on them. In computing the future value of an annuity, it is necessary to know (1) the interest rate, (2) the number of payments (receipts), and (3) the amount of the periodic payments (receipts).

To illustrate the computation of the future value of an annuity, assume that you invest $2,000 at the end of each year for three years at 5% interest compounded annually. This situation is depicted in the time diagram in **Illustration G.6**.

ILLUSTRATION G.6 **Time diagram for a three-year annuity**

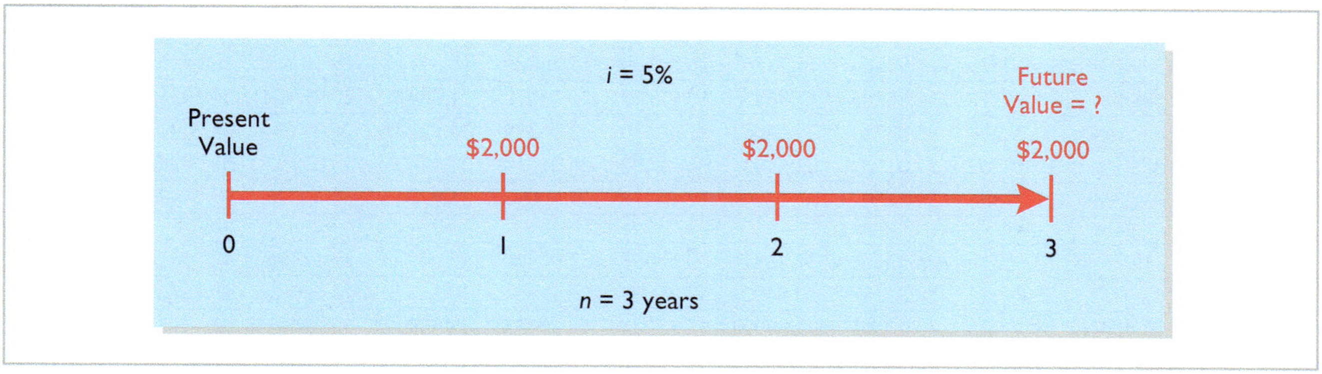

The $2,000 invested at the end of year 1 will earn interest for two years (years 2 and 3), and the $2,000 invested at the end of year 2 will earn interest for one year (year 3). However, the last $2,000 investment (made at the end of year 3) will not earn any interest. Using the future value factors from Table 1, the future value of these periodic payments is computed as shown in **Illustration G.7**.

ILLUSTRATION G.7
Future value of periodic payment computation

Invested at End of Year	Number of Compounding Periods	Amount Invested	×	Future Value of 1 Factor at 5%	=	Future Value
1	2	$2,000		1.10250		$2,205
2	1	2,000		1.05000		2,100
3	0	2,000		1.00000		2,000
				3.15250		**$6,305**

The first $2,000 investment is multiplied by the future value factor for two periods (1.1025) because two years' interest will accumulate on it (in years 2 and 3). The second $2,000 investment will earn only one year's interest (in year 3) and therefore is multiplied by the future value factor for one year (1.0500). The final $2,000 investment is made at the end of the third year and will not earn any interest. Thus, $n = 0$ and the future value factor is 1.00000. Consequently, the future value of the last $2,000 invested is only $2,000 since it does not accumulate any interest.

Calculating the future value of each individual cash flow is required when the periodic payments or receipts are not equal in each period. However, when the periodic payments (receipts) are **the same in each period**, the future value can be computed by using a future value of an annuity of 1 table. **Table 2** is such a table.

Table 2 shows the future value of 1 to be received periodically for a given number of payments. It assumes that each payment is made at the **end** of each period. We can see from Table 2

TABLE 2 **Future Value of an Annuity of 1**

(*n*) Payments	4%	5%	6%	7%	8%	9%	10%	11%	12%	15%
1	1.00000	1.00000	1.00000	1.0000	1.00000	1.00000	1.00000	1.00000	1.00000	1.00000
2	2.04000	2.05000	2.06000	2.0700	2.08000	2.09000	2.10000	2.11000	2.12000	2.15000
3	3.12160	3.15250	3.18360	3.2149	3.24640	3.27810	3.31000	3.34210	3.37440	3.47250
4	4.24646	4.31013	4.37462	4.4399	4.50611	4.57313	4.64100	4.70973	4.77933	4.99338
5	5.41632	5.52563	5.63709	5.7507	5.86660	5.98471	6.10510	6.22780	6.35285	6.74238
6	6.63298	6.80191	6.97532	7.1533	7.33592	7.52334	7.71561	7.91286	8.11519	8.75374
7	7.89829	8.14201	8.39384	8.6540	8.92280	9.20044	9.48717	9.78327	10.08901	11.06680
8	9.21423	9.54911	9.89747	10.2598	10.63663	11.02847	11.43589	11.85943	12.29969	13.72682
9	10.58280	11.02656	11.49132	11.9780	12.48756	13.02104	13.57948	14.16397	14.77566	16.78584
10	12.00611	12.57789	13.18079	13.8164	14.48656	15.19293	15.93743	16.72201	17.54874	20.30372
11	13.48635	14.20679	14.97164	15.7836	16.64549	17.56029	18.53117	19.56143	20.65458	24.34928
12	15.02581	15.91713	16.86994	17.8885	18.97713	20.14072	21.38428	22.71319	24.13313	29.00167
13	16.62684	17.71298	18.88214	20.1406	21.49530	22.95339	24.52271	26.21164	28.02911	34.35192
14	18.29191	19.59863	21.01507	22.5505	24.21492	26.01919	27.97498	30.09492	32.39260	40.50471
15	20.02359	21.57856	23.27597	25.1290	27.15211	29.36092	31.77248	34.40536	37.27972	47.58041
16	21.82453	23.65749	25.67253	27.8881	30.32428	33.00340	35.94973	39.18995	42.75328	55.71747
17	23.69751	25.84037	28.21288	30.8402	33.75023	36.97351	40.54470	44.50084	48.88367	65.07509
18	25.64541	28.13238	30.90565	33.9990	37.45024	41.30134	45.59917	50.39593	55.74972	75.83636
19	27.67123	30.53900	33.75999	37.3790	41.44626	46.01846	51.15909	56.93949	63.43968	88.21181
20	29.77808	33.06595	36.78559	40.9955	45.76196	51.16012	57.27500	64.20283	72.05244	102.44358

that the future value of an annuity of 1 factor for three payments at 5% is 3.15250. The future value factor is the total of the three individual future value factors was shown in Illustration G.7. Multiplying this amount by the annual investment of $2,000 produces a future value of $6,305.

The demonstration problem in **Illustration G.8** shows how to use Table 2.

ILLUSTRATION G.8 **Demonstration problem—Using Table 2 for *FV* of an annuity of 1**

John and Char Lewis's daughter, Debra, has just started high school. They decide to start a college fund for her and will invest $2,500 in a savings account at the end of each year she is in high school (4 payments total). The account will earn 6% interest compounded annually. How much will be in the college fund at the time Debra graduates from high school?

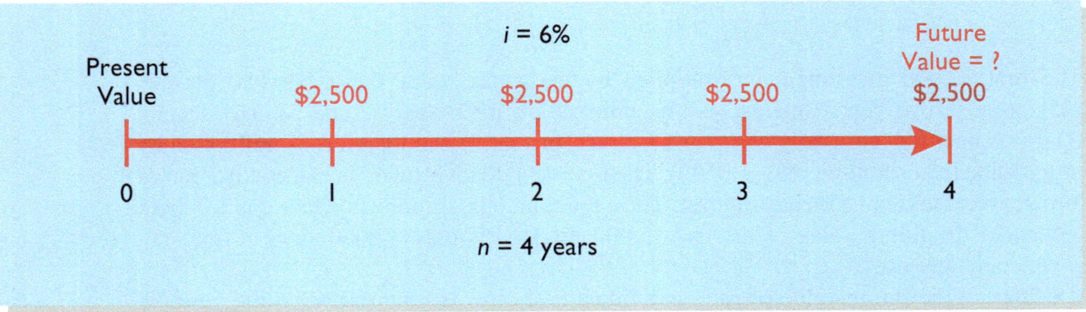

Answer: The future value factor from Table 2 is 4.37462 (4 payments at 6%). The future value of $2,500 invested each year for 4 years at 6% interest is **$10,936.55** ($2,500 × 4.37462).

Present Values

LEARNING OBJECTIVE 2

Compute present values.

Present Value Variables

The **present value** is the value now of a given amount to be paid or received in the future, assuming compound interest. The present value, like the future value, is based on three variables: (1) the dollar amount to be received (future amount), (2) the length of time until the amount is received (number of periods), and (3) the interest rate (the discount rate). The process of determining the present value is referred to as **discounting the future amount**.

Present value computations are used in measuring many items. For example, the present value of principal and interest payments is used to determine the market price of a bond. Determining the amount to be reported for notes payable and lease liabilities also involves present value computations. In addition, capital budgeting and other investment proposals are evaluated using present value computations. Finally, all rate of return and internal rate of return computations involve present value techniques.

Present Value of a Single Amount

To illustrate present value, assume that you want to invest a sum of money today that will provide $1,000 at the end of one year. What amount would you need to invest today to have $1,000 one year from now? If you want a 10% rate of return, the investment or present value is $909.09 ($1,000 ÷ 1.10). The formula for calculating present value is shown in **Illustration G.9**.

Present Value (PV) = Future Value (FV) $\div (1 + i)^n$

ILLUSTRATION G.9
Formula for present value

The computation of $1,000 discounted at 10% for one year is as follows.

$$\begin{aligned} PV &= FV \div (1+i)^n \\ &= \$1{,}000 \div (1+.10)^1 \\ &= \$1{,}000 \div 1.10 \\ &= \$909.09 \end{aligned}$$

The future amount ($1,000), the discount rate (10%), and the number of periods (1) are known. The variables in this situation are depicted in the time diagram in **Illustration G.10**.

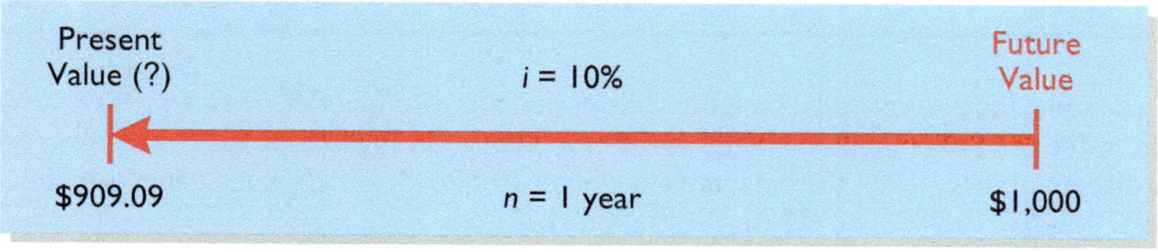

ILLUSTRATION G.10
Finding present value if discounted for one period

If the single amount of $1,000 is to be received **in two years** and discounted at 10%, the formula $PV = \$1{,}000 \div (1 + .10)^2$ is used, where $(1 + .10)^2$ is equal to 1.21 (1.10 × 1.10). Its present value is $826.45 ($1,000 ÷ 1.21), depicted in **Illustration G.11**.

ILLUSTRATION G.11

Finding present value if discounted for two periods

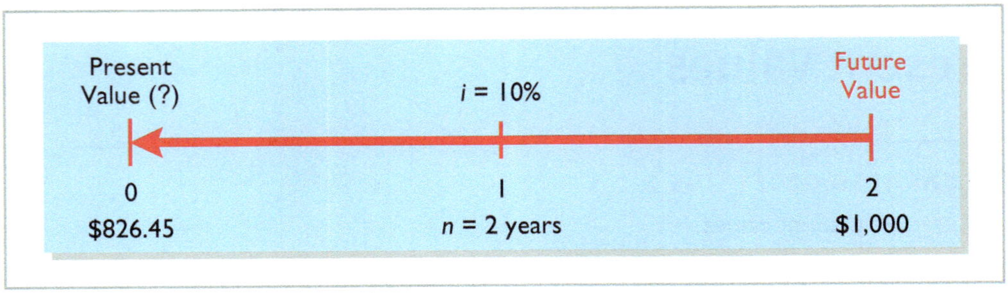

The present value of 1 may also be determined through tables that show the present value of 1 for *n* periods. In **Table 3**, *n* is the number of discounting periods involved. The percentages are the periodic interest rates or discount rates, and the 5-digit decimal numbers in the respective columns are the present value of 1 factors.

When using Table 3, the future value is multiplied by the present value factor specified at the intersection of the number of periods and the discount rate.

TABLE 3 Present Value of 1

(*n*) Periods	4%	5%	6%	7%	8%	9%	10%	11%	12%	15%
1	.96154	.95238	.94340	.93458	.92593	.91743	.90909	.90090	.89286	.86957
2	.92456	.90703	.89000	.87344	.85734	.84168	.82645	.81162	.79719	.75614
3	.88900	.86384	.83962	.81630	.79383	.77218	.75132	.73119	.71178	.65752
4	.85480	.82270	.79209	.76290	.73503	.70843	.68301	.65873	.63552	.57175
5	.82193	.78353	.74726	.71299	.68058	.64993	.62092	.59345	.56743	.49718
6	.79031	.74622	.70496	.66634	.63017	.59627	.56447	.53464	.50663	.43233
7	.75992	.71068	.66506	.62275	.58349	.54703	.51316	.48166	.45235	.37594
8	.73069	.67684	.62741	.58201	.54027	.50187	.46651	.43393	.40388	.32690
9	.70259	.64461	.59190	.54393	.50025	.46043	.42410	.39092	.36061	.28426
10	.67556	.61391	.55839	.50835	.46319	.42241	.38554	.35218	.32197	.24719
11	.64958	.58468	.52679	.47509	.42888	.38753	.35049	.31728	.28748	.21494
12	.62460	.55684	.49697	.44401	.39711	.35554	.31863	.28584	.25668	.18691
13	.60057	.53032	.46884	.41496	.36770	.32618	.28966	.25751	.22917	.16253
14	.57748	.50507	.44230	.38782	.34046	.29925	.26333	.23199	.20462	.14133
15	.55526	.48102	.41727	.36245	.31524	.27454	.23939	.20900	.18270	.12289
16	.53391	.45811	.39365	.33873	.29189	.25187	.21763	.18829	.16312	.10687
17	.51337	.43630	.37136	.31657	.27027	.23107	.19785	.16963	.14564	.09293
18	.49363	.41552	.35034	.29586	.25025	.21199	.17986	.15282	.13004	.08081
19	.47464	.39573	.33051	.27615	.23171	.19449	.16351	.13768	.11611	.07027
20	.45639	.37689	.31180	.25842	.21455	.17843	.14864	.12403	.10367	.06110

For example, the present value factor for one period at a discount rate of 10% is .90909, which is the value used to compute $909.09 ($1,000 × .90909) in Illustration G.10. For two periods at a discount rate of 10%, the present value factor is .82645, which is the value used to compute $826.45 ($1,000 × .82645) in Illustration G.11.

Note that a higher discount rate produces a smaller present value. For example, using a 15% discount rate, the present value of $1,000 due one year from now is $869.57 ($1,000 × .86957), versus $909.09 at 10%. Also note that the further in the future that the future value is, the smaller the present value. For example, using the same discount rate of 10%, the present value of $1,000 due in **five years** at 10% is $620.92 ($1,000 × .62092). The present value of $1,000 due in **one year** is $909.09, a difference of $288.17.

The following two demonstration problems (**Illustrations G.12** and **G.13**) illustrate how to use Table 3.

ILLUSTRATION G.12

Demonstration problem—Using Table 3 for *PV* of 1

Suppose you have a winning lottery ticket and the state gives you the option of taking $10,000 3 years from now or taking the present value of $10,000 now. The state uses an 8% rate in discounting. How much will you receive if you accept your winnings now?

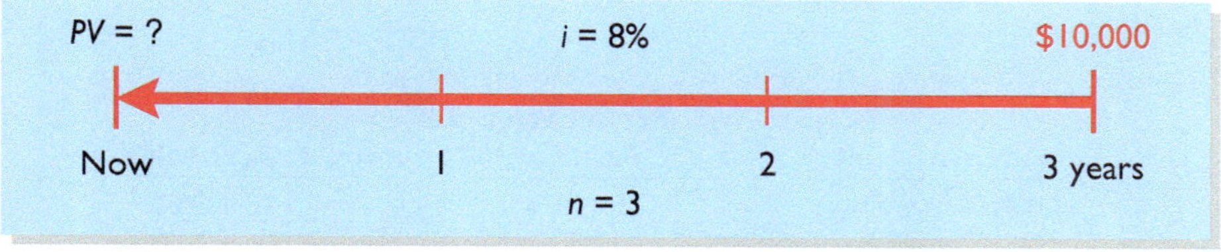

Answer: The present value factor from Table 3 is .79383 (3 periods at 8%). The present value of $10,000 to be received in 3 years discounted at 8% is **$7,938.30** ($10,000 × .79383).

ILLUSTRATION G.13

Demonstration problem—Using Table 3 for *PV* of 1

Determine the amount you must deposit today in your super savings account, paying 9% interest, in order to accumulate $5,000 for a down payment 4 years from now on a new car.

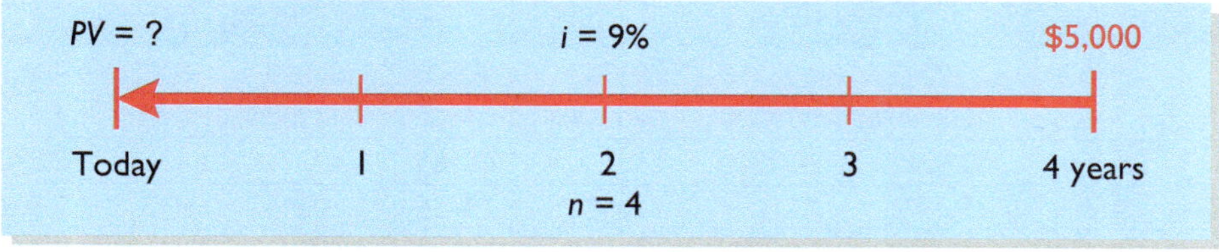

Answer: The present value factor from Table 3 is .70843 (4 periods at 9%). The present value of $5,000 to be received in 4 years discounted at 9% is **$3,542.15** ($5,000 × .70843).

Present Value of an Annuity

The preceding discussion involved the discounting of only a single future amount. Businesses and individuals frequently engage in transactions in which a series of equal dollar amounts are to be received or paid at evenly spaced time intervals (periodically). Examples of a series of periodic receipts or payments are loan agreements, installment sales, mortgage notes, lease (rental) contracts, and pension obligations. As discussed earlier, these periodic receipts or payments are **annuities**.

The **present value of an annuity** is the value now of a series of future receipts or payments, discounted assuming compound interest. In computing the present value of an annuity, it is necessary to know (1) the discount rate, (2) the number of payments (receipts), and (3) the amount of the periodic receipts or payments. To illustrate the computation of the present value of an annuity, assume that you will receive $1,000 cash annually for three years at a time when the discount rate is 10%. This situation is depicted in the time diagram in **Illustration G.14**. **Illustration G.15** shows the computation of its present value in this situation.

ILLUSTRATION G.14

Time diagram for a three-year annuity

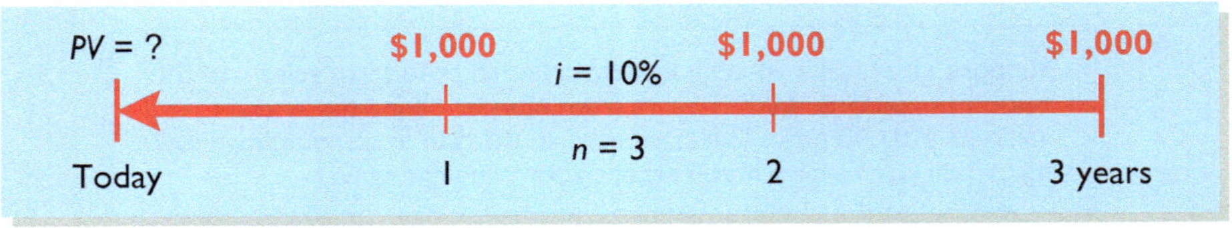

ILLUSTRATION G.15

Present value of a series of future amounts computation

Future Amount	×	Present Value of 1 Factor at 10%	=	Present Value
$1,000 (1 year away)		.90909		$ 909.09
1,000 (2 years away)		.82645		826.45
1,000 (3 years away)		.75132		751.32
		2.48686		**$2,486.86**

This method of calculation is required when the periodic cash flows are not uniform in each period. However, when the future receipts are the same in each period, an annuity table can be used. As illustrated in **Table 4**, an annuity table shows the present value of 1 to be received periodically for a given number of payments. It assumes that each payment is made at the end of each period.

TABLE 4 Present Value of an Annuity of 1

(*n*) Payments	4%	5%	6%	7%	8%	9%	10%	11%	12%	15%
1	.96154	.95238	.94340	.93458	.92593	.91743	.90909	.90090	.89286	.86957
2	1.88609	1.85941	1.83339	1.80802	1.78326	1.75911	1.73554	1.71252	1.69005	1.62571
3	2.77509	2.72325	2.67301	2.62432	2.57710	2.53130	2.48685	2.44371	2.40183	2.28323
4	3.62990	3.54595	3.46511	3.38721	3.31213	3.23972	3.16986	3.10245	3.03735	2.85498
5	4.45182	4.32948	4.21236	4.10020	3.99271	3.88965	3.79079	3.69590	3.60478	3.35216
6	5.24214	5.07569	4.91732	4.76654	4.62288	4.48592	4.35526	4.23054	4.11141	3.78448
7	6.00205	5.78637	5.58238	5.38929	5.20637	5.03295	4.86842	4.71220	4.56376	4.16042
8	6.73274	6.46321	6.20979	5.97130	5.74664	5.53482	5.33493	5.14612	4.96764	4.48732
9	7.43533	7.10782	6.80169	6.51523	6.24689	5.99525	5.75902	5.53705	5.32825	4.77158
10	8.11090	7.72173	7.36009	7.02358	6.71008	6.41766	6.14457	5.88923	5.65022	5.01877
11	8.76048	8.30641	7.88687	7.49867	7.13896	6.80519	6.49506	6.20652	5.93770	5.23371
12	9.38507	8.86325	8.38384	7.94269	7.53608	7.16073	6.81369	6.49236	6.19437	5.42062
13	9.98565	9.39357	8.85268	8.35765	7.90378	7.48690	7.10336	6.74987	6.42355	5.58315
14	10.56312	9.89864	9.29498	8.74547	8.24424	7.78615	7.36669	6.98187	6.62817	5.72448
15	11.11839	10.37966	9.71225	9.10791	8.55948	8.06069	7.60608	7.19087	6.81086	5.84737
16	11.65230	10.83777	10.10590	9.44665	8.85137	8.31256	7.82371	7.37916	6.97399	5.95424
17	12.16567	11.27407	10.47726	9.76322	9.12164	8.54363	8.02155	7.54879	7.11963	6.04716
18	12.65930	11.68959	10.82760	10.05909	9.37189	8.75563	8.20141	7.70162	7.24967	6.12797
19	13.13394	12.08532	11.15812	10.33560	9.60360	8.95012	8.36492	7.83929	7.36578	6.19823
20	13.59033	12.46221	11.46992	10.59401	9.81815	9.12855	8.51356	7.96333	7.46944	6.25933

Table 4 shows that the present value of an annuity of 1 factor for three payments at 10% is 2.48685.[1] This present value factor is the total of the three individual present value factors, as shown in Illustration G.15. Applying this amount to the annual cash flow of $1,000 produces a present value of $2,486.85.

The following demonstration problem (**Illustration G.16**) illustrates how to use Table 4.

ILLUSTRATION G.16

Demonstration problem—Using Table 4 for *PV* of an annuity of 1

Kildare Company has just signed a capitalizable lease contract for equipment that requires rental payments of $6,000 each, to be paid at the end of each of the next 5 years. The appropriate discount rate is 12%. What is the present value of the rental payments—that is, the amount used to capitalize the leased equipment?

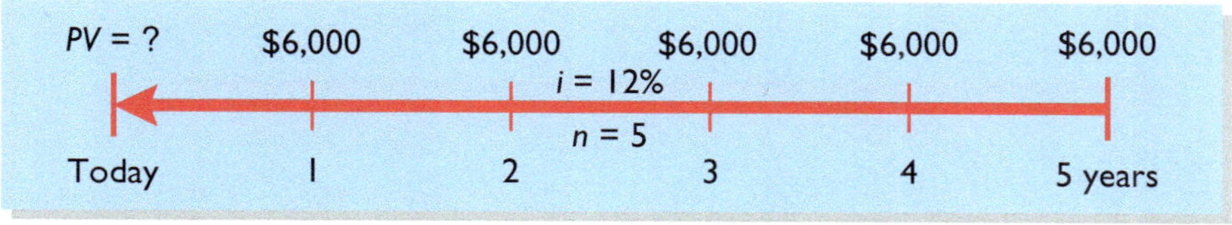

Answer: The present value factor from Table 4 is 3.60478 (5 payments at 12%). The present value of 5 payments of $6,000 each discounted at 12% is **$21,628.68** ($6,000 × 3.60478).

Time Periods and Discounting

In the preceding calculations, the discounting was done on an annual basis using an annual interest rate. Discounting may also be done over shorter periods of time such as monthly, quarterly, or semiannually.

When the time frame is less than one year, it is necessary to convert the annual interest rate to the applicable time frame. Assume, for example, that the investor in Illustration G.14 received $500 **semiannually** for three years instead of $1,000 annually. In this case, the number of periods becomes six (3 × 2), the discount rate is 5% (10% ÷ 2), the present value factor from Table 4 is 5.07569 (6 periods at 5%), and the present value of the future cash flows is $2,537.85 (5.07569 × $500). This amount is slightly higher than the $2,486.86 computed in Illustration G.15 because interest is computed twice during the same year. That is, during the second half of the year, interest is earned on the first half-year's interest.

Present Value of a Long-Term Note or Bond

The present value (or market price) of a long-term note or bond is a function of three variables: (1) the payment amounts, (2) the length of time until the amounts are paid, and (3) the discount rate. Our example uses a five-year bond issue.

The first variable (dollars to be paid) is made up of two elements: (1) a series of interest payments (an annuity) and (2) the principal amount (a single sum). To compute the present

[1]The difference of .00001 between 2.48686 and 2.48685 is due to rounding.

value of the bond, both the interest payments and the principal amount must be discounted—two different computations. The time diagrams for a bond due in five years are shown in **Illustration G.17**.

ILLUSTRATION G.17 **Time diagrams for the present value of a bond**

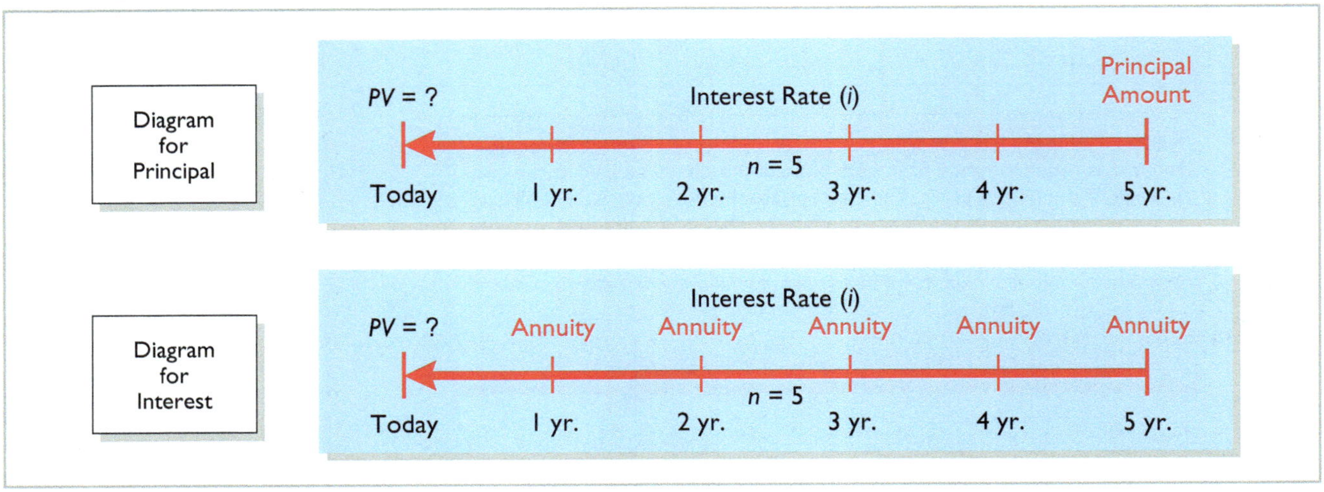

When the investor's market interest rate is equal to the bond's contractual interest rate, the present value of the bonds will equal the face value of the bonds. To illustrate, assume a bond issue of 5%, 10-year bonds with a face value of $100,000 with interest payable **annually** on January 1. If the discount rate is the same as the contractual rate, the bonds will sell at face value. In this case, the investor will receive (1) $100,000 at maturity and (2) a series of ten $5,000 interest payments ($100,000 × 5%) over the term of the bonds. The length of time is expressed in terms of interest periods—in this case—10, and the discount rate per interest period, 5%. The time diagram in **Illustration G.18** depicts the variables involved in this discounting situation.

ILLUSTRATION G.18 **Time diagram for present value of a 5%, 10-year bond paying interest annually**

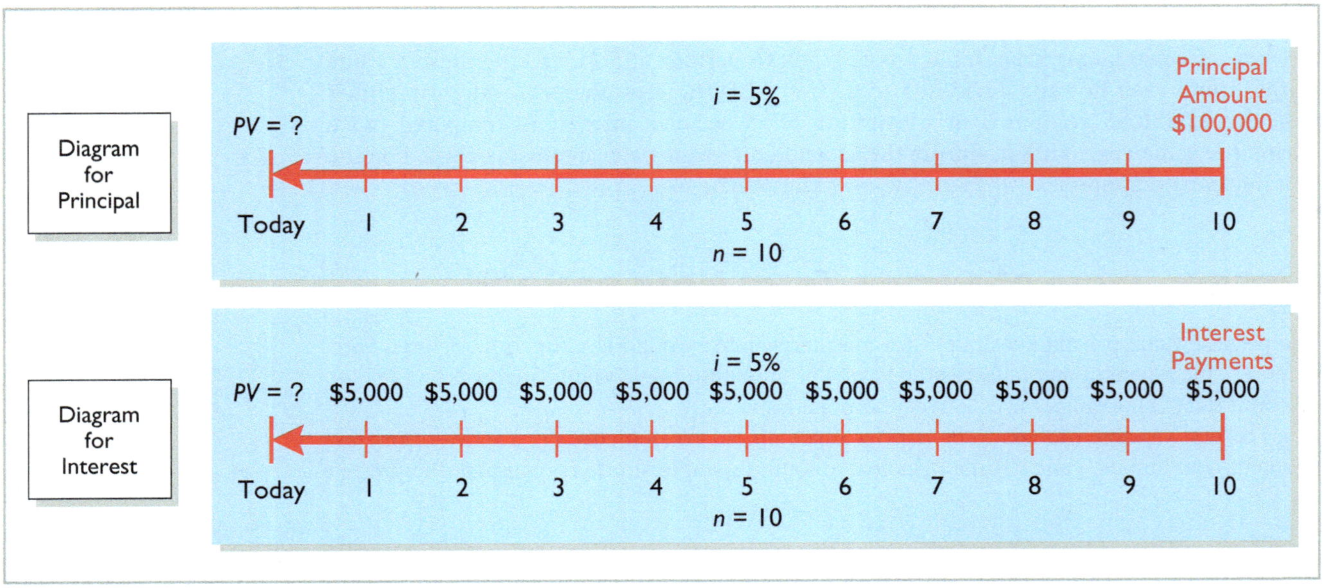

Illustration G.19 shows the computation of the present value of these bonds.

ILLUSTRATION G.19
Present value of principal and interest—face value

5% Contractual Rate—5% Discount Rate	
Present value of principal to be received at maturity	
$100,000 × *PV* of 1 due in 10 periods at 5%	
$100,000 × .61391 (Table 3)	$ 61,391
Present value of interest to be received periodically over the term of the bonds	
$5,000 × *PV* of 1 due periodically for 10 periods at 5%	
$5,000 × 7.72173 (Table 4)	38,609*
Present value of bonds	**$100,000**

*Rounded

Now assume that the investor's required rate of return is 6%, not 5%. The future amounts are again $100,000 and $5,000, respectively, but now a discount rate of 6% must be used. The present value of the bonds is $92,639, as computed in **Illustration G.20**.

ILLUSTRATION G.20
Present value of principal and interest—discount

5% Contractual Rate—6% Discount Rate	
Present value of principal to be received at maturity	
$100,000 × .55839 (Table 3)	$55,839
Present value of interest to be received periodically over the term of the bonds	
$5,000 × 7.36009 (Table 4)	36,800
Present value of bonds	**$92,639**

Conversely, if the discount rate is 4% and the contractual rate is 5%, the present value of the bonds is $108,111, computed as shown in **Illustration G.21**.

ILLUSTRATION G.21
Present value of principal and interest—premium

5% Contractual Rate—4% Discount Rate	
Present value of principal to be received at maturity	
$100,000 × .67556 (Table 3)	$ 67,556
Present value of interest to be received periodically over the term of the bonds	
$5,000 × 8.11090 (Table 4)	40,555*
Present value of bonds	**$108,111**

*Rounded

The above discussion relied on present value tables in solving present value problems. Calculators may also be used to compute present values without the use of these tables. Many calculators, especially financial calculators, have present value (*PV*) functions that allow you to calculate present values by merely inputting the proper amount, discount rate, periods, and pressing the PV key. We discuss the use of financial calculators in a later section.

Capital Budgeting Situations

LEARNING OBJECTIVE 3

Compute the present value in capital budgeting situations.

The decision to make long-term capital investments is best evaluated using discounting techniques that recognize the time value of money. To do this, many companies calculate the present value of the cash flows involved in a capital investment.

To illustrate, Nagel-Siebert Trucking Company, a cross-country freight carrier in Montgomery, Illinois, is considering adding another truck to its fleet because of a purchasing opportunity. **Navistar Inc.**, Nagel-Siebert's primary supplier of overland rigs, is overstocked and offers to sell its biggest rig for $154,000 cash payable upon delivery. Nagel-Siebert knows that the rig will produce a net cash flow per year of $40,000 for five years (received at the end of each year), at which time it will be sold for an estimated salvage value of $35,000. Nagel-Siebert's discount rate in evaluating capital expenditures is 10%. Should Nagel-Siebert commit to the purchase of this rig?

The cash flows that must be discounted to present value by Nagel-Siebert are as follows.

Cash payable on delivery (today): $154,000.

Net cash flow from operating the rig: $40,000 for 5 years (at the end of each year).

Cash received from sale of rig at the end of 5 years: $35,000.

The time diagrams for the latter two cash flows are shown in **Illustration G.22**.

ILLUSTRATION G.22 **Time diagrams for Nagel-Siebert Trucking Company**

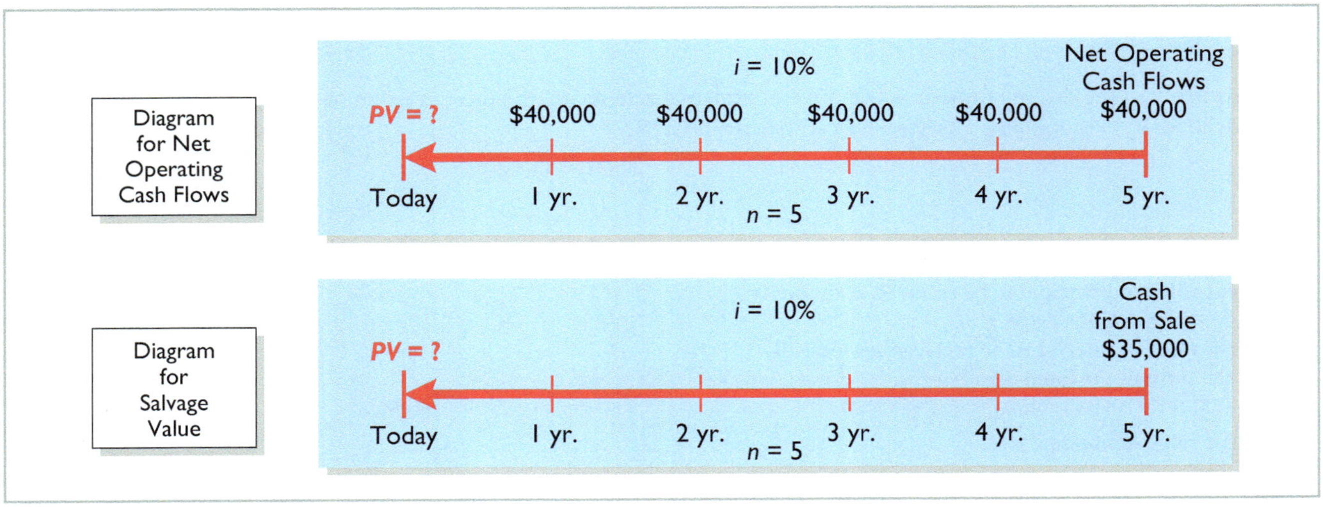

Notice from the diagrams that computing the present value of the net operating cash flows ($40,000 at the end of each year) is **discounting an annuity** (Table 4), while computing the present value of the $35,000 salvage value is **discounting a single sum** (Table 3). The computation of these present values is shown in **Illustration G.23**.

ILLUSTRATION G.23

Present value computations at 10%

Present Values Using a 10% Discount Rate	
Present value of net operating cash flows received annually over 5 years	
$40,000 × PV of 1 received annually for 5 years at 10%	
$40,000 × 3.79079	$ 151,631.60
Present value of salvage value (cash) to be received in 5 years	
$35,000 × PV of 1 received in 5 years at 10%	
$35,000 × .62092	21,732.20
Present value of cash **inflows**	173,363.80
Present value of cash **outflows** (purchase price due today at 10%)	
$154,000 × PV of 1 due today	
$154,000 × 1.00000	(154,000.00)
Net present value	**$ 19,363.80**

Because the present value of the cash receipts (inflows) of $173,363.80 ($151,631.60 + $21,732.20) exceeds the present value of the cash payments (outflows) of $154,000.00, the net present value of $19,363.80 is positive, and **the decision to invest should be accepted**.

Now assume that Nagel-Siebert uses a discount rate of 15%, not 10%, because it wants a greater return on its investments in capital assets. The cash receipts and cash payments by Nagel-Siebert are the same. The present values of these receipts and cash payments discounted at 15% are shown in **Illustration G.24**.

ILLUSTRATION G.24

Present value computations at 15%

Present Values Using a 15% Discount Rate	
Present value of net operating cash flows received annually over 5 years at 15%	
$40,000 × 3.35216	$ 134,086.40
Present value of salvage value (cash) to be received in 5 years at 15%	
$35,000 × .49718	17,401.30
Present value of cash **inflows**	$ 151,487.70
Present value of cash **outflows** (purchase price due today at 15%)	
$154,000 × 1.00000	(154,000.00)
Net present value	**$ (2,512.30)**

Because the present value of the cash payments (outflows) of $154,000.00 exceeds the present value of the cash receipts (inflows) of $151,487.70 ($134,086.40 + $17,401.30), the net present value of $2,512.30 is negative, and **the investment should be rejected**.

The above discussion relied on present value tables in solving present value problems. As we show in the next section, calculators may also be used to compute present values without the use of these tables. Financial calculators have present value (PV) functions that allow you to calculate present values by merely identifying the proper amount, discount rate, periods, and pressing the PV key.

Using Financial Calculators

LEARNING OBJECTIVE 4

Use a financial calculator to solve time value of money problems.

Business professionals, once they have mastered the underlying time value of money concepts, often use a financial calculator to solve these types of problems. To use financial calculators, you enter the time value of money variables into the calculator. **Illustration G.25** shows the five most common keys used to solve time value of money problems.[2]

ILLUSTRATION G.25

Financial calculator keys

where:

N = number of periods
I = interest rate per period (some calculators use I/YR or i)
PV = present value (occurs at the beginning of the first period)
PMT = payment (all payments are equal, and none are skipped)
FV = future value (occurs at the end of the last period)

In solving time value of money problems in this appendix, you will generally be given three of four variables and will have to solve for the remaining variable. The fifth key (the key not used) is given a value of zero to ensure that this variable is not used in the computation.

Present Value of a Single Sum

To illustrate how to solve a present value problem using a financial calculator, assume that you want to know the present value of $84,253 to be received in five years, discounted at 11% compounded annually. **Illustration G.26** depicts this problem.

ILLUSTRATION G.26

Calculator solution for present value of a single sum

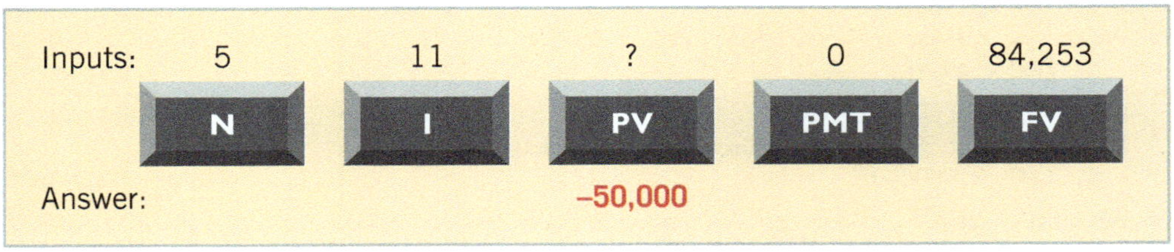

Illustration G.26 shows you the information (inputs) to enter into the calculator: N = 5, I = 11, PMT = 0, and FV = 84,253. You then press PV for the answer: −$50,000. As indicated, the PMT key was given a value of zero because a series of payments did not occur in this problem.

Plus and Minus

The use of plus and minus signs in time value of money problems with a financial calculator can be confusing. Most financial calculators are programmed so that the positive and negative cash flows in any problem offset each other. In the present value problem above, we identified the $84,253 future value initial investment as a positive (inflow); the answer −$50,000 was shown as a negative amount, reflecting a cash outflow. If the 84,253 were entered as a negative, then the final answer would have been reported as a positive 50,000.

Hopefully, the sign convention will not cause confusion. If you understand what is required in a problem, you should be able to interpret a positive or negative amount in determining the solution to a problem.

Compounding Periods

In the problem above, we assumed that compounding occurs once a year. Some financial calculators have a default setting, which assumes that compounding occurs 12 times a year. You must determine what default period has been programmed into your calculator and change it as necessary to arrive at the proper compounding period.

[2]On many calculators, these keys are actual buttons on the face of the calculator; on others, they appear on the display after the user accesses a present value menu.

Rounding

Most financial calculators store and calculate using 12 decimal places. As a result, because compound interest tables generally have factors only up to five decimal places, a slight difference in the final answer can result. In most time value of money problems, the final answer will not include more than two decimal places.

Present Value of an Annuity

To illustrate how to solve a present value of an annuity problem using a financial calculator, assume that you are asked to determine the present value of rental receipts of $6,000 each to be received at the end of each of the next five years, when discounted at 12%, as pictured in **Illustration G.27**.

	N	I	PV	PMT	FV
Inputs:	5	12	?	6,000	0
Answer:			−21,628.66		

ILLUSTRATION G.27
Calculator solution for present value of an annuity

In this case, you enter N = 5, I = 12, PMT = 6,000, FV = 0, and then press PV to arrive at the answer of −$21,628.66.

Future Value of a Single Sum

Now let us look at an investment to illustrate how to solve a future value problem using a financial calculator. Assume that you will invest $20,000 today into a fund and you intend to leave it there for 15 years. The fund earns 7% interest. **Illustration G.28** shows how to compute the future value of the fund at the end of year 15.

	N	I	PV	PMT	FV
Inputs:	15	7	20,000	0	?
Answer:					−55,180.63

ILLUSTRATION G.28
Calculator solution for future value of single sum

In this case, you enter N = 15, I = 7, PV = 20,000, PMT = 0, and then press FV to calculate the future value of −$55,180.63.

Future Value of an Annuity

You can use a financial calculator to solve a future value of an annuity problem for an annuity investment. Assume that you will invest $8,000 into a fund at the end of each of the next eight years. The fund earns 9% interest. **Illustration G.29** shows how to compute the future value of the fund at the end of the eighth year.

	N	I	PV	PMT	FV
Inputs:	8	9	0	8,000	?
Answer:					−88,227.79

ILLUSTRATION G.29
Calculator solution for future value of an annuity

In this case, you enter N = 8, I = 9, PV = 0, PMT = 8,000, and then press FV to determine the future value of −$88,227.79.

Internal Rate of Return

You can also use these same calculator keys to compute the internal rate of return of an investment that has equal cash flows. Suppose that a purchase of a piece of equipment with a seven-year life requires an initial investment of $54,000, has positive cash flows of $7,800 per year, and has an estimated salvage value of $11,000. The computation is shown in **Illustration G.30**.

ILLUSTRATION G.30

Calculator solution for internal rate of return

Inputs:	7	?	–54,000	7,800	11,000
	N	I	PV	PMT	FV
Answer:		4.52%			

In this case, you enter N = 7, PV = −54,000 (we entered as a negative, since it is an outflow), PMT = 7,800, FV = 11,000, and then press FV to determine the answer of 4.52%. Notice that the advantage to this approach is that you arrive at a much more precise result, rather than the rough approximation provided by the present value tables. To determine the internal rate of return using your calculator for an investment with unequal cash flows, you need to employ the cash flow key (CF) and the internal rate of return key (IRR). The use of these function keys varies across calculators, so you should consult the user manual for your calculator or the manufacturer's website for specific information.

Useful Applications of the Financial Calculator

With a financial calculator, you can solve for any interest rate or for any number of periods in a time value of money problem. Here are some examples of these applications.

Auto Loan

Assume you are financing the purchase of a used car with a three-year loan. The loan has a 9.5% stated annual interest rate, compounded monthly. The price of the car is $6,000, and you want to determine the monthly payments, assuming that the payments start one month after the purchase. This problem is pictured in **Illustration G.31**.

ILLUSTRATION G.31

Calculator solution for auto loan payments

Inputs:	36	9.5	6,000	?	0
	N	I	PV	PMT	FV
Answer:				–192.20	

To solve this problem, you enter N = 36 (12 × 3), I = 9.5, PV = 6,000, FV = 0, and then press PMT. You will find that the monthly payments will be $192.20. Note that the payment key is usually programmed for 12 payments per year. Thus, you must change the default (compounding period) if the payments are other than monthly.

Mortgage Loan Amount

Say you are evaluating financing options for a loan on a house (a mortgage). You decide that the maximum mortgage payment you can afford is $700 per month. The annual interest rate is 8.4%. If you get a mortgage that requires you to make monthly payments over a 15-year period, what is the maximum home loan you can afford? **Illustration G.32** depicts this problem.

Inputs:	180	8.4	?	–700	0
	N	I	PV	PMT	FV
Answer:			71,509.81		

ILLUSTRATION G.32

Calculator solution for mortgage amount

You enter N = 180 (12 × 15 years), I = 8.4, PMT = –700, FV = 0, and then press PV. With the payments-per-year key set at 12, you find a present value of $71,509.81—the maximum home loan you can afford, given that you want to keep your mortgage payments at $700. Note that by changing any of the variables, you can quickly conduct "what-if" analyses for different situations.

Review

Learning Objectives Review

1 Compute interest and future values.

Simple interest is computed on the principal only, while compound interest is computed on the principal and any interest earned that has not been withdrawn.

To solve for future value of a single amount, prepare a time diagram of the problem. Identify the principal amount, the number of compounding periods, and the interest rate. Using the future value of 1 table, multiply the principal amount by the future value factor specified at the intersection of the number of periods and the interest rate.

To solve for future value of an annuity, prepare a time diagram of the problem. Identify the amount of the periodic payments (receipts), the number of payments (receipts), and the interest rate. Using the future value of an annuity of 1 table, multiply the amount of the payments by the future value factor specified at the intersection of the number of periods and the interest rate.

2 Compute present values.

The following three variables are fundamental to solving present value problems: (1) the future amount, (2) the number of periods, and (3) the interest rate (the discount rate).

To solve for present value of a single amount, prepare a time diagram of the problem. Identify the future amount, the number of discounting periods, and the discount (interest) rate. Using the present value of a single amount table, multiply the future amount by the present value factor specified at the intersection of the number of periods and the discount rate.

To solve for present value of an annuity, prepare a time diagram of the problem. Identify the amount of future periodic receipts or payments (annuities), the number of payments (receipts), and the discount (interest) rate. Using the present value of an annuity of 1 table, multiply the amount of the annuity by the present value factor specified at the intersection of the number of payments and the interest rate.

To compute the present value of notes and bonds, determine the present value of the principal amount and the present value of the interest payments. Multiply the principal amount (a single future amount) by the present value factor (from the present value of 1 table) intersecting at the number of periods (number of interest payments) and the discount rate. To determine the present value of the series of interest payments, multiply the amount of the interest payment by the present value factor (from the present value of an annuity of 1 table) intersecting at the number of periods (number of interest payments) and the discount rate. Add the present value of the principal amount to the present value of the interest payments to arrive at the present value of the note or bond.

3 Compute the present value in capital budgeting situations.

Compute the present values of all cash inflows and all cash outflows related to the capital budgeting proposal (an investment-type decision). If the **net** present value is positive, accept the proposal (make the investment). If the **net** present value is negative, reject the proposal (do not make the investment).

4 Use a financial calculator to solve time value of money problems.

Financial calculators can be used to solve the same and additional problems as those solved with time value of money tables. Enter into the financial calculator the amounts for all of the known elements of a time value of money problem (periods, interest rate, payments, future or present value), and it solves for the unknown element. Particularly useful situations involve interest rates and compounding periods not presented in the tables.

Glossary Review

Annuity A series of equal dollar amounts to be paid or received at evenly spaced time intervals (periodically). (p. G-5).

Compound interest The interest computed on the principal and any interest earned that has not been paid or withdrawn. (p. G-2).

Discounting the future amount(s) The process of determining present value. (p. G-7).

Future value of an annuity The sum of all the payments (receipts) plus the accumulated compound interest on them. (p. G-5).

Future value of a single amount The value at a future date of a given amount invested, assuming compound interest. (p. G-3).

Interest Payment for the use of another person's money. (p. G-1).

Present value The value now of a given amount to be paid or received in the future, assuming compound interest. (p. G-7).

Present value of an annuity The value now of a series of future receipts or payments, discounted assuming compound interest. (p. G-9).

Principal The amount borrowed or invested. (p. G-1).

Simple interest The interest computed on the principal only. (p. G-2).

WileyPLUS

Many additional resources are available for practice in WileyPLUS.

Brief Exercises

(Use tables to solve exercises BEG.1 to BEG.23.)

Compute the future value of a single amount.

BEG.1 (LO 1) Jozy Altidore invested $6,000 at 5% annual interest, and left the money invested without withdrawing any of the interest for 12 years. At the end of the 12 years, Jozy withdrew the accumulated amount of money. (a) What amount did Jozy withdraw, assuming the investment earns simple interest? (b) What amount did Jozy withdraw, assuming the investment earns interest compounded annually?

Use future value tables.

BEG.2 (LO 1) For each of the following cases, indicate (a) what interest rate columns and (b) what number of periods you would refer to in looking up the future value factor.

1. In Table 1 (future value of 1):

	Annual Rate	Number of Years Invested	Compounded
Case A	5%	3	Annually
Case B	12%	4	Semiannually

2. In Table 2 (future value of an annuity of 1):

	Annual Rate	Number of Years Invested	Compounded
Case A	3%	8	Annually
Case B	8%	6	Semiannually

Compute the future value of a single amount.

BEG.3 (LO 1) Liam Company signed a lease for an office building for a period of 12 years. Under the lease agreement, a security deposit of $9,600 is made. The deposit will be returned at the expiration of the lease with interest compounded at 4% per year. What amount will Liam receive at the time the lease expires?

Compute the future value of an annuity.

BEG.4 (LO 1) Bates Company issued $1,000,000, 10-year bonds. It agreed to make annual deposits of $78,000 to a fund (called a sinking fund), which will be used to pay off the principal amount of the bond at the end of 10 years. The deposits are made at the end of each year into an account paying 6% annual interest. What amount will be in the sinking fund at the end of 10 years?

Compute the future value of a single amount and of an annuity.

BEG.5 (LO 1) Andrew and Emma Garfield invested $8,000 in a savings account paying 5% annual interest when their daughter, Angela, was born. They also deposited $1,000 on each of her birthdays until she was 18 (including her 18th birthday). How much was in the savings account on her 18th birthday (after the last deposit)?

BEG.6 (LO 1) Hugh Curtin borrowed $35,000 on July 1, 2020. This amount plus accrued interest at 8% compounded annually is to be repaid on July 1, 2025. How much will Hugh have to repay on July 1, 2025?

Compute the future value of a single amount.

BEG.7 (LO 2) For each of the following cases, indicate (a) what interest rate columns and (b) what number of periods you would refer to in looking up the discount rate.

Use present value tables.

1. In Table 3 (present value of 1):

	Annual Rate	Number of Years Involved	Discounts per Year
Case A	12%	7	Annually
Case B	8%	11	Annually
Case C	10%	8	Semiannually

2. In Table 4 (present value of an annuity of 1):

	Annual Rate	Number of Years Involved	Number of Payments Involved	Frequency of Payments
Case A	10%	20	20	Annually
Case B	10%	7	7	Annually
Case C	6%	5	10	Semiannually

BEG.8 (LO 2) **a.** What is the present value of $25,000 due 9 periods from now, discounted at 10%?

b. What is the present value of $25,000 to be received at the end of each of 6 periods, discounted at 9%?

Determine present values.

BEG.9 (LO 2) Messi Company is considering an investment that will return a lump sum of $900,000 6 years from now. What amount should Messi Company pay for this investment to earn an 8% return?

Compute the present value of a single amount investment.

BEG.10 (LO 2) Lloyd Company earns 6% on an investment that will return $450,000 8 years from now. What is the amount Lloyd should invest now to earn this rate of return?

Compute the present value of a single amount investment.

BEG.11 (LO 2) Robben Company is considering investing in an annuity contract that will return $40,000 annually at the end of each year for 15 years. What amount should Robben Company pay for this investment if it earns an 8% return?

Compute the present value of an annuity investment.

BEG.12 (LO 2) Kaehler Enterprises earns 5% on an investment that pays back $80,000 at the end of each of the next 6 years. What is the amount Kaehler Enterprises invested to earn the 5% rate of return?

Compute the present value of an annual investment.

BEG.13 (LO 2) Dempsey Railroad Co. is about to issue $400,000 of 10-year bonds paying an 11% interest rate, with interest payable semiannually. The discount rate for such securities is 10%. How much can Dempsey expect to receive for the sale of these bonds?

Compute the present value of bonds.

BEG.14 (LO 2) Assume the same information as BEG.13 except that the discount rate is 12% instead of 10%. In this case, how much can Dempsey expect to receive from the sale of these bonds?

Compute the present value of bonds.

BEG.15 (LO 2) Neymar Taco Company receives a $75,000, 6-year note bearing interest of 4% (paid annually) from a customer at a time when the discount rate is 6%. What is the present value of the note received by Neymar?

Compute the present value of a note.

BEG.16 (LO 2) Gleason Enterprises issued 6%, 8-year, $2,500,000 par value bonds that pay interest semiannually on October 1 and April 1. The bonds are dated April 1, 2020, and are issued on that date. The discount rate of interest for such bonds on April 1, 2020, is 8%. What cash proceeds did Gleason receive from issuance of the bonds?

Compute the present value of bonds.

BEG.17 (LO 2) Frazier Company issues a 10%, 5-year mortgage note on January 1, 2020, to obtain financing for new equipment. Land is used as collateral for the note. The terms provide for semiannual installment payments of $48,850. What are the cash proceeds received from the issuance of the note?

Compute the present value of a note.

BEG.18 (LO 2) If Colleen Mooney invests $4,765.50 now and she will receive $12,000 at the end of 12 years, what annual rate of interest will Colleen earn on her investment? (*Hint:* Use Table 3.)

Compute the interest rate on a single amount.

BEG.19 (LO 2) Tim Howard has been offered the opportunity of investing $36,125 now. The investment will earn 11% per year and at the end of that time will return Tim $75,000. How many years must Tim wait to receive $75,000? (*Hint:* Use Table 3.)

Compute the number of periods of a single amount.

Compute the interest rate on an annuity.

BEG.20 (LO 2) Joanne Quick made an investment of $10,271.38. From this investment, she will receive $1,200 annually for the next 15 years starting one year from now. What rate of interest will Joanne's investment be earning for her? (*Hint:* Use Table 4.)

Compute the number of periods of an annuity.

BEG.21 (LO 2) Kevin Morales invests $7,793.83 now for a series of $1,300 annual returns beginning one year from now. Kevin will earn a return of 9% on the initial investment. How many annual payments of $1,300 will Kevin receive? (*Hint:* Use Table 4.)

Compute the present value of a machine for purposes of making a purchase decision.

BEG.22 (LO 3) Barney Googal owns a garage and is contemplating purchasing a tire retreading machine for $12,820. After estimating costs and revenues, Barney projects a net cash inflow from the retreading machine of $2,700 annually for 7 years. Barney hopes to earn a return of 9% on such investments. What is the present value of the retreading operation? Should Barney Googal purchase the retreading machine?

Compute the maximum price to pay for a machine.

BEG.23 (LO 3) Snyder Company is considering purchasing equipment. The equipment will produce the following cash inflows: Year 1, $25,000; Year 2, $30,000; and Year 3, $40,000. Snyder requires a minimum rate of return of 11%. What is the maximum price Snyder should pay for this equipment?

Determine interest rate.

BEG.24 (LO 4) Carly Simon wishes to invest $18,000 on July 1, 2020, and have it accumulate to $50,000 by July 1, 2030. Use a financial calculator to determine at what exact annual rate of interest Carly must invest the $18,000.

Determine interest rate.

BEG.25 (LO 4) On July 17, 2019, Keith Urban borrowed $42,000 from his grandfather to open a clothing store. Starting July 17, 2020, Keith has to make 10 equal annual payments of $6,500 each to repay the loan. Use a financial calculator to determine what interest rate Keith is paying.

Determine interest rate.

BEG.26 (LO 4) As the purchaser of a new house, Carrie Underwood has signed a mortgage note to pay the Nashville National Bank and Trust Co. $8,400 every 6 months for 20 years, at the end of which time she will own the house. At the date the mortgage is signed, the purchase price was $198,000 and Underwood made a down payment of $20,000. The first payment will be made 6 months after the date the mortgage is signed. Using a financial calculator, compute the exact rate of interest earned on the mortgage by the bank.

Various time value of money situations.

BEG.27 (LO 4) Using a financial calculator, solve for the unknowns in each of the following situations.

a. On June 1, 2019, Jennifer Lawrence purchases lakefront property from her neighbor, Josh Hutcherson, and agrees to pay the purchase price in seven payments of $16,000 each, the first payment to be payable June 1, 2020. (Assume that interest compounded at an annual rate of 7.35% is implicit in the payments.) What is the purchase price of the property?

b. On January 1, 2019, Gerrard Corporation purchased 200 of the $1,000 face value, 8% coupon, 10-year bonds of Sterling Inc. The bonds mature on January 1, 2029, and pay interest annually beginning January 1, 2020. Gerrard purchased the bonds to yield 10.65%. How much did Gerrard pay for the bonds?

Various time value of money situations.

BEG.28 (LO 4) Using a financial calculator, provide a solution to each of the following situations.

a. Lynn Anglin owes a debt of $42,000 from the purchase of her new sport utility vehicle. The debt bears annual interest of 7.8% compounded monthly. Lynn wishes to pay the debt and interest in equal monthly payments over 8 years, beginning one month hence. What equal monthly payments will pay off the debt and interest?

b. On January 1, 2020, Roger Molony offers to buy Dave Feeney's used snowmobile for $8,000, payable in five equal annual installments, which are to include 7.25% interest on the unpaid balance and a portion of the principal. If the first payment is to be made on December 31, 2020, how much will each payment be?

Determine internal rate of return.

BEG.29 (LO 4) Renolds Corporation is considering two alternative investments in excavating equipment. Investment A requires an initial investment of $184,000, has positive cash flows of $27,500 per year, and has an estimated salvage value of $21,000. Investment B requires an initial investment of $234,000, has positive cash flows of $32,800 per year, and has an estimated salvage value of $19,000. Each piece of equipment is expected to have a 12-year useful life. Use a financial calculator to determine the internal rate of return of each project to decide which is more desirable. (Round to two decimal places, e.g., 9.74%.)

Just-in-Time Processing and Activity-Based Costing

Appendix Preview

Traditional costing systems are not the best answer for every company. Some companies have suspected that their traditional costing systems were masking significant differences in their real cost structure, so they sought a new method of assigning costs. These searches by companies for ways to improve operations and gather more accurate data for decision-making have resulted in the development of powerful management tools, including just-in-time (JIT) processing and activity-based costing (ABC). The objective of this appendix is to explain these two management tools.

Appendix Outline

LEARNING OBJECTIVES

1 Explain just-in-time (JIT) processing and activity-based costing (ABC).	• Just-in-time processing • Activity-based costing
2 Apply activity-based costing to a manufacturer.	• Identify and classify activities and assign overhead to cost pools • Identify cost drivers • Compute activity-based overhead rates • Allocate overhead costs to products • Comparing unit costs • Benefits of ABC • Limitations of ABC

Just-in-Time Processing and Activity-Based Costing

LEARNING OBJECTIVE 1

Explain just-in-time (JIT) processing and activity-based costing (ABC).

Just-in-Time Processing

Traditionally, continuous process manufacturing has been based on a **just-in-case** philosophy: Inventories of raw materials are maintained *just in case* some items are of poor quality or a key supplier is shut down by a strike. Similarly, subassembly parts are manufactured and stored *just in case* they are needed later in the manufacturing process. Finished goods are completed and stored *just in case* unexpected and rush customer orders are received. This philosophy often results in a "**push approach**," in which raw materials and subassembly parts are pushed through each process. Traditional processing often results in the buildup of extensive manufacturing inventories.

Primarily in response to foreign competition, many U.S. firms have switched to **just-in-time (JIT) processing**. JIT manufacturing is dedicated to having the right amount of materials, parts, or products just as they are needed. JIT first hit the United States in the early 1980s when automobile companies adopted it to compete with foreign automakers. Many companies, including **Dell**, **Caterpillar**, and **Harley-Davidson**, now successfully use JIT. Under JIT processing, companies receive raw materials **just in time** for use in production, they complete subassembly parts **just in time** for use in finished goods, and they complete finished goods **just in time** to be sold. **Illustration H.1** shows the sequence of activities in just-in-time processing.

ILLUSTRATION H.1 **Just-in-time processing**

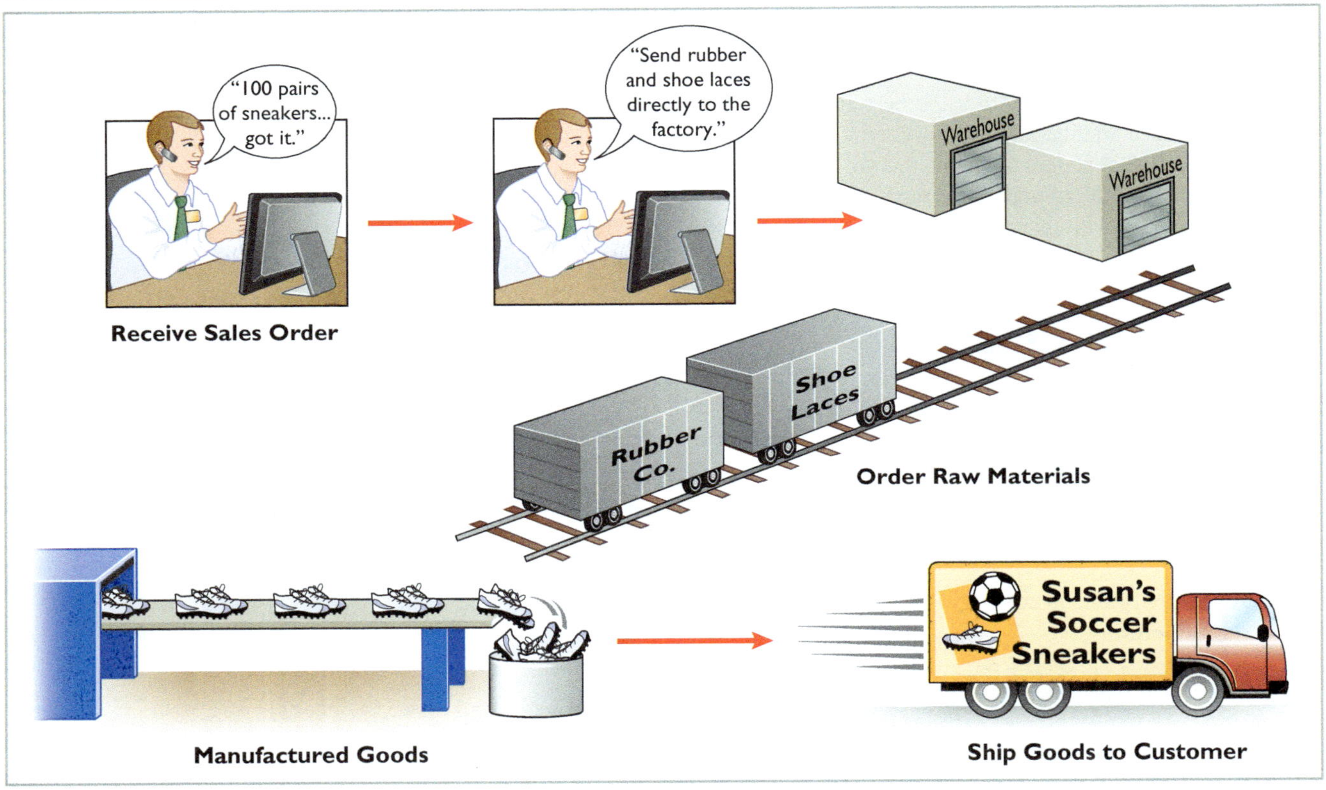

Objective of JIT Processing

A primary objective of JIT is to eliminate all manufacturing inventories. Inventories have an adverse effect on net income because they tie up funds and storage space that could be put to more productive uses. JIT strives to eliminate inventories by using a "**pull approach**" in manufacturing. This approach begins with the customer placing an order with the company, which starts the process of pulling the product through the manufacturing process. A computer at the final workstation sends a signal to the preceding workstation. This signal indicates the exact materials (parts and subassemblies) needed to complete the production of a specified product for a specified time period, such as an eight-hour shift. The next-preceding process, in turn, sends its signal to other processes back up the line. The goal is a smooth continuous flow in the manufacturing process, with no buildup of inventories at any point.

Elements of JIT Processing

There are three important elements in JIT processing:

1. **Dependable suppliers.** Suppliers must be willing to deliver on short notice exact quantities of raw materials according to precise quality specifications (even including multiple

deliveries within the same day). Suppliers must also be willing to deliver the raw materials at specified workstations rather than at a central receiving department. This type of purchasing requires constant and direct communication. Such communication is facilitated by an online computer linkage between the company and its suppliers (see **Helpful Hint**).

2. **A multiskilled work force.** Under JIT, machines are often strategically grouped into work cells or workstations. Much of the work is automated. As a result, one worker may operate and maintain several different types of machines.
3. **A total quality control system.** The company must establish total quality control throughout the manufacturing operations (see **Helpful Hint**). Total quality control means **no defects**. Since the pull approach signals only required quantities, any defects at any workstation will shut down operations at subsequent workstations. Total quality control requires continuous monitoring by both line employees and supervisors at each workstation.

HELPFUL HINT

Buyer leverage is important in finding dependable suppliers. Companies like GM and GE have more success than smaller companies.

HELPFUL HINT

Without its emphasis on quality control, JIT would be impractical or even impossible. In JIT, quality is engineered into the production process.

Benefits of JIT Processing

The major benefits of implementing JIT processing are as follows.

1. Significant reduction or elimination of manufacturing inventories.
2. Enhanced product quality.
3. Reduction or elimination of rework costs and inventory storage costs.
4. Production cost savings from the improved flow of goods through the processes.

The effects in many cases have been dramatic. For example, after using JIT for two years, a major division of **Hewlett-Packard** found that work in process inventories (in dollars) were down 82%, scrap/rework costs were down 30%, space utilization improved by 40%, and labor efficiency improved 50%. As indicated, JIT not only reduces inventory but also enables a company to manufacture a better product faster and with less waste.

One of the major accounting benefits of JIT is the elimination of separate raw materials and work in process inventory accounts. These accounts are replaced by **one account**, Raw and In-Process Inventory. All materials and conversion costs are charged to this account. The reduction (or elimination) of in-process inventories results in a simpler computation of equivalent units of production.

Activity-Based Costing

Activity-based costing (ABC) focuses on the activities required to produce a product or perform a service. An ABC system is similar to conventional costing systems in accounting for direct materials and direct labor, but it differs in regard to manufacturing overhead.

A conventional cost system uses a **single unit-level** basis to allocate overhead costs to products. The basis may be direct labor or machine hours used to manufacture the product. The assumption in this approach is that as volume of units produced increases, so does the cost of overhead. However, in recent years the amount of direct labor used in many industries has greatly **decreased**, and total overhead costs resulting from depreciation on expensive equipment and machinery, utilities, repairs, and maintenance have significantly **increased**.

In ABC, the cost of a product is equal to the sum of the costs of all activities performed to manufacture it. ABC recognizes that to have accurate and meaningful cost data, **more than one basis** of allocating activity costs to products is needed.

In selecting the allocation basis, ABC seeks to identify the **cost drivers** that measure the activities performed on the product. A **cost driver** may be any factor or activity that has a direct cause–effect relationship with the resources consumed. **Illustration H.2** lists examples of activities and possible cost drivers.

Two important assumptions must be met in order to obtain accurate product costs under ABC:

1. All overhead costs related to the activity must be driven by the cost driver used to assign costs to products.
2. All overhead costs related to the activity should respond proportionally to changes in the activity level of the cost driver.

ILLUSTRATION H.2

Activities and cost drivers in ABC

Activity	Cost Driver
Ordering raw materials	Ordering hours; number of orders
Receiving raw materials	Receiving hours; number of shipments
Materials handling	Number of requisitions; weight of materials; handling hours
Production scheduling	Number of orders
Machine setups	Setup hours; number of setups
Machining (fabricating, assembling, etc.)	Machine hours
Quality control inspections	Number of inspections
Factory supervision	Number of employees

For example, if there is little or no correlation between changes in the cost driver and consumption of the overhead cost, inaccurate product costs are inevitable. We provide an example of the use of ABC later in this appendix.

Activity-based costing may be used with either a job order or a process cost accounting system. The primary benefit of ABC is more accurate and meaningful product costing. Also, improved cost data about an activity can lead to reduced costs for the activity. In sum, ABC makes managers realize that it is **activities**, and not products, that determine the profitability of a company—a realization that should lead to better management decisions.

Applying Activity-Based Costing

LEARNING OBJECTIVE 2

Apply activity-based costing to a manufacturer.

In this section, we present a simple case example that compares activity-based costing with traditional costing. It illustrates how ABC eliminates the distortion that can occur in traditional overhead cost allocation. As you study this example, you should understand that ABC does not *replace* an existing job order or process cost system. What ABC does is to segregate overhead into various cost pools in an effort to provide more accurate cost information. As a result, ABC supplements—rather than replaces—these cost systems.

Assume that Atlas Company produces two abdominal fitness products—the Ab Bench and the Ab Coaster. Each year, the company produces 25,000 Ab Benches but only 5,000 Ab Coasters. Each unit produced requires one hour of direct labor, for a total of 30,000 labor hours (25,000 + 5,000). The direct labor cost is $12 per unit for each product. The direct materials cost per unit is $40 for the Ab Bench and $30 for the Ab Coaster.

Atlas also expects to incur annual manufacturing overhead costs of $900,000. Atlas allocates overhead using a single predetermined overhead rate based on the 30,000 direct labor hours it expects to use. Thus, the predetermined overhead rate is $30 per direct labor hour ($900,000 / 30,000 direct labor hours).

Since both products require one direct labor hour per unit, both products are allocated overhead costs of $30 per unit under traditional costing. **Illustration H.3** shows the total unit costs for the Ab Bench and the Ab Coaster.

With this information, we can now calculate unit costs under ABC for the Ab Bench and the Ab Coaster. Activity-based costing involves the following four steps.

1. **Identify and classify the activities** involved in the manufacture of specific products and **assign overhead to cost pools**.
2. **Identify the cost driver** that has a strong correlation to the costs accumulated in each cost pool.
3. **Compute the activity-based overhead rate** for each cost pool.
4. **Allocate overhead costs to products** using the overhead rates determined for each cost pool.

ILLUSTRATION H.3

Total unit costs—traditional costing

	Atlas Company	
Manufacturing Costs	Ab Bench	Ab Coaster
Direct materials	$40	$30
Direct labor	12	12
Overhead	30	30
Total direct cost per unit	$82	$72

Identify and Classify Activities and Assign Overhead to Cost Pools (Step 1)

Activity-based costing starts with an analysis of the activities needed to manufacture a product or perform a service. This analysis should identify all resource-consuming activities. It requires documenting every activity undertaken to accomplish a task. Atlas Company identifies five activity cost pools: manufacturing, setups, purchase ordering, product development, and property and plant.

Next, the company assigns overhead costs directly to the appropriate activity cost pool. For example, Atlas assigns all overhead costs directly associated with machine setups (such as salaries, supplies, and depreciation) to the setup cost pool. **Illustration H.4** shows the five cost pools, along with the estimated overhead assigned to each cost pool.

ILLUSTRATION H.4

Activity cost pools and estimated overhead

Atlas Company	
Activity Cost Pools	Estimated Overhead
Manufacturing	$500,000
Setups	100,000
Purchase ordering	50,000
Product development	200,000
Property and plant	50,000
Total	$900,000

Identify Cost Drivers (Step 2)

After costs are assigned to the activity cost pools, the company must identify the cost drivers for each cost pool. The cost driver must accurately measure the actual consumption of the activity by the various products. To achieve accurate costing, a **high degree of correlation** must exist between the cost driver and the actual consumption of the overhead costs in the cost pool.

Illustration H.5 shows the cost drivers that Atlas Company identifies and their total expected use per activity cost pool.

Availability and ease of obtaining data relating to the cost driver is an important factor that must be considered in its selection.

ILLUSTRATION H.5

Cost drivers and their expected use

Activity Cost Pools	Cost Drivers	Expected Use of Cost Drivers per Activity
Manufacturing	Machine hours	50,000 machine hours
Setups	Number of setups	2,000 setups
Purchase ordering	Number of purchase orders	2,500 purchase orders
Product development	Products developed	2 products developed
Property and plant	Square footage	25,000 square feet

Compute Activity-Based Overhead Rates (Step 3)

Next, the company computes an **activity-based overhead rate** per cost driver by dividing the estimated overhead per activity by the number of cost drivers expected to be used per activity. **Illustration H.6** shows the formula for this computation.

ILLUSTRATION H.6

Formula for computing activity-based overhead rate

$$\frac{\text{Estimated Overhead per Activity}}{\text{Expected Use of Cost Drivers per Activity}} = \text{Activity-Based Overhead Rate}$$

Atlas Company computes its activity-based overhead rates by using the estimated overhead per activity cost pool, shown in Illustration H.4, and the expected use of cost drivers per activity, shown in Illustration H.5. These computations are presented in **Illustration H.7**.

ILLUSTRATION H.7

Computation of activity-based overhead rates

Atlas Company

	A	B	C	D	E	F
1		Atlas Company				
2	Activity Cost Pools	Estimated Overhead	÷	Expected Use of Cost Drivers per Activity	=	Activity-Based Overhead Rates
3	Manufacturing	$500,000		50,000 machine hours		$10 per machine hour
4	Setups	100,000		2,000 setups		$50 per setup
5	Purchase ordering	50,000		2,500 purchase orders		$20 per order
6	Product development	200,000		2 products developed		$100,000 per product
7	Plant and property	50,000		25,000 square feet		$2 per square foot
8	Total	$900,000				
9						

Allocate Overhead Costs to Products (Step 4)

In allocating overhead costs, the company must know the expected use of cost drivers **for each product**. Because of its low volume and higher number of components, the Ab Coaster requires more setups and purchase orders than the Ab Bench. **Illustration H.8** shows the expected use of cost drivers per product for each of Atlas Company's products.

ILLUSTRATION H.8 **Expected use of cost drivers per product**

Activity Cost Pools	Cost Drivers	Expected Use of Cost Drivers per Activity	Expected Use of Cost Drivers per Product: Ab Bench	Ab Coaster
Manufacturing	Machine hours	50,000 machine hours	30,000	20,000
Setups	Number of setups	2,000 setups	500	1,500
Purchase ordering	Number of purchase orders	2,500 purchase orders	750	1,750
Product development	Products developed	2 products developed	1	1
Property and plant	Square feet	25,000 square feet	10,000	15,000

To allocate overhead costs to each product, Atlas multiplies the activity-based overhead rates per cost driver (Illustration H.7) by the number of cost drivers expected to be used per product (Illustration H.8). **Illustration H.9** shows the overhead cost allocated to each product.

ILLUSTRATION H.9 **Allocation of activity cost pools to products**

Atlas Company

	Ab Bench			Ab Coaster		
Activity Cost Pools	Expected Use of Cost Drivers per Product ×	Activity-Based Overhead Rates =	Cost Allocated	Expected Use of Cost Drivers per Product ×	Activity-Based Overhead Rates =	Cost Allocated
Manufacturing	30,000	$10	$300,000	20,000	$10	$200,000
Setups	500	$50	25,000	1,500	$50	75,000
Purchase ordering	750	$20	15,000	1,750	$20	35,000
Product development	1	$100,000	100,000	1	$100,000	100,000
Property and plant	10,000	$2.00	20,000	15,000	$2.00	30,000
Total costs allocated (a)			$460,000			$440,000
Units produced (b)			25,000			5,000
Overhead cost per unit [(a)÷(b)], rounded			$18.40			$88.00

Under ABC, the overhead cost per unit is $18.40 for the Ab Bench and $88.00 for the Ab Coaster. We see next how this per unit amount substantially differs from that computed under a traditional costing system.

Comparing Unit Costs

Illustration H.10 compares the unit costs for Atlas Company's Ab Bench and Ab Coaster under traditional costing and ABC.

ILLUSTRATION H.10 **Comparison of unit product costs**

	Ab Bench		Ab Coaster	
Manufacturing Costs	**Traditional Costing**	**ABC**	**Traditional Costing**	**ABC**
Direct materials	$40.00	$40.00	$30.00	$ 30.00
Direct labor	12.00	12.00	12.00	12.00
Overhead	30.00	18.40	30.00	88.00
Total direct cost per unit	$82.00	$70.40	$72.00	$130.00
	Overstated $11.60		Understated $58.00	

The comparison shows that unit costs under traditional costing are different and often misleading. Traditional costing overstates the cost of producing the Ab Bench by $11.60 per unit and understates the cost of producing the Ab Coaster by $58 per unit. These differences are attributable to how Atlas allocates manufacturing overhead across the two systems. Thus, ABC helps Atlas avoid some negative consequences of a traditional costing system, such as overpricing its Ab Benches and thereby possibly losing market share to competitors. Atlas has also been sacrificing profitability by underpricing the Ab Coaster.

Benefits of ABC

The primary benefit of ABC is **more accurate product costing**. Here's why:

1. **ABC leads to more cost pools** being used to assign overhead costs to products. Instead of one plantwide pool (or even departmental pools) and a single cost driver, companies use numerous activity cost pools with more relevant cost drivers. Costs are assigned more directly on the basis of the cost drivers used to produce each product.
2. **ABC leads to enhanced control over overhead costs.** Under ABC, companies can trace many overhead costs directly to activities—allowing some indirect costs to be identified as direct costs. Thus, managers have become more aware of their responsibility to control the activities that generate those costs.
3. **ABC leads to better management decisions.** More accurate product costing should contribute to setting selling prices that can help achieve desired product profitability levels. In addition, more accurate cost data could be helpful in deciding whether to make or buy a product part or component, and sometimes even whether to eliminate a product.

Activity-based costing does not change the amount of overhead costs. What it does do is allocate those overhead costs in a more accurate manner. Furthermore, if the scorekeeping is more realistic and more accurate, managers should be able to better understand cost behavior and overall profitability.

Limitations of ABC

Although ABC systems often provide better product cost data than traditional volume-based systems, there are limitations:

1. **ABC can be expensive to use.** The increased cost of identifying multiple activities and applying numerous cost drivers discourages many companies from using ABC. Activity-based costing systems are more complex than traditional costing systems—sometimes significantly more complex. So companies must ask, is the cost of implementation greater than the benefit of greater accuracy? Sometimes it may be. For some companies, there may be no need to consider ABC at all because their existing system is sufficient. If the costs of ABC outweigh the benefits, then the company should not implement ABC.
2. **Some arbitrary allocations continue.** Even though more overhead costs can be assigned directly to products through ABC's multiple activity cost pools, certain overhead costs remain to be allocated by means of some arbitrary volume-based cost driver such as labor or machine hours.

Review

Learning Objectives Review

1 Explain just-in-time (JIT) processing and activity-based costing (ABC).

JIT is a manufacturing technique dedicated to producing the right products at the right time as needed. One of the principal accounting effects is that a Raw and In-Process Inventory account replaces both the raw materials and work in process inventory accounts. ABC is a method of product costing that focuses on the activities performed to produce products. It assigns the cost of the activities to products by using cost drivers that measure the activities performed. The primary objective of ABC is accurate and meaningful product costs.

2 Apply activity-based costing to a manufacturer.

In applying ABC, it is necessary to compute the overhead rate for each activity by dividing total expected overhead by the total expected usage of the cost driver. The overhead cost for each activity is then assigned to products on the basis of each product's use of the cost driver.

Glossary Review

Activity-based costing (ABC) A costing system that focuses on the activities required to produce a product or perform a service. (p. H-3).

Cost driver Any factor or activity that has a direct cause-effect relationship with the resources consumed. (p. H-3)

Just-in-time (JIT) processing A processing system dedicated to having the right amount of materials, parts, or products arrive as they are needed, thereby reducing the amount of inventory. (p. H-2).

WileyPLUS

Many additional resources are available for practice in WileyPLUS.

Exercises

EH.1 (LO 1) Sam Snead has formulated the following list of statements about contemporary developments in managerial accounting.

JIT processing and ABC.

1. Just-in-time processing results in a push approach; that is, raw materials are pushed through each process.
2. A primary objective of just-in-time processing is to eliminate all manufacturing inventories.
3. A major disadvantage of just-in-time processing is lower product quality.
4. A primary benefit of activity-based costing is more accurate and meaningful product costing.
5. A major advantage of activity-based costing is that it uses a single unit-level basis, such as direct labor or machine hours, to allocate overhead.

Identify each statement as true or false. If false, indicate how to correct the statement to make it true.

EH.2 (LO 2) Mordica Company identifies three activities in its manufacturing process: machine setups, machining, and inspections. Estimated annual overhead cost for each activity is $150,000, $325,000, and $87,500, respectively. The cost driver for each activity and the expected annual usage are number of setups 2,500, machine hours 25,000, and number of inspections 1,750. Compute the overhead rate for each activity.

Compute activity-based overhead rates.

EH.3 (LO 2) Writing Major Instrument, Inc. manufactures two products: missile range instruments and space pressure gauges. During April, 50 range instruments and 300 pressure gauges were produced, and overhead costs of $94,500 were estimated. An analysis of estimated overhead costs reveals the following activities.

Compute overhead rates and assign overhead using ABC.

Excel

Activities	Cost Drivers	Total Cost
1. Materials handling	Number of requisitions	$40,000
2. Machine setups	Number of setups	27,500
3. Quality inspections	Number of inspections	27,000
		$94,500

The cost driver volume for each product was as follows.

Cost Drivers	Instruments	Gauges	Total
Number of requisitions	400	600	1,000
Number of setups	200	300	500
Number of inspections	200	400	600

Instructions

a. Determine the overhead rate for each activity.

b. Assign the manufacturing overhead costs for April to the two products using activity-based costing.

c. Write a memorandum to the president of Major Instrument explaining the benefits of activity-based costing.

Compute product cost using traditional costing and ABC.

EH.4 (LO 2) Kowalski Company manufactures a number of specialized machine parts. Part Compo-24 uses $35 of direct materials and $15 of direct labor per unit. Kowalski's estimated manufacturing overhead is as follows.

Materials handling	$150,000
Machining	180,000
Factory supervision	138,000
Total	$468,000

Overhead is applied based on direct labor costs, which were estimated at $200,000.

Kowalski is considering adopting activity-based costing. The cost drivers are estimated at:

Activity	Cost Driver	Expected Use
Materials handling	Weight of materials	50,000 pounds
Machining	Machine hours	20,000 hours
Factory supervision	Direct labor hours	12,000 hours

Instructions

a. Compute the cost of 1,000 units of Compo-24 using the current traditional costing system.

b. Compute the cost of 1,000 units of Compo-24 using the proposed activity-based costing system. Assume the 1,000 units use 2,500 pounds of materials, 500 machine hours, and 1,000 direct labor hours.

Assign overhead to products using ABC and evaluate decision.

EH.5 (LO 2) Writing Schultz Electronics manufactures two large-screen television models: the Royale which sells for $1,600, and a new model, the Majestic, which sells for $1,300. The production cost computed per unit under traditional costing for each model in 2020 was as follows.

Traditional Costing	Royale	Majestic
Direct materials	$ 700	$420
Direct labor ($20 per hour)	120	100
Manufacturing overhead ($38 per DLH)	228	190
Total per unit cost	$1,048	$710

In 2020, Schultz manufactured 25,000 units of the Royale and 10,000 units of the Majestic. The overhead rate of $38 per direct labor hour was determined by dividing total expected manufacturing overhead of $7,600,000 by the total direct labor hours (200,000) for the two models.

Under traditional costing, the gross profit on the models was Royale $552 or ($1,600 – $1,048), and Majestic $590 or ($1,300 – $710). Because of this difference, management is considering phasing out the Royale model and increasing the production of the Majestic model.

Before finalizing its decision, management asks Schultz's controller to prepare an analysis using activity-based costing (ABC). The controller accumulates the following information about overhead for the year ended December 31, 2020.

Activities	Cost Drivers	Estimated Overhead	Expected Use of Cost Drivers	Activity-Based Overhead Rate
Purchasing	Number of orders	$1,200,000	40,000	$30/order
Machine setups	Number of setups	900,000	18,000	$50/setup
Machining	Machine hours	4,800,000	120,000	$40/hour
Quality control	Number of inspections	700,000	28,000	$25/inspection

The cost drivers used for each product were:

Cost Drivers	Royale	Majestic	Total
Purchase orders	17,000	23,000	40,000
Machine setups	5,000	13,000	18,000
Machine hours	75,000	45,000	120,000
Inspections	11,000	17,000	28,000

Instructions

a. Assign the total 2020 manufacturing overhead costs to the two products using activity-based costing (ABC) and determine the overhead cost per unit.

b. What was the cost per unit and gross profit of each model using ABC?

c. Are management's future plans for the two models sound? Explain.

Company Index

A

Abercrombie and Fitch, 19-6
Ace Hardware, 6-24
Adelphia, 1-9
adidas, 9-36, 15-31, 19-18
Advanced Micro Devices, 13-7, 21-3
Ag-Chem, 8-27
Ahold NV, 3-58
AIG, 1-6
Alaskan Airlines, 21-2
Alcoa (Aluminum Company of America), 13-29, 14-32
Allegiant Airlines, 19-15
Alliance Atlantis Communications Inc., 17-43
Alphabet Inc., 1-11, 1-25, 4-25
Aluminum Company of America (Alcoa), 13-29, 14-32
Amazon.com, 1-3, 1-45, 2-44, 3-57, 4-57, 5-3, 5-5, 6-46–6-47, 8-47, 9-39, 10-44, 11-39, 14-36, 15-40, 16-33, 17-56, 18-49, 18-50, 19-17, 22-1, 22-2, 23-9, 24-8
American Airlines, 11-4, 19-4, 22-9
American Cancer Society, 13-3
American Express, 9-5, 9-12, 11-2, 23-5
American LaFrance, 20-3
American Van Lines, 25-6
AOL, 16-9
Apple Inc., 1-3, 1-4, 1-10, 1-34, 1-44, 2-43, 3-4, 3-55, 4-40, 4-56, 4-62, 5-39, 5-52, 6-33, 6-46, 8-35, 8-46, 9-27, 9-28, 10-18, 10-44, 11-38–11-39, 12-30, 13-2, 13-3, 13-24, 13-33, 13-35, 14-14, 14-16, 14-26, 14-36, 15-6, 15-30, 15-40, 16-32, 17-2, 17-42, 17-56, 18-49, 18-50, 19-18
Armour, 23-11
AT&T, 1-3, 16-9, 18-7, 19-4, 22-3
Avis, 10-1, 10-8

B

Baan NV, 3-58
BabyCakes NYC, 24-1, 24-2, 24-4
the balance, 24-49
The Balanced Scorecard Institute, 26-45
Bank of America, 9-10
Bank One Corporation, 2-23
Barnes & Noble, 18-42
Barriques, 8-1, 8-3, 8-8, 8-12
Ben & Jerry's, 20-3
Berkshire Hathaway, 14-10
Best Buy, 1-8, 3-12, 3-28, 5-54, 10-23, 14-3
Beverly Hills Fan Company, 23-38
BHP Billiton, 10-23
Bill and Melinda Gates Foundation, 1-25
BMW, 19-18, 23-17
Bob's Red Mill, 24-2
Boeing, 23-8
Boeing Capital Corporation, 10-6
Boeing Company, 10-15, 19-14, 19-17, 20-3
Bogan Communications, 11-18
Boise Cascade, 10-10
BorderStylo LLC, 10-20
Box, 17-15
BP, 6-14
Briggs And Stratton, 25-27
BrightFarms, 22-4
Bristol-Myers Squibb, 6-12, 18-8
Budget, 10-1
Burton Snowboards, 19-9

C

Campbell Soup Company, 6-12, 10-9, 19-4, 27-15, 27-35
Cargill Inc., 13-3
Carnival Corporation, 27-2
Caterpillar Inc., 6-1, 6-2, 6-13, 21-7
CBS, 10-20
Center Ice Consultants, 21-3
Cerberus, 15-2
Chase, 2-23, 26-18
Chevron, 10-10
Chicago Bears, 2-6
Chicago Cubs, 2-6
Chipotle, 19-6
Chrysler, 15-1, 26-15
Cisco Systems, 4-15, 6-47, 9-20, 14-20, 18-8, 25-15
Citicorp, 1-10
Citigroup, 1-10
Clif Bar & Company, 1-5, 1-47
Clorox, 23-1
The Coca-Cola Company, 1-3, 1-45, 1-47, 2-44, 3-55, 4-56, 5-52, 5-53, 6-46, 8-46–8-47, 9-39, 10-44, 11-8, 11-39, 13-34, 14-36, 15-40, 16-33, 17-56, 18-49, 19-7, 19-18, 21-1, 22-42, 22-43, 24-20, 25-27
Columbia Sportswear Company, 1-1–1-2, 17-43
Commercial Capital LLC, 9-39
Commonwealth Edison, 14-5
Computer Associates International, Inc., 25-49
ConAgra Foods, 5-19, 14-3
ConocoPhilips, 10-23
Conservation International, 26-15
Continental Bank, 10-6
Costco Wholesale Corp., 5-13, 17-5
Countrywide Financial Corporation, 9-18
Craig Consumer Electronics, 6-5
Credit Suisse Group, 2-11
Crocs, Inc., 1-9
Current Designs, 19-1, 19-2, 19-4, 19-7, 19-11, 19-38, 20-39, 21-42, 22-40, 23-36, 23-37, 24-45, 25-46, 26-42, 27-32
Cypress Semiconductor Corporation, 17-43

D

Daimler-Benz, 15-2
DaimlerChrysler, 15-2
Deere & Company, 9-19
Dell, 2-13, 6-3, 19-4, 19-16, 27-1
Dell Financial Services, 10-6
Delta Air Lines, 3-3, 3-10, 8-28, 10-15, 23-14, 26-17
Dewey & LeBoeuf LLP, 1-7
Dick's Sporting Goods, 19-10
Discover, 9-11
Dow Chemical, 21-3
DPR Construction, 19-6
Duke Energy Co., 22-3, 25-6, 25-20
Dun & Bradstreet, 18-9
DuPont, 15-3, 15-4, 21-3

E

Earthlink, 14-5
Eastman Kodak, 16-5, 17-1
eBay, 5-20
Eli Lily, 8-4, 25-27
Enron, 1-6, 1-24, 5-20, 13-4, 18-8, 19-4
Equifax, 9-2
ExxonMobil Corporation, 1-10, 6-14, 8-19, 19-16, 20-3, 21-3, 23-11, 27-1

F

Facebook, 1-3, 13-1, 13-5, 13-13, 14-3, 14-14, 19-5
Fannie Mae, 2-23, 3-14
Federal Bureau of Investigation (FBI), 1-3
Federal Express, 19-4
Fiat/Chrysler, 1-47
Fireeye, 17-15
Fitch, 18-17
Flightserve, 22-16
Ford Motor Company, 1-10, 5-4, 6-4, 6-17, 10-23, 15-1, 19-16, 21-16, 22-9, 25-18
Fox Broadcasting, 10-20, 25-9

G

GAP Inc., 1-9, 19-16
General Dynamica Corp., 18-4
General Electric (GE), 1-5, 5-11, 14-3, 19-5, 19-18, 20-9, 21-11
General Mills, 10-9, 18-9, 21-3
General Motors Corporation (GM), 1-4, 9-28, 11-5, 15-1, 15-3, 15-14, 16-5, 18-7, 18-36, 19-4, 19-16, 20-4, 23-1, 23-17
Gillette Company, 16-9
Glassmaster Company, 26-44
Global Reporting Initiative, 19-19
Goldman Sachs, 1-10, 20-18
Goodyear, 23-15
Google, 3-28, 10-20, 10-21, 13-1–13-3, 13-7, 18-3
Green Bay Packers, 2-1, 2-45
Groupon, 3-1
Gulf Craft, 21-30
Gulf Oil, 13-5

H

Hain Celestial Group, 2-9
HealthSouth, 1-6
Hershey, 21-6
Hertz Car Rental, 10-1
Hewlett-Packard (HP), 19-4, 19-15, 19-17, 23-8, 26-16
Hilton Hotels, 10-6, 19-17, 22-3
H.J. Heinz Company, 14-20
Holland America Line, 27-1, 27-2, 27-9
Home Depot, 1-3, 6-4, 6-24, 10-4
Honda, 25-17
Honeywell International, 18-7
Household International, 7-12

H&R Block, 21-4
Hughes Aircraft Co., 18-4
Human Rights Watch, 19-18

I

IBM, 5-20, 13-3, 13-6*n*.1, 13-24, 14-10, 18-5, 18-7, 19-17, 26-4
Ice Pro, 21-3
IHS, 20-10
IKEA, 23-10
Inditex SA, 19-16
The Institute of Management Accountants (IMA), 19-41, 20-41
Intel, 1-47, 19-16, 21-3, 21-17
InterContinental, 10-6
Intuit Inc., 7-1, 7-4
IT&T, 1-1

J

J. Crew, 1-9
J. Walter Thompson, 21-3
J.C. Penney Company, Inc., 9-4, 9-27, 9-32, 17-5
Jiffy Lube, 21-4
Jif Peanut Butter, 21-30
John Deere Capital Corporation, 10-6
Jones Soda Co., 21-1, 21-3
Jostens, Inc., 26-16
J.P. Morgan Leasing, 10-6
JP Morgan Chase, 9-10

K

Kaiser, 21-3
Kellogg Company, 18-9, 20-3, 21-3, 21-10, 21-12, 21-13, 21-15, 21-16, 21-18–21-23, 22-10, 26-11
Kmart, 3-57, 23-38
Kohl's Corporation, 8-34, 17-5
Kraft Foods, 26-11
Kraft Heinz, 24-20
Kroger Stores, 5-4, 6-12, 22-9

L

Lease Finance Corporation, 10-6
Leslie Fay, 6-5, 6-48
Lockheed Martin Corp., 4-15, 10-15
Louis Vuitton Moët Hennessy, 1-3, 1-48, 2-47, 3-60, 4-62, 5-56, 6-49, 8-50, 9-42, 10-47, 11-42, 13-38, 14-39, 15-43, 17-60, 18-52
Lucent, 19-4

M

Mackinac Center for Public Policy, 24-47
Macy's, Inc., 25-18
Madison Square Garden, 24-8
Major League Baseball Players Association, 1-5
Manville Corp., 11-6
Marcus Corporation, 4-27
Marriott Hotels, 10-6, 10-9, 22-3, 25-6
Massachusetts General Hospital, 22-3
MasterCard, 9-11, 9-12
Maxwell Car Company, 15-1
Mayo Clinic, 20-18, 21-3
McDonald's Corporation, 1-10, 1-47, 10-18, 10-33, 13-3, 15-12, 17-49, 26-3
McDonnell Douglas, 19-17
McKesson Corporation, 5-3, 6-48, 8-28
Medtronic, Inc., 15-6
Mercedes, 23-17
Merrill Lynch, 1-10
Method Products, 23-1, 23-8
MF Global Holdings Ltd, 2-1, 2-21, 13-4
Microsoft Corporation, 1-4, 5-11, 5-20, 10-18, 10-23, 13-2, 17-1, 17-17, 18-36, 19-2
Minnesota Mining and Manufacturing Company (3M), 9-29, 11-33
Mitsubishi, 16-35
Mobile Iron, 17-15
Moody's, 18-9, 18-17
Morgan Stanley, 16-13
Morrow Snowboards, Inc., 5-6
Motorola, 6-12, 18-4
MSN, 18-50
Museum of Contemporary Art (Los Angeles, California), 24-24

N

NBC, 10-20
NBCUniversal, 25-9
NEC, 3-58
Nestlé, 1-47
Netflix, 18-50
NetJets, 22-16
Newton Industries, 19-41
NFL, 10-20
Nike, Inc., 1-3, 4-27, 9-8, 9-36, 13-3, 13-4, 13-6, 13-8, 13-14, 14-3, 14-9, 14-14, 18-15, 18-40, 19-17
Nissan, 23-17, 27-1
Nordstrom, Inc., 4-28, 9-13, 18-41

O

Obsidian Energy, 2-9
Office Depot, 5-3
Oracle, 7-4, 19-6
Oral-B Laboratories, 23-1

P

Parmalat, 8-49, 17-12
Penske Automotive Group, 26-17
PepsiCo, Inc., 1-3, 1-4, 1-11, 1-25, 1-45, 2-44, 3-3, 3-55, 4-56, 5-4, 5-52, 5-53, 6-14, 6-46, 8-46–8-47, 9-39, 10-44, 11-8, 11-39, 13-3, 13-34, 14-5, 14-18, 14-36, 15-40, 16-33, 17-56, 18-49, 21-1, 21-3
Phantom Tac, 19-18
Philip Morris International, 15-6
Pilgrim's Pride, 5-19, 24-20
Pratt and Whitney, 20-9
PriceWaterhouseCoopers, 20-18
Princeton University, 24-24
The Procter & Gamble Company (P&G), 1-10, 10-22, 13-8, 16-9, 18-4, 19-10, 23-1, 25-15, 26-4
Prudential Real Estate, 1-10

Q

Quad Graphics, 20-3
Quaker Oats, 6-14, 21-30, 23-1

R

Radio Shack, 2-43
Razor & Tie Music, 12-1
Red Cross, 1-25
Reebok International Ltd., 6-12, 13-16
REI (Recreational Equipment Incorporated), 5-1, 5-3, 5-7, 5-11
REL Consultancy Group, 4-27
Renault, 23-17, 27-1
Rent-A-Wreck, 10-1–10-4, 10-8, 10-20, 10-45
Republic Carloading, 4-22
Rhino Foods, Inc., 4-1
Rite Aid, 9-2
Rolling Stones, 22-20
Royal Ahold, 8-49
Royal Dutch Shell, 6-14, 10-20, 21-3

S

SafeNet, 13-8
Safeway, 8-5
The Sage Group, 7-4
Salvation Army, 13-3
Samsung, 19-6
San Diego Union-Tribune, 26-45
San Diego Zoo, 25-12
SAP AG, 7-4, 19-16
Sara Lee, 19-7
Satyam Computer Services, 8-49
Seattle Seahawks, 21-2
Securities and Exchange Commission (SEC), 16-34, 17-57
Sherwin Williams, 21-3
Siebel Systems, 25-17
Siemens AG, 25-27
Simon Properties, 15-6
Skechers USA, 9-10, 9-19
Skype, 5-20
Small Business Administration, 20-42
Sony, 1-47, 6-19
Southwest Airlines Co., 3-3, 3-10, 4-24, 22-2
Sports Illustrated, 11-4
Sprint Corporation, 11-4
Standard & Poor's, 14-6, 15-40, 18-9, 18-17
Stanley Black & Decker Manufacturing Company, 6-12, 11-7
Starbucks, 1-25, 6-12, 26-1, 26-2, 26-15
Subway, 10-20
Sunbeam, 23-5
SUPERVALU, 14-27

T

Target Corporation, 3-57, 6-4, 7-21, 8-19, 17-5, 18-47, 23-2
Tecumseh Products Company, 27-34
Tektronix Inc., 14-12
Tesla Motors, 1-5, 4-25, 23-17
Texaco Oil Company, 9-27
The Limited, Inc., 14-20
3M (Minnesota Mining and Manufacturing Company), 9-29, 11-33
Time Warner, Inc., 1-5, 16-1, 16-7, 16-9, 16-10, 24-5
Time Warner Cable, 15-4
Tootsie Roll, 1-13
Topps Company, Inc., 18-38
Toyota, 1-47, 19-15, 19-16
Trek, 1-10, 23-10
Tribeca Grand Hotel, 25-1, 25-2
True Value Hardware, 6-4
Turner Broadcasting, 16-7, 16-9
21st Century Fox, 16-2

U

U-Haul, 22-6
Unilever, 15-12, 23-1, 26-18
Unitd States Steel Corp., 15-3
United Airlines, 1-5, 3-10, 11-5, 16-5, 17-1, 22-2, 26-17, 26-19
United Parcel Service (UPS), 18-7
U.S. Navy, 26-4
United States Steel, 22-9, 22-10

United Stationers, 5-3
USAir, 15-3
US Bancorp Equipment Finance, 10-6
USX, 21-3

V

Van Meter Inc., 14-1
Verizon Communications, 15-6, 18-7, 27-8
Visa, 9-11, 9-12, 9-13
Vodafone/Mannesmann, 1-47
Volkswagen, 23-17

W

Wachovia, 9-5
Walgreen Drugs, 5-3, 6-12
Wal-Mart Stores, Inc., 1-3, 1-10, 1-45, 2-44, 3-57, 4-57, 5-2, 5-3, 5-52, 6-4, 6-18, 6-24, 6-46–6-47, 8-19, 8-47, 9-39, 10-44, 11-39, 13-34, 14-20, 14-36, 15-40, 16-33, 17-5, 17-56, 18-47, 18-49, 18-50, 19-17, 26-18
The Walt Disney Company, 1-5, 3-3, 4-26, 10-13, 10-23, 14-15, 20-1, 20-3, 20-13, 21-3
Warner Brothers Motion Pictures, 21-3, 21-30
Waste Management Inc., 2-23
Wells Fargo Bank, 8-3, 9-5, 9-10, 19-17
Wendall Company, 19-40
Wendy's International, 6-12
Wenonah Canoe, 19-1, 19-38
Whitehall-Robins, 9-1
Whole Foods, 19-6
World Bank, 26-4
WorldCom, Inc., 1-6, 1-24, 8-9, 10-6, 13-4, 18-8, 18-14

X

Xerox, 19-4
XM Satellite Radio Holdings, 24-15

Y

Yahoo-Edgar Online, 17-57
Yahoo! Finance, 16-33
Yahoo! Inc., 18-9
Yale Express, 4-22
Young & Rubicam, 21-3

Subject Index

A

ABC (activity-based costing), 19-16, 23-5
Accelerated-depreciation method, 10-12
Accounts, 2-2–2-3. *See also specific types*
  chart of, 2-13
  correct titles for, 2-9
  three-column form of, 2-11
Accounting, 1-3–1-11
  accrual- vs. cash-basis, 3-3
  activities of, 1-3–1-4
  assumptions in, 1-9–1-10
  and budgeting, 24-3
  building blocks of, 1-6–1-11
  career opportunities in, 1-24–1-26
  cost, 20-3
  ethics in, 1-6–1-7
  financial, 1-5, 19-3, 19-4
  generally accepted accounting principles, 1-8
  importance of, in business, 1-1–1-2
  managerial, *see* Managerial accounting
  measurement principles, 1-8–1-9
  payroll, 11-9–11-23
  and quality of earnings, 18-7
  responsibility, *see* Responsibility accounting
  users of accounting data, 1-4–1-6
Accounting cycle, 1-13, 4-19–4-22, 5-15–5-17. *See also specific steps in cycle*
Accounting equation, 1-11–1-20
  assets in, 1-11
  liabilities in, 1-11–1-12
  owner's equity in, 1-12–1-13
  in transaction analysis, 1-13–1-20
Accounting information systems (accounting systems), 1-13, 7-1–7-22
  cash payments journal, 7-17–7-19
  cash receipts journal, 7-11–7-15
  computerized, 7-3–7-4
  and cybersecurity, 7-21–7-22
  general journal, 7-20–7-21
  general ledger, 7-3–7-4
  IFRS and GAAP for, 7-44
  manual, 7-5
  purchases journal, 7-15–7-17
  in QuickBooks, 7-1–7-2
  sales journal, 7-9–7-11
  special journals, 7-8–7-22
  subsidiary ledgers, 7-5–7-8
Accounting period, closing entries in, 4-12
Accounting principle, changes in, 18-6–18-7
Accounting reports, 1-4. *See also* Financial statements
Account numbers, 7-8
Accounts payable, 1-11
  on budgeted balance sheet, 24-21
  for statement of cash flows, 17-11, 17-29
  transaction analysis for, 1-17–1-18
Accounts payable (creditors') subsidiary ledger, 7-6–7-7
Accounts receivable, 9-2–9-13
  on budgeted balance sheet, 24-21
  disposing of, 9-11–9-13
  net, 9-6
  recognizing, 9-2–9-4
  for statement of cash flows, 17-10, 17-28
  valuing, 9-5–9-11
Accounts receivable (customers') subsidiary ledger, 7-6–7-7
Accounts receivable turnover, 9-20, 18-19–18-20
Accruals, 3-5
  adjusting entries for, 3-13–3-20
  of interest receivable, 9-16–9-17
Accrual-basis accounting, 3-3
Accrued expenses, 3-5, 3-14–3-17
Accrued revenues, 3-5, 3-13–3-14
Accumulated depreciation, 4-25, 17-28, 24-21
Accumulated Other Comprehensive Income, 13-17
Accumulated profit or loss, 13-37, 14-38
Accuracy, in financial reporting, 2-23
Activity base, 20-12, 20-13
Activity-based costing (ABC), 19-16, 23-5
Activity index, 22-3, 25-10
Added value, 19-4
Additions and improvements, 10-5
Adjustable interest rates, 15-12
Adjusted cash balance, 8-25
Adjusted trial balance, 3-20–3-24, 4-5–4-8, 5-24
Adjusting entries, 3-2–3-20
  in accounting cycle, 5-15–5-17
  for accruals, 3-13–3-20
  in bank reconciliation, 8-25
  for deferrals, 3-6–3-12, 3-24–3-27
  IFRS and GAAP for, 3-58–3-59
  for merchandising companies, 5-15–5-17
  need for, 3-5
  prior period, 14-12–14-13
  relationships of, 3-17–3-19, 3-27
  in special journals, 7-9, 7-20
  types of, 3-5–3-6
  and value of company, 3-1–3-2
  on worksheet, 4-5–4-8, 5-29
  from worksheets, 4-11
Admission by investment, 12-19–12-21
Admission by purchase of an interest, 12-18–12-19
Admission of partners, 12-18–12-21
Advertising, 1-16–1-17
Affiliated company, 16-8, 16-9
Agents, of corporations, 13-3
Aggregated data, 1-4
Aging schedule, 9-9
Aging the accounts receivable, 9-8, 9-9
Airlines, costs and profits of, 19-15
Allowances-
  purchase, 5-9, 5-26
  sales, 5-12–5-13, 5-27
Allowance for Doubtful Accounts, 9-10
Allowance method, 9-6–9-10
Amortization, 10-18–10-19
  of bond discount, 15-9, 15-20–15-22
  of bond premium, 15-10, 15-22–15-23
  effective-interest method, 15-20–15-23
  straight-line, 15-17–15-19
Analysis of information, 1-4
Annual depreciation, prorating, 10-9
Annual interest rate, 9-15
Annual rate of return method, 27-18–27-19
Anshutz, Philip, 27-15
Appel, Jennifer, 12-6
Applied manufacturing overhead, 20-20–20-22
Arm's-length transactions, 9-3
Articles of co-partnership, 12-6
Articles of incorporation, 13-5
Assets-
  in accounting equation, 1-11
  on classified balance sheet, 4-23–4-26
  current, 4-24, 17-10–17-11
  depreciation of, 3-8–3-10, 10-7
  in double-entry system, 2-4
  fixed, 4-25, 10-3, 17-17
  intangible, 4-25–4-26, 10-18–10-23
  investment of, in partnership, 12-19–12-20
  net, 12-19, 12-22, 14-19
  noncash, 13-12, 17-10–17-11
  noncurrent, 17-13–17-14
  operating, 25-24, 25-25
  other, 4-25
  of partnerships, 12-3, 12-7–12-8
  for payment of partner withdrawal, 12-22–12-23
  pension, 11-22
  property, plant, and equipment, *see* Plant assets
  return on, 18-24
  total, 10-3, 13-16, 14-4, 18-12
Asset misappropriation, 8-18
Asset turnover, 18-24–18-25
Asset turnover ratio, 10-22–10-23
Associate investments, 16-35
Associations of individuals, in partnerships, 12-3
Assumptions-
  accounting, 1-9–1-10
  financial reporting, 3-28–3-29
  net present value method, 27-9–27-10
Auditing, 1-25
Auditors, internal, 8-9
Audit trail, 7-4
Authorized stock, 13-7
Auto industry, debt in, 15-1–15-2
Automation, 20-13
Available-for-sale securities, 16-11–16-13, 18-5
Average collection period, 9-20, 18-20
Average-cost method, 6-8, 6-11–6-12, 6-22
Average investment, 27-19
Average operating assets, 25-25

B

Background checks, 8-10
Bad debt expense, 9-5–9-7. *See also* Uncollectible accounts
Balanced scorecard, 19-17, 26-17–26-20
Balance sheet, 1-20–1-22
  budgeted, 24-20–24-21
  classified, 4-23–4-28, 4-59–4-60, 5-21–5-22, 16-16–16-17
  comparative, 17-6
  current liabilities on, 11-8
  effect of cost flow methods on, 6-13–6-14
  and errors in inventory accounting, 6-16–6-17

horizontal analysis of, 18-11
investments on, 16-15
leased assets on, 15-17
merchandising and manufacturing costs on, 19-13
net change in cash on, 17-14, 17-26
for partnerships, 12-11
ratio analysis, 18-17
receivables on, 9-19
recovery of bad debts on, 9-7–9-8
stockholders' equity section of, 13-17–13-18
trading securities on, 16-12
transfer to worksheet, 5-24, 5-31
unpaid notes payable on, 15-13
vertical analysis of, 18-12
from worksheet, 4-10
write-off of bad debts on, 9-7
Balancing amount, 17-30
Balsam, Craig, 12-1–12-2
Bangladesh, 19-18
Banks, 8-20, 8-23–8-24
Bank accounts, 8-19–8-26
electronic funds transfer system, 8-21
making deposits, 8-19–8-20
reconciling, 8-22–8-26
statements, 8-21–8-22
writing checks, 8-21
Bank charge expense, 8-25
Bank reconciliations, 8-19, 8-22–8-26, 9-4
Bank statements, 8-21–8-22
Barnum, P.T., 1-6
Basic accounting equation, 1-11
Batch jobs, 20-3
Batteries, for electric cars, 23-17
Beginning inventory, errors in, 6-15
Beginning work in process, 19-11, 21-10, 21-18
Best-efforts contracts, 13-7*n*.2
Bezos, Jeff, 22-1, 23-9
Blank, Arthur, 1-4
Board of directors, 19-5
Bonds, 15-2–15-12
amortization of, 15-17–15-23
amortizing the discount, 15-9, 15-19–15-22
amortizing the premium, 15-10, 15-22–15-23
discount/premium on, 15-7–15-11
at face value, 15-7
green, 15-12
hot market for, 15-6
issued for cash, 17-14, 17-25
issuing, 15-3–15-4, 15-7–15-11
market price of, 15-5–15-6
price quoting for, 15-4, 15-7
recording transactions with, 16-4–16-5
redeeming, 15-11–15-12
safety of, 16-5
trading, 15-4
types of, 15-3
Bond amortization, 15-17–15-23
effective interest method, 15-20–15-23
straight-line, 15-17–15-19
Bond certificates, 15-3
Bond indentures, 15-3
Bonding of employees, 8-9
Bond interest expense, 15-20, 16-4
Bond interest paid, 15-10, 15-20
Bond issues-
at a discount, 15-7–15-9
at face value, 15-7
at a premium, 15-8–15-11
procedures for, 15-3–15-4
Bonds payable, 17-13, 17-25, 17-29
Bonuses-
on admission of a partner, 12-20–12-21
as fringe benefits, 11-10
stock bonus programs, 14-1–14-2
on withdrawal of a partner, 12-22–12-23
Books, reconciling items per, 8-24
Book errors, 8-24, 8-25
Bookkeeping, 1-4
Book (carrying) value-
for bonds issued at discount, 15-8
and depreciation, 10-7, 10-10, 10-11
for partnership assets, 12-20
for prepaid expenses, 3-10
in repair, retain, or replace decision, 23-14
Book value per share, 14-18–14-20
Borrowing, cost of, 15-8–15-10
Bowerman, Bill, 13-3
Boyle, Gert, 1-1–1-2
Boyle, Tim, 1-2
Break-even analysis, 22-14–22-18
Break-even point, 22-12, 22-14–22-15, 22-20–22-21
Brock, Paula, 25-12
Budgets, 24-3. *See also specific budgets*
flexible, 25-6–25-13
standards vs., 26-4
static, 25-4–25-6
Budgetary control, 25-1–25-13
defined, 25-3–25-4
flexible budgets, 25-6–25-13
in hospitality sector, 25-1–25-2
static budget reports, 25-4–25-6
Budgetary optimism, 24-9
Budgetary planning, 24-1–24-25
budgeted balance sheet, 24-20–24-21
budgeted income statement, 24-15–24-17
cash budget, 24-17–24-22
direct labor budget, 24-13–24-14
direct materials budget, 24-10–24-13
effective budgeting, 24-3–24-6
manufacturing overhead budget, 24-14–24-15
master budget, 24-6–24-7
in nonmanufacturing companies, 24-22–24-25
production budget, 24-9–24-10
and profitability, 24-1–24-2
sales budget, 24-8–24-9
selling and administrative expense budget, 24-15
Budgetary slack, 24-6
Budget committee, 24-4–24-5
Budgeted balance sheet, 24-20–24-21
Budgeted income statement, 24-15–24-17
Budgeting-
and accounting, 24-3
benefits of, 24-3
effective, 24-3–24-6
in nonmanufacturing companies, 24-22–24-25
participative, 24-5–24-6
zero-based, 24-20
Budget period, length of, 24-4, 24-6
Budget reforecasting, 25-12
Budget reports, 25-3–25-7, 25-11–25-13
Budget shortfalls, 24-24
Budget variance, 25-4
Buffett, Warren, 14-10, 18-1, 18-2
Buildings, 10-4, 17-13, 17-24, 17-29, 24-21
Burden, 19-8
Business-
accounting and success in, 19-1–19-2
importance of accounting in, 1-1–1-2
internal control and size of, 8-11
inventory management and success of, 6-1–6-2
"winning" at, 4-1–4-2
Business component, discontinued, 18-4
Business documents, 5-11
Business plans, 24-4
Business transactions. *See also* Transaction analysis
analyzing, 1-13–1-20
in double-entry system, 2-4–2-6
incorrect/inappropriate recording of, 2-9
purchasing, 5-6–5-10
sales, 5-11–5-15
in subsidiary ledgers, 7-7
Buyer, freight costs incurred by, 5-8
By-laws of corporations, 13-5

C

Calendar years, 3-3
Callable bonds, 15-3
Canceled checks, 8-22
Capacity, 23-7, 26-6
Capital-
corporate, 13-4, 13-9–13-10
cost of, 27-9
legal, 13-8
owner's, 1-12, 2-5
paid-in, 13-9, 13-11, 13-17, 14-7, 14-12
and par value, 13-8
for proprietorship, 1-9
total, 12-22
working, 11-8
Capital accounts, in partnerships, 12-19, 12-23
Capital budgeting, 27-1–27-20
annual rate of return method, 27-18–27-19
cash flow information for, 27-3–27-4
cash payback, 27-4–27-6
in cruise industry, 27-2
with intangible benefits, 27-11–27-13
internal rate of return method, 27-16–27-18
for mutually exclusive projects, 27-13–27-14
net present value method, 27-6–27-16
post-audit of projects, 27-15–27-16
and risk analysis, 27-14–27-15
Capital credit, partners', 12-20
Capital deficiency (partnership liquidation), 12-13, 12-15–12-18
Capital expenditures, 10-5, 27-18
Capital ratios, for partnerships, 12-9–12-10, 12-12
Capital stock, 13-17
Careers in accounting, 1-24–1-26
Carpenter, Jake Burton, 19-9
Carrying value, *see* Book value
Carrying (book) value method, 15-11
Cash, 8-27
on budgeted balance sheet, 24-21
and depreciation, 10-7
fictitious uses and sources of, 17-12
and fraud, 8-11
investments of, 16-2
net change in, 17-14–17-15
reporting, 8-27–8-28
for statement of cash flows, 17-30
Cash-basis accounting, 3-3
Cash budget, 24-17–24-22

Cash controls, 8-11–8-19
  disbursements, 8-14–8-16
  petty cash fund, 8-16–8-19
  point-of-sale system for, 8-1–8-2
  receipts, 8-12–8-14
Cash disbursements, 8-14–8-16, 24-17, 24-19
Cash dividends, 14-3–14-4
Cash equivalents, 8-27
Cash flows. *See also* Statement of cash flows
  ability to generate, 17-3
  assumptions about, 27-9
  for capital budgeting, 27-3–27-4
  classification of, 17-3–17-4, 17-7
  equal annual, 27-5, 27-7
  free, 17-17–17-18
  net annual, 27-5, 27-10
  at not-for-profit organizations, 24-23
  unequal annual, 27-5, 27-8
Cash management, 17-1–17-2, 24-20
Cash payback period, 27-5
Cash payback technique, 27-4–27-6
Cash payments, 12-14, 17-20–17-24
Cash payments (cash disbursements) journal, 7-17–7-19
Cash purchases, 1-15, 1-16
Cash (net) realizable value, 6-18, 9-6, 9-16
Cash receipts-
  on cash budget, 24-17, 24-19
  in direct method, 17-20–17-21
  internal controls for, 8-12–8-14
  transaction analysis for, 1-18–1-19
Cash receipts journal, 7-11–7-15
Cash register documents, 5-11
Cash resources, dividends and, 14-3
Cash withdrawals, transaction analysis for, 1-18
Castle, Ted, 4-1, 4-2
CEO (chief executive officer), 19-5, 19-6
CFO (chief financial officer), 19-5
Change in accounting principle, 18-6–18-7
Channel stuffing, 18-8
Charter, corporate, 13-5–13-6
Charter flights, 22-16
Chart of accounts, 2-13
Checks, 8-7, 8-14, 8-21–8-25
Check register, 8-15
Chenfield, Cliff, 12-1–12-2
Chief executive officer (CEO), 19-5, 19-6
Chief financial officer (CFO), 19-5
China, 12-4
Chrysler, Walter, 15-1
Cichanowski, Michael, 19-1–19-2
Claims, fictitious, 8-5
Classified balance sheet, 4-23–4-28
  IFRS and GAAP for, 4-59–4-60
  investments on, 16-16–16-17
  for merchandising companies, 5-21–5-22
Closely held corporations, 13-3. *See also* Privately held corporations
Closing entries-
  in accounting cycle, 5-15–5-16
  for merchandising companies, 5-15–5-16, 5-28–5-29
  for partnerships, 12-8–12-9
  posting, 4-14–4-15
  preparing, 4-12–4-14
  in special journals, 7-9, 7-20
Closing the books, 4-11–4-19
  post-closing trial balance, 4-16–4-18
  posting closing entries, 4-14–4-15
  preparing closing entries, 4-12–4-14
  with virtual closes, 4-15
Code of ethical standards, 19-17–19-18
Collaboration, 25-15
Collections, 24-18
Collection agents, 11-4
Collusion, 8-11
Columbus, Christopher, 1-4*n*.2
Commercial substance (exchanges), 10-23–10-24
Common costs, 25-21
Common-size analysis, *see* Vertical analysis
Common stock, 13-6, 13-10–13-12
  allocating cash dividends to, 14-4–14-7
  and book value per share, 14-18–14-19
  on budgeted balance sheet, 24-21
  at charter, 13-6
  earnings per share for, 14-17–14-18, 18-26
  net income available to holders of, 14-15
  no-par value, 13-11–13-12
  paid-in capital, 13-9
  par value, 13-10–13-11
  for services or noncash assets, 13-12
  for statement of cash flows, 17-13–17-14, 17-25, 17-29
Communication, 1-3, 1-4, 8-4
Company, responsibility accounting for, 25-14
Comparability, 3-28
Comparative balance sheets, 17-6
Competition, 25-15
Completed jobs, 20-15–20-20
Completeness, 3-28
Complete statement of comprehensive income, 18-6
Component depreciation, 10-47
Compound entries, 2-9
Comprehensive income, 5-21, 18-5–18-7
Comprehensive income statement, 5-21, 16-13
Computerized accounting systems, 7-3–7-4
Computer recycling, 3-17
Concentration of credit risk, 9-19–9-20
Confirmatory value, 3-28
Conservatism, 6-17
Consigned goods, ownership of, 6-6
Consistency, 3-28, 6-14
Consolidated financial statements, 16-8–16-9
Constant percentage rate (amortization), 15-20
Constraints, theory of, 19-16
Construction of buildings, 10-4
Consumer cooperatives (co-ops), 5-1–5-2
Contingent liabilities, 11-6–11-7, 11-41
Continuous 12-month budgets, 24-4
Contra account for bonds at a discount, 15-8
Contra asset accounts, 3-9
Contractual interest rate, 15-3, 15-7
Contractual restrictions, on retained earnings, 14-12
Contra revenue accounts, 5-13
Contra stockholders' equity account, 13-14
Contributed capital, *see* Paid-in capital
Contribution margin (CM), 22-11, 22-15–22-16, 22-19, 23-17
Contribution margin ratio (CVP analysis), 22-13–22-14, 22-16, 22-19
Control-
  budgetary, *see* Budgetary control
  internal, *see* Internal control
Control accounts, 7-6–7-8, 20-8, 20-10, 20-16
Control activities, 8-4
Control environment, 8-4
Controllability of items, 25-16
Controllable margin, 25-21, 25-24–25-25
Controllable revenues and costs, 25-15, 25-20–25-23
Controllable variance, overhead, 26-14, 26-23–26-24
Controllers, 13-4, 19-5
Controlling, as management function, 19-4
Controlling interest, 16-8
Convergence, 1-8
Conversion costs, 21-10, 21-14, 21-20
Convertible bonds, 15-3
Co-ops, 5-1–5-2
Coordination, of activities, 24-3
Co-ownership of property, 12-3
Copyrights, 10-19
Corporate capital, 13-4, 13-9–13-10
Corporate social responsibility, 1-23, 4-26, 19-18, 26-15
Corporations, 1-10, 13-1–13-19, 14-1–14-20
  book value per share for, 14-18–14-20
  characteristics of, 13-3–13-5
  corporate capital, 13-9–13-10
  dividends for, 14-2–14-9
  forming, 13-5–13-6
  "going public" for, 13-1–13-2
  income statements for, 14-16–14-17
  multinational, 1-46
  reasons for investing, 16-2–16-3
  stock bonus programs, 14-1–14-2
  stockholder rights, 13-6
  stockholders' equity on financial statements, 13-17–13-19, 14-11–14-16
  stockholders' equity statements for, 14-18
  stock issues, 13-6–13-9
  stock splits, 14-9–14-11
  stock transactions, 13-10–13-17
  subchapter S, 12-4
Corporation income statement, 14-16–14-17
Correct cash balance, 8-25
Correcting entries, 4-19–4-22, 7-9, 7-20
Corruption, 8-18
Cost(s). *See also specific types*
  in computation of depreciation, 10-8
  of copyrights, 10-19
  in CVP analysis, 22-11
  in FIFO vs. weighted-average method, 21-22–21-23
  of franchises, 10-20
  in managerial accounting, 19-7–19-10
  in noncash transactions, 13-12
  of patents, 10-19
  of plant assets, 10-3–10-6
Cost accounting, 20-3
Cost accounting systems, 20-3–20-7
Cost behavior analysis, 22-2–22-7
Cost centers, 25-18, 25-20
Cost constraints, 3-30
Cost drivers, 21-7
Cost flows, 5-4–5-6, 21-4
Cost flow assumptions and methods-
  average-cost, 6-11–6-12
  effects of, 6-12–6-14
  first-in, first-out, 6-9–6-10
  in inventory costing, 6-8–6-12
  last-in, first-out, 6-10–6-11
  in perpetual inventory systems, 6-20–6-22
Costing-
  activity-based, 19-16, 23-5

inventory, *see* Inventory costing
job order, *see* Job order costing
operations, 21-16
tradeoffs between systems, 21-16–21-17
for units completed and units in process, 21-15
Cost method, 13-14–13-15, 16-6–16-7
Cost of borrowing, 15-8–15-10
Cost of capital, 27-9
Cost of direct materials purchases, 24-11
Cost of ending inventory, 6-9–6-12
Cost of goods available for sale, 6-9
Cost of goods manufactured, 19-11–19-12
Cost of goods manufactured schedule, 19-12, 20-20–20-21
Cost of goods purchased, 19-11
Cost of goods sold-
and entries for jobs completed, 20-16–20-17
in merchandising operations, 5-3
in periodic system, 6-8, 6-10–6-12
under periodic system, 5-25
under perpetual system, 5-11
transfer to, 21-8
and variances, 26-16
and year-end balance, 20-21–20-22
Cost principle (historical cost principle), 1-8–1-9, 3-29, 10-3, 13-12
Cost reconciliation schedule, 21-15, 21-21–21-22
Cost-volume-profit (CVP) analysis, 22-10–22-24
break-even analysis, 22-14–22-18
components, 22-10–22-11
CVP income statement, 22-11–22-14
margin of safety, 22-20–22-21
target net income, 22-18–22-19
Cost-volume-profit (CVP) graph, 22-16–22-17, 22-19
Cost-volume-profit (CVP) relationships, 22-1–22-24
break-even analysis, 22-14–22-18
cost behavior analysis, 22-2–22-7
CVP analysis, 22-10–22-14
margin of safety, 22-20–22-21
mixed costs analysis, 22-7–22-10
regression analysis, 22-21–22-24
and revenue–profit relationship, 22-1–22-2
target net income, 22-18–22-19
Credits, 2-3–2-7, 2-21
Credit balance, 2-3
Credit cards, 9-12–9-13, 11-1–11-2, 23-5
Credit crisis, 9-18
Crediting accounts, 2-3
Creditors, 1-5, 1-12, 12-10, 13-18
Creditors' subsidiary ledger, 7-6–7-7
Credit purchases, 1-16–1-17, 7-16
Credit ratings, 18-17
Credit risk, 9-19–9-20, 16-5
Credit sales, 7-9–7-10
Credit terms, 5-9
Cross-footing a journal, 7-14
Cruise industry, capital budgeting in, 27-2
Cumulative dividends, 14-5
Current assets, 4-24, 17-10–17-11
Current liabilities, 11-1–11-9
analysis of, 11-8–11-9
bond interest payable, 15-7
on classified balance sheet, 4-26–4-27
credit card debt, 11-1–11-2
current maturities of long-term debt, 11-5
noncash, 17-11–17-12
notes payable, 11-3–11-4
reporting, 11-6–11-8
sales taxes payable, 11-4
unearned revenues, 11-4–11-5
Current ratio, 11-8–11-9, 18-16, 18-19
Curvilinear behavior, of costs, 22-5
Customers-
cash receipts from, 17-21
collections from, 24-18
as external users, 1-5
Customer perspective (balanced scorecard), 26-18–26-19
Customers' subsidiary ledger, 7-6–7-7
Cutoff rate, 27-9
CVP analysis, *see* Cost-volume-profit analysis
CVP graph, 22-16–22-17, 22-19
CVP income statement, 22-11–22-14
CVP relationships, *see* Cost-volume-profit relationships
Cybercrime, 7-4, 7-21
Cyber security risks, 7-21–7-22

D

Data access, accounting software, 7-4
Days in inventory, 6-18, 18-21
Death of partner, 12-23–12-24
Debenture bonds, 15-3
Debits, 2-3–2-7, 2-21
Debit balance, 2-3
Debiting accounts, 2-3
Debt. *See also* Uncollectible accounts
in auto industry, 15-1–15-2
bad debt expense, 9-5–9-7
credit card, 11-1–11-2
long-term debt, 11-5
Debt financing, 15-15–15-16
Debt investments, 16-2–16-5, 16-11–16-14
Debt masking, 15-15
Debt to assets ratio, 15-14, 18-21–18-22
Debt to equity ratio, 18-22
Decentralization, 25-14
Decision making, in capital budgeting, 27-4. *See also* Management decision-making
Declaration date (cash dividends), 14-3–14-4
Declared dividends, 14-3
Declining-balance depreciation, 10-11–10-12
Deductions, payroll, 11-10–11-12
Deferrals, 3-5–3-12, 3-24–3-27
Deficit, 14-12
Defined-benefit plans, 11-23
Defined-contribution plans, 11-22–11-23
Department(s), 21-8, 25-14
Depletion (natural resources), 10-17–10-18
Depletion cost per unit, 10-18
Deposits, bank, 8-19–8-20, 8-22, 8-24
Deposits in transit, 8-23
Depreciable assets, 3-8–3-10, 10-7
Depreciable cost, 10-9
Depreciation-
accelerated, 10-12
accumulated, 4-25, 17-28, 24-21
adjusting entries for, 3-8–3-10
component, 10-47
computing, 10-7–10-8
declining-balance method, 10-11–10-12
and income taxes, 10-13
of plant assets, 10-7–10-14
revising periodic estimates of, 10-13, 10-14
for statement of cash flows, 17-9, 17-23, 17-29
straight-line method, 10-9–10-10, 10-12
total expense, 10-12
units-of-activity method, 10-10–10-12
Depreciation rate, 10-9
Depreciation schedule, 10-9
Detail, in budgets vs. long-range plans, 24-6
Diary, recording in, 1-3
Differential analysis, 23-3. *See also* Incremental analysis
Direct fixed costs, 25-21
Directing, as management function, 19-4
Direct issues of stock, 13-7
Direct labor, 19-7, 24-13
Direct labor budget, 24-13–24-14
Direct labor price standard (direct labor rate standard), 26-5
Direct labor quantity standard (direct labor efficiency standard), 26-6
Direct labor standards, 26-5–26-6
Direct labor variances, 26-11–26-15
Direct materials, 19-7, 24-19
Direct materials budget, 24-10–24-13
Direct materials price standard, 26-5
Direct materials quantity standard, 26-5
Direct materials standards, 26-5
Direct materials units required for production, 24-10
Direct materials units to be purchased, 24-10
Direct materials variances, 26-7–26-12
Direct method (statement of cash flows), 17-7, 17-19–17-26
investing and financing activities, 17-24–17-25
net change in cash, 17-26
operating activities, 17-19–17-24
Direct write-off method, 9-5–9-6
Disbursements, 8-14–8-16, 24-17, 24-19
Disbursements journal, 7-17–7-19
Disclosures, clarity of, 5-20
Discontinued operations, 18-4
Discounts-
bond, 15-7–15-9, 15-17–15-22
on bonds payable, 15-8, 15-18
"Korean," 1-8
purchase, 5-9–5-10, 5-26
sales, 5-13–5-14, 5-27
Discounted cash flow methods, 27-6. *See also specific types*
Discount period, 5-9
Discount rate (NPV method), 27-6, 27-9
Dishonored notes, 9-17
Disinvestments, 1-19
Disposal-
of accounts receivable, 9-11–9-13
of discontinued business component, 18-4
of notes receivable, 9-16–9-17
of plant assets, 10-14–10-17, 17-9–17-10, 17-23
of treasury stock, 13-15–13-16
Dividends, 14-2–14-9
ability to pay, 17-3
cash, 14-3–14-4
cumulative, 14-5
and free cash flow, 17-17
IFRS and GAAP for, 14-38
liquidating, 14-3
for preferred stockholders, 14-4–14-6, 14-15–14-17
stock, 14-7–14-9
from stock investments, 16-7, 16-8
Dividends in arrears, 14-5

Divisions, in responsibility accounting, 25-14
Division of labor, 7-7, 7-9
Documentation procedures, 8-7, 10-6, 21-5
Dollar signs, use of, 2-22
Dollar-value LIFO, 6-8*n.*1
Dot-com bubble, 18-2
Double-declining-balance method, 10-11
Double-entry system, 2-4–2-6
Double taxation, 13-5
Drawings (by owners), 1-12, 1-19, 2-5, 4-11, 4-14
Dual disclosures, 18-4
Dual posting, 7-20
Duties-
  rotating, 8-9, 8-10
  segregation of, 8-6–8-7, 9-4, 9-7

E

Early warning system, budgeting as, 24-3
Earnings. *See also* Retained earnings
  employee earnings record, 11-13–11-14
  gross, 11-10, 11-18
  from investment income, 16-3
  management of, 5-19
  price-earnings ratio, 14-17*n.*2, 18-26
  quality of, 18-7–18-9
Earnings per share (EPS), 14-16–14-17, 18-25–18-26
Earnings statement, 1-20. *See also* Income statement
Ebbers, Bernie, 10-6
Economic entity assumption, 1-9–1-10, 3-29
Economic life, 3-1
Effective-interest amortization, 15-20–15-23
Effective-interest rate, 15-20
Electric cars, 23-17
Electronic funds transfers (EFTs), 8-14, 8-25
Electronic payments, reconciliation of, 8-24
Electronic spreadsheets, *see* Worksheets
Elimination, of unprofitable segments/products, 23-15–23-17
Employees, partners vs., 12-10
Employee compensation, *see* Payroll accounting
Employee earnings record, 11-13–11-14
Employee Retirement Income Security Act (ERISA), 11-22
Employee stock ownership plan (ESOPs), 1-5
Employee theft, 8-18
Employer payroll taxes, 11-16–11-18
Employer-provided pension plans, 11-22–11-23
Ending inventory-
  in budgeting process, 24-9, 24-11
  cost of, 6-9–6-12
  errors in, 6-15–6-16
  work in process, 19-12
Enterprise resource planning (ERP) systems, 7-4, 19-16
Entry-level software, 7-3–7-4
EPS (earnings per share), 14-16–14-17, 18-25–18-26
Equal Employment Opportunity Act, 26-3
Equipment-
  on budgeted balance sheet, 24-21
  business decisions about, 10-1–10-2
  cash purchases of, 1-15
  cost of, 10-4–10-5
  property, plant, and, 4-25
  repairing, retaining, or replacing, 23-14–23-15
  for statement of cash flows, 17-13, 17-24–17-25, 17-29
Equity financing, 15-15–15-16
Equity method (stock investments), 16-7–16-8
Equivalent units of production-
  FIFO method for, 21-17–21-23
  on production cost report, 21-13–21-14
  weighted average method for, 21-9–21-11, 21-22–21-23
Erikson, Gary, 1-5
ERISA (Employee Retirement Income Security Act), 11-22
ERP (enterprise resource planning) systems, 7-4, 19-16
Errors-
  in bank accounts, 8-23–8-24
  in beginning inventory, 6-15
  book, 8-24, 8-25
  correcting entries for, 4-20–4-22
  and faithful representation, 3-28
  inventory, 6-15–6-17
  irregularities vs., 2-21, 2-22
  subsidiary ledgers for identification of, 7-7
  in trial balances, 2-22
ESOPs (employee stock ownership plan), 1-5
Estimating-
  depreciation, 10-13, 10-14
  inventories, 6-22–6-24
  overhead, 20-12
  uncollectible accounts, 9-6, 9-8–9-10
Ethics issues-
  appearance of liquidity, 4-26
  approval of requisitions, 20-8
  arm's-length transactions, 9-3
  available-for-sale securities, 16-13
  comparing cash from operations to net income, 17-3
  completion percentages, 21-10
  cyber security, 7-4
  depletion understatement, 10-18
  disclosure of details, 5-20
  earnings management, 5-19
  and economic entity assumption, 1-9
  errors in statements, 4-19
  expectations for EPS, 14-17
  financial manipulations, 1-7
  in financial reporting, 1-6–1-7, 5-11
  grace period for finance charges, 9-12
  income and inventory, 6-5
  inventory fraud, 6-4, 6-16
  make-or-buy decision, 23-9
  managerial accounting, 19-17–19-18
  meeting standards, 26-4
  motivating employees, 11-10
  non-owner managers, 13-5
  occupational fraud, 8-18
  overstatement of value, 2-11
  overstating market value, 16-13
  partnership agreements, 12-6
  partnership liquidations, 12-12
  petty cash control, 8-16
  purchase price allocation, 10-7
  safety improvements, 27-13
  software for curbing fraud, 7-4
  specific identification method, 6-8
  telecommunications to remote areas, 19-14
  treasury stock purchase, 13-15
  unrealistic budgets, 24-6
European Union, 1-8
Evaluation of companies, *see* Financial statement analysis
Exchange of plant assets, 10-23–10-25
Exotic Newcastle Disease, 25-12
Expanded accounting equation, 1-12–1-13
Expected input and output, budget based on, 24-23
Expenditures-
  capital, 10-5, 27-18
  for plant assets, 10-2–10-14
  revenue, 10-5
Expenses-
  accrued, 3-3, 3-14–3-17
  bad debt, 9-5–9-7
  bank charge, 8-25
  bond interest, 15-20, 16-4
  in capital budgeting, 27-3
  in double-entry system, 2-5–2-6
  operating, 5-8, 5-19, 5-20, 17-22–17-23
  other expenses and losses, 5-19
  owner's equity decrease from, 1-12
  payroll, 11-14–11-15
  prepaid, 3-5–3-10, 3-25–3-26, 17-11, 17-28
  recognizing, 3-3–3-4
  on single-step income statement, 5-20
  total depreciation, 10-12
  transaction analysis for, 1-17
Expense recognition principle, 3-4, 3-5, 3-30
Expense reports, fraudulent, 8-9
External transactions, 1-14
External users, 1-5

F

Face value-
  of bonds, 15-3, 15-4, 15-7
  of notes, 9-16
Factors, 9-11–9-13
Factory labor costs, 20-6, 20-10–20-12, 21-7
Factory overhead, 19-8
Fair Labor Standards Act, 26-3
Fair value-
  for equity securities, 16-10, 16-12, 16-14
  for partnership assets, 12-7–12-8
  for plant assets, 10-7
Fair value principle, 1-9, 3-29
Faithful representation, of financial information, 1-8, 3-28
FASB, *see* Financial Accounting Standards Board
Favorable variances, 26-8, 26-22
Federal Bureau of Investigation (FBI), 1-25
Federal Insurance Contribution Act (FICA), 11-11
Federal Trade Commission, 1-5
Federal unemployment taxes, 11-16
Federal Unemployment Tax Act (FUTA), 11-16
Fees, 11-10
FICA (Federal Insurance Contribution Act), 11-11
FICA taxes, 11-10, 11-11, 11-16
FIFO, *see* First-in, first-out
FIFO (first-in, first out) method for equivalent units, 21-17–21-23
Finance, careers in, 1-10
Finance charges, 9-12
Financial accounting, 1-5, 19-3, 19-4
Financial Accounting Standards Board (FASB), 1-8, 1-48
  authority of, 19-18
  comprehensive income requirements, 18-5*n.*1
  definitional structure of, 2-46

on direct method, 17-7
on financial instrument accounting, 9-41, 11-42, 15-42, 16-35
financial statement presentation project of, 4-60, 14-38, 17-59
financial statement structure project of, 5-55, 18-52
framework for accounting standards of, 7-44, 11-42, 15-42
revenue recognition project of, 3-59
Financial budgets, 24-6, 24-7
Financial information, in management decision-making, 23-3
Financial markets, 1-46
Financial performance measures, 25-21, 26-19
Financial perspective (balanced scorecard), 26-18–26-19
Financial pressure, in fraud triangle, 8-3
Financial reporting, 3-28–3-30
Financial statements, 1-4, 1-20–1-24. *See also individual statements*
accuracy of, 2-23
from adjusted trial balance, 3-21–3-24
adjusted trial balances on, 4-8
consolidated, 16-8–16-9
current liabilities on, 11-6–11-9
depreciation on, 3-9–3-10
effect of cost flow methods on, 6-12–6-14
going beyond, 1-23
intangible assets on, 10-22–10-23
inventories on, 6-17–6-20
investments on, 16-10–16-18
long-term liabilities on, 15-14–15-17
manufacturing costs in, 19-10–19-14
for merchandising companies, 5-17–5-23
monthly, 20-21
natural resources on, 10-22–10-23
for partnerships, 12-11–12-12
plant assets on, 10-22–10-23
receivables on, 9-18–9-21
stockholders' equity on, 13-17–13-19, 14-11–14-16
time periods for, 3-3
totaling worksheet columns for, 4-9
from worksheets, 4-10–4-11
Financial statement analysis, 18-1–18-28
horizontal, 18-9–18-12
IFRS and GAAP for, 18-51–18-52
quality of earnings, 18-7–18-9
ratio analysis, 18-14–18-28
sustainable income, 18-3–18-7
vertical, 18-9–18-10, 18-12–18-14
Financial statement fraud, 8-18
Financing activities, 17-3, 17-4, 17-13–17-14, 17-24–17-25
Financing section (cash budget), 24-17, 24-19
Finished goods, 6-3
Finished goods inventory, 6-3, 20-15–20-16, 21-8, 24-21
First-in, first-out (FIFO), 6-8–6-10, 6-12–6-14, 6-20–6-21
First-in, first out (FIFO) method for equivalent units, 21-17–21-23
First-in, still here (FISH), 6-10
Fiscal year, 3-3
Fixed assets, 4-25, 10-3, 17-17. *See also* Plant assets
Fixed costs-
and controllable margin, 25-24–25-25
in CVP relationship, 22-3–22-4
and elimination of unprofitable segments/products, 23-16–23-17
in flexible budget, 25-10
identifying, 22-9–22-10
in incremental analysis, 23-5, 23-7
for investment centers, 25-23
in manufacturing overhead budget, 24-15
mixed costs as, 22-7, 22-8
for profit centers, 25-21
static budget reports for, 25-5
Fixed interest rates, 15-12
Fixed ratios (income), 12-9, 12-10
Flexible budgets, 25-6–25-13
case study of, 25-9–25-11
developing, 25-9
and manufacturing, 25-17
in responsibility accounting, 25-20
uses of, 25-7–25-9
Flexible budget reports, 25-11–25-13
FOB (free on board), 5-8
FOB destination, 5-8, 6-5
FOB shipping point, 5-8, 6-5
Food production, 22-4
Footing a journal, 7-14, 7-15
Forensic accounting, 1-25
For-profit corporations, 13-3
401(k) plans, 11-22
Franchises, 10-20
Fraud, 8-3–8-4
altered checks, 8-7
bank reconciliation, 9-4
cash as susceptible to, 8-11
fake expense reports, 8-9
fake invoices, 8-6
fictitious claims, 8-5
fictitious uses and sources of cash, 17-12
in hotel housekeeping, 8-10
and IFRS, 8-48–8-49
inventory, 6-4, 6-6, 6-16
net income, 10-6
occupational, 8-18
and payroll accounting, 11-18
reimbursement requests, 8-7
sales commissions, 8-8
software to curb, 7-5
statistical indicators of, 18-14
and stock options, 13-8
theft of merchandise, 5-12
Fraud triangle, 8-3
Free cash flow, 17-17–17-18, 18-22–18-23
Free on board (FOB), 5-8
Free shipping, 23-9
Freight costs, 5-8, 5-26
Freight-in, 5-26
Fringe benefits, 11-18, 11-20–11-23. *See also* Payroll accounting
Full disclosure principle, 3-30, 17-5
Funds, availability of, 27-4
FUTA (Federal Unemployment Tax Act), 11-16

G

GAAP, *see* Generally accepted accounting principles
Gains-
on disposal of business component, 18-4
on disposal of plant assets, 10-15–10-16
on exchange of plant assets, 10-24–10-25
other revenues and gains, 5-19
realized, 12-12, 16-16–16-17
unrealized, 16-11, 16-16–16-17
Gamification, 25-25
Geneen, Harold, 1-1
General journal, 2-8–2-10
adjusting entries in, 3-18–3-19
closing entries in, 4-12, 4-14
posting to ledger from, 2-12
and special journals, 7-8, 7-9, 7-20–7-21
General ledger, 2-10–2-13
chart of accounts in, 2-13
and post-closing trial balance, 4-16–4-18
posting to, 2-12, 7-9, 7-10, 7-14, 7-20
standard form of account in, 2-11
and subsidiary ledger, 7-6, 7-7
General ledger accounting systems, 7-3–7-4
Generally accepted accounting principles (GAAP), 1-8
for accounting information systems, 7-44
and accrual-basis accounting, 3-3
for adjusting accounts, 3-58–3-59
and capital on balance sheets, 13-17
for classified balance sheet, 4-59–4-60
for dividends, 14-38
and effective-interest method, 15-20
for financial statement analysis, 18-51–18-52
and fraud, 8-48–8-49
IFRS vs., 1-47–1-48
for income statements, 18-8
for inventories, 6-48
for investments, 16-35
for liabilities, 11-41–11-42, 15-41–15-42
for merchandising operations, 5-54–5-55
for plant, property, and equipment, 10-46–10-47
for receivables, 9-41
recording process for, 2-46
for revenue/expense recognition, 3-4
for statement of cash flows, 17-58–17-59
and stockholders' equity, 13-36–13-37
General management, careers in, 1-10
General partners, 12-4
Gift cards, accounting for, 3-12
Global Reporting Initiative, 19-19
Global Responsibility Report, 26-15
Going concern assumption, 3-29, 10-7
Goods in transit, ownership of, 6-5–6-6
Goodwill, 4-26, 10-18, 10-20
"Google Glass," 10-20
Governmental accounting, 1-25
Governmental budgets, 24-24
Grace period, 9-12
Graham, Benjamin, 18-2
Green, selling, 5-14
Green bonds, 15-12
Greenhouses, urban, 22-4
Gross earnings, 11-10, 11-18
Gross margin, 5-18
Gross profit, 5-18–5-19
Gross profit method, 6-23
Gross profit rate, 5-18, 18-25

H

Hackers, 7-21
Hacktivists, 7-21
Health insurance, 11-21–11-22
Held-to-maturity securities, 16-11
High-low method (CVP), 22-7–22-9

Historical cost principle (cost principle), 1-8–1-9, 3-29, 10-3, 13-12
Honored notes, 9-16
Horizontal analysis, 18-9–18-12
Hospitality sector, budgetary control in, 25-1–25-2
Human behavior, 8-11, 24-5–24-6, 25-16
Human resource controls, 5-12, 8-9–8-10, 11-18
Human Rights Watch, 19-18
Hurdle rate, 27-9

I

IAASB (International Auditing and Assurance Standards Board), 8-49
Iacocca, Lee, 15-1
IASB, *see* International Accounting Standards Board
Ideal standards, 26-4
Identification of economic events, 1-3, 1-4
IFRS, *see* International Financial Reporting Standards
Ig Nobel Prize, 8-49
IMA, *see* Institute of Management Accountants
IMA Statement of Ethical Professional Practice, 19-18
Impairments, 10-13
Imprest system, 8-16
Incentives, 19-17, 23-5, 25-25
Income, 6-5
  available to common stockholders, 14-17
  comprehensive, 5-21, 18-5–18-7
  investment, 16-3
  net, *see* Net income
  from operations, 5-19
  other comprehensive, 5-55
  for partnerships, 12-8–12-11
  pro forma, 18-8
  residual, 25-26–25-27
  sustainable, 18-3–18-7
Income and loss ratio, 12-8
Income ratios-
  at admission/withdrawal of partner, 12-20–12-21, 12-23
  at liquidation of partnership, 12-14
  in partnerships, 12-9–12-10
Income statement, 1-20–1-22
  budgeted, 24-15–24-17
  comprehensive, 5-21, 16-13
  corporate, 14-16–14-17
  CVP, 22-11–22-14
  effect of cost flow methods on, 6-12–6-13
  and errors in inventory accounting, 6-15–6-16
  horizontal analysis of, 18-11–18-12
  leased assets on, 15-17
  merchandising and manufacturing costs in, 19-11
  for merchandising companies, 5-17–5-21
  multiple-step, 5-18–5-20, 5-22
  operating activities on, 17-4
  ratio analysis, 18-18
  single-step, 5-20–5-21
  and statement of cash flows, 17-6, 17-19
  sustainable income on, 18-5
  transfer to worksheet, 5-24, 5-29–5-31
  under- and overapplied overhead on, 20-22
  variances on, 26-16–26-17
  vertical analysis of, 18-13
  from worksheet, 4-10
Income summary, 4-12
Income taxes-
  cash payments for, 17-23–17-24
  for corporations, 13-5, 14-16
  and depreciation, 10-13
  payroll deductions for, 11-10–11-12
Income taxes payable, 17-11–17-12, 17-29
Incremental analysis, 23-1–23-17
  and activity-based costing, 23-5
  for make-or-buy decisions, 23-8–23-10
  management decision-making process in, 23-3–23-6
  for repairing, retaining, or replacing equipment, 23-14–23-15
  for sell-or-process further decisions, 23-10–23-13
  for special orders, 23-6–23-7
  for sustainability decisions, 23-1–23-2
  for unprofitable segments or products, 23-15–23-17
Incremental revenue, 23-11
Indefinite life, 10-18
Independent internal verification, 8-8–8-9
  of bank reconciliations, 9-4
  of cash uses and sources, 17-12
  and inventory fraud, 6-6
  of net income, 10-6
  of payroll expenses, 11-18
  and statistical indicators of fraud, 18-14
  and stock options, 13-8
Indirect fixed costs, 25-21
Indirect issues of stock, 13-7
Indirect labor, 19-7
Indirect manufacturing costs, 19-8
Indirect materials, 19-7
Indirect method (statement of cash flows), 17-6–17-16
  investing and financing activities, 17-13–17-14
  net change in cash, 17-14–17-15
  operating activities, 17-9–17-13
  worksheet for, 17-26–17-30
Industry averages (norms), 18-9, 18-15, 18-19
Information, for internal control, 8-4
Information technology, 1-47
Insiders, cybercrime by, 7-21
Institute of Management Accountants (IMA), 19-18, 19-41, 20-41
Insurance, 3-8, 11-21–11-22
Intangible assets, 10-18–10-21
  accounting for, 10-18–10-20
  on classified balance sheet, 4-25–4-26
  and research and development costs, 10-21
  statement presentation and analysis of, 10-22–10-23
Intangible benefits, of capital projects, 27-11–27-13
Intended use of land, 10-3
Intercompany comparisons, 18-9, 18-15, 18-19
Interest (business), 12-18–12-19, 16-8
Interest (financial), 3-15
  accrued, 3-15
  on bonds, 15-5, 15-16, 16-4
  on buildings, 10-4
  cash payments for, 17-23
  computing, 11-3
  on notes receivable, 9-15
  on partners' capital, 12-10–12-11
Interest rates, 9-15
  for bonds, 15-3, 15-7–15-8, 15-20
  market, 15-5, 15-7
  for mortgages, 15-12–15-13
Interest receivable, 9-16–9-17
Interest yield, 27-16
Interim periods, 3-3
Internal auditors, 8-9
Internal control, 8-1–8-28
  with accounting software, 7-4
  bank accounts for, 8-19–8-26
  for bank reconciliations, 9-4
  components of, 8-4
  and fraud, 8-3–8-4
  and inventory fraud, 6-6
  limitations of, 8-10–8-11
  for net income, 10-6
  over cash, 8-1–8-2, 8-11–8-19, 17-12
  for payroll, 11-18–11-20
  principles of, 8-4–8-10
  and reporting of cash, 8-27–8-28
  and Sarbanes-Oxley Act, 1-24, 1-48, 3-5
  and statistical indicators of fraud, 18-14
  and stock options, 13-8
  and theft of merchandise, 5-12
Internal process perspective (balanced scorecard), 26-18–26-19
Internal rate of return (IRR), 27-16, 27-17
Internal rate of return (IRR) method, 27-6, 27-16–27-18
Internal Revenue Service (IRS), 1-5, 1-25, 10-13, 11-12, 11-18
Internal transactions, 1-14
Internal users, 1-4–1-5
International Accounting Standards Board (IASB), 1-8, 1-48
  definitional structure of, 2-46
  on financial instrument accounting, 9-41, 11-42, 15-42, 16-35
  financial statement presentation project of, 4-60, 14-38, 17-59
  financial statement structure project of, 5-55, 18-52
  framework for accounting standards of, 7-44, 11-42, 15-42
  on liabilities, 11-41
  revenue recognition project of, 3-59
International Auditing and Assurance Standards Board (IAASB), 8-49
International Financial Reporting Standards (IFRS), 1-8, 1-47–1-48
  for accounting information systems, 7-44
  for adjusting accounts, 3-58–3-59
  and capital on balance sheets, 13-17
  for classified balance sheet, 4-59–4-60
  for dividends, 14-38
  for financial statement analysis, 18-51–18-52
  and fraud, 8-48–8-49
  for inventories, 6-48
  for investments, 16-35
  for liabilities, 11-41–11-42, 15-41–15-42
  for merchandising operations, 5-54–5-55
  for plant, property, and equipment, 10-46–10-47
  for receivables, 9-41
  recording process for, 2-46
  for statement of cash flows, 17-58–17-59
  and stockholders' equity, 13-36–13-37
Interpretation of information, 1-4
Intracompany comparisons, 18-9, 18-15, 18-19
Inventoriable costs, 19-8
Inventory(-ies), 6-1–6-24

beginning, 6-15
business success and management of, 6-1–6-2
classifying, 6-3–6-4
days in, 6-18, 18-21
determining quantities, 6-4–6-6
ending, 6-9–6-12, 6-15–6-16, 19-12, 24-9, 24-11
errors in accounting for, 6-15–6-17
estimating, 6-22–6-24
excessive levels of, 6-19
financial effects of inventory methods, 6-7–6-15
in financial statements, 6-17–6-20
finished goods, 6-3, 20-15–20-16, 21-8, 24-21
IFRS and GAAP for, 6-48
and income, 6-5
just-in-time, 6-3–6-4, 19-16
merchandise, 6-3
periodic system for, 5-5, 5-24–5-31, 6-8–6-9
perpetual system, *see* Perpetual inventory system
physical, 5-4, 5-6, 6-4
raw materials, 24-21
for statement of cash flows, 17-10–17-11, 17-28
work in process, 19-11, 19-12, 20-8, 20-12

Inventory costing, 6-7–6-15
consistency concept in, 6-14
cost flow assumptions, 6-8–6-12
financial statement and tax effects of methods, 6-12–6-14
lower-of-cost-or-net realizable value, 6-17–6-20
perpetual system, 6-20–6-22
specific identification method, 6-7–6-8

Inventory turnover, 6-18–6-20, 18-20–18-21
Investee, 16-6
Investing activities-
cash flows from, 17-3, 17-4
direct method for, 17-24–17-25
indirect method for, 17-13–17-14
noncash, 17-5

Investments, 16-1–16-18
associate, 16-35
on classified balance sheet, 4-25
debt investments, 16-2–16-5, 16-11–16-14
with dividends, 14-6
on financial statements, 16-10–16-18
IFRS and GAAP for, 16-35
long-term, 16-15
by owner, 1-12, 1-15
in partnerships, 12-19–12-20
reasons for making, 16-3–16-4
short-term, 16-15
stock investments, 16-6–16-10, 16-14
in technology, 16-1–16-2

Investment centers, 25-18, 25-20, 25-22–25-26
Investment portfolio, 16-6
Investors, 1-5, 1-10
Invoices, 5-7, 5-11, 8-6
Involuntary withdrawal, 12-21
IRR (internal rate of return), 27-16, 27-17
Irregularities, 2-21, 2-22
IRR (internal rate of return) method, 27-6, 27-16–27-18
IRS, *see* Internal Revenue Service

J

JIT (just-in-time) inventory, 6-3–6-4, 19-16
Jobs, 20-3, 21-3
Job cost sheet, 20-7, 20-8, 20-14–20-16
Job order cost flow, 20-4–20-5, 20-17–20-18, 21-5
Job order costing, 20-1–20-22
advantages and disadvantages, 20-19–20-20
applied manufacturing overhead in, 20-20–20-22
assigning manufacturing costs in, 20-7–20-12
cost accounting systems, 20-3–20-7
jobs completed and sold in, 20-15–20-20
for movie studios, 20-1–20-2
predetermined overhead rates in, 20-12–20-15
for service companies, 20-18–20-19

Job order cost systems, 20-3–20-4
process cost systems vs., 21-3–21-5
standard cost accounting system with, 26-20–26-23

Joint costs, 23-12
Joint products, 23-11
Journals, 2-7–2-10. *See also* General journal
cash payments (disbursements), 7-17–7-19
cash receipts, 7-11–7-15
cross-footing, 7-14
footing, 7-14, 7-15
posting to, *see* Posting
purchases, 7-15–7-17
sales, 7-9–7-11
simple and compound entries in, 2-9
special, *see* Special journals

Journalizing, 2-8–2-9
adjusted trial balances, 4-5
adjusting entries, 3-18–3-19, 4-11
bond transactions, 15-4, 15-7
cash payments transactions, 7-17–7-19
cash receipts transactions, 7-12–7-14
closing entries, 4-12–4-14, 5-28–5-29
credit purchases, 7-16
credit sales, 7-9–7-10
in general journal, 7-20
illustration of, 2-14–2-19
manufacturing costs, 21-6–21-9
special journals for, 7-9, 7-20
with standard cost accounting system, 26-20–26-22

Just-in-time (JIT) inventory, 6-3–6-4, 19-16

K

Knight, Philip "Phil," 1-4, 13-3, 13-4
"Korean discount," 1-8

L

Labor costs, 19-7
and conversion costs, 21-10
direct, 24-13
factory, 20-6, 20-10–20-12, 21-7
process vs. job order cost systems for, 21-4

Labor price variance (LPV), 26-12, 26-13, 26-15
Labor quantity variance (LQV), 26-12–26-14
Labor unions, 1-5
Labor variances, 26-11–26-15
Land-
as plant assets, 10-3–10-4, 10-7
for statement of cash flows, 17-13, 17-24, 17-29

Land improvements, 10-4
Large stock dividend, 14-8
Last-in, first-out (LIFO), 6-10–6-11
dollar-value, 6-8*n*.1
financial statement and tax effects, 6-12–6-14
in GAAP and in IFRS, 6-48
in periodic inventory systems, 6-8
in perpetual inventory systems, 6-21–6-22

Last-in, still here (LISH), 6-9
LCNRV (lower-of-cost-or-net realizable value method), 6-17–6-20
Lean manufacturing, 19-15
Learning and growth perspective (balanced scorecard), 26-18–26-19
Leases and leasing, 10-6, 15-16–15-17
Ledgers, 2-10–2-13. *See also* General ledger; Subsidiary ledgers
proving, 7-10, 7-15, 7-17, 7-19
with standard cost accounting system, 26-22

Legal capital, 13-8
Legal existence, of corporations, 13-3, 13-5
Legal life, patent, 10-19
Legal restrictions on retained earnings, 14-12
Lenders, 9-18
Leonardo da Vinci, 1-4*n*.2
Lessee, 15-16
Lessor, 15-16
Leveraging, 18-24
Liabilities (financial)-
in accounting equation, 1-11–1-12
on bank statements, 8-22
on classified balance sheet, 4-23, 4-26–4-27
contingent, 11-6–11-7, 11-41
current, 4-26–4-27, 11-1–11-9, 15-7, 17-11–17-12
and dividends in arrears, 14-5
in double-entry system, 2-4
IFRS and GAAP for, 11-41–11-42, 15-41–15-42
long-term, *see* Long-term liabilities
noncurrent, 17-13–17-14
payroll, 11-14–11-15
pension, 11-22
total, 18-12

Liability (legal), in partnerships, 12-3, 12-4
Licenses, 10-20, 13-5–13-6
Life insurance benefits, 11-21–11-22
Life of a corporation, 13-4
LIFO, *see* Last-in, first-out
LIFO conformity rule, 6-14
Limited liability, 1-10, 12-4, 13-3
Limited liability companies (LLCs), 12-4
Limited liability partnerships (LLPs), 12-4
Limited life, 10-18, 12-3
Limited partners, 12-4
Limited partnerships (Ltd., LP), 12-4
Limited resources, 27-13
Linear cost assumption, 22-5, 22-6
Line positions, 19-5, 19-6
Liquidation, 12-12–12-18, 14-3
Liquidity, 4-27, 11-8–11-9
Liquidity ratios, 18-15–18-16, 18-18–18-21
LISH (last-in, still here), 6-9
LLCs (limited liability companies), 12-4
LLPs (limited liability partnerships), 12-4
Loans, bad, 9-18
Long-range planning, 24-6
Long-term debt, 11-5
Long-term debt due within one year, 11-5
Long-term investments, 4-25, 16-15
Long-term liabilities, 11-3, 15-1–15-23
bonds, 15-2–15-12
on classified balance sheet, 4-27–4-28
debt in auto industry, 15-1–15-2
effective-interest amortization, 15-20–15-23

Long-term liabilities (*Continued*)
on financial statements, 15-14–15-17
notes payable, long-term, 15-12–15-13
postretirement benefits, 11-23
straight-line amortization, 15-17–15-19
Long-term notes payable, 15-12–15-13
Losses-
accumulated, 13-37, 14-38
from discontinued operations, 18-4
on disposal of plant assets, 10-16, 17-9–17-10, 17-23
on exchange of plant assets, 10-24
and margin of safety, 22-20
net, *see* Net losses
other expenses and, 5-19
realized, 12-12, 16-16–16-17
unrealized, 16-11, 16-16–16-17, 18-5–18-6
Lower-of-cost-or-net realizable value (LCNRV), 6-17–6-20
Lowry, Adam, 23-1, 23-2
LPs (limited partnerships), 12-4
LPV, *see* Labor price variance
LQV (labor quantity variance), 26-12–26-14
Ltd. (limited partnerships), 12-4

M

Machine hours, 20-13, 21-7
Machine time used, 21-7
McKenna, Erin, 24-1, 24-2
MACRS (Modified Accelerated Cost Recovery System), 10-13
Madoff, Bernard, 8-26
Mail receipts, cash, 8-14
Make-or-buy decisions, 23-8–23-10, 23-17
Maker (promissory notes), 9-13
Management-
acceptance of budget by, 24-4
benefits of budgeting for, 24-3
careers in, 1-10
controllable costs for, 25-15
of corporations, 13-4–13-5
functions of, 19-3–19-6
performance evaluations by, 25-16
Management accounting, *see* Managerial accounting
Management by exception, 25-15
Management consulting, 1-25
Management decision-making-
about repairing, retaining, or replacing equipment, 23-14–23-15
for eliminating unprofitable segments, 23-15–23-17
incremental analysis for, 23-3–23-6
make-or-buy decisions, 23-8–23-10
sell-or-process further decisions, 23-10–23-13
on special orders, 23-6–23-7
on sustainability, 23-1–23-2
Managerial accounting, 1-5, 1-25, 19-1–19-19
in business success, 19-1–19-2
cost concepts in, 19-7–19-10
financial accounting vs., 19-3, 19-4
managers' functions in, 19-3–19-6
manufacturing costs, 19-7–19-8, 19-10–19-14
organizational structure, 19-5–19-6
trends in, 19-14–19-19
Manual accounting systems, 7-5
Manufacturing companies, 19-7–19-8
budgets for merchandisers vs., 24-22
classifying inventory in, 6-3–6-4
flexible budgets for, 25-17
process cost systems for, 21-3
sales budget for, 24-8
value chain of, 19-15–19-16
Manufacturing costs, 19-7–19-8. *See also* Job order cost flow; Process cost system
accumulating, 20-4–20-7, 20-17
assigning, 20-4, 20-7–20-12, 20-17, 21-5–21-9
in balance sheet, 19-13
cost concepts, 19-9–19-10
cost of goods manufactured, 19-11–19-12
in CVP analysis, 22-11
in income statement, 19-11
indirect, 19-8
in job order cost system, 20-4, 20-7–20-12, 20-17, 21-4, 21-5
journal entries for, 21-6–21-9
in process cost system, 21-4–21-9
static budget reports for, 25-5
total, 19-12, 20-20–20-21
Manufacturing overhead, 19-7, 19-8, 20-6
applied, 20-20–20-22
and conversion costs, 21-10
journal entries for, 21-7
process vs. job order cost systems for, 21-4
standards for, 26-6
variances for, 26-14–26-15
Manufacturing overhead budget, 24-14–24-15
Margin (income) measure, 25-24
Margin of safety, 22-20–22-21
Margin of safety ratio (CVP), 22-20–22-21
Marketable securities, 16-15
Marketing, 1-10
Market interest rate, 15-5, 15-7
Market price, 14-20
Market value of bonds, 15-5–15-6
Mark-to-market accounting, 16-11
Marshall, John, 13-2
Master budget, 24-6–24-7, 25-7
Matching principle, *see* Expense recognition principle
Materials-
addition of, in production, 21-13, 21-20
equivalent units for, 21-20
Material bad debts, 9-6
Materials costs, 19-7
direct materials, 24-11
journal entries for, 21-6–21-7
process vs. job order cost systems for, 21-4
raw, 20-5, 20-8–20-10
Materiality, 3-28, 10-5, 25-16
Materials price variance (MPV), 26-9–26-11, 26-16
Materials quantity variance (MQV), 26-10, 26-11
Materials requisition slips, 20-8, 21-6
Materials variances, direct, 26-7–26-12
Maturities, long-term debt, 11-5
Maturity date-
for bonds, 15-3, 15-11–15-12
for notes receivable, 9-14–9-15
Maturity value, notes receivable, 9-16
Mayor, David, 19-18
Measurement principles, 1-8–1-9, 3-29
Medicare taxes, 11-11
Members (LLCs), 12-4
Merchandise, theft of, 5-12
Merchandise inventory, 6-3
Merchandise purchases budget, 24-22–24-25
Merchandising companies, 5-1–5-31
accounting cycle for, 5-15–5-17
budgeting in, 24-22–24-23
classifying inventory in, 6-3
cost of goods in, 19-11–19-13
flow of costs in, 5-4–5-6
forms of financial statements for, 5-17–5-23
IFRS and GAAP for, 5-54–5-55
operating cycles in, 5-3–5-4
periodic inventory system for, 5-24–5-31
recording purchases of merchandise, 5-6–5-10
recording sales of merchandise, 5-11–5-15
voting rights at, 5-1–5-2
worksheets for, 5-23–5-24, 5-29–5-31
Merchandising profit, 5-18–5-19
Mergers and acquisitions, 1-47
Mineral deposits, 10-17
Minimum rate of return, 25-27
Misallocation of workers, 26-13
Mixed costs, 22-6–22-10, 22-21–22-24
Modified Accelerated Cost Recovery System (MACRS), 10-13
Monetary unit assumption, 1-9, 3-29
Monitoring, for internal control, 8-4
Monthly budget data, 25-10
Monthly responsibility reports, 25-22
Mortgages, 15-12–15-13
Mortgage bonds, 15-3
Mortgage notes payable, 15-12
Motivation, budgeting to improve, 24-3
Movie studios, job order costing in, 20-1–20-2
Moving-average method, 6-22
MPV (materials price variance), 26-9–26-11, 26-16
MQV (materials quantity variance), 26-10, 26-11
Multinational corporations, 1-47
Multiple-step income statement, 5-18–5-20, 5-22
Murdoch, Rupert, 16-2
Murdock, Wilbert, 11-1–11-2
Music industry, partnership in, 12-1–12-2
Mutual agency, 12-3
Mutually exclusive projects, 27-13–27-14

N

Nasdaq, 13-13
National credit card sales, 9-12–9-13
Nation-states, cybercrime by, 7-21
Natural resources, 10-17–10-18, 10-22–10-23
Negotiable instruments, 8-20
Net annual cash flow, 27-5, 27-10
Net assets, 12-19, 12-22, 14-19
Net cash from operating activities, 17-3, 17-5
Net change in cash, 17-14–17-15, 17-26
Net income, 1-21
available to common stockholders, 14-15
converting, from accrual to cash basis, 17-7, 17-9–17-13, 17-20–17-24
on CVP income statement, 22-12, 22-13
and drawings, 4-14
and elimination of unprofitable segments/products, 23-15
and fraud, 10-6
on multiple-step income statement, 5-19
net cash from operating activities vs., 17-3, 17-5
for partnerships, 12-3, 12-8–12-11
in sell-or-process further decisions, 23-11
target, 22-18–22-19
and trading securities, 16-11
on worksheet, 4-9, 4-11

Net losses, 1-21
  and elimination decisions, 23-15
  for partnerships, 12-3, 12-8–12-11
  and retained earnings, 14-11–14-12
  on worksheet, 4-9, 4-11
Net pay, 11-12–11-13, 11-18
Net present value (NPV), 27-6, 27-7, 27-10–27-11, 27-14
Net present value (NPV) method, 27-6–27-16
  comprehensive example, 27-10–27-11
  discount rate in, 27-9
  and intangible benefits, 27-11–27-13
  internal rate of return method vs., 27-18
  for mutually exclusive projects, 27-13–27-14
  and post-audit of capital projects, 27-15–27-16
  for projects with equal annual cash flows, 27-7
  for projects with unequal annual cash flows, 27-8
  risk analysis, 27-14–27-15
  simplifying assumptions in, 27-9–27-10
Net (cash) realizable value, 6-18, 9-6, 9-16
Net sales, 5-18, 18-10, 18-13
Net 30, 5-9
Network compatibility of software, 7-4
Neutrality, 3-28
No capital deficiency (partnership liquidation), 12-13–12-15
Nominal accounts, 4-12. *See also* Temporary accounts
Noncash activities, 17-4–17-5
Noncash assets, 13-12, 17-10–17-11
Noncash current liabilities, changes to, 17-11–17-12
Noncontrollable revenues and costs, 25-15
Noncurrent assets, 17-13–17-14
Noncurrent liabilities, 17-13–17-14
Nonfinancial information, in decision-making, 23-3
Nonfinancial performance measures, 25-21, 26-17, 26-19
Nonlinear behavior, of costs, 22-5
Nonmanufacturing companies, 24-22–24-25
Nonoperating activities, 5-19–5-20
Nonpayment of deficiency, partnership with, 12-17
Non-recurring charges, 18-4
No-par value stocks, 13-8, 13-11–13-12
Normal balances, 2-4, 2-7
Normal capacity, 26-6
Normal range, 22-5. *See also* Relevant range
Normal standards, 26-4
Notes payable, 1-12, 11-3–11-4, 15-12–15-13
Notes receivable, 9-3, 9-13–9-18
  computing interest on, 9-15
  disposing of, 9-16–9-17
  maturity date for, 9-14–9-15
  recognizing, 9-15–9-16
  valuing, 9-16
Notes to financial statements, 9-19–9-20, 17-5
Not-for-profit corporations/organizations, 24-24
Not sufficient funds (NSF) checks, 8-25
NPV, *see* Net present value
NPV method, *see* Net present value method
NSF (not sufficient funds) checks, 8-25

O

Objectives, 24-3, 26-18, 26-19
Obsolescence, 10-7
Occupational fraud, 8-18
Oil reserves, 10-17
Operating activities-
  cash flows from, 17-3, 17-4
  direct method, 17-19–17-24
  indirect method, 17-9–17-13
Operating assets, 25-24, 25-25
Operating budgets, 24-6, 24-7
Operating cycles, 4-24, 5-3–5-4
Operating expenses-
  cash payments for, 17-22–17-23
  freight costs as, 5-8
  on multiple-step income statement, 5-19, 5-20
Operations, discontinued, 18-4
Operations costing, 21-16
Opportunity, in fraud triangle, 8-3
Opportunity costs, 23-4, 23-9
Ordinary repairs, 10-5
Organizational structure, 19-5–19-6, 24-3
Organization charts, 19-5, 25-18
Organization costs, 13-6
Organizations with partnership characteristics, 12-3–12-5
Organized crime, cybercrime and, 7-21
Other assets, reporting, 4-25
Other comprehensive income, 5-55
Other expenses and losses, 5-19
Other receivables, 9-3
Other revenues and gains, 5-19
Outstanding checks, 8-23, 8-24
Outstanding stock, 13-18
Overapplied manufacturing overhead, 20-21–20-22
Over budget (term), 25-7
Overhead. *See also* Manufacturing overhead
  and conversion costs, 21-10
  factory, 19-8
  flexible budget report on, 25-8
  journal entries for, 21-7
  predetermined, 20-12–20-15, 20-17
  process vs. job order cost systems for, 21-4
  standard predetermined rate, 26-6
  static budget report on, 25-7
Overhead controllable variance, 26-14, 26-23–26-24
Overhead variances, 26-14–26-15, 26-23–26-24
Overhead volume variance, 26-14, 26-24
Over-the-counter cash receipts, 8-12–8-14
Owners-
  and corporations, 13-2
  investment of cash by, 1-15
  in proprietorship, 1-9
Owner's capital, 1-12, 2-5
Owner's equity. *See also* Corporate capital
  in accounting equation, 1-12–1-13
  on classified balance sheet, 4-23, 4-28
  decreases in, 1-12–1-13
  in double-entry system, 2-4–2-5
  increases in, 1-12, 1-16
Owner's equity statement, 1-20–1-22, 4-10
Ownership, 6-4–6-6, 14-7
Ownership rights, 13-3, 13-6

P

Pacioli, Luca, 1-4*n*.2
Paid absences, 11-21
Paid-in capital, 13-9, 13-17
  in excess of par value, 13-11
  and net losses, 14-12
  and stock dividends, 14-7
Paper (phantom) profit, 6-13
Parent company, 16-8, 16-9
Participative budgeting, 24-5–24-6
Partners, 12-4
  admission of, 12-18–12-21
  withdrawal of, 12-21–12-24
Partners' capital statement, 12-11
Partnerships, 1-9–1-10, 12-1–12-24
  admission/withdrawal of partners, 12-18–12-24
  forming, 12-2–12-8
  liquidation of, 12-12–12-18
  in music industry, 12-1–12-2
  net income/net loss in, 12-8–12-12
Partnership agreements, 12-6
Partnership dissolution, 12-3
Partnership liquidation, 12-12–12-18
Par value stock, 13-8, 13-10–13-11, 14-9
Patents, 10-19
Payee, 8-20, 9-13
Payment(s)-
  bank reconciliation of, 8-24
  of deficiency, 12-16–12-17
  for direct materials, 24-19
  of payroll, 11-15–11-16
  from petty cash fund, 8-16–8-17
  transaction analysis for, 1-17–1-18
Payment date (cash dividends), 14-4
Payout ratio, 14-14–14-15, 18-26–18-27
Payroll accounting, 11-9–11-23
  determining payroll, 11-10–11-13
  employer payroll taxes, 11-16–11-18
  filing/remitting payroll taxes, 11-18–11-19
  and fraud, 11-18
  fringe benefits, 11-20–11-23
  internal control for, 11-19–11-20
  recording payroll, 11-13–11-16
Payroll deductions, 11-10–11-12
Payroll register, 11-14
Payroll taxes, 11-16–11-19
Payroll tax expense, 11-15
PCAOB (Public Company Accounting Oversight Board), 8-3
Pensions, 11-22–11-23, 18-7
Pension recipients, 11-22
P-E (price-earnings) ratio, 14-17*n*.2, 18-26
Percentages, 18-15
Percentage change, 18-11
Percentage of receivables basis (uncollectibles), 9-8, 9-9
Performance evaluation, 25-15–25-17, 26-4
Performance obligations, 3-3, 3-10
Period costs, 19-8
Periodic depreciation, 10-13, 10-14
Periodic inventory systems, 5-5, 5-24–5-31, 6-8–6-9
Periodicity assumption, 3-3. *See also* Time period assumption
Permanent accounts, 4-12, 4-16–4-17
Perpetual inventory systems, 5-4–5-17, 6-8
  in cost accounting systems, 20-3
  cost flow methods in, 6-20–6-22
  entries for periodic system vs., 5-27–5-28
  merchandising entries with, 5-16–5-17
  recording purchases under, 5-6–5-10
  recording sales under, 5-11–5-15
Petty cash fund controls, 8-16–8-19
Phantom profit, 6-13
Pharmaceutical companies, receivables management for, 9-1–9-2

Physical controls, 5-12, 8-7–8-8
Physical custody, 8-6
Physical inventory, 5-4, 5-6, 6-4
Physical units, 21-13
Physical unit flow, 21-13, 21-19–21-20
Pickard, Thomas, 1-4
Plan administrators, 11-22
Planning-
 budgetary, *see* Budgetary planning
 long-range, 24-6
 as management function, 19-4, 24-3
Plant and equipment, 10-2. *See also* Plant assets
Plant assets, 4-25, 10-1–10-26
 business decisions about equipment, 10-1–10-2
 depreciation of, 10-7–10-14
 disposal of, 10-14–10-17
 exchange of, 10-23–10-25
 expenditures for, 10-2–10-6
 loss on disposal of, 17-9–17-10, 17-23
 statement presentation and analysis of, 10-22–10-23
P&L (profit and loss) ratio, 12-8
Point-of-sale (POS) systems, 8-1–8-2
Ponzi schemes, 8-26
Post-audit of capital projects, 27-15–27-16
Post-closing trial balance, 4-16–4-18
Posting, 2-12
 of adjusting entries, 3-18–3-19, 4-11
 cash payments journal, 7-18, 7-19
 cash receipts journal, 7-14–7-15
 of closing entries, 4-12, 4-14–4-15, 5-28–5-29
 of correcting entries, 4-21
 dual, 7-20
 illustration of, 2-14–2-20
 job cost sheet, 20-8
 purchases journal, 7-16–7-17
 sales journal, 7-10, 7-11
 special journals for, 7-8, 7-20
Postretirement benefits, 11-21–11-23
Practical range, 22-5. *See also* Relevant range
Predetermined overhead, 20-12–20-15, 20-17
Predictive value, 3-28
Preemptive right, 13-6
Preferred dividends, 14-4–14-6, 14-15–14-17
Preferred stock, 13-12–13-13, 14-4–14-7, 14-19
Premium-
 on bonds, 15-8–15-11, 15-19, 15-22–15-23
 on stock, 13-11
Prenumbering documents, 8-7
Prepaid expenses (prepayments), 3-5
 adjusting entries for, 3-6–3-10
 alternative treatment of, 3-25–3-26
 for statement of cash flows, 17-11, 17-28
Price-earnings (P-E) ratio, 14-17*n*.2, 18-26
Price variances-
 labor, 26-12, 26-13, 26-15
 materials, 26-9–26-11
Pricing, FIFO vs. weighted-average method and, 21-23
Principal (bond), 15-5, 15-16
Principal (mortgage), 15-13
Prior period adjustments, 14-12–14-13
Private accounting, 1-25. *See also* Managerial accounting
Privately held corporations, 13-3
Probable contingencies, 11-6
Process cost flow, 21-5, 21-6
Process cost system, 20-3, 21-1–21-23
 assigning manufacturing costs, 21-6–21-9
 equivalent units, 21-9–21-11, 21-17–21-23
 job order cost systems vs., 21-3–21-5
 process cost flow, 21-6
 production cost report, 21-12–21-17
 for service companies, 21-4
 at small businesses, 21-1–21-2
 uses of, 21-3
Product(s)-
 job costing in decisions about, 20-4
 sell-or-process further decisions for, 23-10–23-13
 unprofitable, elimination of, 23-15–23-17
Product costs, 19-8, 19-10
Production, inventory and, 6-3
Production budget, 24-9–24-10, 24-12
Production cost report, 21-12–21-17, 21-22, 21-23
Production department, 26-11, 26-14
Product warranties, 11-7
Profit(s). *See also* Cost-volume-profit (CVP) relationships
 accumulated, 13-37
 equation for, 22-15
 gross, 5-18–5-19
 merchandising, 5-18–5-19
 paper (phantom), 6-13
 relationship of revenue and, 22-1–22-2
 retained, 13-37, 14-38
Profitability, 24-1–24-2, 27-5, 27-18
Profitability index, 27-14–27-16
Profitability ratios, 18-16–18-18, 18-23–18-27
Profit and loss (P&L) ratio, 12-8
Profit and loss statement, 1-20. *See also* Income statement
Profit centers, 25-18, 25-21–25-22
Profit margin, 18-24
Pro forma income, 18-8
Promissory notes, 9-13. *See also* Notes receivable
Property, plant, and equipment, 4-25, 10-2, 10-46–10-47. *See also* Plant assets
Proportion, 18-15
Proprietorships, 1-9
Pro rata basis, 14-2
Prorating annual depreciation, 10-9
Proving ledgers, 7-10, 7-15, 7-17, 7-19
Provisions, 11-41–11-42
Public accounting, 1-24–1-25
Public companies, 13-1–13-2
Public Company Accounting Oversight Board (PCAOB), 8-3
Publicly held corporations, 13-3
Purchases-
 of buildings, 10-4
 of merchandise, 5-6–5-10
 recording, 5-6–5-10, 5-26
 transaction analysis for, 1-15–1-16
 of treasury stock, 13-14–13-15
Purchase allowances, 5-9, 5-26
Purchase discounts, 5-9–5-10, 5-26
Purchase invoice, 5-7
Purchases journal, 7-15–7-17
Purchase of an interest (partnerships), 12-18–12-19
Purchase price, intangible asset, 10-19
Purchase returns, 5-9, 5-26
Purchasing activities, segregation of, 8-6
Purchasing department, 26-11

Q

Qualitative decision-making factors, 23-5
Quality of earnings, 18-7–18-9
Quantity variances-
 labor, 26-12–26-14
 materials, 26-10, 26-11
Quarterly dividend rate, 14-3
Quarterly tax reports, 11-18

R

Rates, 18-15
Ratios, 18-14
Ratio analysis, 18-14–18-28
 comprehensive example, 18-17–18-28
 liquidity ratios, 18-15–18-16, 18-18–18-21
 long-term liabilities, 15-14–15-15
 profitability ratios, 18-16–18-18, 18-23–18-27
 solvency ratios, 18-16, 18-18, 18-21–18-23
Rationalization, in fraud triangle, 8-3
Raw materials, 6-3, 19-7
Raw materials costs, 20-5, 20-8–20-10
Raw materials inventory, 24-21
R&D (research and development) costs, 10-21
Real accounts, 4-12. *See also* Permanent accounts
Real estate, 1-10
Real estate taxes payable, 1-12
Realization, partnership, 12-12
Realized gains and losses, 12-12, 16-16–16-17
Reasonable assurance concept, 8-10
Reasonable possible contingencies, 11-6
Receivables, 9-1–9-21
 accounts receivable, 9-2–9-13
 on financial statements, 9-18–9-21
 IFRS and GAAP for, 9-41
 notes receivable, 9-13–9-18
 for pharmaceutical companies, 9-1–9-2
 types of, 9-3
Reconciling bank accounts, 8-22–8-26
 entries from, 8-25–8-26
 illustration of, 8-24–8-25
 procedure for, 8-22–8-24
Reconciling items, on statement of cash flows, 17-27–17-30
Record date (cash dividends), 14-4
Recording process, 2-1–2-23, 5-26–5-28
 accounts in, 2-2–2-3
 activities in, 1-3, 1-4
 for bond transactions, 16-4
 chart of accounts, 2-13
 debits and credits in, 2-3–2-7
 for employer payroll taxes, 11-17–11-19
 illustrated, 2-13–2-18
 importance of organized, 2-1–2-2
 journal in, 2-7–2-10, 2-19–2-20
 ledger in, 2-10–2-13, 2-20
 for payroll, 11-13–11-16
 with periodic inventory system, 5-25–5-28
 with perpetual inventory system, 5-6–5-15, 5-27–5-28
 posting in, 2-12, 2-19, 2-20
 for purchases of merchandise, 5-6–5-10, 5-26
 for sales of merchandise, 5-11–5-15, 5-27
 for special and general journals, 7-9, 7-20
 steps in, 2-7–2-8
 for stock transactions, 16-6–16-8
 trial balance in, 2-21–2-23
 for write-off of uncollectible debt, 9-7

Recordkeeping, 8-6
Recovery of uncollectible accounts, 9-7–9-8
Recycling, 3-17, 21-11
Redeeming bonds, 15-11–15-12
Regression analysis, 22-8, 22-21–22-24
Regular partnerships, 12-4
Regulations, government, 13-5, 26-3
Regulatory agencies, 1-5
Reimbursement requests, fraud involving, 8-7
Reinvestment, 27-9
Related activities, 8-6
Relevance, 1-8, 3-28
Relevant costs and revenues, 23-4, 23-7, 23-14, 23-15
Relevant range, 22-5–22-6, 25-10
Remittance advice, 8-20
Remote contingencies, 11-6
Repairs, ordinary, 10-5
Report preparation software, 7-4
Repurchase of shares, 13-16
Required rate of return, 27-6, 27-9, 27-17, 27-19
Research and analysis, budgeting, 24-3–24-4
Research and development (R&D) costs, 10-21
Reserves, 13-36, 14-38
Residual claims, 13-6
Residual equity, 1-12. *See also* Owner's equity
Residual income, 25-26–25-27
Residual value, 10-8, 10-47
Responsibility, 8-5
Responsibility accounting, 25-13–25-27
  controllable vs. noncontrollable revenues/costs, 25-15
  investment centers, 25-22–25-26
  performance evaluation, 25-15–25-17
  responsibility centers, 25-18–25-22
  responsibility reporting system, 25-17–25-18
  and ROI vs. residual income, 25-26–25-27
Responsibility centers, 25-16, 25-18–25-22
Responsibility reporting system, 25-17–25-18
Restricted cash, 8-27–8-28
Restructuring charges, 18-4
Retailers, 5-3, 24-8
Retail inventory method, 6-24
Retained earnings, 13-9, 13-37, 14-11–14-13
  on budgeted balance sheet, 24-21
  payment of cash dividends from, 14-3
  prior period adjustments, 14-12–14-13
  on statement of cash flows, 17-14, 17-25, 17-29–17-30
  and stock dividends, 14-7
  on stockholders' equity statement, 14-18
  and stock splits, 14-9
Retained earnings restrictions, 14-12
Retained earnings statement, 14-13
Retained profits, 13-37, 14-38
Retirement of plant assets, 10-15
Retiring partner, bonus to, 12-22–12-23
Returns, 5-9, 5-12–5-13
Return on assets, 18-24
Return on common stockholders' equity (ROE), 14-15, 18-23
Return on investment (ROI), 25-23–25-27
Revenues, 1-12, 1-16. *See also* Sales revenue (sales)
  accrued, 3-3, 3-13–3-14
  in allowance method, 9-6
  in capital budgeting, 27-3
  controllable, 25-15, 25-20–25-23
  in double-entry system, 2-5–2-6
  incremental, 23-11
  noncontrollable, 25-15
  other revenues and gains, 5-19
  recognizing, 3-3–3-4
  relationship of profit and, 22-1–22-2
  relevant, 23-4, 23-7, 23-14, 23-15
  for service companies, 20-19
  on single-step income statement, 5-20
  from stock investments, 16-8
  unearned, 3-5, 3-10–3-11, 3-26–3-27, 11-4–11-5
Revenue expenditures, 10-5
Revenue recognition principle, 3-3–3-5, 3-30, 18-8
Reversing entries, 4-19, 4-22, 4-29–4-30
Risk, 8-10, 27-4
Risk analysis, 8-4, 27-14–27-15
Robotic workers, 22-9
Rodgers, Aaron, 2-1
ROE (return on common stockholders' equity), 14-15, 18-23
ROI (return on investment), 25-23–25-27
Rolling Stones, 22-20
Rowlings, J.K., 10-18
Ryan, Eric, 23-1, 23-2

S

Safe cash payments schedule, 12-14. *See also* Schedule of cash payments
Safety improvements, 27-13
Salaries, 3-16–3-17, 11-10, 12-10–12-11. *See also* Payroll accounting
Salaries and wages payable, 1-12
Sales activities (sales)-
  of bonds, 16-4
  of merchandise, 5-11–5-15
  of plant assets, 10-15–10-17
  of receivables, 9-11
  recording, 5-11–5-15, 5-27–5-28
  segregation of purchasing and, 8-6
  of stocks, 16-7
  of treasury stock, 13-15–13-16
Sales budget, 24-8–24-9, 24-12
Sales budget report, 25-4–25-5
Sales commissions, 8-8
Sales discounts, 5-13–5-14, 5-27
Sales dollars-
  break-even point in, 22-14, 22-15
  contribution margin ratio in, 22-16
  margin of safety in, 22-20
  target net income in, 22-19
Sales forecasts, 24-4
Sales invoices, 5-11
Sales journal, 7-9–7-11
Sales returns and allowances, 5-12–5-13, 5-27
Sales revenue (sales), 5-3, 5-18
  and controllable margin, 25-24
  credit card, 9-12–9-13
  income statement presentation of, 5-18
  net, 5-18, 18-10, 18-13
Sales taxes payable, 1-12, 11-4
Sales units-
  break-even point in, 22-14, 22-15
  target net income in, 22-18–22-19
Salvage value, 10-8, 10-10, 10-11
SAP ERP, 7-4
Sarbanes-Oxley Act (2002)-
  and accounting software, 7-4
  and accuracy of financial reports, 2-23
  code of ethical standards based on, 19-17
  and corporation management, 13-4
  and ethics, 1-6
  and fraud, 8-3–8-4, 8-48–8-49
  and human resources, 8-10
  and internal auditor's job, 1-25
  and internal control, 1-24, 1-48, 3-5
Schedule of cash payments, 12-14
Schultz, Howard, 26-2
SEC, *see* Securities and Exchange Commission
Secured bonds, 15-3
Securities-
  available-for-sale, 16-11–16-13, 18-5
  held-to-maturity, 16-11
  marketable, 16-15
  trading, 16-11–16-13, 18-5
Securities and Exchange Commission (SEC), 1-5, 1-8, 1-25, 8-26, 13-5, 15-15, 16-13, 16-34, 18-8
Segments, 23-15–23-17, 25-14
Segregation of duties, 8-6–8-7, 9-4, 9-7
Seller, freight costs for, 5-8–5-9
Selling and administrative costs, 22-11
Selling and administrative expense budget, 24-15, 25-5
Sell-or-process further decisions, 23-10–23-13
Sensitivity analysis, 27-14
Services, 1-17, 13-12
Service companies-
  balanced scorecard for, 26-19
  budgeting in, 24-23–24-24
  charter flights by, 22-16
  flexible budgets for, 25-9, 25-12
  free shipping, 23-9
  incentives to close credit cards, 23-5
  job order costing in, 20-18–20-19
  and managerial accounting, 19-14–19-15
  operating cycles for, 5-3
  process cost systems for, 21-4
  revenue for, 20-19
Service revenue, 20-19
Shareholders' equity, 13-9. *See also* Corporate capital
Short-term investments, 16-15
Short-term paper, 16-15*n*4
Significant variances, 26-16
Simple entries, 2-9
Single-step income statement, 5-20–5-21
Sinking fund bonds, 15-3
"Slush" funds, 8-16
Small businesses, 21-1–21-2, 24-4
Small stock dividend, 14-8
Social responsibility, *see* Corporate social responsibility
Social Security, 11-21
Social Security taxes, 11-11
Software, 7-3–7-4
Sold jobs, 20-15–20-20
Solvency ratios, 18-16, 18-18, 18-21–18-23
South Korea, 1-8
SOX, *see* Sarbanes-Oxley Act (2002)
Special journals, 7-8–7-22
  cash payments, 7-17–7-19
  cash receipts, 7-11–7-15
  effects on general journal, 7-20
  purchases, 7-15–7-17
  sales, 7-9–7-11
Special orders, 23-6–23-7

Specific identification method (inventory), 6-7–6-8
Split-off points, 23-18
Staff positions, 19-5–19-6, 24-23
Stakeholders, 1-7
Standards. *See also* Standard costs
across companies, 26-2
budgets vs., 26-4
government, 26-3
ideal vs. normal, 26-4
variances from, 26-7–26-20
Standard costs, 26-1–26-24
accounting system for, 26-20–26-23
balanced scorecard, 26-17–26-20
direct labor variances, 26-11–26-15
direct materials variances, 26-7–26-11
manufacturing overhead variances, 26-14–26-15
overhead controllable variances, 26-23–26-24
overhead volume variances, 26-24
reporting variances from, 26-16–26-20
setting, 26-4–26-7
and standards across companies, 26-2
and standards vs. budgets, 26-4
Standard cost, job order accounting system, 26-20–26-23
Standard cost accounting system, 26-20–26-23
Standard hours allowed, 26-14, 26-23
Standard predetermined overhead rate, 26-6
Stated value, 13-8, 14-9
Statement of cash flows, 1-20, 1-21, 1-23, 17-1–17-33
analyzing, 17-17–17-18
and cash management, 17-1–17-2
classification of cash flows, 17-3–17-4, 17-7
direct method for, 17-7, 17-19–17-26
format of, 17-5–17-6
IFRS and GAAP for, 17-58–17-59
indirect method for, 17-6–17-16, 17-26–17-30
preparation of, 17-6–17-16, 17-19–17-26
ratio analysis, 18-18
significant noncash activities, 17-4–17-5
T-account approach, 17-31–17-33
usefulness of, 17-3
worksheet for, 17-26–17-30
Statement of comprehensive income, 14-38, 18-3, 18-5–18-6
Statement of earnings, 11-15
Statement of operations, 1-20. *See also* Income statement
State unemployment taxes, 11-17
Static budgets, 25-4–25-6
Static budget reports, 25-4–25-7
Stocks, 13-6–13-9. *See also* Common stock
authorized, 13-7
capital, 13-17
issued for cash, 17-14, 17-25
issuing, 13-6–13-9
no-par value, 13-8, 13-11–13-12
outstanding, 13-18
par value of, 13-8, 13-10–13-11, 14-9
preferred, 13-12–13-13, 14-4–14-7, 14-19
of tech companies, 17-15
treasury, 13-14–13-17
Stock bonus programs, 14-1–14-2
Stock certificates, 13-6, 13-7
Stock dividends, 14-7–14-9
Stockholders-
limited liability of, 13-3
ownership rights of, 13-6
preferred, 14-4–14-5
Stockholders' equity, 4-28, 13-9. *See also* Corporate capital
cash dividends and, 14-4
contra account for, 13-14
and disposal of treasury stock, 13-16
effect of dividends on, 14-8–14-9
effect of stock splits on, 14-9
on financial statements, 13-17–13-19, 14-11–14-16
and IFRS/GAAP, 13-36–13-37
return on, 14-15, 18-23
and statement of cash flows, 17-13–17-14
in vertical analysis, 18-12
Stockholders' equity statement, 14-14, 14-18
Stock investments, 16-6–16-10
Stock option plans, 13-8
Stockpiling, 24-11
Stock quotes, reading, 13-13
Stock splits, 14-9–14-11
Stoppleworth, Kerry, 8-1–8-2
Straight-line amortization, 15-17–15-19
Straight-line depreciation, 10-9–10-10, 10-12
Su, Vivi, 9-1–9-2
Subchapter S corporations, 12-4
Subsidiary (affiliated) company, 16-8, 16-9
Subsidiary ledgers, 7-5–7-8
job cost sheets as, 20-8, 20-10
posting from cash receipts journal to, 7-14, 7-15
posting from purchases journal to, 7-16–7-17
Summa de Arithmetica, Geometria, Proportione et Proportionalite (Luca Pacioli), 1-4*n*.2
Sunk costs, 23-4, 23-14
Supplementary schedule to statement of cash flows, 17-5
Suppliers, cash payments to, 17-21–17-22
Supplies, 1-15–1-16, 3-7–3-8
Sustainability, decisions about, 23-1–23-2
Sustainability reporting, 8-4, 10-23
Sustainable Apparel Coalition, 1-2
Sustainable income, 18-3–18-7

T

Tabular summaries, 2-3
T-accounts, 2-3, 17-21, 17-31–17-33
Take-home pay, 11-12. *See also* Net pay
"Tapping the cookie jar," 9-10
Target net income, 22-18–22-19
Taxes and taxation-
as accounting area, 1-25
on corporations, 13-5
and depreciation, 10-13
double taxation, 13-5
effect of cost flow methods on, 6-12–6-14
on employers, 11-16–11-19
FICA, 11-10, 11-11
income, *see* Income taxes
for partnerships, 12-3
payroll, 11-10–11-12, 11-16–11-19
real estate taxes payable, 1-12
sales taxes payable, 1-12, 11-4
Taxing authorities, 1-5
Tech company stock, 17-15
Technology, investments in, 16-1–16-2
Temporary accounts, 4-12, 4-17–4-18
Theft, 5-12, 8-18
Theory of constraints, 19-16
Three-column form of account, 2-11
Tilton, Glenn, 26-19
Times interest earned, 18-22–18-23
Times interest earned ratio, 15-14–15-15
Timeliness, 3-28
Time period assumption, 3-3–3-6, 3-29, 3-58
Time span, cost controllability and, 25-15
Time tickets, 20-10
Time value of money, 15-5, 23-5, 27-5, 27-8
TLV (total labor variance), 26-12, 26-13
TMV (total materials variance), 26-9
Top management, performance evaluations, 25-16
Total assets, 10-3, 13-16, 14-4, 18-12
Total capital, 12-22
Total conversion costs, 21-14
Total cost of goods manufactured, 19-12
Total cost of trading securities, 16-11
Total costs-
fixed, 22-3–22-4, 22-8
in job order vs. process cost systems, 21-5
mixed, 22-6
variable, 22-3
Total costs accounted for, 21-15, 21-22
Total costs to be accounted for, 21-15, 21-22
Total depreciation expense, 10-12
Total fair value, 16-11
Total labor variance (TLV), 26-12, 26-13
Total liabilities, 18-12
Total manufacturing costs, 19-12, 20-20–20-21
Total materials variance (TMV), 26-9
Total overhead variance, 26-14
Total quality management (TQM), 19-16
Total standard cost per unit, 26-6–26-7
Total units accounted for, 21-13
Total units to be accounted for, 21-13
Total variance, 26-8
TQM (total quality management), 19-16
Traceable costs, 25-22
Trademarks, 10-19, 10-20
Trade names, 10-19
Trade receivables, 9-3. *See also* Accounts receivable; Notes Receivable
Trading on the equity, 18-24
Trading securities, 16-11–16-13, 18-5
Transaction analysis, 1-13–1-20, 2-14–2-18. *See also* Business transactions
Transfers, in process costing, 21-8, 21-18
Transportation bills, correcting entries for, 4-22
Transposition error, 2-22
Treasurers, 13-5, 19-5
Treasury stock, 13-14–13-17
Trend analysis, *see* Horizontal analysis
Trial balances, 2-21–2-22
adjusted, 3-21–3-24
limitations of, 2-22
outdated information in, 3-5
post-closing, 4-16–4-18
on worksheet, 4-4–4-8, 5-24, 5-29
Triple bottom line, 19-18
True cash balance, 8-25
Trustees (bonds), 15-3

U

Unamortized Discount on Bonds Payable, 15-18
Uncertainty, with current liabilities, 11-6–11-7
Uncollectible accounts, 9-5–9-11
allowance method, 9-6–9-10
direct write-off method, 9-5–9-6

Uncollectible accounts expense, 9-5
Underapplied manufacturing overhead, 20-21–20-22
Under budget (term), 25-9
Understandability, 3-28
Underwriting, 13-7–13-8
Unearned revenues, 3-5
adjusting entries for, 3-10–3-11
alternative treatment of, 3-26–3-27
as current liabilities, 11-4–11-5
Unemployment taxes, 11-17
Unfavorable variances, 26-8, 26-22
Unit contribution margin (CVP analysis), 22-12, 22-15–22-16, 22-19
Unit conversion cost, 21-14
Unit costs-
fixed, 22-4
for job order vs. process cost systems, 21-5
variable, 22-3, 22-7–22-8, 22-15
United Nations, 22-4
U.S. Commerce Department, 17-2
Units-of-activity depletion, 10-17
Units-of-activity depreciation (units-of-production method), 10-10–10-12
Unit production costs, 21-14–21-15, 21-20–21-21
Units completed, 21-15, 21-17
Unit selling price, 22-15
Units in process, costing for, 21-15
Units started, 21-17
Unlimited liability, 12-3
Unprofitable segment elimination decisions, 23-15–23-17
Unrealized gains and losses, 16-11, 16-16–16-17, 18-5–18-6
Unsecured bonds, 15-3
Unusual items, 18-8–18-9
Useful financial information, 3-28
Useful life, 3-8, 10-5–10-6, 10-8, 10-19, 27-7
Users of accounting data, 1-4–1-6

V

Vacations, required, 8-9, 8-10
Valuation-
of accounts receivable, 9-5–9-11
cost allocation vs., 10-7
of notes receivable, 9-16
Value chain, 19-15–19-16
Variable costs-
classification of mixed costs as, 22-7–22-8
and controllable margin, 25-24–25-25
in CVP relationship, 22-3
in flexible budget, 25-8, 25-10
identifying, 22-9–22-10
in incremental analysis, 23-5
in manufacturing overhead budget, 24-15
unit, 22-3, 22-7–22-8, 22-15
Variances from standards, 26-7–26-20
direct labor variances, 26-11–26-15
direct materials variances, 26-7–26-12
journalizing, 26-20–26-22
manufacturing overhead variance, 26-14–26-15
overhead, 26-23–26-24
reporting, 26-16–26-20
significant, 26-16
Venture capital firms, 12-4
Verifiability, 3-28
Verification, independent internal, *see* Independent internal verification
Vertical analysis, 18-9–18-10, 18-12–18-14
Virtual closes, 4-15
Voluntary restrictions, on retained earnings, 14-12
Voluntary withdrawal, 12-21
Voting rights, 5-1–5-2
Vouchers, 8-15
Voucher register, 8-15
Voucher system controls, 8-15–8-16

W

Wages, 3-16–3-17, 11-10, 26-13. *See also* Payroll accounting
Wage and Tax Statement (Form W-2), 11-19
Warehousing systems, robotic, 22-9
Warranties, product, 11-7
Wear and tear, 10-7
Weighted-average method, 21-9–21-11, 21-22–21-23
Weighted-average unit cost, 6-12
Weighting, in balanced scorecard, 26-19
West, Laura, 7-1, 7-2
West, Paul, 7-1, 7-2
Wholesalers, 5-3
Wind farms, 27-15
Wireless service providers, 27-8
Withdrawal by payment from partnership assets, 12-22–12-23
Withdrawal by payment from partners' personal assets, 12-22
Withdrawal of partners, 12-21–12-24
Withholding tax table, 11-12
Work force, 26-13, 26-14
Working capital, 11-8
Work in process, 6-3
beginning, 19-11, 21-10, 21-18
in job order vs. process costing, 21-5
in weighted-average method, 21-10
Work in process inventory, 19-11, 19-12, 20-8, 20-12
Worksheets, 4-2–4-11
for merchandising companies, 5-23–5-24, 5-29–5-31
preparing adjusting entries from, 4-11
preparing financial statements from, 4-10–4-11
for statement of cash flows, 17-26–17-30
steps in preparing, 4-3–4-9
Write-off, of uncollectible account, 9-7

Y

Years, fiscal vs. calendar, 3-3
Year-end balance, 20-21–20-22

Z

Zero-based budgeting, 24-20
Zero-interest bonds, 15-5
Zoological Society of San Diego, 25-12
Zuckerberg, Mark, 13-1, 13-2

RAPID REVIEW
Chapter Content

ACCOUNTING EQUATION (Chapter 2)

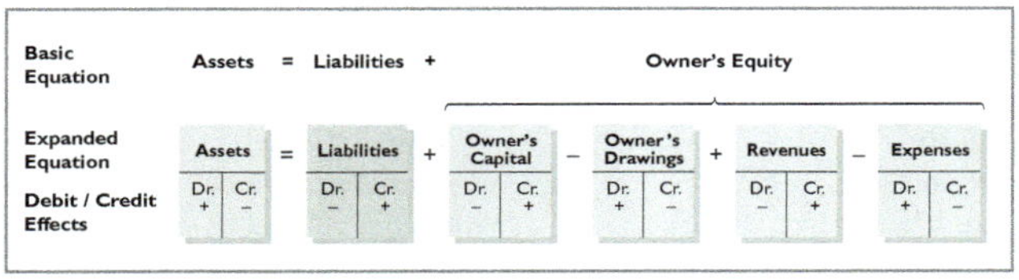

ADJUSTING ENTRIES (Chapter 3)

	Type	Adjusting Entry	
Deferrals	1. Prepaid expenses 2. Unearned revenues	Dr. Expenses Dr. Liabilities	Cr. Assets Cr. Revenues
Accruals	1. Accrued revenues 2. Accrued expenses	Dr. Assets Dr. Expenses	Cr. Revenues Cr. Liabilities

Note: Each adjusting entry will affect one or more income statement accounts and one or more balance sheet accounts.

Interest Computation

Interest = Face value of note × Annual interest rate × Time in terms of one year

CLOSING ENTRIES (Chapter 4)

Purpose: (1) Update the Owner's Capital account in the ledger by transferring net income (loss) and Owner's Drawings to Owner's Capital. (2) Prepare the temporary accounts (revenue, expense, Owner's Drawings) for the next period's postings by reducing their balances to zero.

Process

1. Debit each revenue account for its balance (assuming normal balances), and credit Income Summary for total revenues.
2. Debit Income Summary for total expenses, and credit each expense account for its balance (assuming normal balances).

   STOP AND CHECK: Does the balance in your Income Summary account equal the net income (loss) reported in the income statement?

3. Debit (credit) Income Summary, and credit (debit) Owner's Capital for the amount of net income (loss).
4. Debit Owner's Capital for the balance in the Owner's Drawings account, and credit Owner's Drawings for the same amount.

   STOP AND CHECK: Does the balance in your Owner's Capital account equal the ending balance reported in the balance sheet and the owner's equity statement? Are all of your temporary account balances zero?

ACCOUNTING CYCLE (Chapter 4)

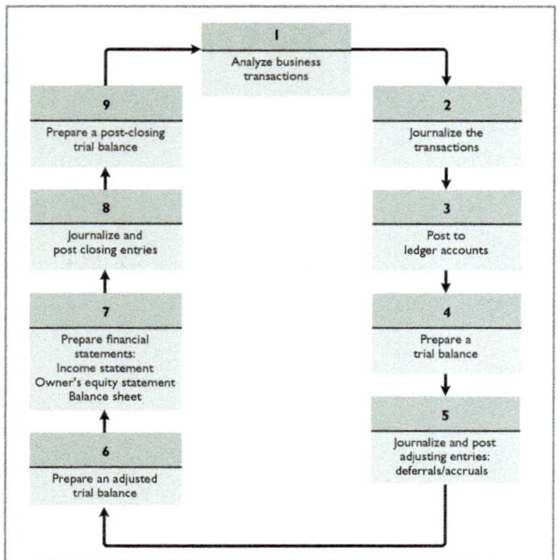

Optional steps: If a worksheet is prepared, Steps 4, 5, and 6 are incorporated in the worksheet. If reversing entries are prepared, they occur between Steps 9 and 1.

INVENTORY (Chapters 5 and 6)

Ownership

Freight Terms	Ownership of goods on public carrier resides with:	Who pays freight costs:
FOB shipping point	Buyer	Buyer
FOB destination	Seller	Seller

Perpetual vs. Periodic Journal Entries

Event	Perpetual	Periodic*
Purchase of goods	Inventory Cash (A/P)	Purchases Cash (A/P)
Freight (shipping point)	Inventory Cash	Freight-In Cash
Return of goods	Cash (or A/P) Inventory	Cash (or A/P) Purchase Ret. and All.
Sale of goods	Cash (or A/R) Sales Revenue Cost of Goods Sold Inventory	Cash (or A/R) Sales Revenue No entry
Sales returns and allowances	Sales Ret. and All. Accounts Receivable Inventory Cost of Goods Sold	Sales Ret. and All. Accounts Receivable No entry
Sales discounts	Cash Sales Discounts Accounts Receivable	Cash Sales Discounts Accounts Receivable
End of period	No entry	Closing or adjusting entry required

*Covered in appendix.

Cost Flow Methods

- Specific identification
- First-in, first-out (FIFO)
- Weighted-average
- Last-in, first-out (LIFO)

FRAUD, INTERNAL CONTROL, AND CASH (Chapter 8)

The Fraud Triangle

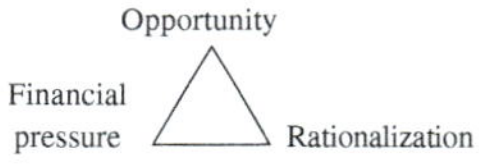

Principles of Internal Control Activities

- Establishment of responsibility
- Segregation of duties
- Documentation procedures
- Physical controls
- Independent internal verification
- Human resource controls

Bank Reconciliation

Bank	Books
Balance per bank statement Add: Deposit in transit Deduct: Outstanding checks Adjusted cash balance	Balance per books Add: Unrecorded credit memoranda from bank statement Deduct: Unrecorded debit memoranda from bank statement Adjusted cash balance

Note: 1. Errors should be offset (added or deducted) on the side that made the error.
2. Adjusting journal entries should only be made on the books.

STOP AND CHECK: Does the adjusted cash balance in the Cash account equal the reconciled balance?

RAPID REVIEW
Chapter Content

RECEIVABLES (Chapter 9)

Methods to Account for Uncollectible Accounts

Direct write-off method	Record bad debt expense when the company determines a particular account to be uncollectible.
Allowance methods: **Percentage-of-sales**	At the end of each period, estimate the amount of credit sales uncollectible. Debit Bad Debt Expense and credit Allowance for Doubtful Accounts for this amount. As specific accounts become uncollectible, debit Allowance for Doubtful Accounts and credit Accounts Receivable.
Percentage-of-receivables	At the end of each period, estimate the amount of uncollectible receivables. Debit Bad Debt Expense and credit Allowance for Doubtful Accounts in an amount that results in a balance in the allowance account equal to the estimate of uncollectibles. As specific accounts become uncollectible, debit Allowance for Doubtful Accounts and credit Accounts Receivable.

PLANT ASSETS (Chapter 10)

Presentation

Tangible Assets	Intangible Assets
Property, plant, and equipment	Intangible assets (patents, copyrights, trademarks, franchises, goodwill)
Natural resources	

Computation of Annual Depreciation Expense

Straight-line	$\dfrac{\text{Cost} - \text{Salvage value}}{\text{Useful life (in years)}}$
Units-of-activity	$\dfrac{\text{Depreciable cost}}{\text{Useful life (in units)}} \times$ Units of activity during year
Declining-balance	Book value at beginning of year × Declining balance rate* *Declining-balance rate = 1 ÷ Useful life (in years)

Note: If depreciation is calculated for partial periods, the straight-line and declining-balance methods must be adjusted for the relevant proportion of the year.
Multiply the annual depreciation expense by the number of months expired in the year divided by 12 months.

SHAREHOLDERS' EQUITY (Chapter 13)

Comparison of Equity Accounts

Proprietorship	Partnership	Corporation
Owner's equity Owner's capital	Partner's equity Name, Capital Name, Capital	Stockholders' equity Common stock Retained earnings

No-Par Value vs. Par Value Stock Journal Entries

No-Par Value	Par Value
Cash Common Stock	Cash Common Stock (par value) Paid-in Capital in Excess of Par—Common Stock

DIVIDENDS (Chapter 14)

Comparison of Dividend Effects

	Cash	Common Stock	Retained Earnings
Cash dividend	↓	No effect	↓
Stock dividend	No effect	↑	↓
Stock split	No effect	No effect	No effect

BONDS (Chapter 15)

Premium	Market interest rate < Contractual interest rate
Face Value	Market interest rate = Contractual interest rate
Discount	Market interest rate > Contractual interest rate

INVESTMENTS (Chapter 16)

Comparison of Long-Term Bond Investment and Liability Journal Entries

Event	Investor	Investee
Purchase / issue of bonds	Debt Investments Cash	Cash Bonds Payable
Interest receipt / payment	Cash Interest Revenue	Interest Expense Cash

Comparison of Cost and Equity Methods of Accounting for Long-Term Stock Investments

Event	Cost	Equity
Acquisition	Stock Investments Cash	Stock Investments Cash
Investee reports earnings	No entry	Stock Investments Revenue from Stock Investments
Investee pays dividends	Cash Dividend Revenue	Cash Stock Investments

Trading and Available-for-Sale Securities

Trading	Report at fair value with changes reported in net income.
Available-for-sale	Report at fair value with changes reported in the stockholders' equity section.

STATEMENT OF CASH FLOWS (Chapter 17)

Cash flows from operating activities (**indirect method**)

Net income			
Add:	Losses on disposals of assets	$ X	
	Amortization and depreciation	X	
	Decreases in current assets	X	
	Increases in current liabilities	X	
Deduct:	Gains on disposals of assets	(X)	
	Increases in current assets	(X)	
	Decreases in current liabilities	(X)	
Net cash provided (used) by operating activities			$ X

Cash flows from operating activities (**direct method**)

Cash receipts (Examples: from sales of goods and services to customers, from receipts of interest and dividends on loans and investments)	$ X	
Cash payments (Examples: to suppliers, for operating expenses, for interest, for taxes)	(X)	
Net cash provided (used) by operating activities		$ X

PRESENTATION OF NON-TYPICAL ITEMS (Chapter 18)

Prior period adjustments (Chapter 14)	Statement of retained earnings (adjustment of beginning retained earnings)
Discontinued operations	Income statement (presented separately after "Income from continuing operations")
Changes in accounting principle	In most instances, use the new method in current period and restate previous year's results using new method. For changes in depreciation and amortization methods, use the new method in the current period but do not restate previous periods.

RAPID REVIEW
Chapter Content

MANAGERIAL ACCOUNTING (Chapter 19)

Characteristics of Managerial Accounting

Primary users	Internal users
Reports	Internal reports issued as needed
Purpose	Special purpose for a particular user
Content	Pertains to subunits, may be detailed, use of relevant data
Verification	No independent audits

Types of Manufacturing Costs

Direct materials	Raw materials directly associated with finished product
Direct labor	Work of employees directly associated with turning raw materials into finished product
Manufacturing overhead	Costs indirectly associated with manufacture of finished product

JOB ORDER AND PROCESS COSTING (Chapters 20 and 21)

Types of Accounting Systems

Job order	Costs are assigned to each unit or each batch of goods
Process cost	Costs are applied to similar products that are mass-produced in a continuous fashion

Job Order and Process Cost Flow

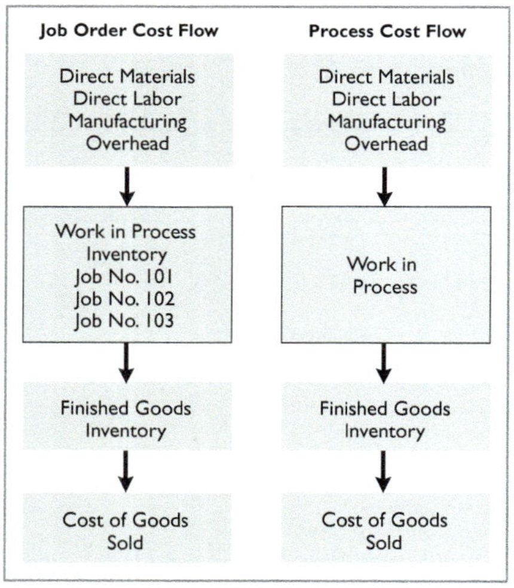

COST-VOLUME-PROFIT (Chapter 22)

Types of Costs

Variable costs	Vary in total directly and proportionately with changes in activity level
Fixed costs	Remain the same in total regardless of change in activity level
Mixed costs	Contain both a fixed and a variable element

CVP Income Statement Format

	Total	Per Unit
Sales	$XX	$XX
Variable costs	XX	XX
Contribution margin	XX	$XX
Fixed costs	XX	
Net income	$XX	

Unit contribution margin = Unit selling price − Unit variable costs

Break-even point in units = Fixed costs ÷ Unit contribution margin

Required sales in units for target net income = (Fixed costs + Target net income) ÷ Unit contribution margin

RAPID REVIEW
Chapter Content

INCREMENTAL ANALYSIS (Chapter 23)

1. Identify the relevant costs associated with each alternative. **Relevant costs** are those costs and revenues that differ across alternatives. Choose the alternative that maximizes net income.
2. **Opportunity costs** are those potential benefits that are given up when one alternative is chosen instead of another one. Opportunity costs are relevant costs.
3. **Sunk costs** have already been incurred and will not be changed or avoided by any future decision. Sunk costs are not relevant costs.

BUDGETS (Chapter 24)

Components of the Master Budget

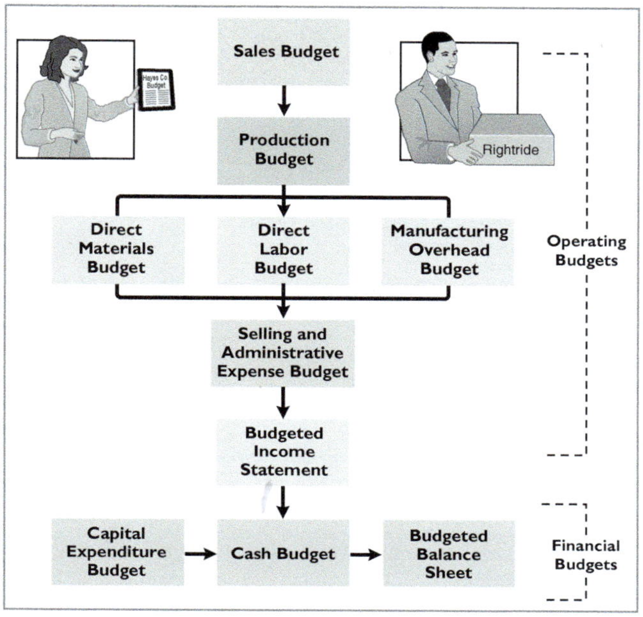

RESPONSIBILITY ACCOUNTING (Chapter 25)

Types of Responsibility Centers

Cost	Profit	Investment
Expenses only	Expenses and Revenues	Expenses and Revenues and ROI

Return on Investment

Return on investment (ROI) = Investment center controllable margin ÷ Average investment center operating assets

STANDARD COSTS (Chapter 26)

Standard Cost Variances

Total materials variance = Materials price variance + Materials quantity variance

Total labor variance = Labor price variance + Labor quantity variance

Total overhead variance = Overhead controllable variance + Overhead volume variance

Balanced Scorecard

Linked process across perspectives:

Financial → Customer → Internal Process → Learning and Growth

Materials price variance = $AQ \times AP$ − $AQ \times SP$

Materials quantity variance = $AQ \times SP$ − $SQ \times SP$

Labor price variance = $AH \times AR$ − $AH \times SR$

Labor quantity variance = $AH \times SR$ − $SH \times SR$

***Overhead controllable variance** = Actual overhead − Overhead budgeted

***Overhead volume variance** = Fixed overhead rate × (Normal capacity hours − Standard hours allowed)

*Appendix coverage

CAPITAL BUDGETING (Chapter 27)

Annual Rate of Return

Annual rate of return = Expected annual net income ÷ Average investment

Cash Payback

Cash payback period = Cost of capital investment ÷ Annual cash inflow

Discounted Cash Flow Approaches

Net Present Value	Internal Rate of Return
Compute net present value (a dollar amount). If net present value is zero or positive, accept the proposal. If net present value is negative, reject the proposal.	Compute internal rate of return (a percentage). If internal rate of return is equal to or greater than the minimum required rate of return, accept the proposal. If internal rate of return is less than the minimum rate, reject the proposal.

RAPID REVIEW
Financial Statements

Order of Preparation

Statement Type	Date
1. Income statement	For the period ended
2. Retained earnings statement	For the period ended
3. Balance sheet	As of the end of the period
4. Statement of cash flows	For the period ended

Income Statement (perpetual inventory system)

Company Name Income Statement For the Period Ended		
Sales		
Sales revenue	$ X	
Less: Sales returns and allowances	X	
Sales discounts	X	
Net sales		$ X
Cost of goods sold		X
Gross profit		X
Operating expenses		
(Examples: store salaries, advertising, delivery, rent, depreciation, utilities, insurance)		X
Income from operations		X
Other revenues and gains		
(Examples: interest, gains)	X	
Other expenses and losses		
(Examples: interest, losses)	X	X
Income before income taxes		X
Income tax expense		X
Net income		$ X

Income Statement (periodic inventory system)

Company Name Income Statement For the Period Ended			
Sales			
Sales revenue		$ X	
Less: Sales returns and allowances		X	
Sales discounts		X	
Net sales			$ X
Cost of goods sold			
Beginning inventory		X	
Purchases	$ X		
Less: Purchase returns and allowances	X		
Net purchases	X		
Add: Freight-in	X		
Cost of goods purchased		X	
Cost of goods available for sale		X	
Less: Ending inventory		X	
Cost of goods sold			X
Gross profit			X
Operating expenses			
(Examples: store salaries, advertising, delivery, rent, depreciation, utilities, insurance)			X
Income from operations			X
Other revenues and gains			
(Examples: interest, gains)		X	
Other expenses and losses			
(Examples: interest, losses)		X	X
Income before income taxes			X
Income tax expense			X
Net income			$ X

Retained Earnings Statement

Company Name Retained Earnings Statement For the Period Ended	
Retained earnings, beginning of period	$ X
Add: Net income (or deduct net loss)	X
	X
Deduct: Dividends	X
Retained earnings, end of period	$ X

STOP AND CHECK: Net income (loss) presented on the retained earnings statement must equal the net income (loss) presented on the income statement.

Balance Sheet

Company Name Balance Sheet As of the End of the Period			
Assets			
Current assets			
(Examples: cash, short-term debt investments, accounts receivable, inventory, prepaids)			$ X
Long-term investments			
(Examples: investments in bonds, investments in stocks)			X
Property, plant, and equipment			
Land		$ X	
Buildings and equipment	$ X		
Less: Accumulated depreciation	X	X	X
Intangible assets			X
Total assets			$ X
Liabilities and Stockholders' Equity			
Liabilities			
Current liabilities			
(Examples: notes payable, accounts payable, accruals, unearned revenues, current portion of notes payable)			$ X
Long-term liabilities			
(Examples: notes payable, bonds payable)			X
Total liabilities			X
Stockholders' equity			
Common stock			X
Retained earnings			X
Total liabilities and stockholders' equity			$ X

STOP AND CHECK: Total assets on the balance sheet must equal total liabilities and stockholders' equity; and, ending retained earnings on the balance sheet must equal ending retained earnings on the retained earnings statement.

Statement of Cash Flows

Company Name Statement of Cash Flows For the Period Ended	
Cash flows from operating activities	
(*Note:* May be prepared using the direct or indirect method)	
Net cash provided (used) by operating activities	$ X
Cash flows from investing activities	
(Examples: purchase / sale of long-term assets)	
Net cash provided (used) by investing activities	X
Cash flows from financing activities	
(Examples: issue / repayment of long-term liabilities, issue of stock, payment of dividends)	
Net cash provided (used) by financing activities	X
Net increase (decrease) in cash	X
Cash, beginning of the period	X
Cash, end of the period	$ X

STOP AND CHECK: Cash, end of the period, on the statement of cash flows must equal cash presented on the balance sheet.

RAPID REVIEW
Using the Information in the Financial Statements

Ratio	Formula	Purpose or Use
Liquidity Ratios		
1. Current ratio	$\frac{\text{Current assets}}{\text{Current liabilities}}$	Measures short-term debt-paying ability.
2. Acid-test (quick) ratio	$\frac{\text{Cash + Short-term investments + Accounts receivable (net)}}{\text{Current liabilities}}$	Measures immediate short-term liquidity.
3. Accounts receivable turnover	$\frac{\text{Net credit sales}}{\text{Average net accounts receivable}}$	Measures liquidity of receivables.
4. Inventory turnover	$\frac{\text{Cost of goods sold}}{\text{Average inventory}}$	Measures liquidity of inventory.
Profitability Ratios		
5. Profit margin	$\frac{\text{Net income}}{\text{Net sales}}$	Measures net income generated by each dollar of sales.
6. Asset turnover	$\frac{\text{Net sales}}{\text{Average total assets}}$	Measures how efficiently assets are used to generate sales.
7. Return on assets	$\frac{\text{Net income}}{\text{Average total assets}}$	Measures overall profitability of assets.
8. Return on common stockholders' equity	$\frac{\text{Net income − Preferred dividends}}{\text{Average common stockholders' equity}}$	Measures profitability of owners' investment.
9. Earnings per share (EPS)	$\frac{\text{Net income − Preferred dividends}}{\text{Weighted-average common shares outstanding}}$	Measures net income earned on each share of common stock.
10. Price-earnings (P-E) ratio	$\frac{\text{Market price per share of stock}}{\text{Earnings per share}}$	Measures ratio of the market price per share to earnings per share.
11. Payout ratio	$\frac{\text{Cash dividends declared on common stock}}{\text{Net income}}$	Measures percentage of earnings distributed in the form of cash dividends.
Solvency Ratios		
12. Debt to assets ratio	$\frac{\text{Total liabilities}}{\text{Total assets}}$	Measures percentage of total assets provided by creditors.
13. Times interest earned	$\frac{\text{Net income + Interest expense + Income tax expense}}{\text{Interest expense}}$	Measures ability to meet interest payments as they come due.
14. Free cash flow	Net cash provided by operating activities − Capital expenditures − Cash dividends	Measures the amount of cash generated during the current year that is available for the payment of additional dividends or for expansion.